SCIENCE IN THE LAW

FORENSIC SCIENCE ISSUES

By

David L. Faigman
University of California
Hastings College of the Law

David H. Kaye
Arizona State University
College of Law

Michael J. Saks
Arizona State University
College of Law

Joseph Sanders
University of Houston
Law Center

AMERICAN CASEBOOK SERIES®

WEST GROUP

A THOMSON COMPANY

ST. PAUL, MINN., 2002

American Casebook Series, and the West Group symbol
are registered trademarks used herein under license.

COPYRIGHT © 2002 By WEST GROUP
              610 Opperman Drive
              P.O. Box 64526
              St. Paul, MN 55164–0526
              1–800–328–9352

All Rights Reserved
Printed in the United States of America

ISBN 0–314–26326–8

TEXT IS PRINTED ON 10% POST CONSUMER RECYCLED PAPER

For Susan
      (DLF)

For Miranda
      (DHK)

For Roselle
      (MJS)

For Mary
      (JS)

*

Preface

For the rational study of the law the black
letter man may be the man of the present, but
the man of the future is the man of statistics
and the master of economics.

— Oliver Wendell Holmes[1]

The intellectual life of the whole of western
society is increasingly being split into two
polar groups. . . . Literary intellectuals at one
pole — at the other scientists. . . . Between
the two a gulf of mutual incomprehension.

— C.P. Snow[2]

Judges and lawyers, in general, are not known for expertise in science and mathematics. Nor is science a subject given significant attention in American law schools. The reasons are manifold. Despite Justice Holmes' prescient and often-quoted statement, the legal profession has perceived little need for lawyers to have a grounding in the scientific method. Indeed, law students, as a group, seem peculiarly averse to math and science. The American educational system is partly at fault, for students routinely divide, or are divided, into two separate cultures early in their training. Students who display a talent in math and science typically pursue careers in medicine, engineering, biology, chemistry, computer science, and similar subjects. Students with less inclination toward quantitative analysis very often go to law school. It is perhaps not surprising that the student who excels in the humanities soon learns that the best job opportunities for a graduate in Nineteenth Century Russian Literature can be found through law school. Whatever its origins, the legal profession today is a particularly salient example of a literary culture that remains largely ignorant of scientific culture.

Increasingly, however, there are signs that a "third culture" is emerging in the law.[3] This third culture would be one that integrates a sophisticated understanding of science into legal decisionmaking. Perhaps the most visible sign of this emerging integration is the United States Supreme Court's decision

---

1. Oliver Wendell Holmes, Jr., *The Path of the Law*, 10 HARV. L. REV. 457, 469 (1897).
2. C.P. Snow, *The Two Cultures and the Scientific Revolution* 3 (Rede Lecture 1959).
3. Cf. JOHN BROCKMAN, THE THIRD CULTURE (1995) (chronicling the emergence of a "third culture" in society generally, through the increasing numbers of scientists writing for a general audience); STEVEN GOLDBERG, CULTURE CLASH: LAW AND SCIENCE IN AMERICA (1994) (exploring the many contexts in which law and science overlap in practice).

in *Daubert v. Merrell Dow Pharmaceuticals, Inc.*[4] The Court, for the first time in its history, considered the standard for evaluating the admissibility of scientific expert testimony. Briefly, the *Daubert* Court held that under the Federal Rules of Evidence, trial court judges must act as "gatekeepers," and evaluate the validity of the basis for proferred scientific expertise before permitting the expert to testify. In two subsequent cases – *General Electric Co. v. Joiner*[5] and *Kumho Tire Ltd. v. Carmichael*[6] – the Court further explicated the obligations that this gatekeeping role demands. These obligations were codified in the Federal Rules of Evidence in 2000. Moreover, states have increasingly followed the Supreme Court's lead, with many adopting *Daubert* outright, and still others incorporating the insights of *Daubert's* validity standard into their preexisting tests for admission of expert testimony.

Application of the *Daubert* standard requires an understanding of scientific research. Whether the Court intended to change the way the law responds to scientific evidence, or had more modest expectations, is impossible to know. Without doubt, however, the many judges, lawyers and scholars who have written on the decision have discovered a revolution of sorts. This revolution is one of perspective, and it affects profoundly not only the judges who guard the gate, but also the lawyers who seek to enter through it.

Until *Daubert,* courts had applied a variety of tests, with most courts being deferential to the scientists in their respective fields of expertise. This role was most closely associated with the general acceptance test articulated in *Frye v. United States.*[7] *Frye* instructed judges to admit scientific evidence only after it had achieved general acceptance in its field. The *Daubert* Court, in contrast, found that the Federal Rules of Evidence require judges themselves to determine the scientific validity of the basis for expert testimony. The shift in perspective is subtle yet profound. Whereas *Frye* required judges to survey the pertinent field to assess the validity of the proffered scientific evidence, *Daubert* calls upon judges to assess the merits of the scientific research supporting an expert's opinion. Implicitly, as well, the *Daubert* standard contemplates that lawyers will have sufficient expertise to explain the science to judges when they make admissibility arguments. The *Daubert* perspective immediately raised the spectre, as Chief Justice Rehnquist decried it, of judges assuming the role of "amateur scientists."[8] The gatekeeping role, he feared, was one most judges were ill-suited to fill.

Daubert has not come to mean that judges must be trained as scientists to carry out admissibility decisions. No one expects judges to join physicists soon in the search for grand unified theories.[9] But there is considerable space between being a trained scientist and being ignorant of science. Although *Daubert* does not expect judges and lawyers to be scientists, it does expect them to be sophisticated consumers of science. This book was formulated with that goal in mind. It is intended to introduce students to the rigors and details

---

4. 509 U.S. 579, 113 S.Ct. 2786, 125 L.Ed.2d 469 (1993).

5. 522 U.S. 136, 118 S.Ct. 512, 139 L.Ed.2d 508 (1997).

6. 526 U.S. 137, 119 S.Ct. 1167, 143 L.Ed.2d 238 (1999).

7. 293 F. 1013 (D.C. Cir. 1923).

8. 113 S.Ct. at 2800 (Rehnquist, C.J., concurring in part and dissenting in part).

9. See generally STEVEN WEINBERG, DREAMS OF A FINAL THEORY: THE SEARCH FOR THE FUNDAMENTAL LAWS OF NATURE (1992).

underlying scientific expert testimony. This book offers an entry point to a host of scientific fields that are highly relevant to the law. It is not intended to provide simple "answers" or final "conclusions." Instead, it is designed and organized to acquaint aspiring lawyers with scientific fields that will be crucial to their practices.

This volume is part of a special student edition of a much larger work intended for a professional audience, our four volume treatise, MODERN SCIENTIFIC EVIDENCE: THE LAW AND SCIENCE OF EXPERT TESTIMONY (2d ed. 2002). There are three volumes in the student edition. The first volume, *Standards, Statistics and Research Issues*, concentrates on the background issues in both law and science that lie behind the sundry contexts in which experts are employed. The second volume, *Social and Behavioral Science Issues*, is organized around substantive topics in the social and behavioral sciences. The third volume, *Forensic Science Issues*, concentrates on an array of important forensic subjects. We hope that the three volumes will be of service either standing alone or as companions to regular texts in a variety of classes, ranging from social science in law to forensic science classes. More fundamentally, we hope that the process of educating lawyers and judges regarding the scientific method will begin in law school. If *Daubert* stands for the proposition that judges and lawyers must henceforth understand science well enough to integrate it successfully into the law, then the educational process that will allow this to occur must begin in law school.

The chapters follow one of two formats. Several chapters provide general overviews of the subject. Most chapters, however, are divided into two sections, one dedicated to the legal relevance of the particular field and the second concerned with the state of the art of the research in that field. The first section is authored by the editors and the second is authored by one or more eminent scientists. The sections on the state of the science are all written largely following a similar organizational scheme. We asked the contributors to discuss the scientific questions or hypotheses posited by the researchers, the methods brought to bear to study these hypotheses, the areas of scientific agreement, the areas of scientific disagreement, and the likely future directions for scientific research in the area. Some scientific topics lend themselves to this scheme better than others. Nonetheless, our guiding objective was to make the science accessible to the non-scientifically trained generalist.

Daubert, perhaps, represents nothing more, *or less,* than that the legal culture must assimilate the scientific culture. As compared to the sciences, the law obviously has different objectives, values, and time tables in which to work. The law should not, nor could it, adopt the scientific perspective wholly and without qualifications. Science is merely a tool that the law can and must use to achieve its own objectives. Science cannot dictate what is fair and just. We can confidently conclude, however, that science has become, and will forever more be, a tool upon which the law must sometimes rely to do justice.

David L. Faigman
David H. Kaye
Michael J. Saks
Joseph Sanders

February, 2002.

*

Acknowledgments

At the conclusion of THE ADVENTURES OF HUCKLEBERRY FINN, Huck states, ". . . and so there ain't nothing more to write about, and I am rotten glad of it, because if I'd a knowed what a trouble it was to make a book I wouldn't a tackled it and ain't agoing to no more."[1] We, perhaps, suffer Huck's lament more than he, for he never knew the pain of periodic supplements, as are planned for these volumes. However, we have had the immeasurable assistance of a score of colleagues and students who have made our task less trouble. We wish to thank all of the people who contributed so much to both the first and second editions.

At the University of California, Hastings College of the Law, we wish to thank our colleagues Mary Kay Kane, William Schwarzer, Roger Park, and Eileen Scallen for their support, encouragement and comments on various parts of this book. In addition, much is owed the student research assistants who spent innumerable hours on the project, including Tamara Costa, Kathryn Davis, Jamie Tenero, Paula Quintiliani, Amy Wright, Ali Graham, Cliff Hong, Lucia Sciaraffa, Faith Wolinsky and Sara Zalkin. Finally, we owe a considerable debt to Ted Jang and, especially, Barbara Topchov for secretarial support.

At Arizona State University, College of Law, we thank Gail Geer, Sonja Quinones and Rosalind Pearlman for secretarial support and Vivian Chang and James Pack for research assistance.

At the University of Iowa, College of Law, we thank research assistants "Max" Wilkinson, Alec Hillbo, and Patricia Fowler.

At the University of Houston Law Center, we wish to thank the students in the Spring 1996 Scientific Evidence seminar who did much in assisting on the toxic tort sections of the of the first edition: Angela Beavers, Chris Blanton, Armi Easterby, Nellie Fisher, Stephanie Hall, Jim Hildebrandt, Lynn Huston, Preston Hutson, Dino Ioannides, Candice Kaiser, Bill Long, Helen O'Conor, Ruth Piller, Larry Pinsky, John Powell, Jane Starnes, Donna Woodruff, and Kirk Worley. On the second edition, we extend our grateful appreciation to the research assistance of William Campbell, Mary Chapman, Alison Chein, Cynthia DeLaughter, Linda Garza, Linda Glover, Jamie Liner, Laura Moore, Jason Pinkall, Scott Provinse, Amanda Snowden and Angela Williams. Special thanks goes to Bethany Fitch who helped to cite check and proof read the manuscript.

Outside of our respective home institutions, we have had the generous assistance of many colleagues and institutions. At the Federal Judicial Center, we wish to thank Joe Cecil for his support and encouragement of this project. We are also indebted to Bert Black, for both his assistance in identifying authors and his generous sharing of ideas on a variety of topics.

*

---

[1] MARK TWAIN, ADVENTURES OF HUCKLEBERRY FINN 363 (Random House 1996).

List of Contributors

Edith D. Balbach is a postdoctoral fellow at the Institute for Health Policy Studies, University of California at San Francisco, where she studies issues related to youth and tobacco.

Alfred A. Biasotti (1926–1997), M.S. in Criminalistics, U.C. Berkeley, was a criminalist, supervising criminalist, and administrator from 1951 to 1990, retiring as Assistant Chief of the Bureau of Forensic Sciences, California Department of Justice. He helped establish the California Criminalistics Institute; authored numerous articles on firearms and toolmark identification; was a Fellow of the American Academy of Forensic Sciences; and a distinguished member of the Association of Firearm and Toolmark Examiners. He passed away on June 24, 1997, from complications associated with Parkinson's Disease.

Stuart Bondurant received his B.S. in Medicine and his M.D. from Duke University. He interned and completed his residency in Internal Medicine at Duke University Medical Center and the Peter Bent Brigham Hospital in Boston. He served in the United States Air Force as a research internist and chief medical officer in the Acceleration Section of the Aeromedical Laboratory at Wright–Patterson Air Force Base. Dr. Bondurant was a member of the faculty of the School of Medicine at Indiana University Medical Center and was Chief of the Medical Branch of the Artificial Heart–Myocardial Infarction Program at the National Heart Institute. Dr. Bondurant was also Professor and Chair of the Department of Medicine prior to serving as President and Dean of Albany Medical College in Albany, New York. In 1979 he became Professor of Medicine and Dean of the School of Medicine of the University of North Carolina at Chapel Hill. In July 1994 he retired as Dean and on leave of absence from UNC-CH served as Director of the Center for Urban Epidemiologic Studies of the New York Academy of Medicine. He is currently Professor of Medicine and Dean Emeritus at the School of Medicine of the University of North Carolina at Chapel Hill. During his career, Dr. Bondurant has served as an officer of many organizations and societies including President of the American College of Physicians, the Association of American Physicians, and the American Clinical and Climatological Association, Acting President of the Institute of Medicine of the National Academy of Sciences, Vice President of the American Heart Association and of the American Society for Clinical Investigation, Chairman of the Board of the North Carolina Biotechnology Center, Chair of the Council of Deans of the Association of American Medical Colleges, and Chair of the Association of American Medical Colleges. From 1989 to 1995 he served as Chair of the North Carolina Governors Commission on the Reduction of Infant Mortality.

Dr. Bondurant has also served as advisor to the National Institutes of Health, the Veterans Administration, the Department of Defense, and the Department of Health and Human Services. He is a Master of the American College of Physicians, and a Fellow of the Royal College of Physicians of Edinburgh and of the Royal College of Physicians of London. He holds an Honorary Doctor of Science Degree from Indiana University, the Citizen Laureate Award of the Albany (New York) Foundation, and the 1998 Thomas Jefferson Award of the Faculty of the University of North Carolina. He received the David P. Rall Award of the Institute of Medicine of the National Academy of Sciences in 2000.

Eugene Borgida, Ph.D. is Professor of Psychology and Law at the University of Minnesota, Twin Cities. He is also a Morse–Alumni Distinguished Teaching Professor of Psychology. In addition, Borgida is Adjunct Professor of Political Science and serves as Co–Director of the University's Center for the Study of Political Psychology. He has served as Associate Dean of the College of Liberal Arts and as chair of the Psychology Department. Borgida is a Fellow of the APA and APS, and on the Board of Directors for APS and the Social Science Research Council. He has published on a variety of research issues in psychology and law and in social psychology, and his work has been funded by NIMH, NIH, and NSF.

C. Michael Bowers practices dentistry and law in Ventura, CA. He has been a Deputy Medical Examiner for the Ventura County Coroner's Office since 1988. He is a diplomate of the American Board of Forensic Odontology.

Robert M. Bray is the director of the Substance Abuse Epidemiology, Prevention, and Risk Assessment Program at Research Triangle Institute in Research Triangle Park, North Carolina, where he has been since 1980. Previously, he was a faculty member at the University of Kentucky. He holds B.S. and M.S. degrees in psychology from Brigham Young University and a Ph.D. in social psychology from the University of Illinois, Urbana–Champaign. He is a member of the American Psychological Association and the American Public Health Association. He served on the Committee on Drug Use in the Workplace for the National Research Council, Institute of Medicine. His recent work has focused on substance use epidemiology and related problems in military and civilian populations. He has directed the 1982, 1985, 1988, 1992, 1995, and 1998 Worldwide Surveys of Substance Use and Health Behaviors Among Military Personnel and is currently conducting the 2001 survey in the series. He also was coordinator of analytic reports for the 1988 and 1990 National Household Surveys on Drug Abuse (NHSDAs) and is currently directing the National Analytic Center, a project focused on analyzing data from the NHSDA and other substance abuse datasets. Dr. Bray directed the Washington, DC, Metropolitan Area Drug Study (DC*MADS), a 6-year comprehensive project of the prevalence, correlates, and consequences of drug abuse in household and nonhousehold populations (including people who are homeless or institutionalized, adult and juvenile offenders, clients entering treatment programs, and new mothers). He is the principal editor of a book, published by Sage Publications, based on findings from DC*MADS and titled DRUG USE IN METROPOLITAN AMERICA. Dr. Bray is co-editor of THE PSYCHOLOGY OF THE COURTROOM.

Diana Burgess, Ph.D. is a senior research associate in Strategic Growth Initiatives in the Consumer Insights division of General Mills. She has conducted research on sexual harassment, gender stereotyping and political participation. Currently, she is conducting organizational research on knowledge sharing and knowledge seeking within General Mills. She also is conducting pro bono research for the National Campaign to Prevent Teen Pregnancy.

Stephen J. Ceci, Ph.D., holds a lifetime endowed chair in developmental psychology at Cornell University. He studies the accuracy of children's court-room testimony, and is the author of over 300 articles, books, and chapters. Ceci's honors include a Senior Fulbright–Hayes fellowship and a Research Career Scientist Award. In 1993 Ceci was named a Master Lecturer of the American Psychological Association. He is currently a member of seven editorial boards and a fellow of six divisions of the APA, and of the American Association of Applied and Preventive Psychology, British Psychological Society, and American Psychological Society. His book (co-written with Maggie Bruck) JEOPARDY IN THE COURTROOM: A SCIENTIFIC ANALYSIS OF CHILDREN'S TESTIMONY (1995) is an American Psychological Association bestseller and winner of the William James Book Award by APA. He is a senior scientific advisor to the Canadian Institute for Advanced Research. Ceci is a member of the National Academy of Sciences Committee on Behavioral, Cognitive, and Sensory Sciences, and a member of the American Psychological Society's Board of Directors. He is past president of Division 1 (General Psychology) of APA. In 2000 Ceci received the Lifetime Distinguished Contribution Award from the American Academy of Forensic Psychology.

Michael R. Chial is Professor of Audiology in the Department of Communicative Disorders at the University of Wisconsin–Madison. His doctorate is from the University of Wisconsin–Madison. For 20 years he has worked with the American National Standards Institute and is currently working with the Audio Engineering Society to develop technical standards for forensic applications of audio recordings. He is past associate editor of the JOURNAL OF SPEECH AND HEARING RESEARCH, and Fellow of the American Speech–Language–Hearing Association and the American Academy of Audiology.

Dennis J. Crouch is the interim director at the Center for Human Toxicology, University of Utah, where he has been employed since 1977. He is also a research assistant professor at the University of Utah's College of Pharmacy, Department of Pharmacology and Toxicology. He received a B.S. degree from Western Illinois University, Macomb, Illinois, in 1971; received graduate training at the University of Utah, 1980–1981 in biochemistry and pharmacology; and received a M.B.A. degree from Utah State University, Logan, Utah in 1989. From May 1990 through November 1991, he was at the National Institute on Drug Abuse. He was responsible for administrative aspects of the National Laboratory Certification Program for forensic laboratories and research on the impact of occupational drug testing on drug use patterns, transportation safety, and business. He is a member of the California Association of Toxicologists, Society of Forensic Toxicologists, and the International Association of Forensic Toxicologists, as well as a fellow of the American Academy of Forensic Sciences. Mr. Crouch has published over 50 peer-reviewed scientific articles on therapeutic drug monitoring, analytical toxicology, forensic toxicology, drugs and driving, and workplace drug testing. Current research interests include alcohol and other drug use in transportation safety, evaluating the impact of workplace testing programs on businesses, monitoring of laboratories performing workplace testing, GC/MS, LC/MS, and MS/MS analyses of drugs of abuse.

Russellyn S. Carruth is an Adjunct Professor of Law at the University of Pittsburgh School of Law, where she teaches in the environmental law clinic.

She practiced law with the firm of Burr, Pease & Kurtz in Anchorage, Alaska from 1974–1995. Her practice included toxic torts litigation, which involved issues of admissibility of scientific evidence. Since retiring from private practice, she has taught environmental law at the University of Medicine and Dentistry of New Jersey, School of Public Health, where she is an Adjunct Assistant Professor. She has written and spoken on legal/scientific issues, including the admissibility of scientific evidence in litigation. She serves on the Board of the Society of Risk Analysis Section on Risk Law. She received her B.A. degree from University of California at Berkeley in 1966 and J.D. from University of California at Davis in 1974.

Shari Diamond, a social psychologist and attorney, is a Professor of Law and Psychology at the Northwestern University School of Law and a Senior Research Fellow at the American Bar Foundation. She has practiced intellectual property law at Sidley & Austin. She was a member of the Panel on Evaluation of DNA Forensic Evidence and the Panel on Sentencing Research for the National Academy of Sciences. Professor Diamond was President of the American Psychological Association's Division of Psychology and Law, received the APA's Distinguished Contributions to Research in Public Policy Award, and was Editor of the LAW & SOCIETY REVIEW.

Patricia L. Dill completed her Master of Science degree in Social Psychology at Mississippi State University in 1997 and currently is a doctoral student in Health Psychology at University of Missouri–Kansas City. She also is currently a Health Communication Intern at the National Cancer Institute. Her research interests include prevention and intervention of alcohol use (particularly DUI offenders) and tobacco use, treatment of obesity, and health behavior, with a focus on community and public health interventions.

John P. Foreyt, Ph.D., received his Ph.D. in clinical psychology in 1969 from Florida State University and completed his clinical internship at the University of Southern California Medical School. He served on the faculty at Florida State University until 1974 when he moved to Baylor College of Medicine, Houston, Texas. He is currently Professor there in the Department of Medicine and Department of Psychiatry. He is the Director of the DeBakey Heart Center's Behavioral Medicine Research Center, Department of Medicine. He is a member of the Medical Scientist Staff, Internal Medicine Service, The Methodist Hospital, Houston, Texas. Dr. Foreyt is a Fellow of the Society of Behavioral Medicine, a Fellow of the Behavioral Therapy and Research Society, and a Fellow of the Academy of Behavioral Medicine Research and other professional organizations. He also is an honorary member of the American Dietetic Association. Dr. Foreyt is currently a member of the editorial boards of: *Eating Disorders, Obesity Research, Journal of Cardiopulmonary Rehabilitation, American Journal of Health Promotion, Journal of Behavioral Medicine, American Journal of Health Promotion*, and *Diabetes, Obesity and Metabolism*. Dr. Foreyt has published extensively in the areas of diet modification, cardiovascular risk reduction, eating disorders, and obesity. He has published 15 books and more than 230 articles in these areas.

Patricia Frazier received her Ph.D. in Social Psychology and Counseling Psychology in 1988 from the University of Minnesota. She currently is an Associate Professor in the Counseling Psychology and Social Psychology programs at the University of Minnesota. Dr. Frazier is past Associate Editor of LAW AND HUMAN BEHAVIOR and past chair of the Courtwatch Committee of the Society for the Psychological Study of Social Issues. Her research interests include sexual victimization and the interface between psychology and the law, particularly the use of expert testimony in rape trials.

David A. Freedman is Professor of Statistics, University of California, Berkeley, California. He is the author of many works on probability theory and statistics, including a widely used elementary textbook. He is a member of the American Academy of Arts and Sciences.

Gary L. French is Senior Vice President and Director of Litigation and Regulation Practice with Nathan Associates Inc., Arlington, Virginia. He earned his Ph.D. in economics from the University of Houston and then taught economics, finance, and statistics as a member of the faculties at three universities.

James C. Garriott is a toxicology consultant in San Antonio, Texas. He holds a Ph.D. in Toxicology and Pharmacology, and is a diplomat of the American Board of Forensic Toxicology, Inc. He served as the chief toxicologist for Dallas County, Texas from 1970 to 1982, and then held the same position at Bexar County, Texas until retiring in 1997. He was also professor at the University of Texas Health Science Centers of Dallas and San Antonio. Dr. Garriott is the author of over 100 articles and book chapters in the toxicology literature, as well as co-author and editor of two toxicology reference books and is on the editorial review board of four toxicology and forensic journals. He is recognized for his knowledge and expertise in the forensic toxicology of ethyl alcohol, and he edited the text Medicolegal Aspects of Alcohol, now in its third edition. Dr. Garriott was the 1993 recipient of the Alexander O. Gettler award for outstanding achievements in analytical toxicology by the American Academy of Forensic Sciences.

David W. Gjertson, Ph.D., is Associate Professor of Biostatistics and Pathology, UCLA, and chair of the Parentage Testing Unit of the Standards Program Committee of the American Association of Blood Banks.

Stanton A. Glantz, a professor of medicine at the University of California at San Francisco and a member of the Institute faculty. He also served as a consultant to OSHA.

Bernard D. Goldstein is the Dean of the University of Pittsburgh's Graduate School of Public Health. He served as the Director of the Environmental and Occupational Health Sciences Institute, a joint program of Rutgers, The State University of New Jersey and the University of Medicine and Dentistry of New Jersey (UMDNJ)–Robert Wood Johnson Medical School from 1986–2001. He was the Chair of the Department of Environmental and Community Medicine, UMDNJ–Robert Wood Johnson Medical School from 1980–2001. He was the first Principal Investigator of the Consortium of Risk Evaluation with Stakeholder Participation (CRESP). Dr. Goldstein earned his B.S. degree at the University of Wisconsin in 1958 and his M.D. degree at New York University School of Medicine in 1962. He is a physician, board certified in Internal Medicine and Hematology; board certified in Toxicology. Dr. Goldstein's past activities include Member and Chairman of the NIH Toxicology Study Section and EPA's Clean Air Scientific Advisory Committee; Chair of the Institute of Medicine Committee on the Role of the Physician in Occupational and Environmental Medicine, the National Research Council Committees on Biomarkers in Environmental Health Research and Risk Assessment Methodology and the Industry Panel of the World Health Organization Commission on Health and Environment. He is a Member of the Institute of Medicine where he has chaired the Section on Public Health, Biostatistics, and Epidemiology and he has been a Member of the Institute of Medicine Committee on Environmental Justice: Research, Education, and Health Policy Needs. He is the author of over two hundred articles and book chapters related to environmental health sciences and to public policy.

Grant Harris is a Research Psychologist at the Mental Health Centre, Penetanguishene, Ontario, Canada. He is also an adjunct Associate Professor of Psychology at Queen's University, Kingston. He obtained a B.Sc. from the University of Toronto, and his Ph.D. in Experimental Psychology from McMaster University. He first worked at the Penetanguishene Mental Health Centre in 1974 and rejoined the staff in 1980. He was, for several years, responsible for the development and supervision of behavioral programs on maximum security units for dangerous and assaultive men. Since joining the Research Department in 1988, he has been awarded several research grants and has conducted extensive scientific research on violent and criminal behavior, psychopathy, and sexual aggression and deviance. He is (together with Vernon Quinsey, Marnie Rice and Catherine Cormier) an author of the recent book, *Violent Offenders: Appraising and Managing Risk* published by the American Psychological Association. In 1997, with colleagues from MHCP's Research Department, Dr. Harris received the Amethyst Award for Outstanding Achievement in the Ontario Public Service.

Patricia A. Hastings, Ph.D., York University, is currently on staff at DecisonQuest in Washington, D.C.

Kirk Heilbrun is Professor and Chair, Department of Clinical and Health Psychology, MCP Hahnemann University, and Lecturer in Law, Villanova Law School. He received his A.B. from Brown University in 1975 and his Ph.D. from the University of Texas at Austin in 1980. He is past-president of both the American Psychology–Law Society and the American Board of Forensic Psychology. He is the author of PRINCIPLES OF FORENSIC MENTAL HEALTH ASSESSMENT (forthcoming, Klumer/Plenum) as well as a number of articles in related areas.

Roger C. Herdman, born in Boston, MA, September 22, 1933; Phillips Exeter Academy, 1951; Yale University, Magna Cum Laude, Phi Beta Kappa, BS, 1955; Yale University School of Medicine, MD, 1958. Interned at the University of Minnesota. Medical Officer, US Navy, 1959–1961. Thereafter, completed a residency in pediatrics and continued with a medical fellowship in immunology/nephrology at Minnesota. Held positions of Assistant Professor and Professor of Pediatrics at the University of Minnesota and the Albany Medical College between 1966–1979. In 1969, appointed Director of the New York State Kidney Disease Institute in Albany. During 1969–1977 served as Deputy Commissioner of the New York State Department of Health responsible for research, departmental health care facilities and the Medicaid program at various times. In 1977, named New York State's Director of Public Health. From 1979 until joining the US Congress's Office of Technology Assessment (OTA) was a Vice President of the Memorial Sloan–Kettering Cancer Center in New York City. In 1983, named Assistant Director of OTA and then Acting Director and Director from January 1993–February 1996. After the closure of OTA, joined the National Academy of Sciences' Institute of Medicine as a Senior Scholar, directed studies on a national trust fund for graduate medical education, medical and ethical issues in organ transplantation, the safety of silicone breast implants, and the VA National Formulary. After completing those studies was appointed Director of the IOM's National Cancer Policy Board in August 2000. He also works on Institute relations with the U.S. Congress and chairs the National Academies' Institutional Review Board.

Charles R. Honts is the Department Head and a Professor of Psychology at Boise State University and Editor of The Journal of Credibility Assessment and Witness Psychology. He is the recipient of grants from the U.S. Office of Naval Research and from the Royal Canadian Mounted Police to conduct research on the psychophysiological detection of deception. He is a Forensic Psychological Consultant to numerous public agencies in the United States in Canada. He has been a licensed polygraph examiner for 25 years.

Herbert Hovenkamp is the Ben V. & Dorothy Willie Professor of Law at the University of Iowa. He is the author of Federal Antitrust Policy: the Law of Competition and its Practice (1994), co-author of Antitrust Law (rev. ed.1995–1999), and many other works on anti-trust law, the law of property, legal history, and the history of law and science and law and economics.

James I. Hudson, M.D. is an Associate Professor of Psychiatry at Harvard Medical School and an Associate Psychiatrist at McLean Hospital, Belmont, Massachusetts. He is an author of more than 150 articles in the areas of eating disorders, fibromyalgia, psychopharmacology, the neurophysiology of sleep, and the issues of trauma and memory. He is currently engaged in studies of the genetic epidemiology of affective spectrum disorder, and of new medications for mood, anxiety and eating disorders.

Jennifer S. Hunt, Ph.D. is an Assistant Professor of Psychology at the University of Nebraska–Lincoln. Her research investigates the ways that pre-existing expectations, including stereotypes, influence people's thoughts and behavior. Her current work is examining the effects of stereotypes on health judgments, as well as the influence of individuating information on stereotype activation. In addition, she is investigating how cultural variations in beliefs about the justice system affect legal participation.

Melissa L. Hyder is currently a doctoral student in the Interdisciplinary Ph.D. program in Clinical Health Psychology at the University of Missouri–Kansas City. She received her B.A. in Psychology from Rockhurst University in 1999. Her research interests include physical activity, sports medicine, and childrens' obesity and nutrition.

William G. Iacono, is Distinguished McKnight University Professor, Professor of Psychology, University of Minnesota, Director, Clinical Science and

Psychopathology Research Training Program, recipient of the American Psychological Association's Distinguished Scientific Award for an Early Career Contribution to Psychology, the Society for Psychophysiological Research's Distinguished Scientific Award for an Early Career Contribution to Psychophysiology, Past–President of the Society for Psychophysiological Research (1996–97) and former Member, Department of Defense Polygraph Institute's Curriculum and Research Guidance Committee.

Kristina Kelly is a doctoral candidate at the University of Minnesota, Twin Cities. Her research interests include the psychology of gender and the study of health judgment and decision-making. She is currently investigating how social and cultural factors affect women's behaviors and cognitions, and in particular, how these factors influence the ways that women explain their own behavior in health and non-health domains.

Raymond D. Kent is Professor of Speech Science in the Department of Communicative Disorders, University of Wisconsin–Madison. His doctorate is from University of Iowa and he did postdoctoral work in speech analysis and synthesis at the Massachusetts Institute of Technology. He has edited or written eleven books, including THE ACOUSTICAL ANALYSIS OF SPEECH (with Charles Read, 1992), and is past editor of the JOURNAL OF SPEECH AND HEARING RESEARCH. He holds an honorary doctorate from the University of Montreal Faculty of Medicine, is a Fellow of the Acoustical Society of America, the International Society of Phonetic Sciences, and the American Speech–Language–Hearing Association, and has earned Honors of the American Speech–Language–Hearing Association.

John C. Kircher is an Associate Professor of Educational Psychology, University of Utah. He specializes in the use of computer, psychometric, and decision theoretic methods for assessing truth and deception from physiological recordings. He pioneered the development of the first computerized polygraph system and has collaborated with David C. Raskin and Charles R. Honts since 1977 on research and development of methods for the physiological detection of deception.

John J. Lentini is a fire investigator and chemist who manages the fire investigation division of Applied Technical Services of Marietta, Georgia. He is a fellow of the American Academy of Forensic Sciences and the American Board of Criminalistics, holds certificates from the National Association of Fire Investigators and the International Association of Arson Investigators. He chairs the ASTM Committee Responsible for developing forensic science standards, and is a principal member of the National Fire Protection Association's Technical Committee on Fire Investigations. Mr. Lentini has investigated more than 1500 fires, and analyzed more than 20,000 samples of fire debris.

Paul S. Lowengrub is a consulting economist and financial expert with Nathan Associates, Arlington, Virginia. He earned his Ph.D. in economics and finance from Arizona State University, and taught economic and finance courses for a year at The American Graduate School of International Management.

David T. Lykken is Professor of Psychology, University of Minnesota, author of A TREMOR IN THE BLOOD: USES AND ABUSES OF THE LIE DETECTOR, (2d ed. 1998), recipient of the American Psychological Association's Award for a *Distinguished Contribution to Psychology in the Public Interest* (1991) and for *Distinguished Scientific Contributions for Applications of Psychology* (2001), Past-President of the Society for Psychophysiological Research (1980–81), and recipient of that Society's *Award for Distinguished Scientific Contributions to Psychophysiology* (1998).

John Monahan, a clinical psychologist, holds the Doherty Chair in law at the University of Virginia, where he is also a Professor of Psychology and of Legal Medicine. He has been a Guggenheim Fellow, a Fellow at Harvard Law School and at the Center for Advanced Study in the Behavioral Sciences, and a Visiting Fellow at All Souls College, Oxford. He was the founding President of the American Psychological Association's Division of Psychology and Law and received an honorary doctorate in law from the City University of New York. Monahan has won the Isaac Ray Award of the American Psychiatric Association, has been elected to membership in the Institute of Medicine of the National Academy of Sciences, has been appointed to the Committee on Law and Justice of the National Research Council, and has directed the MacArthur Research Network on Mental Health and the Law. His work has been cited frequently by courts, including the California Supreme Court in *Tarasoff v. Regents* and the United States Supreme Court in *Barefoot v. Estelle*, in which he was referred to as "the leading thinker on the issue" of violence risk assessment.

Jeffrey W. Morris, M.D., Ph.D., is the former Director, Long Beach Genetics and Clinical Associate Professor of Pathology, University of California, Irvine. He serves as a member of the Parentage Testing Ancillary Committee, College of American Pathologists and is a past Chairman, Committee on Parentage Testing of the American Association of Blood Banks.

John E. Murdock, M.C. in Criminalistics, U.C. Berkeley, is a Senior Firearms and Toolmark Examiner with the Bureau of Alcohol, Tobacco, and Firearms, San Francisco Laboratory Center. Author of a number of articles on firearms and toolmark examination, he is past president of the California Association of Criminalists, an emeritus member of the American Society of Crime Laboratory Directors, and a distinguished member of the Association of Firearm and Toolmark Examiners.

Robert Nadon, Ph.D., is Associate Professor of Psychology at Brock University in St. Catharines, Ontario, Canada. Actively engaged in both research and teaching, Dr. Nadon has published extensively on hypnosis, with particular interest in personality and methodological issues. He is a Fellow of the Society for Clinical and Experimental Hypnosis, a past Research Fellow of the Canadian Social Sciences and Humanities Research Council, an Advisory Editor for the INTERNATIONAL JOURNAL OF CLINICAL AND EXPERIMENTAL HYPNOSIS, and a Consultant Editor, for CONTEMPORARY HYPNOSIS.

Michael Nash, Ph.D., is Associate Professor at the University of Tennessee and is actively engaged in clinical training, research, and teaching. He is Editor in Chief of the INTERNATIONAL JOURNAL OF CLINICAL AND EXPERIMENTAL HYPNOSIS, Past President of Division 30 of the American Psychological Association, Fellow of both the Society for Clinical and Experimental Hypnosis and the

American Psychological Association, and is a Diplomate of the American Board of Professional Psychology. Dr. Nash has published extensively on the effects of sexual abuse, short-term psychotherapy, and hypnosis. Dr. Nash is Co–Editor with Dr. Fromm of the classic text on experimental hypnosis, Contemporary Hypnosis Research, and his research and writing have earned him numerous awards.

Paul Oliva, B.A., M.A. is a former senior clinical research technician in the Biological Psychiatry Laboratory at McLean Hospital, Belmont, Massachusetts.

Joseph L. Peterson, D.Crim., is Professor of Criminal Justice at the University of Illinois at Chicago. His research has tracked the evolution of the forensic sciences over the past thirty years, focusing on the quality of results emanating from crime laboratories, ethical dilemmas facing scientists, and the impact of science on legal decision making. Previously, he served as Executive Director of the Forensic Sciences Foundation and directed the criminal justice research center at John Jay College of Criminal Justice in New York.

Henry Petroski, Ph.D., P.E., is Aleksandar S. Vesic Professor of Civil Engineering and Professor of History, Duke University, Durham, North Carolina.

Harrison G. Pope, Jr., M.D. is a Professor of Psychiatry at Harvard Medical School and Chief of the Biological Psychiatry Laboratory at the McLean Hospital Alcohol and Drug Abuse Research Center in Belmont, Massachusetts. He is an author of more than 300 published papers on a range of topics in psychiatry, including eating disorders, mood disorders, psychiatric diagnosis, substance abuse, psychopharmacology, and the current debate about trauma and memory. Dr. Pope currently devotes most of his time to research and teaching.

Walker S. Carlos Poston II, M.P.H., Ph.D. received his Ph.D. from the University of California-Santa Barbara and an M.P.H. from the University of Texas Houston Health Sciences Center. He is Co–Director of Behavioral Cardiology Research at the Mid America Heart Institute and Assistant Professor in the Clinical Health Psychology Interdisciplinary Ph.D. program at the University of Missouri–Kansas City. His research focuses on understanding genetic and environmental contributions to cardiovascular disease and obesity, particularly in minority populations. Dr. Poston has been the principal or co-investigator on several funded studies examining health outcomes in obesity treatment and the epidemiology of hypertension and obesity in African Americans. He has published nearly 80 articles and book chapters focusing on obesity and cardiovascular disease and has presented his work in national and international scientific forums. Dr. Poston is a fellow of the North American Association for the Study of Obesity and a member of the American Heart Association's Council on Epidemiology and Prevention and the Society of Behavioral Medicine.

Martine Powell, Ph.D. is a Senior Lecturer in the School of Psychology, Deakin University, Melbourne Australia. She has been conducting research in the area of child eyewitness memory, as well as training programs in investigative interviewing, for the past ten years. She has also trained and worked as a clinical psychologist, specializing in the treatment of child abuse and neglect.

Norman Poythress is a Professor in the Department of Mental Health Law & Policy, Florida Mental Health Institute, University of South Florida. He received his A.B. from Indiana University in 1969 and his Ph.D. from the University of Texas at Austin in 1977. He is past-president of the American Psychology–Law Society (Division 41 of the American Psychological Association). In 1990, he received the American Academy of Forensic Psychology's Award for Distinguished Contributions to Forensic Psychology. He is a coauthor of PSYCHOLOGICAL EVALUATIONS FOR THE COURTS: A HANDBOOK FOR MENTAL HEALTH PROFESSIONALS AND LAWYERS, as well as numerous articles on the interaction of mental illness and the criminal justice system.

Gabrielle F. Principe is a National Institute of Mental Health Postdoctoral Fellow at Cornell University. She was educated at Temple University and the University of North Carolina at Chapel Hill, where she received her doctorate in developmental psychology. Her research examines factors affecting the accuracy and retention of young children's memories for salient personal experiences.

David C. Raskin is Professor Emeritus, University of Utah and Editor of Psychological Methods in Criminal Investigation and Evidence and Co–Editor of Electrodermal Activity in Psychological Research. He has been the recipient of numerous grants and contracts from the National Institute of Justice, U.S. Department of Defense, U.S. Secret Service, and U.S. Army Research and Development Command to conduct research and development on psychophysiological detection of deception. He was the Co–Developer of the first computerized polygraph system. He was Past President Rocky Mountain Psychological Association and is an Elected Fellow in the American Psychological Association, American Psychological Society, American Association for Applied and Preventive Psychology. He has served as a Forensic Psychological Consultant to numerous federal and local agencies and legislative bodies in the United States, Canada, Israel, United Kingdom, and Norway. He has been a licensed polygraph examiner for 27 years.

Marnie Rice is Director of Research of the Mental Health Centre, Penetanguishene, Ontario, Canada. She is Professor of Psychiatry and Behavioural Neurosciences at McMaster University, Associate Professor of Psychology at Queen's University, and Scientific Director of the Centre for the Study of Aggression and Mental Disorder. She has been awarded several research grants and has over eighty publications including three coauthored books on the topics of violent and criminal behavior, sex offenders, psychopaths and arson. Dr. Rice obtained her honours B.A. in Psychology from McMaster University; a Master's Degree from the University of Toronto; and a Ph.D. in Clinical Psychology from York University. She was the 1995 recipient of the American Psychological Association's award for Distinguished Contribution to Research in Public Policy, and the 1997 recipient of a Government of Ontario Amethyst Award for Outstanding Contribution by an Ontario Public Servant.

D. Michael Risinger is a Professor of Law at Seton Hall University School of Law; B.A. Magna Cum Laude, Yale University, 1966, J.D. Cum Laude, Harvard Law School, 1969.

Victor L. Roggli received a B.A. degree in Biochemistry and Environmental Engineering from Rice University in Houston Texas in 1973, and doctor of medicine degree from Baylor College of Medicine in 1976. He completed residency training in pathology at Baylor Affiliated Hospitals in 1980, and is board certified in Anatomic and Clinical Pathology. Dr. Roggli has published more than 120 articles in peer reviewed journals, approximately half of which deal with asbestos or asbestos-related diseases. He has also published 21 chapters in textbooks and is the author/editor of three books, including Pathology of Asbestos–Associated Diseases.

Daniel L. Rubinfeld is Robert L. Bridges Professor of Law and Professor of Economics at the University of California, Berkeley. He has been a fellow of the National Bureau of Economic Research, the Center for the Advanced Study in the Behavioral Sciences, and the Simon Guggenheim Foundation.

Sara Rzepa is a graduate student in the Psychology Department at York University in Toronto, Ontario, Canada. Her research interests include jury decision making and she is currently involved in research on jury decision making in trials involving battered women who have killed their abusers.

Regina A. Schuller, Ph.D. is Associate Professor of Psychology at York University in Toronto, Ontario, Canada. She is actively engaged in both research and teaching and in 1995 received York's President's Prize for Promising Scholars. Her research interests focus on the impact of social science framework testimony, in particular, expert testimony pertaining to battered women and on juror/jury decision processes. She also serves on the editorial board of LAW & HUMAN BEHAVIOR AND PSYCHOLOGY, PUBLIC POLICY, AND LAW.

George F. Sensabaugh, Jr., is Professor, School of Public Health, University of California at Berkeley. He was a member of the National Academy of Sciences' Committee on DNA Technology in Forensic Science and its subsequent Committee on DNA Forensic Science: An Update.

Christopher Slobogin is Stephen C. O'Connell Professor of Law at the University of Florida Levin College of Law, an affiliate professor with the Department of Psychiatry at the University of Florida, and an adjunct professor at the Florida Mental Health Institute, a department of the University of South Florida. Professor Slobogin received an A.B. from Princeton University, and a J.D. and LL.M. from the University of Virginia. He has served as chair of the American Association of Law Schools Section on Mental Disability and Law, Reporter for the American Bar Association's Standards on Criminal Responsibility, editor or reviewer for Behavioral Science & the Law, Law & Human Behavior, the American Journal of Psychiatry, and Psychology, Public Policy & Law, and as the Director of the University of Virginia's Forensic Psychiatry Clinic. He has authored a casebook and a treatise on mental health law, as well as numerous articles in the area.

John L. Solow is Associate Professor of Economics at The University of Iowa, where he has been a member of the faculty for over twenty years. He received his B.A. in economics from Yale University, and his M.A. and Ph.D. in economics from Stanford University.

Tomika N. Stevens is currently an advanced student in the Law–Psychology Program at Villanova Law School and MCP Hahnemann University, where she is a candidate for Juris Doctorate (2003) and Doctor of Philosophy, Clinical Psychology (2004). She received her A.B. from Princeton University in 1997.

David A. Stoney has a Ph.D. in Forensic Science from the University of California, Berkeley, where he worked on the statistical modeling of fingerprint identifications. He worked for six years at the Institute of Forensic Sciences, Criminalistics Laboratory, in California before joining the faculty of the University of Illinois at Chicago. After serving as Director of Forensic Sciences for eight years he left to become Director of the McCrone Research Institute in Chicago, a not-for-profit corporation dedicated to teaching and research in microscopy and microscopic analysis.

John Thornton, D.Crim., is an Emeritus Professor of Forensic Science at the University of California at Berkeley. He worked in an operational crime laboratory for 15 years and taught at Berkeley for 24 years. He also has taught forensic science in Colombia, Israel, Mexico, India, and the People's Republic of China. He is a past president of the California Association of Criminalists and past chairman of the Criminalistics Section of the American Academy of Forensic Sciences.

Lawrence M. Tierney, Jr. is a professor of medicine at the University of California at San Francisco. He received his M.D. From the University of Maryland in 1967, and did his residency in internal medicine at Emory University and the University of California at San Francisco. After two years in the U.S. Navy, he joined the faculty at the latter institution, where he is Professor of Medicine. He served as director of the residency training program as well of the third and fourth year medical student clerkships, and is also Associate Chief of the Medical Service at the San Francisco Veterans Affairs Medical Center. He has won over twenty major teaching awards, and has been invited on five separate occasions to address the UCSF medical school's graduating class. He is the senior editor of Current Medical Diagnosis and Treatment, a textbook in its 42nd edition, and has published numerous articles in medical journals, his principal interests being clinical decision-making, medical education, and evidence-based medicine.

Daniel Wartenberg received a Ph.D. degree in Ecology and Evolution from the State University of New York at Stony Brook in 1984 and then was a Fellow in the Interdisciplinary Programs in Public Health at the Harvard School of Public Health. He joined the faculty of the Robert Wood Johnson Medical School of the University of Medicine and Dentistry of New Jersey (UMDNJ) in Piscataway, New Jersey in 1986 where he is currently Professor and Chair of the Doctoral Committee for the UMDNJ School of Public Health. He serves on the New Jersey Commission on Radiation Protection, is a member of the National Council on Radiation Protection and Measurement, and served on both the National Academy of Sciences Committee and the National Institute of Health's Working Group addressing the possible health effects of electric and magnetic fields. Dr. Wartenberg has investigated a variety of methodological issues related to the study of magnetic fields and cancer, and has conducted two meta-analyses of the magnetic field and childhood cancer studies. Currently, he is completing a study of children with unusually high magnetic field exposures that he has identified using geographic information system (GIS) technology. In addition to his work on magnetic fields, he also conducts research on risk assessment, the effects of exposure to toxic chemicals and the investigation of disease clusters.

Noel S. Weiss received an M.D. degree from Stanford University School of Medicine and an M.P.H. and Dr. P.H. from the Harvard School of Public Health. In 1973, after two years at the National Center for Health Statistics, he joined the faculties of the University of Washington School of Public Health and Community Medicine and the Fred Hutchinson Cancer Research Center. He served as Chairman of the Department of Epidemiology at the University of Washington from 1984–1993. While the majority of his research has been in the area of cancer (he was awarded an Outstanding Investigator grant from the National Cancer Institute for the period 1985–1999), he has maintained an interest in and written extensively on epidemiologic methods and clinical epidemiology.

Gary Wells is Professor of Psychology and Distinguished Professor of Liberal Arts and Sciences at Iowa State University, Ames, Iowa. His experiments and papers on eyewitness testimony have appeared in scientific psychology's premiere journals.

Summary of Contents

———

Table of Contents

*

Table of Cases

References are to section and note.

*

SCIENCE IN THE LAW
FORENSIC SCIENCE ISSUES

*

CHAPTER 1

THE GENERAL ASSUMPTIONS AND RATIONALE OF FORENSIC IDENTIFICATION

by

John I. Thornton* & Joseph L. Peterson**

Table of Sections

* John Thornton, D.Crim., is an Emeritus Professor of Forensic Science at the University of California at Berkeley. He worked in an operational crime laboratory for 15 years and taught at Berkeley for 24 years. He also has taught forensic science in Colombia, Israel, Mexico, India, and the People's Republic of China. He is a past president of the California Association of Criminalists and past chairman of the Criminalistics Section of the American Academy of Forensic Sciences.

** Joseph L. Peterson, D.Crim., is Professor of Criminal Justice at the University of Illinois at Chicago. His research has tracked the evolution of the forensic sciences over the past thirty years, focusing on the quality of results emanating from crime laboratories, ethical dilemmas facing scientists, and the impact of science on legal decision making. Previously, he served as Executive Director of the Forensic Sciences Foundation and directed the criminal justice research center at John Jay College of Criminal Justice in New York.

Westlaw Electronic Research

See Westlaw Electronic Research Guide preceding the Summary of Contents.

—————

§ 1–1.0 INTRODUCTION

The identification of items of physical evidence is a routine practice in any forensic laboratory. These identifications are not, however, made in a vacuum of the intellect. They are made in a conglomerate and frequently disheveled atmosphere of science, inference, knowledge, supposition, assumption, rationalization, and bias. In an ideal world, all forensic endeavors would be true palaces of clarity, constructed and imbued only with the purest scientific spirit and unsullied by less noble considerations. Alas, it is not to be. In short, forensic science is subject to the same real-world considerations as any other applied science. Being caught permanently in the crossfire of the adversary system has not made matters any better.

Most forensic examinations are conducted in government-funded laboratories, usually located within law enforcement agencies, and typically for the purpose of building a case for the prosecution. Police agencies investigate most crime scenes and recover the evidence that is submitted to the laboratory for analysis and interpretation. Laboratory resources are limited, however, and priorities dictate which evidence is examined and in what order. The laboratory procedures followed in examining evidence and the content of laboratory reports are determined by local practice and professional guidelines. Quite apart from these organizational factors, the properly trained forensic scientist attempts to remain independent from various pressures that may influence the scientist to bias results. The courts set standards for assessing the reliability and admissibility of scientific evidence. The evidence that is presented before the court may also be reviewed by defense counsel,

whose ability to interpret and possibly re-examine that evidence is severely limited by resources available to hire independent experts. Forensic examiners who deliver court testimony may engage opposing experts in their effort to explain to the court the significance of their examinations.

If forensic science is to maintain a high quality ethic in the conduct of its affairs, the processes by means of which forensic identifications are effected must be understood and controlled. This applies to those processes that are noble as well as those that are less so. The assumptions and rationale of forensic identifications are of critical importance in bringing coherence to this important subject.

Forensic science is, in many ways, an untidy, scruffy sort of discipline. In an anthropomorphic sense, it has dirty fingernails and hair growing out of its ears. Those using forensic science have had trouble in deciding what they want from it, and those practicing it have had trouble deciding what they will allow themselves to become. In any discussion of forensic science, it is inevitable that when focusing on one aspect, another aspect will, amoeba-like, bulge out somewhere else. Forensic science is not a subject that lends itself well to orderly analysis, and anyone who attempts to confine in a close space the general assumptions and the rationales of the forensic sciences is certain to be a very busy shepherd.

This situation arises because physical evidence is without scope or dimension. Physical evidence runs the gamut from the commonplace to the virtually unique, and the forensic scientist is expected to deal with it all. At one time or another, virtually anything can represent a form of physical evidence, from badger hairs to billiard balls, from bloodstains to bullets. This diversity in the form of physical evidence makes forensic science a necessarily messy, disheveled sort of thing. The forensic scientist has no control over what constitutes physical evidence—it is thrust upon him by the vagaries of life itself.[1]

Forensic science has historically been troubled by a serious deficiency in that a heterogeneous assemblage of technical procedures, a pastiche of sorts, however effective or virtuous they may be in their own right, has frequently been substituted for basic theory and principles. There are, nevertheless, certain features of forensic science that are common to all forensic examinations—common denominators that cut across the various disciplines that comprise the totality of the forensic sciences.

§ 1–1.0

1. The authors are forensic scientists, but only one sort of forensic scientist—they are criminalists. The reader of this work will understand that there are many other types of forensic scientists—forensic accountants, forensic linguists, forensic engineers, and experts in everything from pornography to potholes.

The present writers do not presume to understand or even appreciate all of the issues that pertain to every facet of what we broadly call "forensic science." The comments here center around physical evidence in connection with criminal matters, because that is what the author understands best.

§ 1–1.1 What Makes Something "Forensic?"

An analysis of the term forensic science will help us understand what is meant by the term. "Forensic" comes to us from the Latin *forensus*, meaning "of the forum." In Ancient Rome, the forum was where governmental debates were held, but it was also where trials were held. It was the courthouse. So forensic science has come to mean the application of the natural and physical sciences to the resolution of conflicts within a legal context. "Science" also comes to us in a roundabout fashion from the Latin *scire*, meaning "to know." The classical definition of science is that it is an orderly body of knowledge with principles that are clearly enunciated. This definition will suffice for many of our purposes, but will collapse when it is applied to some specific physical evidence types. Again, this will be discussed in more detail below.

What then, of the forensic *scientist*? The single feature that distinguishes forensic scientists from any other scientist is the expectation that they will appear in court and testify to their findings and offer an opinion as to the significance of those findings. The forensic scientist will, or should, testify not only to what things *are*, but to what things *mean*. Forensic science is science exercised on behalf of the law in the just resolution of conflict. It is therefore expected to be the handmaiden of the law, but at the same time this expectation may very well be the marina from which is launched the tension that exists between the two disciplines.

§ 1–1.2 What Is Expected of the Forensic Sciences?

The clients of the forensic sciences—the police, the attorneys, and the courts—have somewhat conflicting expectations of what science is likely to provide. By and large, forensic science is selfishly viewed in strictly utilitarian terms, i.e., how is this going to help me? Although the police may aggressively pursue their investigations, they will, with a minimum of ritual whining, generally accept what a forensic laboratory is able to provide. The courts are interested in forensic science only from the standpoint of how science may be used by the trier of fact to resolve technical issues.

But there is a fundamental conflict here. The classical goal of science is the production of *truth*, while the goal of law is the achievement of *justice*.

Few forensic scientists harbor serious misgivings about the expectation of good science on the part of their clients, be they the police, the prosecution, or the defense bar; indeed, most forensic scientists are rather cynical on this point. The clients want good science and the truth if it will help their case. If good science and the truth will not help their case, they will willingly settle for poor science and something less than the absolute truth.

Most forensic scientists accept the reality that while truthful evidence derived from scientific testing is useful for establishing justice, justice may nevertheless be negotiated. In these negotiations, and in the just resolution of conflict under the law, truthful evidence may be subordinated to issues of fairness, and truthful evidence may be manipulated by forces beyond the ability of the forensic scientist to control or perhaps even to appreciate fully.

§ 1–1.3 Subordination of "Scientific Truth" to "Legal Truth"

Forensic scientists recognize that they are but the hired help, and that forensic science is but the handmaiden of the legal system. The validity of facts testified to in a court of law by non-expert witnesses is perpetually subject to challenge. When facts are introduced into a court of law by a scientist, however, they are likewise subject to the same challenge. Scientific "truths" are established when the validity of a proposition is proven to the satisfaction of a prudent and rational mind. Legal "truths" are not established by the exercise of the scientific method, but by the processes of the adversary system.

The role of physical evidence in the administration of justice may reasonably be described as follows: Science offers a window through which the law may view the technological advances of our age. Science spreads out a smorgasbord of (hopefully) valid facts and, having proudly displayed its wares, stands back. The law now picks out those morsels that appear most attractive to it, applying selection criteria that may or may not have anything to do with science. These selection criteria may appear sensible, even obligatory to the law, but may appear illogical or even whimsical to science.

Having discussed the part that forensic science plays in the broader drama of the administration of justice, we may now proceed to address how this role is played out.

§ 1–2.0 COMPARISON

Physical evidence at the scene of a crime may serve to associate that scene with a particular individual. Such evidence frequently is termed *associative evidence*. A fingerprint of the suspect at the crime scene is the archetypal example. If the suspect's fingerprints are found at the crime scene, he is unquestionably (or as nearly unquestionable as things get) associated with the scene in some way. The suspect may have had legitimate access to the scene, or the suspect may have been at the scene at some previous time, but the issue of the fundamental presence of the suspect at the scene is essentially unassailable. Associative evidence works both ways—something belonging to the suspect may be found at the scene, or something from the scene may later be found on or in the possession of the suspect after the suspect has left the scene. An example of the latter is a bloodstain of a victim on the clothing of the suspect. The forensic scientist undertakes to compare evidence found at the crime scene to evidence known to belong to a suspect.

§ 1–2.1 Class and Individual Characteristics

In the comparison of physical evidence, it is often helpful to make use of the concepts of *class characteristics* and *individual characteristics*. Class characteristics are general characteristics that separate a group of objects from a universe of diverse objects. In a comparison process, class characteristics serve the very useful purpose of screening a large number of items by eliminating from consideration those items that do not share the characteristics common to all of the members of that group. Class characteristics do not, and cannot, establish uniqueness. Individual characteristics, on the other hand, are those exceptional characteristics that may establish the uniqueness of an object. It should be recognized that an individual characteristic, taken in isolation, might not in itself be unique. The uniqueness of an object may be established by an ensemble of individual characteristics. A scratch on the surface of a bullet, for example, is not a unique event; it is the arrangement of the scratches on the bullet that mark it as unique.

An example of a class characteristic is "red." The characteristic "red" separates red items from those of all other colors. Class characteristics may be chained together to further refine the screening or elimination process.[1] "Red Buick" will instantly exclude from consideration any other vehicle, but will not distinguish among a sub-population of red Buicks. There is a fundamental mathematical foundation to this type of elimination, which resides in the "either/or" logic of Boolean algebra. Any vehicle that is not a red Buick may be eliminated because it is "either" of another manufacturer "or" it is of some other color.

An example of an individual characteristic would be the VIN number of the vehicle. The license plate number might be an individual characteristic, but the remote possibility exists that there would be some duplication of license plate numbers among different states and possibly between different countries. Examples of a few other class and individual characteristics for a number of evidence categories are given in Table 1.

Table 1. Class and Individual Characteristics

Class Characteristic	Individual Characteristic
Fingerprint pattern (e.g., loop, whorl, arch).	Ridge ending, bifurcation, dot.
Number of lands and grooves of a firearm.	Striations on the surface of a fired bullet.
Thickness of a shard of glass.	Irregular fracture margin.
Width of a prying tool (e.g., screwdriver).	Striations within the toolmark.
Tread pattern of an automobile tire.	Cuts and tears acquired through use.

The trick is to recognize class and individual characteristics for what they are, and not to confuse the two. Frequently this is easily accomplished. In other instances, however, this is not easily realized, and may call upon and challenge the experience of the examiner. An example of this is to be found in the area of handwriting examination. An examiner may note an unusual letter formation, which in the experience of that examiner seems to be unique. The natural tendency would be to categorize the letter form as an individual characteristic, as an idiosyncratic expression of the writing of a particular person to the exclusion of all other people. But it may be that every schoolchild in a Bulgarian town was taught to execute that particular letter formation. The characteristic may be obscure, but it is still a class characteristic, not an individual characteristic, and should be given only the weight that a class characteristic deserves and not the additional weight that ordinarily would be given to an individual characteristic.

Individual characteristics may arise out of different considerations. They may result from natural phenomena which are poorly understood or not

§ 1–2.0

1. It should be apparent that the "class" in "class characteristic" and the "class" in "clas-sification" are derived from the same root.

understood at all, such as the origin of fingerprints, or earprints, or lip prints. They may arise from manufacturing processes, which are understood but which are unintentional in their expression, such as marks associated with the machining of tools. Or they may reflect the career and history of an item after the manufacturing process—the use and the abuse of the item. Examples of the latter would be uneven wear and tear on the patterned sole of a shoe, or a screwdriver that has suffered some damage by having been used as a prying tool.

In the process of the comparison of an evidence item and an exemplar item, the analyst typically will check to see that the class characteristics agree before proceeding to the individual characteristics. It would be senseless, for example, to spend hours examining the striations on two bullets if one was a .22 caliber bullet and the other was a .38 caliber bullet. It is not obligatory in every case, however, to ensure that the class characteristics between the two items agree. For example, in the comparison of fingerprints, the class characteristic of pattern might not be apparent in a fragmentary fingerprint. The individual characteristics, i.e., the detailed pattern of the fingerprint ridges, may nevertheless be compared and an identification effected. If the patterns were apparent, however, one would not proceed to a comparison of the fingerprint ridges if one print was a loop and the other was a whorl.

§ 1–2.2 Features

Forensic scientists are concerned, even obsessed, with features. A feature is a quality, property, or trait that is used to characterize an object or a source. Some features are dichotomous, that is, they are either present or absent. Other features are quantifiable, and may take on values which are continuous, quasi-discrete, or discrete. Of whatever sort, it must be recognized that some features are rather ephemeral in how they are perceived and recognized by the eye and the mind. These include some of the features upon which we rely the most in forensic practice—visual, two-dimensional images of the features in shoeprint impressions, fingerprint minutiae, handwriting characteristics, and firearms striae. These features may be evaluated and tested, but the manner in which these patterns are recognized by the human mind is not well understood.

Forensic scientists are (hopefully) adept at recognizing features by means of which items are identified, e.g., pine pollen under the microscope, 00 Buckshot, a Greek "ε" in handwriting. It is reasonable to ask what are the limits that apply to the ability to identify things by sight. (Further analysis may of course follow). The answer is that we don't really know, but almost certainly the number of things that can be identified by the inspection of visible features alone would number in the thousands. One possibly appropriate analogy is Chinese characters. The ability to recognize two or three thousand characters will allow a person to read a Chinese newspaper. Scholars may, on the other hand, recognize upwards of ten thousand.

§ 1–2.3 Feature Independence

The soundness of a hypothesis increases when the prediction it makes is supported by several lines of evidence that have no relationship to one another. This is the condition of independence. If, on the other hand, one feature of the evidence is correlated with another feature, then the observation of one can predict, to a greater or lesser extent, the second feature. This is the condition of dependence.

If features are dependent, the forensic scientist is not justified in multiplying the frequencies of their individual occurrences to calculate the discriminating power of the features for the purpose of determining identity of source. For forensic identifications, the most valuable features are those that are demonstrably independent. Studies testing the independence of features exist for only a few evidence categories (e.g., blood types, glass density and refractive index, and gunshot residue). Where no studies exist, which is true for the preponderance of physical evidence types, prudence argues for caution in the interpretation of the evidence.

§ 1–3.0 IDENTIFICATION AND INDIVIDUALIZATION

Forensic science is classically described as being concerned with the analysis, identification, and interpretation of physical evidence. We find that in the English language, there are two somewhat different connotations associated with the term *identification*. In one sense, identification refers to the process of placing an item in a category. One may say, "I identified the specimen as an *Ursus horribilis*." That will establish that the animal is a grizzly bear. We now know that the animal is not a polar bear, or a panda, or a Himalayan Sun bear. But at this point, the bear could be any one of a number of grizzly bears. In the same sense of the word, one may identify a specimen of *Cannabis sativa*, or one may identify an automobile as a red Buick.

But rarely is the forensic scientist satisfied with this level of identity. In most situations, it is desirable to extend the level of discrimination beyond merely placing the item in a category. It is not sufficient to identify a firearm as a Smith & Wesson, if the issue is whether that *particular* firearm, to the exclusion of all other Smith & Wesson firearms, was responsible for having fired the fatal bullet. It is not sufficient to identify a vehicle as a red Buick if the issue is whether that particular red Buick is the one that ran down a hit-and-run victim.

To extend the discrimination to the level desired, i.e., uniqueness, the concept of *individualization* is required. Individualization is the process of placing an object in a unit category which consists of a single unit. Individualization implies uniqueness; identification, strictly speaking, does not require it. As discussed below, though individualization is clearly the goal toward which forensic science strives, it can be achieved only in a probabilistic sense, of reducing uncertainty to the smallest possible amount.

But in everyday usage, the term identification often is used when the concept of individualization is intended. One may hear testimony of the sort, "I identified the latent fingerprint as having been made from the right ring finger of the defendant." The intent of the witness here is to declare clearly that the latent fingerprint was that of the defendant, to the total exclusion of all other fingers of all of the other people in the world. The use of the term "identified" here is not the most precise usage of the word; the term "individualized" would be more felicitous. But the use of term "individualization" and various other forms of the word would only confuse matters. If, in response to the question, "Did you have occasion to identify the suspect's fingerprint on the knife?" the witness were to answer, "No, I individualized it," communication would be thwarted and the listener confused.

This is a constraint imposed by our language, and there is probably no feasible remedy. Forensic scientists are accustomed to the use of the term identification when what actually is meant is individualization, and few forensic scientists will go to the bother of correcting another person who uses the terms casually.[1] It should be appreciated, however, that the process of identification means one thing to the forensic scientist, and another thing to the botanist or the zoologist.

§ 1–3.1 Identification Processes v. Comparison Processes

In the "identification" mode, the forensic scientist examines an item of evidence for the presence or absence of specific characteristics that have been previously abstracted from authenticated items. Identifications of this sort are legion, and are conducted in forensic laboratories so frequently and in connection with so many different evidence categories that the forensic scientist is often unaware of the specific steps that are taken in the process. It is not necessary that those authenticated items be in hand, but it is necessary that the forensic scientist have access to the abstracted information. For example, an obscure 19th Century Hungarian revolver may be identified as an obscure 19th Century Hungarian revolver, even though the forensic scientist has never actually seen one before and is unlikely ever to see one again. This is possible because the revolver has been described adequately in the literature and the literature is accessible to the scientist. Their validity rests on the application of established tests which have been previously determined to be accurate by exhaustive testing of known standard materials.

In the "comparison" mode, the forensic scientist compares a questioned evidence item with another item. This second item is a "known item." The known item may be a standard reference item which is maintained by the laboratory for this purpose (e.g., an authenticated sample of cocaine), or it may be an exemplar sample which itself is a portion of the evidence in a case (e.g., a sample of broken glass or paint from a crime scene). This item must be in hand. Both questioned and known items are compared, characteristic by characteristic, until the examiner is satisfied that the items are sufficiently alike to conclude that they are related to one another in some manner, or, alternatively, until the examiner is satisfied of a lack of commonality.

In the comparison mode, the characteristics that are taken into account may or may not have been previously established. Whether they have been previously established and evaluated is determined primarily by (1) the experience of the examiner, and (2) how often that type of evidence is encountered. The forensic scientist must first determine what the characteristics are to be compared, then determine the weight to be ascribed to them, and then decide upon the number of matching characteristics that must be noted before a conclusion can be reached. This is more easily said than achieved, and may require *de novo* research in order to come to grips with the

§ 1–3.0

1. In the ensuing discussion, "identification" will be used in the more-or-less common use of the word, despite the fact that uniqueness is implied.

significance of observed characteristics. For example, a forensic scientist compares a shoe impression from a crime scene with the shoes of a suspect. Slight irregularities in the tread design are noted, but the examiner is uncertain whether those features are truly individual characteristics unique to this shoe, or a mold release mark common to thousands of shoes produced by this manufacturer. Problems of this type are common in the forensic sciences, and are anything but trivial.

In a strict sense, the identification mode is actually a form of the comparison mode. The identification mode does in fact involve a comparison, but a comparison of an evidence item with a hypothetical ideal instead of a tangible example.

§ 1–3.2 Explicable Differences

Differences exist between all objects, even those that are exceedingly similar in their outward appearance. The document examiner does not expect replicate signatures from one person to be totally superimposable; the firearms examiner does not expect replicate test firings from a particular firearm to agree in every striae on the surfaces of the two bullets. It follows, then, that total agreement between evidence and exemplar is not to be expected; some differences will be seen even if the objects are from the same source or the product of the same process. It is experience that guides the forensic scientist in distinguishing between a truly significant difference and a difference that is likely to have occurred as an expression of natural variation.

But forensic scientists universally hold that in a comparison process, differences between evidence and exemplar should be explicable. There should be some rational basis to explain away the differences that are observed, or else the value of the match is significantly diminished.

A danger exists that, once the examiner has become satisfied that a match does exist between the evidence and the exemplar, any differences will be dismissed as trivial and insignificant. A different, and more forgiving, set of criteria may be employed to rationalize away the differences than that originally employed in establishing the match. This is a situation where the training and experience of the examiner is at a premium, and the examiner must be attentive to the natural tendency to defend one's opinion against any and all challenges.

§ 1–4.0 EVALUATION OF SOURCE

The forensic scientist often is called upon to compare evidence items to determine whether they did, or could have, come from the same source. Consider, for example, a case where a hair is found in an automobile suspected of having been used as the getaway car in a bank robbery. The hair is recovered by a police investigator, and the forensic laboratory is requested to compare the hair with exemplar hair of a suspect. The issue of identity here is not a question of "What is it?", but rather is a question of "Where did it come from?"[1] Here it is *identity of source* that occupies our attention, not *identity of the object*.

<hr />

§ 1–4.0

1. The question has been phrased here in a commonly encountered but inelegant fashion. A more precise formulation of the appropriate question would be "Given the undeniable fact that this is a hair, from whom did the hair originate?"

The concept of identity of source presents some other complications, arising from the fact that there is not just one singular relationship between an object and its source.[2] An object may be related to its source because of *production* considerations, or because of *segment* considerations, or because of *alteration*, or because of considerations of *spatial location*; often the relationships operate alone, but situations commonly arise in which the relationships are interwoven, with no single relationship dominating the tapestry.

Production considerations are straightforward. The source produces the object, and the composition of the raw material utilized in the production are then expressed in the object. An example would be a sample of glass in which the principal components of silica, soda, and lime also contained, inadvertently, traces of the elements Manganese, Iron, and Copper. Finding these elements in an evidence sample of glass at the same concentration as the putative source would establish a relationship between the evidence and the source. (Whether the same concentration of these elements establishes *uniqueness* to the evidence is another matter.)

A segment relationship exists when a source is somehow dismantled and parts of the whole are somehow scattered. If a fragment of glass located at the scene of a hit-and-run accident is found to match an irregular edge of a broken headlight of the vehicle belonging to the suspect, a relationship between the evidence and the source is thereby established. In this instance, the composition of the glass as dictated by production considerations is not relevant.

An alteration relationship exists when a source is an agent or a process that alters or modifies an object. For example, in the commission of a burglary, a surface is acted upon by a prying tool. In this process, the surface is marked in a unique fashion by the tool. Subsequent comparison of the marks at the scene with test marks from the suspected tool may establish that a particular tool, to the total exclusion of all other tools in the world, was responsible for the evidence marks. In this sense, the tool may be viewed as having altered the otherwise pristine surface; the *tabula rasa* of the surface has now been altered so as to register a unique signature of the responsible tool.

The fourth type of relationship between a putative source and an object is the relationship of spatial location. A "source" may be a point in space as well as a tangible physical object. Just as a river has a source, an object of evidence may have its origin at a particular spatial location. For example—was the shooter in front of the murder victim, or behind? Does the broken glass on the roadway indicate the specific point of impact to a hit-and-run victim?

§ 1–4.1   "Same as That" vs. "Born of That"

A useful tool in the conceptualization of physical evidence is the "same as that" versus "born of that" dialectic which comes to us from the Sanskrit.

---

2. The entire landscape of how criteria are established for association and exclusion, as well as how physical evidence is conceptualized by the forensic scientist, has been developed elegantly by Chesterene Cwicklik, *An Evaluation of the Significance of Transfers of Debris: Criteria for Association and Exclusion*, 44 J. Forensic Sci. 1136 (1999).

The Sanskrit word *tatsam* means "same as that." The word *tadbhav* means "born of that." Ancient Indian philosophers found the two concepts to be useful, and indeed the concepts appear to have a good deal of utility in how physical evidence can be regarded.

In the comparison of two items of physical evidence, the evidence may be of the "same as that" type, or of the "born of that" type. An obvious example of the "born of that" type is a fired bullet. The bullet may be identified as having been fired through a particular gun barrel, to the total exclusion of all other gun barrels in the world. In a literal as well as figurative sense, the bullet has been "born" of the gun barrel. But when cocaine is identified, the analyst is comparing a set of observations derived from the evidence against a set of observations derived from known cocaine. The chemical reactivity of the unknown is the same as that of known cocaine, as is the mass and infrared spectrum. So the unknown is the "same as that," i.e., the known cocaine, and the identification is thereby effected. Physical evidence can almost always be ascribed to one or the other of these appellations, and the effort in doing so is frequently rewarded in terms of the clarity with which the evidence may be regarded.

§ 1–4.2   Uniqueness

Forensic scientists have struggled with the concept of uniqueness, but then so have others–philosophers, logicians, Boolean algebra mathematicians, and rare coin dealers. Each of these groups has made an uneasy peace with the concept.

It is generally held that no two snowflakes are exactly the same.[3] Based on the same type of not very rigorous observation, it is held that no two fingerprints have ever been found to have the same ridge positioning. In the same fashion, no two firearms have ever been found that have exactly the same configuration, and no two panes of glass have ever been observed to fracture into shards of identical shape and size.[4] Observations such as these have gradually become tenets of the beliefs of the forensic scientist of the uniqueness of all objects. In some quarters, these tenets have been scooped up and extended into a single, all-encompassing, generalized principle of uniqueness, which states that "Nature never repeats itself."[5]

---

3. This is, of course, not known with certitude to be true. Indeed, snowflakes that are indistinguishably alike have been reported. N.C. Knight, *No Two Alike?* 69 BULL. AM. METEOROLOGICAL SOC'Y 496 (1988) (finding "apparent contradiction of the long-accepted truism that no two snow crystals are alike.") For a less-than-serious discussion of the uniqueness of snowflakes within a forensic context, *see* John I. Thornton, *The Snowflake Paradigm*, 31 J. FORENSIC SCI. 399 (1986).

4. In practice, uniqueness is more an assumption than an observation. Most areas of forensic practice provide no occasion for testing the assumption, because examiners do not compare evidence in any one case to evidence in every other case. The one exception is fingerprints, where an evidence print is systematically compared to a huge database of other

prints. Examiners of firearms and broken glass have no comparable system and therefore no comparable opportunity for detecting coincidental matches. Where systematic studies are undertaken to look for identical snowflakes, or indistinguishable forensic evidence, such as handwritten signatures, the findings unsettle the assumptions. *See* John Harris, *How Much Do People Write Alike? A Study of Signatures*, 48 J. CRIM. L & CRIMINOLOGY 647 (1958). DNA typing has taken a radically different approach, sidestepping this difficult problem by making no heroic assumptions and instead calculating probabilities of coincidental matches.

5. This is an ancient dogma, and has seen many expressions. Leibniz said: "... it is necessary, indeed, that each monad [object] be different from each other. For there are never in nature two beings which are exactly alike

This principle is probably true, although it would not seem susceptible of rigorous proof. But the general principle cannot be substituted for a systematic and thorough investigation of a physical evidence category. For convenience in discussion, one may posit that no two snowflakes are alike, but it does not immediately follow that no two shoe soles are alike, since snowflakes are made in clouds and shoes are not. If it is absolutely true that no two shoe soles are alike, the basis for this uniqueness must rest on other grounds, and those grounds must be identified and enunciated.

§ 1–5.0   SCIENCE AND THE SCIENTIFIC METHOD

The scientific method and how it is invoked and applied has occupied the thoughts of many of the world's greatest intellects, and the present authors do not presume to attempt to join their company.[1] But an understanding of the basic tenets of the scientific method is essential to the understanding of how a forensic scientist approaches or *ought* to approach problems.

§ 1–5.1   Science

There is a difference between *science* and the *scientific method*, a difference that even scientists may not fully appreciate. The latter is generally the means to the former, but the two concepts are at best loosely related. The classical definition of a science is "an orderly body of knowledge with principles that are clearly enunciated." While this definition will suffice for most purposes, it is generally conceded that a few other qualifiers may be necessary. For example, additional requirements commonly added specify that the subject be susceptible of testing, and that it be reality-oriented. When these two additional provisos are added, religion, for example, fails to qualify, regardless of how clearly its principles have been enunciated or how orderly those principles may appear.

§ 1–5.2   Scientific Method

The scientific method, on the other hand, is not a body of knowledge; it is a way of looking at things. The scientific method has been embraced by the modern world because of its incredible power and utility—it is useful for answering many questions concerning the real world. Prior to the modern era, the explanation of many natural phenomena was based on the exercise of the imagination. Thunder was Thor tossing lightning bolts through the heavens. Demented people were possessed by evil spirits.

and in which is it not possible to find an internal difference." GOTTFRIED W. VON LEIBNIZ, MONADOLOGY, Section ix, 4th lettre a' Clarke, sect. 4/6 (1951). And, in particular reference to physical evidence, Kirk and Grunbaum have stated: "... all items of the universe are in some respect different from other similar items, so that ultimately it may be possible to individualize any object of interest...." Paul L. Kirk & Benjamin W. Grunbaum, *Individuality of Blood and Its Forensic Significance, in* LEGAL MEDICINE ANNUAL 288 (Cyril Wecht ed., 1968).

§ 1–5.0

1. Reference works on the history of science, and the philosophy of science, are legion. A good primer is to be found in KARL POPPER, CONJECTURES AND REFUTATIONS: THE GROWTH OF SCIENTIFIC KNOWLEDGE (5th ed. 1989). A painless introduction to the scientific method is to be found in ROBERT PIRSIG, ZEN AND THE ART OF MOTORCYCLE MAINTENANCE 107–111 (1974).

Gradually, progressive thinkers began to look for intrinsic evidence of the truth of various propositions, and this skepticism eventually spawned the development of the scientific method. The foundation of the scientific method, the most fundamental aspect, is the formulation and testing of hypotheses.[2] Since the laws of nature do not change from day to day, certain phenomena should therefore be repeatable, with a predictable outcome. This is a fundamental premise of the scientific method, but its practical application to forensic problems is not as straightforward as might be imagined.

Little of what goes on in forensic science resembles the classical description of how science develops theories, tests hypotheses, and revises its ideas and understandings.[3] That is partly because the scientific method is a description of pure, or basic, science (knowledge building), while forensic science is an *applied* science. Ideally, forensic scientists would apply the best knowledge borrowed from basic research that *has* employed the scientific method. Additional reasons are discussed below.

§ 1–5.3 Induction and Deduction

Many forensic identifications involve deductive processes, *a la* Sherlock Holmes, through the application of relevant generalizations to a particular set of circumstances. Induction is a type of inference that proceeds from a set of specific observations to a generalization, called a premise. This premise is a working assumption, but it may not always be valid. A deduction, on the other hand, proceeds from a generalization to a specific case, and that is generally what happens in forensic practice. Providing that the premise is valid, the deduction will be valid. But knowing whether the premise is valid is the name of the game here; it is not difficult to be fooled into thinking that one's premises are valid when they are not.

Forensic scientists have, for the most part, treated induction and deduction rather casually. They have failed to recognize that induction, not deduction, is the counterpart of hypothesis testing and theory revision. They have tended to equate a hypothesis with a deduction, which it is not. As a consequence, too often a hypothesis is declared as a deductive conclusion, when in fact it is a statement awaiting verification through testing.

§ 1–5.4 Failure of the Forensic Sciences to Consistently Appreciate the Implications of the Scientific Method

The validity of the scientific method is unassailable; no rational person takes issue with its utility in problem solving. But that does not mean that "science" as it is practiced in the real world is infallible. The scientific method is the means by which much of what we believe has come to be discovered. What we do with that discovered knowledge is another matter. The scientific

---

2. Hypothesis is one of a number of related words of Greek origin that are curiously but consistently pronounced in English in such a manner as to obscure their meaning. *Thesis* denotes an idea or a proposition, and in logic is construed to mean a proposition that may be advanced without proof. *Hypo-* is the Greek root for "less than." The word would be more easily understood if we pronounced it as *hypo-*

thesis, which we don't. In the same fashion, we say *an-tith-esis* instead of the more meaningful *anti-thesis*, and *synth-esis* instead of the more descriptive *syn-thesis*. (*Anti-*, "against," and *syn-*, "with.")

3. For further discussion of the scientific method, *see Science in the Law: Standards, Statistics and Research Issues,* Chapter 2.

method has given us the collective knowledge essential to various scientific disciplines—chemistry, physics, geology, botany, biology, etc. It has set the stage for the exercise of science. It sits there, as a way of learning something that would otherwise be unknown, waiting for someone—anyone—to invoke its power.

But those individuals engaged in "scientific" work rarely study the scientific method. To be sure, those engaged in research are expected to pick up the scientific method somewhere along the way; for the most part scientists don't study the implementation of the scientific method. Philosophers of science think about the scientific method. Basic research scientists use it to generate new knowledge. Applied scientists typically study the knowledge that the scientific method has managed to accumulate. For example, the chemist studies the hydrogen bond, and the biologist studies the double helix of DNA, but rarely does either receive instruction concerning the scientific method *per se*. It is not only possible, but indeed is generally the case, that a person with a Bachelor's Degree in chemistry, geology, biology, or other scientific discipline, has not had a single college lecture on precisely how the scientific method works.

This ultimately works against the best interests of the forensic scientist, who ordinarily does not learn much about how undiscovered information is brought to light. If one wishes to know something about the hydrogen bond or the double helix of DNA, one can after all consult books on those subjects. But if one wishes to understand a unique event in which physical evidence plays a role, one must improvise, using the scientific method as the engine to generate that knowledge.

The failure of scientists in general, and of forensic scientists in particular, to understand how knowledge is acquired and applied, leads to abuse. The problem lies in the fact that the forensic sciences are frequently concerned with unique or highly unusual events. Most other scientific disciplines are concerned with the usual and the typical, and with the manner in which things generally happen. The forensic sciences, on the other hand, are concerned with the unusual and the atypical, and with the ways that things generally do not happen. This requires a change of emphasis, away from the commonplace and toward the unknown. This in return requires a return to the scientific method to answer questions concerning the physical evidence.

Consider an instance in which the relevant physical evidence consists of a broken jar of peanut butter. Looking in the index of a textbook on forensic science under "p" for peanut butter will be to no avail. There are undoubtedly experts on peanut butter, but they are probably few and far between, or expensive, or uninterested in forensic problems, or all of the above. The forensic scientist has no alternative but to learn something about peanut butter. The forensic scientist is unlikely ever to have another peanut butter case in his career, but the necessity of becoming an expert on peanut butter has been thrust upon the examiner. Formal education will provide only a direction; it is the scientific method that will provide the truth. If the scientist understands the scientific method poorly, or does not have the wit or patience to apply it properly, errors of judgment can easily occur. This point seems to have eluded the legal profession entirely—the circumstances surrounding many cases are so unusual, or so specific to a particular case, that a research regimen will be required. It may not be particularly sophisticated research. But it is research nevertheless, and the scientific method, whether full-blown or truncated, must be invoked in how this research is executed.

Also, there is a critical distinction between an observation and its interpretation. An observation is a determination or measurement made under a controlled set of conditions. Interpretation, on the other hand, is the intellectual endeavor that assigns a meaning to the observation in the light of scientific knowledge. These two elements may be summarized as "What things are," and "What things mean." It is an evasion of the responsibility of the forensic scientist to state what something "is" without accompanying that opinion, whenever possible, with a statement as to what it "means." This is not a usurpation of the province of the court. To give a court an opinion without attempting to provide the ability to place that opinion in a sensible perspective would be a disservice to the legal system. The court could be convinced of the technical soundness of the opinion, but would be forced to guess as to how that opinion should be factored into the totality of the case. From the standpoint of the court, or a jury, this would be equivalent to listening to an obscure Japanese *noh* drama without the benefit of the plot.

§ 1–5.5 Substitution of Intuition or Experience for Defensible Scientific Fact

Virtually everyone agrees that an expert's bare opinion, unsupported by factual evidence, should be inadmissible in a court of law. And yet, precisely that sort of testimony is allowed every day in courts throughout the country by judges who believe that every statement uttered by a person with a scientific degree or employed by an agency called "scientific" is therefore a scientific opinion. Courts permit expert testimony from those with specialized knowledge. But how is a court to gauge such knowledge? The answer generally lies in the education and experience of the prospective witness.[4] A convenient means is to look for a measure of scientific education, and a university degree in a scientific discipline will ordinarily meet that test.

With an educational requirement satisfied, a court will then look at experience. But experience is very difficult to evaluate. The more experience the better, but rarely is there any effort exerted to distinguish between 10 years of experience and 1 month of experience repeated 120 times, or 1 month of experience spread out over 10 years.[5] Furthermore, some experts exploit situations where intuition or mere suspicions can be voiced under the guise of experience. When an expert testifies to an opinion, and bases that opinion on "years of experience," the practical result is that the witness is immunized against effective cross-examination. When the witness testifies that "I have

4. One of the many myths that is promulgated by the legal system is that *voir dire* and cross-examination, together with judicial discretion, will cull out the scientifically lame and halt. Certainly that does occur. More often, however, the court will not know whether the expert witness received superior grades in relevant courses at a flagship university, or had a "C" average on a football scholarship at some institution that no one in the courtroom has ever heard of. How often is a *curriculum vitae* checked in the course of a trial? How often is a

perjury charge leveled at expert witnesses who puff up their credentials?

5. A knowledgeable, well-prepared attorney could probably smoke out this point, although whether he or she would win points with a jury is debatable. The fact that forensic scientists get away with this unjustified reliance on experience as often as they do may be a sad reflection on just how few knowledgeable, well-prepared attorneys there are.

never seen another similar instance in my 26 years of experience …,'' no real scrutiny of the opinion is possible. No practical means exists for the questioner to delve into the extent and quality of that experience. Many witnesses have learned to invoke experience as a means of circumventing the responsibility of supporting an opinion with hard facts. For the witness, it eases cross-examination. But it also removes the scientific basis for the opinion.

Consider the following exchange on cross-examination:

Question	Answer	Translation
Is this situation unusual?	I have never seen a similar instance.	You don't know what I have seen and what I haven't, so I can say this and get away with it.
What is the basis of your opinion?	My 26 years of experience in the field.	It's really a surmise on my part. I believe it to be true, but I can't really tell you why I think that. It's really more of an impression that I have than anything else but I can't say that it's a surmise or a vague impression, could I?
Can you tell us how many cases of this type you have examined?	Many hundreds.	I don't know, and I certainly don't know how many of them would support my current position, and I might not be able to tell even if I went back and pulled the files.
Can you supply us with a list of all those cases?	Oh, no, I don't think so. They go back many years.	No way. You don't have any way of smoking those cases out of me, and even if I was ordered to do so, I could come up with plenty of reasons not to comply.
Can you supply us with the raw data on all those cases?	I don't think so. Some of them were when I was in my previous job. And some might be on microfilm. And it would take weeks or months to locate all of them.	Not a chance.
Were those cases subjected to independent scrutiny for technical correctness?	All of them were reviewed by my supervisors. I don't have any reason to believe that their review wasn't adequate.	No. And also, now you're going to have to argue with those nameless, faceless supervisors that I have alluded to but haven't identified.

Testimony of this sort distances the witness from science and the scientific method. And if the science is removed from the witness, then that witness has no legitimate role to play in the courtroom, and no business being there. *If there is no science, there can be no forensic science.*

Experience is neither a liability nor an enemy of the truth; it is a valuable commodity, but it should not be used as a mask to deflect legitimate scientific scrutiny, the sort of scrutiny that customarily is leveled at scientific evidence of all sorts. To do so is professionally bankrupt and devoid of scientific legitimacy, and courts would do well to disallow testimony of this sort. Experience ought to be used to enable the expert to remember the when and the how, why, who, and what. Experience should not make the expert less responsible, but rather more responsible for justifying an opinion with defensible scientific facts.

§ 1–5.6 Legal Skepticism Concerning Case–Oriented Research

While many cases will of necessity require a mini-research project to adequately deal with the physical evidence, forensic scientists are frequently frustrated at the lack of respect accorded by courts to their efforts. Courts often have been skeptical of research that is directed toward a particular case. Courts frequently disallow testimony by an expert concerning some experiment specifically conducted to answer an issue raised in a particular case because the experiment did not faithfully duplicate *all* of the conditions of the incident in question, e.g., the temperature or humidity isn't known, or the origin of the test materials may not be identical in all respects to the original evidence. The same court may, however, allow another expert to testify to some vague generalizations based on experience with *none* of the conditions specified or even enunciated. This is lamentable. If legitimate research is accepted in connection with, for example, dinosaurs, or the archeology of Egypt, it is unreasonable to summarily condemn well-crafted research that may not be able to duplicate every fanciful parameter of the investigation. Courts should recognize that the questions posed by case-oriented research are often helpful to the trier of fact, and that the research conducted to answer those questions may be as elegant as any other type of research.

§ 1–6.0 STANDARDS OF OPERATION, STANDARDS OF PERFORMANCE

The forensic sciences require adherence to standards of operation and of performance.[1] These standards must be clearly enunciated and must be, at least in their basic form, the consensus of opinion of workers in that particular subject area. Stated differently, forensic scientists are not entitled to indulge whims in the conduct of their work. They must adhere to performance norms which have been previously laid down. A forensic scientist who adopts an extreme position that runs counter to the flow of prevailing opinion on a subject, or who enters an area in which operational norms have not been established, has a burden even greater than usual to justify that position in the light of good scientific practice.

A problem arises when the forensic scientist is confronted with a unique problem, a problem not previously encountered and unlikely ever to occur

---

§ 1–6.0

1. The notion of standards is certainly not new. In a surprisingly scientific view of things for 450 B.C., Mo Tzu said that:

> For any doctrine, some standard must be established. To expound a doctrine without a standard is like determining the directions of sunrise and sunset on a revolving potter's wheel. In this way the distinction of right and wrong and benefit and harm cannot be

clearly known. Therefore for any doctrine there must be the three standards:

(1) There must be a basis or foundation,

(2) There must be an examination,

(3) There must be practical application and interpretation.

Wing-Tsit Chan (ed.), A SOURCEBOOK IN CHINESE PHILOSOPHY 222 (1963).

again in the career of that scientist. This situation arises more commonly than might be thought. The forensic scientist is asked to characterize or examine some peculiar substance—a sample of peanut butter, or a physical match between two minute broken pieces of pine needle, or to extract from tissue or bodily fluids some new drug. The analyst cannot go to a textbook on forensic science for a direct answer. Instead, the analyst must look beyond the horizons of the forensic science discipline and acquire the knowledge necessary to deal with the problem at hand.

But while there may not be established procedures in the forensic laboratory for each one of the myriad of materials that could possibly represent physical evidence in a particular case, there are nevertheless standards of scientific endeavor which are applicable to every situation: 1) personal bias must be subdued, 2) the problem must be tacked down emphatically, 3) a hypothesis must be posed, 4) experiments must be conducted to test the hypothesis, 5) if necessary to clarify an issue, subordinate hypotheses must be developed and tested, 6) conclusions must rest on evidence from the experiments. In addition, the analyst must possess at least a threshold conversancy with the subject. A chemist attempting to identify a plant fragment would be lost; likewise would be a botanist attempting to identify a mineral.

§ 1–6.1 Reliability, Validity, Precision, and Accuracy[2]

The methods utilized by the forensic scientist must be shown by appropriate scientific research to be reliable, valid, precise, and accurate. In general usage by the lay public, these terms have somewhat vague and overlapping meaning, but to the scientist their meanings are clear.

Reliability refers to the extent to which a measuring instrument produces the same result when it is used repeatedly to measure the same object or event. If a bathroom scale reports different weight when the same person stands on it repeatedly, then it lacks even reliability. Thus, a parade of forensic scientists who make the same subjective judgment, or a series of machines that give the same readings in response to the same evidence sample, can only be said to be reliable. *Validity* refers to the degree to which a measuring instrument measures what it purports to measure. A reliable watch set to California time will not be valid in Massachusetts or Guam. Even a bathroom scale that is highly reliable will not be valid if it is used to measure intelligence. Similarly, forensic scientists or machines that are in agreement may be highly reliable (in agreement with each other) without being valid (without reaching the correct answer). They can all be wrong.

Accuracy implies conformity to a standard. If one accepts the bullseye of a dartboard as the standard, and if all of the darts hit the bullseye, then accuracy has been achieved. If, on the other hand, all of the darts hit the board in a one inch cluster at 7 o'clock but 4 inches from the bullseye, then the accuracy is poor. *Precision* refers to the refinement of a measure. How precise a measure needs to be depends on the task at hand. The nearest whole pounds will suffice to weigh players on a football team; it is too gross a measure for weighing samples of drugs.

2. John Keenan Taylor, Quality Assurance of Chemical Measurements (1987); G. Kateman & F.W. Pijpers, Quality Control in Analytical Chemistry (1981).

§ 1–6.2 Expression of Certainty of Opinions

Forensic scientists have an obligation to express their opinions in a manner which is as clear as possible. A disservice is rendered to the legal system if the court, jury, or client attorney is forced to guess as to the certainty to which the expert's conclusions are intended.

In most instances, the forensic scientist will be unable to express an opinion in terms of mathematical probabilities. There are few exceptions. Because allele frequencies are known for many populations, a DNA analyst may be able to state something along the lines of "the alleles in this bloodstain may be expected to occur randomly once in 1.2 billion Caucasians, in 0.8 billion Blacks, and in 1.4 billion Hispanics." The ability to express an opinion in a quantifiable fashion is limited to just a few physical evidence categories. But in most physical evidence categories, there simply are no defensible probability models that may be applied, and conclusions must be framed verbally rather than mathematically. Moreover, the difference is not merely one of expression, but of the basis of the opinion. While for DNA analysis there are data on which to base objective probability calculations, for most forensic sciences examiners have to intuit their own subjective probability estimates. This is often a frustration to the user of the opinion—court or jury—who would prefer a more finite expression of certainty (and uncertainty).

Any opinion rendered by a forensic scientist must have in it an associated or embedded statement as to the conviction of the scientist as to the reliance that may be placed on the opinion. In practice, this is difficult to achieve. An opinion may be emphatic, e.g., "A comparison of the questioned text with the exemplar writing reveals sufficient agreement to establish the suspect as having written the questioned text." Or it may justifiably be far less than emphatic, e.g., "A comparison of the questioned text with the exemplar writing reveals some minimal agreement with respect to handwriting characteristics; the amount of agreement is insufficient to establish the suspect as having written the questioned text." The user of the opinion—court, jury, or bar—is understandably interested in knowing where on the continuum of relative certainty the forensic scientist would have his or her opinion pegged. But problems exist with nomenclature, and problems exist in communicating the certainty with which the scientist has embraced the opinion. In one study,[3] researchers asked test subjects to ascribe a mathematical probability , 0 to 1, to the phrase "quite likely." The mean response was 0.79. The mean response for the phrase "quite unlikely," was, however 0.11. The two values should add up to unity. This asymmetry in how common verbal phrases are associated with probability is common in our language. Slow, reluctant efforts are being made within the forensic sciences, however, to standardize to a greater extent the language in which opinions are couched.[4]

§ 1–6.3 The Mismeasure of Evidence

Everyone connected with the justice system expects forensic science to be infallible. It is not. The law would prefer hard facts, inviolate and certain. But

---

3. S. Lichtenstein & J. Newman, *Empirical Scaling of Common Verbal Phrases Associated with Numerical Probabilities*, 9 PSYCHONOMIC SCI. 563 (1967).

4. D. A. Rudram, *Interpretation of Scientific Evidence*, 36 SCI. & JUST. 133 (1996).

science, however pure it may be in the abstract, must be practiced in the real world by fallible human beings using imperfect tools. The standard expectation that pertains to any forensic endeavor is that the work is exemplary. The analyst is expected to deliver quality work, and anything else will be criticized or even rejected. But to consistently deliver quality work over a long period of time will require an enormous dedication of resources—time, effort, care, and money. Consistently high quality work can be provided, but the cost will be high. Quality work on a shoestring is an oxymoron. If adequate resources are not provided and an error in analysis or interpretation occurs, typically the blame is placed on the analyst rather than the withholder of resources.

Techniques exist by means of which error may be measured and managed, but error is never entirely absent. Any forensic scientist who believes that he or she will complete a satisfying and rewarding professional career without making a serious mistake will eventually be taught otherwise, and will suffer treble recompense for their arrogance. The trick is to try to keep the error out of the courtroom. Most mistakes in the laboratory are the result of inexperience, inadequate training of the analyst, the analyst being in a hurry, or the analyst simply wanting to please and be helpful. Some errors are inherent in the nature of evidence and limitations of analytical methods.

It is possible to *minimize* the possibility of error, however. The means typically employed to accomplish this are an ensemble of techniques—the technical review of the work of the forensic scientist, proficiency testing, accreditation of laboratories, and certification of analysts

§ 1–6.4 Proficiency Testing as a Means of Ensuring Quality in Technical Procedures

Proficiency testing is a means by which the preceding qualities can be measured. Evidence created by one laboratory (the "manufacturer") may be submitted to forensic scientists for their testing and their results can be compared with the known values from the manufacturer. To use this procedure effectively, the analyst is not informed of the "true" answer until after the test has been completed. In this manner, errors, or potential sources of error, may be identified.

Error is a concept that causes a good deal of consternation in the minds of forensic scientists. Modern science embraces error forthrightly—error is measured and is managed. Forensic science in general, however, has tended to deal with error by burying its head in the sand; clearly it will not be permitted to continue to do so in the future.

Proficiency testing, the most appropriate means for the identification of sources of error, is unpopular with forensic science practitioners in general because of a widespread belief that a missed proficiency testing sample will be used to discredit them in court. This belief is not entirely without justification. The potential exists that in court, counsel for the opposing side will in a self-serving fashion misconstrue, pervert and abuse a missed proficiency test. Certainly in a court of law, where testimony is given in response to posed questions, and where the witness ordinarily is unable to exercise any significant control over the issues under discussion, the ability of an expert witness to defend against this type of supposed self-righteous indignation is severely hampered.

Consequently, many forensic scientists view proficiency testing with considerable anxiety because they fear that a single, isolated substandard proficiency test will compromise their entire career.[5] Under the adversary system of justice it is the legitimate function of opposing counsel to attempt to discredit the testimony of the expert witness, whether the witness is correct or not, and whether or not the attorney personally believes that the witness is correct. It is the function of the expert, on the other hand, to be technically correct just as often as is humanly possible, and in recognition of this fact most forensic scientists consent, somewhat reluctantly and with trepidation, to a program of proficiency testing. Increasingly, however, forensic scientists have come to recognize that the solution to the issue of proficiency testing lies not in avoidance, but in acceptance. Proficiency testing is simply the cost of doing business in the forensic science profession; it cannot be avoided.

A point that has eluded the legal system, however, is that proficiency testing samples may be made so easy that everyone would get them correct, or they could be made so difficult that no one would get them correct. To ferret out error, proficiency tests should be of varying degrees of difficulty, arranged so as to represent a reasonable challenge to the analyst. Additionally, some proficiency tests should be *extremely* challenging, designed to severely tax the skills, knowledge, and ingenuity of the analyst. In the casual parlance of the forensic science community, these are referred to as "stinker" tests. It is to be expected that no analyst will achieve perfect results on these particularly challenging tests, and a less-than-perfect performance on those tests should garner no blame on the part of the analyst. The analyst, however, has reason to suspect that in court his nose will be rubbed in the muffed test, and that he will be unfairly stigmatized.

§ 1–6.5 Signal Detection Theory and Proficiency Testing

Signal detection theory (SDT) is a means for reviewing decision-making in forensic examinations and is designed to disentangle the two components of accuracy in ambiguous decision situations: 1) the examiner's diagnostic/discrimination abilities, and 2) the decision threshold of the examiner. Two examiners with identical technical skills will arrive at different answers if they employ different threshold criteria in terms of what constitutes an identity or a match.[6] Discrimination ability is actually determined by two components—the examiner's technical skills and the quality of the evidence itself. Technical ability is dependent upon the examiner's training, the laboratory's resources (instrumentation, equipment, etc.), and the types of tests being performed. Decision threshold will similarly be influenced by two factors: prior probability (or expectancies) of a positive conclusion, and utilities associated with a particular outcome (what might be termed motivation). What is the frequency that a comparison yields a positive (match) or negative

---

5. Forensic scientists are often quite touchy on this issue. Forensic scientists, when questioned about proficiency tests they have taken, would like to be able to ask their cross-examiner, "Have you ever lost a case? It doesn't matter if it was years ago, it doesn't matter if the case was hopeless to begin with, it doesn't matter that you were tired, or simply didn't have time to prepare adequately, or were ham- pered by a lack of investigative resources. The question to you is: Have you ever lost a case? Because if you have, then how could you possibly expect this jury to accept anything you say?"

6. Victoria L. Phillips et al., *The Application of Signal Detection Theory to Decision–Making in Forensic Science,* 46 J. FORENSIC SCI. 294 (2001).

(nonmatch) conclusion? What are the real world consequences of an examiner's conclusion that items do or do not share a common origin? The forensic scientist's conclusions can have profound consequences for parties involved.

Lower decision thresholds will yield more "hits" but will also produce more false positives. Higher decision thresholds will produce more correct rejections, but more false negatives. We know, too, with forensic evidence that certain types of evidence, such as fingerprints, bear features more reliably measured and interpreted than evidence such as handwriting that is less distinctive and has more variability from the same source. (A person's signature will vary slightly every time they write it.) Examiners may employ criteria that are not published, agreed upon, or for that matter clearly articulated. It would be extremely helpful to the field of forensic science to know if variations in decisional accuracy are the result of differences in examiners' backgrounds and training, or merely the employment of different decision thresholds. Do decision thresholds vary among forensic specialties, or might the thresholds vary for the same examiner depending upon the case or the types of other evidence present? Peterson et al.[7] have found that examiners in different laboratories prepare exclusionary reports at very different rates, compared with the fraction of time they may conclude their findings are merely inconclusive. There are many factors that influence examiners' projected estimates of likely matches—from the presence of suspects in cases to the use of computerized data bases that may have already assigned a priority value to an item of evidence in terms of its degree of fit with the unknown sample.

What SDT can do is assist in sorting out the "raw diagnostic skill" of examiners from "decision thresholds". The capabilities of examiners with different backgrounds, training and experience may be determined. The factors that cause decision thresholds to rise or fall could be studied. No systematic study yet exists to determine if the organizational home of a forensic examiner (e.g., government examiner or defense expert) influences the decision thresholds employed. A major change that would be needed to enable proficiency testing data to be of greater utility in something like SDT would be to have examiners give their conclusions a "confidence rating" (perhaps on a scale of certainty from 1 to 10) which could help set the decision thresholds used by different examiners. We would also need to introduce changes to enable the data from the same individuals or laboratories to be linked over successive examinations. It would also be helpful to have an expert rating/assessment of the level of difficulty of the test being administered. There are many reasons why SDT should be employed by the forensic field to aid in research on forensic science decision making.

§ 1–7.0   ISSUES OF PROFESSIONAL PRACTICE

§ 1–7.1   Documentation of Findings

Forensic science cannot be viewed solely in terms of its products; it is also judged by the legitimacy of the processes by which evidence is examined and

7. Joseph L. Peterson et al., Forensic Evidence And The Police (National Institute of   Justice, 1984).

interpreted. Any opinion rendered by a forensic scientist in a written report or in court testimony must have a basis in fact and theory. Without such a basis, any conclusions reached are bereft of validity and should be treated with derision.

The forensic scientist must always bear the burden of responsibility of justifying an opinion, and the work that has led to that opinion. If this work is not properly documented, it deserves to be rejected. It is not within the prerogatives of the forensic scientist to waive this requirement, and no one has the right to release the forensic scientist from this burden. Notetaking and other forms of documentation are as important to the forensic scientist as a proper grounding in chemistry, biology or other discipline. In general, documentation to support conclusions must be such that in the absence of the original examiner, another competent examiner could evaluate what was done and interpret the data. The standard here, which should be met, is whether an entry in laboratory notes would be intelligible to another analyst without additional explanation.

§ 1–7.2   Statistical Basis for Evidence Evaluation

Behind every opinion rendered by a forensic scientist there is a statistical basis. We may not know what that basis is, and we may have no feasible means of developing an understanding of that basis, but it is futile to deny that one exists.

In the forensic sciences, there is an incredible amount of difficulty attached to the development of a statistical basis for evidence evaluation.[1] It is not because the forensic science community lacks the wit to develop these statistics or is too lazy to commence the process. It is because the types of examination that are often conducted in forensic laboratories do not lend themselves to analysis by conventional statistics.[2] There are exceptions, however, as in blood group typing, DNA typing, and some aspects of gunshot residue models.

The lack of such data has consequences that help us to better appreciate what forensic individualization science aims to do and what it is able to achieve. The most common and coherent theory of forensic identification is that where there is a high degree of variation among attributes (of toolmark striations, writing, friction ridges on skin, and so on), then where a "match" is observed the probability that the match is coincidental rather than reflecting a shared source will be very small. Forensic sciences that have such data can actually calculate the probability of a coincidental match, and report that probability to the judge and jury. Forensic individualization sciences that lack actual data, which is most of them, have no choice but to either intuitively

---

§ 1–7.0

1. C.G.G. Aitken & D.A. Stoney, The Use of Statistics in Forensic Science (1991).

2. The late Paul Kirk put it thusly:

[Forensic science] is concerned with the unlikely and the unusual. Other sciences are concerned primarily with the likely and the usual. The derivation of equations, formulas, and generalizations summarizing the normal behaviour of any system in the universe is a major goal of the established sciences.... Mathematical analysis is even more necessary for interpreting the significance of each fact that is elicited relative to the evidence. However, we do not yet know how to make such an analysis, despite technical success in determining the actual facts of a crime through study of physical evidence.

Paul L. Kirk, *Criminalistics*, 40 Science 367 (1963).

estimate those underlying probabilities and calculate the coincidental match probability from those subjective probabilities, or simply to assume the conclusion of a minuscule probability of a coincidental match (and in fact they do the latter). Moreover, since the basis of all forensic identification is probability theory, examiners can never really assert a conclusion of an "identification to the exclusion of all others in the world," but at best can only assert a very small (objective or subjective) probability of a coincidental match. Those forensic scientists who claim to have identified something "to the exclusion of all others in the world" are offering more of a hope or an overstatement than an opinion that rests on a scientifically meaningful basis. Most, or at least many, forensic scientists understand this well enough that they can explain it to a judge or jury if someone were to ask them to do so. It is ironic that those areas of forensic science that have real underlying data offer more modest statements of individualization, while those limited to subjective or impressionistic data make the strongest statements, sometimes of absolute certainty. Finally, the probabilistic basis of forensic identification means that debates over whether there really literally are "no two alike" in some area of forensic science are not relevant to the real issue in an identification: what the probability is of a coincidental match.

§ 1–7.3   Personal Bias in Observation and Interpretation

Personal bias and the influence of expectations caused by knowing "too much" about a case have an unknown impact on the judgments of forensic scientists. Well trained and well managed forensic scientists try to reduce it to a very low level, but no prudent scientist would claim that it was forever absent.[3] Bias that would cause the forensic scientist to embrace a position concerning the guilt or innocence of an accused is clearly improper. That sort of bias is easily recognized for its evil *en se*, however. More insidious is the sort of bias in which an analyst will engage to protect findings once they have been developed, or where the results of a test are expected to the extent that the expected results are observed even when they are absent or only marginally present. For example, an analyst might present data in a graphical form in which small effects appear major by stretching the axis. It is possible that the analyst might not even be consciously aware of the implications of these types of delinquencies. The potential exists here for diverse sorts of rationalization, with the consequent application of a more forgiving set of criteria when faced with unexpected results.

This type of bias is nurtured by the analyst working in an atmosphere where external sources of feedback are not in place. The remedy is to have the work of the analyst reviewed by peers or supervisors, where subtle and insidious mechanisms of bias may be unveiled and brought to light.

To diminish personal bias, forensic scientists can make use of many of the same sorts of checks that are utilized in many other scientific disciplines, *viz.*, blind proficiency testing, replicate testing within the laboratory or in another laboratory, confirmation of observations by other analysts, and marking of

---

3. *See* Michael Risinger, Michael Saks, Robert Rosenthal & William Thompson, *The* Daubert/Kumho *Implications of Observer Effects in*   *Forensic Science: Hidden Problems of Expectation and Suggestion*, Cal. L. Rev. (forthcoming).

samples in a manner so that the outcome of a particular test cannot be anticipated.[4]

§ 1–7.4 Physical Evidence Is Not the Property of One Side or the Other

Good science requires that physical evidence not be considered as chattel; it is not the exclusive property of one side or the other in a contested matter, but must be held in trust for both sides. The side that gets to it first must recognize a responsibility to conserve and to preserve the evidence for an independent examination by the other side. Whether or not a jurisdiction accepts this as a legal procedural rule, it is an ethical principle of forensic science and a maxim of science in general.

§ 1–8.0 SUBJECTIVE TESTS VS. OBJECTIVE TESTS

Many of the examinations conducted in a forensic science laboratory are rather subjective. A subjective test[1] calls upon the experience of the examiner for the proper interpretation of the test results. This is a troublesome area for the forensic scientist, or at least it *should* be. Clearly it is a troublesome area for the courts and for attorneys.

"Subjectivity" typically occurs in two stages of forensic science individualization. First, the examiner makes a complex judgment as to whether there is a match. Second, the examiner must estimate the improbability of occurrence of such a match in order to evaluate the likelihood that the questioned and the known share a common source or match as a matter of coincidence. The first of these steps could and perhaps some day will be done by optical scanners and computers. For now it is done by the exercise of human perception and cognitive processing to compare patterns, and that makes it "subjective." These cognitive tasks actually are something that humans generally are extremely good at. The second stage is more troublesome and should be the heart of the problem for forensic science and for law. This second stage is interpretation of the meaning of a match. That problem is that in order to estimate the probability, or improbability of something, one needs data about the population from which it came—more precisely, data about each of the elements on which comparison has been made—and the appropriate statistical calculus must be applied. For every area of forensic identification science (except DNA typing), because there exist no relative frequency data ("objective probabilities"), examiners have no choice but to intuit, to rely on "experience," in other words, to guesstimate what those values are and therefore to reach judgments of the probability of a coincidental match based on what literally are known as "subjective probabilities." This second stage involves human judgmental tasks that humans are generally quite poor at.[2]

Of course, the classical definition of subjective raises at least the possibility of caprice, of personal bias, of conditioning by the personal characteristics of the mind of the analyst, and of other motivation, which might range from

---

4. *See generally id.*

§ 1–8.0

1. Webster's NEW COLLEGIATE DICTIONARY gives, as the second definition of the word subjective, the following: "**2.** Exhibiting or af-fected by personal bias, emotional background, etc.; as a *subjective* judgment." (Italics in original).

2. *See* the considerable body of research on decision heuristics.

the merely inexplicit to the wholly sinister. But this is an unfortunate consequence of the English language, rather than a fundamental defect of reason. The opposite of subjective is *objective*,[3] which carries the connotation of detachment and impartiality. But the cliché "a lack of objectivity" does not reflect back on the antonym "subjectivity," but implicitly suggests personal bias.

There is a tendency to view subjective tests with some measure of skepticism or even distrust. But not all forensic tests are equivalent in the amount of subjectivity that is involved. Two issues are involved. The first issue is how much subjectivity exists, and the second issue is whether a higher level of subjectivity is correlated with a higher level of unreliability.

Cognitive scientists have developed methods for studying subjective phenomena and have produced massive amounts of research for well over a century.[4] Relevant to the problem of subjective judgment in many areas of forensic work, that research has studied the conditions under which such judgments are more stable and consistent within and across observers as well as the factors that produce distortions in the perception of complex stimuli, methods of eliciting judgments that maximize sensitivity and consistency, and ways of translating subjective experience into objective criteria.[5]

Ironically, given the importance of subjective judgments in the forensic sciences, there has not been much research into the implications of subjective testing, nor much borrowing from cognitive science research (as there has been in other fields involving subjective pattern recognition, such as radiology and sonar). The factors that could be expected to influence subjectivity—the nature of the task, the nature of the evidence, training, experience, alienation, fatigue, the potential for rationalization when confronted with apparent error, indifference on the part of laboratory administrators, an inclination to please one's superiors—have not been addressed within the forensic science profession. Reliability and validity of subjective judgments can be measured. But in forensic science, little work has been done on the problem. As we begin a new millennium, this remains one of the major challenges to the forensic sciences.

It is possible to construct an array of physical evidence types, and indicate roughly how much subjectivity is to be expected, as in Figure 1.[6] At the lower end might be a jigsaw-like "physical match" of two items, where the fit of

---

3. Webster's NEW COLLEGIATE DICTIONARY gives, as the second definition of the word objective, the following: "**2.** Exhibiting or characterized by emphasis upon or the tendency to view events, phenomena, ideas, etc., as external and apart from self-consciousness; not subjective; hence, detached; impersonal unprejudiced; as, an *objective* discussion; *objective* criteria." (Italics in original).

4. For some older examples, *see* G.T. FECHNER, ELEMENTS OF PSYCHOPHYSICS (originally published 1860; H.E. Alder trans., 1966); L.L. Thurstone, *Attitudes Can be Measured*, 33 AM. J. SOCIOLOGY 529 (1928); H. Gulliksen, *Measurement of Subjective Values*, 21 PSYCHOMETRIKA 229 (1956).

5. *See* D.M. GREEN & J.A. SWETS, SIGNAL DETECTION THEORY AND PSYCHOPHYSICS (1966); LAWRENCE BARSALOU, COGNITIVE PSYCHOLOGY: AN IN-

TRODUCTION FOR COGNITIVE SCIENTISTS (1992); MICHAEL SUELZER, ANALYSES OF HUMAN QUANTITATIVE JUDGMENT: MODELS OF SEQUENTIAL MAGNITUDE ESTIMATION (1991); DANIEL ALGOM, PSYCHOPHYSICAL APPROACHES TO COGNITION (1992); and work appearing in such journals as: PERCEPTION AND PSYCHOPHYSICS, COGNITIVE PSYCHOLOGY, COGNITIVE SCIENCE, and PATTERN RECOGNITION. *See also* Victoria L. Phillips et al., *The Application of Signal Detection Theory to Decision–Making in Forensic Science*, 46 J. FORENSIC SCI. 294 (2001).

6. The designations given here are merely approximations; some disagreement within the forensic science community would be expected. This is particularly true if it is someone's personal ox that is being gored.

irregular margins indicates convincingly that the two items were at one time joined. Here the interpretation rests squarely on the items themselves—the objects—hence the examination would rank low in terms of subjectivity. At the other extreme, the comparison of an evidence bullet and a test fired bullet would rank high in terms of subjectivity; here the interpretation has much to do with the training, the experience, and the notions of the examiner.

Figure 1
Relative Subjectivity in Various Forensic Science Specialties

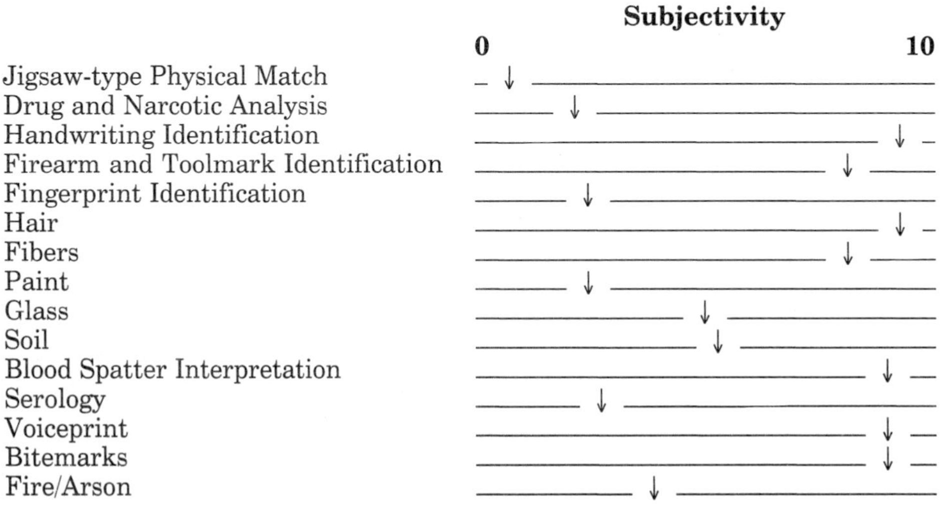

Subjectivity

Specialty	0 ——— 10 (approx. position)
Jigsaw-type Physical Match	~0
Drug and Narcotic Analysis	~1
Handwriting Identification	~8.5
Firearm and Toolmark Identification	~8
Fingerprint Identification	~2
Hair	~8.5
Fibers	~8
Paint	~2
Glass	~4.5
Soil	~5
Blood Spatter Interpretation	~9
Serology	~2
Voiceprint	~9
Bitemarks	~9
Fire/Arson	~4

§ 1–9.0 VULNERABILITY OF PHYSICAL EVIDENCE CATEGORIES IN LIGHT OF *DAUBERT* CRITERIA

§ 1–9.1 Daubert Criteria

In *Daubert v. Merrell Dow Pharmaceuticals*,[1] the U.S. Supreme Court interpreted the criteria for the admissibility of scientific evidence under the Federal Rules; the implications of this decision have been extensively discussed elsewhere in this work.[2] It is of some interest, however, to see how various evidence categories size up when viewed in the light of these criteria.

The *Daubert* court says that the scientific wheat may be winnowed from the scientific chaff by careful attention to four criteria:

1) Whether a theory or technique can be (and has been) tested.

2) Whether the theory or technique has been subjected to peer review and publication (as a means of helping to expose weaknesses in methodology and analysis, as *Daubert's* discussion of these criteria goes on to explain).

3) The known or potential rate of error, and the existence and maintenance of standards controlling the technique's operation.

4) Finally, "general acceptance" can yet have a bearing on the inquiry.

§ 1–9.0

1. Daubert v. Merrell Dow Pharmaceuticals, Inc., 509 U.S. 579, 113 S.Ct. 2786, 125 L.Ed.2d 469 (1993).

2. For a detailed review of the implications of the *Daubert* decision for scientific evidence, see *Science in the Law: Standards, Statistics and Research Issues*, Chapter 1.

Criterion (4) would tend to "grandfather" in many types of forensic examinations. For example, firearms identification is so firmly entrenched that it is unlikely that courts will look askance at it, despite the fact it would be sorely tried to comply with criteria (1) and (3). Criterion (2), if it is understood as most courts have understood it, namely, as being satisfied merely by the fact of publication in peer reviewed journals, is unlikely to pose a problem for most evidence categories. It is in connection with criteria (1) and (3) that *Daubert* poses a threat to many evidence categories. The "known or potential rate of error" alluded to in criterion (3) simply has not been established for the majority of forensic examinations, nor are there good mechanisms in place for attempting to do so. Criterion (1) speaks to whether a method can be (or has been) tested for its validity and for its applicability. Many forensic examinations have been evaluated, but by flawed testing methods. The issue is not whether a particular approach has been tested, but whether the sort of testing that has taken place could pass muster in a court of science. If not, then that approach may not have a legitimate claim to the indulgence of a court of law.

In view of the fact that no one has previously attempted to do so, it may be of some benefit to view a number of types of forensic science evidence, assessing them in terms of subjectivity and in terms of *Daubert* criteria (1) and (3). Although this is attempted here for just a few evidence types, this kind of assessment could be accomplished for virtually every category of physical evidence.

§ 1–9.2 Forensic Identification Subspecialties

§ 1–9.2.1 Blood and Other Physiological Fluids[3]

Subjectivity: Moderately low.

Reliability in the minds of forensic scientists: High. The reliability may be determined with considerable confidence by means of proficiency testing.

Vulnerability to attack in the light of Daubert *criteria (1) and (3)*: Moderately low.

Early in the 20th Century it was recognized that the blood of humans displayed a host of genetic markers, some of which could be demonstrated in dried bloodstains. Principal among these markers was the ABO blood group system, and for many years this was the only blood group system for which reliable typing methods for a dried stain were available.

Then, in the middle 1960s, a number of serum isoenzyme and serum protein groups were successfully typed in dried stains; this marked an epoch in the history of forensic serology. To ABO typing was added Phosphoglucomutase (PGM), Esterase D (EsD), Erythrocyte Acid Phosphatase (EAP), Glyoxalase (Glo), Adenylate Kinase (AK), Haptoglobin, Group Specific Compo-

3. John I. Thornton, *DNA Profiling*, 67 Chemical & Engineering News (Nov. 20, 1989); Lawrence Kobilinsky, *Deoxyribonucleic Acid Structure and Function—A Review, in* Forensic Science Handbook, Vol. III, 287 (Richard Saferstein ed., 1993); John S. Waye & Ronald M. Fourney, *Forensic DNA Typing of Highly Polymorphic VNTR Loci, in* Forensic Science Handbook, Vol. III, 358 (Richard Saferstein ed., 1993); George F. Sensabaugh & Edward T. Blake, *DNA Analysis in Biological Evidence: Applications of the Polymerase Chain Reaction, in* Forensic Science Handbook, Vol. III 416 (Richard Saferstein ed., 1993). *Also see* Chapters 25 and 26.

nent (Gc), and others. While ABO typing was capable of discriminating between individuals at a level of 15 to 48%, the isoenzyme and serum protein groups could typically discriminate between individuals at a level of a few percent down to as refined a level as 0.001%.

All of this was essentially rendered obsolete in the early 1980s, with the introduction of DNA (Deoxyribonucleic acid) typing. DNA typing has eclipsed conventional blood typing, and is widely viewed as being one of the two most important advances in forensic science in the 20th Century.[4] DNA typing is capable of exceedingly high discrimination, and in favorable circumstances it can be shown that only one person in several billion could have been the source of the evidence bloodstain. The highest discrimination is given by the typing procedure referred to as Restriction Fragment Length Polymorphism (RFLP). Another technique, Polymerase Chain Reaction (PCR), is applicable where the evidence is limited or where the DNA has been partially degraded by environmental factors. A further adaptation of the PCR method involves Short Tandem Repeats (STRs).

DNA typing has been subjected to the most rigorous scrutiny by the courts, presumably because its discriminating power is so great and so much is at stake when a suspect is associated to a crime scene only through DNA typing. Or perhaps because (at least some) modern courts or lawyers are more literate about science than they were in the past.

DNA analysts seem to have embraced the premise that they had best be very careful with their statistics, because, if they aren't, their work will be rejected. If this paradigm becomes the standard, then many other evidence categories, whose statistical underpinnings have yet to be developed, are in deep trouble.

The reliability of DNA testing may be determined by proficiency testing,[5] through which *Daubert* criteria (1) and (3) may be satisfied. Testing of this

---

4. The other would be the automated, computerized single fingerprint identification system.

5. Proficiency testing is discussed in greater detail elsewhere in this chapter in connection with specific types of physical evidence, but to clarify the issue of proficiency testing, it is a quality assurance practice in which an analyst is given a known sample, and processes that sample in accordance with the procedures that he or she normally employs. The analyst is not aware of the correct or expected results until after the test has been concluded. The test is therefore conducted "blind." In some instances it may be possible to conduct "double blind" testing, where the analyst is not aware that the sample is a proficiency test. This is not always feasible in forensic practice, however, where the analyst normally has the prerogative to inquire as to the integrity of the evidence, discuss the manner of collection, and explore other extrinsic issues that might relate to the interpretation of the evidence. In the forensic sciences, much of the proficiency testing that is done is accomplished through Collaborative Testing Services (CTS), a private company established in 1971 that is engaged in a

wide variety of interlaboratory testing in both the industrial and forensic sectors. As stated in their literature, "all of the tests are designed to assist organizations in achieving and maintaining quality control objectives." More than 2000 laboratories in the United States and laboratories in 50 countries participate in one or more CTS testing programs. CTS first became engaged in crime laboratory proficiency testing in the mid-1970s when the Forensic Science Foundation (FSF) first received grants from the U.S. Justice Department to develop such a program. CTS became a subcontractor, manufacturing specimens and analyzing test results. This resulted in the publication J. L. Peterson, E. L. Fabricant, K.S. Field & J.I. Thornton, CRIME LABORATORY PROFICIENCY TESTING PROGRAM (United States Department of Justice, 1978) that, in turn, stimulated a number of important quality assurance initiatives in the forensic laboratory field. It was also in 1978, with the conclusion of Federal grant support for this testing, that CTS joined with FSF and the American Society of Crime Laboratory Directors (ASCLD) to continue the program on a fee per test specimen basis.

sort will determine whether the methods used are adequate and whether the techniques used by a particular analyst were proper. There is little if any opportunity for the rationalization of incorrectly reported results when proficiency testing samples are processed according to the methods typically employed in the laboratory. Some indication of the error rate for the typing of bloodstains is known for both DNA typing and conventional serological methods.

Physiological fluids other than blood include semen, urine, perspiration, milk, feces, and tears. With the exception of semen, there is rarely any attempt to do anything more than to identify the nature of the material. The non-proteinaceous fluids, i.e., urine, perspiration, and tears, contain little in terms of biological markers of a particular person. While blood group substances have been recovered successfully from these materials, doing so is rarely attempted and even more rarely accomplished.

Semen occurs frequently in cases of sexual assault, and is a valuable form of physical evidence. The identification of a stain as a semen stain may be achieved by a combination of methods, including the demonstration of the enzyme acid phosphatase, the demonstration of the semen-specific protein p30, or the demonstration of intact spermatozoa by means of microscopy. In most instances, semen stains can be subjected to DNA analysis, with a high degree of individuality established. In cases of aspermic or vasectomized males, where no intact spermatozoa are to be found, conventional serology may narrow down the possible contributors to a few percent of the population.

As with blood evidence, the reliability of the testing may be determined by means of proficiency testing. Testing of this sort will determine whether the methods used are adequate, and whether the techniques used by a particular analyst were proper. This type of testing ordinarily will satisfy the *Daubert* criteria (1) and (3).[6]

Beginning with blood and physiological fluids, we will briefly summarize the results of collaborative testing (CTS) proficiency tests of crime laboratories over the past twenty-two years. Participants grew from 75 laboratories in 1978 to 484 participants in 1999—more than a six-fold increase. From 1978 to 1999, more than 50 blood and physiological fluid exercises were distributed to laboratories with participation rates (laboratories receiving samples and actually returning results) increasing from 45% in the first set of samples (78–91) to above 70% in samples from 1992 through 1999. In the tests up through those issued in 1991, laboratories engaged in conventional serological testing, and from 1992 onward, laboratories had the option of testing their DNA proficiency. Participants were commonly issued two or more stains. Typically a stain of known source (from a victim or suspect) and one or more stains of unknown origin found at a crime scene, on a garment, or some other location of importance to the investigation. Laboratory results were compared with

6. While the results of CTS proficiency testing gives an *inkling* of the potential or real error rate that *Daubert* calls for, for several reasons these results cannot be construed as the true error rate. Participation in CTS proficiency testing is voluntary and arguably in-volves only the better and more progressive forensic laboratories. Additionally, in many laboratories the CTS tests are treated in an entirely different manner than routine physical evidence.

values provided by the manufacturer of the proficiency test. The laboratories were asked to determine if the stains could have shared a common origin.[7]

Laboratories improved their typing of biological stains using conventional serological techniques during the course of the testing, correctly typing stains about 94% of the time in the period 1978–1991, but greater than 98% of the time since then. Using these conventional methods, laboratories correctly ascertained the source of bloodstains about 89% of the time and were incorrect about 6% of the time. In terms of comparing the source of biological and bloodstain *mixtures*, laboratories were only successful about 83% of the time, and were incorrect 11% of the time. In terms of errors, laboratories more frequently stated that stains *could have* had a common source (when they didn't) than concluding they *didn't*, when in fact they *did*. Mistakes were not as often due to mistyping as they were to the failure of laboratories to employ enough systems to distinguish the samples. Secretor status testing was one area in particular where laboratories performed poorly and which led to improper determinations of common origin. While the introduction of isoenzyme and serum protein systems in the late 1970s led to substantial improvement over straight ABO testing in determinations of source, the introduction of DNA typing in the 1990s provided another quantum level boost in the ability of laboratories to distinguish biological stains.

In the early years of proficiency testing using DNA typing, although determinations of common source were generally correct, they were not perfect. Progressively, though, test results improved. In tests in 1995–96 where laboratories used both conventional serological techniques and DNA typing, a sizeable percentage (from one-fifth to one-half) of laboratories respectively failed to distinguish stains using conventional serology, but using RFLP and PCR, less than 1% of results were inconsistent with manufacturers' specifications. Laboratories did experience some difficulty in simulated sexual assault cases in determining the origin of DNA present in male and female fractions of vaginal swabs. In the mid to late 1990s, typically 98–99% of replies were correct, with occasional tests where 2–3% of exercises produced inconclusive results. The 1999 test was one of those where less than 1% of replies were in error but around 3% were inconclusive. Clearly, the introduc-

7. As explained by Joseph L. Peterson & Penelope Markham, *Crime Laboratory Proficiency Testing Results, 1978–1991, II: Resolving the Questions of Common Origin*, 40 J. Forensic Sciences 1009, 1009 (1995), "criterion/unit of measurement ... is the comparison, whereby one or more questioned (unknown origin) samples were compared with one or more standard (known) samples." An exercise involving a single known stain and four stains of unknown origin would entail four comparisons, and the results of each comparison was tallied (did it agree or disagree with the manufacturer's value or was the result inconclusive?). Thus, because of the way correct and incorrect examiner decisions are summarized, readers must be cautious to avoid being misled into an exaggerated impression of accuracy, depending upon the test design. For example, suppose an examiner must compare a ques- tioned evidence item to two known exemplars, one of which is shares a common source with the questioned evidence. If the examiner associates the questioned item with the wrong exemplar, there will be an accuracy of 0% (one false positive and one false negative). If the materials contained not two but four exemplars, and the examiner made the same mistake as before, now the accuracy rate would be counted as 50% (one false positive, one false negative, and two correct non-associations). If the materials contained not four but eight exemplars, and the examiner made the same mistake as previously, now the accuracy rate would be counted as 75% (one false positive, one false negative, and six correct non-associations). And so on. Consequently, the more similar in design the tests are that are being compared, the more meaningful the comparisons will be.

tion of DNA typing has enabled laboratories to be much more accurate in differentiating and associating biological stains.

§ 1–9.2.2   Glass[8]

Subjectivity: Low.

Reliability in the minds of forensic scientists: Moderately high to high.

Vulnerability to attack in the light of Daubert *criteria (1) and (3):* Moderately high.

In crimes against the person, glass may be broken inadvertently as a result of violent activity. In crimes against property, glass may be purposely broken in order to gain entry. Whether the evidence consists of window glass or beverage bottle glass, automobile headlight glass or a makeup mirror, it may be characterized by physical and optical properties.

The direction of force applied to a broken window can ordinarily be determined with a high degree of certainty, as can the direction of travel of a bullet. The time interval between the breaking of the glass and the collection of the evidence cannot be determined, except in accordance with common sense observations of the extent of accumulation of dust, soil, or other debris.

The greatest number of glass evidence cases, however, involve very small fragments of broken glass that are recovered in the clothing or shoes of a suspect. These fragments are compared on the basis of density, refractive index, fluorescence under short-wavelength ultraviolet illumination, and elemental composition.

Prevailing opinion is that a match in each of these properties indicates a moderate to high probability that the exemplar and evidence samples have shared a common origin. Fluorescence may in some instances eliminate some glass samples from consideration, but rarely contributes significantly to the issue of commonality of source. Elemental composition is primarily of value in those relatively uncommon instances in which a maverick element, serving as a highly characteristic appellation, occurs in the glass. Density and refractive index are useful because they can be determined on very small quantities of glass, and are susceptible to small changes in the composition of glass. Refractive index may be determined at more than one wavelength of light, resulting in the acquisition of information on the dispersion of the glass. Refractive index and dispersion, together with density, represent the minimum testing that can be justified. Elemental composition alone can never form the basis of an opinion concerning commonality of source.

Most forensic laboratories accept the so-called *Miller Criteria*,[9] which state that for two samples of glass to be consistent with having shared a common origin, they must agree to within ±0.0010 g/cc with respect to density, and in refractive index to within ±0.0002 for the nD line and

---

8. Elmer T. Miller, *Forensic Glass Comparisons, in* 1 FORENSIC SCIENCE HANDBOOK (Richard Saferstein ed., 1982); David A. Stoney & John I. Thornton, *Glass Evidence, in* SCIENTIFIC AND EXPERT EVIDENCE (Edward J. Imwinkelried ed., 1981).

9. Named for Elmer Miller, the FBI analyst who devoted virtually his entire professional career to the forensic study of glass. *See* Elmer T. Miller, *supra* note 8.

± 0.0004 for the n_C and n_F lines. (n_D, n_C and n_F are different wavelengths of light).

It is not possible to give a mathematical probability that an evidence sample has shared a common origin with an exemplar sample. No probability model has ever been developed to do so. It is possible, however, to compare the density and refractive index of an evidence sample of glass against a database of these properties to assess whether the sample is a rather prosaic type of glass or is uncommon. This will not deliver a probability, but will enable the analyst to tender an opinion concerning how common those particular values are and to perform a t-test on the hypothesis that the glass samples do not come from the same source.

Blind-trial studies of the incidence of error in forensic laboratories undertaking this type of examination are lacking, but no rational person would claim that the incidence of error is nil. The error rate as countenanced in the *Daubert* criterion (3) is unknown.

Nineteen different glass comparison exercises were distributed to participating laboratories over the twenty-two years of CTS testing. Laboratories participating in testing grew from 63 laboratories to 107 in 1999. Laboratories were typically asked to compare two or more glass chips and to determine if they could have shared a common origin.[10] Laboratory performance on these samples ranged widely, depending upon the difficulty of the exercise. Typically laboratories were correct from 90 to 98% of the time, but in about a quarter of the tests labs substantially disagreed with the manufacturer's specifications. Three of the problematic exercises involved samples that were produced by the same manufacturer, using the same process, but at different times and/or locations. Such samples had very similar compositions and physical measurements but were, in fact, of different sources. Some of these samples only differed in refractive index measurements to the fourth or fifth decimal place, which exceeded the technical capacity of some laboratories. These tests illustrate well the dilemma of forensic laboratories when examining items such as glass that have been mass produced using stringent quality controls that yield products that will be widely distributed, but which have almost identical properties. Laboratories also experienced difficulty when the test samples gathered from the "crime scene" had actually originated from <u>two</u> different sources, one of the same origin as glass found on a suspect's shoe and one different. Almost a quarter of laboratories failed to complete measurements on all samples. As a result, half of these laboratories reported the sample could have a common source and half said they didn't; the completely correct response would have noted both types of glass.

Laboratories improved their measurements of glass over time; e.g., their refractive index measures were much "tighter" in later tests than in earlier ones. Such dramatic improvements in refractive index measurements were not always matched by comparable improvements in other methods (color, UV fluorescence, elemental analysis). As in other exercises, the success of laboratories in interpreting this type of physical material was influenced substantially by the difficulty of the test, as in cases where the manufacturer of the proficiency tests issued samples of very similar, but not identical, origin, or

10. *See supra* note 7.

when they mixed pieces of different types of glass in the same sample which made for a much more challenging proficiency test. The fact, though, that the proficiency advisory committee decided to issue such challenging samples can be interpreted to mean that glass evidence in actual forensic cases will occasionally involve such complexities.

§ 1–9.2.3   Hair Evidence[11]

Subjectivity: Very high.

Reliability in the minds of forensic scientists: Low.

Vulnerability to attack in the light of Daubert *criteria (1) and (3):* High.

In an exclusionary mode, hair is a rather good form of evidence. If the evidence hair is blond, straight, and twelve inches long, it may be emphatically eliminated as having originated from a person whose exemplar hair is black, curly, and two inches long. In an inclusionary mode, however, hair is a miserable form of evidence. The most that can be said about a hair is that it is consistent with having originated from a particular person, but that it would also be consistent with the hair of numerous other people. Stronger opinions are occasionally expressed, but they would not be supportable. An exception would be where the hair was forcibly removed from the skin. In this instance, it may be possible to extend the amount of information given up by the hair by recovering and amplifying the DNA from the root.

Hair is examined under the optical microscope, in much the same manner that it was examined at the beginning of the century. With the exception of DNA typing, there have been no significant advances in how hair evidence is examined. Not even the scanning electron microscope, with its much greater resolving power, has significantly advanced hair comparison.

Human hair can be rather easily distinguished from animal hair, however, and animal hair of different genera can generally be distinguished reliably by a suitably trained and experienced examiner.

A probability model has been advanced for the interpretation of hair evidence.[12] This model, however, has received a cool reception from the forensic science community. While some aspects of this model are demonstrably valid, criticism of the model has been persuasive.

The validity of hair evidence is susceptible of objective testing, although this has not been accomplished on a scale and in such a manner as to satisfy *Daubert.* The error rate of hair examination is unknown.[13]

In the early sets of proficiency exercises issued by CTS in the 1980s, laboratories, on average,[14] disagreed with the manufacturer in about 8% of their comparisons, and were inconclusive in another 18%. The incorrect

---

11. Richard Bisbing, *The Forensic Identification and Association of Human Hair, in* 1 FORENSIC SCIENCE HANDBOOK (Richard Saferstein ed., 1982).

12. Barry D. Gaudette, *An Attempt at Determining Probabilities in Human Scalp Hair Comparison,* 19 J. FORENSIC SCI. 599 (1974); Barry D. Gaudette, *Probabilities and Human Pubic Hair Comparisons,* 21 J. FORENSIC SCI. 514 (1976); Barry D. Gaudette, *Some Further*

Thoughts on Probabilities and Human Hair Comparisons, 23 J. FORENSIC SCI. 758 (1978).

13. In the wake of *Daubert,* at least one court has found hair identification evidence to be so defective as to require vacating a conviction based on hair identification. Williamson v. Reynolds, 904 F.Supp. 1529 (E.D.Okla.1995).

14. *See supra* note 7.

determinations were distributed equally between situations where laboratories reported hairs could have shared a common origin when they didn't, and vice versa. Because of difficulties of selecting completely homogeneous samples, and the possibility of "overlapping characteristics" between the victim and suspect samples, the proficiency advisory committee cautioned that in many situations an inconclusive response may be the most appropriate reply. As a result of these difficulties in preparing a fair, yet challenging, proficiency test, CTS discontinued issuing these types of samples in 1989.

§ 1–9.2.4 Fiber Evidence[15]

Subjectivity: High.

Reliability in the minds of forensic scientists: Intermediate.

Vulnerability to attack in the light of Daubert *criteria (1) and (3):* Moderately high.

Fibers may be encountered at the scenes of crimes, where they may be transferred from one item to another. Typically this is in the case of violent contact between two individuals, where fibers from a garment of one individual are transferred to the garment of the other individual. Depending on the type of fiber, this transfer may be in one direction, or may be in both directions. Forensic scientists have almost universally accepted the *Locard Exchange Principle*. This doctrine was enunciated early in the 20th Century by Edmund Locard, the director of the world's first crime laboratory, in Lyon, France. Locard's Exchange Principle states that with contact between two items, there will be an exchange of microscopic material. This certainly includes fibers, but extends to other microscopic materials such as hair, pollen, paint, and soil.

Fibers may be of animal or vegetable origin, or may be synthetic. Examples of animal fibers are wool, mohair, and angora. Examples of vegetable fibers are cotton and linen. The principal synthetic fibers are nylon, polyester, acrylic, and rayon. Animal fibers are hairs utilized in the fabrication of cloth. A wool fiber, for instance, is termed a wool fiber even though fundamentally it is a sheep hair. The identification of animal fiber as to species is by means of the microscope. Other than the morphology of the hair, there are no techniques available at the present time to distinguish one type of animal fiber from another. Further characterization of the animal fiber may be achieved, in the case of fibers that have been dyed, by an assessment of the hue and the degree of saturation (i.e., intensity of the color) of the fiber; this may be accomplished in a strict comparison mode or by means of microspectrophotometry.[16]

Vegetable fibers are identified by their microscopic appearance, and by various staining reactions. No instrumental techniques exist for their identification, nor is the scanning electron microscope of any particular advantage. The identification of vegetable fibers is considered by the forensic science

15. James Robertson (ed.), FORENSIC EXAMINATION OF FIBERS (1992); Barry D. Gaudette, *The Forensic Aspects of Textile Fiber Examination, in* 2 FORENSIC SCIENCE HANDBOOK (Richard Saferstein ed., 1988).

16. This is an unusually expressive word. *Micro-*, "small." *spectro-*, "appearance." *photo-*, "light." *metry-*, pertaining to "a means of measurement." So microspectrophotometry is "a means of measuring the appearance of light in a small specimen".

community to be straightforward, although the more obscure vegetable fibers, e.g., sisal, jute, Manila hemp, rarely are encountered and therefore are not likely to be recognized immediately by the analyst. White cotton fibers are so ubiquitous in our environment, however, they are virtually without significance as evidence; typically they are ignored unless there are circumstances that impart to them some special significance.

Synthetic fibers are abundant and represent the single most important type of fiber evidence. The means for the identification and comparison of these synthetic fibers are more diverse. Microscopic examination is essential for morphology and for the assessment of hue. But since these fibers are polymers, they may be approached by instrumental means as well. Fourier Transform Infrared Microspectrophotometry is ideally suited for this purpose, and is non-destructive. Pyrolysis-gas chromatography is perhaps even *more* discriminating, but this test is of a destructive character.

Many synthetic fibers have a characteristic cross-sectional appearance, which may enable the analyst to associate a fiber with a particular manufacturer. This type of examination is only as good as the library of known fibers that is available for reference, however. The major manufacturers of synthetic fibers maintain such libraries—certainly of their own fibers, and, for the purpose of guarding against patent infringement, the fibers of some of their competitors. A comprehensive library of the cross-sectional appearance of synthetic fibers is, however, something that is not ordinarily available to the typical forensic laboratory.

The validity of fiber identification techniques is susceptible of objective testing, although this has not been accomplished on a scale and in such a manner as to satisfy *Daubert*. The error rate of fiber examination is unknown. The validity of the interpretation of the significance of a match in fiber evidence has not been subjected to systematic testing of the sort countenanced by *Daubert*.

Laboratories subscribing to the sixteen CTS proficiency exercises generally were asked to identify the types of fibers presented and to answer a question about the origin or two or more fibers.[17] Labs were presented with both natural and synthetic fibers used in cordage, clothing, the home and in automobiles. Laboratories employed a range of microscopical, chemical and analytical techniques in their examinations. With respect to identification methods, most laboratories performed them quite well, but on occasion misidentified both natural and synthetic fibers. Laboratories sometimes were unable to perform the particular test that would have distinguished fibers, while in other cases they failed to make appropriate observations and interpretations of their data. Of great concern were those few laboratories unable to distinguish between generic classes of fibers, as between polyester and nylon. In some situations, even though laboratories failed to correctly identify the particular fiber category, they were nonetheless able to note differences between one or more fibers and to correctly answer the common origin question.

On the initial eight tests that asked laboratories to determine if two or more fibers originated from the same source, correct comparisons hovered

17. *See supra* note 7.

around 85%, while for the latter eight challenges, correct comparisons exceeded 90% and, in three tests, exceeded 95%. Similarly, prior to 1990 the rates of incorrect inclusions and exclusions were 10% and higher, while in the 1990s laboratories made fewer outright mistakes and more often failed to distinguish fibers by submitting inconclusive results. In the 1980s, laboratories made more errors and reported fibers could have shared a common origin when they didn't, but in the latter period incorrect inclusions and exclusions were balanced. Two notable exams occurred where a substantial percentage of laboratories were unable to distinguish between two types of nylon fibers (nylon 6 and nylon 6.6) and could not distinguish a dog hair from a mixture of mohair and alpaca hairs. The nylon fibers could have been differentiated by melting point tests that labs, not arriving at the correct conclusion, failed to perform. For the animal hairs/fibers exercise, many of the labs giving an inconclusive result simply because they did not have the expertise to distinguish such samples (which rarely are presented to crime labs as evidence). It appears labs were generally able to distinguish fibers that were clearly different, but had difficulty with samples where the fibers were similar but had slight differences in delustering agent, color or construction.

§ 1–9.2.5 Fingerprint Evidence[18]

Subjectivity: Moderately low.

Reliability in the minds of forensic scientists: High.

Vulnerability to attack in the light of Daubert *criteria (1) and (3):* Low.

Fingerprints are held up as the ultimate yardstick of uniqueness. When spectroscopists and organic chemists wish to label an area of the infrared spectrum that is capable of uniquely identifying a chemical, they refer to the "fingerprint area" of the spectrum. When molecular biologists refer to the form of DNA typing that demonstrates the seemingly unique character of DNA, they have chosen to call it "DNA fingerprinting."

The palmar surfaces of the hands and fingers, and the dorsal surfaces of the feet and toes, possess ridges. These ridges have a detailed geometry which is considered to be unique to each person. This assumption of uniqueness is based on (1) empirical evidence, and (2) probability models. The empirical evidence for the uniqueness of fingerprints generally takes the form of: "No two people have ever been found to have the same fingerprints." This statement is certainly true, but it does call out for a qualifier which is seldom appended. It should be recognized that while fingerprints are assumed to be unique, to the exclusion of everyone else in the world, no one is actually intercomparing the fingerprints of everyone in the world. A more precise statement would be: "To the extent that the effort has been made to intercompare fingerprints, no two people have ever been found to have the same fingerprints." Actually, the effort has been considerable, though by no means exhaustive, and no two fingers have ever been found in which the ridges match.

Since the early days of fingerprint identification, fingerprint analysts have agonized over the issue of how many fingerprint characteristics are needed to establish an unequivocal identification. The bottom line is that we

---

18. Robert D. Olsen, Scott's Fingerprint Mechanics (1978). *See also* Chapter 2.

still do not know. In the United States, some number between eight and twelve matching characteristics has been widely advanced as the criterion for identification.[19] There is no magic number, but there is a loose convention. While twelve matching characteristics has been adopted as representing a rigorous identification, what twelve matching characteristics really means is simply that the fingerprint examiner can stop counting and write the report.

But if twelve matching characteristics represent a rigorous identification, what about eleven? The answer is, yes, that would still constitute an identification. What about one? The answer is no. What about ten? What about nine? Fingerprints at crime scenes vary in clarity and in the expanse of the fingerprint area expressed. As the number of matching characteristics falls, the righteousness of the identification is diminished. Dogma, as currently expressed, is that eight matching characteristics, if they are clear and unambiguous, are adequate for an identification.[20] Six matching characteristics, however, would be sufficient justification for police investigators to channel virtually all of their investigative effort toward that one person.

It should be understood how fingerprint analysts have arrived at this position. If twelve matching characteristics are required, no one will come forward with an instance of apparent misidentification. If the number is dropped to eleven, the same situation applies. Ten characteristics, the same result. But this is a slow march toward disaster. At some point, a misidentification would certainly ensue. Every fingerprint examiner has seen fingerprints from two different people that have shown three or four matching characteristics in a local area (although accompanied by many dissimilarities as well). At the number eight, fingerprint examiners have exhausted all of their enthusiasm for having the number lowered.

Although eight or more characteristics might be required for an identification, a fingerprint at a crime scene that matched that of a suspect in six, or five, or perhaps even four characteristics would still represent valuable investigative information. A five-point fingerprint would not satisfy anyone in terms of an absolute identification, but it would certainly justify investigative effort being channeled into the investigation of that one suspect.

So eight matching characteristics, if they are clear and unambiguous, will serve for purposes of identification. A problem, however, is that if the evidence print can be gleaned for no more than eight characteristics, it is likely that the print suffers from some lack of clarity. Evidence fingerprints that possess only eight characteristics, but with those eight characteristics being brilliant and unequivocal, are not commonly encountered. So at the same time that the criterion for identification is being relaxed, the ambiguity of each characteristic is being augmented.

Most fingerprint technicians embrace the "One Dissimilarity Doctrine," which says that a single unexplained dissimilarity precludes an identification. This doctrine was first enunciated in the early days of fingerprint comparison as a means to allay any skepticism about the validity of this form of identification. It was enunciated as a *legal* doctrine, however, not a *scientific*

---

19. There is no worldwide consensus. Elsewhere, the number varies, and may be as high as sixteen.

20. Some bold and venturous examiners might place the number at six; other examiners would view this as teetering on the brink of recklessness.

one. There is no scientific basis for the doctrine. The doctrine has the ring of "fairness" to it, but there is no scientific support, one way or the other, for assuming the validity of the doctrine. In practice, the doctrine is abused or violated constantly. Whenever a fingerprint analyst encounters a fingerprint with a dozen or so matching characteristics and one dissimilarity, he will invariably rationalize the dissimilarity somehow, even if the rationalization is contrived.

Misidentifications based on fingerprint evidence are quite rare, but they do occur, invariably the result of human error. In most instances the sin has been one of misfeasance, with an indistinct evidence fingerprint being misidentified by an examiner who is inexperienced, or in a hurry, or simply anxious to help a police investigator. In a very few instances the sin has been one of malfeasance. It has happened that fingerprint examiners have lost their ethical compass and have reported a fingerprint identification when there was none, and cases are not unknown where a police officer has unscrupulously substituted other fingerprints for evidence fingerprints ostensibly recovered from a crime scene.

Latent fingerprint examiners generally performed very well on the seventeen CTS latent fingerprint proficiency tests over the past twenty-two years.[21] Rates of correct identifications are among the highest of any evidence category, usually in the 98%–99% range. Normally, examiners would receive one or more latent finger or palm prints from a "crime scene" and would be asked if one or more prints could be associated with a set of known prints either from a suspect or the elimination prints of a victim. Actual misidentifications are very rare, amounting to fewer than 0.5% of comparisons. There are three areas of notable exception: 1) situations where the examiner linked the latent to the correct ten fingerprint card, but then designated the wrong finger. These mistakes are usually attributed to carelessness. 2) in another test, laboratories failed to intercompare several latents *with each other*. That is, latents from several different scenes could not be associated with a known set of prints, but were all left by the same individual. In one test, examiners reported only 8% of the intercomparison identifications that were present. 3) the highest rate of incorrect values was in an exercise where the latent prints included those that were taken from twin brothers and 22% of participants made "erroneous identifications." More than 40% of respondents in this exercise failed to identify one or more of the questioned prints. As noted above, the proficiency advisory committee believed many identifications were missed (that is examiners failed to make an identification that was present) due to "procedural restrictions regarding the number of points observed before an identification is established."

§ 1–9.2.6 Soil and Mineral Evidence[22]

Subjectivity: Intermediate to moderately high.

Reliability in the minds of forensic scientists: Moderately low.

21. *See supra* note 7.

22. John I. Thornton, *Forensic Soil Characterization in* PROGRESS IN FORENSIC SCIENCE (Andreas Machly & Ray Williams, eds., 1986);

Raymond C. Murray, *Forensic Examination of Soil, in* 1 FORENSIC SCIENCE HANDBOOK (Richard Saferstein, ed., 1982).

Vulnerability to attack in the light of Daubert *criteria (1) and (3):* Moderately high.

Soil is the superficial, weathered covering of the earth. It occurs with moderate frequency as physical evidence, but tends to be underestimated and underutilized by criminal investigators. Soil and minerals are characterized by density, by elemental composition, and by the identification of the parent minerals by means of the polarized light microscope. Even if there is a very high degree of accord in these properties, the most that can be said about soil and mineral evidence is that it is consistent with having shared a common origin with a particular exemplar sample.

The skills required for these types of examinations are rarely seen in those individuals whose training has been in chemistry or the biological sciences. People with specialized training in mineralogy and petrology, those branches of geology concerned with the identification of minerals, rarely enter the province of forensic science. As a consequence, few forensic scientists have the requisite inventory of skills necessary to accomplish examinations of this sort.

The validity of soil and mineral analysis is susceptible of objective testing, although this has not been accomplished on a scale and in such a manner as to satisfy *Daubert*. The error rate for these types of examinations is unknown.

§ 1–9.2.7 Handwriting[23]

Subjectivity: Very high.

Reliability in the minds of forensic scientists: Variable depending upon the nature and extent of the writing, but generally considered to be no better than Intermediate in terms of reliability.

Vulnerability to attack in the light of Daubert *criteria (1) and (3):* High.[24]

Arguments that the identification of handwriting is a science are weak, to the point of being indefensible. Certainly handwriting identification has its scientific elements. It is reality oriented, it involves specialized knowledge, observations are made under controlled conditions, and in some instances hypotheses can be formulated and then tested.

But at that point handwriting identification parts company with other, established scientific disciplines. The classical, and probably outdated, definition of a science is that it is an orderly body of knowledge with principles that can be clearly enunciated.[25] The principles by means of which the handwriting of a particular person can be distinguished from the handwriting of another have not been clearly enunciated. Handwriting identification is more of an art, or a technical skill, than a science.

23. Richard L. Brunelle, *Questioned Document Examination, in* 1 FORENSIC SCIENCE HANDBOOK (Richard Saferstein ed., 1982). *See also* Chapter 3.

24. A growing number of courts have determined that handwriting identification evidence fails the *Daubert* test and cannot be regard as a science, and have therefore limited or excluded expert testimony by asserted handwriting experts. The case law is reviewed in Chapter 28, § 1.0.

25. Even here, however, some "fuzziness" exists. While this definition satisfies most demands placed on it, it isn't entirely satisfactory. By this definition, science could arguably be applied to library science, astrology, secretarial science, stamp collecting, and the law.

It does not follow, however, that because handwriting identification is not a science that it is devoid of validity. Handwriting identification conducted by a skilled practitioner may possess a high degree of validity. The fact that something is more of an art than a science does not automatically render it disreputable; physicians may diagnose influenza, for example, based on very little information and having applied little or no science in the process. The challenge, of course, is to demonstrate with systematic empirical data (e.g., proficiency tests) that one does reach correct results and therefore is a skilled practitioner. There is no other way to distinguish the skilled from the incompetent.

Handwriting is identified by a comparison of slant, the proportionality of letters to one another, the manner in which letters are formed, and individual letter characteristics. As school children, we are all taught to write in a particular manner. We are expected to emulate the so-called "copybook style" of writing, in which every letter is made in a particular fashion, and in which every letter is of the same size, and every upper and lower loop letter extends above or below the line to the same extent.[26] If the handwriting instruction that school children received was successful, everyone's handwriting would appear the same and no one could ever be identified. But people typically depart from the copybook style by adopting idiosyncratic characteristics that, given time and practice, develop into habits. It is this deviation from copybook style that enables the handwriting examiner to identify the writing of a particular person.

The real problem in handwriting identification is that writing is a dynamic activity. A person's handwriting differs from heroin or a shard of glass. Writing involves numerous muscles and bones that may or may not be acting in concert at a given moment, along with a variable amount of concentration or nonchalance on the part of the writer. This places a great premium on the collection of adequate exemplar handwriting, to document the range and variation of the known writing of the individual. This is not a trivial problem. Added to this, some individuals have little skill in writing, with the result that their exemplar handwriting does not display much in the way of ingrained habit. Without a substantial infusion of ingrained habit, the writing of that person cannot be identified.

The validity of handwriting comparison is susceptible of objective testing. This type of testing has in fact been attempted, although it is arguable whether this testing has been accomplished on a scale and in such a manner as to satisfy *Daubert*. Moreover, a fundamental assumption, the theory of uniqueness in handwriting, has been called into doubt.[27] The true error rate of handwriting comparison under various conditions is unknown, but the available data would not inspire a great deal of confidence.[28]

The sixteen CTS questioned document proficiency tests reviewed for this chapter included both exercises where examiners compared questioned and known signatures and writings to determine the authorship of written materi-

---

26. Numerous copybook styles exist in the United States, such as the Palmer, the Zaner–Bloser, the New Laurel, and the D'Nealian. Different copybook styles come in and out of vogue, like hemlines or sunspot activity.

27. *See* John Harris, *How Much do People Write Alike? A Study of Signatures*, 48 J. Crim. Law & Criminology 647 (1958).

28. The empirical research is reviewed in Chapter 3.

als, and other cases where laboratories were asked to examine mechanical impressions, inks and photocopying (rubber stamps, printing, etc.).[29] Examiners made few mistakes with the mechanical impression evidence, with fewer than 5% of responses in error; however, a substantial proportion (10% or more) of replies fell into the inconclusive category. Here, there was a tendency for laboratories to give an inconclusive reply, particularly where the correct response would have been to exclude the materials as having a common source. Another exercise involving different inks was easily deciphered by all laboratories. With respect to handwriting comparisons, examiners performed very well on the more straightforward tests with correct results approaching 100%. However, in other slightly more challenging tests, a very high percentage of replies (25% and more) were inconclusive. Laboratories also incorrectly associated an author with questioned samples as high as 10% of the time. There was also a high percentage of inconclusives, particularly where the examiner should have excluded a known set of writing but didn't (by saying they couldn't be eliminated as a source). Examiners lacked sophistication in more complicated cases involving multiple authors. That is, they correctly noted one suspect had authored a portion of a document, but failed to mention that a second author penned other sections of the same document.

§ 1–9.2.8 Narcotics and Drugs of Abuse[30]

Subjectivity: Low.

Reliability in the minds of forensic scientists: High.

Vulnerability to attack in the light of Daubert *criteria (1) and (3):* Low.

Narcotics and drugs of abuse may be considered together as a group, because identical measures are used for their identification. Each chemical species is capable of being characterized because each material has a unique molecular structure. This structure can be probed with a number of analytical methods, the principal ones being ultraviolet and infrared spectrophotometry, mass spectroscopy, gas chromatography, liquid chromatography, nuclear magnetic resonance, functional group reactivity and optical crystallography. Each of these approaches is extensively utilized in chemistry and other disciplines, and each has a demonstrated history of reliability.

The *Daubert* criteria (1) and (3) may be satisfied by means of proficiency testing.

A total of 42 drug proficiency tests were offered by CTS to subscribing forensic laboratories from 1978 to 1999.[31] Usually the tests challenged laboratories to identify one or more drugs in the presence of other mixtures/diluents. In some cases laboratories were also asked to quantitate the sample if a drug was found. The number of laboratories participating in testing increased more than six-fold over the twenty-two years of testing, with more than five hundred laboratories enrolled in drug tests in 1999. Response rates increased substantially over this two-decade period, with rates hovering in the 50% to 60% range in the 1980s, increasing to 80% and higher in the late 1990s.

---

29. *See supra* note 7.

30. Clarke's Isolation and Identification of Drugs (2d ed., A.E. Moffet ed., 1986); Jay A. Siegel, *Forensic Identification of Controlled*

Substances *in* 2 Forensic Science Handbook (Richard Saferstein, ed., 1988).

31. *See supra* note 7.

Samples were generally of four types: samples containing a single controlled drug; those containing more than one controlled substance; those with one or more controlled drugs mixed with noncontrolled drugs; and those containing only noncontrolled drugs.

Laboratories generally performed very well in these proficiency tests, correctly identifying the controlled substance in the sample about 96% of the time. The rate of successful identifications increased about three percentage points in the past nine years, compared with the previous eleven years. In fourteen of the exercises 100% of the laboratory replies correctly identified the drug in question. Where errors were made, it was far more common for labs to fail to identify a drug that was present (false negative) than to erroneously report a drug present when it wasn't (false positive). Laboratories did not perform as well with <u>mixtures</u> where, after identifying the primary controlled drug present, labs would sometimes fail to identify the remaining controlled and/or noncontrolled drugs present. In fact, when the success rate of identifying these other noncontrolled drugs is incorporated, the overall successful rate of identification drops about ten percentage points. Laboratories were successful in identifying opiates, stimulants, and depressants about 97% of the time, but had less success with hallucinogens where they were correct about 89% of the time. Laboratories were not particularly successful quantitating drugs, with only about half to two-thirds of labs even attempting quantitation (many local labs do not regularly perform such tests) and, of these, about 10% producing values outside the limits of acceptability.

§ 1–9.2.9   Voiceprints[32]

Subjectivity: Very high.

Reliability in the minds of forensic scientists: Low.

Vulnerability to attack in the light of Daubert *criteria (1) and (3):* High.

Voiceprints, the application of the voice spectrograph to questioned recordings of speech, have failed to garner a significant following outside the community of voiceprint specialists. The forensic science community in general has withheld a certain measure of respect from this type of evidence, and courts have struggled also with the problem of attributing to these procedures the proper extent of reliance.

Voiceprint evidence may eventually satisfy *Daubert*, but at the present time it would be quite vulnerable to *Daubert* criteria (1) and (3), and may have some problems with criteria (2) and (4) as well. The testing of the reliability of voiceprints that was initially conducted has been soundly criticized on the basis of weakness of methodology; it remains to be seen if voiceprints can recover from these false starts.

§ 1–9.2.10   Bitemarks[33]

Subjectivity: Very high.

Reliability in the minds of forensic scientists: Variable, but often low.

---

32. *See* Chapter 6.

33. Irvin M. Sopher, Forensic Dentistry (1976); Lester L. Luntz and Phyllys Luntz, Handbook for Dental Identification (1973). *See also* Chapter 5.

Vulnerability to attack in the light of Daubert *criteria (1) and (3):* Moderately high.

Bitemark evidence falls within the province of the forensic odontologist. Many bitemark cases involve evidence that is straightforward and unambiguous. In these instances, a photograph (or in some instances a cast) of the bitemark may be shown in juxtaposition with a test impression made by the teeth of a suspect, and the extent of agreement is apparent to everyone, jury included. The only question that remains at that point is the likelihood that another bite is an equally good match, something that has not been tested. In other instances, however, the evidence marks are obscure, or fragmentary, or susceptible to some negotiation or interpretation. In these instances, forensic odontologists have been more successful in convincing courts of the legitimacy of their opinions than they have been in convincing other forensic scientists. Other forensic scientists who routinely compare pattern evidence, e.g., shoeprint evidence, often have difficulty in seeing the agreement claimed by bitemark specialists. The bitemark specialists attribute this blindness to the fact that the other pattern specialist is not a dentist, and therefore is unable to properly interpret the patterns caused by teeth. The pattern specialists counter with the charge that this is The Emperor's New Clothes Syndrome, and the discussions quickly deteriorate. Significant areas of disagreement exist which have not yet been resolved within the forensic science community.

Nevertheless, forensic odontologists have been quite active in promulgating criteria for the identification of bitemarks, and have pursued a vigorous program for the certification of those engaged in this practice.

The *Daubert* criteria (1) and (3) may be satisfied by proficiency testing.

§ 1–9.2.11   Arson and Fire Evidence[34]

Subjectivity: Moderately low.

Reliability in the minds of forensic scientists: Moderately high.

Vulnerability to attack in the light of Daubert *criteria (1) and (3):* Moderately low.

In the minds of many forensic scientists, the analysis and identification of arson accelerants and of other fire-related phenomena are roughly coextensive with the analysis and identification of drugs and narcotics. Both areas are fundamentally aspects of chemical analysis. The instrumental methods of analysis for the two areas are virtually identical, and the comments above in § 9.2.8 hold as well for the characterization of arson accelerants.

Arson evidence consists of more than the identification of hydrocarbon accelerants, however. The character of heat-crazed glass, the temperature at which various items melt, the processes by which fires progress, are all areas, which involve some application of subjective judgment. In these areas of greater subjectivity, training and experience on the part of the analyst will play a large part.

The *Daubert* criteria (1) and (3) may be satisfied by proficiency testing.

34. Charles C. Midkiff, *Arson and Explosive Investigation, in* 1 FORENSIC SCIENCE HANDBOOK (Richard Saferstein ed., 1982). *See also* Chapter 7.

Laboratories experienced difficulties with the flammable proficiency tests, with the fraction of acceptable/correct results varying considerably.[35] The number of laboratories participating in these tests rose about threefold over the twenty-two years of testing. While laboratories generally performed well in identifying accelerants, of concern was the fact that they reported finding flammables present in more than 10% of samples when in fact none was present in tests up through 1990. A low point of performance also was a sample issued in 1992 in which fewer than 25% of laboratories correctly identified turpentine applied on either of two samples of Oak flooring burned with a Bunsen burner. Only 10% of labs correctly found the turpentine on both samples. In another sample involving cotton swabs, first soaked with water and then soaked with lighter fluid, an average of 90% of laboratories correctly identified a "light or medium petroleum distillate" on the two samples. In another sample involving several different classes of flammables applied to simulated fire debris, almost 90% identified kerosene, only about 60% correctly identified the class #1 lighter fluid, and only about half were able to identify the components of a mixture of gas and fuel oil. Problematic recovery techniques were blamed where samples contained wide boiling ranges of petroleum distillates. In exercises containing blank samples (containing no distillates) an average of 1–2% of laboratories incorrectly reported the presence of an ignitable fluid even though they contained only distilled water. Laboratories had success stating that a volatile was present, or that two distinct samples contained flammables not of the same source, but were unable to correctly identify the classes of petroleum products present. In another case containing three different types of volatiles, a high (about 95%) percentage of labs could identify kerosene and mineral spirits, but fewer that 80% identified lamp oil.

§ 1–9.2.12 Toolmark and Firearms Evidence[36]

Subjectivity: High.

Reliability in the minds of forensic scientists: High.

Vulnerability to attack in the light of Daubert *criteria (1) and (3):* Moderate.

Toolmark and firearms evidence has always suffered from the fact that the examination of these types of evidence is highly subjective, and cannot fall back upon a body of independently-derived scientific knowledge.

There is a lack of objective standards in the interpretation of toolmark and firearm evidence. Despite three-quarters of a century, no systematic and comprehensive attempt to codify standards for a minimum toolmark or firearms match has been published. This cannot, however, be attributed to professional lassitude. It reflects instead the nature of toolmark and firearms evidence and the uniqueness of each tool or gun barrel. The markings on the surface of a bullet, for example, are unique because the barrel of the weapon is unique. The very notion of uniqueness thwarts attempts to generalize and categorize, processes which are necessary prolegomena to the development of objective standards.

35. *See supra* note 7.

36. J. Howard Mathews, 1 Firearms Identification (1962); 2 Firearms Identification (1962), 3 Firearms Identification (1973); Julian S.

Hatcher, Frank J. Jury & Jac Weller, Firearms Investigation, Identification, and Evidence (1977). *See also* Chapter 4.

The problem is not that there are no objective criteria to be applied to the interpretation of toolmark and firearms evidence, but that the criteria, which do exist, are so diffuse. The information that the toolmark and firearms examiner uses to establish that a bullet was fired from a particular weapon or that the mark was created by a particular screwdriver is in large part based on experience that does not, and cannot, come out of books. Consequently it is difficult to transfer one examiner's ability to interpret the microscopic images to another person. Each examiner has to build up a background of experience. A standard of proficiency and a level of expertise may indeed be achieved, but it is very difficult to effectively test the examiner. Nevertheless, it is not impossible.

Not all aspects of toolmark and firearms evidence are wholly subjective. The weight of a bullet, its diameter, the width of a toolmark, are all examples of objective features. So are the fine striae on the surface of a bullet. Ten different firearms examiners looking through a comparison microscope will see the same configuration of striae. They may be recorded photographically or by means of contour analysis. Ten people drawn from the general public, given a few minutes of instruction on what to look for, also will see the same striae.

Up to this point, the examination is objective. But now, with striae on the evidence bullet and test fired bullet matching under the microscope, the question becomes one of whether the *extent* of matching of striae justifies a conclusion that both projectiles were fired from the same weapon. This step involves a high degree of subjectivity, but the opinion of the examiner is not made in a vacuum. The matching of striae on bullets or in toolmarks is a form of pattern recognition, and like many other examples of pattern recognition it is harder to describe the process than to perform. But the successful matching of striae is actually the *product*, not the *process*.

Restricting the discussion to firearms evidence, the process begins with the examination of a number of consecutively fired bullets from a single weapon, noting the similarities in the striae on the surfaces of the bullets, and noting the dissimilarities as well. Some dissimilarities are to be expected, and the extent of both accord and discord must be determined. The next step is to examine bullets fired from other weapons of the same manufacture and model. Profound dissimilarities are to be expected in this situation, and again the nature and number of these dissimilarities must be determined. Any attack on the validity of firearms evidence would have to address the accord in the former instance and the lack of it in the latter.

This process of examination of known weapons and projectiles may, in the case of a new firearms examiner, be repeated for scores of cycles before the examiner begins to forge a notion of uniqueness. The process is subjective, but criteria for the identification of striated evidence do exist as the projection of a gestalt of past experience. Training of this sort is probably more systematic in its application than any course of instruction that any of us have received on, for example, how to distinguish our own house from others on the street.

The *Daubert* criteria (1) and (3) may be satisfied by proficiency testing.

Firearms constitute a major portion of cases crime laboratories receive in violent crimes. Laboratories participating in tests grew from about 50 laboratories in 1978 to almost 300 in 1999, practically a six-fold increase.[37] Laboratories typically performed their comparisons well, with a fairly low rate of incorrect comparisons (2–3%), but with a substantial percentage (10–13%) of inconclusive responses. There were two exercises where inconclusive responses exceeded 50% of replies. The majority of scenarios involved tests in which examiners were asked to compare test fired bullets and/or cartridge cases with evidence projectiles found at the scenes of crimes. There were also three cases in which laboratories were asked to estimate the approximate distance between the cloth provided and the muzzle of the firearm used to fire the bullet. Laboratories generally performed well on these exercises, although many reported they would not issue a formal report in such cases if they did not have the actual weapon and ammunition to perform their own tests (which they did not in these cases).

Most of the inconclusive replies occurred in situations where bullets/cartridge cases were actually of *different* origin, but laboratories did not report proper results. The high rate of inconclusive replies may be attributed to the fact that laboratories were not issued a firearm to perform their own test fires, the difficulty of the test and clarity of the instructions given laboratories. In most scenarios, however, the manufacturer checked about 10% of specimens before they were issued to laboratories to insure they were suitable for comparison. While acknowledging that an inconclusive reply is sometimes the appropriate response to ambiguous evidence, "it is not when sufficient data for a conclusive answer is available." As with other examination areas, it is clear the field lacks firm criteria/thresholds for distinguishing cases of common origin from inconclusives from those of different origin.

Laboratories were invited to examine a wide variety of toolmarks over the study period; they ranged from marks made by screwdrivers, bolt cutters, drill bits, hammers, and hand stamps. In some cases the manufacturer supplied the suspect tool to participants, but in many cases laboratories were given only test marks. In such situations, the manufacturer would check all or a percentage of the marks to insure an identification was (or was not) indicated. The number of participating laboratories grew from 79 in 1981 to 247 in 1999, a three-fold increase. Early in testing around 50% of laboratories returned replies, but in the late 1990s, upwards of 75% returned answer sheets.

Typically, fewer than 5% of replies were incorrect, with many with rates as low as 1%. One test involved the comparison of a suspect handstamp impression in lead with four other hand stamp impressions, and only two of 178 responding laboratories incorrectly reported none of the suspect tools making impressions 1 through 4 had made the mark. Another exercise involving boltcutters asked if either of two copper wires had been cut with the tool. One had and one hadn't and only three of more than 300 reported comparisons were incorrect. Still, some exercises gave laboratories particular problems as did one involving groove joint pliers where 12% of replies incorrectly excluded the supplied tool as having made the marks on a stem of a doorknob. An additional 37% of replies were inconclusive. All marks had been examined before sample mailing to insure they were of sufficient quality for identification. Another exercise involved a pair of pliers and five cut wires and examiners were asked if the pliers could have cut the wires. 40% of

---

37. *See supra* note 7.

replies were inconclusive, where laboratories should have excluded the pliers as having made the marks. Often, examiners were reluctant to offer a firm conclusion because they reported they were unsure if the blade of the tool might have undergone changes between the times the different markings had been made. Another theme that extended throughout many of the tests was the suggestion (by the advisory committee) that examiners review/reevaluate their identification criteria. Because there was an effort to review exercises before they were issued to insure the marks were "identifiable", it became evident examiners were employing different criteria for concluding two or marks were made by the same tool.

Appendix I

Glossary

Accuracy. Conformity to a standard of correctness.

Alteration relationship. Exists when a source is an agent or a process that alters or modifies an object.

Associative evidence. Physical evidence at the scene of a crime that may serve to connect that scene with a particular individual.

Class characteristics. General characteristics that separate a group of objects from a universe of diverse objects.

Forensic science. Science exercised on behalf of the law.

Identification. Refers to the process of placing an item in a category. In common usage, including among forensic scientists, this term is used even when *individualization* is what is meant.

Individual characteristics. Those exceptional characteristics that may establish the uniqueness of an object.

Individualization. The process of placing an object in a category which consists of a single, solitary unit. Individualization implies uniqueness; *identification* does not require it.

Precision. The refinement of a measure to a greater or lesser degree.

Production considerations. The source produces the object, and the composition of the raw material utilized in the production are then expressed in the object. Finding these elements in an evidence sample at the same concentration as the putative source would establish a relationship between the evidence and the source.

Proficiency testing. A quality assurance practice in which an analyst is given a known sample and processes that sample in accordance with usual procedures. The analyst is not aware of the correct or expected results until after the test has been concluded.

Reliability. The extent to which a measuring instrument produces the same result when it is used repeatedly to measure the same object or event.

Segment relationship. When a source is somehow dismantled and parts of the whole are somehow scattered. The parts retain a relationship to the whole.

Spatial location. A type of relationship between a putative source and an object. A "source" may be a point in space as well as a tangible physical object.

Validity. Refers to the degree to which a measuring instrument measures what it purports to measure.

Appendix II
Bibliography

General

P. DEFOREST, AN INTRODUCTION TO CRIMINALISTICS (1983).

B. FISHER, TECHNIQUES OF CRIME SCENE INVESTIGATION (2000).

H. LEE, CRIME SCENE HANDBOOK (2001).

R. SAFERSTEIN, HANDBOOK OF FORENSIC SCIENCE (VOL. 1 1982, VOL. 2 1988, VOL. 3 1993).

R. SAFERSTEIN, AN INTRODUCTION TO FORENSIC SCIENCE (2000).

ENCYCLOPEDIA OF FORENSIC SCIENCE (J. Siegel ed., 2000)

B. TURVEY, CRIMINAL PROFILING (1999).

Blood and Other Physiological Fluids

I. ALCAMO, DNA TECHNOLOGY (2000).

S. BAXTER, *Immunological Identification of Human Semen*, 13 MED. SCI. & LAW 155 (1973).

T. BEVEL & R. GARDNER, BLOODSTAIN PATTERN ANALYSIS (1997).

E. BLAKE & G. SENSABAUGH, *Genetic Markers in Human Semen: A Review*, 21 J. FORENSIC SCI. 784 (1976).

E. BLAKE, J. MIHALOVICH, R. HIGUCHI, P. WALSH & H. ERLICH, *Polymerase Chair Reaction (PCR) Amplification and Human Leukocyte Antigen (HLA)-DQ⌈CD Oligonucleotide Typing on Biological Evidence Samples: Casework Experience*, 37 J. FORENSIC SCI. 700 (1992).

J. BUTLER, FORENSIC DNA TYPING (2001).

B. CULLIFORD, THE EXAMINATION AND TYPING OF BLOOD STAINS IN THE CRIME LABORATORY (1971).

C. COMEY & B. BUDOWLE, *Validation Studies on the Analysis of the HLA DQ⌈CD Locus Using the Polymerase Chain Reaction*, 36 J. FORENSIC SCI. 1633 (1991).

M. FARLEY & J. HARRINGTON, FORENSIC DNA TECHNOLOGY (1991).

E. GIBLETT, GENETIC MARKERS IN HUMAN BLOOD (1969).

P. GILL, A. JEFFREYS & D. WERRETT, *Forensic Application of DNA "Fingerprints,"* 318 NATURE 577 (1985).

H. HARRIS & D. HOPKINSON, HANDBOOK OF ENZYME ELECTROPHORESIS IN HUMAN GENETICS (1976).

R. JONAKAIT, *Will Blood Tell? Genetic Markers in Criminal Cases*, 31 EMORY LAW J. 833 (1982).

R. Jonakait, *Genetic Analysis in Forensic Science*, 29 J. Forensic Sci. 948 (1984).

S. Kaye, *The Acid Phosphatase Test for Seminal Stains*, 41 J. Crim. L. & Criminol. 834 (1951).

S. Kind, *The Acid Phosphatase Test*, in 3 Methods of Forensic Science (A. Curry ed., 1964).

L. Kobilinsky, *Deoxyribonucleic Acid Structure And Function—A Review*, in 3 Forensic Science Handbook (R. Saferstein ed., 1993).

H. Lee, *Identification and Grouping of Bloodstains*, in 1 Forensic Science Handbook (R. Saferstein ed., 1982).

H. Lee & R. Gaensslen, *Forensic Serology*, in 1 Advances in Forensic Science (1985).

A. Jeffreys, V. Wilson & S. Thein, *Hypervariable "Minisatellite" Regions in Human DNA*, 314 Nature 67 (1985).

D. Kaye & G. Sensabaugh, Reference Guide on DNA Evidence (1998).

F. Lundquist, *Medicolegal Identification of Seminal Stains Using the Acid Phosphatase Test*, 50 Arch. Pathol. 395 (1950).

National Research Council, DNA Technology in Forensic Science (1992).

O. Prokop & G. Uhlenbruck, Human Blood and Serum Groups (1969).

R. Reynolds, G. Sensabaugh & E. Blake, *Analysis of Genetic Markers in Forensic DNA Samples Using the Polymerase Chain Reaction*, 63 Anal. Chem. 2 (1991).

G. Sensabaugh, *Isolation and Characterization of a Semen–Specific Protein from Human Seminal Plasma: A Potential New Marker for Semen Identification*, 23 J. Forensic Sci. 106 (1978).

G. Sensabaugh, *Biochemical Markers of Individuality*, in 1 Forensic Science Handbook (R. Saferstein ed., 1982).

G. Sensabaugh & E. Blake, *DNA Analysis in Biological Evidence: Applications of the Polymerase Chain Reaction* in 3 Forensic Science Handbook (R. Saferstein ed., 1993).

J. Waye & R. Fourney, *Forensic DNA Typing of Highly Polymorphic VNTR Loci*, in Forensic Science Handbook (R. Saferstein ed., 1993).

J. Wolson & W. Stuver, *Simultaneous Electrophoretic Determination of Phosphoglucomutase Subtypes, Adenose Deaminase, Erthrocyte Acid Phosphatase, and Adenylate Kinase Enzyme Phenotypes*, 30 J. Forensic Sci. 904 (1985).

B. Wraxall, *Forensic Serology*, in Scientific and Expert Evidence (2d ed., E. Imwinkelried ed., 1981).

Glass

M. Dabbs & E. Pearson, *The Variation in Refractive Index and Density Across Two Sheets of Window Glass*, 10 J. Forensic Sci. Soc'y 139 (1970).

W. Fong, *The Value of Glass as Evidence*, 18 J. Forensic Sci. 398 (1973).

M. Houck, Mute Witness: Trace Evidence Analysis (2001).

S. McJunkins & J. Thornton, *Glass Fracture Analysis: A Review*, 2 Forensic Sci. 1 (1973).

E. Miller, *Forensic Glass Comparisons, in* 1 Forensic Science Handbook (R. Saferstein ed., 1982).

S. Ojena & P. DeForest, *A Study of the Refractive Index Variations Within and Between Sealed Beam Headlights Using a Precise Method*, 17 J. Forensic Sci. 409 (1972).

K. Smalldon & C. Brown, *The Discriminating Power of Density and Refractive Index for Window Glass*, 13 J. Forensic Sci. Soc'y 307 (1973).

D. Stoney & J. Thornton, *Glass Evidence, in* Scientific and Expert Evidence (2d ed., E. Imwinkelried ed., 1981).

D. Stoney & J. Thornton, *The Forensic Significance of the Correlation of Density and Refractive Index*, 29 For. Sci. Inter. 147 (1985).

J. Thornton & P. Cashman, *Glass Fracture Mechanisms: A Rethinking*, 31 J. Forensic Sci. 818 (1986).

J. Thornton, *The Use of k Values in the Interpretation of Glass Density and Refractive Index Data*, 34 J. Forensic Sci. 1323 (1989).

F. Tooley, the Handbook of Glass Manufacture (1974).

Hair Evidence

C. Aitken & J. Robertson, *The Value of Microscopic Features in the Examination of Human Hairs: Statistical Analysis of Questionnaire Returns*, 31 J. Forensic Sci. 546 (1986).

C. Aitken & J. Robertson, *A Contribution to the Discussion of Probabilities and Human Hair Comparisons*, 32 J. Forensic Sci. 684 (1987).

H. Anderson, *A Simple Scheme for the Individualisation of Human Hair*, 17 Microscope 221 (1969).

P. Barnett & R. Ogle, *Probabilities and Human Hair Comparison*, 27 J. Forensic Sci. 272 (1982).

R. Bisbing, *The Forensic Identification and Association of Human Hair, in* 1 Forensic Science Handbook (R. Saferstein ed., 1982).

B. Davis, *Phases of the Hair Growth Cycle*, 194 Nature 694 (1962).

M. Eddy & J. Raring, *Technique in Hair, Fur, and Wool Identification*, 15 Proc. Penn. Acad. Sci. 164 (1941).

S. Garn., *Types and Distribution of the Hair in Man*, 53 Ann. N.Y. Acad. Sci. 498 (1951).

B. Gaudette & E. Keeping, *An Attempt at Determining Probabilities in Human Scalp Hair Comparison*, 19 J. Forensic Sci. 599 (1974).

B. Gaudette, *Some Further Thoughts on Probabilities and Human Hair Comparisons*, 23 J. Forensic Sci. 758 (1978).

B. Gaudette, *A Supplementary Discussion of Probabilities and Human Hair Comparisons*, 27 J. Forensic Sci. 279 (1982).

J. Glaister, A Study of Hairs and Wool Belonging to the Mammalian Group of Animals Including a Special Study of Human Hair Considered from the Medico-Legal Aspect (1931).

J. Glaister, *Contact Traces*, 7 J. Forensic Med. 44 (1960).

L. Hausman, *Structural Characteristics of the Hair of Mammals*, 54 Amer. Naturalist 496 (1920).

L. Hausman, *A Comparative Racial Study of the Structural Elements of Human Head Hair*, 59 Amer. Naturalist 529 (1924).

L. Hausman, *Histological Variability of Human Hair*, 18 Amer. J. Phys. Anthrop. 415 (1934).

K. Hoffman, *Statistical Evaluation of the Evidential Value of Human Hairs Possibly Coming from Multiple Sources*, 36 J. Forensic Sci. 1053 (1991).

M. Houck, Mute Witness: Trace Evidence Analysis (2001).

D. Hrdy, *Quantitative Hair Form Variation in Seven Populations*, 39 Amer. J. Phys. Anthrop. 7 (1973).

P. Kirk, Human Hair Studies. *I. General Considerations of Hair Individualization and Its Forensic Importance*, 31 J. Crim. L. & Criminology 486 (1940).

S. Niyogi, *A Study of Human Hairs in Forensic Work—A Review*, 9 J. Forensic Med. 27 (1962).

S. Niyogi, *A Study of Human Hairs in Forensic Work*, 2 Proc. Canad. Soc. For. Sci. 105 (1963).

M. Trotter, *A Review of the Classifications of Hair*, 24 Amer. J. Phys. Anthrop. 105 (1938).

C. von Beroldingen, G. Sensabaugh & H. Erlich, *DNA Typing from Single Hairs*, 1988 Nature 332 (1988).

R. Wickenheiser & D. Hepworth, *Further Evaluation of Probabilities in Human Scalp Hair Comparisons*, 35 J. Forensic Sci. 1323 (1990).

Fiber Evidence

R. Bressee, *Evaluation of Textile Fibre Evidence: A Review*, 32 J. Forensic Sci. 510 (1987).

R. Cook & C. Wilson, *The Significance of Finding Extraneous Fibers in Contact Cases*, 32 Forensic Sci. Int'l. 267 (1982).

L. Forlini & W. McCrone, *Dispersion Staining of Fibers*, 19 Microscope 243 (1971).

R. Fox & H. Schuetzman, *The Infrared Identification of Microscopic Samples of Man–Made Fibers*, 13 J. Forensic Sci. 397 (1968).

B. Gaudette, *The Forensic Aspects of Textile Fiber Examination*, in 2 Forensic Science Handbook (R. Saferstein ed., 1988).

M. Grieve, *Fibers and Forensic Science–New Ideas, Developments, and Techniques*, 6 Forensic Sci. Rev. 59 (1994).

M. Grieve, *The Role of Fibers in Forensic Science Examinations*, 28 J. Forensic Sci. 877 (1983).

M. GRIEVE & L. CABINESS, *The Recognition and Identification of Modified Acrylic Fibers*, 29 FOR. SCI. INT'L. 129 (1985).

M. GRIEVE, J. DUNLOP & P. HADDOCK, *An Assessment of the Value of Blue, Red, and Black Cotton Fibers as Target Fibers in Forensic Science Investigations*, 33 J. FORENSIC SCI. 1331 (1988).

M. GRIEVE, J. DUNLOP & P. HADDOCK, *Transfer Experiments with Acrylic Fibers*, 40 FORENSIC SCI. INT'L. 267 (1989).

M. GRIEVE, *Fibres and Their Examination in Forensic Science*, in 4 FORENSIC SCIENCE PROGRESS (A. Maehly & R. Williams eds., 1990).

M. HOUCK, MUTE WITNESS: TRACE EVIDENCE ANALYSIS (2001).

R. JANIAK & K. DAMERAU, *The Application of Pyrolysis and Programmed Temperature Gas Chromatography to the Identification of Textile Fibers*, 59 J. CRIM. LAW, CRIMINOLOGY & POLICE SCI. 434 (1968).

A. LONGHETTI & G. ROCHE, *Microscopic Identification of Man–Made Fibers from the Criminalistics Point of View*, 3 J. FORENSIC SCI. 303 (1958).

C. LOWRIE & G. JACKSON, *Recovery of Transferred Fibers*, 50 FOR. SCI. INT'L. 111 (1991).

J. ROBERTSON, C. KIDD & H. PARKINSON, *The Persistence of Textile Fibers Transferred During Simulated Contacts*, 22 J. FORENSIC SCI. SOC. 353 (1982).

K. SMALLDON, *The Identification of Acrylic Fibers by Polymer Composition as Determined by Infrared Spectroscopy and Physical Characteristics*, 18 J. FORENSIC SCI. 69 (1973).

M. TUNGOL, E. BARTICK, & A. MONTASER, *Analysis of Single Polymer Fibers by Fourier Transform Infrared Microscopy: The Results of Case Studies*, 36 J. FORENSIC SCI. 1027 (1991).

Fingerprint Evidence

J. ALMOG & A. GABAY, *A Modified Super Glue Technique—The Use of Polycyanoacrylate for Fingerprint Development*, 31 J. FORENSIC SCI. 250 (1986).

J. ALMOG, A. HIRSHFELD & J. KLUG, *Reagents for the Chemical Development of Latent Fingerprints: Synthesis and Properties of Some Ninhydrin Analogues*, 27 J. FORENSIC SCI. 912 (1982).

D. ASHBAUGH, QUANTITATIVE-QUALITATIVE FINGER RIDGE ANALYSIS (1999).

F. CHERILL, THE FINGERPRINT SYSTEM AT SCOTLAND YARD (1954).

J. COWGER, FRICTION RIDGE SKIN (1983).

H. CUMMINS & C. MIDLO, FINGER PRINTS, PALMS AND SOLES (1976).

B. DALRYMPLE, J. DUFF & R. MENZEL, *Inherent Luminescence of Fingerprints by Laser*, 22 J. FORENSIC SCI. 106 (1977).

F. GALTON, FINGER PRINTS (1892).

HOME OFFICE SCIENTIFIC RESEARCH AND DEVELOPMENT BRANCH, MANUAL OF FINGERPRINT DEVELOPMENT TECHNIQUES (1986).

H. LEE AND R. GAENSSLEN, ADVANCES IN FINGERPRINT TECHNOLOGY (1991).

R. MENZEL, *The Development of Fingerprints*, in SCIENTIFIC AND EXPERT EVIDENCE (2d ed., Edward Imwinkelried ed., 1981)

A. MOENSSENS, FINGERPRINTS AND THE LAW (1969).

A. MOENSSENS, FINGERPRINT TECHNIQUE (1971).

R. OLSEN, SCOTT'S FINGERPRINT MECHANICS (1978).

D. STONEY & J. THORNTON, *A Critical Analysis of Quantitative Fingerprint Individuality Models*, 31 J. FORENSIC SCI. 1187 (1986).

H. WILDER & B. WENTWORTH, PERSONAL IDENTIFICATION (1918).

Soil and Mineral Evidence

W. GRAVES, *A Mineralogical Soil Classification Technique for the Forensic Scientist,* 24 J. FORENSIC SCI. 323 (1979).

C. HURLBUT, DANA'S MANUAL OF MINERALOGY (18th ed.1971).

W. McCRONE & J. DELLY, THE PARTICLE ATLAS (1973).

R. MURRAY & J. TEDROW, FORENSIC GEOLOGY, EARTH SCIENCES AND CRIMINAL INVESTIGATION (1975).

R. MURRAY, *Forensic Examination of Soil*, in 1 FORENSIC SCIENCE HANDBOOK (R. Saferstein ed., 1982).

J. THORNTON & F. FITZPATRICK, *Forensic Characterization of Sand*, 20 J. FORENSIC SCI. 460 (1975).

J. THORNTON & A. McLAREN, *Enzymatic Characterization of Soil Evidence*, 20 J. FORENSIC SCI. 674 (1975).

J. THORNTON, *Forensic Soil Characterization*, in 1 FORENSIC SCIENCE PROGRESS (A. Maehly & R. Williams eds., 1986).

Handwriting

R. BRUNELLE, *Questioned Document Examination*, in 1 FORENSIC SCIENCE HAND-BOOK (R. Saferstein ed., 1982).

MAUREEN CASEY, *Questioned Document Examination*, in MODERN LEGAL MEDI-CINE, PSYCHIATRY, AND FORENSIC SCIENCE (W. Curran, A. McGarry & C. Petty eds., 1980).

J. CONWAY, EVIDENTIAL DOCUMENTS (1959).

E. ELLEN, THE SCIENTIFIC EXAMINATION OF DOCUMENTS (1989).

W. HARRISON, SUSPECT DOCUMENTS (2nd ed.1966).

W. HARRISON, FORGERY DETECTION: A PRACTICAL GUIDE (1964).

O. HILTON, SCIENTIFIC EXAMINATION OF QUESTIONED DOCUMENTS (Revised ed. 1982).

O. HILTON, *How Individual are Personal Writing Habits?*, 28 J. FORENSIC SCI. 683 (1983).

O. HILTON, *The Evolution of Questioned Document Examination in the Last 50 Years*, 33 J. FORENSIC SCI. 1310 (1988).

J. KELLY, *Questioned Document Examination*, in SCIENTIFIC AND EXPERT EVIDENCE (2d ed., Edward Imwinkelried ed., 1981).

J. LEVINSON, QUESTIONED DOCUMENTS (2000).

T. MCALEXANDER, J. BECK & R. DICK, *The Standardization of Handwriting Opinion Terminology*, 36 J. FORENSIC SCI. 311 (1991).

R. MUEHLBERGER, *Identifying Simulations: Practical Considerations*, 35 J. FORENSIC SCI. 368 (1990).

C. MITCHELL, *Handwriting and Its Value as Evidence*, J. ROYAL SOC. OF ARTS 81 (1923).

R. MORRIS, FORENSIC HANDWRITING IDENTIFICATION (2000).

A. OSBORN, QUESTIONED DOCUMENTS (2nd ed.1929).

D. PURTELL, *Modern Handwriting Instructions, Systems, and Techniques*, 8 J. POLICE SCI. & ADMIN. 66 (1980).

E. SMITH, PRINCIPLES OF FORENSIC HANDWRITING IDENTIFICATION AND TESTIMONY (1984).

F. WHITING, *Inconclusive Opinions: Refuge of the Questioned Document Examiner*, 35 J. FORENSIC SCI. 938 (1990).

Narcotics and Drugs of Abuse

F. BAILEY & H. ROTHBLATT, HANDLING NARCOTIC AND DRUG CASES (1972).

D. BERNHEIM, DEFENSE OF NARCOTICS CASES (1983).

C. FULTON, MODERN MICROCRYSTAL TESTS FOR DRUGS (1969).

T. GOUGH, THE ANALYSIS OF DRUGS OF ABUSE (1991).

E. HORWOOD, ANALYTICAL METHODS IN FORENSIC CHEMISTRY (1990).

M. KURZMAN & D. FULLERTON, *Drug Identification*, in SCIENTIFIC AND EXPERT EVIDENCE (2d ed., E. Imwinkelried ed., 1981).

T. MILLS, W. PRICE, P. PRICE & J. ROBERSON, INSTRUMENTAL DATA FOR DRUG ANALYSIS (1981–1994).

R. SAFERSTEIN, *Forensic Applications of Mass Spectrometry*, in 1 FORENSIC SCIENCE HANDBOOK (R. Saferstein ed., 1982).

J. SIEGEL, *Forensic Identification of Controlled Substances*, in 2 FORENSIC SCIENCE HANDBOOK (R. Saferstein ed., 1988).

R. SMITH, *Forensic Applications of High–Performance Liquid Chromatography*, in 1 FORENSIC SCIENCE HANDBOOK (R. Saferstein ed., 1982).

I. SUNSHINE, HANDBOOK OF ANALYTICAL TOXICOLOGY (1969).

J. YINON, FORENSIC MASS SPECTROMETRY (1987).

Voiceprint

R. BOLT, R. COOPER, E. DAVID, P. DENES, J. PICKETT & K. STEVENS, *Speaker Identification by Speech Spectrograms: A Scientist's View of its Reliability for Legal Purposes*, 47 J. ACOUSTICAL SOC. AMER. 597 (1970).

R. Bolt, F. Cooper, E. David, P. Denes, J. Pickett & K. Stevens, *Speaker Identification by Speech Spectrograms: Some Further Observations*, 54 J. Acoustical Soc. Amer. 531 (1973).

H. Hollien, the Acoustics of Crime: the New Science of Forensic Phonetics (1990).

L. Kersta, *Speaker Recognition and Identification by Voiceprints*, 40 Conn. Bar J. 586 (1966).

L. Kersta, *Voiceprint Identification*, 196 Nature 1253 (1962).

L. Kersta, *Voiceprint Identification Infallibility*, 34 J. Acoustical Soc. Amer. 1978 (1962).

B. Koenig, *Spectrographic Voice Identification: A Forensic Survey*, 79 J. Acoustical Soc. Amer. 2088 (1986).

B. Koenig, *Spectrographic Voice Identification*, 13 FBI Crime Lab Digest 105 (Oct.1986).

National Academy of Sciences, On the Theory and Practice of Voice Identification (1979).

K. Thomas, *Voiceprint—Myth or Miracle*, in Scientific and Expert Evidence (2d ed., Edward Imwinkelried ed., 1981).

O. Tosi, Voice Identification: Theory and Legal Applications (1979).

O. Tosi, *Voice Identification*, in Scientific and Expert Evidence (2d ed., E. Imwinkelried ed., 1981).

O. Tosi, H. Oyer, W. Lashbrook, C. Pedrey, J. Nicol & E. Nash, *Experiment on Voice Identification*, 51 J. Acoustical Soc. Amer. 2030 (1972).

O. Tosi, *Fundamental of Voice Identification*, in Modern Legal Medicine, Psychiatry, and Forensic Science (W. Curran, A. McGarry & C. Petty eds., 1980).

Voice Identification and Acoustic Analysis Subcommittee (VIAAS), *Voice Comparison Standards*, 41 J. Forensic Identification 373 (1991).

Bitemarks

American Board of Forensic Odontology, *Guidelines for Bite Mark Analysis*, 112 J. Amer. Dental Assoc. 383 (1986).

J. Beckstead, R. Rawson & W. Giles, *A Review of Bite Mark Evidence*, 99 J. Amer. Dental Assoc. 69 (1979).

B. Benson, J. Cottone, T. Bomberg, & N. Sperber, *Bite Mark Impressions: A Review of Techniques and Materials*, 33 J. Forensic Sci. 1238 (1988).

J. Camerson & B. Sims, Forensic Dentistry (1974).

Outline of Forensic Dentistry (J. Cottone & S. Standish eds., 1982).

G. Gustafson, Forensic Odontology (1966).

W. Harvey, Dental Identification and Forensic Odontology (1976).

W. Hyzer & T. Krauss, *The Bite Mark Standard Reference Scale ABFO No. 2*, 33 J. Forensic Sci. 498 (1988).

L. Levine, *Bitemark Evidence*, 21 Dental Clinics of N. Am. 145 (1977).

L. Luntz & P. Luntz, Handbook for Dental Identification (1973).

R. Rawson, R. Ommen, G. Kinard, J. Johnson & A. Yfantis, *Statistical Evidence for the Individuality of the Human Dentition*, 29 J. Forensic Sci. 245 (1984).

R. Rawson, G. Vale, E. Herschaft, N. Sperber & S. Dowell, *Analysis of Photographic Distortion in Bite Marks: A Report of the Bite Mark Guidelines Committee*, 31 J. Forensic Sci. 1261 (1986).

R. Rawson, G. Vale, N. Sperber, E. Herschaft, & A. Yfantis, *Reliability of the Scoring System of the American Board of Forensic Odontology for Human Bite Marks*, 31 J. Forensic Sci. 1235 (1986).

I. Sopher, Forensic Dentistry (1976).

N. Sperber, *Forensic Odontology*, in Scientific and Expert Evidence (2d ed., E. Imwinkelried ed., 1981).

Arson and Fire Evidence

T. Aldridge & M. Oates, *Fractionation of Accelerants and Arson Residues by Solid Phase Extraction*, 31 J. Forensic Sci. 666 (1986).

J. Andrasko, *The Collection and Detection of Accelerant Vapors Using Porous Polymers and Curie Point Pyrolysis Wires Coated with Active Carbon*, 28 J. Forensic Sci. 330 (1983).

B. Beland, *Comments on Fire Investigation Procedures*, 29 J. Forensic Sci. 191 (1984).

W. Bennett & K. Hess, Investigating Arson (1984).

D. Berry, Fire Litigation Handbook (1984).

D. Berry, *Characteristics and Behavior of Fire*, 34 Def. Law. J. 243 (1985).

P. Kirk, Fire Investigation (3rd ed., J. DeHaan ed., 1991).

Law Enforcement Assistance Administration (LEAA), Arson and Arson Investigation (1978).

D. Mabley, Arson Investigation and Prosecution (1982).

C. Midkiff, *Arson and Explosive Investigation*, in 1 Forensic Science Handbook (R. Saferstein ed., 1982).

V. Reeve, J. Jeffrey, D. Weihs, & W. Jennings, *Developments in Arson Analysis: A Comparison of Charcoal Adsorption and Direct Headspace Injection Techniques Using Fused Silica Capillary Gas Chromatography*, 31 J. Forensic Sci. 479 (1986).

R. Smith, *Mass Chromatographic Analysis of Arson Accelerants*, 28 J. Forensic Sci. 318 (1983).

S. Swab, Incendiary Fires: A Reference Manual for Fire Investigators (1983).

Toolmark and Firearm Evidence

Association of Firearm and Toolmark Examiners (AFTE), Glossary (1980).

A. Biasotti, *A Statistical Study Of the Individual Characteristics of Fired Bullets*, 4 J. Forensic Sci. 34 (1959).

A. BIASOTTI, *The Principles of Evidence Evaluation as Applied to Firearms and Tool Mark Identification*, 9 J. FORENSIC SCI. 428 (1964).

D. BURD & P. KIRK, *Tool Marks: Factors Involved in Their Comparison and Use as Evidence*, 32 J. CRIM. LAW & CRIMINOLOGY 679 (1942).

D. BURD & R. GREENE, *Tool Mark Comparisons in Criminal Investigations*, 39 J. CRIM. LAW & CRIMINOLOGY 379 (1948).

D. BURD & R. GREENE, *Tool Mark Examination Techniques*, 2 J. FORENSIC SCI. 297 (1957).

G. BURRARD, THE IDENTIFICATION OF FIREARMS AND FORENSIC BALLISTICS (1962).

P. CECCALDI, *The Examination Of Firearms and Ammunition*, *in* 1 METHODS OF FORENSIC SCIENCE (F. Lundquist ed., 1962).

J. DAVIS, TOOL MARKS, FIREARMS, AND THE STRIAGRAPH (1958).

W. DEINET, *Studies Of Models Of Striated Marks Generated by Random Processes*, 26 J. FORENSIC SCI. 35 (1981).

C. GODDARD, *Scientific Identification of Firearms and Bullets*, 17 J. CRIM. LAW, CRIMINOLOGY & POLICE SCI. 254 (1926).

E. FLYNN, *Toolmark Identification*, 2 J. FORENSIC SCI. 95 (1957).

J. GUNTHER & C. GUNTHER, THE IDENTIFICATION OF FIREARMS (1935).

J. HATCHER, F. JURY & J. WELLER, FIREARMS INVESTIGATION, IDENTIFICATION, AND EVIDENCE (1957).

M. JOSSERAND & J. STEVENSON, PISTOLS, REVOLVERS, AND AMMUNITION (1967).

D. MACPHERSON, BULLET PENETRATION (1994).

J. MATHEWS, FIREARMS IDENTIFICATION (Vols. 1–2, 1962; Vol. 3, 1973).

E. MATUNAS, AMERICAN AMMUNITION AND BALLISTICS (1979).

W. ROWE, *Firearms Identification*, *in* 2 FORENSIC SCIENCE HANDBOOK (R. Saferstein ed., 1988).

E. SPRINGER, *Toolmark Examination—A Review of Its Development in the Literature*, 40 J. FORENSIC SCI. 964 (1995).

R. WILHELM, *General Considerations of Firearms Identification and Ballistics*, *in* SCIENTIFIC AND EXPERT EVIDENCE (2d ed., Edward Imwinkelried ed., 1981).

CHAPTER 2

FINGERPRINT IDENTIFICATION

Table of Sections

A. LEGAL ISSUES

Westlaw Electronic Research

See Westlaw Electronic Research Guide preceding the Summary of Contents.

A. LEGAL ISSUES

§ 2–1.0 THE JUDICIAL RESPONSE TO PROFFERED EXPERT TESTIMONY ON FINGERPRINT IDENTIFICATION

Fingerprint identification evidence presents post-*Daubert* courts with a paradox. On the one hand, most if not all of the claims made by or on behalf of fingerprint examiners enjoy widespread and unquestioning belief among the lay public, including the bench and the bar. On the other hand, surprisingly little conventional science exists to support the claims of the fingerprint examination community. The latter point is sufficiently well appreciated within the fingerprint community that, following the decisions in *Daubert*[1] and *Kumho Tire*,[2] the National Institute of Justice was asked to support research to test the validity of some of their most important assertions, which thus far have gone largely untested. "The participants in the [National Institute of Justice Fingerprint Research Advisory Panel] included practicing latent print examiners, researchers, and senior administrators from Federal, State, and private forensic science laboratories. They reached a consensus that the field needs ... [b]asic research to determine the scientific validity of individuality in friction ridge examination...."[3] On the one hand, strong intuitions have convinced several generations of fingerprint examiners that all of their beliefs about the nature of fingerprints and about fingerprint identification are correct. On the other hand, they can point to remarkably little hard data from systematic tests of the validity of those claims. How are courts to resolve insuperable challenges to the unchallengeable?

Today, a thoughtful and scientifically literate[4] proponent of expert fingerprint identification testimony, compelled by a thoughtful and scientifically literate opponent to demonstrate the validity of fingerprint identification claims in front of a thoughtful and scientifically literate judge, would face a

---

§ 2–1.0

1. Daubert v. Merrell Dow Pharmaceuticals, Inc., 509 U.S. 579, 113 S.Ct. 2786, 125 L.Ed.2d 469 (1993).

2. Kumho Tire Co. v. Carmichael, 526 U.S. 137, 119 S.Ct. 1167, 143 L.Ed.2d 238 (1999).

3. National Institute of Justice, Forensic Friction Ridge (Fingerprint) Examination Validation Studies (March, 2000). Although this solicitation for research proposals was original-

ly scheduled for publication in August, 1999, the FBI arranged to delay its release until after the trial of United States v. Mitchell. The case and the incident are discussed *infra*, at § 1.2.

4. By "scientifically literate" we mean nothing more (nor less) than having an understanding of how to ask empirical questions and how to evaluate the answers offered to those questions.

number of serious difficulties. The seminal cases admitting fingerprint evidence in American courts paid so little attention to the foundation of the asserted science that they offer no help in evaluating the admissibility of fingerprint identification evidence under *Daubert* and *Kumho Tire.* Proficiency testing does not support the claimed error rate of zero or of the unanimity of opinion asserted by fingerprint examiners.[5] Many of the most basic claims of fingerprint identification have never been tested empirically, and the field's most thoughtful research and scholarship have concluded that, in the strong form in which they usually are presented, those claims in fact are unprovable.[6] The most central beliefs of the public and the legal profession are irrelevant to the task at hand in most fingerprint identification cases.[7] The judgments whether a match exists or not and whether the latent and the known share a common origin or not have not evolved beyond subjective appraisal.[8] Finally, while the practical and realistic goal of fingerprint identification would be to make probability statements about the likelihood that a latent print which appears to match a suspect's rolled print actually came from someone *other than* the suspect (that is, the probability of a coincidental match), the fingerprinting field eschews probability statements as an "ethical" offense, and demands that its members offer only opinions of an absolute and certain nature or give no opinion.[9]

The greatest challenge, of course, is faced by the thoughtful and scientifically literate judge who has to decide whether to admit or exclude the fingerprint examiner's expert testimony. Some judges have simply taken judicial notice of the truth of the fingerprint community's beliefs, which—in the context of challenges brought under new law designed to encourage rigorous gatekeeping—would seem to be an acknowledgment of and response to the lack of more conventional scientific evidence on the issue.[10] A judge who

---

5. *See* David Grieve, *Possession of Truth,* 46 J. FORENSIC IDENTIFICATION 521 (1996) (Editor of the leading fingerprint examination journal lamenting that in the first proficiency test of fingerprint examiners, "... one in five [experts] would have provided damning evidence against the wrong person" and that only 44% of 156 examiners offered correct answers to all of the fingerprints in the test.). *See also* Collaborative Testing Services, Inc., Forensic Testing Program: Latent Prints Examination, Report No. 9808 (1998) (unpublished report). The few subsequent proficiency tests that have been conducted have the error rate averaging around 0.5%.

6. "It is unfortunate that this approach carries the implication that a complete correspondence of two patterns might occur...." "... it is impossible to offer decisive proof that no two fingerprints bear identical patterns." HAROLD CUMMINS & CHARLES MIDLO, FINGER PRINTS, PALMS AND SOLES: AN INTRODUCTION TO DERMATOGLYPHICS 154 (1943). *See also* David Stoney, *What Made Us Ever Think We Could Individualize Using Statistics?,* 31 J. FORENSIC SCI. SOC'Y 197 (1991).

7. *See infra* § 2.1.2[3][b]. Because most comparisons are between fragments of prints, the question that needs to be asked is whether

portions of two people's fingerprints can be so alike that examiners mistake one person's print as belonging to the other person. Since such errors can occur and have occurred, the questions move on to: what are the probabilities of such errors under varying conditions.

8. *See infra* § 2.3.1[1].

9. *See infra* § 2.1.2[7].

10. *E.g.,* United States v. Mitchell, Crim. No. 96–407 (E.D.Pa., *Daubert* hearing held July 7–13, 1999); State v. McGee, No. 99–CR–277 (Superior Court of Carroll County, Ga., *Daubert* hearing held October 27, 2000). Were there adequate solid research, courts could cite it and explicate it. Moreover, it is not clear whether the courts relying on judicial notice are treating the question as one of adjudicative or legislative fact. If they are taking judicial notice of adjudicative fact (under Federal Rule of Evidence 201 or a state equivalent) they must find that the adjudicative fact at issue is "not subject to reasonable dispute" and (in a criminal case) must instruct the jury that it has the discretion to accept or reject the judicially noticed fact. Yet this kind of judicial notice seems inapplicable because the very reason for taking judicial notice on this issue is that conventional scientific evidence is lacking.

takes *Daubert's* commands seriously would be hard pressed to write a coherent opinion justifying a decision to admit the expert opinion.[11] Indeed, because fingerprint identification has been both oversold and under-researched it is a prime candidate for exclusion for the most conventional of reasons for requiring expert testimony to cross a high threshold in order to enter the courtroom, namely, that the jury will give it excessive weight. Some judges might feel that because their duty is to obey the law, where *Daubert* is the law the lack of data or other rigorous evidence underlying fingerprint identification claims compels them to rule that the fingerprint expert may not testify.[12] However, the very ubiquity of the public's implicit belief in the validity of fingerprint identification evidence will cause many judges to think twice before excluding the expert testimony, though perhaps not for reasons of law or science. The professional skepticism of normal scientists requires them to postpone belief until the data are sufficient to support belief. Similar postponement of belief by courts would mean that in the case at bar the expert opinion would not enter, and that has its own consequences. Still other judges might conclude that they somehow "know" the claims are correct[13] and *that* belief, however it was arrived at, it might be argued, satisfies *Daubert*.[14]

None of these is a happy resolution. Perhaps courts will begin to find more creative and practical solutions to this boggling dilemma.[15] One possibility is partial admission: the expert is allowed to testify to similarities and differences between the questioned and the known evidence, but may not offer an ultimate opinion of identification or non-identification.[16] Another possibility might be to require, as a condition of admission, that examiners

If, on the other hand, these courts are taking judicial notice of legislative fact they are on firmer legal ground because this latter type of judicial notice is applicable to facts that usually are anything but indisputable (*see* Federal Rule of Evidence 201, Advisory Committee's Note). Yet judicial notice of legislative fact is appropriate only for decisions that are being made as a matter of law, and which therefore would be subject to *de novo* review on appeal, which would be contrary to the Supreme Court's holding in General Electric Co. v. Joiner, 522 U.S. 136, 118 S.Ct. 512, 139 L.Ed.2d 508 (1997). Clearly, there are some legal as well as scientific conundrums to be resolved.

11. *See infra* § 2.3.1[1] (Considering the possible application to fingerprint methods of some of the criteria courts used to evaluate DNA typing: "Woe to fingerprint practice were such criteria applied!")

12. An example is Judge Seay's assessment of hair identification evidence in the habeas corpus review of Williamson v. Reynolds, 904 F.Supp. 1529 (E.D.Okla.1995). But that is a rare example. Other judges faced with forensic sciences that similarly failed to pass *Daubert* muster have striven to find ways to keep the evidence from being excluded. *See, e.g.,* United States v. Starzecpyzel, 880 F.Supp. 1027 (S.D.N.Y.1995) (concluding that because forensic handwriting examiners flunked *Daubert*, they were not doing science; because they were

not doing science they did not have to pass muster under *Daubert*; therefore they were permitted to testify).

13. Scientists, and other logical people, would ask: how can one "know," when the problem is a paucity of data?

14. Query whether this is simply judges engaging in the same *ipse dixit* that the Supreme Court has prohibited experts from engaging in. General Electric Co. v. Joiner, 522 U.S. 136, 118 S.Ct. 512, 139 L.Ed.2d 508 (1997).

15. Some solutions simply may not be available to the judicial management of these problems, though they could be managed through proper legislation. For example, it might be expedient to grant temporary admission, that is, temporarily stay the operation of *Daubert* against a particular expertise or field of expertise, and permit continued admission of expert opinions for a limited number of years to permit belated empirical testing of the field's claims, after which period admission would be conditioned on producing the required evidence of validity. But it is hard to imagine how this can be done by courts making case-by-case decisions to admit or exclude.

16. This has occurred in many cases where the testimony of forensic handwriting examiners has been offered. *See* discussion of cases at 2 MODERN SCIENTIFIC EVIDENCE § 28–1.4.2.

give scrupulously accurate portrayals of the limitations of their field and their conclusions.[17] Another solution might be judicial instruction of the jury about the limitations of a field, notwithstanding popular beliefs to the contrary.[18] If nothing else, courts should have no objection to the opponent of admission offering to the jury evidence of the weakness or lack of confirmatory science, in order to assist the jury in determining the weight that should be given to the expert's opinion.[19]

Though we hesitate to venture a guess as to the eventual outcome of this period of questioning the heretofore unquestionable, we will say this much. One likely and beneficial scenario would be that the belated empirical research sparked by the fingerprint community's fear of exclusion under *Daubert* and *Kumho Tire* will result in knowledge that will lead courts not to exclude but to require fingerprint identification expert witnesses to remain within the bounds of those data, to become aware of and be candid about the field's limitations, and to refrain from making unsupportable exaggerations– some of which virtually define the field in the popular imagination.

§ 2–1.1 Admissibility Prior to *Daubert*

Expert testimony based upon fingerprints to prove identity is admitted in every jurisdiction of the United States.[20] That much is well known. The details of judicial acceptance of the technique during the second decade of the Twentieth Century are far less well known. This evidentiary development was characterized by meager judicial scrutiny combined with relatively rapid spread of acceptance among numerous jurisdictions. That swiftness is somewhat surprising considering that fingerprint identification presented the courts with a claim that was still novel (infinite and absolute individualization) in a remarkably strong form (infallibility).[21] And rapid considering the recent shortcomings and abandonment of anthropometry, the first child of scientific attempts at individualization, which had made essentially the same claims.[22]

17. Thus, if the data do not exist to support assertions of absolute identification, or an opinion is based on subjective probability guestimations or intuition or leaps of faith, the witness must say so as part of the opinion.

18. Compare the court's instruction in United States v. Starzecpyzel, 880 F.Supp. 1027 (S.D.N.Y.1995).

19. As the Supreme Court explained in *Daubert*: "Vigorous cross-examination, presentation of contrary evidence, and careful instruction on the burden of proof are the traditional and appropriate means of attacking shaky but admissible evidence."

20. *See* Annotation, *Fingerprints, Palmprints, or Bare Footprints as Evidence*, 28 A.L.R. 1115 (1953); and *infra* note 28.

21. Recall that once these concepts were accepted on behalf of fingerprint identification, numerous other forensic individualization areas made the same claim by analogizing themselves to fingerprints.

22. Anthropometry, or *bertillonage*, developed in the early 1880s by Alphonse Bertillon,

a clerk in the Paris prefecture of police, relied on the measurements of 11 different physical features of prisoners to determine if they had prior arrests in spite of their giving aliases to the police. Anthropometry marked the birth of forensic individuation techniques. Although anthropometry and fingerprints share the same underlying theory, fingerprints involve many more than 11 features, the features are more likely to be independent, and therefore less likely to be in violation of the statistical principle that is at the heart of all forensic individualization. And, obviously, fingerprints can be used not only to identify and catalog suspects once they are arrested, but can be used to help find suspects who left their fingerprints at a crime scene. Bertillon's system became controversial when it was thought that some prisoners were found who, contrary to the theory, had indistinguishable anthropometric measurements. *Bertillonage* would have been replaced by fingerprinting anyway, given the latter's greater convenience and unrivaled usefulness for investigative purposes. For a history of these matters, *see* JÜRGEN THORWALD,

Case law upholding the admission of fingerprint evidence begins in 1911 with *People v. Jennings*,[23] in Illinois. Within the decade New Jersey,[24] New York,[25] Nevada,[26] and Texas[27] joined Illinois in approving the admissibility of fingerprint evidence. These initial jurisdictions established the rationale for admissibility. Little more than the passage of time seems to have been necessary for eventual universal acceptance. In the next ten years 12 more states joined. And by the end of the 1930s all but five states were formal members of the club.[28]

THE CENTURY OF THE DETECTIVE (1965); *see also* John I. Thornton, *Criminalistics—Past, Present, Future* 11 LEX ET SCIENTIA 1 (1975).

23. People v. Jennings, 252 Ill. 534, 96 N.E. 1077 (Ill.1911).

24. State v. Cerciello, 86 N.J.L. 309, 90 A. 1112 (N.J.Err. & App.1914).

25. People v. Roach, 215 N.Y. 592, 109 N.E. 618 (N.Y.1915).

26. State v. Kuhl, 42 Nev. 185, 175 P. 190 (Nev.1918).

27. McGarry v. State, 82 Tex.Crim. 597, 200 S.W. 527 (Tex.Crim.App.1918).

28. Following are the initial appellate cases in various jurisdictions admitting expert testimony on identification based on fingerprint examinations. In other jurisdictions, fingerprint evidence came to be admitted without specific judicial authorization.

Second Circuit: United States v. Perillo, 164 F.2d 645 (2d Cir.1947);

Seventh Circuit: United States v. Dressler, 112 F.2d 972 (7th Cir.1940);

Eighth Circuit: Duree v. United States, 297 F. 70 (8th Cir.1924);

Ninth Circuit: Stoppelli v. United States, 183 F.2d 391 (9th Cir.1950);

Tenth Circuit: United States v. Fujii, 55 F.Supp. 928 (D.Wyo.1944); Fujii v. United States, 148 F.2d 298 (10th Cir.1945);

Alabama: Leonard v. State, 18 Ala.App. 427, 93 So. 56 (1922);

Arizona: Moon v. State, 22 Ariz. 418, 198 P. 288 (Ariz.1921);

Arkansas: Hopkins v. State, 174 Ark. 391, 295 S.W. 361 (Ark.1927);

California: People v. Van Cleave, 208 Cal. 295, 280 P. 983 (Cal.1929);

Connecticut: State v. Chin Lung, 106 Conn. 701, 139 A. 91 (Conn.1927);

Florida: Martin v. State, 100 Fla. 16, 129 So. 112 (Fla.1930);

Georgia: Lewis v. State, 196 Ga. 755, 27 S.E.2d 659 (Ga.1943);

Idaho: State v. Martinez, 43 Idaho 180, 250 P. 239 (Idaho 1926);

Illinois: People v. Jennings, 252 Ill. 534, 96 N.E. 1077 (Ill.1911);

Iowa: State v. Steffen, 210 Iowa 196, 230 N.W. 536 (Iowa 1930);

Kentucky: Hornsby v. Commonwealth, 263 Ky. 613, 92 S.W.2d 773 (Ky.1936); Ingram v. Commonwealth, 265 Ky. 323, 96 S.W.2d 1017 (Ky. 1936);

Maryland: Debinski v. State, 194 Md. 355, 71 A.2d 460 (Md.1950);

Massachusetts: Commonwealth v. Bartolini, 299 Mass. 503, 13 N.E.2d 382 (Mass.1938);

Michigan: People v. Chimovitz, 237 Mich. 247, 211 N.W. 650 (Mich.1927); People v. Les, 267 Mich. 648, 255 N.W. 407 (Mich.1934);

Mississippi: Willoughby v. State, 154 Miss. 653, 122 So. 757 (Miss.1929);

Missouri: State v. Richetti, 342 Mo. 1015, 119 S.W.2d 330 (Mo.1938);

Nevada: State v. Kuhl, 42 Nev. 185, 175 P. 190 (Nev.1918); State v. Behiter, 55 Nev. 236, 29 P.2d 1000 (Nev.1934);

New Jersey: State v. Cerciello, 86 N.J.L. 309, 90 A. 1112 (N.J.Err. & App.1914);

New Mexico: State v. Johnson, 37 N.M. 280, 21 P.2d 813 (N.M.1933);

New York: People v. Roach, 215 N.Y. 592, 109 N.E. 618 (N.Y.1915);

North Carolina: State v. Combs, 200 N.C. 671, 158 S.E. 252 (N.C.1931);

Ohio: State v. Viola, 82 N.E.2d 306 (Ohio App. 1947);

Oklahoma: Stacy v. State, 49 Okla.Crim. 154, 292 P. 885 (Okla.Crim.App.1930);

Oregon: State v. Smith, 128 Or. 515, 273 P. 323 (Or.1929);

Pennsylvania: Commonwealth v. Loomis, 270 Pa. 254, 113 A. 428 (Pa.1921);

Texas: McGarry v. State, 82 Tex.Crim. 597, 200 S.W. 527 (Tex.Crim.App.1918);

Vermont: State v. Watson, 114 Vt. 543, 49 A.2d 174 (Vt.1946);

Washington: State v. Bolen, 142 Wash. 653, 254 P. 445 (Wash.1927);

West Virginia: State v. Johnson, 111 W.Va. 653, 164 S.E. 31 (W.Va.1932);

Wyoming: Waxler v. State, 67 Wyo. 396, 224 P.2d 514 (Wyo.1950).

These cases, germinal not only for fingerprint identification but for many other forensic individualization techniques, invested virtually no effort assessing the merits of the proffered scientific evidence, but merely cited treatises on criminal investigation, or general approval of science, or, soon, other cases admitting it.

In *Jennings*, expert opinion based on fingerprints was the sole ground of identification. The court recognized the novelty of the expertise at issue, noting that "the courts of this country do not appear to have had occasion to pass on the question." In upholding the admissibility of fingerprint expertise, the *Jennings* court cited two general encyclopedias,[29] three treatises on crime investigation methods,[30] and one recent English case.[31] Nowhere in the opinion, however, does the court articulate the basis of the expertise it is evaluating, or discuss any scientific evidence in support of the expertise, or illuminate the technique's theoretical premises, or explain why one should believe that fingerprint examiners can do what they claim the ability to do. Nor do the cited sources fill that gap.[32] In addition, the court also referred to four experts who testified on behalf of fingerprint identification, each of whom had been studying or practicing fingerprint examination for three to four years before the trial. But the court's opinion shares nothing of what, if anything, they had to say on the question at issue.

Here is the totality of what the court had to say in its review of the science:

> These authorities state that this system of identification is of very ancient origin, having been used in Egypt when the impression of the monarch's thumb was used as his sign manual, that it has been used in the courts of India for many years and more recently in the courts of several European countries; that in recent years its use has become very general by the police departments of the large cities of this country and Europe; [of] the great success of the system in England, where it has been used since 1891 in thousands of cases without error. . . .[33]

Based on the preceding, the *Jennings* court concluded:

> We are disposed to hold from the evidence of the four witnesses who testified, and from the writings we have referred to on this subject, that

29. 10 ENCY. BRITANNICA 376 (11th Ed., 1910–11); 5 NELSON'S ENCYCLOPEDIA 28.

30. HANS GROSS, CRIMINAL INVESTIGATION 277 (Adams' Transl., 1907); LEONHARD F. FULD, POLICE ADMINISTRATION 342 (1909); ALBERT OSBORN, QUESTIONED DOCUMENTS 479 (1910).

31. *In re Castleton's Case*, 3 Crim. App. 74.

32. Nor would one expect them to. With the possible exception of Osborn's treatise on handwriting (which is discussed at some length at 2 MODERN SCIENTIFIC EVIDENCE § 28) they do not even purport to be presentations of the basic science underlying techniques of crime investigation.

33. *Supra* note 4, at 547. The allusion to "thousands of cases without error" obviously begs the question of validity. In actual disputed cases it rarely if ever is possible to tell whether the identification was correct or not; that is why the issue was before the factfinder. This has been a major problem in validating many forensic techniques. *See* discussions of this problem in CONGRESSIONAL OFFICE OF TECHNOLOGY ASSESSMENT, THE SCIENTIFIC VALIDITY OF POLYGRAPH TESTING: A RESEARCH REVIEW AND EVALUATION (1983); John Thornton, *Courts of Law v. Courts of Science: A Forensic Scientist's Reaction to* Daubert, 1 SHEPARD'S EXPERT AND SCIENTIFIC EVIDENCE QUARTERLY 480 (1994). Take *Jennings* as an example: how might one confirm whether that fingerprint identification was correct or not?

there is a scientific basis for the system of finger print identification, and that the courts are justified in admitting this class of evidence;....[34]

The second American case to consider the admissibility of fingerprint evidence, *Cerciello*, neither cited nor explained anything whatsoever concerning the expertise at issue. This court's scientific assessment was nothing more than a generalized endorsement of scientific progress:

> [I]ts admission as legal evidence is based upon the theory that the evolution in practical affairs of life, whereby the progressive and scientific tendencies of the age are manifest in every other department of human endeavor, cannot be ignored in legal procedure, but that the law, in its efforts to enforce justice by demonstrating a fact in issue, will allow evidence of those scientific processes which are the work of educated and skillful men in their various departments....[35]

The court's legal reasoning amounted to this: the admission of expert opinion, "one of the prominent exceptions of the general rules of evidence," was permitted on so many other matters that the court could hardly exclude one more; moreover, the jury would give the testimony whatever weight was appropriate.

The *Roach* court did no more than to cite *Castleton*[36] and *Jennings*, commenting of the latter that "The opinion of Chief Justice Carter in that case contains an instructive and learned discussion of this whole subject." The opinion offers no citations to any scientific materials or any discussion of the principles claimed to be the foundation of the technique. The court focused on the "qualifications" of the witness rather than the content of the science.[37] The court reasoned: "In view of the progress that has been made by scientific students and those charged with the detection of crime in police departments ... we cannot rule as a matter of law that such evidence is incompetent."

In Texas, the *McGarry* court rested its opinion squarely on *Jennings*, literally adopting the Illinois opinion as its own. After quoting at length[38] from *Jennings*, *McGarry* held simply: "We conclude that the evidence of the witness was admissible."[39]

The quality of judicial scrutiny of fingerprint evidence rarely exceeded that of *Jennings*, and sometimes it fell far shorter. While some cases made reference to actual early scientific works on fingerprints,[40] others cited Mark Twain's novel, PUDDIN' HEAD WILSON, as authority for the infallibility of fingerprint evidence,[41] or appealed to far higher authority:

> "God's finger print language," the voiceless speech, and the indelible writing on the fingers, hand palms, and foot soles of humanity by the All–Wise Creator for some good and useful purpose.... [namely,] the ulti-

---

34. *Supra* note 23, at 550.

35. *Supra* note 24, at 314.

36. *Supra* note 31.

37. "Before testifying to his opinion as to the identity ... the witness explained fully his qualifications, specified the circumstances upon which he predicated his opinion, and swore that he was able to express an opinion with reasonable certainty." *Roach, supra* note 25, at 623.

38. *McGarry, supra* note 27, at 528–530.

39. *Id.* at 603.

40. Notably, FRANCIS GALTON, FINGER PRINTS (1900); WILLIAM HERSCHEL, THE ORIGIN OF FINGER PRINTING (1916); H. FAULDS, GUIDE TO FINGER-PRINT IDENTIFICATION (1905).

41. State v. Kuhl, 42 Nev. 185, 175 P. 190 (Nev.1918); Stacy v. State, 49 Okla.Crim. 154, 292 P. 885 (Okla.Crim.App.1930).

mate elimination of crime ... [by] unquestionable evidence of identity in all cases.[42]

Before long, courts had ample precedents from sister jurisdictions to cite as authority for the infallibility of fingerprint evidence. Popular and judicial intuitions about fingerprints are so strong that not a case can be found that entertains any serious doubt about the scientific perfection that has been achieved by fingerprint examination.[43]

A modern court, compelled to apply the conventional scientific criteria outlined in *Daubert*, would find no help in these earlier cases. Indeed, it may be precisely the easy and rapid admission in those early cases that brings us to the post-*Daubert* dilemmas that today's courts are beginning to face. Because the forensic sciences have no tradition of research, little if any institutional support for doing research, and generally no cognate fields in academia or industry to do the research for them, once they are admitted to court their efforts to test themselves or prove themselves all but cease.[44] Had the early courts been more thoughtful and demanding, there would be less left untested and unproved today. And that research is likely to come into being only if today's courts are thoughtful and demanding.[45]

§ 2–1.2 Post-*Daubert* Challenges in Federal Courts

Modern cases have raised, and modern courts have responded to, challenges to fingerprint identification expert evidence under *Daubert* rather haltingly. The first of these was *United States v. Sherwood*,[46] in which the defense belatedly challenged the district court's admission of the testimony of a fingerprint expert without having first conducted a *Daubert* analysis. The Ninth Circuit reviewed the district court's decision for plain error.[47] But the defendant conceded so many of the *Daubert* factors that the court of appeals concluded on the strength of the defendant's concessions themselves that the district court's failure to conduct a 104(a) hearing was not error:

> Sherwood admits that [the expert witness's] technique is the generally-accepted technique for testing fingerprints and that fingerprint comparison has been subjected to peer review and publication. Furthermore, Sherwood admits that Dunn's testimony would aid the jury in determining the kidnappers' identity, thereby satisfying the second prong of the

---

42. *Kuhl*, quoting approvingly from Frederic Augustus Brayley, Brayley's Arrangement of Finger Prints Identification and Their Uses, for Police Departments, Prisons, Lawyers, Banks, Homes, Trust Companies ... and in Every Branch of Business where an Infallible System of Identification is Necessary (1909). In fairness to the *Kuhl* court it must be noted that its opinion was perhaps the most erudite, citing some of the most scholarly works on fingerprints—as well as some of the silliest.

43. *See* Stevenson v. United States, 380 F.2d 590 (D.C.Cir.1967).

44. An Assistant U.S. Attorney has argued that it is unfair to criticize forensic sciences "for failing to develop a rigorous empirical defense of [their] theories and methods" because they "had not had any particular reason to conduct validity studies because their testi-

mony was being admitted without them." J. Orenstein, *Effect of the* Daubert *Decision on Document Examinations From the Prosecutor's Perspective*, 1 Forensic Science Communications (October 1999), at http://www.fbi.gov/programs/lab/fsc/backissu/oct1999/abstrctf.htm.

45. While the results of such research will be unlikely to lead to ultimate exclusion, it is likely to lead to a tempering of the astounding claims made by fingerprint and other forensic examiners, such as the claim of error rates of zero.

46. 98 F.3d 402 (9th Cir.1996).

47. "[B]ecause [the defendant] failed to make a specific objection to the expert testimony regarding the prints ... review [was] limited to plain error analysis." *Id.* at 408.

Daubert test. Consequently, the district court did not commit actual error in admitting [the expert witness's] testimony.[48]

If the defendant had conceded virtually every issue it had raised by its *Daubert* challenge, there may well have been nothing left for the court to decide, particularly under a deferential standard of review. Still, the Court of Appeals opinion is about as perfunctory as one could imagine. The merits of the science received no scrutiny at any level. The court made no effort to assess–or, indeed, even to find and cite–studies purporting to establish the scientific foundation on which the techniques of fingerprint identification purports to stand. Had it done so, it would have been illuminating to see what the court found and what it made of what it found.

An oblique reference to the core assumptions of fingerprint identification was made in *United States v. Salameh*.[49] This case involved an appeal of convictions in the World Trade Center bombing case. The fingerprint issue went not to the heart of the theory or validity of fingerprint identification, but only to whether a fingerprint expert was able to determine the manner in which a person held a notebook (from which one might infer that the person whose fingerprints were on the notebook made the terroristic writings that were in it). The defense argued that a fingerprint expert's expertise did not include conclusions about the orientation of a person's grip on a notebook. In rejecting that challenge, the court concluded that the expert's "testimony regarding the placement of [the defendant's] hand on the notebook was based on the same well-accepted scientific foundation as her identification of his fingerprints."[50] Though this is the essential reasoning that supports the court's holding, it hardly seems to be more than a throw-away line. It is hard to fathom what the foundation that is offered to support claims of fingerprint identity could have to do with the orientation of a hand in holding an object. The allusion to the "well-accepted scientific foundation" of fingerprint identification doubtless is a reflection of popular cultural beliefs about fingerprint identification because the opinion neither cites nor makes any reference to any source that addresses that proposition. Putting that aside and focusing on the expertise that was called into question by the task at hand in this case[51]– the position of a hand holding an object–nothing is offered to support the asserted expertise beyond the court's reliance on the *ipse dixit* of the expert. The opinion does nothing to relieve one's curiosity about whether fingerprint examiners do or do not have any special skill in reaching conclusions about the orientation by which an object has been held.

In *United States v. Malveaux*[52] the defendant appealed a bank robbery conviction on several grounds. The one of interest here is his claim that "the district court erred by admitting expert fingerprint testimony because the government did not meet its burden under the *Frye* test."[53] The court first noted that *Frye* has been displaced by *Daubert*. The court then summarily disposed of the defendant's claim: "[W]e conclude that [the defendant's]

---

48. *Id.*

49. 152 F.3d 88 (2d Cir.1998).

50. *Id.* at 129.

51. *Kumho Tire* (explaining that assessments of the dependability of an expertise must be addressed to the specific task em-

ployed in the case at bar, and not be based on a general, global, vague, set of skills.)

52. 208 F.3d 223 (9th Cir.2000)(unpublished).

53. *Id.*

contention is without merit because the record reflects that the expert's testimony was based on scientific techniques and advanced a material aspect of the government's case."[54] The court was silent on the basis for concluding that these techniques were scientific, by which the court presumably meant that identification by fingerprints withstands a *Daubert* challenge because the techniques used are valid. In addition, however, the court states somewhat paradoxically that challenges to validity go to weight and not to admissibility, and are therefore for the jury to evaluate. *Daubert*, of course, stands for the proposition that in order to be admissible expert evidence must be sound, a gatekeeping decision that is for the judge to make.[55]

The first case in which a serious and timely *in limine* challenge was made to the foundational claims of fingerprint identification, and in which a *Daubert* hearing was held, was *United States v. Mitchell.*[56] At the *Daubert* hearing, both the proponent and the opponent offered briefs, witnesses, and arguments that attempted to provide the court with real information about the strengths and the weaknesses of the claims of fingerprint identification.

Because the district court wrote no opinion to accompany its ruling, details are somewhat hard to come by, and this discussion relies on the reports of participants other than the judge.[57] The proponent's major witnesses at the *Daubert* hearing were Bruce Babler,[58] Donald Ziesig,[59] David Ashbaugh,[60] Bruce Budowle,[61] and Stephen Meagher.[62] Called by the opponent were James Starrs,[63] Simon Cole,[64] and David Stoney.[65]

The proponent's witnesses explained the process of fingerprint identification and their theories of why it is believed sound by fingerprints examiners and should be by the court as well, despite limited conventional scientific testing. They presented a variety of such arguments, including the fact that identical twins do not have identical fingerprints,[66] the argument that 100

---

54. *Id.*

55. *Id.* at n. 5 ("[t]o the extent that [the defendant] questions the validity of the fingerprint comparison, this is a question of weight and credibility that properly went to the jury.")

56. United States v. Mitchell, Crim. No. 96–407–1 (E.D.Pa., judgment entered February, 2000). A previous trial and conviction resulted in a reversal, reported at 145 F.3d 572 (3d Cir.1998).

57. Query what is signified by the judge's failure to write an opinion in so noteworthy a hearing, and whether the failure of the district judge to give reasons for his conclusion will not in itself require the Court of Appeals to remand. Our sources are: Press Release, Office of the U.S. Attorney for the Eastern District of Pennsylvania (Sep. 13, 1999); Simon Cole, *The Myth of Fingerprints*, LINGAFRANCA, Nov.2000, at 54; *Fingering Fingerprints: Fingerprints, the Touchstone of Forensic Science, Have Never Been Subjected to Proper Scientific Scrutiny*, THE ECONOMIST, Dec. 16, 2000, at 69; and a summary at http://onin.com/fp/daubert_links.html#CASE1.

58. A Professor of Physical Anthropology from Marquette University.

59. An engineer at Lockheed–Martin Corp.

60. A Sergeant in the Royal Canadian Mounted Police.

61. Bruce Budowle, a senior scientist at the FBI Laboratory in Quantico, who holds a doctorate in genetics.

62. Latent Print Unit Chief at the FBI Laboratory.

63. Professor of law and forensic science at George Washington University and co-author of ANDRE MOENSSENS ET AL., SCIENTIFIC EVIDENCE IN CIVIL AND CRIMINAL CASES (4th ed.1995).

64. A sociologist and historian of science, and author of SIMON A. COLE, SUSPECT IDENTITIES: A HISTORY OF FINGERPRINTING AND CRIMINAL IDENTIFICATION (2001).

65. Director of the McCrone Research Institute in Chicago, holds a doctorate in forensic science, and is the author of the scientific section of this chapter, Part B: Scientific Status.

66. However, query which way this fact cuts. It implies that fingerprints are determined by unknown random or non-random forces in addition to whatever genetic forces may be operating.

years of fingerprint casework constitutes empirical testing, efforts at developing statistical models of fingerprint identification, and they claimed that the error rate in fingerprint identification is zero.[67] Ashbaugh offered the theory that he has developed in an effort to articulate a foundation for fingerprint identification that can meet modern scientific standards. In addition, the government offered the findings of two studies conducted for the purposes of this hearing.

The witnesses for the opponent pointed to the subjectivity and lack of standards, lack of conventional scientific testing of the hypotheses at the root of belief in absolute identification by fingerprints, and that fingerprint casework does not constitute testing because it is not designed to falsify the examination.[68] These witnesses also pointed to errors demonstrated by proficiency testing and errors which have been found in actual cases. The debate between the experts also involved the issue of counting points of similarity between known and questioned prints (and that while point-counting is rejected by American examiners, they nevertheless engage in it in whatever idiosyncratic way each one chooses).[69]

Two studies conducted by the government in reaction to the challenge raised in this case are noteworthy on several levels. First of all, the fact that such research had not been conducted before, and had to be rushed into being for this hearing is itself astonishing. Most fields of normal science could pull from the shelf dozens or hundreds, if not thousands, of studies testing their various hypotheses and contentions, which had been conducted over the past decades or century, and hand them to the court. The need to conduct such studies at such a late date would seem to be a dilemma for the proponents (do we go to court without the studies, or do we conduct them and thereby underscore the fact that until now such research had not been done) and would seem to confirm a major point being made by the opponents.

67. As witness Budowle explained: "I don't think error rates is the right approach. I think errors are the right approach in reviewing errors in improving upon them, discussing them and fixing them is an absolutely important thing to do. But using them to calculate an error rate is meaningless and misrepresents the state of the art." Witness Meagher argued that if error is divided into "methodological error" (the errors made by the technique) and "examiner error," all of the errors would be found to be a result of the latter, and therefore the technique of fingerprint examination is flawless; it is certain examiners who err. These statements reflect the culture of fingerprinting practice which protects its doctrine by attributing errors to individual examiners, rather than by asking what might have been flawed in the field's methods. Witness Cole commented that this was like "saying automobiles have an extremely low 'scientific' crash rate. It's only when we put drivers behind the wheel that they crash." The most interesting question is why the proponents of fingerprint identification think that having a zero error rate is so essential that they will go to such lengths to insist on the proposition, while normal sciences consider error unavoidable and most of them have routine ways to measure and take account of error.

68. Put simply, rarely is it possible to test whether an examiner in a real case is correct or incorrect. In scientific research a study is designed so that the hypothesis at issue is made falsifiable and can be tested. If the process withstands the effort at falsification, the hypothesis thereby gains strength.

69. Prof. Starrs criticized the fingerprint field for "the claim of absolute certainty ... the failure to carry out controlled empirical data searching experimentation, a failure to recognize the value of considerations of the error rate." He also criticized "the lack of objectivity and uniformity and systemization with respect to standards, if any, of the fingerprint analysis. It is a miasma. It just has absolutely no basis at all in solid science. There's [not] even a modicum of scientific certainty in the way in which they conduct themselves."

One of the studies conducted by the government for the *Daubert* hearing in this case employed the two actual latent and the known prints that were at issue in the case. These prints were submitted to 53 state law enforcement agency crime laboratories around the country for their evaluation. Though, of the 35 that responded, most concluded that the latent and known prints matched, eight said that no match could be made to one of the prints and six said that no match could be made to the other print. This disagreement is significant, given the professional ideology of fingerprint examiners, which asserts that they are so conservative in reaching conclusions that no one of them would declare a match unless it were certain that every other examiner who looked at the same prints would also declare them a match.[70] This first test of that belief had to be shocking to the field. The FBI reacted by sending annotated blow-ups of the prints to those examiners who judged the prints unmatchable, showing the points of claimed similarity, and asking them to reconsider their original conclusion. Apparently each of these examiners then adopted the FBI's view of the prints.

A second study was an effort to obtain an estimate of the probability that one person's fingerprints would be mistaken for those of another person, at least to a computer system designed to match fingerprints. The FBI asked Lockheed–Martin, the manufacturer of its AFIS (automated fingerprint identification system), to help it run a comparison of the images of 50,000 single fingerprints against the same 50,000 images, and produce a similarity score for each comparison. The point of this exercise was to show that the similarity score for an image matched against itself was far higher than the scores obtained when it was compared to the others. As James L. Wayman,[71] later commented in a working paper discussing the case: "The comparison of images to themselves lead, of course, to extremely high scores, which researchers called the 'perfect match' score. Because in life fingerprints are always changing, no real comparison of two different images of the same finger will ever yield such a high score. By adopting, as the definition of 'in common,' the score obtained by comparison of identical images, the government very strongly biased any results in the government's favor."[72] A test more faithful to the task at hand would have used two different images of the same fingers, and no doubt would have obtained more modest result.

In a further effort to supply the data needed to answer the question about the task-at-hand–which in *Mitchell* and in most fingerprint cases, involves smeared and fragmentary latent prints–the FBI re-ran the study using cropped prints. This effort, presumably, suffered from the same flaw as the initial one, as well as sparing the computer some of the most nettling

---

70. *See* Simon Cole, *What Counts for Identity? The Historical Origins of the Methodology of Latent Fingerprint Identification*, 12 SCIENCE IN CONTEXT 56 (1999). This is a sensible goal for an endeavor that relies so heavily on subjective judgment. *See infra* § 2.3.1[1] ("The criteria for absolute identification in fingerprint work are subjective and ill-defined.") Perhaps the best indication of how troubling the findings were is that the government reportedly initially tried to withhold its findings from the defense.

71. Director, U.S. National Biometric Test Center at the College of Engineering, San Jose State University, which tests biometric identification systems.

72. James L. Wayman, *Daubert* Hearing on Fingerprinting: When Bad Science Leads to Good Law: The Disturbing Irony of the *Daubert* Hearing in the Case of U.S. v. Byron C. Mitchell (2000), available at http://www.dss.state.ct.us/digital/news17/bhsug17.htm and http://www.engr.sjsu.edu/biometrics/publications_daubert.html.

problems of trying to determine where on a finger or hand a fragment came from and its orientation.

"In short," Wayman observed, "nothing in the government study or testimony gives us any indication of the likelihood that the crime scene fingerprints were falsely identified as belonging to the defendant Mitchell or, more broadly, that any latent fingerprints might be falsely identified."[73]

Following the hearing, the district judge made no written order or opinion and gave no verbal explanation about his ruling of evidentiary reliability. He merely stated his conclusions from the bench: that the fingerprint expert testimony was admissible, that its probative value outweighed its prejudicial impact, and that the defense was prohibited from presenting witnesses to the jury who would testify about the general flaws in fingerprint identification. The only expert witnesses permitted to the defense were fingerprint examiners who would testify to their specific conclusions in this case.[74]

An interesting postscript to the *Mitchell* case is the discovery after trial and conviction that the FBI had prevailed upon the National Institute of Justice to delay release of its request for research proposals to test important beliefs about fingerprint identification[75] until after the conclusion of Mitchell's trial.[76] Thus, at the same time the FBI was telling the *Mitchell* court that everything that needed to be known to confirm the reliability of fingerprint identification already was known, they were telling the NIJ to delay the process of funding research aimed at answering some of the unknowns, studies that it was hoped would be useful in defending against future challenges. This stratagem could eventually carry the proceedings back to a new *Daubert* hearing.[77]

Another federal case that considered a challenge to the admissibility of expert testimony on fingerprint identification is *United States v. Havvard.* [78]In contrast to the array of expert witnesses presented to the judge in the *Mitchell* court's *Daubert* hearing, the parties to *Havvard* offered the judge

---

73. *Id.* Wayman, it should be noted, believes that at the end of the day fingerprints will be proven to be reliable enough to warrant admission as evidence. But, he writes, "I'm saddened, however, that the government's case had to rest on such shoddy science. I'd certainly prefer to see good law resulting from good science. We must strive to do better." *Id.*

74. Note that, with respect to attacking the weight to be given to fingerprint identification generally, the *Mitchell* court's conception of the division of responsibility for evaluation of evidence is the opposite of the *Malveaux* court, 208 F.3d 223 (9th Cir.2000)(unpublished), which held that such attacks went exclusively to weight and were for the jury. Neither court reflects the conventional view reiterated in *Daubert*, which is that expert evidence is subject first to gatekeeping review by the court, and second, if the court rules the evidence admissible, to the weight of the evidence. (*Daubert*: "Vigorous cross-examination, presentation of contrary evidence, and careful instruc-

tion on the burden of proof are the traditional and appropriate means of attacking shaky but admissible evidence.") It should matter to a factfinder whether the error rate of an identification technique is a fraction of a percent or 20 percent, even if the court regards neither level of error sufficient to exclude the expert testimony.

75. *See supra* note 3.

76. *See Fingerprints: No Marquis De Queensbury Rules for the F.B.I.*, Sci. Sleuthing Rev., Fall 2000, at 8.

77. Not to mention the possible imposition of sanctions on those who conspired to hide relevant information from the court. It is particularly ironic that a judicial truth-seeking proceeding would motivate members of one government agency to undertake to delay scheduled knowledge-building work of another government agency in order to prevent relevant information from coming to light.

78. 117 F.Supp.2d 848 (S.D.Ind.2000).

only a single expert: Stephen Meagher, the same FBI Latent Print Unit Chief who had testified in the *Mitchell* hearing. Upon ruling in favor of admission, and giving his reasons orally, Judge Hamilton reduced his reasons to "written form at the government's request because it may be useful to other courts."[79]

The defendant argued that "there is no reliable statistical foundation for fingerprint comparisons and no reliable measure of error rates in latent print identification, especially in the absence of a specific standard about the number of points of identity needed to support an opinion as to identification."[80] The government, in response, argued that "fingerprint identification is so well-established that the court should not even hold a hearing on the issue."[81]

To summarize the opinion in a nutshell, the *Havvard* court generally answered each scientific question not by pointing to research data but instead to assurances that the adversary process was operating.

Judge Hamilton began by reminding readers of the massive cultural acceptance of beliefs about fingerprint identification: "The court's decision may strike some as comparable to a breathless announcement that the sky is blue and the sun rose in the east yesterday."[82] "Nevertheless," the opinion continues," *Daubert* and *Kumho Tire* invite fresh and critical looks at old habits and beliefs."[83]

The so-called *Daubert* factors are entirely appropriate for the evaluation of empirical claims such as those made by fingerprint examiners about the nature of fingerprints and their own skills, and the court applied the factors to those claims. Unfortunately, while most of the *Daubert* factors invoke aspects of the scientific method, for each one of them the *Havvard* court substituted the crime investigation or litigation process.

On the issue of falsification, and whether the techniques are testable or have been tested, the court wrote that:

> They have been tested for roughly 100 years. They have been tested in adversarial proceedings with the highest possible stakes–liberty and sometimes life. The defense has offered no evidence in this case undermining the reliability of the methods in general. The government points out correctly that if anyone were to come across a case in which two different fingers had identical fingerprints, that news would flash around the legal world at the speed of light. It has not happened in 100 years.[84]

The court assumes that no special research effort is needed, that in the course of ordinary casework errors would become apparent. One must ask what

---

79. *Id.* at 850.

80. *Id.*

81. *Id.* at 851.

82. *Id.* at 849. The court makes an important point here. Although the color of the sky and the rising of the sun, at least at these casual levels of precision, are apparent to anyone who looks, the accuracy of fingerprint identifications is not at all obvious, and the claims are anything but vague and general. And yet, as the court suggests, many members of the public and the bar, as well as the bench, regard these matters as being equally obvious and certain. This is precisely why *Daubert* requires judges to undertake a skeptical, scientifically disciplined gatekeeping role. It cannot be enough to say that something is "common knowledge," that "everyone knows" something to be true. Indeed, if those statements are so, it should be easy to support them with unusually solid, rather than unusually weak, evidence. It is too easy to be lulled into accepting our uninformed or misinformed assumptions.

83. *Havvard* at 849.

84. *Id.* at 854. *But see infra* § 2.3.2.

opportunity ordinary casework affords for falsification. It is not obvious how such fortuitous testing is likely to occur. For example, where a suspect's prints are compared to crime scene prints, the circumstances do not permit such a test. In normal casework, when a match is found, the search ends, and there is no chance of finding further matches. The usual process might often or typically prevent rather than create a test of the hypothesis. A more serious problem is that this is not the relevant hypothesis given the usual task-at-hand. The more practical question is: given fragmentary or distorted latent prints and examiners of varying skills and differing judgment, how often are false positive errors made? Mistaking one person's prints for those of another person has occurred in both actual cases and in proficiency testing.[85] Normal science would pose the following sorts of questions: What is the probability of an erroneous match? Under what circumstances are errors more likely or less likely to occur?[86] And then designs research to find answers.

On the issue of "peer review and publication" the court stated:

> Next, the methods of identification are subject to peer review. [A]nother qualified examiner can compare the objective information upon which the opinion is based and may render a different opinion if warranted. In fact, peer review is the standard operating procedure among latent print examiners.

> *Daubert* refers to publication after peer review, which is important in evaluating scientific evidence because it shows that others qualified in a field have evaluated the method or theory outside the context of litigation and have found it worthy of publication. The factor does not fit well with fingerprint identification because it is a field that has developed primarily for forensic purposes. The purpose of the publication factor is easily satisfied here, however, because latent fingerprint identification has been subject to adversarial testing for roughly 100 years, again in cases with the highest stakes possible. That track record provides far greater assurance of reliability than, for example, publication of one peer-reviewed article describing a novel theory about the cause of a particular disease at issue in a civil lawsuit.[87]

The *Havvard* court confuses the process of fundamental knowledge building in a science with the quotidian practice of examiners checking each other's work.[88] The community of science subjects work to peer review and publica-

---

85. For examples of false positive errors (erroneous matches), *see* State v. Caldwell, 322 N.W.2d 574 (Minn.1982); James E. Starrs, *A Miscue in Fingerprint Identification: Causes and Concerns*, 12 J. OF POLICE SCI. & ADMIN. 287 (1984); David Grieve, *Possession of Truth*, 46 J. FORENSIC IDENTIFICATION 521 (1996); and the web page of latent print examiner Ed German which, among other information, presents current examples of erroneous identifications, at http://onin.com/fp/problemidents.html.223

86. Or, as Prof. Wayman puts the question: "What is a reasonable estimation of the chance of an error when comparing fingerprint images of reasonable size, position and quality? The answer, based on sound science, could have been, 'Reasonably low'. Unfortunately, the gov-

ernment's answer, disguised in the forms and terminology of 'statistical estimation', was absurd." *Supra* note 72.

87. *Havvard* at 854.

88. What exactly they are checking in a process that is essentially subjective is hard to know. *See* § 2.1.2[3][b] and [c] The peer "reviewer" most likely is seeing whether the two examiners' two subjective judgments reach the same result. This can be valuable if the review is conducted blind, but far less valuable if the second examiner knows what the first examiner concluded (for example, where the second examiner is given the two assertedly matching prints and is asked to confirm the match.) *See* Risinger et al., *The* Daubert/Kumho *Implica-*

tion in part because "submission to the scrutiny of the scientific community ... increases the likelihood that substantive flaws in methodology will be detected."[89] Regardless of whether a field was "developed primarily for forensic purposes"—or primarily for treating sick patients, or primarily for developing construction materials, or primarily for selecting people with aptitude to become pilots—one still can ask the field whether it has a research literature of some kind testing its beliefs and practices, how well designed those studies are (the principal function of peer review and publication referred to by *Daubert*), and what the studies found. Only one field in the preceding sentence is unable to produce numerous studies which a court could review to enable it to evaluate the field's various claims.

On the issue of error rates, the court wrote:

> Another *Daubert* factor is whether there is a high known or potential error rate. There is not. The defense has presented no evidence of error rates, or even of any errors. The government claims the error rate for the method is zero. The claim is breathtaking, but it is qualified by the reasonable concession that an individual examiner can of course make an error in a particular case. *See* Moenssens, et al., Scientific Evidence in Civil and Criminal Cases, at 516 ("in a great number of criminal cases" defense experts have undermined prosecution by showing faulty procedures or human errors in use of fingerprint evidence). Most important, an individual examiner's opinion can be tested and challenged for error by having another qualified examiner compare exactly the same images the first one compared. *See also Daubert*, at 596 ("Vigorous cross-examination, presentation of contrary evidence, and careful instruction on the burden of proof are the traditional and appropriate means of attacking shaky but admissible evidence.").
>
> Even allowing for the possibility of individual error, the error rate with latent print identification is vanishingly small when it is subject to fair adversarial testing and challenge.[90]

The issue of error rate was discussed above, in relation to *Mitchell*. In *Havvard* the court concludes that the error rate is "vanishingly small" though it cites no relevant research on the issue, but has essentially accepted the notion that the error rate is zero—except when errors are made. Finally, the court again bases its belief in low or no error on the workings of the adversary process.

Despite the lack of systematic empirical answers to the empirical questions before it, and its repeated need to fill those gaps in scientific knowledge by appeal to the adversary process, the court ended up concluding that the proffered expert testimony "satisfies the standards of reliability in *Daubert* and *Kumho Tire*. In fact, after going through this analysis, the court believes that latent print identification is the very archetype of reliable expert testimony under those standards."[91]

The court's analysis overlooks the task-at-hand concerns of *Kumho Tire*, whereby the focus of inquiry would have centered on data illuminating the

tions of Observer Effects in Forensic Science: Hidden Problems of Expectation and Suggestion, CAL. L. REV. (forthcoming).

89. *Daubert* at 593.

90. *Havvard* at 854.

91. *Id.* at 855.

capability of a field to provide reliable opinions about the precise expert task at issue in the case (which in this case is never specified, but in most cases: "Latent prints are usually prints of only a relatively small portion of the friction ridges on a particular finger. Latent prints can also vary widely in terms of the quality and clarity of the image.").[92]

United States v. Joseph[93] betrays even less curiosity about the empirical or theoretical basis of identification by fingerprints—no discussion of the logic of the challenged fingerprint identification techniques, no data, no citations to research, no attempt to justify the proponent's claims, nothing beyond the conclusory assertion that "fingerprint analysis has been tested and proven to be a reliable science over decades of use for judicial purposes." No hearing was held; the court made its decision on written submissions or argument on the motion; and the challenged method passed muster under *Daubert* and *Kumho Tire* because the court says so. Interestingly, the court granted funds to enable the defense to hire its own fingerprint expert to assist in challenging the weight to be given the government's fingerprint expert witness during trial.

In addition to *Mitchell*, *Havvard* and *Joseph*, challenges have been brought in a number of other cases, but those involved no published opinions, and often involved no written orders or even *Daubert* hearings.[94] This topic illustrates the difficulty some judges have in framing clear empirical questions and being reasonably rigorous in their evaluation of what are offered as empirical answers. Add to that the difficulty of putting aside assumptions so widely held in the general culture and adopting in their place an attitude of suspended judgment and honest agnosticism on the question under scrutiny. These cases are problematic because, whatever *Daubert* stands for, it is not question-begging.

§ 2–1.3 Post-*Daubert* Challenges in State Courts

No state court challenges to the fundamental admissibility of fingerprint expert evidence have been published, though several motions have apparently taken place. They dispose of the issue by refusing to hold a hearing, by refusing to authorize funds for the opponent's proposed scientific witnesses, by taking judicial notice of the validity of basic propositions about fingerprints, or by finding that state law has no means for challenging non-novel scientific evidence.[95]

92. *See* § 2.1.2[3].

93. 2001 WL 515213 (E.D.La.2001).

94. Brief summaries of cases involving challenges to the admissibility of fingerprint experts can be found on a web page maintained by latent print examiner Ed German, supplied mostly by assistant U.S. attorneys, can be found at http://onin.com/fp/daubert_links.html. As of this writing the list includes these additional federal cases: United States v. Alteme, Case No. 99–8131 (S.D. Fla., proceedings on the motion held Apr. 3–6, 2000); United States v. Obanion, Criminal No. DKC–98–0442 (D. Md., proceedings on the motion held Jun., 2000); United States v. Williams, Criminal No. 00–5263T (W.D. Wash., proceedings on the mo-tion held Jul. 7, 2000); United States v. Rogers, Criminal No. CR–90–1BR (E.D.N.C., proceedings on the motion held Dec. 6–7, 2000); United States v. Ressam, Criminal Action No. CR99–666C (W.D. Wash., proceedings on the motion held Mar. 12, 2001).

95. People v. Torres, No. BA145133 (Superior Court of the County of Los Angeles, Oct. 10, 2000) (denied motion without a hearing); People v. Nawi, No. 176527 (Superior Court of the County of San Francisco, Oct. 10, 2000) (denied motion to obtain defense witnesses for a hearing on admissibility); Georgia v. McGee, No. 99–CR–277 (Superior Court of Carroll County, Oct. 27, 2000) (taking "judicial notice of the fact that the fingerprints of each human

A Montana case illustrates how the evaluation of a fairly novel scientific claim is at once both different from and yet very similar to evaluating a claim that has long been assumed true. In this situation as well, we see the difficulty courts are having as they try to follow the unfamiliar mission on which *Daubert* sends them. Montana adopted *Daubert* as its own rule in *State v. Moore*.[96] In *Montana v. Cline*,[97] an FBI fingerprint expert testified concerning the age of a latent thumb print. The age of the print was essential to the outcome of the case, because it would help a jury choose between competing theories of the case offered by the government and the defense. The defendant appealed, *inter alia*, on the ground that scientific evidence does not support the witness's claim that the age of a print can be determined. The Montana Supreme Court held that the testimony on the fingerprint's age did satisfy the *Daubert* criteria (or, more precisely, it upheld as not clearly erroneous the trial court's implicit decision that a valid basis existed for making the age determination). The following portions of the court's opinion are relevant to its *Daubert* review. The Montana Supreme Court encountered a number of problems on the way to reaching its decision.

On the issue of whether *Daubert* applies only to novel scientific evidence, the *Cline* court wrote:

> [W]e do not consider fingerprint evidence in general to be novel scientific evidence. However, in the present case the issue is whether it is possible to determine the age of a fingerprint utilizing magnetic powder. We apply the *Daubert* standard to this case because we consider fingerprint aging techniques in this context to be novel scientific evidence. Certainly all scientific expert testimony is not subject to the *Daubert* standard and the *Daubert* test should only be used to determine the admissibility of novel scientific evidence.[98]

This certainly misstates the rule announced in *Daubert*,[99] though it may now be the law of Montana. And it is questionable whether it follows the Montana Supreme Court's own adoption of *Daubert*. If *Daubert* was to be so limited in Montana, there is no Montana case that says so directly, no case that acknowledges that Montana is rejecting this aspect of the United State Supreme Court's view in *Daubert*, and no case that offers any reasons or analysis suggesting why it would make sense to limit *Daubert* gatekeeping in this way. The *Cline* court appears to think that it is bound to this position by its prior adoption of *Daubert*, though there is nothing in *Moore,* and certainly none in *Daubert* itself, supporting such an interpretation.

---

being are different from those of any other human being and that said individual fingerprints are permanent and that they are not altered by the passing of time or by degenerative physical disorder or traumatic event; That the fingerprint identification of individuals has been accepted as accurate by all state and Federal courts of the United States as well as by the courts throughout the entire world for at least the past 80 years. . . ."); People v. Ake, No. CM14979 (Superior Court of Butte County, California, May 7, 2001) (holding that *Frye*, not *Daubert*, controls in California, that *Frye* limits only new or novel scientific evidence and that fingerprinting is not new).

96. 268 Mont. 20, 885 P.2d 457 (1994).

97. 275 Mont. 46, 909 P.2d 1171 (Mont. 1996).

98. *Id.* at 55.

99. "[W]e do not read the requirements of Rule 702 to apply specially or exclusively to unconventional evidence. Of course, well-established propositions are less likely to be challenged than those that are novel, and they are more handily defended." *Daubert*, n. 11, at 593.

On the issue of whether *Daubert* is a less or a more liberal test than *Frye*, the *Cline* court stated:

> When we adopted the *Daubert* test in *Moore*, we specifically noted the continuing vitality of *Barmeyer* as that case pertained to the scientific evidence. In *Barmeyer* we held that "it is better to admit relevant scientific evidence in the same manner as other expert testimony and allow its weight to be attacked by cross-examination and refutation."[100] In *Barmeyer*, we rejected the "general acceptance" test, holding that it was not in conformity with the spirit of the new rules of evidence.[101]

> In *Daubert*, the United States Supreme Court also rejected the "general acceptance" standard in favor of the more liberal test embodied in Rule 702, Fed.R.Evid.[102]

> We noted that Rule 702, Fed.R.Evid., still requires the district court to screen such evidence to ensure that any and all scientific testimony or evidence admitted is not only relevant, but reliable.[103]

> In adopting the *Daubert* test, we concluded that "before a trial court admits scientific expert testimony, there must be a preliminary showing that the expert's opinion is premised on a reliable methodology."[104]

An important tension exists not only among these statements, but within *Daubert* itself. *Daubert's* holding that FRE 702 requires the testimony of a scientific expert witness to be grounded on a sound scientific basis cannot co-exist with the notion that the Federal Rules necessarily set a lower threshold than *Frye* would.[105] Taking the scientific issue in the present case, suppose it were generally accepted among fingerprint examiners that they could reckon the age of a fingerprint but that the empirical research testing their ability to do so did not support that contention, or showed that they could not. The former fact would win admission for the testimony under *Frye*, but the latter fact would lead to its exclusion under *Daubert*.

On the merits of the issue whether fingerprint experts can reckon the age of latent fingerprints, the *Cline* court held:

> In this case, the State established the necessary foundation regarding the issue of determining the age of fingerprints. [The expert witness] referenced and quoted a number of scientific treatises on fingerprint technology. The treatises established that while the age of a latent print cannot be established with complete accuracy, experienced examiners can proffer an opinion regarding the age of a latent print based on the examiner's experience and investigation. The District Court, although not applying the *Daubert* criteria, correctly found that this was an area where experts could disagree, that the testimony would be subject to cross-examination, and that the credibility of the witnesses and the weight of their testimony should be for the jury to decide, not the court.

100. Barmeyer v. Montana Power Co., 202 Mont. 185, 657 P.2d 594, at 598 (1983) (quoting United States v. Baller, 519 F.2d 463, 466 (4th Cir.1975)).

101. *Cline, supra* note 97, at 55 (quoting *Moore, supra* note 96).

102. *Id.* (quoting *Moore, supra* note 96).

103. *Id.* (quoting *Moore, supra* note 96).

104. *Id.* at 56 (quoting *Moore, supra* note 96).

105. *See* Science in the Law: Standards, Statistics and Research Issues, Chapter 1.

How accurately fingerprint examiners are in their estimation of the age of a print, and whether that accuracy is within the tolerances required by a court, would seem to be a relatively easy inquiry to frame. But the answer to that question cannot be discerned from the court's opinion. The expert's testimony, to the extent it is reflected in the opinion[106] supplies no answer, and the court cites none of the studies to which it alluded. Whether or not the data alluded to—in which the witness "referenced and quoted a number of scientific treatises on fingerprint technology"—adequately supported the claims of asserted expertise is the critical inquiry under *Daubert*. There is, of course, a world of difference between someone asserting something in a treatise and that assertion being a conclusion based on sound empirical evidence. Had the Montana court's opinion summarized the relevant data, or at least cited the relevant studies, it would have been far more persuasive, as well as more helpful to other courts that may face the same issue. As it stands, the opinion has the ring of considerable equivocalness.[107]

The opinion mentions that an affidavit supporting the defense contention that the age of latent prints cannot be determined with sufficient accuracy was provided by Prof. Andre Moenssens[108] in support of a defense motion for a new trial. Similarly, the present chapter suggests that divining the age of a fingerprint is "not generally possible, although some indications may be provided in extreme cases...."[109] And one recent article reviewing studies of the question concludes that the dating of a fingerprint is largely a speculative endeavor.[110] Thus, there is at least a serious difference of opinion in the expert community.[111] The need for an open-eyed examination of the actual data would seem to be essential. This case should make it apparent why it behooves a court to state the basis for its opinion with more documentation and thoughtfulness than is found in the this case.

All of the post-*Daubert* cases thus far remain foreshadowing. One day a thoughtful challenge to fingerprint identification will be met with a thoughtful defense of it in front of a thoughtful judge, and a thoughtful opinion will issue. That opinion will be extremely interesting, because *Daubert* and fingerprinting are somewhat like the mythical collision between an irresistible force (*Daubert/Kumho*) and an immovable object (belief in the infallibility of fingerprint identification).[112]

---

106. "I think this is a fresh latent print probably about a month or two old. But, again, there is leeway either way." *Cline, supra* note 97, at 54.

107. "... cannot be established with complete accuracy ... [but] ... examiners can proffer an opinion ... an area where experts could disagree...." That one "can" venture an opinion says nothing about the reliability versus speculativeness of the opinion.

108. Prof. Moenssens is a former fingerprint examiner, now a professor of law and the director of a forensic science institute at the University of Missouri at Kansas City, and the author of Fingerprints and the Law (1969), Fingerprint Techniques (1971), and co-author of Scientific Evidence in Civil and Criminal Cases (4th ed., 1995).

109. *See infra* § 2.2.4. If certain rare circumstance do permit a reliable estimate, did those conditions exist in this case at bar? *Kumho Tire* and logic would require such consideration.

110. *See* materials cited *infra* § 2.2.4, especially Charles Midkiff, *Lifetime of a Latent Print: How Long? Can You Tell?* 43 J. Forensic Identification 386 (1993).

111. And possibly no difference of opinion. Are there data on only one side of this question and a testifying expert too eager to help "his side" win its case, or data pointing in different directions which support different conclusions?

112. At the end of the day, the most defensible position is likely to be that there is considerable probative value in fingerprint comparisons, but that the field has cultivated an

B. SCIENTIFIC STATUS

by

David A. Stoney*

§ 2–2.0 THE SCIENTIFIC BASIS OF EXPERT TESTIMONY ON FINGERPRINT IDENTIFICATION

§ 2–2.1 Introductory Discussion of the Science

§ 2–2.1.1 The Scientific Questions

Fingerprints have become synonymous with the concept of absolute identification. They are applied in two ways: to establish personal identity and to prove that an individual touched a surface.

Questions of personal identity typically arise upon arrest or death. The person's fingerprints are taken and compared with previously existing fingerprint records. Historically this process depended on systematic manual classification using detailed codes based on the grosser aspects of the fingerprint patterns. Hard-copy fingerprint records were filed according to these codes building an ordered reference set. Thereafter, questions of personal identity could be addressed by coding a person's fingerprints and searching the fingerprint files under the corresponding codes. This process is now computerized and the traditional codes have been replaced by various image and comparison algorithms. Using either system, after fingerprint records are retrieved a direct manual comparison process is performed by a fingerprint expert to establish identity or exclusion.

Scientific questions related to the use of fingerprints for personal identification are:

1. How specific are identifications made by comparing fingerprint records?

2. Do the salient features of fingerprints (as recorded) remain constant throughout life?

3. How can fingerprint records be stored and retrieved efficiently and reliably?

The other application of fingerprints is in the proof that an individual touched a surface. These "latent" fingerprints first must be located on a surface. Often they must be rendered visible by treatment with powders or

---

illusion of infallibility that is unsupported by available data and theory. The courts might come to require fingerprint expert witnesses to bring their claims into closer alignment with what is actually known and not known, so that juries have a chance to more accurately assess the probative value of the evidence and not be overwhelmed by a fingerprint examiner's "aura of infallibility."

* Dr. Stoney has a Ph.D. in Forensic Science from the University of California, Berkeley, where he worked on the statistical modeling of

fingerprint identifications. He worked for six years at the Institute of Forensic Sciences, Criminalistics Laboratory, in California before joining the faculty of the University of Illinois at Chicago. After serving as Director of Forensic Sciences for eight years he left to become Director of the McCrone Research Institute in Chicago, a not-for-profit corporation dedicated to teaching and research in microscopy and microscopic analysis.

chemicals. This process is called fingerprint development. Following development of the prints, their location is documented and they are collected, often by physically lifting the print from the surface using tape and placing the tape onto a card. Subsequently the print is compared to fingerprint records of individuals to test for identity of source. Candidate "suspects" for comparison are selected either directly through case investigations, or through computer searching. Regardless of how the candidates for comparison are selected, a manual comparison by a fingerprint expert follows.

Scientific questions regarding fingerprints as proof that an individual touched a surface are:

4. What procedures are best to develop fingerprints on what surfaces?

5. How should fingerprints be collected and documented?

6. Were the fingerprints deposited contemporaneously with the alleged offense? How old are the prints?

7. Can fingerprints be forged or planted?

8. Does the absence of a person's fingerprints prove non-touching?

9. How absolute are identifications that are made by comparing developed fingerprints with fingerprint records?

10. What criteria are needed for a fingerprint to have utility other than for identification?

11. How can fingerprint records be accessed to select candidates for comparison?

12. Are fingerprint comparison practices reliable and/or scientific according to prevailing legal standards?

The questions posed arise in the day-to-day interaction of fingerprint practices, police investigation and the legal process. The depth of scientific study and the relevance to legal issues varies. It is useful to re-group the questions as follows.

[1] Specificity, Constancy and Reliability

This issue relates to questions 1, 2, 9 and 12. Questions 1 and 9, concerned with the specificity of fingerprint identifications, are of utmost importance. Question 2, whether fingerprints are a constant attribute throughout life, is necessary to justify the comparison of records taken at different times. These issues are central to both scientists and the law. There is considerable scientific research and experience to address the question of constancy throughout life.[1] The questions of specificity have received surprisingly little scientific attention.[2] There are various reasons for this, including

§ 2–2.0

1. Harold Cummins & Charles Midlo, Finger Prints, Palms and Soles (1943); James F. Cowger, Friction Ridge Skin: Comparison and Identification of Fingerprints 146–149 (1983); Blanka Schaumann & Milton Alter, Dermatoglyphics in Medical Disorders 1–12 (1976).

2. David A. Stoney & John I. Thornton, *A Critical Analysis of Quantitative Fingerprint Individuality Models*, 31 J. Forensic Sciences 1187 (1986); David A. Stoney, *Measurement of Fingerprint Individuality, in* Advances in Fingerprint Technology, 2nd Edition (Henry C. Lee & Robert E. Gaensslen eds., 2001).

(1) the professional practice of rendering an opinion only when it is absolute, (2) the history of public and legal acceptance of fingerprint practices, (3) the intuitively convincing variation seen in fingerprints, and (4) the difficulty of defining the scientific problem sufficiently for systematic study. Question 12, regarding issues of reliability and scientific status is of direct legal concern.

[2] Value of Fingerprints Other Than for Identification

This issue relates to Question 10. Circumstances arise where there is legal interest in fingerprints when no identification has been made as, for example, where they could be offered to show that someone *other than the defendant* was present at a crime scene, had handled a document, etc. As such the *exclusionary value* of a fingerprint becomes important. Another circumstance is where the *placement of the fingerprint* in itself has important legal significance. Examples are where the placement of fingerprints allow reconstruction of how a weapon was handled or who was sitting where. Under these conditions, even if an identification is not possible, a fingerprint that *may* be from one or more persons, and *is not or probably is not* from one or more others, may be of probative value. There has been very little scientific consideration of these issues, largely due to the professional practice of rendering opinions only when there is an absolute identification.

[3] Time of Deposition of the Fingerprints

This issue relates to Question 6. The value of fingerprints as proof in specific case circumstances often is linked to the question of when the touching occurred or, equivalently, how long the fingerprints have been present on the receiving surface. There are two general approaches to address this: relative or absolute. Relative methods are intuitively suggested by case circumstances when timing can be related to events such as when a surface was cleaned, the breaking of a window, bleeding, or the deposition of additional prints. Absolute determinations are not generally possible, although some indications may be provided in extreme cases by consideration of the fingerprint development method and specific case circumstances.

[4] Fingerprint Development

This issue relates to Questions 4 through 8. Recently the technical procedures of fingerprint development and collection (Questions 4, 5) have received considerable scientific study as new methods for fingerprint visualization have emerged.[3] The legal significance of this research is limited, however, because if a print is found, often it does not matter how, technically, it was recovered. Legal concerns do arise relating to the failure to search properly for fingerprints and the failure to locate (or the possible destruction of) fingerprints that could have produced exonerating evidence. Scientists have essentially restricted their attention to developing protocols for fingerprint development that maximize the possibility and efficiency of recovering prints.

3. ADVANCES IN FINGERPRINT TECHNOLOGY, 2nd   eds., 2001).
Edition (Henry C. Lee & Robert E. Gaensslen

The technical method of fingerprint development also influences the attempt to answer Question 6, how long fingerprints have been on a surface. Scientists have conducted experiments that address some aspects of this question and some, occasionally useful, generalizations can be made. Most of the scientific studies, however, have compared the efficacy of different development methods under controlled conditions. In a particular case the (unknown) contingencies of print deposition and other uncontrolled conditions preclude inferences based on these studies.[4]

Similarly, the law often is concerned with the possibility of inferring from the absence of fingerprints that no touching occurred (Question 7). There is no scientific basis for such an inference: depending on the condition of the hands and the nature of the contact, no detectable, usable fingerprint necessarily results from touching.

The question of forgery or planting of fingerprints (Question 8) is naturally of concern, both legally and scientifically. Setting aside the intentional falsification of evidence by investigators or laboratory personnel (fingerprint fabrication), the question of prints being planted, transferred or forged to implicate an innocent individual remains. At issue are the possibility of such prints and the detectability of their fraudulent nature during scientific examination. There is little systematic research in these areas, but there is a body of collective experience that has been reviewed recently.[5]

[5] Storage and Retrieval of Records

This issue relates to Questions 3 and 11. Although there is considerable scientific and commercial interest in mechanisms for the storage and retrieval of fingerprint records, the legal questions that arise are of very limited scope. Efficiency of the investigative process is affected by these procedures, but the conclusions drawn by the fingerprint examiners are independent of what methods were used to retrieve the stored prints. Recently, in civil actions for false imprisonment, issues have arisen regarding the failure of an electronic computer search to locate the actual offender's fingerprint records. This failure was only recognized years later when a second, supplementary search was conducted.[6]

Having given an overview of the key questions of legal and scientific concern, we will next describe the scientific methods that are used to address these questions. After this background material the specific areas of scientific agreement and disagreement will be discussed.

§ 2–2.1.2 The Scientific Methods Applied in the Research

The first three parts of this section are: [1] Fingerprint Recording and Processing, [2] Fingerprint Filing and Record Retrieval, and [3] Fingerprint Examination, Comparison and Interpretation. Different physical locations and

---

4. Charles R. Midkiff, *Lifetime of a Latent Print How Long? Can You Tell?*, 43 J. FORENSIC IDENTIFICATION 386 (1993). *See also* materials cited *infra* note 36.

5. Pat A. Wertheim, *Detection of Forged and Fabricated Latent Prints*, 44 J. FORENSIC IDENTIFICATION 652 (1994); Pat A. Wertheim, *Integrity Assurance: Policies and Procedures to Prevent Fabrication of Latent Print Evidence*, 48 J. FORENSIC IDENTIFICATION 431 (1998).

6. Newsome v. James, 968 F.Supp. 1318 (N.D.Ill.1997).

different personnel are often involved in these three aspects of fingerprint work.[7] The next three parts of this section focus on the basis for absolute identification: [4] The Generalized Case for Absolute Identification, [5] Counting Minutiae or Points of Comparison, and [6] Statistical Bases. The final two parts of the section discuss [7] Professional Rejection of Qualified Identifications and [8] Uses Other Than for Identification.

Fingerprints are reproductions of the ridged skin surface of the fingers (or palm) resulting from the transfer of oil or other matter to the receiving surface. A typical well-recorded fingerprint is shown in Figure 1.

7. The material in the first two sections can be found discussed in more detail in Lee & Gaensslen, *supra* note 3; Cowger, *supra* note 1.

Figure 1

Bear in mind that the absence of fingerprints does not necessarily indicate that a person did not touch the item or surface. Depending on the type and condition of the surface, the state of the finger and the manner of contact, prints may or may not be left and, if left, they may or may not be of sufficient clarity and extent to have any useful value.

[1] Fingerprint Recording and Processing

Fingerprint records of individuals traditionally have been prepared by carefully inking a person's fingers with printing ink and rolling the fingers onto a standard "10–print" card. Direct electronic recording of fingerprints increasingly is used.

Latent fingerprints are discovered at crime scenes by various methods. Technicians may focus on specific areas where relevant fingerprints are likely to be found (such as items known to have been moved during a burglary) or there may be a more general search. The most traditional method to *discover* prints is searching with a flashlight held at a grazing angle to a surface. A modern variation is the use of laser light.

The most traditional processing method to *discover and visualize* fingerprints is dusting with fingerprint powder. Fingerprint powder adheres to the perspiration, oils and extraneous matter that are present on the fingers and that often transfer to surfaces during touching. Powders are most effective on smooth, clean, *non*-porous surfaces such as glass. After the passage of time the oily materials comprising the fingerprint may dry, leading to a poorer adherence of the powder.

Prints developed by powder may be photographed, but they are often *lifted* using tape, without prior photography. The tape is pressed onto the print and the surrounding surface. It is then pulled off, taking the powder with it. Powder adheres not only from the print, but from the background surface, often recording surface details such as scratching, printing or rain spots. The tape lift is transferred to a glossy card. Areas on the cards are provided for a technician's notes and sketch.

Another frequently encountered type of fingerprint development involves fuming. A traditional fuming method uses iodine, which absorbs into the oils present in perspiration and turns a brown color. This color fades with time, so photography is essential. Currently the widely used fuming method is cyanoacrylate or "super-glue" fuming. The fume turns fingerprints white. These prints are permanent and they can then be dusted and lifted for convenience. Super glue fuming is a particularly efficient and versatile processing method. It is applicable to surfaces that create problems for powder methods, such as plastic bags, highly polished surfaces, and textured surfaces.

A third widely used type of fingerprint development involves chemical color reactions. On porous surfaces, notably paper, the chemical *ninhydrin* is often employed, developing purple fingerprints. Ninhydrin will develop very old prints as well as recently deposited ones. Bloody fingerprints can be visualized or enhanced using other chemical methods.

Today there are many alternative chemical treatments, specialized powders and optical enhancing methods. Some may allow subsequent lifting, others can be documented only through photography. These specialized techniques have extended capabilities to recover prints on surfaces that previously had been nearly impossible, such as on adhesive surfaces and between successive layers of overlapping duct tape. Fingerprints may be detectable by one method and undetectable by another. Proper use of the methods involves consideration of the order of application and the type of documentation necessary for each.[8]

The extent of note-taking during fingerprint processing varies considerably. Frequently this is influenced by time constraints. Processing may occur at crime scenes, or alternatively portable items (including automobiles) may be recovered and processed in a laboratory setting. Depending on local policies the personnel involved may be police officers, crime scene technicians, fingerprint technicians or forensic laboratory personnel. Ideally, notes should provide documentation of what areas or items were processed, what processing methods were used, when the processing was done and how many latent lifts were recovered from each item or area. On the fingerprint lifts themselves should be a full description of the print's original location, with a sketch where appropriate.

[2]   Fingerprint Filing and Record Retrieval

Traditionally the inked fingerprint cards of individuals have been physically filed according to a code that was developed during the early part of the century. This has been quite effective but has now been almost completely surpassed by computerized methods. Both are in use and small sets of hard copy files are often kept at the police department level.

Manual codes are based on the gross pattern features of fingerprints, rather than the fine detail. A set of grosser observations on each finger yield incredible variety of fingerprint classes and sub-classes when combined. Electronic "codes" vary with the particular proprietary algorithms used by the various computer systems, but much more of the finer detail within a print is used for coding. Inked fingerprint cards can be "read" optically by a computer or direct, live-scanned images can be used for input. Key features of the general pattern and local detail are extracted and serve as the basis for coding. This provides enough information so that prints of individual fingers can be processed efficiently. Optical images of the fingerprints themselves also are stored on most systems.

When *crime scene* prints (in contrast to inked prints) are to be entered into a computerized system they are first individually examined by technicians who prepare the prints for automated input. This step is necessary because latent fingerprints vary considerably in their clarity, contrast and size. A common procedure is for prints to be enlarged and traced. The tracing is then photographically reduced and this tracing, rather than the original print, is optically read by the computer. Alternatively, some systems project the crime scene print onto a screen and the technician interactively indicates the locations and nature of the fingerprint detail.

Once records have been filed (manually or electronically) they may be retrieved by the codes or simply by the name of the person the prints were taken from. In *manual systems* a record typically would be retrieved under

---

8. Lee & Gaensslen, *supra* note 3; Olivier Ribaux et al. *"Goldfinger": An Expert Computer System for the Determination of Fingerprint Detection Sequences*, 43 J. FORENSIC IDENTIFICATION 468 (1993); S. A. Hardwick et al., *Fingerprints (Dactyloscopy): Sequential Treatment* *and Enhancement, in* ENCYCLOPEDIA OF FORENSIC SCIENCE 877 (J. Siegel et al. eds., 2000); S. K. Branble & J. S. Brennan, *Fingerprints (Dactyloscopy): Chemistry of Print Residue, in* ENCYCLOPEDIA OF FORENSIC SCIENCE 866 (J. Siegel et al. eds., 2000).

two circumstances. The first is where a person's prints have been taken and their identity is to be checked against the previous fingerprint records. The new prints are coded and records with the same code are retrieved for manual comparison. The second circumstance is where prints have been found at a crime scene *and* a particular suspect has been developed through case investigation. The suspect's fingerprint records would then be retrieved to allow comparison with the crime scene prints. A third, more remote, possibility would be a case where an entire set of ten prints was left at a crime scene. These could be coded and this code could then be used to retrieve candidate records. *Notably absent* in the manual system was a method to go directly from single crime scene fingerprints to the selection of candidate ten-print cards from the fingerprint files. *In computerized systems* this additional capability is achieved because single crime scene prints can be entered and records can be searched. Typically the search provides a listing of candidates, ranked by a comparison algorithm. Candidate cards are retrieved (physically or on-line) and direct comparisons are made by a fingerprint examiner. In no sense is the computer doing the ultimate comparison of suspects' and crime scene prints. The process is not the same and the task is not part of the computer's design. Rather, the computer helps in the selection of candidates. The retrieval of records by the computer in no way compromises a later identification, nor does it impart any degree of proof.

Failure to recognize the latter point can be a source of confusion. One example is the view that fingerprint examiners alter or create evidence when they use tracings of crime scene prints, or designate the location and nature of fingerprint details. These practices involve expert judgment and do indeed substitute the expert's interpretation of the fingerprint for the actual evidence. As noted above, however, the search merely retrieves candidates for comparison. The actual comparison is conducted by the fingerprint examiner using the actual fingerprint evidence, not the representations used for computer searching.

[3]   Fingerprint Examination, Comparison and Interpretation[9]

[a]   *Examination of Fingerprints*

Fingerprint examiners may or may not be involved in fingerprint processing. Often they will receive inked prints taken following arrest along with latent lifts that were processed and collected from crime scenes by others. Certification of Latent Print Examiners is conducted by examination through the International Association for Identification. This is an excellent and well-motivated program.[10]

Fingerprints are examined visually by fingerprint examiners under low power magnifiers (typically 5 to 10X). Photography may be substituted for

---

9. The material in this section can be found discussed in more detail in Cowger, *supra* note 1; David R. Ashbaugh, *The Premises of Friction Ridge Identification, Clarity, and the Identification Process*, 44 J. Forensic Identification 499 (1994); David R. Ashbaugh, Quantitative-Qualitative Friction Ridge Analysis (1999);

Christophe Champod, *Edmond Locard—Numerical Standards and "Probable" Identifications*, 45 J. Forensic Identification 136 (1995).

10. International Association for Identification, Secretary of the Latent Print Certification Board, 545 Nixon St., St. Charles, IA 50240.

direct examination under lenses, or may be included as part of the fingerprint development procedure (as, for example, with the use of colored filters to optically enhance a fingerprint).

Fingerprints are reproductions of the ridged skin surface of the fingers and palm. Important features are the overall patterns formed by the ridges and the discontinuities in individual ridges (see Figure 1). The patterns form the basis for the traditional fingerprint classification methods. A fingerprint card, with a person's ten fingerprints, is assigned a detailed filing code based on the ten patterns. Automated coding of fingerprint cards for computerized storage, with modified coding methods, eventually will replace the traditional methods. The legal significance of this change (in most contexts) is negligible.[11]

[b]　Comparison of Fingerprints

When comparing two fingerprints the patterns of the ridges are used for orientation, but the comparison itself is done by noting the relative positions within the pattern where individual ridges branch or terminate. These ridge discontinuities are known as *fingerprint minutiae*. Examiners compare the type of minutiae (forks or ending ridges), their direction (loss or production of a ridge) and their relative position (how many intervening ridges there are between minutiae and how far along the ridges it is from one minutiae to the next). More subtle variations in the ridge form and ridge path are also included in the comparison.

With *latent* fingerprints found on surfaces (as opposed to standard, inked fingerprints) the initial examination addresses the suitability of the print for productive examination. The print is evaluated for clarity and for the amount of detail present. It is common for prints to be graded subjectively (for convenience) into three groups according to their "value" for identification: identifiable, no value, or possible value.

Some prints are unambiguously identifiable. Their clarity and detail are sufficient to meet prevailing standards and, if the person who made the print were found, identification would be forthcoming (barring rather extreme contingencies, such as severe scarring of the person's finger). Other prints may be poorly defined, smudged or fragmented to such a degree that a conclusion of "no value for identification" is justified. Prints of "possible value" for identification are common and the designation is capable of causing confusion when the legal community presses the scientist to decide if a given print is really identifiable or not. When examining a print, some of the detail seen may or may not be from the finger that produced the print. Smudging, dirty surfaces, dirty fingers and contingencies of fingerprint deposition all contribute to the incomplete transfer of the finger's detail and the introduction of specious or artifactual detail. Some of the actual and artifactual detail is recognizable as such, but there is always a residual set of details that may or may not be actually on the finger that made the print. During the comparison process it may become apparent that what was believed to be an artifact or an indistinct portion of the print does, in fact, correspond to an actual feature of a suspect's fingerprint. Thus, in practice, the designation of

---

11. *But see supra* note 6.

possible value often remains until an identification is made. In the extreme, a print originally judged to be of no value for identification may later be identified.

Fingerprint comparison involves juxtaposition of two prints by a variety of possible means. Initially, the overall pattern of the ridges in the crime scene print is examined, together with any small groups of minutiae or particularly characteristic features of the print, such as scars or creases. The goal is to develop an initial search criterion that will allow efficient screening of the candidate reference fingerprints from the inked fingerprint cards, or from the electronic image database. (Formal definition of this criterion is not made, and several different criteria may be tried in difficult cases.) With the criterion in mind the reference fingerprints are considered, one by one, searching for a corresponding set of details. If each of a candidate's ten fingers is rejected then an exclusion results: the latent fingerprint was not made by the fingers represented on the card. If one or more of the candidate's fingers meet the initial search criterion then the comparison continues. Additional minutiae are sought that bear a specific, well-defined relationship to initial ones, expanding the set of corresponding detail. Minutiae must agree in their type, orientation and relative position. Comparison of relative position includes, in effect, comparing the paths and form of all of the ridges between the two minutiae.

During the comparison process allowance must be made for differences arising from the normal contingencies of printing.[12] In general, the poorer the quality of the print, the greater the extent of these differences. As differences are encountered the question arises of whether these differences are "real," meaning they represent an actual difference in the fingers that made the prints, or "apparent," meaning that they have been introduced by the contingencies associated with the printing or developing process. The term *explainable differences* often is used for differences that may have arisen by these contingent means. The term does *not* mean that the examiner has a specific explanation for why a particular difference exists; rather it means that the difference is of the type commonly seen among prints that have originated from the same finger. An example of this sort is where, due to differences in the amount of ink or finger pressure, ending ridges may appear to be forks or vice versa.

In fingerprint comparison judgments of correspondence and the assessment of differences are wholly subjective: there are no objective criteria for determining when a difference may be explainable or not. The fingerprint examiner's judgment is based on a variety of considerations, including:

- the clarity of the fingerprint,
- familiarity with the types of differences that are seen routinely in fingerprints from one individual,
- familiarity with how the fingerprint development process may affect the print's appearance,
- the presence and nature of other corresponding or discrepant detail in the comparison.

12.   Ashbaugh (1999), *supra* note 9, at 109–136.

[c] Interpretation of Fingerprint Comparisons

The criteria for absolute identification of an individual through fingerprint comparison are wholly dependent on the professional judgment of a fingerprint examiner.[13] When a fingerprint examiner determines that there is *enough* corresponding detail to warrant the conclusion of absolute identification, then the criteria have been met. Many fingerprint examiners will have a second examiner review their identification, and some laboratories have made this their official policy. The formality and independence of this re-examination process varies. Usually a second examiner will know the result of the first examination, but will be asked to make an equally formal evaluation of the print.

The process of fingerprint examination and comparison has recently been articulated by Ashbaugh[14] and his terminology has gained some acceptance within the fingerprint community. There are four steps to his process, following the acronym ACE–V for Analysis, Comparison, Evaluation and Verification. In the *Analysis* step the poorer quality, latent fingerprint is examined to assess the quality and quantity of detail that is present. This includes evaluation of the clarity of the print, what part of the hand it may have come from, different kinds and levels of detail, and distortions arising from numerous causes. In the *Comparison* step the print is compared with a candidate reference print. The *Evaluation* step results in the formation of the examiner's opinion, and the *Verification* step is the re-examination of the prints by a second fingerprint examiner.

[4] The Generalized Case for Absolute Identification

The argument for absolute identification begins with the observation of the extreme variability of fingerprint minutiae, even among identical twins. (In addition to overall genetic factors,[15] detail in fingerprints is determined by the highly variable dynamics of fetal hand development.) The extreme variability among fingerprints is readily appreciated if one takes prints from different individuals and an attempt is made to successively find a correspondence of a small group of three, then four, then five minutiae. To illustrate the point, correspondence of three minutiae may well be found when comparing two prints. A correspondence of four minutiae might well be found upon diligent, extended effort when comparing the full set of prints of one individual with those from another person. For a legitimate correspondence of five points between different individuals it might mean searching for weeks among many different individuals. A correspondence of six points might be a lifetime's search. Unfortunately, although there is extensive collective experience among casework examiners,[16] there has been no systematic study such as that described above.

Nonetheless, the fingerprint examiner's opinion of absolute identification is a logical extension of this process, including as its final step a "leap of

13. Charles R. Kingston & Paul L. Kirk, *Historical Development and Evaluation of the "12 Point Rule" in Fingerprint Identification*, 186 INT'L CRIM. POLICE REV. 62 (1965); COWGER, *supra* note 1; Ashbaugh (1994), *supra* note 9; Champod, *supra* note 9.

14. Ashbaugh (1994), *supra* note 9.

15. DANUTA Z. LOESCH, QUANTITATIVE DERMATOGLYPHICS (1983).

16. ANDRE A. MOENSSENS, FINGERPRINT TECHNIQUES 262 (1971).

faith" where, in the critical, experienced (but subjective) judgment of the examiner, it is *inconceivable* that the fingerprint could have come from another person's finger.

Important factors that enter into the professional judgment of an absolute identification are:

- the extent of the print (area and number of minutiae),
- the clarity of the print,
- the presence or absence of dissimilarities, and
- the examiner's training, experience and ethics.

[5]   Counting Minutiae or Points of Comparison

The *number* of corresponding minutiae, or "points," is a convenient, somewhat objective feature to use when discussing fingerprint comparisons. For many years the use of the *number of points* has been discussed and debated among the profession, with the key focus being, "Should there be a formally established minimum number of 'points' that is needed for an absolute identification?" and, "If so, what is this number?"[17]

Although the number of points is a convenient summary of a comparison, it is insufficient and incomplete. Lacking are the consideration of (1) the clarity of the minutiae, (2) the finer details that are present in minutiae, scars, or on the ridges themselves, and (3) allowance for differences in "value" that would account for unusual or special features of minutiae. In the United States these features are subjectively evaluated by fingerprint examiners. After much consideration and debate, there is (explicitly) no minimum number of points necessary for an identification.[18] Many other countries, however, *do* have a minimum point requirement for legal admissibility. In the United Kingdom, for example, there was for about 80 years a standard that required at least 16 points. This practice was discontinued in 2001.[19]

Nonetheless, there is at least historical agreement that twelve corresponding simple ridge characteristics are sufficient to prove identity.[20] In the United States it is generally regarded that six minutiae are too few for absolute identification. Seven or eight generally are regarded as enough, *if they satisfy an experienced examiner*.[21]

More recently questions have arisen regarding whether or not it is appropriate to count minutiae at all. This topic is considered more fully, *infra*, in the section on areas of scientific disagreement.

[6]   Statistical Bases

From a statistical viewpoint, the scientific foundation for fingerprint

17.   Kingston & Kirk, *supra* note 13; Champod, *supra* note 9; Ian W. Evett & Ray L. Williams, *A Review Of The Sixteen Points Fingerprint Standard In England And Wales*, 46 J. Forensic Identification 49 (1996).

18.   Champod, *supra* note 9.

19.   Christophe Champod, *Fingerprints (Dactyloscopy): Standard of Proof, in* Encyclopedia of Forensic Science 884 (J. Siegel et al. eds., 2000).

20.   Kingston & Kirk, *supra* note 13; Champod, *supra* note 9.

21.   Cowger, *supra* note 1.

individuality is incredibly weak. Beginning with Galton[22] and extending most recently to Champod[23] and to Meagher, Budowle and Zeisig[24] there have been a dozen or so statistical models proposed.[25] These vary considerably in their complexity, but in general there is much speculation and little data. Champod's recent work is the exception, bringing forth the first realistic means to *predict* frequencies of occurrence of specific combinations of ridge minutiae. Scientifically, the next step would be to assess the accuracy of the predictions. No such work currently is being done. Champod's work does support *rejection* of simple minutiae counts as a realistic summary of fingerprint individuality. This is because the specific portion of the finger that the print comes from and the specific nature of each minutiae have a highly significant effect on the observed frequencies of occurrence.

[7]　Professional Rejection of Qualified Identifications

Fingerprint examiners abhor qualified, "probable," identifications—to the degree that offering such opinions, except under extraordinary conditions (such as being directly ordered to do so by the court), is considered unethical by the profession.[26] In essence, *the profession* refuses *en bloc* to give testimony unless it is absolutely sure of an identification.[27] This remains despite the scientifically obvious continuity between the extremes of *no value* and *absolute identification*. In other countries practices of (legally) excluding fingerprint evidence below a conservatively large "point threshold" establishes essentially the same thing, but in the United States the accepted norm has not been determined by the courts, but rather by independent regulation within the fingerprint profession. (A more complete discussion of this topic appears, *infra*, in the section on Areas of Scientific Disagreement.)

[8]　Uses Other Than for Identification

Apart from *identification*, fingerprints can have value for two other purposes: *exclusion* and *reconstruction*. Prints have exclusionary value when it can be determined that a specific individual *did not* make them. In general, all identifiable prints also have exclusionary value, but some non-identifiable prints do as well. An example of the latter instance is where a pattern

22. Francis Galton, Finger Prints 100–113 (1892; reprinted 1965).

23. Christophe Champod, *Reconnaissance Automatique Et Analyse Statistique Des Minuties Sur Les Empreintes Digitales* (1995) (unpublished Ph.D. dissertation, University of Lausanne, Switzerland); Christoph Champod & Pierre Margot, *Computer Assisted Analysis Of Minutiae Occurrences On Fingerprints*, in Proceedings of the International Symposium on Fingerprint Detection and Identification 305 (J. Almog & E. Springer eds., 1996).

24. S.B. Meagher, B. Budowle & D. Ziesig, 50K vs. 50K Fingerprint Comparison Test (1999) (unpublished study submitted as evidence in United States v. Byron Mitchell, Crim. No. 96–407 (E.D. Pa., hearing of July 8, 1999)); J. L. Wayman, *When Bad Science Leads To Good Law: The Disturbing Irony Of*

The Daubert *Hearing In The Case Of U.S. v. Byron C. Mitchell*, Biometrics Publications, http://www.engr.sjsu.edu/biometrics/publications_daubert.html; *see also* discussion in Stoney, *supra* note 2.

25. David A. Stoney & John I. Thornton, *supra* note 2; Stoney, *supra* note 2; Champod, *supra* note 23; Cummins & Midlo, *supra* note 1.

26. Ashbaugh (1994), *supra* note 9; Champod, *supra* note 9; Christophe Champod & Ian Evett, *A Probabilistic Approach to Fingerprint Evidence*, 51 J. Forensic Identification 101 (2001).

27. "Absolutely sure," therefore, is really a statement about the examiner's subjective probability judgment.

element, such as a (target-shaped) whorl, is present in the crime scene fingerprint and the individual in question lacks this pattern on all of his fingers.[28] Examinations for exclusion are dependent on complete, clear, inked prints from the individual and clear prints from the crime scene. Each possible area on the person's prints must be searched for correspondence with the crime scene print, so if the inked print set is incomplete (lacking, for example, the tips or edges of the fingers), then the examination may be inconclusive.

Exclusion results only when all areas of the person's hands have been searched and rejected. This can be very time consuming. Particular attention is given, therefore, to the overall pattern of the crime scene print, the presence of conspicuous ridge characteristics, or anything that will allow efficient screening of the different areas of the inked prints. When such indications are absent the search may be prohibitively laborious. If one proceeds systematically, however, the examinations often are *possible*. The results may be inconclusive due to the quality of the crime scene prints or reference prints, or due to incomplete reference prints.[29]

Fingerprints also have value for *reconstruction* of a crime inasmuch as they indicate where and what was touched and, from evidence of smearing or deformation, *how* the touching occurred. The position of a print, along with neighboring prints or smudges, is thus frequently important and requires documentation. This may be in the form of photographs, sketches or written notes. In the absence of sufficiently detailed documentation, a successful determination of the original position often can be made by comparison of the surface detail recorded on the fingerprint lift with the original surface.

Documentation of fingerprint examinations and comparisons has historically been quite limited. Often report forms are used which indicate the items examined, the examinations requested, and the results of the examination. Statements of results typically are limited to the presence or absence of a specific individual's fingerprints, usually, but not always, with reference to the individual latent lift cards. Examiners usually initial the lift cards and inked fingerprint records when identifications have been made, indicating the date and case number along with the person and finger that were identified.

More progressive documentation of fingerprint examinations is beginning to emerge, with some departments requiring a record for each latent print on each lift showing whose prints were compared and the results of each comparison (whether an identification, an exclusion, or an inconclusive or omitted examination).[30]

§ 2–2.2 Areas of Scientific Agreement

Most of the material in the sections that follow can be found discussed in more detail in the basic references in the margin.[31] More specific citations are supplied where appropriate.

28. MOENSSENS, *supra* note 16, at 258.

29. COWGER, *supra* note 1, at 173–181.

30. The Illinois State Police, for example, employ a "Fingerprint Matrix" form that documents these aspects of the examination. *See also* Becki Daher, *Documentation of Latent Print Comparisons* 50 J. FORENSIC IDENTIFICATION 119 (2000).

31. COWGER, *supra* note 1; Lee & Gaensslen, *supra* note 3.

§ 2–2.2.1 Constancy of Patterns

Fingerprint patterns remain constant throughout life with the exceptions of (1) distortion of the pattern due to growth, (2) temporary damage to the superficial skin surface, and (3) permanent damage due to scarring of the underlying tissues of the skin.[32] Scarring, once it occurs, generally enhances, rather than detracts from, the individuality of the print. (Scars are permanent, comparatively rare, and originate in a non-systematic way. They have an abrupt appearance within the fingerprint pattern, with a specific dimension, shape and relationship to the surrounding minutiae.)

§ 2–2.2.2 Sufficiency of Identifying Details

Comparison of a set of inked fingerprints taken from a person on one occasion with those taken on another provides a certain means of proving or disproving identity. The chance of duplication of this intricate pattern is conceived to be so small that it may be ignored. There is no known instance of failure among many, many attempts.[33] A single well-recorded fingerprint is universally considered to contain more than enough detail for this proof. (For this point of scientific agreement, we are specifically referring to clearly recorded impressions of large portions of the finger(s), in contrast to the full domain of latent fingerprints where the size and clarity of the detail vary over a considerable range.)

§ 2–2.2.3 Storage and Retrieval

Ten-print fingerprint records can be reliably coded and filed by manual methods so that any possible corresponding records can be retrieved efficiently and reliably checked for correspondence.[34]

Computerized methods that accomplish the same process also are reliable, have greater efficiency and can be applied not only to inked, ten-print records, but also to individual inked fingerprints and to crime scene fingerprints (when the latter are sufficiently clear and extensive).[35]

§ 2–2.2.4 Crime Scene Prints

Physical and chemical procedures are well-established that allow for efficient, systematic discovery and recovery of fingerprints from crime scenes or items of evidence.

Fingerprint lifts and photographs almost always reveal sufficient detail regarding the surface where the print was found so that, should the issue arise, the original location of the print can be established by comparison of the lift or photograph with the surface.

Absent extraordinary circumstances, or independent events (such as cleaning), the age of a fingerprint cannot be determined.[36] In general, as

32. Cummins & Midlo, *supra* note 1; Cowger, *supra* note 1; Schaumann & Alter, *supra* note 1.

33. Federal Bureau of Investigation, The Science of Fingerprints: Classification and Uses (1984), at iii-iv.

34. Cowger, *supra* note 1.

35. Lee & Gaensslen, *supra* note 3.

36. Midkiff, *supra* note 4; Alan L. McRoberts & Kurt E. Kuhn, *A Review of the Case Report, Determining the Evaporation Rate of Latent Impressions on the Exterior Surfaces of Aluminum Beverage Cans*, 42 J. Forensic Identification 213 (1992); the original case report is, James F. Schwabenland, *Determining the*

prints age, they become more difficult to recover by powder methods. Fingerprints recovered chemically from paper could have been deposited at any time (they could be extremely old or extremely recent).

The absence of fingerprints does not indicate that a person did not touch the item or surface with their exposed fingers. Whether or not fingerprints are left depends on the condition of the surface, the condition of the fingers, and the dynamics of touching.

Fingerprints recovered from crime scenes or items of evidence often contain sufficient detail for absolute identification of the person making the print. Often the existence of sufficient detail, or its absence, is unambiguous. For some prints, however, it may not be possible to determine if the print is identifiable or not (before comparison) because of the ambiguity between artifactual detail in the print and genuine reproduction of the skin surface.

§ 2–2.2.5 Identification and Interpretation

Fingerprints from the same finger vary routinely due to the contingencies of printing: the amount and type of residue on the fingers, the nature of the receiving surface, and the nature of contact between the finger and the surface. Allowance for this variation is made during fingerprint comparisons and is an essential part of the process. Study of these variations by direct experiment and through casework provides the expertise required to make the necessary allowances.[37]

Counting the number of minutiae is a useful, but incomplete, method of describing the individuality present in a print. Even with this qualification, sixteen clear corresponding minutiae are (more than) sufficient for "absolute" identification.

Fingerprints that contain sufficient detail for identification also contain more than sufficient detail for exclusion.

§ 2–2.2.6 Training, Experience and Ability of Fingerprint Examiners

Fingerprint examiners differ in their level of training, experience and ability.[38] This means that for a given fingerprint case examination, a more experienced or more highly skilled examiner may well be convinced of (and report) an absolute identification, whereas less experienced or less skilled examiners may conclude (and report) that they are unable to make an identification.

Evaporation Rate of Latent Impressions on the Exterior Surfaces of Aluminum Beverage Cans, 42 J. FORENSIC IDENTIFICATION 85 (1992); William C. Sampson & Glenn C. Moffett, *Lifetime of a Latent Print on Glazed Ceramic Tile*, 44 J. FORENSIC IDENTIFICATION 379 (1994); Ernest W. Moody, *The Development of Fingerprint Impressions on Plastic Bags over Time and under Different Storage Temperatures*, 44 J. FORENSIC IDENTIFICATION 266 (1994).

37. *See* especially Ashbaugh (1999), *supra* note 9, at 109–136. *See also* John Thornton, *The One–Dissimilarity Doctrine in Fingerprint Identification*, 306 INT'L CRIM. POLICE REV. 1 (March, 1977); William F. Leo, *Distortion versus Dissimilarity* 48 J. FORENSIC IDENTIFICATION 125 (1998).

38. Pat A. Wertheim, *The Ability Equation*, J. FORENSIC IDENTIFICATION (1996).

§ 2–2.3   Areas of Scientific Disagreement

§ 2–2.3.1   The Question of Standards and the Basis for Concluding an Absolute Identification

[1]   Criteria Range from Self–Evident to Subjective and Untested

The criteria for absolute identification in fingerprint work are subjective and ill-defined. They are the product of probabilistic intuitions widely shared among fingerprint examiners, not of scientific research.[39] Outside of the fingerprint profession this is generally unappreciated.

Given the above, it is remarkable that fingerprints are idealized as *the standard* for conclusions of absolute identity. This situation has come about through historical public and legal acceptance of fingerprint practice, combined with the intuitively convincing variation present in fingerprints.[40] Considering this tradition, the successful application of subjective methods, and the inherent difficulties in rendering the process objective, it would be difficult to fault current practices. There is, however, a mixing of scientific, legal and political judgments leading to this conclusion. This can be quite problematic when fingerprints are then held up as the standard to judge performance in other disciplines (notably DNA typing). Fingerprint identifications are a popularly held concept based on subjective criteria and empirically successful practice. They are not the product of conventional scientific experimentation and statistical evaluation.

There is no room for rational debate over the sufficiency of a reasonably complete, well recorded, fingerprint for absolute identification. This is based on the intense variability seen in even small areas of prints, together with the observed correspondence of a much larger area, leading to the judgment that it is inconceivable that the fingerprint could have come from another person's finger. *Conceptually*, this subjective judgment is probabilistic: the chance of duplication of this intricate pattern is conceived to be so small that it may be ignored.

As the area of the finger represented or the clarity of the print diminishes, however, there necessarily comes a point where absolute identification is no longer justified on these subjective grounds. Where is this point? There is surprisingly little with which to answer, yet the issue is one that is continually faced within the profession. The criteria for absolute identification are wholly dependent on the subjective professional judgment of a fingerprint examiner. When a fingerprint examiner determines that there is *enough* corresponding detail to warrant the conclusion of absolute identification, then the criteria have been met. Period.[41]

---

39. *See* David A. Stoney, *What Made Us Ever Think We Could Individualize Using Statistics?*, 31 J. FORENSIC SCIENCE SOC'Y 197 (1991); COWGER, *supra* note 1, at 146–149; Stoney, *supra* note 2.

40. Simon A. Cole, *Witnessing Identification: Latent Fingerprinting Evidence and Expert Knowledge*, 28 SOCIAL STUDIES OF SCIENCE, 687(1998); Simon A. Cole, *What Counts for Identity?: The Historical Origins of the Methodology of Latent Fingerprint Identification*, 12 SCIENCE IN CONTEXT 139 (1999).

41. Ashbaugh (1999), *supra* note 9, at 103, 144–148.

Efforts to assess the individuality of DNA blood typing make an excellent contrast.[42] There has been intense debate over which statistical models are to be applied, and how one should quantify increasingly rare events. To many, the absence of adequate statistical modeling, or the controversy regarding calculations, brings the admissibility of the evidence into question. Woe to fingerprint practice were such criteria applied!

Much of the discussion of fingerprint practices in this and preceding sections may lead the critical reader to the question, "Is there any scientific basis for an absolute identification?" It is important to realize that an absolute identification is an opinion, rather than a conclusion based on scientific research. The functionally equivalent scientific conclusion (as seen in some DNA evidence) would be based on calculations showing that the probability of two different patterns being indistinguishably alike is so small that it asymptotes with zero, and therefore, for practical purposes, is treated as if it were zero. The scientific conclusion, however, must be based on tested probability models. These simply do not exist for fingerprint pattern comparisons.

[2] The Absence of Suitable Measurements Creates Vague and Flexible Criteria

Counting corresponding minutiae has been an inherent part of fingerprint comparisons since they were first scientifically studied by Galton.[43] The limitations of a minutiae count have long been recognized and, over the last few decades, the traditional use of a specific threshold number of minutiae has been rejected on the grounds that there is no scientific basis for this practice.[44] Most recently some leading practitioners have denounced and denied the practice of counting minutiae entirely.[45] This view is founded in the fear that if one merely counts minutiae one will be distracted from properly comparing all aspects of the print.[46] Stating the deficiencies of minutiae point counts, however, does not bring one closer to having a suitable replacement measure.

The next place to look for a measurement of the value of a fingerprint comparison would be to the statistical models. As noted earlier, about a dozen models for quantification of fingerprint individuality have been proposed.[47] None of these even approaches theoretical adequacy, however, and none has been subjected to empirical validation. Apart from illustration of the intense variability in fingerprint patterns, and the inability of simple minutiae counts to quantify this variability, these models *occupy no role* in the routine professional practice of fingerprint examination. Indeed, inasmuch as a statis-

42. Stoney, *supra* note 39.

43. Galton, *supra* note 22.

44. Champod, *supra* note 19; Evett & Williams, *supra* note 17; P. Margot & E. German, *Fingerprint Identification Breakout Meeting "Ne'urim Declaration,"* in Proceedings of the International Symposium on Fingerprint Detection and Identification (J. Almog & E. Springer eds., 1996).

45. *See* the excellent discussion by John Thornton, Setting Standards in the Comparison and Identification (May 9, 2000) (transcription of presentation at the 84th Annual Training Conference of the California State Division of International Association for Identification, Laughlin, Nevada), available at www.latentprints.com.

46. Ed German, www.onin.com/fp.

47. Stoney & Thornton, *supra* note 2; Champod, *supra* note 23; Stoney *supra* note 2.

tical method would suggest qualified (non-absolute) opinions, the models are rejected on principle by the fingerprint profession.

What, then, are the standards in fingerprint identification practice? Any unbiased, intelligent assessment of fingerprint identification practices today reveals that there are, in reality, no standards. That is, the amount of correspondence in friction ridge detail that is necessary for a conclusion of identity has not been established. There is an even more basic deficiency, however. We have no methodology in place that is capable of *measuring* the amount of correspondence in a fingerprint comparison. And there is a third, corollary deficiency. We have no methodology in place that is capable of measuring the amount of detail that is available in a fingerprint for comparison to another. In summary we cannot:

> measure the amount of detail in a (single) fingerprint that is available to compare,
>
> measure the amount of detail in correspondence between two fingerprints, or
>
> objectively interpret the meaning of a given correspondence between two fingerprints

Controversy exists regarding the first two of the above points. Specifically, it is asserted that the Analysis phase and the Comparison phase[48] of the fingerprint examination process are objective.[49] This assertion is based on the idea that when a specific fingerprint is being considered, that print is constant and whatever characteristics it has are present and unvarying. This is oblique to the issue, confusing alternative usages of the word "objective."[50] Fingerprint examiners may be looking at the same print, but the process of determining how much detail is present and whether that detail corresponds within allowable limits is explicitly subjective. Specifically, there are no objective standards in the Analysis phase regarding the determination of what detail is reliable. Examiners rely, quite appropriately, on their expert assessment of distortions and the contingencies of printing in order to determine what portions of the print are reliable representations of the detail that is present on the finger that made the print. Similarly, there are no objective standards in the Comparison phase that determine the allowances that can be made for the minor "explainable" discrepancies that are inherent in fingerprints. Again, examiners rely, quite appropriately, on their expert assessment of these discrepancies and based on their training, experience and skill they determine the tolerances that are applied in the Comparison phase.

AFIS computer technology holds promise to provide some objectivity in these areas, but AFIS has been and remains restricted to the task of screening millions of prints and efficiently selecting candidates for fingerprint compari-

---

48. The Analysis, Comparison and Evaluation steps are discussed *supra*, at § 2.1.2.

49. *See*, for example, Ashbaugh (1999), *supra* note 9, at 148; German, *supra* note 46; Stephen B. Meagher, testimony at *Daubert* Hearing, United States v. Mitchell, Crim. No. 96–407 (E.D.Pa., testimony of July 8, 1999). *See also*, B. Darymple, *Fingerprints (Dactyloscopy): Identification and Classification, in* EN-CYCLOPEDIA OF FORENSIC SCIENCE 975 (J. Siegel et al. eds., 2000).

50. For example, Ashbaugh (1999), *supra* note 9, at 148, states, "The comparison is objective, others must be capable of seeing the physical attributes one sees. If one feels his or her objectiveness has been compromised due to the consultation, one should ask a third party to carry out the verification."

son.[51] Although this is an important, effective and indeed, revolutionary task, the comparison itself is reserved for the individual fingerprint examiner. The examiner applies a personal, subjective criterion that, despite all its historical precedent, legal acceptance and public confidence, is both vague and flexible.

Current practices are supported by legal and professional tradition, empirical success in millions of cases and professional self-regulation. Critical judgment is applied to the comparison examination process and to the rendering of opinions, but there is no justification based on conventional science: no theoretical model, statistics or empirical validation process.

Recognition of the above deficiencies does not mean that the fingerprint practices are discredited, that they have no foundational basis, or that the process is necessarily unreliable. The question of legal reliability is, however, a reasonable one to ask. Legal scrutiny of fingerprints is, after more than 80 years of uncritical public and judicial acceptance, entirely appropriate.

§ 2–2.3.2   Questions of Standard Practices, Proficiency Testing, Self–Regulation and Empirical Validation

One of the most controversial areas of disagreement surrounds the question of whether fingerprint procedures have been empirically validated during their long use. There are a number of related issues and topics including proficiency testing, self-regulation among the fingerprint profession, and the lack of standard practices.

One extreme (but widely held) view is that since no two fingerprints from different individuals have ever been found to be alike, with more than 100 years of experience, the empirical validity of fingerprints is established. This statement is based on the individuality of complete fingerprints and as such is nearly meaningless to the process of latent fingerprint examination. Left out is the reality that fingerprint comparisons involve prints with widely varying quality and quantity of ridge detail, ranging from near-perfect reproductions of a finger's friction ridge skin to blurred smudges that may show no ridge detail at all. The issue is not the finding of two fingerprints that are alike, but rather the finding of prints from two different fingers that can be mistakenly judged to be alike by a fingerprint examination.

Here one runs into a fundamental problem, since neither the education of fingerprint examiners, nor the process of fingerprint examination is standardized. There is a voluntary certification process,[52] which, when linked to hiring practices, serves a gatekeeping function in many jurisdictions. In no practical sense, however, can we consider the performance of fingerprint examiners to be uniform. Fingerprint examiners differ in their level of training, experience and ability, causing differences in opinions regarding the same evidence.[53]

In this context, consider the assertion that the fingerprint process has been empirically validated because there have never been prints from two different fingers that have been mistakenly judged to be alike by a fingerprint examiner. This is simply not true. Mistakes have been made in casework[54] and

---

51. The one attempt to use AFIS for a fingerprint model resulted in disastrously erroneous results due to biases and deficiencies in the research design. *See supra* note 24.

52. *Supra* note 10.

53. *See* § 2.2.6.

54. For example, State v. Caldwell, 322 N.W.2d 574 (Minn.1982); James E. Starrs, *A Miscue in Fingerprint Identification: Causes and Concerns*, 12 J. OF POLICE SCI. & ADMIN. 287

in proficiency tests.[55] These mistakes, however, are subject to dismissal for a variety of reasons, such as:

(a) the specific examiner making the mistake was unqualified or incompetent

(b) the materials submitted for examination were incomplete,

(c) a novice was given the proficiency test as a training exercise.

In the face of demonstrable error, many in the fingerprint profession would simply explain that such errors would not be made by properly qualified fingerprint examiners. This may be true, but this means that the validation experiment itself is deficient. In effect, because the circumstances of the experiment were not sufficiently controlled, the outcome can be explained away. Similarly, when errors are made in casework (and subsequently discovered), the profession has seen the issue as exclusively one of examiner error, adopting the practice of "sacrificing the examiner" and saving the appearance of infallibility.[56]

In reality the current fingerprint examination processes are inextricably linked with the human examiner and one cannot separate the human error of the examiner (whatever the cause) from the reliability of fingerprint evidence. It has been widely and explicitly asserted that this separation is possible and that therefore fingerprint evidence has a zero error rate.[57]

Another problem with the assertion of empirical validity based on the absence of mistakes is that there is no established mechanism to uncover the mistakes. How would it be established that an error in a fingerprint identification occurred? Unless there is re-examination by a higher authority such mistakes are not uncovered. (And then when they are, as noted above, the error is attributed to a deficient examiner, not to any unreliability in the process.)

For the reasons discussed, we can set aside the experience and asserted infallibility of fingerprint examination practices as a foundation for reliability. What about more specific, objective validation studies of the (subjective) fingerprint practices? Although such tests are feasible, they have not been conducted. In the absence of such controlled, scientific testing, proficiency test results and cases of practitioner error have been cited as evidence to demonstrate the *unreliability* of the process. This evidence is disconcerting, but it in no way amounts to a fair empirical test of fingerprint identification practices. The problem is this: to test a process, the process itself must be defined or regulated in a way that the outcome of the test can be linked back to the process. We have a vague and flexible process in fingerprint identification. It varies with the individual examiner. If any examiner fails a test, this can be attributed to that particular examiner, leaving the process untested. Until we sufficiently define the process, no error rate can be measured and the process cannot be validated.

(1984); For current cases *see* Ed German, *supra* note 47.

55. David Grieve, *Possession of Truth*, 46 J. FORENSIC IDENTIFICATION 521 (1996); Champod *supra* note 19, at 889.

56. Cole, *supra* note 40.

57. For example, Bruce Budowle, testifying at *Daubert* hearing in United States v. Mitchell, Crim. No. 96–407 (E.D.Pa., hearing held July 7–13, 1999).

§ 2–2.3.3   The Question of Opinions of Qualified Association

As discussed in preceding sections, qualified, "probable" identifications are not accepted as valid, reportable opinions by the fingerprint profession.[58] To any scientist it is nevertheless obvious that between the two extremes of "no value" and "absolute identification" there must be some middle ground. In the absence of a well-defined scientific resolution of this problem (such as credible scientific models to support qualified associations) the fingerprint profession has adopted what amounts to an independent regulatory practice. Once ethically forbidden without exception, qualified identifications now are allowed by the fingerprint profession only under very narrow circumstances. They cannot be offered voluntarily. Suppose, for example, some poor quality fingerprints are found on a cash box at a burglary. Examination shows that the prints are "probably" from one of two defendants. The laboratory or police report would avoid conveying this finding, stating simply that "No identification was made." If called to testify, attorneys representing the other defendant might well press the fingerprint examiner to give the opinion that prints are "probably" from the first defendant. Specific allowance was made in professional ethical codes to avoid the dilemma of a choice among the alternatives of a professional ethics violation (for giving the qualified opinion), perjury (for lying about it), or contempt of court (for refusing to give it). To remain ethical the examiner must essentially offer the opinion under protest and must fully qualify the response as being outside of routine professional practice.

The abhorrence for qualified, "probable" identifications arises from a number of sources. Fundamentally, there is concern that the fact-finder would place undue weight on the evidence. It is argued that when examiners offer only absolute identifications, defendants are given the benefit of the doubt. (For the most part this latter point is true, although in some cases, such as that described above, what is a conservative lack of evidence against one may, of course, be prejudicial to others.) There is also concern that the practice of offering qualified opinions would compromise the popular acceptance of the infallible certainty of fingerprint identifications.[59] Furthermore, the practice would necessarily lead to probability questions such as, "How likely is it that a random person could have made this print?" As discussed above, there are no reasonable data and no scientific model that would allow an answer. Indeed, the practice of refusing even to consider qualified opinions is so uniform that there is no body of professional experience upon which to build.

The final leap-of-faith to absolute identification is thus an essential element of fingerprint practice. If fingerprint identification had an acceptable quantitative basis in theory or empirical validation criteria, then qualified (non-absolute) associations would be a necessary scientific byproduct. Legal admissibility, of course, would be another matter, but at least the scientists would be doing science and leaving standards of admissibility to the courts.

§ 2–2.3.4   The Question of Exclusionary Value

There is some limited divergence of opinion over how extensive a finger-

---

58. The material in this section can be found discussed in more detail in Champod, *supra* note 9 and Champod & Evett, *supra* note 26.

59. Cole, *supra* note 40.

print must be to have exclusionary value.[60] Some examiners hold closely to the view that for an exclusion to be *possible* a fingerprint *must* be identifiable. This is erroneous. The issues involved are the clarity of the prints, the completeness of the reference prints and the amount of time available to study them. The crime scene prints must be clear enough to be unambiguous in their detail (we must be able to conclude that the absence of certain details means that a person did not make the print). The reference prints from the individual must also show *all* surfaces of the fingers and palms completely (otherwise the missing portions could be the source of the print).[61] An opinion of exclusion results only after all possible areas of the person's hands have been screened for possible correspondence with the print. When a print is unidentifiable (and often when it is identifiable) this can be very time consuming.

Controversy arises from several sources. One is that the time required of the fingerprint examiner is prohibitive, hence the examination is "not possible" as a practical (rather than scientific) matter. Exacerbating this is that, from a prosecution point of view, such an examination often is considered pointless. (From a defense point of view, of course, the existence of *someone else's* fingerprint in a key location may be of considerable importance.) A third source of controversy is that, when a fingerprint is unidentifiable, comparison of a print for exclusion might lead to the discovery of some corresponding detail, but not enough for a conclusive identification. This raises the specter of a *possible* identification, which as discussed above, is outside the scope of routine professional practice. This difficulty is resolved, in accordance with professional practice, by offering the opinion that "I could neither identify nor exclude this print as being made by the subject"—and offering nothing further.

§ 2–2.3.5   The Possibility of Forged or Planted Fingerprints

The question of forgery or planting of fingerprints is naturally of concern, both legally and scientifically. Setting aside the intentional falsification of evidence by investigators or laboratory personnel, the question of prints being planted, transferred or forged to implicate an innocent individual remains. Scientific debate has centered on whether fingerprint examiners could detect forged prints, if encountered. This discussion, of course, must consider the degree of scrutiny that a print receives during routine examination. The issue is resolved not so much by technical means as by practical considerations. It is extremely impractical to forge a fingerprint and to do so successfully would require an unusual amount of specific knowledge. Fabrication of prints by those having this special knowledge has, however, occasionally occurred.[62]

§ 2–2.3.6   Fingerprint Documentation and Reporting

As mentioned earlier, the extent of note-taking and reporting of finger-

---

60. Very little formal treatment of this subject has been made. *See*, for example, Cowger *supra* note 1, at 129–131, 173–174; Andre A. Moenssens, Fingerprints and the Law 115–116 (1969); and Moenssens *supra* note 16, at 258.

61. These sets of comprehensive inked reference prints are referred to as "major case prints." *See* Pat Wertheim, *Inked Major Case Prints*, 49 J. Forensic Identification 468 (1999).

62. Wertheim (1994 and 1998), *supra* note 5; Moenssens, *supra* note 16.

print processing and comparison varies considerably.[63] Frequently, the notes and reports that are available are insufficient to document fully what was processed, where prints were found, what comparisons were made, and what the results of these comparisons were. Indeed, to some extent, prevailing practices have the effect of hiding this information. Related controversies may arise. These are, for the most part, subject to legal, rather than scientific debate, but some discussion of the science is helpful to appreciate the significance of issues that might otherwise be overemphasized or overlooked.

Available documentation may fail to show the original position of a print with sufficient accuracy to establish the needed proof or to fully explore possible defense arguments. Under these circumstances scientists usually can conduct a comparison of the fingerprint lifts or photographs directly with the original surface in order to acquire the needed information.

Documentation of the results of comparisons is invariably complete with regard to identifications of the suspect. Reports may or may not mention identifications of co-defendants, victims and other individuals; or the presence of any prints that are definitely not the suspect's. Indirectly, there may be reference to the number of identifiable prints, or to prints of value (or possible value) for identification. The existence of these prints may help determine whether it would be worthwhile requesting a re-examination of the fingerprints for exclusions.

Given the prevailing professional practices, very seldom will reports refer to prints that might be from the suspect. (These would be prints where the examiner cannot make a definite conclusion that the print either is or is not from the suspect.) A typical approach would be to report that "no identification of the suspect's prints could be made," a statement that although true, leaves unsaid the actual results of the comparison. (Is there agreement, as far as it goes, with the suspect? Or is there absolute, apparent, or possible exclusion? Or are the prints simply too poor to compare, given time constraints?)

§ 2–2.3.7 Omission of Fingerprint Processing and Disposal of Latent Lifts

Another primarily legal controversy arises regarding the destruction (or possible destruction) of evidence through the omission of fingerprint processing or the disposal of latent fingerprint lifts.[64] There is some scientific input into these issues and, as with the preceding section, it offers some help in defining the legal controversy.

As an example, consider a case where a loaded gun has been found in an automobile glove compartment. An arrest is made and the gun is booked directly into property, without a request for fingerprint processing. The defense later argues that by failing to process the gun for fingerprints and by its subsequent handling, exonerating fingerprint evidence may have been

63. Moenssens *supra* note 16, at 109–112; Cowger *supra* note 1, at 85–88; Richard H. Fox and Carl L. Cunningham, Crime Scene Search and Physical Evidence Handbook 47–59 (1973). *See also supra* note 30.

64. I have frequently encountered cases where these issues have been of concern to defense counsel. However, I am unaware of any judicial opinions regarding the issue or any written discussion of the issue in the forensic science literature.

destroyed. Several findings could be construed as exonerating: finding no fingerprints of the suspect, finding someone else's fingerprints, or finding the defendant's fingerprints in some location on the gun (such as the barrel) that would support the suspect's statement regarding its use (e.g., "I was hammering in a stake with the butt when the gun went off accidentally"). Scientifically, the first of these would be specious because the absence of fingerprints would not indicate that a person did not touch an item. The other two findings are a scientifically reasonable basis on which to make the legal argument.

Related arguments can occur regarding the disposal of latent lifts, or latent lifts that have become lost. Suppose a police department submits fingerprints to the laboratory and receives the finding that the prints are of "no value" (meaning no value for identification of the suspect). Subsequently the police department discards the latent lifts or they are lost. There is a scientifically valid argument that exonerating evidence may have been destroyed, as there may have been value for exclusion or reconstruction.

§ 2–2.4   Future Directions

When this chapter was originally written (1996) the future directions were summarized briefly:

> It is unlikely that any significant current research will affect fingerprint practices over the next several years. We can anticipate that additional means of detecting fingerprints and more efficient methods of electronic processing will develop. At the academic level, there is a continuing low-level of effort into the statistical modeling of the variation in fingerprint minutiae. This has been made more feasible by the electronic storage of fingerprint patterns, and eventually models will be developed and tested. Even so, it is unlikely that these models will be readily accepted as a basis for fingerprint identification methodology.

The earlier version also noted that with respect to the scientific basis of fingerprint comparisons that there was

> ... no prevailing scientific debate on these issues. For such a critically important discipline in forensic science there certainly ought to be. But among fingerprint professionals little point is seen in it. They would argue that the subjective standards used for identification are conservative (based on their historical record), and that there is no need for objective scientific research. The argument would continue that scientific inadequacies in the statistical models render them irrelevant to real-world practice. Since the current practices have a sufficient scientific basis to be both functionally effective and to be legally accepted, where is the impetus for scientific research? Outside the profession there is the unchallenged popular perception that fingerprints are the epitome of individual variation and that they must be individual, so what point is there in debate or study? Even the reality of the issues arising from fingerprints of diminishing size and quality has not disturbed this popular perception.

Happily we can now report that this situation has changed: we have active debate in the scientific, fingerprint practitioner and legal communities. Although the body of the fingerprint profession still sees scientific research on fingerprint individuality as unnecessary,[65] the forensic science community has explicitly recognized the need.[66] More importantly, the legal community has begun to critically examine the scientific status of fingerprint practices. We can now confidently predict significant changes in both the legal perspective on fingerprint evidence and the scientific foundations for fingerprint practices.

These changes will not reveal any startling deficiencies in the capability of fingerprints to absolutely identify individuals. They may not even change much in the way of how fingerprints are examined, compared and interpreted. The changes will nonetheless be fundamental. We will have scientifically valid systems in place to ensure reliability and we will have replaced the naive wholesale acceptance of fingerprint evidence with a critical awareness of the issues necessary for reliable proof.

From the scientist's perspective, there are two conceptual routes to this end. One is to approach fingerprint evidence by developing realistic models that will:

measure the amount of detail in a (single) fingerprint that is available to compare

measure the amount of detail in correspondence between two fingerprints

objectively interpret the meaning of a given correspondence between two fingerprints

These models will have flaws. They will be unable to incorporate all of the fingerprint examiner's expertise, and they will not fully incorporate the finer details that are represented in fingerprints. But they will be testable, and we will have science.

The second conceptual approach is to empirically test the reliability of fingerprint practices as they are currently conducted. A meaningful test will require

an *a priori* definition of the process itself

a set of fingerprint examiners of acknowledged, unquestionable, "consensus," expertise to conduct the process in the test

a realistic set of fingerprint test cases, covering a wide range of quality and extensiveness in the prints.

Neither of these approaches is particularly easy, and neither is likely to be cooperatively entered into by the fingerprint profession, but they are feasible and ultimately the issues are of paramount legal importance.

Steps will be necessary to translate the results of either of these approaches into reliable fingerprint practices. If objective measurements follow from the first approach, the methodology used for the examination, comparison and interpretation of fingerprints could be radically changed. This may seem attractive, but I suspect that such a procedural change is unnecessary. It presumes that things are bad, when in fact they are vague and flexible.

65. *See, e.g.,* David Grieve, *Baiting Laws with Stars,* 48 J. Forensic Identification 426 (1998).

66. National Institute of Justice, Forensic Sciences: Review of Status and Needs 28–31 (1999).

Out of the second approach there will be demonstrable reliability of fingerprint identifications when there is some minimal level of detail present in the fingerprints. Narrower, though still subjective, bounds will be placed on the identification criterion. To translate the results of this approach to reliability in the routine professional practice we need a method to ensure that any given fingerprint examiner is operating within the consensus norms that have been validated by experiment. This might follow a certification process, but I suspect that more explicit, ongoing external review is appropriate. This type of review is also appropriate to address the post-conviction issues that are sure to arise. One option is to use the acknowledged (and now tested!) panel of experts to review *any questioned casework, past or present.* If this were done a pattern of three outcomes would develop. Firstly, the work of nearly all fingerprint examiners in nearly all cases would be found to be well within the professional (and now tested) norms. Secondly, some very few cases would be uncovered where, even among the best of the best, there is controversy regarding the sufficiency of the identification. This result will produce professional debate and have the benefit of refining and narrowing the consensus norms. This result will also create interesting legal issues to be resolved. Thirdly, the work of some fingerprint examiners would be found to be either erroneous, fraudulent or outside the consensus norms.

The argument may be encountered that the above system is essentially in place, operating department-by-department, when fingerprint identifications are checked by colleagues or supervisors. This view is incorrect. Two things are missing. First there are no established, tested, normative practices. Second there is no mechanism in place to ensure local adherence to the these practices.

Appendix I

Glossary

ACE–V. An acronym for the four articulated steps in fingerprint examination: Analysis, Comparison, Evaluation and Verification.

AFIS. An acronym for automated fingerprint identification systems. These computerized databases allow retrieval fingerprint records that show electronic codes similar to a crime scene print. The system selects candidates for subsequent manual comparisons by fingerprint experts.

Analysis. The preliminary assessment of the quality and quantity of friction ridge detail present in a friction ridge print. This includes examination of distortions, clarity, availability of detail for comparison, the possible part of the hand from which the print came and any internal indications of unreliability in the print. (As formally defined in the ACE–V fingerprint examination process. *See* ASHBAUGH, QUANTITATIVE-QUALITATIVE FRICTION RIDGE ANALYSIS (1999).)

Anatomical aspects (in fingerprint analysis). Determination, based on the consideration of a single print, which finger or what part of the palm that the print came from.

Bifurcation. A synonym for "fork," used to describe the form of a minutae that is present where there is a branching of a ridge.

Classification of fingerprints. The process of assigning codes to fingerprints so that they can be efficiently organized, stored and retrieved. Historically conducted manually using prints from an individual's ten fingers. Now also performed electronically and on single fingerprints.

Cold search. Beginning with a single crime scene print, the process of searching a large database of reference prints for a matching print.

Comparison. The systematic comparison of all available friction ridge detail in the unknown, or latent print, to the detail present in the known, or reference print. (As formally defined in the ACE–V fingerprint examination process. See ASHBAUGH *supra.*)

Cyanoacrylate fuming. A fingerprint visualization technique, also known as super-glue fuming, which uses this chemical and is effective on a wide range of surfaces.

Deposition distortion. Distortions in a print caused by the pressure of deposition, generally resulting in a flattening and broadening of each ridge.

Development of fingerprints. Fingerprint development, or visualization, is the process of rendering invisible prints visible. It may employ optical, chemical or physical methods.

Development medium distortion. Distortions in a print caused by the method used to render the print visible.

Distortions. See Deposition Distortion, Development medium distortion, Matrix distortion, Pressure distortion, Substrate distortion.

Elimination prints. Fingerprints taken for reference purposes from persons (other than the offender) who had access to a crime scene or to items of evidence. Any fingerprints taken as evidence are first compared with the elimination prints to eliminate the possibility that the prints are from these persons.

Evaluation. The answering of two questions by the expert: (1) Is there agreement between the latent and reference prints? and (2) Is the agreement sufficient to eliminate all possible donors in the world except this one? (As formally defined in the ACE–V fingerprint examination process. *See* ASHBAUGH *supra.*)

Exclusion of fingerprints. A conclusion that a fingerprint did not come from a specific individual.

Exclusionary value. A judgement concerning a fingerprint's suitability for excluding that any particular person could have made it.

Explainable differences in fingerprints. Differences of a type routinely occurring among prints made by the same finger.

Fingerprints. Reproductions of the ridged skin surface of the fingers (or palm) resulting from the transfer of oil or other matter to a surface.

First level detail. General overall friction ridge pattern shape, e.g. circular, looping, arching or straight. (As formally defined in the ACE–V fingerprint examination process. *See* ASHBAUGH *supra.)*

Hypothenar. The portion of the palm along the side between the little finger and the wrist.

Identification of fingerprints. The process of assigning the origin of a fingerprint to a specific individual.

Incipient Ridges. Fine, underdeveloped ridges that lack pores.

Interdigital. The upper portion of the palm at the base of the digits.

Latent fingerprints. Fingerprints that are invisible under normal viewing conditions. Latent fingerprints are rendered visible by fingerprint development methods.

Lift card. A small card used to hold pieces of tape that have lifted developed fingerprints from their original surface.

Lifting of fingerprints. Removal of a fingerprint from its original surface, typically using tape after the print has been dusted with fingerprint powder.

Major Case Prints. The result of inking and recording of every existing area of friction ridge skin present on the hands and fingers.

Magnabrush. A magnetic fingerprint dusting tool that employs iron filings mixed with fingerprint powder.

Matrix. The substance of which the fingerprint is composed, e.g. sweat, oils, blood.

Matrix distortion. Distortions resulting from the nature or behavior of the substance of which the fingerprint is composed.

Minutiae. The fine structure of fingerprint consisting of the individual branchings and terminations of ridges.

Ninhydrin. A chemical used to develop latent fingerprints, especially on paper. Ninhydrin reacts with amino acids in fingerprints producing a reddish purple color.

Number of points. The number of minutiae or other details seen in a fingerprint.

Palmar. Relating to the palm of the hand.

Patterns of fingerprints. The overall geometry of the ridges in a fingerprint, especially useful for classification and for registration of prints prior to detailed comparison.

Plantar. Relating to the sole of the foot.

Points v. Minutiae or other details seen in a fingerprint.

Powder development of fingerprints. A long-standing method of visualizing fingerprints based on the adherence of powder to perspiration, oils or other extraneous matter that has been transferred from the fingers to a surface.

Pressure distortion. A smearing type of distortion caused by horizontal movement of the finger when the print is made.

Qualified fingerprint identification. A less than certain opinion concerning whether a particular person made a fingerprint.

Radial. Toward the thumb side of the hand.

Second level detail. The specific paths of the ridges. This includes the minutiae (or points), but also includes the path of scars, incipient ridges, and flexion creases. (As formally defined in the ACE–V fingerprint examination process. *See* ASHBAUGH *supra*.)

Substrate. The surface on which the print is found.

Substrate distortion. Distortions introduced due to the nature of the substrate. These can result from flexibility, shape, deformation or surface contamination.

Super-glue. See Cyanoacrylate fuming.

Ten-print card. The card used to record inked reference fingerprints of an individual.

Thenar. The area of the palm nearest the thumb.

Third level detail. The small shapes on the ridge, the relative location of pores, and the small details contained in accidental damage to the friction ridges. (As formally defined in the ACE–V fingerprint examination process. *See* ASHBAUGH *supra*.

Ulnar. Toward the little finger part of the hand.

Verification. The peer review by another expert conducted as a quality assurance step. (As formally defined in the ACE–V fingerprint examination process. *See* ASHBAUGH *supra*.)

CHAPTER 3

HANDWRITING IDENTIFICATION

by

D. Michael Risinger*

Table of Sections

A. LEGAL ISSUES

* Professor of Law, Seton Hall University School of Law; B.A. *Magna Cum Laude*, Yale University, 1966, J.D. *Cum Laude*, Harvard Law School, 1969. Portions of this chapter appear in D. Michael Risinger (with Michael J. Saks) *Science and Nonscience in the Courts: Daubert Meets Handwriting Identification Expertise*, 82 Iowa L. Rev. 21 (1996); D. Michael Risinger, Mark P. Denbeaux & Michael J. Saks, *Brave New "Post-*Daubert *World"—A Reply to Professor Moenssens*, 29 Seton Hall L. Rev. 405 (1998); and D. Michael Risinger, *Defining the "Task at Hand": Non–Science Forensic Science after* Kumho Tire v. Carmichael, 57 Wash. & Lee L. Rev. 767 (2000).

Westlaw Electronic Research

See Westlaw Electronic Research Guide preceding the Summary of Contents.

————————

A. LEGAL ISSUES

§ 3–1.0   THE JUDICIAL RESPONSE TO PROFFERED EXPERT TESTIMONY ON HANDWRITING IDENTIFICATION BY COMPARISON OF HANDS

§ 3–1.1   Introductory Note

Document examiners do many things. They examine typewriting for signs of idiosyncratic typeface alignment and wear which might indicate a common origin for two documents. This task is a form of toolmark analysis best considered in connection with that chapter. They analyze ink to reveal its physical and chemical properties, a task best considered in connection with the subject of forensic chemistry. In addition, they scrutinize the alignment of printed lines and the overlap of handwritten lines to determine if words or phrases have been after-inserted, and they analyze the composition, method of production, and watermark of paper in order to ascertain probable origin and, in some cases, age. These functions may, in some applications, involve elements of chemistry, but in addition they almost always depend on specialized knowledge of manufacturing processes and manufacturer specifications not unlike that employed in firearms identification concerning the relative number, spacing, pitch and direction of twist, of grooves and lands in various makes of rifled barrels.

All of these functions generally share the strengths and weaknesses otherwise associated with toolmark evidence, forensic chemistry, and the like. They are not, however, what this chapter is about. This chapter concerns the asserted skill that historically formed the foundation of the document examiner's trade, and still comprises a surprisingly high percentage of the everyday work of document examiners both in and out of court.[1] This is the asserted

—————

§ 3–1.0

1. For instance, in his January 1993 testimony in In Matter of Requested Extradition of

Smyth, 826 F.Supp. 316 (N.D.Cal.1993), an international extradition case involving an alleged IRA terrorist, Special Agent Richard M.

ability to determine the authorship *vel non* of a piece of handwriting by examining the way in which the letters are inscribed, shaped and joined,[2] and comparing it to exemplars of a putative author's concededly authentic handwriting.

The balance of this section provides a discussion of the history of the courts' response to such asserted expertise.[3]

§ 3–1.2 Early Legal History

The notion that handwriting can be used to identify its author is very old,[4] as is the notion that a person can learn to make such an identification by study. Attempts to develop a system of such expertise appear to have started in Italy and France in the seventeenth century,[5] and by 1737 were well enough accepted in France to have been incorporated into the law. The Code du Faux (Code Concerning Forgeries) contained detailed provisions for regulating the collection of exemplars and their presentation to handwriting identification experts, which from the context of the code we may conclude formed a professional cadre of fair number.[6] However, no such claimed expertise then existed in the English speaking world. As we shall see, in Anglo–American courts a corps of asserted experts came into existence only after lawyers persuaded the courts to accept the idea that such an expertise might exist.[7]

Experts of any kind did not play a large role in litigation during the common law period, and when they occasionally did testify, they did so without a clearly defined set of legal principles governing their qualifications

Williams, an FBI questioned documents examiner with 17 years of experience, testified that "the bulk of" his work dealt with handwriting. Transcript at 231, on file with author. Nearly 90% of recent reported cases involving questioned document examiners concerned handwriting identification. *See infra* § 1.4, note 42.

2. That is, by examining the characteristics of what is sometimes called the "static trace" left behind by the dynamic act of writing.

3. A more extensive review of the legal history of handwriting identification expertise can be found in D. Michael Risinger, Mark P. Denbeaux & Michael J. Saks, *Exorcism of Ignorance as a Proxy for Rational Knowledge: The Lessons of Handwriting Identification "Expertise"*, 137 U. Pa. L. Rev. 731, 751–771 (1989).

4. Huntington Hartford quotes Aristotle as observing that "[J]ust as all men do not have the same speech sounds, neither do they have the same handwriting." Huntington Hartford, You Are What You Write 43 (1973) (quoting Aristotle, On Interpretation, Part I).

5. The earliest treatise in this line, of a definite graphological cast, appears to be Camillo Baldi, Trattato Come Da Una Lettera Missiva Si Conoscano La Natura, e Qualità Dello Scrittore (Milano, Geo. Batt Bidelli, 1625) [An Essay on the Means of Examining the Character and Qualities of a Writer from His Letters.] On

graphology more generally, *See* § 2.2.2, note 62.

6. *See generally* Francois Serpillon, Code du Faux, ou Commentaire sur l'Ordonnance du Juillet, 1737, Avec Une Instruction pour les Experts en Matiere de Faux (Lyon, Gabriel Regnault, 1774).

7. It appears certainly true that there was no cadre of such experts in England, and that the common law courts were strangers to such expertise. However, the same may not have been true in the ecclesiastical courts. *See* Philip Floyer, The Proctor's Practice in the Ecclesiastical Courts 103 (Worrall, London, 1744), under the title "Evidence": "Where either party would produce any writing and give it in evidence, it must be exhibited with an allegation, and so proved. The Hand of a party signing may be proved by letters, or other his handwriting, which are to be exhibited by an allegation, and being proved, Proctors or Approved Writers are to be assigned by the Judge to compare the same, who are to give Verdict thereon." This appears to describe more of a special jury practice than proof by expertise. Proctors were the cadre of practitioners in the Arches courts (which included Admiralty and the Ecclesiastical Courts), but who might qualify to sit as an "Approved Writer" is both fascinating and totally unclear.

or their use. It was not until 1782, in the case of *Folker v. Chadd*,[8] that a reported decision affirmed the propriety of the use of such "skilled witnesses,"[9] although the practice at trial was of course much older. The earliest trial use of skilled witnesses of which we have a record occurred in the trial of the Earl of Pembroke for the murder of Nathaniel Cony in 1678[10] (though it does not appear to have been regarded as a novelty in that case).

Until the very end of the 18th century, every example of expert testimony in the English speaking world involved witnesses whose expertise had primary application to practical affairs outside the courtroom, such as the physicians in the Earl of Pembroke's case or the engineers in *Folker v. Chadd*. If expertise in general then played a small role in the law, claimed expertise limited to issues that were or might be involved in court cases (what one might call a dominantly forensic expertise), was non-existent. The first such forensic expertise allowed into the courtroom was handwriting identification expertise. Thus, handwriting identification expertise is the oldest "forensic science" although it did not secure a place in the common law courtroom until nearly a century after its introduction into French proceedings.

When handwriting identification expertise finally did enter the common law courtroom, it did so haltingly.[11] In 1792, Lord Kenyon, sitting as a trial judge, allowed two postal inspectors proffered by one of the parties to testify concerning authorship by comparing known exemplars of one party's handwriting to a document whose authorship was at issue in the case.[12] However, the next year Kenyon reversed himself and in two cases held such testimony inadmissible.[13] In the 1802 case of *R. v. Cator*[14] the court held that a postal inspector might give an opinion as to whether a signature was in a "feigned hand" by examination of the signature alone, but could not compare hands. This position was reaffirmed by a divided court in *Doe d. Mudd v. Suckermore*[15] in 1836, and it was not until an 1854 statute was construed to authorize it that handwriting identification expertise became admissible in English courts.[16]

8. 3 Dougl. 157, 99 Eng.Rep. 589 (K.B. 1782).

9. In the 18th century the term "skilled witness" covered everyone we would today refer to as an expert. The term seems to have become recently used to refer to practical, as contrasted with scientific, experts. See, *e.g.*, the original Advisory Committee Note to Fed. R. Evid. 702.

10. *The Trial of Philip, Earl of Pembroke and Montgomery, at Westminster, for the Murder of Nathaniel Cony* (1678), in 6 COBBETT'S COMPLETE COLLECTION OF STATE TRIALS 1310 (1810). It appears that by the 1640s, surgeons were often, though by no means always, called upon to take part in coroners' inquests. Interestingly, the oldest surviving documentation of the practice currently known appears in the Maryland colonial records. *See* Helen Brock & Catherine Crawford, *Forensic Medicine in Early Colonial Maryland, 1633–83, in* LEGAL MEDICINE IN HISTORY (M. Clark & C. Crawford eds., 1994). In addition to the Earl of Pembroke's case, there were two other *notorious* 17th century trials in which expert testimony was given: *The Trial of Robert Green, Henry Berry,*

and Lawrence Hill, at the Kings–Bench, for the murder of Sir Edmundbury Godfrey (1679), in 7 COBBETT'S COMPLETE COLLECTION OF STATE TRIALS 159 (1810); and *The Trial of Spencer Cowper, Ellis Stephens, William Rogers, and John Marson, at Hertford Assizes, for the Murder of Mrs. Sarah Stout* (1699), 13 A COMPLETE COLLECTION OF STATE TRIALS 1105 (T.B. Howell ed., 1812). The expertise involved in all three trials was medical expertise. *See generally* T.R. FORBES, SURGEONS AT THE BAILEY: ENGLISH FORENSIC MEDICINE TO 1878 (1985).

11. This story is told in more detail in Risinger et al., *supra* note 3, at 751–771.

12. Goodtitle d. Revett v. Braham, 4 Term Rep. 497 (1792).

13. Carey v. Pitt, *Esq.*, Peake Add Cas. 130 (1793); Stranger v. Searle, 1 Esp. 14 (1793).

14. 4 Esp 117 (C.P. 1802)

15. 5 A. & E. 703 (K.B. 1836).

16. Common Law Procedure Act, 1854, 17 & 18 Vict., ch. 125, § 27; *See* Risinger et al., *supra* note 3, at 757–758, especially n. 116.

§ 3–1.3   Admissibility in American Jurisdictions

The story in the United States is even more complex. Until the passage of the English statute, most American jurisdictions followed English practice and rejected such expertise. There were some significant exceptions, however. In the 1836 case of *Moody v. Rowell*,[17] Massachusetts became the first common law jurisdiction[18] to authorize the use of such asserted expertise. The rationale of the *Moody* case is telling. Up to that time, in all Anglo–American jurisdictions, handwriting had been formally authenticated as to authorship by the recognition testimony of non-expert witnesses who were familiar with the putative author's handwriting, supplemented on occasion by direct jury comparison between challenged documents and other, authentic, writings of the putative author which might happen to be in the case for other purposes. This was taken to be such weak evidence that, without evaluating the validity of the proffered experts' claims to expertise, the *Moody* Court ruled that such asserted expert testimony should be admitted because it could not be any worse than what was traditionally relied on.[19] This seems to be the dominant rationale for the allowance of such testimony in those states which followed Massachusetts' lead over the next fifty to seventy-five years. While by 1900 a substantial majority of American jurisdictions accepted such testimony,[20] the prevailing attitude may be best exemplified by the opinion of the New York Court of Appeals in *Hoag v. Wright*,[21]

> The opinions of experts upon handwriting, who testify from comparison only, are regarded by the courts as of uncertain value, because in so many cases where such evidence is received witnesses of equal honesty, intelligence and experience reach conclusions not only diametrically opposite, but always in favor of the party who called them.[22]

While some courts continued to reject such expertise, and most which allowed it remained skeptical, a group of professional experts was growing up and beginning to seek greater respectability. It is ironic that when expert handwriting identification testimony was first declared admissible in America and England, there were no experts. That is to say, the lawyers seeking to utilize such testimony had to proffer various witnesses who were willing to assert a kind of *ad hoc* expertise acquired as a side effect of being something else, such as a postal inspector or a bank teller. No practicing forensic

---

17.   34 Mass (17 Pick.) 490 (1835).

18.   Louisiana's version of the French Civil Code provided for resort to handwriting experts, but it is not clear that at the time of its statehood there were any such experts in Louisiana. *See* Risinger et al., *supra* note 3, at 761, n.133.

19.   This was the rationale urged by the dissenters in Doe d. Mudd v. Suckermore. The *Moody* court concluded that "this species of evidence, though generally very slight, and often wholly immaterial, is competent evidence." 34 Mass (17 Pick.) at 498.

20.   The earliest authority for the admission of such testimony in each U.S. jurisdiction is set out chronologically in Appendix 3 to Risinger et al., *supra* note 3, at 788. (There is an error in that Appendix. The earliest date for Arkansas should be 1920, on the authority of Murphy v. Murphy, 144 Ark. 429, 222 S.W.

721. In addition, there is evidence of unchallenged use of such experts as early as 1910 in Arkansas (Strickland v. Strickland, 95 Ark. 623, 129 S.W. 801) and 1932 in Wyoming (State Bd. of Law Exam'rs v. Strahan, 44 Wyo. 156, 8 P.2d 1090), and perhaps 1835 in Ohio, based on Bank of Muskingum v. Carpenter's Adm'rs, 7 Ohio 21, where such evidence is adverted to in the reporter's summary of evidence but is not mentioned in the opinion. (Prof. Andre Moenssens called attention to these cases.))

21.   174 N.Y. 36, 66 N.E. 579 (N.Y.1903).

22.   *Id.* at 581. *See also* Miles v. Loomis, 75 N.Y. 288 (1878); Mutual Benefit Life Ins. Co. v. Brown, 30 N.J.Eq. 193 (1878), aff'd, 32 N.J.Eq. 809 (1880); In re Fuller's Estate, 222 Pa. 182, 70 A. 1005 (Pa.1908).

document examiner today would concede any expertise to such witnesses.[23] When the legal system agreed to accept such testimony, however, it created a demand which was to be met by people who turned their entire attention to filling it. Not surprisingly, that resulted in people setting out to create a standard theory and practice giving the appearance of "science." Among the first of those people was Charles Chabot,[24] who, despite his name, was English. He was originally a lithographer by trade, but developed an interest in handwriting identification about the time such expert testimony was gaining admissibility in English courts. It is unclear how much he was influenced by contemporary French theory and practice, but in 1871, at the urging of his lawyer-disciple Edward Twistleton (who wrote a lengthy theoretical introduction to the book), he published THE HANDWRITING OF JUNIUS PROFESSIONALLY INVESTIGATED, which was the first book in English to assert that there was a science of handwriting identification,[25] and to illustrate its methodology.[26]

In the United States three books were published in the 1890s, Persifor Frazer's THE MANUAL OF THE STUDY OF DOCUMENTS (1894),[27] William E. Hagan's DISPUTED HANDWRITING (1894)[28] and Daniel T. Ames' AMES ON FORGERY (1899),[29] but the event that was to turn handwriting identification expertise from ugly duckling to swan was the publication in 1910 of Albert S. Osborn's QUESTIONED DOCUMENTS, with an introduction by John Henry Wigmore.

Osborn's book, Osborn's personality, and Osborn's relationship with Wigmore, are the cornerstones upon which respect for asserted handwriting

23. See, e.g., ALBERT S. OSBORN, QUESTIONED DOCUMENTS 286–287 (2d ed., 1929).

24. Chabot and his contemporary Frederick G. Netherclift were the first full time handwriting identification consultants in England, both beginning their practices in the mid–1850s after earlier careers in engraving and lithography. Two short reports by Netherclift on aspects of the Junius controversy appear in Chabot's book. Chabot, at any rate, was a significant enough character in mid-Victorian London to have rated an entry in the Dictionary of National Biography.

25. Twistleton refers to Chabot's work as a "scientific demonstration." CHARLES CHABOT, THE HANDWRITING OF JUNIUS PROFESSIONALLY EXAMINED 220(Edward Twistleton ed. 1871).

26. Id. The subject matter to which Chabot applied his methods was the authorship of the anonymous "Junius" letters, famed in the political controversy of late 18th century England. Interestingly, although Albert S. Osborn was a great admirer of the theoretical aspects of both Twistleton's and Chabot's writing in this book (See ALBERT S. OSBORN, QUESTIONED DOCUMENTS 34–35(1910); OSBORN, 2d ed., supra note 23, at 1000), he disagreed with Chabot's conclusion that the Junius letters were written by Sir Philip Francis, asserting that Chabot and Twistleton had been misled by "improper standards" and "planted" documents. Id. Osborn seemed to favor John Horne Tooke as Junius. After the publication of his book, Cha-

bot's testimony in the Tichborne Claimant case (the O.J. Simpson case of Victorian England) brought him to the attention of the general public.

Note that while Chabot's book was the first book in English on the subject, it was not the first written source in English. In 1850, in Massachusetts, under the authority of Moody v. Rowell, Nathaniel D. Gould, a teacher of penmanship for 50 years, was called on behalf of the prosecution in the famous trial of Harvard Professor Dr. John W. Webster for the murder of Dr. George Parkman. Since this trial was a sensation in its day, a verbatim transcript was made and published. In his preliminary testimony, Mr. Gould sets out the two basic principles of the field, which he claims to have derived from his own observation and reflection. See REPORT OF THE TRIAL OF JOHN WEBSTER, PHONOGRAPHIC REPORT 116 (2d ed. revised, 1850).

27. PERSIFOR FRAZER, THE MANUAL OF THE STUDY OF DOCUMENTS (Lippincott, Philadelphia, 1894)(retitled BIBLIOTICS, OR THE STUDY OF DOCUMENTS, in the 1901 Third Edition). Frazer's book was to have no lasting influence, as its main original theses were totally rejected by Albert Osborn and his followers. See OSBORN, 2D ED., supra note 23, at 990.

28. W.E. HAGAN, DISPUTED HANDWRITING (1894).

29. D.T. AMES, AMES ON FORGERY (1899).

identification expertise in the United States was built.[30] As to Osborn's book, it set out the theory and practice of the claimed expertise so comprehensively that it is fair to say that all treatments of the subject since have simply been rearrangements or expansions of Osborn's 1910 book.[31] As to his personality, he was clearly a man of exceptional intelligence and critical abilities, but with a blind spot. He had a kind of mystical faith in the ability of the human mind to create a system of analytical expertise for the solution of virtually any class of problem. And, while he could be laudably skeptical regarding the claims of others,[32] he never seemed to notice that most of the generalities upon which he built his own system lacked empirical verification.[33] Nevertheless, he had faith in himself and his vision, and the ability to sell others on that vision, whether the audience was a jury, a group of students, or an audience of lawyers or judges. His most significant convert was Wigmore, the most influential figure in evidence theory of the last hundred years. Together, Osborn and Wigmore conducted a quarter century public relations campaign on behalf of "scientific" handwriting identification expertise as practiced by Osborn and described in his book.

The ultimate triumph of this vision was finally insured by the Lindbergh Baby kidnaping case, *State v. Hauptmann*, in 1936. Osborn was the chief witness called to testify that Bruno Richard Hauptmann had written all of the ransom notes found or sent after the abduction of the son of Charles A. Lindbergh. The public seemed to need to believe Hauptmann was guilty, wanted him convicted, and was grateful to those who supplied the evidence. Osborn became a celebrity. In the half century after the affirmance of *Hauptmann*,[34] no reported opinion rejected handwriting expertise, nor was much skepticism displayed towards it. Rather, it became universally accepted as scientific and dependable. This may be best summed up by the following quotation from Judge Cohalan dissenting in the 1977 case *In re Estate of Sylvestri*,[35] which contrasts sharply with the criticism found in *Hoag v. Wright*: "Since that rather cynical observation was made by our highest court in *Hoag*, examiners of questioned documents, as handwriting experts prefer to be called, have attained more respectable standing in the courtroom"[36] As a New Jersey court observed in 1957,[37] after the *Hauptmann* case, handwriting

30. It also did not hurt that the book received a glowing review from Roscoe Pound, another of the legal giants of the era, in the Harvard Law Review, 24 HARV. L. REV. 413 (1910).

31. This includes Osborn's own 1929 second edition, *supra* note 23, which had surprisingly little new information on handwriting identification theory or practice. Most of its material on those topics is taken verbatim from the 1910 edition, *supra* note 26. Note that the text reference is only to the orthodox non-graphological literature. See *infra* § 2.2.2, note 62.

32. Notably, graphologists, who claim to be able to determine personality traits from handwriting. *See* the quote from OSBORN, 2d ed., at 442–444, set out in Risinger et al., *supra* note 3, at n. 13.

33. *See* § 2.3.

34. State v. Hauptmann, 115 N.J.L. 412, 180 A. 809 (N.J. 1935).

35. 55 A.D.2d 916, 390 N.Y.S.2d 598 (1977).

36. 390 N.Y.S. 2d at 600. Judge Cohalan's observation is literally accurate, but may have been intended sarcastically, since Cohalan was dissenting from a 2–1 decision (without opinion) finding that the conclusion of an asserted handwriting expert, contradicted by another such expert, was sufficient of itself to support a jury verdict of forgery in the face of contrary testimony by three disinterested witnesses to the signature. No such skepticism was entertained by the Court of Appeals in affirming the majority, however. Matter of Sylvestri, 44 N.Y.2d 260, 405 N.Y.S.2d 424, 376 N.E.2d 897 (Ct.App.1978).

37. Morrone v. Morrone, 44 N.J.Super. 305, 130 A.2d 396 (App.Div.1957).

identification expertise could no longer be regarded as "the lowest order of evidence, and ... accorded little evidential weight."[38]

§ 3–1.4   Recent Developments

Two events stimulated a reevaluation of handwriting identification expertise. The first was the publication of an article (Risinger et al.[39]) in the University of Pennsylvania Law Review in 1989, pointing out the lack of empirical validation of the claims of the expertise. The other was the U.S. Supreme Court's 1993 decision in *Daubert v. Merrell Dow Pharmaceuticals, Inc.*,[40] rejecting previous approaches to acceptability of expertise under the Federal Rules of Evidence, and putting in play the validity of claims to scientific expertise[41] even for long accepted subjects. As a result there has been a flurry of litigation in the last seven years over the validity of handwriting identification expertise, resulting in several written decisions, all in criminal cases and all in federal courts:[42] *United States v. Starzecpyzel*,[43] *United States v. Ruth*[44] (hereafter, *Ruth I*), *United States v. Velasquez*,[45] *United States v. Jones*,[46] a second opinion in *United States v. Ruth*[47] (hereafter,

38. 130 A.2d at 400. Osborn recognized the centrality of the *Hauptmann* case. Concerning it, he wrote in 1940, "[i]t can be correctly stated that in that little one hundred year old courtroom at Flemington, N.J., the scientific examination and proof of the facts in document cases was nationally recognized and firmly established as a New Profession." Albert S. Osborn, *A New Profession*, 24 J. Am. Jud. Soc. No. 1 (1940), reprinted in Albert S. Osborn, Questioned Document Problems (2d ed., Albert D. Osborn ed., 1946), at 311. For a similar evaluation, *see* James V.P. Conway, Evidential Documents (1959), at 210.

39. *Supra* note 3.

40. 509 U.S. 579, 113 S.Ct. 2786, 125 L.Ed.2d 469 (1993).

41. And, ultimately, "non-scientific" expertise as well. *See* Kumho Tire Co. v. Carmichael, 526 U.S. 137, 119 S.Ct. 1167, 143 L.Ed.2d 238 (1999).

42. It seems fair to say that controversy continues to surround the efforts of some academics and courts to come to grips with the perplexing issues involved in evaluating the reliability of proffered handwriting identification expertise. Given the intensity and public nature of this controversy, what is truly surprising is not the relatively small number of cases in which the issues have been examined, but the large number of cases in which the issues have simply been ignored by all sides, court and counsel alike. Since the date of the decision in Daubert v. Merrell Dow Pharmaceuticals, Inc. the presence of questioned document examiner testimony has been noted in more than 300 reported cases, and nearly 90% of these have involved handwriting identification. Yet so far as can be determined from the opinions, dependability issues have been raised

in only nine federal cases noted in the text. In the state courts, where the bulk of the cases arise (split about evenly between criminal and civil cases) only two reported opinions (one criminal and one civil) reflect the possible existence of significant reliability challenges to any aspect of standard document examiner practice. The single possible criminal case exception, Basinger v. Commonwealth, 2000 WL 724037 (Va.Ct.App.2000), appears to have been cursory both in the way the issue was raised and in its disposition. In the single civil case, Estate of Acuff v. O'Linger, 56 S.W.3d 527 (Tenn.Ct.App.2001), the appeals court affirms the trial court's allowance of document examiner testimony after a reliability hearing, but reverses the trial court's decision based on that testimony, finding it insufficient as a matter of law to constitute clear and convincing evidence of forgery, given the other evidence in the record. Compare with In Re Sylvestri, *supra* note 36. Other than this, there is nothing, which is startling, especially in regard to criminal cases, given the controversies in federal court. While it is true that in some cases the non-expert evidence is so strong that mounting an attack on the reliability of the expertise might arguably be thought to be useless and a waste of resources, there are other cases, including criminal cases, where the handwriting identification is central and yet no challenge has been mounted.

43. 880 F.Supp. 1027 (S.D.N.Y.1995).

44. 42 M.J. 730 (U.S. Army Ct.Crim.App. 1995).

45. 64 F.3d 844 (3d Cir.1995).

46. 107 F.3d 1147 (6th Cir.1997).

47. 46 M.J. 1 (U.S.Ct.App., Armed Forces, 1997).

Ruth II), *United States v. Paul*,[48] *United States v. Hines*,[49] *United States v. Battle*,[50] *United States v. Santillan*,[51] *United States v. Rutherford*,[52] and *United States v. Fujii*.[53] Before turning to the cases, however, we must address the potential impact of *Kumho Tire v. Carmichael*.[54]

§ 3–1.4.1   Implications of *Kumho Tire v. Carmichael*

Kumho Tire is dealt with elsewhere in this work in some detail,[55] but for present purposes it is enough to point out two things: First, the court found a general obligation under Fed. R. Evid. 702 to determine that proffered expertise is sufficiently reliable that its admission can properly be said to aid the trier of fact in the task at hand, independent of whether that proffered expertise is appropriately classified as either "novel" or "scientific." And second, the proper focus is not on the dependability of the expertise in some global sense, but its dependability in its application to the task at hand. The question is whether the practitioners of the expertise can be shown to be able to do *what they are claiming to do in the particular case*. This latter point is important to proper understanding of *Kumho Tire*, and to proper treatment of claimed handwriting identification expertise. As evidence from research accumulates in the future, it may well show that questioned document examiners, or some subgroup of them with particular training, are good at some tasks (such as determining that a signature was not written by the person whose name the signature reflects[56]) and bad at others (such as identifying the actual

48. 175 F.3d 906 (11th Cir.1999).

49. 55 F.Supp.2d 62 (D.Mass.1999).

50. 188 F.3d 519 (10th Cir.1999).

51. 1999 WL 1201765 (N.D.Cal.1999).

52. 104 F.Supp.2d 1190 (D.Neb.2000).

53. 152 F.Supp.2d 939 (N.D.Ill.2000). Two other federal cases—United States v. McVeigh, 1997 WL 47724 (D.Colo., Transcript, 1997) (Oklahoma City Bombing Case) and United States v. Brown, No. CR–184 ABC (C.D.Cal. Dec. 1, 1999)—have also involved reliability challenges, but did not result in written opinions. Judge Matsch's decision in *McVeigh*, which was that unless document examiners could satisfy the requirements of *Daubert*, their testimony would be limited to pointing out similarities between the questioned document and the known exemplars, but not to give a conclusion about the authorship of the questioned document, has been influential, even though it was promulgated without formal opinion. (It was also influential in the *McVeigh* case itself, since the prosecution chose not to call its document examiner rather than to try to satisfy *Daubert*.)

McVeigh also illustrates the problem of defining what constitutes a "reported" "opinion" in the days of databases. The oral argument that led to Judge Matsch's decision is reported at 1997 WL 47724. The colloquy, though extensive, does not reveal sufficient facts to determine exactly what task was at issue in the

case, beyond the fact that some documents were going to be attributed to Defendant McVeigh by a document examiner after comparing them with known samples of McVeigh's handwriting. There may have been an issue of printing comparison, or printing to cursive comparison, but that is not clear. Clearly, Judge Matsch does not formulate the specific task at hand with the particularity required by *Kumho Tire*, but his result has been very influential, as evidenced by its impact on United States v. Hines and subsequent cases. *See* the discussion of *Hines*, *infra* at § 1.4.3; and United States v. Santillan, *infra* at § 1.4.3. United States v. Brown, which was decided by order without opinion, and is currently unreported in any sense, is also discussed, *infra* at § 1.4.3, for the sake of completeness.

Another federal case was decided after this chapter manuscript was completed. In *United States v. Saelee*, 162 F.Supp.2d 1097 (D.Alaska 2001), the District Court excluded the expert testimony of the government's document examiner in its entirety.

54. 526 U.S. 137, 119 S.Ct. 1167, 143 L.Ed.2d 238 (1999).

55. *See* 1 Modern Scientific Evidence § 1.3.4. *See also* D. Michael Risinger, *Defining the "Task at Hand": Non–Science Forensic Science After* Kumho Tire v. Carmichael, 57 Wash. & Lee L. Rev.767 (2000).

56. This sentence was written before learning that there was to be a fourth Kam study which deals with this task, and lends some

author of the forged signature). Evidence with regard to dependability for one task does not establish dependability for the other, and courts have generally failed to keep this in mind, or even manifest an awareness of the problem. After *Kumho Tire* they are obliged to.

Kumho Tire emphasizes that the test for non-science expertise is to be "flexible,"[57] and is to be reviewed by an "abuse of discretion" standard,[58] but reaffirms the observation made in *General Electric v. Joiner*[59] that the *"ipse dixit"* of the expert is insufficient.[60] Further, as pointed out by Justice Scalia in his concurrence, it is clear that failure to inquire into reliability with sufficient care and particularity may constitute an "abuse of discretion" in a given case.[61] With these points in mind, we turn to the issues of handwriting identification reliability reflected in the cases.

§ 3–1.4.2 Admissibility of Asserted Handwriting Expert Testimony Before *Kumho Tire*

United States v. Starzecpyzel[62] is the original handwriting expertise reliability case of the modern era. In that case Roberta and Eileen Starzecpyzel were charged with having stolen various works of art from Roberta's elderly (and now senile) aunt. They claimed that the paintings were a gift made prior to the aunt's impairment. Part of the evidence against them was the proposed testimony of a questioned document examiner who, after examining numerous authentic signatures of the aunt on checks and other documents, concluded that the aunt's signatures on deeds of gift for the artwork were forgeries. He did not claim to be able to identify either defendant as the forger.

Judge McKenna of the U.S. District Court for the Southern District of New York held an extensive hearing on the state of knowledge concerning the reliability of such asserted expertise. Judge McKenna's opinion examines the claims of handwriting identification expertise to scientific status at length, and rejects them.[63] Having done this, however, he concludes that since such experts are not practicing a science within the meaning of *Daubert*, *Daubert's*

---

support to the claim of marginal superiority of some experts over lay persons, at least in some contexts, in performing this particular task, at least under test conditions. *See* the preliminary observations on that study, *infra* at § 2.3.6[4].

57. 526 U.S. 137, 119 S.Ct. 1167, 143 L.Ed.2d 238 (1999), at 141, 145 and 150. In my chapter on a legal taxonomy of expertise, at 1 MODERN SCIENTIFIC EVIDENCE § 2, I have suggested that standards of reliability should depend on the kind of expertise, the kind of case and the kind of issue upon which it is being proffered. Without repeating all that was said there, I suggested that when an expertise was being offered by the prosecution in a criminal case on an issue of "brute fact guilt" such as identity, and when the expertise was of the kind where errors in normal practice were not unambiguously revealed to the practitioner by unmistakable circumstances, there should be an especially high degree of proof of dependability before the results of the application of such claimed expertise are allowed before a jury.

58. *Kumho*, at 247; following General Electric Co. v. Joiner, 522 U.S. 136, 118 S.Ct. 512, 139 L.Ed.2d 508 (1997).

59. *Id.*

60. *Id.* at 146.

61. *Kumho* at 158–159 (Scalia, J., concurring).

62. 880 F.Supp. 1027 (S.D.N.Y.1995). In keeping with the severest punctilio of disclosure, it should be noted that one defense expert at the *Daubert* hearing in this case was the author's friend and co-author and one of the editors of this treatise, Dr. Michael J. Saks, and that the author was a consultant to the defense.

63. "Were the Court to apply *Daubert* to the proffered FDE testimony, it would have to be excluded. This conclusion derives from a straightforward analysis of the suggested *Daubert* factors—testability and known error rate, peer review and publication, and general acceptance—in light of the evidence adduced at the *Daubert* hearing." 880 F.Supp. 1027, 1036.

validation requirements therefore do not apply. He then, as already noted, analogizes such a proffered expert to a harbor pilot who learns to do something dependably by experience. As to whether the prosecution's expert would be allowed to testify to his conclusion that the signatures on the documents which were the subject of the prosecution were forgeries, based on his examination of the numerous genuine signatures of the putative victim, the court says that the defense had "presented no evidence, beyond the bald assertions [of its experts], that FDEs [forensic document examiners] cannot reliably perform this task. Defendants have simply challenged the FDE community to prove that this task can be done reliably. Such a demonstration of proof, which may be appropriate for a scientific expert witness, has never been imposed on 'skilled' experts."[64] Judge McKenna then declares himself persuaded that the inferences as to genuineness of the signature at issue in the case before him "can be performed with sufficient reliability to merit admission".[65]

It should be clear that Judge McKenna's bifurcated standard of reliability based on the classification of proffered expertise as "science or non-science" with higher standards applied to science, does not survive *Kumho Tire*.

Finally, it should be noted, however, that, in anticipation of the particularization focus of *Kumho Tire*, Judge McKenna emphasized that the only claimed skill he was dealing with in the opinion was the skill of comparing a known signature with a questioned signature to determine whether the questioned signature was really signed by the person whose name was reflected, and not any other asserted skill or global claim of expertise. This point has generally been lost on later courts and commentators, who have tended to treat *Starzecpyzel* as if it dealt with global validity.

In *Ruth I*,[66] the Court of Military Appeals faced two issues, one dealing with the reliability of forensic handwriting identification and the other with a claim that the defense was denied due process of law by not being allowed to

---

64. *Id.* at 1046. The implication that the ultimate risk of non-persuasion as to reliability is ever on the opponent of a proffer of evidence is startling, in light of Fed. R. Evid. 104 and the general notion that the party seeking admission must convince the court affirmatively of admissibility once the issue is seriously put in issue. Actually, Judge McKenna seems to have been aware of the problems that would be created by formally placing the burden of persuasion on the opponent of a proffer. The actual position taken by his opinion on that issue is ambiguous and unclear, and, one must conclude, intentionally so. In the only explicit discussion of the issue, he concedes that Professor Berger takes the (standard) position that the burden is on the proponent of admissibility, citing Margaret A. Berger, *Evidentiary Framework, in* REFERENCE MANUAL ON SCIENTIFIC EVIDENCE (1995). *Starzecpyzel* at 1031. He then cites an unexamined single line claim to the contrary from the middle of an article by a products liability practitioner whose main position is that *Daubert*'s effect should be viewed as allowing more to be admitted, not less. *Id.*,

citing Arvin Maskin, *The Impact of Daubert on the Admissibility of Scientific Evidence: The Supreme Court Catches Up with a Decade of Jurisprudence*, 15 CARDOZO L. REV. 1921 (1994). However, Judge McKenna attempts not to choose between these two positions, characterizing the question before him as "legal" rather than factual, as if that made the problem go away. *Id.* His later language from the passage cited in the text of this article seems to show his functional adoption of the problematical Maskin position, however, even though, as the text indicates, he goes on to say that he is affirmatively persuaded that handwriting identification testimony "can be performed" with "sufficient reliability to merit admission." *Starzecpyzel*, 880 F. Supp. at 1046.

65. *Id.* Judge McKenna went on to fashion a jury instruction to be given in advance of the expert's testimony to explain that the testimony was not the result of a scientific process, so that the jurors would have no misconceptions in that regard. Id., Appendix I, at 1050–1051.

66. United States v. Ruth, 42 M.J. 730 (U.S. Army Ct.Crim.App.1995).

call its own expert to testify before the jury concerning the weaknesses of handwriting identification expertise. We will return to that issue in due course.[67] As to the reliability challenge, the *Ruth I* court first noted that handwriting expertise had been accepted in the military courts "for at least the past forty-four years."[68] It then declared that *Daubert* did not apply to nonscientific expertise, cited *Starzecpyzel* to establish the nonscientific nature of questioned document examination, and then declared "it has been generally understood that expert testimony on handwriting comparison can assist panel members by focusing their attention on minute similarities and dissimilarities between exemplars that panel members might otherwise miss when their perform their own visual comparison ... It is largely in the location of these similarities and differences that a professional documents examiner has an advantage over panel members."[69] As authority for this the court pointed to no data of any kind, but to an unpublished opinion in *United States v. Buck*,[70] and concluded on this basis that the challenged handwriting identification testimony was admissible as helpful to the trier of fact under Fed. R. Evid. 702. This unanalyzed global approach is now clearly unavailable after *Kumho Tire*. What it reflects, as much by implication as explicitly, is a combination of what may be called the "sufficient experience"[71] test, which emphasizes experience without testing to see if it has actually resulted in the claimed skill, and the "guild" test,[72] in which the existence of an organized

67. *See infra* § 1.4.4.

68. 42 M.J. at 732.

69. 42 M.J. at 733.

70. 1987 WL 19300 (1987).

71. The "sufficient experience" approach is first set out in Edward J. Imwinkelried, *The Next Step after Daubert: Developing a Similarly Epistemological Approach to Ensuring the Reliability of Non–Scientific Testimony*, 15 Cardozo L. Rev. 2271, 2292–2294 (1994). *See also* Lisa M. Agrimonte, *The Limitations of* Daubert *and Its Application to Quasi–Scientific Experts, A Two Year Case Review of* Daubert v. Merrell Dow Pharmaceuticals, Inc. *113 S.Ct. 2787 (1993)*, 35 Washburn L.J. 134, 152–156(1995); and L. Timothy Perrin, *Expert Witness Testimony: Back to the Future*, 29 U. Rich. L. Rev. 1389, 1457–1462 (1995).

To be fair to Professor Imwinkelried, the test was set out as a preliminary step in an article pointing out the difficulties of formulating reliability tests for non-scientific expertise, especially "clinical" or "experience-based" expertise. Professor Imwinkelried himself well understood that *Daubert* in its general aspects required gatekeeping vigilance as to all expertise. Unfortunately, the approach he set out was easily embraced by proponents of the *status quo ante Daubert*, since all that it required was the testimony of the witness that he had had lots of experience, and that much of it was in circumstances substantially like those in the case at hand. (*See, e.g.,* testimony of Grant R. Sperry, *infra* notes 96–99) Practitioners of all sorts of questionable claimed skills can pass this test. It is not that the test is not sufficient for some kinds of expertise in some circum-

stances. It works fine for what I have called "everyday summarizational" experts, who testify to such things as industry practice from their years in an industry. *See* Chapter 2.

The problem is that it supplies little in the way of validation for what I have called "translational" experts, who claim that they can translate their experience into particular adjudicative inferences, such as handwriting identification experts. Here, we must worry about the reliability of not only the subjective data base, but also the subjective translational system applied to it. In short, merely showing up at the scene after auto accidents, even hundreds of times, is a weak warrant to believe a witness's inferences about what happened in the accident itself.

72. The "guild" test goes beyond the "sufficient experience" test by focusing inquiry on the existence of a group that certifies training, experience and methodology. Acceptance by such a group establishes reliability. Note this is not the "*Frye* Test" applied to non-scientific expertise, since in the absence of such group acceptance an individual witness might be found reliable for other reasons, but, like the *Frye* test, acceptance by such a group guarantees admissibility. The problem, of course, is that astrology can pass this test. For the most extended and explicit assertion of the guild approach *see* Andre M. Moenssens, *Handwriting Identification Evidence in the Post-*Daubert *World*, 66 UMKC L. Rev. 251, 291–292(1998). *See also* Thomas M. Reavley & Daniel A. Petalas, *A Plea for Return to Evidence Rule 702*, 77 Texas L. Rev. 493 (1998); Daniel J. Capra, *The*

group which supervises accreditation (and an expert's membership in it) is taken as a sufficient warrant to infer reliability for admissibility purposes. As we will see, elements of these two approaches, usually conflated,[73] have commonly been invoked in an effort to justify admission of claimed handwriting identification expertise, and we will henceforth refer to this conflated rendition simply as the "guild test".

It is important to note what application of expertise was being claimed reliable in *Ruth I*. It was not the ability to determine if a signature was genuine, as was the case in *Starzecpyzel*. It was the much more questionable ability to attribute the authorship of a very small sample of writing (like a forged signature) to a particular person based on comparison to examples of the asserted forger's true writing.[74]

The facts in *Ruth* are these. Some person or persons had put together a get-rich-quick scam which worked like this:[75] Someone opened a bank account in Lichtenstein in the fictitious name "William Cooper" using a falsified copy of a passport. They then gained access to the personnel and pay records of 30–35 American soldiers stationed at a base in Bamberg, Germany. Using the information on bank accounts in those records, they sent letters to the (American) banks of the soldiers directing wire transfers of the complete balance of their accounts to the "William Cooper" account at "one a.m Eastern Time Zone on 01 May 1992". The letters were apparently typed, with handwritten signatures. The scheme was uncovered when the banks were told by their depositors that the letters were fraudulent. (it is not completely clear whether this was before or after any transfers, but appears to have been before, as a result of bank inquiries concerning these unusual balance transfer directives).

Daubert *Puzzle*, 32 Ga. L. Rev. 699, 741–746(1998); and J. Brook Lathram, *The "Same Intellectual Rigor" Test Provides an Effective Method for Determining the Reliability of All Expert Testimony, Without Regard to Whether the Testimony Comprises "Scientific Knowledge" or "Technical or Other Specialized Knowledge,"* 28 U. Memphis L. Rev. 1053 (1998). *See also* (or perhaps *cf.*) Peter B. Oh, *Assessing Admissibility of Nonscientific Expert Evidence under Federal Rule of Evidence 702,* 64 Def. Couns. J. 556 (1997)(explicitly advocating the *Frye* test for non-scientific evidence); Agrimonte, *supra* note 71, at 155. The practical (though often inexplicit) adoption of the guild test by courts is dealt with in connection to numerous cases discussed *infra* at §§ 1.4.2 and 1.4.3.

73. As will become apparent in the discussion of the cases *infra*, one often has to infer the test implicitly being used from the Court's recitation of training, experience and guild membership, followed by a conclusory declaration of reliability.

74. Standard Osbornian theory of handwriting identification holds the latter a much easier task than the former. *See* D. Michael Risinger with Michael J. Saks, *Science and Nonscience in the Courts:* Daubert *Meets Hand-*

writing Identification Expertise, 82 Iowa L. Rev. 21, 73 (1996). In this regard, consider the following quotations from three of the most respected authorities in the standard document examination literature: "It is much easier to show that a fraudulent signature is not genuine than it is to show that such a writing is actually the work of a particular writer," Osborn, Questioned Documents, 2d Ed., *supra* note 24. [If the questioned document is not in the natural hand of the forger] "... the entire problem is an extremely difficult one, and if not handled carefully and cautiously, can lead to serious errors." Ordway Hilton, *Can the Forger be Identified from His Handwriting?,* 43 J. Crim. L., Criminology and Police Sci. 547, 547, 548, 555 (1953). And "... while it is often possible to express and justify a definite opinion as to whether a signature is genuine or forged, it is rarely that the identity of the forger can be established by comparing the handwriting of the forgery and specimens of the handwriting of suspects." Wilson R. Harrison, Suspect Documents: Their Scientific Examination 374(1966).

75. The true crime narrative here given is reconstructed from the statements of fact in both the *Ruth I* and *Ruth II* opinions. I have avoided burdening the text with specific notes to each sentence.

Suspicion fell upon Private Joseph M. Durocher and Specialist Jeffrey A. Ruth, who were personnel action clerks in Bamberg with access to the relevant bank information. Durocher was interrogated, and apparently cooperated with prosecutors, confessing to the scheme and implicating Ruth. Durocher's testimony was the main evidence against Ruth. The only corroboration of Durocher's story was a questioned document examiner's testimony that Ruth signed one of the thirty-odd forged signatures on letters to banks, and that Ruth wrote one (but not all) of the signatures of William Cooper on the applications used to open the bank account in Lichtenstein.

By now the reader will see the problem. Under a proper *Kumho Tire* approach, the issue would have been "what if anything establishes that questioned document examiners can reliably identify the writer of a small sample of writing comprised of only 14–16 letters, under circumstances where the writing might or might not represent an attempt to simulate the writing of the named signatory (since whoever created the scam had access to records containing their actual signatures), and where there is a high circumstantial likelihood of disguise of some sort being utilized in the writing in any event." This question was clearly neither asked nor answered by the court in *Ruth I*.

A similar problem is presented by *United States v. Velasquez*.[76] Again, the case presents both a reliability challenge and a challenge to the exclusion of a counter-expert, and again, discussion of the latter issue is deferred to a later section. As to the reliability issue, the case involved the conviction of Velasquez for a violation of 21 U.S.C. 848, engaging in a continual criminal enterprise involving 5 people or more, which carries a very long sentence. The only evidence establishing that five people rather than three were involved in the alleged drug scheme was testimony by a government questioned documents examiner that mailing labels used to ship drugs had been written at least partly by two alleged coparticipants of defendant. Thus, under a proper *Kumho Tire* approach, the issue would be, "What establishes that questioned document examiners can reliably attribute authorship of individual parts of a document, the whole of which is extremely short, to particular individuals" or something of that nature. Again, this question was neither asked nor answered by the *Velasquez* court, which once again adopted without analysis and by default what was functionally the "guild" test. The *Velasquez* court's "reliability" analysis consists of merely reciting the document examiners training and experience, and her own assertion that she had performed the analysis properly, and declaring that this established sufficient reliability.[77] Again, *Kumho Tire's* emphasis on reliability of expertise in regard to the task to which it is applied in the particular case would seem to dispose such a "guild test" as a dispositive approach, especially when applied globally, as it was in *Velasquez*.

In many ways the 6th circuit opinion in *United States v. Jones*[78] is the standard against which all other unsatisfactory treatments of reliability issues

76.   64 F.3d 844 (3d Cir.1995)

77.   The *Velasquez* court initially took the position that *Daubert* did not apply to handwriting because it was not science, 64 F3d at 45, citing *Starzecpyzel*, but then claimed that "in an exercise of caution" it would review the proffered expertise "for qualifications, reliability and fitness (sic) as those factors have been explicated in *Daubert*." *Id.* It then proceeds

never to mention any reliability criteria beyond the testimony of the document examiner as to the very standard practice which was the subject of the challenge, and her experience. *Id.* at 850–851.

78.   107 F.3d 1147 (6th Cir.1997). The facts of the true crime narrative that is to follow are taken from the Court of Appeals opinion in

in any area must be judged. And it sets a very high standard of unsatisfactoriness indeed. In *Jones*, a thief obtained a credit card promotional mailing sent to Kathleen Jones's daughter's husband's aunt and uncle, on whose property the daughter and her husband lived in a house trailer. The thief then rented a postbox in the name of a third party (who happened to be a co-worker of the defendant), and filled out the credit card application, requesting that the card be sent to the postbox. When the card arrived, items were charged on it to the tune of $3748.00 over a two week period. When the credit card company came looking, somebody pointed a finger at Kathleen Jones. Part of the evidence against Jones[79] was testimony by a questioned document examiner. The exact nature of that testimony is obscured a little by the Court of Appeals right from the beginning, since the opinion states in paragraph 3 that the document examiner's testimony was that "Jones's signature was on: (1) the credit card application; (2) a post-office box registration form for the post-office box to which the card was sent; and (3) two Howard Johnson's motel registration forms, which contained the fraudulently procured number at issue."[80] However, Jones's signature was on none of these documents. What was on the documents was what purported to be the signature of the aunt, which the questioned document examiner attributed to Jones. So the core *Kumho Tire* reliability issue was in *Jones* virtually the same as in *Ruth* and close to the one in *Velasquez*, and as in those cases, it was neither asked nor answered. However, the way in which it was not answered is what raises *Jones* to new heights of unsatisfactory judgecraft.

The opinion first appropriately spends a page disposing of a trivial challenge to the authentication of an exemplar.[81] It then spends over five pages discussing the standard of review to be applied[82] (this was prior to the Supreme Court's opinion in *General Electric Co. v. Joiner*[83]). It then spends two pages and a half deciding that *Starzecpyzel* was right, handwriting expertise is not science, so *Daubert* is irrelevant.[84] (This was prior to *Kumho Tire*, of course). The Court then says "Without relying on *Daubert*, we now address whether handwriting analysis constitutes "technical, or other specialized knowledge" under the Federal Rules of Evidence and whether the expert handwriting analysis offered in this case was sufficiently reliable"[85] On these core issues of the case the court spends less than two and a half pages.[86] In this sparse treatment the court initially makes two points it appears to think are persuasive on issues of general reliability: (1) Other courts and commenta-

---

Jones, supplemented to resolve minor ambiguities by the briefs of the parties at trial and on appeal and the transcript of the trial, on file with the author. Exact footnotes have been omitted to avoid burdening the text.

79. There was other evidence against Jones independent of the handwriting identification. In addition to the coincidence that the postbox was in the name of a co-worker whose purse had been rifled when Jones was around, there was an identification of Jones by the motel clerk, and an identification of her (by her daughter) from a bank camera photo (at a bank where she had no account) showing her doing a transaction at the approximate time the credit card was used to obtain money from that bank. Indeed, one significant issue, had

the courts bothered to go into the issues properly, would have been whether the document examiner was privy to such information, and its effect on his conclusion, consciously or unconsciously. *See* Saks, *supra* note 74, at 64 and accompanying notes.

80. 107 F.3d at 1149.

81. *Id.* at 49–50.

82. *Id.* at 1150–1156.

83. 522 U.S. 136, 118 S.Ct. 512, 139 L.Ed.2d 508 (1997).

84. 107 F.3d at 1156–1159.

85. *Id.* at 1159.

86. *Id.* at 1159–1161.

tors have uniformly found or assumed that handwriting identification expertise is (globally) a proper subject of court testimony, and that the appellant is therefore "asking us to do what no other court we have found has done,"[87] and (2) "The Federal Rules of Evidence themselves suggest that handwriting analysis is a field of expertise."[88] In trying to justify this latter statement, the court sets out an egregious version of what I call "the Rule 901(b)(3) fallacy,"[89] and flagrantly misquotes the rule in order to do it.

As is well known, Fed. R. Evid. 901(a) sets out the general standard for authentication of any evidence whatsoever, and 901(b) gives a non-exhaustive list of acceptable recurrent means of satisfying the general requirements of rule 901(a) for "evidence sufficient to support a finding that the matter in question is what its proponent claims."[90] One way of doing this is set out in 901(b)(3) "Comparison by the trier of fact or by expert witnesses with specimens which have been authenticated." This is the full text of the rule. It is neither limited to documents (much less handwriting), nor does it reference them. In common practice it has been applied whenever an area of expertise, from fingerprints to DNA analysis, is shown or conceded to be reliable to make such comparisons under the standards of 702.[91] However, 901(b)(3) most certainly does not contain any suggestion that because there is a claim that an expert is comparing specimens, the existence of rule 901(b)(3) means that he or she meets the reliability requirements of rule 702. This is flagrantly backward reasoning, whether applied to handwriting identification expertise or anything else. Pursuant to *Daubert* and *Kumho Tire*, the existence of reliable expertise must be determined under Fed. R. Evid. 702. If reliable expertise involving comparison of exemplars is found to exist under the standards of 702, then 901(b)(3) may be referenced to establish its sufficiency for authentication purposes (assuming the expertise involves a comparison of standards).

The mistaken argument from 901(b)(3) just given is the standard form of the fallacy often put forward in prosecution briefs.[92] The *Jones* court, however, takes it one step further (presumably as a result of an embarrassing failure to read the actual text of the rule) when it says that 901(b)(3) provides for authentication of a document by "[c]omparison by ... expert witnesses with specimens which have been authenticated."[93] It then compounds its error by claiming that if handwriting identification expertise were excluded "there would be no place for expert witnesses to compare writing on one document with that on another in order to authenticate a document. In other words, appellant's approach *would render Rule 901(b)(3) meaningless.*"[94] Perhaps this would be true if the rule said what the court apparently thinks it says, but plainly, it does not.

87. *Id.* at 1159.

88. Id.

89. Fed. R. Evid. 901(b)(3).

90. Presumably, by implication, it is what its proponent claims *that makes the evidence relevant to a fact which is rendered material by the applicable substantive law.*

91. *See* Wright & Gold, Federal Practice and Procedure, Evidence, § 7102 at nn. 2–15 (collecting cases applying Rule 901(b)(3)).

92. See, *e.g.,* the government attempt to sell this argument in United States v. McVeigh, 1997 WL 47724 (D.Colo., Transcript, 1997), at 15–17. Judge Matsch catches the fallacy, at 16.

93. 107 F.3d at 1159.

94. *Id.* (Emphasis supplied.)

To its credit, the court does realize, in instinctive anticipation of *Kumho Tire*, that what it has written does not "guarantee the reliability or admissibility of this type of testimony in a particular case. Because this is non-scientific testimony its reliability largely depends on the facts of each case."[95] However, it then sets out an approach to "reliability" which deals with actual reliability almost not at all. Perhaps not surprisingly, it adopts a global combination of the "experience" test and the "guild test."

Jones was, of course, as already noted, not the first court to adopt the "guild" test. However, it is in the details which the *Jones* court seems to believe help justify an inference of reliability where the unintentional humor of the opinion shows forth most strongly. After describing a fairly normal training history for a government questioned document examiner, the court notes that his primary job responsibilities consist of the "examination and comparison of questioned handwriting."[96] The court then notes that the witness estimated that throughout his career, he had conducted "well over a million comparative examinations. J.A. [joint appendix] at 154. In addition he has published numerous articles in the field and testified approximately 240 times in various courts. J.A. at 155. To put it bluntly, the federal government pays him to analyze documents, the precise task he was called upon to do in the district court."[97]

This may be the first case on record in which a person's government job description has been taken as evidence of the reliability of asserted expertise. Even more starkly, the passage illustrates the credulity of the court, and the collision between the court's approach and any even mildly skeptical approach to the dependability of information. This witness testified to conducting "well over a million comparative examinations".[98] If he had been doing document examination 18 hours a day every day for 50 years, he would still have to have done more than three comparative examinations per hour to reach a million.[99] Yet the court swallows the testimony without hesitation and cites it as substantiation for the reliability of his expertise. The *Jones* court then continues as follows: "See Imwinkelried, 15 CARDOZO L. REV. at 2292–93 (stating that the reliability of non-scientific expert testimony increases with the more experience an expert has had and the similarity of those experiences to the expert's testimony)."[100] However, the cited article makes no such sweeping statement at the cited pages or anywhere else.[101]

95. *Id.* at 1160.

96. *Id.*

97. *Id.*

98. Lest the reader believe that some transcription error has been made, the trial transcript does indeed reveal this to have been Mr. Sperry's Testimony.

99. The real circumstances are even more extreme. Mr. Sperry began his training (a two year course) in 1979. Transcript of Testimony, United States v. Jones, No. Cr 3–95–24 (E.D.Tenn. June 29, 1995), at 121 (on file with the author). Thus, at the time of trial, June 1995, he had 16 year of experience, 14 of which were post-training. This more than triples his actual hourly output, to over nine for every

waking hour. Yet, besides his "well over a million comparative examinations" he also testified to having been assigned to "73,[or] 7400 cases" Transcript, at 123. This works out to at least one and a quarter cases, every day including Sundays and holidays, without a break, for all 16 years, including his training period.

100. 107 F.3d at 1160.

101. Which is not surprising, because this is the kind of unsophisticated global universal statement which Professor Imwinkelried would generally not make. The article does take the position that some kinds of inferences must be based on much experience as a precondition to any claim to reliability, but never says that such experiences alone guarantee or even necessarily increase accuracy in all cases.

The court then continues its unaccountable course by asserting that "handwriting examiners themselves have recognized the importance of experience"[102] (no doubt true), but it supports this with a quote from an article in the Journal of Forensic Document Examination which actually claims that the bulk of document examiner experience with handwriting forms is gotten outside the professional sphere and is common with the rest of the world. "For handwriting examiners, this experience comes mainly from the exposure we have to handwriting throughout the course of our life, the majority of which normally would occur before specializing in forensic handwriting examination."[103]

It is on these grounds, coupled with the fact that the document examiner described the process by which he arrived at his conclusions, that the court declared, "given Sperry's various training experiences, his job responsibilities, his years of practical experience, and the detailed nature of his testimony in this case, the court did not abuse its discretion by admitting his testimony."[104]

If *Jones's* careless handling of both sources and reasoning is unusual, *United States v. Paul*[105] is in some ways stranger still. In *Paul*, the Court of Appeals statement of the facts and history of the case is precise and pertinent, and will be set out here in its entirety.

I. FACTS

In May 1996, an unidentified person who stated that he was a bank investigator telephoned Ed Spearman, branch manager of Wachovia National Bank (Wachovia) at Atlanta, Georgia, and warned him that someone intended to leave a note at the bank in an attempt to extort money from the bank. The "investigator" instructed Spearman to follow the directions in the note. Spearman contacted bank security and the Federal Bureau of Investigation (FBI), who advised him to contact the agency immediately if he received an extortion demand. On the following morning, a security camera outside the entrance to Wachovia Bank videotaped a man, wearing a scarf and sunglasses, place an envelope under the front door of the bank. Inside the envelope, addressed to Spearman, was an extortion note that directed Spearman to deliver $100,000 to the men's restroom of a downtown Atlanta McDonald's restaurant. The note threatened violence if Spearman did not follow the instructions and make the payment. Spearman notified bank security and the FBI.

The investigating agents developed a plan to arrest the extortionist: an FBI agent, acting as Spearman, would drive Spearman's car to the McDonald's and place a briefcase in the men's restroom, while surveillance agents would watch the restroom and arrest the person who took the briefcase.

In executing the plan, FBI Agent Eric Bryant testified that upon his arrival at the McDonald's, he entered the men's restroom, observed appellant Sunonda Paul in a restroom stall, left a briefcase and exited the

102. 107 F.3d at 1160.
103. *Id.*, quoting Bryan Found & Doug Rogers, *Contemporary Issues in Forensic Handwriting Examination: A Discussion of Key Issues in the Wake of the* Starzecpyzel *Decision*, 8 J. Forensic Document Examination 1, 26 (1995).
104. 107 F.3d at 1161.
105. 175 F.3d 906 (11th Cir.1999).

restroom. FBI surveillance agents testified that they later saw Paul sitting at a table near the restroom. As Bryant left the McDonald's, surveillance agents observed Paul enter the restroom again and then attempt to leave the establishment with the briefcase in his backpack. When confronted, Paul told the agents that he was in the area to visit a nearby gym and had stopped at the McDonald's for breakfast. He also told them that he decided to take the briefcase after he found it in the restroom. Paul, however, was dressed in casual street clothing and had no gym clothes or athletic equipment in his possession. The agents arrested him.

II. PROCEDURAL HISTORY

A grand jury indicted Paul on one count of bank extortion, in violation of 18 U.S.C. § 2113(a), and Paul pleaded not guilty. Prior to trial, Paul moved in limine to exclude FBI document examiner Larry Ziegler's testimony regarding handwriting analysis. The district court, however, denied Paul's motion at the pretrial hearing.

The demand note left at Wachovia was the key evidence in determining whether Paul was the extortionist. Although FBI agents examined the videotape to determine the identity of the person who delivered the note, they could not identify the person conclusively. Consequently, the FBI conducted fingerprint and handwriting analysis tests on the note to establish the identity of the extortionist. A fingerprint expert concluded that the latent prints on the note and envelope did not match Paul's fingerprints.

Ziegler, the FBI document examiner, compared the handwriting on the note and the envelope to Paul's handwriting samples and concluded that Paul was the author of both. Specifically, Ziegler asked Paul to write the word restaurant. In the presence of an FBI agent, Paul misspelled the word as follows: "restaurant." In the extortion note the extortionist misspelled the word restaurant the same way. Ziegler also asked Paul to write out "Spearman." Paul spelled it "Sperman," the same way the extortionist had addressed the envelope.[106]

What is odd about this is that the Court seems to have turned the case into one concerning the dependability of reasoning about the authorship of a document from mis-spellings in exemplars, without realizing that this is not necessarily an expertise issue, its proper role in document examiner practice is somewhat controversial even in document examiner literature, and it has little to do with the reliability of assignment of authorship based on comparison of form.

Suppose an investigator with no claimed skill in document examination notices what appears to him to be unusual misspellings in a typed robbery note. (The same mis-spelling, say, that was in the robbery note in Woody Allen's movie, "Take the Money and Run," which said (in part) "I am pointing a gub at you.") Acting on other information, he obtains a search warrant for the residence of a suspect and discovers numerous documents, typed or not, in which the suspect refers to "gubs" in contexts which clearly

---

106. *Id.* at 908–909.

indicate he meant guns ("The NRA is right to oppose gub control legislation"). Virtually every court would receive such evidence authenticated by the investigator, though he claims no special knowledge about the uncommonness of this particular misspelling of "gun." Such a case raises interesting issues of jury notice and the accuracy of jury notice in regard to base rate occurrences of mis-spellings derived from common experience, but not of *Daubert/Kumho* reliability of expertise. Exactly how much a document examiner ought to rely or be influenced by mis-spellings is a subject of some controversy, and, as noted above, there have been warnings in document examiner literature against assuming uncommonness and making too much of misspellings.[107] All of this appears to have escaped the notice of the Court of Appeals, however, since these issues are never mentioned in the rest of the opinion.

Of course, though it is not explicitly noted by the court, the questioned document examiner in the case did perform a comparison-of-form analysis in addition to noting the misspellings, and it was that identification by comparison of form which was the subject of Paul's reliability objection. The court deals with that objection as follows:

1. Admissibility of Handwriting Analysis

Paul argues that Ziegler's testimony is not admissible under the *Daubert* guidelines because handwriting analysis does not qualify as reliable scientific evidence. His argument is without merit. In *Daubert*, the Supreme Court held that Federal Rule of Evidence 702 controls decisions regarding the admissibility of expert testimony. The Supreme Court declared that under rule 702, when "[f]aced with a proffer of expert scientific testimony ... the trial judge must determine at the outset pursuant to Rule 104(a), whether the expert is proposing to testify to (1) scientific knowledge that (2) will assist the trier of fact to understand or determine a fact in issue." *Daubert*, 509 U.S. at 592. The Supreme Court stated that "[t]he inquiry envisioned by Rule 702 is, we emphasize, a flexible one" and that "Rule 702 ... assign[s] to the trial judge the task of ensuring that an expert's testimony both rests on a reliable foundation and is relevant to the task at hand." *Daubert*, 509 U.S. at 594, 597. The Court also listed several factors to assist in the determination of whether evidence is scientifically reliable. *See Daubert*, 509 U.S. 592–95.

Many circuits were split at the time of trial, however, on whether *Daubert* should apply to nonscientific expert testimony. Some held that the application of *Daubert* is limited to scientific testimony, while others used *Daubert* 's guidance to ensure the reliability of all expert testimony presented at trial. Compare *McKendall v. Crown Control Corp.*, 122 F.3d 803 (9th Cir.1997) (limiting the application of *Daubert* to the evaluation of scientific testimony); with *Watkins v. Telsmith, Inc.*, 121 F.3d 984 (5th Cir.1997) (holding that the application of *Daubert* is not limited to scientific knowledge).

Recently, however, in *Kumho Tire Company, Ltd. v. Carmichael*, the Supreme Court held that *Daubert*'s "gatekeeping" obligation, requiring the trial judge's inquiry into both the expert's relevance and reliability,

---

107. *See* Risinger et al., *supra* note 3, at 770–771 and authorities there cited.

applies not only to testimony based on "scientific" testimony, but to all expert testimony. *Kumho*, 526 U.S. 137, 119 S.Ct. 1167, 1174, 143 L.Ed.2d 238 (1999). The Court further noted that rules 702 and 703 give all expert witnesses testimonial leeway unavailable to other witnesses on the presumption that the expert's opinion "will have a reliable basis in the knowledge and experience of his discipline." *Kumho*, 526 U.S. 137, 119 S.Ct. at 1174 (citing *Daubert*, 509 U.S. at 592). Moreover, the Court held that a trial judge may consider one or more of the specific *Daubert* factors when doing so will help determine that expert's reliability. *Kumho*, ___ U.S. at ___, 119 S.Ct. at 1175. But, as the Court stated in *Daubert*, the test of reliability is a "flexible" one, and *Daubert*'s list of specific factors neither necessarily nor solely applies to all experts or in every case. *Kumho*, ___ U.S. at ___, 119 S.Ct. at 1175 (citing *Daubert*, 509 U.S. at 594). Alternatively, *Kumho* declares that "the law grants a district court the same broad latitude when it decides how to determine reliability as it enjoys in respect to its ultimate reliability determination." *Kumho*, ___ U.S. at ___, 119 S.Ct. at 1171 (citing *General Electric Co. v. Joiner*, 522 U.S. 136, 118 S.Ct. 512, 139 L.Ed.2d 508 (1997)) (stating that courts of appeals are to apply "abuse of discretion" standard when reviewing district court's reliability determination).[108]

And that is the totality of the court's review of district court's decision on the reliability issue. The careful (or even careless) reader will have noted that, beyond declaring in the second line of the passage that Paul's "argument is without merit", the court never addresses the reliability issue, or addresses what if anything was before the district court which would have rendered its determination of reliability not an abuse of discretion. There is no formulation of the "task at hand", no description of a reliability test, no reference to information before the district court or the district court's reasoning concerning reliability, nothing.

Having assumed the conclusion of sufficient reliability with no analysis of the issue whatsoever, the rest of the opinion on admissibility follows as a matter of course, finding after a recitation of the experts credentials, that the testimony of a qualified expert could assist the trier of fact, and that its prejudicial effect did not substantially outweigh its probative value.[109] All of this is based on the assumed conclusion to the reliability issue never explicitly addressed, but, given the recitative as to credentials, what emerges in the end is functionally the guild test.

And to complete the Court of Appeals reliability opinions extant as of this writing, we turn to *United States v. Battle*.[110] Battle was accused of coming from New York to Kansas to set up a drug distribution operation. The evidence against him was voluminous, and involved many witnesses and many episodes. The handwriting identification testimony figured in a single episode not particularly central to the case, but relevant nevertheless because, if believed, it would establish that Battle received money surreptitiously from an

---

108. 175 F.3d at 909–910 (footnotes and some parallel citations omitted).

109. *Id.* at 911.

110. 1999 WL 596966 (10th Cir.1999). Once again, the narrative here given is drawn from the facts given in the Court of Appeals opinion. Specific footnotes have not been inserted to spare the reader, but can be easily inserted if required.

out of state source under suspicious circumstances. Western Union had a record of a money transfer showing a "Tyler Evans" as the sender and "Anthony Jenkins" as the receiver. The questioned document examiner was called to testify that he had examined exemplars of Battle's signature given when Battle was booked and, in his opinion, Battle signed the name "Anthony Jenkins" to the money transfer.

As usual, the court fails to realize that the document examiner is testifying to one of the subtasks in handwriting comparison most likely to be unreliable. There are 11 letters in "Shawn Battle" and 14 in "Anthony Jenkins" (which was signed only once). They share no capital letters and only 4 small letters (e, h, n, and t) and no letter combinations. One sample is in a presumably normal signature hand and the other is not unless someone named "Anthony Jenkins" in reality signed his own name. If the 10th circuit had done what the Supreme Court did in *Kumho Tire*, it would have examined the reasons to believe or to doubt the accuracy of such a claimed identification. But though it cites *Kumho Tire* in a pro forma way, it does no such thing. It merely recites the document examiner's credentials (the guild test again) and declares that "[o]ur study of the record on appeal convinces us that McPhail's proffered testimony met the reliability and relevancy test of *Daubert*."[111] The opinion manifests some discomfort about its own conclusion, however, as it goes on to say "Be that as it may, in any event any error in this regard is, in our view, harmless error when the evidence is considered as a whole."[112]

§ 3–1.4.3 Admissibility of Asserted Handwriting Expert Testimony After *Kumho Tire*[113]

If the district court opinion in *Starzecpyzel* started the judicial struggle with handwriting identification reliability, the opinion in *United States v. Hines*[114] contrasts sharply with the run of Court of Appeals opinions in taking the reliability issue seriously.

On January 27, 1997, someone robbed the Broadway National Bank in Chelsea, Massachusetts, using a demand or "stick up" note, and escaped. The teller who was robbed, Ms. Jeanne Dunne, described the perpetrator as a dark skinned black man with a wide nose and medium build. Ms. Dunne is white, and the court characterized the description as "as close to a generic identification of an African American male as one can imagine." Later, Dunne failed to pick Hines out of a mugbook where his picture appeared, and failed to positively identify him from an eight picture photo spread, though she said Hines "resembled" the robber. Months later, however, she picked Hines out of a lineup, and positively identified him at trial.

The main corroboration of this eyewitness identification came from an FBI questioned document examiner who compared the robbery note with exemplars of Hines' handwriting and concluded that Hines had written the note. A trial on this evidence ended in a hung jury. Before the retrial, Hines

---

111. *Id.* at **4.

112. *Id.*

113. The opinions in *Paul*, *Battle* and *Hines* all were published after *Kumho Tire*, but sufficiently close in time that their failure to

properly digest and apply it is perhaps understandable.

114. 55 F.Supp.2d 62 (D.Mass.1999).

moved to disallow the document examiner testimony based on lack of sufficient reason to find it reliable under *Daubert*. The court (Judge Gertner), granted the motion in part, and wrote the published opinion during and after the second trial, which also resulted in a hung jury, in order to explain its ruling and give guidance to the parties in the event of a third trial.

As previously noted in regard to *Daubert*, Judge Gertner identifies what she takes to be a "mixed message" in both *Daubert* and in *Kumho Tire*, with the emphasis on reliability pointing in the direction of more rigor in the evaluation of expertise under rule 702 and the emphasis on "the uniqueness of the trial setting, the 'assist the trier' standard and flexibility" doing the opposite.[115] Nevertheless, the court concludes that the main emphasis is on insuring sufficient reliability, and that the Supreme Court "is plainly inviting a reexamination even of 'generally accepted' venerable, technical fields" such as handwriting identification.[116]

Which the court then proceeds to do, with a number of caveats. On what she has seen at the hearing which she held, and in writing, she seems inclined to bar the questioned document examiner testimony in its entirety. However, "[t]his handwriting challenge was raised at the eleventh hour. The hearing was necessarily constrained by the demands of the imminent trial and the schedules of the experts. The Court was unwilling on this record to throw out decades of 'generally accepted' testimony."[117]

In addition, the "compromise solution" Judge Gertner accepts was derived "largely from case law that pre-dated *Kumho*."[118] In other words, the court was not entirely comfortable that she had fully digested and applied the broader implications of *Kumho Tire* which might have been inconsistent with this compromise.

In any event, Judge Gertner proceeds to distinguish between a questioned document examiner's testimony comparing the robbery note with the exemplars and identifying similarities and differences, and testimony concerning the document examiner's inferences of authorship based on those similarities. In sum, she allows the former and bars the latter, essentially adopting the similar approach of Judge Matsch in the Oklahoma City bombing case, *United States v. McVeigh*, which she quotes.[119]

There is a certain commonsense appeal to this approach. The document examiner's extensive experience looking at handwriting may have sensitized the expert to the perception and identification of similarities or differences which an ordinary person might not notice, and at any rate the document examiner will be free to spend more time isolating such similarities and differences than we could expect jurors to do pursuant to their own examination during deliberations. Viewed this way, a document examiner appears to become a sort of summarizational witness,[120] and the notion of "expertise" becomes much less central to their function.

However, there is a serious problem with this, especially if the document examiner is allowed to recite her credentials, titles and job descriptions. By

---

115. *Id.* at 65.
116. *Id.* at 67.
117. *Id.*
118. *Id.*

119. *Id.* at 70, quoting decision of Judge Matsch, discussed *supra* at note 53.

120. *See* Science in the Law: Standards, Statistics and Research Issues, Chapter 2.

identifying a similarity or difference, the examiner is inevitably perceived as asserting the *significance* of those similarities or differences in regard to assigning authorship, so that the conclusions which are barred are easily inferred. In practice, this is profoundly true, since document examiners who believe they have identified the author of a writing by comparison will normally point out *only* similarities, and if differences are called to their attention they will dismiss them as not being significant or "real" differences, but merely manifestations of "individual variation."[121] Nevertheless, the Solomonic compromise of Judges Matsch and Gertner is clearly an improvement over surrendering the gatekeeping function entirely to the guild, as most other courts have done.[122] And there is evidence that it is becoming common practice, as reflected in *United States v. Santillan*,[123] *United States v. Rutherford*,[124] and *United States v. Brown*.[125]

In *Santillan*, the defendant, Rogelio Santillan, was charged with conspiracy to distribute false immigration documents. According to the opinion of the court, the prosecution's document examiner proposed to testify "that she has identified, using control samples of defendant's handwriting, Santillan's handwriting on numerous 'questioned' documents."[126] Note that, more than seven months after *Kumho Tire,* in an opinion referring to *Kumho Tire*,[127] this is as much information as we are given on the "task at hand" in the case before the court. Clearly, the requirements of *Kumho Tire* are not yet dependably appearing on the radar screens of the lower courts.

In any event, Judge Jensen then goes on to deal with the reliability issue globally. After briefly reviewing (and criticizing)[128] the extant research data, the court adopts the *Hines/McVeigh* approach.[129]

In *United States v. Rutherford* defendant Kent Rutherford was charged with bank fraud involving a scheme dealing with a "sale barn" and check. By reference to the opinion, this is all that one could tell. However, an inquiry to the defense attorney in the case reveals that someone registered at a cattle sale as one "George Hipke," a real person of repute. The imposter then purchased an expensive lot of cattle and paid for them with a check bearing the signature "George Hipke." He then removed the cattle. As would be expected, the crime came to light when the real George Hipke learned of the check from his bank.

Rutherford was a retired banker. Exactly why he was charged is a bit unclear, since the people at the sale barn said he was not the person who

---

121. This was one of the main problems that led Judge McKenna to conclude that handwriting identification was not science. *See* the extended discussion in *Starzecpyzel*, 880 F.Supp. 1027, at 1031–1033.

122. Or perhaps not. If the law of unintended consequences holds, some court operating under the *Hines/McVeigh* approach is likely to disallow cross examination of a document examiner on known error rates, such as the 8% document examiner error rate shown on one task in Kam IV, on the ground that they are not giving an opinion, even though their implied opinion is clear to the whole courtroom. For a full discussion of Kam IV, *see infra* § 2.3.6[4].

123. 1999 WL 1201765 (N.D.Cal.1999).

124. 104 F.Supp.2d 1190 (D.Neb.2000).

125. No. CR–184ABC (C.D.Cal. Dec. 1, 1999).

126. 1999 WL 1201765, at *1.

127. *Id.* at *1.

128. *Id.* at *3. Judge Jensen seems especially troubled that Dr. Moshe Kam, the government's chief researcher on handwriting expertise issues, refused to share his raw data.

129. *Id.* at *4.

tendered the check. However, the theory was that he was the mastermind, who sent somebody else to pay for the cattle with a pre-signed check. The proposed expert testimony was that Rutherford in fact signed a "buyer registration form" in Hipke's name, that as to the check bearing George Hipke's purported signature, Hipke did not sign it (a fact that was actually not disputed), and that there was a strong probability that Rutherford did sign it, and that as to a "load out" sheet from Columbus Sale Barn, the inscriptions on the bottom of the sheet were probably written by Rutherford. Once again, although *Kumho Tire* is cited, there is no further attempt to formulate the separate tasks involved in this scenario, or to examine them individually. This is perhaps a bit surprising, given the extensive nature of the *Daubert/Kumho* hearing that was undertaken.[130] And once again, the main task at issue is the attribution of authorship of a forged signature based on the limited amount of writing involved in the signature, though in this case there were two signatures to work with.

In any event, after criticizing the highly suggestive way in which the problem was presented to the expert by the government in obtaining his original opinion,[131] the court ultimately adopts the *Hines/McVeigh* approach, allowing the proffered expert to testify only by pointing out similarities and differences, and not allowing any explicit opinions concerning authorship or probability of authorship.

Additionally, in the unreported case of *United States v. Brown*,[132] another check forgery case involving an attempted attribution of authorship of the forged signature, the court also adopted the *Hines/McVeigh* approach by order without opinion after holding a *Daubert/Kumho* hearing.

Finally, in *United States v. Fujii*, Judge Gottschall of the Northern District of Illinois has rendered the first decision in a handwriting identification case in modern times which excludes document examiner testimony completely. She has also written the first opinion on asserted handwriting identification expertise to manifest a proper *Kumho Tire* "task at hand" approach.

In this case, there was an allegation that defendant Masao Fujii had been involved in a scheme to obtain the fraudulent entry into the United States of two Chinese nationals. Certain immigration forms filled out in hand printing had been tendered in connection with their attempted entry at John F. Kennedy airport in New York City in December of 1999. As evidence of Fujii's participation, the prosecution sought to call an Immigration and Naturalization Service document examiner, who would testify that she had compared the printing on the forms with exemplars of printing by Fujii, and that in her opinion Fujii printed the fraudulent forms. The defense objected on *Daubert/Kumho* grounds, and a hearing was held on the issue.

In her opinion Judge Gottschall notes that in general "[h]andwriting analysis does not stand up well under the *Daubert* standards."[133] However, as to general issues of reliability, she concludes that "this court need not weigh

---

130. In keeping with the highest demands of complete disclosure it is here noted that the defense expert in this case was the author's friend, co-author, and one of the editors of this treatise, Dr. Michael J. Saks.

131. 104 F.Supp.2d at 1193.

132. No. CR 99–184 (C.D.Cal., order dated Dec. 1, 1999), on file with author.

133. *Id.* at 3.

in on this question, for whether handwriting analysis *per se* meets the *Daubert* standards, its application to this case poses more significant problems."[134] This is for two reasons. First, virtually all data on document examiner dependability in identifying the author of handwriting has dealt with cursive and not printed writing. The single recorded proficiency test involving hand printing[135] revealed a 45% error rate on that test. Perhaps more importantly, however, Fujii is a native Japanese who learned to print in English as a second language in Japan. The defense called as a witness Mark Litwicki, Director of Loyola University's English as a Second Language program, who had substantial experience with teaching English to Japanese students in both the United States and Japan. The essence of his testimony was that Japanese learn to print in English only after years of training in the exact copying of Japanese characters where "uniformity of characters 'is an important and valued principle of Japanese handwriting'," that they "spend many years attempting to maximize the uniformity of their writing," that this carried over into their learning to write in English, and that "it would be very difficult for an individual not familiar with the English handwriting of Japanese writers to identify the subtle dissimilarities in the handwriting of individual writers."[136]

Considering all this, the court concludes:

Does Ms. Cox [the document examiner] have any expertise which would allow her to distinguish between unique characteristics of an individual Japanese handprinter and characteristics that might be common to many or all native Japanese handprinters? In an analysis that depends entirely on what is similar between writing specimens and what is different, it would seem to this court essential that an expert have some ability to screen out characteristics which might appear eccentric to the writer, compared with native English printers, but which might in fact be characteristic of most or all native Japanese writers, schooled in English printing in Japan, in printing English. There is no evidence on the record that Ms. Cox has such expertise or has even considered the problem Mr. Litwicki has pointed out.

Considering the questions about handwriting analysis generally under *Daubert*, the lack of any evidence that the identification of handprinting is an expertise that meets the *Daubert* standards and the questions that have been raised–which the government has not attempted to answer–about the expert's ability to opine reliably on handprinting identification in dealing with native Japanese writers taught English printing in Japan, the court grants the defendant's motion [to exclude].[137]

Judge Gottschall's opinion is a masterful example of particularized "task at hand" analysis under the standards of *Kumho Tire*. It provides a model for other courts in how to approach the reliability of specific applications of claimed handwriting identification expertise, and all forms of non-science forensic science.

---

134. *Id.*

135. The 1986 Forensic Sciences Foundation test, the results of which are reported in Risinger et al., *supra* note 3, at 746–747, and also *infra* at § 2.3.1, and testified to in *Fujii* by

Dr. Michael J. Saks as one of the expert witnesses for the defense.

136. *Fujii* at 5, quoting Litwicki.

137. *Id.* at 5–6.

It is interesting to note that in this set of twelve federal cases (including *McVeigh* and *Brown*), only eight of the twelve trial judges involved held full-scale reliability hearings,[138] and of those who did, seven out of eight manifested substantial reservations about handwriting identification expertise even on a global level.[139] Contrast this with the Court of Appeals judges who heard these cases, all of whom were institutionally insulated from *having* to come to grips with the actual state of knowledge concerning handwriting identification by cold records and appendices, and *all* of whom felt comfortable brushing off reliability challenges with some version of the "guild" test. The inertia of a venerable tradition of admissibility appears to be a powerful incentive to turn a blind eye to the evidence on the asserted expertise. In light of *Kumho Tire*, perhaps even appellate judges will have to pay attention to the issues raised by these cases.

§ 3–1.4.4   Counter-testimony on FDEs' Claimed Skills

Another issue which was dealt with in three of these cases, *United States v. Ruth*,[140] *United States v. Velasquez*,[141] and *United States v. Paul*,[142] is the standard for admissibility of evidence tending to show the weaknesses of handwriting identification expertise after a questioned document examiner has been allowed to give testimony concerning the identification of the author of disputed handwriting in support of the prosecution in a criminal case. Stated this way, it would seem that a criminal defendant should have wide latitude in presenting counter-evidence, not merely through cross examination of the government's questioned document examiner, but through his own witnesses. *Daubert* itself emphasized the role of such counter-testimony as an important check on the unwarranted impact of expert testimony that managed to make it over the rule 702 hurdle in spite of some doubts about its reliability.[143] Nevertheless, the handwriting cases are split 1–1 with one tie on the admissibility of such evidence. And there is nothing to account for this result except the courts' varying attitudes, since the proposed counter-expert was the same in each case and proposed to give largely the same testimony in each. One might even go so far as to say that these cases were decisions on the acceptability of Professor Mark P. Denbeaux.[144]

It is important before examining these cases to know what Professor Denbeaux claims to have information about which the average juror would

---

138. *Ruth, Velasquez, Jones* and *Battle* were disposed of at trial either without hearing or on voir dire of the government's proposed expert.

139. Judges McKenna, Matsch, Gertner, Jensen, Collins, Bataillon and Gottschall. Only Judge Tidwell, the trial judge in *Paul*, seemed unconcerned. Apropos all this, consider the following quotation from Judge McKenna's opinion in *Starzecpyzel*: "If forensic document examination does rely on an underlying principle, logic dictates that the principle must embody the notion that inter-writer differences, even when intentionally suppressed, can be distinguished from natural variation. How FDEs might accomplish this was unclear to the Court before the hearing, and largely remains so after the hearing." 880 F.Supp. at 14–15.

140. 46 M.J. 1 (U.S. Ct. App., Armed Forces, 1997).

141. 64 F.3d 844 (3d Cir.1995).

142. 175 F.3d 906 (11th Cir.1999).

143. "Vigorous cross-examination, *presentation of contrary evidence*, and careful instruction on the burden of proof are the traditional and appropriate means of attacking shaky but admissible evidence." 509 U.S. 579, at 596, 113 S.Ct. 2786, 125 L.Ed.2d 469 (emphasis supplied).

144. In the spirit of full disclosure, it should be noted that Mark P. Denbeaux is a colleague, co-author, and longtime close friend of the author.

not have, and what he does not claim. Professor Denbeaux has examined every empirical study on the reliability of handwriting expertise, and can review this literature, what it means and what it does no mean, for the jury. Further, he has studied the standard literature produced by questioned document examiners to explain what they claim to be doing, and he can summarize this literature, and further identify what he, upon reflection and evaluation, has concluded are the main weaknesses of the methodology there set out: high subjectivity, and no criteria to determine if any given similarity or difference between the questioned writing and the known exemplars is significant (an individualizing characteristic) or insignificant (merely intra-writer variation). Finally, he generally asserts that he can point out unac-counted-for dissimilarities between the questioned writing and the exemplars which are as apparently meaningful as the similarities upon which the document examiner witness has relied for identification. However, Professor Denbeaux claims no special skill at determining authorship or lack of author-ship of any document as a result of similarities and dissimilarities. Indeed, his whole point is that it is doubtful whether those who claim such expertise possess it. Further, he makes it clear that he has never undergone whatever training document examiners undergo, and he is not a document examiner. He never asserts that any person did or did not in fact write any questioned document, and eschews any claim of special skill in that regard.

In *Ruth II*, the presiding judge at the court martial refused to authorize the defense to call Denbeaux. Instead, he directed the defense to attempt to cross-examine the government's document examiner first, using material from Risinger et al.[145] The trial attorney made no attempt to cross-examine the document examiner using the published information, and the Court of Mili-tary Appeals ruled that by this lapse counsel had failed to demonstrate that Denbeaux's testimony would have been "relevant and necessary," and so the judge did not abuse his discretion in denying the defense request for the production of Professor Denbeaux.

The Court of Appeals for the Armed Forces granted discretionary review limited to this issue. It was clearly uncomfortable with the handling of the issue by the Court of Military Appeals, given the intervening decision in *Velasquez* from which it quoted extensively on the general point that Den-beaux was an appropriate witness. Nevertheless, it affirmed the conviction, shifting grounds somewhat. The trial judge had invited the defense attorney to renew his motion to call Denbeaux at the close of the testimony of the prosecution's document examiner, and this the defense attorney had failed to do. It was *this* failure, not the cross examination failure, which the Court of Appeals found rendered the actions of the trial judge not to be "an abuse of discretion." So *Ruth II* is in fact a non-decision, with the court of appeals apparently adopting the analysis of *Velasquez*.

In *Velasquez,* the Third Circuit declared that the trial court's refusal to allow Denbeaux to testify after the prosecution was allowed to present identification testimony by a document examiner was an abuse of discretion.[146]

---

145. Risinger, et al., *supra* note 3.

146. Though the decision predated *Joiner*, the court stated the standard as follows: "We review the trial court's ruling on the admissi-bility of Professor Denbeaux's testimony for abuse of discretion," *Velasquez* at 847–848, though it went on to observe: "[B]ut to the extent the district court's ruling turns on an

The court observed that "[t]he mere fact that the Professor is not an expert in conducting handwriting analysis to identify particular scriveners of specified documents does not mean that he is not qualified to offer expert testimony criticizing the standards of the field."[147] In doing this, the Court rejected the most extreme version of the "guild test," which would hold that not only may guild members testify, but only guild members may criticize. The court then found that "sufficient evidence exists to show that the Professor had 'good grounds' for his rejection of handwriting analysis," and further found that Denbeaux's "criticisms of the field of handwriting analysis generally, as well as Ms. Bonjour's analysis in this case, would have assisted the jury in determining the proper weight to accord Ms. Bonjour's testimony,"[148] and that its exclusion was not harmless because, Denbeaux's testimony "very well might have affected the jury's verdict on Count VIII."[149]

However, in *Paul* the 11th Circuit reached a different result, on even more compelling facts. You will recall that the case involved an extortion directed at a bank officer, and Mr. Paul was the gentleman arrested after he picked up the briefcase with the money in a McDonald's restaurant men's room and put it in his backpack. His story was that he just picked up what appeared to be an abandoned or lost briefcase. The main evidence contradicting this was the document examiner's identification of Paul as the writer of the extortion note. Paul was tried and both the document examiner and Denbeaux were allowed to testify. That trial ended in a hung jury. At the retrial the judge concluded upon government objection that Denbeaux's testimony would not be helpful to the trier of fact and barred him from testifying. This time the jury convicted Paul. On appeal, the circuit court disposed of Denbeaux in four paragraphs. They dismissed his academic research in the literature, saying that "his skill, experience, training and education as a lawyer did not make him any more qualified to testify as an expert on handwriting analysis than a lay person who read the same articles." The rest of the opinion concentrated mainly on Denbeaux's lack of qualifications as a document examiner, thereby adopting the extreme "guild test," essentially holding that only those who are members of the guild may present testimony skeptical of its claims. (This would imply that only card carrying astrologers may criticize astrology.) The opinion then concluded, "because Denbeaux was not an expert on the limitations of handwriting analysis, the district court's exclusion of his testimony did not prejudice Paul." Unaccountably, the opinion does not mention the contrary conclusions, reasoning and result of the Third Circuit in *Velasquez*, or the apparent adoption of the *Velasquez* reasoning by the Court of Appeals in *Ruth II*.

What are we to say of the *Paul* opinion? True it is that Denbeaux is an "educational expert," one called to give the jury information derived from study which they might not be aware of, and which they therefore might not properly take into account. In this way he is like an experimental psychologist

---

interpretation of a Federal Rule of Evidence our review is plenary," *id*. at 848. However, the court never quarreled with the District Court's specific construction of a rule. Rather, it addressed what a court should be mindful of "in exercising its discretion," *id*. at 848, and concluded that Denbeaux's testimony "should have been admitted," *id*. at 848, and should

have been admitted "as a matter of law," *id*. at 852, which is another rubric for describing an abuse of discretion.

147. *Id*. at 851.

148. *Id*. at 852.

149. *Id*.

testifying about the problems of eyewitness identification. It is also true that some courts, and even commentators, have had problems with the acceptance of purely educational experts, though the irony is that, at least when it comes to courts, there is a certain asymmetry in their perception of the problem, with the government generally gaining admission of its educational experts and the defendant often not.[150] However, most attempts to account for the rejection of the experimental psychologist in the eyewitness cases center around some notion that the jury is somehow competent from experience to evaluate lay testimony without needing any supplementation from a person claiming to have special knowledge. While these objections are increasingly regarded as extremely weak,[151] they would seem to disappear altogether when the witness the jurors are supposed to evaluate is being presented as an expert. There is nothing about their presumed general experience which would even notionally prepare them to evaluate the weaknesses of claims being made by the expert. An intuition about the untenability of a blanket rule excluding educational counter-expertise in such a situation probably lay behind the Court of Appeals reliance on Denbeaux's lack of guild qualifications. Presumably, someone with those guild qualifications could testify to alert the jury to the weaknesses of the claims of the field, except there are no guild members who believe that there are such weaknesses. The result of *Paul*, if followed, is not only that handwriting experts may testify, but that they are virtually unchallengeable, even though there is plenty of rational reason to be skeptical of many of their claims.

§ 3–1.4.5 Law Review Literature

Before undertaking a review of the empirical research which has been published concerning the accuracy of handwriting identification by questioned document examiners, a word should be said about the scholarly literature. There are two long articles which must be read by anyone interested in the issues raised by this chapter. They are Andre Moenssens, *Handwriting Identification in a Post–Daubert World*,[152] and Risinger, Denbeaux and Saks, *Brave New Post Daubert World—Reply to Professor Moenssens*.[153] In general I will not try to summarize these articles, in part because they should be read and evaluated on their own merits together, and in part because Professor Moenssens' article is in large part an attack on the work of Professors Risinger, Denbeaux and Saks, and Professor Moenssens would never agree with any summary that I might attempt. Among much, much else, the Moenssens article contains the most explicit embracement of what is essentially the guild test to be found in the literature (though he would probably object to the label), and the *Reply* examines at length the weaknesses of that approach.

The reader may also be interested in two commentaries that appear in FORENSIC SCIENCE COMMUNICATIONS, the online journal of the Federal Bureau of

---

150. *See* discussion in D. Michael Risinger, *Navigating Expert Reliability: Are Criminal Standards of Certainty Being Left on the Dock?*, 64 ALBANY L. REV. 99, 131–134 (2000).

151. *See* evolution of the case law on eyewitness experts, reviewed in SCIENCE IN THE LAW: SOCIAL, AND BEHAVIORAL SCIENCE ISSUES, Chapter 8.

152. Andre Moenssens, *Handwriting Identification Evidence in the Post-*Daubert *World*, 66 UMKC L. REV. 251 (1998).

153. D. Michael Risinger et al., *Brave New "Post-*Daubert *World"—A Reply to Professor Moenssens*, 29 SETON HALL L. REV. 405 (1998).

Investigation. One of them, by Michael J. Saks, outlines three types of research which—if conducted and depending upon the findings—could provide an informed, empirical, basis for the claims of forensic document examiners.[154] The second is by Jamie Orenstein,[155] who was the Assistant U.S. Attorney who handled the document examination evidence in the case of *United States v. McVeigh*, where the court refused to allow the expert opinion testimony of FDEs unless and until they could establish their dependability at a *Daubert* hearing, which the government declined to try to do. In what is ostensibly an essay on behalf of the admissibility of FDE opinion testimony, Orenstein concedes the lack of sufficient current evidence on that evidence, and discusses what prosecutors can do to prove handwriting authorship without the testimony of FDEs.

B.   SCIENTIFIC STATUS

§ 3–2.0   THE SCIENTIFIC STATUS OF HANDWRITING IDENTIFICATION EXPERTISE

§ 3–2.1   Introduction

Handwriting identification experts believe they can examine a specimen of adult handwriting and determine whether the author of that specimen is the same person as or a different person than the author of any other example of handwriting, as long as both specimens are of sufficient quantity and not separated by years or the intervention of degenerative disease. They further believe that they can accomplish this result with great accuracy, and that they can do it much better than an average literate person attempting the same task. They believe they can obtain these accurate findings as the result of applying an analytical methodology to the examination of handwriting, according to certain principles which are reflected in the questioned document literature.[1] They believe that this literature explains how to examine handwriting for identifying characteristics, and that by applying the lessons taught by this literature in connection with their experiences in various training exercises and in real world problems, they learn to identify handwriting dependably.

This chapter will examine the justifications for these beliefs, to determine if there exists any evidence that they are true.

§ 3–2.2   Areas of Agreement: The Possibility of a Science of Handwriting Identification

The main goal of all forensic identification, including handwriting identification, is individualization. Individualization is the establishment that a

154. J. Orenstein, *Effect of the* Daubert *Decision on Document Examinations From the Prosecutor's Perspective*, 1 FORENSIC SCIENCE COMMUNICATIONS (Oct., 1999), at http://www.fbi.gov/programs/lab/fsc/backissu/oct1999/abstrcte.htm.

155. M. J. Saks, *Planning the Trip from Folk Art to Science: Why and How*, 1 FORENSIC SCIENCE COMMUNICATIONS (Oct., 1999), at http://www.fbi.gov/programs/lab/fsc/backissu/oct1999/abstrctf.htm.

§ 3–2.0

1. What Osborn referred to as "true methods," ALBERT S. OSBORN, QUESTIONED DOCUMENTS 6(2d ed.1929); and David Ellen refers to as "standard methods" and "proper method", DAVID ELLEN, THE SCIENTIFIC EXAMINATION OF DOCUMENTS: METHODS AND TECHNIQUES 9(1989).

person or object now held is the same person or object associated with a past event in a particular way, to the exclusion of all other candidates. The major source of individualization evidence is what we may call a tagged residue.[2] A tagged residue exists when a person or thing leaves behind some residue of its presence at a relevant time and place, which residue contains information that can be used to conclude (with varying certitude) that a particular person or thing produced the residue. In addition, even when individualization is not confidently possible, exclusion may occur when a decision can be made that a particular source did not produce the tagged residue.

The notion of tagged residues is broader and covers more phenomena than one might at first glance conclude. For instance, eyewitness identification is a special example of the use of tagged residue information. In that case, the residue is not specifically physical, but exists as a memory in the mind of the identifier. Nevertheless, whether we are dealing with mental images or photographs or physical impressions or traces of bodily fluid, all tagged residue situations present some common characteristics and problems. The hope is that the information in the residue may be processed in such a way that one can properly conclude that one and only one object or person could have caused the residue. This hope is in one sense doomed, since all information about such factual relations is probabilistic. Thus, as Hume knew, for any identification whatsoever there is some residual probability of error. On the other hand, under some conditions, the probability of particular identification may be so great that it would be nearly deranged to worry about the probability of error.

The question becomes, what are the main circumstances that affect, or ought to affect, our confidence in particularized identification from a tagged residue, or in exclusion of an item or person as the source?

The main factors appear to be the following: First, what about the residue counts as a relevant characteristic bearing on specific identification (individualization). This question inevitably entails, consciously or unconsciously, some notion of separability and independence[3] of characteristics and some notion of base rate incidences of those characteristics in the population of candidates for the source of the residue.

Second, referring to the particular person or object that in fact caused the residue as the source, we have the problem of potential intra-source variation. Residues from the same source may differ each time a residue is caused. For instance, the passage of a bullet through the barrel of a gun not only leaves marks from the barrel on the bullet, it changes the barrel slightly by friction, so that marks left on the next bullet may be slightly different.

---

2. The term "tagged residue" to describe this class of phenomena is a neologism. No functionally similar term exists in the forensic science literature.

3. In regard to handwriting, Albert S. Osborn was much more willing to assume total independence of characteristics than some of his successors have been. Compare OSBORN, 2d ed., *supra* note 1, at 229 et. seq. with W.R. HARRISON, SUSPECT DOCUMENTS: THEIR SCIENTIFIC EXAMINATION (1958) at 306–307; and ORDWAY HILTON, SCIENTIFIC EXAMINATION OF QUESTIONED DOCUMENTS, at 9, n. 11 (revised ed., 1982; reprinted 1993). However, all seem confident that in practice there is sufficient individuality to distinguish any two adults' handwriting dependably if the samples presented are large enough. With questioned writings, of course, in contrast to known exemplars, the writing sample often consists of very little.

Third, referring to the people or objects that might have caused the residue as candidates, we have the problem of inter-candidate similarity, that is, more than one object may have been capable of causing a residue indistinguishable from the one at hand in one or all dimensions. Thus, given two nearly new screwdrivers of the same size and make, the blades may be so much alike, and the wood on a jimmied windowsill may retain detail so imperfectly, that is impossible to tell which blade left marks on the sill.

Failure to accurately separate important from unimportant characteristics, accurately assess dependence and reflect accurate notions of base rate within the candidate population, whether conscious, analytic and quantified, or unconscious, impressionistic and unquantified, can obviously lead to error, though the fact that the conclusion is error may not be obvious. Failure to properly deal with the effects of intra-source variation or inter-candidate similarity is a further important potential source of error.

These problems are present in all tagged residue situations, though they may be at their most troublesome in the area of handwriting identification. It is obvious that each time a person writes, the individual letters are not formed with mechanical similarity to previously made letters. That creates a protean problem of intra-source (i.e., intra-writer) variation. Less obvious is that it may be that some writers write so much alike that their writing cannot be distinguished confidently, at least with limited samples.[4] This renders inter-candidate (inter-writer) similarity a significant problem. It seems fair to say that when intra-source variation, or inter-candidate similarity, or both, rise to a substantial level, dependable individualization becomes impossible.

In principle, there is nothing in the nature of a tagged residue problem that prevents a science of tagged residue individualization from being developed. For a source of asserted factual knowledge to qualify as scientific in the central modern sense, it must be the product of an enterprise displaying certain characteristics. Chief among these are:[5]

1. A systematic encouragement for gathering and publishing reproducible sense observations.

2. A taxonomy for organizing such observations which lends itself to dependable reproducibility of observation, and to quantification.

3. A process of hypothesis generation which results in statements about the world and its interrelationships which are consistent with all known observations and which are potentially amenable to falsification through empirical observation.

4. An established regime which attempts to falsify new hypotheses empirically (and which is rewarded for doing so).

Moreover, although it is not a logical *sine qua non* of science, there is virtually universal recognition that academic institutions will play a signifi-

---

4. John Harris, *How Much Do People Write Alike? A Study of Signatures*, 48 J. Crim. L. & Criminology 647 (1958).

5. For an expanded discussion, *see* D. Michael Risinger, Mark P. Denbeaux & Michael J.

Saks, *Brave New "Post-Daubert World"—A Reply to Professor Moenssens*, 29 Seton Hall L. Rev. 405, 435–439 (1998).

cant role in the practice of science and the training of scientists in nearly every area.[6]

Some tagged residue individualization processes, such as DNA typing, are sciences, because they are the application of knowledge gained through the process of science. Indeed, there might some day be a science of handwriting identification, and some small first steps have been made in that direction.[7] However, what forensic document examiners do is not science. There is nothing in the enterprise which results in or encourages organized reporting and publication of observations in reproducible form. There is no agreed taxonomy of sufficient refinement to yield dependably quantified data, or dependably comparable observations of any refinement. There has been no theoretical revision of any significance in nearly a century, and there is no professional encouragement or reward for attempts to falsify those theories that exist.

§ 3–2.2.1   Proposed Principles of Handwriting Identification

The foundational principles of the expertise, as they were characterized by the expert relied upon by the prosecution in *Starzecpyzel*, are that no two people write exactly alike, and that no one person writes the same word exactly the same way twice.[8] It is most important to note that these two

---

6. By contrast, handwriting identification has no academic base. Training is by apprenticeship, and there is no standardization of training enforced either by any licensing agency or by professional tradition. Nor is there a single accepted professional certifying body. THE ENCYCLOPEDIA OF ASSOCIATIONS lists five different organizations: the National Association of Document Examiners; the National Bureau of Document Examiners; the World Association of Document Examiners; the Independent Association of Questioned Document Examiners and the American Society of Questioned Document Examiners. At least three of these organizations claim to grant certifications of competence. A glance at the credentials listed by document examiners advertising in various directories aimed at lawyers will quickly reveal at least four or five more such organizations. In an appendix to Andre Moenssens, *Handwriting Identification Evidence in the Post-*Daubert *World*, 66 UMKC L. REV. 2 (1998), Prof. Moenssens lists no fewer than 55 membership organizations involving persons who may claim competence in handwriting identification, many of which grant certifications of competence. (Moenssens describes these organizations in detail. *See id.* at 332–343).

The American Society of Questioned Document Examiners, which one might characterize as the organization of the Osbornian establishment, is generally most vocal and aggressive in claiming its membership's superiority and, in fact, one object of the Moenssens article is to lend support to that claim. However, the certification testing program of its child, the American Board of Forensic Document Examiners (co-sponsored by the American Academy of Fo-

rensic Sciences) described by Mary Wenderoth Kelly (a member of that certifying board) in her testimony in United States v. Starzecpyzel, 880 F.Supp. 1027 (S.D.N.Y.1995), leaves much to be desired. It was based on the administration of five from a pool of only seven or eight different test problems, only two or three of which involve handwriting identification. The same problems were used year after year on an honor system where they were sent to the candidates for certification through their teaching mentor, and left with them for a month unsupervised before the answers were returned. *Starzecpyzel Daubert* hearing transcript of testimony, 2/28/1995 at 48–59 (Kelly direct), at 175–192 (Kelly cross), 3/1/95 at 249–260 (Kelly cross), on file with the author. (Note: there may have been some changes in that certification procedure since Kelly's testimony as a result of criticisms like this one, but what, if any, the changes are is unclear, since the organization does not easily share information).

7. *See, e.g.,* references collected in D. Michael Risinger et al., *Exorcism of Ignorance as a Proxy for Rational Knowledge: The Lessons of Handwriting Identification "Expertise,"* 137 U.PA.L.REV. 731 739, n. 31 (1989); and those referred to in *Starzecpyzel*, 880 F.Supp. 1027, n. 7, and *see* particularly the National Institute of Justice funded project described *infra*, § 2.4.2.

8. Mary Wenderoth Kelly, quoted by Judge McKenna in *Starzecpyzel*, 880 F.Supp. 1027, 1032. At the time of her testimony Ms. Kelly was a document examiner with the Cleveland Police Department with 13 years of experience.

general principles are in their strong form non-science metaphysical statements (though statements with an oddly commonsensical appeal). On some level, no two things can be *exactly* alike, and it is this intuition that underlies both statements. However, what science is concerned with is not metaphysical sameness, but *perceivable* similarities and differences that can be used to accurately assess common origin. When so recast, the statement that no two people write so alike that the differences are imperceptible is not intuitively obvious, nor is the claim that no one ever writes the same word so similarly that the differences are imperceptible. These forms are subject to potential testing by scientific methods, but they have been subjected to virtually no testing, and the small amount of data available do not provide much support for them. These were among the main reasons why Judge McKenna declared handwriting identification expertise to be non-science in *Starzecpyzel*.[9]

What really occurs in practice is an example of the same kind of clinical empiric that also underlies eyewitness identification, and many other everyday processes. Such a process is at root probabilistically derived, just as is formal science, but with two important differences. First, it is not based on standardized measurements of any precision, and second, the database of examples that defines which characteristics are common and which are unusual is not public, recorded for all who will take the time to see and evaluate. Rather, it is private, based on the experiences of the individual practitioner over a long period of time, and stored internally in such a way that many or most of the individual data may be beyond conscious recall. The problem with such a process is that it is only as good as the unexaminable personal database of the practitioner, and the practitioner's not-fully-explainable method of deriving answers to such problems as, in the case of handwriting identification, what constitutes significant intra-writer variation and inter-writer similarity. The practitioner's opinion may be given the appearance of an explanation by pointing out similarities (or differences) between the questioned document and the exemplars, and by assertions that such characteristics are, in the practitioner's experience, common or uncommon. Arguably, however, any opinion of common authorship will have some similarities to support it, and any differences can be assigned to intra-writer variation (usually called "natural" variation[10]).

§ 3–2.2.2   A Summary of Handwriting Identification Practice

Handwriting identification theory does have some process principles and some general rules which are at least not counter-intuitive, and which, if followed, cut the ring down somewhat on saying just anything. The following is an attempt to give a fair summary of the main outlines of those asserted principles and that process in regard to its two most common general applications, signatures and anonymous writings:[11]

She was a director of the American Society of Questioned Document Examiners and a Fellow in the Questioned Document Section of the American Academy of Forensic Sciences. She is certified by the American Board of Forensic Document Examiners and at the time of her testimony served on that board as Vice President and Chair of the Committee on Testing. *Id.*, 2/28/95 at 17–19 (Kelly Direct).

9. *Id.* at 1033–1034, 1038.

10. *See* the discussion in *Starzecpyzel* at 1031–1033.

11. No effort has been made to deal comprehensively with every area of handwriting examination doctrine. For instance, there is no specific treatment of disguise, juvenile handwriting, etc. The purpose of the text is to give

1. There is signal in a handwriting trace which will allow an observer to establish who wrote it dependably under conditions which are usually (but not always) present.[12]

2. This is because of the development of many personal characteristics in handwriting over time which combine to make a virtually unique individual pattern,[13] which can be determined by observation of sufficient examples of the handwriting to derive the pattern[14] even in the face of inevitable variation around the pattern in any given piece of writing.[15]

3. This individual pattern is almost impossible to duplicate undiscoverably even by someone of skill trying to do so, because the variables are too numerous and inconspicuous, and also because the unconscious conflicting personal habits of the writer will manifest themselves either from the beginning or in a very short time.[16]

4. Even when it cannot be established positively who left the trace, information in the trace may excluded a candidate writer.[17]

5. The best way to dependably extract information from the trace is not by gestalt exam, which is not totally useless but often misleading,[18] but by a system of atomized analysis of elements.[19]

6. Atomized analysis breaks the trace down into components, some of which are measurable, some not.[20] The usual system is a frankly incomplete taxonomy[21] with many categories not suited to objective measurement, or to only imprecise estimate.[22]

7. Handwriting questioned documents are either signatures alone, or other more or less extended writing, with or without signatures.

8. Signatures generally are the most personal and uniform of writings,[23] though some people may have more than one signature for different uses or contexts.[24]

the reader unfamiliar with orthodox handwriting examination doctrine a fair sample of its main positions and methodologies.

12. ALBERT S. OSBORN, QUESTIONED DOCUMENTS (1910) at 200–208. The first edition of OSBORN'S QUESTIONED DOCUMENTS has been chosen as the primary source of footnotes to emphasize its foundational status. Only on the rare occasions where some later book offered a clear qualification or variation is that other referenced. However, anyone wondering whether the main outlines of the summary given here still reflect current theory need only compare it to Ordway Hilton's article on the subject in 13 ENCYCLOPEDIA AMERICANA (1992), at 765. Other works thoroughly examined in preparing this summary include: CHARLES CHABOT, THE HANDWRITING OF JUNIUS PROFESSIONALLY EXAMINED (Edward Twistleton ed., John Murray and Sons, London, 1871), WILLIAM E. HAGAN, DISPUTED HANDWRITING, (Banks & Bros., Albany, 1894); D.T. AMES, AMES ON FORGERY (Bancroft–Whitney, San Francisco, 1899) OSBORN, 2d. ed., supra note 1; ALBERT S. OSBORN, QUESTIONED DOCUMENT PROBLEMS (2d ed., Albert D. Osborn ed., 1946);

F. BREASTED, CONTESTED DOCUMENTS AND FORGERIES (1932); ORDWAY HILTON, THE SCIENTIFIC EXAMINATION OF QUESTIONED DOCUMENTS (1956); HILTON, supra note 3; J.V.P. CONWAY, EVIDENTIAL DOCUMENTS, (1959); HARRISON, supra note 3; L. CAPUT, QUESTIONED DOCUMENT CASE STUDIES (1982); ELLEN, supra note 1.

13. OSBORN, 1st ed., at 197.

14. Id. at 196, 231.

15. Id. at 196–197, 231.

16. Id. at 237–238.

17. Id. at 19.

18. Id. at 206, 244–245, 262–263.

19. Id. at 30, 209, 242–243, 253.

20. Id. at 110.

21. Id. at 209.

22. Id. at 209.

23. Id. at 210; see also HILTON, supra note 3, at 168, n. 4.

24. OSBORN 1st ed., supra note 12, at 210.

9. When dealing with a signature, two questions are commonly asked: Did the person whose name is reflected sign it (is it genuine)? And did some other particular person sign it if it is not genuine? Under most circumstances determining whether or not a signature is genuine is the easier task to perform.[25]

10. On the issue of genuineness, start with the questioned signature,[26] and observe:

    a. the signature as a whole, determining the dominant general underlying handwriting system it represents[27] (if possible; everybody learned some system to start, though some people have been exposed to more than one system even when learning by virtue of moving between schools or cultures).[28]

    b. the size of the writing compared to usual signatures of people in general on comparable documents.[29]

    c. location of words in regard to the (real or imaginary) signature line: above, below, trending up or down.[30]

    d. any oddities of letter alignment relative to the words, above or below the general alignment.[31]

    e. proportion of parts: the ratio of the height to the width of the various lowercase "minimum" letters (like a, o, I, c, etc.) and the base parts of the other lower case letters;[32] the proportion of tall lower case letters above the base line to the height of minimum letters;[33] the proportion of lower case letter extensions below the baseline to minimum letters,[34] and any divergences and oddities from the general pattern for individual letters;[35] proportion of capitals to minimums, and the height-width ratio of capitals.[36]

    f. slant of writing measured with glass protractor or goniometer,[37] with any divergences from general slant for individual letters

---

25. *Id.* at 13.

26. Actually, Osborn takes the position that it is best to start with an analysis of the known standards before examining the questioned signature, but concedes this is often not possible in practice. OSBORN 1st ed., *supra* note 12, at 243–244.

27. *Id.* at 190, 263.

28. *Id. See generally* ch. 11.

29. *Id.* at 144–145.

30. *Id.* at 142.

31. *Id.* at 123–124, 142.

32. *Id.* at 146.

33. *Id.* at 145–148, 215, 309–310.

34. *Id.* at 246.

35. *Id.*

36. *Id.* at 145–148, 215, 309–310.

37. *Id.* at 150–154, 246. Harrison supplies the word "goniometer." HARRISON, *supra* note 3, at 330. Harrison asserts that by his date of publication (1959) most writing submitted to his laboratory in England had such variable

slant (called "slope" by him) that it was not worth trying to measure. *Id.*

Here we must consider the role in document examination of that cornerstone of modern science, actual measurement in reproducible quantified standard units of measurement. Osborn had a chapter on measuring instruments in both editions of his book, and the characteristics we are dealing with, such as proportion of parts of various letters, are potentially subject to standard quantified measurement, with mathematical expression of central tendency and variation, etc. In this regard Osborn was on some level aware of the potential value of measurement, and wrote: "The various parts of an ordinary signature when carefully measured bear a certain proportion to each other that with most writers is found to be surprisingly uniform ... when a considerable amount of writing is in question and an adequate amount of standard writing is supplied for comparison, a system of measurements covering a sufficient number of features and examples may be very forceful evidence ... any system of averages, to be reliable, must be

noted. Some slants may be nearly chaotic.[38]

     g.   presence or absence of lines connecting words or initials, and their form.[39]

     h.   presence and placement of punctuation relative to initials.[40]

     i.   character and construction of connections between letters: smalls to smalls and capitals to smalls.[41]

     j.   initial strokes, presence or absence, and how formed.[42]

     k.   presence and placement of any pen lifts within words,[43] and whether they result in discontinuities (spaces) between letters in the middle of words.[44]

based on an adequate number of examples." Osborn 1st Ed. at 146. However, Osborn then goes on to say, "Evidence based on the very great number of measurements necessary to show a very slight divergence is not usually of much weight in this or any similar inquiry, because it is practically impossible for court and jury to review and verify the basis of such an opinion. If the difference is apparent by inspection, then the measurements are of value in making definite what is apparently a fact without such proof." *Id.* at 146–147. In the rest of the book, Osborn recommended the actual quantified measurement of very few handwriting characteristics (as opposed to typewriting, for instance), slant being primary among them. Though Osborn occasionally refers to the "size", "position" and "distance" of characteristics (for instance, *id.* at 246–247, 309–310), in practice all characteristics but slant seem to have been subject to rough subjective estimation with no precise standard measurement at all. Instead, visual charts are relied upon to illustrate assertions of "size," "position" and "distance". Certainly there is no indication in the *Hauptmann* trial testimony of Osborn, his son, or any of the other experts, of actual quantified measurement of characteristics. Albert S. Osborn testimony, 1/11/35, *Hauptmann* transcript at 881–1008; Albert S. Osborn testimony, 1/14/35, at 1009–1051; Elbridge W. Stein testimony, 1/14/35, at 1074–1153; John F. Tyrell testimony, 1/15/35, at 1154–1247; Herbert J. Walter testimony, 1/15/35, at 1248–1271; Harry M. Cassidy testimony, 1/16/35, at 1279–1301; Wilmer T. Souder testimony, 1/16/35, at 1301–1336; Albert D. Osborn testimony, 1/16/45, at 1337–1386; Clark Sellers testimony, 1/16/35, at 1386–1432. Actual measurement appears to play no greater role in standard practice today than in 1935. As Ordway Hilton said in his 1974 Preface to a facsimile edition of Bibliotics, "While certain workers continued to urge the use of measurements, the method has virtually been discarded as too time consuming for the little value which might be derived from it." Persifor Frazer, Bibliotics ii(3d ed.1901, reprinted 1974). Frazer was one of the few who champi-

oned actual measurements. It is regrettable that his view was rejected.

Interestingly, one of the earliest exercises in analytic handwriting identification in the United States involved an attempt to be quite precise both in measurement and mathematics. In the famous Howland Will Case of 1865, which involved a claim to the substantial Howland fortune by the infamous Hetty Green (then Hetty Howland Robinson), Hetty was accused of forging by tracing the signature on the will upon which she relied. Renowned Harvard mathematician Benjamin Peirce and his (later) even more renowned son Charles Sanders Peirce were hired to examine the signature on the will. They devised a method which relied on defining the beginning point of downstrokes, of which there were 30 in the signature. Comparing 42 genuine Sylvia Ann Howland signatures, each to all others (which gave 25,830 comparisons), they determined that any given downstroke start position would coincide using their measurement system only about one time in five. They then compared the challenged will signature with the signature claimed to be the tracing model and found perfect coincidence of the start position of all 30 downstrokes. Using their previous examination to provide the base rate data, they gave the random match probability of one divided by 5 to the 30th power, or one over 2666 followed by 10 zeros. Benjamin Peirce then asserted that "so vast an improbability is practically an impossibility. Such evanescent shadows of probability cannot belong to real life. . . . It is utterly repugnant to sound reason to attribute this coincidence to any cause but design." *See* Louis Menand, *She Had To Have It: The Heiress, The Fortune and the Forgery*, The New Yorker, April 23 & 30, 2001, at 62–70.

38.   Harrison, *supra* note 3, at 330.

39.   Osborn 2d ed. *supra* note 1, at 143.

40.   *Id.*

41.   Osborn 1st ed., *supra* note 12, at 225–226.

42.   *Id.* at 220.

43.   *Id.* at 121–123.

44.   *Id.*

l. forms of each individual letter: general pictorial style, existence of loops, retraces, decorations and flourishes, open tops, etc., with observation of variation in form as letters are repeated;[45] whether variation correlates with position in the word, beginning or middle;[46] forms of endings of terminal letters,[47] method of crossing t's,[48] presence and form of i-dots,[49] etc. Generally, some judgement should be made concerning the rarity of those characteristics (like undotted i's) which diverge from the underlying system.[50] Look also for abbreviated letters (letters only partially made or suggested) which are likely to be relatively personal characteristics.[51]

m. Consider the dynamics that created the static trace.[52] Try to infer pen position and arm and finger movements from line quality[53] (much harder now that nib pen writing is uncommon).[54]

i. direction of stroke—this detail was revealed by shading in the days of nib pens, and was not analyzed separately by Osborn, since stroke direction was then both obvious and apparently more standard. Non-standard stroke direction is not mentioned in Osborn's first edition and is mentioned only twice in the second edition.[55] With the coming of ball point pens and the degeneration of standard writing discipline, stroke direction appears to have taken on a more important role in attempted identification, especially of block printing, and principals for its inference from various characteristics of the static trace have been proposed.[56]

ii. speed—by looking at smoothness and length of curves, classifying writing from slow to rapid (sometimes has evidence of both in different parts).[57]

iii. blunt or pointed beginning or ending strokes showing drawn starts and stops, or flying starts and stops.[58]

iv. muscle movement[59] (very hard to infer accurately absent nib pen).

v. pen alignment[60] (very hard to infer accurately absent nib pen).[61]

vi. pen pressure—shown by depth of pen indentation into

---

45. *Id.* at 246–247.

46. HARRISON, *supra* note 3, at 301.

47. OSBORN 1st ed. *supra* note 12, at 220, 248.

48. *Id.* at 218–219, 248.

49. *Id.* at 248.

50. *Id.* at 228; expanded upon in OSBORN 2d ed., *supra* note 1, at 264–266.

51. OSBORN 1st ed., *supra* note 12, at 247; elaborated upon in OSBORN 2d ed. *supra* note 1 at 253–257.

52. OSBORN 1st ed., *supra* note 12, at 106.

53. *Id.*

54. HILTON, *supra* note 3, at 156; HARRISON, *supra* note 3, at 330.

55. OSBORN 1st ed. at 360, 408. Both these mentions are in regard to photographic illustrations without further discussion in the text.

56. ELLEN, *supra* note 1, at 15–18. *See also* HILTON, *supra* note 3, at 211.

57. OSBORN 1st ed., *supra* note 12, at 110, 113, 117.

58. *Id.* at 248.

59. *Id.* at 105–109.

60. *Id.* at 128, 242.

61. HILTON, *supra* note 3, at 156.

paper, heaviness of ink, width of line, etc.[62]

vii. impulse—sudden changes of direction, may require magnification to be counted accurately, can be counted for individual up strokes and downstrokes.[63]

viii. impulse grades into tremor—rapid shaking (important to note on what strokes present, since tremor of old age or nervousness may be less on up strokes or final stroke than tremor of fraud resulting from trying to draw a facsimile under pressure).[64]

ix. general line impression: flowing, free, rhythmic, halting, slow or drawn.[65]

n. keep alert for retouching, and pen stops or lifts at angles, or on first or last stroke, or other unnatural places.[66]

11. At this point, even without exemplars, a signature may be classified as suspicious if it appears slow and drawn with blunt beginning and ending strokes, much retouching, odd pen lifts, many angular di-

---

62. OSBORN 1st ed., *supra* note 12, at 132–134. This is as good a place as any to talk about the great cleavage in the handwriting identification community, the gulf between the orthodox Osbornians and the graphology-influenced practitioners. The orthodox Osbornians reject any role for theories developed by those seeking to read personality characteristics from handwriting in the identification of authorship, citing, ironically, the absence of validation for those theories. The graphology-oriented practitioners tend to believe in graphology, but they assert that one doesn't have to believe specific character traits are revealed by handwriting in order to gain useful insights into identification from graphological studies. While both Osbornians and graphological practitioners assert that inferences concerning dynamic aspects of writing from the trace can be important in identification of authorship, graphological practitioners tend to make them primary, with many paying particular attention to pen pressure. A number of further ironies must be reported in this regard. First, while it is true that the Orthodox Osbornians have occupied most prominent positions in the document examiner community in the last ninety years, and have controlled the membership of the American Society of Questioned Document Examiners and certification by the American Board of Questioned Document Examiners, there may be a greater number of graphologically-oriented practitioners doing everyday work in court, being heavily represented in the numerically larger membership of organizations such as the National Association of Document Examiners, the World Association of Document Examiners and the Independent Association of Questioned Document Examiners. Second, it was only the more scientifically oriented of the graphologists, and none of the Osbornians, who performed any empirical studies on the

handwriting phenomenon worthy of the name empirical from the 1920s to the 1980s, even going so far as to develop a specially instrumented pen called a graphodyne to record the dynamic aspects of writing as it was taking place, the forerunner of today's digitized pressure tablets used in academic motor control studies which utilize handwriting as a convenient motor control phenomenon. *See generally*, H. HARTFORD, YOU ARE WHAT YOU WRITE (1973), especially his account of C. A. Trip's invention of the graphodyne, at 107–108. Third, recent academic studies tend to indicate that the dynamic aspects of handwriting may indeed be more dependably indicative of individual authorship than other characteristics, though those studies have the advantage of analyzing the dynamic characteristics directly as they are performed, not by way of problematical inference back from the static trace. *See* 3/1/95 *Starzecpyzel Daubert* hearing testimony of Dr. George Stelmach, transcript pages 386–387, on file with the author. Finally, since government laboratories tend to be officially Osbornian, if there are few data on the dependability of identification of authorship by Osbornian practitioners, there are none on the dependability of graphologically oriented practitioners. For a description of this universe from a thoroughly Osbornian perspective (which excoriates even the mild credit where credit is due given graphologists in this footnote), *see generally* Moenssens, *supra*, note 6. For a response, *see Reply*, *supra* note 5, at 483–486.

63. OSBORN 1st ed., *supra* note 12, at 111–114.

64. *Id.* at 116–121.

65. *Id.* at 109–110.

66. *Id.* at 248–249.

rection changes on what would usually be curves, coupled with tremor on other strokes, especially if all of this occurs in a signature which does not appear erratic and out of control on a gross level.[67]

12. To reach a firmer conclusion, one needs exemplars of genuine signatures, preferably from documents of like kind and like formality from the same time period during which the questioned signature was alleged to have been signed.[68] In addition, the examiner should know any claimed circumstances surrounding the making of the questioned signature that might affect the value of an exemplar, such as age or disease.[69] There should be as many exemplars as possible up to about 50–75,[70] though in some circumstances even one, sufficiently close in time will be enough to expose a crude forgery.[71]

13. The known exemplars should be analyzed just like the questioned signature, and a range of variation for each dimension should be determined, though it usually cannot be quantified, but can be observed by juxtaposition of letter examples.[72] If the characteristics of the known exemplars are consistent in every respect with the questioned signature, then it is genuine unless it can be shown to be a tracing,[73] though even a tracing should usually show evidence of being drawn rather than written.[74] If there are significant divergences it is not genuine, though what makes a divergence significant, how many divergences are necessary and how to weigh them is not quantified.[75] It is a fact-sensitive judgment, and even one inexplicable difference might show that the signature is not genuine.[76]

14. It is much harder to determine accurately who wrote a spurious signature than to determine that it is spurious.[77] This is because a forger is either simulating, tracing from a model, or writing with no model of the true signature. In a tracing, no personal writing of the forger is present, and an attempt at simulation will usually suppress individuality enough in the short space of a signature that no conclusions can be drawn.[78] Only when someone signs another's name in the signer's own usual hand is identification a significant possibility, and even then the small amount of writing and the usual presence of some disguise makes a positive identification difficult.[79] However, there may be enough in a signature to exclude a person as a candidate. For instance, if the signature requires more skill and muscle control than the candidate can

---

67. *Id.* at 18, 245.
68. *Id.* at 18, 22.
69. *Id.* at 23–24, 216.
70. *Id.* at 19.
71. *Id.*
72. *Id.* at 203, 243. *See also supra* note 37.
73. *Id.* at 257–260, 266–301, 308.
74. *Id.* at 267.
75. *Id.* at 212, 214–215.
76. *Id.* at 281.
77. *Id.* at 13–14.
78. *Id.*

79. HARRISON, *supra* note 3 at 387. How uncommon it is to be able to make such a positive identification from the one or two words in such a signature is apparently the subject of some controversy among practitioners, since many of them apparently undertake to do it rather frequently. *See* the discussion of United States v. Ruth, United States v. Jones, and United States v. Battle, supra at § 1.4.2; and United States v. Rutherford, *supra* at § 1.4.3. However, the authorities in the field are uniformly skeptical. *See* the quotations set out *infra at* § 2.3.7, note 177.

muster as determined by a sufficient set of exemplars, exclusion would be justified, because one cannot write with more skill than one has.[80]

15. Moving beyond signatures, affirmative identification of the writer of a questioned document depends on both the quantity of the questioned writing, and the quantity and quality of authentic exemplars of a candidate's writing that can be obtained.[81] Natural exemplars showing unselfconscious writing from about the time of the making of the questioned writing are best,[82] but demand exemplars may do if the questioned document is sufficiently recent and if care is taken to guard against disguise in the demand exemplars by the amount required, variations in speed of production required, etc.[83]

16. The analysis of both the questioned and the known writing will be done as above in regard to signatures.[84] In addition, such habits as the layout and margins of the writing on the page will be added.[85] If sufficient peculiarities correspond between the two writings and there are no significant differences, the writer of the exemplars will be established as the writer of the questioned writing.[86] Which peculiarities are rare enough to be significant, which ones are independent of each other in their occurrence, how many are necessary, and how to weight them is not defined, but the following general principles are instructive:

     a. System characteristics of writing systems, foreign and domestic, cannot establish identity, even in combination.[87] Thus an examiner must be conversant with a wide range of such systems and their characteristics.[88]

     b. The most diagnostic idiosyncrasies are those which diverge furthest from the underlying system, which are inconspicuous,[89] and which are not common products of carelessness or the desire for speed (such as open o's and omitted i-dots).[90]

     c. Each case is different and must be judged on its own particular circumstances.[91]

§ 3–2.3   Areas of Disagreement: Testing Document Examiner Expertise

Nothing in the above is mystical or visibly implausible, but, as previously noted, that does not a science make. As sensible as much of it seems, none of the assertions are self-validating, and all are amenable to formal empirical

---

80. Osborn 1st ed., *supra* note 12, at 110–112.

81. *Id.* at 321.

82. *Id.* at 18–19.

83. *Id.* at 24–25. Different authors have elaborate notions of the best ways to take demand exemplars. Compare Osborn 2d ed. *supra* note 1, at 33–34, with Harrison, *supra* note 3, at 442–451, and Hilton, *supra* note 3, at 310–322. Note that both Osborn and Harrison refer to these writings as "request writings" and Hilton refers to them as "request standards," but I have used the term "demand" because in practice that is what is involved in the usual case. They are usually

given under court order and failure to cooperate can result in being jailed for contempt.

84. Osborn 1st ed. at 322.

85. *Id.* at 142–143.

86. *See* Osborn 1st ed. *supra* note 12, at 211.

87. *Id.* at 169, 206, 210, 214.

88. *Id.* at 214.

89. *Id.* at 210, 308.

90. *Id.* at 261.

91. *Id.* at 308; *see generally* Osborn 2d ed. *supra* note 1, at 249–269.

testing which has never been undertaken. Even the assertion that an atomistic analysis leads to better results is not inevitable, as any baseball player whose swing was harmed by a bad batting coach could tell you. And the notion that a learned technique of such analysis, with so many elements of subjective judgement, in an area where clear evidence of accurate conclusions is often not available, will enable all or most people completing such training to give accurate conclusions on both hard and difficult problems, is dubious.

This is not to say that all identification by comparison of hands is necessarily inaccurate. Common experience, once again, confirms that under some circumstances we can recognize a writer by handwriting. There is a tagged signal present, at least sometimes, but how specific or dependably perceived it is in various circumstances is subject to debate. It may be that document examiners, or some of them, pick up a not-fully-analyzable knack of accurate identification of handwriting just by being exposed to a lot of it. It may be that the atomized analysis called for by their method of practice improves the accuracy of some or all of them a little or a lot.

Since such a practical expertise does not have the internal validation of a developed science, it requires the external validation given to an instrument, a black box process, that may or may not lead to dependable results. Here is where science can again come into play, because science can examine the dependability of the results of such a process even when the process is not science. Beyond their own assertions,[92] however, what evidence, if any, exists

92. In *General Electric Co. v. Joiner* and again in *Kumho Tire*, the Supreme Court of the United States warned the courts against the admission of proffered expert testimony based solely on the "ipse dixit of the expert," Kumho Tire Co. v. Carmichael, 526 U.S. 137, 157, 119 S.Ct. 1167, 143 L.Ed.2d 238 (1999), quoting *General Electric v. Joiner*, 522 U.S. 136, 146, 118 S.Ct. 512, 139 L.Ed.2d 508 (1997). We must distinguish among three types of evidence derived by reference to the experts "own assertions," to use the phrase in the text. The first type is simply self faith: "We know we're good because we believe we are," or, "we know we're accurate because we follow the revealed true method in reaching our results." The second type is anecdotal: "In such and such a case, I identified the right person, or was right concerning the forged nature of the document." These anecdotes can further be divided into a number of varieties: The first variety is: "I know I was right because other evidence in the case established the facts independently." In these cases, the examiner almost always, in today's practice, may have known these facts before the examination, so that the handwriting conclusions may be more the result of revelation to the examiner of other facts than the examiner's independent analysis. For example, the opinions in the Lindbergh case are all subject to this suspicion. The second variety is: "the trier of fact agreed with me." Obviously, there may be ego gratification in this, but this factor alone does not establish accuracy. The third variety is "after

my opinion, the defendant confessed, or pleaded guilty, or otherwise admitted I was right." The problem with these anecdotes is that guilty pleas do not very clearly prove factual accuracy, and that the confession or admission cases are usually built on other evidence, which tends to make them overlap with the first kind of anecdote. All of these various versions of "taking the expert's word" as evidence of validity, are weak proxies for a third type of more defensible self-belief, based on a gold standard of empirically unmistakable knowledge of authorship against which the examiners may compare their conclusions, such as harbor pilots have in their actual practice, but which document examiners usually do not. The real risk is that the examiners themselves will make more out of the proxy feedback and self-affirmation than it is rationally worth. That is not to say that there is no anecdotal evidence of value. There are well known cases of miscarriage by document examiners, the existence of which contradicts at least the more extravagant claims concerning the dependability of the expertise, such as those attributed to FBI document section chief Ronald Furgerson by David Fisher in his book *Hard Evidence* that all "180" "certified" document examiners in the United States would reach the same conclusions in any given case as he would. *See* DAVID FISHER, HARD EVIDENCE (1995) at 196. *Vide* Albert S. Osborn's grandson Russell Osborn's mistaken authentication of Clifford Irving's Howard Hughes forgery (*see* STEPHEN FAY et al., HOAX 129–133(1973)), the Hitler Diaries hoax,

to show that document examiners can accurately identify or exclude authorship by comparison of hands, or do so better than the average person?

The answer is, relatively little. In an article published in 1989 in the UNIVERSITY OF PENNSYLVANIA LAW REVIEW, Risinger, et al. reported a full literature search[93] and turned up only one published study bearing on the question, plus five unpublished studies carried out by the Forensic Sciences Foundation (FSF).[94] The only published study, Inbau's *Lay Witness Identification of Testimony*,[95] had such a small number of participants and was so methodologically flawed, that it yielded no informative data on any issue. Though Risinger et al. sparked controversy, in the years since there have been only a handful of new studies: one readministration of one of the FSF studies utilizing a control group of non-document examiner subjects,[96] two more relevant FSF studies,[97] and three published studies and one unpublished study by Dr. Moshe Kam and his colleagues, commissioned by the FBI.[98] All of these

etc. *See generally*, K.W. RENDELL, FORGING HISTORY (1994). The data summarized, *infra*, from the Forensic Sciences Foundation's proficiency studies, showing high rates of disagreement among document examiners, raise grave doubts about the validity such claims. On the other side, there are equally remarkable successes which suggest that under the right conditions and in the best hands, handwriting comparison can do remarkable things. *Vide* the proof of Michele Sindona's 1981 return to the U.S. through the writing on one customs card among thousands in an assumed name (confirmed by a fingerprint on the card), and the 1956 capture of Joseph LaMarca, the Peter Weinberger kidnapper, by identification of his handwriting from among millions of public records documents. In both these cases there was a very striking and easily recognized peculiarity in the handwriting. *See* FISHER, HARD EVIDENCE, *supra*, at 196–198.

93. In their article, *The "Principle of the Drunkard's Search" as a Proxy for Scientific Analysis: The Misuse of Handwriting Test Data in a Law Journal Article*, 1 INT'L J. OF FORENSIC DOCUMENT EXAMINERS 7 (1995), Oliver Galbraith, Craig S. Galbraith and Nanette G. Galbraith criticize the thoroughness of that search, and their title is even taken from the punch line to an old joke meant to ridicule the search as having looked where it was convenient to look rather than where the answer lay. Ironically, Risinger et al., *supra* note 6, took the unusual step of describing in some detail their literature search strategy, and it was a thoroughgoing one. The easiest way to prove that Risinger et al. overlooked important research, of course, would be simply to come forward with it. Despite years of grousing, neither the Galbraiths nor anyone else has yet cited a single empirical study or other test data bearing on the issue of handwriting examiner accuracy which existed at the time Risinger et al. was published which was not addressed in that article.

94. In 1975, under a grant from the Law Enforcement Assistance Administration, the Forensic Sciences Foundation (FSF) set out to create proficiency tests for forensic expert specialties, among them handwriting identification. The results of the 1975 pilot test were later reported in JOSEPH L. PETERSON, ELLEN L. FABRICANT & KENNETH S. FIELD, CRIME LABORATORY PROFICIENCY TESTING RESEARCH PROGRAM, FINAL REPORT (1978). A permanent yearly testing program was begun in 1978 and a handwriting component was added in 1984. *See* Risinger et al., *Exorcism*, *supra* note 7, at 740. These tests were "operated and maintained by Collaborative Testing Services, Inc." (a contract consultant in test design) "with assistance provided by the Forensic Sciences Foundation," and technical supervision "by the Proficiency Advisory Committee, a committee of the American Society of Crime Laboratory Directors." *See* the Introduction to Crime Laboratory Proficiency Testing Program, Questioned Documents Analysis, Report No. 89–5 (1989). These tests are referred to collectively as the "FSF studies."

95. 34 Ill. L. Rev. 433 (1939).

96. Reported in Galbraith et al., *supra* note 93.

97. FSF tests, 1988 and 1989.

98. Moshe Kam, Joseph Wetstein & Robert Conn, *Proficiency of Professional Document Examiners in Writer Identification*, 39 J. FORENSIC SCI. 5 (1994)(hereinafter Kam I); Moshe Kam, Gabriel Fielding & Robert Conn, *Writer Identification by Professional Document Examiners*, 42 J. FORENSIC SCI. 778 (1997)(hereinafter Kam II); Moshe Kam, Gabriel Fielding & Robert Conn, *The Effects of Monetary Incentives on Document Examination Professionals*, 43 J. FORENSIC SCI. 1000 (1998)(hereinafter, Kam III). In addition, there is an as yet unpublished paper, Moshe Kam, Kishore Gummadidala, Gabriel Fielding & Robert Conn, Signature Authenticaion by Forensic Document Examiners (hereinafter, Kam IV) (on file with the author).

will be examined in turn.[99]

§ 3–2.3.1   Forensic Sciences Foundation Proficiency Tests: 1975–1987

The results of the original Forensic Sciences Foundation (FSF) studies may or may not have yielded significant data, depending on one's perspective. The studies were designed as proficiency tests for government crime laboratories. They were taken only by a voluntarily self-selected group of such laboratories who, for each test, decided to request the test materials and to return their results. The necessity of having comparable test materials administered to each participating laboratory meant that the test materials had to be photocopies rather than original documents, and the test takers all knew that they were taking a test rather than working on a real case. The FSF itself officially took the position that the results were not necessarily representative of the actual level of performance in the field. However, the FSF could not have regarded the tests as so problematical as to be meaningless, or they would not have continued to administer them, and they have been continued under the supervision of the American Society of Crime Laboratory Directors.

Beyond these considerations, there is the ever-present problem of test design itself. Designing meaningful studies to test the validity and reliability of a diagnostic process like handwriting identification is not as easy as it might at first appear.[100] As we have seen, a process such as handwriting identification presents a number of potential subtasks dealing with variables such as writing instruments, forgery of various sorts, age, health, and so forth. No single test can map the abilities of any one practitioner, or any group of practitioners. A great many tests (certainly more than have yet been designed and administered) would be necessary to know what, if anything, they can do accurately, and under what conditions. A complete testing regime would have tests which covered the entire spectrum of conditions and difficulties. In addition, the law not only cares about the likely accuracy of results by putative experts, but also about whether the results obtained and testified to by experts leads to more accurate conclusions than would result if the jurors did the comparisons directly without such testimony. "Expertise" exists only if there is a significant accuracy advantage of the putative expert over the average juror. Thus, the tests ideally should be administered to control groups of ordinary people to see if such an accuracy advantage exists.

With these caveats in mind, following is a summary of the tests and results available to Risinger et. al. through 1987 as the FSF reported them.[101]

99. Because the forensic document examination field's body of systematic empirical literature is so meager, averaging a little more than one study every two years since the publication of *Exorcism*, and virtually none in the century of practice before that, the close examination of each new study is warranted.

100. *Vide* the problems Kam et al. have had in design, resulting in a steady refinement from Kam I through Kam IV. *See* discussion of the Kam studies, *infra* at § 2.3.6.

101. In Risinger et al. there are extensive footnotes to specific pages of the FSF reports for virtually each line of text. These have been omitted and, further, no such notes have been inserted in regard to the more recent FSF studies. The FSF reports are short and not easily obtainable. If the reader does not obtain them, page references obviously are useless; if the reader manages to obtain them, page references are unnecessary.

[1] The 1975 Test

In 1975, the participating laboratories were given a letter made up of both handwriting and typewriting. In addition, they received four examples of handwriting written by four different people. The problem was to determine whether the handwriting on the questioned document was written by any of the four "suspects." In reality, the questioned letter had been written by one of the suspects. Of the seventy-four laboratories that responded:

66 (89%) correctly identified the writer of the questioned letter.

1 (1%) gave a partially correct and partially incorrect answer (attributing part of the writing in the questioned letter to the right "suspect" but another part to another "wrong" suspect).

4 (5%) asserted that they could not reach any conclusion from the materials supplied them.

3 (4%) identified the wrong person.

[2] The 1984 Test

In 1984 participating labs were supplied with three handwritten letters containing bomb threats, supposedly received by the news media and then followed by terrorist bombings. The labs were also given two pages of known handwriting samples for each of six suspects (a total of twelve pages). They were to determine if the three questioned letters had all been written by the same person, and whether any or all of the questioned letters had been written by any of the suspects. Two of the threat letters were in fact written by one person, who was not among the suspects and whose actual known writing was not given to the labs. The other threat letter was written by one of the suspects whose exemplars were in his normal hand, but who had tried to simulate the writing of the other two threat letters when producing *his* threat letter.

Forty-one labs requested the test materials but only twenty-three submitted answers. Of those:

17 (74%) perceived the difference in authorship of letter 3.

6 (26)% said erroneously that the same person wrote all three threat letters.

23 (100%) failed to recognize that letter 3 was written by one of the suspects for whom they had known writings.[102]

---

102. Judging from comments at a meeting of the Document Examination Section of the American Academy of Forensic Sciences (February, 1996, Nashville, TN), this question and the finding of 100% error is the single greatest object of complaint by questioned document examiners concerning the FSF tests, a complaint that has some validity, but not as much as they assert. The usual form of their objection appears to be something like, "we don't claim to be able to determine the authorship of a writing made while trying to imitate some other person's writing." (Such an attempt is called "simulation" or "simulated forgery" in normal document examiner parlance.) First, as the authorities cited at § 2.2.2, point number 14, *supra*, demonstrate, the orthodox Osbornian position is not that such attribution of authorship is categorically impossible, but merely that it is extremely difficult, because attempting to imitate someone else's writing is an effective way to disguise one's own writing, and may be so effective at suppressing individ-

[3] The 1985 Test

Participating laboratories were given twelve checks all having signatures in the same name. They were asked to decide which, if any, of the signatures were made by the same person. In fact, two of the twelve had been signed by the real person whose name appeared on them. Of the remaining ten, one was an attempted freehand forgery by a person without known experience as a forger; another was a tracing. The remaining eight were signed by eight different people in their own normal handwriting. Forty-two labs requested test materials and only thirty two returned them. Of those:

13 (41%) gave correct results

2 (6%) wrongly attributed one of the forgeries to the real signatory.

10 (31%) reported that they were unable to reach conclusions.

7 (22%) were substantially wrong, making errors beyond a single misattribution of authorship.

[4] The 1986 Test

The 1986 test involved handwriting. Participating labs were told to assume that police had stopped a car with three known occupants. In the car they found a hand-printed holdup note and other evidence linking the note to a holdup apparently committed by only one person. The labs were given a copy of the holdup note. They were also given a copy of handwriting exemplars from the three occupants of the car. Suspect 1 had actually printed the holdup note. Suspect 2 had not, Suspect 3 had not printed the holdup note either, but he was a document examiner whose hand printed exemplar was an attempt to simulate the printing on the holdup note. Forty-eight labs requested materials and thirty-one returned reports. Of those:

uality that identification is impossible. Second, many examiners are willing to do such attributions in practice. *See* discussions of *Ruth, Jones,* and *Battle, supra* at § 1.4.2 and *Rutherford, supra at* § 1.4.3. The real underlying complaint concerning Question 2 in the 1984 FSF test seems to be that the skill of the simulator was unusual, and even though the writing was in a fairly generous amount, the simulator managed to suppress all identifying characteristics. (It should be noted that there is no specific evidence the simulator in fact was unusually skilled. The argument is circular: since we couldn't identify the writer, he or she must have been exceptionally skilled.) Although this confirms empirically the possibility of false negatives already admitted by Osbornian theory in such cases, this level of skill (if it was exceptional) may be rare enough that the meaning of the universal failure of examiners on this question might be overstated, especially in aggregating it with the results of other tests or questions. However, standard Osbornian theory holds that the act of simulation suppresses individuality even for unskilled simulators. *See* quotes from Albert Osborn, Ord-

way Hilton, and Wilson R. Harrison set out *infra* at § 2.3.7, at note 177. Certainly the results of Kam IV seem to indicated that document examiners are good at identifying simulations by naive and unskilled simulators as not genuine. *See* the discussion of Kam IV, *infra* § 2.3.6[4]. However, there was no test was given to see if document examiners could attribute authorship of those simulations to the actual writer under the same conditions.

As to aggregation, it is true that all aggregation strategies applied to the FSF data are inherently flawed, since no one knows exactly how to measure either the ease or difficulty of a test task, or its statistical incidence in normal practice. However, it appears that more problems in the FSF studies as a whole come from what was assumed to be the easy end of the spectrum, so that the inclusion of the occasional hard task in an aggregation seems not as artificial as excluding it completely. Beyond aggregation objections, there can be no objection to asking the question and observing the results. In addition, it is at least a start to defining the outer limits of whatever expertise, if any, actually exists.

4 (13%) gave correct answers.

3 (9%) said that none of the authors of the exemplars had written the hold-up note.

10 (32%) were unable to reach any conclusions.

14 (45%) assigned authorship to the forger.

[5] The 1987 Test

Because of document examiner complaints concerning the difficulty of prior tests, the FSF decided to make the 1987 test easy. As its report of results said, "This test was designed to be a relatively easy and straightforward test, because of complaints about previous test design. All the writings in this test were natural and free of disguise." In this test, participating laboratories were given a copy of a handwritten extortion note. Exemplars of the handwriting of four persons were also supplied, one of whom actually had written the extortion note. The problem was to determine which, if any, of the "suspects" had written the extortion note. Fifty-five laboratories requested materials and thirty-three responded with reports. Of those:

17 (52%) correctly identified the writer of the extortion note.

1 (3%) incorrectly eliminated the correct suspect, asserting that none of the suspects wrote the extortion note.

0 (0%) incorrectly identified an innocent person as the author.

15 (45%) responded that their results were inconclusive.

§ 3–2.3.2 The Risinger et al. Evaluation of the 1975–1987 FSF Studies

Here is what Risinger et al. said in evaluating the above results:

What do all five FSF studies taken together suggest? A rather generous reading of the data would be that in 45% of the reports forensic document examiners reached the correct finding, in 36% they erred partially or completely, and in 19% they were unable to draw a conclusion. If we assume that inconclusive examinations do not wind up as testimony in court, and omit the inconclusive reports, and remain as generous as possible within the bounds of reason, then the most we can conclude is this: Document examiners were correct 57% of the time and incorrect 43% of the time.

But let us turn to more meaningful readings of the aggregate data. The pilot test in 1975 may have been unrealistically easy, like a line-up with four beefy white policemen and a skinny black person. Did this task present any real difficulty at all? There is no way of knowing whether a group of lay persons would have done any less well, since none was tested. Omitting the 1975 data, the examiners were correct 36% of the time, incorrect 42%, and unable to reach a conclusions 22% of the time. Even these results are biased in favor of accuracy because of the intentional ease of the 1987 test. Disguised handwriting fooled them all and forged printing fooled two-thirds of those who hazarded an opinion about it.

Now consider the effect on the aggregate results of the laboratories that requested test materials but did not return them. More likely than not, these non-respondents bias the results further in favor of correct conclusions. Some of the non-responding labs, no doubt, did not even perform the tests due to the press of daily business. But some others very likely performed the tests and then did not return their reports. Assuming that an examiner who has worked on an answer and then decides not to return it has serious doubts about its accuracy, then the sample of respondents is composed of an unrepresentatively large proportion of those who obtained—or at least think they obtained—correct answers.

If a correct answer consists of a report containing correct conclusions returned pursuant to requested and submitted test materials, then of the total submissions to laboratories in the 1984 through 1987 tests, only 18% gave wholly accurate responses (without the 1987 test the figure drops to 13%).

Finally, consider the possible effect on any aggregate conclusions of the fact that, of the more than 250 ... laboratories that perform handwriting examination (not to mention a large number of private practitioner document examiners), only a fraction even ordered test materials in the first place. It is at least arguable that, by self-selection, the sample is inherently biased in favor of the more conscientious and capable practitioners to begin with. If this is true, the reported results would overstate the accuracy of the handwriting examination field generally.

The 1984, 1985, and 1986 tests presented examiners with a variety of challenges. The results should provide anyone with cause for concern. The examiners who returned reports on the analysis disagreed among themselves a good deal of the time, suggesting limited reliability, and many of the opinions offered were incorrect, suggesting limited validity.

In addition, the studies failed to reveal that certification or experience enhanced accuracy. The 1987 Proficiency Advisory Committee Comments state that "[a]s usual, there were no correlations between right/wrong answers and certification, experience, amount of time devoted to document examination and length of time spent on this test." Consider what this independence means for a court's likely assumptions about whether to admit a proffered expert and for the weight a fact finder is expected to give such testimony. A court is likely to assume that an examiner who is certified, who has been on the job for many years, whose caseload is nothing but document examination, and who has spent a lot of time examining the evidence, is especially likely to have something useful to say to a jury. Yet these data provide no support for these assumptions. Examiners who are uncertified, have little experience, work on document examination only part time, and spend little time on the particular document, are just as likely to be right as someone with more impressive qualifications. Does any of this suggest the existence of expertise?

These are the sorts of findings about the nature and limits of asserted handwriting identification expertise about which both document examiners and the courts need to know but which could not have been known before such studies were undertaken. Though they are not without flaws, these studies represent a step toward systematic and scientific evaluation of the claimed capabilities of this asserted expertise. Perhaps some of the considerably larger number of needed tests yet to be designed and administered would show document examiners faring better, but on the present record we must say that the underpinnings of the "expertise" have degenerated from no data to negative data.

Finally, we cannot emphasize too strongly that from the viewpoint of the law each of these studies suffers from a major omission: the absence of a control or comparison group of lay test-takers. If a jury can compare handwriting no worse than proffered "experts," then the expertise does not exist. For any given task, the level of performance of professional document examiners may be no better than that of layperson. Indeed, lay persons might perform some tasks consistently better than "experts." While such superiority may seem intuitively improbable, it remains a logical possibility and one not without analogues in other areas. For now, the kindest statement we can make is that no available evidence demonstrates the existence of handwriting identification expertise.[103]

§ 3–2.3.3   The Galbraiths' Critique of *Exorcism* and Their Proposed Reanalysis of the FSF Studies

The Galbraiths' main explicit criticisms of Risinger et al. can be summarized as follows:

1. All the FSF studies are methodologically so flawed that they cannot be used as a proper basis for drawing substantive conclusions.[104] Risinger et al. failed to recognize this and as a result of that failure they drew inappropriate conclusions.[105]

2. Even if the data were any good, the way Risinger et al. analyzed the data was wrong.[106]

3. A proper examination of the data (which the Galbraiths claim to do in reexamination) would result in reclassification of many document examiner responses to the tests from incorrect to correct and reveal their performance to be better than Risinger et al. reported.[107]

We will examine each of these criticisms in turn.

The Galbraiths begin their criticisms by invoking "the four types of validity issues identified by Cook and Campbell" in their well respected book, QUASI-EXPERIMENTATION: DESIGN & ANALYSIS ISSUES FOR FIELD SETTINGS.[108] Unfortunately, while there are important criticisms to be made of the methodology of the FSF studies, the Cook & Campbell framework adopted by the Galbraiths is largely inapposite. The Galbraiths confused cause-effect studies (experiments and quasi-experiments) with research aimed more simply at measuring some skill or ability. Cook & Campbell make clear that their validity constructs address problems of inferring that a treatment (independent variable)

---

103. Risinger et al., *supra* note 7, at 747–751 (footnotes omitted).

104. Galbraith et al., *supra* note 93, at 9.

105. *Id.* at 8, 16.

106. *Id.* at 11.

107. *Id.* at 11.

108. THOMAS D. COOK & DONALD T. CAMPBELL, QUASI-EXPERIMENTATION (1979).

caused the observed effects in a dependent variable.[109] The FSF tests were simply trying to measure accuracy of performance (much like testing how well marksmen can hit targets). They were not testing which of two or more treatment conditions produced better performance (such as testing which of two training methods produced more accurate marksmen). Cook and Campbell's book is concerned with the methodological problems of the latter. The FSF studies are of the former kind. The Galbraiths struggled to apply cause-effect methodological issues to research that aimed instead to measure a single variable, test performance, making no attempt to draw causal inferences because there were no independent variables. A far more apt research tradition to inform a critique of the FSF studies would have been the literature of psychometrics (i.e., testing). Moreover, virtually all of the methodological objections raised by the Galbraiths were, in fact, dealt with by Risinger et al., either in the text or in footnotes. In the few instances where this is not true, it is generally because the Galbraiths' objections are inapposite. Their fundamental misreading of Cook and Campbell leads the Galbraiths repeatedly into confusion.

For instance, the Galbraiths assert that one ought to discount or disregard the results of question 2 on the 1984 test (which all examiners got wrong) because of "insufficient co-variation."[110] The Galbraiths assert that "in designing or evaluating *any* test or experiment (such as the FSF tests) one must make sure that there is, or will be, sufficient covariation in the data, that is, variation in the test results must be observed in order to relate the results to the issue under investigation."[111] This is simply untrue in the universal form in which it is expressed; it depends upon what the issue under investigation is. While true for cause-effect studies (which Cook & Campbell were discussing), it is not for more basic skill measurement studies (which we, the FSF, and the Galbraiths are discussing). If all we want to know is "can most human beings hold their breath for ten seconds" the fact that a test administered to 100 humans results in *all* participants holding their breath for ten seconds in no way undermines the validity of the result, statistically or any other way. It is true, as Risinger et al. discussed at length, that tests that are too easy or too hard can lead to results which may be misinterpreted. It is also true that a single test designed to discriminate levels of skill has been unsuccessful if everyone does equally well or equally poorly. However, as Risinger et al. point out, handwriting identification is not a unitary operation, but rather presents "a broad variety of circumstances and tasks. Tests must be designed carefully to present discriminations of meaningful difficulty and variety. Only results from such tests could begin to paint a picture of what both lay people and experts can and cannot do...."[112] Within the context of such a testing regime, it is not a criticism that some particular question or

---

109. *Id.* This is evident throughout the book. But consider the following specifics: The second sentence of the preface: "The designs serve to probe causal hypotheses about a variety of substantive issues in both basic and applied research." *Id.* at ix. The title of the first chapter: "Causal Inference and the Language of Experimentation." The word causation appears in 6 out of 10 section headings within the first chapter. *Id.* at v. The first sentence of the first chapter: "The major pur-

pose of this book is to outline the experimental approach to causal research in field settings." *Id.* at 1.

110. Galbraith et al., *supra* note 93, at 9, 14.

111. *Id.* at 9 (emphasis supplied).

112. *Id.* at 742. Ironically, the Galbraiths' own footnote 14 makes the same point in very similar terms.

subtlest was so hard that none of the experts could do it. By themselves such data are not meaningless, as the Galbraiths seem to claim concerning Question 2 on the 1984 test. In combination with other data such results can help determine the limits of the expertise which were not known before the data were developed.[113]

Methodological misdirections aside, the Galbraiths' main critical thrust, in both parts one and two, is that Risinger et al. erred by accepting the response classifications that had been given to answers in the FSF studies initially *by the responding document examiners themselves* and then *by the FSF in its own summary of results*. Specifically, they claim that many responses that the document examiners labeled "inconclusive" when examining what turned out to be a true author's writings, ought to be treated as correct answers because the explanatory remarks accompanying the answers can be taken to indicate some level of belief that the writer of the exemplar may have written the questioned writing. They assert that these responses should be treated as examples of "qualified opinion" rather than bet-hedging "inconclusives."[114]

Even assuming the validity of their classifications of the data, however, the results do not mean what the Galbraiths go on to claim. They claim to have discovered 18 additional truly correct answers out of 192 total responses.[115] However, all but one of these answers newly classified as correct occurred in response to the two clearly easiest tests, 1975 and 1987.[116] Indeed, 13 of the new corrects were on the 1987 test alone, changing the performance on that test from 52% correct by the reckoning of Risinger et al. (based on the FSF classification) to 91% correct (based on the Galbraith reclassification). Secondly, the Galbraiths discard respondents who actually returned the test but criticized the test materials and checked off "inconclusive." These, they argue, ought to be treated as non-responses,[117] and, they argue even more vigorously, no conclusion can ever be fairly made from a non-response.[118] They then throw out the bad results of question 2 from 1984 (which they do not like for the "lack of co-variation" reasons discussed above, that is, all responses were wrong).[119] Finally, they aggregate all the results even though the dead easy 1975 test accounted for nearly 2½ times the number of responses of the next most responded-to test, and more than three times the

---

113. The Galbraiths also dispute the propriety of any cogitation on how non-responses may have resulted in sample biasing which overstated the skills of document examiners as a whole. They rightly point out that the biasing results of self selection might plausibly have run the other way. The main disagreement between Risinger et al. on the one hand and the Galbraiths on the other seems really to be about who should bear the burden of persuasion and the risk of non-persuasion. The stance of Risinger et al. is clearly that validity is to be treated as unproven until there are sufficient unambiguous data supporting it. The position of the Galbraiths is that one should not doubt validity and "indict the whole field" without affirmative proof of invalidity. The Galbraiths' position appears close to that

adopted by Judge McKenna in *Starzecpyzel*, and the opposite of the law's usual view that the burden is on the proponent of the evidence, as well as that of science that the burden of persuasion is on the one making the claim that some phenomenon exists.

114. The Galbraiths show no examples of moving "inconclusives" to the "totally wrong" column.

115. Galbraith et al., *supra* note 93, at 13.

116. *Id.* at 13.

117. *Id.* at 11.

118. *Id.* at 10.

119. *Id.* at 11.

responses of the hard 1984 test. Based on these adjustments, they claim that document examiners were correct 75% of the time.[120]

The fact remains, however, that the examiners did well at some tasks and poorly on others. The Galbraiths' own analysis (pertinent data reproduced as Table 1 below) shows that, out of six tasks with data sufficient to conduct significance tests, the document examiners could not even exceed *chance* accuracy in two of the six tasks. Think about that finding. Even where the experts do exceed chance performance, is *chance* the criterion of expertise? If a driver manages to stay on the right side of the median stripe more often than chance, if a piano student hits the correct notes more often than chance, if a student scores above sheer guessing on an exam—are they to be regarded as "experts"? And the Galbraiths found that document examiners did not even perform at that level on one third of the tests they took.

Table 1

Comparison of Expertise Against Chance
(Correct Versus Incorrect)

Exam Year (Question)	Observed Proportion Correct		Chance Proportion Correct	Exact Probability		Conclusion
	(M1)	(M2)		(M1)	(M2)	
1975	0.9429 (66/70)	0.9469 (70/74)	0.2000	0.0001	0.0001	Experts outperform chance
1984 Q1	0.5652 (13/23)	0.5652 (13/23)	0.2500	0.0174	0.0174	Experts outperform chance
1984 Q2	0.0000 (0/23)	0.0000 (0/23)	0.1429	0.0575	0.0575	Experts no different than chance
1985	0.5900 (13/22)	0.5517 (16/29)	0.0002	0.0001	0.0001	Experts outperform chance
1986	0.1905 (4/21)	0.2500 (7/28)	0.2500	0.2652	0.5000	Experts no different than chance
1987	0.9444 (17/18)	0.9375 (30/32)	0.2000	0.0001	0.0001	Experts outperform chance

Source: Galbraith et al., *supra* note 92, Table 3.

Put simply, beating chance hardly establishes expertise. Even by the law's generous definition, in order to have expertise one must be able to outperform non-expert average jurors.[121] On that issue, even the Galbraiths concede that no statistically meaningful data existed when Risinger et al. was

---

120. *Id.*

121. Also, even if it could be shown that a proffered expert outperforms jurors, if both do terribly, with lay persons being right one time in a thousand and experts one time in a hundred, such expertise still may not be dependable enough for admission.

published.[122] In an attempt to remedy this absence of data, the Galbraiths administered the 1987 FSF test to two groups of non-experts to see how their performance compared to the document examiners who had been tested earlier. We will analyze those results below, but first we will complete the review of FSF proficiency test data by reporting the results of the 1988 and 1989 tests.

§ 3–2.3.4 Forensic Sciences Foundation Proficiency Tests: 1988–1989

Since the publication of Risinger et al., only two more relevant FSF studies appear to have been undertaken that we have been able to obtain. In 1988 and in 1989 the FSF again administered handwriting identification proficiency tests to document examiners at crime laboratories.[123] The results of the 1988 and 1989 FSF studies have never been published by the FSF,[124] but summary reports containing the results were issued to participating laboratories by the Forensic Sciences Foundation, and those findings are published below

[1] The 1988 Test

The test design for the 1988 FSF proficiency test in handwriting identification was as follows: The written instructions told the labs to assume the following case scenario: Four complaints were received from (four separate) physicians' offices about shipments of narcotics that were not received. The delivery service produced four receipts (Q1–Q4) each containing a signature in the name of a secretary for one each of the four physicians. Each secretary denied writing her own signature or any of the others. (The same driver had apparently made all the deliveries.) Handwriting samples from the four

---

122. "[T]here certainly has been a shortage of studies comparing handwriting identification expertise to non-expertise...." Id. n. 7 at 7; "admittedly sparse history of carefully controlled empirical studies...." *Id.* at 7.

123. In 1990, after the existence of Risinger et al., *supra* note 7, became widely known, FSF quit testing on handwriting identification and began testing on such topics as rubber stamp identification (1990) and photocopying machine identification (1991). There was arguably a "handwriting" element in the 1992 test. However, comparison of form had little to do with obtaining the correct results. One could determine that the signature on the top (white) purchase order copy (copy 1) was photocopier generated and not hand signed, by direct examination without reference to exemplars (if appropriately skilled). The "carbonless carbon" on the yellow copy signature could then be determined to be a tracing of the photocopy signature by observing the ankles stylus indentation on the photocopied signature of the white copy, and the exact correspondence between the stylus indentation and the carbonless carbon signature. The determination that a particular one of the exemplars

provided had been the signature from which the photocopy on the white purchase order had been generated might be called a "comparison of form" problem, but since perfect superimposition was the key to this determination, it is not a comparison of the kind under consideration in this article. (About three quarters of the 90 respondents identified the right exemplar as the source of the photocopy, but the other quarter simply said nothing, and since they were not explicitly asked, these non-responses cannot be counted as errors, given the fact that most of them correctly identified the signature on copy 1 as a photocopy and that on copy 2 as a tracing over of the photocopy, which resolved the issue of genuineness about which they *were* asked). There have been rumors that proficiency tests with handwriting components have been renewed in recent years, but we have not been able to verify this or obtain the results of any which have been administered.

124. Their first general publication was in the first edition of this treatise. They were, however, printed and distributed to the heads of participating laboratories and others, and were thus "semi-published."

secretaries (labeled K1–K4) and the driver for the delivery service (K5) were requested. The delivery service also sent along two other receipts bearing signatures of "unknown persons."

The labs were supplied with six receipts acknowledging the receipt of goods. Receipt Q1 bore the signature "Sharon D. Clayborne" but in fact was written by Richard D. Osbourn, the driver. Receipt Q2 bore the signature "Lisa D. Bridgeforth" and in fact was signed by Lisa D. Bridgeforth. Receipt Q3 bore the signature "Cynthia Y. Boone" but in fact was written by Richard D. Osbourn, the driver. Receipt Q4 bore the signature "Joanna Neuman" and in fact was signed by Joanna Neuman. Receipt Q5 bore the signature "Linda N. Ninestine" and was not written by any of the five people who provided exemplars. Finally, receipt Q6 was signed "Linda D. Wentworth", but in fact was written by Richard D. Osbourn, the driver.

Sharon D. Clayborne, Lisa Bridgeforth, Cynthia Y. Boone, and Joanna Neuman each provided exemplars in which they signed their own names a number of times, and also signed all the other names appearing on the receipts a number of times. Richard D. Osbourn gave exemplars in which he signed all the names appearing on the receipts a number of times. These exemplars were provided to the labs through photographs.

These materials were submitted to seventy-three labs and returned by forty-nine.[125]

125. Before examining the results of these tests, it is necessary to say something about the test design as reflected in the FSF report. The report fails to set out crucial information concerning the test design necessary to evaluate the difficulty of the task presented to the takers of the test. Fair inference from the report, however, indicates that there were in fact people named Lisa D. Bridgeforth and Joanna Neuman who signed the receipts bearing those names, and signed them in their normal signature hands. In addition, it appears that these two gave their exemplars of their own names in their normal signature hands. (If these things are not as stated in the text, the test is one of the worst that could be designed in terms of the standard internal precepts of the asserted expertise. It is a virtual postulate that signatures are special as to design, speed of execution, uniformity, etc. If supposedly authentic questioned signatures, and especially if assuredly known exemplars, are signatures by people for whom the writing is not a habitual signature, but represent someone else's name, the whole exercise would be, in the internal terms of the discipline, grossly and unfairly misleading to the test takers.) If anything appears to correspond to reality in this field, it is that signatures are usually special manifestations of handwriting. It seems reasonable to believe that as a result of repetition, and psychological factors creating a personal stylistic identification with one's own signature, normal signatures are the most individual and uniform parts of a person's writing. This is not to say that signatures cannot be disguised. Nor is it to say that normal signa-

tures of two people with the same name cannot evolve into confusingly similar forms. *See* Harris, *supra* note 4. It is merely to say that it would presumably be rare for the normal signature of one person to look at all like another dissimilarly named person signing that name either in the second person's usual handwriting or in a disguised hand where no real signatures of person number one were available to imitate. Thus it would appear that perfect scores on Q2 and Q4 were, or ought to have been, giveaways.

In addition, the examiners being tested knew which of the sets of exemplars were from each secretary, and which set of exemplars was from the delivery man Osbourn. If they assumed that the original Clayborne and Boone signatures were natural signatures if genuine (as they had a right to do) and if they further assumed or concluded that the real Clayborne and Boone exemplars bore natural Clayborne and Boone signatures (as they had a right to do), then it would become a simple thing to eliminate all the secretarial exemplars as candidates for signing the Clayborne and Boone signatures, since none of the exemplar signatures would be likely to resemble the signatures on the receipts in any arguably significant way. This would reduce the question in regard to Q1 and Q3 to "did Osbourn sign these or not?" The difficulty of that question is presumably somewhat dependent on the nature of the writing presented (which was not reproduced in the report), but the results might also very well be influenced by the fact that Osbourn was the only candidate for those

For reasons set out more fully in the footnote, the 1988 FSF test must be approached with a substantial grain of salt. Each identification is not an independent event, but rather, the test presented two connected sets of issues, one set relatively easy and one set somewhat more difficult. The easy set of issues asked: which if any of these secretaries signed a receipt bearing her name in her normal signature hand? The harder set asked: Of the four signatures left over after disposing of question one, which if any was signed by Richard Boone.

Not surprisingly, out of forty-eight responding labs,[126] all got each response to Q1 substantially right,[127] all but three got each response to Q2 substantially right,[128] and all but one got the answers to Q3 right. (The exception, Lab 531, eliminated Osbourn as the author of Q3.) A 49th lab was unable to reach any conclusions on any of the queries, and marked everything "inconclusive."

Apparently, Joanna Neuman has some significant intra-writer or "natural" variation in her signature, because the responses to Q4 were surprising. Out of 48 responses, 22 were right, but five were wrong in affirmatively excluding the real Joanna Neuman. Twenty-one gave various versions of "inconclusive," ranging from seven leaning toward Neuman to three leaning toward another writer. Our inclination in dealing with these responses is to throw out the inconclusives and to say that in this particular case, nearly a fifth of examiners with definite opinions were wrong. Clearly, even signatures are no guarantee of absolutely easy problems.

Up to this point the errors have been false negatives, assertions that the true writer did not write the questioned signature. Q5 presents the more troubling problem (for the legal system, especially in a criminal context) of false positives. (However, it should be noted that in a forgery case, an error asserting that a signature is not genuine when it is in fact genuine has is

signatures left in the pool, and exterior circumstances already cast suspicion on him. Thus, his identification as the author may have resulted from the design of the test, not from the information derived from his handwriting.

Finally, the test takers might assume (as one respondent explicitly did) that the secretaries were unlikely to be in a position to sign receipts for deliveries to other doctors, which tends to convert the question in Q5 and Q6 to a question of whether or not the "Linda Ninestine" and "Linda D. Wentworth" signatures were signed by Osbourn or not. The elimination of Osbourn as the signer of the "Linda Ninestine" signature was likely to be made easier by the fact that presumably the signature was signed by a real Linda Ninestine in her real signature hand, and the Richard Osbourn exemplars would not only fail to resemble it, the examiners would already have concluded what Richard Osbourn's attempts at fake signatures looked like from Q1 and Q3. This would also assist them in identifying Osbourn as the author of the "Linda D. Wentworth" signature.

On the other hand, they might decide that since Osbourn signed all the other receipts not signed by known secretaries, he was likely to have signed Q5 also. All this raises the question of bias resulting from the presentation of unnecessary context information. Why not just present the exemplars marked questioned and known, and ask who wrote what, if anything?

126. One lab, #517, counted as responding by FSF, responded "inconclusive" to every part of every question, and in its narrative report protested the structure of the test. While we do not believe that inconclusives are categorically meaningless, under these conditions they are, and we have eliminated this lab from consideration.

127. That is, with one exception, all answered either "did not write" or "probably did not write" to each of the secretaries and "did write" or "probably wrote" to the driver Osbourn. The one exception was lab 539, which said Osbourn probably wrote Q1, but responded "inconclusive" to all the secretaries.

128. Labs 522, 539 and 542 failed to identify the true author of the signature, answering "inconclusive" to her.

wrongly inculpatory and in the legal context could be thought of as a false positive.) This time, only 17 labs were right,[129] but even among this group, the use of "probably did not" instead of "did not" rose in comparison to the answers to the previous questions. Only three labs manifested confidence that Osbourn did not write Q5. On the other hand, three labs affirmatively indicated Osbourn *did* write Q5,[130] and one lab (528) said Sharon D. Clayborne wrote Q5. Twenty-seven labs responded "inconclusive" to the Q5 questions, and in general these were unqualified inconclusives (not leaders in the Galbraith sense). Thus false positives made up 19% of the affirmative responses, and 25% of the responses with a confident finding.

Finally, as to Q6, there were 42 correct, two inconclusives that leaned toward Osbourn, three inconclusives, and one wrong exclusion of Osbourn (lab 514).

Thus, one can say that on the easy problems (Q1–Q3), document examiners gave 144 responses, of which 140 (97.2%) were correct or substantially correct, and 1 (0.5%) was an affirmative false exclusions, and 3 (2.5%) were inconclusive. Including Q6 as an easy problem, there were 192 responses, of which 181 (94.3%) were correct, 2 (1%) were affirmative false exclusions, and 9 (4.7%) were inconclusive. On the harder problems (Q4 and Q5), however, document examiners gave 96 responses, of which 39 (40.6%) were correct or substantially correct, nine (9.4%) were incorrect and 48 (50%) were inconclusive. Of the 48 answers reflecting firm conclusions on the harder problems, 19% were wrong, and of the 96 responses, only 41% were affirmatively right. The examiners did very well (but not perfectly) on the easy questions and substantially less well on the more difficult questions. And, as usual, there was no administration to a control group of non-experts to attempt to find out the relative performance advantage, if any, of experts over non-experts.

[2] The 1989 Test

If document examiners might find some comfort in the 1988 results, at least as to the easier tasks, the 1989 results were less comforting. The test was designed to see how well examiners deal with adolescent handwriting. The participating labs were asked to assume that during the final week of the school year, a high school teacher found the tires on her car slashed in the school parking lot. A handwritten note was found on the windshield. The teacher reported the matter to her principal, who in turn notified the police. On advice of the police, the teacher searched exam papers of her students and identified five students whose writing she thought similar to the threatening note. The principal refused, however, to release these exam papers to the police. The police therefore advised the teacher to ask those students to write the contents of the note to dictation five times on separate sheets of paper. Unfortunately, the instructions were misunderstood, and the writings of each

129. One lab was counted as right even though it had one inconclusive instead of five exclusions.

130. Labs 516, 522, and 545. Lab 507 responded by saying that Osbourn wrote the signature also, but the accompanying narrative comments were inconsistent with an affirmative ID of Osbourn. Although this response was counted as a misidentification by the FSF, it seems to have been a typographical error, and we have not counted it. Lab 545 was counted as indicating Osbourn, even though it amended the answer from "probably" to "possibly."

student were made on only one sheet of paper. The students have since dispersed for the summer and are not available to provide additional writings. Along with these facts, the labs were provided with photographs of the note (Q) and the exemplars from the five students (K1–K5), and asked to determine if Q was written by any of the writers of K1–K5.

The questioned document and the five exemplars had been generated in the following way: The questioned document had been written by a 15 year-old female tenth grader. Sixteen other tenth grade students ages 14–16 were asked to write exemplar sheets, and the five appearing closest to the questioned document in the opinion of the testers were used as the exemplars. Three points must be made. Sixteen people is a small set from which to hope to get five confusingly similar handwritings. We are not told if the person who selected the five exemplars claimed any expertise. And none of the people who wrote the exemplars wrote the threatening note.

The test materials were submitted to seventy-two labs of which fifty-three returned the answer sheets. Of those, thirteen labs answered "inconclusive" to every exemplar, and one answered "other" with no specific explanation. Of the thirty-nine remaining labs which offered an opinion actually including or excluding anybody, sixteen misidentified one of the writers of the exemplars as the culprit. (Three more leaned that way). That's 41% false positives.[131]

§ 3–2.3.5   The Galbraith Administration of the 1987 FSF Test to Non–Experts

The Galbraiths obtained copies of the 1987 FSF handwriting test materials, and administered them twice, first to a group of 32 varied non-experts who received the materials in photocopy form, and then (much later) to a group of 33 who were given photographs of the materials. There are some methodological questions about the administration of these tests. We are told neither about the exam conditions, the time allotted, nor the instructions given to the non-experts tested. We do not know if they were administered in a way designed to prevent potential cuing. Further, it is likely that the non-expert test takers suffered from problems of varying motivation, which are discussed in more detail in regard to the Kam et al. study, below. In addition, it seems possible that the non-experts were less likely to feel free to hedge their bets with some sort of inconclusive answer, perhaps not regarding such an answer as acceptable in the same way professional document examiners might regard it as acceptable.[132]

---

131. Or 49% using the Galbraith methodology of including leaders. A strong defender of handwriting experts might say that this is the wrong way to look at the data. Each decision as to each exemplar should be treated as a separate judgment. Thus, the 39 responding labs made 195 judgements of inclusion or exclusion, of which only 16 were wrong. However, a strong critic could counter by saying two things: first, the judgements are clearly not independent. The more you are sure one wrote the note, the more you are sure the other four did not. Second, the important thing in an expertise is not absence of errors, for then a refusal to answer would be counted as estab-

lishing the existence of the expertise. The important thing is how often one makes a judgment which is wholly correct when given the opportunity. In this case, 72 labs were given the opportunity, and only 23 unambiguously did the job right. Of these various ways to view the data, we will stick to the position that ours is most meaningful, since it emphasizes the percentage of experts whose responses could lead to court testimony and who would then give mistaken inculpatory testimony: 41%.

132. This may reflect the instructions, or absence of instructions, on this issue.

However, taking the data at face value, some interesting details emerge. First, even the lay people did significantly better than chance.[133] Second, if the FSF classification is utilized, the performance of the non-experts and the experts is virtually identical for true positives (17 out of 33 for the "experts," 16 out of 32 and 17 out of 33 for the two groups of non-experts). However, the non-experts were significantly worse when it came to false positives (34%, versus none for the document examiners). Finally, if we accept the Galbraith reclassification (and exclusion), document examiners significantly outperformed lay persons as a group (91% correct, no false positives, 3% false negatives; against 58% correct, 34% false positives, 8% false negatives). While these two limited and non-comparable administrations of these test materials cannot establish anything with any certainty, they seem to suggest that, at least as to the easiest tasks of handwriting comparison, the experts may have an approach which guarded against affirmative errors. The experts were no more affirmatively accurate than about half the "non-expert" population, but they were significantly less inaccurate than the other half. Any more confident conclusion as to whether this advantage truly exists, and whether it exists in relation to other more difficult tasks, must await further research.

§ 3–2.3.6 The Studies by Kam and Associates

In this section we begin examination of the studies undertaken by Dr. Moshe Kam and his colleagues under various FBI grants. But a word of caution as we start. Circumstances overtake us all, and if my interpretation of *Kumho Tire* is accurate, all but one of these studies have been rendered only tangentially relevant. That is because Kam I and Kam II were purposely designed to test aggregate global skills, and not to allow isolation of, much less identification of, subtasks such as identifying the handwriting of the foreign-born, adolescent handwriting, the handwriting of the aged and infirm, and so on, and Kam III was based on a readministration of Kam II. Only Kam IV is designed to test something that might be a "task at hand" in an actual case, (determination of signature authenticity). In addition, it must be emphasized that none of these studies address that most recurrent and controversial asserted skill, the ability to assign authorship based on extremely limited amounts of writing, in various contexts. With this in mind, we turn to Kam I.

[1] Kam, Watson & Conn (1994) ("Kam I")

Under a research contract with the FBI, Kam, Watson and Conn designed a test intended to determine whether some professional document examiners had handwriting identification skills significantly better than those of non-experts.[134] Forty-five Drexel University undergraduates copied five test samples on to five sheets of paper. Thirteen of them copied one or another of the samples an extra time. All used their normal handwriting. Fourteen of the students wrote with whatever they had brought with them. Eighteen of the students wrote with medium point Bic pens supplied by the researchers. Thirteen students "randomly swapped pens with each other" between writings, but we are not told what the original source and type of their pens

133. Galbraith et al., *supra* note 93, data table 4 at 16.

134. Kam, Wetstein & Conn, *supra* note 98, at 7–8. All the test design information is on these two pages.

were.[135] This procedure resulted in 238 documents, from which 86 documents were randomly selected as the test materials. These randomly selected 86 documents represented the work of exactly 20 writers. These 86 were then tagged with a "non-trivial" code which would allow the holder of the code to connect each document to a particular writer.

The test consisted of handing each person taking the test the 86 documents and telling them to go into a room with a table and sort them into piles representing the work of a single writer per pile. Test subjects were not told how many writers were represented in the 86 documents, and no time limits were imposed on them. There were two groups of test subjects: seven FBI document examiners (presumably chosen by the FBI to take the test) who were administered the test in Washington, D.C. by being handed the materials and given the instructions by one of their own supervisors; and ten graduate students in the Drexel graduate engineering and MBA programs who were selected in an unspecified manner to participate, and who had the test materials administered to them by their "supervisors" (whatever this may mean in the context of graduate students).[136]

A perfect performance on the test would yield 20 piles, each containing from one to six documents. Each pile would contain all the documents written by a single writer and only the documents written by that writer. There were two possible types of error: a participant could put a document in a new pile when there was already a pile for that author's work. This type of error the authors called over-refinement—making distinctions that were not there.[137] Or a participant could put a document in a pile containing the work of another author. This type of error the authors called under-refinement— failing to make a distinction that should have been made.[138] Of the two, the authors observed that under-refinement errors were perhaps "more significant, since they represent a confusion between two writers," that is, they create the risk of false positives, as opposed to the risk of false negatives resulting from over-refinement.[139]

Since the test materials were not reproduced, we have no first hand way of judging whether this sorting test was inherently easy or difficult. However, since the samples were generated with no attempt to apply any standards of pictorial similarity, it would seem to be like matching photos of twenty randomly selected humans of all races and sexes: that is, many of the subtask matches would seem likely to have presented trivial challenges. In addition, as previously noted, the harder tasks are subject to confusion by virtue of the effect of the uncontrolled variable of writing instrument variation. Differences in result between two test takers may actually reflect different assumptions concerning the test structure and the meaning assigned to writing instrument

135. It is unclear why all were not simply supplied with medium Bics from the beginning. This variation in ink or pencil types introduced a variable into the study's design having unknown impact and no apparent relevance to the issue of identification from form. For example, it may have created a distraction which the non-experts were more susceptible to, leading to inflated differences in scores between experts and non-experts.

136. The form of test administration was selected to impress upon the participants "the importance that their respective institutions attach to these experiments." We suspect that the FBI document examiners were more impressed with this message than the graduate students.

137. *Id.* at 8.

138. *Id.*

139. *Id.* at 9.

variation. In addition, we also do not know what relationship there is between the skills necessary for this test and the skills brought to bear in real-life document examination tasks, since document examiners are not called upon to do this kind of sorting task in their ordinary work. However, the ability to accurately perceive diagnostic patterns of similarity and difference in the writing represented by the test materials would seem likely to be common to both the test and to many kinds of real-life problems. At any rate, both test groups took the same test and the object was to see if there were differences in performance between the two, at least as to this test, for whatever reason.

The results obtained by the FBI document examiners are so good that one is tempted to conclude that the task was globally an easy one, especially given the differences in performance between easy and hard tasks which seem to be shown in the FSF studies. It may also be that the seven examiners selected to take the tests by the FBI were otherwise reputed to be the best in their employ. Nevertheless, taken at face value, their performance was impressive: five of the seven were perfect and the other two had only two errors each, one making one extra pile and having one incorrect inclusion, and the other making two extra piles.[140]

It is also true that the performance of the non-expert test takers was, in the aggregate, clearly inferior to that of the FBI document examiners. However, there is another uncontrolled variable which may account for much of the difference: test-taker motivation. Clearly, knowing the growing controversy over the bare existence of any such expertise, the FBI document examiners realized that the foundation of their careers may have been at stake when they took the test. The graduate students had nothing at stake beyond some varying individual notions of personal pride at doing the best job they could, if that.[141] In line with this, the striking thing about the performance of the graduate student group was its extreme bimodality. Four of the ten made only between 9 and 14 total errors, averaging 11, which were mainly errors of over-refinement (too many piles, one person's writing counted as two persons' writing).[142] Additionally, half of the graduate students made only 2 or 3 errors of under-refinement, assigning the authorship of a document to the wrong person, and one of the FBI examiners made one such error.[143] If the top

---

140. *Id.* at 10.

141. It would be interesting to know how much time was actually spent doing the tests by the members of each group, since there were no imposed time limits, but those data are not provided and, indeed, were not kept. In his phone conversation with one of the editors, Professor Kam indicated that he was present for each of the graduate student runs, and that all expended some hours on the task. However, according to Professor Kam, the test was designed after enquiry to document examiners concerning their notions of how long tasks take, to be a full working day's project for a document examiner, so there is some mild reason to believe that the document examiners spent significantly more time than the graduate students on the task, but there are no actual data to that effect.

One can argue that it is exactly the difference in motivation to expend time examining and comparing details of questioned writings and known exemplars that justifies the admission of document examiner testimony, since the lay jury is not likely to spend the time analyzing the material assuredly necessary for peak performance even if they could perform as well as document examiners if they spent the time. This is an interesting notion, analogous to the rationale for allowing testimony regarding summaries of voluminous material. Cf. Fed. R. Evid. 1006. How this fits in with our usual notions of expertise is not clear. At this juncture there is insufficient information on the contours of both lay and document examiner accuracy to justify rethinking the role of or justification for allowing such expertise.

142. *Id.*

143. *Id.*

40% of non-experts represented the properly motivated performance of non-experts, the differences in performance between the experts and non-experts, while perhaps statistically significant, is less significant in practical terms.

At the other end of the performance scale, the bottom 40% of the graduate student group made between 31 and 45 errors, averaging 38.5.[144] One person made 21 extra piles (41 total piles) and then assigned 24 of the remaining 45 documents to the wrong piles. Another made a total of 58 piles (38 extra) and assigned 6 of the remaining 28 to wrong piles. (One suspects that there was a subset of 21 or 22 documents in the set of test materials which could have been given to almost anyone as a virtually unfailable test.)

A note on the method of administering the test to the FBI agents: First, we know that the tests were administered "in Washington, D.C." and that they were "administered through the agents' supervisors." But we do not know from the published record exactly what this means. Certain obvious questions concerning the method of administering the test to the FBI agents present themselves. Were the test materials sent to Washington and kept there during the period necessary for the seven test runs, without the presence of a representative of Kam et al.? If so, this might severely undermine the validity of the results, raising as it does the distinct possibility of collaboration by substantially interested parties uncommitted to the standards of academic science. Further, while we are told that the test subjects were told nothing about the characteristics of the test materials and how they were generated, we are not told if their supervisors or others in the FBI were given such information. After all, the test was developed pursuant to an FBI contract with Prof. Kam to study the methods of handwriting experts with an eye to developing a computerized scanner which could perform this work as a screening tool. If people in the FBI had information about the characteristics of the test materials, the possibility of intentional or unintentional disclosures cannot be ignored. Finally, there is the matter of the "non-trivial code" with which the test materials were inscribed, which allowed them to be matched later for statistical analysis. If it consisted merely of a randomly generated number which matched an identification key kept at all times by the researchers in Philadelphia, fine. However, if to make their computer work easier they embedded the identification information in the code itself, the entire test was compromised if the materials were sent to the FBI without researcher proctoring.

One of the editors contacted Professor Kam, who graciously filled in many of the missing details.[145] Professor Kam told us that no one in the FBI was given any information on the characteristics of the database from which the test materials were drawn, or on how they were selected. It was true that the tests were administered in Washington by sending the materials to an FBI contact after giving him instructions on how to administer the test. He was to administer the test to one agent, then return the results of the sorting to Prof. Kam for scoring. Further, as to the code, it did consist of a randomly generated number, and to guard against those who had already taken the test sharing any useful tips with those who had not, the coding to the 86 papers was changed each time they were sent to Washington for administration.

144. *Id.*

145. Telephone interview by Michael J. Saks (Autumn, 1994).

However, since there was nothing in the actual design of the test which would insure that the test materials were not photocopied the first time they were sent to the FBI by someone who gained access to them during the substantial time they were available for the first administration of the test, collaboration on the test by the FBI document examiners cannot be procedurally ruled out. On the other hand, the performance of the FBI document examiners was remarkable even if there was collaboration, though the results under those circumstances would be attributable only to the group, or to the best performer in the group.[146]

Where does this leave us? If the level of graduate student performance and its variation are the product of motivational differences and the artifactual impact of the writing instruments, the data could no longer be taken to support a marginal performance advantage in the experts. These artifacts cannot be ruled out as insignificant. Kam III was an effort to examine this issue, but does not lay it to rest (*see infra* at § 2.3.6[3]) If the variations mirror reality, then we potentially have an even stranger situation (but it is also consistent with the results of the Galbraith study). It may be that average people have a wide range of knacks, ranging from good to poor. It may be that, at least as to easy tasks, the expert is a lot better than half the non-experts but not much better than the other half. (This might simply result from people in the half of the non-expert population with the knack comprising most of those drawn to the work of document examination in the first place.) In the face of harder tasks, there is reason to believe tentatively that the marginal advantage may break down. What should be the law's response to a situation like that? The law is not well equipped to put such a situation into its usual paradigm, which assumes a substantial skill break between all members of the expert group and the overwhelming majority of the randomly selected population.

[2]   Kam, Fielding & Conn (1977) ("Kam II")

Between the beginning of May and the end of September 1996, Kam, Fielding and Conn administered a test of their own design to three groups of

---

146. Before speaking to Professor Kam, we thought that there was some reason to believe that the test administration was over-supervised, not under-supervised. In 1993, Agent Richard Williams testified in a proceeding in San Francisco that he was one of the test subjects, and that during the administration of the tests he was surrounded by people in white coats with clipboards asking him questions about what was going through his mind as he did the test. *See* Williams testimony, In Matter of Requested Extradition of Smyth, 826 F.Supp. 316 (N.D.Cal.1993), transcript at 127. He referred to the test as a "quick and dirty" sorting. *Id.* at 125. If the tests were conducted in this way, they would appear not to have been double blind, and the phenomenon of "Clever Hans" cuing (named after the famous German horse that was thought capable of solving arithmetic problems until he was tested under careful procedures which prevented subtle cues from reaching him) cannot be ruled out. However, at the time of his testimony Williams was trying to diminish the significance of the fact that *any* mistakes had been made by the professionals. In addition, he may not actually have been one of the 7 test subjects (though he insistently testified that he was, *id.* at 127) but merely one of those document examiners "interviewed at length after the testing" to try to determine the mental processes behind document examiner performance. *See* Kam I, *supra* note 101, at 13. It seems very likely that these interviews were conducted around an examination of the test materials, and that this is what Williams was involved in, not an actual run of the test itself. Williams' testimony does give rise to questions concerning the way these materials are presented to courts by document examiner witnesses, and the lengths to which they may go to bend the meaning of the tests in a desired direction.

about 35 questioned document examiners each, a group of eight document examiner trainees, and a group of 41 untrained non-experts.[147]

Before we look at the published results of these tests, let us examine the test design, and the limits of what we might expect that it can and cannot tell us. First, like Kam I, this is a multi-document sorting test of a type

147. All details of the Kam II test procedures are drawn from pages 779–781 of that eight-page article, *supra* note 98. Because the material is so short, specific footnote references to page are omitted as unnecessary and burdensome to the reader.

The test materials were generated as follows: 150 persons, ages 20 to 27, were selected by an unknown protocol to provide writing samples and they agreed to do so. Each writer worked on a wide and well lit table in a classroom setting. Each writer generated 12 documents on 8½ x 11 in. 20 lb. white paper, copying three short assigned texts four times each. Each used pens supplied by the test designers. All writers were given both blue medium Bic pens and black medium Bic pens, and told to use both colors, switching "every 2–3 documents", so each writer created both blue and black documents in no exact fixed ratio or order. This resulted in 1800 documents, four each of three texts by 150 writers. Thirty of those writers were then selected (presumably at random) and all the documents generated by those thirty (360 documents) were placed in a set. These documents were then random number coded for writer identity. Random documents were then drawn from the set of 360 until 6 documents by 6 different writers was obtained— that is, after drawing the first document, if the second document was by the same writer, it was returned to the pool and another was drawn, and so forth, until a set of 6 documents by 6 different writers was obtained, which documents could represent randomly any text and either color ink. This set of 6 was then labeled "Unknown A1". The same process was repeated until 12 such sets were obtained (Unknowns A1 ... A12) which together contained 72 documents in 12 sets of 6 each, each of the six by a different writer in each set. The remaining 288 documents were then randomly distributed into 12 sets referred to as "database packages" (database A1 ... A12), each containing 24 random documents. The use of the label "unknown" was somewhat problematical. Among document examiners, "unknown" is the label given to a document of unknown authorship to be compared with standards of known authorship. In the Kam II test, none of the documents in either the "unknown" sets or the "database" sets were unknowns in this sense. They were in fact functionally the same from that perspective: both sets were known to the testers and unknown to the test takers. The test was thus the same kind of sorting test involved in Kam I. A simi-

lar process was undertaken with the remaining documents not in set A, generating a set B. with the same subset characteristics, and so on for set C, until there were five such universes, A–E, containing 12 6–document "Unknown" sets each and 12 24–document "database" sets each. Each test participant was tested by randomly selecting a Universe A–E, then within that Universe randomly selecting an "unknown" set from the 12, and randomly selecting a "database" set from the 12, explaining to the test subject that the "unknown" sets contained 6 writings by 6 different writers without disguise, and asking the test participant to determine whether any document or documents in the "database" set of 24 were written by any writer represented in the "unknown" set. Here we have a problem in figuring out the limiting conditions of the sets so generated. This is because the report of the study is a bit hazy on this point. It is inexplicit whether, once "Unknown A1" was generated, the writers there represented were removed, so that set A2 would have six writers who were different from each other and also all different from the ones in set A1, or whether the process was simply repeated on all the *documents* remaining after the generation of set A1, in which case set A2 could, in theory, contain the exact same writers as A1. It appears that the latter must be the case, because with 12 sets of 4, one would need 48 writers to have no overlaps, and there were only 30 writers in the pool. But in that case, it is possible (though unlikely) that each set A1 thru A12 represented exactly the same 6 writers, since each writer had generated 12 documents. Similarly, in regard to the "database" sets, in the event of the distribution just described, *a fortiori*, no "database" set would, or could, contain a document truly matching one in an "unknown" set. This theoretical (and very remote) possibility is only important to understand the real meaning of the first three tables in the Kam II report. These tables are obviously descriptive of the distribution of matches in the actual tests as given to the participants, not of the probability of such matches resulting from the distribution process described above. Thus, while there is a statistical probability that some test might be administered which had no true matches, in the 154 tests actually run there was always at least one true positive match. Similarly, at the other extreme, though there is a remote possibility of as high as 18 true matches, in the actual 154 tests administered there were never more than 10.

encountered rarely if at all in actual practice.[148] This is not to say the results are meaningless. As noted elsewhere in regard to the similar characteristics of Kam I, "the ability to accurately perceive diagnostic patterns of similarity and difference in the writing represented by the test materials would likely be common to both the test and to many kinds of real-life problems."[149] It is merely to caution against simple extrapolation to actual practice without further thought.

Second, there are problems of motivation. Professional document examiners would be expected to put in more focused effort, given that their careers (and the fate of their profession) are in some sense on the line, than would students. This was a serious problem with Kam I.[150] However, in Kam II, the designers have made a commendable attempt to correct for this by offering the non-experts a schedule of monetary rewards and penalties. Unhappily, the schedule of rewards and penalties utilized was particularly unfortunate and problematical. The non-experts were told that they would receive a $25 participation fee, and that their payment would not go below this regardless of actual performance. They were then told they would receive an additional $25 for each true positive match, that they would lose $25 for each false positive match, that they would lose $10 for failing to see a true match, and that they would gain nothing for accurately rejecting a non-match. This payoff schedule can be schematically represented by Table 2.

Table 2

The Payoff Matrix Used in Kam II for Non-experts

		Reality	
		Match	Non–Match
Decision	Match	True Positive +25 (Very Good)	False Positive –25 (Very Bad)
	Non-Match	False Negative –10 (Bad)	True Negative 0 (Indifferent)

Under this regime, if their objective was to maximize their payoff, the non-experts would guess a match whenever it appeared to them to be as likely as a non-match. This is because, over the long run, it would appear that such

---

148. Kam states that the "format was selected to resemble a multi-suspect case in which extensive examination of documents was required," Kam II at 780, but in fact, because there were multiple documents in each comparison set, none of which were known as to origin by the examiner, it resembles no real case. Perhaps it would be better if real cases were presented to examiners in this blind a fashion, but they are not. *See* D. Michael Risinger & Michael J. Saks, *Science and Nonscience in the Courts:* Daubert *Meets Handwriting Identification Expertise,* 82 Iowa L. Rev. 21, 64(1996).

149. *Id.* at 60.

150. *Id.* at 61.

a strategy would at least break even, whereas guessing "no match" on such an evaluation would lose an average $5 per guess over the long run. Plus, there was no real incentive to avoid false positives for fear of actually losing something they already had at the beginning of the test, because they were guaranteed their starting $25 no matter how bad their performance. This reward schedule seems guaranteed to make the non-experts risk-preferring regarding finding matches, even in the face of instructions that they should declare a match only if they were really, really sure. And this effect is on top of the well-known tendency for a most people to become risk preferring in circumstances of potential high rewards and low costs, regardless of rational odds (sometimes referred to as the "lottery effect").[151]

In contrast to this, the document examiners entered the test under quite a different effective payoff schedule. For one thing, they knew that the worst thing they can do on any proficiency test is to commit a false positive error.[152] (This risk averseness to false positives on known tests is not necessarily present in normal practice.[153]) Secondly, for the document examiners, a correct discovery of a non-match is also a highly desirable indicator of affirmative expertise. The incentive matrix for document examiners taking the Kam II test might be represented as in Table 3:

151. Daniel Kahneman & Amos Tversky, *Prospect Theory: Analysis of Decision Under Risk*, 47 ECONOMETRICA 263 (1979); Lola L. Lopes, *Remodeling Risk Aversion, in* ACTING UNDER UNCERTAINTY: MULTIDISCIPLINARY CONCEPTIONS 267 (George M. von Furstenberg ed., 1990); Lola L. Lopes, *When Time is of the Essence: Averaging, Aspiration and the Short Run*, 65 ORG. BERHAVIOR & HUMAN DECISION PROCESSES 179 (1996); Amos Tversky & Daniel Kahneman, *Advances in Prospect Theory: Cumulative Representation of Uncertainty*, 5 J. RISK & UNCERTAINTY 297 (1992).

152. *See* Moenssens, *supra* note 6, at 315. This is because such a false positive in the real world can result in the conviction of an innocent criminal defendant, a result the official ideology of our criminal justice system disvalues much more than an inaccurate acquittal, as reflected in the requirement of proof beyond a reasonable doubt. Thus, to commit such an error on a proficiency test undermines the status of the expertise in the eyes of the law, and must be avoided at all costs *in tests*.

153. Whether false positives must be as stringently avoided in actual practice is a different issue. It cannot be stated too often that any superiority on the part of document examiners under test conditions will not necessarily carry over to practice, where the pressures on

document examiners, as on other forensic practitioners, are to make matches that confirm positions already arrived at by other investigators, a fact recognized by Moenssens. Consider the following: "[E]ven where crime laboratories do employ qualified scientists, these individuals may be so imbued with pro-police bias that they are willing to circumvent true scientific investigation methods for the sake of 'making their points'.... Unfortunately, this attitude is even more prevalent among some 'technicians' (non-scientists) in the crime laboratories, for whom the presumption of innocence disappears as soon as police investigative methods focus on a likely suspect." Andre Moenssens, *Novel Scientific Evidence in Civil and Criminal Cases: Some Words of Caution*, 84 J. CRIM. L. & CRIMINOLOGY 1, 5 (1993). And further: "The temptation to fabricate or to exaggerate certainly exists. All experts are tempted, many times during their careers, to report positive results when their inquiries come up inconclusive, or indeed to report a negative result as a positive when all other investigative leads seem to point to the same individual. Experts can feel secure in the belief that their indiscretions will probably never come to light." *Id.* at 17.

Table 3
The Implicit Payoff Matrix in Kam II for Experts

Decision		Reality	
		Match	Non–Match
	Match	True Positive (Very Good)	False Positive (Extremely Bad)
	Non-Match	False Negative (Bad)	True Negative (Good)

Thus, in a situation of equipoise, the reward structure would impel experts toward declaring a non-match, and the non-experts toward declaring a match. Hence, the non-experts and the experts took the tests under incentive structures which would be predictably expected to yield more false positives for the non-experts[154] even under equally accurate probability judgements about authorship.[155]

Third, and somewhat unaccountably, is the "ink color" variable. This problem was also present in Kam I. Why the writers of the exemplars were asked to use two different color inks is not at all clear, and the effects on the results, or on the aggregate results between groups, cannot be assumed *a priori* to be trivial. As noted elsewhere, this "introduced a variable into the study's design having unknown impact and no apparent relevance to the issue of identification from form."[156] Nevertheless, this is probably best regarded as simply another subtask variable of the variety inevitably present in the tests as designed, for reasons explained below.[157]

Fourth, passing beyond ink color to a much more serious problem, once again Kam et al. have apparently created the possibility that the document examiners, or some of them, had helpful information about the test in advance of its administration,[158] because apparently the earlier document examiner test subjects got to go over the results of their tests at some point before the next document examiner groups were tested.[159] Kam says he

154. To correct for this, future tests should impose high disincentives on the non-experts for false positive responses, substantially higher than the reward for true positives, and equalize the value of true negatives and false negatives (missed matches).

Scientists who study decision-making of the sort done by forensic scientists, an area of research called "Signal Detection Theory," have developed ways of measuring the raw acuity of examiners separate from the subjective threshold that an observation must cross in order for examiners to decide that what they have observed is a submarine or a tumor or a handwriting "match." Such research has found that incentives for preferring to err in one way (a false negative: failing to detect a tumor) rather than another (a false positive: seeing a tumor where none is) typically have considerable impact on where the psychological threshold is placed, regardless of the raw perceptual accuracy of the examiner. *See* John A. Swets, *The Science of Choosing the Right Decision*

Threshold in High–Stakes Diagnostics, 47 Am. Psychologist 522 (1992); Victoria Phillips, Michael J. Saks & Joseph Peterson, *Signal Detection Theory and Decision-making in Forensic Science*, 46 J. Forensic Sciences 294 (2001).

155. Kam III administered the Kam II test materials to four sets of layperson under four different incentive schemes in an attempt to meet these criticisms. *See* discussion of Kam III, *infra* § 2.3.6[3].

156. *See* Risinger & Saks, *supra* note 148, at n. 142.

157. *See* the discussion under our fifth consideration *infra*, text accompanying note 160.

158. *See* the discussion, *supra* § 2.3.6[1], of this problem in regard to Kam I, which renders it impossible to know if individual performances are in fact group performances in regard to the document examiners tested.

159. It is not fully explicit that this was the case. What Kam says is, because "unknown"

protected against this having any effect by making sure that no pairing of a set of "unknowns" and a set of "data base" documents was ever used twice. However, it should be obvious by now that quite a lot of useful test design information might be gleaned in such a debriefing session. For instance, if you know how the data base was generated, you can figure out pretty quickly how rich or poor in true matches the tests are likely to be, that is, what the rough probabilities are of maximum and minimum numbers of true positives, information not available to the non-experts, who might be expected to assume a universe much richer in matches, which might encourage guessing. And note that, while the document examiners were divided into three regional groups for statistical purposes, the members of at least the Northeast group were tested in at least two different sub-groups at two different times, with their results being aggregated statistically. It seems especially unnecessary to have run the tests in such a way as to create this problem, since all that was necessary was to collect all the data before conducting any post-mortems.

Fifth, and finally, the actual tests presented an unknown variety of subtasks in an unknown distribution. In addition, some important varieties of subtask were clearly absent from the test, and as to those, the test can generate no direct data of any kind. Like the Kam I universe of writing exemplars, the much larger and more controlled universe generated for Kam II was generated with no attempt at isolating subtasks (comparing two exemplars with similar but unusual "class characteristics," for instance, such as the handwriting of two German immigrants of similar age and sex). Any given such subtask *might* have been present somewhere in some run of the test, but we don't know which were, which weren't, or when. This is not necessarily a criticism, but it must be kept in mind when determining what the test can tell us. Each test was a little different, presenting a different set of challenges, and the most that can be said is that the challenges are likely to be typical of a certain range of comparison situations. They are also unlikely to mirror those encountered in litigation. This is because many of the subtask problems are likely to be trivial, like distinguishing between two randomly selected humans of all races and sexes, since the exemplars were generated with no apparent attempt to make the set of materials richer in confusingly similar exemplars than random life would be.[160] Most importantly, some very critical subtasks were not under test at all, such as the effects of forgery or disguise, the particular problems of signatures or adolescent handwriting, or those of the elderly or infirm, or the like. However, with these limitations in mind, and within the range of aggregate subtasks present in the tests, the tests can generate important data, and would be expected to generate the following types of data:

and "database" pairings were never repeated "(e)ven if correct results from an early test were fully known to all test-takers in a later session, this information was practically useless. We do not believe that any attempt was made to record or share results from our tests between test-takers. However, if such attempts were made, they could not affect the results in a meaningful way." Kam II at 779. We take this to mean that results were provided the test takers at some point in advance of the next group of tests. (In order to make sure this was what happened, repeated attempts have been made to obtain explicit clarification from Dr. Kam, both by e-mail and by regular mail, but Dr. Kam has not responded. Under the circumstances we proceed on the assumption that what was written was what happened.) This is one more illustration of the hidden pitfalls of human testing that may not be immediately apparent to a researcher more accustomed to computer modeling.

160. *See* the discussion, *supra* § 2.3.6[1], of the same problem in regard to Kam I.

- The aggregate performance of the professional document examiner group as to true positives, false positives, true negatives and false negatives.

- The aggregate performance of each subgroup of professional document examiners as to the same categories of result.

- The aggregate performance of the trainee group as to the same categories of result.

- The aggregate performance of the non-expert group as to the same categories of result.

- The distribution of performances among the professional document examiner group (best score, worst score, distribution in between, as to all categories of result).

- Same for subgroups.

- Same for trainees.

- Same for non-experts.

Indeed, these data are so important that, with a small domain like 154 tests, one might expect to see a frequency distribution, or even a data table giving each taker's (unidentified by name) individual scores, as was done in Kam I. In the Kam II report, however, all that is given is aggregate performance of groups, and that only in numerical averages. There is no distribution information given at all, even in the form of standard deviation values. It's not that this information does not exist or was not available to Kam et al. It just is not given. Important information is hidden (unintentionally or otherwise) behind the few aggregate statistics provided.[161]

161. Think of what this means. We do not know how well the best lay people performed, or how poorly the worst document examiners performed. Kam et al. know, but no one else does. Even the aggregate data establish that there is no significant difference in average performance in regard to true positives. (Note that the proper conclusion is "no significant difference," not "accept" the null hypothesis as Kam et al. mistakenly conclude in Kam II (tables 10, 11, 13, 15, and accompanying text). A null hypothesis is only a starting point. Based on evidence, it can be rejected. But the failure to reject it as false is not the equivalent of "accepting" it as true.) In this particular study it is in regard only to false positives, the most dangerous type of error, that document examiners have a significant aggregate advantage. However, without distribution information, we do not know if, for instance, the best half of the non-experts is as good or better at avoiding false positives as the worst half of the document examiners. Averages can conceal important variations.

This is not as farfetched as it might sound. The data from the Galbraith study and from Kam I tended to indicate that non-experts were bimodal in their accuracy distribution, including false positives. If that trend were to hold in Kam II, the best of the non-experts could still be better than the worst of the experts, but the average for non-experts would be dragged down by the truly poor performance of the worst of the non-experts. Similarly, the high average for document examiners could conceal a cluster of very poor performers on the low end. We are well aware that the test design, which resulted in each test administered being different from every other, and each test participant therefore taking a somewhat different test, makes statements about comparative individual performance problematical, absent some way to rate the relative difficulty of particular tests. Nevertheless, other moments of performance distributions have as much claim to meaning from these data as the one Dr. Kam chose to publish, and cannot be derived without the data. These data exist but were not published. What is worse, Dr. Kam was repeatedly requested to provide it to us and others, and repeatedly refused. For details, *see* Risinger et al., *supra* note 5, at 431–33 and accompanying notes. Finally, pursuant to an agreement, and consistent with general federal policy on data produced under federal contracts, Professor Kam and the FBI agreed to disclose the data to Dr. Michael Saks (March 28, 2000), but more than a year later, and after several reminders to send the data, the FBI explicitly reneged on its promise. Un-

The reader will have seen by now why Kam's conclusion that the results of Kam II "lay to rest the debate over whether or not the professional document examiners possess writer-identification skills absent in the general population" is more than a small exaggeration. A more proper conclusion would be that under test conditions not replicating actual practice in significant ways, and as to an undefined range of subtasks not including many of the most important ones of actual forensic practice, the aggregate average performance of document examiners in correctly identifying actual matches was virtually identical to layperson (layperson correctly matched authors 87.5% of the time, compared to 87.1% for experts), but document examiners were better at avoiding false positives than non-experts (layperson mistook a non-match for a match 38.3% of the time compared to 6.5% for experts), and the latter findings may be an artifact of the varying incentive and disincentive regimes applying to the two groups, perhaps compounded by other factors. More importantly, there is nothing to show that this relative advantage when performing on what is known to be a test, even if real, is robust enough to continue in the face of expectancy and suggestion effects (properly) excluded from the test, but present in normal practice. Only tests specifically directed toward this issue, or a regime of blind proficiency testing, can answer this.

[3]   Kam, Fielding & Conn (1988) ("Kam III")

Responding to criticisms concerning the confounding effect of the monetary incentives given to lay test subjects in Kam II, Kam Fielding and Conn administered the Kam II test to four groups of 32–34 Drexel University College of Engineering sophomores, 87% of whom were receiving financial aid (and therefore might arguably respond sensitively to changes in monetary incentives.). One group repeated the Kam II test with its original reward scheme intact, that is, the subject was guaranteed $25 for participation, and beyond that, correct matches gained $25, inaccurate declarations of match lost $25, failure to declare a match when one was present lost $10, and accurately declaring a non-match neither gained or lost (*see* extensive description and criticism *supra* at § 2.3.6[2]). The other three groups each took the test under different incentive schemes, which were as follows:

> Group 2: correct matches gained $25, inaccurate declarations of match lost $25, failure to declare a match when one was present lost $25, accurate declaration of a non-match neither gained nor lost. $25 minimum participation fee guaranteed.
>
> Group 3: correct matches gained $25, inaccurate declarations of match lost $50, failure to declare a match when one was present lost $5. Accurate declaration of non-match neither gained nor lost. $25 minimum participation fee guaranteed.
>
> Group 4: Participant starts with a bank of $100. Correct matches neither gain nor lose, inaccurate declarations of match lost $25, failure to declare a match when one was present lost $25. Accurate declarations of non-match neither gain nor lose. $25 minimum participation fee guaranteed.

der such circumstances, one can be forgiven for suspecting that the distribution data would show bimodality for the performance of the non-experts and poor performance by a significant cluster of document examiners.

Kam III does not give performance data for each group, merely aggregate numbers for all four groups combined regarding "hit rate" (actual accurate declarations of match as a percent of possible accurate declarations of match) and "wrong association rate" (inaccurate declarations of match as a percent of possible inaccurate declarations of match). However, Kam III does compare those rates between individual groups statistically, and finds that, as to hit rate and wrong association rate, there were no statistically significant difference among any of the four test groups. However, there is a small impediment to any general conclusion that incentive schemes, even incentive schemes at this level of reward, and which incorporate a gain floor, do not significantly influence test-taker behavior. The aggregate performance of the four new test groups was significantly better than the original Kam II lay group. The hit rate was insignificantly lower, but the new wrong association rate was significantly better (0.227 compared with 0.338, a 41% better performance at avoiding wrong associations.) Kam III attributes this to the aggregate tendency of the new groups to declare fewer affirmative matches of any kind, as if this were an explanation. But to what do we attribute this new reticence? Both reward scheme 3 and reward scheme 4 would each seem to encourage risk averseness in declaring matches of any kind, which is what was observed in the aggregate data, as compared to Kam II. So the conclusion that the different incentive schemes did not significantly affect lay performance is hardly established by Kam III.

Finally, it should be noted that none of the tested incentive schemes had the characteristics of the scheme recommended, *supra*, in § 2.3.6[2], note 154. Number 3 came closest, by penalizing false positives more harshly than it rewarded true positives, but the penalty differential was not severe enough, and the scheme did not equalize the value of accurately perceiving a match and accurately perceiving a non-match (true positives and true negatives).

[4]   Kam, Gummadidala, Fielding & Conn ("Kam IV")

Between May and November of 1998, pursuant to their FBI contract, Dr. Moshe Kam and his associates initiated the first study ever designed to test the abilities of document examiners against the abilities of ordinary people in regard to a specific task that is actually a task commonly undertaken by document examiners in normal practice. A number of preliminary observations must be made before dealing with the details and results of that study.

First, the task selected for examination, determining whether a signature is genuine (written by the person whose name is reflected by the signature) or non-genuine (not written by the person whose name is so reflected) is *sui generis* according to the standard theory of handwriting examination used by document examiners. This is because real signatures are regarded as a category of writing separate from all other writing insofar as it is common for them to manifest a high degree of personally unique characteristics, resulting from a combination of repetition and emotional or stylistic investment. If document examiners are right about this (and it is neither counter-intuitive nor in conflict with existing empirical evidence), then it would be error to generalize from skill levels shown in this study to similarly high skill levels in separate and more difficult tasks, such as identifying the actual author of a concededly inauthentic signature.[162] This is in no way a criticism of design of the study. One must start somewhere, and it makes a certain sense to start with the easiest definable task and work on from there.

Second, the study is currently unpublished. Ordinarily we would be reticent to summarize and comment on the results of research in advance of publication by the researchers. However, in this case, we believe an exception to that general rule is in order. It has been more than two years since the completion of the study, and there is no indication that as yet it has even been submitted for publication. It would be unfortunate if this important study were for whatever reason to remain unknown. In addition, the study has in fact been published, in a manner of speaking. A complete draft was produced and relied upon by Dr. Kam in connection with his testimony in the *Daubert/Kumho* hearing in *United States v. Rutherford*. If the study is in good enough shape to be proffered in order to influence a court's decision on document examiner reliability, it is in good enough shape to be described and evaluated for the interested public.

Determining the authenticity of a signature is an important task in many legal contexts, such as, *inter alia*, the probate of wills and, perhaps most commonly, asserted cases of check forgery. Broadly speaking, inauthentic signatures can be generated in three general ways. The forger can be in possession of a blank check, say, but have no model of an authentic signature to try to simulate. Signatures generated under those conditions, whether in the normal hand of the forger or in some sort of disguised hand, usually present trivial problems for determining authenticity. The new study (preliminarily titled "Signature Authentication by Forensic Document Examiners" and hereafter referred to as Kam IV) wisely did not include such circumstances.[163] Another possible way in which inauthentic signatures are generated is when the forger has a model of a genuine signature to use in attempted simulation and, in addition, is experienced in forgery, that is, has done simulations often before and has at least come to believe that they have mastered simulation skills sufficiently to do a good job. Kam IV was not designed to examine document examiner or non-document examiner skills in detecting forgeries under such conditions.

The final category of non-genuine signatures involves what we may call naive forgers, that is, people who have a model of a genuine signature for purposes of simulation, but who have no previous experience in forgery. Kam IV was designed to deal only with forged signatures of this type.[164] Note that the study could have been designed only to deal with such signatures, simply

162. Note that this lack of generalizability is not symmetrical. To the extent significant error rates are shown on this task, it is fair to infer, at least tentatively, that error rates on harder tasks would be at least as high and probably higher, whereas good performance on this task is extremely weak evidence concerning good performance on other tasks. And it must always be kept in mind that performance under test conditions may not measure performance under the normal conditions of practice, which are subject to substantial forces of expectation and suggestion.

163. One weakness of Kam I and Kam II was that the tests included a substantial though not exactly known number of such trivial tests. *See* discussion of those studies, *supra*. The design of Kam IV avoids this.

164. One detail of the procedure for generating test materials might have undermined this to an unknown degree. All simulations were generated by only 7 simulators, and since, on average, they had to do 25 simulations each, they would of necessity have become relatively experienced simulators by the end of the process. Whether they became better simulators is another question.

by insuring that all questioned signatures presented to participants were of this type. However, again wisely, the test was designed to present both authentic and inauthentic signatures, so it is in reality two subtests, one involving the ability to declare accurately that a naive forgery is a forgery, and the other the ability to declare accurately that a genuine signature is genuine.

Within certain limits,[165] the test design was quite well conceived. Test materials were generated as follows: 64 people provided 12 signatures each in their own names on 12 identical pieces of paper, according to a procedure well designed to obtain their normal everyday signature. These 64 sets of 12 were then each randomly divided in two, yielding 64 sets of six signatures to be used as "known authentic signatures" (like six randomly selected cancelled checks from a particular person), and 64 sets of 6 to form the basis for the "questioned signatures". It was then randomly determined how many, if any, authentic signatures would be removed from each set, to be replaced by simulations. Two sets were to have none removed (they remained all genuine), 7 sets one removed, 17 sets two removed, 21 sets 3 removed, 12 sets 4 removed, 4 sets 5 removed, and one set was to have every signature replaced by a simulation.

The simulations were then generated as follows. Seven people with no prior experience with signature simulation were hired to do all the simulations. Sets were randomly selected and assigned to a simulator, who had unlimited time to examine the six genuine signatures in the "known" set, and to generate one or at most two simulations by whatever method seemed best to the simulator. If two simulations were required, the set was then assigned to another simulator to generate one of the two simulations. If more than three simulations were required, two or three simulators were used, with no more than two signatures per simulator allowed in any given set. Care was taken to make sure the simulations were indistinguishable from the originals in every way except handwriting. A test consisted of handing a test subject a randomly selected set of "known signatures" and the associated set of "questioned signatures" and explaining that the known signatures were real normal signatures and each of the questioned signatures might be either genuine or a simulation. The subjects were provided with a microscope, a light source and a hand-held magnifier. The ordinal scale of certainty represented by ASTM standard E1658 was explained to them, and the subjects were then asked to determine whether each questioned signature was genuine by the standards of the top two degrees of certainty in that standard, a simulation by reference to the bottom two degrees, or to declare themselves "unable to determine."

165. Explicit detailed evaluations of the limits of the test design will await the publication of the study. However, the main ones are the ages of the providers of both the genuine signatures and the simulated signatures (19–30, with an apparent skew toward the lower end of that age range), the incentive scheme for the non-expert test subjects (which once again does not mimic the incentives for the professional document examiner test subjects), and the allowance of the simulators to select for themselves the best method of simulation from a variety of potential methods explained to them before they undertook their simulations (including backlighting, carbon paper, overhead projection and, presumably but not explicitly, freehand simulation). Signatories of a different age group might have displayed more or less intra-writer variation in their signatures. The problems of incentives have already been discussed in connection with Kam II and Kam III, *supra*, and the problems presented by the unknown variation in simulation method are addressed below. Also, there was once again an unnecessary ink-color variability.

The test was administered to three groups of professional document examiners, all of whom were either members of the American Society of Questioned Document Examiners or of the Southwestern Association of Forensic Document Examiners. In addition, an unknown number were certified by the ASQDE's associated certification board, the American Board of Forensic Document Examiners. The total number of document examiner test subjects was 69.

In addition, the test was administered to 50 non-experts connected in various ways to Drexel University, who were selected to resemble the educational profile of the document examiner subjects.

The resulting performance was summarized in Table 4.

Table 4. Results from the "Kam IV" Study

	Research Participant's Decision:					
	"Questioned Signature is Genuine"		"Questioned Signature May or May not be Genuine"		"Questioned Signature is Not Genuine"	
Ground Truth	FDEs	Non–FDEs	FDEs	Non–FDEs	FDEs	Non–FDEs
Questioned Signature: Genuine	85.89%	70.00%	7.05%	4.30%	7.05%	26.10%
Questioned Signature: Not Genuine	0.49%	6.47%	3.45%	1.40%	96.06%	92.00%

Exact data are not given in the draft, merely statistical summaries, but a likely typical numerical distribution can be extracted from what is given, and is useful to illustrate approximately what the actual data set might have looked like. What follows is thus a typical distribution approximately consistent with the summaries given, but the real distribution is likely to have varied from these numbers by a few either way, and so what follows is for illustrative purposes only.

The universe of possible tests was comprised of 64 potential tests, which contained 384 potential judgements (6 x 64), containing 53.64% genuine signatures (206 out of 384) and 46.36% simulated signatures (158 out of 384). While individual test sets were potentially subject by random draw to as many as three repetitions between the three document examiner test groups (the lay group was tested all at once, and therefore not subject to test set repetition), we can be reasonably assume that both in the case of the 69 document examiners total 414 judgments, or the lay persons total 300 judgments, the distribution between genuine signatures and simulations should track the distribution in the total test pool fairly closely. So for illustrative purposes it is fair to say assume there were likely about 224 times document examiners faced genuine signatures. Assuming this, of those genuine signatures, the document examiners accurately identified 192 as genuine. But they expressed no opinion as to 16 of those genuine signatures, and they affirmatively misidentified 16 of them as simulations. Similarly, using the same assumptions, the document examiners faced approximately 190 simulations, and they got 177 right, offered no opinion on 12, and made only one error.

In the case of non document examiners, they may fairly be taken to have faced about 162 genuine signatures. Of these, they got about 113 right. They expressed no opinion at a lower rate than document examiners (4.3% of the time, or about 7 cases), and they declared genuine signatures to be simulations 42 times (about 26%). Clearly, intra-writer variation creates a serious problem, making many genuine signatures appear questionable.[166] Though document examiners did better in sorting this out, they still had a fairly high rate of error.

Lay test subjects faced about 138 simulations. They correctly identified about 127 of these as simulations. Again, they responded that they admitted inability to determine genuineness less than the document examiners (in only 2 cases), and they wrongly declared more simulations to be genuine than did the document examiners (9 times, as opposed to the document examiners single error in a larger universe of decisions). However, it also appears fairly clear that most simulations were not very convincing to anyone, since both document examiners and ordinary folks identified more than 90% of them as simulations (96% for document examiners, 92% for ordinary people).

Another way to express the differences in performance between document examiners and non document examiners is to describe the error rate when you hear the conclusion "genuine" or the conclusion "simulation" (omitting any time an examiner is unable to reach a conclusion).[167]

For document examiners, the conclusion "genuine" was given 193 times, which was right 192 times and wrong once. The conclusion "simulation" was given 193 times, and which was right 177 times and wrong 16 times.

With lay persons, the conclusion "genuine" was given 122 times, which was right 113 times and wrong 9 times. The conclusion "simulation" was given 169 times, which was right 127 times and wrong 42 times.

Thus, document examiners were right about 99.5%[168] of the time when they said "genuine" and 92% of the time when they said "simulation." Lay persons were right 93% of the time when they said "genuine" and 75% of the time when they said "simulation."

What conclusions can be drawn from this study? Taken at face value, a reasonable interpretation of the results would be something like this:

- Naive simulators do not on the whole appear to produce very convincing simulations. The overwhelming majority were properly identified as such by both document examiners and lay persons, though document examiners had a marginal advantage 96%–92%.

- Neither document examiners nor lay persons actually declare naive simulations to be genuine very often. However, simulations were found to be genuine by lay persons 6.5% of the time, and by document examiners only a half a percent of the time. The fact that one document examiner declared one of these naive simulations genuine indicates that the expert error rate even for this easy task is not

166. This is consistent with the results of the 1988 FSF test discussed *supra.*

167. Note that these values may differ from those in the table because these do not include inconclusives in the calculations.

168. In the draft, this value is given as 99.2% (0.008 error), which would suggest that FDEs made fewer than 135 declarations of genuiness. This seems unlikely, given the number of tests administered.

vanishingly small, but it is small, both absolutely and compared to the lay group, even though the lay group did not perform poorly itself.

• Intra-writer, or "natural," variation among genuine signatures written by a single person poses serious dangers when trying to determine whether a signature is genuine or simulated. Thus, 8% of what document examiners declared to be simulations were in fact genuine signatures, and 25% of what lay persons similarly declared to be simulations were genuine. While the document examiners were better than the lay persons in this regard, the document examiner error rate on this supposedly easy task is substantial, and much higher that the document examiner literature would lead one to believe.[169] (This conclusion is also consistent with the results of the1988 FSF study, wherein document examiners declared a genuine signature of Joanna Neuman to be not genuine 18.5% of the time (5 of 27 responses).[170])

• Document examiners are significantly better at avoiding being fooled by genuine signature variation than lay persons, and significantly better at most authentication subtasks than are lay persons under these test conditions. However, the advantage may partly be the result of a phenomenon which has by now been repeatedly observed in testing document examiners against ordinary people. Under test conditions, ordinary people seem generally less likely to choose indecision options than document examiners.[171]

However, before generalizing these results to the real world, caveats are in order.

First, none of the Kam tests have yet resolved the incentive problem. All reward schemes for lay subjects used so far would seem to bias lay subjects toward affirmative declarations and away from inconclusives. Both Kam III and internal variations in the reward schemes used in Kam IV have led Kam to conclude that variations in reward schemes do not significantly affect lay test-taker performance. However, Kam III itself contains internal evidence of effect from incentive scheme variation, as we have seen above.[172] Beyond that, it seems virtually certain that *some* reward schemes could change the way lay subjects responded under various levels of uncertainty. None of the schemes used by Kam so far have imposed sufficiently high penalties on affirmative error[173] to mirror document examiner motivation in tests which may affect the continued existence of their profession. However, this caveat is perhaps rendered less serious by the notion that the lay test subjects need not be as motivated to avoid error as the document examiners, merely as motivated to

169. *See, e.g.,* statements of Ron Furgerson, FBI Document Section Chief, quoted *supra* § 2.3, at note 92, and Irby Todd, *Do Experts Frequently Disagree?*, 18 J. FORENSIC SCIENCE 455 (1973).

170. *See supra* § 2.3.3[1].

171. This was observed in the Galbraith et al. study, *supra* note 93, and in Kam II.

172. *See* § 2.3.6[3].

173. Especially error which could be identified as likely to be false positive error in criminal cases, a kind of error which all document examiners know would be the kiss of death if

revealed *in test data.* (As has been discussed above, it is not at all clear that they are equally motivated to avoid such error in real practice.) Interestingly, this asymmetrical motivation to avoid error of a certain type is reduced in the Kam IV test, since erroneous declarations of authenticity and inauthenticity can both lead to false convictions in criminal cases, depending on the case and its facts, though erroneous declarations of authenticity would more commonly have that result, since check forgery is such a common crime.

avoid error as jurors, and the deficiencies of the incentive schemes in the tests are much less clear in this regard.

What is more important, however, are the gross potential differences in document examiner performance between test conditions and real conditions of practice. Put simply, document examiner performance under test conditions is likely to be the best performance of which they are capable, and therefore error rates are likely to the lowest possible error rates under ideal conditions which do not apply to the real world. This is because of two linked variables: motivation and expectancy effects.

It is safe to say that, given the controversy of the last decade, there is not a document examiner in the country who does not understand that high error rates on tests, especially errors which would commonly be false positive errors in criminal cases, could lead to the widespread exclusion of document examiner testimony, and potentially, to the loss of their career. While this would be most clearly true in regard to non-blind proficiency tests, where individual performance might be discovered and compared to group norms, it is true even for tests like the Kam tests, which appear to have been designed to the extent possible to eliminate the potential for identifying and drawing conclusions about individual performance. Under conditions of normal practice, however, it is not at all clear that the sociology of the law enforcement agencies for which most of the document examiners work actually disvalues false positives to the same degree, or that inconclusive responses are as professionally acceptable in practice as on a test. The effect of different contexts with different intrinsic motivations is compounded by the highly suggestive manner in which cases are often presented to document examiners, complete with the theory of the investigators and the non-handwriting reasons for reaching one conclusion or another.[174] It would be startling if these circumstances did not affect performance and, consequently, error rates.

Nevertheless, these caveats are not really criticisms of the Kam IV test itself, and it is up to the legal system to fashion appropriate doctrines to take into account the difficulties in reasoning from the ideal conditions of tests to the predictably different and non-ideal conditions of practice. It may also be up to the legal system to require the conditions of practice to better mirror the ideal[175], but failure as yet to do so cannot be laid at Dr. Kam's doorstep. Post hoc, the results of Kam IV can give some comfort to Judge McKenna, by providing evidence that, under test conditions, document examiners significantly outperform ordinary people in determining signature genuineness (which was the basic task at hand in *Starzecpyzel*).[176] And the same results can frustrate the defense attorneys in the same case, since they would have dearly loved to have had the data on the 8% document examiner error rate even under ideal conditions on the exact task that the document examiner per-

174. *See* the court's comments in United States v. Rutherford set out *infra* note 180.

175. *See generally* D. Michael Risinger, Michael J. Saks, William C. Thompson & Robert Rosenthal, *The Daubert/Kumho Implications of Observer Effects in Forensic Science: Hidden Problems of Expectation and Suggestion*, 90 CAL. L. REV. (Forthcoming, 2002).

176. Or was it? Kam IV deals with the dangers of authentic signature variation with regard to a set of 19–30 year olds. What does this tell us about the dangers of similar variations with regard to infirm elderly persons in the early stages of Alzheimers, which was in fact the issue in *Starzecpyzel*. This simply and clearly illustrates the problems of both over and under-specificity which must be dealt with carefully when formulating the "task at hand."

formed in that case. And the results can give no comfort at all to the judges in all the other intervening cases where document examiner testimony was admitted on a different and more difficult "task at hand" (therefore, presumably at least, subject to much higher error rates), for which there still are no data, particularly attribution of authorship from a signature or other similarly limited sample. Kam IV shows the way. Ten or twenty further similarly designed tests devoted to different tasks will begin finally to map the contours of document examiner skill, and show other clinical forensic disciplines what is needed.

§ 3–2.3.7 Conclusions

In summary, what should we make of the available empirical data concerning handwriting identification expertise? First, any affirmative use of the data to support any hypothesis must be heavily qualified because of the small number of studies that have been conducted and their methodological problems. Even with this in mind, it seems fair to say that such a skill probably exists in some people for some tasks, but probably involves a large amount of inherent talent, and that while training and practice of "the true method" of atomized analysis may lead some people to become more dependable at some tasks, such credentials and experience alone do not necessarily establish the existence of a dependable skill.

Beyond this, if anything appears to be supported by the data, it is that there are many context-defined subtasks involved in handwriting identification, some easy, some very hard. Such skill as exists seems to be undependable even in many of those who have it, when it comes to many hard sub-tasks. Not even the most generous reading of currently available data could support a claim that we know how to define all of those subtasks. In addition, as a practical expertise, handwriting identification differs from many areas (such as Judge McKenna's harbor piloting) in that independent confirmation of the accuracy of one's results does not dependably emerge from everyday practice.

Finally, there is reason to believe that, like eyewitness identification, handwriting identification is strongly influenced by context cuing, that is, by the presentation of extraneous information to the examiner indicating the answer desired and non-handwriting reasons for its being the correct conclusion. Such presentations appear to be the norm in the submission of actual cases to document examiners, as even the materials of the FSF studies reveal.[177] Here the founding fathers of the area were quite sensible, for Hagan, Ames, and Osborn all took strong positions that it was the professional duty of the document examiner to insist that such information not be presented and to take steps to set up modes of consultation to insure against such contamination.[178]

---

177. *See* the discussion of the presentation of extraneous context information by the designers of the FSF studies, and the use of such information by test takers, at *supra* note 125 and accompanying text.

178. [T]he examiner must depend wholly upon what is seen, leaving out of consideration all suggestions or hints from interested parties; and if possible it best subserves the conditions of fair examination that the expert should not know the interest which the party employing him to make the investigation has in the result. Where the expert has no knowledge of the moral evidence or aspects of the case in which signatures are a matter of contest, there is nothing to mislead him, or to influence the forming of an opinion; and while knowing of the case as presented by one side of the contest might or might not shade the opinion formulated, yet it is better that the latter be based

§ 3–2.4 Future Directions

§ 3–2.4.1 Interdependence of Research and Court Decisions

In the first edition of this treatise, this section emphasized that information on the actual contours of document examiner reliability would be forthcoming only to the extent the legal system forced it to be derived and produced in court, and, in its absence, was willing to reject proffered testimony. On this front there has been progress and there is reason to hope for future progress. The response of judges who have actually examined the empirical record in that regard has been overwhelmingly one of troubled concern and skepticism. The Supreme Court's decision in *Kumho Tire v. Carmichael* has made it clear that, at least for the federal courts, the non-scientific nature of a claimed expertise is no excuse for failing to evaluate its reliability by appropriate standards, and that such evaluation must be directed to the reliability of the expertise in the specific "task at hand" at issue in the particular case. Even before the lessons of *Kumho Tire* had been fully internalized, trial judges (in federal court, at any rate) had begun to place substantial restrictions on the kind of testimony that could be given by document examiners in handwriting identification cases under the *Hines/ McVeigh* approach, allowing testimony concerning only similarities and differences, and forbidding conclusions. Unfortunately, this approach is flawed, in that it represents a Solomonic compromise not tied specifically to required *Kumho Tire* "task at hand" analysis and evaluation. *United States v. Fujii*, however, provides an example of proper *Kumho Tire* analysis, and shows the way for the future.

Note that, just because *Fujii* resulted in full exclusion of document examiner testimony in regard to the task of identifying whether a particular Japanese man trained in English as a second language in Japan was the author of a limited amount of handwriting on INS forms, this does not mean that all document examiner testimony should be excluded in regard to every "task at hand." Research can provide a warrant for believing that document examiners possess sufficient skills in regard to particular tasks to warrant admission, at least under test conditions. Kam IV shows for the first time how

entirely on what the writing itself shows, and nothing else.

HAGAN, *supra* note 12, at 85.

No expert should permit himself to be *retained* in the sense in which an attorney is retained, viz., for the purpose of making the most of and winning a case, right or wrong. . . .

When the services of an expert are sought, he should, so far as is possible, avoid knowing the circumstances or the relations of the party asking his opinion as to the case.

AMES, *supra* note 12, at 89.

It should be understood that the chief source of error in these cases is this intense partisan spirit and the spirit of advocacy surrounding the whole proceeding. The scientific examiner deliberately endeavors to keep outside the circle of these influences. Too often the investigation of what is in fact a genuine document, or, of what is in fact a crude forgery, is not taken up as a scientific investigation but every argu-ment and every influence is brought to bear in order to get favorable opinions and assistance from those who can assist in any way. . . .

There is of course certain legitimate information that the qualified examiner should have as to alleged conditions surrounding a document that is questioned but he does not need to know, and should not be told, why this or that should have been done or should not have been done by a testator or why, for other outside reasons, it is reasonable to assume that the alleged act was, or was not, performed. One who examines a document should have information as to the condition of an alleged writer or any alleged surrounding conditions that may have affected the result, or any facts that are a legitimate part of the technical problem which is submitted to him.

OSBORN 2D ED., *supra* note 1, at 2–3.

such specific "task at hand" research can be designed and administered. While one should be hesitant to base too much on a single unreplicated study, and while Kam IV involves only writers between the ages of 19 and 30, it would not be irrational for a judge to be influenced by the results in deciding whether to allow document examiner testimony on the question of signature authenticity, leaving the weight of the testimony to cross examination or counter-testimony concerning the document examiner error rates shown by the research on this, and perhaps other, tasks.

In June of 1998 the Justice Department's National Institute of Justice issued a formal solicitation for proposals for Forensic Document Examination Validation Studies to be funded by the Institute. To date, no results of such studies have been published.[179] However, one can hope that they will follow Kam IV's lead in testing document examiner performance against non-document examiner performance in regard to particular tasks of the kind that are commonly the subject of proffered testimony. After a couple of dozen such studies, we will finally begin to know what document examiner testimony ought to be admissible under *Kumho Tire*, and what ought to be excluded. Until the studies are produced, the proper response under the terms of Fed. R. Evid. 702 and *Kumho Tire* should be total exclusion. If this is true generally, it is even more certain in regard to those tasks clearly recognized as exceptionally problematical by the leading document examiner treatises themselves, such as attributing the authorship of forged signatures, or other very limited examples of writing.

Finally, even good research of the Kam IV variety cannot resolve one huge and protean problem undermining the reliability, not only of document examiner testimony, but potentially of all forensic science: context suggestivity in the way cases are presented to the expert for evaluation. This issue is both serious, and potentially curable, at least to a large degree, by changes in the practice of crime laboratories. Once again, however, crime labs are likely to do only what courts force them to do. And once again, there is at least some mild reason to believe that at least some courts are beginning to notice, as the criticism of the suggestive presentation by investigators to the document examiner in *United States v. Rutherford*[180] shows. Certainly the suggestive way a particular case is presented is an appropriate factor to be considered in any *Daubert/Kumho* reliability determination.[181] Whether courts will become more appropriately sensitive to this in the future remains to be seen. And when, if ever, any of this will percolate into the consciousness of courts in criminal cases to the same degree it already has in some civil case contexts[182] is another question that only time can answer.

179. Instead, the funding was apparently directed toward the development of computerized handwriting identification. *See infra* § 2.4.2.

180. 104 F.Supp.2d 1190, 1193 (D.Neb. 2000) ("FDE Rauscher admitted that he was not given samples of anonymous writings and then given the questioned documents for the purposes of determining which one of the anonymous writers wrote the questioned documents (Tr. 68:18–25). Instead, prior to Rauscher's analysis, the government identified the author of the exemplars (samples) and explained its theory that the writer of the exemplars and the checks was the author of the questioned documents (e.g., check and load out sheet)."

181. *See generally* Risinger, Saks, Thompson & Rosenthal, *supra* note 174.

182. *See generally* D. Michael Risinger, *Navigating Expert Reliability: Are Criminal Standards of Certainty Being Left on the Dock?*, 64 ALBANY L. REV. 99 (2000).

§ 3–2.4.2 Computer Authentication and Identification of Handwriting

It is appropriate to note in closing the current activities of the United State Department of Justice regarding handwriting identification expertise validation. The Federal Bureau of Investigation formed a Technical Working Group on Forensic Document Examination (TWGDOC) in May of 1997.[183] The first task undertaken by TWGDOC was to develop an agreed upon set of standard procedures for performing handwriting comparisons.[184] The National Institute of Justice (N.J.) noted in 1998 that "[s]uch procedures must be based ... on more than community-based agreement. Procedures must be tested statistically in order to demonstrate that following the stated procedures allows analysts to produce correct results with acceptable error rates. This has not yet been done". To date, (May, 2001) TWGDOC has yet to issue a report, at least publicly, or to publish such standards.

In July, 1996, N.I.J. held a "Workshop for Planning a Research Agenda for Questioned Document Examination (now called Forensic Document Examination)."[185] As a result of that workshop, and in recognition that since "the seminal ruling in *United States v. Starzecpyzel* (S.D.N.Y.1995) ... the judicial system has challenged FDEs, especially handwriting identification, to demonstrate its scientific validity and reliability as forensic evidence,"[186] and further recognizing that this had not yet been accomplished, the N.I.J. solicited proposals for research concerning "the statistical validation of the individuality of handwriting,"[187] and the "statistical validation of standard operating procedures for handwriting comparison."[188] To date, no results of such research have been published. However, in an apparent attempt to explore instrumented alternatives to human document examiners, the N.I.J. funded research by a group at the State University of New York at Buffalo. This group has made some progress toward a computerized system which may one day be able to determine if handwriting was authored by a particular person with a defined degree of random match probability, at least under some circumstances. However, the research is still in the developmental stage.[189] Available information concerning both the design of validation tests and their results is not sufficient to evaluate the current state of their research, beyond saying that no claim is made that the system has been developed to the point that it could be confidently used in many recurrent tasks, especially those involving potential disguise. In addition, it appears clear that in any situation where the program must consider a significant number of potential candidates for authorship of a handwriting sample, its current accuracy drops precipitously. Nevertheless, future developments may lead to a system having the proven capacity to replace human document examiners with instrumentally generated information of known high validity and low error rates under the conditions actually applying to particular identification tasks in a particular case.

183. National Institute of Justice, U.S. Department of Justice Solicitation: Forensic Document Examination Validation Studies 2 (June, 1998).

184. *Id.*

185. *Id.*

186. *Id.*

187. *Id.*

188. *Id.* at 3.

189. A visually impressive slide show summary of the research to date may be found at www.cedar.buffalo.edu.NIJ/pres/sld001.htm.

CHAPTER 4

FIREARMS AND TOOLMARK IDENTIFICATION

Table of Sections

A. LEGAL ISSUES

Westlaw Electronic Research

See Westlaw Electronic Research Guide preceding the Summary of Contents.

A. LEGAL ISSUES

§ 4–1.0 THE JUDICIAL RESPONSE TO FIREARMS AND TOOLMARK IDENTIFICATION EXPERT EVIDENCE

Reported judicial examinations of the scientific evidence on which toolmark and firearms examination (formerly, and incorrectly, termed "ballistics") expertise rests are remarkably few, and the resulting opinions tend to be both empty and opaque. While expert evidence on toolmarks and firearms identification is universally admissible,[1] this universal admissibility has come

§ 4–1.0

1. Cases can be found admitting testimony on a wide assortment of tools and tool markings. For some examples: Screwdrivers and

crowbars on doors, sashes, and safes: State v. Wade, 465 S.W.2d 498 (Mo.1971); State v. Brown, 291 S.W.2d 615 (Mo.1956); State v. Eickmeier, 187 Neb. 491, 191 N.W.2d 815

about with virtually no judicial evaluation of the validity of the underlying science or its application. One might have expected the situation to change following *Daubert*,[2] but so far that has not happened.

§ 4–1.1 Toolmark Identification

Apparently the first appellate decision to consider the admissibility of modern toolmark identification expertise was *State v. Fasick*,[3] a 1928 Washington State case which rejected the proffered testimony. In that case, a murder had been committed and the body covered with fir branches cut from nearby trees. The government offered Luke S. May, a pioneering forensic scientist who would become one of the founders of toolmark identification.[4] May had made sample cuttings of fir branches with the suspect's knife and examined the microscopic marks left by the blade, comparing them with the marks left in the branches found covering the body. He concluded that the branches had been cut with the same knife, thus placing the defendant at the crime scene. The trial court initially excluded, but then admitted, May's testimony. The Washington Supreme Court, however, found the logic behind the expert's opinion unconvincing. Wrote the Court: "You could not tell in a thousand years whether the two pieces were cut by the same knife."[5] On rehearing one year later the Court affirmed its initial rejection of toolmark identification expertise.

Eighteen months after deciding *Fasick* and only six months after re-affirming itself, the Washington Supreme Court was presented with remarkably similar evidence from the same expert. This time, in *State v. Clark*,[6] in the context of a rape case, fir boughs and saplings had been cut and used by the rapist to construct a blind from which to attack his victim. Again a knife, again cut fir branches, again Luke May the proffered expert witness. But this time the Court held that expert opinion about whether the defendant's knife cut the branches was evidence that was admissible: "The photomicrographs ... conclusively establish, we are convinced, as doubtless the jury were, that the cuts were made with the same blade."[7] The Washington Supreme Court made no effort to explain its abrupt reversal, and barely even acknowledged the contradictory opinion in *Fasick*, decided only a few months earlier.[8]

(Neb.1971); People v. Perroni, 14 Ill.2d 581, 153 N.E.2d 578 (Ill.1958). Knives on wood: State v. Clark, 156 Wash. 543, 287 P. 18 (Wash.1930). Car tools: Adcock v. State, 444 P.2d 242 (Okla.Crim.App.1968); State v. Smith, 156 Conn. 378, 242 A.2d 763 (Conn. 1968). Hammers: State v. Olsen, 212 Or. 191, 317 P.2d 938 (Or.1957). Bolt cutters used to gain entry or on the stolen material: Souza v. United States, 304 F.2d 274 (9th Cir.1962). Bullets: *see infra* § 1.2. *See generally*, ANDRE A. MOENSSENS, ET AL., SCIENTIFIC EVIDENCE IN CIVIL AND CRIMINAL CASES § 6.27 (1995).

2. Kumho Tire Co. v. Carmichael, 526 U.S. 137, 119 S.Ct. 1167, 143 L.Ed.2d 238 (1999) (hereafter, *Kumho Tire*).

3. 149 Wash. 92, 270 P. 123 (Wash.1928), *aff'd*, 149 Wash. 92, 274 P. 712 (Wash.1929).

4. The dust cover to his semi-autobiographical book on forensic science characterizes May

as "America's Sherlock Holmes." LUKE S. MAY, CRIME'S NEMESIS (1936).

5. *Id.* at 96.

6. 156 Wash. 543, 287 P. 18 (Wash.1930).

7. *Clark*, 156 Wash. 543, 287 P. 18, at 20.

8. Yet the *Clark* court was ebullient in its praise of this new specie of evidence:

Courts are no longer skeptical that by the aid of scientific appliances the identity of a person may be established by finger prints. There is no difference in principle in the utilization of the photomicrograph to determine that the same tool that made one impression is the same instrument that made another impression. The edge on one blade differs as greatly from the edge on another blade as the lines on one human hand differ from the lines on another. This is a progressive age. The scientific means afforded should be used to apprehend the criminal.

In an article written the same year *Clark* was decided, May discussed the case, describing what he had offered to the court. He asserted that he had "conclusively established" that the same knife was used. His inference of that identification was derived by probabilistic reasoning that is familiar[9] in the field of forensic identification:

> Invoking the law of probabilities, using the algebraic formula for determining combinations and permutations, with only one-third of the marks here shown as factors, there would be only "one" chance of there being another blade exactly like this if every one of the hundred million people in the United States had six hundred and fifty quadrillion knives each.[10]

Several years later, after praising the *Clark* Court for making an "outstanding progressive decision," a "significant step forward,"[11] May described the *Clark* opinion as "a precedent which has already been cited in criminal trials in many other states, thereby legally advancing science in its battle against crime." While it may be that *Clark* was called to the attention of some trial judges, the opinion did not, and surprisingly so, become the talisman for the admission of toolmark expert evidence as, say, *Jennings*[12] had become for fingerprints. *Clark* was cited in only two subsequent appellate opinions, and not for propositions that would have pleased Luke May.[13] Somehow *Clark* went from standing for the "conclusive" power of toolmark identification evidence in 1930 to standing for the admissibility of "a less than exact" process in 1985.

There is nothing in the *Clark* opinion that could help a judge in a subsequent case to understand why toolmark evidence was valid and admissible, if indeed it was. The case merely offered the conclusory and unexplained enthusiasm of a Court that only months before had rendered its equal and opposite opinion on the very same question.

After so interesting a start in the case law, the subject of the validity of toolmark identification evidence has had surprisingly little appellate exposure in the decades since. From *Fasick* in 1929 to *Ramirez v. State*[14] in 1989, no other cases excluding toolmark identification evidence are to be found. For 25 years following *Clark,* there are no appellate decisions scrutinizing any aspect of toolmark identification.

Toolmark identification opinions resurfaced in 1955 with *People v.*

Nor do the briefs to the Court give any clues as to what changed from *Fasick* to *Clark*.

9. Michael J. Saks & Jonathan J. Koehler, *What DNA "Fingerprinting" Can Teach the Law About the Rest of Forensic Science,* 13 Cardozo L. Rev. 361 (1991).

10. Luke S. May, *The Identification of Knives, Tools, and Instruments a Positive Science,* 1 Am. J. Police Sci. 246 (1930). This means one chance in 6.5 x 1025 (that is, 6.5 septillion; 6.5 followed by 24 zeroes). May does not explain how he made this calculation, but note that this is far more diagnostic than genetic fingerprinting claims to be.

11. May, *supra* note 4, at 47. Unfortunately, he misses the chance to teach us something

about the difference between the contrast in the court's thinking from *Clark* to *Fasick* because he does not mention *Fasick* at all.

12. People v. Jennings, 252 Ill. 534, 96 N.E. 1077 (Ill.1911).

13. Hansel v. Ford Motor Co., 3 Wash.App. 151, 473 P.2d 219 (Wash.Ct.App.1970) (a case not involving toolmarks at all); State v. Bernson, 40 Wash.App. 729, 700 P.2d 758 (Wash.Ct. App.1985) (for the proposition that "[a]n expert's use of 'could have' or 'possibly' has been allowed in other cases where a less than exact scientific process is involved.").

14. Ramirez v. State, 542 So.2d 352 (Fla. 1989).

Wilkes.[15] In *Wilkes*, the state's expert testified that although ordinarily no more than 25% of the striations correspond when a tool other than the one used in the crime is compared, in this instance 80% of the striations corresponded. He concluded, therefore, that the defendant's drift punch was the one used to help open a safe. In upholding the admission of this testimony, the court cited nothing other than a distant analogy to another case of a burgled safe in which a heel print left on an invoice at the crime scene corresponded to a shoe owned by the defendant.

A year later, in *State v. Brown*,[16] the Missouri Supreme Court upheld the admissibility of toolmark expert testimony based on no citations to legal or scientific authority. Instead, the court rested on being impressed by the expert witness's prior employment by the F.B.I. as an analytical chemist and his hobby of carpentry. The defendant's argument that the testimony was admitted without anything that resembled scientific support was to no avail. The court relied on the notion that trial judges have discretion to admit or exclude expert testimony on myriad subjects, and the jury bears the ultimate responsibility to weigh all the evidence.[17] With so deferential a standard, there really was nothing for the court above to decide.[18]

The next case reviewing the admissibility of toolmark identification appears twenty years later–an appeal from a burglary conviction in North Carolina. This court in this case reasoned: "It seems abundantly clear that ... there can be expert testimony upon practically any facet of human knowledge and experience."[19] It appears that this court mistook the phrase "can be" for "is." Whether an adequate expertise existed yet, *vel non*, was the issue presented. The court simply begged the question, abdicating any judicial responsibility to assure that evidence submitted to the jury has some minimum level of validity. The court merely assumed an expertise into existence.

The first federal court to opine on the question of toolmark admissibility did so in 1978 in *Fletcher v. Lane*.[20] Here, the defendant challenged a toolmark expert's positive identification—of a screwdriver found in the defendant's home as being the one that made prymarks on the victim's door, to the exclusion of all other screwdrivers in the world—as an assertion that could

15. People v. Wilkes, 280 P.2d 88 (Cal.Ct. App.1955).

16. 291 S.W.2d 615 (Mo.1956).

17. On the subject of appellate review, *see* 1 Modern Scientific Evidence § 1–3.6. The U.S. Supreme Court held in General Electric Co. v. Joiner, 522 U.S. 136, 118 S.Ct. 512, 139 L.Ed.2d 508 (1997) that appellate review under *Daubert* is deferential–a dubious legal principle for dealing with scientific principles, which are trans-case. But even *Joiner* does not authorize deference to opinions devoid of reasons, or devoid of reasons having any substance. Moreover, it is doubtful that the actual rule in any American jurisdiction in the past century was that trial judges had the discretion, on a case by case basis, to admit or exclude what they please, without coherent explanation and reviewable only on a test of clear error. For one pre-*Daubert* analysis of the role of law and appellate courts in such matters, *see* Dunagin v. City of Oxford, 718 F.2d 738 (5th Cir.1983).

What these cases may really reflect is the daunting challenge of having to think rationally about those myriad subjects, develop workable legal tests, and apply them consistently. It is easier for the appellate courts to pass the problem to the trial courts and the trial courts to pass the problem to the jury. At least by their terms, *Daubert* and *Kumho Tire* (hereafter, *Kumho Tire*) would seem to have brought an end to such evasions of evaluation, at least by trial judges.

18. The same rationale can be found in State v. Churchill, 231 Kan. 408, 646 P.2d 1049 (Kan.1982).

19. State v. Raines, 29 N.C.App. 303, 224 S.E.2d 232, 234 (N.C.Ct.App.1976) (quoting Stansbury's N.C. Evidence, Subject Matter of Expert Testimony, § 134 at 438).

20. 446 F.Supp. 729 (S.D.Ill.1978).

not be made, that was unsupportable, or at least unsupported, on scientific grounds, and therefore should not have been admitted.[21] The district court converted this challenge from one of scientific validity to one of credibility: "Petitioner's ... contention is essentially an attack on the credibility of the expert testimony. The credibility of a witness is a matter for jury determination...."[22] Again, this seems to be the kind of open door policy that *Daubert* and its progeny have sought to close, or at least to place a gatekeeper in front of.

An example of the error into which courts may fall by so casually scrutinizing expert testimony is provided by *Commonwealth v. Graves.*[23] An expert testified that scratch marks on the neck of a victim of strangulation matched the defendant's fingernail. The defendant challenged this type of identification as lacking sufficient scientific recognition to meet the *Frye* admissibility standard.[24] The Pennsylvania court turned away the challenge, concluding:

> [T]he methods and techniques used ... all were consistent with standards of general scientific acceptance in the field of tool-marks, of which, according to the witnesses, testimony as to finger nail wounds is a part.[25]

But consider this comment on the case:

> The Pennsylvania reviewing court, however, completely failed to recognize that the class characteristics of the fingernail and the scratch marks, although similar, lacked the necessary individual markings to tie the accused's fingernail to the scratch marks on the victim to the exclusion of all others.[26]

In other words, there was no consideration of the possibility by the court, and apparently not be the expert either, that the marks found were characteristic of a large class of fingernails and not of one of the defendant's nails uniquely.

In rare instances a court will reject the opinion of toolmark experts on the ground that a scientific predicate was not established. In *Ramirez v. State*[27] the government sought to prove that the defendant's knife was the murder weapon "to the exclusion of all other" knives in the world by showing that microscopic striations made by the suspect's knife matched microscopic striations on the victim's cartilage. Though in most cases the forensic science expert witness's expert's mere assertion that something can be done reliably is enough for a court, in this case it was not. Neither was the fact that a Kansas court had admitted such testimony,[28] nor an article by the expert

21. *Cf.*, May, *supra* note 10 and accompanying quotation.

22. *Id.* at 731. The same rationale can be found in Potter v. State, 416 So.2d 773 (Ala. Crim.App.1982).

23. 310 Pa.Super. 184, 456 A.2d 561 (1983).

24. Frye v. United States, 293 F. 1013 (App.D.C.1923).

25. *Graves,* 456 A.2d at 566.

26. MOENSSENS, ET AL., *supra* note 1, at 379–380. *See also* James Starrs, *Procedure in Identifying Fingernail Imprint in Human Skin*

Survives Appellate Review, 6 AM. J. FOR. MED. & PATH. 171 (1985).

27. 542 So.2d 352 (1989). Pursuant to reversal and remand, Ramirez was again tried and convicted; again the conviction was reversed and remanded; and the litigation continues as of this writing.

28. State v. Churchill, 231 Kan. 408, 646 P.2d 1049 (Kan.1982). "We reject the state's argument that, since the Supreme Court of Kansas in *Churchill* admitted testimony that a particular knife caused the wound, without a predicate of scientific reliability, we should do likewise." *Ramirez,* 542 So. 2d at 355.

concerning the technique. The Florida Supreme Court held that this testimony was erroneously admitted because "no scientific predicate was established from independent evidence to show that a specific knife can be identified from the marks made on cartilage."[29] Cases requiring an adequate scientific basis to be established before allowing opinions based on that scientific predicate to go to the jury have been rare in the courts' review of toolmark expert evidence.[30]

§ 4–1.2   Firearms Examination

Expert testimony identifying a particular weapon as the one source of both a questioned (crime scene) bullet and known bullets (test firings) is admissible in every American jurisdiction. At least 37 jurisdictions have approved it by appellate opinion.[31] In all others, presumably, admission is a consequence of no challenge having being raised, thereby giving the courts no occasion to consider the admissibility of such evidence. But in no case has careful judicial or legislative scrutiny of the premises and performance of firearms experts occurred.

The earliest cases[32] admitting firearms identification testimony occurred more than 30 years before the admission of fingerprint expert evidence.[33] But these early cases typically permitted non-experts to testify to such matters as the identification of a gunshot as having emanated from a particular type or caliber of firearm based on its sound, or that a certain wound was caused by a firearm of a particular caliber, or that bullets matched based on their weight.

The first case admitting what we may call modern firearms identification evidence–microscopic comparison of striations left on bullets by the characteristics of the barrel of a firearm–was *Commonwealth v. Best*,[34] an opinion written by Justice Oliver Wendell Holmes for the Massachusetts Supreme Judicial Court. The comparisons were made by manually pushing a bullet

29. *Ramirez,* 542 So. 2d at 354.

30. The *Kumho Tire,* task-at-hand, scientific question here is whether this medium (cartilage) is capable of receiving and holding without distortion marks of sufficient detail to permit a reliable toolmark analysis. Perhaps it can, perhaps it cannot. And what are risks of error (false inculpatory opinions or false exculpatory opinions?) associated with the imperfections of the medium. Those are among the concerns a *Daubert/Kumho* court must decide. (Interestingly, Florida was and remains a *Frye* jurisdiction, yet it insisted on a scientific basis as a precondition to admission.) Obviously, the materials with which toolmark experts usually work, metal and wood, are less elastic than cartilage, which is probably less elastic than the materials with which forensic dentists usually work, though forensic dentists are looking at far less microscopic detail than toolmark examiners are.

Though the court does not address the issue, there also is the problem of an opinion that a knife is the murder weapon "to the exclusion of all others" in the world. Though this is a common sort of conclusion among toolmark and other forensic examiners, it does not follow from the probabilistic logic underlying this

form of expertise–see discussion, *supra,* of Luke May and the origins of toolmark analysis, and the discussion, *infra,* of the science, and especially the discussion of objective criteria and the study of known non-matching comparisons, *infra* § 2.4–but is in actuality a "leap of faith" from the improbable and unlikely to the absolute and certain. *See also* the related discussions of all other forensic identification sciences in their chapters in this treatise.

31. *See* E. LeFevre Annotation, *Expert Evidence to Identify Gun from which a Bullet or Cartridge was Fired,* 26 A.L.R.2d 892 (1952); Jay M. Zitter, Annotation, *Admissibility of Testimony that Bullet Could or Might Have Come from a Particular Gun,* 31 A.L.R.4th 486 (1984).

32. *E.g.,* Wynne v. State, 56 Ga. 113 (1876); Dean v. Commonwealth, 73 Va. 912 (1879); Moughon v. State, 57 Ga. 102 (1876); State v. Smith, 49 Conn. 376 (1881); People v. Mitchell, 94 Cal. 550, 29 P. 1106 (Cal.1892); State v. Hendel, 4 Idaho 88, 35 P. 836 (Idaho 1894).

33. People v. Jennings, 252 Ill. 534, 96 N.E. 1077 (Ill.1911).

34. 180 Mass. 492, 62 N.E. 748 (1902).

through the suspect firearm rather than firing it. The defense argued that this comparison was invalid because of changes in the firearm from the time it was allegedly used in a murder and the testing, and the method of testing.[35] Justice Holmes saw no problem:

> We see no other way in which the jury could have learned so intelligently how that gun barrel would have marked a lead bullet fired through it, a question of much importance to the case. Not only was it the best evidence attainable but the sources of error suggested were trifling. The photographs avowedly were arranged to bring out the likeness in the marking of the different bullets and were objected to on this further ground. But the jury could correct them by inspection of the originals, if there were other aspects more favorable to the defense.[36]

By the 1920s, Calvin Goddard had emerged as the "father" of modern forensic firearms identification, and was certainly the most prominent thinker, writer, and expert witness on the subject. Courts which had earlier rejected such expert evidence reversed themselves, at least in part under Goddard's influence. For example, in 1923 the Illinois Supreme Court rejected firearms identification expertise, concluding that identification of a bullet as having been fired by a particular gun was impossible and "preposterous."[37] But in 1930, in *People v. Fisher*[38] the same court reached the opposite conclusion. The principal difference between the two opinions is a lengthy and detailed account of Dr. Goddard's credentials and experience in the latter opinion, as if to say that an expertise, a science, exists in the person of an expert. But, of course, the case became precedent for the technique, not only for the testimony of Calvin Goddard.

The Court of Appeals for the District of Columbia Circuit decided its landmark firearms identification case, *Laney v. United States*,[39] on the same day that it decided the famous case of *Frye v. United States*,[40] in an opinion written by the same Judge Van Orsdel who wrote the *Frye* opinion. But, while *Frye* announced the standard that novel scientific techniques were admissible only when the theory on which they were based had achieved general acceptance in the relevant scientific community, on that same day firearms expertise was tested by an entirely different standard, and perhaps by no standard at all:

> ... the testimony given by the expert witnesses, tending to establish that the bullet, extracted from the head of the deceased, was shot from the pistol found in the defendant's possession, was competent, and the examination in this particular was conducted without prejudicial error....[41]

---

35. More specifically, the defense argued, without rebuttal: (1) greatly divergent pressures between firing a bullet and pushing it, (2) a period of time passed from the date of the murder until the date of testing that allowed rust to form inside the barrel, and (3) shots had been fired through the weapon after the date it allegedly was used in the murder, thereby changing its characteristics.

36. 180 Mass. at 495–96.

37. People v. Berkman, 307 Ill. 492, 139 N.E. 91 (Ill.1923).

38. 340 Ill. 216, 172 N.E. 743 (1930).

39. 294 F. 412 (App.D.C.1923).

40. 293 F. 1013 (App.D.C.1923).

41. *Laney,* 294 F. at 416.

By the late 1920s and early 1930s the trend toward judicial acceptance of firearms identification was clear.[42]

More modern cases have met challenges to firearms identification expertise by referring to the earlier precedents—which themselves make no inquiry of either the *Frye* or the *Daubert* type, but generally concluded merely that relevance is the test of admissibility, and other concerns go only to the weight the jury should accord the testimony.[43]

§ 4–1.3 Post-*Daubert* Decisions

Since the decision of the United States Supreme Court in *Daubert*, only two federal cases have been reported that addressed any aspect of firearms identification. Unfortunately, the issue in both of them is more than a bit tangential to the core scientific claims of firearms identification, yet they illuminate interesting aspects of what courts will or will not require of expert witnesses, at least forensic science expert witnesses.

In *United States v. Corey*,[44] the defendant had been convicted of being a felon in possession of a firearm. The government's expert testified to his opinion that the gun found in the defendant's possession was manufactured by Smith and Wesson in Massachusetts and thus necessarily traveled in interstate commerce. The defendant was arrested in Maine. However, Smith and Wesson also had a manufacturing plant in Maine. The examination of the expert made relatively clear that he had relied heavily on a conversation he had with the manufacturer's historian.[45] In essence the defendant was arguing that the government was trying to avoid the requirements of the business records exception and was introducing hearsay through the expert testimony rules instead.[46] The court rejected this argument, finding that the expert had relied on his general experience and other factors beyond the discussion with the historian.[47] But neither the appellate court nor the trial court seemed able to explain precisely what those bases were: "Agent (sic) Cooney testified that he based the opinion, at least in part, on his own knowledge and expertise as a firearms specialist, both with the ATF and in the private sector.... Further, Cooney confirmed that he had handled '[h]undreds of thousands of firearms,' and had 'examined that type of shotgun ... before.' Thus, as the district court aptly noted, Firearms Enforcement Officer Cooney himself had 'acquired this information over the years.' "[48] The failure of the court to provide a straightforward reason how the expert knew the weapon was manufactured in the Massachusetts plant rather than in the Maine plant suggests that the expert had no reason either, but was of the "it is so because I say it is so" school of expertise. A dissenting judge pointed out that the weapon's serial number could have been checked against the manufacturer's database to determine where it was produced, and that the witness should have been required to

---

42. Two noteworthy opinions come from Kentucky: Jack v. Commonwealth, 222 Ky. 546, 1 S.W.2d 961 (Ky.1928); Evans v. Commonwealth, 230 Ky. 411, 19 S.W.2d 1091 (Ky. 1929). MOENSSENS ET AL. characterize *Jack* as the start of "a truly objective appraisal by the appellate courts" and *Evans* as the "first exhaustive opinion treating firearms identification as a science." MOENSSENS ET AL., *supra* note 1, § 6.18.

43. *E.g.*, State v. Schreuder, 712 P.2d 264 (Utah, 1985); State v. Courtney, 25 Ohio App.3d 12, 495 N.E.2d 472 (Ohio Ct.App.1985).

44. 207 F.3d 84 (1st Cir.2000).

45. *Id.* at 86.

46. *Id.* at 86–87.

47. *Id.* at 89.

48. *Id.* at 90.

base his opinion on that kind of information, of distinctive markings on the weapon. The majority rejected this suggestion, arguing that "such a regimen would reinvent the 'best evidence' requirement which Evidence Rule 703 was designed to relax."[49]

Ramirez v. Artuz,[50] stands as something of a counterpoint to *Corey*. Ramirez was a habeas corpus petitioner who had been convicted of armed robbery. Part of the case against him was the testimony of a witness who recognized the kind of nine-millimeter weapon used by one of the robbers. Such a weapon was later found in the petitioner's apartment. At trial the defendant had proffered expert testimony that the gun in question "looked similar to tens of thousands of guns in the New York metropolitan area and that there was nothing particularly distinctive about a square nose on a nine-millimeter firearm." This gets closer to the main problem of firearms identification, which is the extent to which a weapon can be pinpointed to being a particular one. The smaller the number of such weapons, as identified by the witness, the more likely it was the one owned by Ramirez. The larger the class of weapons that would look like what the witness saw, the less probable that it was the one owned by Ramirez. The trial court excluded the defense expert, and with it the habeas petition. The court relied on the deferential standard of *Joiner* and applied New York's standard for expert evidence admissibility: expert testimony must "help to clarify an issue calling for professional or technical knowledge, possessed by the expert and beyond the ken of the typical juror."[51] Why that standard did not lead to admission in the original case is not clear.

The issues in *Sexton v. State*[52] come much closer to the mark. The defendant was convicted of three counts of aggravated assault with a deadly weapon. Police recovered a total of sixteen shell casings at the scene of the crime, including four nine millimeter shell casings. A search of Sexton's home found twenty-six live nine millimeter cartridges. All of the shell casings were given to Ronald Crumley, a firearm and toolmark examiner. Crumley concluded that all four of the spent shell casings had been fired from the same gun, and that two of the spent shell casings had been cycled through the same magazine as twelve of the live cartridges and the other two spent shell casings had been cycled through the same magazine as twelve of the other live cartridges.

Crumley based these findings on the general theory of toolmark examination.[53] "According to Crumley, if the lips leave a mark on the cartridge, that mark is individual to the magazine, like a fingerprint. Thus, if sufficient magazine marks are left on a shell casing and a live cartridge, a firearm and toolmark examiner can determine, by looking at the two objects under a comparison microscope, whether they were cycled through the same magazine."[54] After a hearing on a motion to bar the expert testimony, the trial court allowed Crumley to testify.

49. *Id.* at 91.
50. 1999 WL 754354 (E.D.N.Y.1999).
51. *Id.* at *5.
52. 12 S.W.3d 517 (Tex.Ct.App.1999).
53. Discussed *supra* as well as in the scientific evidence section of this chapter, *infra* § 2.1.1.
54. *Sexton*, 12 S.W.3d at 519.

The Court of Appeals affirmed the trial court's admission, and based its conclusion that the witness's opinion rested on sufficiently solid ground principally on the citation by Crumley of "three treatises in which magazine marks are mentioned as a way of matching cartridges or shell casings."[55] "[W]hile the treatises may make only sparse mention of magazine marks, it is clear that the literature supports the theory that a magazine can leave identifiable marks on cartridges and shell casings that can be matched to that magazine."[56]

That the "sparse mention" of matching shells to magazines is adequate under a *Daubert*-type test is highly doubtful. Under a proper *Kumho Tire* task-at-hand analysis, the court is correct to focus on magazine marks–and the question of whether that particular task can be performed sufficiently well for admission, rather than on global notions of firearms and toolmark theory and practice. But having framed the right question, the court was satisfied with the most minimal of answers.[57]

As to error rates, Crumley assured the court that, although this was the first time he had attempted to match magazine markings in a case, "there is no possibility of error in matching one set of magazine marks to another. Crumley claims the technique is one-hundred percent reliable and never wrong."[58] The court was untroubled by these extreme and unsupported (by anything but the witness's *ipse dixit*) statements: "[W]hile Crumley's assertion does not conclusively establish the overall reliability of the technique for matching magazine marks [citation omitted], it provides at least some evidence of the possible rate of error, or lack thereof, in the process [citation omitted]."[59]

55. *Id.* at 520.

56. *Id.*

57. According to two firearms and toolmark examiners to whom one of the editors showed relevant portions of the *Sexton* court's opinion, both with far more experience than Crumley, Crumley's statements about linking cartridge casings to a magazine through which they have been cycled would be tenable if and only if the following assumptions are met: First, that Crumley evaluated the magazine in question and determined that the bearing surfaces of the magazine lips were individualistic and had no subclass characteristic influence; in other words, that he determined the manner in which they were manufactured to eliminate the possibility that other magazines produced by the same process would produce the same marks. Second, that if there were subclass influences, Crumley evaluated the manner in which a cartridge rides over the bearing surfaces so that he might be able to distinguish subclass from individualistic characteristics and not mistake one for the other. Third, that Crumley took into account the fact that magazine lip marks generally provide limited information, with striae being unusually small and limited in quantity. Under these conditions, it has happened that some examiners have placed more weight on a small number of matching striae than was warranted. And, fourth, given the above, that Crumley made conservative adjustments to his subjective criteria for identification, in light of the numerical criteria for identification based on matching agreement in known-non-matching toolmarks (see discussion of objective criteria at *infra* § 2.4), so as to reduce the probability of a coincidental match, that is, the probability of declaring a non-matching magazine toolmark to be a match.

58. *Sexton v. State*, 12 S.W.3d 517 (Tex. App.1999).

59. *Id.*, at 521. Though such extreme and absolute pronouncements are common among forensic scientists, they are virtually never uttered or believed by normal scientists who regularly rely on actual data–perhaps because the latter are tempered and sobered by actual data. In firearms and toolmark analysis, errors do occur. *See infra* § 2.3.2. And some kinds of examinations are more error-prone than others. Years of proficiency testing indicated a 12% error rate for firearms and 26% for toolmarks. Joseph L. Peterson & P. N. Markham, *Crime Laboratory Proficiency Testing Results, 1978–1991, II: Resolving Questions of Common Origin*, 40 J. Forensic Sci. 1009 (1995). If inconclusives are omitted from the calculations, the error rates become 1.4% for firearms and 4% for toolmarks. Richard A. Grzybowski & John E. Murdock, *Firearm and Toolmark Identification—Meeting the Daubert Challenge*, 30 ASS'N FIREARM & TOOLMARK EXAMINERS J. 3, 9

The one post-*Daubert* case that raises the core issue at the heart of a *Daubert* challenge to traditional firearms identification, *People v. Hawkins*,[60] was brought, ironically, in a *Frye* jurisdiction, where attacks based on the weaknesses of the underlying science do not carry the opponent of admission as far as they might. In response to the challenge to the scientific basis of firearms identification evidence, the firearms experts did not try to prove the validity of their field by reference to its purported scientific basis so much as they suggested they had gained a special talent for associating bullets with the guns that fired them through repeated observation of guns and bullets. Prosecution experts "conceded that ballistics identification is not an exact science. Rather, ballistics experts develop proficiency by microscopically observing a large number of bullets known to have been fired from the same gun, and from different guns, so that they acquire knowledge of when the similarities of the bullets' striations are sufficient to establish that the bullets were discharged from the same firearm."[61] Obviously there are several empirical claims in those statements which are testable and can be found to be true or not true, but for now they sufficed. In rebuttal the defense introduced two articles by Alfred Biasotti that call for the reform of firearm identifications by developing a statistical database. One expert "conceded that ballistics identification was to some extent more of a skill than a science, an intuition informed by extensive experience."[62] The *Hawkins* court upheld the admissibility of the firearms expert evidence under *Frye*. In a *Daubert* jurisdiction, however, and especially in the wake of *Kumho Tire*, firearms experts ought to be prepared for a different experience. Under *Kumho Tire*, claiming that they are engaged in more of an art than science, and that there is internal consensus about their artfulness, would not be enough.

§ 4–1.4 Conclusion

The case law on the admissibility of toolmark identification and firearms identification expert evidence is typified by decisions admitting such testimony with little, and usually no, reference to legal authority beyond broad "discretion" and an adroit sidestepping of any judicial duty to assure that experts' claims are valid. Appellate courts defer to trial courts, and trial courts defer to juries. Later appellate courts simply defer to earlier appellate courts.

One might have expected the scientific basis of the claims of toolmark and firearms experts, measured by whatever test the courts of a given jurisdiction had devised, to be the central issue in reviewing a challenge to their admissibility. To date, the opinions lack such scrutiny. In the long run, the provisions of *Daubert* seem likely to alter that century-long pattern, and create a new and long overdue body of case law on the subject.

At a practical level, if *Daubert* can do nothing else in the criminal context, it might eventually encourage (or compel) experts to learn the data surround-

---

(1998). What examiner Crumley was dealing with (magazine marks) is a toolmark, not a rifling mark (the marks imparted by gun barrels onto bullets fired through them). Crumley's inexperience with the particular task-at-hand increases the chances that he could make an error, in particular mistaking subclass, or even class, characteristics for individualizing characteristics.

60. 10 Cal.4th 920, 42 Cal.Rptr.2d 636, 897 P.2d 574 (Cal.1995).

61. *Id.* at 588.

62. *Id.*

ing the capabilities and limitations of their fields and to share those data candidly with courts.

B. SCIENTIFIC ISSUES

by
Alfred Biasotti* & John Murdock**

§ 4–2.0 THE SCIENTIFIC BASIS OF FIREARMS AND TOOL-MARK IDENTIFICATION

§ 4–2.1 Introductory Discussion of the Science

Forensic firearms examiners are concerned with such varied tasks as (1) serial number restoration, (2) examination of suspected gunshot residues, (3) function testing of firearms, (4) determination of muzzle to target distance, (5) determining what kind of firearm was responsible for firing recovered bullets or cartridge cases, (6) aiding in the reconstruction of crime scenes through the examination and evaluation of firearms evidence, (7) intercomparison of both unknown evidence and test fired bullets, cartridge cases, and shotshell components with one another, and (8) comparing toolmarks[1] on unfired cartridges and shotshells which can occur when unfired ammunition has been worked through the action of a firearm, as well as on fired bullets, cartridge cases, and shotshell components with test toolmarks produced deliberately on similar items in an attempt to identify whether a particular firearm made toolmarks on evidence items, to the exclusion of all other firearms.

Task number eight overlaps into the area of forensic toolmark examination. Members of this related profession are concerned mainly with attempting to determine whether submitted tools[2] such as screwdrivers, hammers, pliers, drill bits, punches, etc., were used to make toolmarks on portions of a crime scene or on materials found at or related to a crime scene, to the

---

* Alfred A. Biasotti (1926–1997), M.S. in Criminalistics, U.C. Berkeley, was a criminalist, supervising criminalist, and administrator from 1951 to 1990, retiring as Assistant Chief of the Bureau of Forensic Sciences, California Department of Justice. He helped establish the California Criminalistics Institute; authored numerous articles on firearms and toolmark identification; was a Fellow of the American Academy of Forensic Sciences; and a distinguished member of the Association of Firearm and Toolmark Examiners. He passed away on June 24, 1997, from complications associated with Parkinson's Disease.

** John E. Murdock, M.C. in Criminalistics, U.C. Berkeley, is a Senior Firearms and Toolmark Examiner with the Bureau of Alcohol, Tobacco, and Firearms, San Francisco Laboratory Center. Author of a number of articles on firearms and toolmark examination, he is past president of the California Association of Criminalists, an emeritus member of the American Society of Crime Laboratory Directors, and a distinguished member of the Association of Firearm and Toolmark Examiners.

The views expressed in this chapter are those of the authors alone; no endorsement has been sought from the Bureau of Alcohol, Tobacco and Firearms or any other agency or organization.

§ 4–2.0

1. When two objects come into contact, the harder object may mark the surface of the softer object. The tool is the harder object. The relative hardness of the two objects, the pressures and movements, and the nature of the microscopic irregularities on the tool are all factors that influence the character of the toolmarks produced.

2. A tool is defined as an object used to gain mechanical advantage. It also is the harder of two objects, which produces toolmarks when brought into contact with the softer one.

exclusion of all other tools. Typical toolmarks submitted in a non-firearms case would be those found on certain components of homemade bombs, on locks and window or door parts in forced entry cases, and just about anywhere that a tool has been used. The word "tool" must be considered in the broadest possible sense. Thus the steel bumper of a truck backing through an aluminum framed supermarket door may leave toolmarks on the relatively soft aluminum doorframe. The truck and bumper would be the tool and the specific portion of the bumper contacting the aluminum doorframe causing the toolmarks would be the working surface of the tool.

This chapter is concerned with the individualization of firearms and toolmarks and not with the myriad of other tasks, such as those described above, because it is the individualization process that leads to the strong associative evidence which links a defendant to a crime. The defendant is connected to the crime scene by virtue of having possessed a firearm or tool that has been identified as having made toolmarks found on submitted evidence.

§ 4–2.1.1   The Scientific Questions

The individualization of firearms and toolmarks involves the physical comparison of one solid object with another solid object to determine through pattern recognition whether or not they were (1) once part of the same object, (2) in contact with each other, (3) share similar class or individual characteristics.[3]

Physical comparisons of this nature have evolved as distinct forensic disciplines, namely, firearm and toolmark identification, tire and footwear impressions, and latent fingerprint identification.[4] This evolution as separate disciplines has occurred apparently due to differing bodies of background knowledge required, although these comparisons are based on the same physical phenomena, i.e., the imparting or transfer of a presumably unique combination of patterns or contours from one solid surface to another.

---

3. *Class characteristics* are measurable features of a specimen that indicate a restricted group source. They result from design factors, and are therefore determined prior to manufacture. *Individual characteristics*, on the other hand, are marks produced by the random imperfections or irregularities of tool surfaces. These random imperfections or irregularities are produced either incidental to manufacture or are caused by use, corrosion, or damage. They are considered unique to that tool and therefore are believed to distinguish it from all other tools. The individualization process relies on pattern recognition, which results from complex interactions between the eyes and the brain. F. Taroni et al., *Statistics: A Future in Toolmarks Comparison?*, 28 Ass'n Firearm & Toolmark Examiners J. 227 (1996).

4. Alfred A. Biasotti, *Firearms and Toolmark Identification–A Forensic Science Discipline*, 12 Ass'n Firearm & Toolmark Examiners J. 12 (1980); Charles R. Meyers, *Firearms and Toolmark Identification–An Introduction*, 25 Ass'n Firearm & Toolmark Examiners J. 281 (1993).

PHYSICAL COMPARISONS

PATTERN FIT
("Physical Match")

The examination of 2 or more objects either through physical, optical, or photographic means which permits one to conclude whether the objects were either one entity or were held or bonded together in a unique arrangement. Also called Fracture Match.

PATTERN TRANSFER
("Toolmarks and Other Impression Marks")

TWO DIMENSIONAL
(SURFACE/IMPRINT MARKS)

(1) IMPRESSION TYPE* examples:
  (a) finger, palm and foot imprints
  (b) tire and footwear imprints

(2) STRIATED TYPE** examples:
  (a) rubber wiper blade marks on glass
  (b) toolmarks in general which lack depth.

(3) COMBINATION OF (1)&(2)***

THREE DIMENSIONAL
(CONTOUR/IMPRESSION MARKS)

(1) IMPRESSION TYPE* examples:
  (a) tools, shoes, tires or other compression marks
  (b) breechblock, firing pin marks

(2) STRIATED TYPE** examples:
  (a) fired bullets
  (b) chisel, plane and other cut marks

(3) COMBINATION OF (1)&(2)***

---

*   IMPRESSION denotes perpendicular movement of the "tool" relative to the surface marked.
**   STRIATED denotes lateral movement of a "tool" relative to the surface marked or lateral movement of the surface marked relative to the tool.
*** Denotes imprints or marks formed by a combination of lateral and perpendicular movements.

FIGURE 1: A generic classification of contemporary physical comparisons that utilize various forms of pattern recognition to identify two separated objects which were: 1) once part of the same object, 2) in contact with each other, or 3) which share some other class or individual characteristics.

The methodology applied to the various physical comparisons outlined in Figure 1 is directed to recognizing and determining whether or not a particular combination or pattern of surface characteristics is randomly distributed and, if so, whether the agreement between evidence and test grouping is greater than what has been observed in known non-matches.[5]

The methodology necessary to recognize, measure and demonstrate a unique combination of class and individual characteristics among diverse objects varies, depending on the type of objects compared, e.g., fired bullets, cartridge cases, footwear, tire impressions or fingerprints. The fundamental rationale for individualizing a mark or impression, however, is that the pattern or combination of individual characteristics is presumed to be unique to the exclusion of all other possible patterns or combinations of characteristics.

The physical comparisons traditionally and routinely covered under the heading of "firearms and toolmark identification" will be discussed under the two basic physical phenomena of "Pattern–Fit" and "Pattern Transfer" (Figure 1).

The "pattern-fit" category is a simple concept. This category is defined as a "physical match" by the forensic scientist, or the "jigsaw puzzle fit" by the lay person. Most people readily recognize that each piece is unique in completing a puzzle, or that the broken pieces of a once solid object uniquely fit together to make the whole. The unique character of a physical match depends on the complexity of the random contours of the separated surfaces. The greater the complexity of the contours formed by the separated surfaces, the more probable that the match is unique.

The "pattern transfer" category, in contrast, is more difficult to understand and demonstrate. Consequently, identification involving pattern transfer is subject to more challenges and controversies. Toolmarks made by firearm components, other tools, and other solid objects in the "Pattern Transfer" category in Figure 1 are, therefore, the main focus of this chapter. We will discuss both "three-dimensional" (contour/impression) and "two-dimensional" (surface/imprint) toolmarks, recognizing that the fundamental criterion for determining the probability that a toolmark is unique remains the same.

The "three-dimensional" pattern transfer-type marks are further classified into "impression" and "striated" marks.[6] Toolmarks produced by firearm

---

5. *Known non-match*: Toolmarks known to have been made by different tools, or made by the same tool but deliberately placed in a non-matching position.

6. *Impressed toolmarks* are produced when a tool is placed against another object and enough force is applied to the tool so that it leaves an impression. The class characteristics (shape) can indicate the type of tool used to produce the mark. These marks can contain *class* or *individual characteristics* of the tool producing the marks. These also are called *compression marks*. *Impressed toolmarks* consist of contour variations on the surface of an object caused by a combination of force and

motion where the motion is approximately perpendicular to the plane being marked.

Striated toolmarks are produced when a tool is placed against another object and with pressure applied, the tool is moved across the object producing a striated mark. *Friction marks, abrasion marks,* and *scratch marks* are terms commonly used when referring to striated marks. These marks can contain *class* and/or *individual characteristics. Striations* are further defined as contour variations, generally microscopic, on the surface of an object caused by a combination of force and motion where the motion is approximately parallel to the plane being marked.

components and other tools typically are a combination of both impression and striated marks. Toolmarks produced on bullets fired through a gun barrel are primarily striated.

With either two or three-dimensional toolmarks, the primary factor to consider, for individualization purposes, is the nature of the surface suspected of having made the toolmark. The portion of a tool that can come into contact with, and cause markings on other objects, is called the working surface. Toolmarks can be identified as having been made by a specific tool to the exclusion of all other tools only when the responsible working surface has been determined to be unique and therefore capable of making unique or, in other words, individual marks. The examiner uses knowledge of: (1) machining processes, (2) the microscopic appearance of the working surface, and (3) the results of research performed on consecutively manufactured tools in making this determination.

In this context, various parts of firearms are considered simply as tools. For example, the inside of a rifled gun barrel acts as a tool when it marks a bullet fired through it; an extractor acts as a tool when it extracts fired cartridge cases or unfired cartridges from the chamber of a firearm; and a firing pin acts as a tool when it strikes the primer portion of a cartridge, and so on.

Some working surfaces are unique the moment they are produced by the manufacturer. This is because some machining processes such as grinding generally produce a uniquely finished surface. Numerous toolmark studies of ground working surfaces have demonstrated that in most instances a different random distribution of individual characteristics is formed each time a working surface is ground.[7] Other machining processes, such as those where hardened cutters are used, often produce very similar toolmarks on items consecutively manufactured. A good example of this is the persistence of matching toolmarks in .25 auto caliber cartridge case extractor grooves described by Johnson.[8] These similar (sometimes matching) toolmarks are composed of sub-class characteristics.[9] The manufacturer's goal is to produce many items of the same shape that are, within certain tolerances, the same size. They also want each of these items to have an acceptable surface finish or appearance. Items that look the same to the unaided eye are said to have the same class characteristics. The manufacturers are not, however, con-

7. Alfred A. Biasotti & John E. Murdock, *"Criteria For Identification" or "State of the Art of Firearms and Toolmark Identification,"* 16 Ass'n Firearm & Toolmark Examiners J. 16 (1984); S. J. Butcher & P.D. Pugh, *A Study of Marks Made by Bolt Cutters,* 15 J. Forensic Sci. Soc'y 115 (1975); D. J. Watson, *The Identification of Toolmarks Produced from Consecutively Manufactured Knife Blades in Soft Plastic,* 10 Ass'n Firearm & Toolmark Examiners J. 43 (1978); F. H. Cassidy, *Examination of Toolmarks from Sequentially Manufactured Tongue-and-Groove Pliers,* 25 J. Forensic Sci. 798 (1980); D. Q. Burd & A. E. Gilmore, *Individual and Class Characteristics of Tools,* 13 J. Forensic Sci. 390 (1968); Bernard L. Diamond, *The Scientific Method and The Law,* 19 Hastings L.J. 179 (1967).

8. T. Johnson, The Persistence of Toolmarks in R–P .25 Auto Cartridge Case Extractor Grooves, Presented at the Annual A.F.T.E. Training Seminar, Orlando, Florida (May 10–14, 1982). *See* Biasotti & Murdock, *supra* note 7, for illustrations of these toolmarks.

9. *Subclass characteristics* are discernible surface features of an object which are more restrictive than *class characteristics* in that they are: (1) produced incidental to manufacture, (2) are significant in that they relate to a smaller group source (a subset of the class to which they belong), and (3) can arise from a source which changes over time. Examples would include: bunter *marks* (headstamps produced on cartridge cases) produced by bunters made from a common master, *extrusion marks* on pipe, etc.

cerned that many or all of these items may bear toolmarks composed of subclass characteristics depending on the way in which they were manufactured. The firearms and toolmark examiner must be alert to the possibility that evidence toolmarks may have been produced by a tool working surface having subclass characteristics.

A classic example of the evaluation of the working surface of a tool and the determination of the presence of subclass characteristics was reported by Murdock in 1974.[10] In this example, the working surfaces of desk stapler rams from two different brands of desk staplers were evaluated. The ram is the tool in a desk stapler that consists of a hardened piece of metal that comes into contact with a staple when the staple is driven out of the stapler. It was determined that in the finished product, the rams in one brand of desk stapler had unique working surfaces whereas the rams in the other brand of desk stapler had matching subclass characteristics. When new, the desk staplers with the matching subclass characteristics probably would not be capable of leaving unique toolmarks on the top of staples driven from them. After these working surfaces become worn and the subclass characteristics become obliterated, the toolmarks produced by them would be unique.[11]

A tool may have subclass toolmarks near the working surfaces and yet because of the relative position of the subclass toolmarks they have no effect on the ability of that tool to leave unique toolmarks. For example, the teeth on slip joint pliers often are formed by a cutting process that leaves subclass toolmarks. When these teeth grip objects and the tool is used in the normal way, sliding toolmarks (from slippage) often are made 90 degrees from the orientation of the subclass toolmarks. Thus the subclass characteristics have no effect on the unique signature left behind by the pliers teeth. The examiner, must, therefore, for any specific tool, be able to: (1) recognize the presence of subclass characteristics and (2) properly evaluate the significance of subclass toolmarks when they are present by determining whether or not they are influencing the nature of any evidence toolmarks that are under consideration.

Having considered the nature of the tool working surface suspected of being responsible for making an evidence toolmark, a critical question arises. How much agreement is needed between an evidence and test toolmark before a conclusion of identification to the exclusion of all other tools is justified? This is the basic question asked first by science and then by the law. We will discuss how much agreement is needed following a description of the steps taken by an examiner during a typical toolmark comparison case.

§ 4–2.1.2 The Scientific Methods Applied in Firearms and Toolmark Examination

A typical toolmark comparison case usually starts with questioned toolmarks of some sort that are evaluated for evidentiary purposes. The submitted evidence, consisting either of actual objects or pieces of objects or replicas (casts) of suspected toolmarks found on immovable objects, is microscopically

10. John E. Murdock, *The Individuality of Toolmarks Produced by Desk Staplers*, 6 Ass'n Firearm & Toolmark Examiners J. 23 (1974).

11. For a highly favorable evaluation of this forensic research, *see* Crime Laboratory Management Forum 177–178 (R.H. Fox & F.H. Wynbrandt eds., 1976).

examined for toolmarks and any toolmarks found are evaluated in order to determine: (1) what type and configuration of tool was used and (2) whether the toolmarks have potential value for comparison and identification purposes. Toolmarks have potential value for comparison and identification purposes if a sufficient number of microscopic features are present and if they possess sufficient clarity and definition. The toolmarks also are examined for the presence of trace evidence, such as paint.

If tools are submitted for comparison, they are examined for trace evidence and a determination is made as to whether the class characteristics of any specific tool agrees with the class characteristics found in the toolmarks. If the class characteristics agree, test toolmarks are made for comparison with the submitted evidence toolmarks. When test toolmarks are made, every attempt is made to duplicate the general appearance of the evidence toolmarks by varying the tool angles and degree of pressure. This is fairly easy with firearms toolmark evidence since ammunition feeds into and out of firearms in a predictable way that is usually easy to duplicate simply by operating the firearm mechanism in the normal way.

With non-firearm toolmarks, numerous test toolmarks sometimes have to be made because the first test toolmarks produced are sometimes of no value for comparison, since the angles and pressures used did not create test toolmarks having the general appearance of the evidence toolmark(s). Early test marks of no value can be, but certainly do not have to be, discarded when they have been made in a relatively soft material such as lead, which will not generally cause alteration of the tool's working surface. If a relatively soft test material proves to be inappropriate because the right kind of test toolmarks are not being produced, the examiner may have to use some of the same type of material, usually harder than lead, that bears the evidence toolmark(s). If this is a relatively hard material, all test marks made in it should be retained since there is a possibility that making test marks in this harder material may alter the working surface of the tool thereby making future comparisons very difficult. As a general rule, any time the test media show any sign of causing alteration to a tool working surface, all test marks should be retained.

Regardless of the media used for test marks, the goal of test mark production is to vary the angle and pressure of the working surface of the tool so that a test mark is produced by every part of every working surface that could reasonably have been used to produce the evidence toolmark. The examiner stands the best chance of identifying the tool when a comprehensive series of test marks has been prepared, assuming that the four conditions described in the next paragraph are true. It is possible, however, that if a comprehensive series of test marks is not produced, an examiner may falsely exclude the tool.[12] A false inclusion is highly improbable because no matter how many different test marks are produced, the likelihood is remote that any of them will exhibit sufficient agreement for a positive identification if the tool was not the tool used to produce the evidence toolmark. For practical purposes, examiners regard this probability as so small that the probability of a false inclusion is considered to be zero.

---

12. A false exclusion occurs when the tool actually used to produce the evidence toolmark   is excluded.

Appropriately prepared test toolmarks, having the general appearance of the evidence toolmarks, are next compared to one another to see if the tool is capable of leaving reproducible toolmarks. If it is, one would expect to be able to identify the tool as having made the evidence toolmark provided that: (1) it was used to make the evidence toolmark, (2) the responsible working surface has not been damaged since having been used, (3) the evidence toolmark bears sufficient, unique impression or striated markings for identification purposes, and (4) the responsible working surface of the tool consists of an individual surface finish and not merely class or subclass features.

Subclass characteristics are toolmarks that, because of their well defined continuous, often prominent, and sometimes equally spaced appearance without changing significantly over some distance, can be suspected of being found on other similarly manufactured tool working surfaces. The presence of toolmarks of this nature on working surfaces must prompt the examiner to conduct research, such as the desk stapler example cited above, into the effect on individuality caused by their presence.

The retention of only those test toolmarks used for the identification, assuming that the discarded toolmarks were made in test material softer than the tool working surface and caused no changes in the working surface, does not create a bias against an accused. Most tool working surfaces will have a number of surfaces capable of producing toolmarks. For example, one of the authors identified a hack saw blade as being used to produce a series of seven teeth marks on the end of a length of copper pipe that had been fashioned into a pipe bomb. The toolmark identified was a striated mark caused by a sidewise motion of the blade; it was not a cutmark. Many of the hack saw teeth were broken; of the approximately 173 teeth on the blade, only a seven tooth section could have been used! Approximately 300 test marks were made using sheet lead before an identification was made. It was necessary to make this many testmarks because of the saw blade length, the numerous possible blade angles when it traveled sideways during the production of approximately 24 different sets of seven teeth wide marks, and because many teeth were broken. Most of these test toolmarks have no bearing on the identification and could be remade if necessary.

When sufficient agreement is found between the evidence toolmark and a test toolmark, a positive identification of the tool is made to the exclusion of all other tools. All test toolmarks relied upon for the final comparison results must be retained.

The comparison process just described assumes that the examiner has the tool working surface available for comparison so that an evaluation can be made, as described above, to see whether or not it is capable of producing a unique toolmark. Situations occur where an examiner does not have a tool and is simply comparing toolmarks from a series of crimes to see if the crimes are connected. In these situations, if the toolmarks from a series of crimes *are identified* as having been produced by the same tool, the examiner is relying on general knowledge of how the working edges of such tools are produced. For example, the cutting edges of twist drills are finished by grinding. This machining process has been demonstrated to produce a microscopically unique working surface on twist drill cutting edges.[13] A series of twist drill impressions (where the hole is *not* drilled all the way through) from a series of crimes can, therefore, be determined to have been drilled with the same twist drill if sufficient microscopic agreement is present.

When there is, however, a chance that microscopic subclass characteristics, having their origin in the manufacturing process, can be present in the type of toolmarks recovered in a series of crimes, a more cautious approach should be taken. It is not uncommon in these cases for the examiner to write a report that states that sufficient microscopic agreement is present to *suggest* that the same tool made the series of toolmarks, but that a conclusive opinion can be rendered only after an examination of the responsible tool. Once the examiner has the tool, the working surface can be evaluated to determine if the tool produces a unique toolmark, or is one that contains subclass characteristics that are capable of being transferred to toolmarked surfaces.

With respect to toolmarks associated with firearms evidence, Bonfanti and De Kinder have provided a comprehensive summary of the influences of manufacturing processes on the identification of bullets and cartridge cases. Their summary clearly illustrates that not every manufactured tool surface is unique and that firearm and toolmark examiners must consider the possibility of sub class (family) carry over on consecutively manufactured tool working surfaces before positively identifying a toolmark as having been made by one particular tool, to the exclusion of all other tools.[14]

We return now to the issue of how much agreement between crime scene evidence toolmarks and test toolmarks made with a suspect tool is required to determine that the working surface(s) of only one particular tool made the mark.

§ 4–2.2   Areas of Scientific Agreement

The theory of identification, as it relates to toolmarks, adopted by the Association of Firearm and Toolmark Examiners (A.F.T.E.),[15] gives a non-quantitative answer to the question of how much agreement is needed. This theory is reproduced below in its entirety.

Theory of Identification as it Relates to Toolmarks

a) The theory of identification as it pertains to the comparison of toolmarks enables opinions of common origin to be made when the unique surface contours of two toolmarks are in "sufficient agreement."

b) This "sufficient agreement" is related to the significant duplication of random toolmarks as evidenced by the correspondence of a pattern or combination of patterns of surface contours. Significance is determined by the comparative examination of two or more sets of surface contour patterns comprised of individual peaks, ridges and furrows. Specifically,

13. Joseph A. Reitz, *An Unusual Toolmark Identification Case*, 7 Ass'n Firearm & Toolmark Examiners J. 40 (1975).

14. M.S. Bonfanti & J. De Kinder, *The Influences of Manufacturing Processes on the Identification of Bullets and Cartridge Cases–A Review of the Literature*, 39 Sci. & Justice 3 (1999).

15. *Theory of Identification, Range of Striae Comparison Reports, and Modified Glossary Definitions—An AFTE Criteria For Identification Committee Report*, 24 Ass'n Firearm & Toolmark Examiners J. 336 (1992).

the relative height or depth, width, curvature and spatial relationship of the individual peaks, ridges and furrows within one set of surface contours are defined and compared to the corresponding features in the second set of surface contours. Agreement is significant when it exceeds the best agreement demonstrated between toolmarks known to have been produced by different tools and is consistent with the agreement demonstrated by toolmarks known to have been produced by the same tool. The statement that "sufficient agreement" exists between two toolmarks means that the agreement is of a quantity and quality that the likelihood another tool could have made the mark is so remote as to be considered a practical impossibility

However, A.F.T.E. did not define "sufficient agreement" in quantitative terms. Instead, it has adopted the following position statement:

c) Currently the interpretation of individualization/identification is subjective in nature, founded on scientific principles and based on the examiner's training and experience.

Section (c) states in part that the interpretation of individualization/identification is founded on scientific principles. The research directed toward criteria for identification in firearm and toolmark identification was reviewed and discussed by the authors in 1984.[16] All examinations utilizing mathematical models, mechanical models, and actual toolmarks, made with new or used tools, up to 1984 indicated that sufficient agreement of striated or impression toolmarks could be expressed by agreement of a relatively small number of individual characteristics. This research is described in some detail in § 2.4. This research was carried out by adherence to the process known as the scientific method. In this process, variables were limited and observations were made that have allowed examiners to *predict* the ability to individualize "pattern-transfer" toolmarks. This *prediction* has been continually tested empirically and has stood the test of time, resulting in the general principle (Theory) adopted by A.F.T.E. in 1992.[17] The studies leading up to this theory have been peer reviewed, published, and thus have been available for replication by the relevant scientific community of forensic scientists. Nichols reviewed thirty-four articles that pertained to identification criteria for firearm and toolmark identification. These articles included empirical studies of consecutively manufactured barrels, firing pins, breechfaces, assorted tools as well as mathematical and computer models. Although not all of these articles generated quantifiable numbers, Nichols felt that ". . . all of these appear to be based at least in part on the scientific method . . ."[18]

Research conducted by adherence to the scientific method allows *predictions* to be made and thus serves as a guide to future situations, which in this specific instance is the identification of toolmarks. In contrast, most of the day-to-day measuring and careful observation that occurs in firearm and toolmark sections of crime laboratories is essential to the completion of casework, but is not carried out by using scientific methodology. Firearm and toolmark examiners apply science and scientific methods, procedures and instruments in a practical way, but most are more skilled in the art of

16. Biasotti & Murdock, *supra* note 7.

17. *Theory of Identification, supra* note 15.

18. R.G. Nichols, *Firearm and Toolmark Identification Criteria: A Review of the Literature*, 42 J. FORENSIC SCI. 466 (1997).

applying those methods and procedures than they are in the basic sciences involved.[19] Diamond put it succinctly during a discussion of the scientific method, when he said: (1) that the value and truth of science lies in its methods, not its numbers and diagrams; and (2) determinations of specific measurements only define unique observations, but do not allow predictions to be made about future situations.[20]

As stated in section (c) of the A.F.T.E. *Theory of Identification*,[21] "currently the interpretation of individualization/identification is subjective in nature. . . ." Because decisions are based on subjective estimates of probability, the Association of Firearm and Toolmark Examiners has adopted the following range of conclusions to be used when comparing toolmarks.[22]

Range of Conclusions Possible When Comparing Toolmarks

The examiner is encouraged to report the objective observations that support the findings of toolmark examinations. The examiner should be conservative when reporting the significance of these observations. The following represents a spectrum of statements:

1) *Identification*: Agreement of a combination of individual characteristics and all discernible class characteristics where the extent of agreement exceeds that which can occur in the comparison of toolmarks made by different tools and is consistent with the agreement demonstrated by toolmarks known to have been produced by the same tool.

2) *Inconclusive*:

A.   Some agreement of individual characteristics and all discernible class characteristics, but insufficient for an identification.

B.   Agreement of all discernible class characteristics without agreement or disagreement of individual characteristics due to an absence, insufficiency, or lack of reproducibility.

C.   Agreement of all discernible class characteristics and disagreement of individual characteristics, but insufficient for an elimination.

3) *Elimination*: Significant disagreement of discernible class characteristics and/or individual characteristics.

4) *Unsuitable*: Unsuitable for comparison.

The introductory paragraph to the A.F.T.E. *Range of Conclusions Possible when Comparing Toolmarks*, encourages examiners to report the objective observations that support their findings. This means that the examiner is free to express how he feels about the comparative evidentiary value of the toolmark comparisons. For example, a comparison conclusion of inconclusive may be further described as consisting of considerable agreement, such as that described in § 2.1.1, which may allow the examiner to conclude that it is very likely that the submitted tool was the tool used to make the submitted toolmark.

19. Letter from John E. Davis to John Murdock (Dec. 27, 1977) (on file with the author).

20. Diamond, *supra* note 7.

21. *Theory of Identification, supra* note 15.

22. *Id.*

Since the interpretation that forms the basis for these conclusions is subjective, Murdock has suggested a series of questions designed to test the witness's qualifications for making a conclusion of identity when striated toolmarks have been identified.[23] The thrust of these questions is to evaluate the witness's knowledge of the extent of agreement that can be found when comparing striated toolmarks known to have been made by different tools. Some of these questions, together with suggested appropriate responses may be found in Appendix II. A similar line of questioning could also be developed for impression type evidence, including toolmarks. Although these fourteen questions focus on the witness's knowledge of the extent of microscopic agreement that can be found when comparing striated toolmarks known to have been made by different tools, qualified examiners need to demonstrate that they also have spent considerable time studying the extent of agreement in known matches as well as various forms of inconclusive examples.

§ 4–2.3   Areas of Scientific Disagreement

§ 4–2.3.1   Disagreement About the Scientific Foundations

The disagreement that exists in the field centers around whether objective quantifiable standards can be developed as criteria for the identification of toolmarks. While most would probably agree that the development of such criteria is desirable, some consider it impossible. John Davis[24] expressed it this way:

> Since all toolmarks are "unique" in a sense, I doubt that "universal criteria" can be found that would apply to all such marks to permit conclusions purely "objective" in nature. Since even the "application" of predetermined criteria calls for degrees of expertise itself, it is generally my position that the "minimum criteria" required for an identification must themselves vary with the degree of expertise and experience of the examiner and therefore minimum criteria cannot be fixed except in "unstable form."[25]

As early as 1977, however, Davis stated:

> If some day a computer or the like is built which will "look" at bullet striae and plot and evaluate the highs and lows, highlights or shadows, spatial relationships, etc., and "conclude" there is an identity, or a non-identity or a "don't know," perhaps we can call it another "objective" method. But it would be the "art" of the experienced examiners that would be the basis for input into the instrument—not the "science."[26]

Although the day referred to above by Davis in 1977 has not and likely never will arrive, we do have automated comparison systems that select high confidence candidates for comparison by firearms and toolmark examiners.

---

23. John Murdock, *Some Suggested Court Questions to Test Criteria for Identification Qualifications*, 24 Ass'n Firearm & Toolmark Examiners J. 69 (1992).

24. Author of An Introduction to Tool Marks, Firearms, and the Striagraph, *infra* note 35.

25. Personal notes of John E. Davis (April 1984) (on file with the author); personal communications between Davis and the author (June, 1984).

26. Davis, *supra* note 19.

There is no question, however, that conclusions of identity in firearms and toolmarks are possible. The examiner qualified to render such conclusions should be familiar with:

  1. Empirical studies of consecutively manufactured tools.

  2. The significance or impact upon individuality of the various means used to manufacture tool edges or working surfaces.

  3. Theoretical studies where both mechanical and mathematical models have been used to study toolmark consecutiveness.

  4. The quantity and quality of matching agreement found in comparisons of toolmarks known to have been produced by different tools. (Known non-matches.)

The authors sincerely hope that objective quantitative criteria will be developed that can be applied universally to the evaluation of striated toolmarks. Progress in this area is described *infra* § 2.4. Until this is done, however, the correctness of subjective evaluations must continue to be based upon individual expertise gained mostly by training and experience. In addition, a working knowledge of the research that has been done in the four categories listed above will help ensure that conclusions of identity, when made, are fully justified.

§ 4–2.3.2   Disagreement Among Practitioners in Particular Applications

In spite of the research efforts described *supra* §§ 2.2 and 2.4, occasionally forensic experts differ in their opinion about the identification of toolmarks. It has been the authors' experience, limited almost exclusively to striated toolmarks in firearms cases, that many of these disagreements stem from one examiner ascribing too much significance to a small amount of matching striae and not appreciating that such agreement is achievable in known non-match comparisons.

Hodge[27] discusses other sources of error, such as (1) rushing through laboratory examinations due to excessive pressure from investigators, (2) not being thorough, and (3) trying to be helpful. Hodge goes on to discuss some ways to minimize these sources of error.

Will errors continue? We suppose so, but hope that the concept of known non-match comparisons, the thorough understanding of the influence of subclass characteristics, and in-laboratory peer review by skilled co-workers will hold them to an absolute minimum.

Based on present data, the field is in a poor position to calculate error rates. Thornton[28] recently addressed known or potential rate of error by saying that test results hinging on judgment calls do not lend themselves to analysis by conventional statistics. No doubt Thornton was not saying that the products of human judgment cannot be measured statistically, since most if not all of cognitive science does precisely that, but rather that forensic

27. Evan E. Hodge, *Guarding Against Error*, 20 Ass'n Firearm & Toolmark Examiners J. 290 (1988).

28. John I. Thornton, *Courts of Law v. Courts of Science: A Forensic Scientist's Reaction to Daubert*, 1 Shepard's Expert & Sci. Evidence Q. 480 (1994).

science researchers have not managed to calculate them for the forensic specialties like firearm and toolmark comparison that depend in part on subjective judgment. With modern statistical technology, forensic science decision-making could be subjected to quantitative analysis.[29] But to date it has not been.

Some have used the results of the proficiency testing program administered by the Forensic Sciences Foundation as the major information about error rates.[30] Admittedly, this is tempting since they represent virtually the only information collected on a large scale, but it is at the same time a flawed approach. These declared (not blind) proficiency tests were designed to be used by individual crime laboratories as a quality assurance tool and were never intended to be used as the basis for a nationwide study of forensic error rates. Some crime laboratories treat them formally, requiring that they be completed by the due dates so that their results will be among the tabulated data sent out following each test. Other laboratories treat them much less formally, asking only that they be worked on as time permits, and it usually does not. Still other laboratories work harder on the proficiency tests than on their regular caseload, because they are "a test." In addition, some examiners may be more conservative when reporting the results of a declared proficiency test, feeling that they have little to gain but much to lose if they make an error. It has generally been the case that although proficiency test results have been reviewed by a supervisor before being reported, they were not peer reviewed. Peer review is an important process that is widely used in crime laboratories. This process helps prevent errors in casework from seeing the light of day. In cases where the supervisor was not a subject matter expert in the proficiency test subject there would be, essentially, no peer review. In these circumstances, the reported error rates would, therefore, closely approximate an individual examiner's error rate. The American Society of Crime Laboratory Directors' Laboratory Accreditation Board (ASCLD/LAB) approved a program in December 1997 that suddenly moved proficiency test results into a hi-stakes game. In December, 1997 ASCLD/LAB approved the Proficiency Review Program (PRP). Under this program, in ASCLD accredited crime laboratories, the results of an individual's proficiency tests must be released to a Proficiency Review Committee (PRC) established by ASCLD/LAB. The PRC will review the proficiency test results and if a discrepancy is found the laboratory will be notified and appropriate action must be taken. The type of action will depend on the level of discrepancy (class 1, 2 or 3). Failure to properly address the discrepancy may result in sanctions, which could include revocation of ASCLD/LAB Accreditation. It is clear that in such a high stakes game, laboratory administration will do everything possible to ensure that the proficiency test results are correct before reporting them. Prior to the PRC it was a more low-stakes game, with the individual examiners rising or falling on their own merit. The reputation of the laboratory is now at stake. Consequently, we cannot know if pre 1998 proficiency studies overstate or understate the accuracy of examinations. But, it seems

29. Victoria Phillips et al., *Signal Detection Theory and Decision-making in Forensic Science*, 46 J. FORENSIC SCI. 294 (2001).

30. Randolph N. Jonakait, *Real Science and Forensic Science*, 1 SHEPARD'S EXPERT & SCI. EVIDENCE Q. 446 (1994).

fairly certain that post 1998 proficiency studies may overstate the accuracy of examinations.

It would be more instructive if the crime laboratories completing the proficiency tests by the due dates were required to indicate if normal laboratory procedures were followed, whether this included peer review and supervisorial scrutiny, whether the test was used as a test for a trainee, and so on. With this additional information, more meaningful comments could be made about these proficiency test results. Or, better, that they be submitted to examiners as if they were part of the regular caseload—that is, blind proficiency testing.

Moreover, there are inherent difficulties associated with the production of toolmark proficiency tests. Due to the nature of this evidence, each sample is unique. Since there are dynamic forces involved in producing the toolmark samples, there are opportunities for variations between samples. Since all proficiency test subscribers examine unique samples, can widespread test results be used for more than a general indication of error rates? Probably not.[31]

§ 4–2.4 Development of Objective Criteria for Identification

In 1984, we concluded that existing research was insufficient to validate the quantitative objective criteria necessary to conclude that a working surface is unique.[32] To develop these criteria we recommended that examiners be familiar with the extent of agreement, both in quantity and quality, observed in comparisons of toolmarks known to have been produced by different tools. This recommendation, subsequently referred to as known non-match (KNM) comparisons, is an essential part of the non-quantitative theory of identification and the hypothesis adopted by the Association of Firearms and Toolmark Examiners (A.F.T.E.) in 1992.[33]

The authors added a quantitative dimension to this fundamental hypothesis. The probability that a toolmark or working surface is unique can be determined by the number and complexity (i.e., size, shape, depth) of randomly occurring matching individual characteristics in excess of the number of characteristics observed and documented in KNM comparisons.

No probability estimates were calculated for KNM comparisons because determining the maximum number of well defined matching individual characteristics in large statistical samples (i.e., more than 100) of KNMs for a variety of different types of tools is the most direct and conclusive way of

---

31. For further details on proficiency tests and their findings, *see* Joseph L. Peterson & P. N. Markham, *Crime Laboratory Proficiency Testing Results, 1978–1991, I: Identification and Classification of Physical Evidence,* 40 J. FORENSIC SCI. 994 (1995); Joseph L. Peterson & P. N. Markham, *Crime Laboratory Proficiency Testing Results, 1978–1991, II: Resolving Questions of Common Origin,* 40 J. FORENSIC SCI. 1009 (1995). Richard A. Grzybowski & John E. Murdock, *Firearms and Toolmark Identification–Meeting the Daubert Challenge,* 30 ASS'N FIREARM & TOOLMARK EXAMINERS J. 3 (1998), summarized Peterson & Markham's data for firearms and toolmark proficiency

tests as follows: Calculating an error rate based on the total number of decisions reached (that is, including inconclusive responses, which in fact are neither correct nor incorrect), the error rate is 12% for firearms and 26% for toolmarks. But if one calculates an error rate based only on incorrect responses, as Grzybowski & Murdock believe it should be, the results are far better: 1.4% for firearms and 4% for toolmarks.

32. Biasotti & Murdock, *supra* note 7.

33. *Theory of Identification, supra* note 15.

determining that the probability of a false positive identification is beyond a practical possibility.

Probability estimates for the number of matching individual characteristics for known matches[34] and KNMs historically have been based on theoretical assumptions using mathematical calculations unsupported by published empirical studies of actual toolmarks. Consequently, no objective, quantitative, criteria for determining the individuality of toolmarks is presented in any of the leading texts or dissertations on this subject.[35]

The first published empirical study intended to test theoretical probability estimates using actual toolmarks was conducted by Biasotti and published in 1959.[36] Two groups of .38 Special Smith and Wesson revolvers were examined in this study. The first group consisted of sixteen used guns from which six to twelve 158 grain lead bullets were fired. The second group consisted of eight new guns from which six 158 grain lead bullets and six 158 grain metal-jacketed bullets were fired. The data for comparisons made between bullets fired from the same gun were obtained by considering the first bullet as the primary reference, and then comparing the succeeding five test firings with it. This made a total of 400 land and 400 groove impressions compared for the group of sixteen used guns, plus a total of 200 land and 200 groove impressions compared for each group of lead and metal-jacketed bullets from the eight new guns. The data for bullets fired from different guns were obtained by comparing the first bullet from each gun with the first bullet from a different gun, for a total of 36 different combinations, giving a total of 180 land and 180 groove impressions compared for each of the following groups of guns and tests: (1) used, lead bullets, (2) new, lead bullets, and (3) new, metal-jacketed bullets.

Two basic types of data were recorded: (1) the total line count and total matching lines[37] per land or groove impression from which the percent

---

34. *Match* is a term traditionally and commonly used to denote an identification between two physical objects based on the correspondence of an unspecified quantity and quality of randomly distributed individual characteristics. In a general sense, *match* simply means that two things are equal or similar to one another. In forensic identification the term *match* has come to mean that two things share a common origin. For example, two fingerprints being made by the same person, or two toolmarks, one a test and one questioned, being made by the same tool. When two toolmarks match forensically, they have been individualized to a common source; one tool to the exclusion of all others. *See* Biasotti & Murdock, *supra* note 7; Alfred A. Biasotti, *A Statistical Study of the Individual Characteristics of Fired Bullets*, 4 J. Forensic Sci. 34 (1959) (a summary of Biasotti's thesis, Bullet Comparison: A Study of Fired Bullets Statistically Analyzed (1955) (on file with the University of California at Berkeley)); Alfred A. Biasotti, *The Principles of Evidence Evaluation as Applied to Firearms and Toolmark Identification*, 9 J. Forensic Sci. 428 (1964).

35. *See* G. Burrard, The Identification of Firearms and Forensic Ballistics (1934); Jack D. Gunther & C.O. Gunther, The Identification of Firearms (1935); A. Lucas, Forensic Chemistry and Scientific Criminal Investigation (3rd ed.1935); J.S. Hatcher, Textbook of Firearms Investigation, Identification and Evidence (1935); J.S. Hatcher, F.J. Jury & J. Weller, Firearms Investigation, Identification, and Evidence (1957); John E. Davis, An Introduction to Tool Marks, Firearms and the Striagraph (1958); J. Mathews, 1 Firearms Identification (1962); T.A. Warlow, Firearms, the Law and Forensic Ballistics (1996); Brian J. Heard, Handbook of Firearms and Ballistics (1997).

36. Biasotti, *supra* note 34.

37. *Matching lines* is a term used for brevity to denote matching striae either consecutive or non-consecutive which have a unique character, i.e., width, height, length, and contour. *See* Biasotti & Murdock, *supra* note 7; Biasotti, *Principles of Evidence Evaluation*, *supra* note 34; and Biasotti, *A Statistical Study*, *supra* note 34.

matching lines[38] was calculated and (2) the frequency of occurrence of each series of consecutive matching lines[39] for which probability estimates were calculated.

For same gun comparisons, the author strictly held to the criteria for consecutive matching lines, while for different gun comparisons the criteria were liberally interpreted. To add a further subjective bias toward higher consecutive line counts, each land and groove impression of reference bullets from different guns was compared with other land or groove impressions appearing most similar in overall contour and degree of marking.

Probability estimates for the *same* gun comparisons showed a high frequency of two or more consecutive lines; however, more significantly, no more than three consecutively matching lines were found for all lead bullets, or more than four for metal-jacketed bullets from all *different* gun comparisons.

The concept of "consecutiveness" is a simplified way of expressing the matching of a segment of contour, or a pattern of matching individual characteristics in a striated toolmark. These results, therefore, support the validity of the hypothesis adopted by A.F.T.E. and further developed by the authors.

This fired bullet study also demonstrated the unsuitability of using "percent matching lines" as a criterion of identification, particularly for fired bullets where the percent matching striae in known matches can be approximately the same as the percent matching striae found in known non-matches. In this study, bullets fired from different barrels (i.e., "known non-matches") ranged from 15 to 20% matching striae, whereas bullets fired from the same barrel (i.e., "known matches") ranged from 21 to 38% matching striae. These ranges for known matches versus known non-matches were obtained from all the striae on all the bullets compared and appear to offer a criterion for identification. However, because of the difficulty in judging the qualitative agreement of individual striae spread over several land or groove impressions, a percent matching number often can be misleading and may result in a false identification.

Analogous studies have reported up to 28% matching striae in known non-matches produced by the ground working surfaces of tools; i.e., knives, bolt cutter blades, and tongue-and-groove pliers.[40] Striae produced by a ground working surface are typically similar in height, width, spacing (often due to grit size), and lack much three dimensional contour. Therefore they are

38. *Percent matching lines* denotes the percent of matching striae without regard to consecutiveness. *See* Biasotti & Murdock, *supra* note 7; Biasotti, *A Statistical Study, supra* note 34.

39. *Consecutively matching lines* are striae that correspond or match with respect to each striae's width, depth and contour and are of sufficient length to assure that striae are parallel to one another. The term *striae* is today more commonly used than "lines" although the latter term is still used by some to describe striae that are very shallow and thus appear

virtually two dimensional. *See* Biasotti & Murdock, *supra* note 7; Biasotti, *Principles of Evidence Evaluation, supra* note 34; Biasotti, *A Statistical Study, supra* note 34.

Consecutive striae are counted as follows: (a) two-dimensional—only striae that match exactly in relative position and width are counted; (b) three-dimensional—only the ridges are counted and not the valleys between the ridges.

40. Butcher & Pugh, *supra* note 7; Watson, *supra* note 7; Cassidy *supra* note 7.

viewed as two-dimensional parallel "lines."[41] These type of shallow striae, combined with less than a two millimeter wide striated toolmark available for comparison, and the absence of clear class characteristic limits, can result in a false identification if percent match is the only criterion used.[42]

Other published research designed to validate quantitative probability estimates for matching striae have been conducted using mechanical or mathematical models. In one such study[43] a comparison of 1003 positions of known non-match of a 25 striae wide two-dimensional toolmark found that a five consecutive striae match occurred only at one position. No greater consecutive matching occurred and no 4X matching, but a greater number of 3X and 2X matching was found.[44] The features of toolmark depth and contour were not present in those two-dimensional toolmarks and so were not considered in this experiment.

In 1970, Brackett[45] explored the application of mathematical models to the study of striated toolmarks. This work reports an attempt to idealize striated marks in order to develop a theoretical basis (i.e., mathematical model) for their analysis. It is possible to take Brackett's ideal models and convert them into mechanical models which may be compared with actual toolmarks, the goal being to obtain sufficient information to enable establishment of objective criteria of identity of two sets of marks.

Brackett made a finding of great practical importance. Using *actual* consecutive line counts from a randomly selected example from Biasotti's bullet study,[46] he was able to demonstrate that a plot of the distribution of these actual run counts closely approximated those predicted by the general equation (i.e., mathematical model) that he derived. Brackett thus succeeded in deriving an equation which simulates the run distribution[47] properties of actual cases of randomly distributed striae. The importance of this finding is that this equation can be used to generate computer assisted programs capable of studying the effects of such crucial variables as striae density, uniformity or non-uniformity, and randomness, with a speed and efficiency not possible by conventional direct visual comparisons and evaluation. No one, however, has pursued this line of research.

In a review of published efforts from 1990–1994 to make toolmark examinations more objective, Springer[48] concluded that, "the early 1990's shows much promise for the advancement of toolmark comparisons." He suggests that the advancements will be made by automated technology.

Research[49] performed under the direction of the authors following their 1984 *"Criteria for Identification"* or *"State of the Art"* paper[50] was specifically

---

41. *See supra* note 39.

42. Butcher & Pugh, *supra* note 7.

43. Conducted in 1968 by Murdock, Barnett and McJunkins, reported in Biasotti & Murdock, *supra* note 7.

44. "5X" would be shorthand for "five consecutive striae," "4X" for "four consecutive striae," and so on.

45. J.E. Brackett, *A Study of Idealized Striated Marks and Their Comparison Using Models*, 10 J. Forensic Sci. Soc'y 27 (1970).

46. Biasotti, *A Statistical Study, supra* note 34.

47. "Run count" is a term used by Brackett to describe the number of consecutive matching striae. "Run distribution" is a term used by Brackett to describe the number of striae in any given toolmark or portion thereof.

48. E. Springer, *Toolmark Examinations— A Review of Its Development in the Literature*, 40 J. Forensic Sci. 964 (1995).

49. The authors were principal instructors in six forty-hour courses that dealt exclusively with "Firearms and Toolmark Identification Criteria." These were offered by the California Department of Justice Criminalistic Institute

directed at examining actual two and three-dimensional striated and impression toolmarks to determine in KNM comparisons: (1) for striated marks, the maximum percent match and the maximum number of consecutive matching striae, and (2) for impression marks, the maximum number of matching randomly distributed individual characteristics.

The striated toolmark samples studied during the CCI classes consisted of:

> 1) Six 9 mm. Luger metal jacketed test bullets, followed by six lead test bullets fired from ten previously unfired, consecutively rifled, gun barrels. Plastic casts were made of each barrel before tests were fired. Microscopic examination of these casts revealed no subclass characteristics in either the lands or grooves in any of the ten barrels.

> 2) Twelve duplicate sets of striated test marks made with the top and bottom working edges of a previously unused, three-fourths inch wide chisel having a stone-ground working edge.

For the bullet comparisons, the examiners were directed to select and compare "out-of-phase"[51] land and groove marks (fired from the same barrel), or any of the five land and groove marks (fired from different barrels) where the striae appeared most similar in density, width, and contour. Similarly, for the chisel test marks, the examiners were directed to select any test from the same out-of-phase side, or any combination of opposite side tests. These examination procedures were intended to maximize the finding of the highest percent match and highest number of consecutively matching striae for KNM comparisons.

The most significant conclusions that can be drawn from more than a thousand specifically directed, striated KNM bullet and chisel mark comparisons are:

> 1) Not more than three consecutive corresponding three-dimensional striae (i.e., among the bullets) were found, and the few (less than 20) apparent "fours" found lacked exact qualitative agreement[52] in striae width, relative position, or contour.

(CCI) commencing 12/10/90, 4/29/91, 5/11/92, 2/1/93, 12/11/95 and 10/96. Each course averaged twelve students, ranging in experience from one to fifteen or more years, doing comparison microscope examinations of toolmarks generated both by firearms and a hand tool. The goal of these courses was to conduct practical exercises with actual toolmarks to further develop and refine objective, quantitative criteria. John Murdock and Frederic Tulleners (Program Manager for CCI) have conducted these classes annually since 1996.

50. Biasotti & Murdock, *supra* note 7.

51. *Out-of-Phase* refers to two possible situations: (1) two bullets which were fired from the same gun barrel are aligned on the comparison microscope so that the land and groove impressions on these bullets, which were produced by the same lands and grooves in the barrel, are *not* opposite each other. When the

correct corresponding land and groove impressions are opposite one another, the bullets are said to be "in phase." This also is sometimes called *orienting* or *indexing. See* Glossary of the Association of Firearm and Toolmark Examiners (1994), at 76. Or, (2) when two toolmarks are lined up in such a way that they cannot possibly match, such as when clearly defined edges of two toolmarks are offset from each other.

52. *Qualitative Agreement* refers to the degree or extent of the agreement of striae width, relative position and contour. In practice, striae in one toolmark often will come close to matching striae in another toolmark with respect to these comparison parameters. Significant correspondence or agreement is achieved when there is *exact* agreement of these comparison parameters. Close does not count, and *very* closely agreeing striae may be ascribed

2) For striae lacking depth and therefore appearing two-dimensional (i.e., among the chisel marks), not more than five consecutive corresponding striae were found.[53]

3) Percent matching striae ranged from 15 to 30%, which is similar to values reported in previous studies,[54] thus confirming the limited value of percent match as a criterion for identification.

4) The nearly identical range of quantitative values found in all known non-match comparisons for all types of rifled barrels, in addition to striated marks made by the ground working surface of a chisel, demonstrates that the probability for the matching microscopic agreement of randomly distributed striae is fundamentally the same, regardless of the tool used.

Analogous studies of impression type toolmarks, such as firearm breech block markings, or models of randomly distributed individual characteristics of the same or different shape revealed no more than four matching individual characteristics. Even this small degree of chance correspondence observed was possible only if one ignored the exact shape, size, and orientation that was present in each of these randomly distributed individual characteristics. In practice, the examiner would critically evaluate impression characteristics occupying the same relative position for the extent of agreement, and conclude that evidence and test impressions were made by the same surface only where the matching[55] features are sharply defined either wholly or in part.

All research to date supports the hypothesis that it is possible to individualize toolmarks because there are practical probability limits to: (1) the number of randomly distributed consecutive matching striae, and (2) the number of randomly distributed matching individual characteristics in impression toolmarks in known non-match positions. This research also demonstrates that quantitative objective criteria can be applied with a high degree of statistical confidence in determining that a toolmark is unique if the values from KNM comparisons are conservatively applied. The authors, in advocating the following conservative quantitative criteria for identification guidelines, have considered that: (1) there is a probability that a higher number of both single and multiple groups of consecutive matching striae than empirically observed to date could occur in KNM's, (2) the occurrence of multiple groups of consecutive matching striae appearing in the same relative position in any given known non-matching toolmark becomes less probable as the number of groups increases, and (3) there may be some variance between examiners in their subjective interpretation of the qualitative and quantitative agreement observed. With these considerations in mind, the authors' conservative quantitative criteria for identification are:

1) In three-dimensional toolmarks when at least two different groups of at least three consecutive matching striae appear in the same relative position, or one group of six consecutive matching striae are in agreement in an evidence toolmark compared to a test toolmark.

greater significance than is justified, leading to incorrect identifications.

53. Biasotti & Murdock, *supra* note 7.

54. *Id.*; Biasotti, *A Statistical Study, supra* note 34.

55. *See* Biasotti & Murdock, *supra* note 7.

2) In two-dimensional toolmarks when at least two groups of at least five consecutive matching striae appear in the same relative position, or one group of eight consecutive matching striae are in agreement in an evidence toolmark compared to a test toolmark.

For these criteria to apply, however, the possibility of subclass characteristics must be ruled out.

Research conducted thus far indicates that the practical probability limits in known non-matches for impression toolmarks are similar to those found for striated toolmarks. However, more research is needed involving very fine, high density, randomly distributed individual impression characteristics, viewed two dimensionally, before definitive practical probability limits can be stated confidently.

Since this chapter was first published in 1997, there have been several studies which have included an evaluation, using consecutive matching striae, of the numerical criteria for the identification of striated toolmarks proposed above by the authors.[56] No known non-matching (two- or three-dimensional) toolmarks were found in these studies which exhibited agreement in excess of the proposed Biasotti–Murdock criteria.

One indication that the concept of objective quantitative criteria for identification is gaining wider acceptance is that approximately 300 members of the Association of Firearm and Toolmark Examiners (AFTE) voluntarily participated in a four-hour workshop on the subject at their 1999 annual training seminar.[57]

56. Fred Tulleners, Mike Giusto & James Hamiel, *Striae Reproducibility on Sectional Cuts of One Thompson Contender Barrel*, 30 Ass'n Firearm & Toolmark Examiners J. 62 (1998); Jerry Miller & Michael McLean, *Criteria for Identification of Toolmarks*, Ass'n Firearm & Toolmark Examiners J. 15 (1998) (offering a sound description of the history of criteria for identification, the use of IBIS and the scientific method; the authors used IBIS to sort single land impressions of .38 special caliber bullets for comparison; the test firings used in their study were from firearms associated with forensic casework and thus were used firearms); Jerry Miller, *Criteria for Identification of Toolmarks Part II–Single Land Impression Comparisons,* 32 Ass'n Firearm & Toolmark Examiners J. 116 (2000) (extending his IBIS sorted study by examining single land impressions of .25 auto, .380 auto and 9mm calibers; because he limited his studies (Part I and II) to single land impressions, he found that he excluded some known identifications because there was not enough agreement to meet the Biasotti–Murdock criteria; no false identifications were made, however; the test firings used in this study were from firearms associated with forensic casework and thus were used firearms); Jerry Miller, *An Examination of Two Consecutively Rifled Barrels and a Review of the Literature,* 32 Ass'n Firearm & Toolmark Examiners J. 259 (2000) (after reviewing literature dealing with the examination of bullets fired from consecutively rifled barrels, Miller then compared test bullets pushed through two new consecutively rifled gun barrels; after determining that there was no sub class influence, he evaluated the test bullets by using the Biasotti–Murdock numerical criteria for identification described in this chapter; he found that no false identifications would be made using these criteria); Fred Tulleners, David Stoney & James Hamiel, An Analysis of Consecutive Striae on Random and Consecutive Chisels, Paper presented at the annual meeting of the American Academy of Forensics Sciences (Feb.1999) (manuscript submitted to the Journal of Forensic Sciences).

57. Objective Criteria Workshop, presented by Torrey D. Johnson (of the Las Vegas Metro Police Department Forensic Laboratory) in Williamsburg, Virginia (July 18–23, 1999). Each participant performed a number of toolmark "photo comparisons" and were to conclude if the comparisons represented an identification, an elimination or were inconclusive of the AFTE glossary A, B or C type; *see supra* note 15 and accompanying text. The hypothesis for this study was that, when toolmarks are compared, based on corresponding groups of striae, called consecutive matching striae, a level of correspondence exists which provides a satisfactory determination of identity between the marks. If it is possible to establish this level, it is possible to define quantitatively the degree of correspondence that divides inconclusive from identification.

On a more practical level, Bruce Moran has authored two papers which describe how he uses objective quantitative criteria in firearms and toolmark casework and how a typical question and answer session might go in court on the same subject.[58]

§ 4–2.5   Future Directions

It is anticipated that objective quantitative criteria for identification will eventually become widely accepted and used because of the research already conducted and published, plus a commercially available system called the Integrated Ballistic Identification System (IBIS)[59] developed by Forensic Technology Industries of Montreal, Canada, for the comparison of fired bullets and cartridge cases. Barrett reported on the basic concept of the IBIS system in 1991, while Tontarski and Thompson have provided a description of the IBIS system as it was being used in 1998.[60] It has undergone several upgrades since.

The primary purpose of these automated comparison systems, as far as fired bullets are concerned, is to rapidly screen large populations of electronically stored images of fired bullets. From a comparison of the unique features of the stored images, these systems produce a list of bullet images ranked in order of striae agreement. An imaging comparison system called "Drugfire" was developed for cartridge cases by the Federal Bureau of Investigation.[61] Drugfire machines are, however, currently being phased out. They are being replaced across the United States by IBIS machines.

Automated systems do *not* make identifications, or replace the need for an expert examiner. The identification or exclusion of the images generated by these systems must be based on the informed judgement of an examiner comparing real or replica bullets or cartridge cases selected by these systems.

However, these systems will continue to make major contributions toward establishing objective quantitative criteria for identification. Objective criteria such as the number of consecutively corresponding striae, or the percent of corresponding striae, and the effect of variable qualitative dimensions of individual characteristics can be evaluated rapidly for large populations of known non-matches from a variety of different calibers, bullet and cartridge types and manufacturing methods. These automated measurements, which are inherently objective, can therefore be used to increase substantially the

58. Bruce Moran, *The Application of Numerical Criteria For Identification in Casework Involving (Ammunition) Magazine Marks and Rifling Impressions (on Bullets)*, 33 Ass'n Firearm & Toolmark Examiners J. 41 (2001) (including a well-illustrated discussion of sub class toolmarks on ammunition magazine lips); Bruce Moran, *Firearms Examiner Expert Witness Testimony: The Forensic Firearms Identification Process Including Criteria for Identification and Distance Determination*, 32 Ass'n Firearm & Toolmark Examiners J. 231 (2000) (providing helpful discussion concerning skillful and thorough presentation of this subject in court).

59. Technical and other information available from Wayne Baird and Rene Belanger,

Forensic Technology, Inc., 3300 Cavendish Blvd., Suite 400, Montreal, Quebec, Canada H4B 2M8.

60. Michael R. Barrett, *The Microchip and the Bullet: A Vision of the Future*, 23 Ass'n Firearms & Toolmark Examiners J. 876 (1991); Richard E. Tontarski & Robert M. Thompson, *Automated Ballistic Comparison: A Forensic Tool for Firearms Identification–An Update*, 43 J. Forensic Sci. 641 (1998).

61. Robert W. Sibert, *Drugfire: Revolutionizing Forensic Firearms Identification and Providing the Foundation for a National Firearms Identification Network*, 21 Crime Laboratory Dig. 63 (October 1994).

statistical confidence in the range of correspondence observed in direct manual known non-match comparisons.

Beyond this, it is up to individual examiners to become aware of the literature about criteria for identification and use it in their day-to-day casework. Perhaps then it will be possible to come close to the standard espoused by Paul Kirk in his syllabus to his University of California, Berkeley, Course number 151: "In criminalistic practice [forensic science], mistakes are not allowed."[62] In reality, mistakes do occur in forensic science, as in all other professions. All we can do is to try very, very hard to prevent them. It is our belief that the continued development and widespread acceptance of objective quantifiable criteria for identification will hold mistakes to a minimum, especially where limited striae are available for comparison.

With the assumption that firearm/toolmark examiners embrace the concept of quantitative criteria for identification of striated toolmarks using consecutive matching striae, Grzybowski and Murdock have summarized the view of many examiners by concluding that:

> The firearm/toolmark identification field has all the indicia of a science: (1) It is well grounded in scientific method; (2) it is well accepted in the relevant scientific community; (3) it has been subjected to many forms of peer review and publication; (4) it has participated in proficiency testing and published error rates; and (5) it provides objective quantitative criteria that guide the identification process.[63]

62. Paul L. Kirk, Outline of Laboratory Work in Criminology 151 (University of California, Berkeley, 1957, reprinted 1963), at 2.

63. Grzybowski & Murdock, *supra* note 31 (including a basic discussion of the scientific method as well as inductive and deductive reasoning).

Appendix 1

Glossary of Terms

Drawn from a list promulgated by the Association of Firearm and Toolmark Examiners

Accidental characteristic. Term formerly used to mean individual characteristic. See individual characteristics.

Class characteristics. Measurable features of a specimen which indicate a restricted group source. They result from design factors, and are therefore determined prior to manufacture.

Impression. Contour variations on the surface of an object caused by a combination of force and motion where the motion is approximately perpendicular to the plane being marked. These marks can contain *class* and/or *individual characteristics*.

Individual characteristics. Marks produced by the random imperfections or irregularities of tool surfaces. These random imperfections or irregularities are either produced incidental to manufacture or are caused by use, corrosion, or damage. They are unique to that tool and distinguish it from all other tools.

Striations. Contour variations, generally microscopic, on the surface of an object caused by a combination of force and motion where the motion is approximately parallel to the plane being marked. These marks can contain *class* and/or *individual characteristics*.

Subclass characteristics. Discernible surface features of an object that are more restrictive than *class characteristics* in that they (1) are produced incidental to manufacture, (2) relate to a smaller group source (a subset of the class to which they belong), (3) can arise from a source which changes over time. Examples include: bunter marks (headstamps produced on cartridge cases) produced by bunters made from a common master, extrusion marks on pipe, etc.

Tool. An object used to gain mechanical advantage. Also thought of as the harder of two objects which produces toolmarks when brought into contact with each other resulting in the softer one being marked.

Toolmark, impressed. Marks produced when a tool is placed against another object and enough force is applied to the tool so that it leaves an impression. The class characteristics (shape) can indicate the type of tool used to produce the mark. These marks can contain *class* and/or *individual characteristics* of the tool producing the marks. Also called *compression marks*.

Toolmark, striated. Marks produced when a tool is placed against another object and with pressure applied, the tool is moved across the object, producing a striated mark. *Friction marks, abrasion marks*, and *scratch marks* are terms commonly used when referring to striated marks. These marks can consist of either *class* or *individual characteristics*, or both.

Appendix 2

Questions Designed to Test a Witness's Ability to Identify Striated Toolmarks

1. Have you had training in toolmark comparisons?

2. Please describe this training for us. I am especially interested in the specific training you have had that enables you to individualize striated toolmarks.

(Several types of training are possible: (1) regular classroom, (2) organized on-the-job training, and (3) structured self-directed type. All of these can focus on many areas worthy of study such as note taking, photography, tool manufacturing in general, but be unrelated to the individualization process.)

3. When you are comparing striated toolmarks made by tools capable of making unique toolmarks, how much agreement do you require before you can identify a specific tool as having made a specific evidence toolmark?

(An amount that exceeds the best known non-match agreement that I have ever seen, either in my experience or in the literature.)

4. How much agreement do other examiners require?

(This is generally unknown but the answer to #3 above is generally accepted.)

5. What is the standard amount of agreement that is required by the profession of toolmark examiners for an identification?

(There are no objective, quantifiable standards recognized by the profession; but there are individual subjective "standard criteria" built up in the examiners' mind's-eye.)

6. If there are no universally recognized objective, quantifiable standards for the amount of agreement that is required to individualize striated toolmarks, how do you expect this court to evaluate the propriety of your conclusion(s)?

(There are subjective guidelines. There has been a *Theory of Identification* and *Range of Conclusions Possible when Comparing Toolmarks* (*supra* note 15) adopted by the Association of Firearm and Toolmark Examiners.)

7. Would you expect to find some agreement [matching striae] when comparing striated toolmarks known to have been made by different tools?

(The answer is yes.)

8. Isn't it true that there can be, on occasion, a considerable amount of agreement in comparisons of this sort, especially if the width of a shallow (for practical purposes, two-dimensional) mark being compared is quite small [say 2 millimeters or less]?

(The agreement referred to here should be enough agreement to pique an examiner's interest. The answer should be yes, but if no, you could refer the witness to a 1975 article on boltcutters (*supra* note 7) wherein quite a bit of apparent matching striae in known non-match positions are shown; or Murdock & Biasotti's "State of the Art ..." article (*supra* note 7) which also contains illustrations of known non-match agreement.)

9. The match or agreement in this case has been characterized as "_____".

(The person asking the question can either quote from pretrial oral statements or written report(s) describing the nature of the toolmark agreement. The agreement may be described, depending on the examiner, as "significant," "best seen," "textbook," etc.)

10. Since you can get striae agreement in "known non-match" comparisons, how can you be sure that the agreement in this case is any better than remarkable "non-match" agreement. If the agreement in this case is no better than that, it doesn't mean anything does it?

(A witness who has never compared known "non-matches" is in a poor position with respect to this question. A witness who has studied known non-matches probably would say that the agreement exceeds known "non-match" agreement, if it does.)

11. Have you ever *deliberately* compared striated toolmarks that you knew were made by different tools?

(The answer should be yes. "Deliberately" is the key word here. When you do this, you are focusing on known non-match (KNM) agreement. When you find KNM agreement incidental to casework, you are probably not so focused and probably wouldn't take the time to record agreement in KNM positions; most examiners, however, gain some experience in KNM agreement while doing striae comparison casework.)

12. If so, how many of these comparisons have you made and what was the purpose of making comparisons of this sort?

(Approximately _____, for purposes of finding maximum striae agreement in any given KNM position.)

13. Wouldn't you agree that it is important in order to properly evaluate and determine the significance of limited or less than textbook striae agreement to know what the best agreement looks like in known non-match comparisons?

(The answer is yes. This knowledge is best gained by *deliberate* KNM comparisons, and not simply by what the examiner remembers having seen while comparing striae in casework, although some knowledge as mentioned above in #11, is gained in this way.)

14. In order to make a positive identification of striated marks, it seems to me that you have to have an amount of agreement that exceeds the best known non-match agreement. Do you agree?

(Yes. A witness who acknowledges having limited or no experience critically comparing known non-matching striated toolmarks, may not be in a very good position to properly evaluate the significance of the amount of agreement in cases where limited striae are present.)

CHAPTER 5

IDENTIFICATION FROM BITEMARKS

Table of Sections

Westlaw Electronic Research

See Westlaw Electronic Research Guide preceding the Summary of Contents.

A. LEGAL ISSUES

§ 5–1.0 THE LEGAL RELEVANCE OF RESEARCH ON BITE-MARK IDENTIFICATION

The analysis of bitemarks for the purpose of identifying a criminal perpetrator is a specialized task within the broader discipline of forensic odontology. Accordingly, it presents more challenging questions to odontologists and, in turn, to courts. Forensic dentists long have been called upon to identify the remains of victims of disasters by comparing the victims' dentition with dental records.[1] In trying to identify perpetrators of crime, the forensic dentist seeks to compare a suspect's dentition with a latent mark left in the victim's flesh or in some material, usually an edible substance, found at the scene of a crime.[2]

§ 5–1.1 Bitemark Identification and the *Daubert* Factors

Like all forensic identification sciences, the claims of the field of forensic odontology clearly are empirical in nature and therefore amenable to review under *Daubert's*[3] criteria for evaluating scientific claims. Against those criteria, bitemark identification encounters several interesting problems. Clearly the nature of dentition and the asserted skills of forensic dentists are testable. And, although some of the scientific issues and claims in forensic odontology have been tested more extensively than the scientific issues and claims of most forensic individualization sciences, that is largely because most of the other forensic individualization sciences have conducted or been subjected to remarkably little systematic empirical testing.[4] Important issues about the nature of identification by bitemark comparisons remain unresolved.[5]

Some of the research that has been conducted has been published and, if not peer reviewed before publication, certainly has been afterwards. Troublingly, some of the research has not been published or otherwise made public.[6] Recall that, properly understood, "peer review and publication" is concerned with evaluating the methodology of the "testing" referred to above. The published research in forensic odontology is not without flaws, and those flaws will inevitably and properly affect the seriousness with which the findings of those studies are taken.[7]

§ 5–1.0

1. In mass disasters dentists are able to identify 20–25% of the victims. *See infra* § 2.1.1.

2. The two tasks differ in important ways. In the disaster situation, there is a finite number of candidates to identify, and full dentition often is available from the victims as well as from the dental charts. In forensic bitemark cases, the number of potential suspects is huge, the bitemarks include only a limited portion of the dentition, and flesh is a far less clear medium than having the teeth (of the disaster victim) themselves.

3. Daubert v. Merrell Dow Pharmaceuticals, Inc., 509 U.S. 579, 113 S.Ct. 2786, 125 L.Ed.2d 469 (1993).

4. *See, e.g.*, Chapters 2 and 3.

5. Discussed at various places in the Scientific Status section of this chapter, *infra* § 2.0.

6. The results of the fourth round of proficiency testing are reported *infra*, § 2.1.3[1], but the first three have never been published. In fairness to forensic dentists, it must be noted that the program of proficiency testing of other areas of forensic science are never published, but rather are circulated only among members of the field.

7. *See* discussion at various places in the Scientific Status portion of this chapter, *infra* § 2.0.

The error rate in bitemark identification, particularly the rate of false positive errors, appears to be quite high.[8]

Finally, general acceptance is an issue in forensic dentistry with regard to the task of linking crime scene marks to the dentition of a suspect. Not long ago, many, perhaps a majority, of forensic odontologists doubted that they could make pinpoint identifications in more than the rare case. Due to the eager acceptance by judges of bitemark expert testimony,[9] that number has dwindled, but a significant minority of forensic dentists retain their doubts about some of the field's vital claims. Thus, general acceptance in forensic odontology is not nearly so strong as it is in other forensic science fields.

§ 5–1.2 Divergence of Opinions by Bitemark Experts

One pattern that has emerged from the testimony presented in bitemark cases is the persistence of forensic odontologists testifying to contrary opinions. This occurs not only for opinions about the identity of the maker of a bitemark, but also on the question of whether or not a wound was caused by a bite.

In numerous cases, forensic odontologists have disagreed about whether a particular mark on a victim was a bitemark or not.[10] An increasingly well-known article reports on a case in which an injury was initially interpreted as a "possible" bitemark.[11] A suspect was then developed and dental models were taken of his teeth. After comparing the model to the injury, two forensic odontologists "stated that not only was the injury definitely caused by a human bite, but that the individual characteristics of the injury identically matched the suspect's dentition."[12] Thereafter, it was determined through an elaborate series of tests that the injury was not a bitemark after all, even though certain areas "suggested outlines of individual tooth margins."[13] In their article, the authors, both prominent forensic dentists, state the following conclusion:

> [When an injury is initially evaluated, and consideration is given toward the possibility of a human bite origin, *the first question to be asked is,* "Is this truly a bite injury?"] . . . . *If the answer is affirmative, the next two questions are* "What portion or portions of the dental arcade does it represent and what class and individual tooth characteristics does it contain?" These [latter] two questions must be always addressed in sequence, as the application of the second query is wholly dependent upon the answer to the first. *If this process is altered, and the basic presence or*

8. *See infra* § 2.1.3[1].

9. *See* discussion *infra* of People v. Marx and its aftermath.

10. *See, e.g.,* Kinney v. State, 315 Ark. 481, 868 S.W.2d 463 (Ark. 1994) (state and defense experts disagree about whether mark was human bitemark); State v. Holmes, 234 Ill.App.3d 931, 176 Ill.Dec. 287, 601 N.E.2d 985 (Ill.App. 1992) (same); Davis v. State, 611 So.2d 906 (Miss.1992) (same); People v. Noguera, 4 Cal.4th 599, 15 Cal.Rptr.2d 400, 842 P.2d 1160, 1165 (Cal.1992) (same); State v. Kendrick, 47 Wash.App. 620, 736 P.2d 1079 (1987) (Wash. App. same); People v. Smith, 63 N.Y.2d 41, 479 N.Y.S.2d 706, 468 N.E.2d 879 (N.Y.1984) (same); State v. Keko, Case No. 92–3292 (Parish Plaquemines, Louisiana, 1992) (same).

11. K. Sperry & H.R. Campbell, Jr., *An Elliptical Incised Wound of the Breast Misinterpreted as a Bite Injury*, 35 J. Forensic Science 1126 (1990).

12. *Id.* at 1228.

13. *Id.* at 1235.

absence of an actual bite pattern injury is not adequately addressed, the eventual outcome may be disastrous.[14]

The other issue, whether a defendant was the source of a bitemark, has generated at least as much disagreement between experts. Numerous examples of these cases are cited in the margin.[15]

In addition to the above-cited decisions, there have been numerous reports of forensic odontologists reaching opinions that disagreed with the results of DNA and other forensic analysis. Examples of such cases are given in the margin.[16]

The rather frequent disagreement among forensic dentists, more common than among other forensic identification scientists,[17] could be explained in a number of different ways. Bitemark comparisons may be inherently more ambiguous than other identification types. Forensic dentists may simply be

---

14. *Id.* (emphasis added).

15. *See, e.g.,* Milone v. Camp, 22 F.3d 693 (7th Cir.1994) ("at trial much evidence was adduced by both sides concerning whether Milone's dentition matched the bitemark"; defendant "presented several experts of his own to testify that he could not have made the mark found"); Wilhoit v. Oklahoma, 816 P.2d 545 (Ct.Cr.App.Okla.1991) (eleven "well-recognized forensic odontologists" disagree with state's experts that defendant caused the bitemark on victim); Spence v. State, 795 S.W.2d 743 (Tex. Cr.App.1990) ("there was truly a battle between two of today's leading experts in the field of forensic odontology at appellant's trial"); State v. Sager, 600 S.W.2d 541 (Mo.Ct. App.1980) (defendant's two experts disagreed with State's experts); Kennedy v. State, 640 P.2d 971 (Okla.Crim.App.1982) (defendant's expert disagreed with State's expert); Harrison v. State, 635 So.2d 894 (Miss.1994) (defense expert files affidavit on appeal disagreeing with state's expert); Brown v. State, 690 So.2d 276 (Miss.1996) (state and defense experts disagree); Jackson v. Day, 1996 WL 225021 (E.D.La.1996) (defense counsel ineffective for failing to retain forensic odontologist to rebut state's expert; "[at trial,] the state's odontologist expert testified that the bitemarks found on the victim were similar to the dental impressions made by the defendant ... In the habeas record, the defense has presented the court with an affidavit from an odontologist which excludes [the defendant] as producing the dentition relied on by the state at trial"); Case v. Mississippi, 651 So.2d 567 (Miss.1995) (state's expert testifies that marks on victim were bitemarks caused by defendant's dentition; defense expert testifies that he does not know whether marks were bitemarks, let alone what caused them); Banks v. State, 725 So.2d 711 (Miss.1997) (prosecution and defense experts disagree); State v. Richardson, No. A–4255–95T4 (Sup.Ct.N.J.App.Div.1997) (State's expert testifies that defendant's teeth matched a bitemark on the victim's back while defense expert testifies that defendant could not have

made the bitemark); "Other Lehigh Trials Have Had A Steep Price," 1998 WL 12854106, Allentown Morning Call (7/12/98) (reporting on Commonwealth v. Gonzalez, a case in which state's expert concluded that woman could have bitten infant and defense expert concluded that marks were too small to have been caused by defendant).

16. *See, e.g.,* Mississippi v. Gates, No. 5060 (Humphrey Cty. Cir. Ct. 1998) (DNA excludes suspect whose dentition a forensic odontologist stated matched "bite marks" on the victim; case dismissed); Mississippi v. Bourn, No. 93–10,214(3) (Cir. Ct., Jackson County, Mississippi) (DNA, hair analysis and fingerprint analysis excluded suspect whose dentition a forensic odontologist stated matched "bite marks" on the victim); Florida v. Dale Morris (Pasco County, 97–3251 CFAES, 1997) (prosecutors dismiss first degree murder charge after defense odontologists disagree with conclusion of state's experts that a bitemark on victim "matched" defendant's dentition; subsequent to the dental analyses, DNA results excluded the defendant). *See also, Dentist Defends His Advice in Slaying,* Tampa Tribune (3/3/98), 1998 WL 2766563 (dentist matched defendant's teeth to alleged bite on 9-year-old neighbor; "Although renowned Miami forensic odontologist Richard Souviron supported Martin's finding [of a match], they were disputed by two defense-hired experts: Phil Levine of Pensacola and Lowell Levine of Albany, N.Y."); Malcolm Ritter, *Dentists Take a Bite out of Crime; Experts Battle Crooks Using Teeth Marks, Blue Jean Seams,* The Milwaukee Journal Sentinel (6/7/98), 1998 WL 6331555 (reporting that DNA analysis conflicted with opinions of two forensic odontologists; defendant pleads guilty).

17. Whose principal empirical support for their claim of expertise seems to be that they are rarely if ever contradicted by their peers. *See, e.g.,* David Fisher, Hard Evidence 245 (1996). *See* Chapter 2 at § 1.2.

more available to defendants compared to most other forensic scientists, who are more or less exclusively in the employ of the government. Or, relatedly, board-certified forensic odontologists may inadvertently reach conclusions favorable to the party that has retained them[18]—by no means a phenomenon new to the courts. So, whether the fact of frequent disagreement reveals bitemark identification to be a peculiarly unreliable area, or whether areas of expertise that create an illusion of consistency[19] are the more worrisome, is by no means clear.

§ 5–1.3   The Judicial Response to Expert Testimony on Bitemark Identification

Though expert opinion on bitemark identification is one of the newer areas of forensic identification, having arrived in the courts only in the past generation, it was rapidly admitted in many jurisdictions throughout the United States. The great majority of those cases occurred after 1980.[20]

18. *See*, Jon J. Nordby, *Can We Believe What We See, If We See What We Believe?—Expert Disagreement*, 37 J. FORENSIC SCI. 1115 (1992) (disagreement among honest experts often caused by "expectation-laden observations").

19. Behind which hides an equal amount of ambiguity and disagreement.

20. By state:

Cal.:

   People v. Marx, 54 Cal.App.3d 100, 126 Cal.Rptr. 350 (Cal.App.1975).

Conn.:

   State v. Ortiz, 198 Conn. 220, 502 A.2d 400 (Conn. 1985).

Fla.:

   Bundy v. State, 455 So.2d 330 (Fla.1984).

   Bundy v. State, 490 So.2d 1258 (Fla.1986).

   Bundy v. State, 497 So.2d 1209 (Fla.1986).

   Bundy v. State, 538 So.2d 445 (Fla.1989).

Ill.:

   People v. Milone, 43 Ill.App.3d 385, 2 Ill. Dec. 63, 356 N.E.2d 1350 (Ill.App.1976).

   People v. Williams, 128 Ill.App.3d 384, 83 Ill.Dec. 720, 470 N.E.2d 1140 (Ill.App. 1984).

Ind.:

   Niehaus v. State, 265 Ind. 655, 359 N.E.2d 513 (Ind. 1977).

La.:

   State v. Wommack, 770 So.2d 365 (La.App. 2000)

Mich.:

   People v. Marsh, 177 Mich.App. 161, 441 N.W.2d 33 (Mich.App.1989).

Minn.:

   State v. Hodgson, 512 N.W.2d 95 (Minn. 1994).

Miss.:

   Howard v. State, 697 So.2d 415 (Miss. 1997) (holding bitemark expert testimony inadmissible)

   Brooks v. State, 748 So.2d 736 (Miss.1999) (holding bitemark expert evidence admissible)

Mo.:

   State v. Sager, 600 S.W.2d 541 (Mo.App. 1980).

   State v. Kleypas, 602 S.W.2d 863 (Mo.App. 1980).

   State v. Turner, 633 S.W.2d 421 (Mo.App. 1982).

NY:

   People v. Middleton, 54 N.Y.2d 42, 444 N.Y.S.2d 581, 429 N.E.2d 100 (N.Y. 1981).

   People v. Smith, 63 N.Y.2d 41, 479 N.Y.S.2d 706, 468 N.E.2d 879 (N.Y. 1984).

   People v. Smith, 110 Misc.2d 118, 443 N.Y.S.2d 551 (1981).

NC:

   State v. Temple, 302 N.C. 1, 273 S.E.2d 273 (N.C. 1981).

   State v. Green, 305 N.C. 463, 290 S.E.2d 625 (N.C. 1982).

NM:

   State v. Garrison, 120 Ariz. 255, 585 P.2d 563 (Ariz. 1978).

Okla.:

   Kennedy v. State, 640 P.2d 971 (Okla. Crim.App.1982).

RI:

   State v. Adams, 481 A.2d 718 (R.I.1984).

SC:

   State v. Jones, 273 S.C. 723, 259 S.E.2d 120 (S.C. 1979).

Several ironies accompany this legal history. One is that forensic odontologists, perhaps reflecting a grounding in scientific skepticism that is absent from the more traditional forensic identification sciences,[21] were more doubtful about whether the state of their knowledge permitted them to successfully identify a perpetrator "to the exclusion of all others." The history of other areas of forensic identification reveals no similar self doubts. Second, the courts began admitting expert testimony on bitemarks while many prominent forensic odontologists still doubted whether the necessary knowledge existed to permit them to make such identifications accurately. Third, and most remarkable, rather than the field convincing the courts of the sufficiency of its knowledge and skills, admission by the courts seems to have convinced the forensic odontology community that, despite their doubts, they were able to perform bitemark identifications after all.[22]

§ 5–1.3.1 Cases Before *Daubert*

The first case in the United States to confront the admissibility of expert testimony on a bitemark identification was *Doyle v. State*.[23] Doyle was charged with burglary. At the site of the burglary was found a piece of partially eaten cheese. After arresting Doyle, the sheriff asked him to bite a piece of cheese, which the suspect voluntarily did. A firearms examiner compared the two pieces of cheese to try to determine if the questioned and the known tooth marks had been made by the same person. The firearms examiner concluded that they had. At trial a dentist testified that from his own examination of plaster casts of the cheese bitemarks, he also reached the opinion that one and the same dentition had made both sets of bites.[24] The Texas Court of Criminal Appeals upheld the admission of this bitemark opinion testimony.

Although the empirical research necessary to form the scientific ground for such a conclusion had not yet been undertaken,[25] the defense in *Doyle* did not contest admissibility by raising any issue of scientific validity, but instead raised only procedural challenges.[26] Thus, the *Doyle* court did not address the

Tex.:

    Doyle v. State, 159 Tex.Crim. 310, 263 S.W.2d 779 (Tex.Cr.App.1954).

    Patterson v. State, 509 S.W.2d 857 (Tex. Cr.App.1974).

Wis.:

    State v. Stinson, 134 Wis.2d 224, 397 N.W.2d 136 (Wis.App.1986).

21. Compared to examiners of fingerprints, footprints, toolmarks, document examiners, firearms, and so on.

22. In their book on scientific evidence, ANDRE MOENSSENS, ET AL. SCIENTIFIC EVIDENCE IN CIVIL AND CRIMINAL CASES (4th ed.1995), they conclude concerning the relationship between the courts and expert opinion on bitemark identification:

The wholesale acceptance, by the courts, of testimony on bite mark identification has transformed the profession. Whereas prior to 1974 the main thrust of forensic dentistry was to prove identity of persons by means of a comparison of postmortem and antemortem dental records in mass disasters, the

profession has changed direction and is now heavily involved in assisting prosecutors in homicide and sex offense cases. Having received judicial approval of bite mark comparisons, there seems to be no more limit on the extent of forensic odontological conclusions.

Id. § 16.07, at 985.

23. 159 Tex.Crim. 310, 263 S.W.2d 779 (Tex.Crim.1954). Although this was the first appellate consideration of bitemark evidence, the technique had been used for related identification purposes for decades. *See* § 2.0.

24. *See* § 2.0.

25. As leading forensic odontologists today readily note. *See* studies discussed in the Scientific Status portion of this chapter, *infra* § 2.0.

26. The defense raised only the issue of whether obtaining the bitten cheese from the defendant constituted a confession and thereby violated a Texas statute prohibiting obtaining confessions without warning defendants of their likely use.

scientific status of bitemark identification. Nevertheless, another Texas court relied on *Doyle* twenty years later as the basis for rejecting an appellant's contention that bitemark test results were of unproven reliability.[27] Both Texas cases seemed to take admissibility as a given, and neither addressed the scientific issues.

The cornerstone case on the admissibility of bitemark identification was decided the following year, in 1975, in California. This case undertook to grapple with the scientific issues on which admissibility of bitemark identification should turn, but in the end succeeded only in eluding them. *People v. Marx*[28] involved a brutal murder of an elderly woman who had an elliptical laceration on her nose. This mark was judged to be a human bite, and impressions were made of the wound for comparison with a cast of the defendant's teeth.

At trial, three odontologists testified that in their opinion the defendant's dentition matched the bite wound.[29] One of those experts took pains to note that in many other cases he had refused to offer a firm opinion or even to testify about an identification. This case, however, was an exception in that the dentition at issue was extremely unusual and the bitemark was exceptionally well defined. The witness characterized these bite impressions as the clearest he had ever seen, either personally or in the literature. Despite the expert's caution, and unusual case facts emphasizing the rarity of both the dentition and the bitemarks, *Marx* pried open the courtroom door for bitemark identification. Having done so, it became the admission ticket for a far wider and more dubious array of dentition in many subsequent cases.

On appeal, the defense challenged the admission of expert opinions on bite wound identification on the ground that the purported skills were not sufficiently established or generally accepted in the field of forensic dentistry. Thus, under California law following *Frye v. United States*,[30] the admission of such testimony would have been error. The field was, after all, sharply divided over the question of whether they could identify biters by the bitemarks left in crime victims. The California Court of Appeals acknowledged that there was "no established science of identifying persons from bite marks...."[31] Moreover, the theory of bitemark identification is in essence based on an assessment of the probability that two or more people could leave the same bitemark,[32] yet no data existed on those probabilities. How did the Court of Appeals reach its decision to admit the testimony, despite the California Supreme Court's repeated announcement of general acceptance as the governing rule in that state, and its prohibition on evidence based on speculative probability estimates?[33] In several ways.

The Court of Appeals deflected the implications of *Frye,* by interpreting that test in these terms:

27. Patterson v. State, 509 S.W.2d 857 (Tex.Cr.App.1974).

28. 54 Cal.App.3d 100, 126 Cal.Rptr. 350 (1975).

29. Gerry L. Vale et al., *Unusual Three–Dimensional Bite Mark Evidence in a Homicide Case,* 21 J. FORENSIC SCI. 642 (1976).

30. 293 F. 1013 (D.C.App.1923).

31. *Id.* at 353.

32. *See* § 2.1.5[3].

33. People v. Collins, 68 Cal.2d 319, 66 Cal.Rptr. 497, 438 P.2d 33 (Cal.1968).

The *Frye* test finds its rational basis in the degree to which the trier of fact must accept, on faith, scientific hypotheses not capable of proof or disproof in court and not even generally accepted outside the courtroom. *Frye,* for example, involved the lie detector test in which the trier of fact is required to rely on the testimony of the polygrapher, verified at most by marks on a graph, to which the expert's hypothesis gives some relevant meaning.... [Other cases reflect] [t]he same concern that the trier of fact will be overwhelmed by "ill conceived techniques with which the trier of fact is not technically equipped to cope," sacrificing its independence in favor of deference to the expert.[34]

The paradox, of course, is that expert opinion testimony is permitted precisely because it is believed that the expert's understanding exceeds the jury's, and the expert can tell the jury truths that the jury could not otherwise grasp. Be that as it may, the court thus distinguished *Marx* from *Frye* by reasoning that *Frye* applied to evidence that was indecipherable without an expert's interpretation, whereas *Marx* involved models, X-rays, and slides of the victim's wounds and the accused's dentition, all of which were clearly visible for the jurors to view, assess, and verify on their own during court proceedings, without having to rely on the expert odontologist as a necessary intermediary. Forensic odontologists, no doubt, would be astonished to learn that once the pictures are taken and the molds cast, no special expertise or judgment is required to assess whether the wound was made by the defendant's dentition.

The *Marx* court concluded, alternatively, that the requirements of *Frye* *had* been met because the methods used to facilitate the bitemark identification were not really novel:

> [T]he experts did not rely on untested methods, unproven hypotheses, intuition or revelation. Rather, they applied scientifically and professionally established techniques—X-rays, models, microscopy, photography—to the solution of a particular problem which, though novel, was well within the capability of those techniques.[35]

On this view, *Frye* is about the tools, not the meaning of the information collected with the help of the tools. While the reliability of the tools is by no means unimportant, the most fundamental issues in bitemark identification, as with all forensic identification, are (a) whether the population variation in the relevant characteristics is immense, (b) whether in practice that underlying variation is adequately captured by the available tools and evidence, particularly, (c) whether the latent mark has enough distinct variation in it to allow the probability that someone else's dentition may have left the mark to fall comfortably low.[36] None of this essential knowledge was, or usually is, available to the jury. The question the court might well be focusing on, however, is whether that information is even available to the expert.[37]

Ironically, the *Marx* court appears to have believed that an inquiry about or offer of evidence on the probabilities underlying bitemark identifications would be inadmissible in California under the rule of *People v. Collins*.[38] It

---

34. People v. Marx, 54 Cal.App.3d 100, 110–111, 126 Cal.Rptr. 350 (1975).

35. *Id.* at 111.

36. *See* § 2.1.5[3].

37. If it is not, in some form or fashion, then the expert is speculating.

38. 68 Cal.2d 319, 66 Cal.Rptr. 497, 438 P.2d 33 (Cal. 1968).

held that, since the experts never had actual data and did no calculations of probability, but instead remained impressionistic and intuitive, "[n]one of the witnesses engaged in a 'trial by mathematics' [citing *Collins*] on or off the stand. There was no error."

First of all, the *Marx* court overstates the *Collins* prohibition. In *Collins*, a major ground of the inadmissibility of a statistically based identification was that it was based on (a) speculative probabilities (rather than known relative frequencies of the attributes at issue), and (b) a lack of proof that the attributes of interest consisted of independent events,[39] thereby resulting in faulty computations. In short, the evidence lacked essential foundation. Absent these flaws, such evidence might well be admissible. Second, whether a *jury* will be allowed to hear the numbers is one thing. Whether they may be heard *by a court* in deciding a preliminary question such as the admissibility of purported scientific evidence is quite another. Any court following FRE 104 or an equivalent rule plainly is authorized to do so,[40] and any court following *Daubert* apparently has a *duty* to do so.[41] And surely the experts ought to have such data, because those are what their conclusions rely upon.[42]

Most interesting, perhaps, *Marx* is one of the rare cases to realize that much forensic identification evidence invokes much the same reasoning that the California Supreme Court found so troubling in *Collins*. To believe that the experts or the court, in deciding a question of admissibility of expert evidence, should eschew consideration of the underlying data and the statistical inferences to be drawn from those data, is a deeply confused extension of *Collins*. It solves few if any of the problems that *Collins* was concerned with; it merely pretends the problems are not there. The existence and nature of probability data are at the heart of the theory of forensic identification, and a court ought to be scrutinizing them, not insisting that all is well because no one looked at or thought about them.[43]

The following year, in 1976, Illinois had its first occasion to consider the admissibility of bitemark evidence. In *People v. Milone*, the Court of Appeals held it admissible as "a logical extension of the accepted principle that each person's dentition is unique."[44] The court based this on its earlier recognition of the identification of accident victims from their dental records. In this case, expert witnesses disagreed sharply on the question of the validity and utility of bitemark identifications. The testimony of three forensic dentists was offered by the prosecution and four by the defense. The defense experts testified and cited odontological literature showing, at the least, considerable disagreement among forensic odontologists as to whether offenders could be

---

39. In order to apply the multiplication rule to calculate the probability, each component must be uncorrelated with each other component.

40. Moreover, in deciding such preliminary questions, the court "is not bound by the rules of evidence except those with respect to privileges." Fed. R. Evid. 104(a).

41. Among other data to be considered is a technique's "known or potential error rate." *Daubert*, at 594.

42. Compare the work of experts in DNA identification. *See* Chapter 11.

43. DNA evidence is the best example of a field providing the necessary data and probability calculations, and the chief exception to the rule that the evidence offered by the forensic identification sciences resembles the evidence offered in People v. Collins. Forensic odontologists appreciate that these data are needed, and have been developing them. *See* scientific status portion of this chapter, *infra* § 2.0.

44. People v. Milone, 43 Ill.App.3d 385, 2 Ill.Dec. 63, 356 N.E.2d 1350 (Ill.App.1976).

uniquely identified from bites left in the flesh of victims. Notwithstanding the controversy in the record and in the literature, the court found that the general acceptance standard had been met.[45] In contrast to the approach a court would be expected to take today under *Daubert,* the *Milone* court held that questions about the truth of the proposition quoted above—of immense variation and unique identifiability—went to the weight of the expert testimony, not to its admissibility.

By 1978, a California Court of Appeals flatly held that the testimony of three forensic odontologists established that bitemark identification had gained the required general acceptance in the relevant scientific community.[46]

Perhaps the most unusual legal development after *Marx* and before *Daubert* was a suit by the defendant who had been convicted in *People v. Milone.* Paroled after serving nearly twenty years in prison for murder, Milone continues to insist upon his innocence and continues to try to clear his name. In federal court, under both the *Frye* and *Daubert* standards, he has challenged the original decision to admit the expert bitemark testimony. Another murder victim was later found in the same area where the victim in the *Milone* case had been found. A potential bitemark from the second murder victim was linked to a suspect, Macek. The crime scene bitemarks in the two cases were judged by at least one forensic odontologist to be indistinguishable from each other.[47] Macek signed but later withdrew a confession to having killed the victim for whose murder Milone had been convicted.[48] For present purposes, more important than the question of whether or not Macek killed both victims, is the suggestion that the relevant portions of dentition of two different suspects were indistinguishably alike.[49]

The Court of Appeals for the Seventh Circuit expressed sympathy with the Milone's request, in light of the new evidence presented, but declined to rule on the case for want of a constitutional basis for granting relief, and because principles of federalism precluded a federal court from re-examining an issue of fact that is reserved to the states.[50]

§ 5–1.3.2 Cases After *Daubert*

No federal courts have evaluated the admissibility of bitemark expert evidence under the requirements of the Supreme Court's decision in *Daubert.* Several state cases have done so, and are worth comment for an assortment of reasons.

45. Incidentally, as a testament to the power of weak or inapt precedents, the court cited the Texas cases of *Doyle* (which had no data) and *Patterson* (which relied on *Doyle*), as well as California's *Marx* (which dealt with highly unusual dentition, in contrast to the apparently more common dentition of the present case).

46. People v. Slone, 76 Cal.App.3d 611, 143 Cal.Rptr. 61 (1978).

47. The forensic odontologist, later President of the American Academy of Forensic Sciences, had been a defense expert in the *Milone* case and wrote about these cases in, Lowell Levine, *Forensic Dentistry: Our Most Controversial Case, in* 1978 LEGAL MEDICINE ANNUAL (Cyril Wecht, ed.).

48. Discussed in State v. Sager, 600 S.W.2d 541 (Mo.App.1980).

49. Such findings are not unique in the identification sciences. In the present case, however, it might be noted that the comparison was not made using standard methods or procedures because of the full mouth extractions by Macek. The comparisons of the injury to x-rays of pre-extracted teeth hold little similarity to standard comparison procedures of overlaying biting edges onto the injury patterns on the skin.

50. Milone v. Camp, 22 F.3d 693 (7th Cir. 1994).

The bitemark evidence in *State v. Hodgson*[51] consisted of apparent teeth marks in a suspect's arm, which a forensic dentist compared to known molds of the dentition of a murder victim. The dentist testified to "several similarities" between the bitemark on the defendant and the victim's teeth. Defense counsel objected to a question calling for the odontologist's opinion as to whether the bitemark and the victim's teeth matched, and the witness did not state her opinion.

On appeal, the defendant challenged the admission of the bitemark expert evidence on the grounds that it was not generally accepted, and therefore should not have been admitted under Minnesota's version of the *Frye* test, *State v. Schwartz*.[52] On the question of the admissibility of bitemark expert testimony, the Minnesota Supreme Court concluded as follows:

> We note that recently the United States Supreme Court, in *Daubert v. Merrell Dow Pharmaceuticals, Inc.*, held that the Rules of Evidence supersede the *Frye* or general acceptance test for the admission of novel scientific evidence. We need not address the issue of what impact *Daubert* should or will have in Minnesota. Suffice it to say, we are satisfied that basic bitemark analysis by a recognized expert is not a novel or emerging type of scientific evidence.[53]

Thus, the court disposed of the issue simply by holding that bitemark expert evidence was not novel.

Whether non-novel evidence ever was insulated from fresh scrutiny under *Frye*-type tests once the issue of the evidence's unreliability, or its unproven reliability, was raised, has always been doubtful, but it certainly is not supported by any apparent logic. Why should non-novelty, by itself, shelter from re-examination erroneous scientific claims that have lost the support of the field or fields from whence they came? Under any test, the more coherent view is that novelty should serve not as a prerequisite for judicial scrutiny, but as a hair trigger for it. *Daubert* itself had this to say on the role of non-novelty:

> [W]e do not read the requirements of Rule 702 to apply specially or exclusively to unconventional evidence. Of course, well-established propositions are less likely to be challenged than those that are novel, and they are more handily defended.[54]

Though Wyoming is a *Daubert* state, a challenge to bitemark expert evidence received no more consideration there than it had in Minnesota. The defendant in *Seivewright v. State*[55] had been convicted of a burglary during which the burglar had taken a bite out of a block of cheese. At trial an orthodontist who had made an impression of the cheese and of the defendant's teeth testified that the defendant had bitten the cheese. The trial court did not hold a hearing to consider the challenge to bitemark expertise. On

---

51. 512 N.W.2d 95 (Minn.1994).

52. 447 N.W.2d 422 (Minn.1989).

53. *Hodgson, supra* note 51, at 98, citing C. Herasimchuk, *A Practical Guide to the Admissibility of Novel Expert Evidence in Criminal Trials Under Federal Rule 702*, 22 St. Mary's L.J. 181, 210–11 and n. 122 (1990) and Annot.,

77 ALR 3rd 1122 (1977) and (1993 Supp.) for the proposition that bitemark expert testimony is no longer novel.

54. *Daubert*, n. 11, at 593.

55. 7 P.3d 24 (Wyo.2000).

appeal, the Wyoming Supreme Court cited *Daubert, Joiner*[56] and *Kumho Tire*,[57] but did not conclude that an evidentiary hearing is required to hear a challenge to forensic bitemark evidence. Apparently it was enough to cite a number of cases in which such testimony had been admitted. On the other hand, the Court reversed the conviction because the prosecution had not provided a copy of the expert's curriculum vita or his report.

This case reflects two ironies. One, *Daubert* seems to have been adopted in Wyoming in name but not in spirit or practice. Rather than supporting inquiry into the empirical and theoretical underpinnings of bitemark opinions, both the trial and Supreme Court were content to deny a hearing and look to cases of admission in other courts as the basis for gatekeeping. Second, while the failure of the government to provide information on the expert's background and the report of his findings were sufficient for reversal, it is hard to imagine that anything in either the vita or the report could have led to exclusion of the expert's opinion. That is to say, if the heart and soul of the expertise are of no interest or consequence, why would the details of the dentist who reached the opinion, or how he reached the opinion, make any difference?[58]

Mississippi has decided a pair of bitemark cases that are difficult to reconcile with each other or with Mississippi case law on admissibility. Mississippi is not, as of this writing, a *Daubert* state, and asserts that it follows *Frye*,[59] though it is not evident from its bitemark cases that general acceptance was a criterion the Court attended to. Despite its avowed lack of allegiance to *Daubert*, in *Howard v. State*[60] the Mississippi Supreme Court seemed inclined to critically evaluate, rather than blindly accept, the assertions of forensic odontologists concerning the scientific validity and evidentiary reliability of their field's conclusions. The Court wrote:

> This Court has never ruled directly on the admissibility or reliability of bite-mark identification evidence, though it has addressed cases in which bite-mark evidence was an issue. [Citation omitted.] While few courts have refused to allow some form of bite-mark comparison evidence, numerous scholarly authorities have criticized the reliability of this method of identifying a suspect. [Citation omitted.] It is much easier to exclude a suspect through such comparison than to positively identify a suspect. [Citations omitted.]
>
> There is little consensus in the scientific community on the number of points which must match before any positive identification can be announced. [Citation omitted.] Because the opinions concerning the methods of comparison employed in a particular case may differ, it is certainly open to defense counsel to attack the qualifications of the expert, the methods and data used to compare the bitemarks to persons other than the defendant, and the factual and logical bases of the expert's

56. General Electric Co. v. Joiner, 522 U.S. 136, 118 S.Ct. 512, 139 L.Ed.2d 508 (1997).

57. Kumho Tire Co. v. Carmichael, 526 U.S. 137, 119 S.Ct. 1167, 143 L.Ed.2d 238 (1999).

58. Indeed, one member of the Supreme Court dissented that the errors on which the reversal was based were harmless errors.

59. *See* Kansas City Southern Railway Company, Inc. v. Johnson, 798 So.2d 374 (Miss.2001), cert. denied ___ U.S. ___, 122 S.Ct. 43, ___ L.Ed.2d ___ (2001) and cases cited therein.

60. 701 So.2d 274 (Miss.1997).

opinions. Also, where such expert testimony is allowed by the trial court, it should be open to the defendant to present evidence challenging the reliability of the field of bite-mark comparisons. [Citation omitted.] Only then will the jury be able to give the proper weight, if any, to this evidence.

Two years later, in *Brooks v. State*,[61] a trial court admitted bitemark identification expert testimony and the Mississippi Supreme Court affirmed, holding that such evidence was now admissible. The majority opinion contained not the slightest review of the science (so it was not taking the *Daubert* approach), but it also did not look to the status of bitemark individualization among forensic odontologists. The opinion does little more than to announce that bitemark expert testimony is admissible because the Court says so.[62] The only reasoning behind the decision appears to be that the defense is free to cross-examine and offer rebuttal witnesses. This would appear to be no gatekeeping of any kind: everything is admissible so long as the defense is afforded the opportunity to attack the weight of the opinion during trial. Ironically and paradoxically, a concurrence implies that the opinion as consistent with *Daubert* and its progeny:

> The majority view is correct and long overdue. The U.S. Supreme Court recent decisions [citing *Kumho Tire, General Elec. Co. v. Joiner,* and *Daubert*] stress that the federal district courts must be gatekeepers on the admission of expert testimony. I am confident that our learned trial judges will properly determine, on a case-by-case basis, whether an expert may testify to certain matters if the proper procedures are followed by the parties seeking the admission of such expert's testimony.[63]

Like the main opinion, the concurrence is silent on the criteria for all of that confidence and correct gatekeeping, and does not venture to demonstrate any of it.

A dissenting opinion by one justice noted that many questions still surround bitemark identification opinions[64] and, in this instance, the expert who testified for the state.[65]

---

61. 748 So.2d 736 (Miss.1999).

62. "We now take the opportunity to state affirmatively that bite-mark identification evidence is admissible in Mississippi." *Id.* at 739.

63. *Id.* at 747.

64. "1. The timing of the bite mark injury; 2. Enhancement procedures and techniques (note that in this case, West testified that he used ultraviolet light to enhance the wound enabling him to find "several unique marks" that corresponded to the flaws on the back side of Brooks's teeth; this technique is what allowed West to be positive that only Brooks could have made the two indentations); 3. The type of material for test bites or the accuracy of test bites under various mockup conditions; 4. The pressure necessary to produce the various levels of tissue injury under normal and unusual circumstances has not been reliably measured; 5. Manipulation of various types of distortion to produce correction; 6. The problem faced by forensic dentists today is not necessarily one of matching the bite mark to a set of teeth. It is demonstrating whether another set of teeth could have produced the same or similar mark; 7. There is not universal agreement on which injuries are bite mark related; 8. Research on the minimum number of points of concordance or the minimum number of teeth marks needed in a bite mark for certainty is not as well established as the uniqueness of the dentition." *Id.* at 748.

65. Michael West is infamous in forensic dentistry and the courts for asserting conclusions that go well beyond what the data allow, with a confidence unsupported by the data (West is notorious for emphasizing to juries that his conclusions are "indeed and without doubt"), inventing his own unverified technique (which he termed the "West Effect"), and misrepresenting evidence and data to bolster his testimony. For his accumulated misdeeds he has been professionally punished by

Louisiana is a *Daubert* state. In *State v. Wommack*[66] a defendant was convicted of attempted murder and burglary, and the Court of Appeals affirmed. Some of the evidence against the defendant consisted of a bitemark: the victim had bitten her assailant. At trial two experts testified concerning the bitemark on the defendant, an oral-maxillofacial surgeon and a forensic pathologist. They both testified that marks on the defendant's arm came from a human bite, but they did not link the marks specifically to the victim, and they acknowledged the possibility of error and uncertainty in their opinions. On appeal the defendant challenged the experts who testified about the bitemark. The Court of Appeals held that "the *Daubert* standards do no appear to be readily applicable to the present case. Neither expert used complex testing in identifying the wound found on [the defendant's] arm. . . . Expert opinion testimony based upon personal observation and experience is admissible." Here, then, is a court—a year after the Supreme Court held in *Kumho Tire* that all expert evidence, regardless of how it is labeled or characterized, must pass a test suitably calculated to evaluate its validity—which believes that only "complex testing" but not "personal observation and experience" are subject to scrutiny, and that the latter are *ipso facto* admissible.

B. SCIENTIFIC ISSUES

by

C. Michael Bowers*

§ 5–2.0 THE SCIENTIFIC STATUS OF BITEMARK COMPARISONS

§ 5–2.1 Introductory Discussion of the Scientific Status of Bitemark Comparisons

The definition and breadth of forensic odontology has evolved over the centuries and now includes identification by means of dental DNA and salivary DNA.[1] "Odontology" is well established in the European dental language where it means the "study of teeth." The United States counterpart, "Forensic dentistry," is synonymous.

---

the American Academy of Forensic Sciences, the American Board of Forensic Odontology, and the International Association for Identification. *See id.* at 748–50. Some may find the most remarkable things about this to be that with such a record there still are prosecutors who will hire him (owing either to ethical or tactical concerns), defense attorneys who cannot have him declared unqualified, or juries that believe him.

In a civil suit against West for damages in another case in which his fallacious testimony led to an erroneous conviction, a federal court denied West's motion to dismiss. Keko v. Hingle, 1999 WL 155945 (E.D.La.1999).

66. 770 So.2d 365 (La.App.2000).

* Dr. Bowers practices dentistry and law in Ventura, CA. He has been a Deputy Medical Examiner for the Ventura County Coroner's Office since 1988. He is a diplomate of the American Board of Forensic Odontology. The author would like to thank the following for their contributions to this chapter: Iain A. Pretty (University of Liverpool, School of Dentistry), John Holdridge (Justice Center, New Orleans, LA), David Sweet (Director, Bureau of Legal Dentistry, Vancouver, British Columbia), Dr. Duane Spencer (Diplomate of the ABFO), David Averill (Diplomate of the ABFO), Gary Bell (Diplomate of the ABFO), George Gould (Diplomate of the ABFO).

§ 5–2.0

1. David Sweet et al., *PCR-based DNA Typing of Saliva Stains Recovered from Human Skin*, 42 J. FORENSIC SCI. 320 (1997).

The initial United States historical case that utilized dental information occurred during the Revolutionary War period. Paul Revere recognized a prosthetic gold device he had previously constructed for a deceased patriot, General Joseph Warren, an American military casualty from the Bunker Hill engagement.[2] The primary duties of dentists in the medico-legal arena are to help identify the dead, apply dental facts and reliable methods to legal problems regarding identification from bitemarks, and, finally, interpretation of quality issues concerning the practice of dentistry. Dental identification of unknown persons relies on the similarities of anatomical and artificial structures (tooth restorations) and is achieved during a comparison process that focuses on shape and measured physical characteristics. Bitemark identification is a relatively recent arrival on the dental-legal scene.[3] Its inception was promoted by judicial interest in physical evidence left at crime scenes and bitemarks present on the skin of assault and homicide victims.

The materials used by forensic dentists to capture impressions of bitemarks and teeth are products accepted by the American Dental Association for the general practice of dentistry. Manufacturers stringently maintain the stability and physical duplication accuracy of these products. Dental science has progressed tremendously in the latter 20th century in its ability to create exemplars and replicas of dental structures that are used for later comparison analysis. This replication process uses materials commonly seen in dental offices.

Dental evidence collected in a bitemark case falls into two categories: (1) physical evidence that is a concert of photography and dental impression materials, and (2) biological evidence that is derived from serological swabbing of bitemarks on skin and objects that could have trace saliva DNA deposited by the biter.[4] Subsequent analysis of the latter is the realm of the biomolecular expert, while the former is the traditional bitemark venue of forensic dentists. Forensic dentists traditionally make the following postulates: the dental characteristics of teeth involved in biting are unique among individuals and this asserted uniqueness is faithfully transferred and recorded in the injury. Because these postulates and their dental science foundations constitute the field's most controversial scientific predicates, discussion of them will form a large part of this chapter.

§ 5–2.1.1 Areas of Dental Testimony

Forensic dentists testify in court regarding medical evidence involving teeth. This involves areas of both criminal and civil law, when dental testimony might help answer a question that is at issue in the proceedings.

The predominant subject matter in criminal cases includes bitemark analysis, the identification of human remains and the dental aging of known individuals. The latter two are well founded in traditional dental and anthropological science. These use methods derived from studies of developmental dental biology and individuating characteristics of the cranial skeleton, dental structures, and dental restorations.

2. Lester Luntz & Phyllys Luntz, HANDBOOK FOR DENTAL IDENTIFICATION (1973).

3. Doyle v. State, 159 Tex.Crim. 310, 263 S.W.2d 779 (Tex.Crim.App.1954).

4. The effect of salivary DNA on bitemark investigations will be discussed *infra*, §§ 2.1.7[2], [3].

Human identification testimony has been utilized in the United States since the 1800s.[5] This identification of unidentified persons from their dental characteristics is the primary duty of forensic dentists. In mass disaster incidents, dentists can be expected to identify 20–25% of the victims. This is performed with a considerable degree of accuracy, due, in part, to a finite pool of candidates for identification (passenger lists) and the availability of dental records for comparison. This process emphasizes the comparison of postmortem victims to dental restorations placed during a person's life and certain anatomical structures that had been recorded in the course of radiographic examinations by medical and dental practitioners. Occasionally, old photographs showing unusually positioned front teeth may be superimposed onto postmortem images of a decedent's teeth. The forensic dentist conducts a postmortem dental examination to establish physical findings of a decedent in much the same way as with a living patient, and then compares dental records derived from investigative efforts and missing person reports.

Bitemark analysis is a product of the latter half of the 20th century. The small number of dentists in early court bitemark proceedings has increased substantially over the last twenty-five years. This is due, in part, to (1) the acceptance by the forensic odontological community of the notion that questions of reliability of methods and opinions are satisfied by their years of experience, their credentials, anecdotal reporting, and, in a display of circular logic, (2) the fact that the judiciary has allowed them to offer their opinions in trials.[6]

The physical evidence available in a bitemark case is considerably less than in dental identification. The vast array of potential biters can be large due to the fragmentary and diffuse features seen in skin injuries. The likelihood of a coincidental match of a defendant's teeth to a bitemark injury has not been quantified.

The recognition and admissibility of the discipline of forensic odontology rests on a fragile foundation of minimally relevant empirical research and a mountain of casework articles and commentaries. The caselaw evinces little doubt on the part of judges that dentists can play a role in determining questions of fact relevant to identification in particular cases.

Of particular interest to readers may be § 2.1.4, which is intended to summarize the areas of bitemark inquiry and accumulated knowledge into various categories. This should aid the reader in determining how this material compares to the explicit reliability standards of the law announced in *Daubert* and *Kumho Tire*. Section 2.1.7. describes recent technical efforts to improve the accuracy of bitemark opinions and the application of DNA analysis as it relates to this area of forensic investigation. Section 2.1.8 will introduce data and interpretation regarding scientific reliability from a recent

---

5. Luntz & Luntz, *supra* note 2, at 5–15 (narration of the 1850 Massachusetts homicide trial against John White Webster; a charred skull and denture fragments taken from the cellar of the defendant were identified by the first dean of the Harvard Dental School as those of the victim, Dr. George Parkman.)

6. Raymond D. Rawson & S. Brooks, *Classification of Human Breast Morphology Important to Bitemark Investigation*, 5 J. Forensic Sci. 19 (1984).

proficiency examination of dentists who have been certified by the American Board of Forensic Odontology.[7]

§ 5–2.1.2 Training and Professional Forensic Organizations

Unlike forensic pathologists, forensic dentistry is not a recognized specialty of dental practice. It may be best characterized as a subspecialty of the general field of forensic human identification. This is reflected by the lack of full time residency programs in the United States and the part-time nature of forensic dental consultants. By contrast, colleges and universities in Canada, Europe and Australia have one-year fellowships and graduate training (Masters level) devoted entirely to forensic dentistry.

The typical forensic dental expert is either (1) a practicing dentist, (2) retired from dental practice, or (3) a dental educator. The large majority of dental forensic specialists come from the first category.

Dentists have created their own forensic organizations and have joined others. The American Board of Forensic Odontology is recognized by the American Academy of Forensic Sciences (AAFS) which has an Odontology Section with a membership of over 250 dentists. The American Society of Forensic Odontology has a membership of over 900 and meets concurrently with the AAFS once a year.

The ABFO has created Guidelines and Standards for Human Identification and Bitemark Analysis. This compilation has produced some uniformity in the methods and terminology used by dentists. But it silent regarding reliability of comparison methods and opinions,[8] as well as the scientific validity issues often raised in court concerning bitemark methods.[9]

The regulatory nature of the AAFS and the ABFO occasionally come into play when transgressing members are expelled or are otherwise sanctioned for departures from accepted practices or ethical violations.[10]

§ 5–2.1.3 Recognition and Analysis of Human Bitemarks

A contemporary review of bitemark analysis techniques has summarized certain causes of unreliability in bitemark opinions used in court.[11] These

---

7. Founded in 1976, this U.S. organization now has 113 dentists. Thirteen were grandfathered in as Diplomates. The ABFO provides a certification examination to applicants who have met qualifications of actual casework experience, participation in training seminars and presentations at the American Academy of Forensic Sciences (AAFS) meetings, and affiliations with medico-legal agencies.

8. David Sweet & C. Michael Bowers, *Accuracy of Bitemark Overlays: A Comparison of Five Common Methods to Produce Exemplars from a Suspect's Dentition*, 43 J. FORENSIC SCI. 362 (1998). This computer evaluation of four techniques produced recommendations to (1) eliminate hand drawing of a suspect's teeth and (2) use digital images of dental characteristics. These images are placed (after flipping horizontally) onto a picture of a bitemark in order to evaluate concordance or dissimilarities between the two samples.

9. C. Michael Bowers & Gary Bell (eds.), MANUAL OF FORENSIC ODONTOLOGY (3rd ed.2001) (privately published by the American Society of Forensic Odontology).

10. Mark Hansen, *Out of the Blue*, 82 ABAJ 50 (Feb.1996) (Reporting on a trial court rejection of a technique where the prosecution's dental expert positively linked metal rivets on a butcher knife's handle to marks he purportedly observed on the defendant's hand. These observations on the hand occurred during illumination by 450 nanometers visual (and blue) light. The dentist was unable to photograph the marks on the hand, but testified in court with a Xerographic copy of the defendant's hand as evidence of his findings.)

11. Bruce Rothwell, *Bitemarks in Forensic Dentistry: A Review of Legal, Scientific Issues*, 126 J. AM. DENTAL ASS'N (1995).

include: changes in suspects' teeth from subsequent dental disease and treatment, examiner subjectivity that overvalues common tooth characteristics,[12] poor bias control,[13] lack of forensically relevant population studies to establish the frequencies of occurrence of common dental features, the dimensional accuracy of skin as a substrate for bitemark impressions made by these teeth,[14] and the multitude of unvalidated comparison methods and analytical procedures "recognized" and "generally accepted."

The issue of inter-examiner agreement and accuracy was studied briefly in the mid–1970s and its findings have not been altered by later research.[15] Using ideal laboratory conditions and evidence, experienced examiners who studied bitemark patterns in pig skin correctly identified the biter 76% of the time. Another author noted the subjectivity of this comparison process and has suggested that the strongest opinion linking bitemarks to suspects be limited to "possible" until the time comes that bitemark analysis is more satisfactorily tested in relation to reliability, error rate of dentists, and perhaps comes to be conducted pursuant to court appointed, rather than adversarial, expert testimony.[16]

The experimental evaluation of bitemark examiners has been attempted in the United States by the ABFO. It initiated a series of four studies, starting in 1983, and ending in 1999, where Diplomates were sent sets of teeth and a series of actual bitemark photographs. They were asked to evaluate the evidence as they would in a conventional bitemark case. The cases were provided by members who attested to the identification of the true biter through means other than the bitemark evidence. The 1983 test resulted in an attempt to develop a scoring sheet that created values for specific dental features seen as concordant between the suspect and a bitemark. This led to the publication of a scoring system in 1986.[17] The quantitative values were soon discarded as being unreliable.[18] The descriptors of dental features, however, carried over into the later published ABFO Standards and Guidelines for Bitemark Analysis.[19]

In seeking explanations for the unsatisfactorily high error rates, the previous edition of this chapter suggested that "[t]he lack of a proper match [by the examiners] was partly a reflection of the difficulty in recognizing the features found in a bitemark, partly an issue of experience and training in interpreting bitemark characteristics and matching procedures, and partly a

---

12. The common debate between sparring forensic odontologists is (1) the identification value of a bitemark and (2) the degree of concordance of the injury to certain teeth of the defendant. The proof of a positive opinion is not based on any formal population studies that state the frequency of chance random match with other members of a relevant population.

13. The addition of a "dental lineup" of similar sets of teeth to the sample studied by the dentist has never been mandated. Some of the larger DNA labs separate extraction and comparison activities.

14. Duane T. DeVore, *Bitemarks for Identification? A Preliminary Report*, 11 MED. SCI. &

L. 144 (1971). This study is described in detail *infra* at §§ 2.1.5[1], 2.1.6[1].

15. T.W. MacFarlane et al., *Statistical Problems in Dental Identification*, 14 J. FORENSIC SCI. SOC'Y 247 (1974).

16. C. Michael Bowers, *A Statement Why Court Opinions on Bitemark Analysis Should be Limited*, 4 NEWSLETTER OF THE ABFO 4 (Dec. 1996).

17. ABFO, *Guidelines for Bitemark Analysis*, 112 J. AM. DENTAL ASSOC. 383 (1986).

18. ABFO, *Letter*, 33 J. FORENSIC SCI. 20 (1988).

19. *Supra* note 9, at 344.

function of the difficulty in setting up realistic situations.''[20] The situations for the tests were certainly not unusual. An interesting interpretation is that, at the very least, the ABFO's membership may not generally have attained the skill necessary to achieve reliable results. The notion that experience is the key to reliability is a common theme that is seen throughout the literature.

Two subsequent studies performed after 1983 failed to generate publishable results. The difficulties have been described as a combination of poor experimental design and limited analytical prowess by the profession.[21]

The fourth test—the 4th ABFO Bitemark Workshop—was performed in 1999.[22] The results relate to a number of issues raised throughout the history of bitemark analysis in the United States. Following is a summary of the study and its findings.[23]

[1] Proficiency Testing of Board Certified Odontologists

The intent of the study was to determine the ability of board certified forensic odontologists to correctly analyze bitemark evidence in a small population. All 95 board certified diplomates of the American Board of Forensic Odontology were eligible to participate in the study. Of the 60 diplomates who requested and were sent the study material, 26 returned the necessary data by the deadline and were included in the data results.

Complete case material typical of an actual bitemark case was sent to those diplomates requesting to participate. Each diplomate had six months to analyze and anonymously return findings. The study was based on four bitemark cases with known biters whose identity was substantiated by other means. Three of the cases were actual criminal cases where the bitemark was in skin. The fourth case was a fabricated bite into cheese, in which case each examiner was sent a model of the actual cheese in addition to the typical multiple color and black-and-white photographs. In addition to the four sets of models from the known biters each diplomate was sent an additional three dentitions that were selected at random from the laboratory of a unidentified dentist. These seven models made up the population from which the bitemarks were to be identified. Thus, examiners were asked to look at each unknown (3 sets of wound photos and one cheese model) and to compare each of those to the seven known dentitions, in an effort to determine which, if any, of the knowns matched an unknown.

In each case the expert was required to render an opinion in the below three areas. The expert was given the following choices in each of the three areas as defined by the ABFO Standards for Bitemark Terminology.

   1. Wound Analysis—Does the Injury Represent a Bitemark?

     a. Definite bitemark—no doubt that teeth created the pattern

20. David L. Faigman, David H. Kaye, Michael J. Saks & Joseph Sanders, Modern Scientific Evidence: The Law and Science of Expert Testimony, *Identification from Bitemarks: The Scientific Questions: Recognition and Analysis of Human Bite Marks* § 24–2.1.1[2] 171 (1997).

21. None of these studies have been published. The author gleaned this information from personal communications.

22. The ABFO analysis is currently under review for publication by the Journal of Forensic Sciences.

23. This description and analysis is an independent review of the raw data by this author and Dr. David Averill.

b. Probable bitemark—pattern strongly suggests origin from teeth but could be caused by something else

c. Possible bitemark—pattern may or may not have been caused by teeth; could have been caused by other factors

2. Evidentiary Value

a. High forensic value—could support reasonable certainty in identification

b. Medium forensic value—could support possible opinion in identification

c. Low forensic value—would not support a linking

d. No forensic value—should not be used in investigation

3. Degree of Certainty Describing the Link between the Bitemark and the Suspect

a. Reasonable medical certainty—virtual certainty; no reasonable or practical possibility that someone else did it

b. Probably—more likely than not

c. Possible—could be; may or may not be; can't be ruled out

d. Improbable—unlikely to be the biter

e. Incompatible—not the biter

f. Inconclusive—insufficient quality/quantity/specificity of evidence to make any statement of relationship to the biter

For purposes of this study, a positive linkage of the suspect's dentition to the bitemark consisted of those opinions recorded as: reasonable medical certainty, probably, and possible. Negative linkage consisted of: improbable, incompatible, and inconclusive. Conclusions could be correct in two different ways: by correctly linking an unknown bitemark to the suspect who made it (true positives) or by excluding a suspect who did not make the unknown bitemark (true negatives). Conclusions could be incorrect in two different ways: by incorrectly linking an unknown bite to a suspect who had not made it (false positives) or by excluding a suspect as having made an unknown bite when that suspect had in fact made that bite (false negatives). Table 1 graphically depicts these four possible decision outcomes.

Table 1

Four Possible Decision Outcomes

	Reality	
Decision	Suspect bit victim	Suspect did not bite victim
Positive: Suspect bit victim	True Positive	False Positive
Negative: Suspect did not bite victim	False Negative	True Negative

Table 2 summarizes the results of the study. It is important to say something, first, about the meaning of the data and the way they are presented. Suppose one were told that the overall accuracy rate for a test case was 85%. One might conclude from that number that the examiners were doing reasonably well—not as well as one might hope from a forensic science that claims the ability to connect crime scene bitemarks to suspects "to the exclusion of all others in the world," but not terrible either. In truth, however, the performance is far more troubling than is apparent. What is not made evident by that number is the fact that the poorest level of performance that examiners could achieve in this study—if they got every single answer as wrong as they could get it—would still make them appear to be accurate 71% of the time. That is because if an examiner failed to match a bitemark with the correct dentition (one error) and linked it instead with the dentition of an innocent suspect (second error) he still is gets the remaining five dentitions "right" by not erroneously inculpating them.[24]

Table 2

**Error Rates of Forensic Odontology Diplomates
on the Four Test Cases**

	Overall Error Rate (maximum possible error rate = 27%)	False Positive Errors as Percentage of Examiners Offering Opinions	False Negative Errors as Percentage of Examiners Offering Opinions
Case 1	14%	62%	38%
Case 2	7	42	4
Case 3	12	65	15
Case 4	13	65	27
Medians	12.5%	63.5%	22%

Accordingly, Table 2 seeks to convey a more meaningful idea of how well examiners did by relating their performance to how well they could have done—or more to the point, how poorly they did in relation to how poorly they could have done. The median overall error rate[25] is 12.5%—out of a maximum possible error rate of 27%. Thus, examiners came nearly half the way to being as wrong as they could be. More specifically, it is their false positive error rate—the tendency to conclude that an innocent person's dentition matches the bitemark—that accounts for the bulk of that overall error rate. Table 2 indicates how many examiners committed a false positive error in each test case. In their least bad performance, 42% of them gave a conclusion that inculpated an innocent person's dentition. On average, 63.5% of the examin-

24. Once one set of dentition is linked (correctly or incorrectly) to a bitemark, the others are not linked, and therefore are scored as "correct." In other words, given the test design, an examiner could never make more than two mistakes, and all remaining dentitions are scored as "correct." If instead of providing a set of seven dentitions from which to choose, there had been 100, then the overall accuracy rate, using this seemingly straightforward method of counting, could never be lower than 98% correct—one false positive inculpation of an innocent suspect, one overlooked guilty suspect, and 98 remaining dentitions that get scored as "correct." And, thus, the poorest possible performance would be "2% error."

25. That is, the median of the false positives plus false negatives across the four test cases.

ers committed false positive errors across the test cases. If this reflects their performance in actual cases, then inculpatory opinions by forensic dentists are more likely to be wrong than right. They were, however, much less likely to overlook a true biter—reflected in a median false negative error rate of 22%.

These are not novices; these are diplomates, the most accomplished members of the field. But experience provided no assurance of accuracy. The demography of the test takers failed to disclose any correlation between years in forensic practice case work and correct results.

The results confirm Whittaker's earlier findings discussing the difficulties inherent to bitemark identification.[26] The findings of this most recent ABFO study cast serious doubt on earlier conclusions that the field has "produced a significant number of well trained and capable forensic dentists who have accepted guidelines to follow for evidence collection and analysis. The work of these organizations has contributed to the development of a systematic approach capable of producing reliable opinions."[27]

The sections that follow may illuminate the reasons why accuracy has been so disappointing and what steps may improve accuracy and judicial expectations in the future.

§ 5–2.1.4 Scientific Methods Applied to Comparison Techniques

A major aspect of the bitemark comparison process targets the three-dimensional characteristics of the suspect's teeth. Two studies[28] report data suggesting a high degree of variability in these features, and the authors argue that it shows bitemarks to be unique (infinitely variable) among the human population. Unfortunately, there are no studies relating this hypothesis to actual bitemarks on skin or other substrates. In addition, neither study attempted to prove the independent occurrence of each dental feature. The latter study misapplied probability theory to reach a conclusion of uniqueness of any human being.

In practice, the odontologist compares the Questioned bitemark to duplicates (exemplars) of Known teeth. The assortment of exemplar materials and methods in use are well documented in the literature. Computer imaging, hand-traced outlines, Xerographic copying, and wax impressions, among others, are used to duplicate two and three dimensional features of a suspect's teeth. These methods produce an image of the teeth, called an "overlay" since it is transferred to transparent acetate and superimposed (after being flipped horizontally), onto an image of the bitemark. The examiner studies the relationships between the two images, and reaches an opinion about their similarity.

26. David K. Whittaker, *Some Laboratory Studies on the Accuracy of Bitemark Comparisons*, 25 INT'L DENTAL J. 166 (1975).

27. DAVID L. FAIGMAN, DAVID H. KAYE, MICHAEL J. SAKS & JOSEPH SANDERS, MODERN SCIENTIFIC EVIDENCE: THE LAW AND SCIENCE OF EXPERT TESTIMONY, *Identification from Bitemarks: The Scientific Questions: Recognition and Analysis of Human Bitemarks*, § 24–2.1.1[2] 171–72 (1997).

28. Reidar F. Sognnaes & Raymond.D. Rawson, *Computer Comparison of Bitemark Patterns in Identical Twins*, 105 J. AM. DENTAL ASSOC. 449 (1982); Raymond D. Rawson & Ronald K. Ommen, *Statistical Evidence for the Individuality of the Human Dentition*, 29 J. FORENSIC SCI. 245 (1984).

A recent study was completed in an effort to validate the most popular of these methods.[29] This was the first attempt to compare methods in relation to a reference standard. The study obtained sample data (n=30) from plaster dental study casts of a Caucasian population pool, pertaining to tooth position and area of each tooth biting surface (also called a hollow-volume overlay) using a computer-based optical imaging method. The relative rotation of teeth in each sample was obtained using a geometric analysis. Five commonly used bitemark overlay production techniques were analyzed by computer and statistically to determine how accurately each reproduced the shape, size and rotation of the upper and lower front teeth of the research sample. (See Figure 1.) The computer-based method produced digital images of the dental plaster casts that were found to be very accurate. This method was treated as the "gold standard" and the other methods were compared to it.

Figure 1
Overlays Produces from the Same Dental Cast
Using a Variety of Different Techniques
(Note: not to scale)

1 = computer-generated   4 = xerographic method
2 = hand-traced from study cast 5 = radiographic method
3 = hand-traced from wax bite

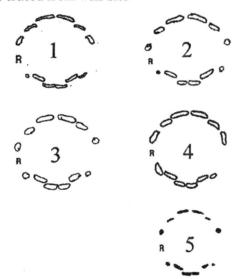

The findings established that there are significant differences among these five methods. The resulting ranking of the various methods is seen in Table 3. The authors suggested that the computer generated bitemark overlays provided the most reproducible and accurate exemplars and recommended that hand tracing of a suspect's teeth be discontinued due to its consistently low ranking for precision in both surface area and rotational accuracy. Findings such as these have played a part in the development and revision of various aspects of bitemark identification practice.[30]

29. *Supra* note 8.

30. RAYMOND JOHANSEN & C. MICHAEL BOWERS, DIGITAL ANALYSIS OF BITEMARK EVIDENCE (2000).

Table 3

Various Overlay Fabrication Techniques Ranked According to Accuracy.

Rank	Area	Rotation
1	Computer-based	Computer-based
2	Radiopaque wax	Xerographic
3	Hand-traced from wax	Hand-traced from wax
4	Hand-traced from study casts	Hand-traced from study casts
5	Xerographic	Radiopaque wax

After Sweet and Bowers (1998)

§ 5–2.1.5 The Scientific Limitations of Bitemark Testimony

The following section describes several scientific issues involving bite-mark analysis. This is presented to illuminate the interface between the rules of scientific admissibility and reliability issues involving forensic dentistry.

[1]   The Accuracy of Skin as a Substrate for Bitemarks

Central to bitemark analysis are the characteristics of the skin receiving the mark, because, in cases of physical assault having skin injuries, the anatomy and physiology of the skin, and the position of the victim, affect the detail and shape of the bitemark. DeVore[31] showed how the positioning of the test bite (actually, it was an inked circle) on a bicep varied depending upon whether the arm was flexed or pronated. (See Figure 2.) What is significant in casework and report writing is the need to experimentally control or establish the amount of positional variation in an actual bitemark case. Use of a live victim in a reenactment is difficult and a deceased individual will not be available. No important papers have been published on this subject since DeVore's in 1971.

31. *Supra* note 14.

Figure 2
Two Identical Marks on Human Skin. The Lower Has Been Distorted by Applying Pressure to the Area (Duplicating Devore's Test).

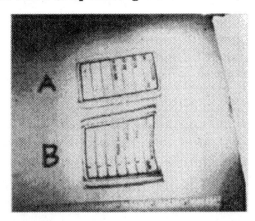

Another issue is the amount of detail present in the bitemark. Skin is a poor impression material. The injury may be a series of reddened bruises at the time of the original photograph. It is rare to see the presence of three-dimensions (i.e., tooth indentations) which could be used for increased detail.

[2] Bruising and Other Considerations

Recognition of the fact that bruising is actually subcutaneous bleeding[32] requires that the investigator not assume that the reddened areas that appear to be teeth are an accurate representation of individual teeth.

Dailey and Bowers[33] describe the shortcomings of attempts by odontologists and other forensic experts to "age" skin injuries according to the degree of discoloration present in the mark. During the process of healing, or skin response to a sufficient force, the bruise will go through color changes before fading from visual recognition. A bruise is an "area of hemorrhage into soft tissue due to the rupture of blood vessels caused by blunt trauma."[34] Using appearance of bruises for the purpose of aging a wound has been judged to be invalid by numerous investigators. A review of research reporting controlled studies of these discolorations over time concluded that, "it would seem unlikely that a bruise could be reliably aged from appearance alone."[35]

The bitemark should be thoroughly analyzed *first*. That means measurements, angles, and other features should be exhaustively studied before the teeth of any suspect(s) are viewed.[36] This provides a modicum of control where the determinations of the forensic value of the bitemark are established prior to the dentist comparing the suspect's dental evidence. The realities of two-

32. J. Curtis Dailey & C. Michael Bowers, *Aging of Bitemarks, A Literature Review*, 42 J. FORENSIC SCI. 791 (1997).

33. *Id.*

34. DOMINICK J. DIMAIO & VINCENT J.M. DI-MAIO, FORENSIC PATHOLOGY (1993).

35. N.E.I. Langlois & G.A.Gresham, *The Aging of Bruises: A Review and Study of the Colour Changes with Time,* 50 FORENSIC SCI. INT'L 227 (1991).

36. Reidar F. Sognnaes, *Forensic Bitemark Measurements*, 55 DENTAL SURVEY 34 (1979).

dimensional (i.e., bruises) bitemarks suggest that finding individualizing (i.e., unique) features in bitemarks is extremely rare. The details of intertooth spaces, rotations, and blank spaces between teeth are the principal features of this type of injury.

[3] The Issue of Individuality of Human Dentition

Another foundation of bitemark analysis is the belief that the total arrangement of a person's dentition creates a dental "profile" of sorts. Attempts to determine, or demonstrate, the uniqueness of human dentition has a history in bitemark analysis that stretches over four decades. The demonstration of uniqueness is a blend of art and opinion. The probability of more than one person producing a similar or identical bitemark in a specific case is the challenge in every bitemark case.[37]

If, however, it can be said that no two humans have the same dentition, the task is made easier, because (putting aside technical problems of the registration and reading of the bitemark[38]) the theoretical probability of a coincidental match becomes zero, and then no probability need be worried about, much less calculated. Legal commentaries from the 1970s and 80s attacked bitemark analysis as a "new and unfounded science of identification"[39] and pointed out that the "uniqueness of the human dentition hasn't been established."[40] The odontology response then and now has been to base its assertion of uniqueness on a small number of journal articles which are less than persuasive in their efforts to prove uniqueness scientifically.[41]

One approach to trying to prove uniqueness has been the comparison of identical twins.[42] The notion is that if "even" identical twins show differences, then every individual on earth "must therefore" be different from every other individual on earth. The logic that goes from the evidence to the conclusion is not especially clear, but we can understand why, as a means of proving uniqueness, it is fundamentally unsound. When it is shown that identical twins do not have identical dentition (or fingerprints, or hair, or anything else), what that establishes is that the genotype for these traits is not isomorphic with the phenotype. Thus, genetics cannot be relied upon as a basis for concluding that these forensically relevant traits vary in accord with all that we know about genetics. Rather, it means that non-genetic, presumably random, factors introduce some disconnection between the genes and their physical expression. Rather than proving that, because identical twins show differences, everyone else must also, it proves that even the attributes of

---

37. John Beckstead et al., *Review of Bitemark Evidence*, 99 J. Am. Dental Assoc. 69 (1979).

38. For example, Rawson & Ommen, *supra* note 28, utilized teeth impressions in wax which were then hand traced and computer analyzed. Because bitemarks in skin were not the target of the 397 sets of wax teeth marks he choose to investigate out of a larger cohort of 1200, the generalizability of the findings to actual bitemarks is questionable.

39. A. Wilkinson & R. Gerughty, *Bitemark Evidence: Its Admissibility is Hard to Swallow*, 12 W. St. U. L. Rev. 519 (1985).

40. Adrian Hales, *Admissibility of Bitemark Evidence*, 51 S. Cal. L. Rev. 309 (1978).

41. Sognnaes & Rawson, *supra* note 28; Rawson & Ommen, *supra* note 28.

42. *See* discussion, *infra* § 2.1.6 [2].

identical twins reflect these random factors and those random factors must be taken into account in determining the probability of a coincidental match. Rather than obviating the need for objective calculations, it brings us right back to the need to calculate probabilities of coincidental matches. The heavy use of probability theory is seen in the seminal bitemark articles of the last four decades.[43] Their implication is that so much variation exists in the morphology and position of teeth that, when the product rule is applied, the probability of two being alike approaches the vanishing point. For example, some authors point to hypothetical frequencies of occurrence of more rare or "uncharacteristic" features, multiply them according to the product rule per Keiser–Neilsen, based on the assumption that these features of higher value are independent of one another , and arrive at vanishingly small probabilities.[44] Keiser–Neilsen was not, however, talking about bitemarks (far more limited representations of dentition) when he introduced the use of the "product-rule"[45] in 1960. He was offering a purely theoretical application of basic notions of probability, assuming that each dental feature was independent of the next and that the product of each frequency of occurrence could be used to establish the frequency of all the features occurring at once. He was actually talking about missing and filled teeth, not bitemarks. Thus, because bitemarks involve many fewer attributes than full sets of teeth, the probabilities can never get as small as Keiser–Neilsen's and the identifications can never be as individuating.

Another problem is that the use of the product rule requires that the separate attributes going into the calculation be independent of each other, otherwise the probability arrived at understates the improbability of the joint occurrence of the attributes. None of studies taking the probability approach to uniqueness of dentition have achieved, or even attempted, to determine whether the attributes of dentition are uncorrelated with each other. To the contrary, some research indicates that the distribution of some tooth positions are less random than others.[46] For example, Figure 3 shows the tooth position data sets for six upper and lower teeth. The frequency of occurrence varies within each upper and lower sample. If each tooth position were occurring independently, the numbers would be similar. For instance, the lower set values of 116.0 and 153.5 are for the two lower front teeth, a considerable difference.[47] The lack of randomness of dental values (shape and position) was reported in a much earlier British paper.[48]

43. S. KIESER-NIELSEN, PERSON IDENTIFICATION BY MEANS OF THE TEETH (1980); Gerald L. Vale, Reidar F. Sognnaes & Thomas T. Noguchi, *Unusual Three–Dimensional Bitemark Evidence in a Homicide Case*, 21 J. FORENSIC SCI. 642 (1976); Rawson & Ommen, *supra* note 28.

44. Rawson & Ommen, *supra* note 28.

45. The product rule applied to dentition states that the probability of the joint occurrence of several attributes is the product of each separate attribute's frequency in the relevant population. This assumes each component occurs independently, something which is not yet known to be true.

46. Rawson & Ommen, *supra* note 28.

47. *Id.*

48. *Supra* note 15.

Figure 3
Number of Different Tooth Positions Found
for Sets of Six Upper and Lower Teeth.

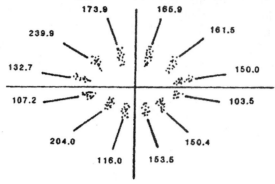

After Rawson et al. (1984).

The largest problem with using probability theory to prove unique individuality is that it is simply incapable of doing so, something that other forensic identification sciences realized some time ago.[49] Probability leads only to probabilities, never to unique, one-of-a-kind certainties. Though it may be the best route to uniqueness, it is incapable of arriving at the desired destination.[50]

What the mathematics of probability can be used for is to calculate the probability of a coincidental match, and that probability can be reported to the trial factfinder. A forensic dentist can never say that the apparent similarity between a bitemark and a suspect's dentition links the suspect with certainty to the crime scene, but the jury could be informed of the probability that a person selected at random would have so similar a match. This is exactly what DNA typing leads to: not assertions of unique matches but a probability of coincidental matches. And that is precisely what other forensic identification sciences such as odontology could do.[51] Unfortunately, forensic dentists have not yet gathered the data to perform these calculations and so their opinions and testimony cannot give such information to factfinders. Thus, while it is true that we could calculate the necessary probabilities based on "missing teeth, pattern of rotation, angulation or position of each tooth . . . if the frequency of certain positions is known for the general population,"[52] the unfortunate state of affairs is that obtaining those frequencies has not yet been accomplished by the field of forensic odontology.

In practice, then, forensic dentists have no choice but to fall back on intuition about frequencies and leaps of inference to reach their conclusions. The forensic dentist intuits the forensic weight (value) that various character-

49. Harold Cummins & Charles Midlo, Finger Prints, Palms and Soles: An Introduction to Dermatoglyphics (1943); David A. Stoney, *What Made Us Ever Think We Could Individualize Using Statistics*, 31 J. Forensic Sci. Soc'y 197 (1991).

50. "It is unfortunate that this approach carries the implication that a complete correspondence of two patterns might occur..." "... it is impossible to offer decisive proof that no two fingerprints bear identical patterns." Cummins & Midlo, *supra* note 49.

51. Michael J. Saks & Jonathan J. Koehler, *What DNA "Fingerprinting" Can Teach the Law About the Rest of Forensic Science*, 13 Cardozo L. Rev. 361 (1991).

52. David L. Faigman, David H. Kaye, Michael J. Saks & Joseph Sanders, Modern Scientific Evidence: The Law and Science of Expert Testimony, *Identification from Bitemarks: The Scientific Questions: Uniqueness of the Human Dentition*, § 24–2.1.1[1], 168(1997).

istics possess. The ABFO Workshop #4 data indicating a high false positive error rate may reflect an over-estimation of the individualizing value of various features. Not all bitemarks have the level of forensic value necessary to identify just one individual. Toolmark terminology was adopted early on by odontologists for discussing the types of dental features seen in bitemarks and the human dentition. A characteristic within a bitemark or in a person's dentition is a distinguishing feature, trait, or pattern. A class characteristic reflects a feature of generic value to a large population. Each human tooth has shape and position features common to the human species. Determining whether an injury is a human bitemark depends on these class characteristics being present in the injury.

Individual dental characteristics are said to be features that are unique to an individual variation within a defined group. The presence of worn, fractured or restored teeth is valued as unique features. If a bitemark possesses the reflection of such a feature, the degree of confidence in a match increases.[53] The odontological literature is silent regarding the frequency of these traits. It is actually rather counter-intuitive to assume enamel chips, fractures, and dental restorations are inherently unique. The shape of human teeth is quite constant in nature and their changes over time is based on common events. The chance occurrence of more than one person having a crooked front tooth is quite large. That is why orthodontists have such large practices.

A frequent refuge for the experienced bitemark expert is the belief that "[t]he controversy seems to hinge on how closely we look at the teeth and teeth marks."[54] This describes the odontologist's rule of thumb protection against false positive bitemark identifications. The weight given to a conclusion is based on the number of characteristics seen in the injury. Probability of a positive match is how many tooth marks are seen, not in the uniqueness value of each individual characteristic of either the defendant or the bitemark injury. Proof of uniqueness is unavailable in the scientific literature.

At the end of the day, the reliability of dental opinion historically is based on intuition derived from the expert's "experience," not scientific data. And the forensic dentist's credibility with the judge or jury generally is based on factors present in the dentist's testimony other than underlying science. These factors include years of experience, demeanor on the witness stand, proper use of terminology, meticulous adherence to procedures (e.g., not forgetting to bring his/her notes), and the like.

§ 5–2.1.6 Scientific Literature on Bitemark Identification

A literature review on the subject of bitemark analysis was presented at the 2000 meeting of the American Academy of Forensic Science in Reno, Nevada.[55] This section gives an overview of the characteristics of and comments on certain seminal articles.

53. *Id.* at 167.

54. *Id.*

55. C. Michael Bowers & Iain A. Pretty, Critique of the Knowledge Base for Bitemark Analysis During the '60's, '70's and Early 80's, Invited address presented at Annual Meeting of the American Academy of Forensic Sciences, Odontology Section (2000).

The material was derived from English language publications from 1960 to 1999. The total number of articles was 120, which contained studies of empirical testing (15%), case reports (40%), technique studies (23%), commentaries (20%), and legal and literature reviews (32%). The 1970s brought out initial articles about bitemarks that were later used in the judicial system to justify the conclusion that bitemark analysis was scientific. The 1980s were the decade of greatest activity. The 90s should be considered the period where biochemical analysis of salivary DNA evidence arrived as the first independent means of confirming or invalidating bitemark opinions. Figure 4 shows the distribution of these papers by general type.

Figure 4

The Bitemark Literature: Number of Publications in Various Categories (1960–1999)

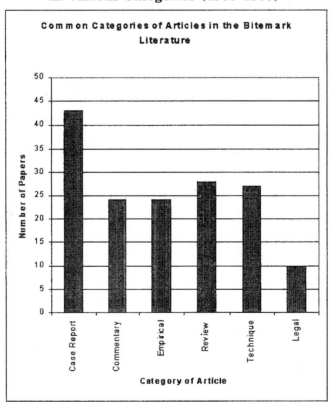

The first thing to note is the limited number of studies,[56] and the second is that only a small subset of these studies report scientific research.

The three scientific limitations and areas of controversy of bitemark analysis have been described earlier in § 2.1.5. The following subsections revisit these issues in relation to the literature obtained by this review.

56. As a contrast, there were 1457 papers on forensic DNA during the same period of time.

[1]   The Accuracy of Skin as a Record of Bitemarks

The bulk of bitemark cases involve injuries on skin. This is not considered a good material on which to record the impression of the biter.[57] The literature shows, however, that the bulk of studies involve bitemarks in inanimate materials. Skin has considerable anatomical variation (e.g. breast tissue versus other locations) and also is affected by posture and movement at the time of biting. The 1971 study by DeVore[58] is the first of only two studies that describe and measured these factors. Figure 2 shows a replication of his simple test where inked stamps were applied at various body locations. In the figure, the lower stamp has been distorted by pressure applied at the bottom of the picture.

DeVore found both shrinkage and expansion of the skin at various positions on the body. The maximum distortion found was 60% expansion at one location. Such variability was seen that the author cautioned about the need to know the exact position of the body at the time of biting before attempting an analysis. This has been generally bypassed in actual practice due to the obvious difficulties in duplicating the dynamics of bitemarks occurring during homicides.

The second extant article on the mechanics of skin distortion appeared in 1974.[59] It reiterated the variable influence body position had on bitemarks in skin. An additional revelation was the effect of healing over time on the shape of bitemarks. The researchers concluded that the changes in bitemark appearance are likely to become greater as the injury grows older. The article ended with the observation that because odontologists were "still ignorant . . . of the conditions during normal biting . . . considerable research is required" to fill that gap in knowledge.

A 1984 article by Rawson and Brooks[60] delineated a classification of breast shapes but provided no additional investigation of the actual distortion values associated with skin. They opined that "the nature of skin and its underlying structures are still of some concern and will probably be a major source of research interest during the next decade."[61]

The questions raised by these three articles remain unanswered. The lack of further research may be attributable to the difficulties of experimental design, issues regarding human research participants, funding, and training. The prevalence of judicial acceptance of bitemark evidence is ironic in light of the cautions expressed in the 1970s that have not been considered since.

[2]   Uniqueness of the Human Dentition

The introduction to this chapter indicated the context of dental identification of human remains, which uses the shape, type, and placement of dental restorations, root canals, and skeletal landmarks as features with individual characteristics. This identification technique has been validated and consistently produces accurate results as evidenced in mass disasters where even

---

57. S.S. Atsu, K. Gokdemir, P.S. Kedici & Y.Y. Ikyaz, *Bite Marks in Forensic Odontology*, 16 J. FORENSIC ODONTOSTOMATOLOLGY 30 (1998); T.J. Stoddart, *Bitemarks in Perishable Substances*, 135 BRIT. DENTAL J. 85 (1973).

58. *Supra* note 14.

59. J.C. Barbanel & J.H. Evans, *Bitemarks in Skin—Mechanical Factors*, 14 J. FORENSIC SCI. SOC'Y 235 (1974).

60. *Supra* note 6.

61. *Id.* at 19.

highly fragmented human remains may be identified dentally and later confirmed by other methods.[62]

Identification from bitemarks, however, is more problematic. It is founded on two postulates: (a) the dental features of the biting teeth (six upper and six lower teeth) are unique, and (b) these dental details can be transferred and recorded in the actual bitemark. These two postulates form the basis for bitemark admissibility as a forensic identification discipline. The overall "uniqueness" of dental characteristics is a common statement in court and in the anecdotal forensic literature. This conclusion is generally accepted though it has not been well tested by research, and it has been subject to considerable criticism.

As discussed earlier, it is impossible to prove uniqueness. It is also unnecessary. Most forensic dentists, however, rely on the unproved and unprovable assumption of uniqueness. The advantage of assuming uniqueness is that it excuses the field from quantitatively analyzing objective dental features seen in bitemarks and human teeth. Such analysis would permit the derivation of probabilities of coincidental matches in actual cases. The "probability of a match" choices now used by dentists in court are offered with no consideration of this vitally important determination, but instead are subjective estimates. Some day, forensic dentistry will follow the lead of DNA typing, forget about "uniqueness," and instead gather the necessary data and calculate the probabilities necessary to inform the factfinder. Indeed, the topic of uniqueness has to advance into the more useful question of coincidental matches, false positive identifications, and scientific proof of conclusions.

Still, the debate over the uniqueness of human teeth is an enduring forensic topic, fueled by a very few articles in the literature. The research that attempted to prove it (the three articles discussed below) explores this path to nowhere. The second and third of the articles are the most often cited as support for the uniqueness claim that forms the foundation of most bitemark opinions.

The first article to consider the statistical treatment of dental features appeared in 1974.[63] MacFarlane et al. studied plaster casts of 200 clinic patients. They developed two categories of features: (a) positive traits were physical shapes and rotations of teeth and (b) negative traits were an absence of teeth. The researchers subjectively inspected the plaster casts and attempted to establish base rates of occurrence of four positive dental features. These features are commonly seen in humans and consisted of (1) the number of teeth and their shapes, (2) any restorations in a front tooth, (3) shape of the jaw, and (4) rotated teeth.

The authors failed to indicate if any of these four features occurred independently of one another, and did not publish their table of results. They used the product rule to establish the likelihood of all four features occurring together and arrived at the value of eight in 100,000 people having teeth who could match a particular dental profile—an over-estimation of improbability due to the apparent violation of the product rule's assumption of indepen-

---

62. The January 31, 2000, Alaska Air crash in Ventura, California, produced multiple positive identifications of victims via dental status, medical status, personal effects, tattoos, fingerprints, and DNA methods.

63. *Supra* note 15.

dence. This figure was introduced in a later trial to much debate and eventual judicial rejection of this statistical method.[64]

The authors evidently reviewed their data and commented that some dental traits appeared to occur randomly in their study while tooth rotation and other traits were dependent. They edited their final conclusions because of this and reduced the frequency values by a factor of four for the dependent dental traits.[65] They did not claim to have confirmed the individuality of human teeth and did not relate bitemarks to their findings.

A study of five sets of identical twins was published in 1982.[66] Although the article stated that efforts were taken to standardize the production of the test bite exemplars, no details are provided. The paper concluded that the dentitions of each pair of twins could be distinguished. The authors went on to extrapolate these findings to the general human population. The fundamental flaw in the essential logic of this approach has been discussed earlier.[67] From a more practical bitemark casework viewpoint, the study is irrelevant to bitemark analysis on skin.

Rawson and Ommen's 1984 study[68] accepted 384 bitemarks in wax from 1200 submitted by contributing dentists. Selection criteria for this subset of the larger sample were not reported. Radiographic prints of the bites were created and then hand traced to produce the outline of the original teeth. This method is not the most accurate, according to a later comparison study.[69]

Several elements of tooth position were then established. It was determined that the minimum number of positions that a tooth can occupy is 150 and the greatest is 239.9. Each tooth's (x, y) coordinate on a graph was multiplied to obtain these values.[70] The authors commented that only five teeth would be necessary for a positive identification (match) of one person from the entire world's population.

Present in this study was the notable use of the product rule. Again, the independence of the dental features examined was not established. But, even if the calculations were correctly based on independent attributes, the notion that if the world population is smaller than the denominator of the fraction produced by the product rule it is thereby proved that no two people on earth can have the same dental profile, is mistaken. This misconstrues the nature of probability. To believe such a conclusion that requires us to assume that God (or Mother Nature)—for some unfathomable reason—gives out only one combination of traits to a customer. The error of this assumption is most easily explained with an illustration.[71] Suppose we have a lottery ticket machine that can produce 1000 differently numbered tickets. On any given

---

64. State v. Garrison, 120 Ariz. 255, 585 P.2d 563 (Ariz. 1978).

65. This important limitation was overlooked by Rawson & Ommen, *supra* note 28.

66. Sognnaes & Rawson, *supra* note 28.

67. *Supra* § 2.1.5[3].

68. *Supra* note 28.

69. *Supra* note 8, at 366. Resolution of the radiographic and hand traced methods are not optimal methods for reproducing images of teeth.

70. Although the article as published actually gives this value as 1.4×10^{14}, and in fact gives similar values for all of its reported probabilities, because probability can take on values only between 0 and 1, we are surmising that the quoted number is actually intended to be raised to a negative power.

71. *See* Michael J. Saks, *Merlin and Solomon: Lesson's from the Law's Formative Encounters with Forensic Identification Science*, 49 HASTINGS L.J. 1069 (1998).

push of the button it will print a ticket numbered at random somewhere between 000 and 999. And suppose we print out 10 tickets. There are, therefore, one hundred times as many numbers that can be printed as there are tickets actually printed. (Similarly, there are 100 times more possible types of dentition than the world's population). What law of nature or mathematics can be used to say that each of those 10 tickets has to be different? The fact is that there is no reason the machine could not print duplicates when drawing at random from its pool of numerical possibilities. The probability of duplication is certainly low (and we can calculate how low), but it is by no means impossible. Consider a different example: There is one chance in 600 billion of any given bridge hand being dealt. Is there any reason to believe that a given hand cannot be dealt again in the next game? Or that it must wait to happen until the other 599,999,999,999 other hands have been dealt? Of course not. Decks of cards, lottery machines and gene pools have no memory for what they did a moment ago.[72]

In present light, this study does confirm that significant variability exists in the human dentition, but not that every person's dentition is distinguishable from every other person's. And, though the article argued only that the human population is unique, the paper often is cited as standing for the more dubious proposition of uniqueness of *bitemarks*. But as Rawson & Ommen commented in their article: "[The question is] whether there is a representation of that uniqueness in the mark found on the skin or other inanimate object."[73]

[3] Analytical Techniques

Empirical testing of methods is an essential basis for confidence in forensic procedures. Bitemark analysis is no exception. The wide variety of comparison techniques allowed by the ABFO is not based on thorough testing to find which are the most accurate. The array of photographic methods, bitemark and suspect exemplar production, and comparison methods are largely unsupported by individual testing and validity testing. The common ground for most dentists, however, is the placement of transparent overlays of the suspect's teeth onto the image of the bitemark. The typical odontologist uses methods that are readily accessible in a dental office. This is mirrored by the technique descriptions and case reports seen in the literature. Occasionally, complex imaging systems are used (e.g. a CT scan to reproduce cross sections of dental casts that give the dentist a look at tooth shape along the length of teeth, or a scanning electron microscope to magnify a single tooth mark), but these are used relatively rarely.

The article by Sweet and Bowers,[74] discussed previously, is the sole example of testing the relative accuracy of different transparent overlay methods. See Table 3. Xerographic and radiographic methods are the ones most commonly used in the literature. This study concluded that the fabrication methods that utilized the subjective process of hand tracing should be discontinued as being the least accurate. It did not correlate any method's advantage or disadvantage in actual bitemark comparisons.

---

72. So long as the deck is kept complete throughout the process (sampling with replacement).

73. *Supra* note 28, at 252.

74. *Supra* note 8.

As a number of legal commentators have observed, bitemark analysis has never passed through the rigorous scientific examination that is common to most normal sciences.[75] The literature does not go far in disputing that claim. Definitive research in these areas remains for the future.

§ 5–2.1.7 Technical Advancements

As explained earlier, the basis of many dental opinions (both in the identification of bodies and in bitemark analysis) is the direct superimposition of Questioned (Q) and Known (K) samples that have sufficient identification value to demonstrate features of common origin or establish an exclusionary result. These direct analysis methods demand rigorous attention to scale dimensions and the detection of photographic distortion, be they radiographs, photographic slides, negatives, or prints, or digital images. These dental techniques are generally analogous to the physical comparison of Q and K evidence in fingerprint, firearms, and toolmark studies.

The process of comparing the Questioned (Q) evidence to the Known (K) evidence is controlled by the ABFO Bitemark Standards and Guidelines. What is evident in the literature and in court is that dentists tend to adopt a method that their professional acquaintances use. Previous articles had talked about the use of digital methods. Sweet and Bowers used a desktop computer and an imaging program called Adobe® Photoshop® to create a transparent *overlay* of the biting perimeters of the teeth (obtained by scanning the dental casts). To review, the older methods included handtracing the tooth perimeters on clear acetate, Xeroxing the dental casts and then tracing the perimeters onto acetate, pushing the dental cast teeth into wax, and the use of X-ray film to capture the teeth impression which had been filled with metallic powder. The following section explains a computer method for bitemark comparison that contains tools which allow for greater control of the bitemark evidence and comparison analysis.

[1] Digital Analysis

Identification disciplines often have the criminalist using a comparison microscope to place the Q and K evidence samples side by side. The loops, whorls, striations, indentations, accidental, and class characteristics present in the evidence samples may then be visually compared. What are difficult to assess, however, in both the crime laboratory and the dental laboratory, are the dimensional parameters of the evidence samples. In dentistry, the traditional ruler and protractor measurements and shape comparison processes are manually derived from evidence photographs and plaster casts of a suspect's teeth. These methods can vary among examiners and are therefore somewhat subjective in nature. Alternatively, some crime lab analysts ignore size comparisons and focus on similarities in class and individual features. In both

75. P. Zarkowski, *Bite Mark Evidence: Its Worth in the Eyes of the Expert*, 1 J. L. & Ethics in Dentistry 17 (1988).

situations, the possibility of error arises from examiner-subjective methods and partial selection of the total physical information available. Additional tools and protocols clearly are needed. The advent of digital technology has provided an opportunity to greatly improve the quality of comparative analyses. Working in digital format has become commonplace due to its many advantages:

- Speed with which digital information can be sent (almost instantaneously).

- Large amounts of digital information can be stored in a very small space.

- Digital images can be enhanced quickly and easily.

- Chain of custody issues are easily handled with digitization.

- Digital information can easily be duplicated and shared worldwide.

- Handling of digital information has proven to be very reliable.

- Standardization of procedures is simplified.

There is no reason why forensic evaluation of dental evidence cannot avail itself of these same advantages.

The recent development of readily available digital imaging software (e.g., Adobe® Photoshop®) and image capture devices such as scanners and digital cameras have created an opportunity to allow the dentist to turn the computer monitor into a comparison microscope with the added benefit of the following functions:

- Accurate means of measuring physical parameters of crime scene evidence.

- Correction of common photographic distortion and size discrepancies.

- Help eliminate examiner subjectivity-better control of image visualization-standardization of comparison procedures.

- Reproducibility of results between separate examiners.

- Electronic transmission and archiving of image data.

- Fabricate exemplars of the evidence and comparison techniques.

- Accurately demonstrate these exemplars to the trier of fact.

Figure 5 shows the background image of a bitemark on pig skin. The "compound overlay" is a digitally captured exemplar of the biter's lower front teeth. The detail present in this experimentally produced comparison shows a high degree of concordance between the exemplars and the injury.

Figure 5

**Digital Image Showing Relationship Between Underlying
Bite Mark and Computer Generated Exemplar of the
Biter's Lower Six Teeth**

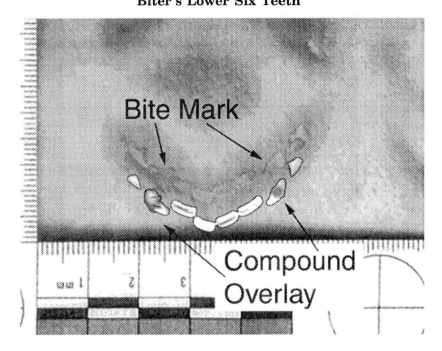

[2] DNA and Bitemark Analysis

Bitemarks have been considered possible sources of serological information since the 1970s. Swabbing of the bitemark area is considered a primary step in evidence collection, and the availability of DNA profiling of the biter's saliva has created a connection between these two areas of forensic identification. But when DNA results are pending in a bitemark case, the optimum protocol is to maintain a separation between the two efforts (physical matching and DNA analysis).

The literature suggests that the investigation of evidence be independent of extraneous information to prevent either intentional or expectational bias.[76] Knowing that the suspect was caught crawling through the window should not add weight to an otherwise inconclusive bitemark (or an ambiguous autorad). Knowing that the suspect's DNA matched should not add weight to an otherwise inconclusive bitemark (or vice versa). The judicial consumer of expert testimony and opinion has a right to expect odontological testing to be independent and blind to other expert conclusions.

[3] Casework Involving both DNA and Bitemark Evidence

Casework involving both forensic dentistry and molecular biology is increasing. Biological and toothmark evidence, when recovered from the same

76. J.J. Nordby, *Can We Believe What We See, If We See What We Believe?—Expert Disagreement*, 37 J. FORENSIC SCI. 1115 (1992).

crime scene, will result in parallel analyses. This section reviews three recently reported instances where both forensic dentistry and molecular biology became intertwined due to the nature of evidence found at the crime scenes. This evidence may be derived from a common origin such as a bitemark on skin which possesses trace amounts of saliva, blood, or semen from the perpetrator. Similarly, an inanimate object connected to the scene might possess toothmarks and biological material that will be compared to physical and genetic data developed from a suspect.

In *State v. White*,[77] a murder victim had been bound and gagged with commercially available duct tape. Marks of five upper teeth were clearly evident on the surface of the duct tape along with the impressions of the lower front teeth showing on the inner cardboard spool. They were presumably made by the assailant using his teeth to tear the tape. A forensic odontologist was retained by the prosecution to compare the pattern in the tape to a suspect's teeth. The suspect had two fractured upper front teeth that compared favorably in size and position to the marks on the tape. Direct physical comparison and a video superimposition of the suspect's dental models were made with a duplicated model of the marks on the tape. The odontology report concluded, with a high degree of confidence, that the suspect's teeth made the indentations in the tape. Prior to the odontologist's analysis, the questioned tape had been swabbed and genomic DNA was obtained and profiled. A DNA report was submitted after the odontological result had been established. The DNA analysis confirmed the odontological findings by concluding that the suspect's salivary DNA was on the duct tape. The odontologist did not become aware of the availability of DNA evidence until after the trial.

In *State v. Brenner*,[78] a total of 22 cigarette butts were recovered from a crime scene as part of a homicide investigation. Small folds were noticed at the end of two filter tips that strongly suggested they were created by the edges of two teeth. The prosecution forensic odontologist opined that a suspect could have made the bitemarks on the filters. The defense odontologist analyzed the same evidence and excluded the suspect. PCR analysis was then performed on saliva recovered from the filter material, and DNA typing eliminated the suspect as the source of DNA on the filtertip.

In *Regina v. Driver*,[79] a murder victim had been sexually assaulted and bitten on her right breast. The body was recovered after being submerged for approximately eight hours in fresh water. A forensic odontologist recorded the bitemark injury and collected salivary DNA from the injury. Additional swabs were taken according to the normal sexual assault protocol established by the pathologist. Once a suspect had been apprehended, the odontologist performed a detailed physical comparison of the bitemark and the suspect's dentition. His conclusion indicated a probable connection between the suspect and the victim's bitemark injury. Later, PCR analysis of genomic DNA obtained from the saliva swabs was performed at a separate laboratory. The results indicated the suspect was the source of the questioned DNA.

77. State v. Wesley White, No. 5941815–3 (Contra Costa County, Cal., Sup. Ct., 1998) (suspect convicted of second degree murder).

78. State v. Brenner, No. FMB01563 (San Bernardino County, Cal., Muni. Ct., East Desert District, Jan.1998), No. 099502556 (San Bernardino Coroner's Case, Jan.1998) (regarding the homicide, case dismissed before trial).

79. Regina v. Terry Grant Michael Driver (Provincial Court, Abbotsford, BC. Canada, Oct. 14, 1995) (defendant convicted of second degree murder).

The impact of DNA analysis in all three cases underscores the persuasiveness of results when both techniques agree. The possibility of a conflict of results also exists.

§ 5–2.2 Areas of Scientific Agreement

Although the field of forensic dentistry is continually at odds over the reliability of bitemark identification conclusions, it has reached consensus on important questions of evidence collection procedure. The areas of agreement regarding these methods are broadly outlined in the ABFO Guidelines and Standards.[80] Refer to Appendices for details regarding these topics.

§ 5–2.2.1 Evidence Collection

The American Board of Forensic Odontology has well accepted protocols on the collection of evidence from both bite suspects and victims. Prior to their inception in 1988, the literature and other forensic organizations had not produced comprehensive measures on these subjects. The American Society of Forensic Odontology has a 20–year history of publishing manuals that were collaborative collections of articles on the breadth of odontology. It should be noted that the 33 contributors to the most recent version[81] all are diplomates of the ABFO. The creative process has been by agreement of the parties and, with the exception of photographic methods and techniques involving dental materials, has not been supported by extensive experimental testing. The process of judicial acceptance of this evidence, however, has developed an appellate history that supports these published ABFO protocols and even unaffiliated forensic dentists follow the concepts.

The collection of bitemark evidence is not solely the realm of dentists. This is particularly the case regarding photographic documentation. Police technicians and forensic pathologists may initially collect the evidence for later evaluation by an odontologist. Errors or omissions of certain procedures, such as specialized casting of a three dimensional bitemark, the proper excision and preservation of tissue, and collection of DNA evidence, generally result in the permanent loss of information. The weight of these transgressions are commonly debated in court.

[1] From the Victim

The collection of bitemark evidence starts with photographic documentation.[82] This may just be a preliminary recording of the general anatomical location of the bitemark. The collection of possible DNA evidence from deposited saliva or blood must take place before any attempts are made to make the bitemark ''cleaner'' or otherwise more photographically acceptable. The swabbing done for salivary DNA is simple and should always be performed. The opportunity may never occur again.

Photography continues afterwards. Bitemark analysis demands that a

80. *Supra* note 9, at 337.

81. *Id.*

82. On the general subject of obtaining evidence from victims, *see* Appendix 1, ABFO

Guidelines on Methods to Preserve Bitemark Evidence.

scale or linear measuring device be placed adjacent to the bitemark[83] and parallel to the skin surface and the camera. Color film and black and white film are considered usual modes of photography. Adjunctive modes of digital, videotape, ultraviolet and alternative photography also are permitted.

The impression or casting of the bitemark completes the process. This is omitted if there are no discernible three-dimensional features seen in the bitemark. Dental materials are used throughout this process, which is both time consuming and demands particular attention to distortion control. The impressions are then used to create dental stone casts of the tissue surface. The availability of these models allows the odontologist to discern indentations created by specific teeth. Tissue removal may then occur in special circumstances and through specific methods that create a rigid framework to minimize later shrinkage of the skin. The sub-surface tissue may contain bruising that reveals additional information. The decision to dissect is made by the pathologist and/or medico-legal authorities.

[2]   From the Suspect

Properly written and signed consent of the individual suspect or an explicit warrant must be obtained prior to collection.[84] This aspect of evidence collection focuses on the visual dental examination, intraoral photography and dental impressions. The use of a scale in appropriate photographs is also expected. It is prudent, but not an ABFO requirement, to examine the suspect for loose teeth, limited jaw opening, or abnormal chewing function. This last commonly is omitted in many odontology reports. The determination of jaw function is mandatory since the physical relationship of the upper and lower teeth in a bitemark must be determined to be anatomically possible.

The suspect's DNA may be obtained during this exam. Swabbing of the oral tissues (inside of the cheek) derives a significant amount of cellular material.

§ 5–2.2.2   Analysis and Comparison of Bitemarks

The general expectations are that odontologists see all the available evidence that is relevant to the bitemark case. Quite often this involves pre-trial discovery challenges to ascertain (1) just how much evidence (usually photographic) is available and (2) full disclosure of the methods and overlay materials from the opposing expert.

The comparison methods that occur follow a standard pattern.[85] The bitemark is the background image that has a properly sized exemplar of the suspect's teeth placed over it. Attempts to standardize terminology are meant to control the variations seen in expert expressions regarding the identification value of bitemarks. This being said, there are many versions of "accept-

---

83. The ABFO No. 2 (Lightning Powder Co., Salem, Oregon) ruler is preferred due to its L-shape and circular reference targets that indicate the proper alignment of the camera to the evidence. These targets allow the image to be rectified and then properly resized to 1:1 (life-size) if there is off-angle distortion present in the original photograph.

84. On the general subject of obtaining evidence from suspects, see Appendix 2. ABFO Guidelines on Methods for the Collection of Suspect Dentition.

85. See Appendix 3, ABFO Guidelines on Methods of Comparing Bitemark Evidence.

able" analyses and comparison methods. The attendant accuracy of each is up to the examiner to decide. The overlays showing the defendant's teeth can range from wax wafers to MRI images.

Agreement exists regarding the "exclusionary value" of bitemark evidence. If the dental characteristics in a bitemark do not have a spatial and/or shape similarity to a suspect, the expected result is an exclusion of the suspect. The other end of the spectrum is also seen, when odontolgists state that only one individual could have made a particular bitemark.

§ 5–2.3   Areas of Scientific Disagreement

The center point of disagreement amongst odontologists is the issue, "what is necessary to support a positive identification from a bitemark?" The odontological literature is silent on the sufficiency of evidence necessary to accomplish this task, yet this positive opinion is permitted to any dentist. Those odontologists who doubt the statement that "bitemarks are as powerful as fingerprints"[86] consider the positive identification of just one person to be quite rare and possible only when remarkable physical detail is present in a bitemark (usually *not* in skin).

The availability of probability theory as a bolster to bitemark identifications is a decades long practice. This flies in the face of aforementioned limitations to "uniqueness" determinations. This continues to be a highly controversial issue among forensic dentists.

The final, and most telling, major disagreement concerns the reliability of bitemark opinions. The proficiency results from the ABFO 4th Bitemark Workshop[87] seriously conflict with decades of assurances by odontologists that scientific reliability is possible and is in effect with bitemark analysis.

§ 5–2.4   Unresolved Issues

What is the threshold quantum of information necessary to diagnose a skin injury as a human bitemark? The bitemark literature considers dental features seen in skin injuries or foodstuffs as "points," or uses synonyms to describe a physical finding pertaining to a tooth. This effort is rather vague since this "point" may be a complete tooth shape, a deeper bite injury showing more three-dimensional information, or only a portion of a tooth that is seen in the injury. The forensic identification value of each "point" is up to the individual dentist. It must be emphasized that many bitemark cases involve nothing more than bruising. The dental examiner must acknowledge that bruising generally creates an area of discoloration that exceeds the dimensions of the compared suspect teeth. The number of "points" necessary to conclude a human bitemark exists is not mandated in the ABFO Guidelines, and in fact is unknown. It is left to the subjective judgment of each examiner. This makes each bitemark case a potential argument between opposing dentists from the very beginning. In unfortunate cases, the question of "whether it is a human bitemark" can take place with the bitemark having been made by just one tooth—if it is a bitemark.

86. Ira A. Gladfelter, Dental Evidence: A Handbook for Police 23 (1975).

87. *See supra* § 2.1.3.

What is the probability that a random match has occurred between a suspect's teeth and a bitemark? The prosecution usually would like to argue that the risk of a coincidental match is so small that it can safely be ignored. The defense usually would like to argue that the risk of a coincidental match is too great not to be taken into account. But at present no one can answer this question in a scientific manner. Any assertion of a small chance is the realm of dentist judgment, even speculation.

How much detail is necessary in a bitemark analysis report?[88] Many experienced odonotologists prepare reports that contain limited and vague information, and which might later be modified at will by the odontologist, just before or even during trial.[89] The typical report contains a list of evidence (usually a single set of dental models of a suspect and bitemark photographs), possibly a copy of the overlay (if one has been used; it is not mandatory) of the suspect's teeth, and a statement regarding conclusions. Other odontologists are of the view that reports must contain specific details of the analyses, indicating exactly what the observations are and how they lead to the examiner's conclusions.

> Proper documentation of image enhancements and color changes performed to evidence photographs. The permitted use of video and digital imaging creates the necessity for the examiner to quantify changes or "improvements" done to an image's color balance, brightness, contrast, and levels of hue and saturation. The lack of "before" and "after values" data makes the duplication of another examiner's efforts problematic at best.

> The amount of photographic distortion that precludes a bitemark analysis. It is common for dentists to receive evidence photographs from a bitemark case. This presents problems if the pictures have been taken improperly. A threshold requirement is that the bitemark be photographically reproduced in a manner that is free of controllable distortion. The literature well documents examples of less than accurate bitemark photographs. Among the common errors are: (1) the improper placement of a scale within the same plane of a bitemark, (2) The camera is not parallel to the plane of the bitemark and (3) the bitemark and the scale are not close enough to each other. The uncorrected acceptance of any of these factors means that the bitemark will not be properly sized and its shape will be distorted. This should preclude any final analysis with a suspect's teeth.

> Estimates of the force necessary to create a particular injury. This is a common question from lawyers and an answer is unattainable. Another variation is "would this injury have caused pain?" Any answers are subjective as the literature is silent to both subjects.

---

88. *See* Appendix 4, ABFO Guidelines for Report Writing.

89. Modifying conclusions or reports before or after they have been written in order to make the findings and conclusions more consistent with other evidence in the case is a practice specifically condemned by the Inspec-

tor General in the investigation of misconduct at the FBI Crime Laboratory. OFFICE OF THE INSPECTOR GENERAL, UNITED STATES DEPARTMENT OF JUSTICE, THE FBI LABORATORY: AN INVESTIGATION INTO LABORATORY PRACTICES AND ALLEGED MISCONDUCT IN EXPLOSIVES–RELATED AND OTHER CASES (1997).

Can a bitemark constitute "Deadly Force?" This is largely a legal question since the dental literature does not contain articles which describe someone dying from a bitemark. Communicable disease may be transmitted by a bite that breaks the skin.

§ 5–2.5 Future Directions

A significant improvement of forensic education is mandatory. The bulk of U.S. forensic odontologists are self-trained products of seminars and week-long meetings. The interface between odontologists and academic programs involving pathology, criminalistics and forensic biology needs to deepen. The availability of forensic "cross-training" in these disciplines and the law would develop clearer understanding of law enforcement and the judiciary's slowly growing requirement of stringently validated protocols for methods and conclusions.

The future work of forensic odontology must focus on reliability testing of procedures, methods, and examiners. Testing the validity of such propositions as "everyone's teeth are unique" and "this bitemark was made by one person in all the world" also are at the top of the list of future work the field must do. Population studies on the lines of what was accomplished in DNA typing would start to distinguish what is commonly seen in a dental profile and what features are seen less often. The assessment of independence among these features must also be undertaken.

The question of coincidental matches between a bitemark and an innocent person must be satisfied. The determinations of "likelihood ratios" to calculate the probability that one set of teeth in a bitemark could randomly match more than one person is an oft quoted wish. The confounding variables found in most bitemark patterns make experimental control that is necessary for these findings very difficult to achieve. The reality is that individualizing (only one person) dental characteristics seldom are seen in bitemarks.

A current belief exists that "the forensic dentist of today often is able to see matching characteristics that are difficult to demonstrate to other less experienced observers or jury member."[90] This axiom has apparently been gored by the ABFO Bitemark Workshop No.4 where the findings suggest that experience has no relationship to the accuracy of bitemark opinions.

The following are several additional issues in bitemark analysis that are of some importance.

What is the threshold quantum of information necessary to diagnose a skin injury as a human bitemark? The bitemark literature considers dental features seen in skin injuries or foodstuffs as "points," or uses synonyms to describe a physical finding pertaining to a tooth mark. This effort is rather vague since this "point" may be a complete tooth shape, a deeper bite injury, or only a portion of a tooth. The forensic value of each "point" is up to the individual dentist. The number of "points" necessary to identify a human's bitemark is not mandated in the ABFO Guidelines and, in fact, is unknown. It is left to the subjective judgment of each examiner.

90. David L. Faigman, David H. Kaye, Michael J. Saks & Joseph Sanders, Modern Scientific Evidence: The Law and Science of Expert Testimony, *Identification from Bitemarks: Bite Mark Guidelines and Studies* § 24–2.4.1, 181(1997).

Considering the enormity of all these limitations, the future may contain a forensic revamping of bitemark analysis testimony where a positive identification is not allowed, but, rather, only a lesser opinion is admissible. On the other hand, if the testing methods of the forensic DNA community (the ability to calculate coincidental matches) can be imported into the odontological context, the future will be brighter.

Appendix 1

ABFO Guidelines on Methods to Preserve Bitemark Evidence

1. Bite Site Evidence

General Considerations—It should be recognized that often the forensic odontologist is not involved in the initial examination and collection of the Bitemark evidence. This does not necessarily preclude the ability of the forensic odontologist to render a valid opinion. The below listed methods are not meant to be an all encompassing list of preservation methods; however, it does list those methods that are used by the diplomates of the ABFO. The use of other methods of documenting the bitemark evidence should be in addition to these techniques.

A. Saliva Swabs of Bite Site

- Saliva swabbings of the bite site should be obtained whenever possible. Obviously, certain circumstances may preclude the collection of this evidence. If the region had been washed prior to the opportunity to swab this procedure would not be possible. If swabbing the area would damage or alter the pattern, it should either not be done or accomplished only after all other preservation methods have been employed.

- It is acceptable to use either cotton tip applicators or cigarette paper to gather this evidence. Other appropriate mediums may be used to collect this information.

- Control swabbings should be taken from other regions or portions of the object or individual that was bitten.

B. Photographic Documentation of the Bite Site

- The bite site should be photographed using conventional photography and following the guidelines as described in the ABFO Bitemark Analysis Guidelines.

- The actual photographic procedures should be performed by the forensic dentist or under the odontologist's direction to insure accurate and complete documentation of the bite site.

- Color print or slide film and black and white film should be used whenever possible.

- Color or specialty filters may be used to record the bite site *in addition to* unfiltered photographs.

- Alternative methods of illumination may be used.

- Video/ digital imaging may be used *in addition* to conventional photography.

- A tripod, focusing rail, bellows or other devices may be utilized.

    1. Lighting

        - Off angle lighting using a point flash is the most common form of lighting and should be utilized whenever possible.

        - A light source perpendicular to the bite site can be utilized *in addition* to off angle lighting; however, care should be taken to prevent light reflection from obliterating mark details in photograph due to "wash out" due to light reflection.

        - A light source parallel to the bite site can be utilized *in addition* to off angle lighting.

        - A ring flash, natural light and/or overhead diffuse lighting can be utilized to off angle lighting.

    2. Scale

        - An ABFO No. 2 scale should be utilized whenever possible.

        - The placement of the scale should follow the guidelines as established in the ABFO Bitemark Analysis Guidelines.

  C. Impressions of Bite Site

    1. Victim's Dental Impressions

        - When the bite site is accessible to the victim's dentition impressions of the victim's teeth should be obtained.

        - Would be useful if victim had bitten the assailant.

    2. Impressions of the Bite Site

        - Impressions of the bite site should be taken when indicated according to the ABFO Bitemark Analysis Guidelines.

        - A backing material should be used to maintain the contour of the impression site.

  D. Tissue Specimens

    1. General Considerations

        - The bite site should be preserved when indicated following proper stabilization prior to removal.

        - The resection of the tissue should follow all other evidence collecting procedures.

        - Tissue Fixative. 10% Formalin is a common fixative used.

2. Evidence Collection of Suspected Dentition

  A. Dental Records

- Whenever possible the dental records of the individual should be obtained in accordance with the ABFO Bitemark Analysis Guidelines.

B. Photographic Documentation of the Dentition

- Photographs of the dentition should be taken by the forensic dentist or by the odontologist's direction.
- A scale such as the ABFO No. 2 scale should be utilized when using a scale in these photographs.
- Video or digital imaging can be used to document the dentition when utilized *in addition* to conventional photography.
- Tripods and/or focusing rails can be used at the discretion of the photographer.
- Extraoral Photographs
- A frontal full face view and a view with the teeth in centric should be taken.
- Intraoral Photographs
- Maxillary and Mandibular occlusal views of the dentition should be taken whenever possible.
- Lateral views of the dentition may be taken.

C. Clinical Examination

1. Extraoral Considerations

- Maximum vertical opening and any deviations should be noted whenever possible.
- Evidence of surgery, trauma and/or facial asymmetry should be noted.
- TMJ function may be checked in addition to the previous observations.
- Muscle tone and balance may also be checked in addition to the previous observations.

2. Intraoral Considerations

- Missing and misaligned of teeth should be noted.
- Broken and restored teeth should be noted.
- The periodontal condition and tooth mobility should be noted.
- Previous dental charts should be reviewed if available.
- Occlusal disharmonies should be noted whenever possible.
- The tongue size and function may be noted *in addition* to the previous observations.
- The bite classification may be noted *in addition* to the previous observations.

D. Dental Impressions

- Dental impressions, following the ABFO Bitemark Analysis Guidelines, should be taken by the forensic dentist or by the odontologist's direction.

- Bite exemplars should be obtained in *addition* to the dental impressions.

E. Saliva Samples

- Saliva swabbings should be obtained if appropriate.

Appendix 2

ABFO Guidelines on Methods for the Collection of Suspect Dentition

Before collecting evidence from the suspect, the odontologist should ascertain that the necessary search warrant, court order or legal consent has been obtained, and should make a copy of this document part of his records. The court document or consent should be adequate to permit collection of the evidence listed below:

1. History

    - Obtain history of any dental treatment subsequent to, or in proximity to, the date of the bitemark.

2. Photography

    - Whenever possible, good quality extraoral photographs should be taken, both full face and profile. Intraoral photographs preferably would include frontal view, two lateral views, occlusal view of each arch, and any additional photographs that may provide useful information. It is also useful to photograph the maximum interincisal opening with scale in place. If inanimate materials, such as foodstuffs, are used for test bites the results should be preserved photographically.

3. Extraoral Examination

    - The extraoral examination should include observation and recording of significant soft and hard tissue factors that may influence biting dynamics, such as temporomandibular joint status, facial asymmetry, muscle tone and balance. Measurement of maximal opening of the mouth should be taken, noting any deviations in opening or closing, as well as any significant occlusal disharmonies. The presence of facial scars or evidence of surgery should be noted, as well as the presence of facial hair.

4. Intraoral Examination

    - In cases in which saliva evidence has been taken from the victim, saliva evidence should also be taken from the suspect in accordance with the specifications of the testing laboratory.

    - The tongue should be examined in reference to size and function. Any abnormality such as ankyloglossia should be noted.

    - The periodontal condition should be observed with particular reference to mobility and areas of inflammation or hypertrophy. Also, if anterior teeth are missing or badly broken down it should be determined how long these conditions have existed.

- It is recommended that, when feasible, a dental chart of the suspect's teeth be prepared, in order to encourage thorough study of the dentition.

5. Impressions

   - Whenever feasible, at least two impressions should be taken of each arch, using materials that meet appropriate American Dental Association specifications and are prepared according to the manufacturer's recommendations, using accepted dental impression techniques. The interocclusal relationship should be recorded.

6. Sample Bites

   - Whenever feasible, sample bites should be made into an appropriate material, simulating the type of bite under study.

7. Study Casts

   - Master casts should be prepared using American Dental Association approved Type II stone prepared according to manufacturer's specifications, using accepted dental techniques.

   - Additional casts may be fabricated in appropriate materials for special studies. When additional models are required, they should be duplicated from master casts using accepted duplication procedures. Labeling should make it clear which master cast was utilized to produce a duplicate.

   - The teeth and adjacent soft tissue areas of the master casts should not be altered by carving, trimming, marking or other alterations.

Appendix 3

Methods of Comparing Bitemark Evidence

A 1994 survey of Diplomates of the American Board of Forensic Odontology indicated that they presently use the following analytic methods in the comparison of bitemark evidence.

1. Generation of Overlays

    A. Acetate tracing directly from models of the suspect.

    B. Acetate tracing indirect from photocopy of model with scale.

    C. X-ray film overlay created from radiopaque material applied to the wax bite.

    D. Alternative methods.

        - Life-sized photos of model printed on acetate film.

        - Greater than life-sized photos of models on acetate.

2. Test Bite Media

    A. Wax exemplars (aluwax, baseplate wax, etc.).

    B. Styrofoam.

    C. Volunteer's skin.

    D. Alternative Methods.

        - Fruits.

        - Clay.

3. Comparison Techniques

    A. Acetate Tracings to life-size photos of wound.

    B. Working study model of teeth to life-size photo of wound.

    C. Working study model to impression of wound or to actual victim.

    D. Acetate overlays of teeth compared to greater than life-size photo of wound.

        - Five times life-size

        - Three times life-size

        - Two times life-size

4. Technical Aids Employed For Analysis

    - Transillumination of tissue.

    - Computer enhancement and/or digitization of mark and/or teeth.

    - Stereomicroscopy and/or macroscopy.

    - Scanning Electron Microscopy.

    - Videotape.

    - Caliper utilization for measurement.

Standards for Bitemark Analytical Methods

1. All Diplomates of the American Board of Forensic Odontology are responsible for being familiar with the most common analytical methods reported in this study.

2. All Diplomates of the American Board of Forensic Odontology should utilize appropriate analytical methods in their analysis of the evidence.

3. A list of all the evidence analyzed and the specific analytical procedures should be included in the body of the final report. All available evidence associated with the Bitemark must be reviewed prior to rendering an expert opinion.

4. Any new analytical methods not listed in the previously described list of analytical methods should be thoroughly explained in the body of the report. New analytical methods should be scientifically sound and duplicated by other forensic experts. New analytical methods should, if possible, be "backed up" with the use of one or more of the accepted techniques listed in these guidelines.

Appendix 4

ABFO Guidelines for Report Writing, Including Terminology

Both in the case of a living victim or deceased individual, the odontologist should determine and record certain vital information.

1. Demographics
   - Name of victim
   - Case Number
   - Date of examination
   - Referring agency
   - Person to contact
   - Age of victim
   - Race of victim
   - Sex of victim
   - Name of examiner(s)

2. Location of Bitemark
   - Describe anatomical location
   - Describe surface contour: flat, curved or irregular
   - Describe tissue characteristics
     - A. Underlying structure: bone, cartilage, muscle, fat
     - B. Skin: relatively fixed or mobile

3. Shape
   - The shape of the bitemark should be described; e.g. essentially round, ovoid, crescent, irregular, etc.

4. Color
   - The color should be noted; e.g. red, purple, etc.

5. Size
   - Vertical and horizontal dimensions of the bitemark should be noted, preferably in the metric system.

6. Type of Injury
   - Petechial hemorrhage
   - Contusion (ecchymosis)
   - Abrasion
   - Laceration
   - Incision

- Avulsion

- Artifact

7. Other Information

- It should be also be noted whether the skin surface is indented or smooth. At some point, the odontologist will evaluate the evidence to determine such things as position of maxillary and mandibular arches, location and position of individual teeth, intradental characteristics, etc. This may or many not be possible at the time of initial examination and will be covered below.

Component Injuries Seen in Bitemarks

Abrasions (scrapes), contusions (bruises), lacerations (tears), ecchymosis, petechiae, avulsion, indentations (depressions), erythema (redness) and punctures might be seen in bitemarks. Their meaning and strict definitions are found in medical dictionaries and forensic medical texts and should not be altered. An incision is a cut made by a sharp instrument and, although mentioned in the Bitemark literature, it is not an appropriate term to describe the lacerations made by incisors.

The term *latent* injury or wound was preferred over occult or trace wound when referring to an injury which is not visible but can be brought out by special techniques.

A Characteristic (as it pertains to Bitemarks)

A *characteristic,* as applied to a bitemark, is a distinguishing feature, trait or pattern within the mark. Characteristics are two types, *class characteristics* and *individual characteristics.*

Class characteristic: a feature, trait or pattern preferentially seen in, or reflective of, a given group. For example, the finding of linear or rectangular contusions at the midline of a Bitemark arch is a class characteristic of human incisor teeth. "Incisors" represent the class in this case. The value of identifying class characteristics is that, when seen, they enable us to identify the group from which they originate. For instance, the class characteristics of incisors (rectangles) differentiates them from canines (circles or triangles). If we define the class characteristics of human bites, we can differentiate them from animal bites. Via class characteristics, we differentiate the adult from the child bite or mandibular from maxillary arch. The original term "class characteristic" was applied to toolmarks and its definition has been modified to make it more applicable to bitemarks.

Individual characteristic: a feature, trait or pattern that represents an individual variation rather than an expected finding within a defined group. An example of this is a rotated tooth. The value of individual characteristics is that they differentiate between individuals and help identify the perpetrator. The number, specificity and accurate reproduction of these individual characteristics determine the confidence level that a particular suspect made the bitemark.

Bitemark Definitions

Bitemark:

- A physical alteration in a medium caused by the contact of teeth.
- A representative pattern left in an object or tissue by the dental structures of an animal or human.

Cutaneous Human Bitemark:

- An injury in skin caused by contacting teeth (with or without the lips or tongue) which shows the representational pattern of the oral structures.

COMMENT: These represent succinct, workable definitions. They lack 100% precision because they exclude the rare cases of denture markings and tooth contact marks without biting action. However, a definition that encompasses all possible tooth/mouth-to-medium contacts would be too cumbersome for practical application.

Description of the Prototypical Human Bitemark

A circular or oval (doughnut) (ring-shaped) patterned injury consisting of two opposing (facing) symmetrical, U-shaped arches separated at their bases by open spaces. Following the periphery of the arches are a series of individual abrasions, contusions and/or lacerations reflecting the size, shape, arrangement and distribution of the class characteristics of the contacting surfaces of the human dentition.

Variations of the Prototypical Bitemark

Variations include additions, subtractions and distortions.

1. Additional features:
   - Central Ecchymosis (central contusion)—when found, these are caused by two possible phenomena:
     - A) positive pressure from the closing of teeth with disruption of small vessels.
     - B) negative pressure caused by suction and tongue thrusting.
   - Linear Abrasions, Contusions or Striations—these represent marks made by either slipping of teeth against skin or by imprinting of the lingual surfaces of teeth. The term *drag marks* is in common usage to describe the movement between the teeth and the skin while *lingual markings* is an appropriate term when the anatomy of the lingual surfaces are identified. Other acceptable descriptive terms include radial or sunburst pattern.
   - Double Bite—a "bite within a bite" occurring when skin slips after an initial contact of the teeth and then the teeth contact again a second time.
   - Weave Patterns of interposed clothing.
   - Peripheral Ecchymosis—due to excessive, confluent bruising.
2. Partial Bitemarks:
   - one-arched (half bites).
   - one or few teeth.

- unilateral (one-sided) marks—due to incomplete dentition, uneven pressure or skewed bite.

3. Indistinct/Faded Bitemarks:

- Fused Arches—collective pressure of teeth leaves arched rings without showing individual tooth marks.

- Solid—ring pattern is not apparent because erythema or contusion fills the entire center leaving a filled, discolored, circular mark.

- Closed Arches—the maxillary and mandibular arch are not separate but joined at their edges.

- Latent—seen only with special imaging techniques.

4. Superimposed or Multiple Bites.

5. Avulsive Bites.

COMMENT: This list excludes variations caused by individual characteristics of the biter's teeth.

Unique and Distinctive

Unique:

This term is variably defined as either one of a kind or rare and unusual. In its most conservative interpretation the following connotations apply:

- such distinctiveness that no other person could have made an identical pattern.

- to the point of persuasion of individuality.

- attributable to only one individual.

- unequaled.

To those who use a more liberal interpretation the following would apply:

- unusual.

- rare.

COMMENT: Forensic odontologists should specify their meaning when they use the word unique.

Distinctive:

- variation from normal, unusual, infrequent.

- not one of a kind but serves to differentiate from most others.

- highly specific, individualized.

- lesser degree of specificity than unique.

COMMENT: A consensus of odontologists indicated that in the hierarchy of the terminology, "unique" implies greater rarity than "distinctive".

Terms Indicating Degree of Confidence
That an Injury is a Bitemark

Possible Bitemark:

An injury showing a pattern that may or may not be caused by teeth; could be caused by other factors but biting cannot be ruled out.

- *criteria:* general shape and size are present but distinctive features such as tooth marks are missing, incomplete or distorted *or* a few marks resembling tooth marks are present but the arch configuration is missing.

Probable Bitemark:

The pattern strongly suggests or supports origin from teeth but could conceivably be caused by something else.

- *criteria:* pattern shows (some) (basic) (general) characteristics of teeth arranged around arches.

Definite Bitemark:

There is no reasonable doubt that teeth created the pattern; other possibilities were considered and excluded.

- *criteria*: pattern conclusively illustrates (classic features) (all the characteristics) (typical class characteristics) of dental arches and human teeth in proper arrangement so that it is recognizable as an impression of the human dentition.

COMMENT: These terms are opinions, representing 3 zones of confidence and do not convey a statistical or mathematical measurement of precision. A lesser quality bitemark can be elevated to definite if multiple bitemarks are present or if amylase is positive (note: this is outdated since it ignores DNA evidence from saliva).

Terms to Indicate That an Injury Represents a Bitemark

Ordinate Ranking of Terms	*Connotation*
• definite	
• positively	no doubt in my mind it is a bitemark
• reasonable medical certainty	virtual certainty;
• highly probable	allows for the possibility
	of another cause, however remote
• probable	more likely than not
• possible	
• similar to	such a mark could have been produced
• consistent with	by teeth but not necessarily and could
• conceivable	have been created by something else,
• may or may not be	no commitment to likelihood.
• cannot be ruled out	
• cannot be excluded	
• unlikely	
• inconsistent	less likely than not
• improbable	

• incompatible	no doubt in my mind it is not a bitemark;
• excluded • impossible	represents something else
• indeterminable • shouldn't be used • insufficient	pattern shows insufficient characterization to comment on teeth as a cause

COMMENT: The above ranked terms are to define the injury itself as opposed to the terms used to describe the degree of certainty that a particular set of teeth caused the wound. Please refer to the "Terms to indicate the Link Between Bitemark and the Suspect(s)" for acceptable terms used to describe the comparison opinion.

Descriptions and Terms Used to Link a Bitemark to a Suspect

A Point, Concordant Point, Area of Comparison, Match, Consistent

Point:

- a singular unit or feature available for comparison or evaluation.
- an area attributable to a tooth.
- a way of counting features.

COMMENT: This term is used as a convenience in reports to address specific components of the bitemark which are being compared to teeth. A point doesn't imply any degree of specificity and (is) not a characteristic.

Concordant Point:

- point seen in both the bitemark and the suspect(s') exemplars.
- corresponding feature.
- comparable element.
- unit of similarity.
- matching point.

Area of Comparison:

- a dynamic or specific region to be compared.
- a complex or pattern made up of a conglomerate of several points or a group of features.

Match:

- nonspecific term indicating some degree of concordance between a single feature, combination of features or a whole case.
- an expression of similarity without stating degree of probability or specificity.

COMMENT: This term "match" or "positive match" should not be used as a definitive expression of an opinion in a Bitemark case. The statement "It is a positive match" or "It is my opinion that the bitemark matches the suspect's teeth" will likely be interpreted by juries as tantamount to specific perpetrator identification when all the odontologist might mean is that a poorly-defined or nonspecific bitemark was generally similar to the suspect's teeth, as it might to a large percentage of the population.

Consistent (compatible) With:

- synonymous to "match," a similarity is present but specificity is unstated.

COMMENT: If used to represent the odontologist's conclusion, the term "consistent with" should be explained in the report or testimony as indicating similarity but implying no degree of specificity to the match. This is necessitated by the fact that our survey showed that this term varied in meaning among odontologists to indicate everything from "possible" to "absolute certainty;" its message is unreliable. However, when used as proposed, it is an acceptable term for those odontologists who are reluctant to suggest culpability of a suspect.

Possible Biter:

- could have done it; may or may not have.
- teeth like the suspect's could be expected to create a mark like the one examined but so could other dentitions.

    criteria: there is a nonspecific similarity or a similarity of class characteristics; match points are general and/or few, and there are no incompatible inconsistencies that would serve to exclude.

COMMENT: This term is approximately synonymous with "consistent with" but has a more universally understandable meaning.

Probable Biter:

- suspect most likely made the bite; most people in the population could not leave such a mark.

    criteria: bitemark shows some degree of specificity to the individual suspect's teeth by virtue of a sufficient number of concordant points including some corresponding individual characteristics. There is an absence of any unexplainable discrepancies.

Reasonable Medical Certainty:

- highest order of certainty that suspect made the bite.
- the investigator is confident that the suspect made the mark.
- perpetrator is identified for all practical and reasonable purposes by the bitemark.
- any expert with similar training and experience, evaluating the same evidence should come to the same conclusion of certainty.
- any other opinion would be unreasonable.

    criteria: there is a concordance of sufficient distinctive, individual characteristics to confer (virtual) uniqueness within the population under consideration. There is absence of any unexplainable discrepancies.

COMMENT: The term reasonable medical certainty conveys the connotation of virtual certainty or beyond reasonable doubt. The term deliberately avoids the message of unconditional certainty only in deference to the scientific maxim that one can never be absolutely positive unless everyone in the world was examined or the expert was an eye witness. The Board considers that a statement of absolute certainty such as "indeed, without a doubt", is unprovable and reckless. Reasonable medical certainty represents the highest order of confidence in a comparison. It is, however, acceptable to state that there is "no doubt in my mind" or "in my opinion, the suspect is the biter" when such statements are prompted in testimony.

Degrees of Certainty Describing
The *Link* Between the Bitemark and Suspect

Terms	*Connotation*
• reasonable medical certainty • extremely probable • high degree of certainty	"virtual certainty; no reasonable or practical possibility that someone else did it"
• very probably • probably • most likely	"more likely than not"
• possible • consistent (with) • can't exclude	"could be; may or may not be; can't be ruled out"
• improbable	"unlikely to be the biter"
• ruled out • excluded • exculpatory • could not have; did not • eliminated • dissimilar • no match; mismatch • incompatible • not of common origin	"not the biter"
• inadequate • inconclusive • insufficient	"insufficient quality/quantity/specificity of evidence to make any statement of relationship to the biter"

• evidence has no probative
   (forensic) value
• unsuitable (should not
   be used)
• non-contributory
• non-diagnostic
	"of no evidentiary value"

COMMENT: Using numbers and percentages to represent opinions is inappropriate unless a specific statistical analysis on a case has been done.

ABFO Standards for "Bitemark Terminology"

The following list of Bitemark Terminology Standards have been accepted by the American Board of Forensic Odontology.

1.   Terms assuring unconditional identification of a perpetrator, without doubt, on the basis of an epidermal bitemark and an open population is not sanctioned as a final conclusion.

2.   Terms used in a different manner from the recommended guidelines should be explained in the body of a report or in testimony.

3.   Certain terms have been used in a nonuniform manner by odontologists. To prevent miscommunication, the following terms, if used as a conclusion in a report or in testimony, should be explained:

- match; positive match.
- consistent with.
- compatible with.
- unique.

4.   The following terms *should not* be used to describe bitemarks:

- suck mark (20% of diplomates still use this antiquated term).
- incised wound.

5.   All boarded forensic odontologists are responsible for being familiar with the standards set forth in this document.

Appendix 5

ABFO Scoring Sheet for Bite Mark Analysis

(Important: Use only with scoring guide, score only reliable information.)

Case Name:

Features Analyzed Discrepancy (if any)	Nbr. of Points	Max.	Mand.

Gross

All teeth in mark present in suspect's mouth	*One per arch	
Size of arches consistent (i.e. mark not larger than dental arch)	*One per arch	
Shape of arches consistent	*One per arch	

Tooth Position

Tooth and tooth mark in same labiolingual position	*One per tooth	
Tooth and mark in same rotational position (whether rotated or normal)	*One per tooth	
Vertical position of tooth regarding occlusal plane matches depth of mark (use only in unusual case)	*One per matching tooth	
Spacing between adjacent marking edges	*One per space	

Intradental Features

Mesiodistal width of tooth matches mark (use only if individual tooth is clearly marked)	*One per tooth	
Labiolingual width of tooth matches mark OR attrition of edge matches mark	**Three per tooth	
Distinctive curvature of tooth incisal edge matches mark (use only in unusual case)	**Three per tooth	
Other distinctive features (fractured teeth, unusual anatomy)	Three per tooth	

Miscellaneous

Suspect has one edentulous arch and this is reflected in bite mark	Three
	Total, each arch:
	Grand Total:

*Three points if feature is significantly distinctive.
**Only in case permitting accurate measurement.

Signature _____   Date _____
2/20/84 Committee on Bite Mark Guidelines

Note: Compilation of "points" was abandoned in January 1988.

CHAPTER 6

TALKER IDENTIFICATION

Table of Sections

A. LEGAL ISSUES

B. SCIENTIFIC STATUS

Westlaw Electronic Research

See Westlaw Electronic Research Guide preceding the Summary of Contents.

A. LEGAL ISSUES

§ 6–1.0 THE JUDICIAL RESPONSE TO PROFFERED EXPERT TESTIMONY ON TALKER IDENTIFICATION

§ 6–1.1 Pre-*Daubert* Decisions

Judicial opinions on the admissibility of talker identification were widely divided before *Daubert*,[1] and following *Daubert* there has been only one additional case that directly considered the admissibility of "voiceprints" or "voice spectrography," though there have been several cases on the periphery of the large central issue. Thus, no consistent or coherent judicial view can be discerned, and whether *Daubert* will guide courts to increased convergence must wait for the future. The patterns and non-patterns of the courts' responses to scientific talker identification is instructive. The accompanying Table 1, Scientific Talker Identification Cases, lists the major talker identification opinions in chronological order, along with certain other information about the cases.

Table I
Scientific Voice Identification Cases:
Holdings, Legal Tests, and Citations to NAS Report

Jurisdiction	Court	Case	Cite	Date	Legal Test*	Held	NAS Report
Military	APP	Wright	17 CMA 183	1967	Reliability	IN	
CA	APP	King	72 Cal.Rptr. 478	1968	Frye-broad	OUT	
NJ	TR	Cary	239 A.2d 680	1970	Frye-broad	OUT	
MN	SC	Trimble	192 N.W.2d 432	1971	none	IN	
FL	APP	Worley	263 So.2d 613	1972	Reliability	IN	
FL	APP	Alea	265 So.2d 96	1972	none + [Reliability]	IN	
CA	APP	Hodo	106 Cal.Rptr. 547	1973	Frye-narrow	IN	
US–DC Cir.	APP	Addison	498 F.2d 741	1974	Frye-broad	OUT	
CA	APP	Law	114 Cal.Rptr. 708	1974	Frye-broad	OUT	
US–EDPA	TR	Sample	378 F.Supp. 44	1974	McC	IN	
MA	SC	Lykus	327 N.E.2d 671	1975	Frye-narrow	IN	
US–4th Cir.	APP	Baller	519 F.2d 463	1975	McC	IN	
OH	APP	Olderman	44 OhioApp.2d 130	1975	Reliability	IN	
US–6th Cir.	APP	Jenkins	525 F.2d 819	1975	McC + [Reliability]	IN	
US–6th Cir.	APP	Franks	511 F.2d 25	1975	McC + [Reliability]	IN	
CA	SC	Kelly	130 Cal.Rptr. 144	1976	Frye-broad	OUT	
US–DC Cir.	APP	McDaniel	538 F.2d 408	1976	Frye-broad	OUT	
NY	TR	Rogers	385 N.Y.S.2d 228	1976	McC + Rel + [Frye]	IN	
PA	SC	Topa	369 A.2d 1277	1977	Frye-broad	OUT	
MI	SC	Tobey	257 N.W.2d 537	1977	Frye-broad	OUT	
US–SDNY	TR	Williams	443 F.Supp.269	1977	Reliab + [Frye-broad]	IN	
MD	SC	Reed	391 A.2d 364	1978	Frye-broad	OUT	

§ 6–1.0

1. Daubert v. Merrell Dow Pharmaceuticals, Inc., 509 U.S. 579, 113 S.Ct. 2786, 125 L.Ed.2d 469 (1993).

US–2nd Cir.	APP	Williams	583 F.2d 1194	1978	McC	IN	
NJ	TR	D'Arc	385 A.2d 278	1978	Reliab or Frye-broad	OUT	
DC	APP	Brown	384 A.2d 647	1978	[Reliability + Frye]	nei-ther	
NY	TR	Collins	405 N.Y.S.2d 365	1978	Reliab + Frye-broad	OUT	
ME	SC	Williams	388 A.2d 500	1978	Reliability–Relevancy	IN	
NY	TR	Bein	453 N.Y.S.2d 343	1982	Reliab + Frye-narrow	IN	no
IN	SC	Cornett	450 N.E.2d 498	1983	Frye-broad	OUT	no
OH	SC	Williams	446 N.E.2d 444	1983	Reliability	IN	no
AZ	SC	Gortarez	686 P.2d 1224	1984	Frye-broad	OUT	yes
RI	SC	Wheeler	496 A2.d 1382	1985	McC	IN	no
LA	APP	Free	493 So.2d 781	1986	Relevancy balance	OUT	slightly
NJ	SC	Windmere	522 A.2d 405	1987	Frye-broad	OUT	no
CO	SC	Drake	748 P.2d 1237	1988	Frye-broad	OUT	no
US–7th Cir.	APP	Smith	869 F.2d 348	1989	Reliability + [Frye]	IN	slightly
US–DHI	TR	Maivia	728 F.Supp.1471	1990	Reliab + Frye-narrow	IN	slightly
US–6th Cir.	APP	Leon	966 F.2d 1455 (table)	1992	McC	IN	no
AK	SC	Coon	974 P.2d 386	1999	Daubert	IN	no

Note: The legal tests are abbreviated as follows: Frye with the relevant fields defined broadly (Frye-broad), or narrowly (Frye-narrow), reliability (reliab) or relevancy (relev), or McCormick weighting (McC). The Court levels are: court of last resort (SC), intermediate court of appeals (CA), trial (TR). Brackets indicate a test a court stated it was applying but where there is no indication in the opinion that the court actually applied that test.

First, we can see from the Table that the extent of agreement in recent years is no greater than in the earliest days of scientific talker identification. Of the first ten courts to consider the technique, six admitted it and four excluded it. The most recent ten to consider it were similarly divided, six for admission and four for exclusion.

Second, we can see that the legal test of admissibility applied by the courts is highly correlated with the holding.[2] Of those courts that applied the classical broad *Frye*[3] test—that is, an understanding of the relevant scientific community as consisting of a range of applicable fields[4] and not merely the one or two narrowly concerned with performing the particular application that constituted the technique at issue—not one admitted expert testimony of talker identification.[5] Of courts that employed a narrow *Frye* test—narrowing

2. Notice that we merely say "correlated." We venture no guess as to whether the rule dictated the conclusion or vice-versa.

3. Frye v. United States, 293 F. 1013 (D.C.Cir.1923).

4. Concerning scientific talker identification, that could mean acoustical engineering, anatomy, electrical engineering, linguistics, phonetics, physics, physiology, psychology, physiology, and statistics—because the technique of voice spectrography made assumptions about or borrowed principles from each of these fields.

5. People v. King, 266 Cal.App.2d 437, 72 Cal.Rptr. 478 (Cal.Ct.App.1968); State v. Cary, 99 N.J.Super. 323, 239 A.2d 680 (Law Div. 1968); United States v. Addison, 498 F.2d 741, (D.C.Cir.1974); People v. Law, 40 Cal.App.3d 69, 114 Cal.Rptr. 708 (Cal.Ct.App.1974); People v. Kelly, 17 Cal.3d 24, 130 Cal.Rptr. 144, 549 P.2d 1240 (Cal. 1976); United States v. McDaniel, 538 F.2d 408 (D.C.Cir.1976); Com. v. Topa, 471 Pa. 223, 369 A.2d 1277 (Pa.1977); People v. Tobey, 401 Mich. 141, 257 N.W.2d 537 (Mich. 1977); Reed v. State, 283 Md. 374, 391 A.2d 364 (Md.1978); People v. Collins, 94 Misc.2d 704, 405 N.Y.S.2d 365 (Sup.Ct.1978); D'Arc v. D'Arc, 157 N.J.Super. 553, 385 A.2d 278 (Ch.Div.1978); Cornett v. State, 450 N.E.2d 498 (Ind.1983); State v. Gortarez, 141 Ariz. 254, 686 P.2d 1224 (Ariz.1984); Windmere, Inc. v. International Ins. Co., 105 N.J. 373, 522 A.2d 405 (1987); People v. Drake, 748 P.2d 1237 (Colo.1988).

the relevant scientific field to those that performed the test at issue—not one excluded the testimony.[6] These two versions of the *Frye* test, and their predictably opposite conclusions, illustrate one of the important criticisms of *Frye*, namely, that defining the relevant scientific fields broadly or narrowly largely dictates the conclusion that will be reached.

Of courts that employed a "relevancy" or "reliability" test—frequently equated, at least in the past, with the test embodied in the Federal Rules of Evidence—eleven admitted[7] talker identification expert testimony and three excluded it.[8] The one case that was decided after and under *Daubert* admitted voice identification expert testimony.[9] The courts varied considerably in what they required for the expertise to be found sufficiently "reliable." Most were satisfied that as long as there was something to be said on behalf of talker identification, that was enough to let it in. One court noted only that the witness was a credentialed expert and cited other jurisdictions that had admitted such testimony.[10] Using a similarly minimal threshold, however, another court excluded the evidence, concluding that its almost presumptive reliability was outweighed by its risk of being given excessive weight by factfinders.[11] Yet another court gave the scientific evidence on the proffered expertise a close and thoughtful examination, much like what the *Daubert* gloss on the Federal Rules would seem to require. That court concluded that talker identification expert testimony was inadmissible.[12]

6. Hodo v. Superior Court, Riverside County, 30 Cal.App.3d 778, 106 Cal.Rptr. 547 (Cal. Ct.App.1973); Commonwealth v. Lykus, 367 Mass. 191, 327 N.E.2d 671 (Mass.1975); People v. Bein, 114 Misc.2d 1021, 453 N.Y.S.2d 343 (Sup.Ct.1982); United States v. Maivia, 728 F.Supp. 1471 (D.C.Hawai'i 1990).

7. United States v. Wright, 37 C.M.R. 447 (1967); Worley v. State, 263 So.2d 613 (Fla. Dist.Ct.App.1972); State v. Olderman, 44 Ohio App.2d 130, 336 N.E.2d 442 (Ohio Ct.App. 1975); People v. Rogers, 86 Misc.2d 868, 385 N.Y.S.2d 228 (Sup.Ct.1976); United States v. Franks, 511 F.2d 25 (6th Cir.1975); United States v. Williams, 443 F.Supp. 269 (S.D.N.Y. 1977); State v. Williams, 388 A.2d 500 (Me. 1978); State v. Williams, 4 Ohio St.3d 53, 446 N.E.2d 444 (Ohio 1983); People v. Bein, 114 Misc.2d 1021, 453 N.Y.S.2d 343 (Sup.Ct.1982); United States v. Smith, 869 F.2d 348 (7th Cir.1989); United States v. Maivia, 728 F.Supp. 1471 (D.C.Hawai'i 1990).

8. People v. Collins, 94 Misc.2d 704, 405 N.Y.S.2d 365 (Sup.Ct.1978); State v. Free, 493 So.2d 781 (La.Ct.App.1986); D'Arc v. D'Arc, 157 N.J.Super. 553, 385 A.2d 278 (Ch.Div. 1978).

9. State v. Coon, 974 P.2d 386 (Alaska 1999), discussed in some detail, *infra* § 1.2.

10. United States v. Smith, 869 F.2d 348 (7th Cir.1989).

11. State v. Free, 493 So.2d 781 (La.Ct. App.1986).

12. People v. Collins, 94 Misc.2d 704, 405 N.Y.S.2d 365 (Sup.Ct.1978). Some excerpts from the opinion:

It should be pointed out that although many of the Courts which admitted Spectrographic Voice Identification have done so based largely on the Tosi study, this study has not been replicated, and there seems to be no other formal experimentation in this area upon which the scientific community can make an informed judgment.

It is certainly reasonable to expect science to withhold judgment on a new theory until it has been well tested in the crucible of controlled experimentation and study.

[T]he entire technique is based substantially on the premise that intraspeaker variability is never as great as inter-speaker variability therefore, while each speaker's voice will be somewhat different each time he renders the same utterance, that difference will never be as great as the difference between the utterances of any two different speakers. It would seem reasonable to suppose that this is true, but this fact has not been proven to the Court's satisfaction.

The testimony however, reveals that there has been no experimentation to show that two different voices will always appear different spectrographically.

Without additional independent proof the Court cannot accept the assumption that inter-speaker variability is always greater than intra-speaker variability.

Other courts employed the McCormick test, weighing the proffered evidence's scientific acceptability against the risks of opaqueness, error, or an exaggerated popular opinion of the technique. Every court employing this test found talker identification expert testimony admissible.[13]

Only one post-*Daubert* opinion exists, and that it discussed at length, *infra* § 1.2.

Finally, one opinion reached its conclusion without employing a discernible legal test.[14]

The refusal of some courts to admit talker identification expert evidence is an exception to the traditional receptiveness of the courts to forensic individuation techniques. Why has talker identification been treated differently? Several interconnected explanations are plausible.

One may be that judges have gradually grown more thoughtful and discerning and less credulous about scientific offerings than their judicial ancestors had been. Numerous courts evaluating talker identification expertise were critical of witnesses testifying on behalf of the technique who were mere technicians rather than educated scientists;[15] or whose livelihoods depended upon continued admission of the technique;[16] or who came from a very small circle of proponents of the technique.[17]

Another factor is that the literature of scientific talker identification, both supporting and questioning the technique, was more quantified and qualified[18] than earlier courts had received about earlier forensic individuation techniques. This is because most of the people involved in talker identification came from fields that had a tradition of empirical testing of their ideas. Indeed, more research was available to the courts about talker identification expertise than for any forensic individuation field that preceded it. This immediately provided the courts with unusual resources with which to comprehend the shortcomings of the technique.[19] When a field provides rigorous self-critiques of its own concepts and techniques, it greatly aids the courts in making a more informed and sober assessment of the field and its likely contribution to the factfinding process.[20] Moreover, controversy tends to

---

13. United States v. Sample, 378 F.Supp. 44 (E.D.Pa.1974); United States v. Baller, 519 F.2d 463 (4th Cir.1975); United States v. Jenkins, 525 F.2d 819 (6th Cir.1975); United States v. Franks, 511 F.2d 25 (6th Cir.1975); People v. Rogers, 86 Misc.2d 868, 385 N.Y.S.2d 228 (Sup.Ct.1976); United States v. Williams, 583 F.2d 1194 (2d Cir.1978); State v. Wheeler, 496 A.2d 1382 (R.I.1985); United States v. Leon, 966 F.2d 1455 (6th Cir.1992) (unpublished).

14. State ex rel. Trimble v. Hedman, 291 Minn. 442, 192 N.W.2d 432 (Minn. 1971).

15. "[The expert witness's] qualifications are those of a technician and law enforcement officer, not a scientist." People v. Kelly, 17 Cal.3d 24, 130 Cal.Rptr. 144, 549 P.2d 1240 (Cal.1976).

16. *Id.* Compare this to the narrow version of the *Frye* test, which essentially asks the practitioners of a technique if they have suffi-

cient confidence in their work that they should be allowed to continue to make a living at it.

17. Of course, these shortcomings do not distinguish talker identification from most other forensic individuation techniques when they were gaining admission to the courts. Indeed, all but the third criticism continues to be true for them.

18. In the sense of limited, restricted, circumspect.

19. The same was true for DNA typing, and was not true for most other forensic individuation techniques.

20. When other fields lack such critiques, is that because there is nothing to question? Or because an uninformed and unquestioning consensus developed among members of the field? And how can courts distinguish between the two possibilities?

precipitate still more research, and a greater volume of research tends to produce a more complex and skeptical impression of the technique in the mind of the court.[21]

In the face of actual data, the courts had a real choice to make. Although the technique could reduce uncertainty in identification, it also was less than perfect. Errors were going to be made, and, unlike some other fields of forensic individuation, talker identification proponents said so.[22] The courts had concrete error rates to evaluate. How good is good enough? How much error is too much? The law provides no standards for making that assessment. Ten percent error may have been viewed by some courts as quite adequate and by other courts as not nearly good enough.

Finally, the courts may have been overwhelmed by the studies. Although more research means a greater potential to understand the scientific questions at issue, it also may have confused some courts, which had limited capacity to interpret and evaluate the empirical studies. If this was the problem, help was on the way.

Unique assistance in evaluating the available data came into being only a decade after talker identification made its first appearance in the courts.[23] Help came in the form of a careful review of scientific talker identification by the National Academy of Sciences.[24] A panel of highly knowledgeable scientists and other experts from diverse relevant fields carefully reviewed the relevant scientific literature and concluded:

> [The assumption] that intraspeaker variability is less than ... interspeaker variability ... is not adequately supported by scientific data.

> Estimates of error rates now available pertain to only a few of the many combinations of situations encountered in real-life situations. These estimates do not constitute a generally adequate basis for a judicial or legislative body to use in making judgments concerning the reliability and acceptability of aural-visual voice identification in forensic applications.[25]

Upon publication of the Report, the FBI ceased performing talker identification for the purpose of offering testimony in court,[26] and it was expected[27] that the courts would stop admitting talker identification expert testimony, at

---

21. This presents a paradox: All else equal, it appears that the better a field studies and critiques itself, the more skeptical the courts seem likely to be of it. The less a field tests its ideas and the more confidently it asserts them, the more positive an impression the courts develop of the field. For a number of the more conventional forensic individuation techniques, there still is no tradition of self-scrutiny or a literature reporting the results of rigorous testing which can inform the courts. At least in terms of their continued acceptance by the courts, those fields have nothing to gain and much to lose by adopting a tradition of inquiry, testing, and skepticism.

22. "Possibly, no combination of methods may ever produce absolutely positive identification or eliminations in 100% of the cases submitted." Oscar Tosi, *The Problem of Speaker Identification and Elimination, in* MEASURE-

MENT PROCEDURES IN SPEECH, HEARING, AND LANGUAGE 399, 428 (Sadanand Singh ed., 1975).

23. Up until that time. There have been two NAS panels formed to review the data on the technique of DNA typing. *See* Chapter 25.

24. The NAS was created during the administration of Abraham Lincoln to provide any agency of the federal government with first rate scientific advice on issues of concern to those agencies. In this instance, the FBI made the request for a review.

25. BOLT ET AL., ON THE THEORY AND PRACTICE OF VOICE IDENTIFICATION (1979).

26. But, as with the polygraph, they continued doing voice spectrographic tests for investigative purposes.

27. *See* ANDRE A. MOENSSENS ET AL., SCIENTIFIC EVIDENCE IN CIVIL AND CRIMINAL CASES 645 (4th ed.1995).

least until the scientific support for it improved.[28] However, of the 12 judicial opinions written since release of the NAS Report,[29] seven admitted the expert testimony while five excluded it. Still more curious, only four cite the Report at all and only one seems to have actually read and learned what the Report had to say. Thus, for the most part, the courts decided the post-NAS cases as if the NAS Report did not exist.[30]

§ 6–1.2   State Decisions Post–*Daubert*

Only one case by a court following *Daubert* has considered the admissibility of expert evidence using voice spectrography. That case, *State v. Coon* (1999),[31] is also the case through which Alaska adopted *Daubert* as its state law.

The defendant in this case was accused of making terroristic telephone calls to the husband of his ex-daughter-in-law. Part of the evidence introduced against him was expert testimony based on voice spectrograph comparisons. The trial court had held this evidence admissible under *Frye* as "generally accepted by courts," and the jury had found the defendant guilty. On appeal Alaska's intermediate appellate court held that the support for admission under *Frye* was inadequate, and remanded for further proceedings on the admissibility issue. The State appealed to the Alaska Supreme Court, which retained jurisdiction but remanded for findings under both *Frye* and *Daubert*. In its decision, the Alaska Supreme Court explicitly adopted *Daubert,* adopted a deferential standard of review, and held the voice spectrograph evidence admissible under the *Daubert* test.

Query whether, when making rulings on the admissibility of scientific evidence as a general matter (that is, whether the science is sufficiently dependable to be admitted, not whether it has sufficient fit to the facts of the particular case at bar), the trial court is in a better position to make the decision than an appellate court. Is verbal testimony by a few witnesses (the typical mode of information gathering by a trial court) a more or a less illuminating method of learning about the underlying basis of the expertise than reading the relevant research literature, with the guidance of counsel in the form of briefs and arguments (the mode of information gathering more often used by an appellate court).[32] The Court suggested that the main advantage of a deferential standard of review lies in the notion that a trial court would have at its disposal more up-to-date information than an appellate court could.[33]

---

28. Few if any of the scientific shortcomings raised by the Report have been solved by subsequent research. *See* discussion *infra* § 2.4.

29. *See* Table 1.

30. Whether this reflects the shortcomings of counsel (for not drawing the courts' attention to the NAS study) or the courts (for not finding it themselves, or not appreciating its value to their decisions), we are unable to say.

31. 974 P.2d 386 (Alaska 1999).

32. For an analysis of the special problems scientific evidence presents to determining the proper standard of review, *see* SCIENCE IN THE LAW: STANDARDS, STATISTICS AND RESEARCH METHODS, Chapter 1.

33. In the present case, this clearly is not what happened. As the opinion states, ". . . no scientific literature was submitted to the trial court for review, but [the voice identification expert] testified about several articles and studies addressing voice spectrographic analysis, and conceded that the reliability of the technique was disputed among members of the relevant scientific community." *Coon*, at 402. A visit to a library by a judicial clerk could unearth a far more complete review of the relevant scientific research than the selective, self-

If the Alaska Supreme Court believed that the trial court was in a better position to gather the evidence, why didn't it make the *Daubert* versus *Frye* decision, remand for the trial court to complete the case consistent with that holding, and let that specific admissibility decision be appealed if and when the parties chose to do so? Since the Supreme Court reviewed the trial court ruling on admissibility for abuse of discretion following the United States Supreme Court's opinion in *Joiner*,[34] (and ruled that the trial court's conclusions were "not an abuse of discretion"), does that mean that the admissibility of voice spectrographic evidence is not settled as a matter of precedent in Alaska, and that the State's trial courts are free to make contrary decisions when the same question of admissibility presents itself in future cases, so long as they make their rulings under the *Daubert* test? Apparently so. From the opinion it appears that the Alaska Supreme Court expects trial courts to make these decisions case-by-case, to contradict each other from time to time, and to be reviewed for abuse of discretion—yet the court hints that somehow (notwithstanding the announced rule) appellate courts will resolve the contradictions before they became an embarrassment, and that in any event the court did not expect this problem to occur very often. The court justifies its approach in part by treating all applications of science as so highly case specific, that the contradictions will be attributable to differences in the case facts.

Oddly, the opinion relied on Rule 703, rather than 702, as the foundation for its *Daubert* analysis, noting that the "commentary to the Alaska Rules of Evidence provides support for the State's view that ... Rule 703 is also a source for an approach broader than the Frye standard."[35] The basic points the Court makes about the dependability of scientific knowledge are entirely reasonable, but finding them in Rule 703 makes little sense. Rule 703 pertains to the facts or data relied on in the *particular* case (that is, the adjudicative facts), not the general scientific background being relied upon (more akin to legislative facts, or empirical authority) and the methods by which the expert may come into possession of those case-specific facts. In addition, query whether *Daubert* really is "broader" than *Frye*.[36] At the same time, the opinion clearly recognizes that its adoption of *Daubert* would lead both to admitting previously inadmissible evidence and excluding previously admissible evidence (and therefore in some situations *Daubert* is "narrower" than *Frye*). The court rejected a number of arguments against the adoption of *Daubert*. It rejected the argument that *Daubert* would place too heavy a burden on trial courts, noting that courts can obtain help by appointing their own experts under Rule 706. It also rejected concerns about adversely affecting the admissibility of traditional forensic evidence like fingerprinting, hand-

serving, and, in this instance, out-of-date sampling of research literature referred to verbally from the witness stand.

34. General Electric Co. v. Joiner, 522 U.S. 136, 118 S.Ct. 512, 139 L.Ed.2d 508 (1997). The Alaska Supreme Court adopted that same position, with one of the four justices dissenting. The dissent emphasized the trans-case nature of scientific evidence, in contrast to the usual adjudicative evidence whose admissibility is being ruled upon. For further discussion of this problem, *see* Chapter 1.

35. *Coon*, 974 P.2d 386 (Alaska 1999). Alaska Rule of Evidence 703 provides: "The facts or data in the particular case upon which an expert bases an opinion or inference may be those perceived by or made known to the expert at or before the hearing. Facts or data need not be admissible in evidence, but must be of a type reasonably relied upon by experts in the particular field in forming opinions or inferences upon the subject."

36. Recent judicial experience and scholarly analysis have eroded that simple equation..

writing, and hair comparison analyses,[37] and about opening the doors to "junk science."[38]

In examining the evidence underlying the claims of voice spectrographic identification, the Alaska Supreme Court conducted a limited and superficial review of the research on which such a decision must depend, doing little more than quoting the trial court's conclusory assertions.[39] Given that no research literature was "submitted" to the trial court, and that court did not ask for any or do any research on its own, unless the court recognized any duty to look beyond the four corners of the record from the trial's hearing on the issue, then by definition the supreme court's review will be limited to the limited review of the science conducted below. As noted above and in the original chapter, few courts have cited the National Academy of Sciences' authoritative review of voice spectrography research, the findings of which led the FBI to withdraw from offering such evidence in courts. *State v. Coon* joins that list of cases that overlooked the major scientific review of the question before them. Thus, despite the *Coon* court's own discussion of the heightened analysis of the science that is called for under a *Daubert* review, its own first outing offers a review of the scientific claims, and a review of the adequacy of the trial court's gatekeeping, that is remarkably meager.

§ 6–1.3   Federal Decisions Post–*Daubert*

No cases involving disputes over "classical" voice spectrography have been reported from the federal courts subsequent to *Daubert*. But other types of voice identification expertise and some more peripheral issues were discussed and debated.

The defendant in *United States v. Salimonu*[40] was found guilty of importing heroin. Among the issues he raised on appeal was the trial court's decision to exclude expert testimony that the voice on the inculpatory tape recordings was not his. The First Circuit affirmed. The trial judge had admitted defense testimony about voice spectrographs, but excluded a linguist's testimony that was based on simply listening to the tapes in question. This expert "admitted that he had no training or special certification in voice identification or comparison, and that he had only engaged in voice recognition procedures two or three times before." Moreover, he "knew of no studies to determine the rate of error for this kind of identification," and conceded that a lay person would be able to discern the same differences between the tapes that he heard.

The defendant in *Virgin Islands v. Sanes*[41] was convicted of robbery and rape. Part of the evidence introduced against him at trial was the victim's identification of his voice. She selected his voice from recordings of several voices. The defendant sought to introduce the testimony of an expert who

---

37. Consult the appropriate chapters in this treatise to see how those asserted expertises have fared, or are expected to fare, under a *Daubert* analysis.

38. Notice that these two arguments—that *Daubert's* standard is so low that it will lead to the admission of junk science and so high that it will exclude forensic science—are at war with each other. They cannot both be true.

39. The opinion gives a more detailed recitation of the expert's background and experience than it does the data on the underpinnings of the technique at issue (for which any facts about the particular expert are irrelevant).

40.   182 F.3d 63 (1st Cir.1999).

41.   57 F.3d 338 (3d Cir.1995).

would have testified about why voice identification is not as accurate as eyewitness identification. The expert was not allowed to give this testimony, but was allowed to testify regarding the distinguishing characteristics of the defendant's voice. With little analysis, the Third Circuit held the trial court had not abused its discretion. Concerning research relevant to the scientific issues in this case, see the discussion of Earwitness Research.[42]

The defendant in *United States v. Jones*[43] had been convicted for distributing cocaine. On appeal, he argued that the trial court had improperly excluded expert testimony on voice identification. The trial court had applied the *Frye* Test, but the Ninth Circuit found that even under *Daubert* the evidence should have been excluded. The expert had developed his voice comparison technique himself, and could not cite any scientific basis for it. He conceded that no scientific studies or published research supported his theory.

The defendant in *United States v. Drones*,[44] sought, and had obtained from the district court, relief for his claim of ineffective assistance of counsel on the grounds that his attorney had failed even to investigate the availability of voice identification expert testimony to evaluate a tape that the government asserted contained the defendant's voice. The court of appeals reinstated the state court verdict. At the habeas hearing, the petitioner's expert stated that he found from his examination that there was "probably elimination" of the defendant as a source of the voice on the recording. According to the expert, this meant that "80% of the comparable words in the samples were dissimilar aurally and spectrographically." The petitioner's expert conceded, however, that there were sundry weaknesses with this technology and that no objective criteria existed by which to check the accuracy of any conclusions an examiner might reach. Also testifying at the hearing, the government's expert echoed these cautionary words, noting that very little research had been done to validate the courtroom use of this technology. The court of appeals concluded that voice identification expertise is not competent evidence. "Given the current state of the law regarding the admissibility of expert voice identification testimony and the expert testimony presented at the evidentiary hearing, we cannot say that counsel's choice of strategy was unreasonable and therefore deficient."

One of the defendants in *United States v. Bahena*,[45] complained that the district court erred in excluding his expert on voice spectrography. The appellate court rejected this argument, and affirmed the convictions of all of the defendants. The court of appeals found that the lower court had not abused its discretion in excluding this particular witness, noting that the expert here had no college degree, was not a member of any professional association and was not familiar with the standard practices in the field of voice identification.

42. *See infra* § 2.2.5.

43. 24 F.3d 1177 (9th Cir.1994).

44. 218 F.3d 496 (5th Cir.2000).

45. 223 F.3d 797 (8th Cir.2000).

B. SCIENTIFIC STATUS

by

Raymond D. Kent* & Michael R. Chial**

§ 6–2.0 THE SCIENTIFIC BASIS OF EXPERT TESTIMONY ON TALKER IDENTIFICATION

§ 6–2.1 Introductory Discussion of the Science

§ 6–2.1.1 The Scientific Questions

[1] Terminology and Basic Concepts

Most people can easily recognize family members, friends, coworkers, and popular figures from the sounds of their voices. This familiar form of personal identification finds forensic application in situations where a voice has been heard by a witness or, even better, a recording has been made of the voice in question. Talker identification may be broadly defined as a decision-making process that relies on properties of the talker's speech signal. The decision-maker's objective is to identify an individual by the characteristics of that individual's speech. The term *talker identification* is used in this chapter because it denotes the task of trying to identify a human talker. Other terms used for this application are *speaker identification* and *voice identification*.

Traunmuller[1] listed four kinds of information contained in the speech signal:

1. *Phonetic quality* refers to the linguistic content of the spoken message, i.e., the essential material from which we derive the information intended by the talker.

2. *Affective quality* is paralinguistic information, meaning that it accompanies the linguistic message of speech and may contribute to the interpretation of that message. Emotional attributes fall into this category.

3. *Personal quality* is extralinguistic, meaning that it is outside the ordinary linguistic aspects of speech. Personal quality is informative about the

* Raymond D. Kent is Professor of Speech Science in the Department of Communicative Disorders, University of Wisconsin–Madison. His doctorate is from University of Iowa and he did postdoctoral work in speech analysis and synthesis at the Massachusetts Institute of Technology. He has edited or written eleven books, including THE ACOUSTICAL ANALYSIS OF SPEECH (with Charles Read, 1992), and is past editor of the JOURNAL OF SPEECH AND HEARING RESEARCH. He holds an honorary doctorate from the University of Montreal Faculty of Medicine, is a Fellow of the Acoustical Society of America, the International Society of Phonetic Sciences, and the American Speech–Language–Hearing Association, and has earned Honors of the American Speech–Language–Hearing Association.

** Michael R. Chial is Professor of Audiology in the Department of Communicative Disorders at the University of Wisconsin–Madison. His doctorate is from the University of Wisconsin–Madison. For 20 years he has worked with the American National Standards Institute and is currently working with the Audio Engineering Society to develop technical standards for forensic applications of audio recordings. He is past associate editor of the JOURNAL OF SPEECH AND HEARING RESEARCH, and Fellow of the American Speech–Language–Hearing Association and the American Academy of Audiology.

The authors thank Lonnie L. Smrkovski for his comments on an earlier draft of this chapter. The opinions expressed herein are solely those of the authors.

§ 6–2.0

1. Hartmut Traunmuller, *Conventional, Biological, and Environmental Factors in Speech Communication: A Modulation Theory*, 18 PERILUS (PHONETIC EXPERIMENTAL RESEARCH, INSTITUTE OF LINGUISTICS, UNIVERSITY OF STOCKHOLM) 1 (1994).

talker, but not the message. The information can include the talker's gender, age, state of health, and individual characteristics.

4. *Transmittal quality* gives perspectival information about the talker's location, including the distance from the one who hears the signal, orientation in space, presence of background noise, and influence of environmental acoustics that may introduce effects such as reverberation.

Talker identification rests on the assumption that intratalker variability (e.g., the variability associated with multiple productions of the same speech sample by a given talker) is less than intertalker variability (e.g., the variability associated with productions of the same speech sample by different talkers). The capability of recognizing a talker is based on two primary sources of intertalker differences: (1) anatomic differences in the size and shape of the speech organs, and (2) subtle individual differences in how speech sounds are made. The former are sometimes called *physiological differences* and the latter *behavioral differences*. Physiological differences generally are not subject to learning effects, whereas behavioral differences often are. A hardware-software analogy also has been used to distinguish these two types of differences among talkers,[2] with physiological factors being compared with the hardware and behavioral factors (including sociolinguistic and psychological factors) with the software. Presumably, the hardware is less easily altered than the software. The speech pattern produced by any one individual is a combination of physiological and behavioral factors. Differences among talkers are therefore a combination of the same factors.

Talker recognition may be subdivided into various approaches: talker recognition by listening (aural recognition), by machine (automatic recognition), and by visual inspection of spectrograms (also known as "voiceprints" or "voicegrams"). These are not necessarily mutually exclusive procedures. Forensic applications commonly make use of both aural recognition and spectrograms, and it is possible to use all three methods in reaching a decision.

This chapter concentrates on the third approach, visual inspection of spectrograms, but some comments will be included on the first and second approaches as well. Visual inspection of spectrograms is the major source of evidence provided by trained examiners. The overarching scientific question is whether an individual talker can be distinguished from a larger group of talkers on the basis of visual patterns in a spectrogram. Because the properties of the spectrogram are essential to an understanding of their use in talker identification, some general comments on spectrograms are in order.

Spectrogram is a generic term for the conventional analysis of sound according to the three dimensions of frequency, time, and intensity. In the typical spectrogram, time is represented along the horizontal axis, frequency (the rate of vibration of a sound component, heard as pitch) along the vertical axis, and intensity (magnitude of a sound component, heard as loudness) as a gray (or darkness) scale. An example of a spectrogram is shown in Figure 1. These visual patterns were introduced as a practical laboratory technique in the 1940s and have been a major source of information in the study of speech.

2. Hisao Kuwabara & Yoshinori Sagisaka, *Acoustic Characteristics of Speaker Individual-* *ity: Control and Conversion*, 16 SPEECH COMMUNICATION 165 (1995).

Terms synonymous with *spectrogram* are *voiceprint*, *voicegram*, and *Sona-gram*™.

The term "voiceprint" was coined by Gray and Kopp[3] and reintroduced by Kersta[4], an early proponent of talker recognition through comparisons of visual patterns. Some writers viewed the "voiceprint" as analogous to the "fingerprint." The term "voicegram" was substituted for voiceprint by others who believed that the term *voiceprint* could be misleading. Whereas a finger can leave a direct physical impression when it is pressed against a surface (hence leaving a genuine "print") the voice is given visual representation only by a series of transformations in which acoustic energy is eventually represented on paper.[5] The term *voicegram* is preferable to *voiceprint* though both have the technical disadvantage of emphasizing "voice" rather than "speech." Although voice certainly is important as the primary energy source of speech, speech is really more than voice. This is one reason why the term *talker identification* is used in preference to *voice identification* in this chapter. Energy from the voice is modified by the speech organs through resonance and other influences. Talker identification generally relies on patterns of speech including characteristics of voice, resonance, and articulation.[6] *Speaker identification* is a frequently used term, which may be gaining prominence.[7]

[a]   Instrumentation and Display

Instruments for this type of speech analysis differ in several respects, but all include components that acquire sound (generally via microphones or audio recorders), edit stored signals, analyze sounds to produce spectrograms, and display results (analog units by means of facsimile technology; digital units by means of video monitors and laser or video printers). Because several systems can be used to make spectrograms, it is reasonable to ask if there are any differences among them that should be considered in the accuracy of talker identification. Unfortunately, very few comparisons of this type have been made, but Hazen[8] reported no differences between the Voiceprint Laboratories 4691C Sound Spectrograph and the Kay Elemetrics Corporation 6061A Sonagraph (neither of these analog devices is now manufactured). While contemporary digital instruments offer greater flexibility and precision

---

3. C. H. Gray & G. A. Kopp, *Voiceprint Identification*, BELL TELEPHONE LABORATORIES REPORT 1 (1944).

4. Lawrence G. Kersta, *Voiceprint Identification*, 196 NATURE 1253 (1962).

5. "Voiceprint" also was used as a trademark by Voiceprint Laboratories, Inc. a manufacturer of speech spectrography equipment. A successor firm, Voice Identification, Inc., retains rights to that trademark and manufactures an analog device (Model 700) favored by some forensic practitioners.

6. The term *Sona-gram* is a trademark of a manufacturer (Kay Elemetrics Corporation) that currently markets two digital spectrographs—the Model 5500 (a dedicated, stand-alone device) and the Model 4300B (designed for use with general-purpose personal computers). A number of other systems, especially

computer programs designed for clinical research and treatment, geophysical and bioacoustical research, music and audio engineering purposes, produce spectrograms as one analysis alternative. *See* Charles Read et al., *Speech Analysis Systems: A Survey*, 33 J. SPEECH & HEARING RESEARCH 363 (1990); Charles Read, et al., *Speech Analysis Systems: An Evaluation*, 35 J. SPEECH & HEARING RESEARCH 314 (1992).

7. A disadvantage to this term is that the word *speaker* has two prominent meanings, one being a human talker and the other being an electroacoustic device such as a loudspeaker.

8. Barry Hazen, *Effects of Differing Phonetic Contexts on Spectrographic Speaker Identification*, 54 J. ACOUSTICAL SOC'Y AM. 650 (1973).

than earlier analog machines, the older devices produced hard-copy records of superior resolution. It has not been studied whether important differences exist among the various devices and computer systems currently used to make spectrograms, a problem complicated by the lack of appropriate recorded reference material (speech and speech-like signals) designed to compare alternative systems.

In this chapter, the term *spectrogram* will be used in the broad sense to include all varieties of visual displays of speech that rely on a conventional three-dimensional analysis of time, frequency and intensity.[9] In customary practice, two types of spectrograms have been used: wide-band and narrow-band. These two types are distinguished by the width of the analyzing filter which can result in different kinds of spectrograms. The bandwidth of the analyzing filter can be likened to a kind of acoustic "window" that is passed along the signal to determine the energy in various frequency regions. The narrower the bandwidth of the analyzing filter, the better the resolution of frequency but the poorer the resolution of time. Briefly, the wide-band spectrogram uses either a 250 or 300 Hz bandwidth filter and is especially useful for speech analysis because it reveals certain acoustic features that have been important in distinguishing among various types of sounds and among different talkers. In particular, the wide-band spectrogram usually is effective in displaying *formants* (acoustical energy constrained to frequency regions by vocal tract resonances). The wide-band spectrogram is particularly useful for the analysis of highly dynamic signals such as speech.[10] Figure 1 illustrates a wide-band speech spectrogram of the utterance "I said stop"; Figure 2 notes landmarks typical of speech sounds in the word "stop." The horizontal axis of both panels is time and the vertical axis is frequency in Hertz (Hz) or cycles per second. The third dimension of the spectrogram is intensity: darker areas represent greater intensity.

---

9. Time is represented from left to right. Frequency is the rate of vibration of a sound stimulus and is expressed in the unit of hertz (Hz), which is the number of cycles of vibration per second. The acoustic energy in adult male speech is essentially contained in a frequency range (bandwidth) of about 50 to 8,000 Hz. However, speech can be understood even with much narrower bandwidths. For instance, telephone bandwidth is on the order of 3,000 Hz (500 to 3,500 Hz). The greatest concentration of speech energy for adult male voices is in the range of about 100 to 2500 Hz. Intensity is one measure of the magnitude or strength of sound energy. It is usually expressed in decibels (dB), a logarithmic scale.

10. Roel Smits, *Accuracy of Quasistationary Analysis of Highly Dynamic Speech Signals*, 96 J. ACOUSTICAL SOC'Y AM. 3401 (1994).

SPECTROGRAM

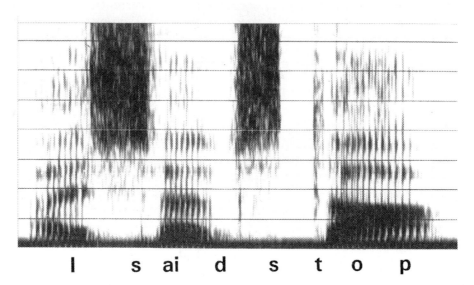

Figure 1. A spectrogram of the utterance, "I say stop." Time is represented on the horizontal axis, frequency on the vertical axis, and intensity as variations in darkness. The horizontal lines indicate frequency intervals of 1 kHz (1000 Hz).

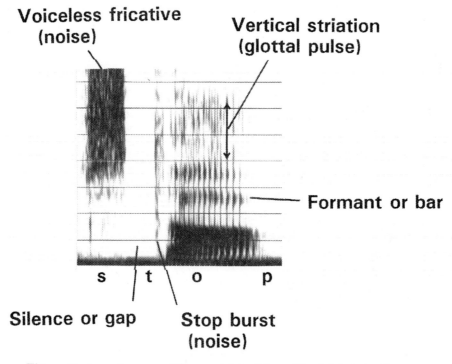

Figure 2. A spectrogram of the word "stop" from Fig. 1, labeled with some acoustic features that might be used in talker identification by spectrogram.

Most of the published scientific papers are based on wide-band analyses of selected words produced by adult male talkers. In this chapter, the wide-band analysis is assumed unless otherwise noted. This is also the common form of analysis used in talker identification from the visual examination of spectrograms. An advantage of many of the contemporary computer-based speech analysis systems is that they offer a range of choices of analysis filter bandwidths. The clarity of formants is influenced by interactions between bandwidth and the frequency characteristics of the speech to be analyzed. Conventional filters 250 or 300 Hz in width are generally suitable for analyzing the speech of adult males, but other bandwidths may be preferable for certain groups, including women, children, some adolescent males, and men with unusually high vocal fundamental frequency (the physical attribute most closely related to what we hear as vocal pitch). Scientific interest in the features of formants that distinguish males, females and children began in the 1940s and continues to the present.[11] Buder,[12] for example, has summarized nearly 90 years of quantitative descriptions of vocal quality. These include simple statistical summaries of fundamental frequency and voice amplitude, long and short term perturbations and covariations in both, and various spectral measures. While many of these pertain to clinical voice disorders, some have been incorporated into currently available instrumentation used in forensic practice. Differences between controlled clinical recording environments and those common to forensic practice may limit application of recent innovations in measurement, but some may prove useful. The essential point is that characteristics of the laboratory analysis should be selected to match talker characteristics in ways that recognize the limitations of recording methods to capture those characteristics.

[b] Decision Objectives

Talker recognition embraces procedures with different decision objectives and assumptions. These include *talker verification* (or authentication), *talker identification*, and *talker elimination*. Talker verification is a test of an identity claim in which a speech sample from an individual is compared to a stored reference sample previously obtained from the individual whose identity is claimed. A common application is security access. A person making the identity claim will be granted access if this person's speech sample is a satisfactory match to a stored pattern. Talker identification is a decision process in which an utterance from an unknown speaker is attributed to one speaker in a known population, such as employees in a high-security facility. Talker elimination is the inverse process of deciding that an utterance from an unknown talker cannot be attributed to a particular speaker in a known population. Most forensic applications involve speaker identification or elimination and these will be the central issues in this chapter.

Talker identification and elimination can be studied experimentally using three different comparison procedures: *closed-set, open-set,* and *discrimina-*

11. W. Keonig et al., *The Sound Spectrograph*, 17 J. Acoustical Soc'y Am. 19 (1946); Gordon E. Peterson & Harold L. Barney, *Control Methods Used in the Study of the Vowels*, 24 J. Acoustical Soc'y Am. 175 (1952); James Hillenbrand et al., *Acoustic Characteristics of American English Vowels*, 97 J. Acoustical Soc'y Am. 3099 (1995).

12. Eugene H. Buder, *Acoustic Analysis of Voice Quality: A Tabulation of Algorithms 1902–1990, in* Voice Quality Measurement (Raymond D. Kent & Martin J. Ball eds., 2000).

tion. Different patterns of correct and incorrect decisions are possible for each procedure. In the closed and open procedures, a sample (exemplar) of speech from an unknown talker (U) is compared to exemplars from some number (N) of talkers whose identities are known (K). Normally, each known talker (K_n) is represented by a single exemplar—in other words, the known talkers are independent of each other. If one of the known talkers (assume it is K_3) is indeed the same as talker U, and if (prior to the experiment) the examiner is informed a match exits, then the procedure is closed. The procedure is open if the examiner is told that the population of known talkers may or may not actually include talker U. A common experimental strategy is to organize comparisons of unknown and known exemplars as pairs following the form: U vs. K_1, U vs. K_2, ... U vs. K_n. Assuming the examiner is required to consider each pair only once, a total of N paired comparisons is possible. Each pair-wise comparison is constrained to one of two decisions: $U = K_n$ (a claimed identification) or $U \neq K_n$ (a claimed elimination). Examiner claims are compared to the actual configuration of pairs (known to the experimenter, but not the examiner). If a claimed identification is wrong, the decision is called a false identification or false positive. If a claimed elimination is wrong, the decision is called a false elimination or false negative.

In the closed-set procedure, the examiner is asked *which* known exemplar matches the unknown sample. Only one claimed identification ($U = K_3$ in this example) can be correct and no more than N–1 claimed eliminations can be correct. There can be only one false elimination because the pairing of U vs. K_3 occurs only once. Up to N–1 false identifications are possible, but because the examiner knows that only one match exists, and because at least one identity claim must be made, the closed-set procedure effectively limits the possible number of false identifications to one.

In the open-set procedure, the examiner is asked *whether* one of the known samples matches the unknown exemplar and (if so), *which* one. If the target is included among the known exemplars, there may be one correct identification, N–1 correct eliminations, one false identification, and one false elimination. In the open procedure with the target talker (K_3 in this example) absent, however, there can be as many as N correct eliminations and one false identification. There can be no correct identification and no false elimination because the target talker is not available for comparison. Comparison of results from open-and closed-set procedures allow study of examiner preferences for claims of elimination or identification, as well as the impact of the spectrographic cues available to the examiner upon decision-making behavior.

Systematic variations of closed and open procedures are possible in which the examiner is either allowed or required to consider each pair more than once, and in which the experimenter manipulates the size and nature of exemplars, the prior probabilities of correct identifications, the examiner's knowledge of those probabilities, or the costs assigned to false identifications and false eliminations. A common variation employs *match trials* in which coded versions of the unknown exemplar are included among the set of known samples, resulting in a comparison of the form U_a vs. U_b. Match trials are single-blind experimental controls intended to index correct identification and false elimination. Experimental variations modify the numbers of possible correct and incorrect decisions, but not the types of error. Distinctions between closed and open procedures are pertinent to laboratory studies, but in forensic practice it may not be possible to know which condition applies.

The discrimination procedure differs from open-set and closed-set procedures in that the examiner is provided with several exemplars produced by one unknown talker and several exemplars produced by a single known talker (N = 1). The examiner's task is to determine whether the two groups of exemplars are *sufficiently similar* to have been produced by the same individual. Match trials can be used in discrimination procedures for the purposes noted above. This procedure can produce correct identifications, correct eliminations, false identifications and false eliminations. Most scientific studies can be classified according to the terms introduced to this point.

Under controlled experimental conditions, correct and incorrect decision outcomes can be described for different identification procedures based upon various data. Rigorous quantitative comparison of decision methods is possible using techniques drawn from signal detection theory[13] and Bayesian statistics. These scientific techniques are similar to those used in research on medical diagnosis.[14]

[c] Acoustic Characteristics

A number of different acoustic characteristics are potentially useful in talker identification. An extensive and detailed listing is not possible in this brief chapter, but some commonly used characteristics can be cited as examples. Tosi et al.[15] considered the parameters of mean frequencies and bandwidths of vowel formants, gaps and type of vertical striations, slopes of formants, duration of similar phonetic elements and plosive gaps, energy distribution of fricatives, plosives, and interformant spaces.[16] Buder[17] identifies other parameters of broader scientific interest. The Voice Identification and Acoustic Analysis Subcommittee of the International Association for Identification (VIAAS–IAI) guidelines[18] specifically mentioned the following: general formant shaping and positioning, pitch striations, energy distribution, word duration, and coupling of the oral and nasal cavities. Other possibilities include inhalation noise, repetitious throat clearing, and vocalized pauses. It should be noted that these are broad categories of acoustic differences and each can include a number of variations or subtypes. The degree to which a given acoustic characteristic may contribute to an identification can vary with

13. *See* John Swets, *Measuring the Accuracy of Diagnostic Systems*, 240 Science 1285 (1988); John Swets & Ronald Pickett, Evaluation of Diagnostic Systems: Models from Signal Detection Theory (1982).

14. Helena C. Kraemer, Evaluating Medical Tests: Objective and Quantitative Guidelines (1992).

15. Oscar Tosi et al., *Experiment on Voice Identification*, 51 J. Acoustical Soc'y Am. 2030 (1972).

16. Individual vowel formants have two primary characteristics: the center frequency of the formant and its bandwidth (spread of energy). Vertical striations relate to the vocal pitch and to irregularities in vocal fold vibrations. Formant slopes refer to changes in the frequency of a formant during a specified time interval. Durations can be determined for a variety of acoustic segments, each of which is defined in terms of one or more acoustic features. Energy distribution typically is described in terms of the major frequency regions of sound energy, e.g., the fricative "s" in the word "stop" has the most high-frequency energy as shown in Figure 1.

17. Buder, *supra* note 12.

18. VIAAS–IAI: Voice Identification and Acoustic Analysis Subcommittee (VIAAS) of the International Association for Identification (IAI), *Voice Comparison Standards*, 41 Forensic Ident. 373 (1991).

the talkers under examination, the quality of the recordings, and the speech sample available for inspection. The various sounds of a language differ in terms of their distinguishing acoustic characteristics, and some research studies indicate that some phonemes (the basic sound elements that distinguish among words) are better for discriminating among speakers than others.[19]

As the preceding discussion reveals, the scientific study of speech represents a number of different disciplines, including physics, physiology, anatomy, and psychology.[20]

[2]   A Model of Talker Identification Variables

A general conceptual model, or theory, would be useful in integrating the data from various studies and in understanding the potential interactions of the factors that influence talker identification. No unified theory of talker identification has been offered in the scientific literature, but we suggest what one might look like here.

19. Francis Nolan, The Phonetic Bases of Speaker Recognition (1983).

20. A very readable account of this multi-disciplinary endeavor is provided by Peter B. Denes & Elliott N. Pinson, The Speech Chain (2nd ed., 1993).

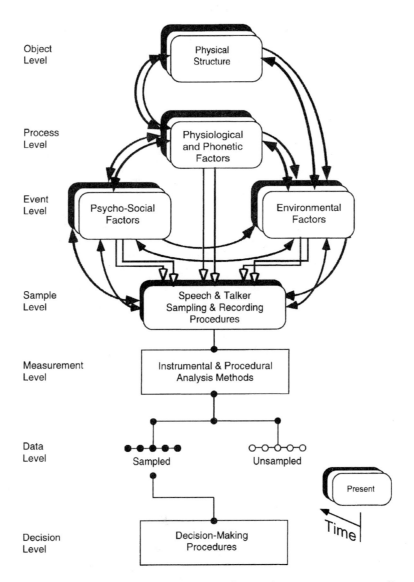

Figure 3. A conceptual model of talker identification by spectrogram, proceeding from events that occur early in the process (top) to those occurring later in the process (bottom). Curved arrows represent mutual influences (interactions) among components of the model and curved boxes represent components for which variabilities are known to exist. The model considers talker identification in regard to several levels, ranging from an object level (anatomy of talkers) to a decision level (at which outcomes of talker identification or elimination are desired). Note the third dimension of time. See text for explanation.

Figure 3 considers talker identification with respect to seven major levels. The first three of these (object, process, and event levels) pertain to spontaneous speech production, and the next (sample level) pertains to actions by which speech is captured or elicited for later comparison. The fifth (measurement) level relates to the methods by which recorded speech is analyzed, resulting in reports of the outcomes of such analyses (data level). The last (decision) level deals with the methods and rules by which various data are compared for the purpose of making a decision. For these purposes, decision outcomes are limited to identification and elimination, with or without qualifications of relative certainty.

The object, process, and event levels all have temporal extent, i.e., they can change with the passage of time. The curved lines with solid arrows linking the components of these levels are intended to suggest interactions or mutual influence among the components. These interactions also can change over time. Process and event levels combine to yield spoken language, depicted here with uncurved lines ending in open arrows.

Object, process, and event level components also are subject to major sources of variability, indicated in Figure 3 by curved boxes. Some of these variances change with time. For example, over relatively long periods of time, the anatomical structures involved in speech production change. An obvious change occurs at puberty when males undergo major changes in laryngeal anatomy. Less obvious are structural changes related to habits of vocal use, environmental agents, aging, and other life events (e.g., changes in dentition). These sources of variability exist both within individuals (over short and long periods of time) and between individuals at any given moment in time. Factors affecting physiological and phonetic variability include general health, state of sobriety or intoxication, and the "rules" underlying various spoken languages. Psycho-social factors include dialect, education and social status, communicative intent, speaking style, and emotional state. Another is the tendency of talkers to reflect the vocal style (changes in vocal loudness, pitch, speaking rate, and patterns of pauses) of those with whom they are communicating.

Environmental factors also can influence speech production. One such effect is the tendency of talkers to increase vocal effort (hence, vocal loudness) as the amplitude of ambient noise increases. This effect (known as the Lombard voice reflex) appears to differ between males and females.[21] Talkers also tend to change certain articulation characteristics in the presence of high levels of background noise or other interference.

The absence of temporal invariance and the presence of variability within and between talkers do not necessarily obviate talker identification if their net impact is small compared to the sources of consistency within the time frames typical of forensic identification. Two conditions seem scientifically necessary to justify talker identification by spectrographic (or any other) methods. First, the effect of interactions among physical structure, physiological and phonetic factors, and psycho-social factors must be consistent within an individual, at least over relatively short periods of time. Further, the patterns of these interactions must be sufficiently idiosyncratic to produce measurable differences among individuals under field conditions. This consistency presumably results in spoken language that differs demonstrably among individuals and is transparent to such factors as vocal disguise.

The fourth major level, sample level, is directly relevant to research design and forensic practice, and therefore is discussed *infra*.[22]

21. Jean–Claude Junqua, *The Lombard Reflex and its Role on Human Listeners and* *Automatic Speech Recognizers*, 93 J. Acoustical Soc'y Am. 510 (1993).

22. *See infra* § 2.1.2[3] Sampling of Talk-

The decision level involves the ways in which data from different speech samples are compared for the purpose of identifying or eliminating individual talkers. Although standards exist to guide the procedures by which data are compared and the decision options that are allowed, standards are not always followed. Moreover, the standards themselves are somewhat arbitrary. The quality of decision-making ultimately is influenced by formal decision rules, the sufficiency of data, the accuracy and precision of measurement, and the thoroughness of procedural controls invoked while sampling speech materials and talkers.

Talker identification may resemble handwriting identification more than it does fingerprint identification. Both speech and handwriting are dynamic events, influenced by structural (anatomical) and physiological factors; both are influenced by developmental changes and by psycho-social factors. Because fingerprints are static (rather than dynamic) events, they are uninfluenced by physiology and psycho-social factors. Fingerprints are not subject to developmental change and (barring serious physical trauma) they do not change with age.

§ 6–2.1.2 Scientific Methods Applied in Talker Identification Research

The scientific evidence on talker identification has been obtained primarily by laboratory experimentation. The basic design of a talker identification experiment involves selection of (a) a group of talkers, (b) a type of speech material (e.g., isolated words, short sentences, or conversation), (c) one or more examiners (who may be trained or untrained), and (d) decision categories used by the examiners. However, many additional details of the experimental design need to be specified.

Because the acoustic signal of speech is shaped by a large number of factors, some of which are not under direct experimental control, the results of experiments often must be interpreted with regard to several interacting factors. The conceptual model or framework, such as that presented in Figure 3, may serve to clarify the major issues underlying talker identification by means of spectrographic comparison.[23] Figure 3 summarizes a number of variables and potential interactions that conceivably influence talker identification by spectrogram comparison.

[1] Variations in Methods

As a result of the manifold decisions that have to be made in designing a single experiment, it is rare that any two published reports on talker identification can be directly compared with respect to size of error. As one major contributor to this field remarked, "the reader should be warned that most of the laboratory experiments on voice identification performed to date share one common characteristic—their results are very hard to compare because experimental conditions among them differ widely and data were reported

ers.

23. With minor modifications, structurally similar models could be constructed for other systems of forensic identification such as those based on fingerprints and handwriting.

differently."[24] The matter becomes further complicated in attempted extrapolations from the laboratory experiments to practical application in forensics (as discussed earlier in this chapter). These differences among laboratory experiments and between laboratory experiments and forensic examinations are major obstacles in the evaluation of the accuracy of talker identification.

[2] Quantity of Sound Studied

One reason for the difficulty of comparing various published studies is that each experiment must severely limit the quantity of evidence examined in comparison to the potential amount of evidence. Speech consists of a number of speech sounds that can be combined to form words. Words, in turn, can be selected to form a potentially infinite number of sentences. On any occasion, a talker may use just a few words. The words available for examination may not be ideal for the purpose of talker identification, because some words contain better cues for identification than others. Some of the most frequently occurring words in English are short in duration and therefore limited in their acoustic cues. These words include: the, of, I, and, you, to, a, in, that, it, is, he, we. Furthermore, a word produced in different phonetic contexts (such as different sentences) will not necessarily have the same acoustic appearance from one context to the next. Finally, the production of a word even in the same context (produced in the same phrase or sentence) may vary from one time to another.

[3] Sampling of Talkers

At the sample level of the model discussed, *supra*,[25] are those procedures used to select talkers to be recorded for forensic comparison, and specification of the speech to be produced by those talkers. Such selections are undertaken in circumstances in which it is normally possible to exercise some control over recording environment, language, and speaking style. If these controls are managed skillfully and thoroughly, some of the event level variances can be minimized, thus providing samples for comparison that are "fair" in the sense that the remaining variances are dominated by the presumably idiosyncratic interactions noted above. Because multiple speech and talker samples cannot be collected at exactly the same moment, temporal variables exist at the sample level. If samples are collected with proper attention to investigative technique, the identities of all but one of the talkers should be known with certainty. (This assumes, of course, that recordings are authentic and have not been edited in any way.)

Once appropriate voice samples have been collected and authenticated, a host of formal observations can be made. Some of these observations result in quantitative measurements based on visual displays of speech, others exist in the form of non-numerical observations of the visual displays themselves, and still others exist in the form of perceptual observations about the audio material under consideration. Sample duration and recording quality limit the observations that are possible. The reports of quantitative and non-quantitative observations form the data used in talker identification. Of the universe

---

24. Oscar Tosi, Voice Identification: Theory and Legal Applications 57 (1979).

25. *See supra* § 2.1.1[2] A Model of Talker Identification Variables.

of potential data based on speech spectrograms, only a subset is used in most forensic situations. Because the subject of most forensic speech analysis is recorded material, and because the method of analysis is instrumental, temporal variances are of minimal importance.

[4] Differences Between Scientific Research and Forensic Application

Finally, it would be helpful to compare the methods used in scientific research and those used in forensic practice. Before doing so, however, we should note that general standards or recommendations have been published for forensic examination.[26] The procedures followed by individual examiners may vary. The following discussion, however, assumes forensic procedures generally consistent with the aforementioned sources. In particular, frequent reference will be made to the guidelines of the Voice Identification and Acoustic Analysis Subcommittee of the International Association for Identification (VIAAS–IAI). These guidelines, published in 1991, are the most recent recommendations for forensic examination.

Published scientific research differs from forensic application in four potentially important respects:

[a] Decision Categories

One difference between scientific studies and typical forensic application is that forensic examiners generally use categories of "no decision" or "uncertain" whereas most published research has required that subjects judging spectrograms choose between identification and elimination. According to VIAAS–IAI, "every examination conducted can only produce one of seven (7) decisions: Identification, Probable Identification, Possible Identification, Inconclusive, Possible Elimination, Probable Elimination, or Elimination".[27] Quantitative criteria based on decisions for the number of comparable words are associated with each of the seven decisions. Apparently, no published large-scale research project has used these decision categories. Consequently, some writers have argued that the accuracy rates in the experimental studies are conservative estimates of the accuracy to be expected in forensic examinations.

---

26. *See* RICHARD H. BOLT ET AL., ON THE THEORY AND PRACTICE OF VOICE IDENTIFICATION (1979); Bruce E. Koenig, *Speaker Identification*, 49 FBI LAW ENFORCEMENT BULLETIN 20 (1980); Bruce E. Koenig, *Spectrographic Voice Identification: A Forensic Survey*, 79 J. ACOUSTICAL SOC'Y AM. 2088 (1986) (letter); Bruce E. Koenig, *Spectrographic Voice Identification*, 13 CRIME LAB DIGEST 105 (1986); LONNIE L. SMRKOVSKI, FORENSIC VOICE IDENTIFICATION (Michigan Department of State Police, 1983); TOSI, *supra* note 24; VIAAS–IAI, VOICE IDENTIFICATION INSTRUCTION MANUAL (n.d.).

27. VIAAS–IAI, *supra* note 18 at 387.

[b]   Visual vs. Visual–Aural Identification

A second difference between the scientific research on talker identification and the forensic situation is that forensic examiners routinely use aural recognition and spectrograms in reaching a decision, but published research articles have rarely, if ever, studied the joint use of aural and spectrographic procedures. Stevens et al.[28] compared spectrographic and aural presentations of stimuli. They found that the percentages of correct responses in both closed and open tests were significantly higher for aural than for visual examination. However, the examiners were not specially trained for visual examination of spectrograms, and the speech samples were brief (although exceeding the minimum number of words recommended by the VIAAS–IAI). Apparently, no published scientific report used a procedure that accords with the customary practice in forensic examination of using trained personnel to conduct combined aural and spectrographic examinations in reaching a decision of identification or elimination. Experiments have been conducted on aural and spectrographic identification separately, but it has not been established how the two methods of examination complement one another in joint application.

As a partial answer to this question, Bolt et al.[29] compared the aural task performance reported by Stevens et al.[30] with the visual spectrogram performance reported by Tosi et al.[31] Bolt et al. concluded, "These results would seem to support the idea that listening and visual examination of spectrograms are comparable as single-mode methods of speaker recognition" (at 118). Bolt et al. also concluded that listening-only experiments on talker identification show that (1) performance is less than perfect, with error scores for best conditions ranging from 5 to 15%; and (2) performance is fairly robust under certain types of degradation (such as filtering and addition of noise). It is not clear from this research to what degree the aural performance of experts in voice identification differs from that of laypersons. Carlson and Granstrom showed that accurate matching of unknown voices speaking different utterances can be done if the samples are sufficiently long. But they also report that listeners differ in this ability.[32] Representative studies on aural identification of talkers are given in the margin.[33] The results of selected studies are summarized in Table 2.

28. Kenneth N. Stevens et al., *Speaker Authentication and Identification: A Comparison of Spectrographic and Auditory Presentations of Speech Material*, 44 J. ACOUSTICAL SOC'Y AM. 1596 (1968).

29. BOLT ET AL., *supra* note 26.

30. Stevens et al., *supra* note 28.

31. Tosi et al., *supra* note 15.

32. Rolf Carlson & Bjorn Granstrom, *An Interactive Technique for Matching Speaker Identity*, 52 PHONETICA 236 (1995).

33. Peter D. Bricker & Sandra Pruzanski, *Effects of Stimulus Content and Duration on Talker Identification*, 40 J. ACOUSTICAL SOC'Y AM.

1441 (1966); FRANK R. CLARKE ET AL., CHARACTERISTICS THAT DETERMINE SPEAKER RECOGNITION (Electronic Systems Division, U.S. Air Force Technical Report ESD–66–636, 1966); Frances McGehee, *The Reliability of the Identification of the Human Voice*, 17 J. GEN. PSYCH. 249 (1937); Frances McGehee, *An Experimental Study in Voice Recognition*, 31 J. GEN. PSYCH. 53 (1944); Irwin Pollack et al., *On the Identification of Speakers by Voice*, 26 J. ACOUSTICAL SOC'Y AM. 403 (1954); William Voiers, *Perceptual Basis of Speaker Identity*, 36 J. ACOUSTICAL SOC'Y AM. 1065 (1964).

Table 2

Summary of Selected Experiments in Talker Identification. Examples for Both Listening (Aural) and Visual (Spectrogram) Experiments Are Shown. Note: Many Important Differences Among the Studies Are Not Represented in This Table, Which Is Intended to Show the General Sizes of Error in Selected Experiments.

Source	Talkers	Examiners	Error rate
LISTENING EXPERIMENTS			
McGehee (1937, 1944)	31 males, 18 females, selected to form panels of 5 talkers.	740 college students (untrained), selected to form 15 panels of listeners.	17 to 87%, depending on time elapsed between first and second sessions.
Pollack et al. (1954)	16, in groups of 2 to 8.	Listeners familiar with the talkers.	5% for normal voiced speech; 70% for whispered.
Bricker & Pruzansky (1966)	10.	16 listeners. familiar with the talkers.	0 to 8% across judges for best condition.
Stevens et al. (1968)	24 highly homogeneous talkers.	6 (untrained).	Closed tests: 6 to 18% false identification; 6 to 8% false identification and 8 to 12% false elimination.
VISUAL EXPERIMENTS			
Young & Campbell (1967)	5 men used as known talkers in each trial.	10 examiners with 2.5 hr. of training.	63% based on two short words excerpted from context.
Stevens et al. (1968)	24 highly homogeneous talkers.	4–6 (untrained).	Closed tests: 21 to 28% false identification; Open tests: 31 to 47% false identification and 10 to 20% false elimination.
Hazen (1973)	50 males.	7 two-person panels trained over several sessions.	Closed tests/same context: 20% Open tests/same context: 7% false identification, 36% false elimination.
Smrkovski (1976)	7 male and 7 female.	4 experts, 4 trainees, 4 novices.	Match/no match decisions: 0% errors for experts and trainees; 5% false identification and 25% false elimination for novices.
Tosi et al. (1972)	Up to 40 in individual experiments; drawn from 250 men selected from 25,000	29 persons trained for one month, working individually or in two- or three-person teams.	For open tests, noncontemporary spectrograms and continuous speech: 6% false identification 13% false elimination.

It is likely that a combination of aural and visual identification procedures would have a lower error rate than either procedure used alone, but the amount of error reduction is unknown. The VIAAS–IAI specifies that in spectrographic/aural analysis, an "aural short-term memory comparison must be conducted...."[34] and this procedure appears consistent with common forensic procedure. Indeed, it is unlikely that examiners who prepare the

34. VIAAS–IAI, *supra* note 18 at 385.

spectrograms for identification purposes would not listen to the tape recordings as part of the process. Forensic standards developed at the German Bundeskriminalamt use a combination of listening and spectrographic analysis.[35] The procedure includes listening and analysis by a phonetician, who identifies and characterizes dialect, pathologic features, and any other idiosyncratic properties. Acoustic analysis is performed both to provide quantitative support to the characteristics determined by listening and to supply additional information. A careful co-registration of the two kinds of analysis would enhance the validity and reliability of identification judgments.

The effects of combined auditory and visual information also have been assessed for the related purposes of speaker verification or identification. This research pertains to circumstances in which both facial and voice information are available. For speaker verification, a system using dual classifiers (acoustic features of the voice and visual features obtained from a lip tracker) outperformed single methods of classification and reduced the error rate of the acoustic classifier from 2.3% to 0.5%.[36] Fusion of audio and video information in a multi-expert decision making machine was accomplished by Duc, Bigun, Bigun, Maitre, and Fischer.[37] They reported a success rate of 99.5% for speaker verification. A general review of audio-visual integration by Chen and Rao also points to the advantages of using both sources of information.[38] These results may be particularly important in the use of videotapes containing both visual and auditory signals relevant to identification of individuals.

[c] Quality of Speech Samples and Authenticity of Recordings

A third difference is that with few exceptions laboratory research has used high-quality speech recording systems with well-established procedures and unquestioned authenticity. Forensic applications frequently must contend with recordings obtained under less than ideal conditions and sometimes of doubtful authenticity. Recordings based on telephone conversations exhibit audio bandwidths ranging from 2000 Hz to about 3500 Hz, depending on a host of factors (telephone handset characteristics, mouth-to-microphone distance, the length of the transmission path, and intervening signal encryption, broadcasting, and switching technologies). Owen described the typical surveillance recording as having "an audio bandwidth of 300 Hz to 6000 Hz, with a maximum dynamic range of 30–50 dB."[39] These specifications are quite poor in comparison to laboratory equipment currently used in scientific studies of speech.[40] Although recent technical improvements permit surveillance record-

35. Hermann J. Kunzel, Sprechererkennung: Grundzuge forensischer Sprachverarbeitung (1987); Hermann J. Kunzel, *Current Approaches to Forensic Speaker Recognition*, Proceedings of ESCA Workshop on Speaker Recognition, Identification, and Verification 135 (Martigny, Switzerland, April 5–7, 1994).

36. P. Jourlin et al., *Acoustic-labial Speaker Verification*, 18 Pattern Recognition Letters 853 (1997).

37. Benoit Duc et al., *Fusion of Audio and Video Information for Multi Modal Person Authentication*, 18 Pattern Recognition Letters 835 (1997).

38. Tsuhan Chen & Ram R. Rao, *Audiovisual Integration in Multimodal Communication*, 86 Proceedings of the IEEE 837 (1998).

39. Tom Owen, *An Introduction to Forensic Examination of Audio and Video Tapes*, 39 J. Forensic Ident. 75 (1989).

40. In some situations, recordings of poor quality can be enhanced by techniques such as amplitude compression or expansion, gating, simple filtering, or more complex processing (for example, adaptive predictive deconvolution, and adaptive noise cancellation) by which some background noise can be removed. *See* Bruce E. Koenig, *Enhancement of Forensic Audio Recordings*, 36 J. Audio Engineering Soc'y 884 (1988), for a discussion of some of these procedures.

ings with much higher quality, many systems now in use remain very limited in quality. Problems with the quality of forensic recording equipment and methods may be complicated by difficulties in obtaining original recordings, for which enhancement is generally more successful.

Another problem facing the forensic specialist is the possibility that tapes submitted for analysis are nonauthentic or have been altered in some way. Owen,[41] Koenig,[42] and Hollien[43] describe procedures and criteria to ascertain the authenticity of audio tape recordings; Gruber, Poza & Pellicano[44] provide detailed treatment of legal and technical issues associated with authentication of audio recordings for evidentiary purposes. Technical authenticity analysis seeks to determine whether a particular recording was made of the events asserted by the parties who produced the recording, and in the manner claimed by those who produced it, and whether it is free from unexplained artifacts, alterations, deletions, or edits.

The issues of technical quality, enhancement and authentication go beyond the scope of this chapter but should be considered as potentially serious issues in forensic talker identification. Tape recordings should be evaluated to ascertain quality and determine authenticity before spectrograms are examined for talker identification. The VIAAS–IAI has recommended criteria for acceptable quality of speech recordings, including presence of speech energy above 2000 Hz.

[d]   Selection of Talkers for Identification Task

A fourth difference pertains to the selection of talkers for whom an identification will be attempted. Scientific experiments generally select talker subsets randomly, that is, without regard to specific similarities to a given reference talker. In contrast, forensic examination usually involves talkers who are selected because their voices have a similarity to a suspect's voice. That is, the talkers are selected to form a reasonable "lineup" of voices. Similarity among voices is not easily determined or described but this factor becomes important in evaluating error rates in talker identification. If talkers are chosen because of a similarity criterion, identification or elimination is expected to be more difficult as compared to a situation in which talkers are drawn randomly.

§ 6–2.2   Areas of Scientific Agreement

It is clear from studies of the acoustic properties of speech that marked differences may occur among various groups of talkers. For example, the acoustic patterns of speech are different among men, women and children, owing largely to differences in the size of the vocal tract, that is, the resonating system of speech that extends from the larynx up through the nose or mouth.[45] Differences within a given age-gender group are not as conspicuous as the differences across age or gender groups, but some differences exist, at least in selected comparisons. It is possible that racial differences exist,[46]

41.   Owen, *supra* note 39.

42.   Bruce E. Koenig, *Authentication of Forensic Audio Recordings*, 38 J. Audio Engineering Soc'y 3 (1990).

43.   Harry Hollien, The Acoustics of Crime (1990).

44.   Jordan S. Gruber et al., *Audio Recordings: Evidence, Experts and Technology*, 48 Am. Jur. Trials 1 (1993).

45.   Donald G. Childers & Ke Wu, *Gender Recognition from Speech. Part II: Fine Analysis*, 90 J. Acoustical Soc'y Am. 1841 (1991); Raymond D. Kent & Charles Read, The Acoustic Analysis of Speech (1992); Ke Wu & Donald G. Childers, *Gender Recognition from Speech. Part I: Coarse Analysis*, 90 J. Acoustical Soc'y Am. 1828 (1991).

46.   Julie H. Walton & Robert F. Orlikoff, *Speaker Race Identification from Acoustic Cues*

but such differences have not been studied extensively. As a general conclusion, one might say that there is a high likelihood that large subgroups of talkers, particularly age-gender subgroups and some dialect subgroups, can be distinguished from one another. It is also known that certain acoustic measures of speech are correlated with physical features such as age, gender, height, and weight of talkers.[47]

The gender of a talker can be determined with high accuracy using information on vocal fundamental frequency and vocal tract length.[48] When an isolated vowel segment was analyzed according to these features, classification by gender was nearly perfect. Classification of individual talkers required information on acoustic parameters associated with vocal tract filtering (formant patterns). Essentially the same pattern of results obtained for male and female talkers, but classification rates were consistently lower for females, who were more likely to be classified as males than males were to be classified as females. This study is one of the very few to address gender differences in the acoustic identification of talkers.

But the essential question for talker identification by spectrograms for the usual forensic application is whether the intertalker differences are sufficient to distinguish *one* individual from a group of talkers of the same gender and roughly the same age. The relevant scientific literature pertains almost exclusively to men. Under conditions comparable to the typical forensic examination, unique identification (0% error rates for both false identification and false elimination in open tests) is unlikely. One expert in the area wrote, "no method or combination of methods will ever yield a positive result (identification or elimination) in 100% of the cases examined."[49] It is also well known that an individual talker never produces speech in *exactly* the same way in different repetitions of what is intended to be the same utterance.[50] Tokens that are recorded in the same session are more similar than tokens recorded in separate sessions.[51] For some acoustic features, intratalker variability can be as great as intertalker variability.[52]

Prospects for talker identification by spectrograms are improved if intertalker variations are large compared to intratalker variations. As will be discussed below, there are several sources of intratalker variation including emotional state, influence of intoxicants, and style of speaking. In addition, some short-term and long-term variations have been noted in the speech patterns of individual talkers.[53] The VIAAS–IAI recommends that the examin-

in the Vocal Signal, 37 J. Speech & Hearing Research 738 (1994).

47. J. Suzuki, *Correlation of Speaker's Physical Factors and Speech*, 41 J. Acoustical Soc'y of Japan 895 (1985).

48. Jo–Anne Bachorowski & Michael J. Owren, *Acoustic Correlates of Talker Sex and Individual Talker Identity Are Present in a Short Vowel Segment Produced in Running Speech*, 106 J. Acoustical Soc'y Am. 1054 (1999).

49. Tosi, *supra* note 24 at 148.

50. Richard H. Bolt et al., *Speaker Identification by Speech Spectrograms: Some Further Observations*, 54 J. Acoustical Soc'y Am. 531 (1973); Bolt et al., *supra* note 26.

51. Aaron E. Rosenberg & Frank K. Soong, *Recent Research on Automatic Speaker Identification*, in Advances in Speech Signal Processing 701 (Sadaoki Furui & M. Mohan Sondhi eds., 1992).

52. James E. Atkinson, *Inter-and Intraspeaker Variability in Fundamental Voice Frequency*, 60 J. Acoustical Soc'y Am. 440 (1976).

53. Werner Endres et al., *Voice Spectrograms As a Function of Age, Voice Disguise, and Voice Imitation*, 49 J. Acoustical Soc'y Am. 1842 (1971); Michael P. Rastatter & Richard D. Jaques, *Formant Frequency Structure of the Aging Male and Female Vocal Tract*, 42 Folia Phoniatrica 312 (1990).

er compare "similarly spoken words within each voice sample to determine the range of intraspeaker variability"[54] and exclude the sample from comparison if considerable variability is observed. Each of the following factors can substantially affect the accuracy of spectrograms as a means of talker identification. In some cases, two or more of these factors may combine to limit the successful application of the method.

§ 6–2.2.1　Signal Transmission and Recording

It is generally agreed that the speech signal of an individual talker can be affected to some degree by a variety of factors and circumstances in addition to robust individual characteristics of the talker such as anatomy and learned speaking habits.[55] The spectrogram is a visual record of an acoustic signal that represents a series of transformations and passages. Speech is a perishable message. The acoustic vibrations of an utterance decay rapidly in the atmosphere and are lost forever except in the memory of a listener or a storage device such as a tape recorder. Before speech can be stored in a tape recorder or computer, it must be transduced from acoustic to electrical or electromagnetic energy. This transduction process itself can degrade the quality of the signal. In addition, if the speech to be recorded is produced in a background of other sounds, these extraneous sounds usually will be recorded along with the speech signal, reducing the signal-to-noise (S/N) ratio. Some general signal quality requirements have been recommended by the VIAAS–IAI.

§ 6–2.2.2　Phonetic Context and Duration

It is commonly accepted that speech samples chosen for use in talker identification by spectrograms should be controlled for phonetic context and should meet minimal requirements for duration. Phonetic considerations are important because speech sounds can be highly adapted to individual phonetic contexts, particularly the adjacent sounds but also more global influences such as stress pattern (stress is the degree of prominence given to syllables in an utterance) and speaking rate.[56] Words that may seem to be similar from their orthographic spelling can in fact be very different in phonetic properties. The VIAAS–IAI requires a minimum of ten comparable words between two voice samples; the Federal Bureau of Investigation requires twenty words.[57] Words can vary greatly in their total length (measured in time), number of syllables, and number of phonetic constituents. Consider, for example, the monosyllable words *a*, *the*, *it* versus the polysyllable words *telephone*, *carefully*, *explosive*. Although the number of words is a convenient index for perceptual and linguistic reasons, it should be recognized that words are not necessarily equal in their potential for talker identification.

Control for phonetic context possibly can be relaxed if talker-sensitive parameters are studied over long durations of speech. However, it should be stressed that such long durations are not always available in forensic applications. The duration of a sample is important to ensure that a sufficient

---

54. VIAAS–IAI, *supra* note 18 at 384.

55. *See* Richard H. Bolt et al., *Speaker Identification of Speech Spectrograms: A Scientists' View of Its Reliability for Legal Purposes*, 47 J. ACOUSTICAL SOC'Y AM. 597 (1970); Bolt et al., *supra* note 50; BOLT ET AL., *supra* note 26; HOLLIEN, *supra* note 43; TOSI, *supra* note 24.

56. BOLT ET AL., *supra* note 26.

57. Koenig, CRIME LAB DIGEST, *supra* note 26.

number of distinguishing features can be identified in the visual pattern. Research on intertalker and intratalker variability among correlation matrices obtained from continuous speech indicates that about 30 seconds is a minimum duration of speech required for the stabilization of the correlation matrices.[58] Assuming an average speaking rate of about 170 words per minute, a 30–second sample of continuous speech should include about 85 words.[59]

§ 6–2.2.3   Disguises and Mimicking

Another point of consensus is that disguises or mimicking of speech can complicate the use of spectrograms in talker identification, and in some situations may preclude comparisons.[60] One of the most damaging disguises is falsetto (a high-pitched voice quality), which can greatly obscure formants in wide-band spectrograms.[61] This result occurs because the harmonics of the falsetto voice become so widely spaced that the conventional wide-band analysis of 250 or 300 Hz resolves the harmonic pattern of the voice rather than the formant pattern. Disguises differ in the degree to which they hinder talker identification by spectrograms. Self-selected vocal disguises have been among the most effective in published research on speaker identification.[62] The VIAAS–IAI recommends that speech samples containing disguises such as falsetto or whispering be eliminated from comparison consideration.

§ 6–2.2.4   Psychological or Physical State of the Talker

The psychological and physical state of the talker exerts a variety of influences on the speech signal. Although emotional state is not straightforwardly associated with a simple set of acoustic effects, different emotions can be distinguished by combinations of acoustic characteristics.[63] For example, Murray and Arnott[64] compared emotions such as anger, fear, sadness and disgust. Speaking rate tends to be accelerated in anger and fear but decelerated in sadness or disgust. The average pitch of the voice tends to be higher in anger and fear but lower in sadness and disgust. Vocal intensity is increased in anger but reduced in sadness and disgust. The range of vocal pitch

---

58. K. Li & G. Hughes, *Talker Differences As They Appear in Correlation Matrices of Continuous Speech Spectra*, 55 J. ACOUSTICAL SOC'Y AM. 833 (1974).

59. This value is given only as an example based on average speech rates; the actual number of words in a time interval can vary widely across talkers and situations.

60. *See* Endres et al., *supra* note 53; Harry Hollien & Robert E. McGlone, *The Effect of Disguise on "Voiceprint" Identification*, 1976 PROCEEDINGS OF THE CARNAHAN CONFERENCE ON CRIME COUNTERMEASURES 30, *reprinted in* 2 NAT'L J. CRIM. DEF. 117 (1976); Kathleen Houlihan, *The Effects of Disguise on Speaker Identification from Sound Spectrograms*, *in* CURRENT ISSUES IN THE PHONETIC SCIENCES 811 (Harry Hollien & Patricia Hollien eds., 1979); Alan Reich, *Detecting the Presence of Disguise in the Male Voice*, 69 J. ACOUSTICAL SOC'Y AM. 1458 (1981); Alan Reich & James Duke, *Effects of Selected Vocal Disguises Upon Speaker Identification by Listening*, 66 J. ACOUSTICAL SOC'Y AM. 1023

(1979); Alan Reich et al., *Effects of Selected Disguises Upon Spectrographic Speaker Identification*, 60 J. ACOUSTICAL SOC'Y AM. 919 (1976).

61. Endres et al., *supra* note 53.

62. Reich et al., *supra* note 60.

63. Michael H. L. Hecker et al., *Manifestations of Task–Induced Stress in the Acoustic Speech Signal*, 44 J. ACOUSTICAL SOC'Y AM. 993 (1968); Iain R. Murray & John L. Arnott, *Toward the Simulation of Emotion in Synthetic Speech: A Review of the Literature on Human Vocal Emotion*, 93 J. ACOUSTICAL SOC'Y AM. 1097 (1993); Klaus R. Scherer, *Vocal Affect Expression: A Review and a Model for Future Research*, 99 PSYCH. BULLETIN 143 (1986); Vivien C. Tartter & David Braun, *Hearing Smiles and Frowns in Normal and Whisper Registers*, 94 J. ACOUSTICAL SOC'Y AM. 2101 (1994); Carl E. Williams & Kenneth N. Stevens, *Emotions and Speech: Some Acoustical Correlates*, 52 J. ACOUSTICAL SOC'Y AM. 1238 (1972).

64. Murray & Arnott, *supra* note 63.

increases in anger and fear but decreases in sadness. Tartter and Braun[65] found that listeners can accurately discriminate recorded speech produced by the same talkers while frowning, smiling or assuming a neutral facial expression. Frowning has the effect of lowering formant frequencies and increasing syllable duration. It appears that emotions have a multidimensional effect on speech. Although rate, voice pitch and intensity changes are especially notable, alterations can occur in the precision of articulation as well.[66] Very few studies of talker identification have manipulated talker emotion as a factor that might influence the accuracy of talker identification. As an additional complication, phonetic characteristics of speech may change with changes in loudness.[67]

A topic related to a talker's emotional state is the psychological stress of an individual from whom speech is recorded. Note that the word *stress* can denote two different concepts in the study of speech. One is the degree of emphasis or accent placed on a particular word or syllable in an utterance. The other meaning is a general psychological or physiological state that occurs as the result of demanding, hazardous, or threatening conditions. Hecker et al.[68] reported that stress could be aurally detected in the speech of some individuals and that acoustic correlates of psychological stress varied across talkers. One of the most frequently observed acoustic correlates was voicing irregularity, or an irregularity in the pattern of glottal vibration (the vertical striations in a wide-band spectrogram). The understanding of the acoustic correlates of psychological stress is incomplete owing to limitations of published research.[69] Much of the research in this area overlaps with research on the study of the emotional correlates of speech patterns.

The influence of alcohol and other substances also may induce changes in speech patterns. Alcohol inebriation is known to influence speech and it appears that some parameters are particularly sensitive to alcohol consumption.[70] Among the typical changes that have been observed in inebriated speech are misarticulations, reduced speaking rate, an increase in the ratio of voiceless to voiced sounds, a change in pitch range (either larger or smaller, depending on the talker) and an increase in pitch variability. It must be kept in mind that the group studies published in the scientific literature show that individual differences occur but the extent of these differences is not established for anything but small samples of talkers. Accordingly, care should be taken in generalizing from the limited data now in print. Moreover, very little

65. Tartter & Braun, *supra* note 63.

66. Murray & Arnott, *supra* note 63.

67. D. Rostolland, *Phonetic Structure of Shouted Voice*, 51 ACOUSTICA 80 (1982).

68. Hecker et al., *supra* note 63.

69. Douglas A. Cairns & John H. L. Hansen, *Nonlinear Analysis and Classification of Speech under Stressed Conditions*, 96 J. ACOUSTICAL SOC'Y AM. 3392 (1994).

70. F. Klingholz et al., *Recognition of Low–Level Intoxication from the Speech Signal*, 84 J. ACOUSTICAL SOC'Y AM. 929 (1988); L. Lester & R. Skousen, *The Phonology of Drunkenness*, PAPERS FOR THE PARASESSION ON NATURAL PHONOLOGY 233 (A. Bruck et al. eds., 1974); G. Niedzielska et al., *Acoustic Evaluation of Voice in Individuals with Alcohol Addiction*, 46 FOLIA PHONIATRICA 115 (1994); David B. Pisoni & Christopher S. Martin, *Effects of Alcohol on the Acoustic–Phonetic Properties of Speech: Perceptual and Acoustic Analyses*, 13 ALCOHOLISM: CLIN. & EXPERIMENTAL RES. 577 (1989); Linda C. Sobell & Mark B. Sobell, *Effects of Alcohol on the Speech of Alcoholics*, 15 J. SPEECH & HEARING RES. 861 (1972); Linda C. Sobell et al., *Alcohol-induced Dysfluency in Nonalcoholics*, 34 FOLIA PHONIATRICA 316 (1982); STEVEN B. CHIN & DAVID B. PISONI, ALCOHOL AND SPEECH (1997).

is known about the interaction of factors such as the talker's emotional state, overall loudness, psychological stress, and the influence of intoxicants.

A talker's health, particularly the status of the upper respiratory tract, can influence speech patterns. One of the most efficient parameters proposed for talker identification relates to nasal sounds,[71] but these sounds are vulnerable to even a mild head cold.[72] Research on this topic is limited, but it seems likely that a talker's health can affect speech patterns. Normal aging processes also can influence speech production in various ways,[73] and it appears that the speech characteristics most predictive of aged speech also are frequently implicated in the speech of persons with neurologic diseases.[74] Therefore, it has been suggested that normal aging and some neurological diseases have similar effects on speech production.[75]

The implication is that the emotional and physical state of a talker ideally would be controlled in forensic applications of talker identification. However, ascertaining these characteristics and replicating them may be extremely difficult and sometimes impossible. Perhaps the best that can be done in most practical situations is to acknowledge that these factors may limit the accuracy of the identification procedure. The number of potentially significant variables makes talker identification more complicated than fingerprint identification.

§ 6–2.2.5 Earwitness Testimony

There is substantial agreement on the ability of witnesses to identify individuals from the sound of their speech. This research does not speak directly to the abilities of forensic experts but rather to general earwitness testimony (i.e., testimony based on recall of auditory events, especially spoken messages uttered at the scene of a crime). Most published earwitness research focuses either on famous voices or unfamiliar voices. Recent research includes studies of memory for voices and studies of the effects of training on earwitness accuracy, both of which are relevant to gauging the role of audition in talker identification.

The recognition of famous voices improves with duration of the voice sample, with the largest gain in performance occurring within the first second and smaller gains thereafter.[76] A similar effect appears to occur for unfamiliar voices. Cook and Wilding reported that recognition memory improved with longer extracts of a stranger's voice but was not affected by increasing vowel variety (i.e., different types of vowel sounds).[77] These authors also concluded

71. Lo–Soun Su et al., *Identification of Speakers by Use of Nasal Coarticulation*, 56 J. ACOUSTICAL SOC'Y AM. 1876 (1974); NOLAN, *supra* note 19.

72. M. R. Sambur, *Selection of Acoustic Features for Speaker Identification*, ASSP–23 IEEE TRANSACTIONS ON ACOUSTICS AND SPEECH SIGNAL PROCESSING 176 (1975).

73. Raymond D. Kent & Robert Burkhard, *Changes in the Acoustic Correlates of Speech Production, in* AGING: COMMUNICATION PROCESSES AND DISORDERS 47 (Daniel S. Beasley & G. A. Davis eds., 1981); Gary Weismer & Julie M. Liss, *Aging and Speech Motor Control, in* HANDBOOK OF AGING AND COMMUNICATION 205 (D. Ripich ed., 1991).

74. W. Ryan & K. Burke, *Perceptual and Acoustic Correlates of Aging in the Speech of Males*, 7 J. COMMUNICATION DISORDERS 181 (1974).

75. *Id.*

76. Stephan R. Schweinberger et al., *Recognizing Famous Voices: Influence of Stimulus Duration and Different Types of Retrieval Cues*, 40 J. SPEECH, LANGUAGE, & HEARING RES. 453 (1997).

77. Susan Cook & John Wilding, *Earwitness Testimony: Never Mind the Variety, Hear the Length*, 11 APPL. COGNITIVE PSYCH. 95 (1997).

that memory for words spoken was not correlated with memory for an unknown voice. In considering these results, Cook and Wilding raise the possibility that there may be a general ability for memory-for-voices. Sheffert, however, reached a somewhat dissimilar conclusion in an experiment designed to determine whether memory for voices is distinct from episodic memory. The results of Sheffert's study were interpreted to mean that "voices are represented in long-term memory as episodic traces that contain talker-specific perceptual information."[78] Essentially the same conclusion was reached by Remez, Fellowes, and Rubin in an experiment in which natural voices were radically transformed to sinewave replicas (i.e., the formants of speech were replaced by sinusoids).[79] The results of the experiment involving six voices indicated that word recognition was affected by changes in voice for several encoding tasks. It was concluded that even with these highly altered stimuli, listeners still were able to identify ten voices. The authors viewed their results as compatible with a model in which phonetic properties of utterances carry information on both words spoken and the individuals who speak them. Although it is premature to make definitive statements, the recent research is consistent with the idea that voice identification improves with the duration of the voice sample, and that talker information is to some degree combined with information on the words spoken in a composite memory trace. These laboratory studies provide some basic information about how well listeners can identify the voices of others.

Work by Elaad, Segev, and Tobin indicates that talker identification ability is affected by training.[80] They compared identification accuracy in a mock theft study involving three listener groups: voice identification experts,[81] individuals who are totally blind, and sighted listeners without special training or experience. The highest accuracy was achieved by the voice identification experts. There also appears to be an effect of nationality on both face and voice recognition, with subjects showing better recognition for faces and voices of their own nationality.[82] The influence of interviewing technique was investigated by Memon and Yarmey in a mock abduction with 77 subjects who rated the abductor's voice for nine speech characteristics and attempted to identify his voice from an audiotaped lineup.[83] No effect of interview type was found.

In a comparison of eyewitness and earwitness identification with respect to calibration and diagnosticity analysis, Olsson, Juslin and Winman reported that earwitness identification is poorer and is characterized by overconfidence

---

78. Sonya M. Sheffert, *Contribution of Surface and Conceptual Information to Recognition Memory*, 60 PERCEPTION & PSYCHOPHYSICS 1141, 1141 (1998).

79. Robert E. Remez et al., *Talker Identification Based on Phonetic Information*, 23 J. EXPERIMENTAL PSYCH.: HUMAN PERCEPTION & PERFORMANCE 651 (1997). A *formant* is a resonance of the vocal tract; a particular pattern of formants characterizes individual speech sounds. A sinusoid is a pure tone, or signal containing energy at a single frequency.

80. Eitan Elaad et al., *Long-term Working Memory in Voice Identification*, 4 PSYCHOL., CRIME & LAW 73 (1998).

81. The subjects were lay individuals with no special training in talker identification.

82. Nathan D. Doty, *The Influence of Nationality on the Accuracy of Face and Voice Recognition*, 111 AM. J. PSYCH. 191 (1998).

83. Amina Memon & A. Daniel Yarmey, *Earwitness Recall and Identification: Comparison of the Cognitive Interview and the Structured Interview*, 88 PERCEPT. & MOTOR SKILLS 797 (1999).

and low diagnosticity of confidence, meaning that the witness's level or feeling of confidence had a poor relationship with accuracy.[84]

A number of issues relevant to earwitness identification have yet to be studied, including the effects of competing signals, the effects of hearing loss and the effects of linguistic accent (in particular, similarities and differences in the accents of talker and listener). Yarmey reviewed the general topic of earwitness voice identification and recommended procedures for voice line-ups.[85] Although careful attention to these procedures can enhance the reliability of voice lineups, the research on earwitness identification points to general concerns about its accuracy. These shortcomings make objective identification by acoustic analysis all the more important in forensic application. This is not to detract from the combined use of perceptual and acoustic methods, as is commonly used in forensic talker identification.

§ 6–2.2.6   Summary

Reviews of talker recognition published within the last five years are cited in the margin.[86] Although these reviews document several steps of progress, they also make it clear that much remains to be done to establish the scientific validity and reliability of talker identification by acoustic methods. Gruber and Poza[87] list several areas in which there are open questions or a significant lack of scientific evidence. These include knowledge about (1) the uniqueness and consistency of voices, (2) the relative value of aural and visual methods of identification, (3) the relative accuracy of laypersons and experts using different methods of identification, (4) the specific features that pertain to visual or aural pattern matching, (5) the criteria used by forensic specialists, (6) error rates and accuracy in real-world forensic situations, and (7) effect of speaker situation on identification and elimination protocols. This is a substantial list of unresolved issues, and although some progress has been made since publication of the Gruber and Poza volume, the list can be repeated today virtually in its entirety as an agenda for future work.

§ 6–2.3   Areas of Scientific Disagreement

Several areas of disagreement have been discussed in the literature on talker identification. Much of the literature is polarized on the relative accuracy of this method for forensic application. Among the most important publications that are generally critical or guarded concerning speaker identification by spectrograms are Bolt et al.,[88] Gruber and Poza,[89] Hollien,[90] Poza,[91]

84. N. Olsson et al., *Realism of Confidence in Earwitness Versus Eyewitness Identification*, 4 J. Experimental Psychol.: Applied 101 (1998).

85. A. Daniel Yarmey, *Earwitness Speaker Identification*, 1 Psych., Public Pol'y & Law 792 (1995).

86. Joseph P. Campbell, *Speaker Recognition–A Tutorial*, 85 Proceedings of the IEEE 1437 (1997); Sadaoki Furui, *Recent Advances in Speaker Recognition*, 18 Pattern Recognition Letters 859 (1997); Frederic A. Gruber & F. T. Poza, *Voicegram Identification Evidence*, 54 Am. Jur. Trials 1 (1995); W. Majewski, *Speaker Recognition in Forensic Applications*, 82 Acustica (Supp. 1) S 230 (1996); Francis

Nolan, *Speaker Recognition and Forensic Phonetics*, in The Handbook of Phonetic Sciences 744 (William J. Hardcastle & John Laver eds., 1997).

87. Gruber & Poza, *supra* note 86.

88. Bolt et al., *supra* note 50; Bolt et al., *supra* note 55.

89. Gruber & Poza, *supra* note 86.

90. Harry Hollien, *The Peculiar Case of "Voiceprints,"* 56 J. Acoustical Soc'y Am. 210 (1971).

91. Fausto Poza, *Voiceprint Identification: Its Forensic Application*, 1974 Proceedings of the Carnahan Crime Countermeasures Conference (University of Kentucky, Lexington, KY).

and Shipp, Doherty and Hollien.[92] Papers that take a more positive view are Black et al.,[93] Kersta,[94] Koenig et al.,[95] and Tosi et al.[96] These papers provide an overview of various disagreements concerning the use of spectrograms in voice identification or elimination.

Perhaps the most significant area of disagreement concerns the degree to which research has established the validity and reliability of talker identification by spectrograms. Much of the disagreement centers on the interpretation of published data on error rates in identification and elimination. Table 2 reports error rates for selected published studies of talker identification that have used either aural or visual (spectrogram) methods. The studies differ considerably in many features, including number of talkers, number and sophistication of judges, exemplars available for examination, and type of decision. These considerable differences preclude direct comparisons among studies, and Table 2 must be interpreted cautiously. The error rates in this table range from 0% to 85%.

The largest and most comprehensive investigation of talker identification by spectrograms was reported by Tosi et al.[97] This study includes the largest talker sample reported in the published literature: 250 men drawn from what was considered by the investigators to be a "homogeneous population" of 25,000 males speaking general American English (students at Michigan State University). The examiners were 29 individuals given a month's training in spectrographic identification. A total of 34,996 identification trials were carried out. The trials were based on subsets of 10 or 40 speakers drawn from the larger sample of 250 talkers. The experiment included several aspects: comparison of open versus closed tests, use of noncontemporaneous reference and test samples, and context variation.

The condition that probably compares most closely with forensic tests is the open test with noncontemporaneous samples extracted from continuous speech. Forensic tests frequently must use conversational speech samples (continuous speech) obtained at different times (noncontemporaneous samples) and from a suspect who may or may not be in the reference sample, or "lineup" of talkers (open test). For this condition, Tosi et al. reported error rates of 6.4% for false identification and 12.7% for false elimination. The examiners also were asked to rate the certainty of their judgments, and Tosi et al. pointed out that 60% of the incorrect judgments were associated with an "uncertain" rating. The authors suggested that if the examiners had been allowed to use a "no opinion" category of decision, the error rates would have fallen to 2.4% for false identification and 4.8% for false elimination.

Other published studies typically have used talker samples of 10–50 in open or closed tests. As noted earlier, it is difficult to make direct comparisons of reported error rates. However, as a general indication of the results, the lowest error rates (best examiner performance) across the experimental

92. Thomas Shipp et al., *Some Fundamental Considerations Regarding Voice Identification*, 82 J. ACOUSTICAL SOC'Y AM. 687 (1987).

93. John W. Black et al., *"Speaker Identification by Speech Spectrograms: Some Further Considerations,"* 54 J. ACOUSTICAL SOC'Y AM. 535 (1973).

94. Kersta, *supra* note 4.

95. Bruce E. Koenig et al., *Reply to "Some Fundamental Considerations Regarding Voice Identification,"* 82 J. ACOUSTICAL SOC'Y AM. 688 (1987).

96. Tosi et al., *supra* note 15.

97. *Id.*

conditions used in major studies published in refereed journals were: 21.6% for comparison of single words spoken in isolation,[98] 18% for comparison of phrases and sentences,[99] 11.9% for open tests involving cue words in the same context.[100] Depending on which study one chooses, the accuracy of identifying one individual from a group of ten similar talkers under optimal conditions may be as good as 100% or as poor as 80%. By contrast, in an open test under less than optimal conditions, the accuracy may be 40% or even lower.

In their influential paper, Bolt et al.[101] remarked that, "Today's consensus suggests that talker identification by voice patterns is subject to error at a high, and as yet undetermined, rate" (at 602). Bolt et al. concluded, "We find, in brief, that spectrographic voice identification has inherent difficulties and uncertainties. Anecdotal evidence given in support of the method is not scientifically convincing. The controlled experiments that have been reported give conflicting results.... We conclude that the available results are inadequate to establish the reliability of voice identification by spectrograms." Nearly 25 years have passed since publication of the Bolt et al.[102] reports, but no research papers that resolve the question of the reliability of spectrographic talker identification have been published. The debate over the reliability of this method centers on studies published before 1980.

One disagreement pertains to the nature of decisions reached in talker identification or elimination. As noted earlier, scientific studies have relied almost exclusively on positive decisions (identification or elimination), but forensic specialists typically use categories such as "probable" or "inconclusive." Because of these differences in decision categories, it is not a simple matter to relate accuracy rates reported in scientific reports to actual practice in forensic application. It has been argued that the accuracy rates in scientific reports are conservative estimates of the accuracy expected in forensic application, especially if a "no-decision" response is used in the latter. However, this is a matter of interpretation, about which controversy is not surprising. The opposite case also can be argued, given that forensic applications often contend with signals of poor quality, uncooperative subjects, and short samples of speech from which exemplars can be extracted.

Some disagreement continues over the vulnerability of the speech signal to some sources of intratalker variation. Some particular points of disagreement are over (a) the signal quality required for identification purposes, (b) the effect of vocal disguises and the emotional or physical state of the talker, (c) the selection of words or phonetic features for purposes of talker identification. But the importance of these disagreements is lessened by the use of forensic procedures such as those recommended by the VIAAS–IAI.

§ 6–2.4   Future Directions

Bolt et al.[103] recommended four main categories of research in talker identification: "the origins and characteristics of variability; the relations between intraspeaker and interspeaker variability; the relations between

98. Martin Young & Richard Campbell, *Effects of Context on Talker Identification*, 42 J. ACOUSTICAL SOC'Y AM. 1250 (1967).

99. Stevens et al., *supra* note 28.

100. Hazen, *supra* note 8.

101. Bolt et al., *supra* note 50 at 602–603.

102. *Id.*; Bolt et al., *supra* note 55.

103. BOLT ET AL., *supra* note 26.

aural and visual examination; and the potential of developments in automated methods of voice identification to make contributions to the understanding and improvement of identification performed by humans" (at 61). This research agenda might very well be reiterated today, only because limited progress has been made in these areas since the publication of the Bolt et al. report.

Clearly, the need remains for large-scale talker identification experiments that use procedures similar to those in forensic settings, specifically, joint use of aural and spectrographic examinations, and the use of probable or inconclusive decisions. Experiments should use spontaneous speech samples[104] as well as samples gathered using the methods of experienced forensic investigators to elicit exemplars from known talkers, which simulate the rate, vocal effort, and emotional state of the "unknown" talker to whom comparisons will be made. The intensity of debate over the validity and reliability of talker identification by spectrograms is rooted largely in the lack of experimental data collected with appropriate procedures and adequate controls.

A likely direction of future research is continued exploration of automated (or semi-automated) talker identification, possibly aided by aural recognition. Automated identification usually is a computer-based procedure. It offers the advantage of a comparatively objective process in which specified parameters are examined algorithmically and, if appropriate, assigned individual levels of statistical confidence. Automated recognition may evolve as a useful supplement to other procedures that involve more direct human observation and decision making.

One example is the linear prediction model in which different parametric representations of speech are derived.[105] An important advantage of automated procedures is the capability for analyses of long samples of speech for which variation in phonetic characteristics may be less important than for brief samples.[106] Of course, long samples of speech are not necessarily available for forensic purposes. Another advantage is the capability for relatively more straightforward statistical comparison between the recorded speech of an unknown talker and data bases drawn from large numbers of talkers and organized in ways that retain information about gender, age, dialect, speaking rate and effort level, and perhaps physiological and psychological state. This is not to say that visual examination of spectrograms should be superseded by automated methods. The pattern recognition abilities of the human visual system are not easily matched by automated systems. Yet visual recognition (like aural recognition) is a legitimate subject of study. Rosenberg and Soong[107] summarized several procedures for automated analysis, but noted that these procedures are more suited to applications in access control (i.e., security) than to speaker identification, primarily because of difficulties with

104. Hazen, *supra* note 8.

105. One of the most promising parameters was the cepstrum, which is the inverse Fourier transform of the amplitude spectrum. Bishu Atal, *Effectiveness of Linear Prediction Characteristics of the Speech Wave for Automatic Speaker Identification*, 55 J. Acoustical Soc'y Am. 1304 (1974). The cepstrum and a number of other computer-implemented analyses in-

volve highly technical issues in mathematics and signal processing. It is not possible to review these matters in this chapter, but it should be noted that they can introduce considerable complexity in discussions of automated talker identification.

106. Li & Hughes, *supra* note 58.

107. Rosenberg & Soong, *supra* note 51.

uncontrolled variability in the latter. But the recent use of automated analysis with fairly large talker samples (e.g., 100 talkers in a study by Liu et al.[108]) holds promise that these techniques could have forensic relevance.

Scientific and statistical techniques used to study forensic talker identification are similar to those employed to assess decision-making in medicine. Research in clinical decision making suggests that performance depends on whether constituent information is combined in a serial or a parallel fashion.[109] In a serial decision strategy, discrete tests are conducted and evaluated one after another, typically using decision rules that dictate later steps on the basis of the outcomes of earlier steps. In a parallel strategy, discrete tests are made independently, and a decision is based on patterns of outcomes from the group of tests. It would be valuable to know how different types of information arising from talker identification can be combined most effectively to yield an ultimate decision of identification or elimination. For example, one approach is a parallel paradigm in which the outcomes of independent decisions are reached with aural identification, identification by spectrograms, and identification by automated methods. The separate decisions can be weighted, then combined into a final decision. Current approaches appear to be more serial in character: decisions are made based on if-then sequential logic suggested in part by procedural requirements. It appears that potential effects associated with the order in which comparisons are made have not been studied formally.

Similarly, additional research is needed to determine the impact on summary decision outcomes of independent replications of talker identifications by examiners with varying degrees of experience. The VIAAS–IAI standards require that an independent opinion be obtained for all decisions other than inconclusive, possible identification, and possible elimination; a third opinion is required when the first and second examiners cannot resolve differences. Post hoc reports suggest such procedures produce very small proportions of errors, and that such errors as do occur tend to be related to poor recordings, high-pitched voices, or an insufficient number of words.[110] However, these observations are based on a limited number of comparisons (2000 talkers). The examiners were sufficiently similar in training and in the analysis tools used to make comparisons that generalizing beyond them is difficult.

Future work should lead to a better specification of the parameters that are most effective in identifying talkers. Much as fingerprint identification is based on distinguishing features such as whorls, talker identification examines particular features in the spectrogram. A number of features are potentially useful, but they probably are not equally sensitive to interspeaker differences. It would be important to know the relative value of various features for the purpose of speaker identification. One example is specification

108. Chi–Shi Liu et al., *A Study on Minimum Error Discriminative Training for Speaker Recognition*, 97 J. Acoustical Soc'y Am. 637 (1995).

109. Martyn L. Hyde et al., *Auditory Test Strategy*, in Diagnostic Audiology (John T. Jacobson & Jerry L. Northern eds., 1991); Robert Turner, *Techniques to Determine Test Protocol Performance*, 9 Ear & Hearing 177 (1988); Robert Turner et al., *Formulating and Evaluating Audiological Test Protocols*, 5 Ear & Hearing 321 (1984); Robert Turner & Donald Nielsen, *Application of Clinical Decision Analysis to Audiological Tests*, 5 Ear & Hearing 125 (1984).

110. Koenig, J. Acoustical Soc'y Am., *supra* note 26.

of formant tracks and other acoustic features that can be obtained from largely automatic procedures. Goldstein,[111] Sambur,[112] and Wolf[113] described certain acoustic characteristics that were useful in distinguishing among small sets of talkers but more work on larger numbers of talkers is needed. Another promising direction is to specify various phonetic characteristics that are candidates for talker identification. These might include formant patterns for vowels and vowel-like sounds, spectra of frication noise, durations of noise segments, perturbations (irregularities) in vocal fold vibrations, and covariation in selected frequency and intensity features. The large talker databases now available could be studied to construct statistical ensembles for some of these features. One recent example of such work produced long-term average speech spectra using standardized procedures and equipment for 13 languages as spoken by both male and female talkers.[114]

Kuwabara and Sagisaka[115] gave an example of a systematic approach to acoustic identification. They specified acoustic features at two levels, as follows:

Voice source:

1. average vocal fundamental frequency (voice pitch),

2. time-frequency pattern of vocal fundamental frequency (also known as the pitch contour),

3. fluctuations in fundamental frequency,

4. glottal wave shape.

Vocal tract resonances:

1. shape of spectral envelope and spectral tilt,

2. absolute value of formant frequencies,

3. time-frequency pattern of formant frequencies,

4. long-term average spectrum of speech,

5. formant bandwidths.

It should be possible to render identification or elimination decisions along different axes or dimensions, and then combine the independent decisions in a statistical decision model. Examples of different dimensions of analysis are the long-term averaged speech spectrum,[116] the cepstrum,[117]

111. Ursula G. Goldstein, *Speaker-Identifying Features Based on Formant Tracks*, 59 J. ACOUSTICAL SOC'Y AM. 176 (1976).

112. Sambur, *supra* note 72.

113. Jared Wolf, *Efficient Acoustic Parameters for Speaker Recognition*, 51 J. ACOUSTICAL SOC'Y AM. 2044 (1972).

114. Denis Byrne et al., *An International Comparison of Long–Term Average Speech Spectra*, 96 J. ACOUSTICAL SOC'Y AM. 2108 (1994).

115. Kuwabara & Sagisaka, *supra* note 2.

116. Atal, *supra* note 105; Mary Lou P. Gelfer et al., *The Effects of Sample Duration and Timing on Speaker Identification Accuracy by Means of Long–Term Spectra*, 17 J. PHONETICS 327 (1989); Harry Hollien & Wojciech Ma-

jewski, *Speaker Identification by Long–Term Spectra under Normal and Distorted Speech Conditions*, 62 J. ACOUSTICAL SOC'Y AM. 975 (1977); H. Kiukaanniemi, *Individual Differences in the Long–Term Speech Spectrum*, 34 FOLIA PHONIATRICA 21 (1982); J. Zalewski et al., *Cross Correlation of Long–Term Spectra as a Speaker Identification Technique*, 34 ACOUSTICA 20 (1975); Byrne, et al., *supra* note 114.

117. Atal, *supra* note 105; James E. Luck, *Automatic Speaker Verification Using Cepstral Measurements*, 46 J. ACOUSTICAL SOC'Y AM. 1026 (1969).

perturbation measures of vocal function,[118] aural recognition,[119] spectrographic examination of specific phonetic features including formant pattern,[120] temporal features,[121] nasal features,[122] and turbulence noise for fricatives.[123] Some examples of multiple-factor analyses are those of Doherty and Hollien.[124] Fuzzy logic is one potential approach to combining information from several features, no one of which in itself always yields an unambiguous decision.[125]

The use of particular features in spectrograms might be enhanced if standards were available for the determination of differences related to anatomical dissimilarities as opposed to differences that reflect learned speaking patterns. Presumably, anatomy is more difficult to change than learned patterns of speech. Research along these lines may eventually establish criteria for feature selection. Nolan listed the following criteria for the selection of parameters in talker identification: high between-speaker variability, low within-speaker variability, resistance to attempted disguise or mimicry, availability, robustness in transmission, and measurability. It would be a major advance in spectrograph talker identification if a consensus were reached on the degree to which features or parameters satisfy these criteria.[126]

Published research pertains almost exclusively to male speakers, especially young to middle-aged men. Very little scientific information has been collected for female speakers, children of either gender, or elderly men. It is interesting to note that individual identity can be determined fairly well even with infant cries.[127] As it stands now, the scientific validation of talker identification pertains to less than half of the population. Moreover, the total number of speakers examined in all published research on spectrogram identification remains small.

Audio tape authentication and enhancement will experience continued refinement through technological improvements. It is important that consensus be reached concerning criteria for authentication and acceptable procedures for enhancement. Efforts by organizations such as the Audio Engineering Society to develop formal technical standards in these areas may increase

118. Philip Lieberman, *Some Acoustic Measures of the Fundamental Periodicity of Normal and Pathologic Larynges*, 35 J. ACOUSTICAL SOC'Y AM. 344 (1963); Ingo R. Titze et al., *Some Technical Considerations in Voice Perturbation Measurements*, 30 J. SPEECH & HEARING RESEARCH 252 (1987); Kim A. Wilcox & Yoshiyuki Horii, *Age and Changes in Vocal Jitter*, 35 J. GERONTOLOGY 194 (1980); Barbara J. Zyski et al., *Perturbation Analysis of Normal and Pathological Larynges*, 36 FOLIA PHONIATRICA 190 (1984).

119. William A. Hargraves & John A. Starkweather, *Recognition of Speaker Identity*, 6 LANGUAGE & SPEECH 63 (1963); Reich & Duke, *supra* note 60; Stevens et al., *supra* note 28; Voiers, *supra* note 33.

120. Goldstein, *supra* note 111; Wiktor Jassem, *Formant Frequencies as Cues to Speaker Discrimination, in* 1 SPEECH ANALYSIS AND SYNTHESIS 41 (Wiktor Jassem ed., 1968); Conrad L. LaRiverie, *Contributions of Fundamental Frequency and Formant Frequencies to Speaker Identification*, 31 PHONETICA 185 (1975); Wolf, *supra* note 113.

121. C. C. Johnson et al., *Speaker Identification Utilizing Selected Temporal Speech Features*, 12 J. PHONETICS 319 (1984).

122. Su et al., *supra* note 71.

123. Conrad L. LaRiviere, *Speaker Identification for Turbulent Portions of Fricatives*, 29 PHONETICA 98 (1974).

124. E. Thomas Doherty, *An Evaluation of Selected Acoustic Parameters for Use in Speaker Identification*, 4 J. PHONETICS 321 (1976); E. Thomas Doherty & Harry Hollien, *Multiple-factor Speaker Identification of Normal and Distorted Speech*, 6 J. PHONETICS 1 (1978).

125. Manfred R. Schroeder, *Speech and Speaker Recognition*, 12 BIBLIOTHECA PHONETICA (1985).

126. NOLAN, *supra* note 19.

127. Gwen E. Gustafson et al., *Robustness of Individual Identity in the Cries of Human Infants*, 27 DEVELOPMENTAL PSYCHOBIOLOGY 1 (1994).

the consistency with which various practitioners manage, describe and report results of efforts to enhance and authenticate recorded speech and other signals pertinent to forensic work.

As noted in the introduction, appropriately designed and recorded materials do not exist to promote comparison among the various instrumental systems used to produce speech spectrograms. Thus, we lack an independent physical reference by which to benchmark instruments used for talker identification by human, semi-automated or fully automated means. Such standards of comparison are common in other areas in which measurement and measurement method are important. This issue may be more technical than scientific, but it would be useful if those working in the area shared a common means by which to certify signal analyses, the results of which may be used in talker identification.

Like other areas of scientific enterprise, research in talker identification is influenced by philosophical, social and economic factors. Philosophical issues include distaste among some scientists for the adversarial and sometimes pecuniary character of the forensic enterprise and discomfort with legal standards of proof that may differ from scientific standards. One social issue involves isolation from the larger scientific community of potentially interesting analysis methods and data generated by law enforcement and intelligence agencies for reasons of national security. Another social issue has to do with reluctance among some scientists to engage in applied research and differences of opinion about the particular areas of science and engineering best qualified to address certain difficult questions. Economic factors may be the most difficult to deal with because the types of studies called for by Bolt et al.[128] and in this chapter will be costly. The fact that so few studies of appropriate scale and complexity have been performed may be due largely to lack of funds.

Finally, in the margin are major sources that are recommended to readers who seek more detailed information on various aspects of talker identification.[129] Tosi's succinct conclusion of a generation years ago seems equally applicable today:

> Possibly, no combination of methods may ever produce absolutely positive identification or eliminations in 100% of the cases submitted. Reasonably, it could be stated that the better the quality and extension of available samples, the better the qualifications of the examiner, and the more comprehensive the cluster of methods used, the better the chance of obtaining reliable decisions in a large percentage of cases.[130]

128. Bolt et al., *supra* note 26.

129. Bolt et al., *supra* note 50; Bolt et al., *supra* note 26; Gruber & Poza, *supra* note 86; Michael Hecker, Speaker Recognition: An Interpretive Survey of the Literature, American Speech-Language-Hearing Association Monograph No. 16 (1971); Hollien, *supra* note 43; Schroeder, *supra* note 125; Oscar Tosi, *The Problem of Speaker Identification and Elimination, in* Measurement Procedures in Speech, Hearing, and Language 399 (Sadanand Singh ed., 1975); *Special Section on Automatic Speaker Recognition, Identification and Verification,* 17 Speech Communication 81 (1995).

130. Tosi, *supra* note 129 at 428–29.

Appendix

Glossary

Acoustic. of or relating to the science of sound, or to the sense of hearing.

Cepstrum. a type of acoustic analysis defined as the Fourier transform of the power spectrum of a signal. The transform is described in terms of *quefrency* (note the transliteration from frequency), which has time-like properties. The cepstrum often is used to determine the fundamental frequency of a speech signal. Voiced speech tends to have a strong cepstral peak, at the first *rahmonic* (note transliteration from harmonic).

Formant. a resonance of the vocal tract, that part of the speech production system that extends from the larynx to the lips or nostrils. A formant is specified by its center frequency (commonly called formant frequency) and bandwidth. Formants are denoted by integers that increase with the relative frequency location of the formants. F1 is the lowest-frequency formant, F2 is the next highest, and so on. The first three formants are most important for speech analysis and perception.

Fricative. a speech sound characterized by a long interval of turbulence noise. Examples are the initial sounds in the words *thin, van, see, zoo, shoe.* Fricatives are often classified as *stridents* or *nonstridents,* depending on the degree of noise energy. Stridents have greater energy than nonstridents.

Harmonic. an integer multiple of the fundamental frequency in voiced sounds. Ideally, the voice source can be conceptualized as a line spectrum in which the energy appears as a series of harmonics. That is, each line represents one harmonic. The harmonics of the voice source are filtered by the vocal tract resonances.

Interformant spaces. the low-energy regions that fall between adjacent formants. Depending on speech characteristics, these spaces can contain noise or other energy, but usually this energy is quite weak. Consequently, the interformant spaces will appear as white or light gray on a spectrogram.

Orthographic spelling. the written representation of a language. Orthographic spelling may be contrasted with a phonetic transcription. The former refers to the common spelling of words with the letters of the alphabet. The latter is a specialized system in which each symbol uniquely represents a speech sound.

Plosive gap. the acoustic interval corresponding to articulatory closure (vocal tract obstruction) for a plosive consonant; it is identified on a spectrogram as an interval of low acoustic energy, conspicuously lacking in formant pattern or noise.

Plosives. speech sounds characterized by a complete obstruction of the vocal tract that may be followed by an abrupt release of air that produces a burst noise. Examples of plosives are the initial sounds in the words *bill, pill, dill, till, gill,* and *kill.*

Signal detection theory. a mathematical theory dealing with the problem of detecting the presence of a signal in a background of noise. Early applications of this theory sought to statistically measure the accuracy of instrumental and sensory systems, independent of biases arising from the decision criteria of observers. Decision criteria are influenced by the observer's knowledge of the prior probabilities of target events (signals), and by the values and costs associated with correct and incorrect decisions. Accuracy is indexed graphically by means of *relative operating characteristic* (ROC) curves, and quantitatively by measures of performance such as $d\_$ and $A\_$. Subsequent applications of the theory have included problems in medical diagnosis, aptitude testing, weather forecasting, automated information retrieval, and forensic identification.

Spectral envelope. the general shape of the spectrum (the distribution of signal energy as a function of frequency). The envelope often is drawn to represent the overall form of the spectrum and may neglect minor deviations from that form.

Spectral tilt. the general orientation of spectral energy, or the slant of the spectral envelope.

Spectrogram. a graph of acoustic analysis consisting of three dimensions. Typically, time is represented on the horizontal axis, the frequency (pitch) of sound on the vertical axis, and the intensity of sound on the gray scale (shades of darkness). This is a basic form of analysis used in acoustic studies of speech, including talker identification.

Vertical striations. the fine-grained lines that run vertically on a wide-band spectrogram and correspond to the vocal pulses of voicing energy. The presence of these striations is an indication of voicing, and their relative pattern describes properties of the voice source, such as vocal pitch and its regularity.

Vocal folds. muscles and associated tissues located in the larynx and capable of vibrating to produce voice.

Vocal tract. the cavities and structures above the vocal folds that are capable of modifying voice and airflow into distinctive sounds of speech; sometimes called the articulatory or articulatory-resonatory system.

Vocal tract resonances. the natural or resonant frequencies of the vocal tract, which can be determined mathematically from a knowledge of the length and shape of the vocal tract; also called formants.

Voice. the tone produced by vibration of the vocal folds and modified by adjustments of the vocal tract; sometimes used in a general sense to refer to human speech.

CHAPTER 7

FIRES, ARSONS AND EXPLOSIONS

Table of Sections

A. LEGAL ISSUES

Westlaw Electronic Research

See Westlaw Electronic Research Guide preceding the Summary of Contents.

A. LEGAL ISSUES

§ 7–1.0 THE LEGAL RESPONSE TO EXPERT TESTIMONY ON FIRES AND EXPLOSIONS

§ 7–1.1 Introduction

Fire and explosion investigation consists of a highly varied mixture of methods, techniques, and principles. Consequently, there is not just one actual or potential body of relevant scientific research on which experts may depend, but many, some of which are more sound and others which are less sound.[1] Fire investigators can be found who rely on such tools as electronic sniffers, accelerant detecting canines, and gas chromatography; examination of electrical arc beads, metallurgical examination, burn patterns, crazed glass, concrete spalling; and consideration of reports of the color of the smoke and the fire, blood chemistry, and other indications from human remains found at the fire scene. Some of these clues are derived from sound science. Others are nothing more than a set of more or less shared beliefs that may or may not be true.[2] An opinion is then reached by these clues being processed through each investigator's personal experience, beliefs and assumptions—in addition to or instead of any well tested model for analyzing fire evidence.[3]

Such profusion presents courts with a dilemma. In considering admissibility, should members of a field of expertise be required to elucidate each of the components on which they rely, and to establish the validity of each component? Or should the courts make a general, global, judgment about the field, and trust the expert, under questioning by counsel, to spell out the details? Historically, the courts generally followed the latter strategy, and experts, once permitted to testify, were given wide latitude to offer opinions based on whatever the expert thought reasonable.[4] The task-at-hand analysis called for

---

§ 7–1.0

1. This state of affairs contrasts with most of the kinds of expertise with which the chapters of this book are concerned. But it is not unique. For example, the testimony of medical examiners or accident reconstructionists depends on the witness bringing together a potentially wide range of principles or assumptions on which an opinion is based.

2. As the field begins to test its beliefs, some are confirmed and others are found to be false. *See infra* § 2.1.1[1].

3. "As circumstantial proof of the incendiary origin of a fire, arson investigators rely most heavily upon a rather amorphous group of so-called burn or arson indicators." ANDRE A. MOENSSENS ET AL., SCIENTIFIC EVIDENCE IN CIVIL AND CRIMINAL CASES 416 (4th ed. 1995).

4. Thus, it is not possible to list the pivotal or leading case by which each jurisdiction permitted each component of the expertise. And after Daubert v. Merrell Dow Pharmaceuticals, Inc., 509 U.S. 579, 113 S.Ct. 2786, 125 L.Ed.2d 469 (1993) (hereafter, *Daubert*), and Kumho

by *Daubert* and elaborated upon by *Kumho Tire* would appear to have brought those carefree days to an end.[5] Task-at-hand analysis requires a court to identify the precise knowledge and skills invoked by an expert witness and to focus its gatekeeping responsibilities on those particular expert claims. The approach elaborated by *Kumho Tire* follows from the logic of *Daubert*. *Daubert* requires a finding of validity of the basis for an expert witness's opinion. That gatekeeping requirement would be defeated if multiple techniques were allowed to hide behind a global claim of expertise. In other words, *Daubert* appears to require that an expertise be unpacked, so that the court can permit those methods and principles it is persuaded are valid, and only those, to be offered to the factfinder. *Kumho Tire* makes that requirement explicit.

Expert testimony on the causes of fires went through a period of initial judicial resistance as being an inappropriate subject matter for expert opinions.[6] Gradually, the courts began to reverse themselves, allowing fire investigators and others to offer expert testimony on causes of fires.[7] The courts came to focus more on the training and experience of the proffered expert rather than on the validity of the proffered expertise, their assumption being that valid knowledge existed and the only issue was whether the witness possessed it in sufficient quantity. Of course, the line that divides enough training and experience[8] from not enough[9] may not be a very bright one. But deciding on an expert witness's "qualifications" is easy compared to evaluating the validity (or lack of validity) of the knowledge held by the field represented by the witness.[10]

As this chapter explains, some of the scientific predicates long relied upon by investigators and admitted by courts were later found by research on those

Tire Co. v. Carmichael, 526 U.S. 137, 119 S.Ct. 1167, 143 L.Ed.2d 238 (1999) (hereafter, *Kumho Tire*) the case law admitting fire and explosion experts under a notion of broad, global expertise has been rendered irrelevant to future fire admission decisions, at least in *Daubert/Kumho* jurisdictions.

5. *See* SCIENCE IN THE LAW: STANDARDS, STATISTICS AND RESEARCH ISSUES, Chapter 1, § 3.4.

6. State v. Watson, 65 Me. 74 (1876) (testimony of a fireman on the spread of fire and aspects of fire behavior excluded as within the scope of common experience); Neal v. Missouri Pac. Ry. Co., 98 Neb. 460, 153 N.W. 492 (Neb. 1915) (fireman's opinion as to where a fire started excluded as invading the province of the jury); People v. Grutz, 212 N.Y. 72, 105 N.E. 843 (N.Y. 1914) (an assistant fire marshal should not be permitted to express his opinion about the origin of a fire because the physical facts could be readily understood by the jury when properly described); Sawyer v. State, 100 Fla. 1603, 132 So. 188 (Fla. 1931) (witness in arson case, in this instance the chief of a fire department, may not as a general rule give an opinion whether fire was of incendiary origin because this is "a question for the jury to determine, and upon which they can usually form their own opinion without any need of expert advice"); Beneks v. State, 208 Ind. 317, 196 N.E. 73 (Ind.1935) (expert witness cannot give his opinion as to origin of fire

because jury can draw conclusions from observable facts that can be testified to by expert).

7. An example of testimony by an "other": Brown v. Eakins, 220 Or. 122, 348 P.2d 1116 (Or.1960) (an electrician who regularly investigated fires was qualified as an expert on the causes of fires, despite lack of any formal fire investigation training).

8. Billings v. State, 503 S.W.2d 57 (Mo.App. 1973) (fireman with 4.5 years experience and investigation of two dozen fires found to be qualified); State v. Wilbur, 115 R.I. 7, 339 A.2d 730 (R.I. 1975) (seven years experience as firefighter, several months arson investigation training, and three years as a fire inspector found qualified).

9. Sperow v. Carter, 8 Pa. D. & C.2d 635 (1957) (a part time fire chief who had been fighting fires for 20 years found not qualified); State v. Barnett, 480 A.2d 791 (Me.1984) (a fire chief with 18 years experience fighting fires, extensive formal training in fire fighting, and fire investigation experience as a consultant to the Air Force and several large corporations found not qualified).

10. For example, consider an astrologer with a successful practice for 25 years, extensive education and training, and numerous certifications and awards.

investigative methods to be less valid than the experts or the courts thought them to be.[11] In some instances, principles of fire investigation that lacked a sound scientific basis led to convictions for arson and homicide by arson that later were vacated.[12]

Consider the courts' responses to some specific elements of fire investigation lore. Concrete spalling has been allowed as conclusive evidence that a fire was started by incendiary means, typically with little or no question raised about the validity of the asserted relationship between spalling and arson.[13] Crazed glass has been relied upon as "indicating a fast spreading fire."[14] Expert testimony about burn patterns has been admitted as providing evidence that a fire was of incendiary origin.[15] These and other beliefs of fire investigators have since been called into doubt by empirical research.[16] Similarly, some courts recently have been admitting dog "alerts" as evidence of arson without requiring hard evidence of the accuracy of the canines, and in particular without considering empirical evidence of the level of false positive errors in the method–data which have given great pause to many arson evidence professionals.[17]

These examples might make clear why courts could profitably unpack this broad area of forensic expertise into its component sub-areas and separately consider the validity of each. Judicial skepticism is expected to return to some of these areas.

§ 7–1.2   Before *Kumho Tire*: Are Fire Experts Subject to *Daubert* Scrutiny?

In deciding whether asserted fire and arson expertise had to be tested under *Daubert,* some courts made a distinction between whether the expert was offered as, or claimed to be, a "scientific" expert, in which case *Daubert* was applied, or whether the expert was sailing under the flag of "technical or other" expertise, in which case the expert was tested by a lesser standard.

The most interesting of these cases is *Michigan Millers Mutual Insurance Corp. v. Benfield.*[18] The Millers had sought a declaratory judgment against its

---

11. *See infra* § 2.1.1[1].

12. *See, e.g.*, State v. Knapp, No. CR78779 (Superior Court of Arizona, Maricopa County, Feb. 11, 1987); State v. Girdler, No. 9809 (Superior Court of Arizona, Maricopa County, Jan. 3, 1991); *see also,* Girdler v. Dale, 859 F.Supp. 1279 (D.Ariz.1994).

13. *See, e.g.*, Reed v. Allstate Ins. Co., 376 So.2d 1303 (La.App. 2d Cir.1979); Security Ins. Co. of Hartford v. Dudds, Inc., 648 F.2d 273 (5th Cir.1981); State v. Danskin, 122 N.H. 817, 451 A.2d 396 (N.H.1982); LeForge v. Nationwide Mut. Fire Ins. Co., 82 Ohio App.3d 692, 612 N.E.2d 1318 (Ohio App.1992); American Mfrs. Mut. Ins. Co. v. General Motors Corp., 582 So.2d 934 (La.App. 2d Cir.1991) (unlike the other cases in this note, the expert drew a negative inference: because there was no spalling, the fire at issue was thought not to have been arson). *But see infra* § 2.2.1[8].

14. McReynolds v. Cherokee Ins. Co., 815 S.W.2d 208 (Tenn.App.1991). *But see infra* § 2.2.1[7].

15. People v. Calvin Thomas, 65 Cal.2d 698, 56 Cal.Rptr. 305, 423 P.2d 233 (Cal.1967); People v. Swain, 200 Cal.App.2d 344, 19 Cal. Rptr. 403 (1962); Commonwealth v. Wisneski, 214 Pa.Super. 397, 257 A.2d 624 (Pa.Super. 1969); State v. Reis P. Kelley, 901 S.W.2d 193 (Mo.App. W.D.1995); State v. Swanson, 1995 WL 238853 (Minn.App.1995); State v. Bouchillion, 1995 WL 75444 (Tenn.Crim.App.1995); State v. Bernier, 1995 WL 70337 (Conn.Super.1995); State v. Haggood, 36 Conn.App. 753, 653 A.2d 216 (Conn.App.1995); Adams v. Tennessee Farmers Mut. Ins. Co., 898 S.W.2d 216 (Tenn.App.1994). *But see infra* §§ 2.1.1[1] and 2.2.1[1].

16. *See infra* § 2.1.1[1].

17. *See infra* § 1.4.

18. The opinion of the United States District Court for the Middle District of Florida, No. 93–1283–CIV–T–17A, is unreported.

insured, Benfield, precluding payment of fire insurance benefits on several grounds, notably that the fire had been intentionally set. The district judge excluded the testimony of the insurance company's expert, finding that his proffered testimony did not meet *Daubert's* reliability criteria, adding that the testimony did not meet the requirements of *Frye*[19] either.

Michigan Millers appealed to the 11th Circuit,[20] arguing that its expert should have been admitted—not because the expertise was scientific, but because it was *not* scientific, therefore should not have been subject to *Daubert*, and should instead be admissible on a lesser standard as "experience-based" expertise.[21] Appellants cited several cases where testimony had been admitted over *Daubert*-based objections.

The International Association of Arson Investigators (IAAI) submitted an *amicus* brief urging the admission of the expert testimony. The brief argued that a fire and arson expert who is qualified by conventional criteria and who is not presenting any novel scientific evidence should not have to pass *Daubert* scrutiny. That argument was based on the clearly mistaken (but surprisingly common) belief that *Daubert* was narrowly focused on novel scientific techniques and methodologies. Since fire investigation is not a novel scientific technique, the *amicus* argued, *Daubert* should not apply.[22] The IAAI brief also argued that fire and arson investigation is neither a science nor strictly based on science, but its asserted validity rests instead on training and experience, and for that reason as well *Daubert* was inapplicable—a view later rejected unanimously in *Kumho Tire*.[23]

In addition, a member[24] of the IAAI, upon seeing the organization's amicus brief, wrote and submitted his own amicus brief, in which he argued that although the field once was unscientific, it has been making important strides in recent years, and that judicial toleration of unscientific arson investigation certainly would not inspire the field to continue to develop itself as an empirically grounded science.[25]

The Court of Appeals applied an analysis following its decision in the case of *Carmichael v. Samyang Tire, Inc.*[26] It concluded that because the fire investigator in question had held himself out as an expert in fire science, *Daubert* criteria did indeed apply to the issue of the admissibility of his testimony, and the Circuit Court upheld the District Court's exclusion of the testimony. The expert had performed no tests, taken no samples, and could not adequately explain how he had reached his conclusion. The court cited

---

19. Frye v. United States, 293 F. 1013 (D.C.Cir.1923).

20. 140 F.3d 915 (11th Cir.1998).

21. "Millers argues that *Carmichael* [v. Samyang Tire, Inc., 131 F.3d 1433 (11th Cir. 1997)] made clear that the *Daubert* criteria apply only to scientific testimony, and the testimony of their expert was not based on scientific principles but rather was based on his years of experience, and on his skill and experience-based observations." *Id.* at 920.

22. *Cf. Daubert*, 509 U.S. at 593 n. 11.

23. The Supreme Court's view implies that these questions could and should be put to those who claim a valid expertise on the basis of training and experience: What knowledge was imparted to you in your training? How can we know if it was valid? What knowledge did you acquire through your experience? How can we know if it was valid? (After all, if training and experience without further inquiry establish expertise, then astrology would be admissible.)

24. John Lentini, author of the scientific status portion of this chapter.

25. Both the IAAI brief and Lentini's brief were placed on the IAAI homepage, at fire-investigators.org/wwwboard.

26. 131 F.3d 1433 (11th Cir.1997), later to be known as *Kumho Tire v. Carmichael*.

General Electric v. Joiner for the proposition that courts are not required to admit opinions based on nothing more than the *ipse dixit* of the expert.[27] On the other hand, it held that the "experience-based" testimony of a different expert, the local fire investigator employed by Sarasota County, could be admitted for the jury's consideration. Because the fire in question was an obvious arson fire, however, the Court set aside the trial court's directed verdict and remanded the case for a new trial.

The case ultimately was settled prior to a second trial, but the repercussions of the case continued to reverberate through the fire investigation community. As a result of the 11th Circuit's reliance on the witness's self-characterization as either a scientific witness or an experience-based witness, some insurance company attorneys began counseling fire investigators to identify themselves as "experience-based" experts, in an effort to avoid scrutiny under *Daubert*.

Still trying to avoid judicial scrutiny of its asserted expertise, the IAAI again submitted an *amicus* brief when *Carmichael v. Samyang Tire* (of which *Benfield* had been progeny), now known as *Kumho Tire Co., Ltd. v. Carmichael*[28] was heard by the United States Supreme Court. Joining an *amicus* brief filed by the International Association of Chiefs of Police, Mothers Against Drunk Driving, the National District Attorneys Association, and numerous other organizations, their brief in *Kumho Tire* argued that the trial judge's gatekeeping responsibility should not serve as an obstacle to testimony based on "technical" or "specialized" knowledge or it would threaten much of the expert evidence that law enforcement organizations offer.[29]

The Supreme Court in *Kumho Tire*, of course, unanimously rejected such arguments. Had the decision gone the other way, and "technical and other specialized" experts were exempted from scrutiny under *Daubert*, their experience, intuition and *ipse dixit* would have been transformed from shortcomings into the very basis of their expertise. As a result of *Kumho Tire*, *Daubert*-based objections to fire investigation testimony not based on good science have increased.[30] Few of the rulings on *Daubert* challenges to fire investigators have reached the appellate level, but decisions affecting admissibility are quickly and widely circulated among fire investigators through trade publications and electronic bulletin boards.

In still another repercussion of the *Benfield* decision, the National Fire Protection Association Technical Committee on Fire Investigations, the committee responsible for the preparation and maintenance of NFPA 921, *Guide for Fire and Explosion Investigations*, received several public proposals to eliminate from the *Guide* any reference to science or the scientific method. (This despite the fact that *Kumho Tire* had rendered that means of evading scrutiny unavailing.) The proponents of this change wanted to substitute the

27. General Elec. Co. v. Joiner, 522 U.S. 136, 118 S.Ct. 512, 139 L.Ed.2d 508 (1997).

28. 526 U.S. 137, 119 S.Ct. 1167, 143 L.Ed.2d 238 (1999).

29. Brief Amici Curiae of Americans for Effective Law Enforcement, Inc.; Criminal Justice Legal Foundation; Grand Lodge of Fraternal Order of Police; International Association of Arson Investigators; International Associa-

tion of Chiefs of Police; Mothers Against Drunk Driving; National Association of Police Organizations, Inc.; National District Attorneys Association; and National Sheriffs' Association; and Police Law Institute, submitted to the United States Supreme Court in Kumho Tire Company, Ltd. v. Carmichael (October 19, 1998).

30. *See infra* § 1.7.

words "systematic approach" for "scientific method." The Technical Committee rejected these proposals, while attempting to deal with the misperception that a scientific fire investigation requires a complete reconstruction of the fire. The 2001 edition of NFPA 921 makes reference to "cognitive" testing as well as experimental testing as a means of testing a hypothesis within the structure of the scientific method. Cognitive testing, as used in this context, means mentally comparing all of the collected data with the proposed hypothesis, and rejecting the hypothesis if it cannot account for all of the data.

The *Benfield* court was not alone in the question it pondered, as fire investigators sought shelter from *Daubert*. Before *Kumho Tire* unanimously resolved the confusion about whether *Daubert's* gatekeeping requirement applied only to the "scientific" prong of Rule 702, or whether it applied to all kinds of expert opinion evidence, a number of courts struggled with the question in the context of fire causation. Typically, these cases relied on an expert's "experience" to substitute for systematic empirical or theoretical knowledge on the facts in dispute, and allowed the asserted expert to testify.[31] After *Kumho Tire* and after the recent revision to Fed. R. Evid. 702 it is doubtful that the cases cited in the margin could be regarded as following the requirements of Federal evidence law.

§ 7–1.3   Other Aspects of Admissibility and Exclusion of Fire Experts

A number of other aspects of the problem of what is required for proffered fire expert testimony to be admitted, some of them hinted at in the *Benfield* discussion, *supra*, are considered next.

§ 7–1.3.1   The Qualifications of the Expert

The Supreme Court's admissibility cases make clear that the admissibility of claimed expertise is distinct from the qualifications of the expert. Qualifications of fire and arson experts vary considerably, and the courts have done little to distinguish among the various kinds of proffered experts, ranging from fire department employees with minimal science training to bachelors level engineers to chemists with doctorates. Suitable qualifications are necessary but not sufficient for the admission of the proffered expert testimony.[32]

---

31. Talkington v. Atria Reclamelucifers Fabrieken BV (Cricket BV), 152 F.3d 254 (4th Cir.1998) (holding *Daubert* inapplicable to expert testimony about the cause of fire in a house, because the defendant acknowledged the testimony was not science and was not based on scientific principles or data, but was based instead on the expert's training and experience); Polizzi Meats, Inc. v. Aetna Life & Casualty Co., 931 F.Supp. 328 (D.N.J.1996) (holding that the lack of any scientific or other systematic empirical basis for their testimony on the origin and cause of fire at insured's building did not preclude testimony of insurer's expert witnesses); Patterson v. Conopco, Inc., 999 F.Supp. 1417 (D.Kan.1997) (holding it acceptable for an expert to "rely on his experience," though he had never actually conducted any tests on whether human hair could sustain

a fire and, presumably, could point to no data on the question); Fireman's Fund Insurance Co. v. Xerox Corp., 30 F. Supp. 2d 823 (M.D.Pa.1998) (holding *Daubert* inapplicable and admitting an expert's opinion on how a fire started at a copy machine, concluding that the expert was "not relying on any particular methodology or technique," and that he had "reached his ... conclusions by drawing upon general electrical engineering principles and his twenty-five years of experience investigating electrical accidents."). For further discussion of experience-based expertise in fire cases, *see infra* § 7–1.3.3.

32. *Cf.* Allstate Ins. v. Maytag, 1999 WL 203349 (N.D.Ill.1999), discussed in more detail *infra*, a case which illustrates reliance on credentials and no scrutiny of the basis of the proffered testimony.

Kumho Tire went further, emphasizing the need to evaluate the precise "task at hand"—the factual issue which expertise is being offered to resolve. The implications of *Kumho Tire* suggests that the proffered expert must be qualified on precisely the expert issue at bar, rather than some general or global expertise in fire investigation.

Though fairly superficial scrutiny usually is involved in passing on qualifications, it may be worth noting that one can only be qualified as an expert in a subject on which an expertise exists. In other words, one cannot be an expert on something in which there is no expertise. Thus, where a technique (e.g., dog sniffing for accelerants) is being challenged, qualifications and admissibility of the expertise will be entangled.

One example of rather stringent scrutiny of qualifications, interwoven with scrutiny of doubtful foundations for the experts' proffered opinions, is *Weisgram v. Marley Co.*,[33] where the Court of Appeals for the Eighth Circuit found the district court's wholesale admission of various types of fire causation experts to constitute reversible error. The Court of Appeals judged all three experts to be "unqualified" and their opinion testimony "speculative." A city fire captain who investigated the fire in the home was held not qualified to give expert testimony as to whether or not the baseboard heater in the home malfunctioned, or how the heater might have ignited other objects, and his opinions were found to be without foundation. A fire investigator's testimony that the baseboard heater was defective and caused the fire was held to be unsupported by sufficient foundation because no studies had been conducted to test the investigator's theory; the Court found that instead it was based on pure speculation. Finally, the Court held that the expert testimony of a metallurgist that thermostat contacts on the baseboard heater were defectively designed was not supported by sufficient foundation because the metallurgist had little knowledge about this particular model heater or this type of heater. Moreover, upon excluding the testimony of these witnesses, the Court of Appeals directed that judgment be entered against the proponent of this expert evidence, which decision was appealed to the United States Supreme Court.

Specifically, the plaintiffs complained that it was "unfair" to direct a verdict against them without giving them a chance to procure admissible expert testimony. The Supreme Court rejected this argument: "Since *Daubert*, ... parties relying on expert evidence have had notice of the exacting standards of reliability such evidence must meet. It is implausible to suggest, post-*Daubert*, that parties will initially present less than their best expert evidence in the expectation of a second chance should their first try fail. We therefore find unconvincing [the plaintiff's] fears that allowing courts of appeals to direct the entry of judgment for defendants will punish plaintiffs who could have shored up their cases by other means had they known their expert testimony would be found inadmissible."[34] On the specific procedural question presented, the Court held "that the authority of courts of appeals to direct the entry of judgment as a matter of law extends to cases in which, on

---

33. 169 F.3d 514 (8th Cir.1999).

34. 528 U.S. 440, 456, 120 S.Ct. 1011, 145 L.Ed.2d 958 (2000).

excision of testimony erroneously admitted, there remains insufficient evidence to support a jury's verdict."[35]

§ 7–1.3.2   Novelty

Occasionally a court mistakenly treats *Daubert* as applying only to "novel" types of expertise, and in effect grandfathers in a non-novel yet questionable expertise by refusing to scrutinize it. The district court in *Polizzi Meats, Inc. v. Aetna Life & Casualty Co.*[36] did so with remarkable vehemence considering that the court was misreading *Daubert*. The defendant insurer refused to pay the plaintiff's claims resulting from a fire that had destroyed its place of business. Aetna asserted that the plaintiffs had set the fire intentionally. In a partial summary judgment motion, the plaintiffs argued that Aetna's experts had not produced "scientific proof" of the cause of the fire, and therefore they should be barred from testifying. The district court held that this "astounding contention is based on a seriously flawed reading of . . . *Daubert*. . . . [which] addressed the standards to be applied by a trial judge when faced with a proffer of expert scientific testimony based upon a novel theory or methodology. Nothing in *Daubert* suggests that trial judges should exclude otherwise relevant testimony of police and fire investigators on the issues of the origins and causes of fires."[37] Apparently the district court overlooked the gloss on novelty given in *Daubert*, namely: "[W]e do not read the requirements of Rule 702 to apply specially or exclusively to unconventional evidence. Of course, well-established propositions are less likely to be challenged than those that are novel, and they are more handily defended."[38]

An even more confused opinion is *Jugle v. Volkswagen of America, Inc.*[39] This case involved a young man who was burned to death in a Volkswagen Jetta. The defendant sought *in limine* to exclude the plaintiff's experts' testimony, but that motion was denied. One expert offered the opinion that the catalytic converter had caused a wax used on the floor pan to ignite, which in turn had caused plastic fuel lines to melt and burn. A second expert offered the opinion that the converter had ignited the fuel lines directly, even though this theory was contradicted by the first expert's data. The *Jugle* court held *Daubert* inapplicable to the expertise or to the opinions at issue in the case. "Because the opinions of Dr. Jacobson and Mr. Cole are not based on novel scientific techniques, the Court need not test their opinions against *Daubert's* four factors."[40] The opinion went on to say that "[t]he Court must, however, still assess the reliability and fit of the proposed experts' opinions,"[41] and for this proposition it quoted the language in *Daubert* which explained that Rule 702's gatekeeping requirements, explicated in *Daubert*, were not limited to novel or unconventional scientific evidence. Finally, the court found the methodology of the experts reliable, though it provided virtually no description of it in the opinion.[42]

35.   *Id.* at 457.

36.   931 F.Supp. 328 (D.N.J.1996).

37.   *Id.* at 336.

38.   *Daubert* n. 11, at 593.

39.   975 F.Supp. 576 (D.Vt.1997).

40.   *Id.* at 580.

41.   *Id.* at 580.

42.   *Id.* at 581.

§ 7–1.3.3 Basis in Experience versus in Empirically Tested Knowledge

It is clear, after *Kumho Tire*, that no expert witness of any kind may pass through the *Daubert* gate unless and until the court is properly satisfied that the testimony is based on valid principles. What is not yet clear is what criteria courts may or must use in making this assessment, especially since they will vary to a greater or lesser extent with the specie of expert evidence being offered.

In the area of fire and arson, as in other areas, courts have been presented with the dilemma of deciding whether expertise must be based on adequate empirical testing or whether a looser accumulation of individual "experience" is sufficient. One such case is *Patterson v. Conopco, Inc.*[43] This was a wrongful death case involving a woman who died from burns and smoke inhalation in a bathroom fire. The decedent's plaintiff's claim was that hair spray made by the defendant had caused this fatal accident. The trial court denied challenges to the expert testimony of a chemist and a fire investigator. The chemist's report concluded that the hair spray contained flammable materials that are easily ignited and will propagate a fire. The fire investigator's testimony purported to explain how the accident could have occurred. The defendant argued that the chemist's conclusion depended on the assumption that human hair by itself could not sustain combustion, a "fact" based only on the chemist's "experience," not any systematic testing. The court held, nevertheless, that it was acceptable for an expert to "rely on his experience" and to take that more casually acquired knowledge into account in forming an opinion.[44] This decision may or may not have survived *Kumho Tire's* emphasis on the need of a court to evaluate the specific "task at hand."

Because *Allstate Insurance Co. v. Maytag Corp.*[45] was decided after *Kumho Tire*, the magistrate judge had no doubt that *Daubert* applied to fire experts, yet he appears to have been content to rely on the credentials and experience of the experts, rather than scrutinizing with particularity the basis of their asserted knowledge, the content of the knowledge, and determining whether it was sufficiently sound that the opinions flowing from it would be dependable. The judge also did not find the objection that one expert's theory of causation was unsupported by any testing to raise any barriers to the witness offering his opinion on causation. On the other hand, the judge did draw some lines. Because the defendant's expert was a mechanical engineer with a great deal of experience with the cooktops which were the disputed source of a house fire, and not an expert in fire causation, the judge limited his testimony to the nature of the cooktop and why in his opinion it could not have been the source of the fire. In admitting the testimony of both experts, the magistrate judge ruled that they were "based on deductions from various known technical facts which appear to have at least a theoretical basis."[46] One might have expected the judge to follow the example of Justice Breyer in

---

43. Patterson v. Conopco, Inc., 999 F.Supp. 1417 (D.Kan.1997).

44. "It is true, as Conopco asserts, that Armstrong's conclusion was based in part on his stated opinion that human hair by itself (i.e. without an outside fuel source) will not sustain combustion and that this view in turn was founded in large part on Armstrong's personal experience. That fact alone, however, does not make it an illegitimate basis for consideration." *Id.* at 1420.

45. 1999 WL 203349 (N.D.Ill.1999).

46. *Id.* at 5.

Kumho Tire and state with some particularity what the underlying knowledge was, and why it was or was not sound.

This is an issue that undoubtedly will continue to be confronted. Courts would be well advised to unpack the claimed "experience" in order to discover what was learned from it and whether that something supports a valid and reliable expert opinion. As stated in the commentary to the recently revised Fed. R. Evid. 702, "the witness must explain how that experience leads to the conclusion reached, why that experience is a sufficient basis for the opinion, and how that experience is reliably applied to the facts."[47]

§ 7–1.4 Accelerant–Detecting Canines

Without requiring evidence of the ability of dogs in general to detect accelerants, or data concerning the accuracy of the particular dog in question, some courts have allowed the dogs' handlers to testify concerning the presence of accelerants at fire scenes based on the "alerts" of their dogs. This has occurred despite the newness of the technique and the applicability of *Daubert* in those jurisdictions.[48] Such research as has been conducted suggests canines used in this capacity are prone to making false positive errors.[49] Accordingly, the professional association of arson investigators has cautioned against reliance on canines for the detection of accelerants.[50]

Though most courts admitting canine accelerant detection evidence have done so without awareness of the research and professional association prohibition on the evidence, the U.S. Court of Appeals for the Second Circuit has gone to considerable lengths to twist the data and the cautions into unrecognizable form so as to uphold a district court's admission of dog sniff evidence. In *United States v. Marji*,[51] the Court of Appeals evaluated the district court's admission of dog alert evidence and found no error.

---

47. Advisory Committee Notes, Amendments to Fed.R.Evid. 702 (effective December 1, 2000).

48. Admission of evidence of dog alert evidence was upheld in: Reisch v. State, 628 A.2d 84 (Del.Supr.1993); State v. Buller, 517 N.W.2d 711 (Iowa 1994). Evidence from canine arson investigation was admitted in other cases, but the admissibility was not challenged. *See e.g.*, Auto–Owners Insurance Company v. Ogden, 667 So.2d 743 (Ala.1995) (table) (aff'd; rehearing denied; all opinions withdrawn); State v. Bernier, 1995 WL 70337 (Conn.Super.1995); In re W.T.B., 771 So.2d 807 (La.App.2000).

49. The Illinois State Police Bureau of Forensic Sciences conducted an experiment in which they placed known quantities of known substances in containers, and tested the sensitivity (how small a sample can be detected) and selectivity (distinguishing accelerants from other pyrolyzed substances) of both dogs and gas chromatographs or mass spectrometers. They found that while one dog did quite well, other dogs "were indicating on the pyrolyzed carpeting and foam padding samples, as well as on pine wood. . . ." They conclude that because dogs are "not very selective," "a positive alert must always be corroborated by the labora-

tory." George Dabdoub et al., *Accelerant Detection Canines and the Laboratory*, 1995 PROCEEDINGS OF THE AMERICAN ACADEMY OF FORENSIC SCIENCES 19. *See* § 2.1.1[2].

50. The International Association of Arson Investigators adopted an official position which stated that until there is sufficient research to confirm that canines actually can discriminate between real accelerants and the wide array of other ignitable compounds, "[a]ny alert or indication not confirmed by laboratory analysis must be considered a false positive . . . for the purposes of origin and cause determination." They concluded: "If the forensic laboratory examination of the sample is negative for the presence of identifiable ignitable liquids, any positive indication by the canine of that sample *must* be deemed as *not relevant*." IAAI Forensic Science Committee Position on the Use of Accelerant Detection Canines, (Sept.1994). *See infra* § 2.1.1[2].

51. 158 F.3d 60, 63 (2d Cir.1998) ("Although the defendant cites some studies and a proposed amendment to the National Fire Protection Association's Guide for Fire and Explosion Investigations to the effect that dog-sniff evidence is not always reliable, all that these

The Court of Appeals seems to have presumed the soundness, and therefore the admissibility, of dog sniff evidence. The Court misconstrues the nature of error rate data when it states that dog alerts are "not always reliable," and it implies that the dogs usually are reliable. The Court essentially begs the empirical question to be decided. Reliability of a technique cannot be measured on an instance-by-instance basis but only in the aggregate, and the aggregate measure inevitably will show some level of accuracy (hits and correct rejections) and some level of inaccuracy (misses and false alarms). By the standard used by this panel, few if any techniques could ever be found so unreliable that they would have to be excluded. When the Circuit Court states that "all that these sources suggest is that special weight should not be assigned to dog-sniff evidence in the absence of any corroborating evidence," it misrepresents what those sources say and what they mean. The fire and arson field regards dog sniff evidence as merely a preliminary screening test that gives leads to an investigator but which ought not be offered as evidence unless and until it has been confirmed by laboratory testing. That is a far cry from cautioning against giving "special weight" "to dog-sniff evidence in the absence of any corroborating evidence." The Court transforms the field's advice that the evidence should be given no weight into a conclusion that it should be given no more than normal weight.

Finally, the Circuit Court concluded that "even if we were to assume arguendo that the district judge's decision to allow this expert testimony was erroneous" the error was harmless. The Circuit Court would have accomplished the same result, while placing itself on ground more consistent with the empirical evidence on dog alerts, to have concluded that, although the district court erred by admitting the dog-sniff evidence without sufficient basis for believing in its dependability, the error was harmless in light of other evidence in the case on the question of the presence of accelerants.

In other cases, courts found the use of dogs to establish the presence of accelerants to be unreliable and therefore inadmissible.[52]

§ 7–1.5   On Whom Can Fire Experts Rely for the Data on Which They Base Their Conclusions?

The case-specific information on which fire and arson experts base their conclusions sometimes includes the observations or inferences of others. To what extent can a fire investigator rely on the statements and conclusions of others? In *Westfield Insurance Co. v. Harris*,[53] a fire marshal relied for most of his information upon the investigator hired by one of the parties, thereby making his own conclusions the product of someone else's investigation and

---

sources suggest is that special weight should not be assigned to dog-sniff evidence in the absence of any corroborating evidence. We conclude that the trial judge did not abuse his broad discretion under *Daubert* in admitting the testimony. We note further that, even if we were to assume arguendo that the district judge's decision to allow this expert testimony was erroneous, there was substantial additional evidence offered at trial demonstrating that an accelerant was used by the defendant to start the fire.")

52. People v. Acri, 277 Ill.App.3d 1030, 214 Ill.Dec. 761, 662 N.E.2d 115 (Ill.App.1996); Carr v. State, 267 Ga. 701, 482 S.E.2d 314 (Ga.1997); Farm Bureau Mutual Insurance Company of Arkansas, Inc. v. Foote, 341 Ark. 105, 14 S.W.3d 512 (Ark.2000) (adopting *Daubert* as the test for admissibility of expert evidence in Arkansas, and finding that dog sniff evidence for the detection of accelerants failed the test).

53. 134 F.3d 608 (4th Cir.1998).

less than independent. In light of this, the district court had the fire marshal's evidence stricken from the record. The Court of Appeals vacated and remanded, holding that "it is within the fabric of the State Fire Marshal's official duties to receive and rely on insurance company information about fires within his jurisdiction."

In *Minersville Safe Deposit Bank & Trust Co. v. BIC Corp.,*[54] the plaintiffs claimed that a fire had been caused by a BIC lighter. Their experts, a fire marshal and an independent fire investigator, based their opinions about causation on the statements of a three year-old boy who said he had started the fire with a lighter. The district court in this case held that reliance on the child's statement was inadmissible hearsay, excluded the experts' testimony, and granted the defendant's motion for summary judgment.

§ 7–1.6 Who Bears the Burden of Proof in a *Daubert* Hearing?

At one level the answer to the question in the heading should be obvious: the proponent of evidence always bears the burden of persuading the court that the conditions for its admission are met. But the question has nevertheless led to confusion in *Daubert* hearings on a variety of expert areas, and one particularly confusing instance arose in the context of a proffer of expert evidence on fire causation.

Maryland Casualty Co. v. Therm–O–Disc, Inc.[55] involved a fire that began in a clothes dryer, allegedly due to a malfunctioning part. The district court initially placed the burden on the opponent of the expert witness to show that the testimony could not meet the requirements of *Daubert*. Here is the Fourth Circuit's recitation of what happened:

> Neither party disputes that, at the beginning of the *Daubert* hearing, the district court told Jim Rothschild, counsel for Therm–O–Disc, "[y]ou have the burden of proof" with regard to Rodems's testimony. However, counsel immediately corrected the district court on this point, and from then forward it appears that the district court understood both the demands of *Daubert* and its own role as "gatekeeper," and conducted the hearing accordingly. Immediately after the objection, the district court withdrew its call for Mr. Rothschild to come forward and show that Rodems's testimony was not admissible, and called Rodems himself to the stand to explain the basis for that testimony. This Rodems did under both direct and cross-examination. After several hours of testimony, the district court determined that, although it had some reservations about the proffered basis for Rodems's opinion, "the defendant has failed to establish ... [that] Mr. Rodems relied upon a scientific principle that was not valid."[56]

Although the Court of Appeals goes to considerable (and confusing) lengths to try to establish both that there is no burden of persuasion in a 104(a) hearing and that the district court did not err because it placed the burden where it was supposed to be, the final sentence in the quotation above—offered in support of the correctness of the district court's hearing process—should leave

54. 176 F.R.D. 502 (E.D.Pa.1997).   **56.** *Id.* at 784.

55. 137 F.3d 780 (4th Cir.1998).

readers wondering if, at the end of the day, the district judge did understand who bore the burden of persuasion, if there is a burden of persuasion.

The confusion in *Daubert* hearings is perhaps understandable, because the first voice heard is that of the *opponent* of proffered expert testimony. This has given some lawyers and judges the impression that the opponent has the burden of convincing the court that the witness does not meet *Daubert's* requirements. This impression may be all the more compelling when the expertise being challenged is a type that has become familiar to the courts. But the correct procedure is the opposite of that.

The opponent of expert evidence need only make a showing sufficient to convince a trial court that the objection to the evidence is not frivolous; this triggers a *Daubert* hearing under Rule 104(a). In a Rule 104(a) hearing on the question of admissibility of expert evidence, "These matters should be established by a preponderance of proof."[57] This statement of a standard of proof implies that the hearing is analogous to a civil bench trial. The proponent has the initial burden of production and the ultimate burden of persuading the court that the proffered expert evidence satisfies Rule 702, as interpreted by *Daubert* and *Kumho Tire*. The trial judge serves as the factfinder.[58] And the judge must believe the expert's opinion by a preponderance of the evidence.[59] Thus, if both parties sat mute, the court would have to rule against the party with the burden of persuasion, namely, the proponent of the evidence. If at the end of the hearing, the evidence on the evidence were in equipoise, again the court would have to rule against the proponent of the evidence.

§ 7–1.7 Nature of Scrutiny Following *Kumho Tire*

Because *Kumho Tire* closed off the major route by which fire and arson experts had been seeking to evade scrutiny under *Daubert*, one might expect courts to be subjecting experts of many kinds, including fire and arson experts, to more rigorous inspections following *Kumho*. Though limited in number, and revealing a ratio of about 50:50 (close scrutiny to relaxed scrutiny), it does seem that the courts are indeed beginning to step up the level of rigor employed in their evaluations of fire and arson expertise under *Daubert* and *Kumho Tire*. It might be misleading to point out that every one of the cases of more vigorous scrutiny and exclusion occurred in the context of a civil action, because almost all of the cases in which the expertise was challenged were civil cases.

In *Weisgram v. Marley*,[60] discussed in greater detail above, the Eighth Circuit Court of Appeals found plain error in the admission of three expert witnesses who had been permitted to testify by the District Court. A fire department officer who investigated the fire in the home was held not qualified to give expert testimony as to whether or not a baseboard heater in the home malfunctioned, or how the heater might have ignited other objects.

57. *Daubert* 509 U.S. at 593 n. 20.

58. Note that Rule 104(a) also provides: "In making its determination [the court] is not bound by the rules of evidence except those with respect to privileges."

59. This still does not answer the question of how much error is too much error to be admissible. For example, would expert predic-

tions that are shown by all of the available evidence on the evidence to be correct only 51% of the time be sufficiently "reliable" to be admissible? Would expert predictions that are wrong more often than they are right be admissible?

60. 169 F.3d 514 (8th Cir.1999).

A fire investigator's testimony that the baseboard heater was defective and caused the fire was held to be unsupported by sufficient foundation because no studies had been conducted to test the investigator's theory. Finally, the Court held that the expert testimony of a metallurgist that thermostat contacts on the baseboard heater were defectively designed was not supported by sufficient foundation because the metallurgist had little knowledge about this type of heater or this particular model heater. The rulings of the Court of Appeals were affirmed by the Supreme Court.[61]

In *Pride v. BIC Corp.*[62] the plaintiff's three experts were excluded by the District Court (following the recommendation of a Magistrate Judge), and the exclusion was upheld by the Sixth Circuit Court of Appeals. The plaintiff's husband had burned to death in a fire which the plaintiff argued had been caused by the defendant's defective cigarette lighter. In a thoughtful and detailed opinion, the Court of Appeals upheld the exclusion of a mechanical engineer, an analytical chemist, and a local fire inspector, all of whose methods it found inadequate to support their opinions.

Werner v. Pittway Corp.[63] was a suit alleging defective smoke detectors. The District Court excluded the plaintiff's expert witness, finding that the expert offered nothing but a "bare conclusion" regarding the type of detector the plaintiffs' used, and offered no explanation whatsoever regarding the reasoning process that would have permitted him to reach this conclusion.

In *Donnelly v. Ford Motor Co.*[64] the plaintiff claimed that his Ford had a defective ignition switch, which caused the automobile fire in which he was injured. The expert's report asserted his experience and his conclusion to "a reasonable degree of engineering certainty" that "any fire in [one of the defendant's vehicles], in which arson has been eliminated as the cause, that has its origin under the driver side dash and in the area of the steering column can be directly linked to the vehicle ignition switch and system."[65] The report lacked any explanation of the expert's reasoning. A supplemental report contained an explanation insofar as the expert rebutted the defendant's experts, but the court held that "is not a substitute ... for setting forth the reasoning or methodology by which he formed the opinions in his own reports...."[66]

Finally, in *Comer v. American Electric Power,*[67] the plaintiff claimed a power surge caused a fire that seriously damaged his house. The defendant power company's expert agreed that arcing in a panel distribution box led to the fire, but the two sides's experts disagreed about the cause of the arcing condition. Awaiting guidance from the Supreme Court in *Kumho Tire*, the district court delayed ruling on the motion until after the jury returned a verdict for the plaintiff. In granting a motion for judgment as a matter of law the court held the plaintiff's expert evidence inadmissible. The court held that the plaintiff's expert's testimony was based only on personal knowledge and experience, lacked a more sound basis, and therefore his opinions were nothing more than unsupported speculation, inadmissible under *Daubert*,

---

61. 528 U.S. 440, 120 S.Ct. 1011, 145 L.Ed.2d 958 (2000).

62. 218 F.3d 566 (6th Cir.2000).

63. 90 F.Supp.2d 1018 (W.D.Wis.2000).

64. 80 F.Supp. 2d 45 (E.D.N.Y.1999).

65. *Id*. at 49.

66. *Id*. at 50.

67. 63 F.Supp.2d 927 (N.D.Ind.1999).

Joiner and *Kumho Tire*. In commenting on the "lack [of] factual, technical, or scientific support,"[68] the court expressed particular disapproval of the expert's flexibility in reaching opinions:

> Indeed, one marvels at the breath-taking ease with which [the expert] offers his 'expert' opinions, surpassed only by his apparent ability to change them based on nothing more than the mere suggestion of counsel. With such an approach, unshackled as it is to any sort of factual, scientific or technical analysis, [the expert's] testimony easily accommodates whatever theory or time interval is needed by his client.[69]

On the other hand, a number of other cases admitted expert witnesses with minimal scrutiny of the methodology and reasoning (if any) underlying the proffered testimony to determine if it rested on a valid, and therefore admissible, foundation. These include the following cases.

Call v. State Industries[70] involved a claim that the defendant's water heater caused the fire that destroyed the plaintiffs' home. The trial resulted in a jury verdict for the plaintiffs. On appeal, the defendant challenged, *inter alia*, the admissibility of the plaintiff's expert witnesses. The Tenth Circuit Court of Appeals offered only a cursory review of the challenged expert testimony, never explaining how it, or the lower court, reached the conclusion that the testimony was reliable, or what factors it used to reach that conclusion. This would seem to be the very abuse of discretion (a failure to explain what factors were used, why they are appropriate, and why they lead a court to its conclusion on admissibility) that Justice Scalia warned against in his concurrence in *Kumho Tire*.

Allstate v. Maytag,[71] discussed in more detail above, relied entirely on the qualifications of the experts and made no assessment of the basis of the proffered knowledge to opine whether a cooktop was the source of a house fire.

Abu-Hashish v. Scottsdale Insurance Co.[72] allowed the defendant's experts to testify from their observations of burn patters that the fire at issue was not accidental, with no deeper scrutiny of how they could infer causation from what they observed.[73]

Cooper v. Toshiba Home Tech. Corp.[74] admitted a plaintiff's expert who would opine that the fire was caused by a defective kerosene heater made by the defendant. The court admitted the expert on the basis that he was qualified, having "written or presented on issues of fire and arson over three hundred times.... [and] he holds a patent for an anti-flareup device for kerosene heaters."[75] As to the expert's failure to test his hypothesis that a flareup had caused the fire in this case, the court held that such testing was not required, but only that "[t]he expert's conclusions simply must not be 'subjective belief or unsupported speculation.' "[76]

68. *Id.* at 937.

69. *Id.* at 935.

70. 221 F.3d 1351 (10th Cir.2000) (Table).

71. 1999 WL 203349 (N.D.Ill.1999).

72. 88 F.Supp.2d 906 (N.D.Ill.2000).

73. Fire and arson experts have subscribed to numerous beliefs about the relation of features of a burned structure's remains and the cause of the fire, recently determined to be unreliable indicators. *See infra* § 2.1.1[1].

74. 76 F. Supp. 2d 1269 (M.D.Ala.1999).

75. *Id.* at 1278.

76. *Id.*

In *United States v. Gardner*,[77] a criminal case, the court engaged in no apparent scrutiny of the government's expert, but merely asserted by ipse dixit that the government's proffered expert met the standard for admission.

§ 7–1.8 State Cases

Three fire cases from the state courts are noteworthy.

In *Mensink v. American Grain*,[78] the Iowa Supreme Court confronted the same question the U.S. Supreme Court did two years later, in *Kumho Tire*, namely, whether (Iowa's version of) *Daubert* applies to all experts or only to "scientific" experts. The plaintiff had been seriously injured by a dust explosion in a grain elevator that was struck by lightning. The plaintiffs argued, *inter alia*, that the elevator could have and should have installed lightning protection devices, and offered a retired professor of electrical engineering to testify to that opinion. The jury found for the plaintiff. The defense appealed, and the case was reversed and remanded on grounds other than the expert witness issue.

As to the expert issue, the defendants argued unsuccessfully that the plaintiffs' expert should have been excluded under *Daubert* because he had no experience with grain elevators, though he had extensive experience in lightning protection. The court also rejected the argument that the basis of the expert's opinion failed *Daubert's* reliability criteria and was inadmissible for that reason. *Daubert* was held to be inapplicable because, the Court concluded, it is limited to "evidence of a complex nature," which the Court took to mean scientific evidence as opposed to "technical or other specialized knowledge." In this case, the expert had considered factors like the type of building construction and topography of the surrounding area, which the court believed were readily understood by lay jurors. This narrow reading of *Daubert* limits it to "complex" or "scientific" expert evidence, and to the explicit *"Daubert* factors:" rather than taking the case to stand for the more general proposition that all expert testimony must be found to be valid before it can be admitted. *Kumho Tire*, of course, took this latter tack, holding that all expert evidence, regardless of how it is labeled, must be found to be valid before it can be admitted. Whether Iowa or other state courts will follow the Supreme Court's broader reading in *Kumho Tire* remains to be seen.

At trial in the Texas case of *Doyle Wilson Homebuilder, Inc. v. Pickens*,[79] the plaintiffs won damages for the value of their 18–month old home which had burned to the ground while they were away. Their theory of the fire was that defective or improperly installed wiring caused the fire, and their claim was brought against the general contractor. Though it reversed on other grounds, the Court of Appeals rejected the defendant's challenge to the admissibility of the plaintiffs' electrical engineer (no challenge having been made against the plaintiffs' other expert, a fire investigator). The case is interesting for the remarkably thoughtful and detailed care the court of appeals gave to reviewing the details of the experts' testimony. Yet despite that detailed care, the court nevertheless accepted without question the soundness of whatever theory or empirical data or experience underlay the

77. 211 F.3d 1049 (7th Cir.2000).   **79.** 996 S.W.2d 387 (Tex.App.-Austin 1999).

78. 564 N.W.2d 376 (Iowa 1997).

opinions offered. This case highlights the difficulty counsel have in seeing that some experts may (or may not) be offering poorly grounded opinion (where in this case counsel for the defense challenged one but not the other expert). And the difficulty judges sometimes have in looking underneath the opinions and procedures of experts to try to discern the validity of the knowledge upon which it purports to stand.

Finally, *In re W.T.B.*[80] involved a Louisiana juvenile who was adjudicated delinquent for setting fire to a high school building. On appeal he argued that the trial court should not have accepted expert testimony that the fire in question was started with an accelerant. An engineer employed by the school's insurer concluded the fire was caused by an electrical problem. But the Louisiana Court of Appeals affirmed. Citing *Daubert*, the court noted that the fire investigator was well qualified and had 23 years training and experience. His opinion was "based upon the pattern of damage in [the area where he determined the fire had started] and the reaction of the dogs used in the investigation that were trained to sniff the presence of accelerants."[81] Since some of the field's beliefs about burn patterns have been found to be fallacious[82] and dog sniff evidence produces what the field regards as an unacceptably high risk of false positive errors,[83] this is a good example of why a court ought not to be relying on vague assurances from the expert witness but should require hard evidence on the soundness of the proffered testimony before admitting it. As to the contradictory report by the insurer's engineer, that was properly treated as competing evidence which the finder of fact has the duty to weigh and judge.[84]

B. SCIENTIFIC STATUS

by

John J. Lentini*

§ 7–2.0 THE SCIENTIFIC BASIS OF EXPERT TESTIMONY ON FIRES, ARSONS, AND EXPLOSIONS

§ 7–2.1 Introductory Discussion of the Science

The scientific study of fires, arsons, and explosions is unique among the forensic sciences for two reasons. First, the fire or explosion tends to destroy the very physical evidence which can be used to establish the cause, so in the

80. 771 So.2d 807 (La.App.2000).

81. *Id.* at 813.

82. *See infra* § 2.1.1[1].

83. *See supra* § 1.4 and *infra* § 2.1.1[2].

84. When a trier of fact "is confronted with a decision of which expert opinion to credit, a determination of the weight of evidence is a question of fact which rests solely with the trier of fact." *Id.*

* John J. Lentini is a fire investigator and chemist who manages the fire investigation division of Applied Technical Services of Marietta, Georgia. He is a fellow of the American Academy of Forensic Sciences and the American Board of Criminalistics, holds certificates from the National Association of Fire Investigators and the International Association of Arson Investigators. He chairs the ASTM Committee Responsible for developing forensic science standards, and is a principal member of the National Fire Protection Association's Technical Committee on Fire Investigations. Mr. Lentini has investigated more than 1500 fires, analyzed more than 20,000 samples of fire debris, and testified on more than 200 occasions.

case of arson, it is first necessary to prove that a crime has been committed. Second, the vast majority of practitioners of this "scientific" endeavor are not scientists and have little, if any, scientific training or education. While there are other forensic disciplines where technical skills learned on the job may provide adequate training (e.g., fingerprints, firearms identification, and handwriting comparison), it is difficult to argue that reasonable conclusions about fires can be drawn by individuals who have a limited understanding of the chemistry and physics of fire pattern development. Yet, the vast majority of practitioners do not possess a bachelors degree. With the exception of the chemists, who spend most of their time in the laboratory and most of their efforts on detecting minute quantities of flammable, combustible, or explosive material, the people who investigate fires and explosions got their experience one fire at a time, as fire fighters, and later as fire investigators. As such, the body of knowledge used by investigators is divided into two parts: the scientific literature and the anecdotal reports of field investigators.

Because of the extensive destruction of physical evidence, those who investigate fires in the field, known as "cause and origin investigators," rely heavily on eyewitness testimony, and in the absence of that, a frequent occurrence, rely even more heavily on their previous experiences in analyzing small bits of evidence. Fire investigation has been likened to putting together a jigsaw puzzle, where the pieces are all scattered, but additionally, the pieces are frequently missing, and those that are present are frequently unrecognizable.

A fire investigator puts this puzzle together and reaches conclusions by comparing observations with expectations. The expectations have been developed from training and experience, but that training and experience may not necessarily have a solid scientific foundation. For this reason, it is imperative that before an investigator's opinion is taken seriously, the efforts taken to "calibrate" the investigator's expectations should be scrutinized. Most importantly, the presumptions which the investigator carries into each fire scene should be determined, as these presumptions will have a significant impact on the expert's credibility.

Observations that one investigator will use to show incontrovertible evidence of an incendiary origin might be found by another investigator to be an unimportant indicator of a secondary event that occurred long after the origin. There are major areas of disagreement on the ability of investigators to "read" burn patterns, particularly in fires that have burned for extended periods of time. There is also disagreement about an investigator's ability to interpret the condition of wires as evidence of electrical arcing, which might have caused the fire or may be a result of the fire. There are numerous other chicken-and-egg problems that arise in fires, due to the destructive nature of the event.

A major consequence of the destruction of the physical evidence is that very few criminal arson cases are brought. Most of the litigation surrounding fires occurs in the civil arena. Insurance companies are much more likely to deny a payment based on the belief that their insured committed arson than is a prosecutor to bring an arson case against that same individual with the same evidence. This is at least partly due to the lower standard of proof in civil cases. Likewise, in cases where a product or service defect is alleged to have caused a fire, the impetus to settle based on overwhelming evidence is frequently absent, because the evidence is seldom overwhelming, at least as compared to other cases. In the case of arson, the first task of the prosecutor is to prove that a crime has been committed–a task that in most other cases is much more easily accomplished, or hardly even necessary.

There is reasonably good agreement among forensic scientists regarding the proper testing of physical evidence in the laboratory. Consensus standards exist for most routine tests of fire debris. Standardization of field practices, however, is still controversial. One impetus for the standardization of the fire investigation field is the realization by fire investigators (and, indeed, most forensic scientists) that standards may be the key to admissibility. Another impetus for standardization springs from efforts at certification of both laboratory and field investigators. Because examinations are required to grant certification, a standard body of knowledge from which to develop such examinations also is required. Field investigator certification began in the mid-eighties, after a five-year development period. Laboratory investigator certification development began in the mid-seventies, but certification did not become universally available until 1993. Field investigators may obtain certification from either the International Association of Arson Investigators (IAAI) or the National Association of Fire Investigators (NAFI). Laboratory analysts may obtain certification from the American Board of Criminalistics (ABC).

§ 7–2.1.1 Field Investigations

Just as the type of evidence examined and the type of people examining the evidence differ from the field to the laboratory, the approach to the scientific analysis of fire behavior is radically different between the field and the laboratory.

[1] Test Burns

During the 1970s and 1980s, the Center for Fire Research at the National Bureau of Standards, now known as the National Institute of Standards and Technology (NIST), conducted hundreds of excellent test burns, and characterized the behavior of fire up to the point of flashover. Flashover is a transitional phase in compartment fires in which temperatures rise to a level sufficient to cause ignition of all exposed combustible items in the compartment. Most structure fires will eventually achieve flashover, unless there is intervention by fire fighters or unless there is an unusual occurrence which allows the release of the fire gases, thus preventing the heat build-up.[1]

In a typical flashover scenario, an item of burning fuel, typically a piece of furniture, releases heat and smoke into the room, but in its early stages, the fire is unaffected by the room itself. This is known as the "free-burning" stage, and the behavior of the fire at this stage is relatively simple and easily explained (heat rises). When the fire begins to interact with its enclosure, its behavior becomes much more complex. As the fire progresses, a layer of hot gases begins to form at the ceiling, and gradually banks down, becoming

§ 7–2.0

1. NATIONAL FIRE PROTECTION ASSOCIATION, STANDARD GUIDE FOR FIRE AND EXPLOSION INVESTI- GATIONS 17 (PUB. NO. 921) (1995) [hereafter, NFPA 921].

thicker and more charged with energy. Once the gas layer reaches a temperature in the neighborhood of 1100 to 1300F, the radiant heat coming from the gas layer is sufficient to ignite common combustibles.[2]

Unfortunately, the work of the Center for Fire Research was aimed at characterizing the behavior of materials up to the point of flashover, for purposes of improving the safety of structures and contents. Of the hundreds of fires conducted, none were examined to look at the aftermath, so there are almost no data from scientifically conducted test burns which give the field investigator any clues about what type of "burn patterns" remain behind after flashover has been achieved.

Other test burns take place on a regular basis, and are usually conducted at weekend seminars sponsored by local chapters of the International Association of Arson Investigators (IAAI). The reproducibility, and therefore, the validity of these tests varies widely from test to test, depending on the dedication of the test organizers. Many of these "burn exercises" are conducted merely to familiarize new investigators with what a flammable liquid pour pattern looks like, and to provide extinguishment exercises for fire crews.[3] The vast majority of burn exercises conducted over the years have been performed with these limited goals in mind. This approach has resulted in many trainees getting a one-sided view of fire investigation which has unfortunately been passed on to each successive generation of investigators.

As a result of criticism of this practice, fire investigation groups are now beginning to try to simulate accidental fires, and to collect more data from the fires they set. A properly instrumented test burn may have as many as two hundred thermocouples and several radiometers collecting data. A typical test burn conducted by professional fire investigators has fewer than ten thermocouples and no radiometers. The behavior of the fire is usually recorded on video tape.

Two types of test burns have been attempted. The vast majority of test burns are set up to test one or more hypotheses about the general behavior of fire. If the test burn is narrowly focused in terms of the questions it seeks to answer, it is possible for useful information to be derived. Frequently, however, because structures that are available to burn are a rare resource, multiple burns are scheduled for the same structure, but the validity of subsequent tests is questionable.

The second type of test burn aims to reconstruct a particular fire, even though it is generally accepted that no two fires are alike, and an exact reconstruction is impossible. A simple change, such as leaving an interior door open when it should be closed, can drastically affect the behavior of a fire. About the best that can be hoped for is to reasonably reproduce a fire in a single compartment. This requires an exact match of interior finish and furnishings, something which is difficult to ascertain after a severe fire. Because of the time and enormous expense ($10,000—$100,000) involved in full scale test burns, they are usually conducted only when there have been multiple deaths or when the damages are in the millions of dollars.

2. *Id.*

3. NATIONAL FIRE PROTECTION ASSOCIATION, STANDARD ON LIVE FIRE TRAINING EVOLUTIONS IN STRUCTURES (PUB. NO. 1403) (1992).

The U.S. Fire Administration released a new report on the study of fire patterns in July of 1997.[4] A Fire Pattern Research Committee conducted ten full-scale fire tests, four at NIST headquarters in Gaithersburg, Maryland, two in residences in Florence, Alabama, and four in residences in Santa Ana, California. All of the test fires were instrumented and recorded, and the results of the tests are presented in a 210–page report. Many of the concepts, investigative systems, dynamics of pattern production, and pattern analysis concepts put forward in NFPA 921 were confirmed by the program's testing. Several of the "old fire investigators' tales" and fire investigation misconceptions that are repudiated in NFPA 921 were also shown to be unsubstantiated by the program testing.

The "old investigators' tales" whose repudiation was confirmed by this testing included:

- Wide V's versus narrow V's (which were erroneously thought to reflect the "speed of a fire")

- Crazing of window glass (which was erroneously thought to indicate rapid heating—it actually indicates rapid cooling—a much less significant phenomenon)

- Char blisters and speed of fire (large, shiny blisters were thought to indicate a rapid fire, while small flat blisters were thought to indicate a slower fire)

- Window sooting/staining (formerly thought to signify the type of fuel that had burned)

- Color of smoke and flame (also thought to be indicative of the type of fuel that was burning)

Throughout the ten test burns, it became apparent that a major factor in fire pattern development, namely ventilation, was the least understood. The study concluded that much more research needs to be directed at studying the effects of ventilation on the development of fire patterns.

[2] Accelerant Detecting Canines

In the early 1980s, the Bureau of Alcohol, Tobacco & Firearms and the Connecticut State Police pioneered the use of accelerant detecting canines. This practice has spread as its efficacy has become more apparent.[5] One of the central problems in fire investigation, particularly in arson investigation, is the location of suitable samples for submission to a laboratory so that the presence of ignitable liquids can be confirmed. Because most of these liquids have an odor, it is surprising that it took as long as it did until the concept of accelerant detecting canines was explored. The canines have the ability to improve the efficiency of a fire investigation, by going straight to the location

4. Federal Emergency Management Agency, U. S. Fire Administration, USFA Fire Burn Pattern Tests–Program for the Study of Fire Patterns (FA 178) (Jul.1997).

5. Melissa F. Smith, Evidentiary Issues Surrounding Accelerants Detected by Canines (August 9, 1993) (Presentation to the Annual Meeting of the American Bar Association); Mi-

chael Kurz et al., *Evaluation of Canines for Accelerant Detection at Fire Scenes*, 39 J. Forensic Sci. 1528 (1994); George Dabdoub et. al., *Accelerant Detection Canines and the Laboratory*, Proceedings of the Annual Meeting of the American Academy of Forensic Sciences 19 (1995).

of the accelerant, and decreasing the likelihood of the submission of negatives to the laboratory, thus saving an enormous amount of resources. Like many scientific advances, however, the law has gotten ahead of it, and there are now individuals testifying as to the presence of ignitable liquids at a fire scene based on "alerts" from their canines, even though the laboratory has failed to confirm the indication. Given that there have been few scientific studies and even fewer published research papers on the subject of canine proficiency, this is a disturbing trend.[6] Most scientists in the fire investigation field hold that unless there is a positive laboratory analysis to confirm a canine alert, the alert is not useful in determining the cause of the fire, and is, therefore, irrelevant, both to the fire investigator and to the trier of fact.[7]

This widely held view has been codified in NFPA 921, discussed below. Because of concern over some misguided court decisions allowing the testimony of dog handlers regarding unconfirmed alerts, the NFPA passed a "Tentative Interim Amendment" (TIA) to its 1995 edition of the Guide for Fire and Explosion Investigations. Fearing that if they waited to voice their concerns in the 1998 edition of the document, the rapidly developing law on the subject would be too hard to change. Consequently, the Technical Committee on Fire Investigations declared (and the NFPA Standards Council agreed) that a "judicial emergency" existed. The TIA stated that the only legitimate uses for a canine were the selection of samples that had a higher probability of testing positive, and the establishment of probable cause for a warrant to search further. The TIA echoed the concerns expressed by the IAAI Forensic Science Committee, and was carried forward into the 1998 and 2001 editions of NFPA 921.[8]

As a result of the publication of the TIA, judges began to follow the guidance of the fire investigation community, and exclude evidence of unconfirmed alerts. In a murder case in Georgia a conviction was overturned because the trial judge allowed testimony about unconfirmed alerts into evidence,[9] and an appellate court in Illinois held that the trial judge appropriately excluded similar evidence.[10]

[3] Sniffers

Dogs were preceded into fire scenes by electronic sniffers, devices which first were developed in order to detect combustible gases in mines and in utility installations. These devices, while useful in eliminating negative samples, are widely believed to be prone to providing false positive alerts. A positive alert by an electronic sniffer is generally not accepted as an indication of the presence of ignitable liquids.

Commercially available electronic sniffers generally incorporate detection devices similar to those used on gas chromatographs. The simplest machines use thermal conductivity detectors. Flame ionization, photoionization and

---

6. State v. Buller, 517 N.W.2d 711 (Iowa 1994).

7. IAAI Forensic Science Committee et. al., *Position on Accelerant Detection Canines* (adopted September, 1994), 45 FIRE & ARSON INVESTIGATOR 22 (1994).

8. *See* NFPA 921, at §§ 12–5.9 and 14–5.3.4.

9. Carr v. State, 267 Ga. 701, 482 S.E.2d 314 (Ga. 1997).

10. People v. Acri, 277 Ill.App.3d 1030, 214 Ill.Dec. 761, 662 N.E.2d 115 (Ill.App.1996).

solid state models have been used. The more complex detectors are sometimes unable to withstand the fire scene environment. Solid state units with comparison modules, sold by Pragmatics, are probably the most popular unit in use today.

§ 7–2.1.2   Laboratory Analysis

[1]   Classification of Petroleum Products

Most of the people with science degrees who are interested in the study of fires conduct their investigations in the laboratory, where they examine samples brought to them by field investigators. The laboratory analysis of fire debris is one area of forensic science where there is a near consensus on methodology and terminology. Because of this consensus, there has been a considerable amount of research published on the characterization of ignitable liquid residues recovered from fire debris. Much of the credit for this general consensus goes to the International Association of Arson Investigators Forensic Science Committee and ASTM Committee E 30 on Forensic Sciences, which publishes Standard Test Methods for the separation and identification of ignitable liquid residues.[11]

The gas chromatograph (GC) has been the primary instrument used in the identification of petroleum based hydrocarbon liquids, which are the most commonly used accelerants. An identification not based at least in part on GC is probably invalid. Gas chromatographic techniques that are significantly at variance with the ASTM standards have a lower likelihood of being valid.

The identification is based on pattern recognition and pattern matching. The "pattern" arises because petroleum distillates are complex mixtures of up to three hundred compounds. There is, for example, no such entity as a "gasoline molecule." Gasoline, and most petroleum distillates, are resolved by the chromatographic column into separate compounds, usually in ascending order by size (molecular weight). The laboratory analyst comes to recognize the patterns produced by particular classes of petroleum products, and the "match" is made by overlaying the chromatogram from the sample extract onto the chromatogram of a known standard.

There is some room for judgment in this pattern matching, and it is for this reason that the use of mass spectrometry, coupled with gas chromatography, has gained much wider acceptance in recent years. While gas chromatography produces a pattern of peaks, the mass spectrometer is capable of identifying the compounds which produce the peaks. With gas chromatography, it may be possible to confuse patterns produced by background materials with patterns of petroleum based accelerants. This will be less likely to happen when gas chromatography/mass spectrometry (GC/MS) is used, since there is much less guesswork about the identity of the compounds causing the peaks on the chart. Caution is still required, however, since a piece of carpeting (or any combustible) breaking down in the process of combustion

11. AMERICAN SOCIETY FOR TESTING AND MATERIALS, STANDARD TEST METHOD FOR IGNITABLE LIQUID RESIDUES IN EXTRACTS FROM SAMPLES OF FIRE DEBRIS BY GAS CHROMATOGRAPHY (PUB. NO. E 1387) (2000); AMERICAN SOCIETY FOR TESTING AND MATE-RIALS, STANDARD TEST METHOD FOR IGNITABLE LIQUID RESIDUES IN EXTRACTS FROM SAMPLES OF FIRE DEBRIS BY GAS CHROMATOGRAPHY/MASS SPECTROMETRY (PUB. NO. E 1618) (2000).

may produce compounds that also are found in petroleum distillates. Thus, ASTM E 1387 and E 1618 advise analysts that merely detecting benzene, toluene, and xylenes, or higher molecular weight aromatics is not sufficient for identifying gasoline. The relative concentrations of all of the compounds of interest must be such that a recognizable pattern is produced.

In recent years, proficiency tests, manufactured by Collaborative Testing Services (CTS) and sponsored by the American Society of Crime laboratory Directors (ASCLD), have revealed that the error rate for laboratories using only gas chromatography is significantly higher (50 to 100% higher) than laboratories using GC/MS.[12] These same CTS studies show a decreasing reliance on GC alone (at least among CTS subscribers–arguably the better laboratories in the field), and may result in future changes in ASTM standards.

[2] Identification (Individualization) of Petroleum Products

Considerable work has been done regarding the individualization of ignitable liquids in order to tie a suspect to a source. Matching of gasolines has been demonstrated, but as a fire progresses and the gasoline becomes more evaporated, the identification becomes more difficult. The most useful components for individualizing a sample of gasoline are, unfortunately, the components which evaporate first in a fire. The individualization of other petroleum distillates has not been extensively studied, due mainly to the difficulty of the task. Unless there is some unusual compound dissolved in the petroleum distillate, identification is generally regarded as difficult, if not impossible.

Recent studies by environmental chemists, attempting to measure the age or source of petroleum discharges, have identified several classes of higher molecular weight compounds, more likely to survive a fire, which can be used for individualization. Considerable additional work is required before this technology will be applicable to fire debris analysis.[13]

§ 7–2.1.3 Sources

[1] Authoritative Publications

The industry standard for fire investigation is known as NFPA 921, STANDARD GUIDE FOR FIRE AND EXPLOSION INVESTIGATIONS.[14] The National Fire Protection Association is a nonprofit organization which promulgates all types of codes related to fires, including building codes, equipment specifications, guidelines for certification of individuals, and a guide for fire investigation. NFPA 921 is produced and maintained using the NFPA consensus process, which has been approved by the American National Standards Institute (ANSI). The Technical Committee on Fire Investigations, which drafted

---

12. COLLABORATIVE TESTING SERVICES, FLAMMABLES ANALYSIS REPORT No. 9716 (1998); COLLABORATIVE TESTING SERVICES, FLAMMABLES ANALYSIS REPORT No. 9816 (1999); COLLABORATIVE TESTING SERVICES, FLAMMABLES ANALYSIS REPORT No. 99–536 (2000).

13. S.A. Stout & A.D. Uhler, *Chemical "Fingerprinting" of Highly Weathered Petroleum Products*, PROCEEDINGS OF THE AMERICAN ACADEMY OF FORENSIC SCIENCES (Feb.2000).

14. *Supra* note 1.

NFPA 921, consisted of twenty-nine individuals, with membership strictly regulated by NFPA guidelines, including specified numbers of public officials, academics, insurance industry representatives and private experts. The general public has the opportunity to comment on all proposed language in the standard, and on all proposed changes. In general, however, only NFPA members are made aware of pending standards. The committee then votes on whether to accept or reject the comments from the individual submitters, some of whom may be members of the committee. The first edition of NFPA 921 was published in 1992, with no dissenting votes from committee members.

When this chapter was first published in 1997, the industry standard for fire investigation was the 1995 edition of NFPA 921, GUIDE FOR FIRE AND EXPLOSION INVESTIGATIONS. As a result of the receipt of more than 150 proposals for changes, the 1998 edition, which became effective in February of 1998, contained many substantial changes and clarifications.

One of the more interesting changes was the removal of the word "misconception" from the titles of many sections. A significant portion of the fire investigation community was offended by the use of the word "misconception" in the first two editions of the GUIDE. Proponents of the change argued that while the misconceptions might exist in some fire investigators' minds, the first two editions had cleared up many of those misconceptions. In most cases, the text of the chapter section was left intact, but the title was changed. For example, the sections entitled "Misconceptions about Char" and "Misconceptions about Spalling" had their titles changed to "Interpretation of Char" and "Interpretation of Spalling." The cautions regarding the potential for misinterpretation of these two artifacts remained in the text.

Another significant change was the removal of the section on certainty of opinions.[15] A consensus within the Committee developed regarding removal of these various levels of certainty. The Committee felt that they had been mistakenly equated by the legal community with burdens of proof–an easy mistake to make since some of the terms and their definitions plainly adopted terminology that borrowed from and tracked legal burden of proof concepts. Whatever the intention of the fire and arson community may have been, they provide an example of how to invite (and get) confusion. An attempt had been made to clear up the confusion between the 1992 and 1995 editions, but it was not successful. Elimination of the terminology altogether was judged to be the best available course. Now there is no standardization of certainty-of-opinion language among fire investigators.

In the 1998 edition, the chapter on electricity and fire and the interpretation of electrical artifacts was significantly expanded and improved. A chapter was added on building fuel gas systems and a large number of references were added to the explanatory material in the appendix.

Between 1998 and 2001, the NFPA received 183 proposals for changing NFPA 921, and over 500 comments on the Technical Committee's handling of those proposals.

15. Discussed in the 1997 edition of this chapter, John J. Lentini, *Fires, Arsons and Explosions: Field Investigations: Certainty of Opinions*, § 26–2.2.1[14], *in* MODERN SCIENTIFIC EVIDENCE: THE LAW AND SCIENCE OF EXPERT TESTIMONY (David L. Faigman, David H. Kaye, Michael J. Saks & Joseph Sanders eds., 1997).

The current edition of NFPA 921, released in February, 2001, includes a rewritten chapter on vehicle fires, and new chapters on fire deaths, human behavior in fires, analytical tools (including computer assisted fire modeling), wildfire investigations and building systems. Additionally, the GUIDE will be organized into three sections outlining what a fire investigator should know, how a fire investigator should conduct a routine investigation, and special topics in fire investigation.

Other significant additions to the 2001 edition include a discussion of spoliation of evidence, and a definition of those necessary activities that should not be considered spoliation, as well as a discussion of the process of elimination, an attempt to come to grips with the so-called "negative corpus" determination.[16]

The Technical Committee and the NFPA as a whole continued to endorse the scientific method as the appropriate way to investigate fires, turning back proposals to eliminate the word "science" in favor of a so-called "systematic" approach.

In late 1997, the Justice Department began working on national guidelines for fire and arson scene investigation. These guidelines were modeled after NATIONAL GUIDELINES FOR DEATH INVESTIGATION, a research report published by the National Institute of Justice (NIJ) in December of 1997.[17] The Technical Working Group assembled by NIJ at first recommended that the Justice Department simply purchase 15,000 copies of NFPA 921 and mail them to the nation's law enforcement agencies and fire departments. This suggestion was not adopted, and work on the national guidelines continued for three more years, culminating in the publication of a finished pamphlet in June 2000.[18] These national guidelines recommend a general procedure for the handling of fire and arson scenes, and specifically direct responsible officials to find a fire investigator capable of conducting a scientific scene inspection according to the recommendations of NFPA 921. The text urges adherence to other nationally accepted standards, such as those published by ASTM.

A similar guide was published at the same time dealing with the responsibilities to explosion or bombing scenes.[19]

Most fire investigators will, on cross examination, concede that NFPA 921 represents the industry standard for the conduct of fire investigations although it is "only a guide." Perhaps the most important concept embodied in NFPA 921 is the recognition that fire investigation must be based upon the scientific method.[20] This may seem obvious, but until recently, fire investigators based their conclusions upon their "technical knowledge" gained through education, training, and experience. The existence of NFPA 921 makes it more difficult for the investigator to rely solely upon anecdotal experience.

16. *See infra*, § 2.2.1[16].

17. NATIONAL MEDICOLEGAL REVIEW PANEL, NATIONAL GUIDELINES FOR DEATH INVESTIGATION (National Criminal Justice Reference Service (NCJ 167568) (1997)).

18. TECHNICAL WORKING GROUP ON FIRE/ARSON SCENE INVESTIGATION, USDOJ, FIRE AND ARSON SCENE EVIDENCE: A GUIDE FOR PUBLIC SAFETY PERSONNEL (June 2000), at http://www.ojp.usdoj.gov/nij/scidocs2000.htm.

19. TECHNICAL WORKING GROUP FOR BOMBING SCENE INVESTIGATION, USDOJ, A GUIDE FOR EXPLOSION AND BOMBING SCENE INVESTIGATION (June 2000), at http://www.ojp.usdoj.gov/nij/scidocs2000.htm.

20. NFPA 921, *supra* note 1, at 9.

As far as other authoritative sources or learned texts in the field, there is only one text that any group of fire investigators will be likely to agree upon as being authoritative, and that is KIRK'S FIRE INVESTIGATION, by John D. DeHaan.[21] This excellent basic text, which is understandable to nonscientists, explains most of the aspects of fire investigation that a typical investigator is likely to encounter. The first edition of this book was authored by Paul Kirk in 1969,[22] and it was the standard reference for over a decade. To appreciate the changes and improvements in the understanding of fire dynamics and fire investigation that have occurred since 1969, a review and comparison of the successive editions of this book is useful. This popular reference text on fire investigation, came out in its 4th Edition in 1997. There were several additions to the text, as DeHaan attempted to bring it more in line with NFPA 921.

[2]   Periodical Literature

There are several periodicals to which fire investigators may subscribe, and the reliability of the information in these periodical varies widely. FIRE TECHNOLOGY, a peer-reviewed journal, generally deals with highly technical aspects of fire behavior, such as computer modeling and the behavior of large liquid pool fires. Very few fire investigation articles have been published in FIRE TECHNOLOGY.

The most widely read fire investigation publication is THE FIRE & ARSON INVESTIGATOR, the official publication of the International Association of Arson Investigators. Publication in this journal may reflect a thorough peer review (for the more technical articles) or simply editorial review (for news reports or "op ed" pieces). Peer review began only in 1996. The IAAI, until then, elected instead to publish more of a newsletter than a scientific journal, in the belief that everyone is entitled to their own opinions and that the exclusion of articles, even highly technical scientific articles, because of the objections of peer reviewers was equivalent to "censorship."Fortunately, that view has changed.

FIRE FINDINGS, an independent publication, contains an interesting mix of fire-related news and reports of tests conducted by the magazine staff. Peer review is spotty, but much useful data can be found in this journal, and it is likely that review will increase as the magazine develops more depth in its editorial staff.

§ 7–2.2   Areas of Scientific Agreement and Disagreement

§ 7–2.2.1   Field Investigations

There are few fields where the ability of experts to disagree after viewing the same evidence is more of a problem than in fire investigation. Because so much of the physical evidence is destroyed by a fire, it is a rare fire that can be examined by more than one expert yet have only one conclusion reached about it. Generally, the more severe the fire, the less likely two individuals are to agree as to its cause. Certainly, the more thorough the investigation and

---

21.   JOHN D. DEHAAN, KIRK'S FIRE INVESTIGATION (4th ed.1997).

22.   PAUL KIRK, FIRE INVESTIGATION (1969).

the more information that is actually collected, the more likely these individuals are to be able to agree as to the cause of a fire.

[1]   The Behavior of Fire

With respect to the behavior of fire, all investigators will agree that there is a fire triangle consisting of heat, fuel, and oxygen. Some investigators will expand the triangle into three dimensions, and describe a fire tetrahedron, the fourth point of which is a sustained chemical reaction.[23] Fire investigators will all agree that heat rises, and that the principal means of fire spread are conduction, convection, and radiation.

When they actually begin to describe how a *particular* fire spread, however, many fire investigators ignore everything but convection, that is, the phenomenon which causes warm air to rise. This phenomenon also causes a fire to spread out in a "V" shaped pattern until it reaches an obstruction. Thus, seeking the bottom of the "V" shaped burn pattern should lead one to the origin.[24]

Unfortunately, this indication of a fire's origin is useful only when the fire is extinguished prior to achieving total room involvement . Once a fire has progressed beyond a certain point, items that were located near the top of the room catch fire and fall down, causing secondary ignitions, and additional "V" shaped burn patterns.[25] These may be falsely interpreted as evidence of a second point of origin. Since everyone agrees that an accidental fire can begin in only one place, multiple points of origin are generally considered to be an indicator of arson.

There is considerable disagreement in the fire investigation community about the ability of fire investigators to determine multiple origins when the fires have burned together. Some fire investigators insist that they have the ability to determine multiple points of origin even if a room has flashed over. They do this by looking at holes in the floor, and because holes in the floor represent "low burns," these are equated with multiple origins. NFPA 921 advises the investigator to be wary of numerous conditions which could result in "apparent" multiple origins.[26]

Low burns are also taken as an indication of the presence of flammable liquids. Since heat rises and fire burns up, the presence of a low burn is sometimes taken as an indication that there was "something" on the floor which held the fire down. While ignitable liquids will accomplish this task, radiation does an equally fine job of burning floors. If total room involvement has been achieved, there is no reason for a floor not to be burned.[27] The failure to take into account the effects of radiation may be a result of a general lack of understanding of this common and important means of heat transfer.[28]

When the floor is burned, there is a tendency on the part of some fire investigators to believe that, unless it has burned in a perfectly uniform manner, radiation can be ruled out as the cause of the low burning. This is

23.   NFPA 921, *supra* note 1, at 10.

24.   *Id.* at 34.

25.   *Id.* at 33.

26.   *Id.* at 129.

27.   *Id.* at 33.

28.   DeHaan, *supra* note 21, at 28.

based on the perception of flashover as being a uniform phenomenon.[29] Actually, the uniformity of the flashover event breaks down within the first few seconds. Additionally, most synthetic floor coverings have a tendency to tear open during a fire, thus leaving parts of the floor exposed and other parts of the floor covered. These alternating exposed and covered areas can result in the production of patterns, particularly on wooden surfaces, which look remarkably like patterns produced by flammable liquids.[30] This is a fact which is not yet accepted by many fire investigators, but the realization of their misperceptions has led to several well publicized reversals of convictions.[31] The 2001 edition of NFPA 921 contains several new photographs of what one would expect a flammable liquid pour pattern to look like, but which were actually created by radiation alone.[32]

The series of test burns conducted under the auspices of the USFA, discussed above, has generated much interesting data, but there has not been unanimous agreement on the correct interpretation of the data. Several comments critical of the series of tests were received by the NFPA Technical Committee on Fire Investigations when it proposed citing the final test report in NFPA 921.[33] Many of these criticisms cited the ''incomplete'' nature of the data, because funds ran out before all of the proposed tests could be completed. These arguments really did not focus on the quality or the interpretation of the data. Other, more legitimate, criticisms of the report focused on its conclusions about the cause of certain types of burn patterns, believed to have been caused by unique ventilation parameters, and on the suggestion of the report's authors that much meaningful data could be found in the depth of the ''calcination'' of gypsum wallboard.

[2] Accidental Fires

The vast majority of fire scene investigators receive their training as ''arson investigators.'' There are many fires, however, that are accidental in nature and which result in civil litigation. The trend toward subrogation in the insurance industry picked up considerable strength in the 1980s and shows no signs of abating. Thus, arson investigators are now called upon to determine accidental causes, with an eye toward pinning the blame on a manufacturer, or a provider of a service, or anyone other than the named insured. Competent investigators have the good sense to call in the appropriate engineering discipline once they have determined that a particular device is located at the origin. Most engineers are unable to determine the origin of a fire, but most fire investigators are unable to independently determine the cause of failure of an appliance or system.

29. Barker Davie, *Flashover*, 11 NAT'L FIRE & ARSON REP. 1 (1993).

30. John D. DeHaan et. al., *The Lime Street Fire*, 43 FIRE & ARSON INVESTIGATOR, Sep. 1992, at 41; NFPA 921, *supra* note 1, at 38.

31. State v. Knapp, No. CR 78779 (Superior Ct. of Arizona, Maricopa County, Feb. 11, 1987); State v. Girdler, No. 9809 (Superior Ct. of Arizona, Maricopa County, Jan. 3, 1991).

32. NFPA 921 (2001), *supra* note 1, at § 4–17.7.2.

33. Technical Committee Documentation, NFPA, Report on Proposals for the Fall, 2000, Meeting, at www.nfpa.org.; Technical Committee Documentation, NFPA, Report on Comments for the Fall, 2000, Meeting, at www.nfpa.org.

[3] Electrical Activity

Fire investigators agree that the electrical system can be used as a fire detector, in that the first point on an energized electrical circuit which is compromised by a fire is likely to be the first and only point on that circuit where arcing occurs.[34] There is some disagreement, however, about the characterization of arcing. There are many fires where one investigator will point to a piece of melted copper and identify it as arcing, while another investigator will look at the same piece and state that the melting of copper was caused by local fire temperatures in excess of the melting point of copper (1981 degrees F). The determination as to whether a bead of melted copper was caused by electrical or thermal activity can usually be resolved through an examination by a practiced electrical engineer.[35]

Some study has been conducted on the examination of arc beads, in order to determine whether they were created in an atmosphere full of smoke or in a smoke-free atmosphere. The theory is that an arc bead created in a smoke-free atmosphere was created toward the beginning of the fire, and may, in fact, have been the cause of the fire.[36] The ability to determine the elemental content of the atmosphere at the time an arc bead was created, however, has not been repeatedly demonstrated, and the significance of the atmospheric chemistry is a subject of debate.[37] Arcing occurs in almost all fires, and almost all arcing events are the result of a fire, rather than the cause of it. The search for the primary arc, however, has resulted in many disagreements among fire investigators and electrical engineers. The fact is that electrical arcing is not responsible for a large number of fires, but an arc can be shown to be a competent ignition source, although the typical arc lasts less than a second. Thus, electrical arcs are often mistakenly blamed for causing fires.[38]

Other electrical sources are frequently cited, correctly or incorrectly, as the cause of a fire. Heat producing appliances (clothes dryers, portable heaters, stoves, and ovens) are the most frequent causes of fires started with electrical energy.[39] Ballasts from fluorescent lights are probably the most frequently falsely accused electrical devices. When we consider the millions of these devices in use, it is not hard to imagine that there will be a ballast found within ten feet of the origin of almost any commercial fire.

Electronic equipment such as computers, stereo systems, and televisions often are blamed for fires. Television sets manufactured in the early 1970s were responsible for a very high number of fires. By 1993, the Consumer Products Safety Commission estimated that incidence was down to 0.4% of all residential fires, 2100 incidents causing 30 deaths.[40]

Each proposed electrical fire cause deserves careful evaluation. Some "indicators" of electrical causation, like some indicators of arson, have been studied and shown to be less valid than previously thought. Oversized fuses or

34. Richard Underwood & John J. Lentini, *Appliance Fires: Determining Responsibility*, 7 NAT'L FIRE & ARSON REPORT 1 (1989).

35. Bernard Beland, *Examination of Electrical Conductors Following a Fire*, 16 FIRE TECH. 252 (1980).

36. Robert Anderson, *Surface Analysis of Electrical Arc Residues in Fire Investigation*, 34 J. FORENSIC SCI. 633 (1989).

37. Bernard Beland, *Examination of Arc Beads*, 44 FIRE & ARSON INVESTIGATOR, Jun.1994, at 20.

38. DeHAAN, *supra* note 21, at 263.

39. U.S. CONSUMER PRODUCTS SAFETY COMMISSION, 1986 NATIONAL FIRE LOSS ESTIMATES (Oct. 1988).

40. DeHAAN, *supra* note 21, at 261.

breakers, unless very much larger than required, are generally incapable of supplying sufficient current to overheat a circuit. The condition of insulation on a cable may yield some information about overcurrent, particularly if the insulation has melted loose from the conductor. A comparison must be made with a similar unheated wire, however, to determine the original tightness of the insulation. The lack of loose insulation does not rule out overcurrent.[41]

The most frequently encountered problem in the examination of electrical evidence is one of cause and effect. Did the wire short and start the fire, or did the fire burn the insulation and cause the wire to short?

[4]   Cause and Effect

The same type of chicken-and-egg, or cause and effect, argument applies to other systems found in buildings, as well. The gas system, for instance, is frequently compromised by a fire, resulting in leaks observed after the fire. It is the goal of the fire investigator to determine whether the leak existed before the fire. This is often a more difficult question than the science is capable of handling, particularly if the leak occurs in a combustible line. Metallurgists can be of some assistance in determining the reason for a fracture, and can sometimes tell whether the metal broke while it was hot or cold.

The compromise of electrical and fuel systems by fire, and the confusion that it creates, is even more evident in vehicle fires. As a general rule, fire investigators will agree that, while fires can start in the engine compartment and move to the passenger compartment, the reverse is seldom true. Some of the early fire investigation literature pertaining to vehicles suggested that almost all vehicle fires were intentionally set, as all of the fires contained certain "indicators" of excessive heat.[42] These texts are now generally regarded as incorrect, as it has been shown that regardless of ignition method, the temperature achieved by a vehicle fire will approach 2000 degrees F, resulting in buckling and warping of body panels, melting and flowing of window glass, and a loss of seat spring temper. Thus, the intensity and duration of a vehicle fire cannot be interpreted as indicating or not indicating the presence of accelerants.[43]

In a structure fire, an investigator who can narrow the origin down to a three by three foot square is considered a hero. In a vehicle fire, a three by three foot square is the starting point, and unless the exact cause can be determined, the fire investigator will be looked upon as a failure. Thus, frequently investigators will seize upon a burned fuel line, or an arced electrical wire as the cause of a fire, when the evidence argues equally that the observed phenomenon is actually an effect.

[5]   Black Holes

Perhaps no type of fire is more difficult to investigate than the "black hole," a structure fire in which everything is reduced to ashes. Despite the

41.   *Id.* at 216.

42.   National Automobile Theft Bureau, Manual for Investigation of Vehicle Fires (1986).

43.   DeHaan, *supra* note 21, at 179.

difficulties of these investigations, fire investigators have been known to claim the ability to detect multiple origins in completely consumed structures, or to state, based on "indicators," that a fire burned hotter than normal or faster than normal.

The studies done by the Center for Fire Research have tended to put to rest the diagnosis of "faster than normal." If a piece of upholstered furniture is ignited, it can bring a room to total involvement within five minutes. Time to flashover as low as ninety seconds has been reported.[44] Once flashover occurs in a particular room, extension into nearby rooms can be exceedingly rapid, involving entire houses in as little as fifteen minutes.

The fire which burns "hotter than normal" has, in the past, been identified by examination of the metals and other noncombustible materials within a structure, in order to get a handle on the temperature which the fire achieved. In 1969, Kirk advised noting melted metals because:

> The investigator may use this fact to his advantage in many instances, because of the differences in effective temperatures between simple wood fires and those in which extraneous fuel, such as accelerant, is present.[45]

Contrast this advice with DeHaan, Kirk's successor, in 1991:

> While such melted metals cannot and should not be used as proof that the fire was incendiary, the fire investigator should note their presence, extent and distribution. Such information can be of help in establishing differences between normally fueled and ventilated accidental fires and those produced by enhanced draft conditions or unusual fuel loads from accelerants in incendiary fires.[46]

Thus, the modern text recognizes what blacksmiths and metallurgists have known for centuries: that increased ventilation can lead to increased temperatures. Despite this knowledge, fire investigators have frequently relied on the presence of melted copper to indicate a hotter than normal (accelerated) fire. This was particularly true of fires where the melting was found at floor level.

Melted steel was considered to be even more indicative of a "hotter than normal" fire. Steel has a melting temperature of 2100–2700 degrees F, depending on its elemental content. Multiple areas in a structure which exhibit melted steel, then, have been considered as indications of the use of flammable liquids to accelerate a fire.

Actually, it has been demonstrated that the flame temperature above a pool of flammable liquid is no greater than the flame temperature of a well-ventilated wood fire.[47] The purpose of an accelerant is to make the fire burn faster, by involving more materials sooner than they would be otherwise involved. These fires do not necessarily burn at higher temperatures. The rate of heat release is higher in an accelerated fire, as the BTUs are released over a shorter period of time. The temperature of the fire, however, and its ability to melt items such as steel and copper, is actually no different from that of an unaccelerated fire.

44. NFPA 921, *supra* note 1, at 18.

45. KIRK, *supra* note 22, at 145.

46. DeHAAN, *supra* note 21, at 173.

47. Richard Henderson & George Lightsey, *Theoretical Combustion Temperature*, 3 NAT'L FIRE & ARSON REPORT 7 (1985).

After the catastrophic Oakland fire of 1991, Lentini, Smith, and Henderson conducted a study to determine the validity of the "indicators of arson." They studied copper, steel, and glass in fifty of the houses that had been burned to completion. Most of the houses exhibited multiple "indicators" of arson, even though they are known to have burned in an accidental fire.[48]

[6] "Melted" Steel

Metallurgical laboratory analysis conducted as a follow-up to the Oakland study revealed that it is not possible to determine by visual inspection alone whether a piece of steel, particularly a small mass piece of steel such as a bed spring, has melted or merely oxidized. This distinction can only be made by microscopic examination of a polished cross section of the metal. Thus, steel that had been characterized as "melting," at temperatures of up to 2700 degrees F, may have actually been exposed to temperatures as low as 1300 degrees F for long periods of time, and gave an appearance that was wrongly interpreted as melting.[49]

[7] Crazed Glass

Glass is another material that changes as a result of exposure to the heat of a fire. Many texts have referred to the crazing of glass as an indication of rapid heating, and one widely circulated handbook went to far as to state that crazed glass was an indicator of nearby accelerants.[50] Crazed glass was also used as an important indicator in the trial of Ray Girdler, whose conviction was later overturned based on new scientific evidence.[51] Experiments conducted after the Oakland fire study revealed that no amount of rapid heating would cause crazing, but that rapid cooling, caused by the application of a water spray, would cause crazing in all cases, whether the glass was heated rapidly or slowly.[52]

[8] Concrete Spalling

Spalling is the explosive chipping up of concrete, caused by the application of heat. This phenomenon has been the subject of more rhetoric, and probably less research, than most of the other issues in fire investigation. It is one of the most misunderstood and improperly used evidentiary features in the field,[53] and was the basis of an unfortunate case in Alabama which resulted in a major punitive damage award against the insurance company which presented spalling as evidence of incendiary origin. In that case, the fire had reduced a two story house to a pile of rubble about a foot deep on top of the concrete slab basement floor. The fire investigator (the second one hired

48. John J. Lentini et al. *Baseline Characteristics of Residential Structures Which Have Burned to Completion: The Oakland Experience*, 28 FIRE TECHNOLOGY 195 (1992).

49. *Id.*

50. JOHN BARRACATO, BURNING, A GUIDE TO FIRE INVESTIGATION 4 (AETNA Casualty and Surety Company) (1986).

51. State v. Girdler, No. 9809 (Superior Ct. of Arizona, Maricopa County, Jan. 3, 1991).

52. John J. Lentini, *Behavior of Glass at Elevated Temperatures*, 37 J. FORENSIC SCI. 1358 (1992).

53. NFPA 921, *supra* note 1, at 27.

by the insurance company) cleared off a narrow area about ten feet in length and discovered that the floor was spalled. He then declared that a "trail of spalling" existed, and was incontrovertible proof of an arson fire. Despite the fact that the defendant's investigator found that the entire slab was spalled, this "trail" evidence was presented, resulting in the court rendering and the Supreme Court upholding the following characterization: "The presentation of his [the investigator's] testimony borders on the perpetration of a fraud upon the Court."[54]

There is an "old school" which holds that concrete spalling is an indication of the presence of flammable or combustible liquids, as well as a cadre of scientists (none of whom have published in a peer reviewed journal) who hold that it is impossible for a flammable liquid to cause spalling.[55] In the middle are the vast majority of fire investigators, who believe that spalling is just another facet of the "burn pattern," which may or may not indicate the presence of a flammable or combustible liquid, depending on the situation. Most fire investigators have seen containers of ignitable liquids which have spilled their contents onto a concrete floor, and in the exact place where the flammable liquid was located, spalling has occurred. The extrapolation of this anecdotal experience to all fires is, of course, an error, as is the contention that flammable liquids cannot cause spalling under any circumstances.

[9]   Colors of Smoke and Fire

Other indicators of unusual fire behavior that have fallen by the wayside include the color of smoke and the color of the flame. When these indicators first were promulgated by the teachers of fire investigation, they were considerably more valid than they are today. Wood and cellulose products tend to have a gray to white smoke, and burn with a yellow flame. Petroleum based products, such as most common ignitable liquids, burn with a sooty orange flame and produce large quantities of black smoke. In the past, it was thus possible to reach conclusions about what was burning, particularly in the early stages of a fire. In the modern structure, however, a large portion of the interior finish and furnishings consists of petroleum based products in the form of plastic films and fibers. A burning couch is just as likely to produce thick black smoke as is a burning pool of flammable liquid.

Once again, it is useful to contrast Kirk in 1969 with DeHaan in 1991. According to Kirk, "The presence of much black smoke, especially in the early stages of a building fire, is highly indicative of the presence and burning of a highly carbonaceous material, typical of many fire accelerants."[56] DeHaan, on the other hand, advises, "The combustion of [such] polymers contributes largely to the formation of greasy or sticky dense soot found at many fire scenes, and is responsible for the dense black smoke more frequently noted during the early stages of structure fires."[57] Not only is smoke color an unreliable discriminant between normal and abnormal fuels, it has lately been

54. United Services Auto. Ass'n v. Wade, 544 So.2d 906 (Ala.1989).

55. Dennis Canfield, *Causes of Spalling Concrete at Elevated Temperatures*, 34 FIRE & ARSON INVESTIGATOR, Jun.1984, at 22.

56. KIRK, *supra* note 22, at 61.

57. DEHAAN, *supra* note 21, at 80.

found that even ordinary wood fires can produce black smoke in the low oxygen conditions which occur following flashover.[58]

[10] Computer Modeling

As a result of the work conducted at the Center for Fire Research, several computer programs have been developed to predict the spread of a fire, given certain assumptions.[59] If certain facts are known about the configuration of the compartments and fuel packages in a building, and the spread of a fire, these can be plugged into the equation, and the initial conditions derived. Since it is the initial conditions that are of most interest in determining the origin and cause of a fire and its spread from that point, this is the best use to which these computer programs can be applied.

There are currently two types of computer modeling programs for fires: zone models and field models. A zone model divides each compartment into an upper zone and a lower zone, and predicts the conditions in each zone as a function of time. Zone models are useful for situations where a rough approximation will do, and have been used to closely predict, for instance, when flashover will occur, given a specific fire on a specific fuel package. Zone models can be run by a proficient modeler in a few hours on a personal computer. A typical zone model assumes that every part of the zone is uniform with respect to temperature and smoke concentration. Consequently, while the model may be able to predict when any sprinkler head might activate, it will be less reliable in predicting the activation of a particular sprinkler head.

Field models (also known as computational fluid dynamics or CFD models) are much more complicated. They divide each compartment into thousands or tens of thousands of small volumes, and calculate the fire's progress through each volume. This makes the field models much more precise, but they are much more difficult to work with compared to zone models. A multi-compartment field model may require the use of a mainframe computer for one to four weeks in order to perform all of the calculations.

The information required for both field and zone models is the same. A good description of the required inputs, as well as the limitations of computer models has been added to the 2001 edition of NFPA 921.

As in other areas of fire investigation, two experts provided with the same program can plug in different assumptions and reach different conclusions about the spread of the fire. This is because of the large number of variables which affect the fire's behavior. Although computer modeling has been touted as a method for testing an investigator's hypothesis, the vast majority of computer models that are likely to be presented to a jury will demonstrate, but not prove, an expert's opinion.

Because of their ability to graphically present the growth of a fire, computer models are becoming commonplace in fire litigation.

---

58. NFPA 921, *supra* note 1, at 21.

59.   HAROLD NELSON, FPETOOL USERS GUIDE (National Institute of Standards and Technology Pub. No. 4439) (1990).

[11] Fatal Fires

Fires that involve fatalities are more likely to become the subject of civil or criminal litigation than fires that cause only property damage. The methodology of investigating a fatal fire is exactly the same as the methodology involved in investigating a property fire, except that there is one important piece of evidence provided in the fatal fire: the body. In those cases where the victim dies at the scene, the body can provide invaluable information as to the condition of the atmosphere at the time of death.

Carboxyhemoglobin (COHb) and blood alcohol readings are imperative for a proper understanding of what occurred. Low carbon monoxide content in a victim's blood suggests that they were rapidly overcome by heat, and died from burn injuries, rather than smoke inhalation, the most common cause of fire death. Higher carbon monoxide concentrations (around 50%), on the other hand, suggest exposure to a gradual build-up of smoke. Still higher levels of CO suggest brief exposure to very high concentrations of toxic smoke. Such exposures are typical of victims found away from the origin of a fire. Those intimate with the originating fire are unlikely to be still breathing by the time the fire produces high concentrations of CO. Fire extending from the room of origin undergoing flashover can rapidly spread deadly concentrations of CO throughout the building.[60]

Low carbon monoxide (CO) concentrations have been used to indicate to a fire investigator that he was looking at an arson, rather than an accidental fire. The problem with this indication is that, like fire damage itself, carbon monoxide poisoning is a result of both the intensity of the exposure (carbon monoxide concentration) and the duration of the exposure. Exposure to a high concentration for a short period of time may result in the same carboxyhemoglobin level as exposure to a low concentration for a long period of time. For instance, exposure to a concentration of 0.05% CO (500 parts per million) for two to three hours will result in a COHb level of 30%. The same result is achieved by exposure to a concentration of 1% CO (10,000 parts per million) for one to five minutes.[61] Of course, a COHb concentration of zero is an indication that the victim was not breathing, and suggests that death may have preceded the fire.

An excellent review of carbon monoxide data compilations has been published by Gordon Nelson.[62]

The effects of incineration can also lead to mischaracterization of the events leading up to the victim's death. Muscle contraction caused by exposure to heat results in a pugilistic pose, which has led investigators to see the victim as fighting off an assailant.[63] Other artifacts of incineration include neck contusions, which have been interpreted as evidence of strangulation, and skull fractures, caused by the expansion of cranial contents, which have been misinterpreted as evidence of bludgeoning.[64] The knowledge and experi-

60. DeHaan, *supra* note 21, at 380.

61. *Id.* at 311.

62. G.L. Nelson, *Carbon Monoxide and Fire Toxicity: A Review and Analysis of Recent Work*, 34 Fire Technology 39 (1998).

63. DeHaan, *supra* note 21, at 308.

64. State v. Girdler, No. 9809 (Superior Ct. of Arizona, Maricopa County, Jan. 3, 1991).

ence of the medical examiner with burn victims should be carefully scrutinized before allowing these sorts of conclusions into evidence.

[12] Explosions

Procedures for investigating an explosion are similar to those used in fire investigations. A more detailed examination of the surrounding area is generally required, particularly in the case of chemical explosions.[65]

Historically, explosions have been difficult to define, because there are several types of explosions, some of which are difficult to distinguish from rapid combustion. For this discussion, let us describe an explosion as an event having the following four characteristics: high pressure gas, confinement or restriction of the pressure, rapid production or release of the pressure, and change or damage to the confining or restricting structure or vessel.

Two major types of explosions may occur: mechanical explosions, such as steam boiler explosions, and chemical explosions, which encompass combustion explosions and the detonation of high explosives.

In a mechanical explosion, no chemical or combustion reaction is necessary, although mechanical explosions caused by boiling liquid and expanding vapor (BLEVE) frequently happen as a result of heating a sealed container of liquid in a fire. If the liquid is flammable, a chemical explosion may follow the mechanical explosion.

Chemical explosions may be caused by the sudden ignition of dusts, gas/air mixtures, or vapor/air mixtures. These are known as combustion explosions. An explosion in a cloud of smoke from a pre-existing fire is known as a backdraft. Most of the explosions described so far are accidental in nature. Explosions fueled by chemicals whose primary function is to explode are more likely intentional.

All explosions, whether mechanical or chemical, are grouped into two categories: low order and high order. Low order explosions are characterized by a widespread "seat" or no "seat," and by the movement of large objects for short distances. High order explosions are characterized by a well defined "seat," where the energy of the explosion creates a shattering effect, and typically a crater. High order explosions tend to project small objects for long distances.

Determination of the origin or epicenter of an explosion is carried out by searching the perimeter of the scene, locating and documenting projected debris, and developing force vector diagrams. This task may be complicated by secondary explosions, which appear to have more than one "origin." Once the origin is observed, conclusions can be drawn about the type of fuel involved and, if necessary, samples selected for laboratory analysis.

While the types of materials involved in commercial or industrial explosions are too numerous to cover in this chapter, the potential fuels for residential explosions are very limited. Unless the explosion is a backdraft, easily recognized by the smoke staining on the projected objects, the potential

65. NFPA 921, *supra* note 1, chapter 13.

sources of fuel are limited to natural and LP gas, and flammable liquid vapors.

NFPA 921 contains an excellent discussion of the techniques of explosion investigation, and a recent National Institute of Justice guide dealing with the responsibilities of responders to explosion or bombing scenes contains much useful information.[66]

[13] Smoke Detectors

According to statistics compiled by the National Fire Protection Association, residential fire deaths in the United States have dropped from a high of 6,015 in 1978 to 3,360 in 1997.[67] The National Smoke Detector Project–a joint project among the Consumer Product Safety Commission, the Congressional Fire Services Institute, the U.S. Fire Administration, and the National Fire Protection Association–issued a major report in October 1994 on the use of home smoke detectors, and characterized the home smoke detector as the fire safety success story of the decade. According to the 1994 report, smoke detectors cut the risk of dying in a home fire by roughly 40%. In the ten years ending in 1995, the death rate from fires in homes with a smoke detector present was 45% lower than the death rate from fires in homes with no smoke detector present.[68]

Of course, once technology comes into being that can save lives, certain failures of the technology become occasions for tort litigation.[69] The National Smoke Detector Project study found that nearly all of the smoke detectors that failed to operate did so because their batteries were either dead or disconnected. Some research, however, has indicated that for certain types of smoldering fires, the most common type of detector, the ionization detector, does not respond as quickly to the large particles generated by smoldering fires as a different type of detector, the photoelectric detector.[70] The general consensus of the scientific community involved in smoke detector research, and the vast majority of the literature,[71] however, supports the proposition that the differences in response time are not significant with respect to smoldering fires, and the ionization detector's faster response to the more immediately dangerous flaming fire makes it the detector of choice. In recent litigation, smoke detector manufacturers have been sued for failing to incorporate a photoelectric detector into their smoke alarms, and the plaintiffs have had some success.[72]

---

66. See supra note 19.

67. 1997 Fire Loss in the US, 92 NFPA JOURNAL, Sept./Oct.1998, at 72.

68. CONSUMER PRODUCT SAFETY COMMISSION, SMOKE DETECTOR OPERABILITY SURVEY: REPORT ON FINDINGS (1994).

69. See Mark Grady, Why Are People Negligent? Technology, Nondurable Precautions, and the Medical Malpractice Explosion, 82 NW. U. L. REV. 293 (1988).

70. R.G. BILL, THE RESPONSE OF SMOKE DETECTORS TO SMOLDERING-STARTED FIRES IN A HOTEL OCCUPANCY (Factory Mutual Research, Norwood, MA) (1988).

71. R. Bukowski & N. Jason (eds.) INT'L FIRE DETECTION BIBLIOGRAPHY 1975–1990 (NIS-TIR 4661, Building and Fire research Laboratory, Gaithersburg, MD) (1991).

72. See, e.g., Gordon v. BRK Brands, Inc., No. 992–0771 (Circuit Ct. of the City of St. Louis, July, 1999) (settled after a $50 million verdict), or Mercer v. Pittway Corp., 616 N.W.2d 602 (Iowa 2000) ($16.9 million trial verdict for compensatory and punitive damages, reversed in part and remanded for new trial).

Most smoke detectors use a small amount of radioactive material to ionize particles of air in the detection chamber. This causes a current to be conducted between two electrodes. The presence of small particles of smoke in the ionization chamber interferes with this passage of current and triggers an alarm. In photoelectric detection chambers, there is a light emitting device and a light detecting device. The light emitting device is aimed away from the detection device, but the presence of smoke particles causes light to be reflected to the detection device, which sets off the alarm. Photoelectric detectors are not as sensitive to particles smaller than one micron (characteristic of flaming fires) as are ionization detectors. Ionization detectors are not as sensitive to particles larger than one micron (characteristic of smoldering fires) as are photoelectric detectors. All fires produce a wide range of particle sizes, and both types of detectors have been evaluated and found to provide adequate warning.[73] It is possible to build a smoke alarm that utilizes both types of detectors, and the argument has been advanced that alarms that incorporate only ionization detectors are therefore dangerous and defective. Unfortunately, when the smoke detector manufacturers put combination units on the store shelves, they stayed there. Consumers seem to be motivated largely by cost in their selection of smoke alarms. Litigation surrounding smoke detector design is likely to continue, but as of this writing, there have been few appellate decisions on the subject.

[14]   Stolen Autos Recovered Burned

This common scenario requires almost no investigation to determine that the fire was intentionally set. The chances that a vehicle happened to catch fire accidentally after it was stolen is almost not worth considering. The question in cases such as this is not whether the car was set on fire, but who did it. If an insurance company can prove that it was their insured who set the fire, or arranged the theft and fire, the company can avoid payment. Historically, this has been difficult to prove.

A new technique, bearing some resemblance to traditional toolmark analysis, purports to be able to determine the "last key used" to move a vehicle. This technique has no support in the relevant scientific community of firearms and toolmark examiners, but has nonetheless proven popular with insurers, and has been admitted over Daubert objections in several jurisdictions. Challenges are rare because the stakes are usually too low to support the involvement of adverse experts to refute the claim of the "forensic locksmith."

The proponents of this technique submitted a proposal to the NFPA to include it as a tool for vehicle fire investigations, but the Technical Committee rejected the proposal because there was no scientific evidence supporting the validity of the technique.[74]

[15]   Presumption of Accidental Cause

Because the individual making the arson case frequently lacks scientific training, the presumptions which that individual carries into a fire scene

---

73. *Ionization Versus Photoelectric: Choosing the Right Smoke Detector*, 30 BUILDING OFFICIAL & CODE ADMIN., Nov./Dec.1996, at 17.

74. *See* Report on Comments, *supra* note 33.

should be closely scrutinized. Just as the assumptions which are plugged into a computer model can affect the outcome of the analysis, so will the assumptions which a fire investigator carries with him into a fire scene affect the outcome of his investigation.

Because of the large amount of evidence destroyed in a fire, it is possible to "prove" almost any fire scene to be the result of arson, if one is bent on doing so. This idea is conveyed by DeHaan: "If an investigator decides that a fire is arson before collecting any data, then only data supporting that premise are likely to be recognized and collected."[75] DeHaan, of course, was inspired by Holmes (Sherlock, not Oliver Wendell), who stated, "It is a capital mistake to theorize before one has data. Insensibly, one begins to twist facts to suit theories, instead of theories to suit facts."[76]

Many fire investigators will state that they carry no presumptions into a fire scene with them, and rely on an objective evaluation of the evidence to reach their conclusions. NFPA 921 urges upon investigators the scientific method of hypothesis development and hypothesis testing. The question is: Should there be a hypothesis before all of the evidence has been observed? It could be argued that the proper presumption to carry into a fire scene is a presumption of accidental cause, i.e., all fires are presumed accidental until proven otherwise. Such a presumption protects the presumption of innocence accorded to individuals. Many states have codified this presumption of accidental cause into the standard jury charge for arson, but whether codified in a particular jurisdiction or not, the fire investigator who fails to apply the presumption of accidental cause to all fires will eventually make an erroneous declaration of arson.

The error will result from a misinterpretation of circumstantial evidence. In nearly every fire case, it is circumstantial evidence which allows the cause of the fire to be deduced. Likewise, in nearly every arson case, the *corpus delicti* is proven by circumstantial evidence, and the jury is read the standard circumstantial evidence charge. Mr. Holmes described the perils of circumstantial evidence in *The Boscombe Valley Mystery*:

> Circumstantial evidence is a very tricky thing. It may seem to point very straight to one thing, but if you shift your own point of view a little, you may find it pointing in an equally uncompromising manner to something entirely different.[77]

In many instances, if there is one survivor of a fire, particularly a fatal fire, and the fire is determined to have been the result of arson, then only one conclusion can be reached—the survivor did it. This is because, in the investigator's "opinion," the survivor's description of events, which typically depict an accidental fire, is "impossible," and therefore, the survivor is lying. This is exactly what happened to Ray Girdler. Judge James Sult, who presided over the first trial and sentenced Girdler to life in prison, wrote in his opinion remanding the case for a new trial:

75. DeHaan, *supra* note 21, at 4.

76. Arthur Conan Doyle, *A Scandal in Bohemia, in* The Annotated Sherlock Holmes (William S. Baring–Gould ed., 1967).

77. Arthur Conan Doyle, *The Boscombe Valley Mystery, in* The Annotated Sherlock Holmes (William S. Baring–Gould ed., 1967).

The newly-discovered evidence would probably change the verdict upon a retrial of this case. Several considerations support this finding: ...

[A]t the trial of the case, the State claimed, based on then understood fire investigation evidence, that Mr. Girdler's account of the fire was impossible and, therefore, false. The new evidence shows that Mr. Girdler's observations of the fire are consistent with a flashover fire of innocent origin.[78]

If the state's investigator had the proper scientific approach to fire investigation, or even admitted the possibility that an explanation other than burning flammable liquids (none were detected in laboratory analysis) existed, the erroneous conviction might have been avoided.

[16] The "Negative Corpus"

Since the advent of scientifically-based fire investigation, one of the thorniest issues for fire investigators has been the determination of fire cause when the evidence has either burned up or been taken from the scene by the firesetter. "Negative corpus," short for negative *corpus delicti* is fire investigator shorthand for the determination that a fire was incendiary based on the lack of evidence of an accidental cause. Such determinations have generally been held in low regard by the proponents of scientific fire investigation, but that has not prevented their introduction into evidence. The case of *Michigan Millers Mutual Insurance Corp. v. Benfield*[79] was a "negative corpus" determination. When fire investigators testify that a fire was intentionally set, "the elimination of all potential accidental causes" is frequently added to other evidence of incendiary activity.

The NFPA Technical Committee on Fire Investigations struggled with the concept of "negative corpus" for several years. Despite the lack of a demonstrable ignition source, many fires can be stated to have been set based on the absence of any other possibilities. The Committee's challenge was to limit the abuse of the negative corpus determination, and to put legitimate determinations of incendiary activity into the context of the scientific method. The result of the Committee's work, published in the 2001 edition of NFPA 921 is as follows:

Process of Elimination. Any determination of fire cause should be based on evidence rather than on the absence of evidence; however, when the origin of a fire is clearly defined, it is occasionally possible to make a credible determination regarding the cause of the fire, even when there is no physical evidence of that cause available. This may be accomplished through the credible elimination of all other potential causes, provided that the remaining cause is consistent with all known facts.

For example, an investigator may properly conclude that the ignition source came from an open flame even if the device producing the open flame is not found at the scene. This conclusion may be properly reached as long as the analysis producing the conclusion follows the Scientific Method as discussed in Chapter Two.

---

78. State v. Girdler, No. 9809 (Superior Ct. of Arizona, Maricopa County, Jan. 3, 1991).

79. 140 F.3d 915 (11th Cir.).

"Elimination," which actually involves the testing and rejection of alternate hypotheses, becomes more difficult as the degree of destruction in the compartment of origin increases, and is not possible in many cases. Any time an investigator proposes the elimination of a particular system or appliance as the ignition source, the investigator should be able to explain how the appearance or condition of that system or appliance would be different than what is observed, if that system or appliance were the cause of the fire.

There are times when such differences do not exist, for example, when a heat producing device ignites combustibles that are placed too close to it, the device itself may appear no different than if something else were the ignition source.

The "elimination of all accidental causes" to reach a conclusion that a fire was incendiary is a finding that can rarely be scientifically justified using only physical data; however, the "elimination of all causes other than the application of an open flame" is a finding that may be justified in limited circumstances, where the area of origin is clearly defined and all other potential heat sources at the origin can be examined and credibly eliminated. It is recognized that in cases where a fire is ignited by the application of an open flame, there may be no evidence of the ignition source remaining. Other evidence, such as that listed in Section 19–3, which may not be related to combustion, may allow for a determination that a fire was incendiary.

In a determination of an accidental cause, the same precautions regarding "elimination" of other causes should be carefully considered.

Note that nowhere in the above quotation does the term "negative corpus" appear.

The above language represents a compromise between the presumption of accidental cause, and the knowledge that in many cases, particularly where the ignition source is an open flame, incendiary fires may leave behind little physical evidence of their cause.[80]

[17] Certainty of Opinions

Few legal issues other than the cause of fires rely so heavily on the opinion of the investigator. Even in the case of explosions, which may be equally destructive or more destructive than fires, the fact that an explosion occurred drastically limits the number of potential causes.

Fire investigators have struggled with the question of certainty for years, raising such questions as whether an investigator's "comfort level" with his opinion should be stronger in a criminal case than in a civil case. On cross examination, many investigators will admit that they are not infallible, yet nevertheless go on to assert that there is no other possible explanation for their observations than what they have offered.

The uncertainty about certainty has generated much discussion in the fire investigation community, as illustrated by the discussion in the previous

80. NATIONAL FIRE PROTECTION ASSOCIATION,   GATIONS (PUB. NO. 921) (2001).
STANDARD GUIDE FOR FIRE AND EXPLOSION INVESTI-

edition of this chapter. Because it seemed impossible to separate a codification of "comfort level" from legal burdens of proof, the Technical Committee on Fire Investigations voted in 1998 to remove the discussion about levels of certainty from the document.

[18] Conflicting Opinions

There is a curious notion in the fire investigation community that every fire investigator is entitled to his own opinion about the cause of a fire. There is even a tacit recognition of the possibility of investigators reaching different conclusions after making the same observations of the same fire scene in the International Association of Arson Investigators CODE OF ETHICS, which includes the rule, "I will remember always that I am a truth seeker, not a case maker."[81]

Unfortunately, due to the lack of scientific training in the discipline, many investigators do not understand the concept of a "professional" opinion. Certainly, very few investigators will grant their physicians the same right to make a misdiagnosis based on their observation of a set of symptoms. If two doctors disagree on a diagnosis, the doctors regard it as their duty to cooperate and attempt to reach the correct conclusion. They would be uncomfortable knowing that one of them was wrong if they did not do so. Such cooperation in the search for the truth, particularly when arson is alleged, is so far a relatively rare occurrence in fire investigations. Fire investigators with differing views most often leave it up to the trier of fact to decide who is right, even though the legal fact finder is likely to be less knowledgeable about the substance of the expert testimony than either investigator.

§ 7–2.2.2 Laboratory Analysis

Unlike the field investigation of fires, there are considerably more areas of agreement and fewer areas of disagreement in the laboratory analysis of fire debris, and since the early 90s, a near consensus has developed in the scientific community regarding the proper techniques to be applied to samples of fire debris in which it is suspected that ignitable liquid residues are contained. Two chemists, looking at the same data from a fire debris sample, are more likely to agree on its interpretation than are two field investigators looking at the same fire scene, but disagreements still occur, and these are usually due to one of the chemists failing to meet industry standards.

[1] Standard Methods of Sample Preparation

The industry standard for the laboratory analysis of fire debris is embodied in ASTM E 1387, STANDARD TEST METHOD FOR IGNITABLE LIQUID RESIDUES IN EXTRACTS FROM SAMPLES OF FIRE DEBRIS BY GAS CHROMATOGRAPHY.[82] A second standard, E 1618, STANDARD TEST METHOD FOR IDENTIFICATION OF IGNITABLE LIQUID RESIDUES IN EXTRACTS FROM SAMPLES OF FIRE DEBRIS BY GAS CHROMATOGRAPHY/MASS SPECTROMETRY[83] also has been adopted by ASTM. It is agreed almost unanimously in the forensic science community that gas chromatography is an

---

81. INTERNATIONAL ASSOCIATION OF ARSON INVESTIGATORS, IAAI CODE OF ETHICS (1949).

82. *Supra* note 11.

83. *Id.*

essential requirement for the identification of common petroleum-based products. Gas chromatography/mass spectrometry and gas chromatography/infrared spectrophotometry, known as "hybrid" techniques, provide more information, but are basically more sophisticated versions of gas chromatography. Gas chromatography has been the accepted method of analyzing petroleum products since the 60s, but there have been considerable improvements in the field. These improvements and variations on the technique of gas chromatography are reported in peer reviewed journals such as the JOURNAL OF FORENSIC SCIENCES, the JOURNAL OF THE FORENSIC SCIENCE SOCIETY, ANALYTICAL CHEMISTRY, and others.

There have also been numerous improvements in sample preparation techniques over the years. These improvements are also likely to be documented in the literature, and most commonly used sample preparation techniques are described in ASTM standards.

Headspace analysis (ASTM E 1388) is the simplest of the sample preparation techniques. This method is rapid, but not highly reproducible, and not highly sensitive to the heavier hydrocarbons such as those found in diesel fuel. The sample is warmed and a syringe is used to withdraw a small volume of the air above the sample, known as the headspace. This headspace is then injected directly into the gas chromatograph.[84]

Steam distillation (ASTM E 1385) is a classical technique which relies on the immiscibility of oil and water. A visible oily liquid can be separated from the sample, and then diluted or injected directly into the gas chromatograph. This technique is time consuming, and is not sensitive to very low concentrations of ignitable liquids, which are often all that remains in fire debris samples. When applied to a sufficiently concentrated sample, the visible liquid that the technique produces, however, can make a very convincing exhibit.[85] When the jury can actually see the recovered liquid, and perhaps smell it and see it burn, they will not likely feel the need to understand the intricacies of gas chromatography.

Solvent extraction (ASTM E 1386) is another classical technique which is highly sensitive, but which has the disadvantage of dissolving materials other than the ignitable liquid residues of interest. It is also dangerous, and destructive of evidence. This is a technique best applied to very small samples and to the problem of determining what was inside a now empty container.[86]

Headspace concentration techniques (ASTM E 1412 and E 1413) employ an adsorbent to trap volatile materials present in the headspace above a warmed sample. These adsorption/elution techniques are highly sensitive, highly reproducible, and the passive headspace concentration technique is both simple to use and essentially nondestructive of evidence. The sample can be analyzed repeatedly, by different laboratories if necessary. Passive heads-

84. AMERICAN SOCIETY FOR TESTING AND MATERIALS,, STANDARD PRACTICE FOR SAMPLING OF HEADSPACE VAPORS FROM FIRE DEBRIS SAMPLES (PUB. NO. E 1388) (1995).

85. AMERICAN SOCIETY FOR TESTING AND MATERIALS, STANDARD PRACTICE FOR SEPARATION AND CONCENTRATION OF IGNITABLE LIQUID RESIDUES FROM

FIRE DEBRIS SAMPLES BY STEAM DISTILLATION (PUB No. E 1385) (1995).

86. AMERICAN SOCIETY FOR TESTING AND MATERIALS, STANDARD PRACTICE FOR SEPARATION AND CONCENTRATION OF IGNITABLE LIQUID RESIDUES FROM FIRE DEBRIS SAMPLES BY SOLVENT EXTRACTION (PUB. NO. E 1386) (1995).

pace concentration is rapidly becoming the "method of choice" in modern forensic science laboratories.[87]

All of the above sample preparation techniques are scientifically valid. Sample size, ignitable liquid concentration, and the analyst's experience and preference will determine which method of separation is selected. Regardless of separation technique, the analytical methods recognized as valid are limited to those involving gas chromatography.

[2] Classification of Ignitable Liquids

Until recently, it was generally believed that ignitable liquids could be placed into one of five major classes[88] or a sixth "miscellaneous" class. Innovations by the petroleum industry, however, made the classification system used by forensic scientists become cumbersome and confusing. Consequently, the ASTM Committee on Forensic Sciences has changed the structure of its classification system to utilize descriptive class names, and to dispense with class numbers. Distinctions within any one of these classes are very difficult, if not impossible.[89] Once an ignitable liquid has been exposed to a fire, its character changes to the extent that its source is very difficult to identify. Some work has indicated that source identification is possible if a sample is less than 30% evaporated (i.e., at least 70% of the original weight remains). There are times, however, when ignitable liquids are mixed, producing a unique pattern which can conceivably be identified with a source.

The exposure of a petroleum distillate to a fire results in its evaporation, with the lower boiling point compounds being preferentially evaporated over the higher boiling point compounds. This results in an increase in the average molecular weight of the mixture. It is also generally recognized that it is not possible to distinguish whether a sample has been exposed to a fire or to room temperature evaporation. A sample of petroleum distillate that has burned to 50% of its original volume or weight will give a gas chromatographic pattern which is indistinguishable from a sample that has evaporated to that point.

[3] Detection of Explosives

Because of the relative rarity of bombing incidents, the cadre of scientists regularly dealing with the detection and identification of explosive residues is very small. Most private laboratories have only primitive explosive detection capabilities, and most state and local government laboratories are not much better equipped. Techniques for explosive detection and identification appear in the literature, but few laboratories are capable of repeating the published analyses. Techniques used by explosives chemists are as varied as the explosives themselves. The following are techniques used in the federal laboratories

87. AMERICAN SOCIETY FOR TESTING AND MATERIALS,, STANDARD PRACTICE FOR SEPARATION AND CONCENTRATION OF IGNITABLE LIQUID RESIDUES FROM FIRE DEBRIS SAMPLES BY PASSIVE HEADSPACE CONCENTRATION (PUB. NO. E 1412) (1994); AMERICAN SOCIETY FOR TESTING AND MATERIALS,, STANDARD PRACTICE FOR SEPARATION AND CONCENTRATION OF IGNITABLE LIQUID RESIDUES FROM FIRE DEBRIS SAMPLES BY DYNAMIC HEADSPACE CONCENTRATION (PUB. NO. E 1413) (1995).

88. Class 1: light petroleum distillates, Class 2: gasoline, Class 3: medium petroleum distillates, Class 4: kerosene, Class 5: heavy petroleum distillates.

89. ASTM E 1387, *supra* note 11.

on a routine basis: thin layer chromatography, gas chromatography, gas chromatography/mass spectrometry with chemical ionization, infrared spectrophotometry, high performance liquid chromatography, energy dispersive x-ray analysis, x-ray diffraction, and capillary electrophoresis, one of the newer techniques.

As in the analysis of petroleum distillates in fire debris, the critical first step in the analysis of explosive residue is the separation of the residue from the debris. The salts which are the products of the explosive reaction are removed from the debris by a cold water extraction, while the unreacted or partially reacted residue of the explosive itself is removed using an organic solvent. These concentrated extracts are then analyzed by one, or usually several, of the above techniques.

For explosions caused by fuels other than chemicals designed to explode, gas chromatography is the usual method of analysis. Gasoline, the most common fuel for explosive vapor/air mixtures, is detected as described previously. More sophisticated gas chromatography is required to detect ethane, which is found in natural gas, but not in sewer gas. Odorization of natural and LP gases is frequently an issue in explosion cases. Quantitation of the odorant level may be accomplished by gas chromatography or through an odor panel. Reagent tubes can be used to detect the ethyl mercaptan or thiopane used to odorize fuel gases.

§ 7–2.3 Future Directions

The laboratory analysis of fire debris is about as "settled" as any forensic science is ever likely to be. The gas chromatograph/mass spectrometer can provide almost total characterization of complex mixtures to allow for unequivocal identification of the petroleum products that are likely to be used as accelerants. The techniques of sample preparation have reached the practical limit of what is desirable to detect. More sensitive levels of detection increase the risk of identifying ignitable liquid residues that are part of the normal background. The simplicity of the techniques available to achieve current levels of detection provides little impetus to improve the techniques. The impetus in the field is generally to improve the quality of work done by laboratories that have yet to adopt techniques that are generally recognized as valid. As the ASTM methods first adopted in 1990 and 1991 come into more widespread use, laboratories that fail to follow these minimum standards can expect to see their results challenged more frequently and more vigorously.

With the lack of a frontier, more laboratory scientists are stepping out into the field, and applying their scientific skills to the understanding of the behavior of fire. The National Fire Protection Association (NFPA) and the National Institute of Standards and Technology (NIST) are both looking at ways to repeat the experiments of the 70s and 80s, but this time, the researchers will look at the aftermath, rather than just the fire itself. Numerous test burns should be recorded in the next few years, and the information which comes out of them should greatly improve the quality of field fire investigation work.

As more canines are brought into the field of accelerant detection, a body of knowledge, including peer reviewed research, is likely to come into being. The use of accelerant detecting canines may free up large amounts of fire investigators' time, allowing overworked state and local officials to concentrate on those fire scenes most likely to result in prosecutable arson cases.

Computer modeling is likely to assume a much larger role in the future, particularly as data come in from more test burns, and can be used to test a model's predictions.

Certification of field investigators by the International Association of Arson Investigators or by the National Association of Fire Investigators is becoming more common. Neither certification program guarantees the competence of the witness or the correctness of his findings, but the programs do serve a useful purpose in encouraging the fire investigation community to identify some areas of agreement and to study areas of disagreement.

Certification of laboratory analysts through the American Board of Criminalistics began only in 1994, so it will be some time before there is a large core of certified fire debris chemists. As more scientists leave the laboratory to do field research in the area of fire behavior, the understanding of fire behavior is likely to improve, and the quality of fire investigations is likely to benefit from the application of a scientist's natural skepticism to the outdated or unsupported beliefs held by many field investigators. While there are still far too many cases of incorrect fire analyses, the profession is moving incrementally toward a more accurate calibration of expectations.

Appendix

Glossary

Accelerant. An agent, often an ignitable liquid, used to initiate or speed the spread of fire.

Arc. A luminous electric discharge across a gap. If the arc generates sufficient energy, an arc bead may be formed. An arc bead is a round globule of re-solidified metal at the point on an electrical conductor where the arc occurred.

Capillary Electrophoresis. An analytical separation technique which utilizes electric charge to separate and analyze sub-milligram quantities of chemical substances. Capillary Electrophoresis is useful in many types of analytical chemistry, including the detection of explosives and gunshot residues.

Compartment Fire. Any fire which occurs inside an enclosure. Once a fire has progressed beyond the initial free-burning stage, it interacts with the floors, walls, and ceilings of the enclosure and behaves differently from a free-burning fire.

Flashover. A transition phase in the development of a compartment fire in which surfaces exposed to thermal radiation reach ignition temperature more or less simultaneously and fire spreads rapidly throughout the space.

Gas Chromatography (GC). An analytical method for separating and identifying mixtures of compounds. A compound's solubility in a stationary phase versus its solubility in a mobile phase allows separation of similar compounds due to subtle differences in physical or chemical properties. Most gas chromatography performed on ignitable liquid residues relies on differences in boiling points to effect the separation. GC is the fundamental first step in the analysis of any ignitable liquid residue. The output of the GC is known as a chromatogram.

Infrared Spectrophotometry (IR). An analytical method which measures the absorbance of radiation having a wavelength slightly longer than the wavelength of visible light. This method is used to characterize the functional groups present in a sample, and is frequently applied to polymers and drugs. The utility of IR is limited in ignitable liquid residue analysis because most ignitable liquids are mixtures, and infrared spectrophotometry requires pure or nearly pure compounds in order to yield meaningful data. The output of the IR spectrophotometer is known as an absorbance spectrum.

Mass Spectrometry (MS). An analytical method that begins with the breaking up of the compounds of interest by the application of chemical or electrical energy, followed by a measurement of the size and number of ions produced in the ionization step. Like other spectral techniques, mass spectrometry requires pure compounds in order to yield meaningful data. The purification for most mass spectral analysis is accomplished via gas chromatography. Typically, the MS is attached to the output side of a gas chromatograph (GC/MS) column. The output of the mass spectrometer is known as a mass spectrum.

Odorization. The addition of small concentrations of substances to a fuel gas in order to make it detectable by smell. The two common fuel gases, natural gas and LP gas, have no odor. Odorants such as ethyl mercaptan or thiophane must be added to fuel gases in order to make them detectable at a concentration not over one-fifth of the lower limit of flammability.

Radiometer. A collection of thermocouples encased in a solid conductive metal jacket (e.g., copper) which is cooled by water. By measuring the voltage difference between the thermocouples exposed to the fire and the thermocouples exposed to the water, and taking into account the surface area of the case, the radiative flux in watts per square centimeter (or kilowatts per square meter) can be measured directly.

Thermocouple. A device consisting of two dissimilar metal wires which convert heat energy into electrical energy. A voltage measuring device is attached to the wires and the temperature at the junction of the wires can be calculated. This is usually accomplished electronically, and the thermocouple readout, known as a pyrometer, reads directly in degrees F or degrees C.

Thin Layer Chromatography (TLC). A chemical analytical procedure which separates compounds by their solubility in a solvent and the tenacity by which these compounds adsorb (adhere) to a thin sheet of silica gel spread out on a glass plate. Once separated, the spots of analyte can be further characterized by exposure to a developing agent, which causes the spots to change color. As in all chromatographic analyses, a comparison is made between a known substance and an unknown substance. TLC may be used for the separation of drugs and explosives, and also for the characterization of dyes in automotive gasoline.

CHAPTER 8

ALCOHOL TESTING

Table of Sections

A. LEGAL ISSUES

Westlaw Electronic Research

See Westlaw Electronic Research Guide preceding the Summary of Contents.

A. LEGAL ISSUES

§ 8–1.0   LEGAL ISSUES IN ALCOHOL TESTING

§ 8–1.1   Introduction

    The need for some method to test whether an individual was intoxicated must have arisen shortly after the first automobile passed a tavern. Statutes criminalizing drunk driving were passed in the first decades of the twentieth century.[1] Before the development of objective tests for intoxication courts had

---

§ 8–1.0

1. Robert J. Schefter, *Under the Influence of Alcohol Three Hours After Driving: The Constitutionality of the (A) (5) Amendment to Pennsylvania's DUI Statute*, 100 Dick. L. Rev. 441,

444 (1996) notes that Pennsylvania passed its first DUI statute in 1909. It prohibited operation of a motor vehicle while intoxicated, without a precise definition of intoxication.

to rely on the testimony of police officers and others concerning behavioral indicia of drunkenness and the presence of alcohol on the breath. Gradually, chemical tests were employed to measure the presence of alcohol in the body. The tests, in turn, generated DUI[2] statutes whose definition of intoxication are based on the results of these tests. Today, every state defines DUI in terms of some concentration of alcohol in the body, usually defined as blood alcohol concentration (BAC).[3] The present chapter focuses on the question of whether test results should be barred because they fail to meet admissibility thresholds for scientific evidence.[4] As the sophistication and accuracy of tests has improved, the admissibility questions that arise in this area have changed. The current essay will focus its attention on contemporary admissibility questions.[5]

2. States vary in the terminology they use to describe their drunk driving laws. Some use the term DUI (driving under the influence) while others use the term DWI (driving while intoxicated). To complicate matters further, in some jurisdictions DUI is a lesser included offence to DWI. *See* United States v. Sauls, 981 F.Supp. 909, 919 (D.Md.1997) (discussing Maryland law).

3. *See* United States v. Sauls, 981 F.Supp. 909, 928–930 (1997) for a state by state listing of the blood alcohol concentrations that are illegal per se and which raise a presumption of intoxication. Traditionally, a BAC of .10% has been the standard for concentrations that are illegal per se. However, there is considerable pressure to lower this level, in part due to research indicating significant impairment at the lower concentration (see scientific discussion below). *See, e.g.,* WEST'S ANN. CAL. VEHICLE CODE § 23152. The federal government has contributed to this pressure with legislation withholding federal highway money from states that do not adopt the lower standard. 23 U.S.C.A. § 410(f)(5). As per se rules and presumptions are applied to individuals with lower blood alcohol concentrations, the constitutionality of such provisions may become more controversial. *See* United States v. Sauls, 981 F.Supp. 909, 921 (D.Md.1997). On the constitutionality of these presumptions and per se rules, *see* James J. Ahern, *Defending DUI and Related Cases*, DUI IL–CLE 1–1, Illinois Institute for Continuing Legal Education (1995); Peter R. Masterson, *The Military's Drunk Driving Statute: Have We Gone Too Far?* 150 MIL. L. REV. 353 (1995).

An interesting Illinois case dealt with the definition of Blood Alcohol Content and ruled that a jury could not presume the defendant was legally intoxicated based upon results of a serum-alcohol concentration test. The relevant statute was interpreted to require that tests be performed on whole blood. People v. Green, 294 Ill.App.3d 139, 228 Ill.Dec. 513, 689 N.E.2d 385, 389 (Ill.App.1997). In this particular case, the defendant's serum-blood alcohol concentration was over .10, but his BAC was .079. *Id.* at 388.

4. The reader may also wish to refer to the discussion in the chapter on drug testing.

5. As in the area of drug testing, a number of other legal issues have arisen with respect to testing for alcohol. These include claims of illegal search and seizure and violation of the privilege against self incrimination. It is well established that the privilege against self incrimination does not apply to procuring physical evidence such as blood, hair, or urine samples. Moreover, if an officer has probable cause to arrest someone for driving while intoxicated, taking a specimen in a reasonable manner is not a Fourth Amendment violation. Schmerber v. California, 384 U.S. 757, 86 S.Ct. 1826, 16 L.Ed.2d 908 (1966); South Dakota v. Neville, 459 U.S. 553, 103 S.Ct. 916, 74 L.Ed.2d 748 (1983). With respect to drunk driving cases, all states have sidestepped constitutional questions by enacting "implied consent" statutes. The premise of these statutes is that possessing a driving license is a privilege, not a right and that the privilege may be suspended if the individual refuses a reasonable request for a blood, breath or urine sample. *See, e.g.,* VERNON'S TEXAS STATUTES AND CODES ANNOTATED, TRANSPORTATION CODE §§ 724.011, 724.031, 724.035; WEST'S ANN. CAL. VEHICLE CODE § 23612. The defendant's refusal is generally admissible in a subsequent trial. *See* State v. Beaton, 516 N.W.2d 645 (N.D.1994).

In *City of Seattle v. Stalsbroten,* 138 Wash.2d 227, 978 P.2d 1059 (Wash. 1999) the defendant argued that the admission of the fact he refused to submit to a field sobriety test (FST) violated his right against self incrimination. He tried to draw the clever distinction between a suspect's performance on a FST, which is not testimonial, and his verbal answer to the question of whether he was willing to take the test, which he claimed was testimonial. The court of appeals agreed, but the Washington Supreme Court reversed. Both the results of the test and the refusal to take the test are not testimonial. "The argument that refusal to take an FST communicates the suspect's belief that the test will produce evidence of his or her guilt confuses reasonable inferences with communica-

As in the drug testing chapter, we have chosen to organize the discussion according to the type of scientific validity question under consideration. Following Giannelli[6] and Faigman, Porter and Saks,[7] we divide the cases into three broad categories. First, there are cases that address the validity of the theory or principle that provides authority for the expert's conclusions. Second, there are cases that address the general technique or procedure that was used to produce the data about which the expert is testifying. Third, there are cases that address the application of the technique on a particular occasion, that is, the specific practices used to obtain the data in the present case.

This formulation has been adopted in a number of cases, decided both before and after the Supreme Court opinion in *Daubert v. Merrell Dow Pharmaceuticals, Inc.*[8] Although these categories offer a useful way to organize the drug cases, one must keep in mind that many cases fall into more than one category. Moreover, the categories interact with each other. There may be theoretical support for some conclusions and not other, similar, conclusions. Underlying principles may support an expert's conclusion if it is based on one analytical technique, but not if it is based on another, less discriminating technique. Ultimately, each admissibility decision involves an

tions." *Id.* at 1063. *See also* McCormick v. Municipality of Anchorage, 999 P.2d 155 (Alaska App.2000) (refusal admissible over a Rule 403 objection).

Some jurisdictions have held that an individual is entitled to consult with a lawyer prior to the drawing of a sample, but there is no federal constitutional right to counsel in these circumstances. *See* ANDRE MOENSSENS, JAMES STARRS, CAROL HENDERSON AND FRED INBAU, SCIENTIFIC EVIDENCE IN CIVIL AND CRIMINAL CASES 214 (1995).

6. Professor Giannelli divided the question of scientific validity into "(1) the validity of the underlying principle, (2) the validity of the technique applying the principle, and (3) the proper application of the technique on a particular occasion." Paul Giannelli, *The Admissibility of Novel Scientific Evidence: Frye v. United States, a Half–Century Later*, 80 COLUM. L. REV. 1197, 1201 (1980).

7. Faigman, Porter & Saks distinguish between (1) "the theory or principle that provides authority for the conclusions that are drawn from the data," (2) "the general technique or procedure that produces the data," and (3) "the specific practices used to obtain the data." David L. Faigman et al., *Check Your Crystal Ball at the Courthouse Door, Please: Exploring the Past, Understanding the Present, and Worrying About the Future of Scientific Evidence*, 15 CARDOZO L. REV. 1799, 1825–27 (1994).

8. 509 U.S. 579, 113 S.Ct. 2786, 125 L.Ed.2d 469 (1993). *See, e.g.,* United States v. Downing, 753 F.2d 1224, 1234 (3d Cir.1985):

Under *Frye*, therefore, courts confronted with a proffer of novel scientific evidence must make a preliminary determination through the introduction of other evidence,

including expert testimony, regarding (1) the status, in the appropriate scientific community, of the scientific principle underlying the proffered novel evidence; (2) the technique applying the scientific principle; and (3) the application of the technique on the particular occasion or occasions relevant to the proffered testimony.

Similarly, in *United States v. Medina,* 749 F.Supp. 59 (E.D.N.Y.1990), Judge Weinstein noted that general theoretical soundness is, by itself, insufficient to permit the introduction of test results. The sample must be properly obtained, the specific laboratory technique must be sound, and on this particular occasion the laboratory must have been careful and accurate in the use of the technique. *Id.* at 62. In *Hartman v. State,* 946 S.W.2d 60, 62 (Tex. Crim.App.1997), the court interpreted Texas Rule of Evidence 702 (identical to the federal rule) to require, a) a valid underlying theory, b) a valid technique applying the theory, and c) proper application of the technique on the occasion in question.

The Supreme Court *Daubert* opinion recognizes the first two categories when it distinguishes between a general theory and technique. Daubert v. Merrell Dow Pharmaceuticals, Inc., 509 U.S. 579, 592–93, 113 S.Ct. 2786, 125 L.Ed.2d 469 (1993). In *Kumho Tire v. Carmichael,* 526 U.S. 137, 119 S.Ct. 1167, 143 L.Ed.2d 238 (1999), the Court distinguishes between the reasonableness of the general technique of using visual and tactile inspection to determine the cause of a tire failure and the specific application of the technique in the case at hand. *Id.* at 154.

examination of all three categories in relationship to each other and to the conclusions drawn by the expert.

§ 8–1.2   Validity of the Underlying Theory or Principle

The routine detection of impairment and intoxication involves the use of a number of tests. They include chemical, biochemical, and gas chromatographic tests designed to measure an individual's BAC, preliminary passive screening tests designed to detect the presence of alcohol, and various field sobriety tests, including horizontal gaze nystagmus, designed to measure the presence of physical impairments typically associated with alcohol consumption. When the results of these tests are used with an appreciation of their limitations, there have been few successful challenges of the underlying theory or principle of the tests.

§ 8–1.2.1   Novel Scientific Evidence

Some jurisdictions apply *Daubert* or *Frye* rules only to novel scientific evidence.[9] Others follow the federal courts and apply the admissibility criteria to all proffered expert evidence, whether or not it is novel.[10] For courts that do make this distinction, admissibility challenges to most alcohol tests are likely to be rejected because the courts conclude that neither the theory nor the general technique of chemical alcohol testing is novel. In *People v. Bury*,[11] the defendant challenged the admissibility of a preliminary alcohol screening (PAS) test because the machine used to conduct the test (an "Alco–Sensor III") had not been generally accepted by the scientific community as required by the California *Kelly/Frye* test.[12] The appellate court rejected this position because the test is not a new scientific procedure that would trigger a *Kelly/Frye* hearing.

In jurisdictions that do not distinguish between novel and non-novel scientific evidence, successful challenges are theoretically possible. For example, in *Hartman v. State*,[13] the court reversed an appellate court decision to admit the results of an intoxilyzer test without conducting an admissibility hearing as required by *Kelly v. State*.[14] However, the difference between these two positions may have relatively little practical significance in alcohol testing cases. As a concurring opinion in the *Hartman* case notes, some scientific theories are so well accepted that they are entitled to judicial notice of their admissibility.[15] Even when tests fall short of this level, a theory or technique

---

9. *See* State v. Cline, 275 Mont. 46, 909 P.2d 1171 (Mont. 1996); Hulse v. Department of Justice, Motor Vehicle Division, 289 Mont. 1, 961 P.2d 75 (Mont.1998) (a *Daubert* analysis is required only for novel scientific evidence in Montana; the state in future cases no longer needs to introduce evidence proving that a horizontal gaze nystagmus test is scientifically valid); Parker v. State, 777 So.2d 937 (Ala. Crim.App.2000) (since gas chromatograph test is not novel, no *Frye* analysis is required).

10. *See* State v. Torres, 127 N.M. 20, 976 P.2d 20 (N.M. 1999) (assessment of admissibility is not limited to novel scientific theories). *See* § 1.2.5.[1] for a discussion of this issue in the horizontal gaze nystagmus context.

11. 41 Cal.App.4th 1194, 49 Cal.Rptr.2d 107 (1996).

12. 49 Cal. Rptr.2d at 110.

13. 946 S.W.2d 60 (Tex.Crim.App.1997).

14. 824 S.W.2d 568 (Tex.Crim.App.1992).

15. *See* Daubert v. Merrell Dow Pharmaceuticals, Inc., 509 U.S. 579, 592 n. 11, 113 S.Ct. 2786, 125 L.Ed.2d 469 (1993). For example, several states have taken judicial notice of the general acceptance or reliability of horizontal gaze nystagmus tests. In *State v. Taylor*, 694 A.2d 907, 910 (Me.1997), for instance, the Maine Supreme Court took judicial notice of the reliability of HGN tests in making determinations of probable cause for arrest and for

may warrant admissibility as a matter of course. Trial courts should not become constantly embroiled in determining the admissibility of scientific theories and techniques that have already been well established.[16]

§ 8–1.2.2 Chemical, Biochemical and Gas Chromatography Tests

The concepts underlying most chemical, biochemical and gas chromatographic tests are sufficiently well-developed that admissibility is rarely challenged on these grounds.[17] In a number of jurisdictions, admissibility is provided for by statute.[18] Occasionally, there is a challenge to preliminary alcohol screening tests such as officer operated breathalyzer tests. However, these challenges generally are unavailing,[19] especially when the test is only used to establish probable cause for arrest or that the individual is impaired rather than establish a specific BAC.[20]

§ 8–1.2.3 Time of Testing

Although the underlying theory of blood tests for alcohol concentration is firmly established, there remains the question of what conclusions one can draw from these tests. The question is generally one of timing. What does a test conducted at some later time tell us about the level of intoxication of the defendant while he was driving. In *Daubert* terms, these questions are generally one of fit; do the results of the study support the conclusion the state wishes to draw about a given individual? However, in the alcohol testing context, the courts generally resolve this issue without resort to a *Daubert*-like analysis.

Alcohol tests may be used in two ways in drunk driving litigation. Because there is a well established relationship between an individual's BAC and his ability to perform mental and physical functions associated with the operation of a motor vehicle, tests may be used to create a presumption that the individual was driving while impaired.[21] Theoretically, when used this way, test results should be supplemented with additional evidence that the

purposes of establishing criminal guilt in DUI cases. A similar result was reached in *Williams v. State*, 710 So.2d 24 (Fla.App.1998), and *State v. Ito*, 90 Hawai'i 225, 978 P.2d 191, 209 (Haw. 1999).

16. *Hartman*, 946 S.W.2d at 63. The concurring opinion emphasized that appellate courts could only resolve questions involving the underlying scientific theory and the general technique applying the theory. Whether the technique has been properly applied on a given occasion must be decided on a case-by-case basis. *Id.* at 64.

17. *See, e.g.,* Jones v. State, 716 S.W.2d 142 (Tex.App.1986) (results of gas chromatography mass spectrometry (GCMS) test admissible. GCMS has achieved general acceptance); State v. Rolfe, 166 Vt. 1, 686 A.2d 949 (Vt. 1996) (results of infrared breath tests admissible).

18. *See, e.g.,* State v. Rolfe, 166 Vt. 1, 686 A.2d 949, 958 (Vt. 1996) (discussing Vt. St. T. 23 § 1203); Barna v. Commissioner of Public

Safety, 508 N.W.2d 220 (Minn.App.1993) (referring to Minn. R. 7502.0700); Texas Dept. of Pub. Safety v. Jimenez, 995 S.W.2d 834, 838 (Tex.App.1999); Henderson v. State, 14 S.W.3d 409, 410 (Tex.App.2000); Scherl v. State, 7 S.W.3d 650, 652 (Tex.App.1999) (State does not have to introduce expert testimony establishing the reliability of the scientific theory underlying the intoxilyzer because the legislature had determined intoxilyzer test results are admissible when performed in accordance with Department of Public Safety regulations [Tex. Transp. Code Ann. § 724.064]). *See also* McKinney's N.Y. Vehicle and Traffic Law § 1195; State v. Maida, 332 N.J.Super. 564, 753 A.2d 1240 (Law.Div.2000).

19. People v. Bury, 41 Cal.App.4th 1194, 49 Cal.Rptr.2d 107 (1996).

20. Verbois v. State, 909 S.W.2d 140 (Tex. App.1995); State v. Bartlett, 130 N.C.App. 79, 502 S.E.2d 53 (N.C.App.1998).

21. *See* § 2 of this chapter.

individual was in fact impaired while driving. In normal circumstances this may be provided by the arresting officer who can testify about the individual's driving behavior at the time of arrest, but in some situations such corroborating evidence may be unavailable. In order to sidestep this problem, most states use test results in a second way. They have enacted provisions making it a per se offence to operate a motor vehicle when the driver's blood alcohol content is above some threshold, usually .10 or more recently .08.[22]

Whether the test results create a presumption or constitute a per se offence, there remains an issue of whether BAC measured at some time after the defendant was driving is evidence of intoxication at the time he was operating a motor vehicle (see § 2.5 *infra*). States have adopted varying positions as to whether extrapolation back to the time of driving (often called "retrograde extrapolation") is required before the state may rely on the test results. Some state statutes require an expert to extrapolate measured BAC back to the probable BAC at the time the defendant was operating the vehicle.[23] However, accurate extrapolations are very difficult if not impossible absent information about the individual's consumption behavior during the period immediately preceding arrest. Faced with this difficulty and the fact that many defendants either do not know or will not reveal their drinking behavior,[24] most jurisdictions do not require extrapolation.[25] Rather, they create a presumption that the results of tests done within a certain time period following the time the individual was driving are equal to or lower than the BAC while driving.[26] Tests done within the relevant time period are

22. *See* MD. TRANSP. CODE. ANN. § 21–902 (Supp.1994); TENN. CODE ANN. § 55–10–401 (1993). These statutes, unlike the statutes discussed in note 29 *infra*, only create a presumption of intoxication at the time the defendant was driving.

23. State v. Geisler, 22 Conn.App. 142, 576 A.2d 1283 (Conn.App.1990) (vacated on other grounds; Connecticut v. Geisler, 498 U.S. 1019, 111 S.Ct. 663, 112 L.Ed.2d 657 (1991)); State v. Dumont, 146 Vt. 252, 499 A.2d 787 (Vt.1985); State v. Ladwig, 434 N.W.2d 594 (S.D.1989).

24. Miller v. State, 597 So.2d 767 (Fla. 1991).

25. State v. Kubik, 235 Neb. 612, 456 N.W.2d 487 (Neb. 1990); State v. Lusi, 625 A.2d 1350 (R.I.1993); Commonwealth v. Wirth, 936 S.W.2d 78 (Ky.1996); People v. Campbell, 236 Mich.App. 490, 601 N.W.2d 114, 117 (Mich.App.1999) ("Pursuant to the plain language of the statute, a chemical test, regardless of the amount of time before the test is actually performed, is assumed to be a reasonable approximation of a person's blood alcohol level at the time of the offense."); Commonwealth v. Zugay, 745 A.2d 639 (Pa.Super.2000). *Zugay* provides an interesting history of Pennsylvania's zig-zag path on the question of extrapolation back. Pennsylvania's DWI statute, like those in most states, permits conviction either under a general provision or through a per se provision. At one point, the state required expert extrapolation testimony when the state relied on the per se provision, but not when it

used the results of the blood test as some evidence under the general provision. Commonwealth v. Modaffare, 529 Pa. 101, 601 A.2d 1233 (Pa.1992). *See* Mireles v. Texas Dept. of Pub. Safety, 993 S.W.2d 426, 430 (Tex.App. 1999) ("Many courts, including this one, have sustained convictions for driving while intoxicated, in which a much higher standard of proof applied, based in part on after-the-fact test results without expert extrapolation evidence. Furthermore, nothing in the Transportation Code requires the Department to present specific extrapolation evidence.").

26. Woods v. State, 593 So.2d 103 (Ala. Crim.App.1991); Williams v. State, 737 P.2d 360 (Alaska App.1987); Ransford v. District of Columbia, 583 A.2d 186 (D.C.App.1990) (in prosecution for per se offense of driving while intoxicated, government need not present expert testimony extrapolating or relating results of blood alcohol test administered after accused's arrest to his blood alcohol level at time of operation of vehicle); Haas v. State, 597 So.2d 770 (Fla.1992) (properly obtained test results reflecting blood-alcohol level of 0.10 or more, standing alone, constitute circumstantial evidence upon which finder of fact may convict accused driver of driving under the influence either by impairment or by virtue of blood alcohol level); State v. Lusi, 625 A.2d 1350 (R.I.1993) (trier of fact may draw inferences from results of breathalyzer test that blood alcohol content at time of test was same as at time of actual driving). *See* Dean G. Zioze,

presumptively admissible,[27] but may be rebutted[28] by defense expert testimony.[29] Questions of whether the test reflects BAC while driving go to weight, not admissibility.[30]

Because of the extrapolation issue, a number of cases are forced to confront the question of whether tests conducted some period of time following the operation of a motor vehicle are admissible, either for conviction under the per se section of the relevant statute or as evidence of impairment at the time of driving. The area is complicated by specific statutory requirements.[31] Many states require tests to be performed within some time certain after arrest or after the defendant was driving a vehicle. Typical are statutes requiring the test to be administered within two[32] or three[33] hours. Tests done after the relevant time period typically do not enjoy the presumption of admissibility[34] and may not be admitted.[35] From a *Daubert* perspective, the

Trier of Fact May Infer Defendant's Blood Alcohol Concentration at Time of Driving From Results of Subsequent Breathalyzer Test, 28 SUFFOLK U. L. REV. 465 (1994).

27. *See, e.g.*, WEST'S ANN. IND. CODE 9–30–6–15.

28. Apparently New Jersey's presumption is irrebuttable. In *State v. Tischio*, 107 N.J. 504, 527 A.2d 388, 397 (N.J. 1987) the court held that extrapolation evidence was not required nor was it admissible.

29. Commonwealth v. Zugay, 745 A.2d 639, 649 (Pa.Super.2000) ("We hold that once the Commonwealth has established that the driver's blood alcohol content reflects an amount above 0.10%, the Commonwealth has made a prima facie case under 75 Pa.C.S. § 373(a)(4). At this point, the defendant is permitted to introduce expert testimony to rebut the Commonwealth's prima facie evidence. If the defendant decides to rebut the prima facie evidence against him with expert testimony, then the Commonwealth may present its own expert to refute this testimony.").

In *Finney v. State*, 686 N.E.2d 133 (Ind.App. 1997), the defendant challenged the constitutionality of the statutory presumption that the results of a test conducted within three hours of the time the defendant was operating a motor vehicle may be related back to the time the defendant was driving. The court rejected the constitutional argument and held that the defendant failed to rebut the presumption in this case. As the *Finney* court indicates, the strongest case for rebutting the presumption would occur when the driver had very recently consumed alcohol and his blood was tested during the absorption phase. Under these circumstances the driver's BAC at the time of testing might be higher than the driver's BAC at the time he was operating the vehicle.

In *State v. Lusi*, 625 A.2d 1350 (R.I.1993), the defendant presented expert testimony to rebut breathalyzer test results indicating a BAC of .11. Although the test indicated a BAC above .10, "Doctor Cohen testified that there

was a 'substantial likelihood' or a 'reasonable likelihood' that Lusi's BAC at the time he was driving the vehicle was less than 0.10 percent." *Id.* at 1352. The trial judge accepted this testimony and found that the arresting officer's observation of the defendant's behavior at the police station was by itself insufficient to support a conviction. Under these circumstances, the Supreme Court held the defendant was entitled to an acquittal. *Id.* at 1357.

30. *See* Miller v. State, 597 So.2d 767 (Fla. 1991). Some states have attempted to sidestep the entire extrapolation problem by criminalizing an excessive BAC at the time of the test. *See* GA. CODE ANN. § 40–6–391(a)(4) (Supp. 1993) defining a BAC of .10 or more within three hours of driving as an offense. KAN. STAT. ANN. § 8–1567(2) (Supp.1993) (.08 within two hours of driving).

31. *See* State v. Pendleton, 18 Kan.App.2d 179, 849 P.2d 143 (Kan.App.1993) (per se provision in statute requires test to be performed within two hours of time defendant was driving).

32. *See* People v. Victory, 166 Misc.2d 549, 631 N.Y.S.2d 805 (N.Y.City Crim.Ct.1995) (the *Victory* opinion has a useful discussion of the history of the Two Hour Rule in New York); ARIZ. REV. ST. § 28–1381.

33. WEST'S ANN. IND. CODE 9–30–6–2.

34. In *Allman v. State*, 728 N.E.2d 230 (Ind.App.2000), the blood test was not done within three hours of the alleged violation, as required by statute (WEST'S ANN. IND. CODE 9–30–6–15). The appellate court held that under these circumstances the state was not entitled to an instruction telling the jury they are permitted to find the defendant's BAC was at least .10% at the time of the violation if the test revealed a BAC this high or higher. Moreover, because the defendant's test results revealed a BAC just over the legal limit and the state did not provide expert testimony relating that BAC to the time of the accident, it did not meet its burden of proof.

question can be posed as one of reliability. When some time has passed does the unreliability of the evidence argue against its admissibility, e.g. is the error rate too high to permit an inference concerning the driver's BAC at the time of driving?

Setting aside specific statutory requirements, the issue in these cases turns on two questions. First, did the defendant have any opportunity to consume alcohol between the time of driving and the time of the test? Obviously, if the answer is yes then a presumption that the defendant's BAC while driving was as high as or higher than that indicated by the test is unwarranted. Thus, it is important for the state to show that the defendant had no opportunity to consume alcohol after arrest.

Second, is the BAC on the test greater or less than legally permissible? If it is greater, then the defendant's BAC at the time of driving can have been lower only if the defendant was still in the absorption phase at the time the test was taken. Note, however, this potential problem confronts all tests that are not taken immediately after the defendant was driving. In *State v. Banoub*,[36] a blood-alcohol test conducted approximately four hours after defendant's driving showed a result of .08. The court concluded that the delay was not "unreasonable" under Florida's requirement that a test be performed in a reasonable manner.[37] The state's expert testified that blood-alcohol level peeks between 45 minutes and three hours after ingestion, depending on the amount of food consumed at the same time.[38] Four hours after being stopped, a driver's BAC should have peaked and should be no higher than at the time of driving, even though a precise extrapolation back to the time of driving is impossible.[39]

If, on the other hand, the defendant's BAC on the test is less than legally permissible, proof that the BAC was above permissible levels while the defendant was operating the vehicle would require an extrapolation back to the time he was driving. We have uncovered no recent cases permitting the state to do this.[40]

In *State v. Daniel*,[41] a test conducted more than two hours after the

---

35. The Michigan DWI statute does not have a provision making admissibility contingent on the time elapsed between driving and the test. Nevertheless, the appellate courts had grafted a two hour reasonableness requirement onto the statute. In *People v. Wager*, 460 Mich. 118, 594 N.W.2d 487 (Mich. 1999), the Supreme Court overruled these cases and held that there is no requirement the test be given within a reasonable time. The prosecutor is not required to introduce expert evidence on the reliability of blood alcohol tests performed over two hours after a defendant's arrest. For a discussion of this case and the general issue of extrapolation, *see* J. Nicholas Bostic, *Alcohol-Related Offenses: Retrograde Extrapolation after Wager*, 79 Mich. B.J. 668 (2000).

A different question is posed by statutes that criminalize a BAC above a certain level for a period of time after one has been driving. With respect to these statutory provisions, a test administered after the period provided for would not be proof of a violation.

36. 700 So.2d 44 (Fla.App.1997).

37. Fla. Stat. 316.1993(1) (1995).

38. *Id.* at 46.

39. *Id.* The defense is entitled to attack this evidence through cross-examination or the introduction of its own expert witnesses who may testify that the test results do not accurately reflect BAC at the time of the offense.

40. Such an extrapolation is sometimes prohibited by statute. *See* Tex. Transp. Code Ann. § 524.035(a)(1) (Vernon Supp.1999) (an administrative law judge may not find a person was operating a motor vehicle with a BAC greater than 0.10 if the person had an alcohol concentration of less than 0.10 at the time the specimen was taken).

41. 132 Idaho 701, 979 P.2d 103 (Idaho 1999).

accident showed the defendant's BAC to be .06.[42] The Idaho DUI statute prohibits the state from prosecuting a suspect when his BAC is less than .10. The state argued that the statute prohibits prosecution only where the test in combination with expert testimony extrapolating the test result back to the time of driving shows the suspect's level to be below .10. The court disagreed and said the plain meaning of the statute prohibits prosecution even when extrapolation indicates a driving BAC in excess of .10.[43] A dissent argued that this ruling will force officers to choose between addressing emergency medical needs of accident victims and obtaining prompt blood tests of potentially alcohol-impaired drivers.[44]

Few courts have addressed the question of whether retrograde extrapolation evidence is sufficiently reliable to pass *Daubert* muster. An exception is *Hartman v. State*.[45] There the Texas Court of Criminal Appeals held that reverse extrapolation evidence offered to relate defendant's breath test results to the time he was driving must meet the relevant reliability standard before it is admissible.[46] On remand the trial court admitted such testimony over the objection of the defendant. Intoxilyzer tests administered within an hour of defendant's arrest measured his BAC at .138. Based on this, but with no information concerning the defendant's drinking history, age, or weight the state's qualified expert testified that at the time of the stop his BAC was between .11 and .15. The appellate court affirmed the decision to admit this testimony.[47] It noted that the expert did not purport to offer a precise blood-alcohol concentration number for the defendant at the time he was driving. The range that he offered took into account such variables as whether the defendant had eaten and his body's unique way of metabolizing alcohol.[48]

§ 8–1.2.4 Breath Tests

The results of breath tests using various devices such as the Intoximeter are routinely admitted. As the technology underlying these instruments has become widespread, some courts hold that the results of a test may be admitted without the foundational testimony of an operator familiar with the technical bases of the instrument, at least where the instrument has been certified by an appropriate state agency.[49]

Extrapolation issues also have risen with respect to breath tests. One controversy that seems to be dying down is the potential for error involved in an extrapolation from a given breath test result to blood alcohol concentration. The question concerns the appropriate ratio one should use when translating breath results into blood alcohol concentrations. The generally accepted ratio is approximately 2,100 to 1,[50] however, individual ratios may

42. *Id.* at 105.

43. *Id.*

44. *Id.* at 106.

45. 946 S.W.2d 60, 63 (Tex.Crim.App. 1997).

46. 946 S.W.2d at 63.

47. Hartman v. State, 2 S.W.3d 490 (Tex. App.1999).

48. Mata v. State, 13 S.W.3d 1 (Tex.App. 1999), reaches the same result. However, in a lengthy dissent, Justice Cadena argued that the expert's testimony in the case was inadmis-

sible because it was based on "average" and "standard" rates and was not focused specifically on the defendant's characteristics. *Id.* at 32.

49. *See* State v. Sensing, 843 S.W.2d 412 (Tenn.1992); Texas Dept. of Pub. Safety v. Jimenez, 995 S.W.2d 834, 838 (Tex.App.1999).

50. That is 2.1 liters of alveolar lung air contains the same amount of alcohol as one milliliter of blood. *See* § 2.3.2 *infra.*

vary depending on a number of factors such as body temperature, atmospheric pressure, and an individual's medical condition.[51] This may pose a problem when the only test evidence of intoxication is from a breath test and the statute defines intoxication in terms of BAC. The legal issue, of course, is whether the breath test overestimates BAC to the detriment of the accused. Today, it is generally agreed that overestimation is a relatively rare phenomenon, in part because the average ratio in post-absorption subjects is closer to 1:2300.[52]

Most states have sidestepped this problem by redefining illegal alcohol levels in terms of both blood and breath concentrations, typically at the 1:2100 ratio.[53] For example, California redrafted its statute in 1990 to define driving under the influence in terms of "grams of alcohol per 100 milliliters of blood or grams of alcohol per 210 liters of breath."[54] Under this revised statute, the California Supreme Court affirmed a trial court's refusal to allow the defendants to show that their personal partition ratio was different from the standard 1:2100 ratio.[55]

It is reported that as of 1997 38 states have passed such laws.[56] Indiana's attempt to enact such a provision was struck down in *Sales v. State*.[57] The court declared the statute was defective as written.[58] In a subsequent opinion, the court held that absent such a statute the state must present evidence to correlate the results of a breath test with the amount of alcohol in the defendant's blood.[59]

Extrapolation issues occasionally arise with respect to other types of tests as well. In *State v. MacCardwell*,[60] the defendant attempted to suppress the results of a plasma-alcohol concentration in part because the ratio used to convert these results to the equivalent blood-alcohol concentration was unreliable.[61] The state's expert testified that the North Carolina State Bureau of Investigation uses a ratio of 1 to 1.18 to convert plasma concentrations into "whole blood results." He testified that 90% of the published studies in journals report conversion ratios from 1 to 1.15 through 1 to 1.21.[62] Using the 1 to 1.18 ratio, the defendants BAC was .107, and using the more conservative 1 to 1.21 ratio it was still .105. The appellate court found that the trial judge did not abuse his discretion in finding the 1 to 1.18 ratio to be reliable, although it was also proper to permit the defendant to admit evidence attacking the conversion ratio.[63]

51. *See* People v. McDonald, 206 Cal. App.3d 877, 254 Cal.Rptr. 384 (1988); State v. Downie, 117 N.J. 450, 569 A.2d 242 (N.J.1990).

52. *See* § 2.3.2 *infra*.

53. *See* Committee on Alcohol and Other Drugs, National Safety Council, 49 Fed. Reg. 48855 (1984). The National Highway Traffic Safety Administration periodically issues specifications for devices to measure breath alcohol. For example, see 58 Fed. Reg. 48705–01 (1993); 63 Fed. Reg.10066–01 (1998).

54. West's Ann. Cal.Vehicle Code § 23152(b); Jacques Garden, *Exclusion of Evidence Concerning 'Partition Ratio' is Proper Because Section 23152 of the California Vehicle Code Does Not Create a Conclusive Presumption of Intoxication, But Rather Defines The Substantive Offense of Driving With A Specified Concentration of Alcohol in the Body: People v. Bransford*, 22 Pepp. L. Rev. 1721 (1995).

55. People v. Bransford, 8 Cal.4th 885, 35 Cal.Rptr.2d 613, 884 P.2d 70 (Cal.1994).

56. Sales v. State, 714 N.E.2d 1121, 1126 (Ind.App.1999).

57. 714 N.E.2d 1121 (Ind.App.1999).

58. *Id.* at 1129.

59. *Id.* at 1011.

60. 133 N.C.App. 496, 516 S.E.2d 388 (1999).

61. *Id.* at 391.

62. *Id.* at 391.

63. *Id.* at 396.

§ 8–1.2.5 Horizontal Gaze Nystagmus (HGN)

[1] Validity/General Acceptance

As defined in *People v. Ojeda*, "Nystagmus is an involuntary rapid movement of the eyeball which may be horizontal, vertical, or rotary.[64] An inability of the eyes to maintain visual fixation as they are turned from side to side (in other words, jerking or bouncing) is known as horizontal gaze nystagmus, or HGN."[65] Proponents of HGN tests believe that alcohol and drug use increases the frequency and amplitude of HGN and cause it to occur at a smaller angle of deviation from forward.[66] Nystagmus tests are not done in a laboratory, but rather are given by police officers in the field or in a police station subsequent to arrest. The results of an HGN test are frequently introduced as part of the state's case in drunk driving prosecutions and they also may be used when an individual is suspected to be under the influence of some other substance and, therefore, are an important part of the drug testing environment.[67]

HGN tests are frequently used as part of longer field sobriety tests or a drug recognition protocol, designed to assist police in determining whether a driver is impaired and, if so, due to what substance. The most widely used protocol, the "drug influence evaluation," was developed by the National Highway Traffic Safety Administration and the Los Angeles Police Department in response to the fact that police officers were encountering drivers who were clearly impaired but whose blood alcohol concentration reading indicated that they were not intoxicated.[68] Participating jurisdictions give

64. *See* John P. Ludington, *Horizontal Gaze Nystagmus Test: Use in Impaired Driving Prosecution*, 60 A.L.R. 4th 1129 (1988).

65. 225 Cal.App.3d 404, 275 Cal.Rptr. 472 (Cal.Ct.App.1990). *See* Joseph R. Meaney, *Horizontal Gaze Nystagmus: A Closer Look*, 36 Jurimetrics J. 383 (1996); Charles R. Honts & Susan L. Amato–Henderson, *Horizontal Gaze Nystagmus Test: The State of the Science in 1995*, 71 N.D. L. Rev. 671 (1995); James Rick Russell, *Judicial Notice of the Validity of Horizontal Gaze Nystagmus in Texas: Emerson v. State*, 2 Tex. Wesleyan L. Rev. 355 (1995); Stephanie E. Busloff, *Can Your Eyes Be Used Against You? The Use of the Horizontal Gaze Nystagmus Test in the Courtroom*, 84 J. Crim. L. & Criminology 203 (1993). HGN is one type of nystagmus. Occasionally, other nystagmus tests are used by law enforcement authorities. *See* Honts & Amato–Henderson, *supra*, at 685.

66. A useful review of the science on HGN can be found in Meaney, *supra* note 65.

67. State v. Klawitter, 518 N.W.2d 577 (Minn.1994) (marijuana); People v. Quinn, 153 Misc.2d 139, 580 N.Y.S.2d 818 (1991) (cocaine); Kerr v. State, 205 Ga.App. 624, 423 S.E.2d 276 (Ga.Ct.App.1992) (cocaine and marijuana—ad-missibility of nystagmus test not challenged). *See* Chapter 36.

68. *See* Jeffrey M. Morgan, *The Admissibility of Drug Recognition Expert Testimony in the Prosecution of Individuals Driving Under the Influence of a Controlled Substance: State v. Klawitter, 518 N.W.2d 577 (Minn.1994)*, 18 Hamline L. Rev. 261, 267 (1994). The protocol includes the following 12 steps a Drug Recognition Expert (DRE) should take: "(1) a breath-alcohol test; (2) an interview with the arresting officer; (3) a preliminary medical examination, including taking the suspect's pulse, to determine whether immediate medical attention must precede further investigation; (4) eye examinations, including nystagmus and convergence tests; (5) motor skills tests; (6) an examination of pulse, temperature, and blood pressure; (7) a pupil measurement under four lighting conditions and an 'ingestion examination,' checking the suspect's nose and mouth for signs of inhalation or smoking; (8) an 'examination for muscle rigidity'; (9) a search for needle marks; (10) questioning of the suspect in which the officer should suggest that the officer knows the suspect has used certain drugs; (11) documentation of the officer's 'expert opinion' of what categories of drugs, if any, have impaired the suspect's ability to

special training to some officers, who then become drug recognition experts (DRE). Most of the controversy concerning scientific validity has surrounded the HGN test, but the other parts of field sobriety tests or the DRE protocol have also raised some admissibility issues, albeit usually in cases involving drugs other than alcohol.[69]

Courts have used both *Frye* and *Daubert* analyses when assessing the admissibility of nystagmus results. In *People v. Leahy*,[70] the California court of appeals held that HGN tests were inadmissible to show intoxication without a *Frye/Kelly* foundational showing that the procedure had achieved general acceptance in the relevant scientific community. The Supreme Court of California affirmed, and in the process decided that California's *Kelly/Frye*[71] "general acceptance" test would not be altered in the aftermath of the *Daubert* decision.[72] The court concluded that HGN is a "new scientific technique" within the scope of the *Kelly* formulation, and therefore could not be admitted absent proof of its general acceptance.[73] It remanded the case for a *Kelly/Frye* hearing. The court made it clear that the state will not always be required to submit the testimony of an expert to show the general acceptance of HGN tests. "[I]n future cases, once the *Kelly* standard has been met, as reflected by a published appellate precedent, the prosecution will not be required to submit expert testimony to confirm a police officer's evaluation of an HGN test."[74]

The Oregon Supreme Court employed a *Daubert* analysis to assess nystagmus in *State v. O'Key*.[75] The trial court held an omnibus hearing and concluded that HGN evidence was not admissible.[76] An appellate court re-

drive; and (12) a toxicological examination." 518 N.W.2d at 579–80.

69. State v. Baity, 140 Wash.2d 1, 991 P.2d 1151 (Wash.2000). See the Drug Testing Chapter for a more complete discussion of DRE protocols. The National Highway Traffic Safety Administration has a number of publications concerning HGN. *See, e.g.,* NHTSA, HORIZONTAL GAZE NYSTAGMUS: THE SCIENCE AND THE LAW, A RESOURCE GUIDE FOR JUDGES, PROSECUTORS, AND LAW ENFORCEMENT (NHTSA, NTS–21, 400 (1999)), discussing both the science and the law with respect to HGN. *See* http://www.nhtsa.dot.gov/people/injury/enforce/nystagmus/hgntxt.html. Visited, March 28, 2001.

70. 22 Cal.Rptr.2d 322 (1993), review granted and opinion superseded, 25 Cal. Rptr.2d 390, 863 P.2d 635 (Cal. 1993).

71. California adopted a *Frye* test in *People v. Kelly*, 17 Cal.3d 24, 130 Cal.Rptr. 144, 549 P.2d 1240 (Cal. 1976).

72. People v. Leahy, 8 Cal.4th 587, 34 Cal. Rptr.2d 663, 882 P.2d 321 (Cal. 1994).

73. *Id.* at 831–32. In *People v. Stoll*, 49 Cal.3d 1136, 265 Cal.Rptr. 111, 783 P.2d 698, 710 (Cal.1989), the court stated, *"Kelly/Frye* only applies to that limited class of expert testimony which is based, in whole or part, on a technique, process, or theory which is new to science and, even more so, the law." The court noted that in determining whether a scientific

technique is "new" for *Kelly* purposes, long standing use by law enforcement is less significant than repeated use, study and testing by scientists. "To hold that a scientific technique could become immune from *Kelly* scrutiny merely by reason of longstanding and persistent use by law enforcement outside the laboratory or the courtroom seems unjustified." *Leahy*, 882 P.2d at 332.

74. 882 P.2d at 336. The Oregon Supreme Court has adopted a similar rule. *See* State v. O'Key, 321 Or. 285, 899 P.2d 663, 673 (Or. 1995) ("Once a trial court has decided that proffered expert scientific testimony is scientifically valid and has admitted such evidence for the particular purpose to which it is directed, and that decision is affirmed by this court in a published opinion, it will become precedent controlling subsequent trials.").

75. 321 Or. 285, 899 P.2d 663 (Or.1995).

76. In the Oregon test, "each eye is checked for three possible clues that the person tested is under the influence of intoxicating liquor: (1) Angle of onset—the more impaired by alcohol that a person becomes, the sooner the jerking will occur as the eyes move to the side (one point is awarded if nystagmus is present when an officer holds a stimulus at a 40–degree angle); (2) maximum deviation—the greater the alcohol impairment, the more distinct the nystagmus is when the eyes are as far

versed. On appeal, the Oregon Supreme Court first determined that HGN is "scientific evidence" and cannot be admitted absent a showing that it meets the requirements of Oregon Rules 702 and 403.[77] Relying on the omnibus hearing below, the court affirmed the appellate court. HGN is admissible scientific evidence under the Oregon test.[78] The court found that the theory underlying the HGN test, that there is a strong correlation between the amount of alcohol a person consumes and the angle of onset of nystagmus, can be and has been tested.[79] The test does suffer from a non-trivial error rate, due in part to the substantial number of factors other than alcohol or drugs that may induce nystagmus.[80] The court noted, however, that research studies indicate the error rate of an HGN test is lower than for other field sobriety tests routinely admitted into evidence and that when properly administered and scored by a qualified officer the test is a reasonably reliable indicator of alcohol impairment even though other causes of nystagmus cannot be ruled out completely.[81] Finally, it concluded that the test had achieved general acceptance in the relevant scientific communities.[82] The court also considered and rejected the defendant's argument that HGN tests

to the side as possible (one point is awarded if endpoint nystagmus is present); (3) smooth or jerky pursuit—a person impaired by alcohol cannot follow a slowly moving object smoothly with his eyes (one point is awarded if jerky pursuit is observed). A score of six points is possible, three for each eye." *Id.* at 674.

77. "The HGN test provides evidence that purports to draw its convincing force from a principle of science, namely, the asserted scientific proposition that there is a causal relationship between consumption of alcohol and the type of nystagmus measured by the HGN test.... The value of HGN testing depends critically on the demonstrated scientific validity of that proposition. Moreover, the proposition that alcohol consumption causes nystagmus possesses significantly increased potential to influence the trier of fact as a 'scientific' assertion." *Id.* at 675.

78. State v. Brown, 297 Or. 404, 687 P.2d 751 (Or.1984), the leading Oregon case interpreting Oregon's version of Rule 702, identified seven non-exclusive factors that may affect a trial court's admissibility decision: "(1) The technique's general acceptance in the field; (2) The expert's qualifications and stature; (3) The use which has been made of the technique; (4) The potential rate of error; (5) The existence of specialized literature; (6) The novelty of the invention; and (7) The extent to which the technique relies on the subjective interpretation of the expert." *O'Key*, 899 P.2d at 677. In addition, the *O'Key* court cited with approval the four factors listed in *Daubert*, and the factors listed in *United States v. Downing*, 753 F.2d 1224, 1238–41 (3d Cir.1985) (the non-judicial uses and experience with the process or technique and the extent to which other courts have permitted expert testimony based on the process or technique). *O'Key*, 899 P.2d at 679–680.

79. *Id.* at 682.

80. The court listed the following potential causes of a "false-positive" nystagmus test: "First, there is a small but significant number of people who have chronic nystagmoid eye movements. Second, people who have high refractive errors could have trouble seeing the test target with their glasses removed and may therefore have problems with the test. Third, many people will have jerky eye movements even with 0.00 percent BAC. Nearly anything that affects the inner ear labyrinth, including alcohol, will cause nystagmus. The evidence in the record shows that about three percent of the population suffers from non-alcohol-induced nystagmus and that, within that group, there are 50 to 100 causes of the phenomenon. Examples of causes of non-alcohol-induced nystagmus include caffeine, nicotine, eyestrain, motion sickness, epilepsy, streptococcus infections, measles, vertigo, muscular dystrophy, multiple sclerosis, influenza, hypertension, sunstroke, changes in atmospheric pressure, and arteriosclerosis. Depressants and convulsants can cause HGN, and sleep loss can change the angle of onset by about five degrees. Non-alcohol-induced nystagmus, however, typically is asymmetrical (one eye only), whereas alcohol-induced nystagmus is the same in both eyes. Officers are trained to look for that aspect." 899 P.2d at 864 (citing Comment, 84 J. CRIM. L. & CRIMINOLOGY at 212). *See* Schultz v. State, 106 Md.App. 145, 664 A.2d 60, 77 (Md.Ct.App.1995) for another list of possible causes of nystagmus.

81. *O'Key*, 899 P.2d at 684.

82. It defined the communities as pharmacology, ophthalmology, optometry, behavioral psychology, highway safety, neurology, and criminalistics. *Id.* at 686.

should be excluded under Rule 403 because their probative value was outweighed by their prejudicial effect or because the introduction of the evidence would unduly prolong trials.[83]

To our knowledge, no court has concluded after a full *Daubert/Frye* analysis that HGN is never admissible because it is not reliable.[84] Several have taken judicial notice of the procedure's general acceptance and/or reliability. In *State v. Taylor*,[85] the Maine Supreme Court took judicial notice of the reliability of HGN tests in making determinations of probable cause for arrest and for purposes of establishing criminal guilt in DUI cases.[86] A similar result was reached in *Williams v. State*[87] and *State v. Ito*.[88]

83. *Id.* at 688–89.

84. New Jersey is one of the most recent jurisdictions to recognize the reliability of the test. State v. Maida, 332 N.J.Super. 564, 753 A.2d 1240 (Law.Div.2000).

Kansas perhaps comes closest to rejecting this evidence. In *State v. Witte*, 251 Kan. 313, 836 P.2d 1110, 1111 (Kan.1992), the court concluded that HGN had not reached general acceptance under the Kansas version of *Frye*. The syllabus prepared by the court said that the state could meet its *Frye* burden "by proving: (1) The reliability of the underlying scientific theory upon which the horizontal gaze nystagmus test is based (i.e., that the nystagmus of the eye is, in fact, an indicator of alcohol consumption to the degree that it influences or impairs the ability to drive); (2) the method used to test horizontal gaze nystagmus is a valid test to measure or perceive that phenomenon, particularly if the method actually conducted by the law enforcement officer administering the test." 836 P.2d at 1111. The state attempted to demonstrate reliability and general acceptance in State v. Chastain, 265 Kan. 16, 960 P.2d 756 (Kan.1998). The state presented the testimony of a psychology Ph.D as to the reliability of the test, but the trial court, nevertheless, excluded the HGN results. The Kansas Supreme Court affirmed. It steadfastly held to its earlier position that HGN had not reached general acceptance. *Id.* at 761. It quoted favorably the following trial court ruling following the expert's testimony:

State v. Witte raises a number of questions, none of which have been answered here today. There are a number of medical conditions which this witness has testified that she is not qualified to answer, medical questions regarding, and these are issues that were specifically addressed in State v. Witte. And questions that were addressed, this appears to be a bootstrapped-type of testing procedure that has not been shown—there are a number of other matters that need to be addressed before the scientific reliability of this testing will be allowed.

Id.

The final position of the Kansas courts awaits a case where the trial judge admits HGN testimony following the testimony of an expert.

In *State v. Borchardt*, 224 Neb. 47, 395 N.W.2d 551 (Neb.1986), the Nebraska Supreme Court found that the trial court erred in admitting an officer's HGN testimony because the record contained no competent evidence the new test is valid. 395 N.W.2d at 558. *Borchardt* was overruled in *State v. Baue*, 258 Neb. 968, 607 N.W.2d 191 (Neb.2000) (results from HGN field sobriety test are admissible for the limited purpose of establishing that the defendant had an impairment which could have been caused by alcohol).

The Supreme Court of Mississippi concluded that the HGN test is a scientific test. Moreover, it concluded that the test is not generally accepted within the scientific community and cannot be used as scientific evidence to prove intoxication or impairment. Its only permissible use is to prove probable cause to arrest and administer an intoxilyzer or a blood test. Young v. City of Brookhaven, 693 So.2d 1355, 1360–61 (Miss.1997). As the court in *Ballard v. State*, 955 P.2d 931 (Alaska App.1998) notes, however, the "Mississippi court's reasoning is simply confused." *Id.* at 938 n. 6. In *Young* there had been no *Frye* hearing below to determining the general acceptance of HGN tests, and the Supreme Court did not engage in a separate analysis of the question. Therefore, its statement that HGN has not reached general acceptance is *ipse dixit. See* N. Laurence Willey, Jr., *Should HGN in DUI be DOA?*, 13 Me. B.J. 60 (1998).

85. 694 A.2d 907 (Me. 1997).

86. 694 A.2d at 910.

87. 710 So.2d 24 (Fla.App.1998) (HGN is not novel scientific evidence and court takes judicial notice that the technique has reached general acceptance under the *Frye* test). *Williams* comes as close as any recent case to holding that HGN does not require expert testimony as a foundation for admissibility. "Although clothed in scientific garb, we recognize the HGN does not involve any particular 'scientific' skill or equipment and for that reason courts have struggled with its classification. Nevertheless, the HGN test is premised on the

Courts have generally fallen into three camps with respect to the admissibility of HGN results. In one camp are jurisdictions that hold results to be inadmissible in the absence of a foundational showing that the procedure has achieved general acceptance (in *Frye* jurisdictions) or is scientifically valid (in *Daubert* jurisdictions). A second group of states required a foundational showing when HGN was first introduced in the jurisdiction, but have concluded that the scientific validity of the procedure is now established and, therefore, independent expert testimony is no longer required.[89] A third group of states have held that HGN is no more scientific than other field sobriety tests and, therefore, never requires expert testimony as a foundation for admissibility.[90]

The majority of recent cases that have addressed the admissibility question have fallen in the first camp.[91] They include, *State v. Baue*,[92] *State v. Chastain*,[93] *State v. Helms*,[94] *Hulse v. Department of Justice, Motor Vehicle Division*,[95] *Commonwealth v. Sands*,[96] *State v. Meador*,[97] *People v. Kirk*,[98] *Ballard v. State*,[99] *State v. Murphy*,[100] and *State v. Torres*.[101] Courts that take this view generally do so because they believe that, unlike most field sobriety tests, HGN rests on little understood scientific principles and the phenomenon is beyond the common understanding of the jury. As the Court in *Murphy* noted, "In our view, the HGN test does differ fundamentally from other field sobriety tests because the witness must necessarily explain the underlying

asserted scientific proposition that the automatic tracking mechanisms of the eyes are affected by drug consumption. Thus, while we are not convinced that the HGN is truly 'scientific,' because its application is dependent on a scientific proposition and requires a particular expertise outside the realm of common knowledge of the average person, we conclude the HGN is 'quasi-scientific' evidence." *Williams*, 710 So.2d at 30.

88. 90 Hawai'i 225, 978 P.2d 191, 209 (Haw.App.1999). The court reached this conclusion primarily by looking to case law from other jurisdictions. It did not stop there, however. It reviewed the admissibility of HGN tests under factors listed in *State v. Montalbo*, 73 Haw. 130, 828 P.2d 1274, 1280 (Haw. 1992), and found the theory and general technique to be reliable.

89. State v. Superior Court, 149 Ariz. 269, 718 P.2d 171 (Ariz.1986); Albert v. State, 236 Ga.App. 146, 511 S.E.2d 244 (Ga.Ct.App.1999).

90. State v. Murphy, 451 N.W.2d 154 (Iowa 1990); Whitson v. State, 314 Ark. 458, 863 S.W.2d 794 (Ark.1993); City of Fargo v. McLaughlin, 512 N.W.2d 700 (N.D.1994). Recently, New Mexico moved from this category to the first category. *See* State v. Torres, 127 N.M. 20, 976 P.2d 20 (N.M.1999).

91. Earlier cases adopting this position include *State v. Cissne*, 72 Wash.App. 677, 865 P.2d 564, 568 (Wash.Ct.App.1994) ("The HGN test is a different type of test from balancing on one leg or walking a straight line because it rests almost entirely upon an assertion of scientific legitimacy rather than a basis of common knowledge." HGN must meet *Frye* test.)

and *State v. Witte*, 251 Kan. 313, 836 P.2d 1110, 1111 (Kan.1992) ("The horizontal gaze nystagmus test is distinguished from other field sobriety tests in that science, rather than common knowledge, provides the legitimacy for horizontal gaze nystagmus testing.... As such, the foundation requirements for admissibility enunciated in *Frye v. United States* must be satisfied.").

92. 258 Neb. 968, 607 N.W.2d 191 (Neb. 2000).

93. 265 Kan. 16, 960 P.2d 756 (Kan.1998).

94. 348 N.C. 578, 504 S.E.2d 293 (N.C. 1998).

95. 289 Mont. 1, 961 P.2d 75 (Mont.1998).

96. 424 Mass. 184, 675 N.E.2d 370 (Mass. 1997). The case contains a useful list of the positions of other jurisdictions as of 1996. Massachusetts has adopted an admissibility standard that is a mixture of *Frye* and *Daubert*. "A party seeking to introduce scientific evidence may lay a foundation either by showing that the underlying scientific theory is generally accepted within the relevant scientific community, or by showing that the theory is reliable or valid through other means." *Id.* at 371.

97. 674 So.2d 826 (Fla.App.1996).

98. 289 Ill.App.3d 326, 224 Ill.Dec. 452, 681 N.E.2d 1073 (Ill.App.1997).

99. 955 P.2d 931 (Alaska App.1998) (*Frye* test).

100. 953 S.W.2d 200 (Tenn.1997).

101. 127 N.M. 20, 976 P.2d 20 (N.M.1999).

scientific basis of the test in order for the testimony to be meaningful to a jury. Other tests, in marked contrast, carry no such requirement."[102]

However, jurisdictions that require an adequate foundation in each case rarely require testimony from someone other than an adequately trained police officer.[103] The position of the court in the recent case of *State v. Baue*[104] is typical: "We conclude that the majority view is sound, and adopt the view that a police officer may testify to the results of HGN testing if it is shown that the officer has been adequately trained in the administration and assessment of the HGN test and has conducted the testing and assessment in accordance with that training."[105]

Other states have reached a similar result by different means. In *Zimmerman v State*,[106] the court reviewed the superior court opinion in *Ruthardt*[107] holding that HGN is generally accepted. It concluded that under the doctrine of *stare decisis* parties in future cases do not have to establish that HGN is reasonably relied upon by experts in the field. Nevertheless, the party wishing to introduce the evidence must present evidence from an expert with specialized knowledge and training in HGN concerning the underlying principles supporting HGN[108]

In sum, the practical difference between those states that require a showing of scientific validity/ general acceptance and those states that say the scientific validity of HGN has been established and does not need to be proven in each new case is quite small. In most of the states that fall into the first category, the testimony of a trained lay person such as a police officer suffices to lay a validity foundation. Moreover, in most of the states in the second category, the state must put an expert (often an officer) on the stand to explain the principles underlying the test, to testify about how the test is conducted, and to aver that proper procedures were performed by a trained individual in the case at bar.

102. 953 S.W.2d at 202–03.

103. One possible exception may be Montana. In *Hulse v. Department of Justice, Motor Vehicle Division*, 289 Mont. 1, 961 P.2d 75 (Mont.1998), the Montana Supreme Court joined states holding that the scientific validity of HGN has been established. Because a *Daubert* analysis is required only for novel scientific evidence in Montana, the state in future cases no longer needs to introduce evidence proving that the test is scientifically valid. Nevertheless, because the scientific principle underlying the test is beyond the range of ordinary experience, the court must conduct a "conventional Rule 702 analysis." *Id.* at 93. This includes a showing that the expert testifying about HGN has undergone special training and possesses an adequate understanding of the technique to render an expert opinion. In addition, the state must show that the officer administering the test is qualified to do so and that he administered the test in the instant case according to established procedures. *Id.* It is not precisely clear in the *Hulse* opinion what training an individual will need in order to qualify as an expert on the scientific principles.

If the point of requiring expert testimony is to provide jurors with a sufficient understanding of the principles underlying HGN to permit them to assess this evidence, then the testimony of a trained officer might well suffice. In *City of Missoula v. Robertson*, 298 Mont. 419, 998 P.2d 144 (Mont.2000), the court found that a municipal court erred in admitting the testimony of a police officer without expert testimony establishing the test's validity. *Id.* at 152. The officer conceded that he lacked the expertise to testify as to the test's reliability. *Id.*

104. 258 Neb. 968, 607 N.W.2d 191 (Neb. 2000).

105. *Id.* at 205. *See* State v. Zivcic, 229 Wis.2d 119, 598 N.W.2d 565, 570 (Wis.App. 1999) ("[a]s long as the HGN test results are accompanied by the testimony of a law enforcement officer who is properly trained to administer and evaluate the test," the evidence is admissible.).

106. 693 A.2d 311 (Del.1997).

107. 680 A.2d 349 (Del.Super.1996).

108. 693 A.2d at 315.

Theoretically, this position is more easily justified in *Frye* jurisdictions, especially those who hold that *Frye* only applies to "novel" scientific evidence. In *Daubert* jurisdictions, where the proponent has the obligation of showing that the theory underlying HGN is sound, it is not clear how a police officer with little more than a few weeks training is in a position to be qualified to offer this opinion. Nevertheless, through various devices, including judicial notice,[109] courts have bowed to the practicalities of the situation and permitted the officer to establish the general reliability of the technique.

In spite of the widespread acceptance of HGN, especially in the alcohol cases, the science underlying the accuracy of the procedure is not deep and the error rate, especially the false positive rate,[110] in everyday applications is not known.[111] The lack of confirmatory double blind laboratory studies is particularly acute with respect to drugs other than alcohol. However, the few cases that have addressed admissibility in non-alcohol contexts have not focused on this point.

[2] Fit

The potentially large false positive rate raises the question of what conclusions an officer should be allowed to draw from a failed nystagmus test or a failed drug recognition evaluation. As discussed in *Daubert*, this is a question of "fit." "[S]cientific validity for one purpose is not necessarily scientific validity for other, unrelated purposes."[112]

Nystagmus and protocol evidence may be admitted for several different purposes: as probable cause for arrest; as evidence of neurological dysfunction; as evidence that the defendant was driving under the influence of intoxicants; and as evidence as to the defendant's level of intoxication. This last type of testimony points up an important difference between alcohol impairment and drug impairment cases. In order to convict someone for driving while intoxicated, the prosecution must prove the defendant's blood alcohol content was above some threshold, most frequently .10. Courts must resolve, therefore, whether the expert can testify, based on HGN tests alone or in combination with other field tests, that the suspect's BAC was above the minimum threshold. A number of states have answered this question in the negative. In *State v. O'Key*,[113] the court held that HGN evidence is admissible

109. *See* State v. Ito, 90 Hawai'i 225, 978 P.2d 191, 209 (Haw.App.1999).

110. *See* Honts & Amato–Henderson, *supra* note 65 at 688–89. A false positive is a result that indicates the suspect has used drugs, when in fact he has not. In statistics this is frequently called a Type I error. A false negative result occurs when a test indicates the suspect has not used drugs, when in fact he has. This is sometimes called a Type II error. Because litigation involving drug testing is almost always concerned with the rights of the accused, the cases focus their attention on the probability of false positives. A "false positive" in this context occurs when an officer determines that the suspect is intoxicated when in fact he is not. A false positive may occur either because the suspect has consumed a drug but is not yet legally intoxicated, or because the suspect suffers from nystagmus due to other causes, e.g., prescription drugs. There is a potential for a second type of false positive in this situation: the officer may conclude the suspect has failed the test when in fact he has passed it.

111. In controlled studies conducted by NHTSA, the error rate is relatively low, in the 10% range. *See* note 171, *infra*.

112. *Daubert*, 509 U.S. at 591. *See* SCIENCE IN THE LAW: STANDARDS, STATISTICS AND RESEARCH ISSUES, Chapter 1 and the Epidemiology Chapter (Chapter 7) for a fuller discussion of "fit."

113. 321 Or. 285, 899 P.2d 663 (Or.1995).

to establish that a person was under the influence of alcohol, but not to establish the individuals's blood alcohol level. Likewise, in *State v. Superior Court*,[114] although the court found HGN test results to be admissible as to the defendant's intoxication, they are not admissible to prove a blood alcohol concentration above .10.[115] The Arizona Supreme Court clarified the role of HGN tests in the absence of blood in *Hamilton v. City Court*, and in the process seemed to describe an even narrower role for HGN testimony.[116] In the absence of any chemical tests, HGN results are admissible only to permit the officer to testify that "based on his training and experience the results indicated possible neurological dysfunction, one cause of which could be alcohol ingestion."[117]

Maryland and Washington also prohibit the use of HGN results to establish level of intoxication. In *Wilson v. State*,[118] the trial court permitted the arresting officer to testify, based on the results of a HGN test, that the defendant's "blood alcohol content was probably point one zero or higher."[119] The appellate court found that this was error.[120] In *State v. Baity*,[121] the court explicitly limited the scope of permitted testimony based on HGN and DRE protocol results.

> We emphasize, however, that our opinion today is confined to situations where all 12–steps of the protocol have been undertaken. Moreover, an officer may not testify in a fashion that casts an aura of scientific certainty to the testimony. The officer also may not predict the specific level of drugs present in a suspect. The DRE officer, properly qualified, may express an opinion that a suspect's behavior and physical attributes are or are not consistent with the behavioral and physical signs associated with certain categories of drugs.[122]

§ 8–1.2.6 Field Sobriety Tests

Police officers very frequently administer field sobriety tests at the scene after stopping someone who they suspect may be intoxicated. The tests

114. 149 Ariz. 269, 718 P.2d 171 (Ariz. 1986).

115. "The arresting officer's 'reading' of the HGN test cannot be verified or duplicated by an independent party. The test's recognized margin of error provides problems as to criminal convictions which require proof of guilt beyond a reasonable doubt. The circumstances under which the test is administered at roadside may affect the reliability of the test results. Nystagmus may be caused by conditions other than alcohol intoxication. And finally, the far more accurate chemical testing devices are readily available." *Id.* at 181. *See e.g.*, State v. Bresson, 51 Ohio St.3d 123, 554 N.E.2d 1330, 1336 (Ohio 1990) (officer may not give an opinion as to the driver's actual BAC); State v. Garrett, 119 Idaho 878, 811 P.2d 488, 491 (Idaho 1991) ("HGN test results may not be used at trial to establish the defendant's blood alcohol level in the absence of chemical analysis of the defendant's blood, breath, or urine.").

116. 165 Ariz. 514, 799 P.2d 855 (Ariz. 1990).

117. *Id.* at 860.

118. 124 Md.App. 543, 723 A.2d 494 (Md. Ct.App.1999).

119. *Id.* at 496–97.

120. *Id.* at 499. In *State v. Ross*, 147 Or. App. 634, 938 P.2d 797 (Or.Ct.App.1997), the court held that HGN results to show a level of intoxication are inadmissible because the legislature has provided that only a chemical test can be used to determine blood alcohol content, and HGN is not a chemical test. Such statutory provisions are typically enacted to reduce the false positive error rate.

121. 140 Wash.2d 1, 991 P.2d 1151 (Wash. 2000).

122. *Id.* at 1160–61 (2000). In an increasingly frequent situation, the defendants in *Baity* apparently were driving while under the influence of both alcohol and other drugs. *Id.* at 1156.

typically involve such procedures as a horizontal gaze nystagmus test, a "walk and turn" test, a "one-leg stand" test, a "finger-count" test, and asking the suspect to write down the letters of the alphabet.[123] Courts are of two minds about this protocol. Many courts carve out the HGN test for special treatment and hold that the remainder of the test is not scientific. Rather, conclusions drawn from performance on tests such as walk and turn and one-leg stand are simply common sense observations not beyond the ken of a layperson and, therefore, do not require expert testimony as a foundation for admissibility.[124]

Volk v United States[125] is a federal case dealing with this question in the aftermath of the Supreme Court's opinion in *Kumho Tire Co. v. Carmichael*.[126] One might argue that although FTS is not scientific, it is technical expert knowledge to which *Daubert's*[127] reliability requirement applies. In *Volk*, the defendant was convicted by a magistrate judge of driving under the influence of alcohol. The defendant argued that the trial court erred in admitting the testimony of the arresting officer based on his administration of a field sobriety test without first holding a pre-trial evidentiary hearing to determine whether the testimony met the requirements of *Daubert*. The district court disagreed. It noted that far from forcing trial courts to follow a specific procedure, *Kumho* afforded them broad discretion.[128]

The officer testified that he had received specialized training on how to conduct field sobriety tests and had performed such tests on approximately 100 individuals.[129] Based on the totality of the defendant's performance on all of the tests, the officer concluded he had probable cause to arrest the defendant for driving under the influence of alcohol.[130] The district court ruled that the officer's foundation testimony was adequate to support the magis-

123. Volk v. United States, 57 F. Supp. 2d 888, 891 (N.D.Cal.1999).

124. State v. Maida, 332 N.J.Super. 564, 753 A.2d 1240, 1246 (Law Div.2000) ("Defendant argues that the clue point system applied by the Officer in this case is also not scientifically reliable, and, therefore, should be excluded. According to Officer Conroy's testimony, the clue point system is just a formal way of translating the number of times the defendant faltered during a particular field sobriety test. There is absolutely no science involved in the clue point system unless counting is considered a scientific technique.") (Note: there are different clues for each test. For example, in the walk and turn test the clues are: Stops while walking; Does not touch heel to toe; Steps off the line; Raises arms for balance; Incorrect number of steps; Trouble with turn (explain); Cannot perform the test. If one steps off the line twice, this will be scored as two clues. An officer can award a maximum of 8 clues for this test.); Cloud v. State, 2000 WL 719405 at *3 (Tex.App.2000) ("These FSTs involve observation of directed, basic tasks and are barely distinguishable from lay observation of undirected behavior"); State v. Cissne, 72 Wash.App. 677, 865 P.2d 564, 568 (Wash.App. 1994) ("The HGN test is a different type of test from balancing on one leg or walking a straight line because it rests almost entirely

upon an assertion of scientific legitimacy rather than a basis of common knowledge." HGN must meet *Frye* test.); State v. Witte, 251 Kan. 313, 836 P.2d 1110, 1111 (Kan.1992) ("The horizontal gaze nystagmus test is distinguished from other field sobriety tests in that science, rather than common knowledge, provides the legitimacy for horizontal gaze nystagmus testing.... As such, the foundation requirements for admissibility enunciated in *Frye v. United States* must be satisfied.").

As noted earlier, some states conclude that the HGN test itself requires no expert testimony. *See* State v. Murphy, 451 N.W.2d 154 (Iowa 1990); Whitson v. State, 314 Ark. 458, 863 S.W.2d 794 (Ark.1993); City of Fargo v. McLaughlin, 512 N.W.2d 700 (N.D.1994).

125. 57 F. Supp. 2d 888 (N.D.Cal.1999).

126. 526 U.S. 137, 119 S.Ct. 1167, 143 L.Ed.2d 238 (1999).

127. Daubert v. Merrell Dow Pharmaceuticals, Inc., 509 U.S. 579, 113 S.Ct. 2786, 125 L.Ed.2d 469 (1993).

128. *Volk*, 57 F.Supp.2d at 894.

129. *Id.* at 895.

130. Subsequently, the defendant registered alcohol levels of .19 or better on two Intoxilyzer tests. *Id.* at 892.

trate's implicit finding that the conclusion the officer drew based on the field sobriety tests was reliable.

The district court made two additional points that are worth mentioning. First, it distinguished the present case from the expert testimony in *Kumho*. It noted that in *Kumho* the district judge was required to assess expert testimony concerning the condition of an allegedly defective tire which was based on a methodology and experience "so foreign to the layperson as to cast doubt on the jury's ability to properly assess its probative value."[131] Here, however, the officer's "knowledge and experience was not grounded in concepts so foreign that a trier of fact would not be capable of properly assessing the probative value of the testimony. Rather, the officer's conclusions—as well as defendant's criticism of these conclusions—was well grounded in assumptions about the levels of coordination and steadiness that are familiar to the layperson."[132] This observation suggests the sensible rule that the time and effort a trial court must expend before ruling on the admissibility of expert testimony is in inverse relationship to the difficulty it may pose to the trier of fact because of the trier's lack of familiarity with the concepts underlying the expert's testimony.

The second point made by the court is that it is permissible for the officer to base his conclusion on the totality of the circumstances. "The fact that one or more of the individual tests may not have been highly probative of defendant's level of intoxication does not necessarily lead to the conclusion that his testimony regarding these tests was not relevant or reliable under FRE 702."[133] This observation clearly puts the court on the side of those who believe that even though each particular piece of evidence upon which an expert bases his opinion may have flaws, nevertheless the expert's opinion may be supported by the weight of all the evidence taken together.[134]

Regardless of the scientific status of field sobriety tests, there is an important question concerning their reliability. If the experimental evidence on HGN is thin, it is even thinner with respect to other parts of the standard FTS protocol. Given this uncertainty concerning error rate, some defendants have argued, apparently to no avail, that this testimony should be excluded on Rule 403 grounds.[135]

§ 8–1.3 General Technique

Even when a scientific procedure is premised on theories or principles that are scientifically valid (under a *Daubert* test) or have achieved general acceptance (under a *Frye* test), it may be called into question because of the way the general principle is implemented. In the area of alcohol testing, general technique requirements are largely a matter of statute. In addition, a few cases focus on more mundane questions concerning the chain of custody.

§ 8–1.3.1 Procedures Mandated by Statute

Questions involving the general technique of tests employed to measure whether and at what level an individual is intoxicated are uniformly governed

131. *Id.* at 896.

132. *Id.*

133. *Id.*

134. On this point, see Justice Stevens concurring and dissenting opinion in *General Elec-*

tric Co. v. Joiner, 522 U.S. 136, 118 S.Ct. 512, 139 L.Ed.2d 508 (1997).

135. City of Milwaukee v. Bell, 238 Wis.2d 447, 617 N.W.2d 907 (Wis.App.2000).

by state statute. The statutes provide for the licensing of laboratories and periodic testing of their procedures.[136] When approved testing apparatus has met relevant testing requirements, results using the apparatus are routinely admitted.[137] These laws generally direct courts to admit evidence of the amount of alcohol or drugs in the breath or blood of individuals operating a motor vehicle.[138] The statutes typically provide that the evidence is admissible if performed in accordance with prescribed testing procedures.[139] These provisions generally cover issues of chain of custody and quality control procedures within the laboratory. When the state has complied with such provisions, the statutes frequently provide for the admissibility of the test results without the presence or testimony of the technician who performed the test.[140] In *State v. Lanser*,[141] the defendant contended that her test results were inadmissible because the person who drew her blood was not called to testify that she was qualified to perform this procedure. The court concluded that this is not required under the Wisconsin statute. The uncontested testimony of the arresting officer, who observed the blood being drawn, along with the blood drawer's entry and signature on the blood result exhibit were sufficient to authenticate that the blood sample was drawn by a qualified person.

§ 8–1.3.2 Chain of Custody

If the proffering party fails to lay a proper foundation for the expert's testimony by demonstrating that a specimen did indeed come from the accused and then accounting for each successive step in handling a specimen, the expert's testimony may be inadmissible. On the other hand, courts are willing to admit testimony concerning test results when gaps in the chain of custody are not so severe as to undermine all probative value.[142]

Chain-of-custody issues rarely appear in DWI cases, and even more rarely

136. *See, e.g.,* Cal. Bus. & Prof. Code § 1220 (West 2001); Cal. Vehicle Code § 23158 (West 2001); Tex. Transportation Code § 524.038 (Vernon 1999); N.Y. Public Health Law, Ch. 45, Art. 5. T. V. (McKinney 1997); N.Y. Vehicle and Traffic Law § 1194(4)(c) (McKinney 1996).

137. *See* Commonwealth v. Smith, 35 Mass.App.Ct. 655, 624 N.E.2d 604, 607 (Mass. App.Ct.1993); State v. Incashola, 289 Mont. 399, 961 P.2d 745 (Mont.1998); State v. Maida, 332 N.J.Super. 564, 753 A.2d 1240 (Law.Div. 2000). *See* Gil Sapir & Mark Giangrande, *Right to Inspect and Test Breath Alcohol Machines: Suspicion Ain't Proof*, 33 J. Marshall L. Rev. 1 (1999) (arguing the defendant's expert should be permitted to examine the machine used to test the defendant).

138. *See, e.g.,* N.Y. Vehicle & Traffic Law § 1195 (McKinney 1995); Mo. Rev. Stat. § 306.117 (1994); Me. Rev. Stat. Ann. tit. 29A, § 2431 (West 1995); Tex. Transp. Code Ann. § 724.063 (West 1996); Md. Code Ann., Courts & Judicial Proc. § 10–306 (1995); Ala. Code § 32–5A–194 (1995); Conn. Gen. Stat. Ann. § 14–227a(c) (West 1995); Barna v. Commissioner of Public Safety, 508 N.W.2d 220, 222 (Minn.App. 1993) (state followed procedures outlined in Minn. R. 7502.0700).

139. In State v. Hiemstra, 6 Neb.App. 940, 579 N.W.2d 550, 558 (Neb.App.1998), the appellate court ruled that the trial court erred in admitting blood tests because the person who drew the defendant's blood was not qualified under Nev. Rev. Stat. § 60–6,201 (1993).

140. Md. Code Ann., Courts & Judicial Proc. § 10–306 (1995). A related question is whether a hospital blood alcohol test report is admissible under a business record exception without the testimony of the laboratory technician who administered the test. In *Baber v. State*, 738 So.2d 379 (Fla.Ct.App.1999), the court answered affirmatively. Similar holdings can be found in *Dixon v. State*, 227 Ga.App. 533, 489 S.E.2d 532 (Ga.Ct.App.1997) and *State v. Todd*, 935 S.W.2d 55 (Mo.App.1996).

141. 604 N.W.2d 305 (Table) (Wis.App. 1999).

142. *See* Paul C. Giannelli, *Chain of Custody and the Handling of Real Evidence*, 20 Am. Crim. L. Rev. 527 (1983); Kenneth J. Hanko, *Chain of Custody and Laboratory Reports in Drug Prosecutions: A Comparative Analysis of Military and Federal Case Law*, 2 Whittier L. Rev. 213 (1980).

are the cases officially published. In *Bransford v. State*,[143] the blood test report contained a certificate indicating that the laboratory was certified to perform a given test, set forth formal procedures for receipt and handling, and detailed the process by which proper chain of custody was ensured. This certificate provided enough proof to establish chain-of-custody and to satisfy foundational elements of business record and public records exceptions to the hearsay rule.

Chain of custody issues are more likely to arise in cases where the defendant is charged with something more serious than DWI. For example, in *Jordan v. State*[144] the defendant was convicted of driving under the influence (DUI) manslaughter. She challenged the admissibility of blood test results on chain of custody grounds. The court noted that in order to bar introduction of relevant evidence due to a gap in the chain of custody the defendant must show that there was a probability of tampering with evidence. The defendant failed to establish such a probability where the state trooper who supplied the blood sample kit, the nurse who obtained sample, and the state's toxicologist, all testified that the kit did not appear to have been tampered with.

Generally, custody defects go to weight not admissibility of results.[145] In a rare successful chain of custody challenge, the court in *Jones v. Summerdale*[146] overturned the defendant's DUI conviction after finding that the reception of results of the blood alcohol test into evidence was reversible error. The state offered the defendant's blood test into evidence without any testimony indicating the reliability of the test, who performed the test, or the circumstances under which the test was performed.[147]

§ 8–1.4 Specific Technique

The line between general and specific techniques is often blurred. Many chain of custody cases, for example, might be thought of as raising questions of specific procedure in a given case. Here, we discuss cases where the procedures followed in a specific case have been called into question.

In a split decision, a Missouri appellate court affirmed the trial court's decision to reinstate the defendant's driver's license because the officer who administered the breathalyzer test failed to check a box on the maintenance report noting that he had checked the simulator's temperature.[148] Although the officer testified that he did in fact check the instrument temperature and simply overlooked the box, apparently the trial court chose not to believe him.

In *Anderson v. Director of Revenue*,[149] the defendant attempted to challenge the results of a breath test machine on the grounds that the state had failed to meet a requirement of a maintenance check within 35 days of its use because the permit number on the maintenance form was inconsistent with the permit number recorded on the form submitted to the Director. The court

---

143. 125 N.M. 285, 960 P.2d 827 (N.M.App. 1998). For a similar result, see *State v. Bernier*, 235 Wis.2d 277, 616 N.W.2d 525 (Wis.Ct.App. 2000).

144. 707 So.2d 816 (Fla.App.1998).

145. Shayer v. Bohan, 708 A.2d 158 (R.I. 1998); Baker v. Gourley, 81 Cal.App.4th 1167, 97 Cal.Rptr.2d 451 (2000).

146. 677 So.2d 1289 (Ala.App.1996).

147. *Id.* at 1291–92.

148. Endsley v. Director of Revenue, 6 S.W.3d 153 (Mo.App.1999).

149. 969 S.W.2d 899 (Mo.App.1998).

found that this was not sufficient evidence to prove the machine had been improperly maintained.[150]

A number of cases turn on whether a machine has been properly calibrated within a reasonable time of its use in the case at hand.[151] In *State v. Bishop*,[152] the court concluded that the state laid a proper foundation for the admission of a breath test by introducing the original log book of calibrations for the breath test machine, the machine's original certification document, a copy of certified monthly standards reports for the machine, a copy of the document certifying calibration solution, and the trooper's testimony that he was certified to conduct breath tests at the time he administered the motorist's breath test. On the other hand, in *Bransford v. State*,[153] the court found that an entry in a log book for the breath testing machine which indicated only that a self-test was performed with test results of . 00% was insufficient for purposes of taking administrative notice to establish that the machine had been properly calibrated.[154]

State v. Mazzuca[155] addresses the question of whether the results of a "deficient" breathalyser test are admissible. On two occasions the defendant blew short breaths into the breathalyser and both times the machine indicated the sample was deficient. However, both times the test indicated that the defendant was legally intoxicated. In a case of first impression, the appellate court affirmed the trial court's refusal to exclude the test results. The state presented an expert who testified that a deficient sample is one in which the subject did not breathe for a long enough period of time to provide a sufficient deep lung air sample, but that had he done so there was no possibility the sample would have produced a lower test value.[156] The court noted that other states which have considered the question have also admitted the results of "deficient" tests.[157]

The results of a breath test for intoxication may be misleading if the defendant has burped, belched or vomited a short time prior to the test. Therefore, some courts have refused to admit the results of breath tests when the officer cannot testify that he observed the defendant for a period of time prior to administering the test to assure that the test is not contaminated in this way.[158] In *State v. Guidera*,[159] the arresting officer noted that he began observing the defendant at 12:05 a.m. and subsequently administered two "alco-sensor" tests. The first was administered 14 minutes later, violating Vermont's 15 minute rule. The court did not reach the question of whether this test would have been inadmissible, because a second test was performed

---

150. *Id.* at 902.

151. The National Highway Traffic Safety Administration periodically issues model specifications for calibrating breath alcohol testing apparatus. *See* 59 Fed.Reg. 67377–01 (1994).

152. 264 Kan. 717, 957 P.2d 369 (Kan. 1998).

153. 125 N.M. 285, 960 P.2d 827 (N.M.App. 1998).

154. *See also*, Davis v. State, 712 So.2d 1115 (Ala.App.1997) (introducing blood alcohol breath test, without first establishing that testing equipment was properly calibrated at time test was performed, was reversible error).

155. 132 Idaho 868, 979 P.2d 1226 (Idaho App.1999).

156. *Id.* at 1228.

157. *See* People v. DeMarasse, 85 N.Y.2d 842, 623 N.Y.S.2d 845, 647 N.E.2d 1353 (N.Y. 1995); State v. Conrad, 187 W.Va. 658, 421 S.E.2d 41 (W.Va.1992).

158. State v. Grindstaff, 1998 WL 126252 (Tenn.Crim.App.1998); State v. Korsakov, 34 S.W.3d 534 (Tenn.Crim.App.2000); State v. Gregory, 1999 WL 756440 (Ohio App.1999) (statute requires 20 minute observation period).

159. 167 Vt. 598, 707 A.2d 704 (Vt.1998).

three minutes later, outside the 15 minute window.[160] In *State v. Cook*,[161] the defendant argued that the results of his Intoximeter 3000 breath test should be excluded because he wore dentures. The Tennessee statute requires, among other things, that a motorist must be personally observed for 20 minutes before taking the test, during which time he did not have any foreign matter in his mouth, consume alcohol, smoke, or regurgitate. The defendant claimed that the dentures were foreign matter. The officer had asked the defendant if he had any foreign matter in his mouth and he replied that he did not. The officer testified that the intoximeter used in the test would have shut down had it detected the presence of mouth alcohol and would have issued a print-out stating "mouth-alcohol." It did neither.[162] The Tennessee Supreme Court held that under these circumstances the trial court did not err when it admitted the results of the breath test.[163]

The specific technique used in a field sobriety test recently came into question in *State v. Homan*.[164] A state trooper performed a set of field sobriety tests prior to arresting the defendant. The officer admitted to deviating from established practice in several ways. For example, he conducted the walk and turn test between his car and the defendant's car which was performed on a gravel covered, uneven surface.[165] He gave the defendant the option to turn either right or left after completing the required number of steps. The Ohio Supreme Court held that the tests had not been administered in strict compliance with standardized procedures and should not have been admitted as evidence of probable cause to arrest the defendant for driving under the influence of alcohol.[166] Nonetheless, the court concluded that the totality of the circumstance surrounding the officer's encounter with the individual may, and in this case did, provide support for the decision to arrest the suspect.[167]

A similar result was reached in *State v. Hall*.[168] The court held that an officer should not be permitted to testify as to the results of an improperly administered walk and turn test. Contrary to these two Ohio opinions, most jurisdictions hold that failures to follow protocols exactly go to weight, not admissibility.[169]

The *Homan* case cites a National Highway Traffic Safety Administration (NHTSA) study for its position that field sobriety tests are reliable only when "the tests are administered in the prescribed, standardized manner."[170] In fact, there appears to be relatively little data on the reliability costs of failing

---

160. 707 A.2d at 705. In *State v. McCaslin*, 894 S.W.2d 310 (Tenn.Crim.App.1994), the testing officer was unable to testify that he had watched the defendant for the requisite twenty minutes prior to a breath test and the test results were found inadmissible.

161. 9 S.W.3d 98 (Tenn.1999).

162. *Id.* at 2.

163. *See also* State v. Jarnagin, 2000 WL 575232 (Tenn.App.2000) (defendant allegedly had cotton in mouth).

164. 89 Ohio St.3d 421, 732 N.E.2d 952 (Ohio 2000).

165. *Id.* at 955.

166. *Id.* at 955.

167. *Id.* at 957.

168. 2000 WL 1061875 (Ohio App.2000).

169. State v. Williams, 1998 WL 803413 at *4 (Tenn.Crim.App.1998) ("The conditions under which the tests were preformed relate to the weight to be afforded the test results, not the admissibility of the results."); Ballard v. State, 955 P.2d 931, 941 (Alaska App.1998); Cantwell v. State, 230 Ga.App. 892, 497 S.E.2d 609 (Ga.Ct.App.1998); Morrissette v. State, 229 Ga.App. 420, 494 S.E.2d 8, 12 (Ga.Ct.App. 1997) (trial court did not abuse its discretion in admitting evidence of field sobriety tests, despite fact that defendant was injured when he performed tests); Johnson v. State, 1997 WL 256828 at *2 (Ark.Ct.App.1997).

170. *Homans*, 732 N.E.2d at 954.

to follow FST protocols exactly.[171] Certainly, there is no data on whether the results of an FST done imperfectly are less reliable than general observations by the officer of the suspect's driving behavior.[172] On the other hand, it is true that we do have some evidence of the reliability of field sobriety tests done properly, according to established protocol by the officer.

Whatever the merits of the *Homan* position, the case underlines the uncertainty with which the courts have approached this type of evidence. If the admissibility of properly performed field sobriety tests do not require expert evidence because they are not "science," why should we exclude poorly performed tests on error rate grounds? The case points to the fact that field sobriety tests and their horizontal gaze nystagmus component occupy a twilight zone between something everyone understands and something that is beyond the ken of the average jury. In this twilight, courts often stumble off in different directions.

§ 8–1.5   Conclusion

Various breath and blood tests quantifying the amount of alcohol in an individual's system have achieved widespread general acceptance as reliable scientific techniques. Horizontal gaze nystagmus tests remain somewhat controversial. In most jurisdictions they are admissible, after a proper foundation has been laid, to show some impairment, but not to show a particular BAC. Field sobriety tests are generally thought to be no more than common sense knowledge and do not require an expert to establish reliability or general acceptance. Unfortunately, there is no substantial body of reliable research on the reliability of either HGN or the other components of field sobriety tests. The prosecution of drunk drivers would benefit from such work.

171. A 1997 NHTSA San Diego study was undertaken to assess the ability of the tests to detect intoxication at the 0.08% BAC, which increasingly is the cutoff level for per se DWI offenses. Overall the correlation (pearson product moment correlation) between the officer's test scores estimated BAC and the BAC indicated by a subsequent blood test was .69. Using a BAC cutoff of 0.08% the officers made false positive errors in slightly more than 10% of the cases and false negative errors in less than 10% of the cases. Their overall success rate (i.e., saying someone's BAC was over 0.08% when, according to the blood test this was true *and* saying someone's BAC was under 0.08% when, according to the blood test, this was true) was 91%. The research design did not systematically vary the quality of the procedures followed by the officers in the study. Jack Stuster and Marcelline Burns, Validation of the Standardized Field Sobriety Test Battery at BACs Below .010 Percent (1998). the study may be accessed at <http://www.nhtsa.dot.gov/people/injury/alcohol/limit.08/!SFSTREP.pdf> (Visited March 30, 2000).

172. In *Homan*, the officer observed erratic driving, that the driver's eyes were "red and glassy," and that her breath smelled of alcohol. The driver admitted she had been consuming alcoholic beverages. *Id.* at 957.

B. SCIENTIFIC STATUS

by
James Garriott*

§ 8–2.0 TESTING FOR ALCOHOL: FORENSIC ISSUES

§ 8–2.1 Introduction

Alcohol testing is the most frequently performed of all analyses in forensic laboratories, and is the most commonly used laboratory result in courts of law. Alcohol-related litigation most often pertains to prosecution of drinking drivers, but also includes civil and other litigation in motor vehicle and industrial accidents, as well as in aircraft and other public transport accidents.

There were 41,900 motor vehicle-related deaths and an estimated 3,500,-000 injuries in the United States in 1996. Estimated costs from the motor-vehicle accidents were $150 billion.[1] Most studies of motor vehicle fatal or non-fatal accidents show drinking driver involvement in about half and in some studies the figure is as high as 75%, leading to the conclusion that there were over 20,000 motor vehicle fatalities and about 1 million disabling injuries resulting from alcohol use by drivers in 1995. Studies of homicides, suicides, or other forms of violent death also show that greater than half involve alcohol.[2] Alcohol misuse was one of nine factors responsible for half of all deaths among U.S. residents, accounting for 100,000 deaths (5%) in 1993.[3]

All 50 states of the United States, as well as most countries of Western Europe and other parts of the world, have statutes regulating driving a motor vehicle while under the influence of alcohol. Additional laws govern use of alcohol under other circumstances, such as public intoxication and use of alcohol in the workplace. Thus, testing for use of alcohol in living or deceased individuals under a variety of circumstances is nearly universal. Whether such testing is performed on body fluids or organ tissues taken at autopsy, or on blood, urine, or breath in living individuals, it is often extremely important and even critical that the alcohol analyses be performed accurately and correctly and that the results are properly interpreted.

This section will review the current state of the art of alcohol testing and discuss the science necessary to properly interpret alcohol results.

* James C. Garriott is a toxicology consultant in San Antonio, Texas. He holds a Ph.D. in Toxicology and Pharmacology, and is a diplomat of the American Board of Forensic Toxicology, Inc. He served as the chief toxicologist for Dallas County, Texas from 1970 to 1982, and then held the same position at Bexar County, Texas until retiring in 1997. He was also professor at the University of Texas Health Science Centers of Dallas and San Antonio. Dr. Garriott is the author of over 100 articles and book chapters in the toxicology literature, as well as co-author and editor of two toxicology reference books and is on the editorial review board of four toxicology and forensic journals. He is recognized for his knowledge and expertise in the forensic toxicology of ethyl alcohol, and he edited the text Medicolegal Aspects of Alcohol, now in its third edition. Dr. Garriott was the 1993 recipient of the Alexander O. Gettler award for outstanding achievements in analytical toxicology by the American Academy of Forensic Sciences.

Dr. Garriott has served as an expert and testified in numerous legal cases involving drug and alcohol toxicology in courts throughout the United States.

§ 8–2.0

1. National Safety Council, U.S. Dep't of Transportation, National Highway Traffic Safety Admin., Traffic Safety Facts, Alcohol (1996).

2. J.C. Garriott, *Drug Use Among Homicide Victims*, 14 Am. J. Forensic Med. Pathology 51–53 (1993); L.E. Norton et al., *Drug Detection at Autopsy: a Prospective Study of 247 Cases*, 27 J. Forensic Sci. 66 (1982).

3. National Safety Council, U.S. Dep't of Transportation, Accident Facts (1994).

§ 8–2.2   Pharmacology and Toxicology of Ethyl Alcohol

Use of alcoholic beverages is so common in most societies that it is usually thought of as a social beverage, and we often lose sight of the fact that it is a drug. It has effects comparable in many ways to more highly respected therapeutic and "recreational" drugs such as tranquilizers, narcotics, sedatives, and hypnotics. Since it is not controlled as a drug, but is available without restriction to all persons of legal age, it comes as a surprise to many that it has pharmacological properties that impact the body similar to narcotic drugs such as morphine and heroin. Alcohol and narcotic drugs are both euphorigenic, are strong central nervous system (CNS) and respiratory depressants, and induce tolerance and physical dependence (addiction). The major distinctions between the two are the strong analgesic effects of narcotics versus the very weak pain-killing action of alcohol, and the weaker potency of alcohol, which requires tens of grams for effectiveness rather than a few milligrams for narcotics. Due to this low potency of ethyl alcohol, high concentrations must be present in the body to be effective, and consequently it affects all organ and biochemical systems of the body.

§ 8–2.2.1   Interpretation of Alcohol Concentrations

For purposes of this discussion and for general reference, it is necessary to understand alcohol concentration units. This is often difficult for the non-chemist, because different units are used by different laboratories in some instances, and other countries use units other than those customarily employed in the United States. Also, breath testing results are expressed as a unique unit of measure. Only two units are generally used in the United States for blood or other body fluid alcohol expressions. These are "milligrams per deciliter (mg/dL)," usually used by clinical or hospital laboratories, and "grams per deciliter (g/dL)." The two are easily interconverted, because there are 1000 milligrams in one gram. Therefore, one need only divide the expression in mg/dL by 1000 to get the grams per deciliter conversion. It should be noted here that almost all state and federal laws define fluid alcohol concentrations in terms of grams per deciliter, the same as grams per 100 mL. Sometimes the shorthand "%"or "g%" may be used (e.g., 0.12%).

Another complication in this matter is the effort underway to force clinical laboratories to use SI units (Système International d'Unités), which are used in medical journals as a matter of policy. This unit bears no resemblance to the conventional metric unit concentrations with which most of us are familiar. The unit is based on the molecular weight of alcohol, 46.07. The conversion factor for the g/dL (%) unit is 217.1. Thus, 0.10 g/dL blood alcohol becomes 21.71 millimoles per Liter (mmol/L) (see Table 1). Although not used for expressions of alcohol for legal purposes, one may encounter SI units for alcohol in medical journals, or in alcohol concentrations done by clinical laboratories.

TABLE 1

Units for Expressing Body Ethyl Alcohol Concentrations*

United States

Blood and fluids:
0.10% (wt/vol) = 0.10 g/100 mL of blood = 100 mg% = 100 mg/dL

Breath:
0.10   g/210 L of breath air is equivalent to 0.10 g/dL blood alcohol
(based on the breath/blood ratio 2100:1)

Europe

1000 ppm (parts per million) (0.10 g/dL) = 0.0948% (wt./wt.).
0.949% (per mille, mg/g, g/Kg) = 1.00 g/L
SI Units:
0.10% (wt/vol) = 21.71 mmol/L

§ 8–2.2.2   Effects of Alcohol on the Central Nervous System

Alcohol affects all systems of the body to some degree, with major acute and chronic effects on the gastrointestinal system, the liver, the cardiovascular system, and the endocrine system. For example, alcoholic liver disease is among the top ten causes of death in the United States. Congestive heart failure and hypertension, chronic gastritis, gastric ulceration, and both acute and chronic pancreatitis, are some additional diseases related to alcohol use. However, the central nervous system (CNS) is the component of the body most severely affected by alcohol. Since this system is the source of any behavioral aberrations due to alcohol, these effects are the most important to consider for medico-legal interpretation of alcohol related situations.

The intensity of the CNS effects of alcohol is proportional to the concentration of alcohol in the blood. These general effects are outlined in relation to alcohol concentrations in Table 2.[4]

TABLE 2

Stages of Acute Alcoholic Influence/Intoxication

BAC G/100 mL	STAGE OF ALCOHOLIC INFLUENCE	CLINICAL SIGNS/SYMPTOMS
0.01–0.05	SUBCLINICAL	Influence/effects not apparent or obvious; Behavior nearly normal by ordinary observation; Impairment detectable by special tests.
0.03–0.12	EUPHORIA	Mild euphoria, sociability, talkativeness; Increased self-confidence; decreased inhibitions;

*All of the above conversions reflect the United States limit for legal intoxication of 0.10 g/dL (0.10 %) blood alcohol concentration

4. K.M. Dubowski, *Stages of Acute Alcoholic Influence/Intoxication*, THE UNIVERSITY OF OKLA. COLLEGE OF MEDICINE (1997).

BAC G/100 mL	STAGE OF ALCOHOLIC INFLUENCE	CLINICAL SIGNS/SYMPTOMS
		Diminution of attention, judgment and control; Some sensory-motor impairment; Slowed information processing Loss of efficiency in finer performance tests.
0.09–0.25	EXCITEMENT	Emotional instability; loss of critical judgment; Impairment of perception, memory and comprehension; Decreased sensitory response and increased reaction time; Reduced visual acuity, peripheral vision and glare recovery; Sensory-motor incoordination and impaired balance; Drowsiness.
0.18–0.30	CONFUSION	Disorientation, mental confusion, dizziness; Exaggerated emotional states (fear, rage, sorrow, etc.); Disturbance of vision (diplopia, etc.) and of perception of color, form, motion, dimensions; Increased pain threshold; Increased muscular incoordination, staggering gait, and slurred speech; Apathy, lethargy.
0.25–0.40	STUPOR	General inertia approaching loss of motor functions; Markedly decreased response to stimuli; Marked muscular incoordination and inability to stand or walk; Vomiting; incontinence of urine and feces; Impaired consciousness, sleep or stupor.
0.35–0.50	COMA	Complete unconsciousness, coma, anesthesia; Depressed or abolished reflexes; Subnormal temperature; Incontinence of urine and feces; Impairment of circulation and respiration; Possible death.
0.45+	DEATH	Death from respiratory arrest.

Copyright by K.M. Dubowski, University of Oklahoma College of Medicine, Oklahoma City, OK. (Garriott, 1997).

Alcohol's effects on the CNS are considerably more pronounced when the blood alcohol level is rising than when falling. This effect is believed to result from so-called acute (functional) tolerance to alcohol, achieved during the course of the intoxication.[5] It has been shown that rats are about twice as tolerant to a moderate alcohol dose at a given brain level 60 minutes after as compared to 10 minutes after the injection.[6] In humans, the magnitude of the effect is also probably a function of the rate the alcohol is consumed. It was observed that the more rapid the rate of drinking, the greater the degree of performance decrements at the same blood alcohol concentration (BAC).[7] An extreme example of acute tolerance was reported in a human patient in whom a maximum blood alcohol level of 0.78 g/dL was found. When the patient reached a level of 0.30 g/dL, she was, by clinical observations, sober.[8]

The frontal lobes of the brain are sensitive to low concentrations of alcohol, resulting in alteration of thought and mood. The early effects of alcohol are often considered stimulant actions, mediated by depression of the reticular activating system, thereby releasing the cortex from selective control and inhibition. Increased confidence, a more expansive and vivacious personality, mood swings, garrulousness, and increased social interactions are characteristic.[9] These effects are actually due to depression of the inhibitory central mechanisms. The intoxicated individual may then act in ways or perform acts he would not ordinarily do. He may become more aggressive and even violent, due to pent-up hostilities, or express abnormal desires and drives normally kept under control. His awareness and self-control are impaired, however, so that in a conflict he is more liable to come out the loser. He is generally an easy target for violent predators. This is attested to by the very high incidence of alcohol intoxication in homicide victims.[10] He may become overconfident and take dangerous risks he would not ordinarily take, such as speeding and reckless driving, greatly increasing his risk of death or injury. Studies of driving accidents and fatalities have shown a risk factor of 12 times greater probability for being involved in a fatal crash for a driver at 0.10 g/dL blood alcohol (the legal limit for DWI in many states) than for a non-drinking driver.[11]

In the early stages of alcohol intoxication, the processes that depend on previous training and experience and that govern self-restraint and inhibition are affected. Memory, fine discrimination, and concentration functions are dulled as the blood alcohol level rises. Vision (occipital lobe) and coordination (cerebellum) become impaired as the blood level approaches 0.10 g/dL. All bodily functions and abilities governed by the brain are progressively impaired. With acute intoxication (characterized by blood alcohol levels in excess

5. E. Mellanby, *Alcohol: Its Absorption into and Disappearance from the Blood Under Different Conditions*, MEDICAL RESEARCH COMM., SPECIAL REPORT SERIES 31 (1919); H. Moskowitz et al., *The Mellanby Effect in Moderate and Heavy Drinkers*, PROC. SEVENTH INT'L CONF. ON ALCOHOL, DRUGS AND TRAFFIC SAFETY (1977); D.B. GOLDSTEIN, PHARMACOLOGY OF ALCOHOL (1983).

6. A.E. LeBlanc et al., *Acute Tolerance to Ethanol in the Rat*, 41 PSYCHOPHARMACOLOGIA 43 (1975).

7. H. Moskowitz, *Alcohol Influences Upon Sensory Motor Function, Visual Perception, and Attention*, in NATIONAL HIGHWAY TRAFFIC SAFETY ADMINISTRATION, ALCOHOL, DRUGS AND DRIV-

ING 49–69, U.S. DEPT. OF TRANSPORTATION, Publication No. HS 801 096, Mar.1974.

8. K.B. Hammond et al., *Blood Ethanol: A Report of Unusually High Levels in a Living Patient*, 226 JAMA 63 (1973).

9. H. Wallgren & H. Barry III, *Actions of Alcohol*, 1 BIOCHEMICAL, PHYSIOLOGICAL, AND PSYCHOLOGICAL EFFECTS 287 (1970).

10. Garriott, *supra* note 2.

11. P.M. Hurst, *Epidemiological Aspects of Alcohol and Driver Crashes and Citation*, in ALCOHOL, DRUGS AND DRIVING, NATIONAL HIGHWAY TRAFFIC SAFETY ADMIN., TECHNICAL REPORT, DOT–HS–801–096 (M.W. Perrine ed., 1974).

of 0.40 g/dL), even autonomic nervous system functions governed by the medulla and the brain stem are affected. This system governs bodily functions such as heart contraction and respiration. At these levels, there may be a risk of death from depression of the respiratory centers.[12]

[1] Impairment of Specific Functions Related to Driving Ability

[a] Vision

Significant decrements of visual acuity occur after alcohol ingestion. Alcohol slows adaptation to both darkness and light, and lowers resistance to glare at blood alcohol levels ranging from 0.09 to 0.15 g/dL.[13] Impairment of discrimination of colors has been observed after alcohol doses of 0.7 g/kg, equivalent to blood alcohol levels of about 0.10 g/dL.[14] Mergler et al. studied the relationship between alcohol consumption and color discrimination capacity in 136 subjects.[15] He found that the prevalence of dyschromatopsia (color blindness or impaired color discrimination) increased with alcohol intake in all age categories, and that heavy drinkers (greater than about 60 drinks per week) consistently presented with dyschromatopsia. Color loss was primarily in the blue-yellow range, but some subjects showed impairment of red-green color discrimination. In another study, subjects with BAC's from 0.07 to 0.16 g/dL exhibited a specific impairment on the function of blue-sensitive cones or their interaction with longer wavelength-sensitive cones.[16]

Diplopia (double vision) is a well-recognized symptom of alcohol intoxication, but few attempts have been made to describe the specific impact of alcohol on fusion. Miller found measurable effects on fusion latency with blood alcohol levels as low as 0.05—0.06 g/dL.[17] Fusion latency is described as the time required to fuse a binocularly visible target. This effect of alcohol is the source of the well-known "double vision" effect.

In a study of alcohol effects on vision, tracking, and division of attention, it was found that when either visual or tracking functions were examined in complex situations requiring simultaneous visual and tracking responses, as occur in actual driving situations, large performance decrements occurred at low blood alcohol concentrations as low as 0.02 g/dL with nearly all subjects exhibiting effects at 0.08 g/dL.[18] Of studies performed measuring visual skills after low doses of alcohol, 12 of 28 found impairment at blood concentrations

---

12. K.M. Dubowski, *Absorption, Distribution, and Elimination of Alcohol: Highway Safety Aspects*, J. STUD. ALCOHOL, supp. 10, 98 (1985).

13. Wallgren & Barry, *supra* note 9.

14. *See id.*; *see also* L. Schmidt & A.G.A. Bingel, *Effect of Oxygen Deficiency and Various Other Factors on Color Saturation Thresholds*, U.S.A.F. SCH. OF AVIATION MED. PROJECT REPORTS, PROJECT NO. 21–31–002 (1953).

15. Mergler et al.,*Colour Vision Impairment and Alcohol Consumption*, 10 NEUROTOXICOLOGY TERATOL 255 (1988).

16. E. Zrenner et al., *Effects of Ethyl Alcohol on the Eelectrooculogram and Color Vision*, 463 DOCTOR OF OPHTHALMOLOGY 305 (1986).

17. R.J. Miller, *The Effects of Ingested Alcohol on Fusion Latency at Various Viewing Distances*, Percept., 50 PSYCHOPHYSIOLOGY 575 (1991).

18. H. Moskowitz, *Alcohol Influences Upon Sensory Motor Function, Visual Perception, and Attention, in* ALCOHOL, DRUGS AND DRIVING, NATIONAL HIGHWAY TRAFFIC SAFETY ADMIN., DOT–HS–801–096, 49 (1974); H. Moskowitz & S. Sharma, *Effects of Alcohol on Peripheral Vision*

of 0.05 g/dL or less.[19] These studies were in the area of oculomotor control, dealing with eye movement and fusion ability.

In summary, studies performed to measure the effects of alcohol on driving-related visual skills, in which more complex visual skills were studied, showed that alcohol's effect is significant. Impairment may occur in some individuals at blood concentrations as low as 0.03 g/dL, and marked impairment occurs in nearly all individuals at concentrations greater than 0.08 g/dL.[20]

[b] Auditory Discrimination

The sense of hearing (auditory) seems to be more resistant to the effects of alcohol than most other senses. Auditory acuity is not generally affected in humans at low blood alcohol levels (less than 0.10 g/dL). Pihkanen and Kauko reported impairment in two out of three tests performed to measure auditory capability at average blood levels of 0.10 g/dL.[21] A large decrement in discrimination between volumes and intensity of sounds, but a less clear effect on ability to detect faint sounds, has been reported.[22]

[c] Other Sensory Effects

Olfactory and taste sensibilities are affected at low doses of alcohol (0.1– 0.2 g/kg). These senses may be affected at blood levels of 0.04 g/dL or greater,[23] and the effect is a reduction in discrimination, or dulling of the senses.

[d] Reaction Time

Alcohol has a well-established and consistent detrimental effect on reaction time. In general, blood levels in excess of 0.07 g/dL consistently impair reaction responses. Blood alcohol levels of from 0.05 to 0.15 g/dL lengthened reaction time in 42% to 82% of subjects.[24]

In slightly more complicated tasks, in which subjects perform more than one attentive task at one time, alcohol doses of 1.0 to 1.2 g/kg, with alcohol levels averaging 0.11 g/dL, increased reaction time by more than 200%.[25] This

---

as a Function of Attention, 16 HUM. FACTORS 174 (1974).

19. H. Moskowitz & C.D. Robinson, *Effects of Low Doses of Alcohol on Driving–Related Skills: A Review of the Evidence, SRA Technologies, Inc.*, U.S. DEP'T OF COMMERCE, NATIONAL TECHNICAL INFORMATION SERVICE (1988).

20. H. Honneger et al., *Storung der Sehscharfe fur bewegte Objekte durch Alkohol*, 7 BLUTALKOHOL 31 (1970); H.W. Newman & E. Fletcher, *The Effect of Alcohol on Vision*, 202 AM. J. MED. SCI. 723 (1941); Moskowitz, *supra* note 18; R.G. Mortimer, *Effect of Low Blood Alcohol Concentrations in Simulated Day and Night Driving*, 17 PERCEPTIVE MOTOR SKILLS 399 (1963).

21. T.A. Pihkanen & O. Kauko, *The Effects of Alcohol on the Perception of Musical Stimuli*, 40 ANNALS MED. EXP. FENN. 275 (1962).

22. E.M. Jellinek & R.A. McFarland, *Analysis of Psychological Experiments on the Effects of Alcohol*, 1 Q. J. STUD. ALCOHOL 272 (1940).

23. Wallgren & Barry, *supra* note 9.

24. O. Huber, *Utersuchungen uber die Veranderung der Fahrtuchtigkeit von Kraftradfahrern nach massigem Alkoholgenuss*, DUTSCH. Z. GES.; A. Izard & G. Saby, *Contribution a l'etude du comportment psychomoteur de l'homme apres absorption de doses moyennes d'alcool*, 23 ARCH. MAL. PROF. 854 (1962); P. Moureau, *Tendances de la legislation belge en ce quie concerne l'intoxication alcoolique et les accidents de roulage*, 4 REV. ALCOOLISME 178 (1957).

25. O. Gruner, *Alkohol und Aufmerksamkeit, Ihre Bedeutung im motorisierten Verkehr*, 44 DTSCH. Z. GES. GERICHTL. MED. 187 (1955); O. Gruner & H. Ptasnik, *Zur Frage der Beeinflus-*

situation may indicate more closely the effects of alcohol on driving skills, since the driver must control the speed and position of the vehicle, as well as monitor outside signals such as traffic lights and signs. The additional demands on the driver's attention and judgment appear to greatly enhance the detrimental effects of alcohol. Many tests have demonstrated effects of alcohol at low to moderate blood levels detrimental to driving-related skills. West et al. found that a moderate dose of alcohol (0.05 g/dL BAC) increased mean time to respond to hazards from 2.5 seconds with no alcohol to 3.2 seconds.[26] The speed, as measured by time required to drive a timed course, was not affected.

[2] Alcohol Impairment of Driving/Piloting Skills

[a] *Motor Vehicle*

In a review of 177 studies of alcohol related impairment, 158 reported impairment of one or more behavioral skills at one or more BAC's.[27] In 35 studies, impairment was found at BAC's of 0.04 g/dL or less, and the majority found impairment below 0.07 g/dL. It was considered that, since the majority of the studies examined only one blood level of alcohol, these results must represent an underestimation of the level at which impairment begins. The studies were categorized into nine behavioral categories: 1) Reaction time; 2) Tracking; 3) Vigilance or concentrated attention; 4) Divided attention; 5) Information processing; 6) Visual function; 7) Perception; 8) Psychomotor skills; and 9) Actual driving skills on the road or in a simulator.

The area showing the greatest impairment effect of alcohol was *divided attention performance*, with some decrements demonstrated at BAC's of less than 0.02 g/dL. This level is the equivalent of ingestion of about one average beer in a 160 pound man. The second greatest impairment was found with *tracking performance*, at or below 0.05 g/dL. Driving has been described as a time sharing task made up of two major types of activity: compensatory tracking and visual search. It is the requirement for divided attention which is particularly sensitive to the effects of alcohol. In one study of the effect of low BAC's on *driving skills* performance, *divided-attention* and *information processing* tasks, impairment began at levels as low as 0.015 mg/dL and increased with increasing BAC's through 0.06 g/dL, the maximum studied.[28]

BAC's of 0.05 g/dL and above produce impairment of the major components of *driver performance*, including *reaction time, tracking, divided attention performance, information processing, oculomotor functions, perception* and other aspects of *psychomotor performance*. Limited tolerance to some of the impairment parameters of alcohol can occur. Studies designed to compare impairment in experienced versus light drinkers have been performed, and results vary with the type of test parameters and with different studies.[29] In a

sung alkoholbedingten Leistungsabfalles durch Laevulosegaben, 95 Munch. Med. Wochenschr 931 (1953).

26. R. West et al., *Effect of Low and Moderate Doses of Alcohol on Driving Hazard Perception Latency and Driving Speed*, 88 Addiction 527 (1993).

27. Moskowitz, *supra* note 18.

28. H. Moskowitz et al., *Skills Performance at Low Blood Alcohol Levels*, 46 J. Stud. Alcohol 482 (1985).

29. *See* G. Chesher & J. Greeley, *Tolerance to the Effects of Alcohol*, 8 Drugs and Driving 93 (1992).

recent on-road study of the effects of alcohol on driving skills in light and heavy drinkers, serious impairment occurred at BAC levels of 0.10 g/dL and higher in all subjects.[30] There was no evidence of any difference between the two groups. Another study compared the performance of alcoholics, heavy drinkers and social drinkers on cognitive tasks while sober and intoxicated.[31] The social drinkers showed gross signs of intoxication at BAC's of 0.10 g/dL and above, while the heavy drinkers and alcoholics showed almost none of these symptoms. However, all groups were equally impaired on the cognitive performance measures. The groups also had equivalent performance levels while sober, negating any chronic deficits in the alcoholic subjects.

The impairment observed experimentally translates to greatly increased probability of the drinking driver to be involved in fatal and non-fatal vehicular accidents. Low blood alcohol levels were associated with increased driver responsibility rates in a multi-state driver fatality study. Whereas drug and alcohol free drivers were responsible in 67.7% of cases, drivers with blood alcohol concentrations of 0.05–0.07 g/dL were responsible in 80.6%, and those with 0.08–0.10 g/dL in 94.4% of cases.[32]

[b] Aviation

Another area of concern for alcohol impairment is in general and military aviation. The effects of alcohol on specific piloting skills have been evaluated extensively, and impairment has been demonstrated at low BAC's.[33] Concentrations as low as 0.015 g/dL may reduce the ability to perform complex psychomotor tasks during the absorptive phase after alcohol ingestion. Concentrations in the range of 0.03 to 0.05 g/dL have been associated with impairment in tracking of radio-frequency signals, airport-traffic-control vectoring, traffic observation and avoidance, and aircraft descent,[34] as well as impairment of short-term memory, decreases in tracking performance during whole-body motion, target tracking, measures of flight coordination and configuration, and complex coordination.[35]

In 30 actual flights, each including four approaches in a single-engine aircraft using an instrument landing system, approximately twice as many major procedural errors and one episode of loss of aircraft control were observed with mean blood alcohol concentrations of 0.04 g/dL.[36] Current Federal Aviation Administration regulations prohibit any crew member of a

---

30. H. Laurell et al., *The Effects of Blood Alcohol Concentration on Light and Heavy Drinkers in a Realistic Night Driving Situation*, RESEARCH REPORT, NH & MRC ROAD ACCIDENT RESEARCH UNIT, UNIVERSITY OF ADELAIDE, SOUTH AUSTRALIA (1990).

31. L.J. Rosen & C.L. Lee, *Acute and Chronic Effects of Alcohol Use on Organizational Processes in Memory*, 85 J. ABNORMAL PSYCHOL. 309 (1976).

32. Terhune et al., *The Incidence and Role of Drugs in Fatally Injured Drivers*, U.S. DEP'T OF TRANSPORTATION, NATIONAL HIGHWAY TRAFFIC SAFETY ADMIN., TRAFFIC SAFETY FACTS, DOT HS–808–065 (1992).

33. J.G. Modell & J.M. Mountz, *Drinking and Flying—the Problem of Alcohol Use by Pilots*, 323 NEW ENG. J MED. 455 (1990).

34. L.E. Ross & J.C. Mundt, *Multiattribute Modeling Analysis of the Effects of a Low Blood Alcohol in Pilot Performance*, 30 HUM. FACTORS 293 (1988); R.S. Rybeck, *Effects of Alcohol on Memory and Its Implications for Flying Safety*, 41 AEROSPACE MED. 1193 (1970).

35. P.C. Tang & R. Rosenstein, *Influence of Alcohol and Dramamine, Alone and in Combination, on Pilot Performance*, 38 AEROSPACE MED. 818 (1967).

36. C.E. Billings et al., *Effect of Ethyl Alcohol on Pilot Performance*, 44 AEROSPACE MED. 379 (1973).

civil aircraft from flying within 8 hours after the consumption of any alcoholic beverage, while under the influence of alcohol, or while having 0.04 percent (by weight) or more alcohol in the blood.[37] Results of performance studies clearly demonstrate piloting skills impairment at and below the permissible limit.

Yesavage and Leirer reported pilot performance impairment even after complete clearance of alcohol from the blood.[38] They demonstrated a "hangover effect" 14 hours after alcohol ingestion to reach a BAC of 0.10 g/dL or greater which resulted in poorer piloting skills performance in all tests administered. The tests were designed to test emergency response by pilots during takeoff and landing procedures.

In summary, most testing for alcohol-related impairment of performance on driving/flying-related skills shows distinct impairment at levels of 0.05 g/dL or even lower. Although few studies have examined the effects at high blood levels, one can logically expect severe impairment of all driving skills, including decreased responsiveness in the driver to hazards and increases in reaction time of several hundred percent as blood concentrations exceed 0.2 and 0.3 g/dL. Surveys of average blood alcohol levels in motor vehicle driver fatalities range from 0.16 g/dL upward.[39]

While driving statutes in Western Europe have long been stringent regarding permissible blood alcohol levels (as low as 0.02 g/dL in Sweden), the United States has traditionally been lenient toward drinking drivers. In 1987, only 21 states had enacted statutes using a BAC to define alcohol levels for purposes of driving a vehicle, and those that did used the 0.10 g/dL legal standard. In the face of high rates of alcohol related fatalities, injuries, and many billions of dollars annually in damages, along with public pressure on states courts and legislatures, the trend has now changed as federal agencies and states tighten drinking driver legislation. As of January, 2001, 54 state jurisdictions have a BAC standard, 34 use the 0.10 standard, and 19 now use the 0.08 legal limit for driving under the influence.[40]

§ 8–2.2.3   Effects of Alcohol in Combination With Other Drugs

[1]   Depressants

Ethyl alcohol has some degree of interaction with a wide spectrum of other drugs. Classically, it exerts a potentiation or synergistic effect when ingested in the presence of other drugs having CNS depressant effects. When alcohol is ingested in the presence of other depressant drugs, such as sedatives, hypnotics, anticonvulsants, antidepressants, tranquilizers, some analgesics, and opiates, a greatly enhanced depressant effect may occur. Pharmaceu-

---

37. Modell & Mountz, *supra* note 33.

38. J.A. Yesavage & V.O. Leirer, *Hangover Effects on Aircraft Pilots 14 hours After Alcohol Ingestion: A Preliminary Report*, 143 Am. J. Psychiatry 1546 (1986).

39. G. Cimbura et al., *Incidence and Toxicological Aspects of Drugs Detected in 489 Fatally Injured Drivers and Pedestrians in Ontario*, 27 J. Forensic Sci. 855 (1982); J.C. Fell & C.E. Nash, *The Nature of the Alcohol Problem*

in U.S. Fatal Crashes, 16 Health Educ. Q. 335 (1989); J.C. Garriot et al., *Incidence of Drugs and Alcohol in Fatally Injured Motor Vehicle Drivers*, 22 J. Forensic Sci. 383 (1977).

40. Revision to Federal Blood Alcohol Concentration (BAC) Standard for Recreational Vessel Operators, 66 Fed. Reg. 1,859 (Jan. 10, 2001) (to be codified at 33 C.F.R. pts. 95 & 177).

tical package inserts and other drug information circulars warn physicians of the dangers of concomitant use of drugs in the above classes and alcohol.

This enhanced intoxication effect of drugs can occur with low levels of alcohol. The effect can be profound, and numerous deaths result from "mixing alcohol and drugs." The severe intoxication that can occur in this manner also may be a significant factor in the incidence of motor vehicle accidents when drivers combine drugs and alcohol.[41] Of 1,882 fatally injured drivers from seven states, drug and alcohol combinations were detected in 11.4 %.[42] These drugs were predominantly cocaine, marihuana, benzodiazepines, and amphetamines. Drugs in combination, other than cocaine (no effect), increased responsibility in crash causation significantly with low (less than 0.10 g/dL) blood alcohol concentrations.

[2] Stimulants

Amphetamines and other CNS stimulants may antagonize the depressant effects of alcohol to some degree, but do not effectively counteract the impaired motor function induced by alcohol.[43] The interaction with cocaine is more complicated, due to the condensation of alcohol and cocaine to form a third drug, cocaethylene, which may have greater potency and a longer half life than cocaine. The concomitant use of alcohol and cocaine may mitigate the detrimental effects of alcohol on performance to some degree. In a study designed to measure the behavioral effects of cocaine and alcohol on human learning and performance, the combined doses of cocaine (4 to 96 mg/Kg) and alcohol (0 to 1.0 g/Kg) attenuated the effects observed with alcohol and cocaine alone.[44] Both doses of cocaine studied, when combined with alcohol, reduced errors in acquisition (learning) to placebo levels. Likewise, the percentage of errors in performance was consistently reduced below that observed with similar doses of alcohol alone. Thus, cocaine may be an effective antagonist to the depressant effects of alcohol, at least in the moderate alcohol dose ranges as used in this study.

[3] Other Drugs

Alcohol may also interact with numerous drugs of other classes. These interactions may occur with agents including antidepressants, salicylates, antidiabetics (oral hypoglycemic agents), insulin, anticonvulsants and even certain food substances, such as mushrooms, among others.[45] These interactions may result in enhanced effects, reduced effects (antagonism), or severe

41. J.C. Garriot & N. Latman, *Drug Detection in Cases of Driving Under the Influence*, 21 J. Forensic Sci. 398 (1976); J. C. Garriot et al., *supra* note 39; G. Cimbura et al., *supra* note 39.

42. Terhune et al., *supra* note 32.

43. E. Martin et al., *The Pharmacokinetics of Alcohol in Human Breath, Venous and Arterial Blood After Oral Ingestions*, 26 Eur. J. Clinical Pharmacology 619 (1984).

44. Higgins et al., *Effects of Cocaine and Alcohol, Alone and in Combination on Human*

Learning and Performance, 58 J. Experiment. Annals of Behavior 87 (1992).

45. F.L. Iber, *Increased Drug Metabolism in Alcoholics, in Advances in Mental Science*, 3 Biological Aspects of Alcohol.; J.K. Wier & V.E. Tyler, *An Investigation of Coprinus Atramentarius for the Presence of Disulfiram*, 49 J. Am. Pharmacology Assoc. 426 (1960); B.W. Hills & H.C. Venable, *The Interaction of Ethyl Alcohol and Industrial Chemicals*, 3 Am. J. Indus. Med. 321 (1982).

toxic effects, such as hypotensive crisis and severe illness, when combined with certain foods or drugs.[46]

§ 8–2.3   Alcohol Testing Procedures

§ 8–2.3.1   Blood and Body Fluids

Blood is the most frequent body fluid tested for alcohol, and most state laws defining legal intoxication are based on blood concentrations. Legal intoxication is also defined in terms of breath concentration directly, which, in the United States, generally equates to a similar blood concentration when a concentration ratio of 2100:1 is assumed.[47] Methods applicable to testing blood can be used generally for all body fluid analysis, including urine, vitreous humor or other specimens obtainable at autopsy including tissue homogenates.

In laboratory practice today, alcohol is commonly measured by only a few accepted procedures. These can be categorized into three general classes: chemical, biochemical, and gas chromatographic methods.[48]

[1]   Chemical Methods

Chemical methods for alcohol analysis are based on oxidation-reduction reactions. By this process, ethyl alcohol is oxidized (oxygen is added) while another reactant is reduced (removal of oxygen or addition of hydrogen). This occurs in the presence of a catalyst or dehydrating agent such as sulfuric acid. Ethyl alcohol, containing one oxygen entity, may be oxidized first by removal of two hydrogen atoms to form acetaldehyde, which becomes acetic acid by the addition of one oxygen atom.

Alcohol, due to its volatility, is conveniently separated from biological samples by various techniques; and after separation, can be quantitatively measured by means of reaction with oxidizing agents such as dichromate, permanganate, or osmic acid. When alcohol is reacted with potassium dichromate in strong sulfuric acid solution, the yellow-orange dichromate ion is reduced to the blue-green chromic ion while alcohol is oxidized to acetaldehyde, acetic acid, or carbon dioxide and water.

These methods have been applied since early in this century, when E.M.P. Widmark developed a procedure for measuring alcohol in blood utilizing a specially constructed spoon for suspending the biological sample over a known quantity of potassium dichromate solution in a stoppered flask.[49] After heating the flask to drive the oxidation reaction, the cooled dichromate was then titrated with standard sodium thiosulfate using potassium iodide and starch as an indicator. Since that time, a number of suitable dichromate methods for determining ethyl alcohol in body fluids have been described and used in testing laboratories.[50]

---

46. F.A. Seixas, *Alcohol and Its Drug Interactions*, 83 Annals Internal Med. 86 (1975).

47. *See* § 8–2.3.2.

48. R.F. Shaw, *Methods for Fluid Analysis*, in Medicolegal Aspects of Alcohol (James C. Garriot ed., 3rd ed.1996).

49. E.M.P. Widmark, *A Micromethod for the Estimation of Alcohol in Blood*, 131 Biochem. Z. 473 (1922).

50. R.N. Harger, *A Simple Micromethod for the Determination of Alcohol in Biological Material*, 20 J. Lab. Clinical Med. 746 (1935); J.M. Cavett, *The Determination of Alcohol in Blood*

Although chemical procedures were used for many decades, and still may be used in some laboratories, they are no longer standard in the field. The procedure's limitations include their total lack of specificity, their labor intensive nature, and the difficulty in adapting them to automation. In the modern forensic laboratory, large volumes of specimens must often be processed for alcohol and other analytes, and the chemical procedures are not suitable for this purpose. In addition, oxidation-reduction methods will react with other oxidizable substances. These substances include methanol, isopropanol, and other alcohols, as well as volatile putrefactive products. For the latter reason in particular, oxidation methods should not be used for forensic alcohol analysis. However, this is not to say they can not produce valid and even accurate results when used properly and with adequate controls, and they can be useful in clinical and non-forensic alcohol testing.

[2]   Biochemical Methods

Biochemical methods for alcohol analysis utilize some form of enzymatic process, as averse to direct chemical processes as discussed above. The result is similar, in that alcohol is converted to acetaldehyde. The acetaldehyde may be further reacted with another enzyme to produce a reactant which can be measured by spectrophotometric or chemical techniques.

Alcohol dehydrogenase (ADH), a liver enzyme, is often used for the measurement of alcohol in biological fluids. In this reaction, alcohol is oxidized to acetaldehyde by ADH in the presence of a coenzyme, nicotinamide adenine dinucleotide (NAD), which is further reduced to NADH. This reduced form can be measured spectrophotometrically at 340nm. In a secondary reaction the NADH can be coupled to a diaphorase-chromagen system producing a red-colored formazan colloidal suspension that may be read spectrophotometrically at 500nm. This procedure can be automated with microprocessor control and print-out providing rapid turn-around time. The enzyme does not react with methyl alcohol or acetone and only reacts to a lesser degree with isopropyl alcohol and butyl alcohol. Bonnichsen and Theorell described the first use of ADH for the analysis of ethyl alcohol.[51]

The ADH enzyme assays for alcohol are now commonly used in hospitals and clinical laboratories. They provide a rapid and accurate blood or serum alcohol analysis.[52] However, due to cross reactivity of ADH with isopropanol and, to a lesser extent, other alcohols, these methods are not completely specific and are often not generally considered acceptable for forensic use.

and Other Body Fluids, 23 J. LAB. CLINICAL MED. 543 (1938); F.L. Kozelka & C.H. Hine, Method for the Determination of Ethyl Alcohol for Medicolegal Purposes, 13 IND. ENGIN. CHEM. (ANNALS ED.) 905 (1941); L.M. Shope and K.M. Dubowski, Ethyl Alcohol in Blood and Urine: A Simple Photomethod for Its Forensic Determination, 32 AMER. J. CLINICAL PATHOLOGY 901 (1952); Sunshine & R. Nenad, A Modification of Winnick's Method for the Rapid Determination of Ethyl Alcohol in Biological Fluids, 25 ANNALS CHEM. 653 (1953); L.W. Bradford, Concepts and Standards of Performance in the Technique of Alcohol Analysis of Physiological Specimens,

reprinted in, PROCEEDINGS OF THE SYMPOSIUM ON ALCOHOL AND ROAD TRAFFIC, INDIANA UNIVERSITY, INDIANAPOLIS, 61 (1958).

51. R. Bonnichsen & H. Theorell, An Enzymatic Method for the Microdetermination of Ethanol, 3 SCAND. J. CLINICAL LAB. INVEST. 58 (1951).

52. H.M. Redetzki & W.L. Dees, Comparison of Four Kits for Enzymatic Determination of Ethanol in Blood, 22 CLINICAL CHEM. 83 (1976).

Whitehouse and Paul reported an enzymatic method that has been adapted to the Abbott Bichromatic Analyzer-l00.[53] Fully automatic, the method can accommodate up to 192 assays per hour. It requires only 2.5 uL of plasma and therefore is applicable to analysis for ethyl alcohol in blood by finger stick.

The EMIT (enzyme multiplied immunoassay technique) procedure is commonly used as commercial kits for drug detection in urine. In the EMIT procedure, a drug is labeled with an enzyme. The labeled drug is bound to an antibody. When this is combined with a specimen such as urine, any drug present in the specimen displaces the labeled drug from the antibody. This activates the enzyme, which is measured by a change in optical density (OD) in the solution.

A rapid and accurate method using the Roche Cobas Bio centrifugal analyzer and the EMIT-st TM serum ethanol assay reagent was described for measuring ethanol in serum. The results correlated well with a commonly used gas chromatograph headspace method.[54] Because of the rapidity and good practicability of this method, the authors concluded that the method is well suited for use in emergency care units of clinical chemistry laboratories.

The enzymatic EMIT ETS PLUS ethyl alcohol assay was designed for use with the new Syva ETS PLUS analyzer for the quantitative analysis of ethanol in human urine, serum, and plasma. The assay had a linear range up to 0.65 g/dL (0.65 %) and a low detection limit of 0.01 g/dL. The linearity of a method verifies its validity over a range of concentrations to be measured. To compare these ranges, the blood alcohol level for legal intoxication is 0.10 g/dL in most states. This method was found to be free of interference from small molecular weight alcohols, aldehydes, ketones, and glycols.[55]

A new upgraded ETS Plus urine and serum ethanol analyzer for analyzing ethanol in urine, serum, and plasma was also found to be accurate.[56] The precision of the ETS PLUS ethyl alcohol assay yielded a coefficient of variation (CV) of 2.6% at a target value of 0.10 g/dL and a CV of 3.2% at a target value of 0.04 g/dL. The coefficient of variation is a measure of the accuracy and repeatability of a procedure, obtained by measuring the same concentrations under the same conditions repeatedly, to yield a percent of variation from the mean.

In 1984, Abbott Laboratories introduced a radioactive energy attenuation (REA) assay for the determination of ethyl alcohol on the TDx analyzer, a microprocessor-controlled automated fluorometer used for fluorescence polarization immunoassay for many therapeutically monitored drugs. In the REA method for ethyl alcohol, the enzyme-catalytic reactions of ADH and diaphorase result in the formation of a reduced iodonitrotetrazolium (INT), a red color chromogen which has an absorbance peak of 492nm. The concentration of ethyl alcohol is proportional to the degree of inner filter effect on the

53. L.W. Whitehouse & C.J. Paul, *Micro-Scale Enzymic Determination of Ethanol in Plasma with a Discrete Analyzer, the ABA–100*, 25 CLINICAL CHEM. 1399 (1979).

54. F. Degel & N. Paulus, *A Rapid and Precise Method for the Quantitation of Ethanol in Serum Using the EMIT-st Serum Ethanol Assay Reagent and a Cobas Bio Centrifugal Analyzer*, 26 J. CLIN. CHEM. BIOCHEM. 351 (1988).

55. S.A. Jortani & A. Poklis, *Evaluation of the Syva ETS Plus Urine Drug and Serum Analyzer*, 17 J. ANNALS TOXICOLOGY 31 (1993).

56. *Id.*

fluorescence produced. No cross-reaction toward methyl alcohol, isopropyl alcohol, or acetone at concentrations that might be expected in toxic situations occurred.[57]

Abbott Laboratories reformulated the ethyl alcohol assay by replacing the iodonitrotetrazolium violet dye (INT) with a thiazolyl blue dye (MTT). The new formulation significantly reduces the variability often found in analysis of postmortem blood with the original REA reagent system. Postmortem blood is often hemolyzed, or partially decomposed, which leads to difficulties and variabilities in results of analytical procedures. Abbott Laboratories recommends a sensitivity limit (lowest concentration level of detection) for ethyl alcohol in postmortem blood by the REA method of 0.015 g/100mL. Determination of ethyl alcohol in serum, fresh whole blood, fresh or postmortem urine, and vitreous humor by REA demonstrated no specimen bias.[58]

A study using this method which compared suspected driving while intoxicated individuals (DWI blood) and postmortem blood specimens (PM blood) determined that a limit of detection of 0.01 g/dL could be applied for DWI blood specimens, while 0.02 g/dL would be recommended as the limit of detection for PM blood specimens.[59] Blood concentrations of 0.01 or 0.02 g/dL are below significance for driving impairment. The legal limit for driving under the influence is 0.10 g/dL in most states, and as low as 0.08 in some.

For forensic applications, biochemical methods for blood alcohol are not usually used due to their lack of total specificity. Isopropyl alcohol and butyl alcohol may interfere in the reaction. Enzyme methods should therefore be confirmed by an alternate technique if results are to be used by the courts, or in any forensic application.[60] However, these automated techniques are used for alcohol analysis universally in hospitals and clinical laboratories. For this reason, these test results will often be used in civil and criminal litigation.

[3] Gas Chromatographic Methods

The most commonly used methods for the forensic analysis of ethyl alcohol are those utilizing gas chromatography. Gas chromatography is a technique for the separation of volatile substances (gases), performed by passing a gas stream over a stationary phase within a metal or glass column (See Figure 1). In gas liquid chromatography (GLC) an inert gas is passed over a liquid phase that is spread as a thin film over an inert solid (such as glass beads). The substance to be analyzed is introduced into the column by injection of the liquid sample through a syringe into the column, where it is volatilized at high temperature, and then passed through the column by an inert, pressurized gas. The detection system at the end of the column senses and measures each substance as it elutes from the column and transmits the signal to a recorder. These detectors are either thermal (detect thermal

57. P.L. Cary et al., *Abbott Radioactive Energy Attenuation Method for Quantifying Ethanol Evaluated and Compared with Gas–Liquid Chromatography and the DuPont ACA*, 30 CLINICAL CHEM. 1867 (1984).

58. P.L. Cary, *Reformulated REA Ethanol Assay Evaluated*, 10 J. ANNALS TOXICOLOGY 38 (1986).

59. Y.H. Caplan & B. Levine, *Evaluation of the Abbott TDx–Radioactive Energy Attenuation (REA) Ethanol Assay in a Study of 1105 Forensic Whole Blood Specimens*, 32 J. FORENSIC SCI. 55 (1987).

60. J.C. Garriott, *Forensic Aspects of Ethyl Alcohol*, 3 CLINICAL LAB. MED. 385 (1983).

changes) or, more frequently, hydrogen flames (flame ionization detectors—FID's). The response from the detector is recorded and is usually manifested as a "peak" or a blip on the curve as each substance leaves the column and is ionized by the flame. The identifying feature for each substance is the retention time (RT) or the time it takes to traverse the column.

Several gas chromatographic methods, such as solvent extraction, protein precipitation, distillation, direct injection, or headspace techniques have been utilized.[61] Earlier methods involving the separation of ethyl alcohol from biological specimens usually entailed solvent extraction, protein precipitation, and distillation. Current methods involve direct injection and headspace techniques.

Direct injection is self descriptive, and means that the sample (blood or urine) is analyzed by directly injecting it onto the column. This occurs after dilution with water and usually another solvent used as the internal standard. The term "headspace" refers to the air sample within the sealed tube containing the blood sample. This air space is at equilibrium with the liquid sample. According to Henry's Law, the solubility of a gas in a liquid solution is proportional to the partial pressure of the gas. The partial pressure is in turn dependent on temperature and atmospheric pressure. All this means that the concentration of the gas (volatile ethyl alcohol) in the head space will be constant and depend on its concentration in the blood sample under controlled temperature conditions and atmospheric pressure.

61. N.C. Jain & R.H. Cravey, *Analysis of Alcohol, 1. A Review of Gas Chromatographic Methods*, 10 J. CHROMATOGR. SCI. 263 (1972); J.W. Wright, *Alcohol and the Laboratory in the United Kingdom*, 28 ANNALS CLINICAL BIOCHEM. 212 (1991); F. Tagliaro et al., *Chromatographic Methods for Blood Alcohol Determination*, 580 J. CHROMATOGR. 161 (1992).

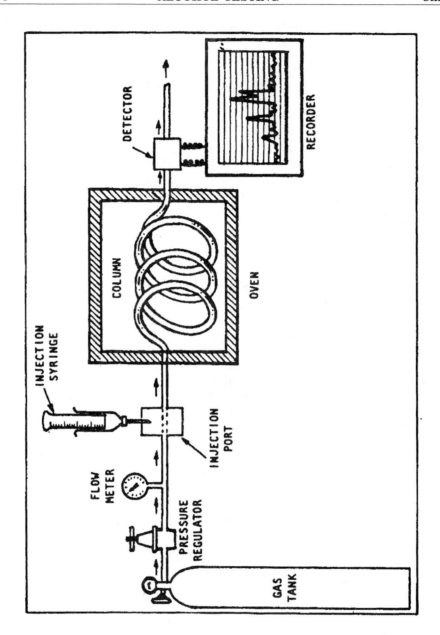

Figure 1.

Diagram showing principles of operation of a gas chromatograph. A sample of liquid or gas is injected into the injection port, usually at high temperature, where it is transferred into the column by an inert gas under pressure and measured by the detector as it comes off the column.

[a] Extraction and Distillation Techniques

One of the earliest methods was that of Cadman and Johns in which they reported a procedure using a Beckman GC–2 gas chromatograph equipped with a thermal conductivity detector (TCD).[62] The extraction technique consisted of pipetting 1 mL blood and 1 mL of n-propyl acetate into a 3 mL screwcapped vial containing 1 g of anhydrous potassium carbonate. The sample vial was mixed and shaken one minute on a mechanical mixer. The sample was centrifuged and a 35 uL aliquot of the n-propyl acetate was injected into the gas chromatograph. Ethyl alcohol standards were prepared by adding measured amounts of ethyl alcohol to blood. This blood was subsequently extracted and chromatographed under the same conditions as that of the unknown samples for quantitation. Extraction procedures have long been superseded by more direct and efficient techniques.

Distillation techniques usually involved separation of ethyl alcohol from the biological specimen by distillation after adding water, along with protein precipitation reagents such as sodium tungstate and sulfuric acid. After distillation, an aliquot was injected into a gas chromatograph.[63] Again, these techniques are rarely used today due to lengthy analysis time.

[b] Direct Injection Techniques

Numerous direct injection methods for the determination of ethyl alcohol in biological specimens by gas chromatography have been published. These techniques may vary according to the preparation of the sample for testing and may consist of (1) direct injection of the sample, (2) protein precipitation and subsequent injection, or (3) dilution of the sample prior to injection. Probably the easiest and fastest is the injection of a diluted sample with an appropriate internal standard into a gas chromatograph equipped with a flame ionization detector. A number of suitable methods have been described,[64] all involving direct injection techniques.

An ultramicro method utilizing direct sample injection was described for identification and quantification of ethyl alcohol in blood and urine.[65] One uL of a mixture of whole blood or urine mixed with equal parts of an internal standard, 1-propyl alcohol, is injected into a gas chromatograph equipped with a flame ionization detector. The column is filled with a precolumn glass insert filled with a loosely packed silanized glass wool plug that acts as a trap for the nonvolatile protein material of the blood or urine samples. The peak area of the alcohol peak and the internal standard peak are measured and compared with known amounts of ethyl alcohol and internal standard, and the concentration of ethyl alcohol present is calculated.

62. W.J. Cadman & T. Johns, *Gas Chromatographic Determination of Ethanol and Other Volatiles from Blood*, NINTH ANNUAL PITTSBURGH CONFERENCE ON ANALYTICAL CHEMISTRY AND APPLIED SPECTROSCOPY, March 1958.

63. J.E. Fox, *Fast Chromatographic Analysis of Alcohols and Certain Other Volatiles in Biological Material for Forensic Purposes*, 97 PROC. EXP. BIOL. MED. 236 (1958).

64. A.S. Curry et al., *Determination of Ethanol in Blood by Gas Chromotography*, 91 ANALYST 742 (1966); B.S. Finkle, *Ethanol-type C Procedure, in* MANUAL OF ANALYTICAL TOXICOLOGY 147 (I. Sunshine ed., 1971); N.C. Jain, *Direct Blood Injection Method for Gas Chromatography Determination of Alcohols and Other Volatile Compounds*, 17 CLIN. CHEM. 82 (1971); J. Solon et al., *Automated Analysis of Alcohols in Blood*, 17 J. FORENSIC SCI. 447 (1972); P. Blume et al., *A Gas Chromatographic Analysis of Ethanol with Identifying Confirmation*, 54 ANNALS BIOCHEM. 429 (1973).

65. B.R. Manno & J.E. Manno, *A Simple Approach to Gas Chromatographic Microanalysis of Alcohol in Blood and Urine by a Direct-Injection Technique*, 2 J. ANNALS TOXICOLOGY 257 (1978).

[c] Headspace Techniques

Headspace techniques are based on Henry's law of physics, which states that the ratio of a dissolved substance in aqueous solution is dependent on temperature, pressure, and concentration in the aqueous medium. These factors, in turn, determine the proportion of the substance in the vapor phase over the liquid, and the volatile substances may be measured by analyzing the vapor which is in equilibrium with a liquid biological specimen. Typically, the blood sample is placed into a vial with appropriate internal standard and sealed with a septum and allowed to stand, usually at 37 degC, until equilibrium is reached. A sample of the headspace is removed from the vial by syringe and injected into a gas chromatograph.

In some methods, sodium chloride is added to the samples in amounts greater than those required for saturation to minimize the variations in the gas-liquid partition ratio of ethyl alcohol.[66] According to the authors, the addition of the salt markedly increases the vapor pressure of ethyl alcohol in the biological samples and permits quantitative analysis of the vapor phase for ethyl alcohol without the preparation of complex standards.

Karnitis and Porter described a method which consists of equilibrating blood with n-propyl alcohol as the internal standard and then injecting the vapors into a 0.125 in. by 6 ft stainless steel column packed with Porapak S.[67] Concentrations were linear over the range 0.00 to 0.35 g/dL blood ethyl alcohol.

Currently, the most widely accepted headspace sampling method is based on one that was developed by Machata using a Perkin–Elmer Multifract F–40 system.[68] This system consists essentially of a gas chromatograph equipped with a flame ionization detector and a special electropneumatic valve dosing system in addition to a conventional injection port for manual sampling; a precision thermostated turntable water bath; and control unit, recorder or printing integrator. The principles of the system are the three basic steps of headspace sampling: (1) equilibration, (2) pressurization, and (3) transfer of a headspace sample onto the column. After equilibrium is established in the vial, a needle connected to the carrier gas inlet is introduced through a rubber cap into the headspace of the vial. If the pressure in the vial is smaller than the carrier gas inlet pressure, part of the carrier gas flow will enter the vial and pressurize it until it reaches the inlet pressure. At this point the carrier gas supply is momentarily cut off for a specified time. This action causes the gas to flow from the vial into the column, barely injecting an aliquot of the headspace. Coefficients of variation below 3% have been reported. Detailed descriptions of the Multifract F–40, F–42, and F–45 are found in manuals published by the Perkin–Elmer Company, and more recently, a detailed procedure was reported by Dubowski.[69]

66. J.E. Wallace & E.V. Dahl, *Rapid Vapor Phase Method for Determining Ethanol in Blood and Urine by Gas Chromatography*, 46 AM. J. CLINICAL PATHOL. 152 (1966).

67. L. Karnitis & L.J. Porter, *A Gas Chromotographic Method for Ethanol in Vapors of Biological Fluids*, 16 J. FORENSIC SCI. 318 (1971).

68. G. Machata, *Determination of Alcohol in Blood by Gas Chromatography Headspace Analysis*, 4 PERKIN ELMER CLINICAL CHEM. NEWSL. 29 (1972).

69. K.M. Dubowski, *Manual for Analysis of*

In addition to the Multifract F–40, F–42, and F–45, the newest automatic headspace sampler is the Perkin–Elmer Model HS–100 mounted on a Sigma gas chromatograph. It combines the simplicity of CRT interaction with the versatility of the microprocessor-control, dual-channel gas chromatograph. The microprocessor control ensures precise thermostating and timing and also allows automatic unattended injection and analysis of up to 100 samples.[70]

§ 8–2.3.2 Breath Testing

[1] Methods for Breath Analysis

Since blood testing requires some degree of invasiveness and the availability of medical personnel, breath alcohol analysis is used much more frequently in most areas. Breath testing is used extensively not only for determining alcohol involvement in motor vehicle violations, but also for other purposes such as testing for alcohol use in the workplace, and in hospitals and drug abuse treatment centers for clinical screening of alcohol use and abuse.

The technology of breath alcohol analysis has evolved from collection of large volumes of breath in balloons and analysis by cumbersome wet chemical methods to automated, portable, microprocessor-controlled instruments which provide immediate results. These instruments are capable of providing reliable results when operated in a non-laboratory environment by individuals with little or no scientific background or training.[71]

[2] Sampling Breath for Alcohol Analysis

Breath testing is a rapid, non-invasive means of determining alcohol concentration and requires only minimal subject cooperation. Alcohol is both infinitely soluble in water and is sufficiently volatile at physiological temperatures to be present in measurable concentrations in deep lung breath. End-expiratory breath is the proper specimen for alcohol analysis, because the terminal portion of a breath expiration reflects the alcohol concentration in arterial blood.[72] Subjects are generally instructed to take a deep breath and provide a steady exhalation into a sampling tube or hose for as long as they are able. During the course of the exhalation, the breath alcohol concentration will increase rapidly until a concentration plateau is reached. Analysis of any portion of the breath sample prior to attaining this plateau will result in a lower breath alcohol concentration. It is therefore standard breath sampling practice to provide a continuous exhalation against moderate pressure and to discard at least the initial two thirds of the sample.[73] The concentration of

Ethanol in Biological Liquids, U.S. Dep't of Transportation, Technical Report, DOT–TSC–NI ITSA–76–4 (1977).

70. S.G. Hurt & B. Welton, *New Microprocessor–Controlled Gas Chromatographs*, 15 Am. Lab. 89 (1983).

71. P.M. Harding, *Methods for Breath Analysis, in* Medicolegal Aspects of Alcohol (J.C. Garriott ed., 1996).

72. American Medical Association, *Alcohol and the Impaired Driver, A Manual on the*

Medicolegal Aspects of Chemical Tests for Intoxication with Supplement on Breath Alcohol Tests, 1970, 1972, reprinted by National Safety Council, 94 (1976).

73. K.M. Dubowski, *Biological Aspects of Breath–Alcohol Analysis*, 20 Clin. Chem. 294 (1974).

alcohol measured in the breath sample may be affected by several factors.

[a] Residual Mouth Alcohol

Alcohol remaining in the oral cavity arising from recent alcohol ingestion, regurgitation of stomach contents containing alcohol or eructation of gas (belching) can contaminate the breath sample and cause falsely elevated results. During the course of exhalation, breath samples contaminated with residual mouth alcohol are characterized by an initial rapid alcohol concentration rise followed by a rapid decline of the concentration to zero or to the baseline breath alcohol concentration.[74] A pre-test alcohol deprivation period of at least 15 minutes provides sufficient time to dissipate residual mouth alcohol, and this waiting period is standard procedure in breath testing.

[b] Condensation Losses

If breath is subjected to a reduction in temperature during or after sampling, its water vapor component will condense and alcohol will be removed from the sample because of it's high affinity for water. This results in a falsely decreased alcohol reading. This potential loss is easily avoided by maintaining the instrument's sample chamber (and any significant length of sampling tubing) at a constant temperature, between 45 and 50 degrees C.

[3] Blood and Breath Relationships

Blood testing results are expressed in terms of grams of alcohol per 210 liters of breath. This does not entail a conversion to actual blood concentration, which had been customary in earlier years, but was often challenged due to known variations in the actual ratios under some conditions. For most purposes, however, the quantity of alcohol in 210 liters of breath air is equivalent to a blood alcohol in the same amount expressed as grams per 100 mL of blood. For example, a breath alcohol of 0.15 g/210L is the same as a blood alcohol of 0.15 g/100 mL (0.15 grams per cent, or 0.15 g/dL). This presumes a blood/breath ratio of 2100:1, or that 2.1 Liters of alveolar lung air contains the same amount of alcohol as one milliliter of blood. A ratio of 2300:1 has been shown to be more accurate in postabsorption subjects, or after complete absorption of alcohol from the gastrointestinal tract.[75] This fact actually works to the benefit of the subject in the postabsorptive phase, however, by giving them a slightly lower reading than if a direct blood alcohol were measured. The potential for variability in the ratio under some absorption circumstances and its influence on interpretation of breath test results have been discussed by other authors.[76]

The actual blood:breath ratio can vary considerably. Prior to complete absorption, the ratio may be much lower, and factors such as variances in

74. K.M. Dubowski, *The Technology of Breath–Alcohol Analysis*, PUBLIC HEALTH SERV., U.S. DEP'T OF HEALTH AND HUMAN SERVS., DHSS No. (ADM) 92–1728 (1992).

75. K.M. Dubowski & B. O'Neill, *The Blood/Breath Ratio of Ethanol*, 25 CLIN. CHEM. 1144 (1979).

76. D.A. Labianca & G. Simpson, *Statistical Analysis of Blood-to-breath Alcohol Ratio Data in the Logarithm-transformed and Nontransformed Modes*, 34 EUR. J. CLINICAL BIOCHEM. 111 (1996).

body temperature may affect the ratio. For example, increases in body temperature will increase the ratio of alcohol, and therefore elevate the breath concentration measured.

[4]　Breath Alcohol Testing Instrumentation

Breath alcohol testing instruments can be classified into three categories: passive alcohol sensor; screening device; and evidential breath tester.

[a]　Passive Alcohol Sensor (PAS)

The PAS is designed to easily and rapidly detect the presence of alcohol. It is most often used by law enforcement officers to screen drivers at roadside sobriety checkpoints. The PAS is a handheld, battery-operated unit which is often housed in a modified police service flashlight.[77] In operation, it is held in proximity to the subject's mouth while an internal fan draws expired breath or air from the vehicle interior into the unit for analysis. No subject cooperation is necessary (thus the term "passive"). If alcohol is detected, its presence, and sometimes an approximate amount, will be displayed.

[b]　Screening Device

Screening devices (also known as preliminary or pre-arrest breath testers) are relatively inexpensive, handheld, portable units which are designed to provide a rapid approximation of alcohol concentration. They are commonly employed by police officers at the scene of traffic offenses where they are incorporated as an adjunct to field sobriety testing to establish "probable cause" for an arrest. These instruments are also used in hospitals[78] and for workplace testing. Lighted panels display a numerical result or an indication as to whether or not a preset alcohol concentration has been exceeded (if the instrument has a "pass/fail" or "pass/warn/fail" display). In many jurisdictions, screening device results are considered unreliable and are not admissible evidence in anything but a probable cause hearing. Even though many of these devices were not originally designed for evidential use, most are capable of producing accurate and reliable results when used properly. Safeguards should be applied, such as a 15 minute waiting period, to avoid interference by mouth alcohol.

A modification of a screening device is the ignition interlock device, which prevents a driver from starting the vehicle if a pre-set alcohol level is detected. This device may be installed as a court-ordered sanction to prevent repeat DWI offenders from continuing to drink and drive.

[c]　Evidential Breath Tester

An evidential breath tester (EBT) is designed to provide accurate, precise, quantitative alcohol results. Results obtained from these devices are generally

---

77. Dubowski, *supra* note 73.

78. M. Falkensson et al., *Bedside Diagnosis of Alcohol Intoxication with a Pocket–Size* *Breath–Alcohol Device: Sampling from Unconscious Subjects and Specificity for Ethanol*, 35 CLINICAL CHEM. 918 (1989).

admissible in court proceedings. The instruments are most often situated at fixed sites such as police stations, but some are designed as mobile units using separate batteries or a vehicle's electrical system to obtain power. Such units have the advantage of providing the capability to measure an alcohol concentration close to the time of a traffic violation and can be used in isolated areas, avoiding lengthy transportation delays before testing.

[5] Potential Challenges to Breath Test Results

Due to frequent use of breath test results in the courts, numerous challenges have been applied in attempts to cast doubt on their validity, or to discredit them altogether. These challenges generally involve allegations that a given breath test result is invalid due to interference with the test by other compounds present in the breath of the defendant at the time, or that the test was improperly applied.

[a] Specificity

It is often alleged that a breath alcohol result is caused wholly or in part due to compounds other than ethyl alcohol in the subject's breath, thus causing a falsely elevated result. The only endogenous compound present in breath which can reasonably be considered to be a potential interferant is acetone. Acetone may be present in elevated concentrations in the breath of diabetics and fasting dieters. The concentrations present are very low except in severe acetonemia in uncontrolled diabetics, and studies have conclusively shown that endogenous acetone will not have a deleterious effect on breath alcohol results.[79] Some other volatile substances may be present in breath, such as the industrial solvents toluene or trichloroethane, due to intensive exposure to paint or other solvent fumes, or in some instances due to deliberate inhalant abuse. However, the amounts of these necessary to pose a possible interference to evidential breath instruments would be extremely high, generally associated with fatal or highly intoxicating blood concentrations. The possible contribution of any exogenous compounds to a breath alcohol result is limited by the physiological restrictions of the potential interferant and the characteristics of the employed detection technology.[80]

[b] Failure to Follow Required Procedure and Documentation

It is of great importance to ascertain that the breath test is conducted in conformance with all applicable rules and regulations. In addition, all steps used in the protocol must be documented. This documentation must show

79. K.M. Dubowski & N.A. Essary, *Response to Breath–Alcohol Analyzers to Acetone*, 7 J. ANNALS TOXICOLOGY 231 (1983); K.M. Dubowski & N.A. Essary, *Response to Breath–Alcohol Analyzers to Acetone: Further Studies*, 8 J. ANNALS TOXICOLOGY 205 (1984); A.L. Flores & J.F. Frank, *The Likelihood of Acetone Interference in Breath Alcohol Measurement*, U.S. DEP'T OF TRANSPORTATION, TECHNICAL REPORT, HS 806 (1985); A.W. Jones, *Breath Acetone Concentrations in Fasting Male Volunteers: Fur-* ther Studies and Effect of Alcohol Administration, 12 J. ANNALS TOXICOLOGY 75 (1988); A.W. Jones, *Breath Acetone Concentrations in Healthy Men: Response of Infrared Breath–Alcohol Analyzers*, 10 J. ANNALS TOXICOLOGY 98 (1986); R.D. Oliver & J.C. Garriot, *The Effects of Acetone and Toluene on Breathalyzer Results*, 3 J. ANNALS TOXICOLOGY 99 (1979).

80. NATIONAL SAFETY COUNCIL, *supra* note 3.

that the instruments have been properly calibrated, maintained and operated by qualified and trained personnel.

[c]   Residual Mouth Alcohol

As previously stated, alcohol in the mouth will result in artificially high test results. Some foreign objects in the mouth, such as chewing tobacco, may trap alcohol and affect the breath test. Mouthwashes, breath sprays, inhalers, and similar products may contain alcohol. If the above are ruled out by observation, and the 15 minute waiting period is observed and documented, any interference with a valid test should not have occurred.

[d]   Instrument Variability

Any kind of instrumentation is subject to some degree of random variability. In approved breath testing instruments, the variability in an instrument's test results is relatively small, varying from coefficients of variation of approximately 0.9% to 3.5%.[81] The standards are set by the Department of Transportation, National Highway Traffic Safety Administration.[82] Equipment must be submitted to NHTSA for evaluation of compliance with these specifications. A list of products conforming to the specifications is published by the NHTSA.

[6]   Detection Technology and Instruments

Current breath alcohol instruments generally utilize one of four types of analytical technology. These detection principles and examples of instruments in which they are employed are listed in Table 3.

TABLE 3
Detection Technology Employed in Breath Alcohol Testing Instruments:

Primary Detection Principle	Instrument
Infrared Spectrometry	BAC DataMaster Intoxilyzer 5000 Intoxilyzer 1400
Electrochemical Oxidation/ Fuel Cell	Alco–Sensor III,IV Alcolmeter S–D2 Alcomonitor Breathalyzer 7410 Intox EC/IR RBT III,IV
Gas Chromatography	Alco–Analyzer 2100
Taguchi Gas Sensor	A.L.E.R.T. Model J4

Breath Alcohol Ignition Interlock Devices 999

---

81. Harding, *supra* note 71.

82. Model specifications for evidential breath testing devices, 49 Fed. Reg. 48,855–48,865 (1984a); Model specifications for calibrating units for breath alcohol testers, 49 Fed. Reg. 48,865–48,872 (1984b); Model specifications for breath alcohol ignition interlocks (BAIIDs), 57 Fed. Reg. 11,772–11,787 (1992); Model specifications for devices to measure breath alcohol, 58 Fed. Reg. 48,705–48,710

Numerous breath alcohol testing instruments have been designed and marketed over the years. Some instruments which are no longer manufactured remain in use in some jurisdictions. The models in Table 3 are in current use, but this list will change from year to year due to new instrument development. All of the instruments described are on the NHTSA conforming product lists for evidential breath testers.

[a] *Infrared Spectrophotometry*

Infrared instruments are the most common type of evidential breath testing devices in use. The underlying principle is that all chemicals absorb infrared radiation at specific wavelengths according to their molecular structure. Ethyl alcohol has infrared absorption in a band from 3.30 to 3.50 microns, which is used by most infrared instruments for its detection. For example, the Intoxilyzer 5000, one of the most widely used evidential breath testing instruments, utilizes a 3.48 micron wavelength for detection of ethanol, and 3.39 for detection of interferents such as acetone.

[b] *Electrochemical Oxidation/Fuel Cell*

The fuel cell is designed to convert fuel and an oxidant into direct current, which serves to quantitate the amount of alcohol. The alcohol is used as the fuel and oxygen from the atmosphere is the oxidant. Alcohol is converted into acetic acid, producing an electric current proportional to the amount of alcohol in the sample. The fuel cells will also react with other alcohols such as methanol, isopropyl alcohol, and to acetaldehyde. The Intox EC/IR (Intoximeters, Inc.) utilizes a fuel cell as the primary technology for alcohol quantitation, and an infrared detector to monitor the breath sample quality and test for interferents. The Breathalyzer 7410 (National Drager) is a hand-held, portable, battery-operated fuel cell instrument. Time and pressure are used to determine adequate breath sampling, and an audible tone and ready light indicate an acceptable sample. Test data can also be downloaded to computers directly.

[c] *Gas Chromatography*

As already discussed, gas chromatography is universally used in analytical laboratories for alcohol and other chemical substance analysis. Currently, only one gas chromatograph designed for breath alcohol analysis is used. The Alco–Analyzer 2100 (U.S. Alcohol Testing of America, Inc.) is designed with a short disposable plastic tubing affixed to the sample port. Breath pressure activates

(1993b); Model specifications for devices to measure breath alcohol, 59 Fed. Reg. 18,839–18,840 (1994a); Model specifications for screening devices to measure breath alcohol in bodily fluids, 59 Fed. Reg. 39,382–39,390 (1994b).

an internal pump which draws breath into the sample loop. A sample size of 10 milliliters is analyzed for alcohol using a Poropak S packing material and a thermal conductivity detector.

[d] Chemical Oxidation/Photometry

The chemical oxidation application was historically used for the first widespread breath alcohol instrumentation used in law enforcement. The breath sample is drawn through an ampoule containing and oxidizing mixture of chemicals. Reaction of alcohol in the breath sample with the mixture causes a change in the absorption characteristics of the solution in ultraviolet light, and this change is measured with a photometer.

The prototype of this instrument was the Breathalyzer. The Breathalyzer was developed by Robert Borkenstein in 1954, and became the predominant instrument used in law enforcement. The Breathalyzer 900A (National Draeger) is designed to pass a fixed volume of breath through the reactant mixture of a solution of potassium dichromate in 50% sulfuric acid. After the reaction occurs, a light source is passed through the ampoule, and the transmission is measured and compared with an unreacted ampoule. The change in transmittance is converted to a linear alcohol concentration scale.

§ 8–2.4 Interpretation of Alcohol Results in Biological Specimens

Testing for ethyl alcohol is the most frequent determination required of laboratories performing toxicology for medical examiners and coroners, as well as in laboratories serving law enforcement agencies. Alcohol is the most common drug found in persons dying of all causes, especially in deaths from violent circumstances,[83] and is the most frequent cause of intoxication in traffic fatalities and in driving offenses. Ethyl alcohol is also one of the leading causes of death resulting from chemical substances, ranking with carbon monoxide and heroin.[84] It is therefore of great importance in forensic autopsy and other forensic investigations to perform accurate analyses for alcohol, using the optimal specimens for this purpose, and to know the significance (and limitations) of alcohol findings in these specimens.

§ 8–2.4.1 Analytical Considerations

The blood or other fluids or tissues taken at a postmortem examination for alcohol analysis are more likely to be contaminated with volatile substances that could potentially interfere with alcohol analysis than are specimens from living subjects. These interfering substances include: methanol and formaldehyde from embalming processes; low boiling decomposition products, such as other alcohols; and abnormal metabolic products, such as acetone, which may be present in deaths resulting from malnutrition or starvation, or in diabetic ketoacidosis. Alcoholic, and sometimes suicidal individuals may

83. Norton et al., *supra* note 2; R.C. Baselt & R.H. Cravey, *Forensic Toxicology, in* TOXICOLOGY, THE BASIC SCIENCE OF POISONS (J. Doull et al. eds., 2nd ed.1980); Garriott, *supra* note 2.

84. J.C. Garriott et al., *Death by Poisoning: a Ten-Year Survey of Dallas County*, 27 J. FORENSIC SCI. 868 (1982); H.L. Taylor & R.P. Hudson, *Acute Ethanol Poisoning: A Two Year Study of Deaths in North Carolina*, 22 J. FORENSIC SCI. 639 (1977); Y.H. Caplan et al., *Drug and Chemical Related Deaths: Incidences in the State of Maryland, 1975–1980*, 30 J. FORENSIC SCI. 1012 (1985).

ingest liquids that contain rubbing alcohol (isopropanol), wood alcohol (methanol), antifreeze (ethylene glycol), or various other volatile solvents, which may result in their death.

When analyzing forensic samples for alcohol, it is essential to utilize a completely specific technique. Volatile organic components would interfere most with the nonspecific oxidation techniques, and least with gas chromatographic procedures, which are designed to separate all low-boiling compounds eluting in the same range as ethyl alcohol. An advantage in analysis of postmortem cases is that a greater choice of specimens is available than in living persons. Whether or not decomposition is present, it is always desirable to analyze additional specimens for optimum interpretation. Blood samples from outside agencies may be taken from corpses under uncertain circumstances, and may be subject to uncertain handling practices. Sample removal, storage and handling practices, and chain of custody must always be considered and evaluated when interpreting alcohol results.

§ 8–2.4.2 Distribution of Alcohol in the Body

Body fluid and tissue distribution of alcohol is a function of water solubility and water content of the compartment. The proportion of alcohol in a tissue will be almost exactly proportional to its water content.

[1] Blood

Blood is the most important of autopsy specimens to analyze for alcohol, and other specimens are usually related to and compared with blood concentrations. The blood itself is subject to variation, depending on site of sampling, collection technique, and other factors to be discussed. In living subjects, venous blood is sampled, usually from the anterior cubital vein of the arm.

After death, sampling is usually from the heart or major vessels. Peripheral blood is more difficult to obtain, but is considered to be more likely to reflect an antemortem blood level due to certain factors which may influence heart blood alcohol concentrations. Arterial blood is up to 40% higher in alcohol concentration than venous blood in the absorptive phase, whereas there is little difference between the two specimens in the postabsorptive phase. Thus blood from the heart or other large blood vessels may differ from venous blood in alcohol concentration at death due to incomplete distribution.[85] Prouty and Anderson analyzed heart and femoral blood in 100 autopsy cases, however, and found the heart/femoral blood ratio to be near unity (0.98).[86] Of 17 cases with differences between the two specimens greater than 20%, only 6 had heart/femoral blood greater than unity. These 6 cases were either in early stages of absorption, or the femoral blood was artifactually low due to low specimen volume in the sample tube. Due to potential variability factors, it is desirable to analyze several specimens comparatively to optimally relate the alcohol concentrations found in a deceased individual to those that would have been present at the time of death.

85. R.B. Forney et al., *The Levels of Alcohol in Brain, Peripheral Blood and Heart Blood Ten Minutes After Oral Administration*, 98 J. PHARMACOL. EXP. THER. 8 (1950); Martin et al., *supra* note 43.

86. R.W. Prouty & W.H. Anderson, *A Comparison of Postmortem Heart Blood and Femoral Blood Ethyl Alcohol Concentrations*, 11 J. ANNALS TOXICOLOGY 191 (1987).

[2] Other Body Tissues

When ingested alcohol is present in the body at autopsy, alcohol is present and can be detected in any soft tissue or fluid. The first specimen chosen should be blood. The most frequent alternate specimen analyzed is vitreous humor. The concentration of alcohol in vitreous humor is not expected to be the same as that in the blood, but the relationship to the blood concentration is well known and therefore usually is confirmatory of blood alcohol levels at death.

The following tissue/blood ratios are typical: brain–0.85; liver–0.80; muscle–0.94; spinal fluid–1.18; serum or plasma–1.16.[87] Literature values for these ratios are usually reported in ranges of concentration ratios found. The preceding ratios are based on values expected at body equilibrium of alcohol. That is, the concentrations that exist about 1–3 hours after the last ingestion of alcoholic beverage. Of course, people do not die at that point only. Therefore, many cases will have ratios either higher or lower than these. Generally when values are lower, the individual was in the preabsorptive phase (having ingested alcohol very recently) of alcohol distribution in the body, and when higher, he was in the postabsorptive phase. As the alcohol becomes absorbed from the stomach and intestines, it distributes to the tissues, and reaches a maximum concentration there about one to three hours after drinking. From that point on, if no more alcoholic beverage is ingested, the values will remain equal to or higher than the blood due to clearance from the blood by metabolism and a lag in redistribution.

[3] Urine

Urine is often sampled at autopsy for toxicology purposes, and may be used in some states in evaluation of drinking drivers. The normal urine to blood ratio is about 1.20, due to the higher water content of urine. Under some conditions, high concentrations of alcohol can be produced artifactually in urine postmortem. Saady et al. permitted urine samples with varying amounts of glucose to sit at room temperature, without preservatives, for up to 20 days, analyzing for ethanol when initially sampled and at intervals.[88] Alcohol was produced in five of the 14 urines, in concentrations of 0.036 to 0.326 in four of the five, and in one, 2.383 g/dL was formed. All of the five samples contained both glucose and yeast. Alcohol did not form in less than 12 hours, and, of course, samples were maintained at room temperature. Conventional refrigeration would be expected to greatly retard or prevent alcohol formation in urine.

Urine alcohol concentration is higher than that of the blood at equilibrium, but may be either higher or lower, depending on the status of absorption. Under usual circumstances in which the samples are sealed and refrigerated soon after autopsy, however, the urine can yield valuable confirmatory information to levels of alcohol found in blood or other specimens. For the above reasons, however, urine alcohol can not be interpreted as an equivalent blood

87. J.C. Garriott, *Analysis for Alcohol in Postmortem Specimens, in* Medicolegal Aspects of Alcohol (J.C. Garriot ed., 1996).

88. J.J. Saady et al., *Production of Urinary Ethanol After Sample Collection*, 38 J. Forensic Sci. 1467 (1993).

alcohol concentration and is not usually used to imply intoxication in legal proceedings.

[4] Vitreous Humor

The vitreous humor of the eye has been used extensively for toxicological analyses in autopsy cases in recent years, and is now recognized as an extremely useful specimen for postmortem alcohol determinations.[89] Its advantages are that it is readily available and easily collected, there is less chance of bacterial contamination than in blood and other organs, and alcohol enters the vitreous and establishes equilibrium about as fast as or faster than in other body compartments. Approximately 2.0 mL of vitreous fluid can be collected from each eye, which is sufficient for alcohol analysis and often for other toxicologic procedures.

The ratio of alcohol concentrations in the blood and vitreous humor is dependent upon the time after ingestion. The time required for the establishment of equilibrium between the two specimens is thought to be about two hours. In experiments reported by Hentsch and Muller,[90] and Garriott,[91] alcohol was given orally to rabbits in a single dose, after which the animals were sacrificed periodically, and vitreous alcohol concentrations were measured. Prior to one hour, the alcohol concentrations were higher in the blood by about 0.05 g/dL but at one to two hours, the two specimens equilibrated, and the concentrations were approximately the same for a short period. After this period, the vitreous humor concentration reached a higher value than blood, and remained so until complete disappearance (Figure 2).

Since the average water contents of blood and vitreous humor are 78% and 99%, respectively, the average vitreous-blood ratio should be about 1.27 when distribution is complete. Ratios higher than this would indicate that the individual was in the postabsorptive phase (greater than two hours after the last alcohol ingestion), while those lower would reflect the preabsorptive phase, or recent alcohol ingestion.

89. R.C. Backer et al., *The Comparison of Alcohol Concentrations in Postmodern Fluids and Tissues*, 25 J. FORENSIC SCI. 327 (1980); Y.H. Caplan & B. Levine, *Vitreous Humor in the Evaluation of Postmodern Blood Ethanol Concentrations*, 14 J. ANNALS TOXICOLOGY 305 (1990); D.J. Pounder & N. Kuroda, *Vitreous Alcohol is of Limited Value in Predicting Blood Alcohol*, 65 FORENSIC SCI. INT'L 73 (1994).

90. R. Hentsch & H.P. Muller, *Tierexperimentelle Untersuchungen uber die Konzentration von peroral zugefuhtem Athanol in Blut und Glaskorper*, 168 ALBRECHT VON GRAEFES ARCH. KLIN. EXP. OPHTHALMOL. 330 (1965).

91. Garriott & Latman, *supra* note 41.

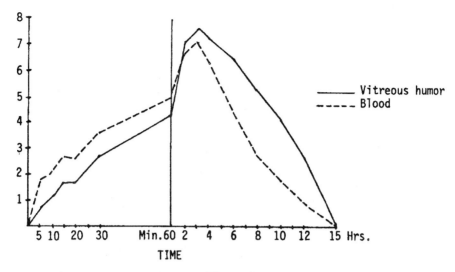

Figure 2.

Comparative blood (dotted line) and vitreous humor (solid line) alcohol concentrations after oral dosing in rabbits. From R. Hentsch & H.P. Muller, *Tierexperimentelle Unterschugen uber de Konzentration von peroral zugefuhrtem Athanol in Blut und Glaskorper*, 168 Albrecht Von Graefes Arch. Klin. Exp. Opthalmol 330 (1965).

§ 8–2.4.3　Postmortem Effects on Blood Alcohol Concentrations

[1]　Diffusion

One of the factors potentially affecting postmortem alcohol determinations is contamination of the specimen by diffusion from another body organ. If one should die shortly after drinking alcoholic beverages, so that the stomach or upper intestine has a high concentration of alcohol, this could continue to diffuse after death into surrounding organs and blood, causing falsely high alcohol concentrations.

The stomach is unlikely to contain much alcohol at the time of death.[92] Backer et al. in a study of 37 autopsy cases with stomach concentrations less than 0.5 g/dL and 23 cases greater than 0.5 g/dL, observed that, in actual cases, only a few stomach alcohol levels exceed 5 g/100 mL.[93] They concluded that the alcohol is absorbed very rapidly from the stomach.

Although alcohol is absorbed from the stomach rapidly, a larger quantity is absorbed from the small intestine. Thus postmortem diffusion into the abdominal cavity could contaminate any abdominal cavity fluid, and surrounding organs. In general, any cavity fluid or blood should be avoided. A combination of heart, femoral, or subclavian blood, vitreous humor and urine, if available, should be used for alcohol analysis, to aid in the interpretation of the state of absorption and in evaluation of the actual blood concentration.

92.　Sunshine & Nenad, *supra* note 50.　　　　**93.**　Backer et al., *supra* note 89.

[2] Sampling Considerations

[a] Antemortem Sampling

Under normal legal blood drawing circumstances, the blood is drawn under supervision of a police officer at a hospital or other suitable location. The arm is cleansed with a non-alcohol containing antiseptic, such as beta-dine, and the blood is collected by venipuncture into a prescribed blood tube. This tube and needle must be sterile, and the tube is usually evacuated (contains a vacuum) so that the blood is drawn into the tube without any action on the part of the individual taking the sample. The tube is usually a commercially available Vacutainer (BD), which contains certain chemical preservatives to stabilize the sample. The almost universally accepted chemicals for this purpose are a mixture of sodium fluoride and potassium oxalate. Sodium fluoride is an effective enzyme inhibiting agent, while the oxalate is an anticoagulant. When present in approximately 2 milligrams per milliliter concentrations, these agents can effectively preserve the blood sample in a sealed vacutainer tube for many months, if the sample is maintained under normal laboratory refrigeration conditions.[94] No substantial gains or losses of alcohol in the sample should occur.

[b] Postmortem Sampling

A source of falsely elevated blood alcohol concentrations in autopsy samples can arise from contamination of the sample with alcohol present in the gastrointestinal tract by passing the syringe needle through it. Although this may be a rare occurrence, it is especially of concern in autopsies involving trauma to the gastrointestinal tract when the heart blood sample is obtained by transthoracic puncture.[95] Winek et al., found 8 cases out of 6000 in which blood alcohol concentrations were falsely elevated due to laceration or transection of the gastrointestinal tract. This problem can be avoided by taking blood from the intact heart chamber, as well as additional samples for comparison, such as vitreous humor and peripheral blood.

[3] Postmortem Decomposition

It is well known that decomposing tissues in the body can lead to production of alcohol. A major problem in forensic alcohol analysis is to determine if the alcohol found was from antemortem ingestion or if all or a portion of the alcohol was produced postmortem. The object is to determine if the subject was intoxicated at the time of his death and, if so, what blood alcohol concentration had been present. Ethyl alcohol formed by postmortem decomposition is the same ethyl alcohol that is ingested in alcoholic beverages. Therefore one cannot analytically distinguish ingested alcohol from alcohol that may have been formed after death.

Many factors have to be considered in making this interpretation. One of the most important considerations is the distribution of alcohol in the body at

94. W.H. Anderson, *Collection and Storage of Specimens for Alcohol Analysis, in* MEDICOLE-GAL ASPECTS OF ALCOHOL (J.C. Garriot ed., 1996).

95. C.L. Winek et al., *The Role of Trauma in Postmortem Blood Alcohol Determination,* 71 FORENSIC SCI. INT'L 1 (1995).

postmortem. The vitreous humor and urine are of utmost value in this determination since glucose (the major substrate for alcohol formation) is usually of very low concentration in these specimens. In most postmortem cases, vitreous humor is present. Urine is less reliably available due simply to the normal periodic (or agonal) emptying of the bladder. In a study of 130 decomposing bodies, vitreous humor was obtained in 70% of cases, while urine was available in only 35%. Vitreous humor was reported to be present until advanced decomposition.[96]

In the mild to moderately decomposed body, the eye chamber is intact, and sufficient vitreous humor can be obtained for alcohol analysis for comparison with blood or urine. If the vitreous humor contains no alcohol, any alcohol found in blood or other body specimens can be assumed to have been formed postmortem. Vitreous humor is generally protected from bacterial contamination and has not been reported to produce endogenous ethanol.

In the intact, decomposing body, ethyl alcohol is usually not formed rapidly, and rarely reaches high levels in blood. In the study of Zumwalt et al.,[97] 24 (80%) of 30 mildly decomposing bodies contained no ethanol, and only one of those found positive could be presumed to have been from postmortem formation. In 23 severely decomposed bodies, three (13%) exhibited endogenously formed alcohol, no alcohol was found in three (13%), while exogenous alcohol was found in seven (30%). No determination could be reached in the remaining ten cases. Twenty-three (17%) of the 130 cases studied had presumed production of alcohol postmortem. Of a total of 23 cases in which presumed endogenous alcohol was found in blood, 19 (83%) had levels of 0.070 mg/dL or less while four cases had 0.110, 0.120, 0.130, and 0.220 mg/dL, respectively. The vitreous humor and urine were used as the criteria for determining the presence of endogenously formed alcohol.[98] In the "fresh" body, refrigerated within four hours of death, no endogenous alcohol was found, even in the presence of bacterial contamination.[99]

[4] Effects of Embalming

The embalmed body has had much of the blood replaced by embalming fluid. Embalming fluids generally contain formalin as the major active component, but also may contain methanol, other alcohols, various odorants, salts, and so forth. Alcohol analysis by gas chromatography will serve to determine if these contaminants are present, and therefore distinguish whether or not the body has been embalmed.

The most prevalent contaminants in embalming fluids are formaldehyde and methanol. Although ethanol may be present in some cavity fluids, it is not a standard component of embalming fluids, and would not be expected to contaminate the vitreous humor. Usually in the embalmed body, vitreous humor will contain a low concentration of methyl alcohol or formaldehyde. Any ethyl alcohol present in the vitreous humor in fresh or embalmed bodies,

96. R.E. Zumwalt et al., *Evaluation of Ethanol Concentrations in Decomposed Bodies*, 27 J. Forensic Sci. 549 (1982).

97. *See id.*

98. *See id.*

99. M.A. Clark & W.D. Jones, *Studies on Putrefactive Ethanol Production, 1. Lack of Spontaneous Ethanol Production in Intact Human Bodies*, 27 J. Forensic Sci. 366 (1982).

other than trace amounts, can be assumed to be the result of antemortem ingestion.

§ 8–2.4.4 Acute Ethyl Alcohol Fatalities

Acute alcohol poisoning or death from overdose of alcohol is a frequent phenomenon. In one 10–year study of a major metropolitan area (Dallas, Texas), 91 cases of acute alcohol overdose were diagnosed, which amounted to 0.3% of all deaths seen, and 8% of all deaths resulting from drugs or toxic agents. These deaths were more frequent than those from any other agent, excepting carbon monoxide and narcotics.[100] In another comparable survey in Maryland, 157 acute alcohol deaths occurred over a 6 year period.[101] These amounted to 9.1% of all deaths due to drugs or other toxic agents. This compared with 13.4% of the cases resulting from acute narcotics overdose. The Medical Examiner's Office of North Carolina determined that 2.5% of all deaths certified in North Carolina over a 24–month period were due to acute alcohol overdose.[102]

The diagnosis of death from acute ethanol poisoning is usually made on the basis of a high blood ethanol level, combined with circumstances consistent with overdose of alcohol. The usually accepted minimum lethal concentration for alcohol in blood is 0.40 g/dL. Lower concentrations are not necessarily inconsistent with death from alcohol overdose, however. Stress from pre-existent disease, reduced individual tolerance to alcohol, and many other factors may result in lower lethal blood alcohol concentrations at death.

While ethanol levels in excess of 0.30 g/dL indicate severe alcohol intoxication with concomitant respiratory depression, there have been numerous observations of individuals driving a motor vehicle with blood alcohol concentrations greater than 0.30 and occasionally greater than 0.40 g/dL, indicating the wide variation in individual tolerance.[103]

§ 8–2.5 Pharmacokinetics and Forensic Extrapolations

In a DWI prosecution, or in civil litigation following injury accidents, it may be necessary for an expert to estimate the alcohol level of a drinking subject at the time of an accident. Often a blood specimen or breath test for alcohol may be taken from one to as long as several hours after the accident. Under these circumstances, an expert may be called to perform a BAC back-extrapolation, based on the test result. To do this properly, a number of factors must be taken into consideration. The most critical are discussed, but the reader would be wise to review a more comprehensive discussion of alcohol physiology and disposition before any attempts are made at extrapolating BAC's.[104] Under ideal circumstances, the BAC at the time of an accident may be estimated by adding the alcohol that would have been cleared from the blood during the waiting period to that determined by analysis. This

---

100. Garriott et al., *supra* note 84.

101. Caplan et al., *supra* note 84.

102. H.L. Taylor & R.P Hudson, *supra* note 84.

103. *See id.*; J. C. Garriott et al., *supra* note 39; G. Cimbura et al., *supra* note 39.

104. A.W. Jones, *Biochemistry and Physiology of Alcohol, in* MEDICOLEGAL ASPECTS OF ALCOHOL (J.C. Garriott ed., 1996); R.C. Baselt, *Disposition of Alcohol in Man, in* MEDICOLEGAL ASPECTS OF ALCOHOL (J.C. Garriott ed., 1996); E.H. Foerster, *Computer Tools for Body Alcohol Evaluation, in* MEDICOLEGAL ASPECTS OF ALCOHOL (J.C. Garriott ed., 1996).

requires only an estimation of the subject's rate of alcohol clearance from the body. This rate may be estimated by use of measured and established ranges in human subjects. The rates vary widely and depend on drinking tolerance and experience, actual BAC and other factors. A study of over 1300 drinking drivers found elimination rates from 0.010 to 0.064 g/dL/Hr, with a mean of 0.022 g/dL/Hr.[105] Dubowski estimated that the mean hourly breath alcohol decrease for adult men lies between 0.0059 and 0.0239 g/230 L/Hr in 95% of subjects.[106] These ranges include extreme rates at both ends, including extremes of tolerance, varied drinking levels and varying circumstances. At elevated blood alcohol concentrations, for example, the rate of clearance is higher than at lower concentrations. The great majority of subjects consuming alcohol under social circumstances, as is usually the case with drinking drivers, clear alcohol at rates between 0.015 and 0.025 g/dL/Hr, and most forensic experts use these ranges for subject extrapolations. It is customary and most scientifically defensible to base these estimates on ranges using established average population metabolism rates, since no one can know the actual rate of metabolism in a given subject without actually measuring it under drinking circumstances similar to those that existed at the time in question. The extrapolation, therefore, is expressed as a value lying between two estimated concentrations.

Recent alcohol ingestion prior to the event in question must be considered in any estimation of BAC's. During alcohol consumption and until peak BAC has been reached, the subject is still in the *pre-absorptive phase*, and after the peak has been reached, he is said to be in the *post-absorptive phase*. The rate of absorption of ingested alcohol is dependent on a number of physiological factors, which include: rate of ingestion, strength of alcohol in the beverage consumed, presence and amount of food in the stomach, physiological state such as general health, stress conditions, and others. Much has been made of these potential factors, but in reality, alcohol consumed under usual social circumstances is absorbed relatively rapidly. The time until peak BAC ranges from 5–105 minutes, and probably occurs in less than 60 minutes in over 90% of subjects.[107] When recent ingestion of alcohol has occurred, the extrapolation process is much more complicated, and the "straight line" extrapolation to a prior point in time is invalid. If this mode were used, it would result in an estimation based on an overshoot of the actual peak BAC, due to the delayed peak resulting from alcohol still being absorbed from the gastrointestinal tract. This would yield a significantly overestimated value. It is essential for an expert familiar with alcohol kinetics to take into consideration all of the circumstances, including kinetics, physiology, consumption history (both recent and remote), and subject parameters, if he is to generate a reasonably accurate interpretation of the subject's state of absorption and BAC at the time of an accident. One must determine as accurately as possible the amount of alcohol consumed in the 1–2 hours prior to the accident. This amount must be either eliminated from the estimation or factored into an

105. W. Neuteboom and A.W. Jones, *Disappearance Rate of Alcohol From the Blood of Drunk Drivers Calculated for Two Consecutive Samples; What do the Results Really Mean?*, 45 FORENS. SCI. INT'L 107 (1990).

106. K.M. Dubowski, *Absorption, Distribution and Elimination of Alcohol: Highway Safety Aspects*, 10 J. STUD. ALCOHOL SUPP. 98 (1985).

107. A.W. Jones, *Status of Absorption Among Drinking Drivers*, 14 J. ANNALS TOXICOLOGY 198 (1990).

absorption/elimination BAC curve. It is also desirable for optimal accuracy to determine the total alcohol consumed over a given period of time. An alcohol kinetics curve can then be generated which should be consistent with the reported blood or breath alcohol concentration (See Figure 3). The physiological parameters, drinking circumstances, absorption time, beverage alcohol content, and other factors to be considered for generation of blood alcohol curves are discussed in the context of a computerized model in more detail elsewhere.[108]

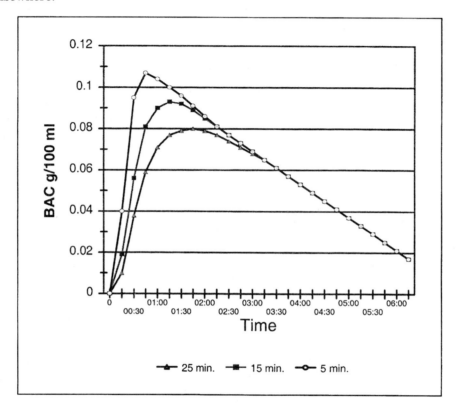

Figure 3.

Effect of absorption time on blood alcohol concentration versus time. From E.H. Foerster, *Computer Tools for Body Alcohol Evaluation, in* MEDICOLEGAL ASPECTS OF ALCOHOL, J.C. Garriott ed. (1996).

108. Foerster, *supra* note 104.

Glossary

Aetaldehyde. Chemical formed from metabolic oxidation of ethyl alcohol in the body. A toxic by-product believed to be largely responsible for the "hangover" effect.

Alcohol dehydrogenase (ADH), a liver enzyme. Enzyme located primarily in cells of the liver, responsible for the metabolic breakdown of ethyl alcohol.

Coefficient of variation. The standard deviation to the mean. An expression of the variability of a system, e.g., a method for analysis.

Depressants. A drug or other chemical substance which depresses the central nervous system, ultimately resulting in sleep, or possibly coma and death from respiratory depression.

Diplopia (double vision). Inability of maintaining focus of objects by both eyes, resulting in double vision. A classic symptom of acute alcohol intoxication.

Direct Injection Techniques. Refers to a means of introducing a sample into the gas chromatograph, in which the sample (e.g., blood) is injected directly into the instrument after mixing with a suitable liquid medium such as water and another solvent for comparison. This solvent is the internal standard.

Dyschromatopsia. Color blindness or impaired color discrimination

Euphorigenic. Term used to define an unusual state or feeling of well-being, usually drug induced. A classic effect of intoxicants such as alcohol and narcotics.

Gas Chromatography. The instrument used to separate chemical mixtures and to determine the components of the mixture. It consists of an injection port, an oven housing a column through which the mixture is passed, pressurized gas to flow through the column, and a detection system.

Headspace. The gas volume in a sealed container in which blood or other fluid has been placed, and maintained under certain conditions to permit an equilibrium to be reached between the gas and the liquid sample. Typically, the headspace gas is used to inject into the gas chromatograph to determine the alcohol content of the blood.

Internal Standard. A chemical substance mixed with the liquid sample (e.g. blood) which has similar characteristics as the substance being analyzed, and which is used to compare with the unknown to determine the quantity present. Typical examples are alcohol as the unknown, contained in a blood sample, and n-propyl alcohol in a standard concentration as the internal standard.

NHTSA. National Highway Traffic Safety Association. A branch of the U.S. Department of Transportation.

Nm. Nanometer. A unit of length one billionth of a meter. Typically used to express characteristic wavelengths of light in the spectrum.

Physical Dependence (addiction). A biochemical adaptation to an exogenous chemical substance under which the body must have the substance present to function normally. When withdrawn, a severe illness may result.

Pipetting. The sampling of a measured volume of substance (liquid) by withdrawal into a calibrated tube (pipette).

Placebo. A non-active substance administered as a control under the same conditions as the test substance in experiments to determine the actual effects of a drug or other substance. Commonly referred to as a "sugar pill".

Sensitivity. A term to define the reliable lower limits of an analytical method.

Stimulants. Drugs or chemicals which stimulate the central nervous system. Typically, these include amphetamines, cocaine, caffeine, and others. Many depressant drugs, such as alcohol, have some initial apparent stimulating effect, but this is usually due to a depression of inhibitory mechanisms.

Système International d'Unitès. SI units. An international system of measure defining concentrations in terms of the molecular weight of the substance. Used primarily in Europe, but medical research and literature in the United States are now using this system for biochemical substances and sometimes for drug and alcohol expressions.

Tolerance. A phenomenon whereby the body becomes less affected by a drug or chemical with increasing use. Classically applied to narcotics and stimulants, where ever increasing doses are required to reach the desired effect.

Vitreous Humor. The fluid contained in the rear, vitreous chamber of each eye. The vitreous has gained favor as a useful specimen for alcohol analysis in autopsy cases.

REFERENCES

American Medical Association. *Alcohol and the Impaired Driver. A Manual on the Medicolegal Aspects of Chemical Tests for Intoxication with Supplement on Breath Alcohol Tests*, 1970, 1972. Reprinted by National Safety Council, Chicago, 1976, [see especially pp. 94–100].

Anderson, William H. and Prouty, Richard W. Collection and Storage of Specimens for Alcohol Analysis, in Medicolegal Aspects of Alcohol, J.C. Garriott ed., Lawyers and Judges Publishing Company, Tucson, AZ, 1996.

Backer, R.C., Pisano, R.V., and Sopher, I.M. The comparison of alcohol concentrations in postmortem fluids and tissues. *J. Forensic Sci.* 25:327–331, 1980.

Baselt, R.C., and Cravey, R.H. Forensic toxicology. p. 663.J. In *Toxicology, the Basic Science of Poisons*, 2nd ed. (J. Doull, C. Klassen, and M. Amdur eds.) MacMillan, New York 1980.

Bjerver, K., and Goldberg, L. Effect of alcohol ingestion on driving ability: Results of practical road tests and laboratory experiments. *Q. J. Stud. Alcohol* 11:1–30, 1950.

Blume, P., Berchild, K.M., and Cawley, L.P. A gas chromatographic analysis of ethanol with identifying confirmation. *Anal. Biochem.* 54:429–433, 1973

Bonnichsen, R., and Linturi, M. Gas chromatography determination of some volatile compounds in urine. *Acta. Chem. Scand.* 16:1289, 1962.

Bonnichsen, R., and Theorell. H. An enzymatic method for the microdetermination of ethanol. *Scand. J. Clin. Lab. Invest.* 3:58, 1951.

Bradford, L.W. Concepts and standards of performance in the technique of alcohol analysis of physiological specimens. Reprinted from the Proceedings of the Symposium on Alcohol and Road Traffic, Indiana University, Indianapolis, pp. 61–79, 1958.

Buijten, J.C. An automatic ultramicro distillation technique for determination of ethanol in blood and urine. *Blutalkohol* 12:393–398, 1975.

Cadman, W.J., and Johns, T. Gas chromatographic determination of ethanol and other volatiles from blood. Read to Ninth Annual Pittsburgh Conference on Analytical Chemistry and Applied Spectroscopy, March 1958.

Caplan, Y.H. and Levine, B. Vitreous humor in the evaluation of postmortem blood ethanol concentrations. *J. Anal. Tox.* 14:305–307, 1990.

Caplan, Y.H., and Levine, B. Evaluation of the Abbott TDx-radiative energy attenuation (REA) ethanol assay in a study of 1105 forensic whole blood specimens. *J. Forensic Sci.* 32:55–61, 1987.

Caplan, Y.H., and Levine, B. The analysis of ethanol in serum, blood, and urine: a comparison of the TDx REA ethanol assay with gas chromatography. *J. Anal. Toxicol.* 120:49–52, 1986.

Caplan, Y.H., Ottinger, W.E., Park, J., et al. Drug and chemical related deaths: Incidences in the stated of Maryland, 1975–1980. *J. Forensic Sci.* 30:1012–1021, 1985.

Caplan, Y.H., Ottinger, W.E., Park, J., et al. Drug and chemical related deaths: Incidences in the state of Maryland, 1975–1980. *J. Forensic Sci.* 30:1012–1021, 1985.

Cary, P.L. Reformulated REA ethanol assay evaluated. *J. Anal. Toxicol.* *10:*38–39, 1986.

Cary, P.L., Whitter, P.D., and Johnson, C.A. Abbott radioactive energy attenuation method for quantifying ethanol evaluated and compared with gas-liquid chromatography and the DuPont ACA. *Clin. Chem.* 30:1867–1870, 1984.

Cavett, J.W. The determination of alcohol in blood and other body fluids. *J. Lab. Clin. Med.* 23:543, 1938.

Chesher, G. and Greeley, J. Tolerance to the effects of alcohol. Alcohol, *Drugs and Driving*, 8:93–106, 1992.

Cimbura, G., Lucas, D.M., Bennett, R.C., et al. Incidence and toxicological aspects of drugs detected in 484 fatally injured drivers and pedestrians in Ontario. *J. Forensic Sci.* 27:855–867, 1982.

Cimbura, G., Lucas, D.M., Bennett, R.C., et al. Incidence and toxicological aspects of drugs detected in 489 fatally injured drivers and pedestrians in Ontario. *J. Forensic Sci.* 27:855–867, 1982.

Clark, M.A., and Jones, W.D. Studies on putrefactive ethanol production. 1. Lack of spontaneous ethanol production in intact human bodies. *J. Forensic Sci.* 27:366–371, 1982.

Curry, A.S., Walker, G.W., and Simpson, G.S. Determination of ethanol in blood by gas chromatography. *Analyst* 91:742, 1966.

Degel, F., and Paulus, N. A rapid and precise method for the quantitation of ethanol in serum using the EMIT-st serum ethanol assay reagent and a Cobas Bio centrifugal analyzer. *J. Clin. Chem. Biochem.* 26:351–353, 1988.

Dubowski, K.M. *Manual for Analysis of Ethanol in Biological Liquids.* U.S. Dept. of Transportation report No. DOT–TSC–NI ITSA–76–4, 1977.

Dubowski, K.M. Absorption, distribution, and elimination of alcohol: Highway safety aspects. *J. Stud. Alc.* Supp 10, 98–108, 1985.

Dubowski, K.M. and Essary, N.A. Breath-alcohol analysis on duplicate samples. In *Alcohol, Drugs and Traffic Safety—T86.* Proceedings of the Tenth International Conference on Alcohol, Drugs and Traffic Safety (P.C. Noordiz and R. Roszbach eds.), Elsevier Science Publishers B.V., Amsterdam, 1987, pp. 373–377.

Dubowski, K.M. and Essary, N.A. Response of breath-alcohol analyzers to acetone. *J. Anal. Toxicol.*, 7:231–234, 1983.

Dubowski, K.M. and Essary, N.A. Response of breath-alcohol analyzers to acetone: Further studies. *J. Anal. Toxicol.*, 8:205–208, 1984.

Dubowski, K.M. and O'Neill, B. The blood/breath ratio of ethanol. *Clin. Chem.* 25:1144, 1979.

Dubowski, K.M. Biological aspects of breath-alcohol analysis. *Clin. Chem.*, 20:294–299, 1974.

Dubowski, K.M. Quality assurance in breath-alcohol analysis. *J. Anal. Toxicol.*, 18:306–311, 1994.

Dubowski, K.M. Stages of Acute Alcoholic Influence/Intoxication, The University of Oklahoma College of Medicine, Oklahoma City, copyright, 1997.

Dubowski, K.M. *The Technology of Breath–Alcohol Analysis.* Public Health Service, U.S. Department of Health and Human Services, DHSS Publication No. (ADM)92–1728, 1992a.

Falkensson, M., Jones, W. and Sorbo, B. Bedside diagnosis of alcohol intoxication with a pocket-size breath-alcohol device: Sampling from unconscious subjects and specificity for ethanol. *Clin. Chem.*, 35:918–921, 1989.

Fell, J.C. and Nash, C.E. The nature of the alcohol problem in U.S. Fatal Crashes. *Health Education Quarterly* 16:335–343, 1989.

Finkle, B.S. Ethanol-type C procedure. pp. 147–149. In *Manual of Analytical Toxicology* (I. Sunshine, ed.). RC Press, Cleveland 1971.

Flores, A.L. and Frank, J.F. The likelihood of acetone interference in breath alcohol measurement. *U.S. Department of Transportation Technical Report HS 806–922*, 1985.

Forney, R.B., Hulpieu, H.R., and Harger, R.N. The levels of alcohol in brain, peripheral blood and heart blood ten minutes after oral administration. *J. Pharmacol. Exp. Ther.* 98:8–9, 1950.

Fox, J.E. Fast chromatographic analysis of alcohols and certain other volatiles in biological material for forensic purposes. Proc. Exp. Biol. Med. 97:236, 1958.

Garriott, J.C. Forensic aspects of ethyl alcohol. *Clin. Lab. Med.* 3:385–396. 1983.

Garriott, J.C. Analysis for alcohol in postmortem specimens, in Medicolegal Aspects of Alcohol, J.C. Garriott, ed. Lawyers and Judges Publishing Company, Tucson, AZ, 1996.

Garriott, J.C. Drug use among homicide victims. *Am. J. Forensic Med. Pathol.* 14:51–53, 1993.

Garriott, J.C. Relationship of vitreous humor and blood alcohol concentrations in rabbits. *Forensic Sci. Gaz.* 7:4–5, 1976.

Garriott, J.C. Skeletal muscle as an alternative specimen for alcohol and drug analysis. *J. Forensic Sci.* 36:60–69, 1991.

Garriott, J.C., and Latman, N. Drug detection in cases of driving under the influence. *J. Forensic Sci.* 21 :398–415, 1976.

Garriott, J.C., Di Maio, V.J.M., and Petty, C.S. Death by poisoning: a ten-year survey of Dallas County. *J. Forensic Sci.* 27:868–879, 1982.

Garriott, J.C., Di Maio, V.J.M., Zumwalt, R.E., et al. Incidence of drugs and alcohol in fatally injured motor vehicle drivers. *J. Forensic Sci.* 22:383–389, 1977.

Garriott, J.C., Di Maio, V.J.M., Zumwalt, R.E., et al. Incidence of drugs and alcohol in fatally injured motor vehicle drivers. *J. Forensic Sci.* 22:383–389, 1977.

Garriott, James C. Drug Use Among Homicide Victims. *Am. J. Forens. Med. Pathol.* 14:234–237, 1993.

Gerichtl. Med. 44:559–577, 1955.

Goldstein, D.B. *Pharmacology of Alcohol*. Oxford University Press, New York, 1983, p. 80.

Gruner, O. Alkohol und Aufmerksamkeit. Ihre Bedeutung im motorisierten Verkehr. *Dtsch. Z. Ges. Gerichtl. Med.* 44:187–195, 1955.

Gruner, O., and Ptasnik, H. Zur Frage der Beeinflussung alkoholbedingten Leistungsabfalles durch Laevulosegaben. *Münch. Med. Wochenschr.* 95:931–933, 1953.

Hammond, K.B., Rumack, B.H., and Rodgerson, D.O. Blood ethanol: A report of unusually high levels in a living patient. *JAMA* 226:63–64, 1973.

Harding, P.M. Methods for Breath Analysis, in Medicolegal Aspects of Alcohol, ed. J.C. Garriott, Lawyers & Judges Publishing Co., Tucson, 1996.

Harger, R.N. A simple micromethod for the determination of alcohol in biological material. *J. Lab. Clin. Med.* 20:746, 1935.

Hearn, W.L., Flynn, D.D., Hime, G.W., et al. Cocaethylene: A unique cocaine metabolite displays a high affinity for the dopamine transporter, *J. Neurochem.* 56(2):698–701, 1991a.

Hearn, W.L., Rose, S. Wagner, J., et al. Cocaethylene is more potent than cocaine in mediating lethality. Pharmacol. Biochem. and Behav. 39(2):531–533, 1991b.

Hentsch, R., and Muller, H.P. Tierexperimentelle Untersuchungen uber die Konzentration von peroral zugefuhrtem Athanol in Blut und Glaskorper. *Albrecht Von Graefes Arch. Klin. Exp. Ophthalmol.* 168:330–334, 1965.

Higgins, S.T., Rush, C.R., Hughes, J.R., et al. Effects of cocaine and alcohol, alone and in combination on human learning and performance. *J. Experiment. Anal. of Behavior* 58:87–105, 1992.

Hills, B.W. and Venable, H.C. The interaction of ethyl alcohol and industrial chemicals. *Am. J. Indust. Med.* 3:321–333, 1982.

Honneger, H., Kampschulte, R., and Klein, H. Storung der Sehscharfe fur bewegte Objekte durch Alkohol. *Blutalkohol* 7:31–44, 1970.

Huber, O. Untersuchungen uber die Veranderung der Fahrtuchtigkeit von Kraftradfahrern nach massigem Alkoholgenuss. *Dutsch. Z. Ges.*

Hurst, P.M. Epidemiological aspects of alcohol and driver crashes and citations. In *Alcohol, Drugs and Driving*, ed. M.W. Perrine, National Highway Traffic Safety Administration, Technical Report, DOT–HS–801–096, 1974.

Hurt, S.G., and Welton, B. New microprocessor-controlled gas chromatographs. *Am. Lab.* 15:89–916, 1983.

Iber, F.L. Increased drug metabolism in alcoholics. *In Advances in Mental Science, vol. 3 Biological Aspects of Alcohol*. (M.K. Roach).

Izard, A., and Saby, G. Contribution a l'etude du comportement psychomoteur de l'homme apres absorption de doses moyennes d'alcool. *Arch. Mal. Prof.* 23, 854–858, 1962.

Jain, N.C. Direct blood injection method for gas chromatography determination of alcohols and other volatile compounds. *Clin. Chem.* 17:82–85, 1971.

Jain, N.C., and Cravey, R.H. Analysis of alcohol. 1. A review of chemical and infrared methods. *J. Chromatogr. Sci.* 10:257–262, 1972a.

Jain, N.C., and Cravey, R.H. Analysis of alcohol. Il. A review of gas chromatographic methods. *J. Chromatogr. Sci.* 10:263–267, 1972b.

Jellinek, E.M., and McFarland, R.A. Analysis of psychological experiments on the effects of alcohol. *Q. J. Stud. Alcohol* 1:272–371, 1940.

Jones, A.W. Breath acetone concentrations in fasting male volunteers: Further studies and effect of alcohol administration. *J. Anal. Toxicol.*, 12:75–79, 1988.

Jones, A.W. Breath acetone concentrations in healthy men: Response of infrared breath-alcohol analyzers. *J. Anal. Toxicol.*, 10:98–101, 1986.

Jortani, S.A., and Poklis, A. Evaluation of the Syva ETS Plus urine drug and serum analyzer. *J. Anal. Toxicol.* 17:31–33, 1993.

Karnitis, L., and Porter, L.J. A gas chromatographic method for ethanol in vapors of biological fluids. *J. Forensic Sci.* 16:318–322, 1971.

Kater, R.M., Carulli, N., and Iber, F.L. Differences in the rate of ethanol metabolism in recently drinking alcoholic and non-drinking subjects. *Am. J. Clin. Nutr.* 22:1608–1617, 1969.

Kozelka, F.L., and Hine, C.H. Method for the determination of ethyl alcohol for medicolegal purposes. *Ind. Engin. Chem. (Anal. Ed.)* 13:905, 1941.

Labianca, D. A. and Simpson, G. Statistical analysis of blood-to-breath-alcohol ratio data in the logarithm-transformed and non-transformed modes. *Eur. J. Clin. Biochem.* 34:111–117, 1996.

Laurell, H., McLean, A.J. and Kloeden, C.N. The effect of blood alcohol concentration on light and heavy drinkers in a realistic night driving situation. NH & MRC Road Accident Research Unit, University of Adelaide, South Australia. Research Report 1/90, 1990.

LeBlanc, A.E., Kalant, H., and Gibbins, R.J. Acute tolerance to ethanol in the rat. *Psychopharmacologia* 41:43–46, 1975.

Lieber, C.S., Rubin, E., and deCarli, L.M. Interactions of ethanol, drug, and lipid metabolism: Adaptive changes after ethanol consumption. In *Advances in Mental Science, vol. 3. Biological Aspects of Alcohol*, (M. K. Roach, W.M. McIsaac, and P.J. Creavan eds.) University of Texas Press, Austin, 1971, pp. 138–167.

Machata, G. Determination of alcohol in blood by gas chromatography headspace analysis *Perkin Elmer Clin. Chem. Newsl.* 4:29–32, 1972.

Manno, B.R., and Manno, J.E. A simple approach to gas chromatographic microanalysis of alcohol in blood and urine by a direct-injection technique. *J.Anal Toxicol.* 2:257–261, 1978.

Martin, E., Moll, W., Schmid, P., et al. The pharmacokinetics of alcohol in human breath, venous and arterial blood after oral ingestions. *Eur. J. Clin. Pharmacol.* 26:619–626, 1984.

Martin, E.W. Table of Drug Interactions. In *Hazards of Medication*. (S.F. Alexander, W.E. Hassan, and D.J. Farage eds). J.B. Lippincott, Philadelphia, p. 415, pp. 430–437, 1971.

Mellanby, E. *Alcohol: Its Absorption into and Disappearance from the Blood Under Different Conditions*. Medical Research Committee, Special Report Series, No. 31, 1919.

Mello, N.K., and Mendelson, J.H. Experimentally induced intoxication in alcoholics. A comparison between programmed and spontaneous drinking. *J. Pharmacol. Exp. Ther.*, 173:101–116, 1970.

Mergler, D., Blain, L., Lemaire, J. et al. Colour vision impairment and alcohol consumption. *Neurotoxicol. Teratol.* 10:255–260, 1988.

Miller, R.J. The effect of ingested alcohol on fusion latency at various viewing distances. Percept. *Psychophysiology.* 50:575–583, 1991.

Modell, J.G. and Mountz, J.M. Drinking and flying—the problem of alcohol use by pilots. *NEJM* 323:455–461, 1990.

Mortimer, R.G. Effect of low blood alcohol concentrations in simulated day and night driving. *Percept. Mot. Skills* 17:399–408, 1963.

Moskowitz, H. Alcohol influences upon sensory motor function, visual perception, and attention. In *Alcohol, Drugs, and Driving*. National Highway Traffic Safety Administration, U.S. Dept. of Transportation publication No. HS 801 096, Mar.1974, pp. 49–69.

Moskowitz, H. and Robinson, C.D. Effects of low doses of alcohol on driving-related skills: A review of the evidence. SRA Technologies, Incorporated, DOT

HS 807 280, U.S. Department of Commerce. National Technical Information Service, Springfield, VA 22161, 1988.

Moskowitz, H. and Sharma, S. Effects of alcohol on peripheral vision as a function of attention. *Hum. Factors*, 16:174–180, 1974.

Moskowitz, H., Burns, M.M. and Williams, A.F. Skills performance at low blood alcohol levels. J. Stud. Alc. 46:482–485, 1985.

Moskowitz, H., Daily, J., and Henderson, R. The Mellanby effect in moderate and heavy drinkers. Proc. Seventh Int. Conf. on Alc. Drugs and Traffic Safety, Melbourne, 23–28 Jan., 1977.

Moureau, P. Tendances de la legislation belge en ce qui concerne l'intoxication alcoolique et les accidents de roulage. *Rev. Alcoolisme* 4:178–180, 1957.

National Safety Council. *Accident Facts*, 1994 ed. Itasca, IL.

National Safety Council Committee on Alcohol and Other Drugs. Recommendations. *Committee Handbook. Committee on Alcohol and Other Drugs*, National Safety Council, Chicago, 1992.

National Safety Council. *Traffic Safety Facts, Alcohol*, U.S. Department of Transportation, National Highway Traffic Safety Administration, 1996. Itasca, IL.

Newman, H.W., and Fletcher, E. The effect of alcohol on vision. *Am. J. Med. Sci.* 202:723–731, 1941.

Norton, L.E., Garriott J.C., and Di Maio, V.J.M. Drug detection at autopsy: a prospective study of 247 cases. *J. Forensic Sci.* 27:66–71, 1982.

Oliver, R.D. and Garriott, J.C. The effects of acetone and toluene on Breathalyzer results. *J. Anal. Toxicol.*, 3:99–101, 1979.

Pihkanen, T.A. and Kauko, O., The effects of alcohol on the perception of musical stimuli. *Ann. Med. Exp. Fenn.* 40:275–285, 1962.

Pounder, D.J. and Kuroda, N. Vitreous alcohol is of limited value in predicting blood alcohol. *Forensic Sci. Int.* 65:73–80, 1994.

Prouty, R.W. and Anderson, W.H. A comparison of postmortem heart blood and femoral blood ethyl alcohol concentrations. *J. Anal. Tox.* 11:191–197, 1987.

Redetzki, H.M., and Dees, W.L. Comparison of four kits for enzymatic determination of ethanol in blood. *Clin. Chem.* 22:83–86, 1976.

Rosen, L.J. and Lee, C.L. Acute and chronic effects of alcohol use on organizational processes in memory. *J. Abnor. Psychol.* 85:309–317, 1976.

Rubin, E. and Lieber, C.S. Alcoholism, alcohol, and drugs. *Science* 172:1097–1102, 1971.

Saady, J.J, Poklis, A., and Dalton, H.P. Production of urinary ethanol after sample collection. *J. Forensic Sci.* 38:1467–1471, 1993.

Schmidt, L. and Bingel, A.G.A. Effect of Oxygen Deficiency and Various Other Factors on Color Saturation Thresholds. U.S.A.F. School of Aviation Medicine Project Reports: Project No. 21–31–002 1953.

Seixas, F.A. Alcohol and its drug interactions. *Ann. Intern. Med.* 83:86–92, 1975.

Shaw, Richard F. Methods for Fluid Analysis, in *Medicolegal Aspects of Alcohol*, 3rd ed. James C. Garriott, editor, Lawyers and Judges Publishing Co., 1996.

Solon, J., Watkins, J., and Mikkelsen, L. Automated analysis of alcohols in blood. *J. Forensic Sci* 17:447–452, 1972.

Starck, H.J. Untersuchungen uber die Verkehrssicherheit alkoholgewohnter Kraftfahrer bei Blutalkoholwerten um 1.5 g-o/00. *Dtsch. Z. Ges. Gerichtl. Med.* 42:155–161, 1953.

Steinberg, M., Nash, J.B., and Walker, J.Q. Quantitation of Alcohols using gas chromatography and a 15% Hallcomid column. *J. Forensic Sci.* 10:201, 1965.

Sunshine, I. Postmortem distribution of ethyl alcohol. Presented at the American Academy of Forensic Sciences, Chicago, Feb.1957.

Sunshine, I., and Nenad, R. A modification of Winnick's method for the rapid determination of ethyl alcohol in biological fluids. *Anal. Chem.* 25:653, 1953.

Takel, H., Nakashima, K., Adachi, O., et al. Enzymatic determination of serum ethanol with membrane-bound dehydrogenase. *Clin. Chem.* 31:1985–1987, 1985.

Taylor, H.L., and Hudson, R.P. Acute ethanol poisoning: a two-year study of deaths in North Carolina. *J. Forensic Sci.* 22:639–653, 1977.

Terhune, K.W., Ippolito, D.L., Hendricks, D.L. at al. The incidence and role of drugs in fatally injured drivers. U.S. DOT, National Highway Traffic Safety Administration, DOT HS 808 065, Oct.1992.

Turkel, H.W. and Gifford, H. Erroneous blood alcohol findings at autopsy, avoidance by proper sampling technique. *JAMA* 164:1077–1079, 1957.

U.S. Department of Transportation, National Highway Traffic Safety Administration. Highway safety programs; Model specifications for evidential breath testing devices. *Federal Register*, 49:48,855–48,865, 1984a.

U.S. Department of Transportation, National Highway Traffic Safety Administration. Highway safety programs; Model specifications for calibrating units for breath alcohol testers. *Federal Register*, 49:48,865–48,872, 1984b.

U.S. Department of Transportation, National Highway Traffic Safety Administration. Model specifications for breath alcohol ignition interlocks (BAIIDs). *Federal Register*, 57:11772–11787, 1992.

U.S. Department of Transportation, National Highway Traffic Safety Administration. Highway safety programs; Model specifications for devices to measure breath alcohol. *Federal Register*, 58:48705–48710, 1993b.

U.S. Department of Transportation, National Highway Traffic Safety Administration. Highway safety programs; Model specifications for devices to measure breath alcohol. *Federal Register*, 59:18839–18840, 1994a.

U.S. Department of Transportation, National Highway Traffic Safety Administration. Highway safety programs; Model specifications for screening devices to measure alcohol in bodily fluids. *Federal Register*, 59:39382–39390, 1994b.

W.M. McIsaac, and P.J. Creaven eds., University of Texas Press, Austin, 1971, pp. 94–110.

Wallgren, H., and Barry, H. III. *Actions of Alcohol, Vol. 1. Biochemical Physiological, and Psychological Effects*. Elsevier, New York, 1970, pp. 287.

West, R., Wilding, J., French, D. et al. Effect of low and moderate doses of alcohol on driving hazard perception latency and driving speed. *Addiction* 88:527–532, 1993.

Whitehouse, L.W., and Paul, C.J. Micro-scale enzymic determination of ethanol in plasma with a discrete analyzer, the ABA–100. *Clin. Chem.* 25: 1399–1401, 1979.

Widmark, E.M.P. A micromethod for the estimation of alcohol in blood. *Biochem. Z.* 131:473, 1922.

Wier, J.K., and Tyler, V.E. An investigation of Coprinus atramentarius for the presence of disulfiram. *J. Am. Pharmacol. Assoc.* 49:426–429, 1960.

Winek, C.L., Winek, C.L., and Wahba, W.W. The role of trauma in postmortem blood alcohol determination. *Forensic Sci. Int.* 71:1–8, 1995.

Yesavage, J.A. and Leirer, V.O. Hangover effects on aircraft pilots 14 hours after alcohol ingestion: a preliminary report. *Am. J. Psychiatry* 143:1546–1550, 1986.

Zrenner, E., Riedel, K.G, Adamczyk, R. et al. Effects of ethyl alcohol on the electrooculogram and color vision. *Doc. Ophthalmol.* 463:305–312, 1986.

Zumwalt, R.E., Bost, R.O., and Sunshine, I. Evaluation of ethanol concentrations in decomposed bodies. *J. Forensic Sci.* 27:549–554, 1982.

CHAPTER 9

DRUG TESTING

Table of Sections

A. LEGAL ISSUES

B. SCIENTIFIC STATUS

Westlaw Electronic Research

See Westlaw Electronic Research Guide preceding the Summary of Contents.

A. LEGAL ISSUES

§ 9–1.0 Legal Issues in Drug Testing

§ 9–1.1 Introduction

Questions concerning the admissibility of tests administered to detect the presence of drugs in individuals have grown along with the growth of the drug problem in the United States. Starting in the early 1980s, urine tests for drugs became commonplace in the criminal justice system, especially in the context of parole and probation revocation and in some pre-trial situations.[1] Testing also occurs in the employment context,[2] in schools,[3] in the military,[4] in

---

§ 9–1.0

1. Kevin B. Zeese, *The Use and Abuse of Drug Tests*, 5 CRIM. JUST. 2 (1991); Jack F. Williams, *Process and Prediction: A Return to A Fuzzy Model of Pretrial Detention*, 79 MINN. L. REV. 325 (1994). Drug testing has come a long way from *People v. Williams*, 331 P.2d 251 (Cal.Super.1958) in which the court admitted into evidence a crude test to detect narcotics use. An examiner visually matched the size of the suspect's pupils with a series of dots on an index card, injected the subject with the chemical Nalline, and measured the pupil size thirty minutes later. Dilated pupils supposedly indicated narcotics use. The case is notable for its liberal application of the *Frye* test. Although the state's experts admitted that the medical profession is unfamiliar with the test, it has been "generally accepted by those who would be expected to be familiar with its use. In this age of specialization more should not be re-

quired." *Id.* at 254. *See Development in the Law, Confronting the New Challenges of Scientific Evidence*, 108 HARV. L. REV. 1481, 1496 (1995).

2. Jan P. Muczyk & Brian P. Heshizer, *A Management Perspective on the Controlled Substance Testing Issue: Management's Newest Pandora's Box*, 2 J.L. & HEALTH 27 (1987–88); Mark A. Rothstein, *Workplace Drug Testing: A Case Study in the Misapplication of Technology*, 5 HARV. J.L. & TECH. 65 (1991); Theresa Casserly, *Evidentiary and Constitutional Implications of Employee Drug Testing Through Hair Analysis*, 45 CLEV. ST. L. REV. 469 (1997); John B. Wefing, *Employer Drug Testing: Disparate Judicial and Legislative Responses*, 63 ALB. L. REV. 799 (2000).

3. *See* Joanna Raby, *Reclaiming Our Public Schools: A Proposal for School-Wide Drug Testing*, 21 CARDOZO L. REV. 999 (1999).

custody disputes,[5] and among athletes.[6] In addition, testing is increasingly used to catch individuals who are driving while impaired.[7] Admissibility of expert testimony remains an issue in all of these areas.[8]

Testing in these areas involves the search for a wide variety of substances (e.g., steroids, marijuana, heroin, cocaine), from different human samples (e.g., hair, blood, urine), using several methodologies (e.g., immunoassays, gas chromatography).[9] Because most of the drugs these tests are designed to detect are controlled substances, the sale and possession of which is illegal, it is not surprising that drug testing raises a wide variety of additional legal issues. They include claims of invasion of privacy,[10] illegal search and seizure,[11] violation of the privilege against self incrimination,[12] denial of due

4. Captain David E. Fitzxkee, *Prosecuting a Urinalysis Case: A Primer*, 1988–Sep. Army Law. 7 (1988); Major Borch, *Court of Military Appeals Decides Role of Judicial Notice in Urinalysis*, 1991–Dec. Army Law. 38 (1991); Major Masterton, *New Rules for Admission of Negative Urinalysis Results*, 1995–Mar. Army Law. 43 (1995); Major Walter Hudson & Major Patricia Ham, *United States v. Campbell: A Major Change for Urinalysis Prosecutions*, 2–May Army Law. 38 (2000).

5. *See* Burgel v. Burgel, 141 A.D.2d 215, 533 N.Y.S.2d 735 (1988).

6. Vernonia Sch. Dist. 47J v. Acton, 515 U.S. 646, 115 S.Ct. 2386, 132 L.Ed.2d 564 (1995); Alan Fecteau, *NCAA State Action: Not Present When Regulating Intercollegiate Athletics—But Does That Include Drug Testing Student Athletes?*, 5 Seton Hall J. Sport L. 291 (1995); Stephen F. Brock et al., *Drug Testing College Athletes: NCAA Does Thy Cup Runneth Over?*, 97 W.Va. L. Rev. 53 (1994); David Galluzzi, *The Doping Crisis in International Athletic Competition: Lessons From the Chinese Doping Scandal in Women's Swimming*, 10 Seton Hall J. Sport L. 65 (2000).

7. Jeffrey M. Morgan, *The Admissibility of Drug Recognition Expert Testimony in the Prosecution of Individuals Driving Under the Influence of a Controlled Substance: State v. Klawitter, 518 N.W.2d 577 (Minn.1994)*, 18 Hamline L. Rev. 261 (1994); Mark Lewis & Betty Buchan, *The Drugged Driver and the Need for a "Per Se" Law*, 72–Aug. Fla. B.J. 32 (1998); Gil Sapir & Mark Giangrande, *Right to Inspect and Test Breath Alcohol Machines: Suspicion Ain't Proof*, 33 J. Marshall L. Rev. 1 (1999); Thomas M. Lockney, *A Comparison of Drinking Driving Law in Norway and North Dakota: More Than a Difference in Penalties*, 76 N.D. L. Rev. 33 (2000).

8. Cain v. Jefferson Parish Dep't of Fleet Management, 701 So.2d 1059 (La.Ct.App.1997) (employment); Nevada Employment Security Dep't v. Holmes, 112 Nev. 275, 914 P.2d 611 (Nev.1996) (same); United States v. Bush, 47 M.J. 305 (C.M.A.1997) (military); Tate v. Hayes, 127 N.C.App. 208, 489 S.E.2d 418 (N.C.Ct.App.1997) (custody dispute); People v.

Shelton, 303 Ill.App.3d 915, 237 Ill.Dec. 12, 708 N.E.2d 815 (Ill.App.Ct.1999) (driving).

9. *See* the discussion by Bray & Crouch in § 2 of this chapter.

10. O'Halloran v. University of Washington, 856 F.2d 1375 (9th Cir.1988); Wilcher v. City of Wilmington, 60 F.Supp.2d 298 (D.Del. 1999) (whether drug testing policy requiring firefighters to give urine specimens under direct supervision of monitor constituted invasion of privacy); Smith v. Fresno Irrigation Dist., 72 Cal.App.4th 147, 84 Cal.Rptr.2d 775 (1999) (construction worker's expectation of privacy was outweighed by irrigation district's legitimate and substantial safety-related reasons for random drug testing).

11. Burka v. New York City Transit Auth., 739 F.Supp. 814 (S.D.N.Y.1990); Skinner v. Rwy. Labor Executives' Assn., 489 U.S. 602, 109 S.Ct. 1402, 103 L.Ed.2d 639 (1989); National Treasury Employees Union v. Von Raab, 489 U.S. 656, 109 S.Ct. 1384, 103 L.Ed.2d 685 (1989); Vernonia Sch. Dist. 47J v. Acton, 515 U.S. 646, 115 S.Ct. 2386, 132 L.Ed.2d 564 (1995); Joy v. Penn–Harris–Madison School Corp., 212 F.3d 1052 (7th Cir.2000) (whether suspicionless drug testing of students involved in extracurricular activities and of students driving to school constitutes an unreasonable search and seizure); Trinidad School Dist. No. 1 v. Lopez, 963 P.2d 1095 (Colo.1998) (suspicionless testing of members of marching band); Chandler v. Miller, 520 U.S. 305, 117 S.Ct. 1295, 137 L.Ed.2d 513 (1997) (statute requiring candidates for higher office in Georga to submit to and pass drug test to qualify for state office did not fit within closely guarded category of constitutionally permissible suspicionless searches). *See* Walker Chandler & Miranda Doming–Krush, *The Constitutional Validity of Suspicionless Drug Testing After Chandler v. Miller*, 28 Stetson L. Rev. 737 (1999).

12. Nottingham v. State, 908 S.W.2d 585 (Tex.Ct.App.1995) (Defendant arrested for driving while intoxicated. Admission of blood test result did not violate defendant's state constitutional privilege against self-incrimina-

process,[13] and of the right to confront witnesses.[14] In addition, drug testing frequently raises chain of custody issues.[15]

The present chapter focuses most of its attention on the question of whether test results should be barred because they fail to meet admissibility thresholds for scientific evidence.[16] However, it will also discuss cases that do not directly address questions of scientific admissibility under a *Daubert* or *Frye* test when the opinions are concerned with the same issues that inform admissibility discussions (e.g., error rates, the opportunity for confirmatory tests).[17]

Given the many cross-cutting currents in this body of law, there are a number of ways in which the cases might be arranged.[18] We have chosen to organize them according to the type of scientific validity question raised by the case. Following Giannelli[19] and Faigman, Porter and Saks,[20] we divide the

tion.); Boling v. Romer, 101 F.3d 1336 (10th Cir.1996) (Colorado statute requiring inmates convicted of offense involving sexual assault to provide state with DNA samples before their release on parole did not compel self-incrimination in violation of Fifth Amendment); Hearn v. Board of Public Edu., 191 F.3d 1329 (11th Cir.1999) (termination for refusing to produce urine for drug test did not violate teacher's privilege against self-incrimination); Nordvick v. Commissioner of Public Safety, 610 N.W.2d 659 (Minn.Ct.App.2000) (implied consent law did not violate right against self-incrimination).

13. Spence v. Farrier, 807 F.2d 753 (8th Cir.1986) (finding use of double EMIT test results as evidence in prison disciplinary hearings not violative of due process); Jensen v. Lick, 589 F.Supp. 35 (D.N.D.1984) (stating that unconfirmed EMIT test results satisfy due process); Wykoff v. Resig, 613 F.Supp. 1504 (N.D.Ind.1985) (holding EMIT test followed by confirmatory "thin layer chromatography" test which indicated use of marijuana, leading to disciplinary action, did not violate due process); Burka v. New York City Transit Authority, 739 F.Supp. 814 (S.D.N.Y.1990) (finding procedure for testing transit employees for marijuana use violated due process); Hearn v. Board of Public Edu., 191 F.3d 1329 (11th Cir.1999) (termination for refusing to produce urine for drug test not a denial of due process); Hill v. Hamilton County Public Hospital, 71 F.Supp.2d 936 (N.D.Iowa 1999) (whether failure to inform nurse of suspicion of illegal drug use after time had passed when she could have produced an exonerating drug is a denial of procedural due process).

14. *See* United States v. Siqueiros, 21 F.3d 1118 (9th Cir.1994) (Probationer challenged the introduction of testimony concerning the results of urine drug tests because original samples had been discarded. Employing a balancing test (the right to confrontation versus the Government's good cause for denying it) the court concluded that the testimony should be admitted. Petitioner's additional sentence

could have been imposed without the positive test results and the samples were lost through no fault of the government.). Compare United States v. Martin, 984 F.2d 308 (9th Cir.1993) (denial of right to retest urine samples a denial of right to confrontation) *and* State v. Wade, 863 S.W.2d 406, 410 (Tenn.1993) (state cannot revoke probation based on unidentified laboratory test indicating probationer had used marijuana without proof of good cause and proof of the reliability of the test result) *with* United States v. Siqueiros, 21 F.3d 1118 (9th Cir. 1994); Jaeger v. State, 113 Nev. 1275, 948 P.2d 1185 (Nev.1997) (probationer was not deprived of right to confront adverse witnesses as to alleged fabrication of drug test result).

15. *See* discussions of chain of custody cases involving drug testing *infra* § 9–1.3.2.

16. This chapter does not include a discussion on the admissibility of tests for alcohol, which is the subject of a separate chapter.

17. *See, e.g., Burka,* 739 F.Supp. at 836. In the process of ruling that the defendant's testing practices constituted an illegal search and seizure and violated plaintiff's due process rights, the court discussed the error rates associated with different types of drug tests.

18. For example, they could be organized by the substance being tested (hair, blood, etc.), by the nature of the controversy (parole revocation, employment, etc.), by the drug (marijuana, cocaine, etc.), or by the type of analysis (radioimmunoassay, gas chromatography, etc.).

19. Professor Giannelli divided the question of scientific validity into "(1) the validity of the underlying principle, (2) the validity of the technique applying the principle, and (3) the proper application of the technique on a particular occasion." Paul Giannelli, *The Admissibility of Novel Scientific Evidence: Frye v. United States, a Half–Century Later,* 80 COLUM. L. REV. 1197, 1201 (1980).

20. Faigman, Porter & Saks distinguish between (1) "the theory or principle that pro-

cases into three broad categories. First, there are cases that address the validity of the theory or principle that provides authority for the expert's conclusions. Second, there are cases that address the general technique or procedure that was used to produce the data about which the expert is testifying. Third, there are cases that address the application of the technique on a particular occasion, that is the specific practices used to obtain the data in the present case.

This formulation has been adopted in a number of cases, decided both before and after the Supreme Court opinion in *Daubert v. Merrell Dow Pharmaceuticals, Inc.*[21] Most relevant with regard to drug testing is Judge Weinstein's opinion in *United States v. Medina.*[22] Judge Weinstein admitted the results of a radioimmunoassay (RIA) hair analysis introduced as part of a probation revocation proceeding. Over the defendant's objection, he concluded that RIA hair analysis is reliable and based on scientific principles of analytical chemistry. Judge Weinstein noted that general theoretical soundness is, by itself, insufficient to permit the introduction of test results. The sample must be properly obtained, the specific laboratory technique must be sound, and on this particular occasion the laboratory must have been careful and accurate in the use of the technique.[23]

Although these three categories offer a useful way to organize the drug cases, a caution is in order. Many cases fall into more than one category. Moreover, the categories interact with each other. There may be theoretical support for some conclusions and not other, similar conclusions. Underlying principles may support an expert's conclusion if it is based on one analytical technique, but not if it is based on another, less discriminating technique. Ultimately, each admissibility decision involves an examination of all three categories in relationship to each other and to the conclusions drawn by the expert.[24]

§ 9–1.2　Validity of the Underlying Theory or Principle

The concepts underlying most chemical drug tests are well developed. The underlying principles supporting techniques such as gas chromatogra-

vides authority for the conclusions that are drawn from the data," (2) "the general technique or procedure that produces the data," and (3) "the specific practices used to obtain the data." David L. Faigman et al., *Check Your Crystal Ball at the Courthouse Door, Please: Exploring the Past, Understanding the Present, and Worrying About the Future of Scientific Evidence*, 15 CARDOZO L. REV. 1799, 1825–27 (1994). For detailed analysis of the levels of abstraction at which science enters the courtroom, see Chapter 1.

21. *See, e.g.*, United States v. Downing, 753 F.2d 1224, 1234 (3d Cir.1985):

Under *Frye*, therefore, courts confronted with a proffer of novel scientific evidence must make a preliminary determination through the introduction of other evidence, including expert testimony, regarding (1) the status, in the appropriate scientific commu-

nity, of the scientific principle underlying the proffered novel evidence; (2) the technique applying the scientific principle; and (3) the application of the technique on the particular occasion or occasions relevant to the proffered testimony.

The Supreme Court *Daubert* opinion appears to adopt at least the first two categories when it distinguishes between a general theory and technique. Daubert v. Merrell Dow Pharmaceuticals, Inc., 509 U.S. 579, 591–93, 113 S.Ct. 2786, 125 L.Ed.2d 469 (1993).

22. 749 F.Supp. 59 (E.D.N.Y.1990).

23. *Id*. at 62. In *Medina*, the evidence was not challenged on these grounds.

24. *See* Comment, *Admissibility of Biochemical Urinalysis Testing Results For the Purpose of Detecting Marijuana Use*, 20 WAKE FOREST L. REV. 391 (1984).

phy/mass spectrometry are rarely challenged.[25] Cases continue to arise, however, concerning tests on hair samples and field sobriety tests, especially horizontal gaze nystagmus tests.

§ 9–1.2.1   Hair

As Judge Weinstein's *Medina* opinion suggests, at the beginning of the 1990s radioimmunoassay (RIA) hair analysis was a relatively new form of forensic proof, not yet recognized by the courts.[26] Hair analysis is attractive to employers, probation officials, and others because, as the court observed, "abstinence for a relatively short period ... purges blood and urine of traces of narcotics. Thus, drug testing of body fluids for drugs using the usual tests only reveals the use of narcotics in the immediate past. RIA hair analysis, by contrast, reveals drug use over a period of months while hair is growing and absorbing drug traces through the blood stream."[27] The *Medina* court found this method to be reliable when used to detect chronic use of a drug. Following *Medina*, courts that have dealt with the question generally agree that such tests are reliable in detecting chronic use of a drug.[28] Occasional drug use presents a more difficult problem.

In *State v. Olea*,[29] the court held that it was harmless error for a trial judge to exclude testimony that defendant tested negative in a hair test designed to detect whether he had used cocaine. The defendant's own expert testified that the test was effective at identifying chronic users, but ineffective in identifying a one-time use.[30] The trial court excluded the evidence on the ground that it was irrelevant to the charge of a single incident of cocaine use.[31]

25. *See, e.g.,* Jones v. United States, 548 A.2d 35 (D.C.1988) (results of EMIT drug test admissible); Jones v. State, 716 S.W.2d 142 (Tex.Ct.App.1986) (results of gas chromatography mass spectrometry [GCMS] test admissible—GCMS has achieved general acceptance); United States v. Bynum, 3 F.3d 769 (4th Cir. 1993); United States v. Vitek Supply Corporation, 144 F.3d 476 (7th Cir.1998); Durham v. State, 956 S.W.2d 62 (Tex.Ct.App.1997); Parker v. State, 777 So.2d 937 (Ala.Crim.App. 2000) (gas chromatograph test not novel, therefore, no *Frye* analysis is required).

26. United States v. Medina, 749 F.Supp. 59 (E.D.N.Y.1990).

27. *Id.* at 60.

28. In *Bass v. Florida Dep't of Law Enforcement*, 627 So.2d 1321 (Fla.Dist.Ct.App. 1993), the plaintiff failed a urine test and was dismissed from her job. She voluntarily underwent further drug testing, including a hair analysis test. The hearing officer refused to admit this evidence. The court of appeals held that radioimmunoassay analysis of human hair to determine cocaine use is generally accepted in the scientific community and thus meets the *Frye* test, still followed in Florida. Therefore, exclusion of the evidence was error. In addition, it was error to exclude the testimony of the plaintiff's expert offering a scientific basis for a false positive reading on the original urine sample. *See In re* Adoption of Baby Boy L, 157 Misc.2d 353, 596 N.Y.S.2d 997 (N.Y.Fam.Ct.1993) (All experts testifying in a *Frye* admissibility hearing agree that RIA analysis of human hair to detect drugs is generally accepted by the toxicological community. Moreover, the witnesses "credibly informed the court—albeit in a technical, scientific manner—that a compound such as cocaine metabolizes in the body system and ultimately produces a peculiar chemical by-product which tends to preserve itself in human hair follicles." *Id.* at 998–99); United States v. Nimmer, 43 M.J. 252 (C.M.A.1995).

29. 182 Ariz. 485, 897 P.2d 1371 (Ariz.Ct. App.1995).

30. *Id.* at 1378.

31. *Id.* The appellate court disagreed with the conclusion that the negative test had no probative weight. It noted that most cocaine users are habitual users. Because the test tended to show that the defendant was not a chronic user, it cast some doubt about his one time use. Nevertheless, this inference was a weak one, rendering the trial court's decision to exclude harmless. *Id.* at 1379.

In *United States v. Nimmer*,[32] the accused was court-martialed for use of cocaine. The evidence against the accused was a urine sample test result that was barely higher than the "positive test" threshold.[33] As part of the defense that either the test was in error or the ingestion was unknowing, the defendant sought the admission of a hair analysis. The defendant's expert was prepared to testify that the hair samples contained no detectable amount of a cocaine metabolite, and that "[b]ased on the inch and half length of the hair, there is no evidence that Mr. Nimmer . . . used cocaine" during the period in question.[34] The trial judge excluded this testimony, based in large part on his finding that although the scientific community generally accepts that chronic cocaine use can be detected by hair analysis, this is not the case with respect to one-time use. Therefore, "[t]here is no reliable evidence that, had this accused used cocaine on the 24th of January, the hypothetical use date referred to in the testimony, that it would have been present in the hair cut from his head on 8 February 1992."[35] The exclusion was affirmed by the Court of Military Review,[36] but remanded for relitigation of the admissibility issue by the Court of Appeals for the Armed Forces.[37] The court instructed the trial judge to consider the factors discussed in *Daubert*:[38] whether the central hypothesis underlying the testimony has been tested,[39] whether the findings have been published and subjected to peer review, the error rate of the techniques in question, and whether those techniques enjoy general acceptance in the scientific community.[40]

In *Nimmer*, the court did not address the question of whether someone could be convicted solely on a hair analysis test.[41] This question was addressed, however, in another military case, *United States v. Bush*.[42] In *Bush*, the defendant was selected for a random drug urinalysis and surreptitiously substituted a saline solution for his urine sample.[43] When this was discovered it was too late to collect another specimen, and instead the Air Force seized a hair sample. Based on this evidence, a general court-martial convicted the

32. 43 M.J. 252 (C.M.A.1995).

33. The reading was 151 nanograms per milliliter, 1 ng/ml above the cut-off level for positive reports using a radioimmunoassay test (RIA) and 51 ng/ml above the cut-off level for a gas chromatography/mass spectrometry test (GC/MS). Apparently both types of tests were used on the sample. *Id.* at 253.

34. *Id.*

35. *Id.* at 254.

36. United States v. Loving, 41 M.J. 213, 229 (C.M.A.1994).

37. 43 M.J. 252 (1995).

38. In *United States v. Gipson*, 24 M.J. 246, 250–51 (C.M.A.1987), superseded by statute as stated in, 37 M.J. 349 (C.M.A.1993), the court determined that the Military Rules of Evidence, patterned after the Federal Rules of Evidence, replaced the *Frye* test with a "reliability" standard, similar to that developed in *United States v. Downing*, 753 F.2d 1224, 1233–37 (3d Cir.1985). This test is basically similar to that announced in *Daubert*. However, unlike *Gipson*, *Daubert*'s reliability analysis

focuses on "the validity of the scientific methodology that led to the evidence." *Id.*

39. The court defined the central hypothesis as follows: "Use of RIA and GC/MS can detect the presence of the metabolite in head hair taken from a single-time user of cocaine." 43 M.J. at 258.

40. *Id.* at 258–59.

41. As the Air Force Court of Criminal Appeals in *United States v. Bush*, 44 M.J. 646, 650 (1996) notes, the question in *Nimmer* is whether the absence of a drug in hair analysis is admissible to show no drug use. The threat is that of a false negative (no drug detected in the hair analysis even though the individual used a drug). This is a different question from whether the presence of a drug is admissible to prove drug use. The threat is that of a false positive (drug detected in the analysis even though the individual did not consume the drug). It is clearly possible to conclude that one conclusion is scientifically reliable while the other is not.

42. 44 M.J. 646 (A.F.Ct.Crim.App.1996).

43. *Id.* at 647.

defendant of use of cocaine. He objected to and appealed the military judge's decision to admit the test, in part because he claimed hair analysis is inadmissible under Mil. R. Evid. 702.[44]

The Air Force Court of Criminal Appeals noted that the question of whether hair analysis alone could be used to prove unlawful use of cocaine was a matter of first impression. The government's F.B.I. expert used a tandem stage quadrapole mass spectrometer (MS/MS) analysis to test the defendant's hair.[45] The court noted that the reason analysis for cocaine in the hair is relatively new is that only recently has technology such as MS/MS analysis permitted the detection and quantifying of substances in minute quantities.[46] Both party's experts agreed that the foundational principles of hair analysis are generally accepted and MS/MS analysis is generally reliable.[47] In this case, both plaintiff and defense experts agreed that cocaine was detected in appellant's hair.

The appellate court noted, "Nothing in the literature submitted by both parties, or in the testimony of the experts, contradicted that, with proper controls, chain of custody, scientific methodology, and instruments of sufficient sensitivity, cocaine found in hair is strongly indicative that cocaine was at some point ingested by the subject, and may properly be considered evidence of wrongful use of that drug. Thus, for all intents and purposes appellant conceded the two principal threshold scientific hypotheses: (a) that cocaine appears in the hair of users; and (b) that scientific analysis using MS/MS (or even GC/MS) instruments can reliably and validly detect that cocaine."[48]

The court concluded, "Mass spectrometer analysis of hair samples is accepted as scientifically reliable in the relevant community of forensic chemistry, has been subjected to peer review, is the subject of a growing body of professional publications, studies, and monographs, and, most important, can be both probative and helpful to the trier of fact."[49]

The experts disagreed primarily on the question of whether passive exposure might explain the results of the analysis of defendant's hair. To lessen this possibility, the government expert washed the defendant's hair in a methanol solution and then tested the wash for the presence of cocaine. The test proved negative.[50] This was evidence that the cocaine discovered in the MS/MS analysis was not the result of passive exposure.

The government's expert also supported his conclusion that the defendant had ingested cocaine based on the ratio of cocaine and cocaine metabolite found in the hair sample. Tests indicated the specimens contained "cocaine and its metabolite, benzoylecgonine at concentrations of 17 and 2.7 nano-

---

44. *Id.* at 648.

45. The court noted that MS/MS represents a quantum advance over GC/MS, the system used in most urinalysis cases. However, the equipment is expensive, costing nearly half a million dollars compared to fifty to seventy-five thousand dollars for a gas chromatography mass spectrometry machine. *Id.* at 651 n. 6.

46. *Id.*

47. Both defense and government experts agreed that ingested cocaine appears in the hair, although there is some uncertainty as to how it gets there. *Id.* at 651. They also agreed that a one-time use of cocaine in moderate quantity might not show up, even on as sensitive machine as a tandem quadrapole mass spectrometer. *Id.*

48. *Id.* at 651.

49. *Id.* at 652.

50. *Id.*

grams per milligram of hair, respectively."[51] As the court noted, this ratio is important because, unlike urinalysis, where metabolized cocaine (benzoylecgonine) is excreted, in hair samples unmetabolized cocaine is typically found in five times the amount of its metabolite. Thus the ratio found in the defendant's hair sample tended to preclude the possibility that the hair was externally contaminated through passive exposure because such contamination would lead to a much higher ratio of cocaine to its metabolite.

The trial judge's decision to admit both a qualitative and quantitative analysis of the defendant's hair was affirmed by the Armed Forces Court of Appeals.[52] The appellate court began by rejecting the defendant's argument that the court should decide the admissibility question "de novo."[53] It refused to view *Nimmer*[54] as an opinion rejecting hair analysis. Rather, *Nimmer* simply called for a *Daubert* hearing preceding the decision whether to admit this type of evidence, something that did occur here.[55]

The defendant argued that hair testing should be used only as a confirmatory test, not the sole test upon which to base a conviction.[56] The court noted that the Society of Forensic Toxicologists (SOFT) harbored some reservations about the use of hair analysis in the workplace and deemed it prudent to have an independent corroboration of a hair analysis results.[57] On balance, however, it found the technique to be sufficiently reliable and valid that the trial judge did not err in admitting it nor was the hair analysis alone insufficient to convict the defendant.[58]

The Nevada Supreme Court also approved the use of hair analysis in *Nevada Employment Security Dep't v. Holmes.*[59] It held that the Nevada Employment Security Department decision to deny a hotel employee unemployment benefits based on a hair analysis indicating she used cocaine in the 90 day period preceding the test was supported by substantial evidence.[60] It overturned a district court determination that "hair drug screens, standing alone, are scientifically unreliable at this time to sufficiently form a legal basis for disqualifying claimants for state unemployment insurance benefits without violating the due process clause of the Fourteenth Amendment of the U.S. Constitution."[61] The court cited other recent cases holding hair analysis to be generally accepted in the scientific community.[62] The Nevada court concluded,

51. *Id.* at 648.

52. *Bush*, 47 M.J. 305 (C.M.A.1997).

53. *Id.* at 309–11. Following *United States v. St. Jean*, 45 M.J. 435, 444 (C.A.A.F.1996), it used the same abuse of discretion standard subsequently adopted by the United States Supreme Court in *General Electric v. Joiner*, 522 U.S. 136, 118 S.Ct. 512, 139 L.Ed.2d 508 (1997).

54. 43 M.J. 252 (1995).

55. 47 M.J. at 309.

56. *Id.* at 310.

57. *Id.* at 312.

58. *Id.* The court noted that there was corroborating evidence in the sense that there was evidence the defendant surreptitiously substituted a saline solution for a urine sample. *Id.* at 310. If the court means to say that in the absence of evidence of deception or avoidance of another test by the defendant the hair anal-

ysis alone would be insufficient to convict, *Bush* has a very limited scope. It appears, however, the court of appeals does not intend such a narrow interpretation. In its closing comments it notes that there is some irony in the fact that the military courts now will accept a conviction based on uncorroborated hair analysis primarily because the defendant thwarted a urinalysis. *Id.* at 312.

59. 112 Nev. 275, 914 P.2d 611 (Nev.1996).

60. For a general discussion of hair analysis in the employment context see Theresa Casserly, *Evidentiary and Constitutional Implications of Employee Drug Testing Through Hair Analysis*, 45 CLEV. ST. L. REV. 469 (1997).

61. *Id.*

62. Bass v. Florida Dep't of Law Enforcement, 627 So.2d 1321, 1322 (Fla.Dist.Ct.App. 1993) (concluding that RIA analysis of hair is generally accepted in the scientific communi-

"RIA testing, especially when coupled with a confirmatory GC/MS test, is now an accepted and reliable scientific methodology for detecting illicit drug use."[63]

In general, the use of hair analysis for drug testing seems well on its way to being accepted by courts, especially in the employment context. In the future, litigation is likely to focus on the particular type of tests conducted and the use of these tests to quantify consumption.

§ 9–1.2.2 EMIT Drug Tests

In the 1980s there were a flurry of cases on the question of whether enzyme multiplied immunoassay technique (EMIT) drug testing of urine was admissible. Some of the earliest cases held that the procedure was inadmissible because it had not achieved general acceptance in the scientific community.[64] However, the great majority of courts concluded that the results of EMIT tests are admissible. The 1988 opinion in *Jones v. United States*[65] collects most of the then existing cases, the great majority of which concluded that EMIT tests were reliable and were generally accepted in the scientific community.[66] Although all recent opinions appear to agree that the general principles underlying EMIT and other drug tests are generally accepted and scientifically valid, considerable disagreement exists concerning the adequacy of a given testing procedure. This issue is best discussed in the next section, general technique.

§ 9–1.2.3 Other Drug Tests

There are very few reported opinions involving challenges to other methods of drug testing. Field tests outside the laboratory would seem to be the most suspect form of testing. However, a field test for cocaine was found to be sufficiently reliable that a police officer was permitted to testify, based on the test, as to the existence of cocaine in the defendant's apartment in *United States v. Blotcher*.[67] On the other hand, a Virginia appellate court

ty); *In re* Adoption of Baby Boy L, 157 Misc.2d 353, 596 N.Y.S.2d 997, 1000 (N.Y.Fam.Ct.1993) (concluding that the process of RIA testing in human hair, when used in conjunction with GC/MS confirmatory testing, "has been accepted by the scientific community as a reliable and accurate method of ascertaining and measuring the use of cocaine by human subjects").

63. *Holmes*, 914 P.2d at 615.

64. Wilson v. State, 697 S.W.2d 83 (Tex.Ct. App.1985) (testimony of operator at trial insufficient to establish scientific acceptance of the EMIT system, including the machine used in the test); Isaacks v. State, 646 S.W.2d 602 (Tex.Ct.App.1983) (same).

65. 548 A.2d 35 (D.C.1988). The *Jones* case has a useful discussion of how an appellate court should proceed in a *de novo* review. "[M]ost appellate courts ... have held that, in determining whether a particular technique or test has general acceptance in the relevant scientific community, the appellate court—like the trial court—may, and often should, pay attention not only to expert evidence of record

but also to judicial opinions in other jurisdictions that have considered the question, as well as to relevant legal and scientific commentaries in which the technique or test has been scrutinized." *Id.* at 41.

66. Lahey v. Kelly, 71 N.Y.2d 135, 524 N.Y.S.2d 30, 518 N.E.2d 924 (N.Y.1987) (EMIT system generally acceptable); Peranzo v. Coughlin, 675 F.Supp. 102 (S.D.N.Y.1987); Harmon v. Auger, 768 F.2d 270, 276 (8th Cir. 1985); Smith v. State, 250 Ga. 438, 298 S.E.2d 482 (Ga.1983) (use of EMIT test results as evidence in probation revocation hearing); People v. Walker, 164 Ill.App.3d 133, 115 Ill.Dec. 268, 517 N.E.2d 679 (Ill.App.Ct.1987) (same); Penrod v. State, 611 N.E.2d 653 (Ind.Ct.App. 1993) (EMIT test has achieved general acceptance).

67. 92 F.3d 1182 (4th Cir.1996) (Table). The officer field tested white flakes in a milky residue on the kitchen sink used by the defendant, allegedly to prepare crack cocaine. The officer testified that the residue tested positive, but he used the entirety of the residue for the test so there was no remaining portion to send

concluded that a trial court erred when it permitted an officer to testify based on the results of a field test for cocaine.[68] However, the court noted that its finding was due to the fact that the record before it contained no evidence that the test had been approved as reliable by the Virginia Division of Forensic Science.[69]

In *Jones v. State*,[70] the defendant challenged a novel use of gas chromatography mass spectrometry (GCMS) to test for succinylcholine—muscle relaxant used to kill defendant's victim. The court outlined the problems with the *Frye* standard of admissibility when applied to rare procedures, but found that GCMS had achieved general acceptance.[71]

The defendant in *State v. Cathcart*,[72] challenged the introduction of expert testimony based on the results of a gas chromatograph mass spectrometer (GC/MS) because the state did not introduce proof of the machine's reliability. At the time there was no New Jersey appellate opinion ruling on the machine's general acceptance. The appellate court affirmed the trial court's decision to admit the evidence. It noted that a proponent of expert scientific testimony may prove its general acceptance in the following three ways: the testimony of knowledgeable experts; authoritative scientific literature; or persuasive judicial opinions.[73] The court cited cases from other jurisdictions,[74] as well as unchallenged use of the results of GC/MS analysis in other New Jersey cases, and concluded the results were admissible absent any evidence offered by the defendant challenging the machine's reliability. Other recent cases continue the trend of finding various drug tests to be generally accepted and scientifically valid.[75] Courts conclude that the tests have reached general acceptance and pass muster under *Daubert*-type analyses.

United States v. Campbell[76] presents an exception to this position. The defendant was convicted by a special court martial of wrongful use of lysergic acid diethylamide (LSD). The Court of Criminal Appeals affirmed but the United States Court of Appeals for the Armed Forces reversed and dismissed.

The evidence upon which the defendant was convicted consisted of three tests of defendant's urine. The first two tests were done over a 4 day period using radioimmunoassay analysis (RIA). Both tests were positive. However, as the court notes, the procedure does not quantify the amount of the drug in a

to a laboratory for further, more reliable testing. *Id.* at *1.

68. Galbraith v. Commonwealth, 18 Va. App. 734, 446 S.E.2d 633 (Va.Ct.App.1994).

69. *Id.* at 637.

70. 716 S.W.2d 142 (Tex.Ct.App.1986).

71. The court argued that Texas should abandon the *Frye* test. "Texas has adopted rules of evidence for criminal cases, effective in September 1986, patterned after the Federal Rules. We think that Texas should follow the cases that have rejected *Frye* and adopt the general relevancy analysis of the rules, with consideration to using the factors set out by *McCormick* as a guideline for analysis." *Id.* at 154. Eventually, Texas followed the court's advice. *See* Kelly v. State, 824 S.W.2d 568 (Tex. Crim.App.1992).

72. 247 N.J.Super. 340, 589 A.2d 193 (N.J.Super.Ct.App.Div.1991).

73. *Id.* at 199.

74. The court cited *Jones v. State*, 716 S.W.2d 142 (Tex.Ct.App.1986).

75. *See* Wood v. State Personnel Board, 705 So.2d 413 (Ala.Ct.App.1997); Anderson v. McKune, 23 Kan.App.2d 803, 937 P.2d 16 (Kan.Ct.App.1997) (latex agglutination immunoassay technique to test for barbiturates); Carter v. State, 706 N.E.2d 552 (Ind.1999) (urinalysis); United States v. Stumpf, 54 F.Supp.2d 972 (D.Nev.1999) (sweat patch).

76. 50 M.J. 154 (1999). The case is discussed in Major Walter Hudson & Major Patricia Ham, *United States v. Campbell: A Major Change for Urinalysis Prosecutions*, 2–May ARMY LAW. 38 (2000).

sample and had not been certified by the Department of Defense as reliable for prosecution under the Uniform Code of Military Justice.[77]

After the two positive RIA test results, defendant's sample was sent to the Northwest Toxicology Laboratory in Salt Lake City, Utah for additional testing using GC/MS/MS (gas chromatography tandem mass spectrometer) methodology. The test showed a level of 307 picograms (one-trillionth of a gram) of LSD per milliliter of urine.[78] The Department of Defense had established a cutoff level of 200 picograms. That is, results indicating less than 200 picograms would be considered negative.[79]

The Northwest Toxicology Laboratory (NTL) was the only facility using this test for the detection of LSD in urine. Although the government's experts testified that the procedure had been subjected to both open and blind testing and the results of the open tests were replicated by two Navy laboratories that performed urine testing for LSD using a different method,[80] the court concluded the government failed to prove the levels or frequence of error which would indicate that a particular GC/MS/MS test reliably detected the presence of LSD metabolites, that the test reliably quantified the concentration of these metabolites, and that the 200 picogram cutoff level was sufficiently high to reasonably exclude the possibility of a false positive and establish the wrongfulness of any use.[81] Therefore, a reasonable factfinder could not conclude that this test excluded the possibility of a false positive, e.g., exposure due to unknown ingestion, or that a person exposed to this amount of the drug would have experienced the physical and psychological effects of the drug.[82]

Critical to the majority's view was the fact that the use of GC/MS/MS to detect LSD in urine samples was novel and was being conducted only by this one laboratory. Apparently this was partly due to the expense of the instrument, which is somewhere around $350,000. The court held out the possibility that in future cases the government may be able to demonstrate the significance of the concentration levels and the reliability of the test.

The opinion is not altogether clear as to what was wrong with this test. It seems, however, that it accepted the theory behind the test and perhaps even the general ability of the GC/MS/MS technique to detect the presence of LSD in urine. What it found most questionable was the potential error rate of the test, i.e., the ability of a 300 picogram result to exclude what it calls false positives.[83] A dissenting opinion argued that the trial court did not abuse is

---

77. *Campbell*, 50 M.J. at 156.

78. *Id.*

79. This very low cut-off is partly due to the fact that the "normal" dose of LSD is between 70 and 100 micrograms (millionths of a gram). The metabolites are further diluted in the body and may emerge in urine in concentrations measured in picograms. *Id.* at 157–158.

80. *Id.* at 157.

81. *Id.* at 161.

82. *Id.* The court held that the prosecution may establish a relationship between test results and the inference of knowing, wrongful use by showing (1) that the "metabolite" is not naturally produced by the body or a substance other than the drug in question; (2) that the cut-off level established for the test and the reported concentration are high enough to reasonably rule out the possibility of unknowing ingestion and to indicate a reasonable likelihood that the user would have experienced effects of the drug; and (3) that the testing methodology reliably detected the presence and reliably quantified the concentration of the drug or metabolite in the sample. *Id.* at 160. The analysis in this case failed the second prong of the test. For a recent case drawing a similar conclusion *see* United States v. Powe, 2000 WL 703684 (N.M.Ct.Crim.App. at *5).

83. These are not necessarily "false positives" in the sense that the urine in fact contains no LSD metabolites. Rather, they are

discretion in admitting the GC/MS/MS results under *Daubert*.[84] Another dissent argued that the majority drew an inappropriate analogy to marijuana cases. In those cases, because of the significant possibility of passive inhalation it is important to establish a minimum threshold sufficiently high to exclude such exposures.[85] In the case of the consumption of a microdot of LSD, however, this is less likely to be an issue.[86]

Ruiz-Troche v. Pepsi Cola of Puerto Rico Bottling Co.[87] raises the interesting question of what types of extrapolation an expert can make given certain toxicological results. In *Ruiz-Troche*, the plaintiff's decedent (Ruiz) and his family were driving in an automobile on a two lane road when he pulled out to pass and collided with an oncoming tractor-trailer rig. The driver and four passengers were killed and a small child sustained permanent brain damage. The jury returned a verdict that assigned 41% of the responsibility for the accident to the truck driver. At trial, the defendant had attempted to introduce an autopsy report indicating that at the time of his death Ruiz's body contained .45 mcg/ml of cocaine and .15 mcg/ml of a cocaine metabolite in its blood, cocaine metabolites in its urine and vitreous humor, and cocaine in its nasal passages.[88] The defendant also attempted to introduce expert testimony based on the autopsy report that Ruiz had snorted 200 milligrams of cocaine within an hour of the accident, that cocaine impairs driving capability and increases the willingness to take risks. A second expert was prepared to testify that Ruiz would not have initiated the fatal passing maneuver had it not been for his cocaine intoxication.[89]

The trial judge excluded the expert testimony as unreliable under *Daubert* and then excluded the autopsy results under FRE 403, concluding that standing alone unexplained, they were more prejudicial than probative.[90] The First Circuit reversed, holding that the trial court abused its discretion in refusing to entertain the expert's dosage and impairment opinion.[91] The opinion was based on studies investigating the "half-life" of cocaine and the time after ingestion at which cocaine and its metabolites reach peak concen-

false in the sense that this very low level of metabolites may be consistent with some type of passive exposure rather than an intentional ingestion of the drug.

84. *Id.* at 168

85. *See* United States v. Harper, 22 M.J. 157 (C.M.A.1986).

86. *Id.* at 164. The Court of Appeals for the Armed Forces granted the government's request for reconsideration and in a short opinion held that the three part test in the original opinion is not necessarily the only means of proving knowing use. United States v. Campbell, 52 M.J. 386 (C.A.A.F. 2000). The government may introduce other, circumstantial evidence to make this proof. In a fairly ambiguous passage, the court holds out the possibility that the government may be able to use the results of a test to show knowing use if it can produce evidence that "can explain, with equivalent persuasiveness, the underlying scientific methodology and the significance of the test results, so as to provide a rational basis for inferring knowing, wrongful use. Such evidence must be

supported by more than an expert's qualifications and generalized theories. It must meet applicable evidentiary standards for scientific and specialized knowledge in terms of reliability and relevance to the specific proposition at issue." *Id.* at 389. It is not entirely clear what the court has in mind, but perhaps it might include expert testimony on the error rate surrounding a given finding and the existence of physiological and psychological effects of ingesting a drug in the dosage suggested by the lower confidence interval of the test result. With respect to this latter possibility, the court went on to hold that the government's expert does not have to introduce scientific evidence tailored to the specific characteristics of the person whose test results are at issue. *Id.*

87. 161 F.3d 77 (1st Cir.1998).

88. *Id.* at 82.

89. *Id.*

90. *Id.* at 79.

91. *Id.* at 85, 86.

trations.[92] The appellate court noted that the literature does not make out an open-and-shut case for the exact amount of cocaine snorted by Ruiz. However, this issue goes to error rate, only one of the factors to be considered when making admissibility decisions. On the other side of the scale, the general theory of cocaine metabolism has been tested and appears to be valid, a substantial literature on point has been published and passed peer review, and the theory appears to have won significant acceptance with the relevant scientific community.[93] The court concluded that the trial judge "set the bar too high."[94] It noted that, "Daubert neither requires nor empowers trial courts to determine which of several competing scientific theories has the best provenance. It demands only that the proponent of the evidence show that the expert's conclusion has been arrived at in a scientifically sound and methodologically reliable fashion."[95] The expert's testimony satisfied this standard.

§ 9–1.2.4 Timing

Occasionally, courts will agree that a test is generally probative as to a suspect's drug use but in a particular case is irrelevant due to timing. In *State v. Olea*[96] the court concluded that any error in excluding evidence that the defendant tested negative on a urine test was harmless. Initially the defendant voluntarily submitted to a test for cocaine use. The specimen tested positive on both an initial screening test and on a second confirmatory test. When told of these results several days later the defendant underwent a urinalysis drug screening test by an independent laboratory. The result was negative. The appellate court noted that the urine test was taken eight days after the original test and said that the test will not detect the presence of cocaine in a person's body if it was last used more than three or four days before the sample was collected.[97]

§ 9–1.2.5 Horizontal Gaze Nystagmus (HGN) and Drug Recognition Evaluation (DRE) Protocol

[1] Validity/General Acceptance

As defined in *People v. Ojeda*, "Nystagmus is an involuntary rapid movement of the eyeball which may be horizontal, vertical, or rotary. An inability of the eyes to maintain visual fixation as they are turned from side to side (in other words, jerking or bouncing) is known as horizontal gaze nystagmus, or HGN."[98] Proponents of HGN believe that alcohol and drug use increases the frequency and amplitude of HGN and cause it to occur at a smaller angle of deviation from forward.[99] Nystagmus tests are not done in a

92. *Id.* at 84.

93. *Id.* at 85.

94. *Id.*

95. *Id.*

96. 182 Ariz. 485, 897 P.2d 1371 (Ariz.Ct. App.1995).

97. *Id.* at 1378.

98. 225 Cal.App.3d 404, 275 Cal.Rptr. 472 (1990). *See* Charles R. Honts & Susan L. Amato–Henderson, *Horizontal Gaze Nystagmus Test: The State of the Science in 1995*, 71 N.D.

L. Rev. 671 (1995); Stephanie E. Busloff, *Can Your Eyes Be Used Against You? The Use of the Horizontal Gaze Nystagmus Test in the Courtroom*, 84 J. Crim. L. & Criminology 203 (1993). HGN is one type of nystagmus. Occasionally, other nystagmus tests are used by law enforcement authorities. *See* Honts & Amato–Henderson at 685.

99. A useful review of the science on HGN can be found in Joseph R. Meaney, *Horizontal Gaze Nystagmus: A Closer Look*, 36 Jurimetrics J. 383 (1996).

laboratory, but rather are given by police officers in the field or in a police station subsequent to arrest. The results of an HGN test are most frequently introduced as part of the state's case in drunk driving cases. However, they may also be used when an individual is suspected to be under the influence of some other substance and, therefore, are an important part of the drug testing environment.[100]

HGN tests are frequently used as part of a longer drug recognition protocol, designed to assist police in determining whether a driver is impaired and, if so, due to what substance. The most widely used protocol, the "drug influence evaluation" was developed by the National Highway Traffic Safety Administration and the Los Angeles Police Department in response to the fact that police officers were encountering drivers who were clearly impaired but whose blood alcohol concentration reading indicated that they were not intoxicated.[101] Participating jurisdictions give special training to some officers, who then become drug recognition experts (DRE). Most of the controversy concerning scientific validity has surrounded the HGN test, but the full protocol has also raised some admissibility issues, albeit usually in cases involving drugs other than alcohol.[102]

[a] Nystagmus

Courts have used both *Frye* and *Daubert* analyses when assessing the admissibility of nystagmus results. In *People v. Leahy*,[103] the court of appeals held that HGN tests were inadmissible to show intoxication without a *Frye/Kelly* foundational showing that the procedure had achieved general acceptance in the relevant scientific community. The Supreme Court of California affirmed, and in the process decided that California's *Kelly/Frye*[104] "general acceptance" test would not be altered in the aftermath of *Daubert*.[105] The court concluded that HGN is a "new scientific technique" within the scope of the *Kelly* formulation, and therefore could not be admitted absent proof of its general acceptance.[106] It remanded the case for a *Kelly/Frye* hearing. The court made it clear that the state will not always be required to

100. State v. Klawitter, 518 N.W.2d 577 (Minn.1994) (marijuana); People v. Quinn, 153 Misc.2d 139, 580 N.Y.S.2d 818 (1991), rev'd, 158 Misc.2d 1015, 607 N.Y.S.2d 534 (N.Y.App. Term.1993) (cocaine); Kerr v. State, 205 Ga. App. 624, 423 S.E.2d 276 (Ga.Ct.App.1992) (cocaine and marijuana—admissibility of nystagmus test not challenged).

101. *See* Morgan, *supra* note 7, at 267. The protocol includes the 12 steps a Drug Recognition Expert (DRE) should take. *See* note 144 *infra* for a list of the factors.

102. State v. Baity, 140 Wash.2d 1, 991 P.2d 1151 (Wash.2000).

103. 17 Cal.App.4th 1796, 22 Cal.Rptr.2d 322 (1993), review granted and opinion superseded, 25 Cal.Rptr.2d 390, 863 P.2d 635 (Cal. 1993).

104. California adopted a *Frye* test in *People v. Kelly*, 17 Cal.3d 24, 130 Cal.Rptr. 144, 549 P.2d 1240 (Cal.1976).

105. People v. Leahy, 8 Cal.4th 587, 34 Cal.Rptr.2d 663, 882 P.2d 321 (Cal.1994).

106. *Id.* at 831–32. In People v. Stoll, 49 Cal.3d 1136, 265 Cal.Rptr. 111, 783 P.2d 698, 710 (1989) the court stated, "*Kelly/Frye* only applies to that limited class of expert testimony which is based, in whole or part, on a technique, process, or theory which is new to science and, even more so, the law." The court noted that in determining whether a scientific technique is "new" for *Kelly* purposes, long standing use by law enforcement is less significant than repeated use, study and testing by scientists. "To hold that a scientific technique could become immune from *Kelly* scrutiny merely by reason of longstanding and persistent use by law enforcement outside the laboratory or the courtroom seems unjustified." *Leahy*, 882 P.2d at 332.

submit the testimony of an expert to show the general acceptance of HGN tests. "[I]n future cases, once the *Kelly* standard has been met, as reflected by a published appellate precedent, the prosecution will not be required to submit expert testimony to confirm a police officer's evaluation of an HGN test."[107]

The Oregon Supreme Court employed a *Daubert* analysis to assess nystagmus in *State v. O'Key*.[108] The trial court held an omnibus hearing and concluded that HGN evidence was not admissible.[109] An appellate court reversed. On appeal, the Oregon Supreme Court first determined that HGN is "scientific evidence" and cannot be admitted absent a showing that it meets the requirements of Oregon Rules 702 and 403.[110] Relying on the omnibus hearing below, the court affirmed the appellate court. HGN is admissible scientific evidence under the Oregon test.[111] The court found that the theory underlying the HGN test, that there is a strong correlation between the amount of alcohol a person consumes and the angle of onset of nystagmus, can be and has been tested.[112] The test does suffer from a non-trivial error rate, due in part to the substantial number of factors other than alcohol or drugs that may induce nystagmus.[113] The court noted, however, that research

---

107. *Leahy*, 882 P.2d at 336. The Oregon Supreme Court has adopted a similar rule. *See* State v. O'Key, 321 Or. 285, 899 P.2d 663, 673 (Or.1995) ("Once a trial court has decided that proffered expert scientific testimony is scientifically valid and has admitted such evidence for the particular purpose to which it is directed, and that decision is affirmed by this court in a published opinion, it will become precedent controlling subsequent trials.").

108. *Id.*

109. In the Oregon test, "each eye is checked for three possible clues that the person tested is under the influence of intoxicating liquor: (1) Angle of onset—the more impaired by alcohol that a person becomes, the sooner the jerking will occur as the eyes move to the side (one point is awarded if nystagmus is present when an officer holds a stimulus at a 40–degree angle); (2) maximum deviation—the greater the alcohol impairment, the more distinct the nystagmus is when the eyes are as far to the side as possible (one point is awarded if endpoint nystagmus is present); (3) smooth or jerky pursuit—a person impaired by alcohol cannot follow a slowly moving object smoothly with his eyes (one point is awarded if jerky pursuit is observed). A score of six points is possible, three for each eye." *Id.* at 674.

110. "The HGN test provides evidence that purports to draw its convincing force from a principle of science, namely, the asserted scientific proposition that there is a causal relationship between consumption of alcohol and the type of nystagmus measured by the HGN test.... The value of HGN testing depends critically on the demonstrated scientific validity of that proposition. Moreover, the proposition that alcohol consumption causes nystagmus possesses significantly increased potential

to influence the trier of fact as a 'scientific' assertion." *Id.* at 675.

111. State v. Brown, 297 Or. 404, 687 P.2d 751 (Or.1984), the leading Oregon case interpreting Oregon's version of Rule 702, identified seven non-exclusive factors that may affect a trial court's admissibility decision: "(1) The technique's general acceptance in the field; (2) The expert's qualifications and stature; (3) The use which has been made of the technique; (4) The potential rate of error; (5) The existence of specialized literature; (6) The novelty of the invention; and (7) The extent to which the technique relies on the subjective interpretation of the expert." *Brown*, 687 P.2d at 759. In addition, the *O'Key* court cited with approval the four factors listed in *Daubert*, and the factors listed in *United States v. Downing*, 753 F.2d 1224, 1238–41 (3d Cir.1985) (the nonjudicial uses and experience with the process or technique and the extent to which other courts have permitted expert testimony based on the process or technique). *O'Key*, 899 P.2d at 679–80.

112. *O'Key*, 899 P.2d at 682.

113. The court listed the following potential causes of a "false-positive" nystagmus test:

First, there is a small but significant number of people who have chronic nystagmoid eye movements. Second, people who have high refractive errors could have trouble seeing the test target with their glasses removed and may therefore have problems with the test. Third, many people will have jerky eye movements even with 0.00 percent BAC. Nearly anything that affects the inner ear labyrinth, including alcohol, will cause nystagmus. The evidence in the record shows that about three percent of the population

studies indicate the error rate of an HGN test is lower than for other field sobriety tests routinely admitted into evidence and that when properly administered and scored by a qualified officer, the test is a reasonably reliable indicator of alcohol impairment even though other causes of nystagmus cannot be ruled out completely.[114] Finally, it concluded that the test had achieved general acceptance in the relevant scientific communities.[115] The court also considered and rejected the defendant's argument that HGN tests should be excluded under Rule 403 because their probative value was outweighed by their prejudicial effect or because the introduction of the evidence would unduly prolong trials.[116]

To our knowledge, no court has concluded, after a full *Daubert/Frye* analysis that HGN is never admissible because it is not reliable.[117] Several

suffers from non-alcohol-induced nystagmus and that, within that group, there are 50 to 100 causes of the phenomenon. Examples of causes of non-alcohol-induced nystagmus include caffeine, nicotine, eyestrain, motion sickness, epilepsy, streptococcus infections, measles, vertigo, muscular dystrophy, multiple sclerosis, influenza, hypertension, sunstroke, changes in atmospheric pressure, and arteriosclerosis. Depressants and convulsants can cause HGN, and sleep loss can change the angle of onset by about five degrees. Non-alcohol-induced nystagmus, however, typically is asymmetrical (one eye only), whereas alcohol-induced nystagmus is the same in both eyes. Officers are trained to look for that aspect.

Id. at 684 (citing Comment, 84 J. Crim. L. & Criminology at 212). *See* Schultz v. State, 106 Md.App. 145, 664 A.2d 60, 77 (Md.Ct. Spec.App.1995) for another list of possible causes of nystagmus.

114. 899 P.2d at 864.

115. It defined the communities as pharmacology, ophthalmology, optometry, behavioral psychology, highway safety, neurology, and criminalistics. *Id.* at 686.

116. *Id.* at 688–89.

117. Kansas is perhaps comes closest to this view. In *State v. Witte*, 251 Kan. 313, 836 P.2d 1110, 1111 (Kan.1992), the court concluded that HGN had not reached general acceptance under the Kansas version of *Frye*. The syllabus prepared by the court said that the state could meet its *Frye* burden "by proving: (1) The reliability of the underlying scientific theory upon which the horizontal gaze nystagmus test is based (i.e., that the nystagmus of the eye is, in fact, an indicator of alcohol consumption to the degree that it influences or impairs the ability to drive); (2) the method used to test horizontal gaze nystagmus is a valid test to measure or perceive that phenomenon, particularly if the method actually conducted by the law enforcement officer administering the test." *Id.* at 1111. The state attempted to demonstrate reliability and general acceptance in *State v. Chastain*, 265

Kan. 16, 960 P.2d 756 (Kan.1998). The state presented the testimony of a psychology Ph.D as to the reliability of the test, but the trial court, nevertheless, excluded the HGN results. The Kansas Supreme Court affirmed. It steadfastly held to its earlier position that HGN had not reached general acceptance. *Id.* at 761. It quoted favorably, the following trial court ruling following the expert's testimony:

State v. Witte, raises a number of questions, none of which have been answered here today. There are a number of medical conditions which this witness has testified that she is not qualified to answer medical questions regarding, and these are issues that were specifically addressed in State v. Witte. And questions that were addressed, this appears to be a bootstrapped-type of testing procedure that has not been shown—there are a number of other matters that need to be addressed before the scientific reliability of this testing will be allowed.

Id. The final position of the Kansas courts awaits a case where the trial judge admits HGN testimony following the testimony of an expert.

In *State v. Borchardt*, 224 Neb. 47, 395 N.W.2d 551 (Neb.1986), the supreme court found that the trial court erred in admitting an officer's HGN testimony because the record contained no competent evidence the new test is valid. *Id.* at 558. *Borchardt* was overruled in *State v. Baue*, 258 Neb. 968, 607 N.W.2d 191 (Neb.2000) (results from HGN field sobriety test are admissible for the limited purpose of establishing that the defendant had an impairment which could have been caused by alcohol).

The Supreme Court of Mississippi concluded that the HGN test is a scientific test. Moreover, it concluded that the test is not generally accepted within the scientific community and cannot be used as scientific evidence to prove intoxication or impairment. Its only permissible use is to prove probable cause to arrest and administer an intoxilyzer or a blood test. Young v. City of Brookhaven, 693 So.2d 1355,

have taken judicial notice of the procedure's general acceptance and/or reliability. In *State v. Taylor*,[118] the Maine Supreme Court took judicial notice of the reliability of HGN tests in making determinations of probable cause for arrest and for purposes of establishing criminal guilt in DUI cases.[119] A similar result was reached in *Williams v. State*[120] and *State v. Ito*.[121]

Courts have generally fallen into three camps with respect to the admissibility of HGN results. In one camp are jurisdictions that hold results to be inadmissible in the absence of a foundational showing that the procedure has achieved general acceptance (in *Frye* jurisdictions) or is scientifically valid (in *Daubert* jurisdictions). A second group of states required a foundational showing when HGN was first introduced in the jurisdiction, but have concluded that the scientific validity of the procedure is now established and, therefore, independent expert testimony is no longer required.[122] A third group of states have held that HGN is no more scientific than other field sobriety tests and, therefore, never requires expert testimony as a foundation for admissibility.[123]

The majority of recent cases that have addressed the admissibility question have fallen in the first camp.[124] They include, *State v. Baue*,[125] *State v. Chastain*,[126] *State v. Helms*,[127] *Hulse v. Department of Justice, Motor Vehicle*

1360–61 (Miss.1997). As the court in *Ballard v. State*, 955 P.2d 931 (Alaska Ct.App.1998) notes, however, the "Mississippi court's reasoning is simply confused." *Id.* at 938 n. 6. In *Young* there had been no *Frye* hearing below to determining the general acceptance of HGN tests, and the supreme court did not engage in a separate analysis of the question. Therefore, its statement that HGN has not reached general acceptance is *ipse dixit*. *See* N. Laurence Willey, Jr., *Should HGN in OUI be DOA?*, 13 ME.B.J. 60 (1998).

118. 694 A.2d 907 (Me.1997).

119. *Id.* at 910.

120. 710 So.2d 24 (Fla.Dist.Ct.App.1998) (HGN is not novel scientific evidence and court takes judicial notice that the technique has reached general acceptance under the *Frye* test). *Williams* comes as close as any recent case to holding that HGN does not require expert testimony as a foundation for admissibility. "Although clothed in scientific garb, we recognize the HGN does not involve any particular 'scientific' skill or equipment and for that reason courts have struggled with its classification. Nevertheless, the HGN is premised on the asserted scientific proposition that the automatic tracking mechanisms of the eyes are affected by drug consumption. Thus, while we are not convinced that the HGN is truly 'scientific,' because its application is dependent on a scientific proposition and requires a particular expertise outside the realm of common knowledge of the average person, we conclude the HGN is 'quasi-scientific' evidence." *Id.* at 30.

121. 90 Hawai'i 225, 978 P.2d 191, 209 (Haw.1999). The court reached this conclusion primarily by looking to case law from other jurisdictions. It did not stop there, however. It

reviewed the admissibility of HGN tests under factors listed in *State v. Montalbo*, 73 Haw. 130, 828 P.2d 1274, 1280 (Haw.1992), and found the theory and general technique to be reliable.

122. State v. Superior Court, 149 Ariz. 269, 718 P.2d 171 (Ariz.1986); Albert v. State, 236 Ga.App. 146, 511 S.E.2d 244 (Ga.Ct.App.1999).

123. State v. Murphy, 451 N.W.2d 154 (Iowa 1990); Whitson v. State, 314 Ark. 458, 863 S.W.2d 794 (Ark.1993); City of Fargo v. McLaughlin, 512 N.W.2d 700 (N.D.1994). Recently, New Mexico moved from this category to the first category. *See* State v. Torres, 127 N.M. 20, 976 P.2d 20 (N.M.1999).

124. Earlier cases adopting this position include *State v. Cissne*, 72 Wash.App. 677, 865 P.2d 564, 568 (Wash.Ct.App.1994) ("The HGN test is a different type of test from balancing on one leg or walking a straight line because it rests almost entirely upon an assertion of scientific legitimacy rather than a basis of common knowledge." HGN must meet *Frye* test.); State v. Witte, 251 Kan. 313, 836 P.2d 1110, 1111 (Kan.1992) ("The horizontal gaze nystagmus test is distinguished from other field sobriety tests in that science, rather than common knowledge, provides the legitimacy for horizontal gaze nystagmus testing.... As such, the foundation requirements for admissibility enunciated in *Frye v. United States* must be satisfied.").

125. 258 Neb. 968, 607 N.W.2d 191 (Neb. 2000).

126. 265 Kan. 16, 960 P.2d 756 (Kan.1998).

127. 348 N.C. 578, 504 S.E.2d 293 (N.C. 1998).

Div.,[128] *Commonwealth v. Sands*,[129] *State v. Meador*,[130] *People v. Kirk*,[131] *Ballard v. State*,[132] *State v. Murphy*,[133] and *State v. Torres*.[134] Courts that take this view generally do so because they believe that unlike most field sobriety tests, HGN rests on little understood scientific principles and the phenomenon is beyond the common understanding of the jury. As the Court in *Murphy* noted, "In our view, the HGN test does differ fundamentally from other field sobriety tests because the witness must necessarily explain the underlying scientific basis of the test in order for the testimony to be meaningful to a jury. Other tests, in marked contrast, carry no such requirement."[135]

However, jurisdictions that require an adequate foundation in each case rarely require testimony from someone other than an adequately trained police officer.[136] The position of the court in the recent case of *State v. Baue*[137] is typical. "We conclude that the majority view is sound, and adopt the view that a police officer may testify to the results of HGN testing if it is shown that the officer has been adequately trained in the administration and assessment of the HGN test an has conducted the testing and assessment in accordance with that training."[138]

Other states have reached a similar result by different means. In *Zimmerman v State*,[139] the court reviewed the superior court opinion in *Ruthardt*[140] holding that HGN is generally accepted. It concluded that under the doctrine of stare decisis parties in future cases do not have to establish that HGN is reasonably relied upon by experts in the field. Nevertheless, the party wishing

128. 289 Mont. 1, 961 P.2d 75 (Mont.1998).

129. 424 Mass. 184, 675 N.E.2d 370 (Mass. 1997). The case contains a useful list of the position of other jurisdictions as of 1996. Massachusetts has adopted an admissibility standard that is a mixture of *Frye* and *Daubert*. "A party seeking to introduce scientific evidence may lay a foundation either by showing that the underlying scientific theory is generally accepted within the relevant scientific community, or by showing that the theory is reliable or valid through other means." *Id.* at 371.

130. 674 So.2d 826 (Fla.Dist.Ct.App.1996).

131. 289 Ill.App.3d 326, 224 Ill.Dec. 452, 681 N.E.2d 1073 (Ill.App.Ct.1997).

132. 955 P.2d 931 (Alaska Ct.App.1998) (*Frye* test).

133. 953 S.W.2d 200 (Tenn.1997).

134. 127 N.M. 20, 976 P.2d 20 (N.M.1999).

135. *Murphy*, 953 S.W.2d at 202–03.

136. One possible exception may be Montana. In *Hulse v. Department of Justice, Motor Vehicle Division*, 289 Mont. 1, 961 P.2d 75 (Mont.1998), the Montana Supreme Court joined states holding that the scientific validity of HGN has been established. Because a *Daubert* analysis is required only for novel scientific evidence in Montana, the state in future cases no longer needs to introduce evidence proving that the test is scientifically valid. Nevertheless, because the scientific principle underlying the test is beyond the range of ordinary experience, the court must conduct a "conventional Rule 702 analysis." *Id.* at 93.

This includes a showing that the expert testifying about HGN has undergone special training and possesses an adequate understanding of the technique to render an expert opinion. In addition, the state must show that the officer administering the test is qualified to do so and that he administered the test in the instant case according to established procedures. *Id.* It is not precisely clear in the *Hulse* opinion what training an individual will need in order to qualify as a expert on the scientific principles. If the point of requiring expert testimony is to provide jurors with a sufficient understanding of the principles underlying HGN to permit them to assess this evidence, then the testimony of a trained officer might well suffice. In *City of Missoula v. Robertson*, 298 Mont. 419, 998 P.2d 144 (Mont.2000), the court found that a municipal court erred in admitting the testimony of a police officer without expert testimony establishing the test's validity. *Id.* at 152. The officer conceded that he lacked the expertise to testify as to the test's reliability. *Id.*

137. 258 Neb. 968, 607 N.W.2d 191 (Neb. 2000).

138. *Id.* at 205. *See* State v. Zivcic, 229 Wis.2d 119, 598 N.W.2d 565, 570 (Wis.Ct.App. 1999) ("[a]s long as the HGN test results are accompanied by the testimony of a law enforcement officer who is properly trained to administer and evaluate the test," the evidence is admissible).

139. 693 A.2d 311 (Del.1997).

140. 680 A.2d 349 (Del.Super.Ct.1996).

to introduce the evidence must present evidence from an expert with specialized knowledge and training in HGN concerning the underlying principles supporting HGN.[141]

In sum, the practical difference between those states that require a showing of scientific validity/general acceptance and those states that say the scientific validity of HGN has been established and does not need to be proven in each new case is quite small. In most of the states that fall into the first category, the testimony of a trained lay person such as a police officer suffices to lay a validity foundation. Moreover, in most of the states in the second category, the state must put an expert (often an officer) on the stand to explain the principles underlying the test, to testify about how the test is conducted, and to aver that proper procedures were performed by a trained individual in the case at bar.

Theoretically, this position is more easily justified in *Frye* jurisdictions, especially those who hold that *Frye* only applies to "novel" scientific evidence. In *Daubert* jurisdictions, where the proponent has the obligation of showing that the theory underlying HGN is sound, it is not clear how a police officer with a few weeks training at most is in a position to be qualified to offer this opinion. Nevertheless, through various devices, including judicial notice,[142] courts have bowed to the practicalities of the situation and permitted the officer to establish the general reliability of the technique.

In spite of the widespread acceptance of HGN, especially in the alcohol cases, the science underlying the accuracy of the procedure is not deep and the error rate, especially the false positive rate, may be substantial.[143] The lack of confirmatory double blind laboratory studies is particularly acute with respect to drugs other than alcohol. However, the few cases that have addressed admissibility in non-alcohol contexts have not focused on this point.

[b] DRE Protocol

As noted above, HGN tests are usually used as part of a longer drug recognition expert (DRE) protocol.[144] The court in *State v. Sampson*,[145] notes

---

141. *Zimmerman*, 693 A.2d at 315.

142. *See* State v. Ito, 90 Hawai'i 225, 978 P.2d 191, 209 (Haw.1999).

143. *See* Honts & Amato–Henderson, *supra* note 98, at 688–89. A false positive is a result that indicates the suspect has used drugs, when in fact he has not. In statistics this is frequently called a Type I error. A false negative result occurs when a test indicates the suspect has not used drugs, when in fact he has. This is sometimes called a Type II error. Because litigation involving drug testing is almost always concerned with the rights of the accused, the cases focus their attention on the probability of false positives. A "false positive" in this context occurs when an officer determines that the suspect is intoxicated when in fact he is not. A false positive may occur either because the suspect has consumed a drug but is not yet legally intoxicated, or because the suspect suffers from nystagmus due to other

causes, e.g., prescription drugs. There is a potential for a second type of false positive in this situation: the officer may conclude the suspect has failed the test when in fact he has passed it.

144. The twelve steps of the DRE protocol are: (1) Breath alcohol test (to verify alcohol was not a factor); (2) Interview of arresting officer by DRE to obtain information about the arrest, actions and statements made by the subject, plus the arresting officer's observations; (3) Preliminary examination and first pulse reading; (4) Eye examination, including nystagmus and convergence tests; (5) Motor skills test, also referred to as divided attention tests or field sobriety tests; (6) Blood pressure, temperature, and second pulse reading; (7) Pupil measurement under four lighting conditions and an "ingestion examination," checking the suspect's nose and mouth for signs of inhalation or smoking; (8) Examination of muscle

that DRE protocols have three major functions: to determine the existence of impairment, to assess whether the cause of the impairment is something other than alcohol or drugs, such as a medical condition, and, if the impairment is caused by drugs, to identify which type of drug most likely produced the impairment.[146]

Several courts have considered whether DRE evidence must pass through the *Frye/Daubert* gate. The *Sampson* opinion reviews recent cases that have considered the issue.[147] *State v. Baity*[148] adopts a position similar to that of earlier cases. Only the nystagmus portion of the protocol is, standing alone, scientific in nature.[149] The court affirmed the trial court conclusion that HGN has achieved general acceptance and set aside the defense argument that the test suffers from a high error rate by saying that this can be shown through cross examination.[150] As to the DRE protocol as a whole, the court concluded that it, as well, had achieved general acceptance in relevant scientific communities.[151]

The *Sampson* court reached a somewhat more guarded conclusion.[152] Two experts testified for the defendant in *Sampson* and both said the DRE had not reached general acceptance in the toxicology community. However, state experts claimed the community considers the protocol to be reliable and valid.[153] The court concluded that "despite the existence of spirited dissent, the DRE protocol has achieved a significant degree of acceptance within the relevant scientific community that weighs in favor of admissibility."[154]

---

rigidity; (9) Inspection for injection sites and third pulse reading; (10) Interrogation, suspect statements, and other observations; (11) Integration of all information as basis for evaluator's opinion; (12) Toxicological examination.

Based on these results, the examiner concludes whether the subject is impaired, if so, whether it is drug related, and the class of drug likely to be causing the impairment. (For example, pupil size is usually normal for depressants but dilated by stimulants.) Usually, a toxicological examination can confirm or rebut the drug classification conclusion. United States v. Everett, 972 F.Supp. 1313, 1316–17 (D.Nev.1997).

145. 167 Or.App. 489, 6 P.3d 543 (Or.Ct. App.2000).

146. *Id.* at 548.

147. *Id.* at 543, 550–51.

148. 140 Wash.2d 1, 991 P.2d 1151 (Wash. 2000).

149. *Id.* at 1157. In *State v. Klawitter*, 518 N.W.2d 577 (Minn.1994), the Minnesota Supreme Court concluded that the protocol as a whole "is not itself a scientific technique but rather a list of the things a prudent, trained and experienced officer should consider before formulating or expressing an opinion whether the subject is under the influence of some controlled substance." *Id.* at 584. The court carved out the HGN and VGN portions of the test, subjected it to *Frye* scrutiny, and said it was admissible. However, it pointed our that the protocol, taken as a whole, works not "to

qualify police officers as scientists but to train officers as observers." *Id.* at 585.

In *Williams v. State*, 710 So.2d 24 (Fla.Dist. Ct.App.1998), the Florida appellate court concluded that the "general portion" of the DRE protocol does not constitute scientific evidence, because the tests and their interpretation are within the common understanding of the lay person. *Id.* at 28. It concluded that the HGN portion of the test was scientific, but because it was not novel science, the test was not subject to greater scrutiny than other parts of the test. *Id.* at 29. The court affirmed admission of the evidence. *Id.* at 37.

See also, People v. Quinn, 153 Misc.2d 139, 580 N.Y.S.2d 818 (Dist.Ct.1991), rev'd on other grounds, 158 Misc.2d 1015, 607 N.Y.S.2d 534 (App.Term 1993) (court assumed DRE protocol was scientific and results admissible).

150. *Baity*, 991 P.2d at 1159.

151. The court included pharmacologists, optometrists, and forensic specialists in defining the relevant communities. *Id.* at 1160.

152. 167 Or.App. 489, 6 P.3d 543 (Or.Ct. App.2000).

153. *Id.* at 553.

154. *Id.* Unlike Washington, Oregon has adopted a version of *Daubert*. *See* the discussion of *O'Key*, *supra*. *See* note 161 *infra* for *Sampson*'s discussion of peer review and publication and error rate. The court also refused to exclude the testimony on Rule 403 grounds. *Id.* at 558.

The only recent federal opinion to consider the issue is *United States v. Everett.*[155] In a case of first impression, the magistrate judge addressed the question of whether the testimony of a drug recognition expert (a Park Service ranger), based on the results of a drug recognition protocol, is scientific evidence governed by *Daubert* and, if so, whether it is admissible.[156]

The court first determined that the ranger's testimony was not scientific. Rather, it was technical in nature and, therefore, not governed by *Daubert*.[157] In light of the Supreme Court's ruling in *Kumho Tire Co. v. Carmichael*,[158] this was wrong. In *Kumho Tire*, the Court held that the trial court must ensure the reliability of all expert testimony, not only that testimony characterized as "scientific." However, the court may use factors other than and in addition to those listed in *Daubert* when making admissibility decisions.[159]

Although the district court in *Everett* concluded that *Daubert* does not control the admissibility of the ranger's testimony, it nevertheless concluded that if the DRE program is found to be "scientific expert testimony" it meets all but possibly one of the *Daubert* factors.[160] The court noted that the weakest link is the potential error rate. Error rate is a complicated issue in this

---

155. 972 F.Supp. 1313 (D.Nev.1997).

156. In *Everett*, a Park Service ranger observed the defendant speeding in the Lake Mead National Recreation Area. He stopped the defendant and noted his eyes were extremely red and his mouth was dry. The ranger questioned the defendant and conducted a series of field sobriety tests. The defendant denied being drunk and this was confirmed by a breath test and the fact that the defendant passed the HGN test. Suspecting that the defendant was under the influence of another drug, the officer took him to the ranger station and conducted a Drug Recognition Evaluation. On the basis of this set of tests the ranger was prepared to testify the defendant was under the influence of marijuana. The defendant argued the testimony was inadmissible on *Daubert* grounds. *Id.* at 1314.

157. *Id.* at 1321. This conclusion depends in part on what the witness is prepared to say.

If the opinion or conclusion is proffered as expert testimony, going to and dispositive of the ultimate issue, that is one use. If it is merely used to find probable cause for the DRE to arrest the subject and require a toxicological exam, that is another use. This Court finds that the DRE can testify to the probabilities, based upon his or her observations and clinical findings, but cannot testify, by way of scientific opinion, that the conclusion is an established fact by any reasonable scientific standard. In other words, the otherwise qualified DRE cannot testify as to scientific knowledge, but can as to "specialized knowledge which will assist the trier of fact to understand the evidence." *Id.* at 1319–20.

It is not clear from this passage what the expert can say. Apparently, the expert can express an opinion as to the probability that

the defendant was under the influence of a particular drug, but not that this opinion reflects a scientific fact. *Id.* at 1324–25.

158. 526 U.S. 137, 119 S.Ct. 1167, 143 L.Ed.2d 238 (1999).

159. The trial court must have the same kind of latitude in deciding how to test an expert's reliability, and to decide whether or when special briefing or other proceedings are needed to investigate reliability, as it enjoys when it decides whether or not that expert's relevant testimony is reliable. Our opinion in *Joiner* makes clear that a court of appeals is to apply an abuse-of-discretion standard when it "review[s] a trial court's decision to admit or exclude expert testimony." 522 U.S. at 138–39. That standard applies as much to the trial court's decisions about how to determine reliability as to its ultimate conclusion. Otherwise, the trial judge would lack the discretionary authority needed both to avoid unnecessary "reliability" proceedings in ordinary cases where the reliability of an expert's methods is properly taken for granted, and to require appropriate proceedings in the less usual or more complex cases where cause for questioning the expert's reliability arises. Indeed, the Rules seek to avoid "unjustifiable expense and delay" as part of their search for "truth" and the "jus[t] determin[ation]" of proceedings. Fed. Rule Evid. 102. Thus, whether Daubert's specific factors are, or are not, reasonable measures of reliability in a particular case is a matter that the law grants the trial judge broad latitude to determine. *Kumho Tire*, 526 U.S. at 152–53. *See* Joiner, 522 U.S. at 143.

160. 972 F.Supp. at 1321. The court reviewed DRE protocols in terms of testability, peer review, general acceptance, potential error rate, and whether the protocol was developed in the shadow of litigation. *Id.* at 1322–26.

context. Laboratory studies produce relatively low error rates in an examiner's ability to identify a class of drugs, but these results are not easily translated into the field. Field studies themselves are compromised in several ways. For example, the suspect often confesses to using a certain drug, contaminating the officer's ability to make a blind assessment.[161] It is not even always clear which error rate is at stake. One relevant error rate is the ability of the examiner to identify the class of drugs ingested by the suspect. As the court notes, this process is similar to what a physician does when conducting a differential diagnosis.[162] Examined from this perspective, we probably know a good deal more about the error rate associated with DRE protocols' ability to identify the type of drug ingested than we do about many differential diagnoses in which the physician attempts to identify a cause for the patient's condition.

The accuracy with which a DRE can identify a class of drugs is important but as the court notes, is rarely the key issue. The statutes in question generally require a finding of being under the influence of "a drug or drugs" and do not require a specific drug identification.[163] Moreover, the DRE's conclusion as to the particular drug ingested is usually confirmed or rebutted by a chemical toxicological test. The error rate that is most relevant is the examiner's conclusion that the defendant was legally impaired due to drug ingestion. Unlike alcohol, where studies have established a correlation between the amount of alcohol in the system and the extent of impairment, the correlation between drug levels and impairment is not well established.[164] Thus, an officer's assessment that the driver was legally impaired cannot be confirmed by a drug test. As the court notes, "apart from and beyond the question of admissibility of the officers testimony regarding the administration of the DRE tests, lies the question of whether the results of the test demonstrate impairment and not mere use."[165] Here, apparently, there is less evidence concerning error rates associated with any level of performance on the protocol. Even were we to have better data, however, there is still the difficult policy decision as to what constitutes an acceptable rate of error, especially false positive error.

The admissibility of drug evaluation protocol results is but one of many areas where the courts are wrestling with the problem of the proper scope of

161. As discussed in the *Sampson* opinion, the literature on the DRE protocol is quite limited. 167 Or.App. 489, 6 P.3d 543, 555 (Or. Ct.App.2000). An original study in Los Angeles by the developers of the protocol found that officers correctly identified someone as impaired 94% of the time and correctly identified the substance 79% of the time. A second 1994 Arizona study found that impairment identifications were correct 91% of the time. Neither of these studies were double blinded, however. A third study at Johns Hopkins was a double blind test using part of the protocol. It found a 92% success rate. The results of none of these studies were published in a peer review journal. One final study was published in such a journal (the Journal of Analytical Toxicology). In this study the DRE officers' success rate was only 51%. The *Sampson* court notes, however, that in the study the researchers did not

use the entire protocol, subjects were given lower than normal doses of drugs, the study was not double blind, the researchers intentionally misled the officers regarding the drugs they would encounter, and the study contained only 18 subjects. *Id.* The *Sampson* court concluded that a sufficient specialized literature exists to satisfy the peer review and publication factor. *Id.* at 556. Moreover, the problem of false positive errors that may occur with respect to the first 11 steps of the protocol will normally be corrected by toxicology results from step 12. *Id.* at 555.

162. 972 F.Supp. at 1322.

163. *Id.*

164. *Id.* at 1317.

165. *Id.* at 1318.

Daubert and *Kumho* and the safeguards that should be placed on testimony for which there is no good error rate data. A clearer picture of the final solution awaits the development of the case law.

[2] Fit

The potentially large false positive rate raises the question of what conclusions an officer should be allowed to draw from a failed nystagmus test or a failed drug recognition evaluation. As discussed in *Daubert*, this is a question of "fit." "[S]cientific validity for one purpose is not necessarily scientific validity for other, unrelated purposes."[166]

Nystagmus and protocol evidence may be admitted for several different purposes: as probable cause for arrest; as evidence of neurological dysfunction; as evidence that the defendant was driving under the influence of intoxicants; and as evidence as to the defendant's level of intoxication. This last type of testimony points out an important difference between alcohol impairment and drug impairment cases. In order to convict someone for driving while intoxicated, the prosecution must prove the defendant's blood alcohol content was above some threshold, most frequently .10. Courts must resolve, therefore, whether the expert can testify, based on HGN tests alone or in combination with other field tests, that the suspect's BAC was above the minimum threshold. A number of states have answered this question in the negative. In *State v. O'Key*,[167] the court held that HGN evidence is admissible to establish that a person was under the influence of alcohol, but not to establish the individual's blood alcohol level. Likewise, in *State v. Superior Court*,[168] although the court found HGN test results to be admissible as to the defendant's intoxication, they are not admissible to prove a blood alcohol concentration above .10.[169] The Arizona Supreme Court clarified the role of HGN tests in the absence of blood in *Hamilton v. City Court*, and in the process seemed to describe an even narrower role for HGN testimony.[170] In the absence of any chemical tests, HGN results are admissible only to permit the officer to testify that "based on his training and experience the results indicated possible neurological dysfunction, one cause of which could be alcohol ingestion."[171]

In the drug context, HGN is only one part of a battery of field sobriety

---

166. Daubert v. Merrell Dow Pharmaceuticals, Inc., 509 U.S. at 591. See Chapter 1 and the Epidemiology Chapter for a fuller discussion of "fit."

167. 321 Or. 285, 899 P.2d 663 (Or.1995).

168. 149 Ariz. 269, 718 P.2d 171 (Ariz. 1986).

169. "The arresting officer's 'reading' of the HGN test cannot be verified or duplicated by an independent party. The test's recognized margin of error provides problems as to criminal convictions which require proof of guilt beyond a reasonable doubt. The circumstances under which the test is administered at roadside may affect the reliability of the test results. Nystagmus may be caused by conditions other than alcohol intoxication. And finally, the far more accurate chemical testing devices are readily available." *Id.* at 181. *See, e.g.,* State v. Bresson, 51 Ohio St.3d 123, 554 N.E.2d 1330, 1336 (Ohio 1990) (officer may not give an opinion as to the driver's actual BAC); State v. Garrett, 119 Idaho 878, 811 P.2d 488, 491 (Idaho 1991) ("HGN test results may not be used at trial to establish the defendant's blood alcohol level in the absence of chemical analysis of the defendant's blood, breath, or urine.").

170. 165 Ariz. 514, 799 P.2d 855 (Ariz. 1990).

171. *Id.* at 860.

tests given by arresting officers.[172] If a trained drug recognition officer concludes that the suspect has failed the protocol, what should the officer be allowed to say on the stand? Conviction of impaired driving due to a substance other than alcohol generally does not require proof of a threshold blood concentration. Perhaps for this reason, courts have been more liberal in allowing officers to testify to the defendant's impairment in drug cases. For example, in *People v. Quinn*,[173] the defendant submitted to the drug influence protocol administered by an officer who was a trained DRE.[174] As part of the protocol, the officer administered both a horizontal and a vertical gaze nystagmus test.[175] No nystagmus was observable, but the officer noted that the defendant was unable to focus her attention on the stimulus. The defendant did fail a number of "divided attention" tests.[176] The defendant challenged the admissibility, under *Frye*, of the officer's testimony concerning 1) the drug influence protocol as a whole, 2) the horizontal gaze nystagmus component of the test, and 3) the officer's qualifications to administer the test and give his opinion at trial. In a lengthy admissibility hearing the court heard evidence from prosecution experts that psychoactive drugs could be classified according to their most observable effects and that based on the results of the protocol a trained individual could "diagnose" the category of drugs taken by an individual with a substantial degree of accuracy.[177] The experts also testified as to the training received by the DRE officer (somewhat in excess of 72 hours).[178] The court held that both the HGN test and the DRE protocol meet the *Frye* standard. Moreover, the court held that the officer "may testify as to the observations he made while testing defendant and give his opinion that she was impaired by cocaine. . . ."[179]

State v. Klawitter,[180] presented a similar question: whether a DRE would be allowed to give an opinion, based on the 12–step drug recognition protocol as to whether the suspect was impaired? The Supreme Court of Minnesota concluded that the DRE could testify that in his opinion the defendant was under the influence of cannabis (marijuana). As in the *Quinn* case, the defendant admitted to the officer that he had taken drugs (marijuana). Unlike, *Quinn*, however, there was no confirmatory drug test.[181] Nevertheless, the court permitted the DRE to give his opinion, based on the results of the

---

172. State v. Klawitter, 518 N.W.2d 577 (Minn.1994).

173. 153 Misc.2d 139, 580 N.Y.S.2d 818 (N.Y.App.Div.1991).

174. During part of the examination, the officer asked the defendant whether she was taking any medication or drugs, to which she responded, "Just coke." *Quinn*, 580 N.Y.S.2d at 819. A subsequent blood test confirmed that she had ingested cocaine as well as diazepam (Valium). *Id.* at 820.

175. A vertical test is the same as the horizontal test except that the stimulus is moved vertically.

176. One of these tests involved taking nine steps down a line on the floor by placing the heal of one foot directly in front of the toe of the other with one's arms at one's side. The

defendant was unable to do this without stepping off the line repeatedly.

177. The state's experts discussed a frequently cited field test conducted in Los Angeles on 173 arrestees. In 94% of the cases in which the DRE opined that an individual was impaired, a drug was found in a fluid sample obtained from the individual. *Quinn*, 580 N.Y.S.2d at 825. As reported in State v. Klawitter, 518 N.W.2d 577 at 581, 79% of the time the DRE correctly identified the specific type of drug.

178. 580 N.Y.S.2d at 828.

179. *Id.*

180. 518 N.W.2d 577.

181. The defendant agreed to provide a urine sample, but apparently was unable to do so. *Id.* at 580.

test, that the defendant was under the influence of marijuana.[182]

In *State v. Sampson*,[183] another DUI case, the appellate court affirmed the trial judge's decision that the procedure and results of the DRE protocol are admissible to show that a defendant was under the influence of a controlled substance.[184] It does not address the question of whether the expert could say more. In *State v. Baity*,[185] however, the court explicitly limited the scope of permitted testimony.

> We emphasize, however, that our opinion today is confined to situations where all 12–steps of the protocol have been undertaken. Moreover, an officer may not testify in a fashion that casts an aura of scientific certainty to the testimony. The officer also may not predict the specific level of drugs present in a suspect. The DRE officer, properly qualified, may express an opinion that a suspect's behavior and physical attributes are or are not consistent with the behavioral and physical signs associated with certain categories of drugs.[186]

Apparently no court has yet held that the results of an HGN test alone would be sufficient to permit an officer to testify that a defendant was legally impaired by a controlled substance.

§ 9–1.3 General Technique

Even when a procedure is premised on theories or principles that are scientifically valid (under a *Daubert* test) or have achieved general acceptance (under a *Frye* test), it may be called into question because of the way the general principle is implemented. In *United States v. Pierre*,[187] the Seventh Circuit suggested a number of approaches that might be taken to ascertain whether a laboratory employs acceptable procedures:

> A court could ask whether the lab's procedures are well designed to yield reliable results. It could arrange for retesting of the samples. If the original specimens are no longer available, a court could inquire whether this lab, in particular, produces reliable results. Such an exercise entails statistical methods. The court needed information on the error rate of PharmChem, the lab that analyzed Pierre's samples.... We assume that reputable labs collect such information, putting samples through their tests on a double-blind basis to find out how frequently their employees err and to learn how to improve their procedures. Pierre might have sought this information from PharmChem. Or perhaps, before engaging a laboratory or renewing its contract, the government submits an assortment of samples containing different drugs (and the statistically appropriate number of samples known not to be contaminated) to see how well the lab distinguishes among them.... If neither PharmChem nor the nor the Executive Branch of government collects this information, Pierre could have asked the district court to distrust PharmChem's reports until the United States put the lab to such a test.[188]

182. *Id.*

183. 167 Or.App. 489, 6 P.3d 543 (Or.Ct. App.2000).

184. 6 P.3d at 558.

185. 140 Wash.2d 1, 991 P.2d 1151 (Wash. 2000).

186. *Id.* at 1160–61.

187. 47 F.3d 241 (7th Cir.1995).

188. *Id.* at 243. The court noted, however, that the existing record offered no reason to believe that the procedures of the lab were unreliable.

As the quoted passage suggests, many cases in this area turn on assessments of error rates, that is, the likelihood that a given procedure will produce an unacceptably high number of "false positive" results. Other cases focus on more mundane questions concerning the chain of custody.

§ 9–1.3.1 EMIT and Other Preliminary Tests

A frequent issue in drug testing cases is whether a given test should, by itself, be sufficient to lead to an adverse legal consequence for the person tested. In the past, this issue was frequently litigated with respect to the use of a single, unconfirmed EMIT test to prove that the suspect took a controlled substance. Some courts held that a single test, unconfirmed by a follow up test is insufficient to support a disciplinary action against a suspect. In *Ferguson v. State Dep't of Corrections*,[189] the Alaska Supreme Court held that an inmate was denied due process when he was withdrawn from a prison industries program immediately after an unconfirmed positive urine EMIT test. The district court in *Jones v. McKenzie*[190] held that the termination of a school bus attendant on the basis of a single EMIT test was arbitrary and capricious, violating the requirements of the Board of Education.[191]

More frequently, courts have concluded that testimony based on a single EMIT test is admissible.[192] Most of these cases, however, involve prison discipline or probation revocation proceedings. A sub-group of the probation cases expressly adopt a lower admissibility threshold. For example, in *In re Johnston*[193] the Washington Supreme Court adopted a "some evidence" standard of admissibility in prison disciplinary hearings.[194] A single failed EMIT test result is some evidence of drug use and, therefore, admissible. The use of this evidence to revoke good time credits does not violate due process. The test results would be admissible even if testimony based on a single positive EMIT test did not meet the *Frye* general acceptance standard.[195] Courts that

---

189. 816 P.2d 134 (Alaska 1991).

190. 628 F.Supp. 1500 (D.D.C.1986).

191. 628 F.Supp. at 1506. In *United States v. Johnston*, 41 M.J. 13 (C.M.A.1994), the defendant offered a "negative" radioimmunoassay (RIA) test of his urine as evidence tending to rebut a charge of marijuana use. The test did in fact show the presence of marijuana metabolites, but at a level below the relatively conservative threshold necessary for a test to be called "positive." The military judge found that a single RIA test is not "a method reasonably relied upon by experts in this particular field to determine the presence or absence of the metabolites of THC by itself, but only in conjunction with further tests ordinarily used under the Department of Defense regulations, that is, the GC/MS [Gas Chromatography/Mass Spectrometry] test." *Id.* at 14–15. Nevertheless, the judge concluded that the evidence was marginally relevant under Rule of Evidence 402. At the time military courts were operating within the confines of *United States v. Arguello*, 29 M.J. 198 (C.M.A.1989), which held on different facts that when the defense introduced a "negative test" (a test showing the presence of a metabolite, but a level below the

"positive" threshold), the government could never rebut the evidence by indicating that the test did show trace amounts of the metabolite. Because of this rule, the military judge excluded the evidence on 403 grounds. The *Johnston* court ended such foolishness by overruling *Arguello*. 41 M.J. at 16.

192. *See* Bourgeois v. Murphy, 119 Idaho 611, 809 P.2d 472 (Idaho 1991) for a discussion of cases going both ways on this question. The *Bourgeois* court expressed doubt as to the adequacy of a single EMIT test, but did not reach the issue because it determined that the defendant correctional facility failed to establish the chain of custody of the prisoner's specimen.

193. 109 Wash.2d 493, 745 P.2d 864 (Wash. 1987) (en banc).

194. *See* Cathryn Jo Rosen, *The Fourth Amendment Implications of Urine Testing For Evidence of Drug Use In Probation*, 55 Brook. L. Rev. 1159 (1990).

195. *See, e.g.*, State v. Ferguson, 72 Ohio App.3d 714, 595 N.E.2d 1011, 1014 (Ohio Ct. App.1991) (the rules of evidence, with the exception of privilege, do not apply to probation revocation proceedings.); Head v. State, 1994

do not specifically announce a special standard for revocation and prison discipline cases also are reluctant to exclude a single unconfirmed EMIT test on general acceptance or scientific validity grounds.[196]

Relatively few recent cases have raised this issue, in part because it is now standard practice to follow an initial screening test with a more accurate follow-up test. For example, in *Nevada Employment Security Dep't v. Holmes*,[197] discussed above, the testing laboratory first tested the individual's hair using a radioimmunoassay hair analysis ("RIA"). In the event of a positive result, a confirmatory gas chromatography/mass spectrometry ("GC/MS") test was performed. If this test also yielded a positive result, the result is reported to the employer. In the *Holmes* case, because of some concerns regarding the chain of custody of the original hair sample, Holmes was tested a second time. Both pairs of tests were positive.[198]

However, the single test question still arises occasionally. In the *Bush* case, the defendant argued that hair analysis should be used only as a confirmatory test for drugs because as implemented its error rate was unknown and because there was insufficient and incomplete documentation of the procedure used in this case. The court rejected each of these arguments.[199]

In *Anderson v. McKune*,[200] a prison inmate challenged disciplinary action taken after he failed a Roche Abuscreen On–Trak drug test (ONTRAK) for barbiturates. He alleged that ONTRAK was unreliable. The district court agreed, granted the prisoner's habeas corpus petition and prohibited the Department of Correction from basing disciplinary actions on the test unless the results were confirmed by a laboratory gas chromatography mass spectrometry test (GC/MS). The ONTRAK test uses a latex agglutination immunoassay technique to test for barbiturates. A urine sample is mixed with an antibody reagent on a test slide. If no barbiturates are detected in the urine sample, the latex reagent forms large particles and the smooth milky appearance of the mixture is changed to include white particles. If sufficient barbiturate levels are in the urine sample, the conjugation is prevented and the mixture remains unchanged.[201] The trial court focused on various notations in the scientific literature identifying ONTRAK as a preliminary test that should be confirmed with a GC/MS test. Moreover, the prison system used ONTRAK only as a preliminary test on its own employees and confirmed

---

WL 520047 (Ark.Ct.App.1994) (court need not determine whether tests meet evidentiary requirements because the rules of evidence are not strictly applicable to revocation proceedings); Higgs v. Bland, 888 F.2d 443 (6th Cir. 1989), appeal after remand, 940 F.2d 664 (6th Cir.1991) (single EMIT test meets "some evidence" standard).

196. Smith v. State, 250 Ga. 438, 298 S.E.2d 482 (Ga.1983); Vasquez v. Coughlin, 118 A.D.2d 897, 499 N.Y.S.2d 461 (N.Y.App. Div.1986). *See also* Jackson v. State, 198 Ga. App. 261, 401 S.E.2d 289 (Ga.Ct.App.1990) (a rare non-prisoner case supporting the admissibility of an unconfirmed immunoassay test for marijuana on somewhat unique facts). The validity of single EMIT tests rarely arises in non-probation cases, perhaps because many states

have statutes requiring confirmatory tests after a positive EMIT test.

197. 112 Nev. 275, 914 P.2d 611 (Nev. 1996).

198. *Id.* at 613. *See also* Goebel v. Warner Transportation, 612 N.W.2d 18 (S.D.2000) (In a case involving the denial of workers' compensation coverage, experts were allowed to testify that plaintiff's use of controlled substances was a substantial factor in causing a truck accident. The testimony was based on an EMIT test followed by a Gas Chromatography–Mass Spectroscopy (GC/MS) test.).

199. 47 M.J. at 311 (C.A.A.F.1997).

200. 23 Kan.App.2d 803, 937 P.2d 16 (Kan. Ct.App.1997).

201. *Id.* at 18.

any positive result with a GC/MS test. Finally, the court noted the subjective nature of the test, whether the mixture's appearance remained milky.

Addressing only the due process issues raised by the habeas petition, the court of appeals reversed. It noted that the inmate claiming violation of his constitutional rights in a habeas proceeding carries the burden of proof.[202] Rights are not denied if the disciplinary decision is supported by "some evidence." Because the district court found the ONTRAK result did provide some evidence of barbiturate use, the inquiry should have ended at that point.[203]

Like many of the cases admitting a single preliminary test result, *Anderson* is best understood as prison discipline case.[204] The "some evidence" standard may support a disciplinary decision based on a test that by itself would not be admissible under a *Frye* or a *Daubert* standard. It would be unlikely for a court to permit an expert to testify as to drug use solely on the basis of an ONTRAK test outside the prison discipline context.

The relevance of *Daubert* recently arose in *United States v. Stumpf.*[205] The government proceeded to revoke Stumpf's supervised release based on a positive test for the use of methamphetamine. The results came from Pharm-Chem sweat patches that the defendant apparently was required to wear. The defendant made an *in limine* motion to exclude these results as scientifically unsound and therefore inadmissible under FRE 702.[206] Federal Rules of Evidence do not apply to supervised release revocation proceedings.[207] The court was unable to find authority that addresses the question as to whether *Daubert* is applicable in this situation.[208] Nevertheless, the court looked to *Daubert* for guidance and found that patch was reliable.[209] It concluded that the device had been tested, it had been the subject of several peer review articles, and had a low error rate.[210]

The question of false positives arose in a somewhat different context in *Wood v. State Personnel Board.*[211] The plaintiff, a former employee of the Department of Corrections, objected to his discharge following a positive drug test. He argued that the Department of Corrections 50–nanogram-per-milliliter standard for a positive test on a marijuana screen established too low a threshold.[212] He noted that the federal standard was 100–nanogram-per-milliliter. The court rejected this argument. It noted that Wood failed to present any evidence that a more stringent standard would have excluded the possibility of a positive test due to inadvertent or unknowing ingestion.[213]

---

202. *Id.* at 19.

203. *Id.* at 20. The court reached the same result in another ONTRAK case, Crutchfield v. Hannigan, 21 Kan.App.2d 693, 906 P.2d 184 (Kan.Ct.App.1995).

204. *See* discussion on p. 522–23 of the first edition of this Treatise.

205. 54 F.Supp.2d 972 (D.Nev.1999).

206. *Id.* at 973.

207. Fed.R.Evid. 1101(d)(3).

208. 54 F.Supp.2d at 973.

209. *Id.* at 974.

210. *Id.* The court sidestepped the question of whether the device had been tested with respect to methamphetamine. It noted the patch had proven highly reliable as a test for the use of cocaine in particular, "and there is no sufficient evidence suggesting that the results for methamphetamine would be any different." *Id.* This observation does appear to raise a question of "fit," but again one must be cautious in generalizing cases such as this to other non-prisoner contexts. *See* State v. Setler, 1998 WL 684246 (Ohio Ct.App.).

211. 705 So.2d 413 (Ala.Civ.App.1997).

212. *Id.* at 418.

213. *Id.*

Moreover, it noted that at least one other jurisdiction had adopted the 50–nanogram-per-milliliter standard.[214]

Testing procedures that involve more than a single EMIT test are almost always found to be admissible, especially if the second test uses a different process.[215] For example, a federal district court granted summary judgment for the prison system in a § 1983 case challenging a testing procedure in which an initial positive EMIT test would be followed by a confirmatory test if the inmate claimed the first test produced a false positive result.[216]

One of the more thorough early discussions of EMIT tests is found in *Peranzo v. Coughlin*.[217] Inmates in New York state prisons moved for a preliminary injunction barring the use of EMIT urinalysis drug test results as the "sole basis" for demonstrating narcotics use in prisoner disciplinary proceedings or parole determinations. Judge Sands held extensive hearings on the reliability of the New York practice of using double EMIT tests, i.e., the same test done twice on a sample, before disciplining an inmate. He cited studies that suggest a single EMIT test may produce an error rate as high as 25%.[218] The court ordered a trial on the merits to determine, among other things, the accuracy of double EMIT tests. In a subsequent opinion in the same litigation, the district court concluded that, "with a 98+% rate of accuracy, the double EMIT testing as performed by DOCS is sufficiently reliable so that the use of the results as evidence, even as the only evidence, in a disciplinary hearing does not offend due process. We further find that the introduction of the results as an element to be considered in parole decisions does not offend due process."[219]

Brown v. Smith is a rare case concluding that double EMIT tests are insufficient.[220] It required the officials at the Attica Correctional Facility to adopt an alternative method of analysis to confirm the initial EMIT results. However, Brown was effectively overruled by *Lahey v. Kelly*, approving a double EMIT procedure.[221]

Despite the courts' reluctance to require a second confirmatory test using a procedure different from EMIT, such a procedure does have merit. A substantial proportion of false positives are due to random testing errors, and a second EMIT test is likely to catch many of these. However, some false positives are systematic errors unique to immunoassay tests, e.g., antibody cross-reactivity with some drugs. Repeating the same test may simply reproduce the same false positive result.[222] Systematic errors are more easily

214. *See* Major v. Cintas/Red Stick, 665 So.2d 153, 155 (La.Ct.App.1995).

215. *See, e.g.,* Wykoff v. Resig, 613 F.Supp. 1504 (N.D.Ind.1985) (EMIT test followed by confirmatory "Thin Layer Chromatography" test).

216. Jensen v. Lick, 589 F.Supp. 35, 39 (N.D.1984).

217. 608 F.Supp. 1504 (S.D.N.Y.1985).

218. *Id.* at 1511.

219. 675 F.Supp. 102, 105 (S.D.N.Y.1987). *See also* Spence v. Farrier, 807 F.2d 753, 756 (8th Cir.1986) (EMIT test with confirmatory second test contains sufficient indicia of reliability to provide some evidence of drug use);

Acuna v. Lewis, 937 F.2d 611 (9th Cir.1991); Weatherly v. Goord, 701 N.Y.S.2d 675, 268 A.D.2d 641 (N.Y.App.Div.2000); Garcia v. Goord, 273 A.D.2d 560, 710 N.Y.S.2d 133 (N.Y.App.Div.2000).

220. 132 Misc.2d 686, 505 N.Y.S.2d 743 (N.Y.App.Div.1985).

221. 71 N.Y.2d 135, 524 N.Y.S.2d 30, 518 N.E.2d 924 (N.Y.App.Div.1987).

222. This produces a problem of "construct validity." One cannot distinguish between results due to the underlying cause (drugs) and results due to the method being used to detect the cause (systematic errors in a given immunoassay technique). *See generally,* Joseph

uncovered if initial EMIT results are confirmed by an alternative chemical test.

Unfortunately, in some states there is little systematic knowledge concerning drug testing laboratory error rates. The American Society of Crime Laboratory Directors (ASCLD) and the ASCLD Laboratory Accreditation Board have recommended that all laboratories perform periodic mandatory proficiency testing as a requirement for accreditation as DNA typing facilities.[223] If similar proficiency testing proposals were uniformly adopted in the drug testing area, it would be possible to ascertain error rates in various laboratories.[224]

§ 9–1.3.2   Chain of Custody

Chain of custody questions are not unique to scientific evidence. However, custody issues are an integral part of the admissibility of drug test results. If the proffering party fails to lay a proper foundation for the expert's testimony by demonstrating that a specimen did indeed come from the accused and then accounting for each successive step in handling a specimen, the expert's testimony may be inadmissible. On the other hand, courts are willing to admit testimony concerning test results when gaps in the chain of custody are not so severe as to undermine all probative value.[225] A few cases provide an overview of the types of issues that may arise.

Bourgeois v. Murphy[226] is an example of a fatal chain of custody gap. The plaintiff, an inmate in an Idaho correctional facility, appealed the imposition of discipline for drug use. The prison system's failure to maintain written documentation concerning the chain of custody of the petitioner's urine sample was a denial of due process.[227]

Blappert v. Dep't of Police,[228] involved the dismissal of a police officer subsequent to a positive test for marijuana. The officer denied using the drug and contended that his specimen had been switched inadvertently with that of someone else. He did not observe a label being attached to the sample and testified it was placed on a crowded counter with a large number of other samples. The technician who collected the specimen was no longer with the testing lab, and no other official from the laboratory testified regarding collection procedures. Under these facts, the court held that there was no

Sanders, *Scientific Validity, Admissibility, and Mass Torts After Daubert*, 78 Minn. L. Rev. 1387, 1402 (1994).

223. Margaret A. Berger, *Evidentiary Framework, in* Federal Judicial Center, Reference Manual of Scientific Evidence 39–117 (1995).

224. *See* Michael J. Saks & Jonathan J. Koehler, *What DNA "Fingerprinting" Can Teach the Law About the Rest of Forensic Science*, 13 Cardozo L. Rev. 361, 368–69 (1991).

225. *See* Paul C. Giannelli, *Chain of Custody and the Handling of Real Evidence*, 20 Am. Crim. L. Rev. 527 (1983); Kenneth J. Hanko, *Chain of Custody and Laboratory Reports in Drug Prosecutions: A Comparative Analysis of Military and Federal Case Law*, 2 Whittier L. Rev. 213 (1980).

226. 119 Idaho 611, 809 P.2d 472 (Idaho 1991).

227. *Id.* at 482. A lack of documentation may not always prove fatal if there is other evidence establishing the chain of custody. *See Wykoff*, 613 F.Supp. at 1513 (Although chain of custody of prisoner's urine sample was not documented in writing, testimony, which established whereabouts of sample from moment it was taken until it was tested, demonstrated that handling of urine sample was adequate so as to afford prisoner due process, absent any evidence that sample was tampered with while unattended.).

228. 647 So.2d 1339 (La.Ct.App.1994).

proper foundation for introducing the test results. Without the drug test there was no legal basis for termination and the officer was reinstated with back pay.[229]

In *Crisco v. State*,[230] the officer testified he purchased a substance from the defendant, placed it in a plastic bag, placed the bag in an envelope to which he attached an evidence submission form on which he described the substance as "one bag of off white powder substance." However, the state crime laboratory report concerning the contents of the envelope described it as "one triangular piece of plastic containing a tan rock-like substance." The court held that the state failed to prove the drug tested was properly authenticated and reversed the conviction for the delivery of methamphetamine. The different descriptions were sufficient to undermine reasonable probability there had been no tampering with or substitution of evidence. Less egregious flaws in the chain of custody do not generally lead to exclusion or a ruling that an adverse outcome based on the test results is a denial of due process.[231] For example, in *Williamson v. Police Board of the City of Chicago*,[232] the court held that in the absence of a tangible suggestion of alteration, the chain of custody of a drug tested urine sample was not broken by the lack of testimony from an officer whose duty it was to transport the specimen from the police property department to the testing laboratory.[233] These "weak links" are frequently said to go to the weight to be given the evidence, not its admissibility.[234]

229. In *Green v. Alabama Power Co.,* 597 So.2d 1325 (Ala.1992), results of blood test indicating plaintiff's decedent had taken cocaine were not admitted due to a break in the chain of custody. Items arriving at the toxicology lab did not correspond exactly to those packaged. "Where a weak link in the chain of custody is found, the weight and credit afforded the evidence, rather than its admissibility, [are] questioned. Where a break in the chain of custody, or a 'missing link' in the chain of custody is shown, the admissibility of the evidence is questioned." *Id.* at 1329.

230. 328 Ark. 388, 943 S.W.2d 582 (Ark. 1997).

231. *See* Saldana v. Coombe, 241 A.D.2d 584, 660 N.Y.S.2d 77 (N.Y.App.Div.1997); Cain v. Jefferson Parish Dep't of Fleet Management, 701 So.2d 1059 (La.Ct.App.1997); Wood v. State Personnel Board, 705 So.2d 413 (Ala.Ct. App.1997); Jordan v. State, 223 Ga.App. 176, 477 S.E.2d 583 (Ga.Ct.App.1996); LoCicero v. Jefferson Parish Dep't of Fleet Management, 722 So.2d 1205 (La.Ct.App.1998); United States v. Brown, 52 M.J. 565 (A.Ct.Crim.App. 1999); People v. Cleveland, 273 A.D.2d 787, 709 N.Y.S.2d 751 (N.Y.App.Div.2000); Sanders v. State, 243 Ga.App. 216, 534 S.E.2d 78 (Ga. Ct.App.2000); McChristian v. State, 70 Ark. App. 514, 20 S.W.3d 461 (Ark.Ct.App.2000). The *McChristian* court distinguished its facts from those in *Crisco*:

Here, the officer described the contents of the evidence envelope as "six rocks" and the chemist's report described it as "a hard off-

white rock-like substance." While in the *Crisco* case there was a difference in descriptions of the color and texture of the substance (white powder substance versus tan rock-like substance), here the difference is only in a specific number of rocks versus a reference to "a hard off white rock-like substance." We view differences in these descriptions, at most, as conflicts in evidence properly weighed by the finder of fact rather than as a failure to prove the authenticity of the cocaine. 20 S.W.3d at 464–65.

232. 182 Ill.App.3d 304, 130 Ill.Dec. 729, 537 N.E.2d 1058 (Ill.App.Ct.1989).

233. *See also* Satchell v. Coughlin, 178 A.D.2d 795, 577 N.Y.S.2d 696 (N.Y.App.Div. 1991). *See* ANDRE A. MOENSSENS ET AL., SCIENTIFIC EVIDENCE IN CIVIL AND CRIMINAL CASES 864–866 (4th ed.1995) for a collection of earlier chain of custody cases involving drug and alcohol testing.

234. As the court in Ballou v. Henri Studios, Inc., 656 F.2d 1147, 1154–55 (5th Cir. 1981):

It is firmly established in this Circuit that the question whether the proponent of evidence has proved an adequate chain of custody goes to the weight rather than the admissibility of the evidence, and is thus reserved for the jury.... Under Fed.R.Evid. 901, once the proponent of the evidence meets the threshold requirement of showing that "in reasonable probability the article has not been changed in any important respect from

A related question that arises in probation revocation cases is whether the written records of a testing laboratory are sufficient to prove the results of a test. In *United States v. Pierre*,[235] the Seventh Circuit noted that the rules of evidence do not apply, and the district judge could rely on written reports of medical tests. The defendant, however, was entitled to go beneath the report and subpoena the laboratory technician.[236]

§ 9–1.3.3 Procedures Mandated by Statute

Many states have enacted statutes that partially govern the admissibility of drug and alcohol tests. These laws generally direct courts to admit evidence of the amount of alcohol or drugs in the breath or blood of individuals operating a motor vehicle.[237] Some states also have legislated in the area of employment testing.[238] The statutes typically provide that the evidence is admissible if performed in accordance with prescribed testing procedures. These provisions generally cover issues of chain of custody and quality control procedures within the laboratory. For example, the Florida statute requires the following:

No laboratory may analyze initial or confirmation drug specimens unless:

1. The laboratory is licensed and approved by the Agency for Health Care Administration using criteria established by the National Institute on Drug Abuse as guidelines for modeling the state drug-testing program.

2. The laboratory has written procedures to ensure chain of custody.

3. The laboratory follows proper quality control procedures, including, but not limited to:

  a. The use of internal quality controls including the use of samples of known concentrations which are used to check the performance and calibration of testing equipment, and periodic use of blind samples for overall accuracy.

  b. An internal review and certification process for drug test results, conducted by a person qualified to perform that function in the testing laboratory.

its original condition," United States v. Albert, 595 F.2d 283, 290 (5th Cir.1979), any doubts raised concerning the possibility of alteration or contamination of the evidence go to the weight and not the admissibility of the evidence.

See also State v. Blevins, 36 Ohio App.3d 147, 521 N.E.2d 1105 (Ohio Ct.App.1987) (breaks in chain of custody go to weight); Levi v. State, 809 S.W.2d 668, 672 (Tex.Ct.App. 1991) (any discrepancy in the source or positive identity of the physical evidence is for the fact-finder to resolve.); Goodwin v. State, 208 Ga.App. 707, 431 S.E.2d 473 (Ga.Ct.App.1993) (same); United States v. Ladd, 885 F.2d 954 (1st Cir.1989); Brooks v. State, 761 So.2d 944 (Miss.Ct.App.2000) (The test of whether there has been a proper showing of the chain of custody is whether there is any reasonable inference of tampering with or substitution of evidence. Small breaks in the chain are not sufficient to raise an inference of tampering.).

235. 47 F.3d 241 (7th Cir.1995).

236. Harris v. United States, 612 A.2d 198 (D.C.1992) (probation violation reports equated with records admitted pursuant to the business records exception to the hearsay rule and, therefore, bear recognized indicia of reliability); United States v. Bell, 785 F.2d 640 (8th Cir.1986); United States v. Pratt, 52 F.3d 671 (7th Cir.1995) (probation officer's report of defendant's urine test admissible); United States v. McCormick, 54 F.3d 214 (5th Cir.1995).

237. *See, e.g.,* N.Y. Vehicle & Traffic Law § 1195 (McKinney 1995); Mo. Rev. Stat. § 306.117 (1994); Me. Rev. Stat. Ann. tit. 29A, § 2431 (West 1995); Tex. Transp. Code Ann. § 724.063 (West 1996); Md. Code Ann., Courts & Judicial Proc. § 10–306 (1995); Ala. Code § 32–5A–194 (1995); Conn. Gen. Stat. Ann. § 14–227a(c) (West 1995).

238. *See* Fla. Stat. ch. 112.0455 (1995); La. Rev. Stat. Ann. 23 § 1601 (West 1995).

c. Security measures implemented by the testing laboratory to preclude adulteration of specimens and drug test results.

d. Other necessary and proper actions taken to ensure reliable and accurate drug test results.[239]

Some statutes specify the types of tests that must be run to minimize error rates.[240] When the state has complied with such provisions, the statutes frequently provide for the admissibility of the test results without the presence or testimony of the technician who performed the test.[241] The statutes typically provide for the appearance of the technician upon timely request by the defendant.[242]

In *Galbraith v. Commonwealth*,[243] the court refused to admit testimony regarding cocaine use based on a field test not approved by the state Division of Forensic Science.[244] Similarly, in *State v. Ross*,[245] the court held that HGN results to show a level of intoxication are inadmissible because the legislature has provided that only a chemical test can be used to determine blood alcohol content, and HGN is not a chemical test. Such statutory provisions are typically enacted to reduce the false positive error rate.

239. FLA. STAT. ANN. § 112.0455(12)(a) (West 1995). *See also* MN. STAT. ANN. § 181.953; OKLA. STAT. ANN. tit. 40 § 557 (West 1995); MD. CODE ANN., COURTS & JUDICIAL PROC. 10–306 (1995); MD. CODE ANN., HEALTH GEN. § 17–214 (1995); ME. REV. STAT. ANN. tit. 29–A § 2431 (West 1995); LA. REV. STAT. ANN. 49 §§ 1005–1006 (West 1995).

240. *See, e.g.*, the following provision in the Connecticut statute:

§ 31–51u. Drug testing: Requirements:

(a) No employer may determine an employee's eligibility for promotion, additional compensation, transfer, termination, disciplinary or other adverse personnel action solely on the basis of a positive urinalysis drug test result unless (1) the employer has given the employee a urinalysis drug test, utilizing a reliable methodology, which produced a positive result and (2) such positive test result was confirmed by a second urinalysis drug test, which was separate and independent from the initial test, utilizing a gas chromatography and mass spectrometry methodology or a methodology which has been determined by the commissioner of public health and addiction services to be as reliable or more reliable than the gas chromatography and mass spectrometry methodology.

(b) No person performing a urinalysis drug test pursuant to subsection (a) of this section shall report, transmit or disclose any positive test result of any test performed in accordance with subdivision (1) of subsection (a) of this section unless such test result has been confirmed in accordance with subdivision (2) of said subsection (a).

In *State v. Johnson*, 26 Conn.App. 553, 603 A.2d 406 (Conn.App.Ct.1992), the Connecticut Court of Appeals rejected a motion to suppress evidence brought by criminal defendants because their conviction for heroin possession was based on a disputed chemical test result. The defendants argued that the test was not as accurate as the gas chromatography, mass spectrometry method provided for in the workplace statute and, therefore, they were denied equal protection. The court found that employees facing drug tests and criminal defendants were not similarly situated. Therefore, § 31–51u does not implicate the equal protection clause. 603 A.2d at 409.

241. MD. CODE ANN., COURTS & JUDICIAL PROC. § 10–306 (1995). For a discussion of one such provision *see* Nicholas J. Weilhammer, *Face to Face: The Crime Lab Exception of Rule 803(8) of the Montana Rules of Evidence and the Montana Confrontation Clause*, 60 MONT. L. REV. 167 (1999).

242. In *State v. Kittrell*, 279 N.J.Super. 225, 652 A.2d 732 (N.J.Super.1995), the defendant challenged the reliability of a drug test, but the trial judge admitted a laboratory certificate which identified cocaine in a bag purchased from the defendant by an undercover officer. The state argued that the defendant must do more than make a blanket challenge; he must point to some specific way in which the laboratory report was tainted before it was required to present the testimony of the laboratory technician. The appellate court agreed but reversed because the state did not follow statutorily mandated pre-trial procedures for ascertaining the nature of the defendant's objection and the admissibility of the laboratory certificate. *Id.* at 736–37.

243. 18 Va.App. 734, 446 S.E.2d 633 (Va. Ct.App.1994).

244. *Id.* at 637.

245. 147 Or.App. 634, 938 P.2d 797 (Or.Ct. App.1997).

§ 9–1.4 Specific Technique

The line between general and specific technique is often blurred. Many chain of custody cases, for example, might be thought of as raising questions of specific procedure in a given case. Here, we discuss cases where the procedures followed in a specific case have been called into question.[246] For example, in *United States v. Hunt*,[247] the Court of Military Appeals reversed a conviction of a private accused of using cocaine because no evidence was admitted as to the actual scientific tests performed on the appellant's urine sample.[248] In *State v. Langley*,[249] the state's laboratory violated Department of Health testing regulations[250] in four separate ways: "1) the laboratory which conducted the blood test did not participate in any proficiency testing program for the particular test used; 2) the test conducted was not approved; 3) no duplicate test was performed; and 4) the initial positive result was not confirmed by any method."[251] The appellate court held that evidence based on this test should have been excluded.

Specific technique issues are also raised when the qualifications of the tester or the calibration of an instrument are challenged.[252] In *Watt v. State*,[253] the state failed to show that the technician who performed drug tests was qualified. It was error to allow testimony based on her analysis.

Whether the expert witness is qualified to offer an opinion is an issue that is sometimes raised with respect to police officers testifying about the results of field sobriety tests.[254] In *Schultz v. State*,[255] the state failed to make a required showing that the officer was qualified to administer a HGN test. In *Duffy v. Director of Revenue*,[256] the court held that a police officer's lack of knowledge as to proper method to score and interpret horizontal gaze nystagmus test results rendered his testimony as to the results inadmissible. However, admitting the testimony was held to be harmless error. In *Common-*

---

246. The quality of laboratory procedures is sometimes litigated outside of the context of admissibility questions. For example, in *Stinson v. Physicians Immediate Care, Ltd.*, 269 Ill.App.3d 659, 207 Ill.Dec. 96, 646 N.E.2d 930 (Ill.App.Ct.1995), plaintiff claimed that the defendant was negligent in performing a drug test on him and reporting a false positive result to his employer. The substance of the allegation revolved around the defendant's laboratory procedures, including failure to use sterile specimen containers, tamper-evident seals, and identifying marks on specimen containers. *Id.* at 931. The court concluded that this claim stated a cause of action and that the laboratory owed a duty to the employees of the firms for whom it did tests.

247. 33 M.J. 345 (C.M.A.1991).

248. *Id.* at 347.

249. 905 S.W.2d 898 (Mo.Ct.App.1995).

250. 19 CSR 20–30.080 (2001), promulgated under the authority of V.A.M.S. § 577.026.

251. 905 S.W.2d at 898.

252. *See* State v. O'Key, 899 P.2d at 670 (Or.1995) (Admissibility is subject to a foundational showing that the officer who administered the test was qualified and that the test

was properly administered and the results were accurately recorded.); State v. Bresson, 51 Ohio St.3d 123, 554 N.E.2d 1330 (Ohio 1990); State v. Ross, 147 Or.App. 634, 938 P.2d 797 (Or.Ct.App.1997).

253. 884 S.W.2d 413 (Mo.Ct.App.1994).

254. The competence of a police officer to testify as to the administration and results of a test is a different question from whether the officer can testify as to the scientific principles underlying the test. In *People v. Leahy*, 8 Cal.4th 587, 34 Cal.Rptr.2d 663, 882 P.2d 321 (Cal.1994), the defendant questioned the competence of a police officer to testify regarding the scientific acceptance of HGN test results. The Supreme Court of California agreed. The officer is not competent to establish general acceptance of HGN in the scientific community or to relate the scientific principles underlying the nystagmus test. However, the court rejected the contention that a qualified police officer would be unqualified to testify about the results of a test. *Id.* at 336.

255. 106 Md.App. 145, 664 A.2d 60 (Md.Ct. Spec.App.1995).

256. 966 S.W.2d 372 (Mo.Ct.App.1998).

wealth v. Sands,[257] the Massachusetts Supreme Court ordered a new trial because the trial court admitted the testimony of an officer as to the defendant's performance on a HGN test without giving the defendant a chance to challenge the officer's qualifications or the procedures he used in administering the test. In *People v. Shelton,*[258] the Illinois appellate court ordered a new trial after it found a police officer's opinion testimony that a motorist was under the influence of drugs, and that drug usage rendered him incapable of driving safely, lacked adequate foundation and was inadmissible because of the officer's limited training in how to detect drug users.[259] Even when an officer is qualified, he may perform a test incorrectly. In *State v. Hall,*[260] the court concluded it was error to admit the testimony of an officer concerning the results of a walk-and-turn test that was improperly administered.

§ 9–1.5 Conclusion

Drug testing has achieved widespread general acceptance as a reliable scientific technique in an array of substantive areas. There simply are no cases challenging properly performed drug tests using sophisticated techniques such as gas chromatography/mass spectrometry. The most active areas of litigation in the drug testing arena deal with HGN and DRE. A fair degree of consensus has developed around the proper role of HGN and DRE testimony in drug cases. However, the error rate associated with these procedures remains in question and thus *Daubert* challenges are likely to continue into the future. Cases involving hair analysis generally conclude that when done properly the results are reliable. It remains to be seen whether hair analysis will come to replace other types of testing in the employment context.

B. SCIENTIFIC STATUS

by

Robert M. Bray* & Dennis J. Crouch**

§ 9–2.0 Drug Use: Evidence From Surveys and Chemical Testing

§ 9–2.1 Introductory Discussion of the Science

The ability to understand and address the Nation's drug problem is dependent, in large measure, on having data that accurately identify and

257. 424 Mass. 184, 675 N.E.2d 370 (Mass. 1997).

258. 303 Ill.App.3d 915, 237 Ill.Dec. 12, 708 N.E.2d 815 (Ill.App.Ct.1999).

259. *Id.* at 823.

260. 2000 WL 1061875 (Ohio.Ct.App.2000).

* Dr. Bray is the director of the Substance Abuse Epidemiology, Prevention, and Risk Assessment Program at Research Triangle Institute in Research Triangle Park, North Carolina, where he has been since 1980. Previously, he was a faculty member at the University of Kentucky. He holds B.S. and M.S. degrees in psychology from Brigham Young University and a Ph.D. in social psychology from the University of Illinois, Urbana–Champaign. He is a member of the American Psychological Association and the American Public Health Association. He served on the Committee on Drug Use in the Workplace for the National Research Council, Institute of Medicine.

His recent work has focused on substance use epidemiology and related problems in military and civilian populations. He has directed the 1982, 1985, 1988, 1992, 1995, and 1998 Worldwide Surveys of Substance Use and Health Behaviors Among Military Personnel

describe drug use behavior. For scientific data about drug use to be of value in the courtroom, there is an underlying assumption that the methods of science provide reliable and valid information. At its heart, science, buttressed with its objective methodology, is intended to assist in the discovery of truth about phenomena. That discovery, however, requires the sifting of evidence from the results of systematic observations, hypotheses, experiments, and tests that are conducted to rule out implausible hypotheses and result in plausible conclusions.[1]

Unfortunately, real-world settings do not always permit the use of optimal study designs and methods that allow one to draw unambiguous conclusions. Such is often the case in studies of drug use; consequently, efforts to determine who is using what drugs and in which contexts can be difficult at times. Two methods most commonly used for learning about substance use are self-reports and biochemical analyses, but, like all scientific methods, each has strengths and limitations. This section briefly examines the benefits and liabilities of these two methods.

§ 9–2.1.1 Strengths and Limitations of Self–Reported Data

Self-reports in which respondents provide data about their behavior form the backbone of most social science approaches to data gathering. Self-report methods rely on respondents' veracity to provide correct information about observations and events. Among self-reports, surveys have been a major vehicle for obtaining data about drug use experiences. The advantage of self-reports about drug use from surveys is that they permit the collection of a

and is currently conducting the 2001 survey in the series. He also was coordinator of analytic reports for the 1988 and 1990 National Household Surveys on Drug Abuse (NHSDAs) and is currently directing the National Analytic Center, a project focused on analyzing data from the NHSDA and other substance abuse datasets. Dr. Bray directed the Washington, DC, Metropolitan Area Drug Study (DC*MADS), a 6–year comprehensive project of the prevalence, correlates, and consequences of drug abuse in household and nonhousehold populations (including people who are homeless or institutionalized, adult and juvenile offenders, clients entering treatment programs, and new mothers). He is the principal editor of a book, published by Sage Publications, based on findings from DC*MADS and titled DRUG USE IN METROPOLITAN AMERICA. Dr. Bray is co-editor of THE PSYCHOLOGY OF THE COURTROOM and has served as an expert witness in several criminal trials.

** Mr. Crouch is the interim director at the Center for Human Toxicology, University of Utah, where he has been employed since 1977. He is also a research assistant professor at the University of Utah's College of Pharmacy, Department of Pharmacology and Toxicology. He received a B.S. degree from Western Illinois University, Macomb, Illinois, in 1971; received graduate training at the University of Utah, 1980–1981 in biochemistry and pharmacology;

and received a M.B.A. degree from Utah State University, Logan, Utah in 1989. From May 1990 through November 1991, he was at the National Institute on Drug Abuse. He was responsible for administrative aspects of the National Laboratory Certification Program for forensic laboratories and research on the impact of occupational drug testing on drug use patterns, transportation safety, and business. He is a member of the California Association of Toxicologists, Society of Forensic Toxicologists, and the International Association of Forensic Toxicologists, as well as a fellow of the American Academy of Forensic Sciences.

Mr. Crouch has published over 50 peer-reviewed scientific articles on therapeutic drug monitoring, analytical toxicology, forensic toxicology, drugs and driving, and workplace drug testing. He routinely provides expert witness testimony in DUI, medical examiner, probation and parole, and a variety of other medicolegal cases. Current research interests include alcohol and other drug use in transportation safety, evaluating the impact of workplace testing programs on businesses, monitoring of laboratories performing workplace testing, GC/MS, LC/MS, and MS/MS analyses of drugs of abuse.

§ 9–2.0

1. Philip J. Runkel & Joseph E. McGrath, RESEARCH ON HUMAN BEHAVIOR: A SYSTEMATIC GUIDE TO METHOD (1972).

rich array of information about the nature and extent of drug use along with information about drug-related consequences and correlates. For example, surveys are used to (a) provide information about the prevalence, trends, patterns, and frequency of use; (b) determine use during selected time periods, such as one's lifetime, or the past year, or the past month; (c) identify the characteristics of users and nonusers; (d) determine the relative popularity of specific individual drugs; (e) identify the route by which drugs are taken (e.g., inhaling, smoking, injecting); (f) assess patterns of use, including whether drugs are taken alone or in combination; (g) examine the reasons and motivations for taking drugs; and (h) assess relationships between drug use and other behaviors, such as criminal involvement and activities. This type of information is not available from any other source than from individuals in various segments of the population. Further, survey content can be modified as needed so that questions are tailored to the specific issues of concern.

To help ensure accurate and precise estimates about drug use and related behaviors, large-scale surveys, such as those described below, use sophisticated sampling techniques for well-defined populations. They also collect demographic information from participants that permits estimates of drug use to be made within population subgroups. Such subgroup data are important in substantiating the need for programs and policies to address drug use problems and for monitoring changes in drug use over time. Because of the richness, uniqueness, and practical utility of surveys, they have become one of the major sources of data for understanding drug use behavior.

Self-reported data are limited, however, by the willingness of respondents to reveal their drug use. In many courtroom and legal situations, respondents may have strong motivations not to report drug use behavior honestly (e.g., arrestees may be fearful that honest reporting about their drug use will aid in their conviction). Thus, self-report measures of drug use can be suspect when respondents recognize that admitting drug use may result in adverse consequences for them or when they are placed in a situation that encourages them to provide socially desirable responses. Several studies, for example, have found systematic underreporting of drug use among arrestees[2] and other groups, such as pregnant women.[3]

Survey results are also subject to the potential bias of self-reports and to the ambiguities caused by questions with varying interpretations. The populations they represent may exclude hard-to-reach subgroups who may be of interest (e.g., homeless people, high school dropouts). In addition, surveys can be relatively expensive to conduct, so sample sizes even in large-scale studies may have too few members of particular subgroups or users of particular drugs to allow for the computation of reliable estimates (e.g., estimating heroin use from surveys of the household population).

In addition to problems of intentional underreporting, there are other potential problems with the validity of survey data, including issues of population coverage and response rates. If the population is not properly

2. James J. Collins & Mary E. Marsden, Validity of Self-reports of Drug Use Among Arrestees (1990) (unpublished manuscript, on file with Research Triangle Institute); Lana D. Harrison, *The Validity of Self-reported Data on Drug Use*, 25 J. OF DRUG ISSUES 91 (1995).

3. National Institute on Drug Abuse (NIDA), PREVALENCE OF DRUG ABUSE AMONG DC WOMEN DELIVERING LIVEBIRTHS IN DC HOSPITALS: 1992 (1995).

represented in the survey or if the response rate is low, biases are introduced that can invalidate the survey results. However, nonresponse adjustments are generally made to credible surveys to help compensate for the potential bias of nonsurveyed persons.

With respect to estimation of trends, consistency over time is an important consideration. In some instances, a systematic or consistent bias in self-reports may still allow valid comparisons between groups or over time. For example, a bias to underreport drug use by survey respondents can still provide useful trend data from surveys. The shape of the curve can be fairly accurate, even though the curve may be uniformly depressed at all points because of underreporting. In this circumstance, it is still possible to make correct assertions about the relative shape of the trend line. Additionally, many of the problems of coverage and response rates can be overcome by the careful design of surveys and the application of vigorous field procedures and statistical adjustments.

Additional information about the validity of self-reports is addressed by Harrison[4] and in a research monograph by Rouse, Kozel, and Richards.[5] A general conclusion emerging from these various reviews is that most people appear to be reasonably truthful (within the bounds of capability) under the proper conditions. Such conditions include believing that the research has a legitimate purpose, having suitable privacy for providing answers, having assurances that answers will be kept confidential, and believing that those collecting the data can be trusted. More relevant to our topic, there is reason to be cautious about self-report data in many legal settings. Persons asked about their substance use after arrest or incarceration may have concerns about the uses to which the data could be put. Hence, in these or similar situations, there may be considerable incentive for drug users to underreport their drug-using behaviors.

The best protection against all these threats to validity is to be aware of them and to deal with them as forthrightly as possible. The major point to be made for present purposes is that, when the circumstances allow the respondent to consider the questions reasonable and justified in terms of purpose, and when respondents can feel reasonably certain that the answers will not be used against them, then self-reports can be sufficiently valid for research and policy purposes. When those conditions are not met—which may often be the case in legal settings—there may well be very substantial underreporting.

Approaches used to encourage truthful reporting include providing explanations of (a) confidentiality and protection of respondents' rights; (b) safeguards to be used in handling the data, such as locked file cabinets for storing identifying information, destruction of such information when it is no longer needed, and presentation of results in aggregate form; and (c) a certificate of confidentiality that authorizes researchers to protect the identity of research subjects by withholding their names and other identifying characteristics from all persons and from courts of law not directly connected with the research.

---

4. Harrison, *supra* note 2.

5. SELF-REPORT METHODS OF ESTIMATING DRUG USE: MEETING CURRENT CHALLENGES TO VALIDITY, (Beatrice A. Rouse et al. eds., 1985).

§ 9–2.1.2 Strengths and Limitations of Chemical Testing Data

Chemical methods that focus largely on urinalyses are considered reasonably objective indicators of drug use and are highly reliable when proper laboratory procedures and methods are followed (see discussion later in this chapter). Drug testing, which began in the 1960s, is generally used to detect and to deter drug use. Testing is done in a number of settings, including the criminal justice system, drug treatment programs, and the workplace. In the criminal justice system, offenders, inmates, and criminal justice employees may be tested to ensure public safety and confidence. Defendants and offenders may be tested at arrest, during incarceration, and as part of supervised release, including probation or parole.

Results of chemical testing are the basic and objective measures of drug use in many studies and in most drug screening and treatment programs. When proper procedures are followed, they give consistent readings and can accurately identify the presence of known drugs or their metabolites in tested specimens. A urinalysis drug test measures the presence of drugs, their metabolites, or both in urine as an indication of recent drug use. When performed according to current professional standards, the tests are very effective in detecting recent drug use.

Measurement problems arise when proper testing procedures are not followed, when contaminants are present either in the drugs or the testing materials, or when the test results are used inappropriately. For example, urine testing does not provide accurate estimates of the prevalence of drug use in specified populations, it does not provide a good measure of the extent of the individual drug use involvement (i.e., use, abuse, dependence), and it is not a good measure of impairment. Moreover, given the low prevalence of positive tests in many populations, it remains plausible that rare and unidentified causes of false positives are operating.

A limitation of urinalysis is that the procedures usually detect only recent use and generally cannot measure patterns or frequency of use. Thus, although appropriate for detecting illicit drug use for a relatively short period, urine data do not contain the richness of context about use that is available from self-reports. Although other chemical methods, such as hair analysis, can potentially trace longer-term patterns of use, data on the measurement properties of this type of analytical technique are still limited.

Test results, either positive or negative, also provide no information on patterns of use, such as frequency, amount, or place of use (e.g., outside the workplace or on the job). In contrast, studies based on self-reports generally inquire into alcohol and other drug use over an extended period of time, frequently the previous month, year, or lifetime. Self-report studies typically ask about the amount and frequency of use to distinguish casual from regular or heavy users and occasionally inquire about the context or social setting in which the drug was used.

Despite some limitations, drug test data, because of their objectivity, are more likely than survey data to be relevant to most judicial proceedings. Nonetheless, surveys are useful in helping to provide a context for understanding broad drug use patterns that are informative to the courtroom both about the general population and about the offender population.

§ 9–2.2   Drug Use Survey Findings for Selected Populations

This section presents information on prevalence and trends in substance use by key segments of the general population and the offender population. Four large-scale survey series provide data that offer useful assessments of drug use behavior: the High School Senior (HSS) surveys and their follow-up component on college-aged youths and young adults; the National Household Survey on Drug Abuse (NHSDA) series; the Worldwide Surveys of Substance Abuse and Health Behaviors Among Military Personnel (MWS); and the Bureau of Justice Statistics (BJS) surveys of jail inmates and State prison inmates. These surveys provide several perspectives about drug use. The HSS surveys, with their follow-up components, furnish data about youths and young adults, a subset of whom are likely to have had an encounter with the law. The NHSDA series offers data on drug use among the general household population, the majority of whom have not engaged in illegal activities. The MWS series contributes data on an important segment of society, the U.S. military. The BJS surveys provide data about drug use among the incarcerated subset of the population.

We also briefly examine selected other sources of data (e.g., the Drug Abuse Warning Network [DAWN] data and the Drug Use Forecasting [DUF] system data) to complement the primary data sources.

The four survey series we review are similar in that they provide estimates of illicit drug use based on self-reports of representative samples of the populations under study. Illicit drug use, as measured in these surveys, involves the use of illegal drugs and the nonmedical use of prescription-type psychotherapeutic drugs. Respondents are typically asked about their use of such drugs in the month or year preceding the survey, as well as during their entire lifetime.

All of the surveys have asked about use of marijuana (including hashish); hallucinogens (including phencyclidine or PCP and lysergic acid diethylamide or LSD); cocaine (including crack); heroin and other opiates; inhalants, such as lighter fluids, aerosol sprays, glue, paint thinners, and cleaning fluids; and nonmedical use of prescription-type psychotherapeutic drugs (i.e., stimulants, sedatives, tranquilizers, and analgesics used without a doctor's prescription or for purposes other than intended). In addition, the surveys have gathered information about alcohol use and cigarette smoking although the measures of these drugs differed somewhat across the different survey series.

§ 9–2.2.1   High School Senior Surveys

The HSS series is an ongoing study of young Americans, conducted by the Institute for Social Research at the University of Michigan.[6] The research design consists of (a) a series of annual, nationwide questionnaire surveys of seniors in high schools, and (b) annual follow-up surveys mailed to subsets of each sample after their graduation. Initial base-year data collection is conducted in approximately 125 to 145 public and private high schools selected to provide an accurate cross-section of high school seniors in the 48 contiguous

---

6. Lloyd D. Johnston et al., MONITORING THE FUTURE: NATIONAL SURVEY RESULTS ON DRUG USE, 1975–1999: SECONDARY SCHOOL STUDENTS (2000); Lloyd D. Johnston, MONITORING THE FUTURE: NA- TIONAL SURVEY RESULTS ON DRUG USE, 1975–1999: COLLEGE STUDENTS AND ADULTS AGES 19–40 (2000).

States. From 14,000 to 17,000 seniors participate each year, and 2,400 participants are selected for follow-up from each senior class. These 2,400 are randomly divided into two separate groups, each numbering about 1,200. Members of one group are invited to participate during the first year after graduation and every 2 years after that; those in the other group are invited to participate during the second year after graduation and every 2 years after that. The result of this approach is that individual participants are surveyed on a 2–year cycle, beginning either 1 or 2 years after graduation. A limitation of this design is that high school dropouts are not included; however, it provides an excellent sample of high school graduates.

The study began with the high school class of 1975, and follow-up surveys began with the graduating class of 1976. Thus, through 1999 the population of interest consists of American men and women aged 18 to 40 who were not high school dropouts. For present purposes, high school seniors and high school graduates aged 19 to 28 are highlighted because sufficient trend data exist for the latter.

Prevalence and Trends in Illicit Drug and Heavy Alcohol Use. In general, there was a long-term gradual decline from the early 1980s to the early 1990s in the proportions of young Americans using illicit drugs. Between 1992 and 1999, however, there was an increase in levels of illicit drug use not seen since the mid–1980s. Figure 9.1 shows trends for any illicit drug use and heavy alcohol use among high school seniors during the month prior to the survey. As shown, more than 30% of the respondents of the high school classes from 1975 through 1982 had used an illicit drug during their senior year, peaking at 39% for the classes of 1978 and 1979. Since that peak, there was a substantial and fairly steady decrease to 14% for the class of 1992, followed by an increase to 18% in 1993, then a steady climb back to 26% for 1997 through 1999. Although the decline in the early 1990s was a notable improvement from the earlier higher rates, still about one in every six or seven seniors had used illicit drugs in the past month in 1992. The upturn from 1993 to 1999 is also a concern in that it signals a shift in progress from the downward decline during the 1980s.

[Figure 9.1. Trends in Substance Use Among High School Seniors, Past 30 Days, 1975–1999 (%)]

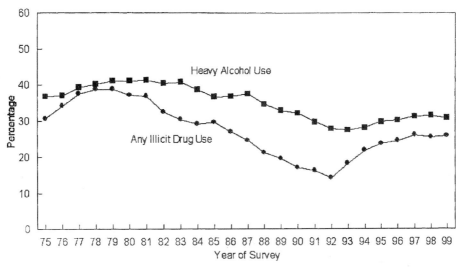

Turning to heavy alcohol use, which is defined as having five or more drinks in a row at least once in the past 2 weeks, Figure 9.1 shows that heavy drinking remained relatively constant from 1975 through the early 1980s, with a prevalence of about 40%. Since that time, it steadily decreased until 1993 and 1994, when some 28% of seniors had five or more drinks in a row at least once in the prior 2 weeks. From 1994 to 1999, the heavy alcohol use rate among young Americans hovered around 30% to 32%. It is of interest to note that rates of heavy drinking during the past month have consistently exceeded the rates of illicit drug use for this same period and decreased at a slower rate during the 1980s. However, they had not increased as much as illicit drug use rates during the 1990s.

The decline in drug use among high school seniors in the 1980s is also evident among the follow-up data for young adults aged 19 to 28, as shown in Figure 9.2. In 1993, about 15% of young adults reported having used an illicit drug at least once in the past 30 days; that statistic was over 25% as recently as 1986, the first year for which the data are available for this age group. Since 1993, the rate had slowly increased to 17% as of 1999. The trend in heavy drinking among young adults has showed little change. During the 14–year period from 1986 to 1999, prevalence stayed at about 35%.[7]

7.   Johnston, *supra* note 6.

[Figure 9.2. Trends in Substance Use Among Young Adults Aged 19 to 28, Past 30 Days, 1986–1999 (%)]

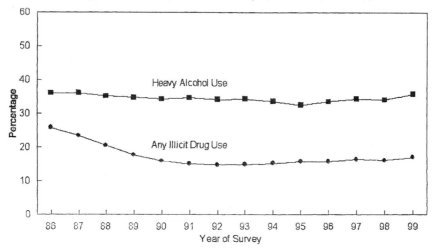

Overall, during the 1980s and early 1990s, there were appreciable declines in the use of a number of the illicit drugs among high school seniors, and between 1986 and 1993 (years for which data are available) there were declines among young adults more generally. Between 1993 and 1999, illicit drug use rates increased, however. Heavy alcohol use showed a decline from 1987 to 1993, followed by a slight increase from 1994 to 1999, among high school seniors. In contrast, it remained fairly constant among young adults.

§ 9–2.2.2   National Household Surveys on Drug Abuse

The NHSDA series provides national-level data about the prevalence, correlates, and trends in the use of illicit drugs, alcohol, and tobacco among members of the U.S. general household population aged 12 years old or older. Surveys have been conducted in 1971, 1972, 1974, 1976, 1977, 1979, 1982, 1985, 1988, and annually since 1990. The National Commission on Marihuana and Drug Abuse sponsored the 1971 and 1972 surveys; the National Institute on Drug Abuse (NIDA) sponsored the NHSDA series from 1974 to 1991; and the Office of Applied Studies (OAS) of the Substance Abuse and Mental Health Services Administration (SAMHSA) began sponsoring the survey series in 1992.

Respondents are selected using a multistage national probability sample of households in the United States. Sampling involves the selection of primary areas (counties), subareas (area segments) within these primary areas, households within subareas, and eligible residents (if any) within these households. The household sampling frame excludes small groups of the general population who do not live in households, such as persons residing in institutions (and, until 1991, persons who were homeless). Data collection procedures have been similar for each NHSDA and include interviewing respondents in their homes. There were changes in the NHSDA questionnaire in 1994, and subsequent adjustments of previous survey data were made to improve comparability to the new questionnaire. Some estimates from 1979 to 1982 are unavailable due to these changes. For questions about use of illicit drugs and alcohol, respondents from 1971 to 1998 marked paper-and-pencil interviewing (PAPI) answer sheets so interviewers could not see the answers of individuals. Beginning in 1999, an interactive, bilingual (English and Spanish), computer-based questionnaire was used. Sample sizes have ranged from 3,200 respondents in 1971 to nearly 70,000 respondents in 1999.[8]

Prevalence and Trends in Drug and Alcohol Use. The percentage of the household population who were current (past month) users of any illicit drug, alcohol, or cigarettes has steadily declined over the past 20 years (see Figure 9.3a and Figure 9.3b). In 1979, approximately 14% of the total household population had used one or more illicit drugs in the past month compared with about 6% in 1998.[9] This represents a striking decline of over 50% during this period. The decreases were more rapid in the earlier part of this period and have since leveled off. Illicit drug use has historically been highest among young adults, and dramatic decreases in the percentage of this group using any illicit drugs in the past month were observed between 1979 and 1998 (38% in 1979 to 16% in 1998). Intermediate rates of use were found for youths; these rates also decreased, but not as rapidly (16% in 1979 to 10% in 1998). Use rates among older adults were the lowest of the three age groups and have shown little change, hovering around 3% to 4% over the period.

[Figure 9.3a, Trends in Illicit Drug Use in the Past 30 Days in the Household Population, by Age Group, 1979–1998 (%)]

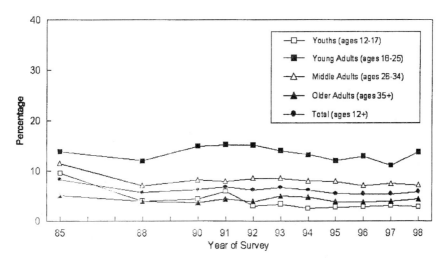

8. SUBSTANCE ABUSE AND MENTAL HEALTH SERVICES ADMINISTRATION (SAMHSA), SUMMARY OF FINDINGS FROM THE 1999 NATIONAL HOUSEHOLD SURVEY ON DRUG ABUSE (2000), *available at* http://www.DrugAbuseStatistics.samhsa.gov/.

9. SAMHSA, NATIONAL HOUSEHOLD SURVEY ON DRUG ABUSE: MAIN FINDINGS 1996 (1998); SAMHSA, NATIONAL HOUSEHOLD SURVEY ON DRUG ABUSE: MAIN FINDINGS 1997 (1999); SAMHSA, NATIONAL HOUSEHOLD SURVEY ON DRUG ABUSE: MAIN FINDINGS 1998 (2000).

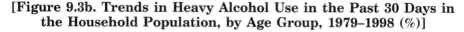

[Figure 9.3b. Trends in Heavy Alcohol Use in the Past 30 Days in the Household Population, by Age Group, 1979–1998 (%)]

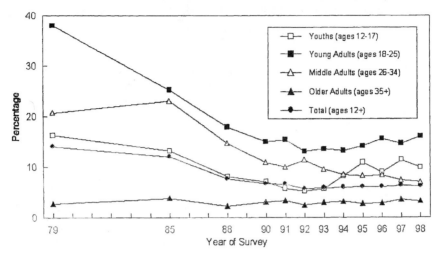

Alcohol use showed a similar pattern with a steady decline in all levels of use from 1979 to 1998 (data not shown). Rates of heavy alcohol use were fairly stable from 1985 to 1998 (years for which data are available). During this period, between 5% and 8% of the total household population were heavy alcohol users. As with illicit drug use, rates of heavy drinking were highest for young adults and lowest for older adults.

Demographic Correlates of Alcohol and Other Drug Use. In 1998, current use of illicit drugs was generally more common among those aged 18 to 25 than among other age groups and more common among men, residents of metropolitan areas, and residents of the West than among other geographic groups. For alcohol use in the past month, rates were significantly greater among those aged 18 to 34 than among other age groups, among men than among women, among whites than among other racial/ethnic groups, among residents of large and small metropolitan areas than among residents of nonmetropolitan areas, and among residents of the Northeast, the North Central, and West regions than among residents of the South.[10]

As shown in Figure 9.3a, in contrast to the overall declining pattern of illicit drug use noted above, youths aged 12 to 17 and young adults aged 18 to 25 showed alarming patterns of increases in use over the past several years. Specifically, rates of use among youths doubled from 5% in 1992 to 11% in 1997, then decreased to 10% in 1998. Young adults showed an upward trend from 13% in 1992 to 16% in 1998. Even though the 1998 rates for these age groups were well below the near-epidemic levels of the late 1970s, they are of considerable concern because of the risks they pose both for health and other forms of unproductive behavior. For example, illegal drugs are associated with premature sexual activity and associated risks of sexually transmitted diseases, delinquency, and involvement in the criminal justice system.[11]

Marijuana has accounted for a significant amount of the flux in these age groups. Other drugs that have contributed to the changing trends, though to a

10. SAMHSA, *supra* note 9.

11. OFFICE OF NATIONAL DRUG CONTROL POLICY (ONDCP), THE NATIONAL DRUG CONTROL STRATE-GY: 2000 ANNUAL REPORT (2000), *available at* http://www.whitehousedrugpolicy.gov/policy/ndcs00/strategy2000.pdf.

lesser extent, have been hallucinogens among youths aged 12 to 17 and cocaine among young adults aged 18 to 25. In addition, there was an increasing trend in new heroin use since 1992. For example, there was over a threefold increase in the estimated number of past month heroin users between 1993 and 1996, with most users under the age of 26.[12]

In addition to assessing trends in illicit drug use and alcohol use, understanding trends in heavy alcohol use are of interest because heavier drinking is related to drinking problems.[13] As shown in Figure 9.3b, rates of past month heavy alcohol use for youths aged 12 to 17 declined sharply from 10% in 1985 to about 3% and held constant at this level from 1994 to 1998. From 1985 through 1991, only adults aged 35 or older had lower rates of heavy alcohol use than youths. Since 1992, youths have had the lowest rate compared to other age groups. Conversely, young adults aged 18 to 25 consistently showed the highest rates of heavy alcohol use; the rate in 1998 (14%) was only slightly lower than the rate in 1991 (15%), although there has been some fluctuation across the years. Heavy alcohol use among middle and older adults continued to decline or stay stable across the period.

§ 9–2.2.3   Military Worldwide Surveys

The MWS series provides data to assess the prevalence, correlates, and trends in alcohol use and illicit drug use among the active-duty Armed Forces. Since 1985, the surveys also have examined the impact of health behaviors other than substance use on the quality of life of military personnel. Burt Associates, Incorporated, of Bethesda, Maryland, conducted the 1980 survey.[14] Research Triangle Institute (RTI) of Research Triangle Park, North Carolina, conducted the 1982, 1985, 1988, 1992, 1995, and 1998 surveys and is currently conducting the 2001 survey.[15] Key trends for the first five surveys are summarized by Bray, Kroutil, and Marsden.[16]

Each MWS has used a similar methodology. The eligible population consists of all U.S. active-duty military personnel from the Army, Navy, Marine Corps, and Air Force stationed throughout the world except recruits, service academy students, persons absent without official leave (AWOL), and persons who have a permanent change of station (PCS) at the time of data collection. A two-stage probability sample has been selected for each survey. The first-stage samples consisted of military installations for each service located throughout the world. The second-stage samples consisted of military personnel stationed at the selected installations who were randomly selected

---

12. SAMHSA, Year-end Preliminary Estimates From the 1996 Drug Abuse Warning Network (1997), *available at* http://www.samhsa.gov/oas/dawn/dwn96toc.htm.

13. Walter B. Clark, & Michael E. Hilton, Alcohol in America: Drinking Problems and Practices in a National Survey (1991).

14. Marvin A. Burt et al., Worldwide Survey of Nonmedical Drug Use and Alcohol Use Among Military Personnel (1980).

15. Robert M. Bray et al., 1982 Worldwide Survey of Alcohol and Nonmedical Drug Use Among Military Personnel (1983); Robert M. Bray et al. 1985, Worldwide Survey of Alcohol and Nonmedical Drug Use Among Military Personnel (1986); Robert M. Bray et al., 1988 Worldwide Survey of Substance Abuse and Health Behaviors Among Military Personnel (1988); Robert M. Bray et al., 1992 Worldwide Survey of Substance and Health Behaviors Among Military Personnel (1992); Robert M. Bray et al., *Trends in Alcohol, Illicit Drug and Cigarette Use Among U.S. Military Personnel: 1980—1992,* 21 Armed Forces & Soc'y 271 (1995); Robert M. Bray et al., 1998 Department of Defense Survey of Health Related Behaviors Among Military Personnel: Final Report (1999).

16. Bray et al. (1999), *supra* note 15.

within pay grade groups. Questionnaires were completed under the direction of civilian research field teams in group administrations at military installations or mailed to eligible respondents who were not available for group sessions. Sample sizes have ranged from approximately 15,000 to 22,000 respondents with response rates ranging from 59% to 81%.

Trends in Alcohol and Other Drug Use. Figure 9.4 presents trends over the seven surveys in the proportions of the total active military force who engaged in illicit drug use and heavy drinking between 1980 and 1998. As shown, there are significant declines in both measures, although the rate of decline varied for each. The percentage of military personnel admitting to having used any illicit drug within the past 30 days declined significantly and markedly from nearly 28% in 1980 to under 3% in 1998.

[Figure 9.4, Trends in Substance Use Among Military Personnel, Past 30 Days, 1980–1998 (%)]

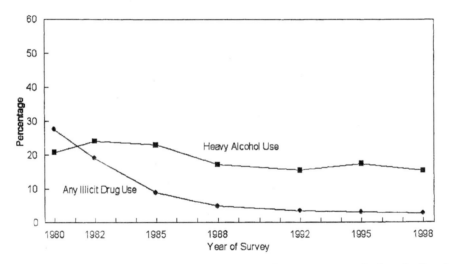

The prevalence of heavy drinking among military personnel also declined significantly between 1980 and 1998, although the decrease was less dramatic than for illicit drug use and that there has been a leveling off of the rate. In 1980, 21% of military personnel reported heavy drinking compared with 15% in 1998. Although heavy drinking does not by itself constitute alcohol abuse, it does indicate drinking levels that are likely to have detrimental consequences, particularly in a group that works with weapons, vehicles, and other dangerous equipment.

The question arises whether these decreases in alcohol and other drug use are an artifact of changes in the demographic composition of the Armed Forces during the 1980s and 1990s, a reflection of general population trends, or the result of military policy. Recruiting and reenlistment successes during this time resulted in a military workforce in 1998 that was somewhat older, had more married personnel, and was better educated than in 1980, characteristics that are associated with a lower likelihood of alcohol and other drug use. For example, 60% of the military force in 1998 were married compared with 53% in 1980; moreover, 61% were over age 25 in 1998 compared with 43% in 1980.[17]

To assess the effect of the changing demographic characteristics on rates of alcohol and other drug use, the 1982, 1985, 1988, 1992, 1995, and 1998 surveys were standardized to the age, education, and marital status distribution of the military population in 1980.[18] Significant declines in any illicit drug use remained after adjusting for demographic changes in the military population. In contrast, much of the decline in heavy drinking observed between 1980 and 1998 was attributable to changes in the demographic composition of the Armed Forces. After the data were adjusted to reflect demographic changes, the rate of heavy drinking in 1998 (19%) did not differ significantly from the rate in 1980 (21%).

Demographic Correlates of Alcohol and Other Drug Use. Data not shown indicate that overall, illicit drug and heavy alcohol use in the military in 1998 occurred among those who were younger, single, and less educated.[19] In addition, men were much more likely to drink heavily than women (17% vs. 4%). The common patterns observed for age, marital status, and educational status were not surprising because marriage and higher educational attainment generally occur with increasing age. Data on marital status indicate that the presence of a spouse was associated with reduced alcohol and other drug use. Among military personnel whose spouses were not with them, illicit drug use rates were similar to what they were among unmarried personnel (6% among spouses not present and 10% among unmarried vs. 3% among spouse present). Rates of heavy alcohol use were above what they were for those who had spouses present (19% among spouses not present and 24% among unmarried vs. 9% among spouses present).

Comparing Military and Civilian Drug Use. Because of the unique mission of the military, the Armed Forces impose rather strict controls over the lives of their members in a number of areas, including alcohol and other drug use. To help gauge the relative magnitude of alcohol and other drug use patterns among military personnel, it is useful to have a civilian comparison group to serve as a benchmark.

Bray, Marsden, and Peterson[20] conducted standardized comparisons of illicit drug use and heavy drinking among military personnel and civilians. Military data were drawn from the 1985 MWS and civilian data from the 1985 NHSDA. The two datasets were equated for age and geographic location of respondents; civilian alcohol and other drug use rates were standardized to reflect the sociodemographic distribution of the military. Standardized comparisons showed that military personnel were significantly less likely than civilians to report having used any illicit drugs during the past 30 days (8% vs. 24%), but they were significantly more likely to be heavy drinkers (21% vs. 11%).

More recently, similar analyses were conducted using data from the 1998 MWS and the 1997 NHSDA.[21] Findings showed the same basic pattern of results as in the 1985 data: Military personnel were still significantly less

---

17. Bray et al. (1999), *supra* note 15; Burt et al., *supra* note 14.

18. Bray et al. (1999), *supra* note 15.

19. *Id.*

20. Robert M. Bray et al., *Standardized Comparisons of the Use of Alcohol, Drugs, and Cigarettes Among Military Personnel and Civilians*, 81 A. J. OF PUB. HEALTH 865 (1991).

21. Bray et al. (1999), *supra* note 15.

likely than civilians to engage in any illicit drug use (3% vs. 11%), but more likely than civilians to drink heavily (14% vs. 10%), especially men aged 18 to 25 (27% vs. 15%).

§ 9–2.2.4 Jail and Prison Inmate Surveys

Two types of surveys sponsored by the Bureau of Justice Statistics (BJS) within the National Institute of Justice (NIJ) provide information about incarcerated persons: (a) surveys of jail inmates and (b) surveys of State prison inmates. The Surveys of Inmates in Local Jails were conducted in 1972, 1978, 1983, 1989, and 1996. Their methodology, which has been similar for each survey, is described by Harlow[22] and Wilson[23] for the 1996 study, which was conducted for the BJS by the U.S. Bureau of the Census. A sample of 431 jails was selected from a universe of 3,328 jails nationwide. The design utilized a two-stage stratified sample in which jails were selected at the first stage based on the size of the male and female populations, and persons within jails were selected at the second stage. A total of 6,133 interviews were completed in 1996 for an overall response rate of 86.3%. Using computer-assisted personal interviewing (CAPI) methods, the interviewers asked inmates about a variety of issues, including individual characteristics, offender behaviors (e.g., current and prior offenses and sentences, criminal histories, detention status), and drug and alcohol use.

The Surveys of Inmates in State and Federal Correctional Facilities were conducted in 1974, 1979, 1986, 1991, and 1997. As with each jail inmates survey, the methodology for the prison inmates surveys has been similar for each survey and is described by Mumola[24] for the 1997 study, which was conducted for the BJS and the Bureau of Prisons by the U.S. Bureau of the Census. The prison inmates survey is actually two surveys: the Survey of Inmates in State Correctional Facilities and the Survey of Inmates in Federal Correctional Facilities (the latter was first conducted in 1991). A sample of 280 State prisons and 40 Federal prisons were selected from a frame of 1,409 State prisons and 127 Federal prisons. This survey used a stratified, two-stage sampling design in which prisons were selected at the first stage based on the gender of the inmate housed at the facility, census region where located, type of facility, security level, and size of the prison population. Persons were selected at the second stage from the sampled prisons. A total of 14,285 interviews were completed for the State survey and 4,041 for the Federal survey for overall response rates of 92.5% and 90.2%, respectively. During the CAPI interviews, inmates reported drug and alcohol involvement along with criminal history, family and employment background, and participation in correctional programs.

Table 9.1 presents data for three survey years for local jail inmates (1983, 1989, 1996), three survey years for State prison inmates (1986, 1991, 1997), and two survey years for Federal prison inmates (1991, 1997). The data focus on lifetime use of drugs (defined as any use of an illicit drug during one's lifetime), regular use of drugs (defined as use at least once a week for at least

22. Caroline W. Harlow, PROFILE OF JAIL INMATES, 1996 (1998).

23. Doris James Wilson, DRUG USE, TESTING, AND TREATMENT IN JAILS (2000).

24. Christopher J. Mumola, SUBSTANCE ABUSE AND TREATMENT, STATE AND FEDERAL PRISONERS, 1997 (1999).

1 month), use in the month prior to the current offense, and use at the time of the offense.[25] Several patterns are clear. Both the jail and the prison surveys show substantial drug use by offenders. From 60% to 83% of jail inmates and prison inmates indicated lifetime use of any drug, and from 42% to 70% reported regular use of any drug. Drugs were used in the month prior to an offense by 55% of jail inmates in 1996 and by 57% of State prison inmates and 45% of Federal prison inmates in 1997. Similarly, drugs were used at the time of the offense by 36% of jail inmates in 1996, by 33% of State prison inmates in 1997, and by 22% of Federal prison inmates in 1997.

25. Allen Beck et al., SURVEY OF STATE PRISON INMATES, 1991 (1993); Caroline W. Harlow, DRUGS AND JAIL INMATES, 1989 (1991); Harlow, *supra* note 22; Mumola, *supra* note 24; Wilson, *supra* note 23.

Table 9.1
Drug Use by Jail and Prison Inmates (%)

Drug Use/Drug	Local Jail Inmates			Prison Inmates					
				1997		1991		1986	
	1996	1989	1983	State	Federal	State	Federal	State	Federal
Ever Used									
Any Drug	82	78	76	83	73	79	60	80	--
Marijuana/Hashish	78	71	73	77	65	74	53	76	--
Cocaine/Crack	50	50	38	49	45	49	37	44	--
Heroin/Opiates[a]	24	19	22	25	16	25	14	26	--
Regularly Used[b]									
Any Drug	64	58	61	70	57	62	42	63	--
Marijuana/Hashish	55	48	55	58	47	52	32	55	--
Cocaine/Crack	31	31	18	34	28	32	21	22	--
Heroin/Opiates	12	12	16	15	9	15	9	18	--
Used in Month Before Offense[c]									
Any Drug	55	44	46	57	45	50	32	56	--
Marijuana/Hashish	37	28	39	39	30	32	19	46	--
Cocaine/Crack	24	24	12	25	20	25	15	20	--
Heroin/Opiates	9	7	8	9	5	10	6	11	--
Used at Time of Offense[c]									
Any Drug	36	27	30	33	22	31	17	36	--
Marijuana/Hashish	19	9	17	15	11	11	6	18	--
Cocaine/Crack	15	14	6	15	9	15	8	10	--
Heroin/Opiates	6	5	6	6	3	6	4	7	--

--Data not collected from Federal prison inmates in 1986.

[a] Heroin only is reported for jail inmates; heroin/opiates are reported for prison inmates.

[b] Use at least once a week for at least 1 month.

[c] Based on convicted jail inmates only in the data shown for the Surveys of Inmates in Local Jails.

Sources: BJS, Survey of Inmates in Local Jails, 1983, 1989, 1996.
BJS, Surveys of Inmates in State and Federal Correctional Facilities, 1986, 1991, 1997.

The patterns of drug use for the jail surveys and the prison surveys were fairly similar across the four types of use and generally indicated that:

- use of any drug for the first two surveys of jail inmates and prison inmates was relatively stable but increased between the second and third surveys;

- marijuana/hashish and cocaine use increased across time for both the jail and prison inmate populations; and

- heroin/opiate use was relatively stable.

Table 9.2 compares lifetime drug use rates across jail and prison offenders and household populations for three age groups (young adults aged 18 to 25, middle adults aged 26 to 34, and older adults aged 35 or older) for the 1986 State prison survey, the 1989 local jail survey, and the 1988 U.S. household population. The more current surveys are not included because the published reports do not contain data for comparable age groups.[26] As shown, across all age groups, members of both jail and prison offender populations are substantially more likely to have ever used drugs than persons in the household population. For example, from 81% to 88% of 18– to 25–year-old inmates reported lifetime drug use compared to 59% of the household population in the 1980s.

26. Beck, et al., *supra* note 25; Harlow, *supra* note 25; NIDA, National Household Survey on Drug Abuse: Main Findings 1988 (1990); Drugs, Crime, and the Justice System: A National Report (Marianne W. Zawitz ed., 1992).

Table 9.2
Comparison of Drug Use, by Age of Offenders and Household Residents (%)

Lifetime Drug Use[a]	Aged 18 to 25			Aged 26 to 34			Aged 35+		
	Local Jail	State Prison	U.S. Household	Local Jail	State Prison	U.S. Household	Local Jail	State Prison	U.S. Household
	1989	1986	1988	1989	1986	1988	1989	1986	1988
Any Drug	81	88	59	83	87	64	65	62	23
Marijuana	76	86	56	74	83	62	58	57	20
Cocaine	50	47	20	57	50	27	42	33	4
Heroin	11	13	*	22	31	2	26	29	1

Note: Information adapted from comparative analysis reported in Zawitz (1992, p. 196).

*Number too small to allow reliable estimates.

[a]Use of any illicit drug one or more times during one's lifetime.

Sources: BJS, Survey of Inmates in Local Jails, 1989.
BJS, Survey of Inmates in State and Federal Correctional Facilities, 1986.
NIDA, National Household Survey on Drug Abuse, 1988.

Overall, drug-related arrests and convictions in the 1980s and early 1990s appeared to be increasing. As noted by Beck et al.[27] and Zawitz[28] the propor-

27. Beck et al., *supra* note 25.

28. DRUGS, CRIME, AND THE JUSTICE SYSTEM: A NATIONAL REPORT, *supra* note 26.

tion of inmates with drug charges as their most serious offense more than doubled from 10% in 1983 to 23% in 1989 among jail inmates and from 9% in 1986 to 21% in 1991 among State prison inmates. In 1991, women in prison (33%) were more likely than men (21%) to be serving a sentence for drug offenses. Black (25%) and Hispanic inmates (33%) were also more likely in 1991 than white inmates (12%) to be serving sentences for a drug offense. Further, drug use was common in 1991 among prison inmates serving time for burglary, robbery, or drug offenses. For example, 56% had used drugs in the month prior to arrest for the current offense, and 31% were using drugs at the time of the offense. Money for drugs motivated more than a quarter of inmates sentenced for robbery, burglary, or larceny in 1991. About 27% of inmates in prison for robbery and 30% of those for burglary reported committing their offense to get money for drugs. About 25% sentenced for drug trafficking in 1991 reported obtaining money for drugs as a motive.

By the late 1990s, drug-related arrests and convictions appeared to continue to be increasing. For example, 22% of local jail inmates in 1996[29] and 22% of State prison inmates in 1998[30] were serving time based on a drug-related charge as their most serious offense. In addition, between 1990 and 1998, there was a doubling in the number of Federal prison inmates serving time because of a drug charge (from 30,470 to 63,011 sentenced inmates).[31] As was the case in 1991, more women (27%) than men (21%) were sentenced to local jails for a drug offense.[32] In State prisons, there was a large increase in drug-related offenses for women such that drug offenders accounted for the largest source of the total growth among female inmates (36%) versus 18% among male inmates.[33] In Federal prisons in 1998, 1 in 10 of the 63,011 prisoners serving time for drug offenses were women.[34] In 1996, about 28% of both blacks and Hispanics compared with 14% of whites were in local jails for a drug offense.[35] In State prisons in 1998, drug offenses accounted for 25% of the total growth among black inmates, 18% among Hispanics, and 12% among whites. The largest numbers of State prisoners in 1998 serving time for drug-related offenses were black (134,800), then Hispanic (51,700) or white (46,-300).[36] Also, there were more whites than blacks or those from other races/ethnicities in Federal prisons (54% were white vs. 45% black and 1.4% other).[37]

As was the case in the 1980s and early 1990s, drug use was common in the late 1990s among inmates serving time for burglary, robbery, or drug offenses. In 1996, 55% of local jail inmates had used drugs in the month before being arrested for their current offense, and 36% were using drugs at the time of the offense,[38] comparable estimates for State and Federal prisoners in 1997 were 57% and 45%, respectively, for use in the month prior to being arrested and 33% and 22% at the time of the offense.[39] Moreover, within local

29. Harlow, *supra* note 22.

30. Allen J. Beck, Prison and Jail Inmates at Midyear, 1999 (Bureau of Justice Statistics, NCJ 181643, 2000).

31. Allen J. Beck, Prisoners in 1999 (Bureau of Justice Statistics, NCJ 183476, 2000).

32. Harlow, *supra* note 22.

33. *Supra* notes 30 and 31.

34. Bureau of Justice Statistics [hereinafter BJS], Compendium of Federal Justice Statistics, 1998 (2000).

35. Harlow, *supra* note 22.

36. Beck, *supra* note 30.

37. BJS, *supra* note 34.

38. Harlow, *supra* note 22.

39. Mumola, *supra* note 24.

jails in 1996 and within State and Federal prisons in 1997, one in six prisoners (about 16% to 19%) said that they committed their offense in order to get money for drugs.[40]

§ 9–2.3 Two Worlds of Drug Use

The data examined from the HSS, the NHSDA, and the MWS paint a very different picture of drug use than the data portrayed by the BJS surveys of jail, State, and Federal prison inmates. They suggest that there may be two very different worlds of drug use represented by these varied populations. A National Research Council (NRC) report concurs with this notion and vividly describes two different worlds of drug use.[41]

> In one world, that of relatively low-intensity consumption (drug *use*) among individuals who can be found in schools and households, drug experience is self-reported more frequently by the wealthy than the less wealthy and by whites than Hispanics or blacks. In this world, there have been steady and cumulatively very marked declines in the prevalence of marijuana use since the late 1970s and of cocaine since the middle 1980s, and heroin use is so rare as to be barely measurable. In another world, that of emergency rooms, morgues, drug clinics, juvenile detention centers, jails, and prisons, in which indicators of intensive drug consumption (*abuse* and *dependence*) are collected: the poor predominate, blacks and Hispanics appearing in numbers much higher than their household or school proportions; marijuana and heroin use are common (though less so in some areas than in the 1970s); and cocaine use increased explosively throughout the 1980s and simply leveled off at high levels in the 1990s.

In addition to data from the jail and prison inmate surveys, an additional useful source of data to examine the extent and trends in the use of heroin and cocaine among hard-core users is the Drug Abuse Warning Network (DAWN) data from hospital emergency departments. DAWN provides semiannual estimates of the number of drug-related visits to hospital emergency departments based on a nationally representative sample of short-stay general hospitals located throughout the coterminous United States. DAWN also collects information on drug-related deaths from selected medical examiner offices. Emergency room estimates are collected from a representative sample of eligible hospitals with oversampling in 21 metropolitan areas. Drug-related death data are produced for more than 40 metropolitan areas.

Prior to 1989, DAWN data were obtained from a set of hospitals that were not statistically representative of any defined population, making it difficult to assess the validity of trends. Since 1989, however, participating hospitals have been representative of defined areas, so trend data can be more reliably assessed.[42] Although most adults aged 26 to 34 and 35 or older in the U.S. general household population in the NHSDA series during the 1980s and 1990s showed declining drug use patterns, that is not necessarily the case for

40. *Id.*; Wilson, *supra* note 23.

41. PREVENTING DRUG ABUSE: WHAT DO WE KNOW? (Dean R. Gerstein & L. W. Green eds., 1993).

42. NATIONAL INSTITUTE ON DRUG ABUSE, ANNUAL EMERGENCY ROOM DATA: 1991 (1992); SAMHSA, ESTIMATES FROM THE DRUG ABUSE WARNING NETWORK: 1992 ESTIMATES OF DRUG-RELATED EMERGENCY ROOM EPISODES (1993); SAMHSA, YEAREND 1999 EMERGENCY DEPARTMENT DATA FROM THE DRUG ABUSE WARNING NETWORK (2000); SAMHSA, DRUG ABUSE WARNING NETWORK: ANNUAL MEDICAL EXAMINER DATA, 1998 (2000).

the heavy or more chronic drug users or those entering the criminal justice system. There is some evidence that the aging of the heavy drug-using cohort of the late 1970s resulted in a shift of the age distribution of the illicit drug-using population. According to DAWN data, among those aged 35 or older there was a 20% to 40% increase in heroin, cocaine, and marijuana/hashish episodes between 1994 and 1996.[43]

In addition, the segment of drug users who visit the hospital for drug-related emergencies may represent the higher risk groups among each age group, thus accounting for the differences in trends indicated by DAWN compared to the general population. From 1990 through 1994, DAWN data showed an alarming increase in drug-related episodes concerning heroin (113% increase), cocaine (78% increase), marijuana (219% increase), and methamphetamine (237% increase). However, rates from 1994 through 1996 either declined or remained stable for these drugs (except for marijuana-related episodes, which continued to increase). Overall drug-related hospital emergency department episodes in 1996 declined significantly from 1994 and 1995.[44]

From 1990 to 1999 overall, the number of total drug-related episodes reported to DAWN increased 49%, from 371,208 to 554,932.[45] Mentions of the four major illicit drugs increased from 1990 to 1999:

- marijuana/hashish (455%, from 15,706 to 87,150);
- methamphetamine/speed (100%, from 5,236 to 10,447);
- heroin/morphine (149%, from 33,884 to 84,409); and
- cocaine (110%, from 80,355 to 168,763).

These increases do not, however, necessarily indicate increased use among the hard-core drug-using population. There are many possible alternative explanations for the cocaine increase, for example, including changes in the extent to which emergency department personnel correctly ascertain the presence of cocaine in a presenting patient; changes in the purity of cocaine may have increased the effective dosage; added adulterants could have increased toxicity; lower prices may have resulted in people taking higher doses; or more new users may be taking cocaine, resulting in "over" reactions to its effects. Nevertheless, the increases in emergency department mentions of cocaine and other drugs throughout the 1990s suggest that use of marijuana, methamphetamine, heroin, and cocaine may not be declining among all subgroups compared with data from the U.S. general household population.[46]

Other less reliable indicators than the DAWN data corroborate the suggestion that illicit drug use may not be declining among all subgroups of the population. One such indicator comes from the Drug Use Forecasting (DUF) system, which was renamed the Arrestee Drug Abuse Monitoring Program (ADAM) in 1997.[47] This system assesses illicit drug use among recent

43. SAMHSA, *supra* note 12.

44. *Id.*

45. SAMHSA, Year-end 1999 Emergency Department Data From the Drug Abuse Warning Network (2000).

46. SAMSHA, *supra* note 8.

47. National Institute of Justice (NIJ), 1995 Drug Use Forecasting: Annual Report on Adult and Juvenile Arrestees (1996); NIJ, Drug Use Forecasting: 1996 annual Report (1996); NIJ, 1997 Drug Use Forecasting: Annual Report on Adult and Juvenile Arrestees: Arrestee Drug Abuse Monitoring Program (1998); Erick

arrestees in selected metropolitan areas. Because of the nature of the data collection procedures, as well as limitations of the design of the system, it is difficult to know what the trends reflect about the larger society. However, the data do show that there are very high levels of illicit drug use among recent arrestees, approaching or even exceeding 50% in some locations. And there is no evidence of any consistent decline in such proportions because the data were first collected in 1986. These findings are supported by those from the BJS inmate surveys described above. In particular, in 1995, the percentages of arrestees testing positive for any drug ranged from 51% to 83% for males and from 41% to 84% for females.[48]

Use of specific drugs also varies by geographic location, a phenomenon that likely reflects the availability and popularity of particular drugs. Methamphetamine use increased significantly between 1990 and 1996 and appeared to be increasing, especially in the western portion of the United States.[49] This finding is consistent with data from the DUF/ADAM Program[50] and findings compiled by an epidemiological workgroup in 20 major metropolitan areas.[51] More specifically, reports from the East and Northeast indicated low use or no increase in the use of methamphetamine, while all western sites reported an increase or high frequency of use, especially among youths and young adults.[52] The 1999 NHSDA and subsequent NHSDAs will provide detailed State-specific trend data so that illicit drug use can be tracked more easily.[53]

Taken together, the data from the HSS, NHSDA, MWS, and BJS surveys, along with those from DAWN and DUF/ADAM, reinforce the idea that there may well be very different worlds of drug use. Hard-core illicit drug use does not appear to be declining, although it seems clear that there are declining numbers of experimental and casual users among the general household and military populations. This suggests a mixed message for the courts. On the one hand, the data are encouraging in that reduced use means that some persons who were at risk of becoming involved in adjudication will not become a burden on the court system. On the other hand, the high rates of use among some groups, the lack of apparent decline among heavier users, and the high levels of use observed in the inmate surveys suggest that drug use is likely to remain a common problem among offenders who enter the court system.

§ 9–2.4 Summary of Survey Findings

The HSS, the NHSDA, and the MWS series all indicate that illicit drug use has generally declined over the past decade or more. The decline is evident among the populations of young people, households, and military personnel. Nevertheless, despite these declines, drug use continues to affect significant proportions of society, a subset of whom are likely to become inmates in jails or prisons. Heavy alcohol use also exhibits negative effects on users, and, unlike illicit drug use, survey findings suggest that its prevalence

D. Wish, *U.S. Drug Policy in the 1990s: Insights From New Data From Arrestees*, 25 INT'N J. OF THE ADDICTIONS 377 (1990).

48. NIJ, DRUG USE FORECASTING: 1996 ANNUAL REPORT, *supra* note 47.

49. SAMHSA, *supra* note 12.

50. *See supra* note 47.

51. NIDA, EPIDEMIOLOGIC TRENDS IN DRUG ABUSE (1996).

52. *Id.*

53. SAMHSA, *supra* note 8.

has not been decreasing. Although surveys of the general population do not provide meaningful estimates of hard-core use of illicit drugs, findings from alternative sources suggest that rates of heavy use of cocaine and heroin may be stable or even increasing.

Although survey findings are useful in helping us understand trends and patterns of use, they do not, of course, predict drug use behavior of individual defendants who face litigation in the courts. Rather, they provide a context for understanding general societal drug use patterns, including those for offender populations. Other more objective indicators of drug use are needed for addressing individual drug use behavior in the courtroom setting. The most accepted objective procedures to detect and identify drugs are chemical tests. The remainder of this chapter reviews the assumptions, procedures, technology, and utility of these tests.

§ 9–2.5   The Pharmacokinetics of Drugs

A knowledge of the basic principles of pharmacology, toxicology, and pharmacokinetics is essential for selecting the specimens to be tested, deciding which drug testing methods to employ, and interpreting drug test results. General pharmacokinetic principles are discussed briefly here. A discussion of toxicology and pharmacology is presented in other chapters of this text (e.g., Chapter 27) and may be found in a variety of textbooks.[54] Collectively, four processes are involved in pharmacokinetics: absorption of drugs into the body, distribution of drugs throughout the body, biotransformation of the drugs, and elimination of the drugs from the body.

Most therapeutically prescribed drugs are taken orally. When taken by mouth, the drug is absorbed into the bloodstream from the gastrointestinal tract. In contrast, drugs of abuse are often self-administered through other routes. For example, marijuana, forms of methamphetamine, and crack cocaine may be smoked. Cocaine is also taken by insufflation or "snorting" the drug into the nasal passages. Intravenous injection is another common method of self-administering heroin, cocaine, and stimulant drugs. Regardless of the route of administration, drugs enter the bloodstream and are distributed throughout the body. During this distribution phase, the drugs are carried to the major organs of the body, the brain and central nervous system, and eventually to muscle, fat, and bone. A number of chemical and biochemical factors (e.g., water or lipid solubility, pH, and chemical structure of the drug) determine the extent of deposition of the drug into each body compartment.

The body contains enzymes designed to biotransform drugs and other ingested toxins. The liver is the primary site of these enzymes that work to modify the drug's chemical structure by usually making it more water soluble and, therefore, more easily eliminated from the body. This process of chemically altering the drug is called "metabolism," and the chemically altered drug is called a "drug metabolite." Most drug metabolites are filtered from the blood by organs, such as the kidney, and subsequently eliminated.

The preceding discussion of absorption, distribution, metabolism, and elimination of drugs is a simplistic overview of a complex series of events.

54. Alfred G. Gilman et al., THE PHARMACO- LOGICAL BASIS OF THERAPEUTICS (8th ed., 1990); Avran Goldstein et al., PRINCIPLES OF DRUG AC- TION (1974); BASIC AND CLINICAL PHARMACOLOGY (G. Bertram ed., 6th ed.1995).

There are numerous creative and even bizarre ways that drug abusers administer drugs. The distribution and rate of distribution of drugs into the various body fluids and tissues are dependent on the drug ingested and the route of administration. Metabolism may occur in body tissues other than the liver, and it may be a multistep biochemical process. Elimination of drugs may occur through numerous routes, such as expired air (e.g., ethanol) and feces (e.g., opiate drugs). However, the pharmacokinetics of each individual drug is somewhat predictable. By knowing the pharmacokinetics of the drug, toxicologists can select the proper specimen(s) to test and can predict the metabolites that should be detected. If a drug is prescribed therapeutically and taken in the recommended doses, the blood drug concentration can be reasonably predicted. The scientific literature also provides sufficient information about drug concentrations in the blood and other tissues to assist in determining whether a toxic or lethal dose of a drug may have been ingested. However (as discussed below), predicting the effects of a drug given its body fluid or tissue concentration, or the dose ingested, is a complex undertaking that should be done with scientific caution.

§ 9–2.6 Specimen Selection

To ensure that comprehensive testing can be performed and that the drug test results can be meaningfully interpreted, the appropriate specimens must be collected. A variety of specimens can be used for testing, including blood, urine, hair, oral fluids, and other body tissues. Specimen selection for postmortem testing, driving under the influence (DUI) testing, and workplace testing are discussed below because this testing often has medicolegal implications.

§ 9–2.6.1 Postmortem Testing

Postmortem toxicology testing may follow deaths from intentional, accidental, and homicidal overdoses or to ensure compliance with prescribed medications, as well as a host of related reasons. Table 9.3 shows the availability of various specimens at autopsy, their utility for drug screening and confirmation/quantitation, and their usefulness for interpretation. (For the purposes of this discussion, drug confirmation and quantitation have not been segregated.) Blood is available for postmortem collection except in extreme circumstances, such as death by fire, if the body is decomposed, or if the body has been embalmed or exhumed. Blood is a valuable specimen because most drugs can be detected in the blood and because, of all specimens, blood drug concentrations often correlate well with dose. Confirmation and quantitation analyses are usually performed using the blood because there is a wealth of scientific literature relating blood drug concentrations to therapeutic use, toxicity, and lethality.[55]

55. Randall C. Baselt, DISPOSITION OF TOXIC DRUGS AND CHEMICALS IN MAN (5th ed.1999); A.H. Stead & A.C. Moffat, *A Collection of Therapeu-* *tic, Toxic and Fatal Blood Drug Concentrations in Man*, 3 HUM. TOXICOLOGY 437 (1983).

Table 9.3 Specimen Availability and Utility for Postmortem Testing

Specimen	Availability[a]	Screen[b]	Confirm/ Quantitate[b]	Interpret[b]
Most Useful Specimens				
Blood	****	****	****	****
Urine	**	****	****	**
Liver	****	**	***	***
Kidney	****	**	***	**
Vitreous Humor	***	***	***	***
Less Useful Specimens				
Brain	***	*	**	**
Gastric Contents	**	**	**	**
History	****	NA	NA	*
Medications	**	NA	NA	*
Syringes and Solid Doses	**	**	***	*
Hair	***	*	*	*

Note: Asterisks (*) provide an indication of the availability and utility of the specimen. The more asterisks, the greater the value.

[a] Availability refers to whether the specimen or evidence can be collected during a medical examiner investigation. Blood is usually available, and urine is less likely to be available.

[b] Utility is ranked for the usefulness of each specimen for screen testing, confirmation/quantitation, and interpretation in postmortem toxicology.

As discussed, many drugs and drug metabolites are excreted from the body in the urine; consequently, their concentrations in the urine usually exceed those found in the blood. This makes urine a useful specimen for drug screening. However, because the urine volume changes from day to day and the excretion of some drugs is dependent on urinary pH, it is difficult to relate urine drug concentrations to specific physiological or toxicological findings.[56] For example, if the deceased had consumed copious amounts of fluids prior to death, the urine would be diluted and the drug concentration reduced. Conversely, if the deceased were dehydrated, urine drug concentrations might be higher than expected for a given dose of drug.

Liver tissue is often collected at autopsy. Because it is the organ responsible for metabolizing many drugs, liver tissue concentrations are often higher than those found in blood. This makes liver tissue a valuable specimen for drug screening. Confirmation and quantitation analyses are also readily performed in the liver due again to the high drug concentrations. There is an extensive body of literature to assist with the interpretation of drugs and their metabolites detected in liver tissue.[57]

Kidney tissue, like liver tissue, may be available for collection at autopsy when blood and urine are not. Drug and metabolite concentrations in the kidneys are usually higher than those found in the blood because the kidneys filter the blood and are a repository for drugs and drug metabolites prior to their elimination in the urine. Interpretation of kidney drug concentrations, however, is somewhat hampered by the lack of literature relating drug dose to tissue concentration.

56. H. Wan et al., *Kinetics, Salivary Excretion of Amphetamine Isomers, and Effect of Urinary pH*, 23 CLINICAL PHARMACOLOGY AND THERAPEUTICS 585 (1978).

57. Baselt, *supra* note 55.

Vitreous humor (eye fluid) is useful for the testing of volatile drugs, such as ethanol, but it has limited utility for general drug screening due to the small volume of the sample (2 to 3 mL).[58]

All other tissues shown in Table 9.3 are less useful to the forensic toxicologist for testing and interpretation. Their usefulness may be limited because they contain minimal concentrations of the drugs, they are difficult to test, or there is little scientific literature to assist the toxicologist in interpreting test results obtained from these specimens.

Drug use and medication histories can provide valuable collaborative information in a death investigation. These histories may assist by focusing the investigation on specific drugs that may have contributed to the death and are often used to support the laboratory's analytical findings. Syringes and solid dose materials serve a similar function in a medical examiner's investigation. In addition, syringes, solid doses, and related materials are easily analyzed by the laboratory because drug concentrations in these materials are extremely high compared to those found in biological specimens. This makes identification and confirmation of drugs in these materials far less complex than in biological specimens.

§ 9–2.6.2 DUI Testing

Table 9.4 shows several biological specimens and their value for testing and interpretation in forensic cases involving drug use and driving. DUI cases present a testing challenge for the forensic laboratory. Unlike medical examiner testing, the subject is living, and as a result, the specimens available for collection are typically limited to blood and urine. The utility of these specimens for screening, confirmation, quantitation, and interpretation was discussed above. Treatment of blood to remove the red blood cells leaves a clear aqueous material called "serum" or "plasma" (depending on the treatment). Plasma and serum specimens are sometimes used in DUI testing and contain drugs at concentrations similar to those found in untreated blood. However, drugs may preferentially partition into the serum, plasma, or red blood cells. Therefore, a distinction must be made between test results from whole blood, plasma, or serum. Plasma and serum may actually be preferable specimens for testing because much of the pharmacokinetic literature relates dose to plasma/serum concentration. Similarly, the performance literature often compares plasma/serum drug concentrations to levels of impairment.

58. MEDICOLEGAL ASPECTS OF ALCOHOL DETERMINATION IN BIOLOGICAL SPECIMENS (James C. Garriott ed., 3rd ed.1996).

Table 9.4 Specimen Availability and Utility for DUI Testing

Specimen	Availability[a]	Screen[b]	Confirm/ Quantitate[b]	Interpret[b]
Blood	****	****	****	****
Plasma/Serum	****	****	****	****
Urine	**	****	****	**
Gastric/Emesis	**	***	***	*
Syringes and Solid Dose Forms	*	**	***	*
Medications	**	NA	NA	*
History	**	NA	NA	**

Note: The number of asterisks (*) indicates the relative value of the method. Methods with more asterisks are considered more reliable than those with fewer asterisks.

[a] Availability refers to whether the specimen or evidence can usually be obtained during a DUI investigation. Blood and plasma/serum are readily collected. Urine is less likely to be available to the investigator.

[b] Utility is ranked as the usefulness of each specimen for screen testing, confirmation/quantitation and interpretation.

Breath has become increasingly popular as a specimen to test for alcohol in DUI cases.[59] However, the vast majority of drugs of abuse are not sufficiently volatile to be detected in breath.

§ 9–2.6.3   Workplace Testing

Workplace drug testing has been primarily performed with urine.[60] There are several advantages to urine testing in workplace programs. It can be collected without the use of invasive techniques, it can be easily tested, and it is an ideal specimen for detecting recent drug use.

The objectives of detecting and deterring drug use differentiate workplace testing from medical examiner and DUI investigations.[61] Federal agencies, such as the Department of Transportation (DOT), have instituted programs to test blood and other tissue following accidents and fatalities.[62] However, this testing is minor in comparison to the mainstream of workplace testing that is performed using urine.

Hair, sweat, and saliva have been advocated as alternative specimens to urine for workplace drug testing. The advantages and disadvantages of these specimens are discussed below.

§ 9–2.7   Chemical Testing Methods

This section discusses the technologies that are commonly used for drug testing. Discussed are thin-layer chromatography (TLC), immunoassay (IA), gas chromatography (GC), high-performance liquid chromatography (HPLC), tandem mass spectrometry (MS/MS), and ion trap mass spectrometry. The description of these techniques is followed by a discussion of the evidentiary value of drug test results obtained using the technologies.

59. UNDER THE INFLUENCE? DRUGS AND THE AMERICAN WORK FORCE (Jacques Normand et al. eds., National Research Council/Institute of Medicine, 1994).

60. *Id.*

61. *Id.*

62. Department of Transportation (DOT), Federal Highway Administration, Drug and Alcohol Testing Programs, 49 C.F.R. pt. 350 (1992).

Testing can be divided into three general categories: (a) screen tests, (b) confirmation tests, and (c) quantitation tests. The function of the screen or qualitative test (see the definitions at the end of the chapter) is to determine whether the sample(s) being analyzed *potentially* contains or does not contain any drugs. Confirmation tests are additional, independent chemical tests used to verify the drug's presence or its absence. Confirmation tests are more accurate and specific than screen tests. Typically, screen tests use methods that are less expensive and less technically challenging than confirmation methods. Screen tests are also less reliable than confirmation tests and are likely to produce some positive results that are not confirmed (i.e., misidentify nonusers as users). Thus, screen tests should be used as indicators of possible drug use, but require a second, more reliable, confirmation analysis to unequivocally establish the presence of the drug. With few exceptions, analyses for medicolegal purposes should include both a screen test and a confirmatory test, and these two independent tests should rely on separate chemical principles to detect and confirm the drug.

Often, confirmation tests are quantitative such that the laboratory can simultaneously establish the drug's chemical identity and determine the amount, or quantity, of drug in the sample. Interpretation of the drug's effect on driving or its toxicity or lethality is problematic without a quantitative measurement.

For workplace drug testing of Federal and DOT-regulated employees, the analytical methods for screening, confirmation, and quantitation are mandated by Federal regulations.[63] However, for the vast majority of forensic analyses, the analytical methods that are used are selected at the discretion of the laboratory. This discretion has led to both positive and negative consequences.[64] Conscientious laboratories are more likely to stay abreast of scientific developments and adopt new testing methods and technologies as they become available. In contrast, less progressive and poorly funded laboratories may select testing methods that are less reliable, and use dated technologies.[65] Drug tests from laboratories using dated methods are less reliable and their results have limited or questionable evidentiary value.

§ 9–2.7.1 Thin–Layer Chromatography (TLC)

TLC and related paper chromatography techniques are very versatile testing methods.[66] Separation of a complex mixture of drugs is achieved with a TLC plate or a paper strip.[67] The TLC plate consists of a thin coating of silica gel (or similar material) on an inert plastic or glass plate.

To use TLC, the drugs must first be extracted from the biological matrix. Biological specimens are aqueous or water containing; therefore, they are not soluble in organic solvents. For example, when water (a biological specimen) is

63. Department of Health and Human Services (DHHS), Mandatory Guidelines for Federal Workplace Testing Programs, 58 Fed. Reg. 6062–72, (1993); DOT, *supra* note 62.

64. Alan H.B. Wu et al., *44 Minimal Standards for the Performance and Interpretation of Toxicology Tests in Legal Cases*, 44 J. Forensic Sci. 515 (1999).

65. *Id.*

66. Clarke's Isolation and Identification of Drugs in Pharmaceuticals, Body Fluids, and Post-Mortem Material, (A.C. Moffat et al. eds., 2d ed.1986).

67. Analytical Procedures for Therapeutic Drug Monitoring and Emergency Toxicology, (Randall C. Baselt ed., 1980); Analytical Methods in Forensic Chemistry, (Matt H. Ho ed., 1990).

mixed with vegetable oil (organic), two layers of liquid are obtained. By adjusting the acidity (pH) of the biological specimen, drugs can be selectively "extracted" or removed from the specimen by an organic solvent, such as chloroform. The organic solvent may then be reduced in volume by evaporation. Evaporation concentrates the drug and improves the likelihood of detection. For example, the blood specimen collected from a DUI suspect contains 1,000 ng/mL of a drug (see definitions at the end of this chapter for units of weight). One mL of the blood is placed in a glass tube, the pH of the blood is adjusted to extract the drug, and 5 mL of organic solvent is then added to the tube. The tube is then capped and mixed. The organic solvent (now containing the drug) is allowed to separate, then it is removed and evaporated to 0.1 mL. The solvent now contains 1,000 ng of drug in a 0.1 mL volume. Therefore, the drug is now 10 times more concentrated in the organic solvent than it was in the original blood specimen. A portion of the organic solvent containing the extracted, and concentrated, drug is then transferred or "spotted" near the bottom of the TLC plate and allowed to dry. The plate is placed in a standing position in a closed glass chamber containing a liquid migration solvent. The volume of migration solvent is adjusted such that it wets the bottom of the TLC plate and then diffuses up the plate. As the solvent migrates up the plate, drugs contained in the spotted extract travel up the plate and are separated. The extent to which the drugs migrate depends on a number of factors, such as the chemical nature of the drug, the components of the migration solvent, and the type of coating on the plate. After the solvent has migrated to the top of the TLC plate, the plate is removed from the chamber and dried. Selective sprays are applied to the plate to visualize the drugs.

The advantages of TLC are that the equipment is inexpensive, 10 to 20 samples can be analyzed simultaneously, minimal training and expertise are required to use the technique, and large numbers of drugs can be tested rapidly and simultaneously. The disadvantages of the TLC procedure are that it lacks the sensitivity to identify most drugs in blood, some experience is needed to interpret the results, and results are strictly qualitative (see Table 9.5).

Table 9.5
Summary of Chemical Testing Methods

Testing Method	Time	Type of Test			Expertise Required	Equipment Cost
		Qualitative (Screen)	Confirmation	Quantitative		
Thin-Layer Chromatography (TLC)	**	**	?	NA	**	*
Immunoassays (IAs)						
Enzyme Immunoassay (EIA)	*	**	*?	NA	*	**
Radioactive Immunoassay (RIA)	**	**	*?	NA	**	**
Fluorescence Immunoassay (FPIA)	**	**	*?	NA	*	**
Gas Chromatography (GC)						
Flame Ionization Detector (FID)	***	***	**	**	***	**
Nitrogen Phosphorus Detector (NPD)	****	****	***	***	****	***
Electron Capture Detector (ECD)	****	****	***	***	****	***
Mass Spectrometry (MS)	*****	*****	*****	*****	*****	*****
High-Performance Liquid Chromatography (HPLC)						
Ultraviolet (UV)	***	**	*	**	***	***
Electrochemical (EC)	****	***	**	***	****	***
Fluorescence	****	**	**	***	****	***
Mass Spectrometry (MS)	*****	*****	*****	*****	*****	*****
Tandem Mass Spectrometry (MS/MS)	*****	*****	*****	*****	*****	*****
Ion Trap Mass Spectrometry (MS)	*****	*****	*****	*****	*****	*****

Note: The number of asterisks (*) indicates the relative value of the method. Methods with more asterisks are considered more reliable than those with fewer asterisks.

? = Questionable value.

NA = Not applicable.

§ 9–2.7.2   Immunoassays (IAs)

In recent years, laboratory-based IA techniques have become widely used to test urine samples for drug abuse.[68] These IA tests are easy to use,

68. COLLEGE OF AMERICAN PATHOLOGISTS & AMERICAN ASSOCIATION OF CLINICAL CHEMISTS, STAN- dards for Accreditation: Forensic Urine Drug Testing Laboratories (1990).

sensitive, rapid, and inexpensive. IA test kits have been marketed for clinical, forensic, probation and parole, and workplace testing.[69] The test kits contain antibodies designed to detect a specific drug or drug metabolite and are based on competition between the drug in the donor's urine and the labeled drug in the test kit for a limited number of antibodies. Commercially available IA kits have drugs with radioactive (RIA), fluorescence (FPIA), and enzyme (EIA) labels.[70] The tests are relatively specific for the target drug or metabolite and are much more sensitive than TLC. Also, the cost per test is comparatively low, no sample pretreatment or extraction is required, limited training is needed to perform the tests, and the tests are easily automated. Because of these features, laboratory-based IA analyses have gained wide acceptance for drug screening in a variety of settings. Unfortunately, in probation, parole, rehabilitation, and similar settings, operators with little scientific background often conduct the tests. These analysts may not be aware of the limitations of the test or how to properly interpret the test results.

A limitation of all IA tests is that they may show antibody cross-reactivity to drugs, drug metabolites, and endogenous compounds with chemical structures similar to the target drug.[71] This problem is exemplified by IA screen tests for amphetamines.[72] Over-the-counter (OTC) drugs, such as phenylpropanolamine, ephedrine, pseudoephedrine, and l-desoxyephedrine (see l-methamphetamine), have remarkably similar chemical structures to amphetamine and methamphetamine and may produce IA-positive screen test results. IA tests are also limited in the number of drugs that they can detect, they must be modified to test specimens other than urine, and the data are often misinterpreted by unqualified technicians. For medicolegal testing, all IA screen test results should be confirmed by an alternate chemical test, and an experienced forensic toxicologist should be consulted to interpret the results.

Concerns about drug abuse and the need for immediate results have created a market for easy-to-use and non-instrumented IA urine screening devices called "on-site" testing devices. Numerous on-site drug testing devices have been described in the literature (e.g., TesTcup®, Triage®, TesTstik®, Rapid Drug Screen®).[73] These devices are immunoassay based, compact (usually ~5 cm by 10 cm), and easily transported and stored; moreover, laboratory equipment is not required to perform the testing. As a result, they are used in remote sites, such as offshore oil-drilling rigs, nuclear facilities, and maritime operations, where use of sophisticated equipment is not practical. Typical drugs tested by the devices include amphetamine, methamphetamine, cocaine metabolite, marijuana metabolite, opiates, and phencyclidine (PCP). For forensic purposes, the devices have been advocated for workplace, criminal justice, and highway safety drug testing. In the workplace, they are used to test employees who must be drug-free as a condition of access to the job site

69. DHHS, *supra* note 63.

70. Olaf H. Drummer, *Review Methods for the Measurement of Benzodiazepines in Biological Samples*, 713 J. Chromatography B, Biomedical Sciences & Applications 201 (1998); Textbook of biopharmaceutical analysis (Robert L. Smith & James T. Stewart eds., 1981).

71. Drummer, *supra* note 70.

72. Michael R. Baylor & Dennis J. Crouch, *Sympathomimetic Amines: Pharmacology, Toxicology and Analysis*, 14 Clinical Chemistry 103 (1993).

73. Dennis J. Crouch, *Alternative Drugs, Specimens and Approaches for Non-regulated Workplace Drug Testing*, in Drug Abuse Handbook 776–93 (1998).

and for use at remote locations where laboratory facilities are not available. In highway safety, on-site devices have been promoted to provide collaborative data in support of field sobriety observations. The devices have several advantages. To conduct the testing, there is no need for a laboratory, sophisticated instrumentation, pretreatment of the urine, or expertly trained personnel. In addition, the test results are usually available within minutes of specimen collection, and the potential for errors that occur when shipping specimens and transcribing data is minimized. Some devices are so cleverly engineered that they serve as both the collection and testing vessel.[74]

The disadvantages of on-site urine screening devices are similar to those of laboratory-based IA tests. The devices are designed to test urine and are not useful for testing other biological matrices. The devices may have cross reactivity to chemically similar drugs, drug metabolites, and endogenous compounds, which often leads to positive screening results that cannot be confirmed. Because the devices are so easy to use, analysts who have limited or no toxicology experience often perform the testing and interpret the test results. An additional disadvantage of the devices is that the results are subjectively interpreted, meaning that the analyst visually reads the results and decides whether to report a positive or negative result. This creates two problems: There is no objective record of the device's results as there are with instrumented IAs; consequently, there are no results for defense review or evidential purposes.

The DHHS has issued draft guidelines that allow the use of on-site IA testing in federally regulated workplace testing programs.[75] This is a major philosophical change in their program. Previously, the DHHS required all screen and confirmation testing to be performed in a single, fully equipped, and fully staffed laboratory.[76] The proposed changes allow a facility to screen urine samples at the point of collection. This screening could be performed using laboratory-based IA methods or on-site testing devices. Confirmation testing would still be performed in a laboratory. At this time, the regulations are in draft form, and public comment is being solicited. It is likely that this change in philosophy will greatly increase the volume of urinalysis testing at the site of collection. It may also increase the litigation surrounding workplace testing because donors may be denied employment or denied access to a work site based on a subjectively read and unconfirmed IA screen test results.

§ 9–2.7.3 Gas Chromatography (GC)

GC is the most widely used and versatile testing technology in the forensic laboratory.[77] GC may be used with a variety of detectors (described below), such as the flame ionization detector (FID), nitrogen phosphorous detector (NPD), electron capture detector (ECD), and mass spectrometry (MS)

74. James Towt et al., *Ontrack Testcup: A Novel, On-site, Muti-analyte Screen for the Detection of Abused Drugs*, 19 J. ANALYTICAL TOXICOLOGY 504 (1995).

75. SAMHSA, *Mandatory Guidelines for Alternative Specimens and Technologies*, available at http://www.health.org:80/workplace/GDLNS–94.htm, 2000b.

76. DHHS, Mandatory Guidelines for Federal Workplace Testing Programs, 53 Fed. Reg. 11970–89 (1988).

77. ANALYTICAL METHODS IN HUMAN TOXICOLOGY: PART 1 (Alan S. Curry ed., 1985).

detector.[78] These detectors vary in specificity, sensitivity, complexity, and cost (see Table 9.5).

Like other types of chromatography, GC is a separation technique. Drugs are isolated from the biological specimen by extraction (see above discussion on TLC). The organic solvent, which may contain a complex mixture of extracted drug(s), is flash vaporized in the GC injector, the drugs are separated by the GC column, and the detector identifies the drugs.

Capillary GC columns are typically 15 to 60 m in length, have an internal diameter of less than 1 mm, and an interior coated with a material that facilitates separation of the drugs. The column is placed in a heated GC oven with one end attached to an injector and the other end to a detector. The injector port is heated and vaporizes the injected drugs. An inert carrier gas, such as nitrogen or helium, sweeps through the injector and the GC column carrying the drugs to the detector. Drugs in the injected specimen extract interact with the column coating to various degrees as the carrier gas sweeps them along. Due to the combination of column temperature, column coating, and the chemical structure of each drug, the mixture of drugs is separated into its individual components. As each drug elutes from the GC column, it produces a response by the detector. The time from injection of the extract onto the column until detection of the drug at the detector is called the drug's "retention time." Retention time is used to qualitatively identify the individual drugs in the extract. The magnitude of the detector response is proportional to the concentration or quantity of the drug in the sample. Thus, GC testing can be used as a qualitative technique to identify the drugs and as a quantitative technique to determine each drug's concentration.

Flame Ionization Detector (FID). One of the most versatile detectors for the analysis of drugs, FID is routinely used by most forensic laboratories for alcohol testing, but it can also be used to analyze for many other drugs. A hydrogen flame maintained in the FID thermally decomposes drug eluting from the GC column. The decomposition creates a change in electrical potential near the flame that is measured and recorded. FIDs are easy to use, inexpensive, reliable, and effective in detecting many drugs. The FID's disadvantages are its lack of specificity and sensitivity (see definitions at the end of this chapter). Because the detector responds to carbon-to-hydrogen bonds, it will detect most organic compounds. FIDs also lack the sensitivity to detect and quantitate many drugs in blood, plasma, or serum samples.[79]

Nitrogen Phosphorus Detector (NPD). The NPD responds only to compounds with nitrogen or phosphorus in their chemical structure, which includes many of the drugs shown in Table 9.6, such as opiates, benzodiazepines, cocaine, PCP, barbiturates, amphetamines, and numerous prescription drugs.[80] Many of these drugs are found in the low ng/mL concentrations (see definitions at the end of the chapter) and cannot be reliably detected by a

78. METHODOLOGY FOR ANALYTICAL TOXICOLOGY (Irving Sunshine & Pater I. Jatlow eds., Vol. II, 1982).

79. DHHS, *supra* note 63; Health Care Financing Administration (HCFA), Clinical Laboratory Improvement Amendments of 1988, 55 Fed. Reg. 20896–20959 (1990); TEXTBOOK OF BIOPHARMACEUTICAL ANALYSIS, (Robert L. Smith

& James T. Stewart eds., 1981); METHODOLOGY FOR ANALYTICAL TOXICOLOGY, *supra* note 78.

80. ANALYTICAL PROCEDURES FOR THERAPEUTIC DRUG MONITORING AND EMERGENCY TOXICOLOGY, *supra* note 67; DHHS, *supra* note 63; DOT, *supra* note 62.

FID. However, the NPD can be 100 to 1,000 times more sensitive than a FID for detection of these drugs. NPDs may be used for screening, confirmation, and quantitation. Moreover, they are relatively inexpensive, sensitive, and selective for drugs that contain nitrogen or phosphorous atoms. Their disadvantages are that they require more expertise to operate than FIDs and, although they are more selective than FIDs, they are less selective than the detectors discussed below.

Table 9.6 Common Over-the-Counter, Prescription, and Abused Drugs

Drug Name	Common or Brand Name	Schedule	Use
Acetaminophen	Tylenol®	OTC	Analgesic
Alfentanil	Alfenta®	II	Analgesic
Alprazolam	Xanax®	IV	Antianxiety
Amitriptyline	Elavil®	Prescription	Antidepressant
Amobarbital	Amytal®	II	Hypnotic—drug of abuse
Amphetamine	Dexedrine®	II	Appetite suppression—drug of abuse
Brompheniramine	Dimetane®	OTC	Antihistamine
Butalbital	Fiorinal®	III	Muscle relaxant
Carbamazepine	Tegretol®	Prescription	Anticonvulsant
Carisoprodol	Soma®	Prescription	Muscle relaxant
Chloral Hydrate	Noctec®	IV	Hypnotic
Chlordiazepoxide	Librium®	IV	Antianxiety
Chlorpheniramine	Chlor–Trimeton®	OTC	Antihistamine
Chlorpromazine	Thorazine®	Prescription	Antipsychotic
Clorazepate	Tranzene®	IV	Antianxiety
Cocaine	Cocaine	II	Local anesthetic—drug of abuse
Codeine	Codeine	II	Analgesic and cough suppression
Desipramine	Norpamin®	Prescription	Antidepressant
Diazepam	Valium®	IV	Antianxiety and anticonvulsant
Digoxin	Lanoxin®	Prescription	Cardiac drug
Diphenhydramine	Benadryl®	OTC	Antihistamine
Doxepin	Sinequan®	Prescription	Antidepressant
Ephedrine	Ephedrine®	OTC or Prescription	Decongestant
Fentanyl	Sublimaze®	II	Analgesic
Fluoxetine	Prozac®	Prescription	Antidepressant
Flurazepam	Dalmane®	IV	Sleep induction
Heroin	Heroin	I	Analgesic—drug of abuse
Hydrocodone	Vicodin®	III	Analgesic and cough suppression
Hydromorphone	Dilaudid®	II	Analgesic
Imipramine	Tofranil®	Prescription	Antidepressant
Lidocaine	Xylocaine®	Prescription	Local anesthetic and cardiac drug
Lorazepam	Ativan®	IV	Antianxiety
Lysergic Acid Diethylamine	LSD	I	Hallucinogen
Maprotiline	Ludiomil®	Prescription	Antidepressant
Meperidine	Demerol®	II	Analgesic
Meprobamate	Miltown®	IV	Sedative
Mescaline	Mescaline®	I	Hallucinogen
Mesoridazine	Serentil®	Prescription	Antipsychotic
Methadone	Dolophine®		Treatment of addiction—analgesic
Methamphetamine	Desoxyn®	II	Appetite suppression—attention deficit disorder—drug of abuse
Methaqualone	Methaqualone	I	Drug of abuse
Methylphenidate	Ritalin®	II	Attention deficit disorder
Methylenedioxyamphetamine	MDA	I	Hallucinogen
Methylenedioxymethamphetamine	MDMA	I	Hallucinogen
Morphine	Morphine	II	Analgesic and drug of abuse
Nortriptyline	Pamelor®	Prescription	Antidepressant
Oxazepam	Serax	IV	Antianxiety
Oxycodone	Percodan®	II	Analgesic and drug of abuse
Oxymorphone	Numorphan®	II	Analgesic and drug of abuse
Paroxetine	Paxil®	Prescription	Antidepressant
Pentazocine	Talwin®	III	Analgesic
Pentobarbital	Nembutal®	II	Sedative
Phencyclidine	PCP	I	Drug of abuse—no accepted medical use
Phenobarbital	Phenobarbital	IV	Anticonvulsant
Phentermine	Ionamin®	IV	Appetite suppression—drug of abuse
Phenylbutazone	Butazolidin®	Prescription	Analgesic
Phenylpropanolamine	Phenylpropanolamine	OTC	Decongestant and appetite suppression
Phenytoin	Dilantin®	Prescription	Anticonvulsant
Prazepam	Centrax®	IV	Antianxiety
Primidone	Mysoline®	Prescription	Anticonvulsant
Procainamide	Procan®	Prescription	Cardiac drug
Propranolol	Inderal®	Prescription	Cardiac drug
Propoxyphene	Darvon®	IV	Analgesic
Pseudoephedrine	Sudafed®	OTC	Decongestant
Salicylate (acetylsalicylic acid)	Aspirin	OTC	Analgesic

Drug Name	Common or Brand Name	Schedule	Use
Sertraline	Zoloft®	Prescription	Antidepressant
Secobarbital	Seconal®	II	Hypnotic
Sufentanil	Sufenta®	II	Analgesic
Temazepam	Restoril®	IV	Hypnotic
Terfenadine	Seldane®	Prescription	Antihistamine
Tetrahydrocannabinol	THC	I	Hallucinogen
Theophylline	Theo–Dur®	Prescription	Asthma treatment
Triazolam	Halcion®	IV	Hypnotic
Thioridazine	Mellaril®	Prescription	Antipsychotic
Trazadone	Desyrel®	Prescription	Antidepressant
Valproic acid	Depakene®	Prescription	Anticonvulsant
Verapamil	Calan®, Isoptin®	Prescription	Cardiac drug

Schedule I, no known medical use.
Schedule II, high abuse potential.
Schedule III, some abuse potential.
Schedule IV, low abuse potential.
Schedule V, low abuse potential. Subject to State and local regulation.
No schedule, "NO" abuse potential.

Electron Capture Detector (ECD). The ECD is used to detect drugs having electronegative elements (halogens) in their chemical structure. Many of the drugs known as benzodiazepines contain chlorine or fluorine and are in this category. Examples of these drugs are Valium®, Librium®, Xanax®, Halcion®, Dalmane®, and Ativan®. The ECD is capable of detecting very low ng/mL concentrations (see definitions at the end of the chapter) of many of these drugs in biological samples. The obvious advantages of this detector are its sensitivity and its selectivity. The disadvantages are that the ECD is not useful for testing other drug classes and considerable operator expertise is required.[81]

Mass Spectrometry (MS). The mass spectrometer is the most versatile GC detector.[82] Several modes of MS detection are available and provide the toxicologist with options similar to the versatility of FID and NPD and to the selectivity of ECD. MS detectors are used for GC testing in the following fashion. When a drug elutes from the GC column, it enters the ionization source of the MS detector. In the ion source, the drug is struck with a beam of electrons that assists in breaking the drug molecule into electrically charged ion fragments. These ion fragments are directed through a mass filter containing four rods (quadrupole) so that they are separated by mass-to-charge. All charged fragments may be detected (as with a FID), or the drug may be chemically treated during the ionization process such that nitrogen-containing drugs are detected. Detection of negatively charged fragments by MS is analogous to what happens with GC–ECD. The MS fragmentation pattern is unique for any given drug. The fragmentation pattern combined with the GC retention time provides a high degree of confidence in the qualitative identification of a drug. For this reason, GC/MS is the most universally accepted confirmation technique available to the forensic toxicologist, and it is the confirmation technique required in Federal workplace testing regulations.[83] GC/MS is also used to quantitate drugs because it is sensitive and extremely selective.[84] GC/MS is not widely used for screening because the analyses are time-consuming, require considerable operator expertise, and the instrumentation is more expensive than that required for

81. DHHS, *supra* note 63; TEXTBOOK OF BIO-PHARMACEUTICAL ANALYSIS (Robert L. Smith & James T. Stewart eds., 1981).

82. FORENSIC APPLICATIONS OF MASS SPECTRO-METRY (Jehuda Yinson ed., 1995).

83. DHHS, *supra* note 63; DOT, *supra* note 62.

84. GC/MS ASSAYS FOR ABUSED DRUGS IN BODY FLUIDS, NATIONAL INSTITUTE ON DRUG ABUSE (NIDA RESEARCH MONOGRAPH 32, DHHS PUBLICATION NO. ADM 80–1014, Rodger L. Foltz et al. eds., 1980).

other screening techniques. Currently, GC/MS analysis is considered the gold standard for forensic testing; nonetheless, many methodological and human errors have been made analyzing for drugs using GC/MS methods.[85]

Despite the advantages and value of GC tests for forensic analyses, there are several limitations. Because sample extraction is required and only one sample can be analyzed at a time, GC techniques are time-consuming compared to TLC or IA. The instruments are complex, computer controlled, and expensive. Consequently, operators must be highly trained in the theory and practice of GC testing. Operation of the more specific and sensitive GC detectors, such as MS detectors, requires additional training. Interpretation of GC, and particularly GC/MS data, requires technical expertise that can only be gained through years of training and instrument operation. Additionally, GC tests cannot be used to readily analyze many drugs and particularly drug metabolites, as described in the following discussion.

§ 9–2.7.4 High–Performance or High–Pressure Liquid Chromatography (HPLC)

Metabolism of drugs by the body (discussed earlier) usually results in compounds that are more water soluble, less volatile, and often not easily analyzed by GC tests without extensive sample preparation. For the analysis of these metabolites and other nonvolatile drugs, HPLC offers an alternative screening, confirmation, and quantitation technique.[86] An HPLC system consists of a high-pressure pump, an injector, solvents, a column, and a detector. The column is typically a metal tube, 10 to 30 cm in length with a 2 to 5–mm internal diameter, that is filled with packing material. The liquid solvent functions like the carrier gas in a GC system. It is pumped through the column and carries the drugs to the detector. Solvent flow rates vary from less than 1 mL/min to over 3.0 mL/min, and pressures of up to 5,000 pounds per square inch may result as the solvent is pumped through the narrow, tightly packed column. An injector is used to introduce the sample extract into the solvent stream. The extract is carried through the column by the solvent and separated into its components. A detector identifies the individual components of the sample. Separation is achieved through interactions of the drug or metabolite with the column packing and the pumped solvent. As in GC testing, qualitative identification of drugs is made by retention time, and the magnitude of the detector response is proportional to the concentration of the drug in the sample extract.

Forensic toxicologists use four types of HPLC detectors: ultraviolet, fluorescence, electrochemical, and mass spectrometry (see Table 9.5).

Ultraviolet (UV). UV detectors are the most commonly used. Many organic compounds, including numerous drugs and their metabolites, absorb UV light. The extent of UV absorbance and the exact wavelength of the

---

85. Joseph H. Autry, NOTICE TO THE DHHS/NIDA–CERTIFIED LABORATORIES (National Institute on Drug Abuse, 1990); Joseph H. Autry, NOTICE TO THE DHHS/NIDA–CERTIFIED LABORATORIES (National Institute on Drug Abuse, 1991); Alan H. Wu, *Mechanism of Interferences for Gas Chromatography/Mass Spectrometry Analysis of Urine for Drugs of Abuse*, 25 ANNALS OF CLINICAL LABORATORY SCI. 19 (1995); Alan H.B. Wu et al., *Minimal Standards for the Performance and Interpretation of Toxicology, Tests in Legal Cases*, 44 J. FORENSIC SCI. 515 (1999).

86. DHHS, *supra* note 63; DOT, *supra* note 62; HCFA, *supra* note 79; ANALYTICAL METHODS IN FORENSIC CHEMISTRY, *supra* note 67; METHODOLOGY FOR ANALYTICAL TOXICOLOGY, *supra* note 78.

absorbance is drug dependent and can be used to detect the drug as it elutes from the HPLC column. The advantage of HPLC with UV detection is that many drugs of interest in forensic toxicology absorb light in the UV range and can be detected and quantitated. A major disadvantage is that many organic molecules found in biological samples, in addition to drugs and drug metabolites, also absorb UV light, so interferences are common.[87]

Fluorescence. Drugs may absorb UV light and also emit light. With a fluorescence detector, the wavelength of the light stimulating the drug molecule may be controlled and the emitted fluorescence monitored. Fluorescence detection can be extremely sensitive for the detection and quantitation of certain drugs, but its use has been limited because few drugs demonstrate native fluorescence and the detector response is often linear through a very limited range.[88]

Electrochemical (EC). EC is a third type of HPLC detector. Many drugs can be made to undergo chemical oxidation or reduction reactions that can be detected by EC detectors. Although extremely sensitive for certain drugs and metabolites, EC detectors are not widely used by forensic toxicologists because they require constant attention and maintenance.[89]

Mass Spectrometry (MS). The MS technique is becoming increasingly popular as a detector for HPLC.[90] Technological developments have reduced instrument costs and complexity, making HPLC/MS more attractive to forensic laboratories.[91] The technology has improved such that columns used for HPLC/MS are typically 5 to 15 cm in length with a 1 to 3–mm internal diameter and solvent flow rates are usually less than 0.5 mL/min. Although several ionization techniques have been introduced as HPLC/MS has evolved, those categorized as atmospheric pressure ionization show the most promise for the analysis of drugs of interest to forensic toxicologists.[92] Electrospray ionization and atmospheric pressure chemical ionization are particularly well suited for the analysis of drugs and drug metabolites.[93]

The HPLC/MS method has numerous advantages. Most drugs and their polar metabolites can be analyzed without derivatization. Analysis times are typically much less than those achieved with the GC/MS method. The MS detector is more sensitive and selective than a UV, fluorescence, or EC detector. Combined HPLC/MS detection is useful for qualitative and quantitative analysis. Due to the pg/mL or pg/mg sensitivity of the HPLC/MS technique, it can be used to detect, confirm, and quantitate drugs in blood, blood stains, hair, sweat, saliva, and a variety of other specimens where low drug concentrations are anticipated. The technique can be used in postmortem, DUI, and workplace testing.

87. ANALYTICAL PROCEDURES FOR THERAPEUTIC DRUG MONITORING AND EMERGENCY TOXICOLOGY, *supra* note 67; DHHS, *supra* note 63; DOT, *supra* note 62.

88. DHHS, *supra* note 63; DOT, *supra* note 62; ANALYTICAL METHODS IN FORENSIC CHEMISTRY, *supra* note 67.

89. DHHS, *supra* note 63; DOT, *supra* note 62; ANALYTICAL METHODS IN FORENSIC CHEMISTRY, *supra* note 67.

90. DHHS, *supra* note 63; DOT, *supra* note 62; ANALYTICAL METHODS IN FORENSIC CHEMISTRY, *supra* note 67; METHODS IN ENZYMOLOGY: MASS SPECTROMETRY (James A. McCloskey ed., Vol. 193, 1990).

91. Yinson, *supra* note 82.

92. Harold Hoja et al., *Applications of Liquid Chromatography–Mass Spectrometry in Analytical Toxicology: A Review*, 21 J. ANALYTICAL TOXICOLOGY 116 (1997).

93. *Id.*

The major limitation of the HPLC/MS technique is its cost. Typical instrument costs are at least twice that of GC/MS detection. In addition, considerable operator expertise is required, the technique is relatively new, and a limited number of methods have been published in the scientific literature. Despite the limitations of the HPLC/MS technique, it has significant advantages over GC/MS analysis and will likely be used increasingly by forensic laboratories.

§ 9–2.7.5   Tandem (MS/MS) and Ion Trap Mass Spectrometry

MS detection is the preferred confirmation used by forensic toxicologists.[94] The tandem mass spectrometry (MS/MS) technique is a promising new form of MS detection that is being used increasingly for the analysis of drug and drug metabolites in biological specimens.[95]MS/MS detection is similar to single-stage MS detection with the following exception. Ions selected during the first mass analysis are further fragmented to produce "product ions" that are selected by a second quadruple mass analysis. Because two mass analyses are performed on the sample, the technique is extremely selective for qualitative identification of drugs and their metabolites. This improved selectivity results in increased sensitivity for quantitation. Therefore, the MS/MS technique can be used to detect very low drug concentrations in specimens that are difficult to analyze, such as blood, hair, sweat, saliva, and body fluid stains. The MS/MS technique can be used with GC or HPLC. Both have applications in drug and drug metabolite analyses. The major limitations of MS/MS are its cost, the operator expertise that is required, and the limited scientific literature on forensic application. Despite the limitations of MS/MS, the technique has significant advantages over MS detection and will likely be used increasingly by forensic laboratories.

As is the case with the MS/MS technique, the ion trap MS technique is not widely used in forensic drug testing. However it has several unique features that make it potentially useful for drug testing. It can be used as a detector for HPLC and for GC and, for the analysis of most drugs, it is usually more sensitive than MS detection. In ion trap MS, ionization and mass analysis of the drug or metabolite takes place in a single chamber. No quadrupole mass filter is used. Some ion trap instruments have additional capabilities that allow for MS/MS-like analysis. Ions selected during the first ion trap analysis can be fragmented to produce product ions that can be selected by a second mass analysis. If desired, ions selected in the second analysis can again be fragmented to produce an additional generation of product ions. This process of analysis, selection, and fragmentation can occur multiple times. Because multiple mass analyses can be performed on the sample, the ion trap MS technique is extremely selective for the qualitative identification of drugs and their metabolites. Its major limitation has been with accurately quantifying drugs and metabolites, especially in biological matrices.

94. David W. Hoyt et al., *Drug Testing in the Workplace: Are Methods Legally Defensible?*, 258 J.A.M.A. 504 (1987).

95. Mike S. Lee & Richard A. Yost, *Rapid Identification of Drug Metabolites with Tandem Mass Spectrometry*, 15 Biomedical & Environmental Mass Spectrometry 193 (1988).

§ 9–2.7.6　Summary and Comparison of Chemical Methods

As discussed above, many methods are available for the detection, confirmation, and quantitation of drugs in biological specimens. Therefore, in many ways, forensic toxicology has become analytical toxicology. This makes forensic toxicology one of the most technical and difficult disciplines for nonscientists to understand. The instrumentation needed to perform the testing is technically sophisticated, and the drugs being prescribed today are more potent and in many cases more toxic than those used previously. Consequently, toxicologists struggle to explain the testing techniques and present their findings in a fashion that is scientifically accurate and yet understandable by the courts.

Table 9.5, presented earlier in the chapter, summarizes the four basic chemical testing methods discussed (i.e., TLC, IA, GC, and HPLC) and their detectors. The table summarizes the methods in terms of the time required to conduct the test, the types of testing methods, the expertise required, and the cost of the equipment needed to perform the test. The most sophisticated methods are GC using a mass spectrometer as the detector (i.e., GC/MS and GC/MS/MS) and HPLC using a mass spectrometer as the detector (HPLC/MS and HPLC/MS/MS). However, these methods are also the most time-consuming, the most costly, and require the most expertise.

Overall, there is a paucity of peer-reviewed scientific literature from which toxicologists, attorneys, and judges can evaluate the scientific merits of drug testing data. The Federal workplace drug testing regulations require that urine be tested, that screening be performed by IA, and that confirmations be conducted using GC/MS.[96] However, few laws specify the testing techniques or the quality of testing needed to support medical examiner and DUI investigations. It is unfortunate that regulations do not define how drug testing should be performed in these and other medicolegal situations because they would help eliminate many of the scientific and legal arguments about the quality and evidentiary value of the drug data. However, even if these laws were in place, laboratories might find compliance difficult given the rapid technological changes in drug testing and the ever-increasing number of drugs available.

A consensus report[97] and research by Hoyt et al.[98] provide some useful guidance for evaluating the quality of medicolegal testing. Their surveys of laboratories, drug testing experts, consultants, and arbitrators rated the legal defensibility of single drug tests and drug screens with confirmation for urinalysis drug testing in the workplace. When only a single test, and no confirmation was performed, IA or TLC tests were rated the least defensible. GC (detector not specified) testing was rated more acceptable than either IA or TLC. The GC/MS test was rated as the most defensible. When two tests were performed, one as a screen and the second as a confirmation, an IA screen followed by an IA confirmation was rated as difficult to defend against legal challenges. IA followed by a confirmation test based on a different

96.　DHHS, *supra* note 63; DOT, *supra* note 62.

97.　B. S. Finkle et al., Technical, Scientific and Procedural Issues of Employee Drug Testing (DHHS Publication No. ADM 90–1684, 1990).

98.　Hoyt, *supra* note 94.

chemical principle, such as GC, was rated as somewhat defensible. An IA or a TLC screen followed by a GC/MS confirmation received the highest scores for legal defensibility. Unfortunately, this survey was published prior to the introduction of the HPLC/MS and the MS/MS techniques.

§ 9–2.8 Method Validation

Experimental data are used to validate the accuracy and reliability of the testing done by forensic toxicologists[99] The selection of a method to test for a particular drug or drug metabolite is at the discretion of the laboratory and depends on the specimen(s) available for testing, the anticipated drug or metabolite concentrations, the laboratory's equipment and personnel, and many other factors. Laboratories must ensure that the method selected can be scientifically defended.[100] Method-validation processes test many features of the method as it is used in, and by, the laboratory. The validation must demonstrate that the method is specific, sensitive, reproducible, and accurate.

§ 9–2.8.1 Qualitative and Quantitative Methods

As stated, a qualitative method is used when the laboratory wishes to determine which drug(s) or metabolite(s) are in a specimen. Both screening and confirmation methods have qualitative components. Typical qualitative screening methods shown in Table 9.5 are TLC, IA, on-site tests, and GC. Currently, GC/MS is the most widely used and accepted qualitative confirmation technique for medicolegal testing. However, HPLC/MS and MS/MS techniques are becoming more popular in forensic testing laboratories and are gaining acceptance.[101] Validation of a qualitative method involves experimentally demonstrating that the method is specific for the drug or metabolite detected and that the method is free from interferences.

A quantitative analysis method is used to determine the amount or the concentration of the drug or metabolite in the tested specimen. Validation of a quantitative method includes experimentally determining the specificity, sensitivity, linearity, precision, and accuracy of the method (see discussion below).[102]

§ 9–2.8.2 Specificity

Specificity is the ability of the technique to discriminate between the drug or metabolite of interest and similar chemicals. An analysis lacks specificity if other substances in the specimen or other drugs with similar chemical structures interfere with the ability of the method to uniquely identify the

99. Darioush Dadgar et al., *Application Issues in Bioanalytical Method Validation, Sample Analysis and Data Reporting*, 3 J. PHARMACEUTICAL & BIOMEDICAL ANALYSIS 89 (1995); DHHS, *supra* note 63; Wolfgang Lindner & Irving W. Wainer, *Requirements of Initial Assay Validation and Publication*, 707 J. CHROMATOGRAPHY B, BIOMEDICAL SCIENCES & APPLICATIONS 1 (1998); TEXTBOOK OF BIOPHARMACEUTICAL ANALYSIS (Robert L. Smith & James T. Stewart eds., 1981).

100. Wu, *supra* note 64.

101. NATIONAL COMMITTEE FOR CLINICAL LABORATORY STANDARDS, GAS CHROMATOGRAPHY/MASS SPECTROMETRY (GC/MS) CONFIRMATION OF DRUGS: PROPOSED GUIDELINES (National Committee for Clinical Laboratory Standards, 1999).

102. Dadgar et al., *supra* note 99; J.R. Lang & S. Bolton, *A Comprehensive Method Validation Strategy for Bioanalytical Applications in the Pharmaceutical Industry: 1. Experimental Considerations*, 9 J. PHARMACEUTICAL & BIOMEDICAL ANALYSIS 357 (1991); Lindner & Wainer, *supra* note 99.

drug of interest. For example, IA and on-site testing devices are designed to detect drugs by class (such as opiates) and often lack the specificity to determine which opiate drug or metabolite is in the specimen. In contrast, MS and MS/MS methods are developed to uniquely identify the particular opiate drug or metabolite in the specimen. Specificity is experimentally determined by analyzing all known compounds that might interfere with an analysis and must be established for confirmation and quantitation methods.

§ 9–2.8.3 Sensitivity

Two sensitivity limits should be established for each quantitative method: the detection limit and the quantitation limit. The drug detection limit is the lowest concentration of the drug or metabolite that can be qualitatively identified. The quantitation limit is the lowest concentration of drug or metabolite that can be accurately quantified. These limits are experimentally established by analyzing specimens containing drug or metabolite at various concentrations until these lower-boundary thresholds are established. The laboratory should not report drug concentrations that are less than the validated quantitation limit, and they should not report the presence of a drug if its concentration is less than the detection limit. For most methods, the minimum concentration at which the drug can be qualitatively identified (or detected) is less than the quantitation limit. Therefore, it may be possible for the laboratory to report with confidence that a drug is present, but they may be unable to report the drug concentration.

§ 9–2.8.4 Linearity

The linearity of a method is established through analysis of a "calibration" or "standard" curve. The laboratory analyzes a series of specimens containing greater and greater concentrations of the drug or metabolite. The instrument response should increase as the concentration of the drug in the samples increases. The linearity of the method is the concentration range through which the instrument response remains linear and accurate quantitative concentrations are obtained. There is a lower concentration (the quantitation limit, discussed above) and an upper concentration limit to the linearity of the method. These limits are a function of several factors, such as the specimen being tested, the extraction efficiency of the method, and the type of detector being used. Only drug or metabolite concentrations in the linear range of the method can be accurately quantified. Therefore, laboratories should not report drug concentrations that are less than or exceed the linear range of the method. A calibration curve should be processed with each quantitative analysis to verify the linearity and to ensure that the sample results are within the linearity of the method.

§ 9–2.8.5 Precision

The precision or reproducibility of a method is a measure of the variability of the analysis. Precision is expressed as intra-(replicate tests within an analysis) or inter-(from day-to-day) assay variability. Intra-assay method precision is determined by experimentally analyzing the same sample at least 10 times in the same analysis. The mean concentration of the replicate analyses is calculated along with the standard deviation. Precision is expressed as the percentage coefficient of variation (%CV), where %CV = standard deviation, divided by the mean, times 100%. Inter-assay precision is experimentally determined by analyzing the same sample (or samples at the same concentration) once per day for a minimum of 5 to 10 days. Inter-assay variability is also expressed as %CV. A method that has greater than 10%CV intra-assay or 20%CV inter-assay variability should be considered suspect. Often, intra-and inter-assay precision are determined at two or three different concentrations in the linear range of the method.

§ 9–2.8.6 Accuracy

Accuracy is a measure of how close the laboratory's result is to the actual drug concentration in the sample. Accuracy is difficult for the laboratory to determine because the actual drug concentration of most samples is not known. Cross-validation of the method by comparing results to those from two or more outside laboratories is sometimes used to establish accuracy. Laboratories enrolled in certification programs can establish the accuracy of their methods by analyzing performance-testing samples (see below).[103] These samples are tested by a number of laboratories and have statistically established drug concentrations. Both the accuracy and precision of the method need to be determined because a method may show excellent precision and poor accuracy; this occurs if the analytical results are reproducible, but the concentration detected is not close to the "known or true" drug concentration. Conversely, a method may be accurate when validated, but imprecise over time.

§ 9–2.9 Good Laboratory Practices

Good laboratory practices are the key to providing drug testing evidence that is scientifically sound and useful to the courts. Such practices include laboratory certification, rigorous chain-of-custody procedures, quality control procedures, quality assurance procedures, and meticulous records. The following section describes recommended good laboratory practices.

§ 9–2.9.1 Laboratory Certification

Currently, there is no widely utilized national certification program for laboratories performing medical examiner or DUI testing. The DHHS-issued *Mandatory Guidelines for Federal Workplace Testing Programs* provide the regulatory framework for the national program that certifies workplace urine-testing laboratories.[104] The requirements of this program have served as a model for local, state, and private-sector certification programs. For the DHHS and similar programs, laboratories are required to have qualified personnel. The personnel must include a director, analysts, and one or more certifying scientists. The director is responsible for managing the laboratory, developing and validating new testing methods, training personnel, writing procedure manuals, monitoring quality control and quality assurance programs, reporting, and interpreting results. Analysts perform the testing. A certifying scientist reviews results from the analyst for clerical and analytical

---

103. College of American Pathologists & American Association of Clinical Chemists, *supra* note 68; DHHS, *supra* note 63.

104. DHHS, *supra* note 76; DHHS, *supra* note 63.

accuracy. Laboratories are required to have secure specimen storage, records, and testing areas. All specimen handling must be recorded on chain-of-custody forms. The certification program requires that screening be performed by laboratory-based IAs and that all confirmation analyses be performed by GC/MS. However, this is being expanded to include HPLC/MS and MS/MS techniques.[105] Validation of the testing methods is required, and records of the daily performance of the methods and equipment must be maintained.

To obtain and maintain certification, the DHHS requires laboratories to analyze performance-testing samples and submit to on-site inspections.[106] Performance-testing samples contain pre-established concentrations of drugs and metabolites, and the laboratory is graded on its ability to accurately screen, confirm, quantitate, and report the correct drug test results in these samples. Failure to obtain, and maintain, an acceptable score on the performance-testing samples precludes initial certification and may result in the probation, suspension, or revocation of certified laboratories. After certification is awarded, laboratories receive performance-testing samples quarterly and are inspected semiannually. On-site inspections are comprehensive and designed to examine all procedures and processes used by the laboratory. Inspectors evaluate the laboratory's written procedures, equipment, security, personnel, specimen-handling and chain-of-custody procedures, security, records, quality control and quality assurance programs, reporting protocols, equipment maintenance, and screening, confirmation, and quantitation methods.

Other laboratory certification programs have been developed for clinical and workplace toxicology testing. Crouch and Caplan[107] and Crouch and Wilkins[108] provided detailed reviews of these programs. The Clinical Laboratory Improvement Act (CLIA) resulted in a Federal program requiring certification of all laboratories testing human specimens for health care purposes.[109] Forensic toxicology laboratories are exempt from this act. The College of American Pathologists and the American Association of Clinical Chemists (CAP/AACC) operate accreditation programs for clinical laboratories, clinical toxicology laboratories, and forensic urine-testing laboratories. Although the CAP/AACC has been successful in establishing standards for workplace urinalysis drug testing and accrediting laboratories, these standards do not address other types of forensic testing.[110] In response to the limited scope of the DHHS and CAP/AACC programs, the Society of Forensic Toxicologists (SOFT) and the American Academy of Forensic Sciences (AAFS) have jointly prepared guidelines for forensic toxicology laboratories that address workplace, medical examiner, and DUI testing.[111] Like the CAP/AACC, these groups have no regulatory authority, and enrollment in their certification programs is strictly voluntary.

105. SAMSAHA, *supra* note 75.

106. DHHS, *supra* note 63.

107. Dennis J. Crouch & Yale H. Caplan, *Monitoring Laboratory Performance, in* THE MEDICAL REVIEW OFFICER'S GUIDE TO DRUG TESTING 163–92 (1992).

108. Dennis J. Crouch & Diana G. Wilkins, *The Certified Laboratory, in* MANUAL FOR ANALYTICAL TOXICOLOGY TRAINING 243–83 (1994).

109. HCFA, Clinical Laboratory Improvement Amendments of 1988, 55 Fed. Reg. 20896–20959 (1990).

110. COLLEGE OF AMERICAN PATHOLOGISTS & AMERICAN ASSOCIATION OF CLINICAL CHEMISTS, *supra* note 68; Lang & Bolton, *supra* note 102.

111. SOCIETY OF FORENSIC TOXICOLOGISTS & AMERICAN ACADEMY OF FORENSIC SCIENCES, FORENSIC TOXICOLOGY LABORATORY GUIDELINES (Society of Forensic Toxicologists, 1991).

Many States and local agencies also administer laboratory certification and accreditation programs. Most of these programs focus on alcohol or workplace urine testing, and few have regulatory authority over DUI, medical examiner, or other forensic testing.

§ 9–2.9.2   Chain-of-Custody Procedures and Documents

Each forensic laboratory must be aware of the legal acceptability, legal admissibility, and scientific defensibility of its chain-of-custody procedures and documents. Laboratories should treat specimens as potential evidence and, therefore, must know the location of the specimen and who has custody of the specimen at all times. Laboratories develop written specimen-handling procedures to ensure that the custody of each specimen is maintained. Transfers of custody are recorded on chain-of-custody forms. The standards to which a laboratory is held for specimen-handling and chain-of-custody documentation depend on the jurisdiction. There is also no consensus among forensic toxicologists about the degree of custody documentation that is needed. However, the laboratory's chain-of-custody documents should contain sufficient detail to re-create the specimen handling through each step of the laboratory's testing.

Forensic laboratories commonly use three chain-of-custody forms: the external specimen form, the internal specimen form, and the aliquot form. The external specimen chain-of-custody form is used to document all custody transfers from the time of specimen collection through receipt of the specimen at the laboratory. Events recorded on the external specimen chain of custody occur before the specimen is received at the laboratory and, consequently, are beyond the control of the laboratory. An internal specimen chain-of-custody form is initiated upon receipt of the specimen at the laboratory and is used to record all specimen and custody transfers that occur within the laboratory. As stated, custody is assumed, and the form initiated, when the specimen is received at the laboratory. Custody is relinquished, and the form is discontinued, if the specimen is transferred to an outside entity or, more commonly, when testing has been completed and the specimen discarded. When laboratory testing begins, small portions of the specimen called "aliquots" are removed from the specimen for analysis. Aliquot chain-of-custody forms are used to record custody transfers of these portions. Laboratories use this form to record the handling of specimen aliquots for screening, confirmation, and quantitation testing. The form is initiated when an aliquot is taken for testing and terminates when that test is completed.

Laboratories accustomed to medicolegal testing are usually familiar with chain-of-custody procedures and forms. However, many laboratories, such as those focusing on clinical toxicology, have little experience with chain-of-custody procedures and frequently do not keep records of custody transfers.

§ 9–2.9.3   Quality Control Samples and Procedures

Generally, laboratories use three types of quality control samples: calibrators (or standards), open controls, and blind controls (see definitions at the end of the chapter). As discussed in the validation section, calibrators are used to establish the instrument response and a calibration curve. Screening calibrators are used qualitatively to determine the instrument response at the specified screening cutoff concentration. The response of each specimen aliquot is compared to that of the calibrator to determine whether the sample is negative or positive. GC/MS calibrators are used both qualitatively and quantitatively. Qualitatively, a confirmation cutoff is set that is analogous to the screening cutoff. The calibration curve becomes the reference to which specimens and other quality control samples are compared and quantified.

Open and blind controls are quality control samples that contain a known drug at a known concentration. These samples are analyzed concurrently with actual specimens and calibrators in an analysis batch. The analyst knows the drug content and concentration of open quality control samples. However, the analyst does not know the identity of blind quality control samples. These samples are placed into the testing batch such that the analyst cannot distinguish them from actual case samples. Screen test quality control samples are used to evaluate the qualitative accuracy of the test. Results are recorded only as positive or negative. GC/MS controls are used qualitatively if the purpose of the analysis is simply to confirm the presence of a drug. If the purpose of the analysis is to quantify the drug or drug(s) present, the quality control samples are also used to assess the quantitative accuracy of the GC/MS analysis.

The laboratory uses quality control procedures and quality control samples to ensure that their testing is reliable.[112] Laboratories establish quality control procedures that are specifically designed for their testing methods, equipment, personnel, and operations. These written procedures establish acceptance criteria for the quality control samples (see below). The procedures may be complex, technically written, and often difficult to interpret when taken out of the context of the laboratory's testing environment. The most simplistic procedures state that no qualitative analysis can be accepted unless the proper qualitative result is obtained on the control sample(s). Simplistic rules for acceptance of quantitative quality control samples require that all quantitative controls must have an analyzed concentration within 20% of their target value. Ten percent or more of the total number of samples analyzed by the laboratory may be quality control samples.

§ 9–2.9.4   Quality Assurance

Federal regulations for workplace testing define quality assurance as a program, "including but not limited to specimen acquisition, security and reporting of results, initial and confirmatory testing and validation of analytical procedures. Quality assurance shall be designed, implemented and reviewed to monitor each step of the process of testing for drugs."[113] The laboratory's quality assurance program should be designed to monitor all aspects of the laboratory with the goal of improving testing accuracy and reliability. Quality control and quality assurance are sometimes used synonymously. As discussed above, a quality control program is used to ensure the

---

112. Crouch & Caplan, *supra* note 107; James O. Westgard & Patricia L. Barry, COST-EFFECTIVE QUALITY CONTROL AND QUALITY PRODUCTIVITY OF ANALYTICAL PROCESSES (American Association for Clinical Chemistry, 1986).

113. DHHS, TRAINING MANUAL OF THE LABORATORY INSPECTORS FOR THE NATIONAL LABORATORY CERTIFICATION PROGRAM (DHHS Publication No. ADM 91–1796, 1991); DHHS, *supra* note 63.

reliability of the testing, while a quality assurance program serves a much broader role in the laboratory.[114]

The list of laboratory equipment requiring quality assurance monitoring to ensure optimum performance is extensive and includes, but is not limited to, the following: analytical balances used for weighing drugs and chemicals; the quality and cleanliness of glassware; the purity of water sources; the temperatures of refrigerators and freezers used for storage of specimens and chemicals; power sources to ensure adequate electrical power to the instruments; ventilation systems; and safety equipment. The laboratory should record each time it performs a quality assurance audit. These records can be used by the laboratory to monitor trends in performance and to identify potential quality problems. Quality assurance records are also a part of each case's records.

§ 9–2.9.5 Records

Laboratory records are evidence and must be meticulously kept. Incomplete records are a liability to the laboratory and inexcusable when forensic testing services are being offered. Laboratory records include all documents associated with each specimen and each analysis performed by the laboratory. Because laboratories use different procedures, it is not possible to present a single, comprehensive list of all documents that a laboratory should be prepared to present and defend. The following are examples of the documents that a laboratory might offer as evidence:[115]

- collection site forms and the external chain-of-custody form;
- forms showing the number and type of specimens received;
- an internal chain-of-custody form for each specimen;
- records showing the label and exact identification of each specimen;
- records showing the condition and volume of each specimen;
- aliquot chain-of-custody forms for screening, confirmation, and quantitation testing;
- quality control records from screening, confirmation, and quantitation testing;
- quality assurance records for all processes and equipment;
- analytical screening and confirmation data, including results for calibrators, controls, and samples;
- records of certifying scientist review for each step in the specimen-handling and analytical processes; and
- the report and conclusions.

These documents should be thorough, signed, and dated at the time each test was performed; moreover, they should be consistent with the written procedures in the laboratory.

114. Crouch & Caplan, *supra* note 107.   **115.** DHHS (1991), *supra* note 113.

§ 9–2.10 Interpretation

Interpreting drug test results is the most problematic aspect of forensic toxicology. Consequently, there are frequent differences of opinion between expert witnesses interpreting the same results. In this section, we discuss interpretation problems faced in medical examiner cases, workplace urine drug tests, and drugs and driving cases.

§ 9–2.10.1 Medical Examiner Cases

Confidence in the interpretation that a drug contributed to the death in a medical examiner case is enhanced when multiple tissues are analyzed and an accurate history of the events surrounding the death is obtained. Three example cases are presented below to illustrate the nature of the problem.

Example 1: Healthy young male. Assume a situation in which the medical examiner suspects that the young man ingested an acute overdose of an antidepressant drug. The following combination of information would verify that interpretation:

- A large concentration of the drug was reported in the gastric contents. This indicates recent ingestion.

- Small concentrations of drug metabolites were detected in the blood and tissues. This suggests that the drug had been consumed recently and had not had time to be extensively metabolized.

- Urine concentrations of the drug and metabolites were not remarkably elevated. This indicates possible acute rather than chronic drug use.

- The young man's medical history indicated availability of the drug.

- A suicide note was found at the scene.

- Anatomical findings were consistent with a drug overdose.

Example 2: Elderly female in poor health. Interpretation of some cases is more problematic than that presented in Example 1. Assume that the medical examiner suspects an acute overdose of the same drug detected in Example 1. However, in this example, the deceased is an 80–year-old female. Her health was poor and her liver functions were diminished. Moreover, the following combination of information would make the interpretation more difficult:

- No gastric contents were available.

- Elevated concentrations of the drug were detected in the blood, but the metabolite concentration was less remarkable. This scenario presents confounding information. Given the small body size and diminished metabolic capacity, one would expect that concentrations might be higher than those in a healthy individual of average size.

- Urine concentrations of the drug and metabolites were not remarkably elevated. Again, these data are difficult to interpret due to the poor health of the woman.

- The medical history of the woman indicated availability of the drug.

- Anatomical findings were consistent with death due to a drug overdose and multiple health problems.

Attributing the death to an overdose of the suspected drug is more problematic in this example due to the health problems of the woman, her diminished capacity to metabolize the drug, and the limited number of tissues tested. The interpretation is further complicated by data from several studies reporting that drugs may "redistribute" after death.[116] This phenomenon may result in changes in blood and tissue and drug and metabolite concentrations after death. These studies demonstrated that postmortem blood collected from different body sites may contain dramatically different concentrations of the drug and its metabolites. They have also shown that blood concentrations of many drugs may be higher in postmortem than in antemortem samples. Blood concentrations of some drugs and metabolites increased 10 or more times apparently due to diffusion of drugs from tissue containing high concentrations of the drugs into the blood.

Example 3: Healthy, middle-aged male being prescribed antidepressant drugs:

- Blood was the only specimen collected; tissues were not collected and urine was unavailable.

- Elevated concentrations of the drug and metabolites were detected in the blood. Metabolite concentrations were less remarkable. In this case, it would be helpful to know whether the concentrations of the drug and its metabolites were in the toxic or lethal range. Even if the concentrations were available, all of the data are from a single specimen.

- The medical history of the deceased indicated availability of the drug, but no additional evidence was found at the scene.

- Anatomical findings were consistent with death due to a drug overdose.

This is a difficult case to interpret because only a single specimen was collected and a limited history was available. Postmortem redistribution of the drug must be considered. A more thorough history and investigation of the circumstances surrounding the death would assist the toxicologist and the medical examiner.

§ 9–2.10.2   Workplace Urine Drug Tests

It would seem that the interpretation of workplace drug cases would be less challenging than the interpretation of medical examiner cases. Unfortunately, this is not always true. Interpretation of urine drug test results can be difficult. Workplace drug testing is forensically unique because the test result may be the only evidence of drug use by the employee. Frequently, this evidence may be an unconfirmed IA test result. Other corroborative information should be factored into the interpretation of these cases, such as use of prescription and over-the-counter (OTC) medications and past drug use history. Unfortunately, this information is usually not available unless the employee challenges the drug test results. Even with MS-confirmed drug test

116. Graham R. Jones & Derrick J. Pounder, *Site Dependence of Drug Concentrations in Postmortem Blood: A Case Study*, 11 J. ANALYTICAL TOXICOLOGY 186 (1987); Richard Prouty & William H. Anderson, *The Forensic Science Implications of Site and Temporal Influences on Postmortem Blood–Drug Concentrations*, 35 J. FORENSIC SCI. 243 (1990).

results, variations in urine volume, potential interferences with the analysis, and the possibility of passive or unknown exposure to the drug must be considered when interpreting the results.

As previously discussed, daily urine volume depends on the subject's degree of hydration. This means that if two subjects excrete the same quantity of a drug over the same time period, the subject with the lesser urine volume (less hydrated) will have a greater urine drug concentration.[117]

Interferences with the analysis continue to be a problem in workplace testing. This is particularly true when confirmation testing is not performed or when a medical review officer does not investigate the case. In many workplace-, probation-, and parole-testing programs, an IA screen is the only analytical testing performed. As discussed earlier, IA tests lack specificity and positive test results can occur from OTC medications and other sources.[118]

Passive inhalation of drugs occurs when an unsuspecting person enters a room where marijuana, cocaine, methamphetamine, PCP, opium, or other drug is being smoked. Drug vapors in the smoke may be inhaled and absorbed into the body. The drug undergoes normal distribution, metabolism, and excretion processes as if it were actively smoked. The dose of drug inhaled is dependent on the concentration of the drug in the smoke, length of exposure, and many other uncontrolled factors. Several authors have published data showing urinary concentrations of drugs following passive inhalation in experimental environments.[119] These data can assist in interpreting urinalysis results, but are limited because most of this research has focused on exposure only to marijuana smoke. It is also difficult to simulate passive exposure conditions. To eliminate the passive inhalation defense, the cutoffs for reporting positive urinalysis drug tests in Federal workplace programs have been set well above the concentrations normally obtained by passive exposure.[120] However, passive inhalation may still be a valid argument when reporting cutoffs are less than those recommended in the Federal programs, if alternate specimens (such as hair) are tested, or if the scientific literature does not address passive inhalation of the drug in question.

Unknowing exposure to drugs has also been a successful defense used by employees. This type of exposure occurs when the employee unknowingly consumes a food or beverage laced with drugs. The most common example of this problem is the innocent consumption of brownies or cake containing marijuana. Exposure to marijuana may also come from consumption of hemp and hemp seed products.[121] Some herbal teas, usually of South American

117. P. Lafolie et al., *Importance of Creatinine Analyses of Urine when Screening for Abused Drugs*, 37 CLINICAL CHEMISTRY 1927 (1991).

118. Joseph H. Autry, NOTICE TO THE DHHS/ NIDA–CERTIFIED LABORATORIES (National Institute on Drug Abuse, 1990); Michael R. Baylor & Dennis J. Crouch, *Sympathomimetic Amines: Pharmacology, Toxicology and Analysis*, 14 CLINICAL CHEMISTRY 103 (1993).

119. Edward J. Cone et al., *Passive Inhalation of Marijuana Smoke: Urine Analysis and Room Air Levels of Delta–9–THC*, 11 J. ANALYTICAL TOXICOLOGY 89 (1987); Mario Perez–Reyes et al., *Pharmacologic Effects of Methamphetamine Vapor Inhalation (Smoking) in Man, in* PROBLEMS OF DRUG DEPENDENCE 1990: PROCEEDINGS OF THE 52ND ANNUAL SCIENTIFIC MEETING OF THE COMMITTEE ON PROBLEMS OF DRUG DEPENDENCE, INC. (Louis Harris ed., NIDA Research Monograph 105, DHHS Publication No. ADM 91–1753, pp. 575–77, 1990).

120. DHHS, *supra* note 63; DOT, *supra* note 62.

121. T. Lehmann et al., *Excretion of Cannabinoids in Urine After Ingestion of Cannabis Seed Oil*, 21 J. ANALYTICAL TOXICOLOGY 373 (1997).

origin, contain cocaine and can produce a positive test for cocaine and its metabolites.[122] Although the Food and Drug Administration banned these teas, they continue to enter the United States. Additionally, prescription drugs, such as codeine, hydrocodone, and hydromorphone, will produce an opiate-positive urine test. Obtaining an accurate case history will assist in interpreting whether passive, unknown, or prescription exposure to the drug are plausible explanations for the positive urinalysis results. The Federal drug-testing programs require that a medical review officer investigate all positive results to protect against taking disciplinary action against employees who may have unknowingly ingested illegal drugs.

As stated above, it is difficult to predict concentrations of drugs or their metabolites in urine because the volume varies and the dose of drug ingested is usually not known. It is especially difficult to predict concentrations of illegal drugs, such as cocaine, methamphetamine, or marijuana, even with a case history because the purity of these street drugs varies considerably. Table 9.7 shows the approximate times that particular drugs may be detected in urine. These detection times will vary with hydration, size of the dose, and frequency of use.

Table 9.7 Urine Detection Time for Selected Drugs and Doses

Drug	Dose	Days Present in the Urine
Amphetamine(s)	Single	1 to 2
Cannabanoids	Single	1 to 2
	Multiple	Several weeks
Cocaine	Single	1 to 3
Opiates (codeine)	Single	1 to 2
PCP	Single	1 to 2

Sources: Baselt & Cravey, 1989; Hawks & Chaing, 1986; Lafolie et al., 1991.

§ 9–2.10.3 Drugs and Driving Cases

DUI cases should be approached as investigations.[123] A driving error, such as a crash or a traffic violation, usually initiates the investigation. Officers at the scene record information about the driving pattern, road conditions, weather conditions, and many other parameters. These officers also make observations about the behavior of the driver. If they suspect the driver is under the influence of alcohol or drugs, the driver may be asked to submit to field sobriety and chemical tests. We focus the discussion on assessment of impairment by the Drug Evaluation and Classification program, drugs commonly found in DUI cases, and the impairing potential of these drugs.[124]

The Drug Evaluation and Classification Program (DEC). The DEC program is designed to train police officers to recognize the behavioral signs of

---

122. Drug Enforcement Administration, *Ice Methamphetamine Analog*, 28 Microgram 1 (1995).

123. National Transportation Safety Board, Safety Study Fatigue, Alcohol, Other Drugs and Medical Factors in Fatal-to-the-Driver Heavy Truck Crashes (Vol. 1, Publication No. NTSB/SS–90/01, 1990).

124. National Highway Traffic Safety Administration, Drug Evaluation and Classification Training Program: The Drug Recognition Technician School: Student Manual (U.S. DOT, 1991).

drug and alcohol impairment and to administer a battery of tests to determine the class of drugs that may have been ingested by the suspect. Drivers suspected of operating a motor vehicle while under the influence and who have a BAC (blood alcohol concentration) less than the legal limit are selected for evaluation. The evaluation includes a series of divided attention tasks, such as Romberg balance, walk and turn, one leg stand, and the finger to nose. In addition, nystagmus, pulse rate, blood pressure, and the oral temperature of the subjects are measured. Results from the divided attention and physiological tests are integrated with observations about the general appearance and attitude of the suspect to predict whether he/she may be under the influence of central nervous system (CNS) depressants, CNS stimulants, hallucinogens, PCP, narcotics, tetrahydrocannabinol (THC), inhalants, or a combination of these drug classes. The accuracy, validity, and sensitivity of these tests are currently being investigated.[125] Although additional data are needed to understand the limitations of the tests, the DEC program can provide strong evidence of drug use if moderate to gross behavioral impairment is present.

Chemical Test Results. Although urine drug test results are useful to demonstrate drug use, they are not useful for establishing impairment to operate a motor vehicle or other complex machine.[126] It is even difficult to predict impairment from a blood drug concentration. This difficulty arises because most studies designed to evaluate drug dose and blood drug concentrations with impairment are laboratory-based performance, driving simulator, or closed-track studies and their results are difficult to extrapolate to actual driving situations. Interpretation is further limited because few drugs have been adequately studied. Inter-subject variability in response to drugs, drug tolerance, drug interactions, and many other factors affect the impairment level shown by subjects. These factors make it impossible at the present time to establish a threshold concentration at which impairment to operate a motor vehicle occurs from most drugs.

Marijuana (THC or its metabolite) was the most frequently detected drug in prevalence studies of the DUI, injured, and fatally injured drivers.[127] Studies have shown that THC or its metabolite was detected in 10% to 15% of these drivers. In a selected population of fatally injured young male drivers, blood from 37% of the drivers contained THC or its metabolite.[128] Performance-based research studies confirm that marijuana use can affect driving.[129]

125. Steven J. Heishman et al., *Laboratory Validation Study of Drug Evaluation and Classification Program: Alprazolam, d-amphetamine, Codeine, and Marijuana*, 23 J. ANALYTICAL TOXICOLOGY 503 (1998).

126. Santo D. Ferrara & Raffaele Giorgetti, METHODOLOGY IN MAN-MACHINE INTERACTION AND EPIDEMIOLOGY ON DRUGS AND TRAFFIC SAFETY (INSTUTO DI MEDICINA LEGALE E DELLE ASSICURAZIONI, 1992).

127. George Cimbura et al., *Incidence and Toxicological Aspects of Drugs Detected in 484 Fatally Injured Drivers and Pedestrians in Ontario*, 4 J. FORENSIC SCI. 855 (1982); Victor C. Reeve et al., STUDY OF THE INCIDENCE OF DELTA-9-TETRAHYDROCANNABINOL (THC) IN FORENSIC BLOOD SAMPLES FROM A CALIFORNIA IMPAIRED DRIVING POPULATION (California State Department of Justice, 1979); Kenneth W. Terhune & James C. Fell, THE ROLE OF ALCOHOL, MARIJUANA, AND OTHER DRUGS IN THE ACCIDENTS OF INJURED DRIVERS (Publication DOT HS, 1–181, 1982).

128. Allan F. Williams et al., *Drugs in Fatally Injured Young Male Drivers*, 100 PUBLIC HEALTH REPORTS 19 (1985).

129. Marcelline Burns & Herbert Moskowitz, *Alcohol, Marihuana and Skills Performance*, 3 ALCOHOL, DRUGS & TRAFFIC SAFETY 954 (1980); Herbert Moskowitz, *Marijuana and Driving*, 7 ACCIDENT ANALYSIS & PREVENTION 323 (1985).

However, some authors have concluded that low blood THC concentrations may actually improve driving performance.[130] Drivers given low doses of THC were thought to be more cautious—at least in research settings.[131] Elevated blood THC concentrations, on the other hand, lead to problems in tracking and integrating information, especially when drivers are confronted with complex divided attention tasks. Additionally, research shows that the combined use of alcohol and marijuana may place drivers at greater risk for accidents than the independent use of either drug.[132]

Cocaine and other stimulant drugs are also routinely detected in drugs-and-driving prevalence studies. Cocaine or its metabolites have been detected in the blood of 10% to 12% of fatally injured drivers.[133] Amphetamines, methamphetamine, and their chemically related OTC drugs were detected in 5% to 10% of the drivers in these studies. Stimulants may improve or adversely affect driving. The use of stimulants by fatigued drivers has been shown to improve performance.[134] Stimulants may also attenuate decrements attributable to low doses of ethanol. However, higher doses of stimulants may lead to greater risk taking, aggressive behavior, aggressive driving, and degraded performance. Driving performance may also be impaired during the "crash" phase or during drug withdrawal.[135] Thus, stimulants may improve or impair driving performance depending on the dose, use pattern, and alertness of the driver.

Some reports show that benzodiazepines are overrepresented in drivers having crashes.[136] Laboratory studies have demonstrated that benzodiazepines affect coordination, steadiness, and reaction time.[137] However, the benzodiazepine performance literature is somewhat ambiguous because impairment has been demonstrated in driving tasks in some studies, but not in others.[138] Studies have variable results depending on the dose and the behavior measured. Interpretation of impairment from benzodiazepine drug test results is a difficult undertaking because there are a number of drugs in this class, their doses vary, tolerance can develop, and their actions vary from inducing sleep and controlling anxiety to controlling seizures. In addition, anxiety has an adverse effect on performance; therefore, when used as prescribed, these drugs could improve the performance of anxious drivers.

130. Hindrick W. Robbe & James W. O'Hanlon, MARIJUANA AND ACTUAL DRIVING PERFORMANCE (National Highway Traffic Safety Administration, DOT, Final Report 808 078) (1993); Williams et al., *supra* note 128.

131. Hindrick W. Robbe, *Marijuana's Impairing Effects on Driving are Moderate when Taken Alone but Severe when Combined with Alcohol*, 13 HUM. PSYCHOPHARMACOLOGY & CLINICAL EXPERIMENTATION 70 (1998); Robbe & O'Hanlon, *supra* note 130.

132. Herbert Moskowitz, *Marijuana and Driving*, 7 ACCIDENT ANALYSIS & PREVENTION 323, (1985); Robbe, *supra* note 131; Robbe & O'Hanlon, *supra* note 130.

133. Dennis J. Crouch et al., *The Prevalence of Drugs and Alcohol in Fatally Injured Truck Drivers*, 38 J. FORENSIC SCI. 1342 (1993); Williams et al., *supra* note 128.

134. Marian W. Fischman et al., *Cocaine Effects in Sleep–Deprived Humans*, 72 PSYCHOPHARMACOLOGY 1 (1980).

135. Everett H. Ellinwood & Arlene M. Nikaido, *Stimulant Induced Impairment: A Perspective Across Dose and Duration of Use*, 3 ALCOHOL, DRUGS & DRIVING 19 (1987).

136. Asbjorg S. Christophersen et al., *Benzodiazepines, Tetrahydrocannabinol and Drugged Driving in Norway* in ALCOHOL AND TRAFFIC SAFETY—T92 1082–87 (1993).

137. John Ingum et al., *Relationship Between Drug Plasma Concentrations and Psychomotor Performance After Single Doses of Ethanol and Benzodiazepines*, 107 PSYCHOPHARMACOLOGY 11 (1992).

138. B. Friedel et al, DIAZEPAM, DRIVING SIMULATOR STUDY, TRAFFIC SAFETY (DOT Final Report DOT HS 807 569) (1990).

Multiple drugs are often encountered in drivers. In fact, it is rare to find a single drug (other than alcohol) in prevalence studies.[139] Interpreting these cases is even more difficult than single drug ingestions because few performance-based studies have addressed the combined impairing effects from multiple drug use. However, studies indicate that even moderate doses of diazepam with alcohol or marijuana with alcohol produced impairment.[140]

Despite the difficulties of interpreting drug test results in DUI cases, it is possible for forensic toxicologists to formulate an opinion about drug impairment in many cases and to support that opinion with the scientific literature. Opinions in DUI cases are best approached with a great deal of caution, and the opinion should be given more credibility when evidence from the investigation, the DEC or behavioral observations, and the chemical test all support the same conclusion. Assessment of driver impairment is also more confidently made when the blood drug concentration, medical history, and drug use history, of the driver are known.

§ 9–2.11　Current and Developing Issues

§ 9–2.11.1　Current Drugs of Forensic Interest

Flunitrazepam (Rohybnol®). Flunitrazepam is not commercially available in the United States. However, it is available in Europe where it is used pre-operatively and as a hypnotic agent. In the United States., flunitrazepam has become known as a "date rape" drug. Due to its hypnotic properties, the drug has been given to subdue unsuspecting victims prior to sexual assaults. The use of flunitrazepam by rapists may be greatly exaggerated. In a study where samples were collected from 334 sexual assault victims suspected of being drugged, flunitrazepam was detected in only 4 cases and other drugs were far more prevalent.[141] Ethanol was detected in approximately one third of the case samples. Cannabinoids, cocaine metabolites, gamma-hydroxybutyrate, and amphetamines were detected in 14%, 9%, 9% and 7% of the case samples, respectively.[142]

Gamma-Hydroxybutyrate (GHB). Like flunitrazepam, GHB has been labeled a "date rape" drug. The study just discussed demonstrated that GHB was used far more commonly in sexual assaults than flunitrazepam.[143] GHB is a naturally occurring and endogenous CNS stimulate that is very similar in chemical structure to gamma-amino butyric acid (an endogenous neurotransmitter). Although it is not commercially available in the United States, GHB is used clinically in other countries as an anesthetic, to treat narcolepsy and to treat alcohol and opiate withdrawal.[144] During the 1980s, GHB was sold in health food stores as a strength enhancer and currently is sold illicitly in the United States for its euphoric and reported aphrodisiac effects. The popularity of the drug has grown rapidly in the 1990s, and it has been identified as a

139. Crouch et al., *supra* note 133; Williams et al., *supra* note 128.

140. Robbe, *supra* note 131; Robbe & O'Hanlon, *supra* note 130.

141. Mamhoud A. ElSohly et al., *Analysis of Flunitrazepam Metabolites and Other Substances in Alleged Cases of Sexual Assault, in* PROCEEDINGS OF THE 50TH MEETING OF THE AMERICAN ACADEMY OF FORENSIC SCIENCES 266–67

(American Academy of Forensic Sciences, 1998).

142. *Id.*

143. *Id.*

144. James Li et al., *A Tale of Novel Intoxication: Seven Cases of Gamma–Hydroxybutryic Acid Overdose,* 31 ANNALS OF EMERGENCY MED. 723 (1998).

causative agent in numerous acute poisonings.[145] Symptoms of GHB poisoning include respiratory depression, agitation, hypotension, and vomiting. Coma and death have been reported from GHB ingestion.[146]

Methamphetamine (Table 9.6). Methamphetamine appears in at least two chemically distinct forms. The l-chemical isomer of methamphetamine has limited abuse potential and is available over the counter as a nasal decongestant. The d-chemical isomer is a controlled substance and a potent CNS stimulant. d-Methamphetamine has been used therapeutically as an anorectic, to combat fatigue, and to treat attention deficit disorder.[147] Methamphetamine (d isomer) has been abused since the 1940s and is currently available under a variety of street names such as "ice," "crank," and "crystal meth".[148] d-Methamphetamine has replaced cocaine in a number of areas as the stimulant drug of choice among drug abusers. Its popularity can be attributed to several factors. It has a longer duration of action than cocaine, it is less expensive than cocaine, and in many areas the supply is greater. It can be easily obtained because it is readily synthesized in clandestine laboratories from over-the-counter drugs, such as ephedrine. The current popularity of the methamphetamine is illustrated by the number of clandestine laboratory seizures associated with its production and by its increased prevalence in poisoned patients. For example, in Utah, the number of clandestine methamphetamine laboratory seizures has more than quadrupled in the past 3 years.[149] In Seattle, reports of methamphetamine use by emergency room patients increased from fewer than 10 in 1991 to 163 in 1995.[150]

The effects of methamphetamine depend on the dose and the frequency of use (see previous discussion of stimulant drugs). Use of therapeutic to moderate doses of methamphetamine result in appetite suppression, arousal, and improved performance. However, chronic use of large doses may produce a progression of effects from restlessness, anxiety, and hyperactivity to psychotic and violent episodes that may be manifested in criminal behavior.[151] Methamphetamine may also adversely affect driving during periods of stimulation from methamphetamine and during the crash phase, which often follows abrupt withdrawal of the drug.[152]

§ 9–2.11.2 Current Specimens of Forensic Interest

Several new specimens, such as meconium, body fluid stains, hair, sweat, and saliva, are being investigated and considered for use in drug testing.[153]

145. DHHS, Centers for Disease Control, *Gamma Hydroxybutyrate Use—New York and Texas, 1995–1996*, 46 Morbidity and Mortality Weekly Report 281–83 (1997).

146. *Id.*

147. Joel G. Hardman & Lee E. Limbird, GOODMAN & GILMAN'S THE PHARMOCOLOGICAL BASIS OF THERAPEUTICS (9th ed.1996).

148. Barry K. Logan et al., *Cause and Manner of Death in Fatalities Involving Methamphetamine*, 43 J. FORENSIC SCI. 28 (1998).

149. Brian Maffly, *Money for the Meth War; Drug Czar Visits State, Rails Against Laws that Make "Poor Man's" Cocaine*, SALT LAKE TRIBUNE, June 3, 1998, at B3.

150. Logan, *supra* note 148.

151. Ellinwood & Nikaido, *supra* note 135.

152. *Id.*

153. SAMHSA, *Mandatory Guidelines for Alternative Specimens and Technologies*, available at http://www.health.org:80/workplace/dtab.htm, 1988a; SAMSHA, *Mandatory Guidelines for Alternative Specimens and Technologies*, available at http://www.health.org:80/workplace/GDLNS–94.htm, 2000b.

Meconium is a baby's first excrement. It accumulates over the last trimester of fetal development and, therefore, may contain drugs that the fetus has been exposed to while in utero. Cocaine metabolites, opiates, nicotine metabolites, and marijuana metabolites have all been identified in meconium.[154] Meconium testing has potential for use in identifying babies born exposed or addicted to drugs and for detecting maternal drug use during pregnancy. Meconium drug test results may be susceptible to challenge because little is known about how drugs are incorporated into meconium, which drugs or metabolites may appear, or what quantity of the drug(s) the mother must take for it to be detected in the baby's meconium.

Dried blood (and other body fluid) stains are a recent addition to the growing list of potential specimens for use in forensic investigations. There is limited research on the detection of drugs in body fluid stains. However, it has shown that many drugs of abuse and some therapeutic drugs can be detected in dried stains from biological specimens.[155] The development of sensitive IA and sophisticated GC/MS, LC/MS, and MS/MS techniques has made it possible to detect and confirm drugs and drug metabolites in dried stains. However, several precautions should be observed when using data from dried stains as evidence. Most laboratories do not have validated methods to screen or confirm drugs and drug metabolites in stains.[156] Likely, there will be little or no scientific data to demonstrate that the drug or metabolite is stable in a dried stain. Similarly, there may be no data available to address the stability of the drug or metabolite on the specific surface or fabric that contained the stain. Stability issues are particularly important when testing is performed months or sometimes years after the stain was deposited. The concentration of a drug or a metabolite in the dried stain cannot be used to predict the concentration in the original liquid specimen without an accurate and reliable method of estimating the initial specimen volume. All reported test results should meet the forensic criterion of testing positive by at least two methods that are based on different chemical principles. This may be a problem when testing small stains because they may not contain sufficient sample for both screen and confirmation testing. It is recommended that dried stains be considered for testing only if no other viable specimens are available.

Hair is another specimen of forensic interest. Numerous toxins, drugs, and drug metabolites have been detected in hair. These include such metals as arsenic, lead, and mercury and the following drugs: heroin, mono-acetylmorphine, morphine, and codeine; cocaine and metabolites; PCP; marijuana and metabolites; methamphetamine, amphetamine, and metabolites; nicotine and metabolites; caffeine and other xanthenes; barbiturates; and benzodiazepines and methadone.[157] There are several advantages to the use of hair as a

154. Enrique Ostrea et al., *Drug Screening of Newborns Meconium Analysis: A Large–Scale Prospective, Epidemiologic Study*, 89 PEDIATRICS 107 (1992); William E. Wingert et. al., *A Comparison of Meconium, Maternal Urine and Neonatal Urine for Detection of Maternal Drug Use During Pregnancy*, 39 J. FORENSIC SCI. 150 (1994).

155. Ira S. DuBey & Yale H. Caplan, *The Storage of Forensic Urine Drug Screen Specimens as Dry Stains: Recovery and Stability*, 41 J. FORENSIC SCI. 845 (1996).

156. Wu, *supra* note 64.

157. Edward J. Cone et al., *Testing Human Hair for Drugs of Abuse. II. Identification of Unique Cocaine Metabolites in Hair of Drug Abusers and Evaluation of Decontamination Procedures*, 15 J. ANALYTICAL TOXICOLOGY 250 (1991); Martha R. Harkey et al., *Simultaneous Quantitation of Cocaine and its Major Metabolites in Human Hair by Gas Chromatography/Chemical Ionization Mass Spectrometry*, 15 J. ANALYTICAL TOXICOLOGY 260 (1991); V. Valko-

specimen for drug testing. Hair can be collected by noninvasive techniques and under direct observation, which helps ensure the identity and integrity of the specimen[158] Although it is sometimes "plucked" from the subject, hair is usually simply cut so the subject feels no discomfort from the collection.

In contrast to blood and urine where occasional use of most abused drugs can only be detected for a short period of time, hair samples may contain a protracted history of the suspect's drug use because drugs incorporated into growing hair reside there until the hair is cut or lost. An additional advantage to hair is that it may be available for collection during exhumations or after deaths caused by traumatic injuries when other specimens are often not available.[159] Hair is readily screened for common drugs of abuse using IA techniques. Confirmation testing is performed with MS or MS/MS techniques.

Despite the advantages of hair as a testing specimen, it has not gained wide acceptance for several reasons. The cost of hair testing may be twice that of urine testing.[160] Also, drug(s) may be deposited onto the surface of the hair by environmental exposure. This may occur during use, but may also occur in nonusers. For example, drugs may be deposited on the hair of nonusers if they are in an area where such drugs as PCP, crack cocaine, methamphetamine, marijuana, hashish, opium, or heroin are volatilized during smoking.[161] External contamination of the hair may also occur tactically when laboratory employees, police officers, and evidence custodians handle seized drugs. The drugs may be inadvertently transferred to the hands and from the hands to the hair. Scientists continue to debate whether washing procedures designed to remove drugs deposited on the hair are totally effective in decontaminating the hair.[162] Also under debate is whether these washing procedures may also remove drugs incorporated into the hair.[163]

The accuracy of hair testing has also been questioned. In a report on the inter-laboratory proficiency testing of hair samples, 14 participating laboratories reported five false positive results and 11 reported false negative results.[164] Little is known about the physiology of incorporation of drugs into hair; even less is known about predicting the dose of the drug consumed or the potential for predicting behavioral effects from a hair-drug concentration. An extremely controversial issue in hair testing is the potential for preferential incorporation of drugs into pigmented hair.[165] This phenomenon implies that there may be racial and hair color biases in hair testing. This topic remains under debate.[166] One often cited study concluded that there is no

---

vic, *Human Hair Growth in* HUMAN HAIR (Vol. I, 1988).

158.   Harkey et al., *supra* note 157.

159.   Crouch, *supra* note 73.

160.   Robert L. DuPont & Werner A. Baumgartner, *Drug Testing by Urine and Hair Analysis: Complementary Features and Scientific Issues*, 70 FORENSIC SCI. INT'L 63 (1995).

161.   Cone et al., *supra* note 157; Martha R. Harkey & Gary L. Henderson, *Hair Analysis for Drugs of Abuse, in* ADVANCES IN ANALYTICAL TOXICOLOGY 298 (1989).

162.   David L. Blank & David A. Kidwell, *Decontamination Procedures for Drugs of Abuse in Hair: Are They Sufficient?*, 70 FORENSIC SCI. INT'L 13 (1995).

163.   *Id.*

164.   Michael J. Welch et al., *Interlaboratory Comparison Studies on the Analysis of Hair for Drugs of Abuse*, 63 FORENSIC SCI. INT'L 295 (1993).

165.   Steven P. Gygi et al., *Incorporation of Codeine and Metabolites into Hair: Role of Pigmentation*, 24 DRUG METABOLISM & DISPOSITION: THE BIOLOGICAL FATE OF CHEMICALS 495 (1996).

166.   *Experts Promote Hair, Sweat Testing Before Congressional Committee*, 12 WORKPLACE SUBSTANCE ABUSE ADVISOR 2 (1998).

racial bias in hair testing, but this study had a number of methodological limitations.[167] That study relied heavily on self-report of cocaine use (self-report is subject to underreporting), did not address hair color differences between the subjects, presented no quantitative hair or urine drug concentrations, and contained no measure of how much cocaine the subjects used.

Sweat also is currently being studied as a forensic specimen. Many drugs of abuse, such as amphetamines and methamphetamine, heroin, marijuana, morphine, methadone, cocaine, and PCP, have been detected in sweat.[168] Sweat is collected with commercially available absorbent patches that adhere to the subject with an adhesive. While the subject wears the patch, it absorbs sweat and drug(s), and their metabolite(s) in the sweat are deposited on the absorbent pad. There are advantages to sweat testing. The patches can be worn for extended periods of a week of more and provide a mechanism for constantly monitoring the subject's drug use. Because they are worn for a week or more, the subjects are not required to have repeated urine sample collections during that time. The patches have a tamper-proof design that ensures they cannot be removed without detection by the monitoring agency. There are also disadvantages to sweat testing. Scientifically, little is known about the deposition of drugs into sweat; therefore, interpreting test results is strictly qualitative. For most drugs, the minimum dose needed for the drug or drug metabolite to be detected in the sweat is not known. The body produces insensible and sensible perspiration. Insensible perspiration is produced as a daily physiological function. Sensible perspiration is produced in response to exercise and body temperature regulation. Both forms of perspiration are collected by the patch and contribute to the deposition of drugs onto a patch. Consequently, the quantity of drug found on the patches is dependent on a number of physiological and life style variables. Another limitation of sweat testing is that sweat patch drug concentrations are similar to blood-drug concentrations and require sophisticated screening and confirmation techniques, such as MS/MS, are required to reliably detect the drugs.

Saliva is a complex fluid produced by several specialized glands. Saliva contains enzymes needed for digestion and serves to moisten the mucus membranes of the upper gastrointestinal (GI) tract.[169] Many drugs of interest to forensic investigators have been detected in saliva: ethanol, amphetamine and other sympathomimetic amines, barbiturates, diazepam, caffeine, heroin, cocaine and metabolites, and cannabinoids.[170] Like hair, an advantage of saliva is that it can be collected noninvasively and under direct observation. Saliva is a filtrate of the blood and, therefore, saliva drug concentrations should reflect blood drug concentrations. For this reason, saliva may prove useful in DUI investigations. Because saliva is primarily water, it is similar to urine and is relatively free of endogenous materials that often interfere with drug screening and confirmation methods. The disadvantages of drug testing in saliva are similar to those of hair and sweat. The pharmacokinetics of most drugs in

167. Tom Mieczkowski & Richard Newel, *An Evaluation of Patterns of Racial Bias in Hair Assays for Cocaine: Black and White Arrestees Compared*, 63 FORENSIC SCI. INT'L 85 (1993).

168. Marcelline Burns & Randall C. Baselt, *Monitoring Drug Use with a Sweat Patch: An Experiment with Cocaine*, 19 J. ANALYTICAL TOXICOLOGY 41 (1995).

169. Edward J. Cone, *Saliva Testing for Drugs of Abuse: Saliva as a Diagnostic Fluid*, 694 ANNALS OF THE NEW YORK ACADEMY OF SCIENCES 91 (1993).

170. Crouch, *supra* note 73.

saliva has not been thoroughly studied. Without a better scientific under-standing of pharmacokinetics and mechanisms of disposition of drugs into saliva, interpreting saliva drug test results remains problematic. Like sweat and hair, often parent drugs, and not drug metabolites are detected in saliva, and drug concentrations are similar to those found in blood. Therefore, sophisticated testing methods are needed to test saliva and the use of simple urine-based IA techniques is ineffective. An additional limitation of saliva as a forensic specimen is that immediately after use drugs ingested orally or smoked may be detected at artificially high concentrations from contamina-tion of the oral cavity.[171] This phenomenon must also be considered when interpreting saliva drug test results.

171. Carol L. O'Neal et al., *Correlation of Saliva Codeine Concentrations with Plasma Concentrations After Oral Codeine Administra-tion*, 23 J. ANALYTICAL TOXICOLOGY 452 (1999).

Glossary

Chemical Testing Definitions

Accuracy Accuracy is a measure of the closeness to the theoretical or true concentration that the laboratory's analysis obtains. Samples analyzed by multiple laboratories or prepared by reference groups are used to assess the accuracy of a method. This term is usually applied to quantitative analysis.

Calibration Curve Also referred to as a "standard curve," the calibration curve is an ascending series of concentrations used to demonstrate the instrument response at each concentration. Generally, the validity of the calibration curve is tested through comparison to a straight-line response by least squares linear regression analysis.

Calibrators Calibrators are quality control samples that may be purchased or prepared by the laboratory and are used to calibrate the testing instruments. These samples are also referred to as "standards" because they may be used to establish a standard curve for the analytical instrument.

Common Expressions of Concentration

—**mg%**: milligram/100 mL of specimen: 1.0 mg% = 1.0 mg of drug / 100 mL of blood

—**mg/dL**: 1.0 milligram/100 milliliters of specimen: 1.0 mg/dL = 1.0 mg%

—**mg/mL**: milligrams/1.0 milliliter of specimen: 1.0 mg/mL = 100 mg%

—**mcg/mL**: micrograms/1.0 milliliter of specimen: 1.0 mcg/mL = 0.001 mg/mL = 0.1 mg%

—**ng/mL**: nanograms/milliliter: 1 ng/mL = 0.001 mcg/mL

—**pg/mL**: picograms/milliliter: 1 pg/mL = 0.001 ng/mL

Controls Controls are quality control samples used to test the accuracy of the calibration or standardization of the analytical instrument. Controls may be purchased or prepared by the laboratory. Monitoring of control values provides the laboratory with information about the daily performance of the assay and trends in the assay performance.

Linearity See calibration curve.

Precision Precision is the reproducibility of the analysis. Precision may be expressed as inter-(from day-to-day) or intra-(repeat analysis on the same day) assay. Performance on quality control samples may be used to express the reproducibility of the analysis.

Qualitative A qualitative analysis is a determination of which drug(s) are contained in a specimen.

Quality Assurance Quality assurance includes all efforts made by the laboratory to ensure the accuracy and validity of its analyses. This includes a comprehensive oversight of all operations of the laboratory from receipt of the evidence for testing through reporting. Examples of quality assurance procedures include quality control, instrument maintenance, records review, analytical data review, specimen identity, and specimen validity verification.

Quality Control Quality control involves those efforts made by the laboratory to ensure the accuracy and validity of each analysis. In practice, quality control of the assay is achieved through ensuring the competency of the reference drug materials, performance of control samples, and calibration of the testing system.

Reference Materials Reference materials are pre-assayed drug materials used to prepare calibrators and controls.

Sensitivity Sensitivity limits are assigned for an analysis as part of validating the method. The limit of quantitation is the lowest concentration of drug that can be accurately quantified. The limit of detection is the lowest concentration of the drug that can be qualitatively identified and is usually less than the quantitative sensitivity limit.

Specificity Specificity is the accuracy of the analysis in qualitatively identifying the drug. An analysis lacks specificity if an endogenous substance or drugs of similar chemical structure interfere with the ability to uniquely identify the drug of interest.

CHAPTER 10

POLYGRAPH TESTS

Analysis

A. LEGAL ISSUES

Westlaw Electronic Research

See Westlaw Electronic Research Guide preceding the Summary of Contents.

A. LEGAL ISSUES

§ 10–1.0 THE LEGAL RELEVANCE OF SCIENTIFIC RESEARCH ON POLYGRAPH TESTS

§ 10–1.1 Introduction

In 1923, in *Frye v. United States*,[1] the United States Court of Appeals for the District of Columbia excluded the defendant's proffer of the results of an early form of the polygraph test because it was not "sufficiently established to have gained general acceptance in the particular field in which it belongs."[2] Seventy years later, in *Daubert v. Merrell Dow Pharmaceuticals*,[3] the United States Supreme Court ruled that *Frye's* "general acceptance" criterion is only one among many factors that federal courts should consider in deciding the determinative question of scientific validity.[4] Following *Daubert*, federal and state courts were asked in case after case to reconsider their approach to polygraphs. In particular, polygraph proponents argued that the *Daubert* standard was inconsistent with excluding this kind of testimony.[5] Some courts agreed with this argument, but most did not. In addition, the United States Supreme Court in 1998 considered the claim that a *per se* rule excluding polygraph testimony in criminal cases violated the Sixth Amendment.[6] The Court rejected the constitutional claim,[7] but five members of the Court noted "some tension" between *Daubert* and a *per se* rule of exclusion of scientific evidence.[8]

Polygraphy, as indicated by its being the subject behind the *Frye* rule, has had a long and mostly troubled history in American courts. Throughout the twentieth century, courts have been, at best, skeptical of polygraph tests and, at worst and more usual, hostile to them.[9] Courts remain wary of the technique. It must be emphasized, however, that polygraphs are used in a wide variety of contexts and under different legal circumstances. Modern courts have begun to consider the value of polygraphs in light of the complex and specific circumstances in which they are offered.[10]

§ 10–1.0

1. 293 F. 1013 (D.C.Cir.1923).

2. *Id.* at 1014.

3. 509 U.S. 579, 113 S.Ct. 2786, 125 L.Ed.2d 469 (1993).

4. *Cf.* United States v. Microtek Int'l Develop. Systems, Inc., 2000 WL 274091 *6 (D.Ore. 2000) (Court concluded that although "[p]olygraphs have come a long way," they are still not reliable enough to admit.). *See generally* Chapter 1.

5. Commonwealth v. Duguay, 430 Mass. 397, 720 N.E.2d 458, 463 (Mass.1999) (Court rejected defendant's argument that Massachusetts' decision adopting *Daubert* test meant that polygraphs were admissible.).

6. United States v. Scheffer, 523 U.S. 303, 118 S.Ct. 1261, 140 L.Ed.2d 413 (1998).

7. *See infra* § 1.4.

8. *Scheffer*, 523 U.S. at 317 (Kennedy, J., concurring in part and concurring in the judgment) (Three Justices, O'Connor, Ginsburg and Breyer, joined Kennedy's opinion that noted this tension. Justice Stevens, the fifth who joined this view, dissented. *Id.* at 319 (Stevens, J., dissenting)).

9. *See* CHARLES A. WRIGHT & KENNETH W. GRAHAM, 22 FEDERAL PRACTICE & PROCEDURE § 5169 n.67 (Supp.1995); *see generally* Charles Robert Honts & Bruce D. Quick, *The Polygraph in 1995: Progress in Science and the Law*, 71 N. DAKOTA L. REV. 987 (1995); Roberta A. Morris, *The Admissibility of Evidence Derived From Hypnosis and Polygraph, in* PSYCHOLOGICAL METHODS IN CRIMINAL INVESTIGATION AND EVIDENCE (David C. Raskin ed., 1989).

10. *See, e.g.*, Ulmer v. State Farm Fire & Cas. Co., 897 F.Supp. 299 (W.D.La.1995) (admitting polygraph evidence after conducting Rule 702–Rule 403 evaluation under *Daubert*);

§ 10–1.2   Admissibility

In general, courts divide into three camps regarding the admissibility of polygraph evidence. First, many courts apply a *per se* rule of exclusion for polygraph evidence. Second, some jurisdictions view polygraph evidence more favorably, and permit it subject to the discretion of the trial court and sometimes only for limited purposes.[11] Third, a significant proportion of jurisdictions permit the parties to stipulate, prior to the test's administration, to the admissibility of the examiner's opinion concerning the results. These three approaches generally describe the division of opinion among courts whether they apply *Frye* or *Daubert* to the evidence. Because courts applying *Daubert* roughly parallel the outcomes of courts applying *Frye*, this section considers the several approaches courts use irrespective of the rule of admissibility they employ. Nonetheless, since the rule of admissibility inevitably affects the *reasons* courts give for their decisions, we explicitly examine these reasons along the way.

§ 10–1.2.1   *Per se* Exclusion

Many courts, especially state courts, maintain a *per se* rule excluding polygraphs.[12] Courts adopting a *per se* rule excluding the use of polygraph evidence base this determination on a variety of reasons. These concerns can be roughly categorized into three principal objections. First, many courts find that polygraphs have not yet been shown to be sufficiently valid or reliable. Second, many courts applying the *Frye* test conclude that polygraph evidence is not generally accepted. And third, a large number of courts believe that the dangers associated with polygraphs are too great.

Although decided long before *Daubert,* the Illinois Supreme Court voiced doubt that polygraphs could meet a scientific validity test: "Almost all courts refuse to admit unstipulated polygraph evidence because there remain serious doubts about the reliability and scientific recognition of the tests."[13] More recently, a federal district court applying the scientific validity test excluded polygraph evidence on the basis of its unreliability.[14] In general, these courts find the subjective nature of the examination,[15] and the slight requirements

State v. Travis, 125 Idaho 1, 867 P.2d 234, 237 (Idaho 1994) (permitting polygraph in Child Protective Act proceedings where sexual abuse is alleged and most of the evidence is second-hand).

11. For example, in *United States v. Piccinonna,* 885 F.2d 1529 (11th Cir.1989) (*en banc*), the Eleventh Circuit held that polygraphs could be admitted for impeachment or corroboration purposes, but any other use had to be the subject of a stipulation. *See infra* § 1.2.4.

12. *See,. e.g.,* State v. Porter, 241 Conn. 57, 698 A.2d 739 (Conn.1997); State v. Shively, 268 Kan. 573, 999 P.2d 952 (Kan.2000); State v. Robertson, 712 So.2d 8, 1998 WL 93283 (La.); Tavares v. State, 725 So.2d 803, 810 (Miss.1998) (*en banc.*); State v. Hall, 955 S.W.2d 198, 207 (Mo.1997); State v. Allen, 252 Neb. 187, 560 N.W.2d 829, 833 (Neb. 1997); People v. Clarence, 175 Misc.2d 273, 669

N.Y.S.2d 161 (1997); Matthews v. State, 953 P.2d 336 (Okla.Cr.App.1998); State v. Sullivan, 152 Or.App. 75, 952 P.2d 100 (Or.App. 1998); Comm. v. Marinelli, 547 Pa. 294, 690 A.2d 203 (Pa.1997); Hall v. State, 970 S.W.2d 137 (Tex. App.1998).

13. People v. Baynes, 88 Ill.2d 225, 58 Ill. Dec. 819, 430 N.E.2d 1070, 1077 (Ill.1981).

14. United States v. Black, 831 F.Supp. 120, 123 (D.N.Y.1993).

15. *See, e.g.,* People v. Anderson, 637 P.2d 354, 360 (Colo.1981) (describing polygraph techniques as "art"); People v. Monigan, 72 Ill.App.3d 87, 28 Ill.Dec. 395, 390 N.E.2d 562, 569 (1979) (objecting to the subjectiveness surrounding the use of the polygraph and the "interpretation of the results"); State v. Frazier, 162 W.Va. 602, 252 S.E.2d 39, 48 (1979) (same).

for qualifying polygraph examiners,[16] to be factors that undermine the value of the test.

Courts also find that polygraph techniques remain highly controversial among "scientific experts" and therefore have yet to achieve "general acceptance." Courts, however, disagree concerning the scope of the "pertinent field" in which polygraphs must gain acceptance in order to be admitted. According to *Frye* itself, the fields of psychology and physiology should be surveyed for general acceptance.[17] Some courts also include polygraph examiners in this field.[18] But other courts specifically reject any reliance on polygraph examiners, because of the examiners' general lack of training and their interest in the outcome.[19]

Relevant to both *Frye* and *Daubert* evaluations of polygraph evidence, the National Academies of Science (NAS) organized a committee to review the scientific evidence on the polygraph in January, 2001. The Committee's report should be available in the Summer of 2002. Committee members' fields of expertise range widely, from biostatistics to psychophysiology.[20] From a *Frye* perspective, NAS's decision to include such a wide spectrum suggests that the "particular field" which should evaluate polygraph validity ranges far beyond polygraph operators or experimental psychologists.[21] This is a lesson worth considering in other scientific evidence contexts. From a *Daubert* perspective, the NAS report will evaluate the scientific basis for polygraphs, a core issue under Rule 702.[22]

Finally, courts express great concern about the effect polygraph evidence has on the trial process. These concerns range from the opinion that polygraphs usurp the jury's traditional role of evaluating credibility[23] to the belief

---

16. *See, e.g., Anderson,* 637 P.2d at 360 ("The absence of adequate qualification standards for the polygraph profession heighten[s] the possibility for grave abuse.").

17. *Frye v. U.S.,* 293 F. 1013, 1014 (D.C.Cir.1923).

18. *See, e.g.,* United States v. DeBetham, 348 F.Supp. 1377, 1388 (S.D.Cal.1972).

19. *See, e.g., U.S. v. Alexander,* 526 F.2d 161, 164 n. 6 (8th Cir.1975) ("Experts in neurology, and physiology may offer needed enlightenment upon the basic premise of polygraphy. Polygraphists often lack extensive training in these specialized sciences."); *but see* United States v. Oliver, 525 F.2d 731, 736 (8th Cir.1975) ("We believe the necessary foundation can be constructed through testimony showing a sufficient degree of acceptance of the science of polygraphy by experienced practitioners in polygraphy and other related experts.").

20. The complete list of expertises includes social psychology, statistics, neuroscience, psychophysiology, biostatistics, systems engineering, memory and cognition, signal detection theory, industrial and organizational psychology, economics, and law.

21. Strictly speaking, the NAS report will not answer the *Frye* question whether polygraph validity is "generally accepted." However,

er, failure of the NAS committee to accept polygraph validity would undoubtedly affect courts' conclusions on this matter.

22. The NAS Polygraph Committee's mandate is to review the use of polygraphs in the area of personnel security. The polygraph is used in this context in two ways. The first is as a screening device, in which the examinee is not specifically accused of anything, and the examiner canvasses broad areas of past conduct that might raise concerns for the respective government agency, such as engaging in acts of terrorism, espionage or spying. Screening is an essentially non-forensic use of the polygraph. However, the polygraph is also used in personnel security to uncover specific acts, such as when a computer disc is missing or a screening test uncovers specific concerns that then narrow the examiner's scope of inquiry. This specific incident form of polygraph examination is essentially the same as occurs when polygraphs are used forensically. The NAS report is expected to examine polygraphs both when used for screening purposes and when employed to investigate specific incidents.

23. *See, e.g.,* State v. Beachman, 189 Mont. 400, 616 P.2d 337, 339 (Mont.1980) ("It is distinctly the jury's province to determine whether a witness is being truthful."); State v. Miller, 258 Neb. 181, 602 N.W.2d 486, 499

that this evidence will overwhelm the jury.[24]

§ 10–1.2.2 Discretionary Admission

Courts agree that *Daubert* applies to polygraph evidence.[25] The biggest change in form, if not in substance, since *Daubert* in regard to polygraphs is the increased number of federal courts that articulate a discretionary standard for this evidence.[26] Several states using a *Daubert*-based validity test have also moved to a standard that leaves polygraph admission within the discretion of trial courts.[27] Leaving discretion to trial courts rather than prescribing a *per se* rule does not seem to have changed practice substantially, however.

For example, in *Cordoba*, the Ninth Circuit held that *Daubert* requires trial courts to evaluate polygraph evidence with particularity in each case.[28] However, district courts applying *Cordoba* usually exclude polygraph evidence.[29] Indeed, courts generally are not sympathetic to proffers of polygraph evidence. They point to high error rates and the lack of standards for administering polygraphs. Moreover, Rule 403 has played a prominent part in courts' particularized analyses of polygraph evidence. Courts cite concerns

(Neb.1999) (noting that polygraphs duplicate purpose of trial).

24. *See, e.g., Alexander,* 526 F.2d at 168 ("When polygraph evidence is offered . . . , it is likely to be shrouded with an aura of near infallibility, akin to the ancient oracle of Delphi."); *Shively,* 999 P.2d at 958 (Court noted that it had long voiced "concern about the weight a jury might place on such evidence."). When the polygraph is proffered in a bench trial, courts may be less concerned with its prejudicial effect. *See, e.g.,* Gibbs v. Gibbs, 210 F.3d 491 (5th Cir.2000) ("Most of the safeguards provided for in *Daubert* are not as essential in a case such as this where a district judge sits as the trier of fact in place of a jury.").

25. *See, e.g.,* United States v. Galbreth, 908 F.Supp. 877, 881 (D.N.M.1995) (analyzing in some detail the application of *Daubert* to polygraph tests); *see also* United States v. Lee, 25 F.3d 997, 998 (11th Cir.1994) (extending *Daubert* to specialized technical equipment). *See generally* James R. McCall, *Misconceptions and Reevaluation—Polygraph Admissibility After Rock and Daubert,* 1996 U.ILL.L.REV. 363.

26. *See* United States v. Posado, 57 F.3d 428, 434 (5th Cir.1995); United States v. Beyer, 106 F.3d 175, 178 (7th Cir.1997); United States v. Williams, 95 F.3d 723, 728–30 (8th Cir.1996); United States v. Cordoba, 104 F.3d 225 (9th Cir.1997); United States v. Call, 129 F.3d 1402 (10th Cir.1997); United States v. Gilliard, 133 F.3d 809 (11th Cir.1998); United States v. Saldarriaga, 179 F.R.D. 140, 1998 WL 324582 (S.D.N.Y.1998); United States v. Marshall, 986 F.Supp. 747 (E.D.N.Y.1997); Meyers v. Arcudi, 947 F.Supp. 581 (D.Conn.1996); United States v. Redschlag, 971 F.Supp. 1371 (D.Co.1997).

27. *See, e.g.,* State v. Brown, 948 P.2d 337 (Utah 1997); State v. Crosby, 927 P.2d 638 (Utah 1996); State v. Porter, 241 Conn. 57, 698 A.2d 739 (Conn.1997).

28. *Cordoba,* 104 F.3d at 229. *See also* Mars v. United States, 25 F.3d 1383, 1384 (7th Cir.1994) ("[W]e have . . . decided to leave the issue of the admissibility of lie-detector evidence up to the individual trial judge, rather than formulate a circuit-wide rule.").

29. In *Cordoba* itself, after the Ninth Circuit remanded the case to the district court for a particularized evaluation, the lower court again excluded the evidence. On appeal, the Ninth Circuit affirmed. United States v. Cordoba, 194 F.3d 1053 (9th Cir.1999). In its opinion, the court reviewed the scientific premises of the polygraph in some detail. The appellate court noted that the district court had found that the polygraph had been subject to testing, albeit with mixed results. *Id.* at 1058. Also, polygraph research had been published in peer reviewed journals. *Id.* The remaining two *Daubert* factors, however, proved the polygraph's undoing. The district court determined that there was no error rate for polygraphs in various contexts, and that the field was badly divided regarding their basic validity. *Id.* at 1059–61. These conclusions, the appellate court found, were well supported. Finally, the district court also concluded that the polygraph exam administered here ran afoul of Rule 403. The Ninth Circuit agreed with this judgment. *Id.* at 1063. *See also* United States v. Microtek Int'l Develop. Systems Div., 2000 WL 274091 (D.Or.2000); United States v. Orians, 9 F.Supp. 2d 1168, 1998 WL 384731 (D.Ariz.1998); United States v. Cordoba, 991 F.Supp. 1199 (C.D.Cal.1998); United States v. Pitner, 969 F.Supp. 1246, 1252 (W.D.Wash.1997).

about infringing on the role of the jury in making credibility assessments,[30] confusion of issues and waste of time,[31] and the problems created if the opposing party does not have a reasonable opportunity to replicate the exam or to have been present when it was given.[32] Courts seem to agree with the Ninth Circuit's conclusion that "[polygraph evidence] still has grave potential for interfering with the deliberative process."[33]

The Fifth Circuit similarly found that its *"per se* rule against admitting polygraph evidence did not survive *Daubert."*[34] The Court explained that *Daubert* changed the evidentiary standard under which the *per se* rule was crafted and, thus, polygraphs would now have to be reevaluated. The court noted "that tremendous advances have been made in polygraph instrumentation and technique in the years since *Frye"* and discussed some of these "advances."[35] Therefore, the court observed, "[w]hat remains is the issue of whether polygraph techniques can be said to have made sufficient technological advance in the seventy years since *Frye* to constitute the type of 'scientific, technical, or other specialized knowledge' envisioned by Rule 702 and *Daubert.* We cannot say without a fully developed record that it has not."[36] The court remanded to the trial court to hold a preliminary hearing to determine this matter.[37]

Several courts find that *Daubert* has not changed their approach to

30. *Orians*, 9 F.Supp. 2d at 1175; *Cordoba*, 991 F.Supp. at 1208; *Pitner*, 969 F.Supp. at 1252.

31. *Gilliard*, 133 F.3d at 815–16; *Pitner*, 969 F.Supp. at 1252.

32. *See Croft*, 124 F.3d at 1120.

33. *Cordoba*, 104 F.3d at 228.

34. *Posado,* 57 F.3d at 429.

Another federal court similarly found that *Daubert* permits a more flexible approach to polygraph evidence than that permitted under the *Frye* test. In United States v. Crumby, 895 F.Supp. 1354 (D.Ariz.1995), the court observed that the historical concern with polygraph evidence has been two-fold, reliability of the test and the prejudicial effect on the jury of admitting it. *Id.* at 1356. The court also noted that good reasons now existed for reconsidering the admissibility of polygraph evidence. These included (1) the fact that in this case the defendant has consistently maintained his innocence and passed a polygraph, (2) *Daubert*, (3) the increase in reliability in the test itself and (4) an alternative vision of the polygraph sketched out in United States v. Piccinonna, 885 F.2d 1529 (11th Cir.1989) (en banc). *Id.* at 1357–58. The court then embarked on an in-depth analysis of the polygraph and found that polygraphy now met the four factors identified in *Daubert. Id.* at 1361. The court placed particular reliance on the scientific research of Dr. David Raskin in reaching its conclusions; the court, however, did not cite or even mention the substantial literature that challenges the validity of polygraph tests. Finally, the court evaluated polygraph evidence under Rule 403, finding that its probative value was not outweighed by unfair prejudice. *Id.* The court stressed several factors as being important in its determination, including in particular that the defendant not the state offered it here and that it would be permitted for a limited purpose. *Id.* at 1363. The court concluded that the defendant could introduce evidence that he took and passed the polygraph if (1) he gave notice to the government, (2) made himself available to a polygraph exam administered by the government, (3) introduced the evidence only to support credibility, if attacked, under Rule 608(a), and (4) the specific questions and physiological data are not introduced into evidence, though the general science of polygraphy may be discussed under Rule 702. *Id.* at 1365. *See also* United States v. Galbreth, 908 F.Supp. 877 (D.N.M.1995) (offering a similar analysis of the issue to that of *Crumby*).

35. *Posado,* 57 F.3d at 434.

36. *Id.* at 433.

37. *Id.* at 436. Lower courts in the Fifth Circuit appear to have embraced their new responsibility to evaluate the admissibility of polygraphs under the specific facts of particular cases. *See, e.g.,* Ulmer v. State Farm Fire & Casualty Co., 897 F.Supp. 299 (W.D.La.1995) (Applying *Posado*, the court permitted the introduction of polygraph results in a civil action in which the defendant insurance company had prompted a Fire Marshall to investigate the plaintiffs for arson; the plaintiffs passed the test administered by a certified, and neutral, examiner.).

polygraph evidence. In *United States v. Black*,[38] for example, the court stated that "nothing in *Daubert* changes the rationale excluding evidence because of reliability concerns."[39] The court concluded that "[a]fter evaluating the standard set forth in the *Daubert* case, premised on Rule 702 of the Federal Rules of Evidence, the Court believes that nothing in *Daubert* would disturb the settled precedent that polygraph evidence is neither reliable nor admissible."[40]

[1] Rule 403

Although not a major part of *Daubert* itself, Rule 403 figures prominently in federal courts' *Daubert* evaluations of polygraph evidence.[41] There is good reason for this, since research indicates that polygraphs are somewhat reliable, but courts are reluctant to find them reliable enough.[42] Since *Daubert's* focus is primarily on relevance, reliability and fit, polygraphs might be thought to meet the basic test. But concerns with this evidence range from friendly and thus invalid tests to invasion of the province of the jury.[43] Rule 403 has permitted courts a more discriminating tool than that permitted by Rule 702 alone. In *Posado*, for example, the court observed that "the presumption in favor of admissibility established by Rules 401 and 402, together with *Daubert's* 'flexible' approach, may well mandate an enhanced role for Rule 403 in the context of the *Daubert* analysis, particularly when the scientific or technical knowledge proffered is novel or controversial."[44] The Sixth Circuit took a similar approach in *Conti v. Commissioner of Internal Revenue*.[45] In *Conti*, the court upheld the lower court's use of Rule 403 to exclude polygraph tests taken unilaterally. The court observed that "the prejudicial effect of [unilateral] polygraph test results outweighs their probative value under Federal Rule of Evidence 403, because the party offering them did not have an adverse interest at stake while taking the test."[46]

Courts, however, have not always used the Rule 403 tool in a discriminating manner. In *United States v. Waters*,[47] the defendant appealed from his conviction for child abuse. The defendant complained on appeal, among other things, that the trial court had erred in refusing to hold a *Daubert* hearing to consider the admissibility of the defendant's polygraph results. At the government's request, the defendant had taken a polygraph, administered by a special agent of the FBI, and had "passed" when asked whether he had ever touched the alleged victim's "private areas in a sexual way."[48]

38. 831 F.Supp. 120 (D.N.Y.1993).

39. *Id.* at 123 (*citing Rea*, 958 F.2d at 1224).

40. *Id.*; *see also* State v. Fain, 116 Idaho 82, 774 P.2d 252, 256 (Idaho 1989) (stating general rule of exclusion, because polygraphs lack validity and reliability).

41. Rule 403 also played a prominent role in admissibility determinations prior to *Daubert. See, e.g., Piccinonna*, 885 F.2d at 1536; Wolfel v. Holbrook, 823 F.2d 970, 972 (6th Cir.1987); United States v. Miller, 874 F.2d 1255 (9th Cir.1989).

42. *See, e.g.*, United States v. Benavidez–Benavidez, 217 F.3d 720 (9th Cir.2000) (District court excluded polygraph evidence for fail-

ing one *Daubert* factor—general acceptance—as well as under Rule 403. Circuit Court ruled that the evidence could pass *Daubert* scrutiny, but be wholly excluded under Rule 403 alone.).

43. *See, e.g.*, United States v. Wright, 22 F.Supp. 2d 751, 755 (W.D.Tenn.1998) (noting concern that polygraphs might "supplant the fact-finding function of the jury").

44. *Posado*, 57 F.3d at 435.

45. 39 F.3d 658 (6th Cir.1994).

46. *Id.* at 663; *see also* United States v. Harris, 9 F.3d 493, 502 (6th Cir.1993).

47. 194 F.3d 926 (8th Cir.1999).

48. *Id.* at 928.

In a cursory analysis, the Eighth Circuit concluded that it did not even have to reach the *Daubert* issue, since "the district court independently excluded the evidence under Fed.R.Evid. 403, which provides for exclusion of evidence 'if its probative value is substantially outweighed by the danger of unfair prejudice, confusion of the issues, or misleading the jury, or by consideration of undue delay, waste of time....' "[49] It is not clear how a *Daubert* analysis can be avoided when balancing probative value against prejudicial effect, since the amount of probative value expert testimony has depends necessarily on the reliability of the evidence. The court cited *United States v. Scheffer*[50] for the proposition that there is substantial disagreement regarding the reliability of polygraphs. But *Scheffer* is not particularly good authority in this case. *Scheffer* was a constitutional challenge in which the Court ruled that it was not unreasonable for the military to adopt a *per se* rule excluding polygraph evidence. Rule 403, in contrast, calls upon courts to conduct a case-by-case evaluation. In *Waters*, there were several factors supporting the polygraph results, at least against government challenges. First, the government had sponsored the test and a government examiner had interpreted it. Second, in a child abuse case such as this, there is little evidence other than the child's statements, evidence not usually deemed the most dependable. The trial court refused even to hold a *Daubert* hearing, and thus never even considered the reliability (and thus the probative value) of the evidence. Without knowing the probative value of the evidence, it is impossible to say that the unfair prejudice is greater.

Rule 403 gives courts the flexibility by which they can manage scientific evidence. Rule 702, among other things, queries the scientific validity of the basis for proffered expert testimony. Yet, in reality, science does not come packaged neatly into "valid" and "invalid" containers. Sometimes, substantial testing will give courts great confidence in the validity of relevant scientific evidence; more usually, however, the testing will leave courts less sure. Rule 403 allows courts to take into account the dangers associated with a particular type of expert testimony as compared to the benefits it offers. Polygraph tests present a particularly appropriate example of the importance of Rule 403 in managing scientific evidence. As the *Posado* court noted, "the traditional objection to polygraph evidence is that the testimony will have an unusually prejudicial effect which is not justified by its probative value, precisely the inquiry required of the district court by Rule 403."[51] At the same time, the *Posado* court noted that polygraphs might possess significant probative value.[52] Hence, courts must now judge the polygraph through the Rule 702 and 403 lenses.

[2] Other Approaches to Discretionary Admittance

In Massachusetts, a *Daubert* state, polygraph evidence is admissible only after the proponent introduces results of proficiency exams that indicate that the examiner can reliably discern truth-telling.[53] The Supreme Judicial Court explained the rule as follows:

49. *Id*. at 930.

50. 523 U.S. 303, 118 S.Ct. 1261, 140 L.Ed.2d 413 (1998).

51. *Posado,* 57 F.3d at 435.

52. *Id.*

53. *Duguay,* 720 N.E.2d at 463.

"If polygraph evidence is to be admissible in a given case, it seems likely that its reliability will be established by proof in a given case that a qualified tester who conducted the test, had in similar circumstances demonstrated, in a statistically valid number of independently verified and controlled tests, the high level of accuracy of the conclusions that the tester reached in those tests."[54]

This requirement, in practice, almost certainly results in the exclusion of most polygraph evidence. Outside of the federal government, polygraph examiners do not undergo routine proficiency tests. Even inside government laboratories, it is somewhat unclear what levels of quality control exist, or whether government records would be readily forthcoming if requested.

Probably the most permissive approach to polygraph evidence occurs in New Mexico. A New Mexico statute "entrusts the admissibility of polygraph evidence to the sound discretion of the trial court."[55] The court in *Tafoya v. Baca*[56] explained the operation of the rule:

"Under [Evidence] Rule 707(d), any party intending to use polygraph evidence at trial must give written notice to the opposing party of his intention. Under Rule 707(g), once such notice has been given, the court may compel ... a witness who has previously voluntarily taken a polygraph test to submit to another polygraph test by an examiner of the other party's choice. If such witness refuses to submit, no polygraph test evidence is admissible at trial. Under [Criminal Procedure] Rule 28(a)(2), a defendant must disclose only those results of a polygraph test which the defendant intends to use at trial."[57]

In addition, New Mexico courts must determine that (1) the polygraph examiner is qualified, (2) the procedures employed were reliable, and (3) the test administered to the subject was valid.[58]

§ 10–1.2.3   Admissibility by Stipulation

By far the most unusual aspect of polygraph evidence is the large part the parties often play in controlling admissibility through stipulation.[59] Although, theoretically, stipulation could be a factor in a wide variety of evidentiary contexts, as a practical matter it is not. This device adds an interesting wrinkle to the problem of the admissibility of scientific evidence.[60]

Although the vast majority of courts routinely exclude the results of polygraph tests, many of these courts qualify this ruling by permitting polygraph results when the parties stipulate to their admissibility prior to the administration of the test.[61] Courts typically premise the decision to permit

54. *Id.* (*quoting* Commonwealth v. Stewart, 422 Mass. 385, 663 N.E.2d 255 (1996)).

55. B & W Construction Co. v. N.C. Ribble Co., 105 N.M. 448, 734 P.2d 226 (N.M.1987).

56. 103 N.M. 56, 702 P.2d 1001 (N.M. 1985).

57. *Id.* at 1005.

58. *Id.* at 1003.

59. *See generally* Note, *Admissibility of Polygraph Test Results Upon Stipulation of the Parties*, 30 MERCER L. REV. 357 (1978).

60. *See also* David Katz, *Dilemmas of Polygraph Stipulations*, 14 SETON HALL L. REV. 285 (1984).

61. *See, e.g., Piccinonna*, 885 F.2d at 1536 ("Polygraph expert testimony will be admissible in this circuit when both parties stipulate in advance as to the circumstances of the test and as to the scope of its admissibility."); *see also* United States v. Gordon, 688 F.2d 42, 44 (8th Cir.1982); Ex Parte Hinton, 548 So.2d 562, 569 (Ala.1989); People v. Fudge, 7 Cal.4th

polygraph results through prior stipulation on principles of estoppel.[62] Some courts also believe that prior stipulations increase the validity of the procedure.[63] Many courts, however, insist that stipulations cannot cure the defects associated with polygraphy.[64] Moreover, absent stipulation, courts uniformly exclude evidence indicating the defendant's willingness[65] or unwillingness[66] to take a polygraph examination.

Most of the courts which permit polygraph results by stipulation require that certain conditions be met. For example, in the widely followed case of *State v. Valdez*,[67] the Arizona Supreme Court established the following four conditions:

(1) That ... counsel all sign a written stipulation providing for defendant's submission to the test and for the subsequent admission at trial of the graphs and the examiner's opinion. . . .

(2) That notwithstanding the stipulation the admissibility of the test results is subject to the discretion of the trial judge. . . .

(3) That if the graphs and examiner's opinion are offered in evidence the opposing party shall have the right to cross-examine the examiner respecting

    a. the examiner's qualifications and training;

    b. the conditions under which the test was administered;

    c. the limitations of and possibilities for error in the technique of polygraphic interrogation; and

    d. at the discretion of the trial judge, any other matter deemed pertinent to the inquiry;

(4) That if such evidence is admitted the trial judge should instruct the jury that the examiner's testimony does not tend to prove or disprove any element of the crime with which a defendant is charged but at most tends only to indicate that at the time of the examination defendant was not telling the truth. Further, the jury members should be instructed that it is for them to determine what corroborative weight and effect such testimony should be given.[68]

1075, 31 Cal.Rptr.2d 321, 875 P.2d 36 (Cal. 1994).

62. *See, e.g.*, Herman v. Eagle Star Ins. Co., 396 F.2d 427 (9th Cir.1968); State v. Olmstead, 261 N.W.2d 880 (N.D.1978); State v. Rebeterano, 681 P.2d 1265 (Utah 1984); McGhee v. State, 253 Ga. 278, 319 S.E.2d 836 (Ga.1984).

63. *See infra* notes 73–74 and accompanying text.

64. *See* United States v. A & S Council Oil Co., 947 F.2d 1128, 1133–34 (4th Cir.1991); United States v. Hunter, 672 F.2d 815, 817 (10th Cir.1982); United States v. Skeens, 494 F.2d 1050, 1053 (D.C.Cir.1974); Pulakis v. State, 476 P.2d 474, 478 (Alaska 1970); Carr v. State, 655 So.2d 824, 836 (Miss.1995); State v. Biddle, 599 S.W.2d 182, 185 (Mo.1980).

65. *See, e.g.*, People v. Espinoza, 3 Cal.4th 806, 12 Cal.Rptr.2d 682, 838 P.2d 204 (Cal.

1992); People v. Mann, 646 P.2d 352, 361 (Colo.1982).

66. *See, e.g.*, Houser v. State, 234 Ga. 209, 214 S.E.2d 893 (Ga. 1975).

67. 91 Ariz. 274, 371 P.2d 894 (Ariz.1962).

68. *Id.* at 900–901. *See also* State v. Souel, 53 Ohio St.2d 123, 372 N.E.2d 1318, 1323–24 (Ohio 1978) (adopting *Valdez* rule); Cullin v. State, 565 P.2d 445, 457 (Wyo.1977) (adopting *Valdez* rule and providing, in cases of stipulation, cross-examination before admitting polygraph evidence); State v. Rebeterano, 681 P.2d 1265, 1268 (Utah 1984) (adopting *Valdez* rule and requiring that the defendant's participation be voluntary). *See generally* Wynn v. State, 423 So.2d 294 (Ala.Crim.App.1982); State v. Milano, 297 N.C. 485, 256 S.E.2d 154 (N.C.1979).

The generous reliance on stipulations to manage polygraph evidence raises substantial analytical difficulties that courts applying *Daubert* and analogous standards of admissibility should consider. Although a factual question, the validity and reliability of polygraph evidence under *Daubert* is, at heart, a legal determination under Rule 104(a).[69] Under the federal rules, judges determine the existence of preliminary facts that are necessary to the application of a particular rule under the preponderance of the evidence standard of Rule 104(a). The admissibility of polygraph evidence thus depends on a judge's preliminary determination that the technique is sufficiently valid to support expert testimony. The fact that the parties are willing to stipulate to polygraph evidence should not free the judge from making this preliminary determination of validity.[70] To be sure, parties regularly stipulate to evidence. But polygraphy is unique, in that the stipulation occurs before the real evidence—the polygraph result—exists. If polygraph results contain too large a margin of error, then a party who stipulates to their admission is playing roulette with his juristic fate. Courts might be reluctant to endorse stipulations that amount to little more than a calculated gamble.

The Illinois Supreme Court asserted that there is an "inconsistency [in] admitting polygraph evidence on the basis of a stipulation since the stipulation does little if anything to enhance the reliability of polygraph evidence."[71] The Illinois court refused to permit the parties to stipulate to the admissibility of results derived from a process that it considered little better than flipping a coin.[72] Other courts, however, find that the stipulation device increases the reliability of the test sufficiently to make it acceptable.[73] According to this view, the stipulation raises the subject's apprehension and leads to the selection of more impartial polygraphers, both factors leading to more accurate results.[74] Whatever the case, notwithstanding the parties' willingness to stipulate, Rules 702 and 403 probably require some preliminary determination that the polygraph test is sufficiently valid and that the agreement to admit the results does not produce excessive unfair prejudice or waste of time.

§ 10–1.2.4 Corroboration and Impeachment Purposes

Many courts do not permit polygraph results as substantive evidence (at least absent stipulation), but permit them for corroboration or impeachment purposes.[75] Several courts allow polygraphs to be used on credibility matters

69. *Daubert*, 509 U.S. at 592 n. 10.

70. *See, e.g.*, Hoult v. Hoult, 57 F.3d 1, 4 (1st Cir.1995) ("We think *Daubert* does instruct district courts to conduct a preliminary assessment of the reliability of expert testimony, even in the absence of an objection.").

71. People v. Baynes, 88 Ill.2d 225, 58 Ill. Dec. 819, 430 N.E.2d 1070, 1078 (Ill.1981) (citing State v. Dean, 103 Wis.2d 228, 307 N.W.2d 628 (Wis.1981)).

72. *See generally Piccinonna*, 885 F.2d at 1537 (Johnson, J., concurring in part and dissenting in part) ("Because the polygraph can predict whether a person is lying with accuracy that is only slightly greater than chance, it will be of little help to the trier of fact.").

73. *See, e.g., Id.* at 1536; Anderson v. United States, 788 F.2d 517, 519 (8th Cir.1986); *Oliver*, 525 F.2d at 737 ; Ex Parte Clements, 447 So.2d 695, 698 (Ala.1984); State v. Montes, 136 Ariz. 491, 667 P.2d 191, 199 (Ariz.1983); *Valdez*, 371 P.2d at 900.

74. *See* United States v. Wilson, 361 F.Supp. 510, 514 (D.Md.1973) (noting that without stipulation the defendant is secure in knowing that unwelcome results can be buried; "[t]his sense of security diminishes the fear of discovered deception, upon which an effective examination depends"); McMorris v. Israel, 643 F.2d 458, 463 (7th Cir.1981) (same).

75. *See, e.g., Piccinonna*, 885 F.2d at 1536.

only when the parties stipulated to this use prior to the examination.[76] Other courts, as noted above, do not allow polygraph results for any purpose, including credibility.[77]

The suitability of employing polygraph evidence for impeachment and corroboration purposes under the federal rules and similar state codes is not obvious. In *Piccinonna,* for example, the court held that polygraph evidence may be introduced "to impeach or corroborate the testimony of a witness at trial."[78] The court established three criteria for such use: (1) notice to the opposing party; (2) reasonable opportunity for the opponent to administer a polygraph to the witness using his own expert; and (3) adherence to Federal Rule 608, which governs evidence proffered to impeach or corroborate a witness.[79]

Rule 608, however, is not well-tailored to this use of polygraph examinations. Rule 608 identifies two kinds of evidence permitted for impeachment and corroboration purposes, as provided under subsections (a) and (b) of the rule.[80] Rule 608(a) allows "opinion and reputation evidence of character." This appears to provide authority, since the proponent of the evidence seeks to introduce "expert *opinion*" on the witness' veracity. Rule 608(a) is ambiguous, however, because it limits opinion evidence to the witness' "*character* for truthfulness or untruthfulness."[81] It is not clear whether polygraph experts

---

76. *See, e.g.,* State v. Souel, 53 Ohio St.2d 123, 372 N.E.2d 1318 (Ohio 1978).

77. *See, e.g.,* United States v. Sanchez, 118 F.3d 192, 195 (4th Cir.1997) ("[P]olygraph evidence is never admissible to impeach the credibility of a witness."); Robinson v. Commonwealth, 231 Va. 142, 341 S.E.2d 159 (Va. 1986); State v. Muetze, 368 N.W.2d 575 (S.D.1985).

78. *Piccononna,* 885 F.2d at 1536.

79. *Id.* Specifically, the court noted as follows:

Rule 608 limits the use of opinion or reputation evidence to establish the credibility of a witness in the following way: "[E]vidence of truthful character of the witness is admissible only after the character of the witness for truthfulness has been attacked by opinion or reputation evidence or otherwise." Thus, evidence that a witness passed a polygraph examination, used to corroborate that witness's in-court testimony, would not be admissible under Rule 608 unless or until the credibility of that witness were first attacked.

Id.

80. Rule 608 provides, in pertinent part, as follows:

(a) **Opinion and reputation evidence of character.** The credibility of a witness may be attacked or supported by evidence in the form of opinion or reputation, but subject to these limitations: (1) the evidence may refer only to character for truthfulness or untruthfulness, and (2) evidence of truthful character is admissible only after the character of the witness for truthfulness has

been attacked by opinion or reputation evidence or otherwise.

(b) **Specific instances of conduct.** Specific instances of the conduct of a witness, for the purpose of attacking or supporting the witness' credibility, other than conviction of crime as provided in rule 609, may not be proved by extrinsic evidence. They may, however, in the discretion of the court, if probative of truthfulness or untruthfulness, be inquired into on cross-examination of the witness (1) concerning the witness' character for truthfulness or untruthfulness, or (2) concerning the character for truthfulness or untruthfulness of another witness as to which character the witness being cross-examined has testified.

FED. R. EVID. 608.

81. FED. R. EVID. 608(a), emphasis added. The Rule 608(a) language closely tracks the "reputation and opinion provision of Rule 405(a)." In fact, the Advisory Committee's Note to Rule 608 refers back to the Note accompanying Rule 405. The Rule 405 Note explains the expansion of the rule from common law practice of limiting character evidence to reputation to the modern approach that allows opinion. The Advisory Committee Note indicates that the word "opinion" was intended to include expert opinion:

If character is defined as the kind of person one is, then account must be taken of varying ways of arriving at the estimate. These may range from the opinion of the employer who has found the man honest to the opinion of the psychiatrist based upon examina-

testify to subjects' characters or, rather, as the much-cited *Valdez* court remarked, only to whether the witness was or was not telling the truth "at the time of the examination."[82] Rule 608 thus does not obviously apply to the situation in which the witness states "X" on the witness stand and the polygrapher testifies as to whether the witness was truthful in saying "X" during the polygraph test. Alternatively, passing or failing a polygraph might be considered a "specific instance of conduct" that indicates the subject's character for truthfulness or untruthfulness. Rule 608(b) regulates the admission of such evidence. But subsection (b) specifically provides that "specific instances of conduct" *cannot* be introduced to support or attack credibility. Specific instances of conduct only can be inquired into on cross-examination. Under Rule 608(b), therefore, a polygraph expert would not be permitted to testify, though the opponent may be permitted to question the witness about the results of the polygraph examination on cross-examination.

§ 10–1.3　Confessions Before, During and After Polygraph Examinations

Courts generally do not exclude confessions made in anticipation of taking, or as a consequence of failing, a polygraph test.[83] Courts do not find the circumstances surrounding polygraph examinations themselves to be unreasonably coercive.[84] However, the circumstances of the polygraph examination might implicate constitutional guarantees[85] and require specific waivers of the right to counsel.[86] In addition, mental incapacity of the subject or extreme and unusual conditions imposed by the examiners, can lead to exclusion of the confession.[87] Even jurisdictions that apply a *per se* rule of inadmissibility allow the use of statements elicited during a polygraph examination, so long as no mention of the polygraph examination is made.[88]

tion and testing. No effective dividing line exists between character and mental capacity, and the latter traditionally has been provable by opinion.

ADVISORY COMMITTEE NOTE TO FED. R. EVID. 405. The kind of expert opinion contemplated by this Note, however, probably does not extend to polygraph testimony, since polygraph experts do not give opinions on "the kind of person" the subject is. Instead, they offer an opinion on whether the subject was or was not lying in response to specific questions.

82. *Valdez,* 371 P.2d at 901.

83. *See, e.g.,* Johnson v. State, 660 So.2d 637 (Fla.1995); Smith v. State,265 Ga. 570, 459 S.E.2d 420 (Ga.1995); State v. Blosser, 221 Kan. 59, 558 P.2d 105 (Kan.1976).

84. *See, e.g.,* People v. Madison, 135 A.D.2d 655, 522 N.Y.S.2d 230 (1987).

85. In *People v. Storm,* 94 Cal.Rptr.2d 805 (2000), the court found that a reasonable person would have believed himself to be in custody "when the polygraph operator told him he had badly flunked the examination." *Id.* at 813. The court of appeal explained that "when appellant was told he had abysmally failed the

polygraph test and therefore was lying when he denied he killed his wife, the only reasonable conclusion appellant could reach was that he was then no longer free to leave." *Id.* at 814.

86. United States v. Leon–Delfis, 203 F.3d 103, 109–112 (1st Cir.2000).

87. *See* People v. Zimmer, 68 Misc.2d 1067, 329 N.Y.S.2d 17 (1972) (subject was emotionally upset, coerced, never read his *Miranda* rights, and was told the polygraph results could be used against him in court); People v. Brown, 96 Misc.2d 244, 408 N.Y.S.2d 1007 (1978) (subject was deprived of sleep and questioned for an excessive length of time); *but see* Keiper v. Cupp, 509 F.2d 238 (9th Cir.1975) (Although the test was conducted in the early morning and the subject was upset and crying, the court held that the test was not "involuntary.").

88. *See* Edwards v. Commonwealth, 573 S.W.2d 640, 642 (Ky.1978); *see also* People v. Ray, 431 Mich. 260, 430 N.W.2d 626 (Mich. 1988) (allowing admissions made before, during or after a polygraph test if the admissions are voluntary); State v. Marini, 638 A.2d 507, 512 (R.I.1994) (same).

§ 10–1.4 Polygraph Evidence and Constitutional Guarantees

Two issues in particular arise concerning the use of polygraph tests under the United States Constitution.[89] Some defendants claim that exclusion of exculpatory polygraph results violates a defendant's Sixth Amendment right to present evidence; other defendants claim that admission of inculpatory polygraph results violates a defendant's Fifth and Fourteenth Amendment rights to due process.[90] In general, courts uniformly hold that the Constitution does not erect *per se* barriers or mandate *per se* admission of polygraph evidence. Instead, courts find that reservations regarding polygraphs are evidentiary concerns that generally do not rise to constitutional dimensions.[91]

In *Scheffer*, the Supreme Court held that a *per se* rule excluding polygraph evidence does not violate the Sixth Amendment right of the accused to present a defense. The Court found that "state and federal lawmakers have 'broad latitude under the Constitution to establish rules excluding evidence from criminal trials.'" Exclusionary rules "do not infringe the rights of the accused to present a defense as long as they are not 'arbitrary' or 'disproportionate to the purposes they are designed to serve.'"[92] The Court held that the rule was not arbitrary in that it was designed to ensure "that only reliable evidence is introduced at trial, [to] preserve[ ] the jury's role in determining credibility, and [to] avoid[ ] litigation that is collateral to the primary purpose of the trial."[93] The rule, the Court concluded, was not "disproportionate in promoting these ends."[94]

According to the Court, the *per se* rule of exclusion had the aim of keeping unreliable evidence from the jury. This "is a principal objective of

89. This section does not address constitutional issues raised by the use of polygraphs in non-evidentiary contexts, such as procedural due process concerns surrounding the use of these tests in the employment context. Under federal law, the Employee Polygraph Protection Act (EPPA), private employers are prohibited from using polygraphs (or any kind of lie detector test), except under certain highly circumscribed circumstances. 29 U.S.C.A. § 2001 et seq. The EPPA, however, does not apply to governmental employers or certain private companies that contract with particular agencies of the government. 29 U.S.C.A. § 2006. *See generally* Veazey v. Communications & Cable of Chicago, 194 F.3d 850, 859 (7th Cir. 1999) ("Congress intended the prohibition on the use of lie detectors to be interpreted broadly."). In addition, many states have anti-polygraph statutes. *See, e.g.,* West's Ann.Cal.Labor Code § 432.2. To the extent state regulations conflict with federal law, the former are preempted by the latter. Stehney v. Perry, 101 F.3d 925, 938 (3d Cir.1996) (finding New Jersey anti-polygraph law preempted by EPPA to the extent the state law prohibited the National Security Agency from administering a polygraph).

90. *See generally* Note, *Compulsory Process and Polygraph Evidence: Does Exclusion Violate a Criminal Defendant's Due Process Rights?*, 12 CONN. L. REV. 324 (1980); Note,

Admission of Polygraph Results: A Due Process Perspective, 55 IND. L.J. 157 (1979).

91. *See, e.g.,* Middleton v. Cupp, 768 F.2d 1083, 1086 (9th Cir.1985) ("We have never held that the Constitution prevents the admission of testimony concerning polygraph verification, although we have expressed an 'inhospitable' leaning against the admission of such evidence as a matter of the federal rules of evidence.").

In *Watkins v. Miller,* 92 F.Supp. 2d 824 (S.D.Ind.2000), the court held that "the prosecutor's suppression of the fact that another suspect failed a polygraph test is ... a Brady violation that is also sufficient by itself to warrant habeas relief." *Id.* at 852. The court explained that "even where exculpatory information is not directly admissible, such as a polygraph result, it may still qualify as Brady material." *Id.* at 851.

92. *Scheffer,* 523 U.S. at 307, (*quoting* Rock v. Arkansas, 483 U.S. 44, 55, 107 S.Ct. 2704, 97 L.Ed.2d 37 (1987)). *But see* Paxton v. Ward, 199 F.3d 1197, 1215–16 (10th Cir.1999) (Court found that the state's *per se* rule excluding polygraphs, applied mechanistically, violated a capital defendant's right to present mitigating evidence at the sentencing phase of the trial.).

93. *Sheffer,* at 307–09.

94. *Id.* at 309.

many evidentiary rules."[95] The government's conclusion that polygraphs were not sufficiently reliable was supported by the fact that "[t]o this day, the scientific community remains extremely polarized about reliability of polygraph techniques."[96]

Justice Kennedy, joined by Justices O'Connor, Ginsburg and Breyer, wrote in concurrence, stating that he would have rested the holding exclusively on "[t]he continuing, good faith disagreement among experts and courts on the subject of polygraph reliability."[97] Justice Kennedy, however, did not agree that the argument that polygraphs usurp the jury's function was especially credible.[98] This argument "demeans and mistakes the role and competence of jurors in deciding the factual question of guilt or innocence."[99] It also, according to Justice Kennedy, relies on the "tired argument," that a jury should not "hear 'a conclusion about the ultimate issue in the trial.' "[100]

Justice Stevens dissented. He began by arguing that the majority's conclusion was inconsistent with *Daubert* which, as lower courts had also read it, gave district judges "broad discretion when evaluating the admissibility of scientific evidence."[101] The core of Stevens' dissent concerned his view that the Court had "all but ignor[ed] the strength of the defendant's interest in having polygraph evidence admitted in certain cases."[102] This interest lay in the defendant's desire to introduce expert opinion that would "bolster his own credibility."[103]

Finally, Justice Stevens argued that polygraph unreliability was greatly exaggerated and that "even the studies cited by the critics place polygraph accuracy at 70%."[104] Moreover, polygraphs compare favorably to many other kinds of evidence that courts routinely admit, including handwriting, fingerprinting and eyewitness identifications. Justice Stevens concluded, "[v]igorous cross-examination, presentation of contrary evidence, and careful instruction on the burden of proof are the traditional and appropriate means of attacking shaky but admissible evidence."[105]

Although *per se* exclusion of polygraph evidence does not violate constitutional guarantees, the Seventh Circuit has held that in jurisdictions in which polygraphs are admissible following stipulation of the parties, prosecutors must provide valid reasons for refusing to stipulate.[106] According to this view, a prosecutor's purely tactical decision to refuse a stipulation concerning polygraph evidence violates due process.[107] In addition, courts hold that due

---

95. *Id.*

96. *Id.* (*citing* MODERN SCIENTIFIC EVIDENCE 565, § 10–2.0, and § 10–3.0 (1997)).

97. *Id.* at 317 (Kennedy, J., concurring in part and concurring in the judgment).

98. *Id.*

99. *Id.*

100. *Id.* (*quoting Id.* at 313, 118 S.Ct. at 1267).

101. *Id.* at 321 (*citing* United States v. Cordoba, 104 F.3d 225, 227 (9th Cir.1997)). Justice Kennedy also agreed that the majority's decision was "in tension" with *Daubert*. *Id.* at 1269 (Kennedy, J., concurring in part and concurring in the judgment).

102. *Id.* at 330 (Stevens, J., dissenting).

103. *Id.*

104. *Id.* at 331 (*citing* Iacono & Lykken, *The Case Against Polygraph Tests*, MODERN SCIENTIFIC EVIDENCE, at 608).

105. *Id.* at 334.

106. McMorris v. Israel, 643 F.2d 458, 466 (7th Cir.1981).

107. *Id. But see* Israel v. McMorris, 455 U.S. 967, 970, 102 S.Ct. 1479, 71 L.Ed.2d 684 (1982) (Rehnquist, J., dissenting from denial of certiorari) (finding the lower court's decision to be a "dubious constitutional holding"); Jones v. Weldon, 690 F.2d 835, 838 (11th Cir.1982) (rejecting *McMorris* holding). Given the

process might also permit defense use of exculpatory polygraph results at the sentencing phase of capital cases. For example, in *State v. Bartholomew*,[108] the Washington Supreme Court held "that polygraph examination results are admissible by the defense at the sentencing phase of capital cases, subject to certain restrictions."[109] These restrictions include, first, that the test be "conducted under proper conditions," and, second, that the examiner be subject to thorough cross-examination by the state.[110]

Constitutional questions also arise when defendants claim that admission of inculpatory polygraph results violate principles of due process. Once again, in general, courts find that the evidentiary standards for polygraph examinations meet constitutional requirements. They hold, however, that the Fifth Amendment privilege against self-incrimination applies to the taking of a polygraph.[111] Thus, courts carefully evaluate a defendant's waiver of right to counsel or right to remain silent in regard to stipulation agreements concerning polygraph examinations.[112] Moreover, under the Fifth Amendment, a defendant's refusal to take a polygraph examination cannot be used against him.[113]

§ 10–1.5 Conclusion

More than most areas of scientific evidence, polygraphs present courts with substantial challenges under the rules of evidence, and implicate most of the panoply of considerations raised by testimony on ostensibly scientifically derived opinion. From the start, given its role in the formulation of the *Frye* test itself, polygraphs have been viewed with suspicion and concern by courts. A principal concern for courts has been defining the "particular field" in which polygraphs belong, especially since they have not been a subject of intense interest among scientists generally. Clearly, polygraphers cannot be the defined field, since they have a peculiar interest in accepting the validity of the trade they ply. Yet, few scientists have studied polygraphs carefully,

Court's holding in *Scheffer*, *McMorris* is unlikely to have much practical effect. Any prosecutor paying the least bit of attention could simply cite the Supreme Court's statement that there is a substantial split in authority over the validity of polygraphs to support a decision not to stipulate to a polygraph examination. *See* Jackson v. State, 997 P.2d 121, 122 (Nev.2000) ("[A]ny party to any criminal or civil action may refuse to agree to the stipulation of a polygraph test for any reason, or no reason at all.").

108. 101 Wash.2d 631, 683 P.2d 1079 (Wash.1984).

109. *Id.* at 1089.

110. *Id.* These two factors come from the *Valdez* test, *infra* note 67 and accompanying text, as adopted in Washington in *State v. Renfro*, 96 Wash.2d 902, 639 P.2d 737 (Wash. 1982).

111. *See* Schmerber v. California, 384 U.S. 757, 764, 86 S.Ct. 1826, 16 L.Ed.2d 908 (1966); *see also* Commonwealth v. Juvenile, 365 Mass. 421, 313 N.E.2d 120, 127 (Mass.1974) ("The polygraph results are essentially testimonial in nature and therefore a defendant could not be compelled initially to take such an examination on the Commonwealth's motion.").

112. *See, e.g.*, People v. Leonard, 421 Mich. 207, 364 N.W.2d 625, 633–35 (Mich.1984) (finding that defendant did not make a knowing waiver of right to counsel at the polygraph examination to which he stipulated); *see also* Patterson v. State, 212 Ga.App. 257, 441 S.E.2d 414, 416 (1994) ("It is not required that the accused have counsel present or act only upon the advice of counsel in order to render a stipulation to the admissibility of the results of a polygraph examination valid and binding upon the accused."); Bowen v. Eyman, 324 F.Supp. 339, 341 (D.Ariz.1970).

113. *See* Melvin v. State, 606 A.2d 69, 71 (Del.1992) ("The trial judge's reliance on [the defendant's] refusal to submit to a polygraph examination violates [his] constitutional right against self-incrimination as guaranteed by the Fifth Amendment to the United States Constitution.").

and some fields in which we would expect interest, such as neuroscience, have ignored the matter entirely.

Under *Daubert*, polygraphs present special challenges. Unlike much expert opinion struggling under *Daubert's* expectations for data, many peer reviewed studies have been conducted testing the validity of polygraphs. As the next two sections make clear, the research completed so far has possibly raised more dust than it has settled. In addition, under Rule 403, courts are particularly concerned with possible prejudice that might accompany expert opinion, ranging from invading the province of the jury to overwhelming it.

Courts are likely to continue to struggle with the issue of polygraphs for some time to come. With the expected publication of an extensive evaluation of polygraphs by a NAS panel, the courts might expect some objective light to be cast on this subject. In addition, the NAS report will hopefully lead to greater interest in polygraphs and other techniques among scientists, prompting the development of psychophysiological or neurological tests that might offer much more powerful techniques than are available given the state of the art today. Almost certainly, the lessons courts learn in this struggle will serve them well in their dealings with other kinds of scientific evidence.

B. SCIENTIFIC STATUS[†]

by

Charles R. Honts*, David C. Raskin**, & John C. Kircher***

§ 10–2.0 THE SCIENTIFIC STATUS OF RESEARCH ON POLYGRAPH TECHNIQUES: THE CASE FOR POLYGRAPH TESTS

§ 10–2.1 Introductory Discussion of the Science

§ 10–2.1.1 Background

Polygraph techniques for the detection of deception and verification of truthfulness have a long history of scientific research, and many prominent

† Scientific opinion about the validity of polygraph techniques is extremely polarized. Therefore, the editors invited scientists from the "two camps" on this issue to present their views. Consistent with classical principles of debate, we have placed the affirmative argument in favor of polygraph tests first. The argument against polygraph techniques, written by Professors Iacono and Lykken, begins at § 10–3.0, infra.

* Professor Honts is the Department Head and a Professor of Psychology at Boise State University and Editor of The Journal of Credibility Assessment and Witness Psychology. He is the recipient of grants from the U.S. Office of Naval Research and from the Royal Canadian Mounted Police to conduct research on the psychophysiological detection of deception. He is a Forensic Psychological Consultant to numerous public agencies in the United States in

Canada. He has been a licensed polygraph examiner for 25 years.

** Professor Raskin is Professor Emeritus, University of Utah and Editor of Psychological Methods in Criminal Investigation and Evidence and Co–Editor of Electrodermal Activity in Psychological Research. He has been the recipient of numerous grants and contracts from the National Institute of Justice, U.S. Department of Defense, U.S. Secret Service, and U.S. Army Research and Development Command to conduct research and development on psychophysiological detection of deception. He was the Co–Developer of the first computerized polygraph system. He was Past President Rocky Mountain Psychological Association and is an Elected Fellow in the American Psychological Association, American Psychological Society, American Association for

psychologists and other scientists have contributed to the existing literature. Following World War II, polygraph testing grew rapidly in its applications within the law enforcement, government, and commercial sectors of our society. This was soon followed by increased scientific research and intense debate within the scientific, legal, and political communities.

Critics as well as supporters of polygraph techniques have pointed out many limitations and misapplications of polygraph techniques.[1] However, we believe that the most vocal critics[2] have grossly overstated the case against the polygraph, in part because of their lack of direct research or experience with the techniques and their applications.[3] Since the fundamental scientific question is the extent to which a psychophysiological test can differentiate truthful from deceptive individuals, much of this section is devoted to that issue and other factors that may affect the various types of polygraph tests in use today.

Scientific research clearly demonstrates that properly conducted polygraph tests have sufficient reliability and validity to be of considerable value to individuals, the criminal justice process, and society. In this chapter, we briefly review the historical development of the polygraph test along with current scientific knowledge concerning the reliability and validity of various polygraph techniques. We discuss the strengths and weaknesses of various approaches and techniques and when their application may or may not be justified on the basis of scientific research. In so doing, we comment on various problems that arise in the field, describe what has been accomplished toward correcting the problems that have plagued attempts to use psychophysiological methods to assess credibility, and suggest ways to improve their accuracy and applications.

Polygraphy is one of the oldest areas of research in applied psychology, and its history is distinguished by the stature of those who have worked in the

Applied and Preventive Psychology. He has served as a Forensic Psychological Consultant to numerous federal and local agencies and legislative bodies in the United States, Canada, Israel, United Kingdom, and Norway. He has been a licensed polygraph examiner for 27 years.

*** Professor Kircher is an Associate Professor of Educational Psychology, University of Utah. He specializes in the use of computer, psychometric, and decision theoretic methods for assessing truth and deception from physiological recordings. He pioneered the development of the first computerized polygraph system and has collaborated with David C. Raskin and Charles R. Honts since 1977 on research and development of methods for the physiological detection of deception.

§ 10–2.0

1. *See, e.g.,* Charles R. Honts, *The Psychophysiological Detection of Deception,* 3 CURRENT DIRECTIONS IN PSYCHOL. SCI. 77 (1994); William G. Iacono & Christopher J. Patrick, *Assessing Deception: Polygraph Techniques, in* CLINICAL ASSESSMENT OF MALINGERING AND DECEPTION 205

(Richard Rogers ed., 1988); David C. Raskin, *The Polygraph in 1986: Scientific, Professional, and Legal Issues Surrounding Applications and Acceptance of Polygraph Evidence,* 1986 UTAH L. REV. 29 (1986); David C. Raskin, *Does Science Support Polygraph Testing, in* THE POLYGRAPH TEST: LIES, TRUTH AND SCIENCE 96 (Anthony Gale ed., 1988).

2. *See, e.g.,* GERSHON BEN-SHAKAR & JOHN J. FUREDY, THEORIES AND APPLICATIONS IN THE DETECTION OF DECEPTION (1990); DAVID T. LYKKEN, A TREMOR IN THE BLOOD (1981); Leonard Saxe, *Detection of Deception: Polygraph and Integrity Tests,* 3 CURRENT DIRECTIONS IN PSYCHOLOGICAL SCIENCE 69 (1994).

3. *See, e.g.,* Charles R. Honts, *Heat Without Light: A Review of Theories and Applications in the Detection of Deception,* 30 PSYCHOPHYSIOLOGY 317 (1993); David C. Raskin & John C. Kircher, *The Validity of Lykken's Criticisms: Fact or Fancy?* 27 JURIMETRICS 271 (1988); David C. Raskin & John C. Kircher, *Comments on Furedy and Heslegrave: Misconceptions, Misdescriptions, and Misdirections, in* ADVANCES IN PSYCHOPHYSIOLOGY 215 (Patrick K. Ackles et. al. eds., vol. 4, 1991).

area.[4] Modern physiological methods for assessing truth and deception began in Italy near the end of the 19th century.[5] In the United States, polygraph techniques were developed as an investigative tool for the law enforcement community, and the early work by Marston[6] and subsequent improvements by Larson[7] and Keeler[8] resulted in a portable polygraph instrument and a general method known as the relevant-irrelevant technique.

§ 10–2.1.2 Psychophysiological Detection of Deception Techniques

[1] The Relevant–Irrelevant Test (RIT)

In the RIT, two types of questions are presented to the subject. Relevant questions directly address the matter under investigation (e.g., "Did you take that $10,000 from the safe?"), whereas irrelevant questions concern neutral topics, such as the subject's name, place of birth or residence, or simple statements of fact (e.g., "Are you sitting down?"). As in all polygraph deception tests, questions must be answered "Yes" or "No." Respiration, electrodermal, and blood pressure responses to the relevant questions are compared to those produced by the irrelevant questions. If the reactions to the relevant questions are generally stronger, the subject is judged to be deceptive to the relevant questions. Conversely, if reactions to the relevant and irrelevant questions are similar in magnitude, the subject is considered truthful to the relevant questions.

The RIT gained widespread use in law enforcement, government, and the private sector in the absence of any credible evidence that it can be used to distinguish truthful and deceptive answers with a reasonable degree of accuracy.[9] Fundamental flaws in the RIT argue strongly against its use in criminal investigations.[10] Most serious is the naive and implausible rationale underlying the test. Although deceptive individuals are likely to produce relatively strong physiological reactions to the relevant questions and be diagnosed as deceptive, many truthful individuals are likely to perceive the relevant questions as more threatening, causing them to react more strongly

4. *See, e.g.*, Roland C. Davis, *Physiological Responses as a Means of Evaluating Information, in* THE MANIPULATION OF HUMAN BEHAVIOR 142 (Albert D. Biderman & Herbert Zimmer eds., 1961); David B. Lindsley, *The Psychology of Lie Detection, in* PSYCHOLOGY FOR LAW ENFORCEMENT OFFICERS 89 (George J. Dudycha ed., 1955); ALEKSANDR R. LURIA, THE NATURE OF HUMAN CONFLICTS (1932); HUGO MUNSTERBERG, ON THE WITNESS STAND (1908); Max Wertheimer & Julius Klein, *Psychologische Tatbestandsdiagnostick*, 15 ARCHIV FUR KRIMINAL-ANTHROPOLGIE UND KRIMINALISTIK 72 (1904). *See also* Paul V. Trovillo, *A History of Lie Detection*, 29 J. CRIM. L. CRIMINOLOGY & POLICE SCI. 848 (1939); Paul V. Trovillo, *A History of Lie Detection*, 30 J. CRIM. L. CRIMINOLOGY & POLICE SCI. 104 (1939) (a two part detailed review of the early history of lie detection).

5. *See, e.g.*, CESARE LOMBROSO, L'HOMME CRIMINEL (2d ed.1895).

6. *See* William M. Marston, *Systolic Blood Pressure Symptoms of Deception*, 2 J. EXPERIMENTAL PSYCHOL. 117 (1917).

7. JOHN A. LARSON, LYING AND ITS DETECTION (1932).

8. Leonarde Keeler, *Scientific Methods of Criminal Detection With the Polygraph*, 2 KAN. B. ASS'N 22 (1933).

9. *See, e.g.*, David C. Raskin et al., *Recent Laboratory and Field Research on Polygraph Techniques, in* CREDIBILITY ASSESSMENT 1 (John C. Yuille ed., 1989).

10. *See, e.g.*, RASKIN (1986), *supra* note 1; David C. Raskin, *Polygraph Techniques for the Detection of Deception, in* PSYCHOLOGICAL METHODS IN CRIMINAL INVESTIGATION AND EVIDENCE 247 (David C. Raskin ed., 1989).

to them. As a result, the RIT can be expected to produce highly accurate decisions on deceptive subjects (true positives) and a large percentage of incorrect decisions on truthful subjects (false positives). Recent research has demonstrated that these predictions are correct. Horowitz, Raskin, Honts, & Kircher reported that only 22% of the innocent subjects in their experiment were able to produce truthful outcomes with the RIT.[11] Another study reported that none of the innocent subjects was able to pass the RIT.[12]

Use of the RIT has declined substantially in recent years, and in most jurisdictions it has fallen into disuse for forensic applications.[13] The Polygraph Protection Act of 1988 essentially eliminated its widespread use by commercial polygraph examiners. Although it offers little protection against false positive errors and the available scientific research argues against its use, the RIT is still employed by polygraph examiners in some federal programs (e.g., Federal Bureau of Investigation and National Security Agency). However, some jurisdictions have recognized the limitations of the RIT and either prohibit its use as evidence[14] or its use for any purpose.[15]

[2] The Control Question Test (CQT)

To overcome the weaknesses of the RIT, Reid devised the control question test (CQT).[16] The CQT differs from the RIT in that physiological reactions to relevant questions are compared to those produced by control (probable-lie) questions. Since control questions are designed to arouse the concern of innocent subjects, it is expected that innocent subjects will react more strongly to them than to the relevant questions. For example, if the subject were suspected of a theft, a control question might be, "During the first 22 years of your life, did you ever take something that did not belong to you?" Control questions are intentionally vague, cover a long period of the subject's life, and include acts that most individuals have committed but are embarrassed or reluctant to admit during a properly conducted polygraph examination. During the pretest review of the questions to be asked on the test, control questions are introduced by the polygraph examiner in such a way that the subject will initially or eventually answer "No" to each of them.

Innocent subjects answer the relevant questions truthfully but are likely to be deceptive or uncertain about their truthfulness when answering the control questions. Therefore, innocent subjects are expected to react more strongly to the control questions than to the relevant questions. In contrast, guilty subjects are expected to be concerned about failing the test because their answers to the relevant questions are deceptive, and they are likely to show stronger reactions to the relevant questions.[17]

11. Steven W. Horowitz et al., *The Role of Comparison Questions in the Physiological Detection of Deception*, 34 PSYCHOPHYSIOLOGY 118 (1997).

12. Frank S. Horvath, *The Utility of Control Questions and the Effects of Two Control Question Types in Field Polygraph Techniques*, 16 J. POLICE SCI. & ADMIN. 198 (1988).

13. OFFICE OF TECHNOLOGY ASSESSMENT, SCIENTIFIC VALIDITY OF POLYGRAPH TESTING: A RESEARCH REVIEW AND EVALUATION (1983).

14. N.M. R. EVID. 707.

15. UTAH CODE ANN. § 34–37–1 (1974).

16. John E. Reid, *A Revised Questioning Technique in Lie Detection Tests*, 37 J. CRIM. L., CRIMINOLOGY & POLICE SCI. 542 (1947).

17. For a more detailed description of the CQT, *see* Raskin, *supra* note 10.

Recently, the term "control question" has been the subject of controversy and confusion in the scientific literature.[18] Control questions are misnamed because they do not function as controls in the strict scientific sense of the term, i.e., they do not elicit reactions that indicate how subjects would react if their answers to the relevant questions were truthful. Rather, they provide an estimate of how innocent subjects would react if their answers to relevant questions were actually deceptive. The fundamental issue is not whether control questions function as controls in the usual scientific sense, but whether they elicit larger reactions than relevant questions from innocent subjects and thereby reduce the risk of false positive errors.

[3]　The Directed Lie Test (DLT)

New question structures and examination procedures have been developed to overcome some of the problems that have plagued traditional comparison question techniques. The most promising of these is the directed lie test (DLT) developed at the University of Utah.[19] The traditional CQT relies on the effectiveness of probable-lie comparison questions that are formulated and chosen by the polygraph examiner to suit each case. Such questions vary considerably and may also be intrusive and ineffective with some subjects. In contrast, the DLT employs a straightforward approach that has clear face validity and uses a relatively small set of simple comparison questions that are much easier to standardize.

The DLT includes questions to which the subject is instructed to lie, e.g., "Before 1998, did you ever make even one mistake?" or "Before 1998, did you ever do something that you later regretted?" The directed-lie questions are introduced during the review of all questions that follows the administration of a number test in which the subject had been instructed to choose a number and lie about the number that was chosen. The subject is told that the number test enables the examiner to determine when the subject is lying and when the subject is answering truthfully. The examiner then explains that the directed-lie questions will ensure that the subject will be correctly classified as truthful or deceptive on the subsequent polygraph test. These procedures reduce the number of false positive errors[20] and increase the standardization and ease of administration of polygraph examinations.[21]

[4]　Guilty Knowledge Tests (GKT)

The concealed knowledge or guilty knowledge test (GKT) is another method for detecting deception.[22] In contrast to the RIT and CQT, the GKT

18.　*See, e.g.,* John J. Furedy & Ronald J. Heslegrave, *The Forensic Use of the Polygraph: A Psychophysiological Analysis of Current Trends and Future Prospects, in* ADVANCES IN PSYCHOPHYSIOLOGY (Patrick K. Ackles et. al., eds. 1991); David T. Lykken, *The Detection of Deception,* 86 PSYCHOL. BULL. 47 (1979); Raskin & Kircher, *supra* note 7; David C. Raskin & John A. Podlesny, *Truth and Deception: A Reply to Lykken,* 86 PSYCHOL. BULL. 54 (1979).

19.　Charles R. Honts & David C. Raskin, *A Field Study of the Validity of the Directed Lie*

Control Question, 16 J. POLICE SCI. ADMIN. 56 (1988); Horowitz et al., *supra* note 11; Raskin, *supra* note 10; Raskin et al., *supra* note 9.

20.　Honts & Raskin, *supra* note 19; Horowitz et al., *supra* note 11.

21.　Honts, *supra* note 1; Raskin, *supra* note 10.

22.　David T. Lykken, *The GSR in the Detection of Guilt,* 43 J. APPLIED PSYCHOL. 385 (1959); Raskin, *supra* note 10.

does not attempt to directly assess the veracity of a person's statements concerning knowledge or involvement in a crime. Instead, this technique is used to determine if the subject is concealing knowledge of details of the crime that would be known only to a guilty person.

The GKT consists of a series of multiple-choice questions, each of which addresses a different aspect of the crime. For example, if the subject is suspected of stealing a ring, a question on the test might be, "Regarding the type of ring that was stolen, do you know if it was: (1) a ruby ring, (2) a gold wedding ring, (3) a pearl ring, (4) a diamond ring, (5) a sapphire ring, (6) a silver and turquoise ring?"[23] A guilty subject who knows the correct alternative is expected to show a relatively strong physiological reaction to that item. However, an innocent subject who has no specific knowledge is not expected to respond differentially to correct and incorrect alternatives.

Typically, only electrodermal responses to the questions are scored, and reactions to the first alternatives are not evaluated because the first item in a series typically produces a large orienting reaction that is independent of any specific knowledge that may be possessed by the subject. Thus, for one multiple-choice question, the probability that the subject's strongest electrodermal response will occur by chance to the correct alternative is 1 in 5, or 20%. With several multiple-choice questions, the chance probability that a subject who has no concealed knowledge will consistently react most strongly to the correct alternatives is exceedingly small.[24]

§ 10–2.2   Areas of Scientific Agreement and Disagreement

§ 10–2.2.1   Survey of the Accuracy of Polygraph Tests

Prior to 1970, virtually no scientific research on the reliability and validity of the CQT in criminal investigation had been conducted. The first scientific study was performed in our laboratory at the University of Utah.[25] By 1983, the Office of Technology Assessment [OTA] had identified 14 analog studies and 10 field studies of the CQT, some of which can reasonably be used to make inferences about the accuracy of control question tests in the field.[26] Lykken reported the first laboratory research on the accuracy of the GKT,[27] and Elaad reported the first field study of the GKT in 1990.[28]

When scientists attempt to assess the usefulness of techniques such as polygraph tests, they are concerned with reliability and validity. In its scientific sense, reliability refers to the consistency of a technique. In studies of polygraph tests, reliability focuses on the consistency of the scoring of the physiological data. Establishing this inter-rater reliability is an important first step in evaluating any test. Reliability and validity are related in that reliability is necessary, but is not sufficient for validity. That is, if a test

23. John A. Podlesny & David C. Raskin, *Effectiveness of Techniques and Physiological Measures in the Detection of Deception*, 15 PSYCHOPHYSIOLOGY 344 (1978).

24. For a detailed description of the GKT, see Raskin, *supra* note 10.

25. Gordon H. Barland & David C. Raskin, *An Evaluation of Field Techniques in Detection of Deception*, 12 PSYCHOPHYSIOLOGY 321 (1975).

26. OTA, *supra* note 13.

27. Lykken, *supra* note 22.

28. Eitan Elaad, *Detection of Guilty Knowledge in Real–Life Criminal Investigations*, 75 J. APPLIED PSYCHOL. 521 (1990).

cannot be scored consistently (reliably), then the scores cannot be valid. The scientific issues surrounding the concept of validity are complex and scientists use the term in several different ways. However, in this context, validity may be considered simply as the accuracy of the polygraph techniques.

The reliability of scoring of the CQT has been studied extensively. Research has clearly indicated that when the performance of competent evaluators is assessed, the reliability of numerical scoring is very high. It is not unusual for agreement on decisions by independent evaluators to approach 100%, and correlational assessments of the reliability of numerical scoring are usually greater than 0.90.[29] The reliability of the GKT has not been reported in the literature, but the simplicity of scoring this test would be expected to produce very high inter-rater reliability. Computer-based statistical decision-making with the CQT is perfectly reliable as long as the computers are functioning properly.[30]

Assessing the validity of polygraph tests is considerably more complex than assessing their reliability. Science has generally approached such problems with different research methodologies that involve conducting research in the laboratory and in the field. Each of these approaches has strengths and weaknesses. The strength of the laboratory approach is that the scientist has control over the situation. Subjects can be randomly assigned to conditions and the scientist knows with certainty who is, and who is not, telling the truth during the polygraph examination. Variables can be manipulated with precision and strong inferential statements can often be made. However, laboratory approaches can be weak in that they may lack realism when compared to the field situation they model.[31]

The main strength of field research is that the scientist can study the phenomenon of interest in real-life settings where realism is not an issue. However, scientific control in field studies can be very difficult. A central issue for field studies is the quality of the criterion of guilt and innocence. This raises questions about how the researchers determined who was truthful and who was deceptive, which is not an easy task. If there had been strong proof of guilt or innocence in the actual cases, polygraph tests would probably not have been conducted.

Neither the laboratory nor the field approach is perfect, so the best strategy is to use both methodologies. To the extent that laboratory studies and field studies converge on the same results, they reinforce and complement each other in determining the true state of the world. The techniques scientists use to overcome the relative weakness of these two methodologies are discussed in the following sections.

29. *See* David C. Raskin, *The Scientific Basis of Polygraph Techniques and Their Uses in the Judicial Process*, *in* RECONSTRUCTING THE PAST: THE ROLE OF PSYCHOLOGISTS IN CRIMINAL TRIALS (Arne Trankell ed., 1982).

30. John C. Kircher & David C. Raskin, *Human Versus Computerized Evaluations of Polygraph Data in Laboratory Setting*, 73 J. APPLIED PSYCHOL. 291 (1988); Charles R. Honts & Mary K. Devitt, *Bootstrap Decision Making*

for Polygraph Examinations: Final Report of DOD/PERSEC Grant No. N00014–92–J–1794, [available from the Defense Technical Information Center, Building 5 Cameron Station, Alexandria, VA 22304–6145].

31. John A. Podlesny & David C. Raskin, *Physiological Measures and the Detection of Deception*, 84 PSYCHOL. BULL. 782 (1977).

[1] Laboratory Studies

[a] Control Question Test

Laboratory research has traditionally been an attractive alternative because the scientist can control the environment. By randomly assigning subjects to conditions, the scientist can know with certainty who is telling the truth and who is lying. Laboratory research on credibility assessment has typically made some subjects "guilty" by having them commit a mock crime (e.g. "steal" a watch from an office), and then instructing them to lie about it during a subsequent test. From a scientific viewpoint, random assignment to conditions is highly desirable because it controls for the influence of extraneous variables that might confound the results of the experiment.[32] The most accepted type of laboratory study realistically simulates a crime in which some subjects commit an overt transaction, such as a theft.[33] While the guilty subjects enact a realistic crime, the innocent subjects are merely told about the nature of the crime and do not enact it. All subjects are motivated to produce a truthful outcome, usually by a cash bonus for passing the test. For example, one such study used prison inmates who were offered a bonus equal to one month's wages if they could produce a truthful outcome.[34]

The advantages of careful laboratory simulations include total control over the issues that are investigated and the types of tests that are used, consistency in test administration and interpretation, specification of the subject populations that are studied, control over the skill and training of the examiners, and absolute verification of the accuracy of test results. Carefully designed and conducted studies that closely approximate the methods and conditions characteristic of high quality practice by polygraph professionals and use subjects similar to the target population, such as convicted felons or a cross-section of the general community, provide the most generalizable results.[35] Laboratory research in general, and credibility assessment in particular, is sometimes criticized for lack of realism, which may limit the ability of the scientist to apply the results of the laboratory to real-world settings. However, a recent analysis reported in the flagship journal of the American Psychological Society examined a broad range of laboratory-based psychological research.[36] The authors concluded, "correspondence between lab-and field-based effect sizes of conceptually similar independent and dependent variables was considerable. In brief, the psychological laboratory has generally produced truths, rather than trivialities."[37] Our position with regard to the high quality studies of the CQT and DLT is similar. We believe that these studies produce important information about the validity of such tests that is not trivial and ungeneralizable, as some critics have claimed. As described below, a recent scientific survey of psychological scientists who work on applied problems in psychology and the law indicates that the vast majority of them share our belief in the value of laboratory studies of the validity of the polygraph.

32. Thomas D. Cook & Donald T. Campbell, Quasi-experimentation: Design & analysis issues for Field Settings (1979).

33. Raskin, *supra* note 29.

34. David C. Raskin & Robert D. Hare, *Psychopathy and Detection of Deception in a Prison Population*, 15 Psychophysiology 126.

35. John C. Kircher et al., *Meta-analysis of Mock Crime Studies of the Control Question Polygraph Technique*, 12 L. & Hum. Behav. 79 (1988).

36. C. A. Anderson et al., *Research in the Psychological Laboratory: Truth or Triviality?*, 8 Curr. Dir. Psychological Sci. 3 (1999).

37. *Id.*

In 1997, a Committee of Concerned Social Scientists filed a Brief for Amicus Curiae[38] with the Supreme Court of the United States in the case of *United States v. Scheffer.*[39] They identified eight high quality laboratory studies of the CQT,[40] the results of which are illustrated in Table 1. These high quality laboratory studies indicate that the CQT is a very accurate discriminator of truthful and deceptive subjects. Overall, these studies correctly classified 91% of the subjects and produced approximately equal numbers of false positive and false negative errors.

Table 1
Results of High Quality Laboratory Studies

Study	Guilty				Innocent			
	n	% correct	% wrong	% Inc.	n	% correct	% wrong	% Inc.
Control Question Tests								
Glinton, et al. (1984)	2	100	0	0	13	85	15	0
Honts, et al. (1994)[a]	20	70	20	10	20	75	10	15
Horowitz, et al. (1994)[b]	15	53	20	27	15	80	13	7
Kircher & Raskin (1988)	50	88	6	6	50	86	6	8
Podlesny & Raskin (1978)	20	70	15	15	20	90	5	5
Podlesny & Truslow (1993)	72	69	13	18	24	75	4	21
Raskin & Hare (1978)	24	88	0	12	24	88	8	4
Rovner, et al. (1979)[c]	24	88	0	12	24	88	8	4
Weighted Means	227	77	10	13	190	84	8	8
Directed Lie Control[d]								
Traditional Control Questions	15	53	20	27	15	80	13	7
Personally Relevant Directed Lie	15	73	13	13	15	87	0	13
Trivial Directed Lie	15	54	20	26	15	67	13	20
Relevant/Irrelevant	15	100	0	0	15	20	73	7
Concealed Knowledge Tests								
Davidson (1968)	12	92	8		36	100	0	
Honts, et al. (1994)[e]	10	80	20		10	90	10	
Lykken (1959)	37	86	14		12	100	0	
Podlesny & Raskin (1978)	10	90	10		10	100	0	
Steller, et al. (1987)	47	85	15		40	100	0	
Weighted Means	116	86	14		108	99	1	

a. Countermeasure Subjects Excluded.
b. Traditional Control Question Subjects Only.
c. Countermeasure Subjects Excluded.
d. Data from Horowitz et al. (1994).
e. Countermeasure Subjects Excluded.

[b] Directed Lie Test

Since the DLT is relatively new, there are fewer studies of its validity. Seven laboratory studies have been conducted, but they are not all of high

38. Charles R. Honts & Charles F. Peterson, Brief of the Committee of Concerned Social Scientists as Amicus Curiae, United States v. Scheffer, in the Supreme Court of the United States (1997). The Amicus was co-signed by 17 individuals holding advanced scientific degrees.

39. 523 U.S. 303, 118 S.Ct. 1261, 140 L.Ed.2d 413 (1998).

40. *See* Avital Ginton et al., *A Method for Evaluating the Use of the Polygraph in a Real–Life Situation*, 67 J. APPLIED PSYCHOL. 131 (1982); Charles R. Honts et al., *Mental and Physical Countermeasures Reduce the Accuracy of Polygraph Tests*, 79 J. APPLIED PSYCH. 252 (1994); Horowitz et al., *supra* note 11; Kircher & Raskin, *supra* note 30; Podlesny & Raskin, *supra* note 31; John A. Podlesny & Connie M. Truslow, *Validity of an Expanded–Issue (Modified General Question) Polygraph Technique in a Simulated Distributed–Crime–Roles Context*, 78 J. APPLIED PSYCHOL. 788 (1993); David C. Raskin & Robert D. Hare, *Psychopathy and Detection of Deception in a Prison Population*, 15 PSYCHOPHYSIOLOGY 126 (1978); Louis I. Rovner et al., *Effects of Information and Practice on Detection of Deception*, 16 PSYCHOPHYSIOLOGY 197 (1979).

quality.[41] The Horowitz et al. study is the most carefully designed and conducted.[42] It used a mock crime that closely approximated the field situation, similar to those described for the CQT in the previous section. The Horowitz study compared the effectiveness of the DLT with the CQT and RIT. Different groups received one of two types of directed lies, personally-relevant directed lies using the procedures previously described or simple directed lies to three of the neutral questions that were used in the RIT. The results indicated that the personal directed lie produced the highest accuracy, except for the RIT with guilty subjects. The outcomes for the four types of tests are presented in Table 2. Among all question structures, the personal directed-lie produced the highest number of correct decisions on innocent subjects and among the three tests that employed comparison questions, it produced the highest number of correct decisions on guilty subjects.

Table 2
Test outcomes of the Horowitz et al. (1997) study

Experimental Groups	Test Outcomes (%)			% Correct Decisions
	Correct	Wrong	Inconclusive	
Guilty				
Relevant-irrelevant	100	0	0	100
Trivial Directed Lie	53	20	27	73
Personal Directed Lie	73	14	13	84
Probable Lie Comparison	53	20	27	73
Innocent				
Relevant-irrelevant	20	73	7	22
Trivial Directed Lie	67	13	20	84
Personal Directed Lie	87	13	0	87
Probable Lie Comparison	80	13	7	86

n = 15 for each of the experimental groups.
The percentage of correct decisions was calculated by excluding inconclusive outcomes.

The U. S. Department of Defense has conducted three sets of studies concerning the validity of the DLT. Barland examined the validity of the Military Intelligence version of the DLT in a mock screening setting with 26 truthful subjects and 30 subjects who attempted deception.[43] All subjects were tested with the DLT; no other techniques were examined. Excluding inconclusive outcomes, Barland's evaluators correctly classified 79% of the subjects. Although this performance appears modest compared to that obtained in

41. Gordon H. Barland, *A Validity and Reliability Study of Counterintelligence Screening Tests*, Unpublished manuscript, Security Support Battalion, 902nd Military Intelligence Group, Fort George G. Meade, Maryland (1981); Department of Defense Polygraph Institute Research Division Staff, *A Comparison of Psychophysiological Detection of Deception Accuracy Rates Obtained Using the Counterintelligence Scope Polygraph (CSP) and The Test for Espionage and Sabotage (TES) question formats* 26 POLYGRAPH 79 (1997); Department of

Defense Polygraph Institute Research Division Staff, *Psychophysiological Detection of Deception Accuracy Rates Obtained Using the Test for Espionage and Sabotage (TES)*, 27 POLYGRAPH 68 (1998); Horowitz et al., *supra* note 11; Sheila Reed, *A New Psychophysiological Detection of Deception Examination for Security Screening*, 31 PSYCHOPHYSIOLOGY S80 (1994).

42. Horowitz et al., *supra* note 11.

43. Barland, *supra* note 41.

Horowitz et al. and the studies reported above for the CQT, it should be pointed out that Barland's study was conducted in a screening setting. By comparison, other mock-screening studies produced near chance performance with probable-lie tests.[44] Therefore, the performance of the directed lie in the Barland study was actually quite strong.

The other two sets of studies on the DLT concern a new test, the test of espionage and sabotage (TES) developed by DODPI for use in national security screening tests. Reed reported three laboratory mock screening studies of the DLT.[45] Following a series of studies that indicated that the national security screening tests of the time were making an unacceptably high number of false negative errors,[46] DODPI attempted to develop a more accurate screening test. It should be noted that the primary concern in conducting national security screening tests is a desire to avoid false negative errors. Following a series of studies that are not publicly available, Reed described the product of DODPI's efforts.

In the first study, the TES test format with only directed-lie comparison questions was tested against two versions of the counterintelligence scope polygraph (CSP) test. One version of the CSP used probable-lie comparison questions (the type of comparison question used in the standard CQT) while the other used directed-lie comparison questions. The TES outperformed both of the CSP formats in terms of correctly identifying guilty subjects. The CSP with directed-lie comparisons was slightly, but not significantly, better at identifying guilty subjects than was the CSP with probable-lie comparisons. The second study produced even higher accuracy for the TES, a directed-lie comparison test format. Little information is provided about the third study, but it also appears to show considerable accuracy for the directed-lie TES. Most recently, DODPI reported a mock espionage/sabotage study that involved 82 subjects.[47] All subjects were tested with the TES. Excluding one inconclusive outcome, the examiners correctly identified 98% of the innocent subjects and 83.3% of the guilty subjects. This study also indicates that the directed-lie TES is extremely successful in discriminating between innocent and guilty subjects.

Abrams reported the only other study of the DLT. Unfortunately that study was so poorly designed and so methodologically flawed that the data are meaningless.[48] Although Abrams and Matte have become outspoken critics of the DLT, their criticisms lack merit and their attacks on the DLT are baseless.[49] Interested readers are referred to the research and commentary by Honts and his colleagues.[50]

44. Gordon H. Barland et al., *Studies of the Accuracy of Security Screening Polygraph Examinations*. Department of Defense Polygraph Institute, Fort McClellan, Alabama. Available *at* http://truth.boisestate.edu/raredocuments/bhb.html (1989); Charles R. Honts, *Counterintelligence Scope Polygraph (CSP) Test Found to be a Poor Discriminator*, 5 FORENSIC REPORTS 215 (1992).

45. Reed, *supra* note 41; also published as Department of Defense Polygraph Institute Research Staff, (1997), *supra* note 41.

46. Gordon H. Barland et al., *supra* note 44; Charles R. Honts, *The Emperor's New Clothes: Application of Polygraph Tests in the American Workplace*, 4 FORENSIC REPORTS 91 (1991); Charles R. Honts, *supra* note 44; Charles R. Honts, *The Psychophysiological Detection of Deception*, 3 CURRENT DIRECTIONS IN PSYCHOLOGICAL SCI. 77 (1994).

47. Department of Defense Polygraph Institute Research Staff (1998), *supra* note 41.

48. Stanley Abrams, *The Directed Lie Control Question*, 20 POLYGRAPH 26 (1991).

49. *See* Stanley Abrams, *A Response To Honts On The Issue Of The Discussion Of Questions Between Charts* 28 POLYGRAPH 223 (1999); John A. Matte, *An Analysis Of The*

[c] Guilty Knowledge Test

There are many published laboratory studies of the GKT, but many of these studies used artificial and unrealistic methods that render the studies useless for providing estimates of accuracy in the field. However, a review of the scientific literature reveals five laboratory studies of the GKT that appear to have methodology realistic enough to allow some generalization to the field.[51] The results of these studies are summarized in Table 3. As with the CQT, the quality laboratory studies of the GKT indicate a high level of accuracy for the technique, but the GKT consistently produces more false negative than false positive errors. This is disturbing because the conditions for the detection of concealed knowledge with the GKT are optimized in the laboratory as compared to the field. In GKT lab studies, the experimenters usually pretest potential items for their salience and memorability by guilty subjects and for their transparency to innocent subjects, i.e., can innocent subjects guess the correct response? Although it might be possible to test the transparency of GKT items in the field, it is not possible to test the memorability of key items. Moreover, there is no clear theoretical basis for judgments about what a guilty person is likely to remember about a crime scene. Those factors likely result in an under-estimation of the field rate of false negative errors when generalizing from laboratory studies of the GKT.

Table 3
The results of studies of the GKT

	Guilty			Innocent		
	n	% Correct	% Wrong	n	% Correct	% Wrong
Laboratory Studies						
Davidson (1968)	12	92	8	36	100	0
Honts et al. (1994)[a]	10	80	20	10	90	10
Lykken (1959)	37	86	14	12	100	0
Podlesny & Raskin (1978)	10	90	10	10	100	0
Steller et al. (1987)	47	85	15	40	100	0
Weighted Means	**116**	**86**	**14**	**108**	**99**	**1**
Field Studies						
Elaad (1990)	48	42	58	50	98	2
Elaad, et al., (1992)	40	53	47	40	97	3
Weighted Means	**88**	**47**	**53**	**90**	**98**	**2**

[a] Countermeasure subjects excluded.

Psychodynamics Of The Directed Lie Control Questions In The Control Question Technique, 27 POLYGRAPH 56 (1998).

50. Charles R. Honts, *The Discussion of Comparison Questions Between List Repetitions (Charts) is Associated With Increased Test Accuracy.* 28 POLYGRAPH 117 (1999); Charles R. Honts, *A Brief Note on the Misleading and the Inaccurate: A Rejoinder to Matte (2000) With Critical Comments on Matte and Reuss (1999),* 29 POLYGRAPH 321 (2000); Charles R. Honts & Anne Gordon, *A Critical Analysis Of Matte's Analysis Of The Directed Lie,* 27 POLYGRAPH 241 (1998); Charles R. Honts et al., *The Hybrid Directed Lie Test, The Overemphasized Com-*

parison Question, Chimeras And Other Inventions: A Rejoinder To Abrams (1999), 29 POLYGRAPH 156 (2000).

51. *See* Park O. Davidson, *Validity of the Guilty–Knowledge Technique: The Effects of Motivation,* 53 J. APPLIED PSYCHOL. 62 (1968); Charles R. Honts, et al., *Mental and Physical Countermeasures Reduce the Accuracy of the Concealed Knowledge Test,* 33 PSYCHOPHYSIOLOGY 84 (1994); Lykken, supra note 22; Podlesny & Raskin, supra note 23; Max Steller et al., *Extraversion and the Detection of Information,* 21 J. RES. IN PERSONALITY 334 (1987).

[2] Field Studies

As noted earlier, the greatest problems in conducting field polygraph studies are the development of criteria for determining who was actually telling the truth and who was lying and the lack of control that the experimenter has over the testing situation. There is a consensus among researchers that field studies should have the following characteristics:

1. Subjects should be sampled from the actual population of subjects in which the scientist is interested. If the objective is to determine the accuracy of a polygraph examination on criminal suspects, then the subjects of the study should be criminal suspects.

2. Subjects should be sampled by some type of random process, and cases must be included independent of the accuracy of the original examiner's decision or the quality of the polygraph charts.

3. The physiological data should be evaluated independently by persons trained and experienced in the evaluation of polygraph tests who employ scoring techniques that are representative of those used in the field. The evaluations should be based only on the physiological data, and the evaluators should not have access to other case information. This provides an estimate of the accuracy of the decisions based solely on the physiological information. However, decisions rendered by the original examiner probably provide a better estimate of the accuracy of polygraph techniques as they are actually employed in the field setting by criminal investigators.

4. The credibility of the subject should be determined by information independent of the polygraph test. Confession substantiated by physical evidence is the best criterion for use in these studies.

[a] Control Question Test

The 1983 OTA review of the scientific literature on polygraph tests identified 10 field studies in the scientific literature that met minimal standards for acceptability.[52] However, none of the 10 studies meets all four of the

52. OTA, supra note 13; the 10 studies included by the OTA were: GORDON H. BARLAND & DAVID C. RASKIN, VALIDITY AND RELIABILITY OF POLYGRAPH EXAMINATIONS OF CRIMINAL SUSPECTS 1 U.S. Department of Justice Report No. 76–1, Contract No. 75–NI–99–0001 (1976); Philip J. Bersh, *A Validation Study of Polygraph Examiner Judgments,* 53 J. APPLIED PSYCHOL. 399 (1969); William A. Davidson, *Validity and Reliability of the Cardio Activity Monitor,* 8 POLYGRAPH 104 (1979); Frank S. Horvath, *The Effect of Selected Variables on Interpretation of Polygraph Records,* 62 J. APPLIED PSYCHOL. 127 (1977); Frank S. Horvath & John E. Reid, *The Reliability of Polygraph Examiner Diagnosis of Truth and Deception,* 62 J. CRIM. L., CRIMINOLOGY & POLICE SCI. 276 (1971); Fred L. Hunter &

Phillip Ash, *The Accuracy and Consistency of Polygraph Examiners' Diagnoses,* 1 J. POLICE SCI. & ADMIN. 370 (1973); Benjamin Kleinmuntz & Julian Szucko, *A Field Study of the Fallibility of Polygraphic Lie Detection,* 308 NATURE 449 (1984); David C. Raskin, 1 RELIABILITY OF CHART INTERPRETATION AND SOURCES OF ERRORS IN POLYGRAPH EXAMINATIONS, U.S. Department of Justice, Report No. 76–3, Contract No. 75–NI–0001. (1976); Stanley M. Slowik & Joseph P. Buckley, *Relative Accuracy of Polygraph Examiner Diagnosis of Respiration, Blood Pressure, and GSR Recordings,* 3 J. POLICE SCI. & ADMIN. 305 (1975); Douglas E. Wicklander & Fred L. Hunter, *The Influence of Auxiliary Sources of Information in Polygraph Diagnoses,* 3 J. POLICE SCI. & ADMIN. 405 (1975).

above criteria for an adequate field study. The overall accuracy of the polygraph decisions in the OTA review was 90% on criterion-guilty suspects and 80% on criterion-innocent suspects. In spite of the inclusion of studies with serious methodological problems, accuracy in field cases was higher than is claimed by some of the most vocal critics.[53]

Subsequent to the OTA study, four field studies of the CQT that meet the criteria for an adequate field study have been reported.[54] As shown in Table 4, they produced a combined estimate of 90.5% accuracy, which is higher than that developed by OTA on the basis of the 10 less rigorous early studies.

Table 4. The Accuracy of Independent Evaluations in High Quality Field Studies of the CQT

Study		Guilty					Innocent		
	n	% Correct	% Wrong	% Inc		n	% Correct	% Wrong	% Inc
Honts (1996)a	7	100	0	0		6	83	0	17
Honts & Raskin (1988)b	12	92	0	8		13	62	15	23
Patrick & Iacono (1991)c	52	92	2	6		37	30	24	46
Raskin et al. (1989)d	37	73	0	27		26	61	8	31
Means	108	89	1	10		82	59	12	29
Percent Decisions		**98**	**2**				**75**	**25**	

a Subgroup of subjects confirmed by confession and evidence.

b Decision based only on comparisons to traditional comparison questions.

c.Results from mean blind rescoring of the cases "verified with maximum certainty" p. 235.

d. There results are from an independent evaluation fo the "pure verification" cases.

It is interesting to note that only in the Patrick and Iacono study did the original examiners perform at a much higher level than the independent evaluators.[55] Patrick and Iacono's original examiners correctly classified 100% of their guilty subjects and 90% of the innocent subjects,[56] which was similar to the performance of the original examiners in the Honts[57] study that used examiners from the same law enforcement agency. Given the general performance of independent evaluators across these high quality field studies, it appears that the performance of the blind evaluators in Patrick and Iacono could be viewed as an outlying data point. Honts provides a discussion of this and other potential problems with the Patrick & Iacono study.[58] If the Patrick & Iacono study is excluded, the remaining three field studies produce an estimate of accuracy of 96%.

53. David T. Lykken, *A Tremor In The Blood: Uses And Abuses Of The Lie Detector* (1998).

54. Charles R. Honts, *Criterion Development and Validity of the Control Question Test in Field Application* 123 J. GENERAL PSYCHOL. 309. (1996); Honts & Raskin, *supra* note 19; Christopher J. Patrick & William G. Iacono, *Validity of the Control Question Polygraph Test: The Problem of Sampling Bias*, 76 J. APPLIED PSYCHOL. 229 (1991); David C. Raskin et al., *A Study of the Validity of Polygraph Examinations in Criminal Investigation*, 1 NAT'L INST. OF JUST. (1988).

55. Patrick & Iacono, *supra* note 54.

56. *Id.*

57. Honts, *supra* note 1.

58. *Id.*

Although the better quality field studies indicate a high accuracy rate for the CQT, all of the data presented in Table 4 were obtained from independent evaluations of the physiological data. That method is desirable for scientific purposes because it eliminates possible contamination (e.g., knowledge of the case facts and the overt behaviors of the subject during the examination) that might have influenced the decisions of the original examiners. Such contamination could distort research designed to determine how much discriminative information was contained in the physiological recordings. However, independent evaluators rarely testify in legal proceedings, nor do they make decisions in most applied settings.

The original examiner renders the diagnosis of truthfulness or deception in an actual case and would testify in court. Thus, accuracy of decisions by independent evaluators is not the true figure of merit for legal proceedings and most other applications. The Committee of Concerned Social Scientists[59] presented the data from the original examiners in the studies reported in Table 4 along with two additional studies that are often cited by critics of the CQT,[60] as shown in Table 5. Those data indicate that the original examiners achieved accuracy rates of 98% on verified innocent suspects and 97% on verified guilty suspects, which are higher than the results from the independent evaluators.

59. Honts & Peterson *supra* note 38.

60. Those two studies are, Benjamin Kleinmuntz & Julian J. Szucko, *A Field Study of the Fallibility of Polygraphic Lie Detection*, 308 Nature 449 (1984), Frank Horvath, *The Effects of Selected Variables on Interpretation of Polygraph Records*, 62, J. Applied Psychol. 127 (1977). Neither of these studies meets the generally accepted requirements for useful field studies but nevertheless they are frequently cited by critics of the CQT as evidence that the CQT is not accurate. The study reported by Benjamin Kleinmuntz and Julian J. Szucko fails to meet the criteria for a useful field study because (1) the subjects were employees who were forced to take tests as part of their employment, not criminal suspects (2) the case selection method was not specified, and (3) the data were evaluated by students at a polygraph school that does not teach blind chart evaluation. Moreover, those students were given only one ninth of the usual amount of data collected in a polygraph examination and were forced to use a rating scale with which they were not familiar. The Horvath study also fails to meet the criteria for a useful study because (1) about half of the innocent subjects were victims of violent crime, not suspects, (2) virtually all of the false positive errors in that study were with innocent victims, not innocent suspects, (3) the independent evaluators were all trained at a polygraph school that does not teach numerical chart evaluation, and (4) cases were not selected at random. Some cases were excluded from the study because of the nature of the charts. An interesting fact that critics almost never mention is that the decisions by the original examiners in the Horvath Study were 100% correct. Also see the discussion in David C. Raskin, *Methodological Issues in Estimating Polygraph Accuracy in Field Applications*, 19, Canadian J. Behaviour. Sci. 389 (1987).

Table 5. Percent Correct Decisions by Original Examiners in Field Cases Using the CQT		
Study	Innocent	Guilty
Horvath (1977)	100	100
Honts and Raskin (1988)	100	92
Kleinmuntz and Szucko (1984)	100	100
Raskin, Kircher, Honts, & Horowitz (1988)a	96	95
Patrick and Iacono (1991)	90	100
Honts (1996)b	100	94
Means	**98**	**97**
a Cases where all questions were confirmed.		
b Includes all cases with some confirmation.		

[b] Directed Lie Test

To date, Honts and Raskin have reported the only field study of the DLT. They conducted polygraph tests of criminal suspects over a 4–year period and obtained 25 confirmed tests in which one personal directed lie was included along with typical probable-lie comparison questions.[61] Each author then performed blind interpretations of the charts obtained by the other author, scoring them with and without the use of the directed-lie question. The results of the Honts and Raskin study indicated that inclusion of the directed-lie question in the numerical evaluation of the charts had a noticeable effect on the confirmed innocent suspects, reducing the false positive rate from 20% to 0%. For the confirmed guilty suspects, it had the slight effect of changing one inconclusive outcome to a false negative. The effects of the directed-lie question on the total numerical scores were more dramatic. Inclusion of the directed-lie comparisons almost doubled the size of the total numerical scores for the confirmed innocent suspects, raising the mean score from +4.7 to +9.0. It had a lesser effect on the scores of the confirmed guilty suspects, lowering them from –13.8 to –11.5. Thus, the directed-lie question raised the mean score for innocent suspects from the inconclusive range into the definite truthful area, while the mean score for guilty suspects remained clearly in the deceptive area. The main impact of the directed-lie question was a reduction in false positive errors.

[c] Guilty Knowledge Test

The only two field studies of the GKT were published in 1990 and 1992.[62] Both are high in quality and meet the four requirements for an adequate field study of polygraph tests described above. The results of those studies are presented in Table 3. Those studies show that the GKT has a very high false negative rate (53%) in field applications. In both studies, more than half of the

61. Honts & Raskin, *supra* note 19.

62. Elaad (1990), *supra* note 28; Eitan Elaad et al., *Detection Measures in Real–Life*

Criminal Guilty Knowledge Tests, 77 J. Applied Psychol. 757 (1992).

guilty criminal suspects passed their GKT examinations, appearing to lack knowledge of the crimes that they had actually committed. In light of the data from laboratory studies and the difficulties in developing good GKT tests as described above, the results of the field studies of the GKT are not at all surprising. Given the extensive literature on the fallibility of eyewitness memory, especially when witnesses are aroused or under stress, it is not surprising that criminals have poor memory for the details of crimes they have committed.[63]

Another factor to consider when evaluating the potential of the GKT as a field polygraph technique is the applicability of the technique to actual cases. In order to conduct a GKT, the examiner must have a number of key items of information from the crime scene to develop the test. Podlesny examined the applicability of the GKT by studying the information available in FBI case files.[64] He estimated that a meaningful GKT could be developed in only 13%–18% of the cases examined. This study suggests that the field applicability of the GKT is extremely limited, even if it had an acceptable level of validity. Given this limitation, demonstrably low accuracy, and strong theoretical reasons why the GKT cannot work properly in the field, it is clear that the GKT is useful only as a vehicle for laboratory research.

§ 10–2.2.2　Countermeasures

Countermeasures are behaviors that an individual may use to attempt to defeat or distort a polygraph test. Countermeasures might be employed either by guilty subjects who are trying to beat the test by appearing truthful or innocent subjects who do not trust the test and want to hedge their bets. Conceptually, countermeasures fall into two major categories, general-state countermeasures that are designed to affect the general mental or physical state of the subject, and specific-point countermeasures that are used to produce physiological changes at specific points during the test. General-state countermeasures include ingestion of drugs, relaxation, and a variety of mental strategies, such as dissociation, self-deception, and rationalization. Specific-point countermeasures include physical and mental maneuvers during and following specific questions in order to increase or decrease physiological reactions to those questions.

Scientists have addressed the problem of polygraph countermeasures, primarily in the laboratory setting. The research clearly indicates that all general-state countermeasures (including drugs) and specific-point counter-measures designed to reduce reactions to relevant questions fail to produce inconclusive or false positive outcomes.[65] However, studies in which subjects have been carefully trained to use specific-point countermeasures to enhance their reactions to control questions have increased false negative rates with both the CQT and the GKT.

63.　Elizabeth F. Loftus & K. Ketcham, Witness for the Defense (1991).

64.　John A. Podlesny, *Is the Guilty Knowledge Polygraph Technique Applicable in Criminal Investigations? A Review of FBI Case Records*, 20 Crime Laboratory Dig. 59 (1993).

65.　*See, e.g.*, Charles R. Honts, *Interpreting Research on Countermeasures and the Physiological Detection of Deception*, 15 J. Police Sci. & Admin. 204 (1987); Raskin, *supra* note 10.

An initial study of the spontaneous use of countermeasures by subjects in mock crime experiments found that countermeasure usage by guilty subjects was high (61% attempted one or more countermeasures), but no guilty subject defeated the test and no innocent subject reported attempting a countermeasure.[66] That study was recently replicated by Honts and his colleagues.[67] In the context of a laboratory study of the CQT, they found that 90% of the guilty and 46% of the innocent subjects reported attempting at least one countermeasure. The spontaneous countermeasures had no significant effects with the guilty subjects, but they did produce a significant effect with innocent subjects. Innocent subjects who attempted a spontaneous countermeasure significantly shifted their scores in the deceptive direction, making it more likely that they would fail the test. It is important to note that providing the subjects with detailed information about the rationale of the control question test and suggestions concerning countermeasures that might be used did not enable them to defeat the test.[68]

[1] Countermeasures and the CQT

A series of studies by Honts and his colleagues examined the effects of specific-point mental and physical countermeasures with the CQT.[69] In these studies, guilty subjects in realistic mock-crime experiments were trained for approximately 30 minutes in the use of one or more of the following countermeasures: biting the tongue, pressing the toes to the floor, mentally subtracting 7s from a number larger than 200. They were fully informed about the nature of the CQT and told that to pass the test they would have to produce larger physiological reactions to the control questions than to the relevant questions. They were instructed to begin their countermeasure as soon as they recognized any control question, stop the countermeasure long enough to answer the question, and resume and continue their countermeasure until the next question began. All subjects were motivated by the promise of a cash bonus if they were successful in producing a truthful outcome.

Across this series of studies, approximately half of the decisions with trained countermeasure subjects were incorrect. There was no significant difference between mental and physical countermeasures, and experienced examiners were unable to detect the use of countermeasures either by inspecting the polygraph charts or by observing the subjects' overt behavior. However, computerized scoring of the polygraph charts outperformed the human evaluators and was more robust in the face of countermeasures. When the discriminant analysis classification model of Kircher & Raskin was applied to these data,[70] the false negative rate was reduced by half.[71] It seems likely that statistical models can be developed to discriminate countermeasure users

66. Charles R. Honts et al., *Effects of Spontaneous Countermeasures on the Physiological Detection of Deception,* 16 J. POLICE SCI. & ADMIN. 91 (1988).

67. Charles R. Honts et al., *Effects Of Spontaneous Countermeasures Used Against The Comparison Question Test,* POLYGRAPH (forthcoming 2001).

68. Rovner et al., *supra* note 40.

69. Charles R. Honts et al., *Effects of Physical Countermeasures on the Physiological Detection of Deception,* 70 J. APPLIED PSYCHOL. 177 (1985); Charles R. Honts et al., *Effects of Physical Countermeasures and Their Electromyographic Detection During Polygraph Tests for Deception,* 1 J. PSYCHOPHYSIOLOGY 241 (1987); Honts et al., *supra* note 40.

70. Kircher & Raskin, *supra* note 30.

71. Honts et al., *supra* note 40.

from innocent subjects and improve this performance. Moreover, it should be noted that all of the countermeasure research data are from laboratory studies because it would be unethical and possibly illegal to train criminal suspects to apply countermeasures in order to defeat law enforcement or defense polygraph examinations in actual criminal cases.[72] Since the task of a countermeasure subject should be easier in the laboratory than in a field setting where the relevant questions are more powerful, the findings of laboratory studies of countermeasures are likely to represent a worst case scenario with regard to the effectiveness of countermeasures.

There is no published research on the effects of countermeasures on the DLT. However, the dynamics and scoring of the DLT are very similar to the CQT, and there is no reason to expect that the DLT is more or less susceptible to countermeasures than the CQT.

[2]   Countermeasures and the GKT

In 1960, Lykken made an effort to train a group of psychologists, psychiatrists, and medical students to beat a GKT.[73] He informed his subjects about the nature of the GKT and instructed them about various maneuvers designed to augment their responses to the incorrect items. Despite the sophistication of the subjects and Lykken's efforts, he failed to produce any effects of countermeasure training. However, subsequent research and analysis discovered a serious methodological flaw in Lykken's research.[74] Elaad's research was somewhat more successful.[75] Significant effects were obtained by having subjects mentally count sheep during the presentation of all of the items on a GKT, but the countermeasure effects were not dramatic.

These results and others that indicate a lack of effects of drugs on the GKT have led some proponents of the GKT to conclude that the GKT is immune to the effects of countermeasures.[76] However, a study by Honts and

72. Lykken attacks polygraph evidence favorable to a defendant by repeatedly reporting the alleged results of an unpublished countermeasures field study that he designed and conducted with the aid of Floyd Fay, an Ohio prison inmate who had failed two polygraphs and was convicted of murder. *See* David C. Raskin, *Science, Competence and Polygraph Techniques*, 8 CRIM. DEF. 11 (1981). Lykken provided Fay with information to train other prison inmates to defeat polygraph tests administered during criminal investigations in the prison and claimed that he and Fay were successful in assisting 23 of 27 guilty prisoners to fool the polygraph. However, they presented no data other than Fay's claims that all of the prisoners he trained according to Lykken's instructions told him that they were guilty and that they took polygraph tests administered by the prison authorities. Fay reported that 23 of his fellow inmates told him they had used the Lykken countermeasure techniques to fool the polygraph. This claim was based on nothing more than undocumented and unsubstantiated claims by a prison inmate about what he claims other admitted felons told him about polygraph tests they claimed to have taken and

beaten. Aside from the ethical issues raised by such a "study," Lykken's report violates all of the requirements for a scientific study put forward by Iacono, Lykken, and everyone else. As one of us told Floyd Fay, "If you can't trust the reports made by a convicted felon, who can you trust?" Interestingly, Fay admitted to one of us that he unsuccessfully used countermeasures on one of the tests that he failed.

73. David T. Lykken, *The Validity of the Guilty Knowledge Technique: The Effects of Faking*, 44 J. APPLIED PSYCHOL. 258 (1960).

74. Honts et al., *supra* note 51; Charles R. Honts & John C. Kircher, *Legends Of The Concealed Knowledge Test: Lykken's Distributional Scoring System Fails To Detect Countermeasures*, 32 PSYCHOPHYSIOLOGY S41 (1995).

75. Eitan Elaad & Gershon Ben–Shakkar, *Effects of Mental Countermeasures on Psychophysiological Detection in the Guilty Knowledge Test*, 11 INT'L J. PSYCHOPHYSIOLOGY 99 (1991).

76. BEN–SHAKAR & FUREDY, *supra* note 2.

his colleagues has shown that conclusion to be incorrect. They examined the effects of pressing the toes to the floor and mentally subtracting 7s on the accuracy of the GKT.[77] Using methods similar to those previously described in studies of countermeasures and the CQT, they informed mock-crime subjects about the nature of the GKT. They told them that in order to pass the GKT they would have to produce larger physiological responses to the non-critical items than to the key items. Subjects were offered a monetary bonus if they could pass their GKT. Ninety percent of the subjects trained in a physical countermeasure and 60% of the subjects trained in a mental countermeasure were able to beat the GKT. The results of this study clearly demonstrate that the accuracy of the GKT is substantially reduced by countermeasures and that the GKT may be even more susceptible than the CQT to the effects of physical countermeasures. However, as with the CQT, the application of the Kircher and Raskin discriminant classification model[78] to these data dramatically improved performance.[79]

§ 10–2.2.3   The Polygraph in Practice

[1]   Application of Comparison Question Tests

Comparison question tests are the most widely used techniques in criminal investigations and judicial proceedings.[80] Almost every major federal, state, and local law enforcement agency employs such tests to reduce the number of suspects so that limited resources can be focused on likely suspects, that is, those who have failed polygraph examinations. Comparison question tests are also used to examine prime suspects and persons formally charged with criminal acts.

In many jurisdictions, prosecutors and defense attorneys make informal agreements that if the suspect or defendant passes a polygraph examination from a competent and well-qualified examiner, the prosecutor will seriously consider dismissing the charges. Alternatively, prior to the conduct of a polygraph examination, prosecutors and defense attorneys may enter into formal stipulations that the results will be admissible as evidence at trial. Under these arrangements, costly trials are often avoided by guilty pleas or dismissals based in part on the results of polygraph tests. Polygraph tests are sometimes used by prosecutors to assess the veracity of individuals involved in the crime who may testify for the prosecution in exchange for immunity or reduced charges if they demonstrate their truthfulness on the polygraph test. Also, some courts use polygraph evidence in post-conviction proceedings, such as sentencing and motions for new trials. A comprehensive compilation and discussion of the federal and state case law and legislation concerning the admissibility of polygraph evidence and the polygraph examiner licensing regulations in the United States was provided by Morris.[81] Honts and Perry and others have provided a summary of the arguments in support of the use

77.   Honts et al., *supra* note 51.

78.   Kircher & Raskin, *supra* note 30.

79.   Honts et al., *supra* note 51.

80.   Raskin (1986), *supra* note 1.

81.   Roberta A. Morris, *The Admissibility of Evidence Derived From Hypnosis and Polygraph, in* PSYCHOLOGICAL METHODS IN CRIMINAL INVESTIGATION AND EVIDENCE 333 (David C. Raskin ed., 1989).

of polygraph tests in legal proceedings.[82]

[2] Application of the Guilty Knowledge Test

Several practical problems prevent widespread use of the GKT, some of which concern the circumstances surrounding many crimes. Consistently choosing details of a crime that are likely to be recognized by the guilty suspect during the test is an insurmountably difficult task for investigators and polygraph examiners. Details of a crime that may seem quite distinctive and memorable to an investigator or polygraph examiner may be unnoticed or forgotten by the perpetrator because of emotional stress, confusion, inattention, or intoxication during the commission of the crime. Thus, the false negative rate of the GKT in criminal investigation is likely to be high.

The utility of the GKT is also limited because innocent subjects frequently are informed about the details of the crime prior to taking a polygraph test. It is common practice for police investigators to disclose details of crimes to suspects in the process of interrogation, for news media to publicize the details of many crimes, and for defense attorneys to discuss the details of police reports and allegations with their clients. Thus, the majority of innocent and guilty criminal suspects obtain knowledge of the critical crime information after the crime was committed, which renders them unsuitable for a GKT.

Many criminal investigations do not lend themselves to the GKT because certain types of crimes characteristically have no special information that is unknown to potential polygraph subjects. Such situations include allegations of forcible sexual assault when the accused claims that the sexual acts were consensual, claims of self-defense in physical assault and homicide cases, and crimes in which the suspect admits having been present at the scene but denies any criminal participation. Because of its high rate of false negative errors and inapplicability in most investigative situations, the GKT is not likely to become a substitute for comparison question tests.

§ 10–2.2.4 General Acceptance of Polygraph Testing by the Scientific Community

Several sources of evidence demonstrate that the validity of polygraph tests is generally accepted in the relevant scientific community. Two valid surveys of the Society for Psychophysiological Research (SPR) directly addressed the general acceptance issue.[83] The SPR is a professional society of scientists who study how the mind and body interact, which makes it an appropriate scientific organization for assessing general acceptance. The Gallup Organization survey was replicated and extended in 1994 by Amato at the

82. Charles R. Honts & Mary V. Perry, *Polygraph Admissibility: Changes and Challenges*, 16 L. & Hum. Behav. 357 (1992); James R. McCall, *Misconceptions and Reevaluation— Polygraph Admissibility After* Rock *and* Daubert, 1996 U.Ill.L.Rev. 363; Edward J. Imwinkelreid & James R. McCall, *Issues Once Moot: The Other Evidentiary Objections to the Admission of Exculpatory Polygraph Examinations*, 32 Wake Forest L. Rev. 1045 (1997).

83. The Gallup Organization, *Survey of the Members of the Society for Psychophysiological Research Concerning Their Opinions of Polygraph Test Interpretations*, 13, Polygraph, 153 (1984); Susan L. Amato, A Survey of The Members of the Society for Psycholphsiological Research Regarding The Polygraphs: Opinions and Implications (1993) (Unpublished Master's Thesis, University of North Dakota, Grand Forks) (on file with authors).

University of North Dakota. The results of those surveys were very consistent. Approximately two-thirds of the doctoral-level members of the SPR who were surveyed stated that polygraph tests are a valuable diagnostic tool when considered with other available information.[84] When only those respondents who described themselves as highly informed about the scientific polygraph literature are considered, the percentage who indicated that polygraph tests are a useful diagnostic tool rose to 83%. Since fewer than 10% reported being involved in conducting polygraph examinations professionally, the results were not influenced by financial interests of the respondents. These findings indicate that there is a great deal of acceptance of polygraph techniques by members of the SPR.[85]

84. Respondents in both surveys gave responses to the following question: Which one of these four statements best describes your own opinion of polygraph test interpretations by those who have received systematic training in the technique, when they are called upon to interpret whether a subject is or is not telling the truth? A) It is a sufficiently reliable method to be the sole determinant, B) It is a useful diagnostic tool when considered with other available information, C) It is of questionable usefulness, entitled to little weight against other available information, D) It is of no usefulness.

85. A third survey of the members of the SPR was reported by Iacono and Lykken in *The Scientific Status of Research on Polygraph Techniques: The Case Against Polygraph Tests,* MODERN SCIENTIFIC EVIDENCE: THE LAW AND SCIENCE OF EXPERT TESTIMONY, (David L. Faigman, David Kaye, Michael J. Saks, & Joseph Sanders eds. 1997); also partially available at William Iacono & David Lykken, *The Validity of the Lie Detector: Two Surveys of Scientific Opinion,* 87 J. APPLIED PSYCH. 426 (1997). Iacono and Lykken are two of the most outspoken critics of polygraph testing. However, the present authors believe that the Iacono and Lykken survey is so flawed and suspect that it cannot be used for any substantive purpose. Problems with the Iacono and Lykken study include: 1) The cover letter for the Iacono and Lykken survey described it as answering questions regarding the admissibility of polygraph evidence in court, rather than the scientific validity of the technique. They inappropriately asked the respondents to make a political and legal judgment rather than a scientific one. Few, if any, SPR members have the legal background to offer an opinion about admissibility. In contrast, Amato and Honts presented the issues in the context of whether or not the SPR should have a formal scientific policy regarding the validity of polygraph testing. 2) Court-ordered discovery and cross-examination in the cases of *State of Washington v. Daniel Gallegos,* 95-1-02749-7 (1996) and *Steve Griffith v. Muscle Improvement, Inc.,* Superior Court of California, sworn deposition 21 April 1998, forced Iacono to reveal that the sample of respondents to the Iacono and Lykken survey

described themselves as very uninformed about the topic of polygraph examinations. Iacono and Lykken's respondents were asked, "About how many empirical studies, literature reviews, commentaries, or presentations at scientific meetings dealing with the validity of the CQT have you read or attended?" Unfortunately, subjects were asked to respond on an unusual non-linear scale. Conversion of the scale units to numbers of items indicates that the average respondent had contact with only 3 items dealing with the validity of the polygraph. Since the responses on this non-linear scale are positively skewed, this means that many more than 50% of the subjects responded that they had contact with fewer than 3 items. In light of the large volume of scientific articles and presentations on this topic (we have either authored or co-authored over 300 such papers and presentations ourselves), these data demonstrate that the Iacono and Lykken sample was relatively ignorant about the science relating to the polygraph; therefore, the subjects were not qualified to offer an opinion about its scientific validity. This information, which Iacono and Lykken chose not to include in either of their publications, would remain hidden were it not for compulsory discovery and cross-examination. 3) Another anomaly in the Iacono and Lykken data analysis makes it impossible to compare some of their results to the other surveys in any meaningful way. In defining their "highly informed" group, Iacono and Lykken included those who chose 4 or higher on their 7–point scale of polygraph knowledge, whereas Amato and Honts included only those who chose 5 and above. This difference in cutting scores makes it impossible to compare these results across the two surveys. Because Iacono and Lykken included relatively ignorant respondents in their highly informed group, their entire analysis is suspect. 4) In their 1997 chapter in this volume, Iacono and Lykken described their survey as a "random sample." However, in their publication Iacono and Lykken revealed that their sampling was not random. They deliberately excluded the authors of this chapter, and possibly other scientific supporters of the polygraph. 5) Because of Iacono and Lykken's unusual and suspicious data analyses and their misrepresentation of the

In November of 2000, Honts, Thurber, and their students conducted a telephone survey of the at-large members of the American Psychology–Law Society (AP–LS). The AP–LS is a particularly relevant scientific group because the members are highly familiar with the nature and difficulty of applied psychology-law research and because they are generally familiar with the legal requirements for the admissibility of scientific evidence. The AP–LS members were asked about a variety of issues concerning polygraph research, general acceptance, and relative validity of the polygraph. The survey required about 10 minutes, and 72% of those contacted agreed to respond. Subjects were told that their responses should take into consideration the use of the comparison question test in forensic situations.

The AP–LS respondents reported having read an average of 14 articles from peer-reviewed publications concerning the polygraph, which is nearly five times the number indicated by the SPR respondents in the Iacono and Lykken survey.[86] The AP–LS members indicated a generally favorable attitude toward the use of laboratory data for estimating the validity of the polygraph in the real world. The majority of the respondents (89%) indicated that laboratory studies should be given at least some weight by policy makers and the courts, and a large number (49%) stated that moderate to considerable weight should be given to laboratory results.[87] This finding strikingly contrasts to the position espoused by Iacono and Lykken, who dismiss such studies. The opinions of the members of the AP–LS about laboratory research are particularly persuasive since they routinely apply the results of science to real-world problems, a process relatively unfamiliar to SPR members whose research is typically theoretically oriented. The vast majority of the AP–LS respondents (91%) believe that it is possible to conduct useful field studies of the polygraph.[88] Nearly all of them (96%) stated that the publication of polygraph studies in peer-reviewed psychology journals is indicative of a

survey in a publication intended for the legal profession, Amato and Honts were concerned that there might be other undisclosed problems with the Iacono and Lykken survey. Under the ethical standards of the American Psychological Association, scientists are required to make their data available for reanalysis by qualified scientists. On March 10, 1997 and subsequent occasions, Amato and Honts wrote Iacono and then Lykken requesting the data from their survey for the purpose of performing an independent reanalysis. To date, they have refused to provide their data. However, Iacono subsequently requested copies of the data from the Amato and Honts survey, which were provided to Iacono within two weeks of the receipt of their request. Iacono and Lykken have said they offered to share their data with Amato and Honts, which is misleading. They offered to provide only the summary data upon which their published analyses were based and would allow Amato and Honts simply to check their calculations. Since they would not permit discovery of other possible irregularities in their analyses and reports nor permit a reanalysis that would allow the results to be compared to the findings of the Amato and Honts survey,

their offer was rejected. Iacono and Lykken's claim that they offered access to their data is simply disingenuous.

86. *See supra* note 85.

87. Respondents were asked the following question: Laboratory mock-crime studies are often used to study polygraph tests. Consider a properly designed and conducted study that employed a realistic mock-crime paradigm (for example a guilty subject goes to an unfamiliar place and takes money from a cash box) and used techniques that are as similar as possible to actual field practice. How much weight should policy makers and courts give to the results of such studies in estimating the validity the polygraph in real world tests? Please choose one of the following: a. No weight, b. Little weight, c. Some weight, d. Moderate weight, e. Considerable weight.

88. Respondents were asked the following question: Do you believe that it is possible to conduct a scientific field validity study of polygraph testing that can yield a useful estimate of the validity of the comparison question test? Yes or No.

general acceptance of the scientific methodology used in those studies.[89]

The AP–LS respondents were also asked about the validity of the CQT. Two approaches were taken to that issue. Respondents were first asked to compare the usefulness of a properly-conducted CQT to seven other types of frequently admitted evidence. The majority of respondents indicated that polygraph results are at least as useful as, or more useful than, psychological opinions about parental fitness, psychological opinions regarding malingering, eyewitness identification, psychological assessments of dangerousness, and psychological assessment of temporary insanity, but are less useful than fingerprint and DNA evidence. They were also asked their opinion of the impact that CQT polygraph evidence would have on the accuracy of judicial verdicts about guilt and innocence. The majority (52%) reported that judicial decision accuracy would be improved by allowing polygraph evidence, while 20% stated that polygraph evidence would have no impact on judicial accuracy. Only 28% indicated that the accuracy of verdicts would decrease if polygraph experts were allowed to testify.

The results of the AP–LS survey present an overall picture that strongly supports the usefulness of polygraph evidence in court. This relevant and knowledgeable scientific community, which is highly experienced with applied research and the requirements of the legal profession, believes that polygraph tests are at least as accurate as many types of evidence currently admitted in court. Moreover, the majority stated that introduction of polygraph evidence would improve the accuracy of judicial decision-making. These results replicate and extend the results reported by Gallup[90] and Amato.[91] They also underscore concerns about the findings reported by Iacono and Lykken.[92]

Another important indicator of the acceptance of the psychophysiological detection of deception in the scientific community is provided by the large number of original scientific studies published in peer-reviewed scientific journals. Studies reporting positive results for the validity of polygraph examinations have appeared in the *Journal of Applied Psychology, Journal of General Psychology, Psychophysiology, Journal of Police Science and Administration, Current Directions in Psychological Science, Psychological Bulletin, Journal of Research in Personality, Law and Human Behavior*, and many others. The review and acceptance process for these journals is lengthy and difficult. The journal editor first sends a submitted article for review by two or three independent scientists who are knowledgeable about the topic and research methods but are not personally involved with the article under consideration. These peer-reviewers comment on the quality of the literature review, the research design, the statistical analyses, the reasonableness of the conclusions drawn, and the appropriateness of the article for publication in the journal. The editor also reviews the article and incorporates the comments and recommendations of the reviewers to make a decision about publication. Minor or extensive revisions are usually required before publication. Manu-

---

89. Respondents were asked the following question: In general, do you believe that studies of the polygraph published in peer-reviewed scientific journals (e.g. PSYCHOPHYSIOLOGY, JOURNAL OF APPLIED PSYCHOLOGY, THE JOURNAL OF GENERAL PSYCHOLOGY) are based on generally accepted scientific methodology? Yes or No.

90. Gallup, *supra* note 83.

91. *Id.*

92. Iacono & Lykken, *supra* note 85.

scripts with unacceptable scientific methods, statistics, or insupportable conclusions are not published (assuming that the methods and data have been honestly and completely reported). For example, the Journal of Applied Psychology has published numerous articles on the psychophysiological detection of deception,[93] even though it rejects 85% of the manuscripts submitted for publication. The publication of numerous articles in mainstream journals of scientific psychology clearly demonstrates that the psychophysiological detection of deception is generally accepted by the community of scientific psychologists. This conclusion was supported by 96% of the AP–LS respondents in the survey described above.

§ 10–2.3   Major Developments and Future Prospects

Major beneficial effects have been produced by improvements in physiological measures and examination procedures and the development and implementation of computer techniques through federally funded research that began at the University of Utah in 1970. By applying the methods and principles of human psychology and psychophysiology, Raskin, Kircher, Honts, and their colleagues refined the pretest interview, improved and developed new test methods, developed better techniques for recording and analyzing the physiological reactions, improved the reliability and accuracy of the numerical scoring system, and developed the first computerized polygraph. The latest version, the Computerized Polygraph System (CPS), is based on the methods and findings of their 30 years of scientific research on the physiological detection of deception.[94] The resulting examination procedures and computer methodology have simplified and improved the standardization of the polygraph examination, enhanced the quality of the polygraph recordings, increased the reliability and accuracy of the polygraph results, and provided higher quality printouts and documentation of the entire procedure. These improvements have generally raised the quality of training and practice of polygraph examiners in agencies such as the US Secret Service, Royal Canadian Mounted Police, other federal, state, provincial, and local law enforcement agencies, and private examiners in the United States, Canada, and many other countries.

93. Some of the articles on the polygraph published in the JOURNAL OF APPLIED PSYCHOLOGY are as follows: P. J. Bersh, *A Validation Study of Polygraph Examiner Judgments*, 53 J. APPLIED PSYCHOL. 399 (1969); P.O. Davidson, *Validity of the Guilty Knowledge Technique: The Effects of Motivation*, 52 J. APPLIED PSYCHOL. 62–65 (1968); E. Elaad, *Detection of Guilty Knowledge in Real–Life Criminal Investigations*, 75 J. APPLIED PSYCHOL. 521–529 (1990); E. Elaad et al., *Detection Measures in Real–Life Criminal Guilty Knowledge Tests*, 77 J. APPLIED PSYCHOL. 757–767 (1992); A. Ginton et al., *A Method for Evaluating the Use of the Polygraph in a Real–Life Situation*, 67 J. APPLIED PSYCHOL. 131–137 (1982); C. R. Honts et al., *Effects of Physical Countermeasures on the Physiological Detection of Deception*, 70 J. APPLIED PSYCHOL. 177–187 (1985); C. R. Honts et al., *Mental and Physical Countermeasures Reduce the Accuracy of Polygraph Tests*, 79 J. APPLIED PSYCHOL. 252–259 (1994); F. S. Horvath, *The Effect of Selected Variables on Interpretation of Polygraph Records*, 62 J. APPLIED PSYCHOL. 127–136 (1977); J, C, Kircher, & D. C. Raskin, *Human Versus Computerized Evaluations of Polygraph Data in a Laboratory Setting*, 73 J. APPLIED PSYCHOL. 291–302 (1988); C. J. Patrick, & W. G. Iacono, *Validity of the Control Question Polygraph Test: The Problem of Sampling Bias*, 76 J. APPLIED PSYCHOL. 229–238 (1991); J. A. Podlesny & C. Truslow, *Validity of an Expanded–Issue (Modified General Question) Polygraph Technique in a Simulated Distributed–Crimes–Roles Context*, 78 J. APPLIED PSYCHOL. 5 (1993).

94. Information about the CPS can be obtained from the Stoelting Company, 620 Wheat Lane, Wood Dale, IL 60191, *at* http://www.stoeltingco.com.

As a result of efforts by scientists and policy makers, many of the most objectionable applications of polygraph tests have been eliminated or severely curtailed by recent legislation and administrative decisions.[95] Along with the reduction in undesirable applications, a large number of the least competent polygraph practitioners were forced to leave the profession. This raised the level of competence and practice in the field and also fostered an increase in research funds and growth of research programs in universities and government agencies. These programs have also served to improve the training and competence of government, law enforcement, and private polygraph examiners.

Automated Test Administration. In an effort to reduce problems that may be associated with examinations performed by human polygraph examiners, Honts and Amato designed a completely automated polygraph test.[96] In the context of a pre-employment screening polygraph examination, they compared the accuracy of polygraph tests conducted by an experienced human polygraph examiner to a standardized examination conducted by tape recording. Automated examination outcomes were significantly more accurate than human-administered examinations. Although these results were obtained from pre-employment type polygraph examinations that are not directly generalizable to forensic settings, they suggest a promising area of research. If similar results can be obtained with forensic polygraph examinations, then a major source of variability and possible bias in polygraph examinations (the examiner) can be greatly reduced. The resulting increase in standardization and decrease in variability would be highly desirable.

The Impact of Outside Issues. Polygraph examiners have long been concerned that outside issues may reduce the accuracy of a polygraph examination. Consider a subject taking a polygraph test for the theft of a small amount of money from a convenience market. The subject had taken the money but is also guilty of a more serious, undiscovered crime of armed robbery and shooting. Many in the polygraph profession believe that the subject's secret concern about the more serious crime might overshadow the relatively minor issue of theft of money and result in a false negative outcome (a guilty person producing a truthful outcome). These examiners attempt to counter the potential effects of outside issues by asking outside-issue questions, e.g., "Is there something else you are afraid I will ask you a question about even though I told you I would not?" Until recently, neither the effects

---

95. The most important development was the passage of the Employee Polygraph Protection Act of 1988, 29 U.S.C.A. §§ 2001–09 (1991). The regulations promulgated by the Department of Labor [29 C.F.R. § 801; 56 Fed. Reg. 9046 (1991)] resulted in the elimination of more than 1 million tests that were conducted each year on applicants for jobs in the private sector and the consequent reduction in the number of polygraph examiners whose primary income was derived from such undesirable and abusive practices. One of us (Raskin) served as the expert for the US Senate Committee on Labor and Human Resources in drafting the legislation and testifying at the Senate hearings.

96. Charles R. Honts & Susan L. Amato, THE AUTOMATED POLYGRAPH EXAMINATION: FINAL REPORT OF U. S. GOVERNMENT CONTRACT NO. 110224–1998–MO. Boise State University (1999). Also reported as: Charles R. Honts & Susan L. Amato, *Human V. Machine: Research Examining The Automation Of Polygraph Testing.* Paper presented at the annual meeting of the Rocky Mountain Psychological Association, Fort Collins Colorado (April, 1999), and Susan L. Amato & Charles R. Honts, *Automated Polygraph Examination Outperforms Human In Employment Screening Context.* Paper presented at the annual meeting of the Midwestern Psychological Association, Chicago, Illinois (May, 1999).

of outside issues nor the effectiveness of outside issue questions had been studied scientifically.

Honts and his colleagues examined the effects of outside issues in a laboratory mock-crime experiment.[97] Half of the subjects stole $1.00 and half did not. Half of the innocent subjects and half of the guilty subjects then committed another crime, the theft of $20.00. All subjects were given a standard CQT concerning only the theft of $1.00. Half of the polygraph tests included two outside issue questions and half contained none. Subjects were told that if they passed their polygraph test, they could keep the money they had stolen. Subjects who stole neither the $1.00, nor the $20.00, were offered a $1.00 bonus if they could pass their polygraph test. Performance was very high for subjects tested with a standard CQT and who did not have the outside issue. With innocent subjects, 91.7% were correctly classified and there were 8.3% false positive errors. With guilty subjects, 91.7% were correctly classified and 8.3% of the outcomes were inconclusive. There were no false negative errors.

The presence or absence of an outside issue produced results that failed to support the traditional beliefs of the polygraph profession. In contrast to the concerns of the polygraph profession, the outside issue manipulation had a minimal and non-significant impact on subjects who stole the $1 (the actual topic of the examination). However, the presence of an outside issue had a major impact on subjects who were innocent of stealing the $1. For those subjects, correct classification rates dropped from 91.7% to 25.0%, a highly significant and powerful result. Furthermore, the outside issue questions were ineffective for detecting the presence of outside issues. These findings might explain some of the variability in false positive errors in field studies of polygraph validity. If the subject population of an agency includes many subjects who have outside issues, then the false positive rate would be expected to be higher and vice versa. The laboratory findings further support the notion that greater confidence can be placed in truthful outcomes of polygraph examinations, whereas failed polygraph examinations should be viewed more cautiously. Finally, the results of the outside issue study suggest that the exact wording of relevant questions is not critical for the detection of subjects who are attempting deception. These results suggest that even if specific details included in a relevant question were incorrect (for example, dates, amounts of money, or specific sexual acts), a subject attempting deception in the matter under investigation would still respond to those relevant questions and would very likely fail the examination. The results are consistent with, and extend the similar findings of Podlesny and Truslow.[98]

§ 10–2.4 Misconceptions About Control (Comparison) Questions

Iacono and Lykken have provided numerous and lengthy arguments attacking the CQT and the DLT while they promote the GKT. Their arguments and analyses rely on a combination of 1) incorrect assumptions and misunderstandings of the conceptual bases of the CQT and DLT, 2) selective

97. Charles R. Honts et al., *Outside Issues Dramatically Reduce The Accuracy Of Polygraph Tests Given To Innocent Individuals*, presented at the American Psychology–Law Society Biennial Meeting, New Orleans, Louisiana (March 2000).

98. Podlesny and Truslow, *supra* note 40.

presentation of the available scientific and professional literature, 3) flawed theoretical speculation based on an incomplete understanding of actual applications of polygraph techniques and other critical aspects of law enforcement investigations and the criminal justice process, and 4) inaccurate and misleading descriptions of virtually all of the research they selected to present (including their own).

The Iacono and Lykken attack on CQT theory centers on the so-called control questions, which they claim "do not serve as strict controls in the scientific sense of this term; the subject's responses to the CQT's control questions do not predict how this subject should respond to the relevant questions if he is answering truthfully."[99] In fact, the control (comparison) questions are designed to predict how the subject would respond to the relevant questions if he were answering *deceptively*.[100] This is the very heart of the CQT and the DLT, and Iacono and Lykken's failure to understand this fundamental principle renders their entire analysis moot. The problem is compounded by their apparent failure to understand how control questions are actually formulated. Rather than demanding great examiner skill, as Iacono and Lykken claim, control questions require only basic knowledge to formulate and properly present to the subject. They also speculate that guilty subjects may react more strongly to the control questions because they encompass other criminal activity that they have not disclosed, thereby beating the test. However, for many laboratory subjects, their lies to the control questions encompass prior criminal acts far more serious than the mock crime, yet they routinely fail the CQT even though there is only a few dollars at stake when they lie to the relevant questions.[101]

§ 10–2.4.1 Inconsistency, Selectivity, and Misrepresentations

Iacono and Lykken change their requirements for valid research studies to fit the current circumstance. When it suits their purpose, they dismiss laboratory studies as useless for estimating polygraph accuracy in real life, stating that only field studies published in peer-reviewed scientific journals are useful. Their position is not supported by the science[102] nor by the opinions of the members of the American Psychology–Law Society as was described above. Furthermore, they ignore a powerful structural analysis demonstrating the fundamental correspondence between the psychophysiological processes underlying laboratory and field polygraphs,[103] as well as a meta-analysis[104] that indicated similar high levels of accuracy of well-executed field studies and laboratory studies that realistically simulate the field polygraph situation. On the other hand, when laboratory findings suit their immediate purposes, Iacono and Lykken frequently rely on carefully selected studies, presentations at scientific meetings, published abstracts, and unpublished studies to support their current argument.

99. Iacono & Lykken, *supra* note 85, at 597

100. See the discussion in John A. Podlesny & David C. Raskin, *Physiological Measures and the Detection of Deception*, 84 PSYCHOLOGICAL BULL. 782 (1977).

101. See the review in John C. Kircher et al., *Meta-analysis of Mock Crime Studies of the Control Question Polygraph Technique*, 12 LAW & HUM. BEHAV. 79 (1988).

102. Anderson et al., *supra* note 36.

103. *See* Raskin, et al., *supra* note 9. *See also* Charles R. Honts et al., *supra* note 51 (reaching a similar conclusion through a different analysis).

104. *See* Kircher et al., *supra* note 101.

When they are unable to find any basis for dismissing studies that contradict their position, Iacono and Lykken resort to more extreme solutions. Lykken testified that studies reporting higher accuracy rates than he claims are possible must have flaws in their research designs or analyses, even though he is unable to identify any flaws.[105] This unsupported backward inference defies science and simple logic. When confronted with the publication of the Honts field study,[106] which contradicted their major arguments against the CQT, they did not re-examine their position. Instead, they resorted to a series of baseless attacks against the editor and the editorial board of a respected peer-reviewed scientific journal that has been published for more than 70 years.[107]

In the 1997 edition of this volume, Iacono and Lykken presented misdescriptions of criminal investigative processes, how polygraphs are used, and the typical circumstances of confessions to create a basis for their argument that it is impossible to accurately assess the accuracy of field polygraph tests. Neither of them has any training or experience in these areas (collectively, we have more than 50 years of such experience), and they employed false assumptions that formed the basis for their erroneous analysis. They claimed that polygraphs are used by police when "there is no hard evidence against a suspect and no arrest has been made" and by defense attorneys when their clients have already "been arrested and there is sufficient evidence to warrant a trial. The rate of guilt thus must be higher for those who are defendants rather than suspects."[108] In reality, the opposites are true. Polygraphs are frequently used by police when they have reason to believe that the suspect is guilty and may confess, and by defense attorneys whose clients may or may have not been arrested or facing trial. Since most criminal cases are resolved by guilty pleas, a large proportion of those who demand a trial are actually innocent. Neither the failure to obtain a confession following a deceptive polygraph nor the suspect passing a polygraph is an automatic end to the investigation of that suspect or any other suspect. The police must continue to pursue investigations in spite of these factors, and many such suspects confess later in the investigation.

Iacono and Lykken used their erroneous assumptions to argue that field studies include only those cases where "a guilty suspect failed a CQT and subsequently confessed ... [but] all polygraph errors in which an innocent person failed a test are omitted ... [and] all cases in which a guilty subject erroneously passed a test would also be excluded. Thus, confession studies rely on a biased set of cases ... where the original examiner was shown to be correct."[109] On the contrary, the field studies presented above in Table 4 included both types of cases where the original examiner was shown to be incorrect. Moreover, their argument inescapably leads to the conclusion that all field studies must show 100% accuracy on guilty and innocent subjects alike. Instead of examining the facts and data related to their assumptions,

105. California v. Parrison and Parrison, San Diego Superior Court, August 20, 1982.

106. Honts, *supra* note 1.

107. William G. Iacono & David T. Lykken, *supra* note 85, at 227 (Pocket Part 2000). Lykken even went so far as to write one of Professor Honts' undergraduate students and suggest there was impropriety in the peer-review process that allowed publication of the Honts study. A copy of this letter is available from Dr. Honts on request.

108. Iacono & Lykken, *supra* note 85, at 599.

109. *Id.* at 602.

Iacono and Lykken then proposed a totally impractical study in which no suspect would be given any test results, none would be interrogated after failing the test, investigators would be deprived of any polygraph outcomes that would help them investigate or solve their cases, and innocent people would be forced to continue as suspects even after passing the polygraph. Such a study raises serious ethical and legal questions.

The above arguments are a variant of an illusory analysis that Iacono invented to attack the field studies based on confessions.[110] He suggested that a sampling anomaly allows a technique with only chance accuracy to produce an estimate that the technique is 90% accurate. Iacono invented a set of circumstances to illustrate this possibility without any data to support his speculation. Although it cannot be tested empirically, Iacono and Lykken have treated this creation as if it were fact. Armed with this unsupported and misleading argument, they confuse triers of fact and lead them to question the value of all field studies of polygraphs. Therefore, Iacono's formulation requires a detailed analysis to expose its fundamental flaws.

Iacono made the following assumptions for his illusory analysis:

1. 400 innocent and 400 guilty criminal suspects are tested.

2. The polygraph is not better than chance in identifying innocent or guilty subjects.

3. Each crime has only two suspects.

4. A guilty suspect is tested first in half of the cases.

5. If the first suspect fails the test, the second suspect will not be tested.

6. Neither innocent suspects nor guilty suspects who pass the test will ever confess.

7. Only 20% of the guilty who are interrogated will confess.

For the illusory analysis to produce the desired result, the following implicit assumptions are required:

8. The polygraph is the only source of information about who is guilty.

9. Guilty people confess only after failing a polygraph test.

Careful examination of Iacono's assumptions yields the following conclusions:

1. A base rate of 50% is statistically neutral, but may not be representative of field conditions. The base rate of guilt in criminal cases varies widely depending upon how and when the polygraph is used. If it is used early in an investigation, there are likely to be many more innocent than guilty subjects; if it is used late in an investigation, there may be many more guilty than innocent subjects. Changes in the base rate will dramatically alter the outcome of the thought experiment.

2. Chance accuracy was assumed for the sake of argument and is contrary to research findings.

110. William J. Iacono, *Can We Determine the Accuracy of Polygraph Tests? in* 4 ADVANCES IN PSYCHOPHYSIOLOGY (J. Richard Jennings et al. eds., 1991).

3. Iacono's assertion that this assumption can be made without a loss of generality is obviously incorrect.

4. This assumption is tenable only if the base rate is 50%, and then only if the order of testing subjects in forensic cases is random. Law enforcement typically tests subjects who are most likely guilty before they test those more likely to be innocent. They never select subjects by a formally random process.

5. This assumption is not in accord with common police practices. If the first suspect fails and does not confess, it is likely that other suspects will be tested. If other suspects pass their tests, more pressure will be brought to bear on the suspect who failed. Further investigation and interrogation often produce a confession from this suspect. Investigations continue until the cases are solved or found to be unsolvable.

6. This assumption is not in accord with standard police practice and forensic experience. The guilty individual may not confess after the polygraph (passed or failed), but may decide to confess later. This often occurs as the result of additional investigation revealing further evidence or as part of an agreement to resolve the case. Recent research suggests that false confessions by innocent people may be a significant problem.[111]

7. This assumption grossly underestimates the confession rate. The Department of Defense reported a confession rate higher than 70% following failed polygraph tests,[112] the Federal Bureau of Investigation reported 56% confessions by deceptive suspects, the U.S. Secret Service reported that 70% of deceptive results were confirmed by admissions and confessions and more than 90% of polygraph examiners' decisions were later confirmed, and the Drug Enforcement Administration reported that 65% confess following a deceptive polygraph result and 85% of those found truthful are later confirmed by investigations.[113]

8. This assumption is also incorrect. There are many other sources of information available to police. Honts and Raskin[114] and Raskin and his colleagues reported field studies in which evidence other than confessions was used to confirm polygraph results,[115] and Honts explored the use of that information in confirming polygraph test outcomes.[116] He found that approximately 80% of case files contained inculpatory information independent of confessions. The assumption that cases are solved only through polygraph tests is clearly not correct, but it is necessary for Iacono's thought experiment to work as described.

111. Saul M. Kassin & Katherine L. Kiechel, *The Social Psychology of False Confessions: Compliance, Internalization, and Confabulation*, 7 PSYCHOLOLOGICAL SCI. 125 (1996).

112. Charles R. Honts, *The Emperor's New Clothes: Application of Polygraph Tests in the American Workplace*, 4 FORENSIC REPORTS, 91 (1991) and the sources cited therein.

113. SCIENTIFIC VALIDITY OF POLYGRAPH TESTING: A RESEARCH REVIEW AND EVALUATION—TECHNICAL MEMORANDUM, 111 (Washington, DC: U.S. Congress, Office of Technology Assessment, OTA–TM–H–15, November 1983).

114. *Supra* note 54.

115. *Id.*

116. *Id.*

9. This assumption is contradicted by data. In the Honts field study,[117] *none* of the confessions that confirmed the innocent subjects was obtained from polygraph testing situations. This analysis clearly reveals that the Iacono illusory analysis is a post-hoc formulation designed specifically to support Iacono's unscientific hypothesis.[118]

In summary, the Iacono analysis lacks logic and contradicts established facts and produces a misleading conclusion. This is sophistry, not science.

§ 10–2.4.2 The Friendly Polygrapher

In discussing law enforcement and privileged polygraph tests, Iacono and Lykken stated, "The more usual case for an evidentiary hearing is one where the defense counsel arranges a privately administered or 'friendly' polygraph test ... there is not a single study demonstrating that friendly tests are valid."[119] This argument was developed by Orne,[120] who speculated that a guilty suspect who takes a non-law enforcement polygraph examination on a confidential basis might beat the test because of a lack of fear that an adverse result will be disclosed to the authorities. This speculation was based solely on the results of an unrealistic laboratory study in which college students were given only card tests and not a CQT.[121] Orne argued that a suspect who expects that only favorable results will be reported has little at stake and is more confident, the examiner is more supportive, and the lack of fear of failure and subsequent disclosure will enable a guilty person to pass the test. However, Raskin demonstrated that the scientific literature provides no support for the friendly examiner hypothesis and generally contradicts it.[122]

As noted above, laboratory studies where there is little at stake routinely produce detection rates of approximately 90%, and laboratory studies using placebos and other procedures designed to make guilty subjects believe they can pass the polygraph test showed no reduction in detection rates even for the GKT, which is easier to beat than the CQT.[123] If Orne's hypothesis were

---

117. *Id.*

118. Iacono's hypothesis is literally "unscientific" in the sense that it cannot be falsified. There is no way to prove that any field study was not the result of processes similar to those invented by Iacono.

119. Iacono & Lykken, *supra* note 85, at 599. Unfortunately, Iacono and Lykken's lack of consistency is not restricted to academic arguments. Although they argue against the CQT and its use by defense attorneys, they themselves devised and performed a CQT on Wounded Knee criminal defendant Russell Means to be presented as evidence for the defense at Means' federal trial in Sioux Falls, South Dakota. This came to light after Lykken testified for the prosecution against the validity of polygraph techniques and the admission of such evidence on behalf of defendant William Wong (*Regina v. Wong*, 33 C.C.C.2d 511 [B.C.S.Ct.1976]. During cross-examination, Lykken admitted under oath that he had never received training in the administration of polygraph tests and he did not believe in them. He admitted that he believed Defendant Means was "guilty of the specific allegations against him ... and was probably lying," but he was prepared to testify on his behalf in court because "in my opinion the application of the standard polygraphic inference rules would lead to the conclusion that he [Means] was telling the truth." Lykken justified his actions by stating, "I felt that Mr. Means deserved and needed all the help he could get ... the test interpreted in the usual way would come out in his favor. It seemed to me possible that it would come out that way precisely because I don't much believe in the test."

120. Martin Orne, *Implications of Laboratory Research for the Detection of Deception, in* LEGAL ADMISSIBILITY OF THE POLYGRAPH 94 (N. Ansley ed. 1975).

121. For a complete description and analysis, see Raskin (1986), *supra* note 1.

122. *Id.*

123. Howard Timm, *Effect of Altered Outcome Expectancies Stemming from Placebo and Feedback Treatments on the Validity of the Guilty Knowledge Technique,* 67 J. APPLIED PSY-.CHOL. 391 (1982).

correct, laboratory studies of the CQT would produce relatively more false negative than false positive errors, which is contrary to the data. Honts reviewed 20 laboratory studies of the CQT with a total of 567 guilty subjects and 490 innocent subjects.[124] The false negative rate was 12% and the false positive rate was 16%. This outcome is opposite to the prediction generated by the friendly examiner hypothesis. Notably, 6 of the 20 studies reported no errors with guilty subjects, even though they had no fear of any negative sanctions associated with failing the test.

Criminal suspects have no assurance that adverse results will remain confidential since most examiners advise them of their rights and obtain a written waiver prior to the test.[125] However, suspects have a great deal at stake. A favorable test may help to obtain a dismissal or acquittal on the charges, and an unfavorable outcome may result in increased legal costs, personal stress, and disruption of their relationship with their defense counsel. These are far greater motivations than the small amount of money guilty subjects have at stake when they routinely fail laboratory polygraph tests. Furthermore, in order to pass a CQT, the guilty suspect must show stronger physiological reactions to comparison (control) questions than to the relevant questions about the allegations. There is no known mechanism or logical argument that explains how a low level of fear or concern about the test outcome can selectively reduce the reactions to the relevant questions so as to produce the pattern of stronger reactions to the comparison questions that is indicative of truthfulness. In fact, fear is not a necessary part of any modern scientific polygraph theory.[126] The laboratory data and logical analysis contradict the "friendly examiner" hypothesis.

There are two published sets of data from tests of criminal suspects that strongly contradict the friendly examiner hypothesis. Raskin presented complete data from 12 years of his confidential CQT examinations for defense attorneys and non-confidential tests for law enforcement, courts, and stipulated situations.[127] He reported that 58% of suspects who agreed in advance that the results would be provided to the prosecution passed their tests, but only 34% of those who took confidential defense tests were able to pass. In addition, the numerical scores were significantly more negative (in the deceptive direction) for confidential tests compared to the more positive scores (in the truthful direction) for non-confidential tests. Honts recently presented a similar, complete set of data from 14 years of confidential and non-confidential examinations.[128] He reported that 70% of the non-confidential tests were passed, while only 44% of the confidential tests were passed. These data also contradict the predictions of the friendly examiner hypothesis. The friendly examiner hypothesis fails on all counts. It is illogical, unsupported by laboratory studies, and contradicted by data from actual field cases.

124. Charles R. Honts, *Is It Time to Reject the Friendly Polygraph Examiner Hypothesis (FEPH)?*, A paper presented at the annual meeting of the American Psychological Society, Washington, D.C (1997, May). Available at: http://truth.idbsu.edu/polygraph/fpeh.html.

125. David C. Raskin, *Polygraph Techniques for the Detection of Deception*, in Psychological Methods in Criminal Investigation and Evidence 255 (D. Raskin ed. 1989).

126. *See* John A. Podlesny & David C. Raskin, *Physiological Measures and the Detection of Deception*, 84 Psychological Bull. 783 (1977); J. Peter Rosenfeld, *Alternative Views of Bashore and Rapp's (1993) Alternatives to Traditional Polygraphy: A Critique*, 117 Psychological Bull. 159 (1995).

127. Raskin (1986), *supra* note 1, at 62.

128. *See* Honts *supra* note 124.

§ 10–2.4.3 The Polygraph and Juries

One of the major issues addressed by the Court in *Scheffer*[129] concerned the potential impact of expert polygraph testimony on jury decisions. Opponents of the admission of polygraph evidence have long argued that such evidence will have an undue influence on jury decision processes, usurp the jury function, confuse the issues, and mislead the jury.[130] However, the majority of justices rejected those arguments in *Scheffer*. Their position is consistent with courtroom experiences in actual cases and the published scientific evidence. Numerous scientific studies have been performed on this topic using mock juries, post-trial interviews with jurors who were presented with expert polygraph testimony, and surveys of prosecutors and defense attorneys in cases where polygraph evidence was presented at trial.[131] The results consistently demonstrate that jurors are cautious with polygraph evidence, and they do not give it undue weight. Also consistent with the majority of the *Scheffer* court, the results show that polygraph testimony does not unduly prolong trials or jury deliberations. Prosecutors and defense attorneys who tried cases with polygraph evidence were highly satisfied with polygraph testimony and they did not believe that it had a disruptive impact on the trials or that the judge or jury disregarded significant evidence because of the polygraph testimony. Like other types of evidence, in some cases juries reached decisions that were contrary to the polygraph evidence. Thus, there are no scientific data to support the claims of critics that polygraph evidence is disruptive to the trial process, and the evidence and our own extensive experience in actual cases supports the usefulness of competent polygraph evidence at trial. More detailed analyses of these studies can be found in Raskin[132] and the Amicus Curiae Brief of the Committee of Concerned Social Scientists submitted in *Scheffer*.[133]

§ 10–2.5 Conclusions

We have spent much of our scientific careers conducting scientific research and development on polygraph techniques for the physiological detection of deception.[134] We have received numerous grants and contracts from

129. *Supra* note 38.

130. *See* M. Abbell, *Polygraph Evidence: the Case Against Admissibility in Federal Criminal Trials*, 15 AM. CRIM. L. REV. 29, 38 (1977).

131. F. Barnett, *How Does a Jury View Polygraph Examination Results?*, 2 POLYGRAPH 275 (1973); Nancy J. Brekke, et al., *The Impact of Nonadversarial Versus Adversarial Expert Testimony*, 15 LAW & HUM. BEHAV. 451 (1991); S.C. Carlson et al., *The Effect of Lie Detector Evidence on Jury Deliberations: An Empirical Study*, 5 POLICE SCI. & ADMIN. 148 (1977); A. Cavoukian & R. J. Heslegrave, *The Admissibility of Polygraph Evidence in Court: Some Empirical Findings*, 4 LAW & HUM. BEHAV. 117 (1980); A. Markwart, & B. Lynch, *The Effect of Polygraph Evidence on Mock Jury Decision–Making*, 7 POLICE SCI. & ADMIN. 324 (1979); Bryan Meyers & Jack Arbuthnot, *Polygraph Testimony and Juror Judgments: A Comparison of the Guilty Knowledge Test and the Con-*

trol Question Test, 27 J. APPLIED SOC. PSYCHOL. 1421 (1997); R. Peters, *A Survey of Polygraph Evidence in Criminal Trials*, 68 A.B.A. J. 161 (1982); L. Vondergeest et al., *Effects of Juror and Expert Witness Gender on Jurors' Perceptions of an Expert Witness*, MODERN PSYCHOLOGICAL STUDIES 1 (1993).

132. Raskin (1986), *supra* note 1.

133. Available through *Polygraph Law Resource Pages* at http://truth.idbsu.edu.

134. In is of interest to note that Raskin initiated the research program at the University of Utah after being asked to testify in 1970 in a capital case in which he criticized prosecution polygraph evidence based on police administration of an RIT. Raskin embarked on a scientific program that he expected would demonstrate that polygraph tests were not accurate. However, results of the first laboratory study of the accuracy of the CQT (see Barland & Raskin, *supra* note 25) contradicted the com-

federal agencies and universities in the United States and Canada for this research, and we have authored hundreds of scientific articles, chapters, books, and scientific presentations on these topics. Two of us have conducted polygraph examinations in more than 2,000 criminal and civil cases, including many of the most celebrated cases of the past three decades, and we have provided expert testimony hundreds of times in federal and state courts. On the basis of the extensive scientific evidence and our personal experiences in actual cases, we firmly believe that polygraph techniques and evidence are of great value to the criminal justice system and the courts. However, general acceptance by our legal system has lagged far behind the science and its applications.

Although virtually all federal, state, and local law enforcement agencies and prosecutors rely heavily on polygraph results, they have routinely opposed the admissibility of polygraph evidence at trial. This has been a major determiner of the long history of rejection by our courts. After the *Daubert* decision, it appeared that there was a new opportunity for the courts to correctly recognize the scientific basis for polygraph techniques.[135] Some influential law review articles argued for admissibility, but a flurry of attempts to admit polygraph evidence met with only limited success.[136] In spite of the strong scientific basis for admitting polygraph evidence at trial, the current status of polygraph evidence in our courts remains relatively unchanged. We believe this is the result of ingrained institutional impediments to the admission of such evidence.

Our judicial system is founded on the premise that jurors have both the ability and sole responsibility to judge the credibility of the testimony of witnesses who appear before them. However, a large and compelling body of scientific literature demonstrates the inability of people, including jurors, to make accurate judgments of credibility.[137] In spite of this evidence, law schools continue to train students in the outmoded, traditional belief, and many courts continue to use it as a basis for excluding polygraph evidence.

Courts often raise the old specter of the "scientific aura" of polygraph evidence overwhelming the jurors and preventing them from properly considering other evidence. The jury research evidence previously described demonstrates the error of that thinking. After considering the available scientific evidence, the majority of the *Scheffer* court rejected the argument that jurors would be unable to give proper weight to polygraph evidence.[138] This has not prevented most courts from continuing to use the old excuse for rejecting polygraph evidence. If there were merit in this argument for exclusion, then all courts should uniformly exclude DNA and fingerprint evidence. This inconsistency is highlighted by the Supreme Court decision in *Barefoot*.[139] Although the Court acknowledged that two-thirds of psychiatric predictions of future dangerous behavior are incorrect, they ignored the opposition of the

monly-held belief about polygraph inaccuracy, and he was obliged by the ethics and principles of science to revise his beliefs to be consistent with the data. Unfortunately, many of today's vocal critics of polygraph maintain their positions in spite of the large body of scientific data to the contrary.

135. *See infra* § 10–1.0.

136. *See* McCall, *supra* note 82; Imwinkelreid & McCall, *supra* note 82.

137. Aldert Vrij Detecting Lies and Deceit (2000).

138. *See supra* note 38.

139. *Barefoot v. Estelle*, 463 U.S. 880, 103 S.Ct. 3383, 77 L.Ed.2d 1090 (1983).

American Psychiatric Association to such testimony and affirmed the admission of a psychiatrist's prediction of future dangerous behavior that resulted in defendant Barefoot being executed. When we compare the handling of polygraph evidence with the routine admission of more influential and sometimes erroneous evidence, it is clear that the courts are biased against polygraph evidence.

Another major impediment for polygraph evidence is the fact that polygraph evidence is almost always proffered by the defendant. Many prosecutors oppose it for this reason and their desire to totally control its use in the criminal justice system, especially when the results of polygraphs they have secretly conducted on prosecution witnesses would be helpful to the defendant. This generally hostile attitude of prosecutors is met with sympathy from the majority of judges who have been drawn from the ranks of former prosecutors.

When all else fails, many courts take refuge in the fact that one party (usually the prosecution) has presented expert testimony that attacks the polygraph. The mere appearance of one inflexible, well-known and well-paid critic of the polygraph provides the excuse for the court to exclude the proffered evidence. Sometimes the expert does not have any scientific credentials to testify in a *Daubert* hearing, but hostile courts will admit and rely on testimony in spite of a record that fails to rebut the scientific basis of the evidence presented by a highly qualified scientific expert.[140] They also may accept an argument that a dispute about the polygraph evidence will become a trial of collateral issues and will consume too much time, even though that argument was also rejected by the *Scheffer*[141] Court. It is time that the courts recognize the legitimate scientific evidence and reject the specious arguments put forth by polygraph critics for personal gain and furtherance of their political agendas.[142]

It is instructive to note that only the New Mexico courts have extensive experience with polygraph evidence. Since 1975, polygraph evidence has been admissible at trial in New Mexico.[143] After eight years of generally positive experience with such evidence in trials, in 1983 the Supreme Court of New Mexico adopted a comprehensive rule that specifies the requirements for admitting polygraph evidence at trial.[144] Although polygraph admissibility has been vigorously challenged by prosecutors numerous times in the 18 years since its adoption, the New Mexico Supreme Court has not reversed its stance. We wonder why almost all other state and federal courts have chosen to ignore the 25 years of positive experience of the New Mexico courts while they continue to exploit all legal devices to exclude polygraph evidence. Clearly, the well-regulated approach to the admission of polygraph evidence has been of

140. *See United States v. Cordoba,* 991 F.Supp. 1199 (1998). The court admitted the testimony of two FBI agents in a *Daubert* hearing. Neither witness had any scientific credentials or training. However, the judge relied on their testimony and openly attacked the uncontradicted scientific testimony of the defendant's expert, whom the judge himself described as "a pioneer psychophysiologist, nationally known scholar in forensic polygraphy, and generally acknowledged as the nation's foremost polygraph expert." We found the court's rulings, to say the least, disheartening.

141. *Supra* note 38.

142. *Supra* note 125.

143. *State v. Dorsey,* 88 N.M. 184, 539 P.2d 204 (1975). Polygraph evidence was admitted by the New Mexico Supreme Court under the constitutional right for a defendant to present a defense.

144. N. M. R. Evid. 707.

benefit to the judicial process in New Mexico courts. There is no logical or practical reason that the situation should be any different in the rest of the United States.

In conclusion, we note that during the summer of 1997 a group of scientists formed the ad hoc Committee of Concerned Social Scientists and submitted a Brief for Amicus Curiae[145] to the United States Supreme Court in *United States v. Scheffer*.[146] That Amicus was signed by 17 professionals with advanced degrees (15 doctoral level). They concluded as follows:

> For the foregoing reasons, the members of the Committee of Concerned Social Scientists respectfully submit that polygraph testing is a valid application of psychological science and that it is generally accepted by the majority of the informed scientific community of psychological scientists as such. Polygraph testing has a known but acceptable error rate that has been well defined by scientific research. Furthermore, there is no scientific evidence that suggests the admission of the results of a polygraph examination before lay jurors will overwhelm their ability to use and value other evidence. Overwhelming the trier of fact is particularly unlikely when the quality and training of the members of a court martial are considered. Many of the traditional objections to the polygraph have been shown by science to be without merit. Although there are problems with the quality of practice in the polygraph profession, such problems are not unique to polygraph tests. They are likely to occur in any situation where a human evaluator is needed to interpret data. In any event, the problems of examiner practice are easily remedied by the traditional means of cross-examination and evidentiary rule.

It is our sincere hope that eventually the courts will recognize the merits and wisdom of this position and accord polygraph evidence its rightful place in the judicial process.

§ 10–3.0 THE SCIENTIFIC STATUS OF RESEARCH ON POLYGRAPH TECHNIQUES: THE CASE AGAINST POLYGRAPH TESTS

by
William G. Iacono* & David T. Lykken**

§ 10–3.1 Introductory Discussion of the Science

Psychophysiological interrogation is based on the plausible assumption that various involuntary physiological reactions to salient questions might

145. *Supra* note 133.

146. *Supra* note 38.

* Distinguished McKnight University Professor, Professor of Psychology, University of Minnesota, Director, Clinical Science and Psychopathology Research Training Program, recipient of the American Psychological Association's *Distinguished Scientific Award for an Early Career Contribution to Psychology*, the Society for Psychophysiological Research's *Distinguished Scientific Award for an Early Ca-*

reer Contribution to Psychophysiology, Past-President of the Society for Psychophysiological Research (1996–97) and former Member, Department of Defense Polygraph Institute's Curriculum and Research Guidance Committee.

** Professor of Psychology, University of Minnesota, author of A Tremor in the Blood: Uses and Abuses of the Lie Detector, (2d ed. 1998), recipient of the American Psychological Association's Award for a *Distinguished Contribution to Psychology in the Public Interest*

reveal truths that the person being questioned is attempting to conceal. Psychophysiological Detection of Deception (PDD) is based on assumptions regarding how guilty and innocent individuals respond differentially to accusatory questions about their involvement in a crime and their character. We shall demonstrate that the assumptions of PDD are in fact implausible, unsupported by credible scientific evidence, and rejected by most members of the relevant scientific community. PDD is widely used in the U.S. both in criminal investigation and for pre- and post-employment screening, mainly by federal police and security agencies. Although claims about its accuracy are unfounded, we shall show that PDD has been embraced by law enforcement agencies because it has utility as an interrogation tool, eliciting confessions or damaging admissions from naïve but guilty suspects. On the other hand, however, we shall show that unjustifiable faith in conclusions based on PDD has permitted sophisticated guilty suspects to escape detection while unsophisticated innocents have been condemned and punished.

Another method of psychophysiological interrogation is for the purpose of detecting the presence of guilty knowledge as opposed to the detection of lying. The Guilty Knowledge Test is used in criminal investigation in Japan and in Israel but is, so far, seldom used in the United States. We shall demonstrate that the assumptions of the Guilty Knowledge Test are quite plausible and that the limited research concerning its validity has so far been encouraging.

§ 10–3.1.1 Background

[1] Instrumentation

The polygraph instrument consists typically of four pens recording physiological responses on a moving paper chart. Two "pneumo" pens, driven by pneumatic belts fastened around the subject's chest and abdomen, record thoracic and abdominal breathing movements. A third pen is connected to a blood pressure cuff or sphygmomanometer around one upper arm. During questioning, this cuff is inflated to partially occlude the flow of blood to the lower arm. Each heart beat then causes this "cardio" pen to briefly deflect while changes in blood pressure cause the entire tracing to move up or down on the chart. The fourth, the GSR or "electrodermal" pen, is connected to two metal electrodes attached to the fingerprint area of two fingers of one hand. This pen records changes in the electrical resistance of the palmar skin, which are caused in turn by sweat gland activity. Thus, the polygraph provides continuous recordings of breathing movements, blood pressure changes, and the sweating of the palms.

The restriction of blood flow in the arm produces ischemic pain after several minutes, which limits the number of questions that can be asked during one "chart" to about ten, after which the cuff pressure must be released. Depending on the polygraph procedure used, a typical test involves several "charts," usually with the same questions repeated in the same or different order, with a rest of several minutes between charts.

(1991) and for *Distinguished Scientific Contributions for Applications of Psychology* (2001), Past–President of the Society for Psychophysiological Research (1980–81), and recipient of that Society's *Award for Distinguished Scientific Contributions to Psychophysiology* (1998).

At the present time, nearly all polygraphic interrogation is intended to determine whether the respondent is answering a specific question or questions deceptively. Contrary to popular belief, however, the polygraph is not a "lie detector." Although some practitioners claim that certain patterns of physiological response recorded on the polygraph chart are specifically indicative of lying,[1] there is no serious scientific support for this view.

Most polygraph examiners, therefore, employ a technique that provides an opportunity to compare physiological responses to different kinds of questions, including questions directly relevant to the issue at hand.

[2]   The Control Question Technique (CQT)

For most forensic applications, a procedure known as the "control question test" is used to evaluate a subject's truthfulness. The CQT is actually a collection of procedures which, although differing from one another slightly in format, all involve the comparison of a subject's responses to relevant questions with responses to interspersed "control" or comparison questions. The CQT is a descendant of the relevant-irrelevant test (RIT), a technique that although widely discredited for criminal applications is still used for employee screening.

The criminal application of the RIT involved two types of questions. The relevant questions focused on the matter of interest and were presented as implicit accusations. In a criminal investigation, the relevant questions usually dealt with a single issue and asked about involvement in an alleged crime, e.g., "Did you rob the First National Bank?" or "Were you involved in any way in the robbery of that bank?" Interposed among these relevant questions were irrelevant questions dealing with innocuous issues unlikely to be of much concern to anyone. Sample irrelevant questions include, "Are you sitting down?" and "Is today Wednesday?" Subjects were expected to answer these questions truthfully, so the physiological responses they elicit served as a baseline against which to compare the responses to the relevant questions. If the responses to the relevant questions were larger than those to the irrelevant queries, then the subject would be deemed deceptive. A truthful verdict required the two types of questions to yield reactions of similar size. The major criticism of this technique is that the irrelevant questions provide no "control" for the psychological impact of being asked the relevant question. The relevant question differs from the irrelevant question both in that it conveys an emotionally loaded accusation and the subject may be lying in response to it. There is no way to determine that a larger response to the relevant question is not due simply to the subject's nervousness about being asked this question. Because of this serious shortcoming, innocent criminal suspects were likely to fail the RIT.

The CQT attempts to improve on the RIT format by keeping the relevant questions and replacing the irrelevant questions with so-called control questions. The control questions refer in a deliberately vague or general way to possible misdeeds from the subject's past, misdeeds that may be chosen so

§ **10–3.0**   Deception 61–71 (2d ed. 1977).

1.   John E. Reid & Fred E. Inbau, Truth and

that they deal with a theme similar to that covered by the relevant question. Typically, qualifying phrasing is added to the control question so that it does not involve the same period of time covered by the relevant question. Examples of control questions used with relevant questions dealing with theft and sexual abuse might be: "Prior to last year, did you ever take something of value from someone who trusted you?" and "Before age 25, did you ever engage in an unusual sex act?"

[a]   Theory of the CQT

Critical to the outcome of the CQT is the manner in which the control questions are introduced. After the relevant questions have been formulated and reviewed, the control questions are presented to the subject with the explanation that they are intended to assess the subject's basic character with regard to honesty and trustworthiness in order to make sure that the subject has never done anything in the past similar to what the subject currently stands accused of doing.[2] The subject is actually told by the examiner that the expectation is that the subject will answer the control questions with a denial. If he or she answers such a question "yes," the examiner responds in a way that suggests disapproval. Thus, the examiner creates a dilemma for the subject by simultaneously creating the expectation that the subject will be honest and yet answer the control questions "no." As Raskin observes, this manipulation "leads the subject to believe that admissions [to the control questions] will cause the examiner to form the opinion that the subject is dishonest and is therefore guilty. This discourages [further] admissions and maximizes the likelihood that the negative answer [to the control question] is untruthful."[3] Raskin goes on to explain that it is important to get the subject to believe that deceptive answers to the control questions "will result in strong physiological reactions during the test and will lead the examiner to conclude that the subject was deceptive with respect to the relevant issues" concerning the alleged crime. However, he acknowledges, "in fact, the converse is true."[4]

CQT theory, therefore, is based on the premise that stronger responses to the control than to the relevant questions indicates that the latter have been answered truthfully. The theory assumes that the guilty person, who must answer the relevant questions deceptively, will be more disturbed by those questions than by the control questions and that his physiological responses will be stronger to the relevant than to the control questions. The theory also assumes that an innocent person, answering the relevant questions truthfully, will be relatively more disturbed by the control questions, because only the answers to these questions involve deception or significant concern.

[b]   Scoring the CQT

Some polygraphers use a "global" procedure to help decide the outcome of the examination. With this approach, the examiner takes into account the

---

2. David C. Raskin, *Polygraph Techniques for the Detection of Deception, in* Psychological Methods in Criminal Investigation and Evidence 247, 254 (David C. Raskin ed., 1989).

3. *Id.* at 255.

4. *Id.*

relative size of the responses to the relevant and control questions as well as all other available information, including the case facts, the subject's explanation of the facts, and his or her demeanor during the examination. Most contemporary practitioners eschew the global approach, preferring instead a semi-objective quantitative method, referred to as "numerical scoring," to decide truthfulness. Each relevant response is compared with the response to an adjacent control question; each such comparison yields a score of –3 if the relevant response is much larger than the control response, a score of +3 if the control response is the much larger of the two, a score of zero if the two responses are about equal, with scores of 1 or 2 for intermediate values. For a typical CQT, the total score might range from +30 to –30 with positive scores interpreted as indicating truthfulness and negative scores indicating deception. Scores in some narrow range about zero, typically between +5 and –5, are interpreted as inconclusive. An increasingly common practice is to feed the polygraph data into a computer that is programmed to score the responses according to some standard algorithm.[5]

[c] The "Stimulation" Test

As part of the CQT, examiners commonly employ a stimulation ("stim") test, the purpose of which is to convince subjects that their physiological responses do in fact give them away when they lie. This procedure is typically administered either prior to asking the first set of CQT questions or after the list of CQT questions has been presented once (i.e., after the first "chart"). Some examiners have the subject select a card from a covertly-marked deck and then instruct him or her to answer "No" to questions of the form: "Is it the 10 of spades?" Because the examiner knows in advance which card was selected, he can ensure that he identifies the correct card irrespective of the subject's polygraphic reaction. Other examiners have the subject choose a number between, say, 1 and 7, and then openly tell the examiner which number was chosen. The subject then is told: "Now when you answer 'No' to the number you selected, I will be able to determine what your polygraphic response looks like when you lie." Some examiners will show subjects the physiological tracings that gave them away in order to prove that they can be detected, perhaps mechanically manipulating the deflection of the pens when the critical item is presented so the subject can easily identify the response. In fact, because people do not show distinctive or characteristic physiological responses when they lie, this form of stim test is also deceptive, falsely suggesting that the examiner has somehow calibrated the test to work optimally on this particular subject.

[d] The Directed Lie Test (DLT): A Variant of the CQT

The DLT is a form of the CQT in which the subject is *instructed* to answer each control question deceptively.[6] "You've told a lie sometime in the past, haven't you? Well, I'm going to ask you about that on the test and I want you to answer 'No.' Then you and I will both know that that answer was

---

5. *Id.* at 260–261; *see also* John C. Kircher & David C. Raskin, *Human versus Computerized Evaluations of Polygraph Data in a Labo-* ratory Setting, 44 J. APPLIED PSYCHOL. 291, 291–302 (1988).

6. Raskin (1989), *supra* note 2, at 271.

a lie and the tracings on the polygraph will show me how you react when you're lying." The DLT is scored in the same way as a standard CQT. Advocates believe that the DLT is an improvement because there is greater certainty that the subject's answers to control questions are false. The DLT involves a slightly different assumption, namely, that innocent persons will be more disturbed while giving—on instruction—a false answer to a question about their past than they will while truthfully denying a false accusation about a crime of which they are currently suspected.

§ 10–3.1.2 The Scientific Questions and Methods

[1] What Branch of Science Is Relevant to the Evaluation of CQT Theory and Application?

Polygraphy is unusual in that it has evolved without formal ties to any scientific discipline. Practitioners are graduates of polygraph trade schools. The faculty at these schools are usually polygraphers or law enforcement professionals. Few are trained as scientists and few have the background necessary to be able to provide competent evaluations of their discipline. As we shall see, even examiners with long experience have no way of knowing how often their decisions are correct. What feedback they do receive is limited to confessions obtained from suspects whom they have diagnosed as deceptive and then interrogated. These events necessarily confirm the examiner's conclusion and, thus, provide the examiner with a grossly misleading impression of consistent accuracy. Because polygraph testing is used for making psychological inferences or diagnoses, we conclude that psychology is the branch of science that is relevant to its evaluation.

[2] Is the CQT a Test?

Standardization and *objectivity* are essential to the definition of a psychological test. A test is considered standardized when its administration and scoring is uniform across examiners and situations. If the outcome of polygraph tests is to be trusted for different subjects and examiners, it is essential that the procedure is always the same. As Anastasi points out, this requirement is "only a special application of the need for controlled conditions in all scientific applications."[7] A technique that is not standardized cannot easily be evaluated; each of its variants would have to be evaluated separately to determine if, as it is generally applied, it is accurate. A test is objective insofar as its administration, scoring, and interpretation are independent of the subjective judgment of a particular examiner.[8] The validity of a test that was not objective would be undermined by individual differences in judgment that varied from one examiner to the next. We conclude that the CQT is neither standardized nor objective and therefore fails to meet the scientific definition of a psychological test.[9]

---

7. ANNE ANASTASI, PSYCHOLOGICAL TESTING 25 (6th ed. 1988).

8. *Id.* at 27.

9. Polygraph examiners, in recognition of this fact, often refer to the CQT as the control question "technique" rather than "test."

[3] Does the CQT Produce Consistent (Reliable) Results?

In psychological science, reliability refers to the likelihood that the test yields results that are consistent and reproducible. Would another examiner score the charts in the same way? Would another test administered to the same subject yield the same results? A test can be reliable and yet inaccurate but a test that is not reliable cannot be accurate.

There are two ways to evaluate the reliability of a polygraph test. *Test-retest* reliability refers to whether the test produces the same result when it is repeated on a second occasion. The other form of reliability, *inter-scorer* reliability, asks whether two examiners can obtain the same result when they independently score the same set of charts. We conclude that inter-scorer reliability can be high (but is not always high in practice) and that test-retest reliability has not been (and probably cannot be) validly assessed.

[4] Is CQT Theory Scientifically Sound?

It is generally agreed that the accusatory relevant questions used in the CQT will tend to produce emotional responses (and associated physiological reactions) in both truthful and innocent suspects. The theory of the CQT is that a truthful suspect will react still more strongly to the comparison questions that refer with deliberate vagueness to possible past misdeeds. We conclude that these "control" questions are not controls in the scientific sense and that the theory of the CQT is not scientifically plausible.[10]

[5] Can CQT Theory Be Tested?

The scientific method requires that hypotheses be testable empirically. In the case of the CQT, these hypotheses are that guilty suspects will consistently display stronger physiological reactions to the relevant (than to the control) questions, and that innocent suspects will consistently be more disturbed by the control questions. We conclude that existing data permit a reasonably fair test of the second hypothesis but that the first hypothesis, concerning the validity of the CQT in detecting deception in guilty suspects, cannot be adequately tested with the available data.

[6] What Scientific Standards Must a Study Satisfy to Provide a Meaningful Appraisal of CQT Accuracy?

There are hundreds of studies on polygraphy, many of which are controversial because of the way they were conducted and the results they obtained. Some of these reports are unpublished, many have been published in polygraph and police trade publications, and many have appeared in scientific journals. Conclusions about polygraphy will depend in part on which of these reports are accepted as scientifically credible. Among this array of papers, how do we decide which to use to evaluate polygraph testing? We conclude that the only studies worth consideration are those that have appeared in peer-reviewed scientific journals.

10. Faced with this valid criticism, proponents now often refer to the CQT as the "comparison question technique."

[7] Is the CQT Accurate (Valid)?

Validity is a synonym for accuracy. Determining the degree to which the examiner's decisions about the truthfulness of subjects agree with ground truth assesses validity. We conclude that the validity of the CQT in detecting truthfulness is negligible and that no acceptable method has yet been implemented for assessing the validity of the CQT in detecting deception.

[8] Can Guilty Persons Be Trained to Use "Countermeasures" to Defeat a CQT?

Countermeasures are deliberately adopted strategies used to manipulate the outcome of a polygraph test. Effective countermeasures should be aimed at enhancing one's response to control questions. This might be accomplished by unobtrusive self-stimulation such as biting one's tongue or thinking stressful thoughts when confronted with this material on a polygraph test. The effectiveness of countermeasures can be determined by instructing guilty subjects on polygraph theory and encouraging them to use these strategies with the appropriate questions as they arise during the examination. By subsequently determining how many of these individuals escaped detection, it is possible to evaluate the effectiveness of different countermeasure maneuvers. We conclude that effective countermeasures against the CQT are easily learned and that no effective means of defeating such tactics have as yet been demonstrated.

[9] Has the Computerization of the CQT Improved its Accuracy?

An increasingly common practice in polygraphy is to use a computer to record the physiological responses of subjects. With some computer systems, software is included to score the physiological data and even interpret it. We conclude that computerization of the CQT lends an aura of objectivity and accuracy that is almost entirely specious.

[10] Why Do Law Enforcement Agencies Use the CQT?

A question that frequently arises concerns why the CQT is used so pervasively if its accuracy is questionable. The simple answer is that under the pressure of taking the CQT, many guilty people confess, thus resolving a case that often could not be resolved through any other means. We conclude that the CQT can be very useful as a tool for inducing confessions (i.e., it has utility) even though its accuracy as a test is negligible.

[11] What Is the Prevailing Scientific Opinion About CQT Theory and Testing?

As will become apparent, it is difficult to provide straightforward answers to many of these questions by conducting scientific investigations. However, polygraph testing, as it is currently practiced, has been around for over forty years, providing ample opportunity for scientists to consider the questions posed here. The views of the relevant scientific community can be surveyed to determine whether there is a consensus of expert opinion regarding the major questions about polygraphy. We provide data showing that the prevailing opinion of the relevant scientific community is that the CQT is not based on sound scientific principles and that the results of CQT should not be relied upon.

[12] Is Polygraph Screening of Federal Employees and Job Applicants Scientifically Justified?

PDD is often used to determine if a job applicant or employee is of good character and would represent a reasonable security risk. There are no credible scientific demonstrations of the accuracy of this PDD application. However, often employees, pressured by polygraphers to divulge everything in their background relevant to such an assessment, make damaging admissions concerning past misbehaviors. We conclude that these tests are used only because employers have found them to be an effective tool for eliciting such information.

[13] Is There an Accurate Psychophysiological Test for Identifying Criminals?

Often scientists are criticized for undermining PDD, thus hampering law enforcement efforts, without offering any workable alternative procedure for identifying criminals. The implication is that scientists find deception detection procedures inherently objectionable and hold a philosophical objection to PDD. In fact there is an alternative to traditional PDD that has a solid scientific foundation, is broadly embraced by scientists, but is ignored by the polygraph profession. We conclude that this alternative, known as the guilty knowledge test, appears to have great promise as a forensic investigative aid.

§ 10–3.2 Areas of Scientific Agreement and Disagreement

§ 10–3.2.1 The Relevant Scientific Community

[1] Scientists at Arms Length

Polygraph tests are psychological tests that use physiological reactions to psychological stimuli (questions) as a basis for inferring a psychological process or state (e.g., deception or guilty knowledge). This means that polygraphic interrogation is a form of applied psychology and, hence, that psychologists constitute the scientific community relevant to polygraph testing. Because polygraphy involves psychophysiological recordings, members of the premier organization composed of psychophysiologists, the Society for Psychophysiological Research, constitute an important part of the relevant scientific community. Members of this organization have been repeatedly surveyed to determine their opinions about polygraph testing.

There is little scientific controversy surrounding the physiological aspects of polygraphy. That is, there is no debate about the adequacy of the instrumentation or the physiological measurements. The controversy about polygraphy concerns its psychological and psychometric aspects, i.e., its properties (e.g., reliability, validity) as a diagnostic technique. Most psychologists are capable of evaluating the psychological principles on which a procedure is based and are knowledgeable about the problems of psychological measurement and should be capable of understanding the scientific questions at issue in this area. Psychologists recognized for distinguished achievement by election as Fellows to the American Psychological Association have recently been surveyed regarding their opinions of polygraph testing. We will review the results of these various surveys near the end of this chapter, after we have completed our analysis of polygraph theory and practices.

[2] Polygraph Examiners Are Not Scientists

It must be stressed that professional polygraph examiners do *not* constitute the relevant scientific community. Few polygraph examiners have any psychological or scientific training. Polygraph schools provide a curriculum lasting from 7 to 12 weeks and the only admission requirement is, in some cases, law enforcement experience. Moreover, even the most experienced polygraph examiner has been systematically misled by the peculiarities of his trade. He seldom discovers for certain whether any given test result is right or wrong. The only certain feedback he does get is when a suspect, whom he interrogates because that suspect "failed" the test, is induced to confess.[11] But these confessions necessarily confirm the test just given. Since suspects are either lying (guilty) or not (innocent), a test as invalid as a coin toss would fail guilty suspects about half the time and some of these would confess after interrogation. Since their experience is thus selectively misleading, polygraph examiners are perhaps the group whose opinions concerning the technique are, paradoxically, of the least value.

§ 10–3.2.2 Why the CQT is Not a Test

[1] Question Construction and Administration Are Not Standardized

As we noted in our description of the CQT, it is not a uniformly applied technique but rather a collection of related procedures. These procedures differ in what kinds of questions, other than relevant and control questions, appear on a test, how questions are ordered and grouped, how best to word relevant and control questions, how to conduct oneself during the interview phases of the interrogation, and how to score and interpret charts. The actual structure of a given CQT depends on what polygraph school a polygrapher attended and the examiner's own preferred practices. The only feature all CQTs have in common is the inclusion of control and relevant questions. Because there is no single CQT format, the CQT is clearly not a standardized procedure.

In order to conduct a CQT, the examiner must review the case facts, consider the subject's account of the case, and decide how best to formulate relevant questions that clearly cover the issue at hand. What is required under these circumstances is a series of subjective assessments regarding question development. Different examiners reach different conclusions about

---

11. William G. Iacono, *Can We Determine the Accuracy of Polygraph Tests?, in* 4 AD- VANCES IN PSYCHOPHYSIOLOGY (J. Richard Jennings et al. eds., 1991).

what questions to ask; this fact again demonstrates the lack of standardization of the CQT.

The examiner also must succeed in deceiving the subject regarding the purpose and function of the control questions. In the case of the CQT, the subject must be led to believe that his being disturbed by these questions might result in his failing the test when, in fact, the reverse is true. In the case of the DLT, he must be led to believe that his directed lie responses will show the examiner what his responses to the relevant questions will be like if he answers the latter questions deceptively; this claim is of course untrue. Failure to adequately deceive the subject in these ways invalidates a basic assumption of the test. Because some examiners are better deceivers than others, and some examinees are more easily deceived than others, this problem represents a serious failure of standardization.

[2]   Subjectivity of Chart Interpretation

The interpretation of the polygraph charts is also problematic. Those employing the global scoring approach are by design using a non-objective, non-standardized procedure. Although numerical scoring is supposed to be based solely on the physiological data, the examiner scoring the chart, just like those adopting the global approach, is aware of the case facts and the subject's behavior during the examination. Patrick and Iacono showed that this information can compromise the examiner's objectivity.[12] Working with real-life cases from a major police agency, the Royal Canadian Mounted Police (RCMP), these investigators found that the examiners often ignored their own numerical scoring when interpreting charts. For instance, when the numerical scoring indicated deception, 18% of the time examiners concluded the test outcome was either inconclusive or truthful. When the scoring fell in the inconclusive range, the examiners actually classified subjects as guilty or truthful 49% of the time.[13]

[3]   Absence of Controlling Standards

In *United States v. Scheffer*,[14] the Supreme Court noted that "there is simply no way to know in a particular case whether a polygraph examiner's conclusion is accurate, because certain doubts and uncertainties plague even the best polygraph exams." We would add that there is no standard in the field regarding what constitutes the "best polygraph exams." The accuracy of a test that is administered with no controlling standards cannot be determined. This is in effect what the court ruled in a *Daubert* hearing in *United States v. Cordoba*.[15] The court, after reviewing manuals and practice codes from various professional polygraph organizations and agencies, and after hearing the testimony of Dr. David Raskin, noted that particular polygraph

---

12. Christopher J. Patrick & William G. Iacono, *Validity of the Control Question Polygraph Test: The Problem of Sampling Bias*, 76 J. Applied Psychol. 229, 229–238 (1991).

13. *Id.* at 233.

14. 523 U.S. 303, 312, 118 S.Ct. 1261, 140 L.Ed.2d 413 (1998).

15. U.S. v. Cordoba, 104 F.3d 225 (9th Cir. 1997).

practices are followed more out of custom or habit than because examiners follow a prescribed set of standards.[16]

§ 10–3.2.3 The CQT Has Unknown Reliability

[1] Inter–Scorer Agreement

The only systematic studies of polygraph reliability have focused on the CQT. There is general agreement that examiners trained in numerical scoring can produce reasonably consistent numerical scores. The Patrick and Iacono findings cited above, however, show that the original examiner, influenced by his knowledge of the case facts, will sometimes disregard the physiological data when reaching a decision. In addition, Patrick and Iacono showed that when another examiner blindly scored the same charts, he would sometimes reach a decision that differed from that of the original examiner. For example, of the 72 charts that the original examiner both scored truthful and judged to be from a truthful person, only 51(71%) were scored truthful by the blind examiner. Because the blind examiner who rescored the charts based his decision solely on the physiological data, the discrepancy in the number of subjects scored truthful by the two examiners roughly reflects the extent to which the original examiner's chart scoring was influenced by his knowledge of the case facts. That is, for the original examiner to score many more charts truthful than the blind examiner who relied exclusively on the physiological data, the original examiner's chart scoring was likely affected by his knowledge of the case facts and therefore was not entirely objective.

16. For instance, the court noted that the Department of Defense Polygraph Institute, which is the most prestigious training facility for polygraphers, "teaches that if a subject fails one relevant question, the subject fails the entire test. Dr. Raskin, however, follows a standard where a subject who fails one relevant question may still pass the test." The court recognized Dr. Raskin as "probably the strongest and best informed advocate of polygraph admissibility" yet expressed the following opinion regarding his testimony about the adequacy of the CQT administered in this particular instance:

The evidence shows, and the court finds, Defendant's test contained many factors which would be considered defects under various versions of industry "standards." The duration and substance of the pre-test interview was not preserved. No tape or video was made of the pre-test interview or the polygraph exam. The examiner didn't calibrate the machine at the prison test site. Although the examiner asked four supposedly "relevant questions," only one was really relevant: two involved undisputed facts, one was marginally relevant, and the wording of the truly relevant question was arguably too ambiguous to be helpful. The examiner found deception in the marginally-relevant question's answer (while Dr. Raskin did not), but the examiner scored it as truthful after obtaining Defendant's explanation for the

answer. The examiner's report was filled with errors and defects: the report was drafted before the test, it did not include a fingertip test, according to Dr. Raskin it lacked attention to detail, it omitted Defendant's response to whether he was under drugs or medication, it misstated the machine used, and it says the stimulation test was done after the first test when it was obviously done first. Although there was movement on a response, the examiner scored the response. The examiner did not record a significant breath. The examiner did not ask if defendant had proper sleep before the exam. The examiner acknowledged the exam was conducted in a poor setting with many distractions. Although each of these occurrences is a defect under various expressions of the industry's standards, Dr. Raskin declined to criticize the test in any meaningful way, and found the test to be entirely acceptable. Confronted with each defect, Dr. Raskin staunchly stuck to his view that the test was reliable and acceptable ... If pro-polygraph's best expert declines to find any fault with an obviously faulty examination, that is strong evidence that there are insufficient controlling standards ... The court finds there are no *controlling* standards to ensure proper protocol or provide a court with a yardstick by which a defendant's examination can be measured. *Id.* at 1207–08 (emphasis added).

The case of the Los Alamos Laboratory scientist accused of mishandling nuclear bomb secrets is illustrative. According to three Department of Energy polygraphers, Dr. Wen Ho Lee passed a polygraph test administered December 23, 1999, but, after suspicions grew that he had passed secrets to China, FBI polygraphers rescored those original charts and concluded that they indicated deception. Nevertheless, when Richard Keifer of the American Polygraph Association examined Lee's polygraph charts, he said "he had never been able to score anyone so high on the non-deceptive scale."[17]

[2]   Test–Retest Agreement

No good scientific data are available that can be used to evaluate the consistency of results when separate CQTs are administered to the same subject by different examiners. A different choice of control questions, a different wording of the relevant questions, even a different manner displayed by the examiner, might influence the emotional responses to the questions and thus change the test outcome, whether computer-scoring is in use or not. Moreover, the CQT relies on the subject's confidence in the accuracy of the procedure; an innocent suspect who has lost confidence in the test may react more strongly to the relevant questions in consequence while a guilty suspect, who has avoided detection on the first test, might be still less disturbed by the relevant questions on the second test. Thus, mistakes on the first test may be likely to be repeated on the second due to their effect on the suspect's confidence. Finally, the psychophysiological phenomenon of habituation could impact repeated testing. Habituation refers to the fact that physiological reactions diminish with repeated exposure to stimuli. It is reasonable to expect that a subject would be less responsive to the questions asked in a second polygraph test, and that such habituated responding might influence the outcome.

In real life, it is not uncommon for a second polygraph to be administered in order to confirm or check the results of the first test. In our experience, these retests provide no useful data about reliability because the polygrapher conducting the second test is always aware of the results of the first test. This knowledge is likely to affect how the examiner conducts and scores the second test; the results of the second test are thus not independent of the results of the first. Under the circumstances, obtaining the same outcome on two polygraph examinations should not be taken as convincing evidence of innocence or guilt.

§ 10–3.3.4   Implausibility of CQT Theory

The scientific plausibility of the CQT can be determined by appraising the psychological assumptions on which it is based. These assumptions, analyzed below, concern what causes the response to relevant questions to be larger or smaller than the response to the "control" or comparison questions.

---

17. *Wen Ho Lee's Problematic Polygraph,* Sharyl Attkisson, http://www.cbsnews.com/ now/story10,1597,157220–41200.shtml (last visited March 27, 2001).

[1] Control Questions Do Not Work for the Innocent

At the heart of the CQT is the assumption that truthful subjects will respond more strongly to the control than the relevant questions. For this to occur, it must indeed be the case, as the proponents of the CQT assert, that innocent subjects will be more disturbed by this question than by the relevant question. As we noted in our discussion of the RIT, it is important that the comparison question that is paired with the relevant question should control for the emotional impact of simply being confronted with an accusatory question. For that to happen, the answer to the comparison question should be just as important to the subject as the answer to the relevant question.

Being asked the relevant questions is likely to evoke large physiological reactions regardless of one's guilt. The theory of the CQT is implausible because the so-called control questions actually used do not serve as strict controls in the scientific sense of this term; the subject's responses to the CQT's control questions do not predict how this subject should respond to the relevant questions if he is answering truthfully.

[2] A Genuine Control Question

How might we design a polygraph test in which the comparison question would provide a true control for the relevant question? One approach would be to lead subjects to believe that they are plausible suspects in two different crimes, both of which bear similar consequences if guilty. However, unknown to the subject, one of the crimes never occurred, so the examiner is certain the suspect did not commit it. A polygraph test containing a true control question could be derived from this scenario by using as the comparison question the "relevant" question pertaining to the nonexistent crime. From the suspect's vantage point, the test would now contain two types of equally threatening relevant questions. The only reason for a stronger response to be elicited by the real relevant question would be because it was answered with a lie. Such genuine control questions are not employed in real life, however.

[3] Polygraphers Cannot Protect the Innocent from Failing the CQT

Proponents of the CQT argue that the apparent imbalance in the emotional impact of the relevant and control questions fails to take into account the subtle manner in which examiners manipulate subjects into believing that the control questions are just as important as the relevant questions to the outcome of the test. Recall from Raskin's characterization of how control questions are introduced to the subject that the examiner attempts to convince the subject that the test will be failed if the control question is answered deceptively and that the subject is manipulated to hold back admissions about material covered by these questions so that he is likely to be answering them deceptively.[18] The assumption is that this manipulation will protect innocent subjects from failing a CQT.

There are several problems with this assumption:

(1) Regardless of how skilled the examiner is, subjects may not be concerned about their responses to the control questions. Subjects might

---

18. Raskin (1989), *supra* note 2, at 254–255.

feel comfortable with their denials to them or, perhaps, because they cannot recall an instance indicating that their response would be untruthful.

(2) Even when the manipulation works exactly as CQT theory requires, it is still the case that the relevant question deals with the material that is of greatest significance, the only material that could directly link the subject to the crime. Given its perceived significance, it is likely to arouse stronger responses than control questions.

(3) The manipulation is obviously difficult to accomplish. It may be impossible to achieve the desired result in many instances, either because the examiner is not skilled enough to deceive subjects in this way or because sophisticated subjects see through the deception.

(4) Finally, any procedure that is predicated on the examiner's ability to deceive the subject in this fashion is vulnerable to the possibility that the suspect may have learned prior to the testing how the procedure is supposed to work and therefore be immune to the requisite deceptions. It is noteworthy that a trained polygraph examiner, who finds himself suspected of some crime, could not be expected to generate a valid CQT, whether innocent or guilty, since he could not be deceived in the required ways.

[4]   How Over–Reacting to Control Questions Makes Guilty Suspects Appear Truthful

Another basic assumption of the CQT is that the deceptive subject will respond more strongly to the relevant than the control question. This assumption requires that suspects not use physical or mental strategies to augment their responses to the control questions. However, as we have already noted, given an explanation of CQT test structure plus coaching on how to willfully enhance physiological reactivity, guilty subjects *can* defeat a CQT. Another problem with this assumption arises from the examiner's attempt, when control questions are introduced, to discourage admissions concerning the topics covered in these questions. If a guilty subject had, for example, a history of undetected criminal activity and kept this secret during the examination, he may indeed be lying in response to the control questions, causing larger responses to these than to the relevant questions. It is important to note that anyone familiar with CQT theory would understand that they should not make admissions to the examiner concerning the content of control questions, and that they should in fact think of the worst transgressions when asked these questions. This simple strategy can be used by anyone to help insure a truthful outcome on a CQT.

[5]   Adversarial vs. "Friendly" CQTs

The notion that a deceptive response to the relevant question will provide a stronger reaction than that to a control question is, according to CQT theory, dependent on the subject's fear of the consequences of detection. If the subject has little to fear, the significance of lying to the relevant question would be diminished and the strength of the physiological reaction to this lie would be reduced. When the police give a CQT, the results of which are public (at least they would be known to the police), the consequences of detection are serious, and the physiological reactivity associated with lying would be expected to be substantial. But such CQTs, administered under adversarial circumstances, seldom become the basis of an evidentiary hearing in court. The more usual case for an evidentiary hearing is one where the defense counsel arranges a privately administered or "friendly" polygraph test. If the subject fails, he has little to lose because the results, protected by attorney-client privilege, will remain secret. If the test is passed, defense counsel releases the results and attempts to get them into evidence in court. Under these "friendly" conditions, the fear of detection assumption is largely violated, responsivity to relevant questions can be expected to be diminished, and guilty suspects are more likely to be scored truthful. There are other reasons why friendly tests have reduced probative value. The fact that there is no assurance that the suspect would not "shop around," taking several tests from different examiners, before achieving a favorable result, indicates further that friendly tests cannot be safely relied upon. When a test is taken under "friendly" circumstances, the examiner knows that he can earn witness fees only if the results are favorable. Without necessarily impugning the integrity of polygraph examiners, this factor would skew the results of such tests.

Despite the fact that the results of friendly, rather than adversarial, tests are likely to be the subject of *Daubert* hearings, research on the validity of polygraph tests has focused on adversarial tests. There is not a single study demonstrating that friendly polygraph tests are valid. Proponents of the polygraph defend the admissibility of friendly tests by claiming that examiners in private practice who conduct tests for both the police and defense attorneys fail about the same proportion of subjects referred from both sources. Besides the fact that polygraph examiners seldom back up such assertions with an independent audit of their own records, thus leaving open the possibility that their claims are inaccurate, to make sense of a finding of equal proportions of failed tests from these two sources requires consideration of the likelihood that subjects from these two settings are guilty. When the police conduct a polygraph test, usually there is no hard evidence against a suspect and no arrest has been made. When a defense attorney offers his client for a polygraph, usually the suspect has been arrested and there is sufficient evidence to warrant a trial. The rate of guilt thus must be higher for those who are defendants rather than mere suspects, and these defendants should be expected to fail CQTs at a rate that is substantially higher than that for suspects tested by the police. For both groups of suspects to fail CQTs at the same rate, a substantial number of guilty suspects would have to pass friendly tests.

[6] The Implausibility of the Directed Lie Test (DLT)

The only differences between the DLT and the standard CQT are as follows: (1) for the CQT, the examiner assumes the control answer is deceptive while, for the DLT, both the examiner and the suspect know that these answers are false; and (2) the subject answers the control questions deceptively on instruction rather than by choice. The DLT assumes that, when instructed to answer falsely a question about some past and trivial misdeed, an innocent suspect will be more disturbed than while truthfully denying his guilt in crime of which he stands accused. Just as for the CQT, the "control" questions are not controls in the scientific sense and there is no discernible reason for supposing that innocent persons will be reliably more disturbed while lying on instruction about some past event than while telling the truth about a recent and serious event that poses a genuine threat.

Proponents of the conventional CQT argue that one of its strengths derives from the fact that control questions are never identified as such to subjects.[19] Indeed, they are deliberately misled to believe that lying to the control questions will generate a deceptive verdict. To the extent that this deception is successful, an advantage of this approach is that unsophisticated guilty subjects may not figure out that it is to their advantage to try to augment their responses to these questions. However, it *is* obvious that even unsophisticated guilty suspects would be able to identify and understand the significance of the directed lie questions. They could easily self-stimulate (e.g., bite their tongues) after each directed lie answer in order to augment reactions to these control questions and thus defeat the test.

§ 10–3.3.5 Intractable Problems Inherent to the Evaluation of CQT Theory

Determining if polygraph theory is testable requires evaluation of the methods that have been used to test it. Two types of studies have been used to determine whether polygraph tests work. In laboratory or analog studies, volunteer subjects, often college students, commit or do not commit mock crimes and are then subjected to polygraph tests. These tests are scored and the percentage of subjects assigned to the innocent and guilty conditions is determined. The great advantage of the analog method is that one has certain knowledge of "ground truth," of which subjects are lying and which are being truthful.

[1] Disadvantages of Laboratory Studies

The disadvantages of laboratory studies include the following:

(1) The volunteer subjects are unlikely to be representative of criminal suspects in real life.

(2) The volunteers may not feel a life-like concern about mock crimes that they have been instructed to commit and about telling lies that they are instructed to tell.

(3) The CQT is an attempt to assess emotions by measuring the physiological reactions associated with lying. Laboratory studies have no way of reproducing the emotional state of a criminal suspect facing possible prosecution for a crime. Compared to criminal suspects, the volunteers are unlikely to be as apprehensive about being tested with respect to mock crimes for which they will not be punished, irrespective of the test's outcome.

(4) The administration of the polygraph tests tends not to resemble the procedures followed in real life. For example, unlike real-life tests,

---

19. Raskin (1989), *supra* note 2, at 254.

which are most often conducted well after the crime took place, laboratory subjects are typically tested immediately after they commit the mock crime. Moreover, in laboratory research, to make the study scientifically acceptable, there is an attempt to standardize the procedure (e.g., all subjects are asked identical questions), a factor that distinguishes these from real-life tests.

The many problems with laboratory studies indicate that their results are not generalizable to real-life applications of polygraph testing. Consequently, these studies cannot be used to determine the accuracy of polygraph tests.

[2] Field Studies

Another approach to evaluating the validity of polygraph tests is to rely on data collected from field or real life settings. Since the original examiner possesses knowledge of the case facts and can observe the demeanor of the suspect during interrogation, this extraneous information might influence his scoring or interpretation of the test. Therefore, field studies have used a design in which different examiners, ignorant of the case facts, "blindly" rescore polygraph charts produced by suspects later determined to have been either truthful or deceptive.

Although free of the disadvantages of the analog design, real life studies must confront the problem of determining ground truth. Most commonly, confessions have been used as the criterion, either establishing that the person tested was lying, because he subsequently confessed, or that some alternative suspect in the same crime, cleared by another's confession, was telling the truth during his polygraph test. Unfortunately, relying on confessions to establish ground truth has serious drawbacks that may not be apparent at first glance. The problem is not with the confession *per se,* but with the consequences of the method used to get the confession.

[a] How Confessions Are Obtained

In CQT studies that have used the confession method to try to estimate polygraph accuracy, confessions are obtained when the examiner interrogates a suspect whom he has scored as deceptive on a just-completed CQT. As indicated above, being told that one has "failed the lie detector" often leads a guilty suspect to conclude that continued denials will be futile and that he may as well confess and make the best deal possible. Because they are obtained pursuant to interrogation after "failing" the CQT, these confessions invariably verify *that* test as accurate. In cases with more than one suspect, such a confession may also clear other suspects; if another suspect has "passed" a CQT prior to the confession, that prior test will also be verified as accurate.

[b] Problems With the Confession Criterion

Because field studies must rely on confessions to determine ground truth, the only cases selected for study are those involving a guilty suspect who failed a CQT and subsequently confessed. All the polygraph errors in which an innocent person failed a test are omitted from the study because, absent a confession, none of these cases would qualify for inclusion. Similarly, because there would be no confession, all the cases in which a guilty subject erroneously passed a test would also be excluded. Thus, confession studies rely on a biased set of cases by systematically eliminating those containing errors and including only those where the original examiner was shown to be correct.

As we noted previously, polygraph scoring is reasonably consistent from one polygrapher to another. Consequently, when this biased set of confession-verified cases, all chosen in such a manner as to guarantee that the original examiner was correct, is rescored blindly by another examiner, it should be no surprise that the second examiner is also correct. Nothing can be concluded about the accuracy of the CQT from a study like this. The consequence of reliance on the confession criterion is that such studies *must* over-estimate the validity of the CQT both in the case of truthful and of deceptive suspects.

[c]   Independent Criteria of Guilt

This problem with confession studies is caused by the fact that the confession obtained following a failed CQT is not independent of the outcome of the CQT. That is, the only way to get a confession is first for the subject to have failed the polygraph. To determine if they could overcome this problem, Patrick and Iacono carried out a field study with the RCMP in Vancouver, British Columbia.[20] These investigators began with 402 polygraph cases representing all of the cases from a designated metropolitan area during a five-year period. Rather than rely on confessions that were dependent on failing a polygraph test to determine ground truth, they searched police investigative files for ground truth information uncovered after the polygraph test was given, such as non-polygraph-related confessions or statements indicating no crime was committed (e.g., something reported stolen was really lost and subsequently recovered by the owner). These authors found only one case out of over 400 that independently established the guilt of someone who took a polygraph test.

It is interesting to consider why it was not possible to establish independent evidence of ground truth for guilty persons in this study. The reason lies in how law enforcement agencies use polygraph tests. Typically, a lie detector test is not introduced into a case until all the leads have been exhausted and the investigation is near a dead end. If one of the suspects fails the test, it is hoped that the subsequent interrogation will lead to a confession, thereby resolving the issue at hand. However, if the test is failed and there is no confession, there will be no new leads to follow, so the police, assuming that the person who failed the polygraph is guilty, do not investigate the case further. Hence, there is almost no opportunity for additional evidence establishing ground truth to emerge. This disappointing finding indicates that, as polygraphy is now employed in law enforcement, it is virtually impossible to establish ground truth in a manner that is independent of polygraph test outcome. Consequently, the accuracy of the CQT for guilty subjects cannot be reliably determined from the research thus far reported.

20.   Patrick & Iacono, *supra* note 12.

[d] Independent Criteria of Innocence

Interestingly, if all the suspects in a case pass a polygraph, because the guilty person could potentially still be identified through further police work, the file is kept active and additional leads are investigated if they arise. Hence, Patrick and Iacono were able to identify 25 cases where no suspect failed a test but where, for example, subsequent police work led to confessions from suspects who never took a polygraph test but whose confession established as innocent those who had.[21] Because these confessions were not dependent on someone having failed a CQT, they could be used to establish the accuracy of the CQT for innocent people by having the physiological charts blindly rescored. The results of this rescoring are presented in the validity section below.

[e] Summary

Laboratory studies, because they do a poor job of simulating the emotionally-laden scenario that exists in real-life criminal investigations, cannot be relied on to estimate polygraph accuracy. Field studies that employ confessions following a failed polygraph also cannot be relied on for this purpose. Credible field studies would be possible, but difficult to implement. To date, no scientifically credible field study of the validity of the CQT in detecting guilty suspects has been accomplished. On the other hand, as Patrick and Iacono showed, because police practices differ between cases that yield at least one failed test and those that yield only passed tests, it is possible to collect data that bears on the accuracy of the CQT for innocent subjects.[22]

§ 10–3.3.6 How to Identify Scientifically Credible Studies

Because the theory of the CQT is so implausible, a heavy burden of proof rests on those who would claim that this procedure can validly distinguish truth from falsehood in the interrogation of criminal suspects. In spite of decades of extensive use in the United States, by federal agencies and local law enforcement, as we have seen, no scientifically acceptable assessment of CQT validity has yet been published. This is due in part to the fact that the real value of the polygraph in criminal investigation is as an interrogation tool, an inducer of confessions, rather than as a decision-making tool or test. Post-test interrogations that elicit a confession necessarily confirm the CQT result that prompted the interrogation. In the absence of systematic evidence concerning the accuracy of CQT results that do *not* lead to confessions, examiners have been able to sustain the belief that all their diagnoses are extremely accurate.

[1] Criteria for a Credible Validity Study

It will be useful to consider the minimum requirements for an acceptable study of CQT validity. These include the following:

(a) Subjects should be a representative sample of suspects tested in the course of criminal investigation.

(b) Since one wishes to estimate with reasonable precision both the CQT's validity in detecting truthful responding and its validity in

---

21. *Id.* at 234.   **22.** *Id.*

detecting deception, test results from at least 100 guilty (deceptive) and 100 innocent (truthful) suspects should be available for the assessment.

(c) For reasons reviewed earlier in discussing the problems of the confession criterion, the innocence or guilt of these study subjects must be determined subsequent to the CQT procedure by investigative methods that are wholly independent of the outcome of the CQT.

(d) Finally, to permit generalizability of the findings, the study would be replicated in a different context (e.g., by a different investigative agency using different examiners).

[2] Plan for a Credible Validity Study

A scientifically credible study of CQT validity might be accomplished by an investigative agency such as the FBI in the following manner:

(1) For a period of months or years, until the necessary number of verified cases had accumulated, *all* suspects under investigation would be given a CQT without post-test interrogation by the examiners.

(2) The test results would be filed separately and not revealed to anyone, including criminal investigators so as not to bias their investigative decisions.

(3) As cases were resolved, the CQT results would be validated against the independent investigative findings.

(4) Should the results prove favorable enough to warrant further study, the project would be replicated by a different investigative agency.

[3] Example of a Non-credible Validity Study

In contrast to this systematic and unbiased research design, we might consider the study by Raskin, Kircher, Honts, and Horowitz of CQT results selected from the files of the US Secret Service.[23] Despite this study's having been completed in 1988, it has not been published in or even reviewed by a scientific journal. Instead, what the authors did must be pieced together from unpublished reports and book chapters in which the procedures and results are selectively presented.

A complication of this study that makes it difficult to compare to others is that it was not possible to verify subjects as truthful or deceptive to all of the questions they were asked on the CQT. Instead, they were classified as "verified deceptive" if at least one CQT question elicited a confession and the answer to no other question could be confirmed truthful. Likewise, they were "verified truthful" if an alternative suspect admitted guilt to the issue covered by a single question and the subject did not admit to guilt on the issues covered by the other questions. Hence, for many subjects, only partial verification of guilt or innocence was obtained.

23. David C. Raskin et al., *A Study of the Validity of Polygraph Examinations in Criminal Investigations* (May 1988) (unpublished manuscript, on file with the University of Utah, Department of Psychology).

From a total of 2,522 CQTs administered, 66 or about 3% resulted in post-test confessions which verified at least one question on the test that prompted the interrogation, and 39 confessions verified the truthfulness of other suspects regarding their response to at least one test question. The 39 verified-truthful CQTs were administered to persons in multiple-suspect cases who were tested prior to some alternative suspect who later confessed. Thus, in this study, only about 4% of the CQTs administered were "verified" as indicating guilt or innocence, and this verification was incomplete, pertaining only to a single relevant question for many of the subjects. The representativeness of these partially verified cases is obviously open to question.

However, a more serious concern is that the method of verification virtually guaranteed that the original examiners' diagnosis would have been correct. That is, the 66 verified deceptive CQTs were verified because the examiner diagnosed deception, interrogated on that basis, and obtained a confession. Similarly, we know that the 39 CQTs verified as truthful by the confession of an alternative suspect would have been classified as truthful by the original examiner, else he would have had little reason to test the alternative suspect who later confessed.

We can therefore conclude that at least 4% of the suspects tested by the Secret Service produced CQT results like those predicted by the theory (deceptive suspects more disturbed by relevant than by control questions, truthful suspects more disturbed by the control questions). We can also conclude that other examiners, asked to score these same polygraph charts, were likely to get results similar to those obtained by the original examiners. But these results are entirely compatible with the assumption that there is no relationship whatever between the veracity of the suspect and his score on the CQT!

Let us suppose that 50% (1,261) of the 2,522 suspects tested were in fact guilty. Let us assume further that the CQT identified deception in these individuals with only chance accuracy. This would result, by chance alone, in 630 of the guilty suspects being classified as deceptive. All or most of these 630 would be interrogated and, as in this case, some 66 of them might confess their guilt. Since some of these 66 would be involved in cases with multiple suspects, their confessions would exculpate the alternative suspects. These alternative suspects were most likely tested and diagnosed truthful prior to the testing of the guilty suspect who confessed, otherwise the suspect who confessed would most likely not have been tested because the guilty party would already have been identified. Note that under these circumstances, the testing of these subjects would be correct 100% of the time even though the test itself has only chance accuracy. If we now take the charts from these cases and have them blindly rescored, because scoring is reliable, we are likely to obtain nearly the same results that the original examiners obtained. However, these results, suggesting near infallibility, are totally misleading and tell us nothing about CQT accuracy.

Raskin et al. emphasize a unique feature of their study as though it represents a significant methodological refinement over other reports. In addition to requiring a confession to substantiate guilt, they also required the presence of "independent corroboration" of the confession in the form of some type of physical evidence. Although this requirement would appear to eliminate the occasional false confession, it does not deal with the fundamental problem inherent in using confessions to establish ground truth. The problem with this requirement is that the corroborating physical evidence is not independent of test outcome. Had the suspect not failed the CQT, there would be no confession, and had there been no confession, there would have been no opportunity to recover the physical evidence. Hence, there is nothing "independent" about the corroborating evidence. Just like the confession, it too is dependent on having failed the polygraph test.

In short, although much has been made of the Secret Service study, as if it had demonstrated a high degree of accuracy for the CQT, when properly analyzed it can be seen to be wholly without probative value. The fact that this study has not been accepted for publication in a peer-reviewed scientific journal illustrates the utility of impartial peer review as a minimum criterion for consideration of scientific claims.

§ 10-3.3.7 CQT Accuracy: Claims of CQT Proponents Are Not Supported

[1] Laboratory Studies

The studies that have achieved publication, although none of them meets the criteria set out above for an adequate validity assessment, do permit certain limited conclusions to be drawn. First, there are a number of studies in which volunteer subjects, usually college students, are required to commit a mock crime and then to lie about it during a CQT examination.[24] Control subjects do not commit the crime and are truthful on the CQT.[25] Instead of fear that failing the CQT will lead to punishment (such as criminal prosecution), subjects in these studies were motivated by a promise of a money prize if they were able to be classified as truthful on the CQT.[26] In these highly artificial circumstances, CQT scores successfully discriminated between the two groups.

When the circumstances are made somewhat more realistic, however, even this mock crime design produces results similar to those reported in the better field studies (discussed below). Patrick and Iacono, for example, using prison inmate volunteers, led their subjects to suppose that their failing the CQT might result in the loss to the entire group of a promised reward and thus incur the enmity of their potentially violent and dangerous comrades.[27] Under these circumstances, nearly half of the truthful subjects were classified erroneously as deceptive.[28] In another study, Foreman and McCauley permitted their volunteer subjects to choose for themselves whether to be "guilty" and deceptive or "innocent" and truthful.[29] Those who elected to be truthful

24. Gordon H. Barland & David C. Raskin, *An Evaluation of Field Techniques in Detection of Deception*, 12 PSYCHOPHYSIOLOGY 321, 321–330 (1975); David C. Raskin & Robert D. Hare, *Psychopathy and Detection of Deception in a Prison Population*, 15 PSYCHOPHYSIOLOGY 126, 126–136 (1978).

25. Barland & Raskin, *supra* note 24; Raskin & Hare, *supra* note 24.

26. Barland & Raskin, *supra* note 24; Raskin & Hare, *supra* note 24.

27. Christopher J. Patrick & William G. Iacono, *Psychopathy, Threat, and Polygraph Test Accuracy*, 74 J. APPLIED PSYCHOL. 347, 348–349 (1989).

28. *Id.* at 350.

29. Robert F. Forman & Clark McCauley, *Validity of the Positive Control Test Using the*

knew that their reward would be smaller but presumably more certain.[30] This manipulation is analogous to crime situations where an individual is confronted with an opportunity to commit a crime with little likelihood of getting caught, e.g., an unlocked car with a valuable item in sight, or a poorly watched-over purse or briefcase, and must decide whether to take advantage of the opportunity. By thus increasing the realism of the test conditions, Foreman and McCauley probably also obtained a more realistic result, with about half of their truthful subjects being erroneously classified as deceptive.

Thus, although mock crime studies with volunteer subjects clearly do not permit any confident extrapolation to the real life conditions of criminal investigation, it does appear that the designs with the greater verisimilitude, which threaten punishment or which merely permit subjects to decide for themselves whether to be truthful or deceptive, demonstrate that the CQT identifies truthful respondents with only chance accuracy.[31]

[2] Field Studies

All reputable scientists acknowledge the importance of the peer-review process as a first line of defense against spurious claims. Studies published in archival scientific journals will have passed the scrutiny of independent scientists knowledgeable in the given area of investigation. No one believes that this process is infallible. Spurious results and dubious conclusions can and do find their way into the scientific literature from time to time. Most scientists consider publication in a peer-reviewed scientific journal to be a necessary but not sufficient basis for the serious consideration of a scientific finding or interpretation. This requirement applies as well to polygraph research as it does to other types of scientific inquiry.

Appearance in a peer-reviewed journal, however, is no guarantee of scientific quality. For example, Honts[32] undertook to evaluate the validity of CQTs administered by the RCMP, using extra-polygraphic criteria of ground truth. The plan was to obtain 75 criminal cases with extra-polygraphic confirmation of guilt and 75 cases in which the suspects had been confirmed to be innocent, also independently of polygraph results. Yet only 13 (rather than the proposed 150) tests were rated as having been strongly confirmed and in all of these cases polygraph-induced confessions of the perpetrator determined ground truth. All of the 7 guilty suspects were scored as deceptive and the 6 innocent suspects were scored either truthful or inconclusive. Apart from these very small and unrepresentative samples, this study failed utterly to assess CQT validity with criteria of ground truth that were independent of the polygraph results, thus guaranteeing a misleading, high accuracy rate. Because this study adds nothing to the sum of our knowledge about the real accuracy of the CQT in criminal investigation, we were surprised that it

Field Practice Model, 71 J. APPLIED PSYCHOL. 691, 691–698 (1986).

30. *Id.* at 693.

31. Raskin et al. do not include these more ecologically valid studies by Patrick and Iacono and Forman and McCauley in their lists of "high quality" laboratory studies (first edition). All but one of the studies they cite is the work of Raskin and his students. The one

study not from their laboratory [Ginton et al., 1984] included only two guilty subjects and thus has no bearing on their calculation of CQT accuracy with guilty subjects in laboratory investigations.

32. Charles R. Honts, *Criterion Development and Validity of the CQT in Field Application*, 123 J. GEN. PSYCHOL. 309–324. (1997).

would be accepted for publication in an archival scientific journal, even the journal edited by a colleague of Honts' at Boise State University. The quality of the peer review that the Honts paper received may be suggested by the following facts: 1) errata were subsequently published to correct obvious arithmetical mistakes pointed out by a reader, 2) the number of subjects in the various groups studied by Honts is inconsistently reported between the published version of this work and the technical report from which the publication was derived,[33] and 3) the *Journal of General Psychology* was ranked 82nd in "impact" among the 97 general psychology journals analyzed by the Institute for Scientific Information.[34]

Four other studies have been published in scientific journals.[35] All four include cases where the verification of guilt and innocence was not entirely dependent on polygraph-induced confessions. In one of these studies, Bersh determined ground truth by relying on the consensus of a panel of attorneys who evaluated the available evidence on each case.[36] Since this evidence included reports of polygraph-induced confessions where they occurred, this criterion is contaminated and, moreover, the evidence did not always permit a confident verdict. In addition, this study, which relied on global chart scoring, did not employ blind chart review. Because the polygraph operators in this study adopted the global approach to chart scoring, their decisions regarding guilt and innocence were based on the same information the panel was given. Given these serious methodological flaws, it is not surprising that the panel and the polygraph operators agreed with each other.

Although not published in a peer-reviewed journal, Barland and Raskin extended the Bersh study using the same research design except that numerical scoring and blind chart review were used.[37] The importance of this study, which its authors have repudiated, is that it reveals that the principal scientific advocate of the CQT, Dr. Raskin, who independently scored all the charts, classified more than half of the innocent suspects as deceptive.[38]

The studies by Horvath and by Kleinmuntz and Szucko both used confession-verified CQT charts obtained respectively from a police agency and

---

33. Although this problem was been pointed out to Dr. Honts in a letter of 15 May 1998, in his reply of 24 May 1998, he refused to explain the discrepancies across these different versions of his work. Dr. Honts refused a request for the data on which this report was based. Letter from Charles Honts to William Iacono (May 24, 1998) (on file with author).

34. Social Sciences Citation Index, 1993, *Journal Citation Reports*. Philadelphia: Institute of Scientific Information. "Impact factor" is a measure of the frequency with which articles published in a journal are actually cited by other authors. For the *Journal of General Psychology*, the average paper was cited only about 0.1 times, indicating that for every 10 articles published by this journal, only one is cited. Hence, scientists ignore most articles in this publication. Competitive peer review occurs in journals that reject most submissions made to them. The field studies that we have identified as the best (which can be found in footnote 1 source, Table 1, p. 608) are published in the *Journal of Applied Psychology* and *Nature*, journals that reject 85% or more of the submissions made to them and whose impact factors rank them as among the very best scientific journals.

35. Philip Bersh, *A Validation Study of Polygraph Examiner Judgments*, 53 J. APPLIED PSYCHOL. 399, 399–403 (1969); Frank Horvath, *The Effect of Selected Variables on Interpretation of Polygraph Records*, 62 J. APPLIED PSYCHOL. 127, 127–136 (1977); Benjamin Kleinmuntz & J.J. Szucko, *A Field Study of the Fallibility of Polygraphic Lie Detection*, 308 NATURE 449, 449–450 (1984); Patrick & Iacono, *supra* note 27; Honts, *supra* note 32.

36. Bersh, *supra* note 35.

37. GORDON H. BARLAND & DAVID C. RASKIN, U.S. DEP'T OF JUSTICE, VALIDITY AND RELIABILITY OF POLYGRAPH EXAMINATIONS OF CRIMINAL SUSPECTS (1976).

38. *Id.*

the Reid polygraph firm in Chicago.[39] The original examiners in these cases did not rely only on the polygraph results in reaching their diagnoses but also employed the case facts and their clinical appraisal of the subject's behavior during testing.[40] Therefore, some suspects who failed the CQT and confessed were likely to have been judged deceptive and interrogated based primarily on the case facts and their demeanor during the polygraph examination, leaving open the possibility that their charts may or may not by themselves have indicated deception. Moreover, some other suspects were cleared by confessions of others, even though the cleared suspects, judged truthful using global criteria, could have produced charts indicative of deception. That is, the original examiners in these cases were led to doubt these suspects' guilt despite the evidence in the charts and proceeded to interrogate an alternative suspect in the same case who thereupon confessed. For these reasons, some undetermined number of the confessions in these two studies were likely to be relatively independent of the polygraph results, revealing some of the guilty suspects who "failed" it. The hit rates obtained in these studies are indicated in Table I.

Table I
Summary of Studies of Lie Test Validity that Were Published in Scientific Journals and that Used Confessions to Establish Ground Truth

	Horvath (1977)	Kleinmuntz & Szucko (1984)	Patrick & Iacono (1991)	Mean
Guilty Correctly Classified	77%	76%	98%	84%
Innocent Correctly Classified	51%	63%	57%	57%
Mean of Above:	64%	70%	77%	70%

In a study by Patrick and Iacono, 65% of the innocent suspects were confirmed as such independently of polygraph results (e.g., the complainant later discovered the mislaid item originally thought to have been stolen).[41] As can be seen in Table I, 43% of these innocent suspects were wrongly classified as deceptive by the CQT. Only one guilty suspect could be confirmed as such from file data independent of CQT-induced confessions; his charts were classified as inconclusive by the CQT. The remaining guilty suspects in the Patrick and Iacono study were all classified solely on the basis of having been scored as deceptive on the polygraph and then interrogated to produce a confession.[42] Understandably, when examiners trained in the same method of scoring independently rescored these charts, they agreed with the original

39. Horvath, *supra* note 35; Kleinmuntz & Szucko, *supra* note 35.

40. Horvath, *supra* note 35, at 129–130; Kleinmuntz & Szucko, *supra* note 35, at 449.

41. Patrick & Iacono, *supra* note 12, at 234.

42. *Id.* at 234.

examiners in 98% of cases.[43] This 98% figure is inflated because only charts that the original examiner decided indicated deception were used in its calculation.[44]

[3] Conclusions

While none of the available studies meet the criteria listed earlier, certain useful conclusions can be drawn. First, the accuracy estimates shown in Table I must all be over-estimates of the real accuracy of the CQT since there was at least some reliance in each study on polygraph-induced confessions as the criterion for ground truth. (Where there is total reliance on the confession criterion, as in the Secret Service study reviewed above, then the apparent accuracy achieved by the examiners who independently rescore the charts is really just a measure of the inter-scorer reliability—an impressively high value but wholly uninformative regarding actual CQT validity.)

Because all the validity estimates are overestimates, a second conclusion permitted by the studies in Table I is that an innocent suspect has little more than a 50% chance of being classified as truthful by an adversarially administered CQT. Thus, had the prosecution offered to drop charges if these suspects passed the polygraph, on the stipulation that adverse results would be admitted as evidence at trial, at least half of these innocent suspects would have heard a polygraph examiner testify before a jury that they had been deceptive in denying their guilt.

Finally, it must be recalled that the polygraph tests involved in these three studies were all administered prior to about 1985, before the existence of an easily-learned method of beating the CQT was widely known.[45] It is a safe assumption that few, if any, of the guilty suspects involved in these four studies employed these effective countermeasures. We know that the 84% average success in detecting deception, shown on the right of Table I, is already an overestimate due to criterion contamination. In the future, as the method to "beat the lie detector" becomes more widely known within the criminal community (instructions on how to beat the polygraph are now available in any public library and also on the internet), we can expect further deflation of the CQT's success in detecting deception.

The burden of proof remains on the advocates of the control question polygraph technique to demonstrate empirically that a method based on such implausible assumptions can have useful accuracy. That proof has not appeared and what relevant data are available, data that permit us at least to

---

43. *Id.*

44. Raskin et al., in DAVID L. FAIGMAN, DAVID H. KAYE, MICHAEL J. SAKS & JOSEPH SANDERS, MODERN SCIENTIFIC EVIDENCE: THE LAW AND SCIENCE OF EXPERT TESTIMONY, 627 (1997), argued that it is the accuracy of the original examiner in these studies summarized in Table I that "is the true figure of merit" when evaluating CQT accuracy because it is the original examiner's decision that would be presented in court. However, when confessions are used to select cases, because a confession can only follow a test scored deceptive by the original examiner, the only cases of the original examiner selected for study will be the ones where he is correct. Citing such figures as legitimate accuracy estimates is thus grossly misleading.

45. Charles R. Honts et al., *Effects of Physical Countermeasures on the Physiological Detection of Deception*, 70 J. APPLIED PSYCHOL. 177, 177–187 (1985); Charles R. Honts et al., *Mental and Physical Countermeasures Reduce the Accuracy of Polygraph Tests*, 79 J. APPLIED PSYCHOL. 252, 252–259 (1994).

set an upper limit on CQT validity, indicate clearly that the accuracy of the CQT is too low for it to qualify as a courtroom aid.

§ 10–3.2.8 How Guilty Persons Can Learn to Produce Truthful CQT Outcomes

Drugs that act to decrease responding in a general way will not normally affect the accuracy of polygraph tests because the CQT is scored by comparing the subject's response to two types of questions. Therefore, successful countermeasures rely on the subject's efforts to artificially augment his response to the control questions. Certain techniques of covert self-stimulation, such as biting the tongue, flexing the toes, or performing mentally stressful arithmetic exercises, can augment the physiological response to a question. To employ such countermeasures, the subject must understand the principle on which the test is based and be able to identify which are the control questions.

Research, as well as a consensus among scientists, supports the view that persons with rather brief training or explanation can covertly self-stimulate so as to augment their responses to CQT control questions, that even experienced examiners cannot detect these countermeasures, and that they may be successful in preventing a guilty suspect from being classified as deceptive on the CQT.[46] There is no good evidence as to how well these countermeasures work under real life conditions and no evidence at all concerning how frequently such countermeasures are successfully employed in real life by sophisticated subjects.

§ 10–3.3.9 Why Computerization Does Not Boost CQT Accuracy

In this increasingly common practice, the physiological responses of the suspect to the questions of a CQT are measured by a computer which then scores the result and compares that score to a table of scores from known truthful or deceptive subjects, stored in the computer's memory. The result of this comparison is a computer-generated statement indicating the probability of truthfulness or deception. For instance, Dr. Raskin testified in *United States v. Clayton and Dalley*, based on a computer determination, that the probability that the defendant was truthful was .993.[47]

Substantial scientific controversy surrounds three assumptions underlying computer scoring:

(1) that the probability of truth or deception in real-world situations can be determined from the score on a CQT (this is the basic assumption of lie detection);

(2) that the scores stored in the computer accurately represent the scores to be expected from truthful or deceptive subjects obtained under circumstances similar to those obtaining in the instant test;

(3) that 50 percent of those who are tested with this instrument are deceptive.

46. Honts et al. 1985, *supra* note 45; Honts et al. 1994, *supra* note 45.

47. United States v. Clayton, U.S. District Court, Phoenix, Arizona, March 22, 1994, No.

92–374–PCT–RCB at 109 (trial transcript of the direct examination of Dr. David Raskin).

To satisfy the second assumption of computer scoring, the database stored in the machine would have to contain the results of polygraph tests administered under real-life conditions to a representative sample of criminal suspects who had been subsequently proven to be innocent, and also a representative sample of suspects later proven to be guilty. Because of the problems of the confession criterion, outlined above, these tests would have to have been verified by some means other than by polygraph-induced confessions. The results of tests administered in the mock crime conditions of laboratory experiments, or tests administered privately to criminal suspects, would not be appropriate to use in this application because such differences in the conditions of testing will yield differences in the distribution and meaning of the scores. It should be emphasized that *no such database currently exists* and that, absent this necessary basis for comparison, the attachment of probability values to results of polygraph tests, whether calculated by a computer or in any other way, is necessarily spurious and misleading. With regard to the third assumption, there is no way of knowing that 50% of those tested will be in fact guilty, nor is it likely that this number does not vary across jurisdictions, settings, and applications. To the extent that considerably fewer or more than 50% of subjects are actually guilty, computer determined probabilities of truthfulness can be quite misleading.

This marriage of the myth of the "lie detector" to the mystique of the computer is a particularly insidious development. When an alleged expert testifies that a defendant's denials of guilt have been scientifically assessed by a computer, which has reported a high probability that these denials are not truthful, one must expect the average juror to give considerable weight to such evidence. However, there does not exist (and may never exist) the database required to yield accurate estimates for computerized chart interpretation. These requirements cannot now be met for criminal suspects tested either under adversarial conditions or privately by an examiner engaged by the defense.

§ 10–3.3.10   The Limited Research on the Directed Lie Version of the CQT

Only two studies are available that examine the accuracy of the DLT. Horowitz et al.[48] conducted a laboratory investigation, which like other laboratory studies, produces results that cannot be generalized to real life because the testing circumstances are too artificial. This leaves a field study by Honts and Raskin[49] as the only investigation that can be used to support the forensic use of the DLT. This study has several important shortcomings. The most serious concerns the use of confessions to establish ground truth. As we have pointed out before, those real-life studies in which tests given to criminal suspects are confirmed by polygraph-induced confessions, and the polygraph charts are later scored blindly by different examiners, must overestimate polygraph accuracy. The other serious shortcomings of this study are that only 12 guilty subjects were included (too small a sample for thorough evaluation of the effectiveness of a new technique) and that the test adminis-

48. Steven W. Horowitz et al., *The Role of Comparison Questions in Physiological Detection of Deception*, 34 PSYCHOPHYSIOLOGY 108–115 (1997).

49. Charles R. Honts & David C. Raskin, *A Field Study of the Directed Lie Control Question*, 16 J. POLICE SCI. & ADMIN. 56–61 (1988).

tered was not a DLT. Instead it was a CQT with one directed lie control question. We can only agree with Honts and Raskin when they concluded their paper with the following remarks: "It is not known whether an examination with only [directed lie control questions] would be valid."[50]

§ 10–3.3.11 Why Law Enforcement Agencies Use Polygraph Tests Despite Their Limitations

Given all of the controversy that exists surrounding polygraph testing, why is it that law enforcement and national security agencies make extensive use of polygraph tests? The answer to this question lies with the fact that they have been found to have considerable utility because of the admissions that some subjects make under the stress of these procedures.

[1] The Polygraph as an Inducer of Confessions

There is no doubt that being told that one has "failed the polygraph" or "seems to be having difficulty with certain questions" is a powerful inducement to confessions or damaging admissions, especially among unsophisticated criminal suspects. Since even innocent suspects have been known to confess in this situation, unsubstantiated confessions pursuant to polygraph testing should be treated with great caution. Examiners often tell suspects that anything they feel guilty about may produce an adverse outcome and, in this way, damaging admissions are often elicited that do not specifically acknowledge guilt in the matter under investigation. Such damaging admissions are sometimes counted as verifications of the polygraph test that produced them; this is, of course, erroneous and may have led to overconfidence in the validity of the CQT. Even if a polygraph technique had only chance accuracy, 50% of the truly guilty would be expected to fail the test and, upon being interrogated, the more unsophisticated of these guilty persons may confess. Those who believe that the utility of polygraphy justifies its use should recognize that the CQT's utility would be even greater if *all* subjects were interrogated as if they had "failed" the test. Guilty suspects who pass the CQT would then not escape interrogation and some of them would respond by confessing.

[2] The Polygraph Test as an Interrogation Tool

The polygraph can also be a useful aid to criminal investigation. Should a suspect exhibit an unusual emotional and physiological response to questions that would not be expected to disturb him if his story is a true one, investigators can be led to look for evidence in new directions. It must be emphasized, however, that the utility of the polygraph in criminal investigation or interrogation does not imply nor depend on the accuracy of the procedure. By the same token, endorsement by scientists that the polygraph might be useful in these ways does not imply that these scientists believe the CQT to be accurate as a test for truth.

An example of a government agency that finds that polygraph testing has utility even though its validity is unproven is the FBI. Despite the FBI's

50. *Id.* at 61.

extensive use of polygraph testing, according to James K. Murphy, former Chief of the FBI Laboratory's Polygraph Unit in Washington, D.C., "The United States Department of Justice and the FBI oppose any attempt to enter the results of polygraph examinations into evidence at trial because the polygraph technique has not reached a level of acceptance within the scientific community and there is no existing standard for training or conducting examinations under which all polygraph examiners must conform."[51]

§ 10–3.3.12 Scientists Are Skeptical of the CQT

We have already stressed that, in the absence of wholly adequate empirical studies of the validity of either the CQT or the GKT, decisions about when and whether to rely on the results of these techniques must be based largely on the scientific plausibility of the respective assumptions on which they are based. For this reason, accurate assessments of the opinions of members of the relevant scientific community, concerning the plausibility of these two techniques, would seem to be of special importance.

In 1994, Amato and Honts reported findings from a survey of the opinions about lie detection of members of the Society for Psychophysiological Research (SPR). This report, based on a response rate of only 30%, was published as an abstract that did not undergo scientific peer review. It followed on the heels of another survey of the members of SPR that also was not published in a scientific journal. Because of these (and other) inadequacies, we conducted new and more extensive surveys of SPR members and also of general psychologists distinguished by election as Fellows of Division 1 of the American Psychological Association (APA1). The results of these surveys, which achieved return-rates of 91% (SPR) and 74% (APA1), were published as a peer-reviewed article in a first-rank journal. These findings show that the vast majority of both groups surveyed expressed grave doubts about the validity of polygraphic lie detection and therefore opposed the introduction of lie test results as evidence in courts. Another recent study found that psychology textbooks express a "strongly negative" opinion of the scientific status of the lie detector. Finally, in September 1999, a panel of senior scientists and engineers from the Department of Energy's weapons laboratories published a detailed appraisal of the scientific status of polygraphy, especially as used in the screening of federal employees. In this section, we review these several sets of data.

[1] Methodologically Flawed Surveys of Scientists

Two prior surveys of members of the Society for Psychophysiological Research (SPR) have been conducted. The first was a 1982 telephone survey of 155 members by the Gallup Organization on behalf of a litigant who wished to introduce into evidence the results of a polygraph test.[52] The unpublished

51. Affidavit of James K. Murphy, Chief of Polygraph, Federal Bureau of Investigation (March 3, 1995) (on file with the authors).

52. The Gallup Organization, Survey of Members of the American Society for Psychophysiological Research Concerning Their Opinion of Polygraph Test Interpretation (1982).

results of this survey are difficult to evaluate because few details have been provided about how the survey was conducted. In particular, there was no indication how many SPR members could not be contacted or refused the telephone poll, information that is essential to evaluating the generalizability of the results.

The second survey, by Amato and Honts,[53] was sent by mail to 450 members of SPR. Only 30% responded. Both surveys asked a single question requiring an appraisal of the "usefulness" of polygraph testing in which respondents were asked to choose one of four statements that best described their "opinion of polygraph test interpretations" to determine "whether a subject is or is not telling the truth." The responses this question received in both surveys is reproduced in Table II.

Proponents of polygraph testing have drawn special attention to the fact that about 60% of respondents in both surveys endorsed alternative "B" indicating that polygraph interpretation "is a useful diagnostic tool." This finding led Amato and Honts to conclude that the membership of SPR consider polygraph tests "useful for legal proceedings,"[54] even though the question does not ask for an opinion concerning the use of polygraph results in court. In fact, the meaning of the response is ambiguous.[55] We have already noted that there is general agreement that polygraph testing has utility as an investigative aid, and there is no reason to suppose that respondents who chose option B considered their response to refer to anything more than investigative applications. Since these surveys made no distinction between the CQT, which most scientists consider to be based on implausible assumptions, and the guilty knowledge test (GKT), which many consider to be scientifically credible, there is also no way of knowing to what type of polygraph test the question refers. Because of the many ambiguities associated with the interpretation of responses to this question coupled with concerns about the representativeness of survey respondents, we undertook our own independent surveys to determine the views of the scientific community concerning deception detection.[56]

53. Susan L. Amato, *A Survey of the Society for Psychophysiological Research Regarding the Polygraph: Opinions and Implications* (1993) (unpublished Master's thesis, University of North Dakota); Susan L. Amato & Charles R. Honts, *What Do Psychophysiologists Think About Polygraph Tests? A Survey of the Membership of the Society for Psychophysiological Research* (1994) (poster presented at the Society for Psychophysiological Research's Annual Meeting).

54. *Id.*

55. Another question on the Amato and Honts survey is less ambiguous in its intent and obtained results indicating substantial doubt about CQT accuracy. It asked: "How accurate is the control question test when administered to a guilty suspect during a crimi-

nal investigation?" Subjects answered on a 1–5 scale anchored with "no better than chance" (i.e., 50%) at the low end and "nearly perfect (100%)" at the high end. The mean response was 3.08, at the approximate midpoint of the scale, corresponding to about 75% accuracy. This accuracy estimate is much lower than the 95% claimed by Raskin, Honts and Kircher, and similar to the upper-bound accuracy estimate we made for criterion guilty subjects in the best field studies on CQT validity (see Table I).

56. William G. Iacono & David T. Lykken, *The Validity of the Lie Detector: Two Surveys of Scientific Opinion*, 82 J. Applied Psychol. 426–433 (1997).

Table II

Opinions of Members of the Society for Psychophysiological Research Regarding the "Usefulness" of Polygraph Test Interpretation in Three Surveys

Response Options:	Gallup (1982)	Amato & Honts (1993)	Iacono & Lykken (1995)
A. Sufficiently reliable method to be the sole determinant	1%	1%	0%
B. Useful diagnostic tool when considered with other available information	61%	60%	44%
*Between "B" and "C"	2%	–	2%
C. Questionable usefulness, entitled to little weight against other available information	32%	37%	53%
D. No usefulness	3%	2%	2%

*Note: Although not offered as an option, in two of the surveys respondents indicated a choice that fell between alternatives B and C.

[2] An Accurate Survey of Society for Psychophysiological Research Members

We conducted a mail survey of a random sample of 50% of the nonstudent members of SPR who had United States addresses according to a SPR membership list provided to us by the Society in October, 1994.[57] To insure anonymity and encourage responsiveness, respondents were asked to return, under separate cover from their questionnaire, a postage-paid post card indicating that they had returned the survey. Those who did not return the postcard received up to three subsequent mailed prompts in an effort to obtain as complete a sample as possible.[58]

Of the 214 SPR members surveyed, 91% returned questionnaires. According to the former US Office of Statistical Standards, response rates of 90% or more can generally be treated as random samples of the overall population and response rates above 75% usually yield reliable results.[59] Significant caution is recommended when response rates drop below 50% as they did in the Amato and Honts survey.[60]

57. Because we conducted the surveys so we could include the results in the MODERN SCIENTIFIC EVIDENCE (1st ed.) chapter to which Raskin, Honts, and Kircher were co-contributors, we did not consider it appropriate to include either them or ourselves in the surveys. In addition, to avoid the possibility that our surveys would be unduly influenced by the inclusion of respondents from our own department (who agree with our views), we eliminated members of our department from both the SPR and APA surveys. The most likely effect of these exclusions was to reduce the overall negativity of the survey results. Because Raskin, Honts, and Kircher are not members of APA, this would be especially true of the APA survey results.

58. A difference between our survey and that of Amato and Honts was that they did not prompt SPR members in an effort to obtain a representative sample. It is possible that had we not prompted our survey subjects, we would have obtained a sample that was more supportive of polygraph testing. To test this possibility, we contrasted the responses of those who responded early to our survey with those who responded late (after prompting). There were no statistically significant differences between these two groups in their opinions to survey questions.

59. *See* MODERN SCIENTIFIC EVIDENCE, *supra* note 44, at § 5–1.0 (1st ed.).

60. *Id.*

Included with each questionnaire was a letter explaining that the survey was prompted in part by *Daubert* and the likelihood that Federal courts might hold hearings to determine the admissibility of polygraph evidence, hearings that would consider in part the general acceptance of the technique by the scientific community. Because *Daubert* hearings are most likely to consider the admissibility of CQT results, respondents were told that all but a few of the survey questions dealt specifically with the CQT.[61]

An abbreviated listing of other key questionnaire items is presented in Table III.[62] The first item asked if respondents would agree that the CQT "is based on scientifically sound psychological principles or theory." Sixty-four percent of SPR members denied that the CQT is based on sound principles. The next two questions inquired separately whether respondents would "advocate that courts admit into evidence the outcome of control question polygraph tests, that is, permit the polygraph examiner to testify that in his/her opinion, either the defendant was deceptive when denying guilt" or "truthful when denying guilt." Over 70% of SPR members would oppose the use of CQT results as evidence in court under either circumstance. Question 5 revealed that respondents were in overwhelming agreement with the "notion that the CQT can be 'beaten' by augmenting one's response to the control questions." For this question, respondents were divided into two groups based on their familiarity with the publication of Honts et al.[63] on countermeasures.

61. Raskin, Honts and Kircher have incorrectly asserted that we have refused to share our survey data, implying that we have something to hide. See Brief of the Committee of Concerned Social Scientists as *Amicus Curiae* in Support of the Respondent, filed in the Supreme Court of the United States, October term 1996 (No. 96–1133), United States v. Scheffer. (Raskin, Honts, Kircher and their colleagues prepared this brief.) In fact, when we offered to share our data with Drs. Honts and Amato in 1997, they rejected the terms of our offer. They then contacted the editor of the journal in which the survey was published, asking him to mediate a data sharing arrangement that satisfied the ethical guidelines of the American Psychological Association. Guided by the journal editor, who characterized our data-sharing proposal as a good-faith effort that he found acceptable, we once again offered to share our data with Honts and Amato. They once again rejected our offer. In April 1998, we requested the data from the Amato and Honts survey. Although they sent copies of the questionnaires completed by those participating in their survey, 22 of the questionnaires were reproduced with such poor quality that the responses to questions on them were illegible. This problem was brought to Dr. Amato's attention in a letter on 4 June 1998. Although she apologized for and promised to correct this problem, despite follow-up phone and mail requests for better reproductions of these questionnaires, we have not yet received them. Consequently, what we received from them is useless because it is not possible to analyze the complete data set to check it for accuracy.

62. Our surveys provided respondents with information about the methods and assumptions of polygraph testing, quoting directly from the work of Raskin, Honts and Kircher when appropriate. We defined each type of polygraph test and gave the rationale underlying each by quoting verbatim Dr. Raskin's characterization of the CQT and the DLT from his past writings. We also provided examples of what hypothetical questions might look like using information from the O.J. Simpson and Unabomber (Ted Kaczynski) cases which were in the news at the time the surveys were done, although in neither case had the trials for these individuals begun. Unfortunately, the Gallup and Amato and Honts surveys did not similarly make unambiguous the terminology used in their polls. Scientists knowledgeable about the methods and problems of psychological testing can evaluate the plausibility and probable accuracy of lie detection, but only if they are clear about the procedures employed and the rationale supporting the use of these tests. The 30% of SPR members who replied to the Amato and Honts survey doubtless included all of the professional polygraphers who belong to that organization (e.g., Raskin, Honts and Kircher themselves) and it is their small and unrepresentative survey that in fact was biased by their failure to describe lie detection techniques so that SPR members who are not polygraphers could offer an informed opinion. An advantage of our survey of APA Fellows was that this distinguished group, none of whom were polygraphers, was able to provide an evaluation of polygraph techniques unmotivated by self-interest.

63. Charles R. Honts et al., *Mental and Physical Countermeasures Reduce the Accuracy of Polygraph Tests*, 79 J. APPLIED PSYCHOL. 252, 252–259 (1994).

Those responding to this question in both groups were almost unanimous in their opinion that the CQT could be beaten in this manner.

Proponents of polygraphy typically assert that the CQT is better than 90% accurate. For example, in *United States v. Clayton and Dalley*,[64] David Raskin testified that an experienced examiner could be expected to identify correctly "about 95% of the deceptive" and "about 90% of the truthful people." As the responses to Question 6 indicate, the SPR membership disagrees with this claim: Only about 25% agree that the CQT is accurate as often as 85% of the time.

For the next item, survey subjects were asked whether, all things being equal, it was more likely that a defendant awaiting trial would pass a friendly test arranged by defense counsel or a test administered by a police examiner. Three fourths of respondents thought a friendly test would be more likely to be passed. The final CQT item results showed that SPR members found it unreasonable for judicial proceedings to give substantial weight to the classification hit rates obtained in mock crime studies.

Table III

Opinions of Members of the Society for Psychophysiological Research about Polygraphy

Questionnaire Item	Percent Agree	Percent Disagree
1. CQT is scientifically sound	36	64
2. GKT is scientifically sound	77	23
3. Would admit failed tests as evidence in court	24	76
4. Would admit passed tests as evidence in court	27	73
5. CQT can be beaten	99	1
6. CQT is at least 85% accurate		
a. for guilty	27	73
b. for innocent	22	78
7. Friendly test more likely to be passed than adversarial test	75	25
8. Reasonable to use laboratory studies to estimate CQT validity	17	83

We also asked the same question that the Gallup poll and Amato and Honts asked. The results are summarized in the third column of Table II. Compared to the earlier surveys, a substantially smaller fraction endorsed option B in our sample and a substantially larger proportion felt that polygraph test interpretations have "questionable usefulness." Possible explanations for these different endorsement frequencies lie with our having made clear that our survey dealt primarily with the CQT (although we did not alter the wording of this question from that of the previous surveys) and our having a representative sample of the SPR membership. Even the minority of SPR members who thought the CQT might be a "useful tool" was unenthusiastic about the CQT. When this selected subset's responses to other questions

64. *Supra* note 47.

were examined, fewer than 40% were found to believe that the CQT's validity was as high as 85% and 51% opposed admitting CQTs as evidence in court. Seventy-three percent thought a friendly test was more likely than an adversarial test to be passed.[65]

[3] A Survey of Distinguished Psychologists

Not all SPR members are psychologists and, indeed, not all of them are scientists. A number of practicing polygraph examiners, including the editor of the trade journal *Polygraph*, for example, hold membership in SPR. To more clearly characterize the opinions of psychological scientists, we thought it appropriate to conduct a similar survey of an elite group of psychologists, persons who had been elected Fellows of the General Psychology Division of the American Psychological Association. Of the 226 Fellows surveyed with addresses in the United States who were still professionally active, 74% responded. This response rate, although quite high for mail survey research,[66] was lower than that in our SPR survey, most likely because this group, honored for their accomplishments by election to the status of Fellow, was less likely to respond because of the demands their careers place on their time.

Table IV
Opinions of Distinguished Members of the American Psychological Association about CQT Polygraphy

Questionnaire Item	Percent Agree	Percent Disagree
1. CQT is scientifically sound	30	70
2. Would admit failed tests as evidence in court	20	80
3. Would admit passed tests as evidence in court	24	76
4. Confident could learn to beat the CQT	75	25
5. CQT is standardized	20	80
6. CQT is objective	10	90
7. If innocent, would take an adversarial test	35	65
8. If guilty, would take a friendly test	73	27
9. DLT is scientifically sound*	22	78

* Asked of half of the APA members.

Abbreviated results of this survey are presented in Table IV. The first three questions were repeated from our SPR survey and replicated the results of that survey by yielding almost identical endorsement frequencies. The

65. Raskin et al. have implied that our obtaining results to the question in Table II that differed from those of the other surveys may be due to our inclusion of illustrative CQT questions that hypothetically could have been used in the O.J. Simpson case. They assert that somehow the mention of Simpson led otherwise rational scientists to instantly develop a negative view of polygraphy as they completed their surveys. Because polygraph testing was not a part of the Simpson trial, it is difficult to see how the mention of Simpson is connected to one's views on polygraphy, and if they were connected, why they would be any more likely to lead to negative than positive views about the polygraph.

66. *See* MODERN SCIENTIFIC EVIDENCE, *supra* note 44, at § 5–4.7.3 (1st Ed.).

fourth question from the Table asked how confident respondents were that they could personally learn to use physical or mental countermeasures to defeat a CQT. Over 70% felt they could do so with moderate to high confidence. The next two questions dealt with whether the administration of the CQT could accurately be considered standardized and was independent of differences among examiners in skill and subjective judgment. The CQT came up short on both counts.

Questions 7 and 8 dealt with the subjects' confidence in the CQT and the friendly polygrapher issue. Subjects were first asked if they personally would take a CQT administered by a police officer if they were *"wholly innocent"* and "the results would be admitted into evidence" before a jury. Only about a third of respondents would be inclined to take such a test, indicating that their confidence that the CQT can be used to fairly assess the truthfulness of innocent individuals is low. The second question required respondents to assume they were *"guilty"* and that their defense attorney arranged a private test by an examiner with expertise equal to that of the police examiner in the preceding question. Would they take this friendly test? Almost three quarters would, indicating that they felt they were risking little under the circumstances.[67] The final question dealt with the scientific justification for the DLT. The APA fellows were overwhelmingly of the opinion that the DLT was not scientifically sound.[68]

67. To determine if those with greater expertise about polygraphy had opinions that differed from those less well informed in our two surveys, we divided our SPR and APA respondents into two groups based on their own appraisal of how informed they were about CQT validity. The results of these analyses are summarized in detail in our journal article. W.G. Iacono & D.T. Lykken, *The Validity of the Lie Detector: Two Surveys of Scientific Opinion*, 82 J. APPLIED PSYCHOL. 426–433 (1997). Briefly, these two groups did not differ in any important respect regarding how they endorsed responses to the questions in Tables II–IV. We also examined the respondents who might be judged as most informed because they reported reading/attending at least six articles/presentations specifically about the accuracy of CQT polygraphy. Even among those in this select group (which made up 23% of the total respondents), there was little enthusiasm for the CQT. For instance, 66% believe the CQT is not based on sound scientific principles and 62% believe that passed CQTs should not be admissible in court. In this regard, it is important to note that the number of papers a scientist has read on CQT validity does not measure the value of his or her opinion about the accuracy of the technique. It would be a mistake to restrict the analysis of scientific opinion to just those few scientists who practice polygraphy or are otherwise involved in this profession. Such individuals, who are likely to consider themselves highly informed and would thus be disproportionately represented in any group selected for familiarity with this topic, are not capable of dispassionate evaluation of polygraph techniques because their livelihood depends on the use of these procedures. Finally, polygraph techniques are based on very simple principles that the vast majority of psychologists are capable of evaluating provided they know what they are. As previously noted, a strength of our surveys is that these principles were presented to respondents by directly quoting from the work of Raskin, Honts and Kircher so there could be no argument regarding whether they were fairly characterized. Our survey results showed that regardless of how well informed respondents were about this topic, most hold decidedly negative views about CQT polygraphy. The Gallup survey of SPR members also failed to find any difference between SPR members who were more versus those who were less informed about polygraph testing. Our findings thus confirm that highly knowledgeable as well as less informed scientists were equally skeptical about the CQT.

68. We have been informed that Honts has been conducting a telephone survey of opinions about polygraphy of the members of the American Psychology and Law Society, a group whose membership includes non-scientists (our informant was a surveyed attorney with no scientific training).

[4] Further Evidence of Scientific Opinion: Attitudes toward Polygraphy in Psychology Textbooks

Honts and colleagues at Boise State University have established a website called the *Journal of Credibility Assessment and Witness Psychology*. One of the few essays to appear on this site was an analysis by Devitt et al. of the treatment of polygraphic detection of deception (PDD) in 37 different introductory psychology textbooks published between 1987 and 1994. This essay reports that "PDD received strongly negative treatment in the texts."[69] Only 16% of the texts provided any positive citations to polygraphy, with the ratio of negative to positive citations exceeding 15 to 1. The authors complain that textbook writers tend to cite mainly critics of the lie detector (including us) and various factual errors are commented upon. The one error cited in the text concerns one author's discussion of the demonstration by Honts et al.[70] that college students can be easily taught to beat the lie detector. That author mistakenly reported that the method taught for producing augmented responses to the control questions involved pressing on a tack in one's shoe. In fact, Honts et al.'s subjects were instructed to press their toes on the floor after answering the control questions.

The tack-in-the-shoe method would undoubtedly work as well or better than the methods employed by Honts et al.[71] Floyd Fay used this technique while serving two years of a life sentence for aggravated murder prior to the discovery of the real killers, which led to his release.[72] Fay's false conviction resulted from testimony that he had failed two stipulated polygraph tests and this led him to make a study of polygraphy while in prison. The institution in which he was incarcerated used the lie detector to adjudicate charges against inmates of violating prison rules. Before his release, Fay managed to train a number of inmates to beat the lie test by pressing on a tack in their shoe after each control question. These and other examples have been reviewed by Lykken.[73]

The main impression left by this review of Devitt et al. is that the authors of psychology textbooks were nearly unanimous in concluding that the lie detector has poor scientific credentials and negligible forensic utility except, perhaps, as an inducer of confessions. As such, this review corroborates the findings from our SPR and APA1 surveys by illustrating that another group of broadly informed psychologists are overwhelmingly negative in their appraisal of polygraph testing.

69. Mary K. Devitt, et al., *Truth or Just Bias: The Treatment of the Psychophysiological Detection of Deception in Introductory Psychology Textbooks*, as 1 J. Credibility Assessment, 9–32 (1997) (This journal is a publication of Charles Honts' website.)

70. Charles R. Honts, et al., *Effects of Physical Countermeasures on the Physiological Detection of Deception*, 70 J. Applied Psychol. 177–187 (1985).

71. This line of research has shown that various techniques can be used to defeat the CQT. In addition to toe pressing, biting the tongue and mentally counting backwards when presented with a control question have been

identified as effective covert methods that enable guilty persons to pass a CQT. Honts et al., *supra* note 70; Charles R. Honts, David C. Raskin, & John C. Kircher, *Mental and Physical Countermeasures Reduce the Accuracy of Polygraph Tests*, 79 J. Applied Psychol. 252–259 (1994).

72. Adrian Cimerman, "They'll Let Me Go Tomorrow," The Fay Case, 8(3) Criminal Defense 7–10 (1981).

73. David T. Lykken, A Tremor in the Blood: Uses and Abuses of the Lie Detector (1981); David T. Lykken, A Tremor in the Blood: Uses and Abuses of the Lie Detector (2nd ed. 1998).

[5]   Summary of Scientific Opinion

These findings make it clear that the scientific community regards the CQT to be an unstandardized, nonobjective technique, based on implausible assumptions, a technique that can be easily defeated by sophisticated guilty suspects, and which is unlikely to achieve good accuracy in detecting either truthfulness or deception. Scientists do not believe that either inculpatory or exculpatory CQT results have sufficient probative value to be introduced as evidence in court and they are especially skeptical about the validity of friendly tests. They do not believe that laboratory studies should be used to estimate CQT accuracy. Further, they do not believe that the recent CQT variant, the Directed Lie Test, provides a credible solution to the defects of the CQT. These same scientists believe that the GKT, in contrast, is scientifically credible.

§ 10–3.3.13   Scientifically Based Forensic Psychophysiology: The Guilty Knowledge Test (GKT)

The major problem with conventional psychophysiological detection of deception (PDD) techniques is that their validity depends on being able to measure complex human emotions to determine if a person is guilty or innocent. Because individual differences in the expression of emotion are substantial, causing the same stimulus to elicit quite different emotions in different people, and specific emotions produce similar physiological reactions, it may never be possible to develop a PDD technique with high accuracy. It is primarily because PDD is an emotion-based assessment that it is not possible to use laboratory studies to gauge accuracy because real life emotion cannot be reproduced adequately in laboratory simulations.

An alternative to PDD involves developing procedures that are not emotion-based. One such technique, the guilty knowledge test (GKT) provides a measure of the cognitive processing associated with memory, something that can be determined using psychophysiological procedures. The GKT answers the question: What does this person know about the crime? Laboratory studies can be used to show how well certain memories can be detected because the assessment of memory in the laboratory does not differ in any important way from the assessment of memory in the field. Two types of measures have been used to assess recognition memory with the GKT. The traditional GKT has involved the measurement of autonomic nervous system responses, especially the galvanic skin response (GSR). More recently, a version of the GKT has been introduced that relies on the monitoring of brain electrical activity.

[1]   Rationale Behind the Traditional GKT

The GKT provides an assessment of an individual's memory about crime relevant information, i.e., knowledge about the crime that the perpetrator would be expected to have. Such "guilty knowledge" can only be assessed in situations in which the examiner knows certain facts about the crime that would also be known to a guilty—but not to an innocent—suspect. These facts or "keys" can be presented in the form of multiple-choice questions: "If you killed Mr. Jones, then you will know where in the house we found his body. Did we find him: In the kitchen? In the basement? In the living room? On the stairway? In the bedroom?" A traditional GKT might involve 5–10 such multiple choice questions, each with keys and foils covering a different memory about the crime.

The GKT assumes that the guilty person's recognition of the correct alternative will cause him to produce a stronger physiological response to that alternative. The incorrect alternatives provide an estimate of what the response to the correct alternative would look like if the subject did not know which alternative was correct; thus, unlike the comparison questions used in the CQT or DLT, the incorrect alternatives of the GKT questions provide genuine controls.

An innocent suspect would have about one chance in five of giving the largest response to the correct alternative in such a five-choice question; thus, the probability of false detection (a false-positive error) on a single GKT item would be 0.20. This probability of error decreases rapidly, however, for each additional GKT item that can be devised; an innocent person would have about 4 chances in 100 of "hitting" on both of two items, 8 chances in 1000 of giving the largest response to the correct alternative on three consecutive items, and so on.

[2] Measuring Brainwaves with the GKT: "Brain Fingerprinting"

In the last decade, scientists have refined the GKT by measuring brain electrical activity rather than the galvanic skin response to assess recognition memory. This GKT application, referred to as "brain fingerprinting" in the popular press, involves attaching electrodes to the scalp and measuring event-related potentials (ERP). An ERP is a brainwave generated every time a person is presented with a discrete stimulus. This complex wave has multiple components, but one aspect of the signal, called the P300 or P3 wave (because it has a latency of over 300 milliseconds and is the third positive component of the ERP), is especially useful for assessing recognition memory. A P300 wave arises every time a stimulus stands out as different from other stimuli a person is presented with. In the context of the GKT, the key alternatives will stand out to the guilty person because they are recognized as guilty knowledge. For the innocent person, none of the alternatives has distinct meaning, so none will evoke a P300 wave.

For the typical adult, the P300 wave has an amplitude of only about 15 microvolts, far smaller than the background electrical activity that is continuously present in the brain. In order to measure P300, the same stimulus must be repeatedly presented, each time recording the brain's electrical response. All the responses to this stimulus are eventually averaged together. The background electrical activity of the brain varies randomly around the time a stimulus is presented. Averaging this random activity causes it to disappear from the averaged signal. Because the ERP is "time locked" to the stimulus (i.e., its shape and latency is the same to every stimulus presentation beginning the moment the stimulus is presented), averaging enhances the ERP signal. Hence, averaging makes it possible to measure accurately this tiny response by strengthening the representation of the ERP while causing the brain's random background electrical activity to fade away. The implications of this for the GKT are several. First, the stimuli must be presented with precise timing and for very short durations. Typically, a computer is used to present them, and they only appear on a computer monitor for about 50 milliseconds. Second, to facilitate averaging, the same stimuli must be presented repeatedly, perhaps 20 or more times. Because a stimulus can be presented every few seconds, this requirement poses few logistical problems because hundreds of stimuli can be presented in a 15–minute recording session.

Because the shape of ERPs vary from person to person, it is important to know what a P300 wave looks like for the given individual. It is also important to make certain that individuals being tested pay attention to the stimuli. Hence, the ERP–GKT includes some special stimuli that the person being tested admits knowledge of and must respond to. Assume, for instance, that one ERP–GKT item deals with knowledge of the weapon used to kill someone. The examiner and the person being tested agree that the item used was not a gun. The actual crime weapon was a hammer. These words, *gun* (the target) and *hammer* (the probe) are flashed every two seconds or so on a computer screen, randomly interspersed with the irrelevant words *knife*, *rope*, and *poison*. The subject is told to press a red response key every time *gun* appears on the screen and a green response key every time another word is presented. This manual response requirement forces the person to pay attention because it compels cognitive processing of each word in order to be able to press the correct key. Because the word *gun* stands out as memorable, when the ERPs to this word are averaged, a distinct P300 wave will be seen. *Knife*, *rope* and *poison* have no special meaning, so ERPs averaged to these words will not contain a distinct P300 wave. The important question concerns whether the probe word *hammer* produces an ERP with a P300 wave that resembles that produced by the target word *gun* or a wave that looks indistinguishable to that of the irrelevant foils. If it resembles *gun*, the subject is attaching special meaning to the presentation of the word representing the murder weapon, i.e., the subject has guilty knowledge. If the ERP resembles that of the foils, there is no evidence of guilty knowledge for the murder weapon. Statistical procedures have been developed to determine the degree to which the ERP to the probe word more closely resembles that of the target or the irrelevant foils. Just as with the regular GKT, the ERP–GKT involves the presentation of multiple items that may include as stimuli words, phrases, and visual displays such as pictures of the crime scene, victim, weapon, etc.

The ERP–GKT has several advantages over the traditional GKT. First, because of the inclusion of the target word, it is possible to determine that the test was properly administered to the subject. We can make this determination by a) showing that the proper button was pressed in response to this word, and b) showing that this word elicits an ERP that is distinctly different from that to the irrelevant foils. If either of these features is absent, the test of the particular subject would not be valid. Second, a built-in control for individual differences in how a person's brain responds to memorable information is included in the test. It would be possible to drop the target condition from the test and simply determine if the probe ERP differs from the irrelevant ERPs. However, we would not know how different it would have to be to signal the typical recognition response of this person's brain. By including the target condition, we know what a given person's recognition response should look like. Third, the ERP–GKT is not dependent on the measurement of autonomic nervous system responses like the GSR. These responses are not always reliably produced and they can be generated by extraneous factors like unintentional movements or provocative thoughts. The ERP is an involuntary response that is always present if the subject is paying attention. Fourth, the ERP–GKT is unlikely to be easily defeated by employing countermeasures. Because ERPs are derived from brain signals that occur only a few hundred milliseconds after the GKT alternatives are presented, and because as yet no one has shown that humans can selectively alter these brain potentials at will, it is unlikely that countermeasures could be used successfully to defeat a GKT derived from the recording of cerebral signals.

[3] Evidence Supporting GKT Accuracy

There are two distinct questions to ask concerning GKT accuracy. The first concerns whether this technique can be used to determine whether someone has recognition memory for an item or event. This question can be answered with laboratory research. The second concerns what items and events it is reasonable to expect a person who has committed a crime to remember. This question is best addressed from field studies that determine what criminals pay attention to and remember as aspects of a crime they commit. As we show below, studies of the GKT are clear in demonstrating that this is a highly accurate technique for determining if an individual recognizes information. However, at present there are no field studies demonstrating what people who commit a crime are likely to remember.[74] Consequently, we can confidently determine whether a subject has recognition memory, but we cannot determine scientifically whether someone who committed a crime should necessarily have certain memories.

[a] Traditional GKT

A virtue of the GKT is that its validity with innocent suspects can be estimated *a priori*. With 5 equally plausible alternatives in each GKT question, an innocent person would have a 20% chance of giving his strongest response to the correct alternative on one question, a 4% chance of appearing guilty on both of two questions, and so on. With a 10–question GKT, if we require five items to be "failed" to classify a person as guilty, more than 99% of innocent suspects can be expected to be correctly classified. The GKT's validity with guilty suspects cannot be predicted with such confidence because we cannot be certain that each suspect will have noticed and remembered all 10 of the items of guilty knowledge.

---

74. Although they were not studies designed to determine what criminals remember from a crime scene, Elaad et al. have carried out field studies using the traditional GKT. Eitan Elaad et al., *Detection Measures in Real–Life Guilty Knowledge Tests*, 77 J. APPLIED PSYCHOL. 757, 757–767 (1992); Eitan Elaad, *Detection of Guilty Knowledge in Real–Life Criminal Investigations*, 75 J. APPLIED PSYCHOL. 521, 521–529 (1990). These studies, carried out in Israel, showed that innocent suspects responded to GKT items as predicted by theory. Guilty suspects seemed to remember about 70% of the guilty knowledge facts used for GKT items, as compared with about 88% for subjects involved in the mock crimes of laboratory studies where the details of the crime scene were still fresh in their minds. The Israeli field studies achieved 97% detection of innocent suspects but only 76% detection of guilty suspects, which has been cited as indicating a defect of the GKT. But this is an erroneous conclusion. Elaad et al. used GKTs with only 1 to 6 items (mean = 1.8), each repeated typically 3 times, so that their detection efficiencies were predictably less than would be expected with GKTs constructed from 6 to 10 different guilty knowledge facts.

The ability of the GKT to detect both innocence and guilt decreases when there are fewer items and also when there are fewer alternatives per item. The validity estimates that have been obtained in the laboratory studies of the GKT that have been published to date have been close to those predicted from the numbers of items and alternatives-per-item used in each study. For instance, a review of eight GKT laboratory studies revealed that the GKT had an accuracy of 88% with guilty study subjects and 97% with innocent subjects.[75]

The GKT is unlikely to be suitable for the investigation of all crimes. Its results will be dependent on what the perpetrator pays attention to and remembers and how well the examiner is able to determine what that may be.[76] Premeditated crimes and those for which it can be determined what exactly the perpetrator did would make good GKT cases. These would include a planned murder, a theft involving unrecovered items, and a sex crime where the victim can give a good account of what happened.[77]

[b] ERP–GKT

The ERP–GKT received its impetus from the work of Dr. Lawrence Farwell. In an initial report by Farwell and Donchin,[78] 20 laboratory subjects were exposed to guilty knowledge about one of two espionage cases. Hence, each subject possessed guilty knowledge regarding one case and not the other. Excluding inconclusive test outcomes, the ERP–GKT was 100% accurate. That is, it was possible to determine for every subject which espionage scenario he was familiar with and which scenario he had no knowledge of by showing that guilty knowledge probes produced ERPs that closely resembled targets when individuals were guilty and that closely resembled irrelevant foils when individuals were innocent. Allen, Danielson, and Iacono[79] carried out three studies of the ERP–GKT using a different method to determine whether a probe ERP better resembled the target or the irrelevant foil ERPs, a method that did not allow for the possibility of inconclusive outcomes. Examining a total of 60 subjects across three studies, they obtained an overall

---

75. LYKKEN, *supra* note 73.

76. Just as fingerprint evidence, when absent at a crime scene, is not exculpating, a passed GKT indicating no recognition of crime scene information also cannot establish innocence. A failed GKT, on the other hand, indicating the presence of knowledge a suspect claims not to have, is potentially as incriminating as fingerprints found at a crime scene.

77. Podlesny et al. have concluded, after a review of FBI files, that only a small fraction of cases would be suitable for GKTs [John A. Podlesny, *Is the Guilty Knowledge Applicable in Criminal Investigations? A Review of FBI Case Records*, 20 CRIME LABORATORY DIG. 59 (1993); John A. Podlesny et al., *A Lack of Operable Case Facts Restricts Applicability of the Guilty Knowledge Deception Detection Method in FBI Criminal Investigations: A Technical Report*, U.S. DEPT. OF JUSTICE, FBI, FORENSIC SCIENCE RESEARCH AND TRAINING CENTER,

QUANTICO, VIRGINIA (1995)]. We expect that a search of Scotland Yard files prior to 1900, when the Galton–Henry system of fingerprint classification was established, would also have failed to find many instances where this powerful forensic tool could be employed retrospectively. When police investigators are trained to search crime scenes for items on which GKT questions might be based, they will in many cases find them.

78. Lawrence A. Farwell & Emanuel Donchin, *The Truth Will Out: Interrogative Polygraphy ("Lie Detection") with Event Related Potentials*, 28 PSYCHOPHYSIOLOGY 531, 531–547 (1991).

79. John J. Allen et al., *The Identification of Concealed Memories Using the Event–Related Potential and Implicit Behavioral Measures: A Methodology for Prediction in the Face of Individual Differences*, 29 PSYCHOPHYSIOLOGY 504, 504–522 (1992).

classification accuracy of 96%. Allen and Iacono[80] later re-analyzed their data using the scoring method of Farwell and Donchin. Excluding inconclusives, they obtained 100% accuracy. Allen and Iacono varied the motivation their subjects had to try to conceal their guilty knowledge and avoid being detected by giving them varying degrees of incentive to try to "beat the test." They found that as incentive was increased, fewer subjects were classified as inconclusive. These results suggest that in real life, the ERP–GKT may work even better than in the laboratory.

Other studies also suggest that the ERP–GKT is likely to work well in the real world. Several clinical studies have been carried out to determine the validity of amnesia claims made by different types of study participants. In one study, four patients with multiple personality disorder (also called dissociative identity disorder) were assessed to determine if the memories of one personality can be recognized by an alter personality that claims amnesia for them.[81] This study involved presenting to the alter personality memorized information learned by the other personality. This memorized information provided the material for the GKT's probe stimuli, while information memorized by the alter personality served as the source of target stimuli. Other meaningless stimuli served as irrelevant foils. The results showed that the alter personalities generated probe ERPs resembling the target ERPs, indicating recognition memory for the alleged amnesic information in all four cases. A similar study evaluated hypnotized individuals with profound recognition memory amnesia. Again, the ERPs to the memory probes closely resembled those of targets, not irrelevant foils.[82]

Farwell and colleagues have also shown the ERP–GKT is likely to be effective in field applications.[83] In one study, subjects admitted to arrests for minor crimes like public drunkenness. They were queried about the details of the event (e.g., who they were with, where they were) and GKT probes, targets, and irrelevant foils were developed. Each subject was tested for guilty knowledge related to his crime and also for guilty knowledge related to a crime of one of the other participants. Again, no errors of classification were evident. In another investigation, individuals reported to a laboratory with a close friend.[84] The friend was interviewed regarding the details of an important event in the life of the study subject, and this information was used to develop memory probes. When subjects were tested, their ERPs to the probe material provided by their friends matched the target ERPs, not those of irrelevant foils. Again, there were no classification errors.

In *Iowa v. Harrington*,[85] the results of an ERP–GKT were introduced in court for the first time as part of an evidentiary hearing. Dr. Farwell administered two separate tests to Terry Harrington, a man who, although

80. John J.B. Allen & William G. Iacono, *A Comparison of Methods for the Analysis of Event–Related Potentials in Deception Detection*, 34 PSYCHOPHYSIOLOGY 234, 234–240 (1997).

81. John J.B. Allen & Hallam L. Movius III, *The Objective Assessment of Amnesia in Dissociative Identity Disorder Using Event–Related Potentials*, 38 INT'L. J. PSYCHOPHYSIOLOGY 21, 21–41 (2000).

82. John J. Allen et al., *An Event–Related Potential Investigation of Posthypnotic Recog-*

nition Amnesia, 104 J. ABNORMAL PSYCHOL. 421, 421–430 (1995).

83. Farwell & Donchin, *supra* note 78, at 531–547.

84. Lawrence A. Farwell & Sharon S. Smith, *Using Brain MERMER Testing to Detect Knowledge Despite Efforts to Conceal*, 46 J. FORENSIC SCI. 1, 1–9 (2001).

85. Harrington v. State of Iowa, PCCV073247, 5 March 2001.

steadfastly maintaining his innocence, was convicted of murder over 20 years ago. Farwell thoroughly investigated the nature of the crime scene, paying particular attention to unusual obstacles the perpetrator would have been confronted by during his flight from the murder scene. This information was not presented at trial, and Harrington claimed no knowledge of these details. Dr. Farwell was able to demonstrate that Harrington's ERP to probe words characterizing these crime facts resembled his ERPs to irrelevant phrases. The target word phrases produced an ERP with a distinct P300 wave, making it distinctly different form the ERPs associated with the other two types of words. Dr. Farwell also tested Harrington on the details of his alibi on the night of the crime. The probe words, representing information Harrington should have remembered about the events surrounding his alibi, evoked an ERP that matched the ERP of the target words and not the ERP of the irrelevant foils. Taken in combination, these results show that Harrington did not have memories related to the commission of the crime but he did recognize information associated with his alibi. The fact that his brain response showed recognition of alibi-relevant information clearly demonstrated that he was able to remember details of the night in question. Judge O'Grady, who held an evidentiary hearing to review the science supporting the ERP–GKT ruled that while the P300 evidence was "arguably merely cumulative or impeaching, it may be material to the issues in the case," but that Harrington "failed to meet his burden to prove that the P300 evidence probably would have changed the result of the trial."[86]

[4] Scientific Opinion

In the surveys conducted by Iacono and Lykken of members of SPR and APA, respondents were asked their opinions regarding the GKT. The results are summarized in Table V. The members of both organizations clearly believed the GKT to have a solid scientific foundation. They also believed that GKT results have probative value. When asked if it was reasonable to believe that a person who failed 8 of 10 GKT items was guilty, the vast majority of both organizations agreed that it was. Finally, asked what was more believable, a failed GKT or a passed CQT administered through a defendant's attorney, respondents found the GKT to offer the more credible result. These results establish two important points. First, scientists find the GKT to be a theoretically sound forensic tool with great potential. Second, scientists are able to distinguish between different forensic uses of psychophysiological procedures. It is not the case that they are opposed in principle to forensic applications of psychophysiology, they are only opposed to those that have a weak scientific basis.

86. *Id.*

Table V
Opinions of Members of the Society for Psychophysiological Research (SPR) and Fellows of the American Psychological Association (APA) about the GKT

Questionnaire Item	Percent Agree	Percent Disagree
1. GKT is scientifically sound.		
SPR	77	23
APA*	72	28
2. Reasonable to believe a suspect is guilty if 8 out of 10 GKT items were failed.		
SPR	72	28
APA*	75	25
3. If a suspect failed a GKT but passed a CQT dealing with the same crime, which result would be more believable?		
GKT result more believable**	73	27

Note: * Asked of half of APA members; ** Asked of SPR members only

§ 10–3.3.14   Polygraph Screening of Federal Employees and Job Applicants

[1]   National Security Screening

In view of the federal Employee Polygraph Protection Act of 1988,[87] which prohibits requiring employees or job applicants in the private sector to submit to polygraph testing, it is ironic that the federal government is the principal employer of polygraph examiners. Applicants for positions with the FBI, CIA, NSA, Secret Service, and similar agencies are required to undergo lie detector tests intended to supplement or substitute for background investigations. Current employees of some of these agencies, military personnel who hold high security clearances, and civil employees of defense contractors doing classified work may be required to undergo periodic tests for screening purposes. The Department of Defense conducted some 17,970 such tests in 1993.[88] Most of these tests, which are based on the relevant/irrelevant polygraph technique, are referred to as counterintelligence scope polygraph tests by the government.

As a consequence of Public Law 106–65 (S. 1059) passed as part of the National Defense Authorization Act of 2000, potentially thousands of scientists and security personnel employed at U.S. weapons labs at Lawrence Livermore, Sandia, or Los Alamos must submit to polygraph tests as part of an effort to improve nuclear security. A relatively new procedure, the Test for

---

87. 29 U.S.C.A. § 2001 et seq. (2000).

88. DEPT. OF DEFENSE POLYGRAPH INSTITUTE, *A Comparison of Psychophysiological Detection of Deception Accuracy Rates Obtained Using the* *Counterintelligence Scope Polygraph and the Test for Espionage and Sabotage Question Formats*, 26 POLYGRAPH 79–80 (1997) (hereafter DoDPI Study 1).

Espionage and Sabotage (TES), or a nearly identical variant of this procedure, the Test for Espionage, Sabotage, and Terrorism (TEST), is used.

As outlined in the recently promulgated Department of Energy (DOE) Rule 709 these counterintelligence polygraph examinations are to be limited to coverage of six topics:[89]

1) espionage,

2) sabotage,

3) terrorism,

4) intentional unauthorized disclosure of classified information,

5) intentional unauthorized foreign contacts, and

6) deliberate damage or malicious use of a U.S. government or defense system.

Rule 709 has a number of interesting features that are similar to those governing the use of polygraph tests by other federal agencies and that are likely to stimulate law suits.[90] These include the following:

- Prospective employees of the DOE or its contractors who refuse to take a polygraph cannot be hired and incumbent employees must be denied access to secret information.

- Using the results of a polygraph test as an "investigative lead" can result in an administrative decision that denies or revokes an employee's access to classified information and may lead DOE to "reassign the individual or realign the individual's duties within the local commuting area or take other actions consistent with the denial of access."

- These tests will be conducted at least every five years and also on an aperiodic basis.

- Public comment on the proposed regulations revealed widespread opinion that "that polygraph examinations have no theoretical foundation or validity." DOE decided, however, that "as a matter of law," the agency is mandated to conduct polygraph examinations, and "is no longer free to act favorably on comments arguing against establishment of a counterintelligence scope polygraph examination program because of information and claims about deficiencies in polygraph reliability."

The TES[91] is a type of DLT that includes four irrelevant questions (e.g., "Do you sometimes drink water?" "Is today ____?") and the following four relevant questions: "Have you committed espionage?" "Have you given classified information to any unauthorized person?" "Have you failed to notify, as required, any contact with citizens of sensitive countries including China?" "Have you been involved in sabotage?" The responses to the relevant questions are compared to the responses to four "directed lie" questions that serve as "controls" or comparisons by providing an example of a response to a known lie. The directed lies are questions that both the examiner and the examinee know will be answered falsely. These four questions are chosen

---

89. Part 709 "Polygraph Examination Regulations'" in Chapter III of Title 10 of the Code of Federal Regulations.

90. In anticipation of the DOE regulations, attorneys representing government employees and employee prospects have indicated a desire to sue the government based on adverse employee decisions made as a result of polygraph examinations.

91. Because the government has published information only on the TES, we will refer to this procedure in the remainder of this section.

from a list of acceptable alternatives, but may include any of the following, which the examinee is directed to answer "No": "Did you ever violate a traffic law?" "Did you ever say something that you later regretted?" "Did you ever lie to a co-worker about anything at all?" Examinees who show greater autonomic disturbance following the questions about espionage and sabotage, than they show following these directed lies, are classified as deceptive.

The field validity of counterintelligence scope polygraph examinations, including the TES, is unknown. However, the Department of Defense Polygraph Institute (DoDPI) has reported two laboratory studies of the validity of the TES.[92] These both employed paid volunteers, 115 of whom were innocent while 60 others were each required to enact simulated acts of espionage or sabotage. Of the innocent subjects, 14 or 12.5% responded in the deceptive direction. Of the "guilty" subjects, 10 or 17% were misclassified as innocent.

It is obviously likely that innocent scientists or other persons with high security clearances would be more disturbed by the TES relevant questions asked during an official screening test than were these volunteers for whom the test carried no threat to their reputations or careers. The disturbance produced by the directed-lie questions, on the other hand, might be expected to be no greater in real-life than in simulated conditions of testing. Therefore, when innocent, loyal government employees with top secret classifications are subjected to the TES, one might expect many more to be classified as deceptive than the 12.5% suggested by the DoDPI studies. The actual rate of false-positive diagnoses is probably close to the 44% level indicated by the real-life studies summarized in Table I.

When DOE scientists are subjected to the planned TES (or TEST), these data indicate that large numbers of innocent employees would be classified as deceptive if the test scores were relied upon. DOE's polygraph examiners avoid any such disastrous result because they know that the base rate of spying (the proportion likely to be spies) among such a highly screened and dedicated group is likely to be tiny. Consequently, they cannot fail 44% or even 12.5% of scientists without undermining their own credibility, creating a personnel management nightmare, and wreaking havoc on employee morale.

Therefore, subjects who are more troubled by "Have you committed espionage?" than by "Did you ever say something that you later regretted?" are invited by the examiner to explain why they might have responded in this way. If the respondent's answer and demeanor satisfy the examiner, his "fail" is converted to a "pass." Thus, by permitting the polygraph operator to be the ultimate arbiter, relying on whatever clinical skills or intuitions the examiner may (or may not) possess, the frequency of false-positive diagnoses is kept to a low value. Nevertheless, if as few as 2% of the 10,000 workers potentially covered by Rule 709 receive final diagnoses of "deception indicated," 200 highly trained but probably innocent scientists would be implicated as spies in the first round of testing.[93]

92. DoDPI Study 1, *supra* note 88; DEPT. OF DEFENSE POLYGRAPH INSTITUTE, *Psychophysiological Detection of Deception Accuracy Rates Obtained using the Test for Espionage and Sabotage*, 27 POLYGRAPH 68–73 (1998).

93. The Department of Defense Polygraph Program report to Congress for Fiscal Year 2000 illustrates how polygraphers adjust the outcomes of their tests to minimize failing anyone. *Department of Defense Polygraph Program Annual Report to Congress, Fiscal Year 2000, Office of the Assistant Secretary of Defense* (2000); available at http://www.fas.org/sgp/othergov/polygraph/dod–2000.html. For fiscal year 2000, 7,688 individuals were given counterintelligence scope polygraph tests but demonstrated "no significant physiological response to the relevant ques-

Although the controversy surrounding the DOE polygraph screening program has focused on the high likelihood that innocent individuals will be judged to be spies, there is little evidence that the program will actually catch spies. The laboratory studies of the TES, which reported only 83% accuracy in identifying persons "guilty" of committing mock-espionage, overestimate accuracy for the real-life guilty in two important ways.

First, consistent with real life screening test practices that help to keep the number failing these tests low, these studies did not conclude that deceptive polygraph tests were in fact failed if, during a post-test interview, an examinee offered information that reasonably justified why the test might be a false positive outcome. However, the design of the studies allowed only innocent test subjects this opportunity to "talk their way out of" a failed test because guilty people were instructed to confess as soon as the examiner confronted them with their deceptive test results. We do not know how many guilty individuals would have been mistakenly judged "false positives" had they been allowed to try to "explain away" the outcome of their examinations.

Second, these DoDPI studies did not account for the likelihood that real spies would use countermeasures to defeat the TES. DOE scientists are not simpletons: if one or two are in fact spies, surely both they and their foreign handlers would have sense enough to be prepared to bite their tongues after each directed-lie question. Thus it is to be expected that the *only* weapons-lab scientists, with their highly specialized skills, who fail the projected DOE polygraph screens, will be truthful, honorable people who cannot offer a plausible excuse for failing their polygraphs. The most likely result of Rule 709 will be their ruined reputations and the government's loss of skilled, dedicated employees.

Besides the facts that these tests are not justified on scientific grounds and that they are clearly biased against truthful employees, there is no evidence that personnel screening tests have any true utility.[94] No spy has ever been uncovered because of a failed polygraph test. Although the government has argued that the admissions individuals make when undergoing these tests provide valuable information, there is no evidence documenting that vital or even important information has been uncovered as a result of polygraph tests. It is possible that employee screening has a deterrent effect in that knowledge that one must pass such tests may discourage would be spies from seeking employment, and it may discourage the currently employed

tions and provided no substantive information." In other words, some undetermined number provided a substantial physiological response but passed because they did not make incriminating revelations. An additional 202 individuals produced significant physiological reactions and provided "substantive information." Of these, 194 received "favorable adjudication" with the remaining 8 cases still pending decisions, with no one receiving "adverse action denying or withholding access" to classified information. These data confirm that the government goes to extreme lengths to ensure no one fails these tests, but they also demonstrate that the tests have no utility.

94. In the Clinton Administration's Joint Security Commission Report ["Redefining Security," A Report to the Secretary of Defense and the Director of Central Intelligence, February 28, 1994, Joint Security Commission, Washington, D.C. 20505; available at http://www.fas.org/sgp/library/jsc/index.html], it is noted that "the most important product of the polygraph process is more likely to be an admission made during the interview than a chart interpretation ... While senior officials at the CIA and the NSA acknowledge the controversial nature of the polygraph process, they also strongly endorse it as the most effective information gathering technique available in their personnel security systems."

from entertaining thoughts about becoming a spy. However, there is no evidence to support such an assertion. Given the ease with which individuals can learn to defeat these tests coupled with the fact that almost no one is judged to have failed them, it is unlikely that they have any serious deterrent effect.[95]

[2] Opinions of DOE National Laboratory Senior Scientists Regarding Employee Screening

Concerned by the requirement that national laboratory employees submit to periodic lie detector tests, a panel of the more senior national laboratory scientists and engineers undertook a detailed appraisal of the existing literature relating to the nature and validity of polygraph screening methods. Sandia's Senior Scientists and Engineers ("Seniors") provide a service to the Laboratories as independent, experienced, corporate evaluators of technical issues. They are available as a group to assist Sandia management with technical reviews of particularly significant issues and programs. Implementation uses subpanels of the Seniors (helped as necessary by other Sandia staff) to conduct the initial, detailed review of issues or programs. The reports of the subpanels are then made available for review by all other Seniors prior to submission to management. The report of the subpanel studying polygraphs and security at Sandia was circulated in the fall of 1999.[96]

These Seniors, whose expertise is in physics, chemistry, or mathematics, do not pretend to be psychologists, psychophysiologists, or psychometricians. But they do know how to read research reports and to evaluate statistical evidence and probabilities. In their Executive Summary, they concluded that

1) There were no adequate studies to support polygraph screening

2) It is impossible to predict what error rates to expect

3) Polygraph testing could drive away existing innocent, talented workers who have provided value to national security programs, and it would deter prospective, talented employment candidates from considering a career in the national laboratories

4) Because few spies are likely to be detected, real subversives may be more likely to become insiders—particularly if over-reliance on polygraph testing leads to reduced emphasis on other security and counterintelligence methods.

§ 10–3.4 Summary of Areas of Agreement: Topics for Future Research

The concept of the "lie detector" is so deeply entrenched in American mythology that it has proved difficult to eradicate. This aspect of American culture has never caught on in European countries although polygraphy is used by law enforcement in Canada, Israel, and Japan. However, CQT results are not admissible in the courts of these countries and, at least in Israel and

---

95. *See* footnote 93 summarizing the DoD Fiscal year 2000 report.

96. Polygraphs and Security, A Study by a Subpanel of Sandia's Senior Scientists and Engineers, October 21, 1999, Sandia, NM; available at http://www.fas.org/sgp/othergov/polygraph/sandia.html.

Japan, police polygraphers seem to prefer to use the GKT where possible, in place of the discredited methods of "lie detection." However, because it is effective, as a "bloodless 3rd degree," in inducing confessions, the polygraph is likely to continue to be valued in police work.

There is general agreement on a number of scientific issues relevant to the use of polygraph tests.

The polygraph machines used to monitor physiological responses, provided they are in good working order, provide adequate recordings.[97]

1) When these physiological signals are computerized, a properly programmed computer can provide an adequate representation of the signals. However, computerized polygraph testing does nothing to resolve any of the controversies surrounding polygraph accuracy because these controversies concern the lack of scientific support for PDD theory and the fact that the results depend on how questions are formulated and asked, unpredictable individual differences in how a person responds emotionally to control and relevant questions, and the likelihood that a guilty person will use undetected countermeasures.

2) PDD procedures are not standardized or objective. This is true about their administration and scoring.

3) The proper administration of a CQT requires the examiner to deceive the examinee by leading the examinee to believe that "failing" the control questions will lead to an deceptive verdict when in fact the opposite is true. Unless innocent people have great concern about failing the control questions, they will inadvertently respond more strongly to the relevant questions and be judged deceptive. Left unresolved is how the test can be valid for an innocent person who is unconvinced by this deception.

4) The comparison or control questions on a CQT or DLT are not controls in the scientific sense in that there is no reason to assume that relevant and control questions have equivalent psychological significance.

5) Basic questions about the reliability or consistency with which polygraph tests produce the same result remain unanswered. In particular, it is not known how likely it is that two different examiners testing the same person would obtain the same result (referred to as test-retest reliability).

6) There are no field studies of CQT accuracy with unambiguous criteria for ground truth that have overcome the confession bias problem. Consequently, there are no studies that both proponents and opponents of polygraph testing can point to as providing a valid estimate of CQT accuracy.

7) Countermeasures can be employed successfully by guilty individuals to pass a polygraph test, and the use of these countermeasures is not detectable.

97. Christopher J. Patrick & William G. Iacono, *A Comparison of Field and Laboratory* *Polygraphs in the Detection of Deception*, 28 PSYCHOPHYSIOLOGY 632–638 (1991).

8) The GKT is a scientifically sound alternative to PDD. Whether based on the measure of autonomic nervous system responses like the GSR or on brain potentials, this technique can accurately determine if someone has recognition memory for information they claim to have no knowledge of.

9) Polygraphers are not scientists, and their opinions regarding polygraph testing are not relevant to how scientists appraise polygraphy. Psychologists, especially those trained in psychophysiology, have the requisite knowledge to evaluate these psychologically based PDD techniques.

10) Personnel screening cannot be scientifically justified. These PDD procedures are biased against the innocent, and have not even been shown to have the kind of utility that the CQT has.

§ 10–3.4.1 The Future of the "Lie Detector"

Because the CQT and its progeny are based on such implausible assumptions, it is unlikely that future research will do more than confirm the present view of the scientific community that these techniques have negligible validity.[98] As we have seen, the fatal defects of the CQT are: (1) innocent suspects are likely to be more disturbed by the relevant questions than by the comparison questions, while (2) sophisticated guilty suspects can easily (and without being detected) self-stimulate so as to augment their responses to the comparison questions and thus to beat the test. Whether scientifically supportable alternative lie detection techniques can be developed remains to be seen. It is well established that cognitive effort produces pupillary dilation and that the greater the effort, the larger the pupillary change. Building on this fact, it has recently been shown that giving a narrative (rather than a Yes or No) answer to a question produces greater pupillary dilation when the answer is deceptive rather than truthful.[99] Although such work requires replication and study in real-life applications, it illustrates that it may be possible to develop instrumental lie detection techniques that circumvent the weaknesses of CQT polygraphy.

§ 10–3.4.2 The Future of the Guilty Knowledge Test

The detection of guilty knowledge, on the other hand, is entirely feasible from a scientific point of view and the limited research so far conducted with the GKT indicates that this technique works just as the theory would predict. The GKT cannot be employed in many situations where lie detection is now used. Its utility is limited to those instances in which the investigator can identify a number of facts about the crime scene that are likely to be recognized by a guilty suspect but not by one without guilty knowledge. But it is important to realize that many celebrated criminal cases, including those involving espionage, could have been solved with dispatch and a high level of statistical confidence had the defendant been administered a GKT.

98. A recent analysis of CQT polygraphy in light of *Daubert* has reached a similar conclusion. Leonard Saxe & Gershon Ben–Shakar, *Admissibility of Polygraph Tests: The Application of Scientific Standards Post–Daubert*, 5 PSYCHOL. L., & PUB. POL'Y, 203 (1999).

99. Daphne P. Dionisio et al., *Differentiation of Deception Using Pupillary Responses as an Index of Cognitive Processing*, 38 PSYCHOPHYSIOLOGY 205–211 (2001).

One example is the case of the missing computer hard drives at the Los Alamos nuclear facility.[100] These laptop drives, about the size of a deck of playing cards, contained nuclear secrets and were missing for as long as six months. They reappeared in a package behind a photocopying machine in one of the nuclear facility buildings. The members of the Los Alamos "X Division" that was entrusted with the security of the drives were flown to Albuquerque for a day and polygraphed, but the mystery regarding who placed the drives behind the photocopier remains unsolved. Had the FBI not publicized the recovery of the drives, the information regarding their whereabouts could have been used to develop a GKT which then could have been administered to X Division personnel. For instance, only the guilty individual would know in what building and room the drive was deposited, that it was placed behind a photocopier, and that it was in a certain type of packaging. The GKT also has screening applications. For instance, notorious FBI spy Robert Hanssen reportedly hacked into a secure computer to access secrets.[101] Hanson and any agent could be routinely asked to take a ERP–GKT where various words and pictures would be flashed, including those associated with information the tested person should not have memory for. Probe words in such a test might include the classified computer password that was last in effect, file names, pictures of computer screens that would have to be processed to access information, and other items that would be salient to someone who gathered information from the computer. To an innocent person, all of these stimuli, mixed in with foils, would evoke no memories or P3 wave. A guilty person, by contrast, would show a P3 recognition response to the probe items.

The GKT has not been used by US law enforcement for two reasons. First, there remains a strong, albeit unjustified, faith in "lie detection" which is so much easier to employ. Secondly, use of the GKT requires that the person who will identify the facts to be used in GKT items must visit the crime scene with the original investigative team. Polygraph examiners do not visit crime scenes and criminalists are not yet being trained to develop GKT items that might later be used by polygraph examiners. It is possible, however, that the apparent possibilities of this technique will come to be exploited in the future. If that time does come, the courts may have occasion to consider such questions as the admissibility of GKT results or whether requiring a suspect to undergo a GKT examination is equivalent to requiring him to permit a photograph or a blood sample to be taken.

§ 10–3.4.3   To Accept the Pro–Polygraph Arguments, One Must Believe

Scientists have often noted that extraordinary claims demand extraordinary supporting evidence. With no solid scientific foundation and a lack of methodologically sound supporting research, the claims that polygraph tests are up to 95% accurate demand close scrutiny. As a convenience to the reader, we conclude by summarizing what would be required to accept the proponents' conclusions about lie detector tests in preference to ours, as follows:

100. *FBI Ends Inquiry in Los Alamos*, New York Times, January 19, 2001.

101. *A Search for Answers: The Suspect; FBI Never Gave Lie Test to Agent Charged as Spy*, New York Times, February 22, 2001.

[1]   Regarding Surveys of the Scientific Community:

That two surveys, one by Amato and Honts and the other by the Gallup organization, neither of which was published in a scientific journal, and neither of which asks directly about the scientific soundness of the CQT or the desirability of using it in legal proceedings, are to be preferred over our surveys of two different scientific organizations, each yielding very similar and overwhelmingly negative results, a study that was published in a scientific journal that regularly rejects over 85% of submitted papers.

That the SPR survey of Amato and Honts, which obtained a response rate of only 30%, did a fairer job capturing the opinions of the relevant scientific community than our survey to which 91% responded.

[2]   Regarding Countermeasures:

That, in real life, subjects cannot be expected to learn how to employ countermeasures despite the widespread availability of information, in the library or on the internet, on how to accomplish this objective and Raskin, Honts and Kircher's published work showing that guilty subjects can successfully employ countermeasures with no more than a half-hour of instruction.[102]

[3]   Regarding the Directed Lie Test:

That the results of the directed lie test, a procedure that has received little systematic scientific study and that is not even generally accepted by the professional polygraph community,[103] meets the *Daubert* standards for credible scientific evidence.

[4]   Regarding Friendly Polygraph Tests:

That polygraph tests arranged by a suspect's defense counsel, the results of which are protected by attorney-client privilege, involve the same degree of fear of detection as adversarial tests administered by the police, the results of which are available to the prosecution.

That friendly tests meet the *Daubert* standard despite the absence of even one empirical study attesting to the accuracy of these tests.

[5]   Regarding Laboratory Studies:

That laboratory studies in which participants are passive recipients of instructions to carry out mock crimes, and which are without the fear of detection that exists in real-life polygraph tests, can be used to accurately estimate the validity of lie detector tests in real life.

102. Besides countermeasure information being available in university libraries, in texts such as this, it is also available in public libraries and bookstores in Lykken's books (cited in footnote 73), and on the worldwide web under www.polygraph.com, www.antipolygraph.org, and www.nopolygraph.com.

103. Responding to a request for information made under the Freedom of Information Act, the Department of Defense Polygraph Institute's Dr. Gordon Barland noted in October of 1996 that "we do not teach, nor do we advocate, [the directed lie test's] use in criminal testing."

[6] Regarding Field Studies:

That those field studies, in which polygraph-induced confessions are the basis for determining ground truth, can be used to estimate CQT accuracy when the only cases selected for study are likely to be the ones that were scored correctly by the original examiner.

[7] Regarding Industry Standards:

That polygraph testing is standardized enough to constitute a scientific test when in fact there are no standards as to what constitutes an acceptable test and the nature of individually administered CQTs varies substantially from one examiner to another.

[8] Regarding Personnel Screening:

That government use of screening tests is justified despite their being strongly biased against the innocent and a complete lack of evidence that they either catch or deter spies.

CHAPTER 11

DNA TYPING*

Table of Sections

A. LEGAL ISSUES

* This chapter is a revised and expanded version of David H. Kaye & George F. Sensabaugh, Jr., *Reference Guide on DNA Evidence*, *in* REFERENCE MANUAL ON SCIENTIFIC EVIDENCE 485 (Federal Judicial Center, 2d ed.2000).

Westlaw Electronic Research

See Westlaw Electronic Research Guide preceding the Summary of Contents.

A.   LEGAL ISSUES

§ 11–1.0   THE LEGAL RELEVANCE OF DNA TESTS

§ 11–1.1   Introduction

Deoxyribonucleic acid, or DNA, is a molecule that encodes the genetic information in all living organisms. Its chemical structure was elucidated in 1954. More than 30 years later, samples of human DNA began to be used in the criminal justice system, primarily in cases of rape or murder. The evidence has been the subject of extensive scrutiny by lawyers, judges, and the scientific community.[1] It is now admissible in virtually all jurisdictions,[2] but

---

§ 11–1.0

1. At the request of various government agencies, the National Research Council em-

paneled two committees for the National Academy of Sciences that produced book-length reports on forensic DNA technology, debate lingers over the safeguards that should be required in testing samples and in presenting the evidence in court.[3] Moreover, there are many types of DNA analysis, and still more are being developed.[4] New problems of admissibility arise as advancing methods of analysis and novel applications of established methods are introduced.

This chapter identifies the legal issues pertaining to the admissibility of and weight of DNA evidence of identity, and it describes the science and technology of forensic DNA analysis.[5] Section 11–1.1 discusses the major objections that have been raised to the admission of DNA evidence. Section 11–1.2 outlines the types of scientific expertise that go into the analysis of DNA samples.

Section 11–2.1 gives an overview of the scientific principles behind DNA typing. It describes the structure of DNA and how this molecule differs from person to person. These are basic facts of molecular biology. The section also defines the more important scientific terms. It explains at a general level how DNA differences are detected. These are matters of analytical chemistry and laboratory procedure. Finally, the section indicates how it is shown that these differences permit individuals to be identified. This is accomplished with the methods of probability and statistics.

The next two sections outline basic methods used in DNA testing. Section 11–2.2 describes methods that begin by using the polymerase chain reaction (PCR) to make many copies of short segments of DNA. Section 11–2.3 examines the theory and technique of the older procedure of measuring restriction fragment length polymorphisms (RFLPs) due to variable number tandem repeats (VNTRs).

Section 11–2.4 considers issues of sample quantity and quality common to all methods of DNA profiling. Section 11–2.5 deals with laboratory performance. It outlines the types of information that a laboratory should produce

with recommendations for enhancing the rigor of laboratory work and improving the presentation of the evidence in court. COMMITTEE ON DNA TECHNOLOGY IN FORENSIC SCIENCE, NATIONAL RESEARCH COUNCIL, DNA TECHNOLOGY IN FORENSIC SCIENCE (1992) [hereinafter NRC I]; COMMITTEE ON DNA FORENSIC SCIENCE: AN UPDATE, NATIONAL RESEARCH COUNCIL, THE EVALUATION OF FORENSIC DNA EVIDENCE (1996) [hereinafter NRC II].

2. For reviews of the challenges to admissibility, see Paul C. Giannelli, *The DNA Story: An Alternative View*, 88 J. CRIM. L. & CRIMIN. 380 (1997) (concluding that courts were too willing to admit an untested technology); David H. Kaye, *DNA Evidence: Probability, Population Genetics, and the Courts*, 7 HARV. J. L. & TECH. 101 (1993) (suggesting that the principal objection to the computations of random match probabilities was exaggerated); William C. Thompson, *Evaluating the Admissibility of New Genetic Identification Tests: Lessons from the "DNA War,"* 84 J. CRIM. L. & CRIMIN. 22 (1993) (reviewing the debate on population

structure but not discussing studies indicating that the effect is generally minor). Some of the leading opinions are reproduced in D.H. KAYE, SCIENCE IN EVIDENCE (1997).

3. *See* D.H. Kaye, *DNA, NAS, NRC, DAB, RFLP, PCR, and More: An Introduction to the Symposium on the 1996 NRC Report on Forensic DNA Evidence*, 37 JURIMETRICS J. 395 (1997); William C. Thompson, *Guide to Forensic DNA Evidence, in* EXPERT EVIDENCE: A PRACTITIONER'S GUIDE TO LAW, SCIENCE, AND THE *FJC MANUAL* 185 (Bert Black & Patrick W. Lee eds., 1997).

4. See NATIONAL COMMISSION ON THE FUTURE OF DNA EVIDENCE, THE FUTURE OF FORENSIC DNA TESTING: PREDICTIONS OF THE RESEARCH AND DEVELOPMENT WORKING GROUP (2000); *infra* § 11–2.1.

5. Leading cases are collected in tables in NRC II, *supra* note 1, at 205–11. For subsequent developments, see D.H. Kaye, *DNA Identification in Criminal Cases: Lingering and Emerging Evidentiary Issues, in* PROCEEDINGS OF THE SEVENTH INTERNATIONAL SYMPOSIUM ON HUMAN IDENTIFICATION 12 (1997).

to establish that it can analyze DNA reliably and that it has adhered to established laboratory protocols.

Section 11–2.6 examines issues in the interpretation of laboratory results. To assist the courts in understanding the extent to which the results incriminate the defendant, it enumerates the hypotheses that need to be considered before concluding that the defendant is the source of the crime-scene samples, and it explores the issues that arise in judging the strength of the evidence. It focuses on questions of statistics, probability, and population genetics.

Section 11–2.7 takes up novel applications of DNA technology, such as the forensic analysis of nonhuman DNA. It identifies questions that can be useful in judging whether a new method or application has the scientific merit and power claimed by the proponent of the evidence. An appendix provides detail on technical material, and the glossary defines selected terms and acronyms encountered in genetics, molecular biology, and forensic DNA work.[6]

§ 11–1.2   Objections to DNA Evidence

The usual objective of forensic DNA analysis is to detect variations in the genetic material that differentiate individuals one from another.[7] Laboratory techniques for isolating and analyzing DNA have long been used in scientific research and medicine. Applications of these techniques to forensic work usually involve comparing a DNA sample obtained from a suspect with a DNA sample obtained from the crime scene. Often, a perpetrator's DNA in hair, blood, saliva, or semen can be found at a crime scene,[8] or a victim's DNA can be found on or around the perpetrator.[9]

In many cases, defendants have objected to the admission of testimony of a match or its implications.[10] Under *Daubert v. Merrell Dow Pharmaceuticals,*

---

6. The glossary defines the words and phrases that are italicized in the text as well as a number of other terms that may be used by experts in these fields.

7. Biologists accept as a truism the proposition that, except for identical twins, human beings are genetically unique. Consequently, in principle, DNA samples can be used to distinguish all individuals who are not identical twins from all other human beings. As discussed *infra* Chapter 26, DNA analysis also can be used to ascertain whether individuals are members of the same family.

8. *E.g.,* United States v. Beasley, 102 F.3d 1440 (8th Cir.1996) (two hairs were found in a mask used in a bank robbery and left in the abandoned get-away car); United States v. Two Bulls, 918 F.2d 56 (8th Cir.1990), *vacated for reh'g en banc, app. dismissed due to death of defendant,* 925 F.2d 1127 (8th Cir.1991) (semen stain on victim's underwear).

9. *E.g.,* United States v. Cuff, 37 F.Supp.2d 279 (S.D.N.Y.1999) (scrapings from defendant's fingernails); State v. Bible, 175 Ariz. 549, 858 P.2d 1152 (Ariz.1993) (blood stains on defendant's shirt); People v. Castro, 144 Misc.2d 956, 545 N.Y.S.2d 985 (Bronx Co.Sup. Ct.1989) (bloodstains on defendant's watch). For brevity, we refer only to the typical case of

a perpetrator's DNA at a crime scene. The scientific and legal issues in both situations are the same.

10. Exclusion of the testimony can be sought before or during trial, depending on circumstances and the court's rules regarding pretrial motions. Pretrial requests for discovery and the appointment of experts to assist the defense also can require judicial involvement. *See, e.g.,* Dubose v. State, 662 So.2d 1189 (Ala.1995) (holding that due process was violated by the failure to provide an indigent defendant with funds for an expert); Cade v. State, 658 So.2d 550 (Fla.Ct.App.1995) (abuse of discretion under state statute to deny defense request for appointment of DNA expert even though there was no showing of specific need, but only the general observation that I can't tell the Court what I'm looking for because "it's so complicated"); State v. Scott, 33 S.W.3d 746 (Tenn.2000) (trial court erred in not appoint an expert for an indigent defendant where the rule requiring a showing of "particularized need" for an expert to assist defense counsel with regard to mitochondrial DNA testing had been shown); NRC II, *supra* note 1, at 167–69; Paul C. Giannelli, Book Review, *The DNA Story: An Alternative View,* 88 J. Crim. L. & Criminology 380, 414–17 (1997)

Inc.,[11] the district court, in its role as "gatekeeper" for scientific evidence, then must assure that the expert's methods are scientifically valid and reliable. Under *Frye v. United States*,[12] the question is narrowed to whether the methods are general accepted in the relevant scientific community.

Because the basic theory and most of the laboratory techniques of DNA profiling are so widely accepted in the scientific world, disputed issues involve features unique to their forensic applications or matters of laboratory technique. These include the extent to which standard techniques have been shown to work with crime-scene samples exposed to sunlight, heat, bacteria, and chemicals in the environment; the extent to which the specific laboratory has demonstrated its ability to follow protocols that have been validated to work for crime-scene samples; possible ambiguities that might interfere with the interpretation of test results; and the validity and possible prejudicial impact of estimates of the probability of a match between the crime-scene samples and innocent suspects. As explained below, some of these objections— particularly those involving probability and statistics—generally have proved more effective than others.

§ 11–1.2.1   Historical Overview

The history of the judicial treatment of DNA evidence can be divided into at least five phases.[13] The first phase was one of rapid and sometimes uncritical acceptance. Initial praise for RFLP testing in homicide, rape, paternity, and other cases was effusive. Indeed, one judge proclaimed "DNA fingerprinting" to be "the single greatest advance in the 'search for truth' . . . since the advent of cross-examination."[14] In this first wave of cases, expert testimony for the prosecution rarely was countered, and courts readily admitted RFLP findings.[15]

In a second wave of cases, however, defendants pointed to problems at two levels—controlling the experimental conditions of the analysis and interpreting the results.[16] Some scientists questioned certain features of the procedures for extracting and analyzing DNA employed in forensic laboratories. It became apparent that determining whether RFLPs in VNTR loci in

---

(criticizing the reluctance of state courts to appoint defense experts and to grant discovery requests); Paul C. Giannelli, *Criminal Discovery, Scientific Evidence, and DNA*, 44 Vand. L. Rev. 791 (1991); Jay A. Zollinger, Comment, *Defense Access to State–Funded DNA Experts: Considerations of Due Process*, 85 Calif. L. Rev. 1803 (1997).

11. 509 U.S. 579, 113 S.Ct. 2786, 125 L.Ed.2d 469 (1993).

12. 293 F. 1013 (D.C.Cir.1923).

13. This history of the judicial reception of DNA evidence is adapted from 1 McCormick on Evidence § 205 (John Strong ed., 5th ed.1999), and Edward J. Imwinkelried & D.H. Kaye, *DNA Typing: Emerging or Neglected Issues*, 76 Wash. L. Rev. 413 (2001).

14. People v. Wesley, 140 Misc.2d 306, 533 N.Y.S.2d 643 (Albany County Ct.1988).

15. Andrews v. State, 533 So.2d 841 (Fla. Ct.App.1988); *Wesley*, 140 Misc.2d 306, 533 N.Y.S.2d 643 (1988); Spencer v. Common-

wealth, 238 Va. 275, 384 S.E.2d 775 (Va.1989) (early version of DQα test properly admitted where "[t]he record is replete with uncontradicted expert testimony that no 'dissent whatsoever (exists) in the scientific community' "); State v. Woodall, 182 W.Va. 15, 385 S.E.2d 253 (1989) (taking judicial notice of general scientific acceptance where there was no expert testimony, but holding that inconclusive results were properly excluded as irrelevant); Thomas M. Fleming, Annotation, *Admissibility of DNA Identification Evidence*, 84 A.L.R.4th 313 (1991).

16. For a comprehensive survey of possible sources of error and ambiguity in VNTR profiling, see William Thompson & Simon Ford, *The Meaning of a Match: Sources of Ambiguity in the Interpretation of DNA Prints, in* Forensic DNA Technology 93 (M.A. Farley & J.J. Harrington eds., 1990).

two samples actually match can be complicated by measurement variability or missing or spurious bands.[17] Despite these concerns, most cases continued to find forensic RFLP analyses to be generally accepted,[18] and a number of states provided for admissibility of DNA tests by legislation.[19] Concerted attacks by defense experts of impeccable credentials, however, produced a few cases rejecting specific proffers on the ground that the testing procedure was not sufficiently rigorous.[20] Moreover, a minority of courts, perhaps concerned that DNA evidence might well be conclusive in the minds of jurors, added a "third prong" to the general acceptance standard.[21] This augmented *Frye* test re-

17. *See* United States v. Yee, 134 F.R.D. 161 (N.D.Ohio 1991), *aff'd sub nom.* United States v. Bonds, 12 F.3d 540 (6th Cir.1993); Anderson, *DNA Fingerprinting on Trial*, 342 NATURE 844 (1989); Thompson & Ford, *Is DNA Fingerprinting Ready for the Courts?*, NEW SCIENTIST, Mar. 31, 1990, at 38; Gina Kolata, *Some Scientists Doubt the Value of "Genetic Fingerprint" Evidence*, N.Y. TIMES, Jan. 29, 1990, at A1 col. 1 (reporting that "[l]eading molecular biologists say a technique promoted by the nation's top law-enforcement agency for identifying suspects in criminal trials through the analysis of genetic material is too unreliable to be used in court"; but the accuracy of this report is seriously questioned in Andre Moenssens, *DNA Evidence and Its Critics—How Valid Are the Challenges?*, 31 JURIMETRICS J. 87 (1990)).

18. *E.g.*, *Yee*, 134 F.R.D. 161 (1991); State v. Pennington, 327 N.C. 89, 393 S.E.2d 847 (N.C.1990) (uncontradicted expert testimony that false positives are impossible); Glover v. State, 787 S.W.2d 544 (Tex.Ct.App.1990) (admissible in light of other decisions where "[a]ppellant did not produce any expert testimony").

19. MD. CODE ANN. CTS. & JUD. PROC. CODE ANN. § 10–915 (Michie Supp.1992) ("In any criminal proceeding, the evidence of a DNA profile is admissible to prove or disprove the identity of any person"); MINN. STAT. ANN. § 634.25 (West Supp.1992) ("In a criminal trial or hearing, the results of DNA analysis . . . are admissible in evidence without antecedent expert testimony that DNA analysis provides a trustworthy and reliable method of identifying characteristics in an individual's genetic material upon a showing that the offered testimony meets the standards for admissibility set forth in the Rules of Evidence."); Kenneth E. Melson, *Legal and Ethical Considerations, in* DNA FINGERPRINTING: AN INTRODUCTION 189, 199–200 (Lorne T. Kirby ed., 1990).

20. People v. Castro, 144 Misc.2d 956, 545 N.Y.S.2d 985, 995 (Sup.Ct.1989) (principles of DNA testing generally accepted, but "[i]n a piercing attack upon each molecule of evidence presented, the defense was successful in demonstrating to this court that the testing laboratory failed in its responsibility to perform the accepted scientific techniques and experiments"); State v. Schwartz, 447 N.W.2d 422,

428 (Minn.1989) ("DNA typing has gained general acceptance in the scientific community," but "the laboratory in this case did not comport" with "appropriate standards"); Colin Norman, *Maine Case Deals a Blow to DNA Fingerprinting*, 246 SCIENCE 1556 (1989); Rorie Sherman, *DNA Tests Unravel?*, NAT'L L.J., Dec. 18, 1989, at 1, 24–25.

Some commentators have assumed or argued that some or all of these issues are aspects of admissibility under Rule 702. *E.g.*, Edward J. Imwinkelried, *The Debate in the DNA Cases over the Foundation for the Admission of Scientific Evidence: The Importance of Human Error as a Cause of Forensic Misanalysis*, 69 WASH. U. L.Q. 19 (1991); Barry C. Scheck, *DNA and Daubert*, 15 CARDOZO L. REV. 1959, 1979–87 (1994); William C. Thompson, *Accepting Lower Standards: The National Research Council's Second Report on Forensic DNA Evidence*, 37 JURIMETRICS J. 405, 417 (1997). This reading of *Daubert* is rejected in *United States v. Shea*, 957 F.Supp. 331, 340–41 (D.N.H.1997), but the protocols of a specific laboratory and the proficiency of its analysts are factors that affect probative value under Rule 403. *See* Margaret A. Berger, *Laboratory Error Seen Through the Lens of Science and Policy*, 30 U.C. DAVIS L. REV. 1081 (1997); Edward J. Imwinkelried, *The Case Against Evidentiary Admissibility Standards that Attempt to "Freeze" the State of a Scientific Technique*, 67 U. COLO. L. REV. 887 (1996).

21. This innovation was introduced in *People v. Castro*, 144 Misc.2d 956, 545 N.Y.S.2d 985 (1989). It soon spread. *See* United States v. Two Bulls, 918 F.2d 56, 61 (8th Cir.1990) ("it was error for the trial court to determine the admissibility of the DNA evidence without determining whether the testing procedures . . . were conducted properly"), *vacated for rehearing en banc, app. dismissed due to death of defendant*, 925 F.2d 1127 (8th Cir.1991); *Ex parte* Perry, 586 So.2d 242 (Ala.1991). For cases declining to graft a "third prong" onto *Frye*, see, for example, State v. Bible, 175 Ariz. 549, 858 P.2d 1152 (Ariz.1993); Hopkins v. State, 579 N.E.2d 1297 (Ind.1991); State v. Ferguson, 20 S.W.3d 485, 495 (Mo.2000); State v. Vandebogart, 136 N.H. 365, 616 A.2d 483 (N.H.1992); State v. Cauthron, 120 Wash.2d 879, 846 P.2d 502 (Wash.1993).

quires not only proof of the general acceptance of the ability of science to produce the type of results offered in court, but also a showing of the proper application of an approved method on the particular occasion.[22] Whether this inquiry is properly part of the special screening of scientific methodology, however, is debatable.[23]

A different attack on DNA profiling that began in cases during this period proved far more successful and led to a third wave of cases in which many courts held that estimates of the probability of a coincidentally matching VNTR profile were inadmissible.[24] These estimates relied on a simplified population-genetics model for the frequencies of VNTR profiles that treats each race as a large, randomly mating population. Some prominent scientists claimed that the applicability of the model had not been adequately verified.[25] A heated debate on this point spilled over from courthouses to scientific journals and convinced the supreme courts of several states that general acceptance was lacking.[26] A 1992 report of the National Academy of Sciences proposed a more "conservative" computational method as a compromise,[27] and this seemed to undermine the claim of scientific acceptance of the less conservative procedure that was in general use.[28]

At this juncture the history was poised to enter a fourth phase. In response to the population-genetics criticism and the 1992 National Academy of Sciences report came an outpouring of both critiques of the report and new studies of the distribution of VNTR alleles in many population groups. Relying on the burgeoning literature, a second National Academy panel concluded in 1996 that the usual method of estimating frequencies of VNTR

---

22. Later, some courts insisted on such a showing as part of the demonstration of scientific soundness required under *Daubert*. *E.g.*, United States v. Martinez, 3 F.3d 1191 (8th Cir.1993).

23. For an analysis concluding that such matters are better handled not as part of the special test for scientific evidence, but as aspects of the balancing of probative value and prejudice, see Margaret A. Berger, *Laboratory Error Seen Through the Lens of Science and Policy*, 30 U.C. DAVIS L. REV. 1081 (1997); *see also supra* note 20.

24. *See* NRC II, *supra* note 1, at 205–11 (exhaustively tabulating cases); David H. Kaye, *DNA Evidence: Probability, Population Genetics, and the Courts*, 7 HARV. J. L. & TECH. 101 (1993).

25. *See* Kaye, *supra* note 24; Thompson, *supra* note 2. In the light of the totality of information on the distribution of various genes in populations, the criticism of the simple random-mating model may have been overblown. *See* Bernard Devlin & Kathryn Roeder, *DNA Profiling: Statistics and Population Genetics*, *in* 1 MODERN SCIENTIFIC EVIDENCE: THE LAW AND SCIENCE OF EXPERT TESTIMONY 710 (David Faigman et al. eds., 1997).

In addition to questioning the model for combining allele frequencies, a few experts testified that no meaningful conclusions can be drawn in the absence of random sampling. *E.g.*, People v. Soto, 21 Cal.4th 512, 88 Cal. Rptr.2d 34, 981 P.2d 958 (Cal.1999); State v. Anderson, 118 N.M. 284, 881 P.2d 29, 39 (N.M. 1994). The Arizona Supreme Court accepted this argument but later retreated from its implications. *See* D.H. Kaye, Bible *Reading: DNA Evidence in Arizona*, 28 ARIZ. ST. L.J. 1035 (1996). The scientific basis for the argument is considered in *id.* and *infra* § 11–2.6.

Another related concern was that the early, nonrandom samples were too small to give good estimates of allele frequencies. This argument generally proved unpersuasive. *E.g.*, United States v. Shea, 957 F.Supp. 331 (D.N.H.1997); People v. Soto, 35 Cal.Rptr.2d 846, 30 Cal.App.4th 340 (Cal.Ct.App.1994), *aff'd*, 21 Cal.4th 512, 88 Cal.Rptr.2d 34, 981 P.2d 958 (1999); State v. Dishon, 297 N.J.Super. 254, 687 A.2d 1074, 1090 (N.J.Super.Ct.App.1997); State v. Copeland, 130 Wash.2d 244, 922 P.2d 1304, 1321 (Wash. 1996).

26. *See* Kaye, *supra* note 24.

27. NRC I, *supra* note 1.

28. *See* D.H. Kaye, *The Forensic Debut of the National Research Council's DNA Report: Population Structure, Ceiling Frequencies and the Need for Numbers*, 96 GENETICA 99 (1995), published in slightly different form in 34 JURI-METRICS J. 369 (1994).

profiles in broad racial groups was sound.[29] In the fourth phase of judicial scrutiny of DNA evidence, the courts almost invariably returned to the earlier view that the statistics associated with VNTR profiling are generally accepted and scientifically valid.[30]

The fifth phase of the judicial evaluation of DNA evidence is well underway. As results obtained with the new PCR-based methods enter the courtroom, it becomes necessary to ask whether each such method rests on a solid scientific foundation or is generally accepted in the scientific community.[31] Sometimes, the answer will be obvious even without an extensive pretrial

29. NRC II, *supra* note 1. The 1996 report provides more refined methods for estimating allele frequencies in ethnic subpopulations.

30. *See, e.g.,* People v. Soto, 21 Cal.4th 512, 88 Cal.Rptr.2d 34, 981 P.2d 958, 974 (Cal.1999) ("Several developments since the filing of *Barney* indicate the controversy over population substructuring and use of the unmodified product rule has dissipated."); People v. Miller, 173 Ill.2d 167, 219 Ill.Dec. 43, 670 N.E.2d 721, 731–32 (Ill.1996) ("while there has been some controversy over the use of the product rule in calculating the frequency of a DNA match, that controversy appears to be dissipating"); Armstead v. State, 342 Md. 38, 673 A.2d 221, 238 (Md.1996) ("the debate over the product rule essentially ended in 1993"); Commonwealth v. Fowler, 425 Mass. 819, 685 N.E.2d 746 (Mass. 1997) (product rule with and without ceilings for VNTRs now meets test of scientific reliability in light of 1996 NRC Report), *departing from* Commonwealth v. Lanigan, 413 Mass. 154, 596 N.E.2d 311 (Mass.1992) (dispute over population structure evinces lack of general acceptance).

Despite these reassuring statements, the "basic product rule" (*see infra* § 11–2.6) is an approximation that is not universally appropriate. A more refined method for handling population structure is available. *See infra* § 11–2.6. The district court in *United States v. Shea,* 957 F.Supp. 331, 343 (D.N.H.1997), held that a random match probability using this F_{ST} adjustment satisfies *Daubert. See also* United States v. Gaines, 979 F.Supp. 1429 (S.D.Fla. 1997). When insufficient data are present to use this method, still other approaches have been proposed. *See infra* § 11–2.6. One such approach was used in *United States v. Chischilly,* 30 F.3d 1144, 1158 n. 29 (9th Cir.1994), to handle the concern that the FBI had insufficient data on VNTR allele frequencies among Navajos. In *Government of the Virgin Islands v. Byers,* 941 F.Supp. 513 (D.Vi.1996), two black men in St. Thomas engaged in "a four-month crime spree" of rape, robbery, kidnaping, and burglary. *Id.* at 514. After one woman was raped a second time by the pair, she identified one as Byers. Byers pled guilty to various charges and testified against an acquaintance, whom the FBI linked to three victims by a three-locus VNTR profile. *Id.* Random match probabilities for African–Americans, whites,

and Hispanics were estimated from the FBI's databases, which did not include inhabitants of St. Thomas. The defendant argued that because the African–American database did not include Afro–Caribbeans, the probabilities were inadmissible. *Id.* at 515. The district court reasoned that:

[A]s the 1996 NRC Report concluded, population subgrouping is important only if we know that the suspect is a member of a particular subgroup. All that was known about the suspect in this case was his race. The victims did not indicate whether he was a transplanted North American, a native St. Thomian, or an immigrant from one of the other Caribbean islands. As recommended by the 1996 NRC Report, the FBI's database for Blacks was used in comparing the defendant's DNA profile since the suspect's race is known in this case. Because investigators did not know the subgroup to which the suspect belonged, there was no need to compare the defendant's DNA profile with any subgroup. The FBI procedure of giving DNA frequency estimations for several different racial groups was more than adequate under the circumstances.

Id. at 522. In our view, the court's reliance on Recommendation 4.1 of the 1996 report was misplaced. Although the victims could not know with certainty whether their assailants were African–American or Afro–Caribbean, the locale of the crimes indicates that the suspect population was dominated by the latter, and that group is not a subpopulation of the African–American population for which a database is available. Consequently, Recommendation 4.3 of the 1996 NRC report would seem to apply. Nevertheless, by crediting FBI testimony that the distribution of VNTR alleles in African–Americans is similar to that in Afro–Caribbeans, the court followed the substance of Recommendation 4.3. *Id.*; *see also* Government of Virgin Islands v. Penn, 838 F.Supp. 1054, 1071 (D.Vi.1993) ("any concern that the St. Thomas' black population's bin frequencies are drastically different from those of the United States black population is unwarranted").

31. *E.g.,* Harrison v. State, 644 N.E.2d 1243 (Ind.1995) (error not to hold *Frye* hearing on PCR-based method). *But see* State v. Scott,

hearing.[32] The opinions are practically unanimous in holding that the more commonly used PCR-based procedures satisfy these standards.[33]

In sum, in little more than a decade, DNA typing has made the transition from a novel set of methods for identification to a relatively mature and well studied forensic technology. However, one should not lump all forms of DNA identification together. New techniques and applications continue to emerge. These range from the use of new genetic systems and new analytical procedures to the typing of DNA from plants and animals. Before admitting such evidence, it will be necessary to inquire into the biological principles and knowledge that would justify inferences from these new technologies or applications.[34] For example, a court's prior approval of RFLP testing by gel electrophoresis or reverse dot blot testing of PCR-amplified fragments containing the HLA DQⵑ gene does not dictate the conclusion that the court also must accept testing at STR loci or mitochondrial DNA sequencing. The newer technologies generally are gaining judicial approval,[35] but a court should not

33 S.W.3d 746 (Tenn.2000) (a state statute providing that "the results of DNA analysis . . . are admissible in evidence without antecedent expert testimony that DNA analysis provides a trustworthy and reliable method of identifying characteristics in an individual's genetic material upon a showing that the offered testimony meets the standards of admissibility set forth in the Tennessee Rules of Evidence" made a hearing on the scientific soundness of mitochondrial DNA testing unnecessary).

32. For example, a procedure may be so similar to accepted protocols that acceptance or validity can be inferred from previous cases. *See* United States v. Johnson, 56 F.3d 947 (8th Cir.1995) (in response to a defense expert's testimony that a police department's variation on the FBI protocol for RFLP–VNTR testing had not been validated, the court held that the variation did not preclude admission where an FBI analyst testified that the difference was of no significance); People v. Oliver, 306 Ill. App.3d 59, 239 Ill.Dec. 196, 713 N.E.2d 727, 734 (Ill.Ct.App.1999) ("the minor variations . . . in the . . . second RFLP test did not render it a new scientific technique for the purposes of *Frye*."). A closer case is *People v. Hill*, 89 Cal.App.4th 48, 107 Cal.Rptr.2d 110, 119 (Ct. App.2001) (PCR-based STR typing is generally accepted, and the particular instrument, "Profiler Plus," used to do it need not be validated because it "does not embrace new scientific techniques"); *cf.* State v. Gore, 143 Wash.2d 288, 21 P.3d 262 (Wash.2001) ("We decline to hold that each time new loci are involved in DNA testing, a *Frye* hearing must be held"). In general, trial courts have considerable "latitude in deciding how to test an expert's reliability, and to decide whether or when special briefing or other proceedings are needed to investigate reliability." Kumho Tire Co., Ltd. v. Carmichael, 526 U.S. 137, 119 S.Ct. 1167, 143 L.Ed.2d 238 (1999).

33. People v. Hill, 89 Cal.App.4th 48, 107 Cal.Rptr.2d 110 (Ct.App.2001) (PCR-based STR typing is generally accepted); People v. Allen, 85 Cal.Rptr.2d 655, 72 Cal.App.4th 1093 (Ct.App.1999) (STR testing); People v. Shreck, 22 P.3d 68 (Colo.2001) (concluding that D1S80 and STR multiplex typing is generally accepted and valid); State v. Roth, 2000 WL 970673 (Del.Super.Ct.2000) (determining that STR analysis satisfies *Daubert*); Commonwealth v. Rosier, 425 Mass. 807, 685 N.E.2d 739 (Mass. 1997) (STR testing); Commonwealth v. Vao Sok, 425 Mass. 787, 683 N.E.2d 671, 672–73 (Mass.1997) (DQⵑ, Polymarker, and D1S80 analysis "meet the test of scientific reliability"); Hughes v. State, 735 So.2d 238 (Miss. 1999) (unspecified PCR method deemed reliable); State v. Jackson, 255 Neb. 68, 582 N.W.2d 317 (Neb.1998) (STR testing); State v. Harvey, 151 N.J. 117, 699 A.2d 596 (N.J.1997) (DQⵑ and Polymarker tests generally accepted); State v. Lyons, 324 Or. 256, 924 P.2d 802 (Or.1996) (DQⵑ admissible under relevancy standard); State v. Moeller, 548 N.W.2d 465 (S.D.1996) (DQⵑ admissible under *Daubert* standard); State v. Gore, 143 Wash.2d 288, 21 P.3d 262 (Wash.2001) (DQ-alpha, polymarker, and D1S80 are generally accepted, as is the basic product rule for these loci).

34. For suggestions to assist in this endeavor, see *infra* § 11–2.7.

35. *See, e.g.,* Adams v. State, 794 So.2d 1049, 2001 WL 410800 (Miss.Ct.App.2001) (mt-DNA sequencing admissible); State v. Underwood, 134 N.C.App. 533, 518 S.E.2d 231 (N.C.Ct.App.1999) (mitochondrial DNA sequencing); State v. Ware, 1999 WL 233592 (Tenn.Crim.App.1999) (unpublished opinion holding that notwithstanding testimony from a defense expert that mt-DNA sequencing had not been adequately validated for forensic use, the FBI's mt-DNA testing was properly admitted under the scientific soundness standard); Mark Curriden, *A New Evidence Tool: First*

confer approval until it is satisfied that the specific technology satisfies the applicable standard.

§ 11–1.2.2 Ascertaining DNA Matches

Even if a generally accepted or valid method of analyzing individuating features of DNA has been employed properly, the interpretation of the laboratory results could be objectionable.

[1] Subjectivity in Ascertaining the Profile

For reasons described in Part B,[36] examiners sometimes disagree as to the profile of a DNA sample.[37] Bona fide disagreements certainly would go to the weight of the evidence and might bear on its admissibility through Federal Rule of Evidence 403.[38] It also can be argued that such disagreements pertain to admissibility under *Daubert*—to the extent that "adequate scientific care" necessitates "an objective and quantitative procedure for identifying the pattern of a sample," and that "[p]atterns must be identified separately and independently in suspect and evidence samples."[39] By and large, however, courts have not been inclined to treat procedures that allow for subjective judgment in ascertaining the profiles as fatal to admissibility.[40]

[2] Measurement Variability and VNTRs

VNTRs are characterized by the variation in their lengths. The measurement process that uses gel electrophoresis ends with pictures that reveals

Use of Mitochondrial DNA Test in a U.S. Criminal Trial, A.B.A.J., Nov.1996, at 18.

36. *See infra* § 11–2.6.

37. *E.g.*, People v. Leonard, 224 Mich.App. 569, 569 N.W.2d 663, 667 (Mich.Ct.App.) (prosecution's academic expert concluded that there was a match at all bands rather than just the three that the state laboratory considered to match), *app. denied*, 456 Mich. 890, 570 N.W.2d 659 (Mich.1997); State v. Jobe, 486 N.W.2d 407 (Minn.1992) (one FBI examiner found a match on the basis of two of four probes, with the other two being inconclusive; another examiner found no match; another scientist called the profiles a "very, very, very significant match"); State v. Marcus, 294 N.J.Super. 267, 683 A.2d 221 (N.J.Super.Ct.App.1996) (defendant's academic expert questioned the results of one probe); State v. Gabriau, 696 A.2d 290, 292 n. 3 (R.I.1997) ("According to [a university geneticist] the laboratory technician had not considered two loci as matches where he himself would have.").

38. For a case questioning whether the disagreement was real, see United States v. Perry, No. CR 91–395–SC (D.N.M. Sept. 7, 1995). There, the district court found a defense expert's suggestions of "lab technicians manipulating samples to achieve false matches" and of an analyst's sizing a band "when no band existed" to be "particularly unprincipled," "the stuff of mystery novels, not science."

39. NRC I, *supra* note 1, at 53. This admonition refers to VNTR profiles. Because the

lengths of the VNTRs cannot be determined precisely, statistical criteria must be used if a statement as to whether bands "match" is to be made. Such criteria are discussed *infra* § 11–2.6, and they might be all that the committee had in mind when it called for an "objective and quantitative procedure." *Cf.* NRC II, *supra* note 1, at 142 ("the use of visual inspection other than as a screen before objective measurement . . . usually should be avoided").

40. *E.g.*, United States v. Perry, No. CR 91–395–SC (D.N.M. Sept. 7, 1995) (stating that "the autorad is a permanent record, and anyone, including defense experts, can conduct an independent measurement of band size. . . ."); State v. Jobe, 486 N.W.2d 407, 420 (Minn. 1992) (observing that "each sample is also examined by a second trained examiner and ultimately the 'match' is confirmed or rejected through computer analysis using wholly objective criteria"); State v. Copeland, 130 Wash.2d 244, 922 P.2d 1304, 1323 (Wash.1996) (suggesting that "complaints about the analyst's ability to override the computer in placing the cursor at the center of a band . . . would be the type of human error going to weight, not admissibility"); *cf.* NRC II, *supra* note 1, at 142 ("if for any reason the analyst by visual inspection overrides the conclusion from the measurements, that should be clearly stated and reasons given").

these variations in the form of "bands" located at different heights on a photographic film.[41] However, just as it is impossible to measure the height of a person to the last decimal place, the measurement process for VNTRs is not perfectly precise. The same DNA fragment can appear at slightly different heights on successive measurements. To account for this measurement variability, most laboratories use a statistically determined *match window*: They declare that two fragments match if the bands appear to match visually, and if they fall within a specified distance of one another.[42] The FBI's match window has been challenged as being too inclusive. Because the window has reasonable, empirically validated error rates,[43] however, these attacks have not prevailed.[44]

Match windows should not be confused with "bins."[45] A "bin" is simply a range of sizes of VNTR fragments, and bins are used to determine the proportion of VNTR alleles of various sizes seen in a database of DNA samples. These proportions then are combined to estimate a profile frequency (the profile typically being composed of six to ten VNTR alleles). For this purpose, the bins used to count allele frequencies should span at least the width of the two adjacent match windows that would lead to a match being declared. Figure 1 shows why.

41. *See infra* § 11–2.3.

42. *See infra* § 11–2.6.

43. *See id.*; Hans Zeisel & David Kaye, Prove It with Figures: Empirical Methods in Law and Litigation 204–06 (1997); D.H. Kaye, *DNA Evidence: Probability, Population Genetics, and the Courts*, 7 Harv. J. L. & Tech. 101 (1994); D.H. Kaye, *The Relevance of Matching DNA: Is the Window Half Open or Half Shut?*, 85 J. Crim. L. & Criminology 676 (1995). *Contra* William C. Thompson, *Evaluating the Admissibility of the New Genetic Tests: Lessons from the "DNA War,"* 84 J. Crim. L. & Criminology 22 (1993); *infra* § 11–2.6.1.

44. *See* United States v. Yee, 134 F.R.D. 161 (N.D.Ohio 1991), *aff'd sub nom.* United States v. Bonds, 12 F.3d 540 (6th Cir.1993); United States v. Jakobetz, 747 F.Supp. 250 (D.Vt.1990), *aff'd*, 955 F.2d 786 (2d Cir.1992); United States v. Perry, No. CR 91–395–SC (D.N.M. Sept. 7, 1995).

45. *See infra* § 11–2.6.3.1.

Figure 1

The relationship between floating bin width and match window

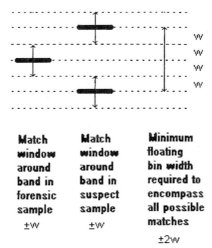

Match window around band in forensic sample ±w	Match window around band in suspect sample ±w	Minimum floating bin width required to encompass all possible matches ±2w

The failure of the FBI to observe this precept prompted the California Supreme Court to affirm the reversal of a conviction for rape and related offenses in *People v. Venegas*.[46] The court recognized the need for a line between mistakes that are so fundamental as to preclude admissibility and less serious errors,[47] but it deemed the use of too narrow a bin width as a fatal methodological flaw under *Frye*.[48]

---

46. 18 Cal.4th 47, 74 Cal.Rptr.2d 262, 954 P.2d 525 (Cal.1998).

47. The court wrote that:

The *Kelly* test's third prong does not, of course, cover all derelictions in following the prescribed scientific procedures. Shortcomings such as mislabeling, mixing the wrong ingredients, or failing to follow routine precautions against contamination may well be amenable to evaluation by jurors without the assistance of expert testimony. Such readily apparent missteps involve 'the degree of professionalism' with which otherwise scientifically accepted methodologies are applied in a given case, and so amount only to '[c]areless testing affect[ing] the weight of the evidence and not its admissibility' . . . .

74 Cal.Rptr. at 284 (citations omitted). *Cf.* State v. Kinder, 942 S.W.2d 313 (Mo.1996) ("argument concerning the manner in which the tests were conducted goes more to the credibility of the witness and the weight of the evidence, which is in the first instance a discretionary call for the trial court and ultimately for the jury").

48. The FBI laboratory determined that defendant's VNTR profile matched the profiles from vaginal swabs and a semen stain, and that the probability of selecting an unrelated individual at random from the Hispanic population with a profile that also matched the samples was approximately 1/31,000. This figure was obtained using the basic product rule with a match window of ±2.5% (74 Cal.Rptr. at 275) and a "fixed bin" width of at least ±3%. *Id.* at 277. The width of these bins was acceptable, since they more than covered the adjacent match windows. However, the FBI examiner also arrived at an estimate of 1/65,000 using the interim ceiling method for combining the allele frequencies and "floating bins" of ±2.5%. *Id.*

The trial court admitted testimony that the probability of a random match was 1/65,000. Figure 1 shows the most extreme bands in a samples from suspects that could be declared to match. These bands are positioned at 5% above and 5% below the band from the forensic sample. Because all bands within this range could be declared to match the band from the forensic sample, the appropriate size of a floating bin is twice the match window around an individual band, or ±5%. One of defendant's experts pointed out that the floating bin should have been at least as wide as two match windows placed end-to-end (±5% rather than

§ 11–1.2.3   Presenting Incriminating DNA Results

Even if the laboratory determination that defendant's DNA matches that found at a crime scene is accurate, the manner in which this finding is presented could be prejudicial. For example, the presentation of a very small "probability of a random match" in the general population, even if validly computed, has been said to be misleading for a variety of reasons. This subsection discusses the legal question of which of the various scientifically defensible probabilities[49] should be admissible in court. Assuming that the probabilities are computed according to a method that meets *Daubert*'s demand for scientific validity and reliability and thus satisfies Rule 702, the major issue arises under Rule 403: To what extent will the presentation assist the jury to understand the meaning of a match so that the jury can give the evidence the weight it deserves? This question involves psychology and law, and we summarize the assertions and analyses that have been offered with respect to the various probabilities and statistics that can be used to indicate the probative value of DNA evidence.

[1]   Should Match Probabilities Be Excluded?

[a]   Are Small Frequencies or Probabilities Inherently Prejudicial?

The most common form of expert testimony about matching DNA takes the form of an explanation of how the laboratory ascertained that the defendant's DNA has the profile of the forensic sample plus an estimate of the frequency of the profile in the population (or the probability that a randomly selected individual in the population will have matching DNA). Many arguments have been offered against this entrenched practice. First, it has been suggested that jurors do not understand probabilities in general,[50] and infinitesimal match probabilities[51] will so bedazzle jurors that they will not appreciate the other evidence in the case or any innocent explanations for the match.[52] Empirical research into this hypothesis has been limited and inconclusive,[53] and remedies short of exclusion are available.[54] Thus, no jurisdiction

---

±2.5%), but the trial court held that the discrepancy merely went to the weight of the evidence.

49.   *See infra* § 11–2.6.

50.   *E.g.,* R.C. Lewontin, *Correspondence,* 372 NATURE 398 (1994).

51.   There have been cases in which the reported population frequencies are measured in the billionths or even trillionths. *E.g.,* Perry v. State, 606 So.2d 224, 225 (Ala.Crim.App. 1992) ("one in 12 billion"); Snowden v. State, 574 So.2d 960, 960 (Ala.Ct.Crim.App.1990) ("'approximately one in eleven billion,' with a 'minimum value' of one in 2.5 billion and a 'maximum' value of one in 27 trillion"); State v. Bible, 175 Ariz. 549, 858 P.2d 1152, 1191 (Ariz.1993) (between one in 60 million and one in 14 billion); State v. Daughtry, 340 N.C. 488, 459 S.E.2d 747, 758–59 (N.C.1995) ("one in 5.5 billion for each of the Caucasion, African–American, and Lumbee populations in North Carolina"); State v. Buckner, 125 Wash.2d 915,

890 P.2d 460, 460 (Wash.1995) ("one Caucasian in 19.25 billion").

52.   *Cf.* Government of the Virgin Islands v. Byers, 941 F.Supp. 513, 527 (D.Vi.1996) ("Vanishingly small probabilities of a random match may tend to establish guilt in the minds of jurors and are particularly suspect."); Commonwealth v. Curnin, 409 Mass. 218, 565 N.E.2d 440, 441 (Mass.1991) ("Evidence of this nature [a random-match probability of 1 in 59 million] . . ., having an aura of infallibility, must have a strong impact on a jury.").

53.   *See* NRC II, *supra* note 1, at 197; Jason Schklar & Shari Seidman Diamond, *Juror Reactions to DNA Evidence: Errors and Expectancies,* 23 LAW & HUM. BEHAV. 159, 181–82 (1999).

54.   Suitable cross-examination, defense experts, and jury instructions might reduce the risk that small estimates of the match probability will produce an unwarranted sense of certainty and lead a jury to disregard other evidence. NRC II, *supra* note 1, at 197

currently excludes all match probabilities on this basis.[55]

A more sophisticated variation on this theme is that the jury will misconstrue the random match probability—by thinking that it gives the probability that the match is random.[56] Suppose that the random match probability p is some very small number such as one in a billion. The words are almost identical, but the probabilities can be quite different. The random match probability is the probability that (A) the requisite genotype is in the sample from the individual tested *if* (B) the individual tested has been selected at random. In contrast, the probability that the match is random is the probability that (B) the individual tested has been selected at random *given that* (A) the individual has the requisite genotype. In general, for two events A and B, P(A *given* B) does not equal P(B *given* A). The claim that it does is known as the fallacy of the transposed conditional.[57]

To appreciate that the equation is fallacious, consider the probability that a lawyer picked at random from all lawyers in the United States is a judge. This "random judge probability" is practically zero. But the probability that a person randomly selected from the current judiciary is a lawyer is one. The "random judge probability" P(judge *given* lawyer) does not equal the transposed probability P(lawyer *given* judge). Likewise, the random match probability P(genotype *given* unrelated source) does not necessarily equal P(unrelated source *given* genotype).

To avoid this fallacious reasoning by jurors, some defense counsel have urged the exclusion of random match probabilities, and some prosecutors have suggested that it is desirable to avoid testimony or argument about probabilities, and instead to present the statistic as a simple frequency—an indication of how rare the genotype is in the relevant population.[58] The 1996 NRC report

---

55. *E.g.*, United States v. Chischilly, 30 F.3d 1144 (9th Cir.1994) (citing cases); Martinez v. State, 549 So.2d 694, 694–95 (Fla.Dist. Ct.App.1989) (rejecting the argument that testimony that "one individual in 234 billion" would have the same banding pattern was "so overwhelming as to deprive the jury of its function"); Hughes v. State, 735 So.2d 238, 262 (Miss.1999) (rejecting general claim that frequencies are prejudicial); State v. Weeks, 270 Mont. 63, 891 P.2d 477, 489 (Mont.1995) (rejecting the argument that "the exaggerated opinion of the accuracy of DNA testing is prejudicial, as juries would give undue weight and deference to the statistical evidence" and "that the probability aspect of the DNA analysis invades the province of the jury to decide the guilt or innocence of the defendant"); State v. Schweitzer, 533 N.W.2d 156, 160 (S.D.1995) (reviewing cases).

56. Numerous opinions or experts present the random match probability in this manner. Compare the problematic characterizations in, *e.g.*, *United States v. Martinez*, 3 F.3d 1191, 1194 (8th Cir.1993) (referring to "a determination of the probability that someone other than the contributor of the known sample could have contributed the unknown sample"), and *State v. Foster*, 259 Kan. 198, 910 P.2d 848 (Kan.1996) (a DNA analyst testified that "the

probability of another person in the Caucasian population having the same banding pattern was 1 in 100,000"), with the more accurate comments of an FBI examiner in *State v. Freeman*, 1996 WL 608328, at *7 (Neb.Ct.App. 1996), *aff'd*, 253 Neb. 385, 571 N.W.2d 276 (Neb.1997), that "[t]he probability of randomly selecting an unrelated individual from the Caucasian population who would have the same DNA profile as I observed in the K2 sample for Mr. Freeman was approximately one in 15 million." For more examples of mischaracterizations of the random match probability, see cases and authorities cited, NRC II, *supra* note 1, at 198 n. 92.

57. It is also called the "inverse fallacy," or the "prosecutor's fallacy." The latter expression is rare in the statistical literature, but it is common in the legal literature on statistical evidence. For an exposition of related errors, see Jonathan J. Koehler, *Error and Exaggeration in the Presentation of DNA Evidence at Trial*, 34 JURIMETRICS J. 21 (1993).

58. George W. Clark, *Effective Use of DNA Evidence in Jury Trials*, PROFILES IN DNA, Aug. 1997, at 7, 8 ("References to probabilities should normally be avoided, inasmuch as such descriptions are frequently judicially equated

noted that "few courts or commentators have recommended the exclusion of evidence merely because of the risk that jurors will transpose a conditional probability,"[59] and it observed that "[t]he available research indicates that jurors may be more likely to be swayed by the 'defendant's fallacy' than by the 'prosecutor's fallacy.' When advocates present both fallacies to mock jurors, the defendant's fallacy dominates."[60] Furthermore, the committee suggested that "if the initial presentation of the probability figure, cross-examination, and opposing testimony all fail to clarify the point, the judge can counter both fallacies by appropriate instructions to the jurors that minimize the possibility of cognitive errors."[61]

No court has excluded a DNA random match probability (or, for that matter, an estimate of the small frequency of a DNA profile in the general population) as unfairly prejudicial just because the jury might misinterpret it as a posterior probability that the defendant is the source of the forensic DNA. One court, however, noted the need to have the concept "properly explained,"[62] and prosecutorial misrepresentations of the random match probabilities for other types of evidence have produced reversals.[63]

[b]   Are Small Match Probabilities Irrelevant?

Second, it has been maintained that match probabilities are logically irrelevant when they are far smaller than the probability of a frame-up, a blunder in labeling samples, cross-contamination, or other events that would

with disfavored 'probabilities of guilt'.... [T]he purpose of frequency data is simply to provide the factfinder with a guide to the relative rarity of a DNA match. . . .").

59. NRC II, *supra* note 1, at 198 (citing McCormick, *supra* note 6, § 212).

60. *Id.* The "defendant's fallacy" consists of dismissing or undervaluing the matches with high likelihood ratios because other matches are to be expected in unrealistically large populations of potential suspects. For example, defense counsel might argue that (a) even with a random match probability of one in a million, we would expect to find 10 unrelated people with the requisite genotypes in a population of 10 million; (b) the defendant just happens to be one of these ten, which means that the chances are 9 out of 10 that someone unrelated to the defendant is the source; so (c) the DNA evidence does nothing to incriminate the defendant. The problem with this argument is that in a case involving non-DNA evidence against the defendant, it is unrealistic to assume that there are 10 million equally likely suspects.

61. *Id.* (footnote omitted). The committee suggested the following instruction to define the random match probability:

In evaluating the expert testimony on the DNA evidence, you were presented with a number indicating the probability that another individual drawn at random from the

[specify] population would coincidentally have the same DNA profile as the [blood stain, semen stain, etc.]. That number, which assumes that no sample mishandling or laboratory error occurred, indicates how distinctive the DNA profile is. It does not by itself tell you the probability that the defendant is innocent.

Id. at 198 n.93. *But see* D.H. Kaye, *The Admissibility of "Probability Evidence" in Criminal Trials—Part II*, 27 JURIMETRICS J. 160, 168 (1987) ("Nevertheless, because even without misguided advice from counsel, the temptation to compute the probability of criminal identity [by transposition] seems strong, and because the characterization of the population proportion as a [random match probability] does little to make the evidence more intelligible, it might be best to bar the prosecution from having its expert state the probability of a coincidental misidentification, as opposed to providing [a simpler] estimate of the population proportion.").

62. United States v. Shea, 957 F.Supp. 331, 345 (D.N.H.1997).

63. *E.g.*, United States v. Massey, 594 F.2d 676, 681 (8th Cir.1979) (in closing argument about hair evidence, "the prosecutor 'confuse(d) the probability of concurrence of the identifying marks with the probability of mistaken identification' ").

yield a false positive.[64] The argument is that the jury should concern itself only with the chance that the forensic sample is reported to match the defendant's profile even though the defendant is not the source. Such a report could happen either because another person who is the source of the forensic sample has the same profile or because fraud or error of a kind that falsely incriminates the defendant occurs in the collection, handling, or analysis of the DNA samples. Match probabilities do not express this chance of a match being reported when the defendant is not the source unless the probability of a false-positive report is essentially zero.

Both theoretical and practical rejoinders to this argument about relevance have been given. At the theoretical level, some scientists question a procedure that would prevent the jury from reasoning in a stepwise, eliminative fashion. In their view, a rational juror might well want to know that the chance that another person selected at random from the suspect population has the incriminating genotype is negligible, for this would enable the juror to eliminate the hypotheses of kinship or coincidence.[65] If the juror concludes that there is little chance that the same genotype would exist in the forensic sample if the DNA originated from anyone but the defendant, then the juror can proceed to consider whether that genotype is present because someone has tried to frame the defendant, or whether it is not really present but was reported to be there because DNA samples were mishandled or misanalyzed.[66] These probabilities, they add, are not amenable to objective modeling and should not be mixed with probabilities that are derived from verifiable models of genetics.[67]

At the practical level, there is disagreement about the adequacy of the estimates that have been proposed to express the probability of a false positive result. The opponents of match probabilities usually argue that an error rate somewhat higher than that observed in a series of proficiency tests should be substituted for the match probability,[68] but the extent to which any such figure applies to the case at bar has been questioned.[69] No reported cases have

64. *E.g.*, Jonathan J. Koehler et al., *The Random Match Probability in DNA Evidence: Irrelevant and Prejudicial?*, 35 JURIMETRICS J. 201 (1995); Richard Lewontin & Daniel Hartl, *Population Genetics in Forensic DNA Typing*, 254 SCIENCE 1745, 1749 (1991) ("probability estimates like 1 in 738,000,000,000,000 . . . are terribly misleading because the rate of laboratory error is not taken into account").

65. *E.g.*, NRC II, *supra* note 1, at 85; NRC I, *supra* note 1, at 88; Russell Higuchi, *Human Error in Forensic DNA Typing*, 48 AM. J. HUM. GENETICS 1215 (1991) (letter). Of course, if the defense were to stipulate that a true DNA match establishes identity, there would be no need for probabilities that would help the jury to reject the rival hypotheses of coincidence or kinship.

66. *E.g.*, Devlin & Roeder, *supra* note 25, § 18–5.3, at 743–44 ("One way to handle the possibility of a laboratory error, which follows the usual presentation of similar types of evidence, is to present the evidence in two stages: Does the evidence suggest that the samples were obtained from the same individual? If so,

is there a harmless reason? Either formal calculations or informal analysis could be used to evaluate the possibility of a laboratory error, both of which should be predicated on the facts of the specific case.").

67. *E.g.*, N.E. Morton, *The Forensic DNA Endgame*, 37 JURIMETRICS J. 477, 480–81 (1997); *cf.* NRC I, *supra* note 1, at 88 ("Coincidental identity and laboratory error are different phenomena, so the two cannot and should not be combined in a single estimate.").

68. *But see* Thompson, *supra* note 20, at 417 (suggesting that "DNA evidence" should be excluded as "unacceptable scientifically if the probability of an erroneous match cannot be quantified").

69. *See, e.g.*, David J. Balding, *Errors and Misunderstandings in the Second NRC Report*, 37 JURIMETRICS J. 469, 475–76, 476 n.21 (1997) ("report[ing] a match probability which adds error rates to profile frequencies . . . would clearly be unacceptable since overall error rates are not directly relevant: jurors must

excluded statistics on proficiency tests administered at a specific laboratory as too far removed from the case at bar to be relevant,[70] but neither has it been held that these statistics must be used in place of random match or kinship probabilities.[71]

[c] Are Match Probabilities Unfairly Prejudicial When They Are Smaller than the Probability of Laboratory Error?

It can be argued that very small match probabilities are relevant but unfairly prejudicial. Such prejudice could occur if the jury was so impressed with this single number that it neglected or underweighted the probability of a match arising due to a false-positive laboratory error.[72] Some commentators believe that this prejudice is so likely and so serious that "jurors ordinarily should receive *only* the laboratory's false positive rate...."[73] The 1996 NRC report is skeptical of this view, especially when the defendant has had a meaningful opportunity to retest the DNA at a laboratory of his choice, and it suggests that judicial instructions can be crafted to avoid this form of prejudice.[74]

[d] Are Small Match Probabilities Unfairly Prejudicial When Not Accompanied by an Estimated Probability of a Laboratory Error?

Rather than excluding small match probabilities entirely, a court might require the expert who presents them also to report a probability that the

assess on the basis of the evidence presented to them the chance that an error has occurred in the particular case at hand," but "[e]rror rates observed in blind trials may well be helpful to jurors."); Berger, *supra* note 20. *But cf.* Thompson, *supra* note 20, at 421 ("While it makes little sense to present a single number derived from proficiency tests as *the* error rate in every case, it makes less sense to exclude quantitative estimates of the error altogether.").

70. *But see infra* § 11–1.1.5.

71. *See* Armstead v. State, 342 Md. 38, 673 A.2d 221 (Md.1996) (rejecting the argument that the introduction of a random match probability deprives the defendant of due process because the error rate on proficiency tests is many orders of magnitude greater than the match probability); Williams v. State, 342 Md. 724, 679 A.2d 1106 (Md.1996) (reversing because the trial court restricted cross-examination about the results of proficiency tests involving other DNA analysts at the same laboratory).

72. *E.g.,* Koehler et al., *supra* note 64; Thompson, *supra* note 20, at 421–22.

73. Richard Lempert, *Some Caveats Concerning DNA as Criminal Identification Evidence: With Thanks to the Reverend Bayes*, 13 CARDOZO L. REV. 303, 325 (1991) (emphasis added); *see also* Richard Lempert, *After the*

DNA Wars: Skirmishing with NRC II, 37 JURIMETRICS J. 439, 447 (1997); Scheck, *supra* note 20, at 1997.

74. NRC II, *supra* note 1, at 199 (notes omitted):

The argument that jurors will make better use of a single figure for the probability that an innocent suspect would be reported to match has never been tested adequately. The argument for a single figure is weak in light of this lack of research into how jurors react to different ways of presenting statistical information, and its weakness is compounded by the grave difficulty of estimating a false-positive error rate in any given case. But efforts should be made to fill the glaring gap in empirical studies of such matters.

The district court in *United States v. Shea*, 957 F.Supp. 331, 334–45 (D.N.H.1997), discussed some of the available research and rejected the argument that separate figures for match and error probabilities are prejudicial. For more recent research, see Schklar & Diamond, *supra* note 53, at 179 (concluding that separate figures are desirable in that "[j]urors ... may need to know the disaggregated elements that influence the aggregated estimate as well as how they were combined in order to evaluate the DNA test results in the context of their background beliefs and the other evidence introduced at trial").

laboratory is mistaken about the profiles.[75] Of course, some experts would deny that they can provide a meaningful statistic for the case at hand, but they could report the results of proficiency tests and leave it to the jury to use this figure as best it can in considering whether a false-positive error has occurred.[76] To assist the jury in making sense of two numbers, however, it has been suggested that an expert take the additional step of reporting how the probability that a matching genotype would be found coincidentally *or* erroneously changes given the random match probability and various values for the probability of a false-positive error.[77]

[e] Are Small Match Probabilities Unfairly Prejudicial When Not Accompanied by an Estimated Probability Involving Relatives?

One commentator has proposed that unless the police can eliminate all named relatives as possible culprits, "the defendant should be allowed to name any close relative whom he thinks might have committed the crime," and the state should use the probability "that at least one named relative has DNA like the defendant's" as the sole indication of the plausibility of the hypothesis of kinship.[78] Whether such numbers should be introduced even when there is no proof that a close relative might have committed the crime is, of course, a matter to be evaluated under Federal or Uniform Rules of

75. Jonathan J. Koehler, *DNA Matches and Statistics: Important Questions, Surprising Answers*, 76 JUDICATURE 222, 229 (1993) ("A good argument can be made for requiring DNA laboratories to provide fact finders with conservatively high estimates of their false positive error rates when they provide evidence about genetic matches. By the same token, laboratories should be required to divulge their estimated false negative error rate in cases where exclusions are reported."). This argument has prevailed in a few cases. *E.g.*, United States v. Porter, 1994 WL 742297 (D.C.Super.Ct.1994) (mem.). Other courts have rejected it. *E.g.*, United States v. Lowe, 954 F.Supp. 401, 415 (D.Mass.1996), *aff'd*, 145 F.3d 45 (1st Cir. 1998).

76. *See* NRC I, *supra* note 1, at 94 ("Laboratory error rates should be measured with appropriate proficiency tests and should play a role in the interpretation of results of forensic DNA typing.... A laboratory's overall rate of incorrect conclusions due to error should be reported with, but separately from, the probability of coincidental matches in the population. Both should be weighed in evaluating evidence."); NRC II, *supra* note 1, at 87 ("[A] calculation that combines error rates with match probabilities is inappropriate. The risk of error is properly considered case by case, taking into account the record of the laboratory performing the tests, the extent of redundancy, and the overall quality of the results."). The district court in *Government of the Virgin Islands v. Byers*, 941 F.Supp. 513 (D.Vi.1996), declined to require proficiency test results as a

precondition for admissibility. *See also* Berger, *supra* note 20, at 1093 ("the rationale for [requiring the prosecution to introduce a pooled error rate] is weak, and ... such a shift would be inconsistent with significant evidentiary policies.").

77. *See* Thompson, *supra* note 20, at 421–22 (footnote omitted):

For example, an expert could say that if the probability of a random match is .00000001 and the probability of an erroneous match is .001, then the overall probability of a false match is approximately .001.... If the probability of an erroneous match is unclear or controversial (as it undoubtedly will be in many cases), then illustrative combinations could be performed for a range of hypothetical probabilities.

This procedure could lead to arguments about the relevance of the values for the "probability of an erroneous match." Depending on such factors as the record of the laboratory on proficiency tests, the precautions observed in processing the samples, and the availability of samples for independent testing, the prosecution could contend that the 0.001 figure in this example has no foundation in the evidence.

78. Lempert, *supra* note 73, at 461. For example, if the defendant named two brothers and two uncles as possible suspects, then the probability that at least one shares a four-locus genotype (with alleles that each occur in 5% of the population) would be about $(2 \times .006) + (2 \times .0000005)$, or about 0.012. *See infra* § 11–2.6.

Evidence 104(b), 401 and 403.[79]

[2] Should Likelihood Ratios be Excluded?

A likelihood ratio expresses how many times more likely it if the defendant is the source of crime-scene sample than if other hypotheses about the origin of the sample are true.[80] The most commonly considered alternative hypothesis is that an unrelated person is the source (coincidence), but likelihood ratios can be calculated with respect to the hypothesis that a close relative is the source (kinship). The 1996 NRC Report offers the following analysis of the admissibility of such ratios:

Although LRs [likelihood ratios] are rarely introduced in criminal cases, we believe that they are appropriate for explaining the significance of data and that existing statistical knowledge is sufficient to permit their computation. None of the LRs that have been devised for VNTRs can be dismissed as clearly unreasonable or based on principles not generally accepted in the statistical community. Therefore, legal doctrine suggests that LRs should be admissible unless they are so unintelligible that they provide no assistance to a jury or so misleading that they are unduly prejudicial. As with frequencies and match probabilities, prejudice might exist because the proposed LRs do not account for laboratory error, and a jury might misconstrue even a modified version that did account for it as a statement of the odds in favor of S [the claim that the defendant is the source of the forensic DNA sample]. [But] the possible misinterpretation of LRs as the odds in favor of identity ... is a question of jury ability and performance to which existing research supplies no clear answer.[81]

Notwithstanding the lack of adequate empirical research, other commentators believe that the danger of prejudice (in the form of the transposition fallacy) warrants the exclusion of likelihood ratios.[82] The issue has yet to be litigated fully.[83]

---

79. Courts may be unwilling to exclude random match probabilities on the basis of uncorroborated arguments about untested relatives. *See, e.g.,* Taylor v. Commonwealth, 1995 WL 80189 (Va.Ct.App.1995) (unpublished) ("Defendant argues that this evidence did not consider the existence of an identical twin or close relative to defendant, a circumstance which would diminish the probability that he was the perpetrator. While this hypothesis is conceivable, it has no basis in the record and the Commonwealth must only exclude hypotheses of innocence that reasonably flow from the evidence, not from defendant's imagination.").

80. *See infra* § 11–2.2.3.1.

81. NRC II, *supra* note 1, at 200–01. A footnote adds that:

Likelihood ratios were used in State v. Klindt, 389 N.W.2d 670 (Iowa 1986) ..., and are admitted routinely in parentage litigation, where they are known as the 'paternity index'.... Some state statutes use them to create a presumption of paternity.... The practice of providing a paternity index has been carried over into criminal cases in

which genetic parentage is used to indicate the identity of the perpetrator of an offense....

Id. at 200 n. 97.

82. *See* Jonathan J. Koehler, *On Conveying the Probative Value of DNA Evidence: Frequencies, Likelihood Ratios, and Error Rates,* 67 COLO. L. REV. 859, 880 (1996); William C. Thompson, *DNA Evidence in the O.J. Simpson Trial,* 67 COLO. L. REV. 827, 850 (1996). *Contra* Koehler et al., *supra* note 64 (proposing the use of a likelihood ratio that incorporates laboratory error).

83. In *State v. Garcia,* 197 Ariz. 79, 3 P.3d 999 (Ct.App.1999), a trial court in Arizona admitted testimony about likelihood ratios in a rape case involving two assailants. Analysis of the semen stain on the victim's blouse indicated that sperm from two males were present. According to the court of appeals, a population geneticist "provided the jury with likelihood ratios (broken down by population subgroups such as Caucasians, African Americans, and the like) for three distinct scenarios involving

[3]   Should Posterior Probabilities be Excluded?

Match probabilities state the chance that certain genotypes would be present conditioned on specific hypotheses about the source of the DNA (a specified relative, or an unrelated individual in a population or subpopulation). Likelihood ratios express the relative support that the presence of the genotypes in the defendant gives to these hypotheses compared to the claim that the defendant is the source. Posterior probabilities or odds express the chance that the defendant is the source (conditioned on various assumptions). These probabilities, if they are meaningful and accurate, would be of great value to the jury.

Experts have been heard to testify to posterior probabilities. In *Smith v. Deppish*,[84] for example, the state's "DNA experts informed the jury that ... there was more than a 99 percent probability that Smith was a contributor of the semen,"[85] but how such numbers are obtained is not apparent. If they are instances of the transposition fallacy, then they are scientifically invalid (and objectionable under Rule 702) and unfairly prejudicial (under Rule 403).

the sources of the DNA mixture found in the stain: (1) victim, defendant and unknown versus victim and two unknowns; (2) victim, defendant and unknown versus defendant and two unknowns; and (3) victim, defendant and one unknown versus three unknowns." *Id.* at ¶ 15. To illustrate the nature of the testimony with simplified numbers for the first set of hypotheses, the calculations might show the chance of the specified DNA types being present was 100 times greater if (a) the DNA came from the victim, the defendant, and a randomly selected person than if (b) it came from the victim and two randomly selected persons.

The trial court admitted this testimony following a *Frye* hearing at which the state's expert testified to general acceptance. The defendant was convicted. On appeal, he argued that the state had not proved that the specific formulas used to calculate the likelihood ratios had been generally accepted. The court of appeals affirmed the conviction, reasoning that both the concept of the likelihood ratio and the specific formulas were generally accepted, as indicated by publications in the scientific literature.

In a petition for review, Garcia suggested that although the use of the likelihood ratio has support in the literature, the particular formulas were not previously published. However, there is no general formula for computing a likelihood ratio. It depends on the specific hypotheses being compared. The likelihood ratio for a mixture with two possible men is different from that for a mixture with three, or four, and so. The same approach produces the appropriate expression in each situation, and arriving at the correct expression is like solving word problems in high school algebra. Everyone agrees that the problems should be solved with formulas derived according to the rules of algebra, but different word problems require different formulas. The use of algebra is generally accepted, but a student can a make a mistake applying those rules.

Although *Garcia* recognizes that the use of likelihood ratios is generally accepted as scientifically valid, the fact remains that an expert can make a mistake in algebraically representing the pertinent conditional probabilities or in working out the algebra that yields the likelihood ratio for a particular problem. Although this sounds like a concern about the implementation of a generally accepted method (so that *Frye* would not apply in most *Frye* jurisdictions), it also can be characterized as a trans-case, major premise (which would require general acceptance). After all, the formulas in *Garcia* easily could be employed in other cases involving a mixture of DNA from one female and two males. There should be little difficulty admitting them under *Daubert*, for the derivation of the formulas is a straightforward algebraic exercise that can be verified by any number of experts familiar with probability theory. Affidavits from a few such experts should be enough to demonstrate the requisite reliability. Under *Frye*, it is more difficult to introduce even an obviously valid result that has yet to be scrutinized by the relevant portion of the scientific community.

84. 248 Kan. 217, 807 P.2d 144 (Kan.1991).

85. *See also* Thomas v. State, 830 S.W.2d 546, 550 (Mo.Ct.App.1992) (a geneticist testified that "the likelihood that the DNA found in Marion's panties came from the defendant was higher than 99.99%"); Commonwealth v. Crews, 536 Pa. 508, 640 A.2d 395, 402 (Pa. 1994) (an FBI examiner who at a preliminary hearing had estimated a coincidental-match probability for a VNTR match "at three of four loci" reported at trial that the match made identity "more probable than not").

However, a meaningful posterior probability can be computed with Bayes' theorem.[86] Ideally, one would enumerate every person in the suspect population, specify the prior odds that each is the source of the forensic DNA and weight those prior odds by the likelihoods (taking into account the familial relationship of each possible suspect to the defendant) to arrive at the posterior odds that the defendant is the source of the forensic sample. But this hardly seems practical. The 1996 NRC Report therefore discusses a somewhat different implementation of Bayes' theorem. Assuming that the hypotheses of kinship and error could be dismissed on the basis of other evidence, the report focuses on "the variable-prior-odds method," by which:

> an expert neither uses his or her own prior odds nor demands that jurors formulate their prior odds for substitution into Bayes's rule. Rather, the expert presents the jury with a table or graph showing how the posterior probability changes as a function of the prior probability.[87]

This procedure, it observes, "has garnered the most support among legal scholars and is used in some civil cases."[88] Nevertheless, "very few courts have considered its merits in criminal cases."[89] In the end, the report concludes:

> How much it would contribute to jury comprehension remains an open question, especially considering the fact that for most DNA evidence, computed values of the likelihood ratio (conditioned on the assumption that the reported match is a true match) would swamp any plausible prior probability and result in a graph or table that would show a posterior probability approaching 1 except for very tiny prior probabilities.[90]

[4] Which Verbal Expressions of Probative Value Should Be Presented?

Having surveyed various views about the admissibility of the probabilities and statistics indicative of the probative value of DNA evidence, we turn to a related issue that can arise under Rules 702 and 403: Should an expert be permitted to offer a non-numerical judgment about the DNA profiles?

Inasmuch as most forms of expert testimony involve qualitative rather than quantitative testimony, this may seem an odd question. Yet, many courts have held that a DNA match is inadmissible unless the expert attaches a scientifically valid number to the figure.[91] In reaching this result, some courts

---

86. *See infra* § 11–2.6.

87. NRC II, *supra* note 1, at 202 (footnote omitted).

88. *Id.*

89. *Id.* (footnote omitted).

90. *Id.* For arguments said to show that the variable-prior-odds proposal is "a bad idea," see Thompson, *supra* note 20, at 422–23.

91. *E.g.*, Commonwealth v. Daggett, 416 Mass. 347, 622 N.E.2d 272, 275 n. 4 (Mass. 1993) (plurality opinion insisting that "[t]he point is not that this court should require a numerical frequency, but that the scientific

community clearly does"); State v. Carter, 246 Neb. 953, 524 N.W.2d 763, 783 (1994) ("evidence of a DNA match will not be admissible if it has not been accompanied by statistical probability evidence that has been calculated from a generally accepted method"); State v. Cauthron, 120 Wash.2d 879, 846 P.2d 502 (Wash.1993) ("probability statistics" must accompany testimony of a match). *Contra* Commonwealth v. Crews, 536 Pa. 508, 640 A.2d 395, 402 (Pa.1994) ("The factual evidence of the physical testing of the DNA samples and the matching alleles, even without statistical conclusions, tended to make appellant's pres-

cite the statement in the 1992 NRC report that "[t]o say that two patterns match, without providing any scientifically valid estimate (or, at least, an upper bound) of the frequency with which such matches might occur by chance, is meaningless."[92]

The 1996 report phrases the scientific question somewhat differently. Like the 1992 report, it states that "[b]efore forensic experts can conclude that DNA testing has the power to help identify the source of an evidence sample, it must be shown that the DNA characteristics vary among people. Therefore, it would not be scientifically justifiable to speak of a match as proof of identity in the absence of underlying data that permit some reasonable estimate of how rare the matching characteristics actually are."[93] However, the 1996 report then explains that "determining whether quantitative estimates should be presented to a jury is a different issue. Once science has established that a methodology has some individualizing power, the legal system must determine whether and how best to import that technology into the trial process."[94]

Since the loci typically used in forensic DNA identification have been shown to have substantial individualizing power, it is scientifically sound to introduce evidence of matching profiles. Nonetheless, even evidence that meets the scientific soundness standard of *Daubert* is not admissible if its prejudicial effect clearly outweighs its probative value. Unless some reasonable explanation accompanies testimony that two profiles match, it is surely arguable that the jury will have insufficient guidance to give the scientific evidence the weight that is deserves.[95]

Instead of presenting frequencies or match probabilities obtained with quantitative methods, however, a scientist would be justified in characterizing every four-locus VNTR profile, for instance, as "rare," "extremely rare," or the like.[96] At least one state supreme court has endorsed this qualitative approach as a substitute to the presentation of more debatable numerical estimates.[97]

ence more likely than it would have been without the evidence, and was therefore relevant.").

92. NRC I, *supra* note 1, at 74. For criticism of this statement, see D.H. Kaye, *The Forensic Debut of the NRC's DNA Report: Population Structure, Ceiling Frequencies, and the Need for Numbers*, 96 GENETICA 99, 104—05 (1995), *reprinted in Human Identification: The Use of DNA Markers* 99, 104–05 (Bruce S. Weir ed., 1995):

> [I]t would not be 'meaningless' to inform the jury that two samples match and that this match makes it more probable, in an amount that is not precisely known, that the DNA in the samples comes from the same person. Nor, when all estimates of the frequency are in the millionths or billionths, would it be meaningless to inform the jury that there is a match that is known to be extremely rare in the general population. Courts may reach differing results on the legal propriety of qualitative as opposed to quantitative assessments, but they only fool themselves when

they act as if scientific opinion automatically dictates the correct answer.

93. NRC II, *supra* note 1, at 192. As indicated in earlier sections, these "underlying data" have been collected and analyzed for many genetic systems.

94. *Id.*

95. *Id.* at 193 ("Certainly, a judge's or juror's untutored impression of how unusual a DNA profile is could be very wrong. This possibility militates in favor of going beyond a simple statement of a match, to give the trier of fact some expert guidance about its probative value.").

96. *Cf. id.* at 195 ("Although different jurors might interpret the same words differently, the formulas provided . . . produce frequency estimates for profiles of three or more loci that almost always can be conservatively described as 'rare.' ").

97. State v. Bloom, 516 N.W.2d 159, 166–67 (Minn.1994) ("Since it may be pointless to

The most extreme case of a purely verbal description of the infrequency of a profile arises when that profile can be said to be unique. The 1992 report cautioned that "an expert should—given ... the relatively small number of loci used and the available population data—avoid assertions in court that a particular genotype is unique in the population."[98] Following this advice in the context of a profile derived from a handful of single-locus VNTR probes, several courts initially held that assertions of uniqueness are inadmissible,[99] while others found such testimony less troublesome.[100]

expect ever to reach a consensus on how to estimate, with any degree of precision, the probability of a random match, and that given the great difficulty in educating the jury as to precisely what that figure means and does not mean, it might make sense to simply try to arrive at a fair way of explaining the significance of the match in a verbal, qualitative, non-quantitative, nonstatistical way."); *see also* Kenneth R. Kreiling, Review—Comment, *DNA Technology in Forensic Science*, 33 JURIMETRICS J. 449 (1993).

98. NRC I, *supra* note 1, at 92.

99. *See* State v. Hummert, 183 Ariz. 484, 905 P.2d 493 (Ariz.Ct.App.1994), *rev'd*, 188 Ariz. 119, 933 P.2d 1187 (1997); State v. Cauthron, 120 Wash.2d 879, 846 P.2d 502, 516 (Wash.1993) (experts presented no "probability statistics" but claimed that "the DNA could not have come from anyone else on earth"), *overruled*, State v. Copeland, 130 Wash.2d 244, 922 P.2d 1304 (Wash.1996); State v. Buckner, 125 Wash.2d 915, 890 P.2d 460, 462 (Wash. 1995) (testimony that the profile "would occur in only one Caucasian in 19.25 billion" and that because "this figure is almost four times the present population of the Earth, the match was unique" was improper), *reconsidered*, State v. Buckner, 133 Wash.2d 63, 941 P.2d 667 (Wash.1997).

100. State v. Zollo, 36 Conn.App. 718, 654 A.2d 359, 362 (Conn.Ct.App.1995) (testimony that the chance "that the DNA sample came from someone other than the defendant was 'so small that ... it would not be worth considering'" was not inadmissible as an opinion on an ultimate issue in the case "because his opinion could reasonably have aided the jury in understanding the [complex] DNA testimony"); People v. Heaton, 266 Ill.App.3d 469, 203 Ill.Dec. 710, 640 N.E.2d 630, 633 (Ill.Ct.App. 1994) (an expert who used the product rule to estimate the frequency at 1/52,600 testified over objection to his opinion that the "defendant was the donor of the semen"); State v. Pierce, 1990 WL 97596, *2–3 (Ohio Ct.App. 1990) (affirming admission of testimony that the probability would be one in 40 billion "that the match would be to a random occurrence," and "[t]he DNA is from the same individual"), *aff'd*, 64 Ohio St.3d 490, 597 N.E.2d 107 (Ohio 1992); *cf.* State v. Bogan, 183 Ariz. 506, 905

P.2d 515, 517 (Ariz.Ct.App.1995) (it was proper to allow a molecular biologist to testify, on the basis of a PCR-based analysis that he "was confident the seed pods found in the truck originated from" a palo verde tree near a corpse); Commonwealth v. Crews, 536 Pa. 508, 640 A.2d 395, 402 (Pa.1994) (testimony of an FBI examiner that he did not know of a single instance "where different individuals that are unrelated have been shown to have matching DNA profiles for three or four probes" was admissible under *Frye* despite an objection to the lack of a frequency estimate, which had been given at a preliminary hearing as 1/400).

In *State v. Hummert*, 188 Ariz. 119, 933 P.2d 1187 (Ariz.1997), VNTR testing performed by the FBI showed that Hummert could have been the source of a semen stain. But the trial court excluded basic product rule estimates of the three-locus profile frequency, and an FBI examiner testified that such a match is "rare" and meant that "[e]ither you're brothers, identical twins, or that would be a very unique experience." 183 Ariz. 484, 905 P.2d 493, 499 (Ariz.Ct.App.1994). A second expert, a geneticist and epidemiologist from the University of California at Berkeley, went further. She testified that "one can, by carefully choosing particular parts of the DNA that vary a lot between people, uniquely identify every person with just a sample of each person's DNA." *Id.* Oddly, the supreme court perceived no testimony that science had established that three-locus VNTR matches demonstrated uniqueness. The majority opinion downplayed the expert testimony, remarking that "[a]t trial, the judge admitted evidence of the match, the criteria for declaring a match, and opinions that Defendant was not excluded by the DNA tests." 933 P.2d at 1189. Later, the opinion recognizes that more was involved—but not much more: "the ... conclusions ... in this case [came] strictly from personal knowledge and study." *Id.* at 1192. The court reasoned such "personal knowledge" need not meet "the apparent trappings of science, the *Frye* rule, and scientific recognition" but rather "need only meet the traditional requirements of relevance and avoid substantial prejudice, confusion, or waste of time." *Id.* at 1195. This "personal knowledge" exception is criticized in D.H. Kaye, *Choice and Boundary Problems in* Logerquist,

With the advent of more population data and loci, the 1996 NRC report pointedly observed that "we are approaching the time when many scientists will wish to offer opinions about the source of incriminating DNA."[101] Of course, the uniqueness of any object, from a snowflake to a fingerprint, in a population that cannot be enumerated never can be proved directly. The committee therefore wrote that "[t]here is no 'bright-line' standard in law or science that can pick out exactly how small the probability of the existence of a given profile in more than one member of a population must be before assertions of uniqueness are justified.... There might already be cases in which it is defensible for an expert to assert that, assuming that there has been no sample mishandling or laboratory error, the profile's probable uniqueness means that the two DNA samples come from the same person."[102]

The report concludes that "[b]ecause the difference between a vanishingly small probability and an opinion of uniqueness is so slight, courts may choose to allow the latter along with, or instead of the former, when the scientific findings support such testimony."[103] Confronted with an objection to an assertion of uniqueness, a court may need to verify that a large number of sufficiently polymorphic loci have been tested.[104]

Hummert, *and* Carmichael, 33 ARIZ. ST. L.J. 41 (2001).

101. NRC II, *supra* note 1, at 194.

102. As an illustration, the committee cited *State v. Bloom*, 516 N.W.2d 159, 160 n. 2 (Minn.1994), a case in which a respected population geneticist was prepared to testify that "in his opinion the nine-locus match constituted 'overwhelming evidence that, to a reasonable degree of scientific certainty, the DNA from the victim's vaginal swab came from the [defendant], to the exclusion of all others.'" NRC II, *supra* note 1, at 194–95 n.84; *see also* People v. Hickey, 178 Ill.2d 256, 227 Ill.Dec. 428, 687 N.E.2d 910, 917 (Ill.1997) (given the results of nine VNTR probes plus PCR-based typing, two experts testified that a semen sample originated from the defendant).

103. NRC II, *supra* note 1, at 195. If an opinion as to uniqueness were simply tacked on to a statistical presentation, it might be challenged as cumulative. *Cf. id.* ("Opinion testimony about uniqueness would simplify the presentation of evidence by dispensing with specific estimates of population frequencies or probabilities. If the basis of an opinion were attacked on statistical grounds, however, or if frequency or probability estimates were admitted, this advantage would be lost.").

104. The NRC committee merely suggested that a sufficiently small random match probability compared to the earth's population could justify a conclusion of uniqueness. The committee did not propose any single figure, but asked: "Does a profile frequency of the reciprocal of twice the earth's population suffice? Ten times? One hundred times?" *Id.* at 194. Another approach would be to consider the probability of recurrence in a close relative. *Cf.* Thomas

R. Belin et al., *Summarizing DNA Evidence When Relatives are Possible Suspects*, 92 J. AM. STAT. ASS'N 706 (1997).

The FBI uses a slightly complex amalgam of such approaches. Rather than ask whether a profile probably is unique in the world's population, the examiner focuses on smaller populations that might be the source of the evidentiary DNA. When the surrounding evidence does not point to any particular ethnic group or geographic area, the analyst takes the random match probability and multiplies it by ten (to account for any uncertainty due to population structure). The analyst then asks what the probability of generating a population of unrelated people as large as that of the entire U.S. (260 million people) that contains no duplicate of the evidentiary profile would be. If that "no-duplication" probability is 1% or less, the examiner must report that the suspect "is the source of an evidentiary sample." Bruce Budowle et al., *Source Attribution of a DNA Forensic Profile, Forensic Science Communications*, July 2000, *available at* http://www.fbi.gov/hq/lab/fsc/backissu/july2000/source.htm. Similarly, the FBI computes the no-duplication probability in each ethnic or racial subgroup that may be of interest. If that probability is 1% or less, the examiner must report that the suspect is the source of the DNA. *Id.* Finally, if the examiner thinks that a close relative could be the source, and these individuals cannot be tested, standard genetic formulae are used to find the probability of the same profile in a close relative. *Id.* What probability permits the analyst to testify that the suspect is the source in this situation, however, is not specified. This type of testimony is questioned in IAN W. EVETT & BRUCE S. WEIR, INTERPRETING DNA EVIDENCE: STA-

§ 11–1.2.5   Proficiency Test Records[105]

In a validation study, the researchers empirically verify the ability of the technology to identify features of DNA molecules. In a proficiency study, the focus is on how competently the laboratory's analysts apply a technology that already has been validated.[106] The purpose of proficiency testing is to uncover difficulties that a particular technician or a particular laboratory might be encountering in applying established methods.

Proficiency testing raises a variety of legal issues. As indicated in the previous section, some commentators have suggested that participation in a program of proficiency testing ought to be a prerequisite to the admission of evidence from a forensic laboratory,[107] that proficiency test results should be admissible to show how likely it is that the laboratory erred in the test at bar,[108] and that random match probabilities ought to be inadmissible unless they are combined with proficiency test results to estimate the probability of a false match. If the second suggestion is followed, and the defense is allowed to introduce evidence of proficiency tests to suggest that the laboratory is prone to err, a further question arises: Should the prosecution be permitted to present testimony that the defense has not retested or even requested the opportunity to retest the samples?[109]

[1]   Is Proficiency Testing a Prerequisite to Admission?

The first suggestion, that courts condition admissibility on proficiency testing, is a departure from the usual practice. As indicated in the previous section, the scientific validity and general acceptance standards relate to the capacity of an analytical procedure to generate accurate results when properly applied, and not to whether the individual or institution using a valid or generally accepted method is skilled and careful or is instead careless and prone to error.[110] Of course, the latter issue can be of paramount importance, but usually it is said to be a matter affecting the weight of the evidence rather than its admissibility.[111]

[2]   When Are Errors on Proficiency Tests Admissible?

The second suggestion, that testimony about proficiency test results be

---

TISTICAL GENETICS FOR FORENSIC SCIENTISTS 108–18 (1998).

105. The discussion in this section is adapted from Imwinkelried & Kaye, *supra* note 13. Proficiency testing of DNA laboratories is described more fully *infra* § 11–2.5.1.3.

106. Proficiency testing in forensic genetic testing is designed to ascertain whether an analyst can correctly determine genetic types in a sample the origin of which is unknown to the analyst but is known to a tester. Proficiency is demonstrated by making correct genetic typing determinations in repeated trials, and not by opining on whether the sample originated from a particular individual. Proficiency tests also require laboratories to report random match probabilities to determine if proper calculations are being made.

107. *See, e.g.,* Scheck, *supra* note 20, at1979–87; Thompson, *supra* note 20, at 417.

108. *See, e.g.,* Koehler, *supra* note 57, at 37–38; Scheck, *supra* note 20, at 1984 n. 93.

109. *Cf.* James Wooley & Rockne P. Harmon, *The Forensic DNA Brouhaha: Science or Debate?*, 51 AM. J. HUM. GENETICS 1164 (1992) (letter urging defense experts who criticize laboratory procedures to do their own tests).

110. United States v. Shea, 957 F.Supp. 331, 340–41 (D.N.H.1997).

111. *See* Imwinkelried, *supra* note 20. In extreme cases, where the laboratory departs so grossly from accepted practices that the reliability of its findings are in serious doubt, the court may well exclude the evidence on the ground that its probative value is too slight to warrant its admission.

used to reveal the chance of error in the case at bar, presupposes that such evidence is admissible at trial. In its 1992 report, a committee of the National Academy of Sciences took the position that "laboratory error rates must be continually estimated in blind proficiency testing and must be disclosed to juries."[112] Some courts then held that when the prosecution introduces testimony about the probability of a coincidentally matching profile, the defendant is entitled to introduce testimony about the laboratory's proficiency tests.[113] Indeed, it has been held that the opponent must be allowed to cross-examine one laboratory representative about errors committed by other analysts at the laboratory.[114]

In contrast, in a report published in 1996, a second committee of the National Academy declined to take a position on whether evidence of laboratory error rates, as estimated from proficiency studies, should be admissible at trial.[115] However, the report's discussion of proficiency testing raises questions about the probative value of such evidence. For example, the report notes that "[t]he pooling of proficiency-test results across laboratories" could mislead a jury and "penalize the better laboratories."[116] It adds that even a test of the same laboratory might be outdated, since the laboratory may have taken corrective action.[117] In these circumstances, the testimony could be vulnerable to an objection under Federal Rule of Evidence 403, which requires the exclusion of evidence whose probative value is substantially outweighed by the dangers of prejudice, confusion of the issues, or undue consumption of time.[118]

A further objection is that the testimony represents inadmissible character evidence.[119] If the theory of logical relevance is merely that the laboratory's past commission of errors increases the probability that the laboratory erred on the occasion in question, then the theory amounts to forbidden character reasoning.[120] It is precisely the theory of logical relevance generally banned by

112. NRC I, *supra* note 1, at 89.

113. *E.g.*, United States v. Porter, 1994 WL 742297 (D.C.Super.Ct.1994).

114. Williams v. State, 342 Md. 724, 679 A.2d 1106 (Md.1996).

115. The report stated that the committee had chosen to limit its remarks to the question of "what aspects of the procedures used in connection with forensic DNA testing are scientifically valid...." NRC II, *supra* note 1, at 185.

116. *Id.* at 86.

117. *Id.* (asserting that "[a] laboratory is not likely to make the same error again"); *see also* NRC I, *supra* note 1, at 120 (recognizing that "errors on proficiency tests do not necessarily reflect permanent probabilities of false-positive or false-negative results").

118. *Cf.* United States v. Lowe, 954 F.Supp. 401, 415 (D.Mass.1996), *aff'd*, 145 F.3d 45 (1st Cir.1998) (rejecting the argument that an expert *must* present an error rate from proficiency tests along with the random-match probability).

119. Edward J. Imwinkelried, *Coming to Grips with Scientific Research in* Daubert's

"Brave New World": The Courts' Need to Appreciate the Evidentiary Differences between Validity and Proficiency Studies, 61 BROOK. L. REV. 1247, 1273–78 (1995). A number of jurisdictions have abolished the character evidence prohibition as it applies to a defendant's character in certain types of cases such as rape or child abuse. See FED. R. EVID. 413–15; CAL. EVID. CODE §§ 1108–09. In these jurisdictions that allow the prosecution to rely on an accused past misconduct as circumstantial proof of the offense that is charged, the defense conceivably could argue that the differential treatment of the accused's inculpatory misconduct and the exculpatory proficiency test results violates the equal protection guarantee. *E.g.*, Nettles v. State, 683 So.2d 9, 12 (Ala.Crim.App.1996). However, the constitutional attacks on character-evidence restrictions on defense evidence have failed. EDWARD J. IMWINKELRIED & NORMAN M. GARLAND, EXCULPATORY EVIDENCE: THE ACCUSED'S CONSTITUTIONAL RIGHT TO INTRODUCE FAVORABLE EVIDENCE Ch. 14 (2d ed.1996).

120. *See, e.g.*, Moorhead v. Mitsubishi Aircraft Int'l, 828 F.2d 278 (5th Cir.1987) (error to admit pilot's low marks at flight school refresher course); *see generally* 1 McCORMICK ON EVIDENCE, *supra* note 13, § 186.

Federal Rule of Evidence 404.[121] Moreover, to the extent that proficiency test results constitute evidence of specific acts introduced to show a general tendency to make mistakes, they seem to run afoul of Rule 405, which forbids this form of proof of character.[122]

This issue is rarely recognized as a character evidence problem in the trial court,[123] but a trial judge might find it difficult to justify overruling a properly phrased character-evidence objection when the theory of relevance is nothing more than a general tendency of the laboratory to make mistakes. If there is a consensus that the jury sometimes needs the proficiency test results as an antidote to overwhelmingly small random match probabilities, then the federal and state rules governing character evidence should be altered to give the trial court the discretion to admit the evidence.[124]

Moreover, both the bench and bar should appreciate that in some circumstances, however, proficiency tests of the laboratory involved in the case should be held admissible without relaxing the ban on character evidence. The ban applies only when the sole theory of logical relevance is that the existence of errors in the past suggests a tendency to err that might affect the result in the case at bar. There might be situations in which the defense can use the test data at trial on an entirely different theory of logical relevance. Assume, for instance, that the experts in a case disagree over whether a peak or a band observed in a DNA test is due to an allele or is an artifact. Evidence that spurious peaks or bands have occurred under similar circumstances in profi-

---

121. Federal Rule 404(a) provides that "[e]vidence of a person's character or a trait of his character is not admissible for the purpose of proving that he acted in conformity therewith on a particular occasion...." Section (b) of the rule recognizes certain exceptions to this blanket rule of exclusion, but none are apposite here. There also is an exception permitting a witness's opponent to impeach the witness by questioning the witness about prior untruthful acts. FED.R.EVID. 608(b). However, those acts relate to the witness's character trait for untruthfulness, rather the trait of competence or proficiency. The Federal Rules expressly carve out the exception for untruthfulness, but there is no comparable exception for the character trait of competence or proficiency.

122. Federal Rule 405(a) provides that "In all cases in which evidence of character or a trait of character of a person is admissible, proof may be made by testimony as to reputation or by testimony in the form of an opinion. On cross-examination, inquiry is allowable into relevant specific instances of conduct." Section (b) permits specific act evidence only when character is "in issue"—a term of art that has no application to the tendency of laboratory personnel to make mistakes in performing DNA tests. See 1 McCORMICK ON EVIDENCE, *supra* note 13, § 187.

123. *But see* United States v. Shea, 957 F.Supp. 331, 344 n. 42 (D.N.H.1997) ("The parties assume that error rate information is admissible at trial. This assumption may well be incorrect. Even though a laboratory or industry error rate may be logically relevant, a

strong argument can be made that such evidence is barred by Fed.R.Evid. 404 because it is inadmissible propensity evidence."); Unmack v. Deaconess Medical Center, 291 Mont. 280, 967 P.2d 783 (Mont.1998) (going to the brink of explicitly holding that the character evidence prohibition bars this type of testimony).

124. Courts also generally have not addressed the impact of the character-evidence ban on expert testimony about the conditions under which eyewitness identifications are likely to be in error. Such testimony is unusual, and exclusion almost invariably is upheld on appeal. In the rare cases where appellate courts have held that the failure to admit the evidence was an abuse of discretion, they have not mentioned the rule against character-evidence. See State v. Chapple, 135 Ariz. 281, 660 P.2d 1208 (Ariz.1983); People v. McDonald, 37 Cal.3d 351, 208 Cal.Rptr. 236, 690 P.2d 709 (Cal.1984). Of course, much of this type of testimony falls outside the character-evidence rule. Thus, the rule does not ban testimony that "weapons focus" interferes with the accuracy of eyewitness identifications any more than it bans testimony that handling DNA samples from the suspect and the crime scene without taking precautions against cross-contamination can produce false matches. On the other hand, testimony that people err in their identifications a specified fraction of the time resembles testimony about the incidence of medical mistakes in hospitals, the safety record of airlines, and the like. These error statistics the law traditionally excludes.

ciency tests of the laboratory on known samples would lend support to the defense theory that the band in the pending case is an artifact. In this situation, proficiency test data are relevant because they provide information about the operating characteristics of the DNA test at that particular laboratory.[125]

[3] Must Proficiency Tests be Used to Modify Random-match Probabilities?

The third suggestion relating to proficiency testing is that random-match probabilities should be inadmissible unless accompanied by or blended with the laboratory's error rate.[126] The 1996 committee observed that combining the two figures "would deprive the trier of fact of the opportunity to separately evaluate the possibility that the profiles match by coincidence as opposed to the possibility that they are reported to match by reason of laboratory or handling error."[127] The committee took the position that "a calculation which combines error rates with match probabilities is inappropriate."[128] The reasoning supporting the committee's position essentially sounds under Federal Rule of Evidence 403.[129] If anything, the Rule 403 objection is more substantial here than when it is urged as a basis for excluding testimony offered to impeach the laboratory's competence. In this situation, the questions about the validity of industry-wide error rates and the staleness of even the laboratory's own tests are equally applicable and call into question the probative worth of the testimony. Moreover, there is a heightened risk that the jury will be confused. Error rates and random match probabilities relate

---

125. Of course, even when the proficiency test data would be admissible and the defense has a legitimate need to discover this type of information, there might be means of satisfying the need other than by furnishing proficiency test results. By way of example, a sampling of the laboratory's case work could meet the need. However, in most cases permitting discovery of proficiency test data may be preferable. It will likely be more convenient for the laboratory to reveal the proficiency test data, since that data has already been compiled and giving the defense access to actual case work could compromise the privacy of the persons involved in those cases. When the defense needs to discover information about the operating characteristics of a laboratory's test for a purpose other than merely establishing the laboratory's general error rate, the data could prove to be admissible at trial; hence, the courts would not be justified in denying discovery of proficiency test results on the ground that such discovery cannot lead to the production of admissible evidence at trial.

126. Combining the random-match probability with the probability of a false-positive laboratory error according the rules governing conditional probabilities would give the jury an estimate of the probability that the laboratory would find a match if the source of the crime-scene DNA were neither the defendant nor a close relative. When random-match probabili-

ties are orders of magnitude smaller than estimates of the chance of a laboratory error of some kind, the possible error rate derived from proficiency testing dominates the combined error risk. As explained in Thompson, *supra* note 20, at 421 n. 59:

> The overall probability that a match will be declared if the samples are from different people is approximately (although not precisely) the sum of the probability of an erroneous match and the probability of a random match. Let S designate that two samples have the same source and $-S$ that they do not; let M designate that two samples have matching DNA profiles and $-M$ that they do not; and let D designate that a match is declared by a DNA analyst following testing. The overall probability of a false match, $P(D|-S)$, is not simply the sum of the probability of a random match, $P(M|-S)$, and the probability of an erroneous match, $P(D|-M)$, but rather, $P(D|-S) = P(D|M)P(M|-S) + P(D|-M)P(-M|-S)$. Because $P(D|M)$ and $P(-M|-S)$ will usually be close to one, however, the sum of the probability of a random match and an erroneous match is close to the overall probability of a false match.

127. NRC II, *supra* note 1, at 85.

128. *Id.* at 87.

129. *See generally* Berger, *supra* note 23.

to distinct hypotheses, and a lay juror may find it difficult to understand the significance of a computation which merges the rates and the probability. That mode of computation could place even greater strain on the jurors' ability to comprehend the body of evidence submitted to them.[130] The few courts that have addressed the argument that error rates should be used to the exclusion of random-match probabilities have not been persuaded.[131]

[4] Is the Opportunity to Retest a Permissible Response to Defense Arguments about Proficiency Testing?

While defense counsel or experts originated the first three suggestions, the fourth suggestion related to proficiency testing has been made by prosecutors. The thrust of this suggestion is that when the defense is allowed to introduce evidence of proficiency tests of the laboratory employing the prosecution expert to suggest that the laboratory is prone to err, the prosecution should be permitted to present testimony that the defense has not retested or even requested the opportunity to retest the samples analyzed by the prosecution expert.[132]

The testimony would be logically relevant on several theories. To begin with, if a defense expert testifies that the laboratory result is untrustworthy, it would be relevant to impeach the defense expert's credibility on the ground that a scientist who truly doubted the accuracy of the analysis normally would have retested the samples to resolve the matter.[133] Inasmuch as replication is a crucial and common feature of scientific inquiry, it could be argued that neglecting to retest is prior inconsistent conduct. On this theory, the defense would be entitled to a limiting instruction to the effect that the expert's failure to retest is not offered to show that the test result is correct, but only to demonstrate that the defense expert is not sincere in asserting that it is flawed.[134]

The probative value of a failure to retest in showing an expert's insincerity, however, is open to question. It is not uncommon for scientists to question in print or otherwise the adequacy of another researcher's experiment before undertaking to replicate it. And even if such opinions were unheard of in the course of ordinary science, the expert may have been retained for the limited purpose of giving an opinion on the adequacy of the testing that was done rather than redoing that testing. Nevertheless, the inference of insincerity

130. *See* Schklar & Diamond, *supra* note 53, 130, at 179 (concluding that separate figures are desirable in that "[j]urors ... may need to know the disaggregated elements that influence the aggregated estimate as well as how they were combined in order to evaluate the DNA test results in the context of their background beliefs and the other evidence introduced at trial.").

131. *E.g.*, Armstead v. State, 342 Md. 38, 673 A.2d 221 (Md.1996) (rejecting the argument that the introduction of a random match probability deprives the defendant of due process because the error rate on proficiency tests is many orders of magnitude greater than the match probability).

132. When the defense argues that the prosecution failed to perform appropriate DNA tests because it feared they would have exonerated the defendant, the prosecution may be permitted to respond that a similar inference can be drawn from the defendant's failure to test material that is made available to it. *See* Hamel v. State, 803 S.W.2d 878, 880 (Tex.Ct.App.1991) (stating that this prosecutorial response is "clearly legitimate" and does not shift the burden of proof to the defendant).

133. This theory does not apply if the defense introduces the proficiency test data by cross-examining the prosecution's experts rather than producing its own expert.

134. FED.R.EVID.105.

need not be particularly strong for the "inconsistent" conduct to be a proper, logically relevant subject for cross-examination.[135]

Second, if the defense expert offers an opinion that the laboratory's results may be in error, the expert's failure to request or conduct an independent test would be relevant to suggest that the jury should give less weight to that opinion.[136] The prosecution could argue to the jury that an expert who fails to use a more definitive and readily available procedure for ascertaining whether the initial test results are correct has not been thorough in evaluating those results, and that such experts deserve little credence because the basis for the opinion is not as complete as it could be. Again, the inference may be debatable, but the standard of relevance, particularly on cross-examination, is lenient.

Third, whether or not a defense expert discusses proficiency tests, the prosecution could argue that the defense failure to retest (or to request a retest) amounts to an admission by conduct by the defendant.[137] The courts have applied the admission-by-conduct theory to a litigant's failure to present evidence when "it would be natural" for the litigant to introduce such testimony.[138] The prosecution might urge that it would be natural for a defendant affected by a false match to seek retesting and that it would be natural for a DNA expert who entertained serious doubts about the accuracy of a prior test to retest the samples.[139]

In short, there are reasonable arguments for permitting the prosecution to raise the issue of retesting when a defendant questions the laboratory's ability to type DNA samples correctly. But even if the inquiry is probative of the insincerity or lack of thoroughness of the expert, or an admission by the defendant, there are potential objections to this counterthrust by the prosecution. One objection is that the inquiry is inconsistent with the prosecution's burden of proof.[140] To reinforce the allocation of the burden to the government, some courts generally forbid prosecution comment on the defense failure to produce evidence.[141] The argument runs that the defense is entitled to rely on the burden and has no obligation to present any evidence at trial. According to this line of argument, it is improper to convert the defense's failure to present testimony into prosecution evidence.[142] Under this line of

---

135. The impeaching statement or conduct "need only bend in a different direction." JOHN M. MCNAUGHT & HAROLD FLANNERY, MASSACHUSETTS EVIDENCE: A COURTROOM REFERENCE 13–5 (1988).

136. Thus, in *People v. Oliver*, 306 Ill. App.3d 59, 239 Ill.Dec. 196, 713 N.E.2d 727 (Ill.Ct.App.1999), the state was allowed to show that a defense expert who questioned the results of DNA tests had done no testing of his own. *See id.* at 736 ("it was proper for the prosecution to bring out on cross-examination that the defense criticisms of the prosecution's expert witnesses were not based on any independent testing that it had done.").

137. 2 MCCORMICK, *supra* note 13, § 264.

138. *Id.* at 174.

139. On this theory, the defense is not entitled to a limiting instruction; an admission by conduct qualifies as substantive evidence.

140. People v. Harbold, 124 Ill.App.3d 363, 79 Ill.Dec. 830, 464 N.E.2d 734, 741 (Ill.Ct. App.1984).

141. Hayes v. State, 660 So.2d 257 (Fla. 1995); People v. Wills, 151 Ill.App.3d 418, 104 Ill.Dec. 278, 502 N.E.2d 775, 777–78 (Ill.Ct. App.1986); State v. Primus, 341 S.C. 592, 535 S.E.2d 152 (S.C.Ct.App.2000).

142. A related argument looks to the privilege against self-incrimination. *Griffin v. California*, 380 U.S. 609, 614, 5 Ohio Misc. 127, 85 S.Ct. 1229, 14 L.Ed.2d 106 (1965), teaches that the prosecution may not comment on the accused invocation of the privilege. However, a prosecutor's statement that the defense has not introduced rebuttal expert testimony would not amount to impermissible comment. Courts have held that similar statements from the prosecution were improper only when the

authority, the defense could bar prosecution comment about the defense's failure to retest the DNA sample. However, even in such a jurisdiction, if the defense overreached, prosecution comment might be permitted as an invited response.[143] In addition, some jurisdictions reject that line of authority and allow comment on the defense's failure to present exculpatory evidence[144] so long as the trial judge clearly instructs the jury that the prosecution has the ultimate burden of proof.

A further objection is that the admission of the testimony is inconsistent with the defendant's attorney-client privilege. A number of jurisdictions apply the attorney-client privilege when, as part of trial preparation, defense counsel hires an expert to evaluate private information from the defendant, such as the defendant's mental or physical condition.[145] The Advisory Committee Note to draft Federal Rule of Evidence 503 endorsed the application of the attorney-client privilege to experts,[146] and some courts have gone to the length of invoking the theory even when the expert did not evaluate information realistically originating from the defendant.[147] Based on these authorities, the defense might contend that the attorney-client privilege applies to a defense expert's retest of a DNA sample. The gist of the objection would be that if the result of a retest would be privileged, it is wrong-minded to penalize the defense for failing to retest.

As with the other suggestions related to proficiency testing, the case law offers little guidance. In principle, it would seem that once the defense has sharpened the issue of the prosecution expert's use of proper test procedures, the prosecution should be allowed to elicit testimony about the defense's failure to retest at least to probe the basis for the expert's opinion and as circumstantial evidence of defendant's belief that retesting would not yield a different result. The fact that the prosecution has the burden of persuasion does not make such inferences impermissible.[148] The constitutional require-

defendant was the only potential witness who could contradict the prosecution. Bergmann v. McCaughtry, 65 F.3d 1372, 1377 (7th Cir. 1995); United States v. Martinez, 937 F.2d 299 (7th Cir.1991). In a case involving DNA, the prosecutor's comments would relate to potential rebuttal testimony by an expert witness rather than any testimony from the accused.

143. Wise v. State, 132 Md.App. 127, 751 A.2d 24 (Md.Ct.App.2000).

144. Van Woudenberg ex rel. Foor v. Gibson, 211 F.3d 560, 570 (10th Cir.2000) ("The prosecutor may ... comment on the defendant's failure to present evidence or call witnesses"); People v. Guzman, 96 Cal.Rptr.2d 87, 80 Cal.App.4th 1282 (Ct.App.2000).

145. Miller v. District Court, 737 P.2d 834, 838 (Colo.1987); State v. Pratt, 284 Md. 516, 398 A.2d 421 (Md.1979); White v. State, 990 P.2d 253 (Okla.Crim.App.1999); State v. Riddle, 155 Or.App. 526, 964 P.2d 1056, 1063 (Or.Ct.App.), *modified*, 156 Or.App. 606, 969 P.2d 1032 (Or.Ct.App.1998); Note, *Disclosures by Criminal Defendant to Defense–Retained Psychiatrist Held Within Scope of Attorney–Client Privilege Which Defendant Does Not

Waive by Pleading Insanity, 9 U. BALT. L. REV. 99, 111 (1979).

146. As enacted, Rule 503 leaves the recognition and development of privileges under federal law to the courts. The original draft would have codified and defined the privileges. Its description of the attorney-client privilege remains useful to courts as they continue to define and refine that privilege.

147. State v. Riddle, 155 Or.App. 526, 964 P.2d 1056 (Or.Ct.App.), *modified*, 156 Or.App. 606, 969 P.2d 1032 (Or.Ct.App.1998) (accident reconstruction expert).

148. Thus, in *Fluellen v. Campbell,* 683 F.Supp. 186 (M.D.Tenn.1987), defense counsel argued that the state's case was weakened by the fact that it failed to have blood tests performed, and the prosecutor remarked in rebuttal "if he thinks that is such good evidence, why didn't he request that it be done?" *Id.* at 89. The federal district court found that "this comment in no way imposed upon the jury a presumption which conflicted 'with the overriding presumption of innocence with which the law endows the accused and which extends to every element of the crime.'" *Id.*

ment for proof beyond a reasonable doubt regulates the quantum of proof the prosecution must present, but no court has invoked the requirement to preclude the prosecution from introducing an otherwise admissible item of evidence. In appropriate circumstances, the majority of courts permit prosecutors to comment on a defendant's failure to produce evidence such as an available witness who would presumably corroborate the defendant's testimony.[149]

Neither should the attorney-client privilege pose an insurmountable barrier. Certainly, the prosecution cannot comment on a defendant's decision to exercise a constitutional privilege,[150] and comment on a defendant's failure to produce a witness is often forbidden when the defendant stands in a privileged relationship with the witness.[151] Consequently, it might be justifiable to apply the attorney-client privilege to a defense expert's actual analysis of material that has become available because of the defendant's exercise of the right to prepare a defense with the assistance of counsel. Perhaps material that both emanates from the defendant and is still confidential would fall into this category. However, these conditions do not seem to be satisfied in this setting. The DNA sample that the defendant suggests has been misanalyzed might be crime-scene material that was not obtained from the defendant, or it could be a sample that the prosecution lawfully acquired from the defendant. In these situations, the attorney-client privilege should not preclude adverse comment on the defense failure to retest.

§ 11–1.3　Relevant Expertise

DNA identification can involve testimony about laboratory findings, about the statistical interpretation of these findings, and about the underlying principles of molecular biology. Consequently, expertise in several fields might be required to establish the admissibility of the evidence or to explain it adequately to the jury. The expert who is qualified to testify about laboratory techniques might not be qualified to testify about molecular biology, to make estimates of population frequencies, or to establish that an estimation procedure is valid.

Trial judges ordinarily are accorded great discretion in evaluating the qualifications of a proposed expert witness, and the decisions depend on the background of each witness. Courts have noted the lack of familiarity of academic experts—such as statisticians or biologists who have done respected work in other fields—with the scientific literature on forensic DNA typing,[152] and on the extent to which their research or teaching lies in other areas.[153]

149. Alan Stephens, Annotation, *Adverse Presumption or Inference Based on Party's Failure to Produce or Examine Family Members Other than Spouse—Modern Cases*, 80 A.L.R.4TH 337, 344 (1990); Alan Stephens, Annotation, *Adverse Presumption or Inference Based on Party's Failure to Produce or Examine Friend—Modern Cases*, 79 A.L.R.4th 779, 785–86 (1990).

150. Most, but not all jurisdictions also forbid comment on the invocation of a statutory or common-law privilege. 1 McCORMICK, *supra* note 13, § 74.1.

151. *See, e.g.*, Alan Stephens, Annotation, *Adverse Presumption or Inference Based on Party's Failure to Produce or Examine Spouse—Modern Cases*, 79 A.L.R.4TH 694 (1990).

152. *See, e.g.*, State v. Copeland, 130 Wash.2d 244, 922 P.2d 1304, 1318 n. 5 (Wash. 1996) (noting that defendant's statistical expert, Seymour Geisser, "was also unfamiliar with publications in the area," including studies by "a leading expert in the field" whom he thought was "a guy in a lab somewhere").

153. *E.g., id.* (noting that defendant's population genetics expert, Laurence Mueller,

Although such concerns may give trial judges pause, they rarely result in exclusion of the testimony on the ground that the witness simply is not qualified as an expert.[154]

The other side of this coin is technicians or scientists with ample expertise in laboratory methods, but less familiarity with population genetics. For example, in *State v. Harvey*,[155] Nathaniel Harvey was convicted of a brutal murder and sentenced to death. A "senior molecular biologist," and "a microbiologist and supervisor of forensic casework" at a private laboratory[156] testified that DNA tests showed that blood samples recovered at the crime scene were genetically comparable to defendant's DNA and that the genotype was common to one–in–1,400 African–Americans.[157] On appeal, Harvey did not dispute the qualifications of these witnesses as experts in the field of DNA testing, but argued that such witnesses, not being statisticians, were not competent to explain the databases and the formula used to derive this figure.[158]

The qualifications of a scientist or technician to testify to statistical estimates should turn on the familiarity of the expert with the methods used,[159] the complexity of those methods, and the extent to which comparable use of such methods is commonplace. The more complex the methods and the less obvious it is that they are appropriate to the problem at hand, the more the expert should be knowledgeable in statistics. The construction of DNA databases and the estimation of genotype frequencies in most cases is not unduly complex.[160] In *Harvey*, the Supreme Court of New Jersey simply observed that "defendant's own expert . . . did not take issue with [the] databases or . . . mathematical formula" and invoked the legal principle that "the competency of a witness to testify as an expert is an issue remitted to the sound discretion of the trial court."[161] On this basis, it concluded that the admission of the biologists' testimony about DNA databases and the frequency of genetic markers in the population was not an abuse of discretion.[162]

"had published little in the field of human genetics, only one non-peer reviewed chapter in a general text, had two papers in the area rejected, was uninformed of the latest articles in the field, had misused a statistical model . . ., had no graduate students working under him, had not received any awards in his field in over ten years, had not received a research grant in about eight years, and made about $100,000 testifying as an expert in 1990–91").

154. *E.g.*, Commonwealth v. Blasioli, 454 Pa.Super. 207, 685 A.2d 151 (Pa.Super.Ct.1996) (professor of ecology and evolutionary biology was said to be qualified, but "barely").

155. 151 N.J. 117, 699 A.2d 596 (N.J.1997).

156. *Id.* at 608.

157. *Id.*

158. *Id.* at 637.

159. *See, e.g.*, People v. Contreras, 246 Ill. App.3d 502, 186 Ill.Dec. 204, 615 N.E.2d 1261, 1265 (Ill.Ct.App.1993) (noting that a "forensic geneticist" with a bachelor's degree in medical technology had "taken master's level courses in genetics and statistics").

160. *But see* NRC II, *supra* note 1, at 133–34 (1996) (suggesting formulas of greater complexity when "the suspect and other possible sources of the sample belong to the same [ethnic] subgroup").

161. 699 A.2d at 637.

162. *Id.* at 637. Likewise, in *State v. Loftus*, 573 N.W.2d 167 (S.D.1997), a prosecution expert from a private company testified to "the possibility of a random match." The defendant argued that although the expert was qualified "in DNA matching techniques," he "was not qualified to give statistical probability DNA opinion because he is not a population geneticist." *Id.* at 173. The South Dakota Supreme Court correctly rejected the proposition that it takes a population geneticist to testify to genotype frequencies. It observed, somewhat cursorily, that "[t]here was ample evidence before the trial court that [the witness] possessed expert qualifications in the area of DNA, which would include statistical DNA probability analysis." *Id.* "Concerning [the expert's] qualifications to present statistical DNA evidence," the Supreme Court wrote only that the expert

Of course, even an expert who is well qualified to testify in a particular field may have unusual views. However, the scientific and legal literature on the objections to DNA evidence is extensive.[163] By studying the scientific publications, or perhaps by appointing a special master or expert adviser to assimilate this material, a court can ascertain where a party's expert falls in the spectrum of scientific opinion. Furthermore, an expert appointed by the court under Federal Rule of Evidence 706 could testify about the scientific literature generally or even about the strengths or weaknesses of the particular arguments advanced by the parties.[164]

B. SCIENTIFIC STATUS

by

David H. Kaye* & George F. Sensabaugh, Jr**

§ 11–2.0 THE SCIENTIFIC STATUS OF DNA TYPING

§ 11–2.1 Overview of Variation in DNA and Its Detection

Deoxyribonucleic acid is a complex molecule that contains the "genetic code" of organisms as diverse as bacteria and humans.[1] This section describes the structure of DNA and how this molecule differs from person to person. It explains at a general level how DNA differences are detected. Finally, the section indicates how it is shown that these differences permit individuals to be identified.

§ 11–2.1.1 DNA, Chromosomes, Sex, and Genes

DNA is made of subunits that include four *nucleotide bases*, whose names are abbreviated to A, T, G, and C.[2] The physical structure of DNA is described more fully in the appendix, but for general purposes it suffices to say that a DNA molecule is like a long sequence of these four letters, where the chemical structure that corresponds to each letter is known as a *base pair*.

"testified that he has published several papers including one focusing on some of the 'statistical methods available for determining whether two DNA samples match.'" *Id.* at 173 n.7.

163. *See, e.g.,* Bruce S. Weir, *A Bibliography for the Use of DNA in Human Identification, in* Human Identification: The Use of DNA Markers 179–213 (Bruce S. Weir ed., 1995); NRC II, *supra* note 1, at 226–39 (list of references).

164. Some courts have appointed experts to address general questions relating to DNA profiling. *E.g.,* United States v. Bonds, 12 F.3d 540 (6th Cir.1993); United States v. Porter, 1994 WL 742297 (D.C.Super.Ct.1994) (mem.). Whether a court should appoint its own expert instead of an expert for the defense when there are more specific disputes is more controversial.

* David H. Kaye is Regents' Professor, Arizona State University College of Law, and Fellow, Center for the Study of Law, Science, and Technology. He was a member of the National Academy of Sciences' Committee on DNA Forensic Science: An Update and was reporter for the Legal Issues Working Group of the National Commission on the Future of DNA Evidence.

** George F. Sensabaugh, Jr., is Professor, School of Public Health, University of California at Berkeley. He was a member of the National Academy of Sciences' Committee on DNA Technology in Forensic Science and its subsequent Committee on DNA Forensic Science: An Update.

§ 11–2.0

1. Some viruses use a related nucleic acid, RNA, instead of DNA to encode genetic information.

2. The full names are adenine, thymine, guanine, and cytosine.

Most human DNA is tightly packed into structures known as *chromosomes*, which are located in the *nuclei* of most cells.[3] If the bases are like letters, then each chromosome is like a book written in this four-letter alphabet, and the nucleus is like a bookshelf in the interior of the cell. All the cells in one individual contain copies of the same set of books. This library, so to speak, is the individual's *genome*.[4]

In human beings, the process that produces billions of cells with the same genome starts with sex. Every sex cell (a sperm or ovum) contains 23 chromosomes. When a sperm and ovum combine, the resulting fertilized cell contains 23 pairs of chromosomes, or 46 in all. It is as if the father donates half of his collection of 46 books, and the mother donates a corresponding half of her collection. During pregnancy, the fertilized cell divides to form two cells, each of which has an identical copy of the 46 chromosomes. The two then divide to form four, the four form eight, and so on. As gestation proceeds, various cells specialize to form different tissues and organs. In this way, each human being has immensely many copies[5] of the original 23 pairs of chromosomes from the fertilized egg, one member of each pair having come from the mother and one from the father.

All told, the DNA in the 23 chromosomes contains over three billion letters (base pairs) of genetic "text."[6] About 99.9% is identical between any two individuals. This similarity is not really surprising—it accounts for the common features that make humans an identifiable species. The remaining 0.1% is particular to an individual (identical twins excepted). This variation makes each person genetically unique.

A *gene* is a particular DNA sequence, usually from 1,000 to 10,000 base pairs long, that "codes" for an observable characteristic.[7] For example, a tiny part of the sequence that directs the production of the human group-specific complement protein (GC)[8] is

G C A A A A T T G C C T G A T G C C A C A C C C A A G G A A C T G G C A [9]

This gene always is located at the same position, or *locus*, on chromosome number 4. As we have seen, most individuals have two copies of each gene at a given locus—one from the father and one from the mother.

A locus where almost all humans have the same DNA sequence is called *monomorphic* ("of one form"). A locus at which the DNA sequence varies among individuals is called *polymorphic* ("of many forms"). The alternative forms are called *alleles*. For example, the GC protein gene sequence has three

3. A few types of cells, such as red blood cells, do not contain nuclei.

4. Originally, "genome" referred to the set of base pairs in an egg or sperm, but the term also is used to designate the ordered set in the fertilized cell.

5. The number of cells in the human body has been estimated at more than 10^{15} (a million billion).

6. If the base pairs were listed as letters in a series of books, one piled on top of the other, the pile would be as high as the Washington monument.

7. The genetic code consists of "words" that are three nucleotides long and that deter-

mine the structure of the proteins that are manufactured in cells. *See, e.g.*, ELAINE JOHNSON MANGE & ARTHUR P. MANGE, BASIC HUMAN GENETICS 107 (2d ed.1999).

8. This "GC" stands for "group complement," and not for the bases guanine and cytosine.

9. The full GC gene is nearly 42,400 base pairs in length. The product of this gene is also known as vitamin D–binding protein. GC is one of the five loci included in the polymarker (PM) typing kit, which is widely used in forensic testing.

common alleles that result from *single nucleotide polymorphisms* (SNPs, pronounced "snips")—substitutions in the base that occur at a given point.[10] In terms of the metaphor of DNA as text, the gene is like an important paragraph in the book; a SNP is a change in a letter somewhere within that paragraph, and the two versions of the paragraph that result from this slight change are the alleles. An individual who inherits the same allele from both parents is called a *homozygote*.[11] An individual with distinct alleles is termed a *heterozygote*.[12]

Regions of DNA used for forensic analysis usually are not genes, but parts of the chromosome without a known function. The "non-coding" regions of DNA have been found to contain considerable sequence variation, which makes them particularly useful in distinguishing individuals. Although the terms "locus," "allele," "homozygous," and "heterozygous" were developed to describe genes, the nomenclature has been carried over to describe all DNA variation—coding and noncoding alike—for both types are inherited from mother and father in the same fashion.

§ 11–2.1.2 Types of Polymorphisms and Methods of Detection

By determining which alleles are present at strategically chosen loci, the forensic scientist ascertains the genetic profile, or *genotype*, of an individual. Genotyping does not require "reading" the full DNA sequence; indeed, direct sequencing is technically demanding and time-consuming.[13] Rather, most genetic typing focuses on identifying only those variations that define the alleles and does not attempt to "read out" each and every base as it appears.[14]

For instance, simple sequence variation, such as that for the GC locus, is conveniently detected using a *sequence-specific oligonucleotide* (SSO) *probe*. With GC typing, probes for the three common alleles (which we shall call A_1,

---

10. In the scientific literature, the three alleles are designated Gc*1F, Gc*1S, and Gc*2, and the sequences at the variable site are shown in Figure 1.

Figure 1. The variable sequence region of the vitamin D-binding protein gene. The base substitutions that define the alleles are shown in bold.

Allele *2: G C A A A A T T G C C T G A T G C C A C A C C C A A G G A A C T G G C A

Allele *1F: G C A A A A T T G C C T G A T G C C A C A C C C A **C** G G A A C T G G C A

Allele *1S: G C A A A A T T G C C T G A **G** G C C A C A C C C A **C** G G A A C T G G C A

See R.L. Reynolds & G.F. Sensabaugh, *Use of the Polymerase Chain Reaction for Typing Gc Variants, in* 3 ADVANCES IN FORENSIC HAEMOGENETICS 158 (H.F. Polesky & W.R. Mayr eds. 1990); A. Braun et al., *Molecular Analysis of the Gene for Human Vitamin–D-binding Protein (Group-specific Component): Allelic Differences of the Common GC Types,* 89 HUM. GENETICS 401 (1992). These are examples of *point mutations.*

11. For example, someone with the Gc*2 allele on both number 4 chromosomes is homozygous at the GC locus. This homozygous GC genotype is designated as 2,2 (or simply 2).

12. For example, someone with the Gc*2 allele on one chromosome and the Gc*1F allele on the other is heterozygous at the GC locus. This heterozygous genotype is designated as 2,1F.

13. However, automated machinery for direct sequencing has been developed and is used at major research centers engaged in the international endeavor to sequence the human genome and the genomes of other organisms. *See* R. Waterston & J.E. Sulston, *The Human Genome Project: Reaching the Finish Line,* 282 SCIENCE 53 (1998). Further improvements in methods for efficient sequencing are on the horizon. *See, e.g.,* David Adam, *Individual Genomes Targeted in Sequencing Revolution,* 411 NATURE 402 (2001) . .

14. For example, genetic typing at the GC locus focuses on the sequence region shown in Figure 1; the remainder of the 42,300 base pairs of the GC gene sequence is the same for almost all individuals and is ignored for genetic typing purposes.

A_2, and A_3) are attached to designated locations on a membrane. When DNA with a given allele (say, A_1) comes in contact with the probe for that allele, it sticks.[15] To get a detectable quantity of DNA to stick, many copies of the variable sequence region of the GC gene in the DNA sample have to be made.[16] All this DNA then is added to the membrane. The DNA fragments with the allele A_1 in them stick to the spot with the A_1 probe. To permit these fragments to be seen, a chemical "label" that catalyses a color change at the spot where the DNA binds to its probe can be attached when the copies are made. A colored spot showing that the A_1 allele is present thus should appear on the membrane.[17]

Another category of polymorphism is characterized by the insertion of a *variable number of tandem repeats* (VNTR) at a locus.[18] The core unit of a VNTR is a particular short DNA sequence that is repeated many times end-to-end. This repetition gives rise to alleles with length differences; regions of DNA containing more repeats are larger than those containing fewer repeats. Genetic typing of polymorphic VNTR loci employs *electrophoresis*, a technique that separates DNA fragments based on size.[19]

The first polymorphic VNTRs to be used in genetic and forensic testing had core repeat sequences of 15–35 base pairs. Alleles at VNTR loci of this sort generally are too long to be measured precisely by electrophoretic methods—alleles differing in size by only a few repeat units may not be distinguished. Although this makes for complications in deciding whether two length measurements that are close together result from the same allele, these loci are quite powerful for the genetic differentiation of individuals, for they tend to have many alleles that occur relatively rarely in the population. At a locus with only 20 such alleles (and most loci typically have many more), there are 210 possible genotypes.[20] With five such loci, the number of possible genotypes is 210^5, which is more than 400 billion. Thus, VNTRs are an extremely discriminating class of DNA markers.

More recently, the attention of the genetic typing community has shifted to repetitive DNA characterized by short core repeats, two to seven base pairs in length. These noncoding DNA sequences are known as *short tandem repeats* (STRs).[21] Because STR alleles are much smaller than VNTR alleles, electrophoretic detection permits the exact number of base pairs in an STR to be determined, allowing alleles to be defined as discrete entities. Figure 2 illustrates the nature of allelic variation at a polymorphic STR locus. The first allele has nine tandem repeats, the second has ten, and the third has eleven.[22]

15. This process of *hybridization* is described in Appendix Part B.

16. The polymerase chain reaction (PCR) is used to make many copies of the DNA that is to be typed. PCR is roughly analogous to copying and pasting a section of text with a word-processor. *See infra* Appendix Part 4.

17. This approach can be miniaturized and automated with hybridization chip technology. *See infra* glossary ("chip").

18. *VNTR* polymorphisms also are referred to as *minisatellites*.

19. We describe one form of electrophoresis often used with VNTR loci *infra* § 11–2.3.

20. There are 20 homozygous genotypes and another $(20 \times 19)/2 = 190$ heterozygous ones.

21. They also are known as *microsatellites*. A valuable reference work that focuses on the STRs now used in forensic typing is JOHN M. BUTLER, FORENSIC DNA TYPING: BIOLOGY AND TECHNOLOGY BEHIND STR MARKERS (2001).

22. To conserve space, the figure uses alleles that are unrealistically short. A typical STR is in the range of 50–350 base pairs in length.

Figure 2. Three Alleles of an STR with the Core Sequence ATTT

ATTTATTTATTTATTTATTTATTTATTTATTTATTT

ATTTATTTATTTATTTATTTATTTATTTATTTATTT

ATTTATTTATTTATTTATTTATTTATTTATTTATTTATTT

Although there are fewer alleles per locus for STRs than for VNTRs, there are many STRs, and they can be analyzed simultaneously.[23] As more STR loci are included, STR testing becomes more revealing than VNTR profiling at four or five loci.[24]

Full DNA sequencing is employed at present only for mitochondrial DNA (mtDNA).[25] *Mitochondria* are small structures found inside the cell. In these organelles, certain molecules are broken down to supply energy. Mitochondria have a small genome that bears no relation to the chromosomal genome in the cell nucleus.[26] Mitochondrial DNA has three features that make it useful for forensic DNA testing. First, the typical cell, which has but one nucleus, contains hundreds of identical mitochondria.[27] Hence, for every copy of chromosomal DNA, there are hundreds of copies of mitochondrial DNA. This means that it is possible to detect mtDNA in samples containing too little nuclear DNA for conventional typing.[28] Second, the mtDNA contains a sequence region of about a thousand base pairs that varies greatly among individuals. Finally, mitochondria are inherited mother to child,[29] so that siblings, maternal half-siblings, and others related through maternal lineage possess the same mtDNA sequence.[30] This last feature makes mtDNA particularly useful for associating persons related through their maternal lineage— associating skeletal remains to a family, for example.[31]

Just as genetic variation in mtDNA can be used to track maternal lineages, genetic variations on the *Y chromosome* can be used to trace

23. The procedures for simultaneous detection are known as *multiplex* methods. *See infra* Glossary ("capillary electrophoresis," "chip"). *Mass spectroscopy* also can be applied to detect STR fragments. *Id.*

24. Usually, there are between seven and fifteen STR alleles per locus. Thirteen loci that have ten STR alleles each can give rise to 55^{13}, or 42 billion trillion possible genotypes.

25. Mitochondrial sequence variations also can be detected with other procedures. *See* Rebecca Reynolds et al., *Detection of Sequence Variation in the HVII Region of the Human Mitochondrial Genome in 689 Individuals Using Immobilized Sequence–Specific Oligonucleotide Probes*, 45 J. FORENSIC SCI. 1210 (2000); M. Stoneking et al., *Population Variation of Human mtDNA Control Region Sequences Detected by Enzymatic Amplification and Sequence-specific Oligonucleotide Probes*, 48 AM. J. HUM. GENETICS 370 (1991).

26. In contrast to the haploid nuclear genome of over three billion base pairs, the mitochondrial genome is a circular molecule 16,569 base pairs long.

27. There are between 75 to 1,000 or so mitochondria per cell.

28. Even so, because the mitochondrial genome is so much shorter than the nuclear genome, it is a tiny fraction of the total mass of DNA in a cell.

29. Although sperm have mitochondria, these are not passed to the ovum at fertilization. Thus the only mitochondria present in the newly fertilized cell originate from the mother.

30. Evolutionary studies suggest an average mutation rate for the mtDNA control region of one nucleotide difference every 300 generations, or one difference every 6,000 years. Consequently, one would not expect to see many examples of nucleotide differences between maternal relatives. On the other hand, differences in the bases at a specific sequence position among the copies of the mtDNA within an individual have been seen. This *heteroplasmy*, which is more common in hair than other tissues, counsels against declaring an exclusion on the basis of a single base pair difference between two samples.

31. *See, e.g.*, Peter Gill et al., *Identification of the Remains of the Romanov Family by DNA Analysis*, 6 NATURE GENETICS 130 (1994).

paternal lineages. Y chromosomes, which contain genes that result in development as a male rather than a female, are found only in males and are inherited father to son. Markers on this chromosome include STRs and SNPs,[32] and they have been used in cases involving semen evidence.[33]

In sum, DNA contains the genetic information of an organism. In humans, most of the DNA is found in the cell nucleus, where it is organized into separate chromosomes. Each chromosome is like a book, and each cell has the same library of books of various sizes and shapes. There are two copies of each book of a particular size and shape, one that came from the father, the other from the mother. Thus, there are two copies of the book entitled "Chromosome One," two copies of "Chromosome Two," and so on. Genes are the most meaningful paragraphs in the books, and there are differences (polymorphisms) in the spelling of certain words in the paragraphs of different copies of each book. The different versions of the same paragraph are the alleles. Some alleles result from the substitution of one letter for another. These are SNPs. Others come about from the insertion or deletion of single letters, and still others represent a kind of stuttering repetition of a string of extra letters. These are the VNTRs and STRs. In addition to the 23 pairs of books in the cell nucleus, another page or so of text resides in each of the mitochondria, the power plants of the cell.

The methods of molecular biology permit scientists to determine which alleles are present. The next two sections describe how this is done. Section 11–2.2 discusses the procedures that can distinguish among all the known alleles at certain loci. Section 11–2.3 deals with the "RFLP" procedures that measure the lengths of DNA fragments at a scale that is not fine enough to resolve all the possible alleles.

§ 11–2.2   DNA Profiling with Discrete Alleles

Simple sequence variations and STRs occur within relatively short fragments of DNA. These polymorphisms can be analyzed with so-called PCR-based tests. The three steps of PCR-based typing are (1) DNA extraction, (2) amplification, and (3) detection of genetic type using a method appropriate to the polymorphism. This section discusses the scientific and technological foundations of these three steps and the basis for believing that the DNA characteristics identified in the laboratory can help establish who contributed the potentially incriminating DNA.[34]

§ 11–2.2.1   DNA Extraction and Amplification

DNA usually can be found in biological materials such as blood, bone,

32. *See, e.g.,* M.F. Hammer et al., *The Geographic Distribution of Human Y Chromosome Variation,* 145 GENETICS 787 (1997). The Y chromosome is used in evolutionary studies along with mtDNA to learn about human migration patterns. *Id.;* M.F. Hammer & S.L. Zegura, *The Role of the Y Chromosome in Human Evolutionary Studies,* 5 EVOLUTIONARY ANTHROPOLOGY 116 (1996). The various markers are inherited as a single package (known as a *haplotype*).

33. They also were used in a family study to ascertain whether President Thomas Jefferson fathered a child of his slave, Sally Hemmings. *See* E.A. Foster et al., *Jefferson Fathered Slave's Last Child,* 396 NATURE 27 (1998); Eliot Marshall, *Which Jefferson Was the Father?,* 283 SCIENCE 153 (1999).

34. The problem of drawing an inference about the source of the evidence DNA, which is common to all forms of DNA profiling, is taken up *infra* § 11–2.6.

saliva, hair, semen, and urine.[35] A combination of routine chemical and physical methods permit DNA to be extracted from cell nuclei and isolated from the other chemicals in a sample.[36] Thus, the premise that DNA is present in many biological samples and can be removed for further analysis is firmly established.[37]

Just as the scientific foundations of DNA extraction are clear, the procedures for amplifying DNA sequences within the extracted DNA are well established. The first National Academy of Sciences committee on forensic DNA typing described the amplification step as "simple . . . analogous to the process by which cells replicate their DNA."[38] Details of this process, which can make millions of copies of a single DNA fragment, are given in the Appendix.

For amplification to work properly and yield copies of only the desired sequence, however, care must be taken to achieve the appropriate biochemical conditions and to avoid excessive contamination of the sample.[39] A laboratory should be able to demonstrate that it can faithfully amplify targeted sequences with the equipment and reagents that it uses[40] and that it has taken suitable precautions to avoid or detect handling or carryover contamination.[41]

§ 11–2.2.2 DNA Analysis

To determine whether the DNA sample associated with a crime could have come from a suspect, the genetic types as determined by analysis of the DNA amplified from the crime-scene sample are compared to the genetic types as determined for the suspect. For example, Figure 3 shows the results of STR typing at four loci in a sexual assault case.[42]

35. See, e.g., COMMITTEE ON DNA TECHNOLOGY IN FORENSIC SCIENCE, NATIONAL RESEARCH COUNCIL, DNA TECHNOLOGY IN FORENSIC SCIENCE 28 (1992) (Table 1.1) [hereinafter NRC I].

36. See, e.g., Michael L. Baird, *DNA Profiling: Laboratory Methods*, in 1 MODERN SCIENTIFIC EVIDENCE: THE LAW AND SCIENCE OF EXPERT TESTIMONY § 16–2.2, at 667 (David L. Faigman et al. eds., 1997); Catherine T. Comey et al., *DNA Extraction Strategies for Amplified Fragment Length Polymorphism Analysis*, 39 J. FORENSIC SCI. 1254 (1994); Atsushi Akane et al., *Purification of Forensic Specimens for the Polymerase Chain Reaction (PCR) Analysis*, 38 J. FORENSIC SCI. 691 (1993).

37. See, e.g., NRC I, *supra* note 35, at 149 (recommending judicial notice of the proposition that "DNA polymorphisms can, in principle, provide a reliable method for comparing samples," "although the actual discriminatory power of any particular DNA test will depend on the sites of DNA variation examined"); COMMITTEE ON DNA FORENSIC SCIENCE: AN UPDATE, NATIONAL RESEARCH COUNCIL, THE EVALUATION OF FORENSIC DNA EVIDENCE 9 (1996) [hereinafter NRC II] ("DNA typing, with its extremely high power to differentiate one human being from

another, is based on a large body of scientific principles and techniques that are universally accepted.").

38. NRC I, *supra* note 35, at 40. The second committee used similar language, reporting that "[t]he PCR process is relatively simple and easily carried out in the laboratory." NRC II, *supra* note 37, at 70. *But see* NRC I, *supra*, at 63 ("Although the basic exponential amplification procedure is well understood, many technical details are not, including why some primer pairs amplify much better than others, why some loci cause systematically unfaithful amplification, and why some assays are much more sensitive to variations in conditions."). For these reasons, PCR-based procedures are validated by experiment.

39. See NRC I, *supra* note 35, at 63–67; NRC II, *supra* note 37, at 71.

40. See NRC I, *supra* note 35, at 63–64.

41. Carryover occurs when the DNA product of a previous amplification contaminates samples or reaction solutions. *See id*. at 66.

42. The initials CTTA refer to these loci, which are known as CPO, TPO, THO, and Amelogenin.

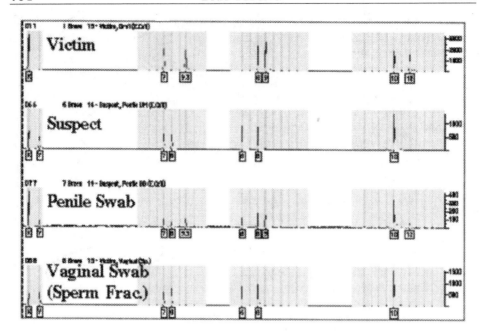

The peaks result from DNA fragments of different sizes.[43] The bottom row shows the profile of sperm DNA isolated from a vaginal swab. These sperm have two alleles at the first locus (indicating that both X and Y chromosomes are present),[44] two alleles at the second locus (consisting of 7 and 8 repeat units), two at the third locus (a 6 and an 8), and one (a 10 on each chromosome) at the fourth.[45] The same profile also appears in the DNA taken from the suspect. DNA from a penile swab from the suspect is consistent with a mixture of DNA from the victim and the suspect.

Regardless of the kind of genetic system used for typing—STRs, Amp–FLPs,[46] SNPs, or still other polymorphisms[47]—some general principles and questions can be applied to each system that is offered for courtroom use. As a beginning, the nature of the polymorphism should be well characterized. Is it a simple sequence polymorphism or a fragment length polymorphism? This information should be in the published literature or in archival genome databanks.[48]

43. The height of (more, precisely, the area under) each peak is related to the amount of DNA in the gel.

44. The X–Y typing at the first locus is simply used to verify the sex of the source of the DNA. XY is male, and XX is female. That these markers show that the victim is female and the suspect male helps demonstrate that a valid result has been obtained.

45. Although each sperm cell contains only one set of chromosomes, a collection of many sperm cells from the same individual contains both sets of chromosomes.

46. "Amp–FLP" is short for "Amplified Fragment Length Polymorphism." The DNA fragment is produced by amplifying a longish sequence with a PCR primer. The longer Amp–FLPs, such as DS180, overlap the shorter VNTRs. In time, PCR methods will be capable of generating longer Amp–FLPs.

47. *See supra* § 11–2.1; *infra* Appendix Part C (Table A–1).

48. Primary data regarding gene sequence variation is increasingly being archived in publically accessible computer databanks, such as GenBank, rather than in the print literature. *See* Victor A. McKusick, *The Human Genome Project: Plans, Status, and Applications in Biology and Medicine, in* GENE MAPPING: USING LAW AND ETHICS AS GUIDES 18, 35 (George J. Annas & Sherman Elias eds.1992). This trend is driven by an explosion of new data coupled

Second, the published scientific literature also can be consulted to verify claims that a particular method of analysis can produce accurate profiles under various conditions.[49] Although such "validation studies" have been conducted for all the discrete-allele systems ordinarily used in forensic work, determining the point at which the empirical validation of a particular system is sufficiently convincing to pass scientific muster may well require expert assistance.

Finally, the population genetics of the marker should be characterized. As new marker systems are discovered, researchers typically analyze convenient collections of DNA samples from various human populations[50] and publish studies of the relative frequencies of each allele in these population samples. These database studies give a measure of the extent of genetic variability at the polymorphic locus in the various populations, and thus of the potential probative power of the marker for distinguishing between individuals.

At this point, the existence of PCR-based procedures that can ascertain genotypes accurately cannot be doubted.[51] Of course, the fact that scientists have shown that it is possible to extract DNA, to amplify it, and to analyze it in ways that bear on the issue of identity does not mean that a particular laboratory has adopted a suitable protocol and is proficient in following it. These laboratory-specific issues are considered in § 11-2.5.

§ 11-2.3   VNTR Profiling

VNTR profiling, described in general terms § 11-2.1, was the first widely used method of forensic DNA testing. Consequently, its underlying principles, its acceptance within the scientific community, and its scientific soundness have been discussed in a great many opinions.[52] Because so much has been written on VNTR profiling, and because the method is being supplanted by more efficient procedures involving discrete allele systems,[53] only the basic steps of the procedure will be outlined here.

1.   Like profiling by means of discrete allele systems, VNTR profiling begins with the extraction of DNA from a crime-scene sample. (Because this

with the fact that most of the detected variation has no known biological significance and hence is not particularly noteworthy.

49.   *Cf.* NRC I, *supra* note 35, at 72 ("Empirical validation of a DNA typing procedure must be published in appropriate scientific journals.").

50.   The samples come from diverse sources, such as blood banks, law enforcement personnel, paternity cases, and criminal cases. Reliable inferences probably can be drawn from these samples.

51.   *See, e.g.,* United States v. Shea, 159 F.3d 37 (1st Cir.1998) (DQA, Polymarker, D1S80); United States v. Lowe, 145 F.3d 45 (1st Cir.1998) (DQA, Polymarker, D1S80); United States v. Beasley, 102 F.3d 1440, 1448 (8th Cir.1996) (DQA, Polymarker); United States v. Hicks, 103 F.3d 837 (9th Cir.1996) (DQA); United States v. Gaines, 979 F.Supp. 1429 (S.D.Fla.1997) (DQA, Polymarker,

D1S80); State v. Hill, 257 Kan. 774, 895 P.2d 1238 (Kan.1995) (DQA); Commonwealth v. Rosier, 425 Mass. 807, 685 N.E.2d 739 (Mass. 1997) (STRs); Commonwealth v. Vao Sok, 425 Mass. 787, 683 N.E.2d 671 (Mass.1997) (DQA, Polymarker, D1S80); State v. Moore, 268 Mont. 20, 885 P.2d 457 (Mont.1994) (DQA), *overruled on other grounds in* State v. Gollehon, 274 Mont. 116, 906 P.2d 697 (Mont.1995); State v. Harvey, 151 N.J. 117, 699 A.2d 596 (N.J.1997) (DQA, Polymarker); State v. Lyons, 324 Or. 256, 924 P.2d 802 (Or.1996) (DQA); State v. Moeller, 548 N.W.2d 465 (S.D.1996) (DQA); State v. Begley, 956 S.W.2d 471 (Tenn. 1997) (DQA); State v. Russell, 125 Wash.2d 24, 882 P.2d 747, 768 (Wash.1994) (DQA).

52.   *See* NRC II, *supra* note 37, at 205–11 (listing leading cases and status as of 1995, by jurisdiction). The first reported appellate opinion is *Andrews v. State,* 533 So.2d 841 (Fla. Dist.Ct.App.1988).

53.   *See supra* § 11-2.2.

DNA is not amplified, however, larger quantities of higher quality DNA[54] are required.)

2. The extracted DNA is "digested" by a *restriction enzyme* that recognizes a particular, very short sequence; the enzyme cuts the DNA at these *restriction sites*. When a VNTR falls between two restriction sites, the resulting DNA fragments will vary in size depending on the number of core repeat units in the VNTR region.[55] (These VNTRs are thus referred to as a *restriction fragment length polymorphism*, or RFLP.)

3. The digested DNA fragments are then separated according to size by *gel electrophoresis*. The digest sample is placed in a well at the end of a lane in an agarose gel, which is a gelatin-like material solidified in a slab. Digested DNA from the suspect is placed in another well on the same gel. Typically, control specimens of DNA fragments of known size, and, where appropriate, DNA specimens obtained from a victim, are run on the same gel. Mild electric current applied to the gel slowly separates the fragments in each lane by length, as shorter fragments travel farther in a fixed time than longer, heavier fragments.

4. The resulting array of fragments is transferred for manageability to a sheet of nylon by a process known as Southern blotting.[56]

5. The restriction fragments representing a particular polymorphic locus are "tagged" on the membrane using a sequence-specific probe labeled with a radioactive or chemical tag.[57]

6. The position of the specifically bound probe tag is made visible, either by autoradiography (for radioactive labels) or by a chemical reaction (for chemical labels). For autoradiography, the washed nylon membrane is placed between two sheets of photographic film. Over time, the radioactive probe material exposes the film where the biological probe has hybridized with the DNA fragments.[58] The result is an *autoradiograph*, or an autorad, a visual pattern of bands representing specific DNA fragments. An autorad that shows two bands in a single lane indicates that the individual who is the source of the DNA is a heterozygote at that locus. If the autorad shows only one band, the person may be homozygous for that allele (that is, each parent contributed the same allele), or the second band may be present but invisible for technical

---

54. "Quality" refers to the extent to which the original, very long strands of DNA are intact. When DNA degrades, it forms shorter fragments. RFLP testing requires fragments that are on the order of at least 20,000–30,000 base pairs long.

55. *See supra* § 11–2.

56. This procedure is named after its inventor, Edwin Southern. Either before or during this transfer, the DNA is *denatured* ("unzipped") by alkali treatment, separating each double helix (*see infra* Appendix, Figure A–1) into two single strands. The weak bonds that connect the two members of a base pair are easily broken by heat or chemical treatment. The bonds that hold a base to the backbone and keep the backbone intact are much stronger. Thus, the double-stranded helix separates

neatly into two single strands, with one base at each position.

57. This locus-specific probe is a single strand of DNA that binds to its complementary sequence of denatured DNA in the sample. *See supra* § 11–2.2. The DNA locus identified by a given probe is found by experimentation, and individual probes often are patented by their developers. Different laboratories may use different probes (i.e., they may test for alleles at different loci). Where different probes (or different restriction enzymes) are used, test results are not comparable.

58. One film per probe is checked during the process to see whether the process is complete. Because this can weaken the image, the other film is left undisturbed, and it is used in comparing the positions of the bands.

reasons. The band pattern defines the person's genotype at the locus associated with the probe.

Once an appropriately exposed autorad is obtained, the probe is stripped from the membrane, and the process is repeated with a separate probe for each locus tested. Three to five probes are typically used, the number depending in part on the amount of testable DNA recovered from the crime-scene sample. The result is a set of autorads, each of which shows the results of one probe.[59] If the crime-scene and suspect samples yield bands that are closely aligned on each autorad, the VNTR profiles[60] from the two samples are considered to match.[61]

§ 11–2.3.1   Validity of the Underlying Scientific Theory

The basic theory underlying VNTR profiling is textbook knowledge. The molecular structure of DNA,[62] the presence of highly polymorphic VNTR loci,[63] and the existence of methods to produce VNTR fragments and measure their lengths are not in doubt.[64] Indeed, some courts have taken judicial notice of these scientific facts.[65] In short, the ability to discriminate between human DNA samples using a relatively small number of VNTR loci is widely accepted.

§ 11–2.3.2   Validity and Reliability of the Laboratory Techniques

The basic laboratory procedures for VNTR analysis have been used in other settings for many years: "The complete process—DNA digestion, electrophoresis, membrane transfer, and hybridization—was developed by Edwin Southern in 1975.... These procedures are routinely used in molecular biology, biochemistry, genetics, and clinical DNA diagnosis...."[66] Thus, "no

---

59. For a photograph of an autorad, see, *e.g.*, NRC II, *supra* note 37.

60. Each autorad reveals a single-locus genotype. The collections of single-locus profiles, one for each single-locus probe, sometimes is called a multi-locus VNTR profile. A "multi-locus probe," however, is a single probe that produces bands on a single autorad by hybridizing with VNTRs from many loci at the same time. It is, in other words, like a cocktail of single-locus probes. Because it is more difficult to interpret autoradiographs from multi-locus probes, these probes have not been used in criminal cases in the United States.

61. Issues that arise in interpreting autoradiographs and declaring matches are considered *infra* § 11–2.6.

62. *See supra* § 11–2.1.

63. Studies of the population genetics of VNTR loci are reviewed in NRC II, *supra* note 37. *See also infra* § 11–2.6.

64. *See, e.g.,* NRC I, *supra* note 35, at 149 (recommending judicial notice of the proposition that "DNA polymorphisms can, in principle, provide a reliable method for comparing samples," but cautioning that "te actual discriminatory power of any particular DNA test will depend on the sites of DNA variation examined"); NRC II, *supra* note 1, at 9 ("DNA typing, with its extremely high power to differentiate one human being from another, is based on a large body of scientific principles and techniques that are universally accepted."); *id.* at 36 ("Methods of DNA profiling are firmly grounded in molecular technology. When profiling is done with appropriate care, the results are highly reproducible.").

65. *See, e.g.,* State v. Fleming, 698 A.2d 503, 507 (Me.1997) (taking judicial notice that "the overall theory and techniques of DNA profiling [are] scientifically reliable if conducted in accordance with appropriate laboratory standards and controls"); State v. Davis, 814 S.W.2d 593, 602 (Mo.1991); People v. Castro, 144 Misc.2d 956, 545 N.Y.S.2d 985, 987 (N.Y.Sup.Ct.1989); cases cited, NRC II, *supra* note 37, at 172 n. 15.

66. NRC I, *supra* note 35, at 38.

scientific doubt exists that [these technologies] accurately detect genetic differences.''[67]

Before concluding that a particular enzyme-probe combination produces accurate profiles as applied to crime-scene samples at a particular laboratory, however, courts may wish to consider studies concerning the effects of environmental conditions and contaminants on VNTR profiling as well as the laboratory's general experience and proficiency with these probes. And the nature of the sample and other considerations in a particular case can affect the certainty of the profiling. The next two sections outline the type of inquiry that can help assess the accuracy of a profile in a specific case.

§ 11–2.4 Sample Quantity and Quality

The primary determinant of whether DNA typing can be done on any particular sample is (1) the quantity of DNA present in the sample and (2) the extent to which it is degraded. Generally speaking, if a sufficient quantity of reasonable quality DNA can be extracted from a crime-scene sample, no matter what the nature of the sample, DNA typing can be done without problem. Thus, DNA typing has been performed successfully on old blood stains, semen stains, vaginal swabs, hair, bone, bite marks, cigarette butts, urine, and fecal material. This section discusses what constitutes sufficient quantity and reasonable quality in the contexts of PCR-based genetic typing[68] and VNTR analysis by Southern blotting.[69] Complications due to contaminants and inhibitors also are discussed. Finally, the question of whether the sample contains DNA from two or more contributors is considered.

§ 11–4.1.1 Did the Sample Contain Enough DNA?

The amount of DNA in a cell varies from organism to organism. The DNA in the chromosomes of a human cell, for example, is about two thousand times greater than that in a typical bacterium.[70] Within an organism, however, DNA content is constant from cell to cell. Thus, a human hair root cell contains the same amount of DNA as a white cell in blood or a buccal cell in saliva.[71] Amounts of DNA present in some typical kinds of samples are indicated in

---

67. OFFICE OF TECHNOLOGY ASSESSMENT, GENETIC WITNESS: FORENSIC USES OF DNA TESTS 59 (1990). The 1992 NRC report therefore recommends that courts take judicial notice that:

[t]he current laboratory procedure for detecting DNA variation (specifically, single-locus probes analyzed on Southern blots without evidence of band shifting) is fundamentally sound, although the validity of any particular implementation of the basic procedure will depend on proper characterization of the reproducibility of the system (e.g., measurement variation) and the inclusion of all necessary scientific controls.

NRC I, *supra* note 35, at 149. The 1996 report reiterates the conclusion that "[t]he techniques of DNA typing [including RFLP analysis] are fully recognized by the scientific community." NRC II, *supra* note 37, at 50. It insists that "[t]he state of the profiling technology and the methods for estimating frequencies and related statistics have progressed to the point where the admissibility of properly collected and analyzed DNA data should not be in doubt." *Id.* at 36.

68. *See supra* § 11–2.2.

69. *See supra* § 11–2.3.

70. A human egg or sperm cell contains half as much DNA; hence, the haploid human genome is about one thousand larger than the typical bacterial genome.

71. A human cell contains about six picograms of DNA. (A picogram (pg) is one trillionth (1/1,000,000,000,000) of a gram.) Sperm cells constitute a special case, for they contain half a genetic complement (that which the father passes along to an offspring) and so contain half as much DNA (about 3 pg). The 3 pg of DNA varies from sperm cell to sperm cell because each such cell has a randomly drawn half of the man's chromosomes. The DNA in a semen sample contains many of these cells; being a mixture of the many combinations, it contains all the man's alleles.

Table A–2 of the Appendix. These vary from a trillionth or so of a gram for a hair shaft to several millionths of a gram for a post-coital vaginal swab. RFLP typing requires a much larger sample of DNA than PCR-based typing. As a practical matter, RFLP analysis requires a minimum of about 50 billionths of a gram of relatively non-degraded DNA,[72] while most PCR test protocols recommend samples on the order of one to five billionths of a gram for optimum yields.[73] Thus, PCR tests can be applied to samples containing ten to five hundred-fold less nuclear DNA than that required for RFLP tests.[74] Moreover, mitochondrial DNA analysis works reliably with DNA from even fewer cells. As noted in section 11–2, cells contain only one nucleus, but hundreds of mitochondria. Consequently, even though there rarely is sufficient DNA in a hair shaft to allow testing with nuclear DNA markers, the mitochondrial DNA often can be analyzed.[75]

These sample-size requirements help determine the approach to be taken for a DNA typing analysis. Samples which, from experience, are expected to contain at least fifty to one hundred billionths of a gram of DNA typically are subjected to a formal DNA extraction followed by characterization of the DNA for quantity and quality. This characterization typically involves gel electrophoresis of a small portion of the extracted DNA. This test, however, does not distinguish human from non-human DNA. Since the success of DNA typing tests depends on the amount of human DNA present, it may be desirable to test for the amount of human DNA in the extract.[76] For samples that typically contain small amounts of DNA, the risk of DNA loss during extraction may dictate the use of a different extraction procedure.[77]

Whether a particular sample contains enough human DNA to allow typing cannot always be predicted in advance. The best strategy is to try; if a

72. RFLP analysis has been performed successfully on smaller amounts of DNA but at a cost of longer autoradiograph exposure times. From the standpoint of the reliability of the typing, what is important is the strength of the banding pattern on the autoradiograph or lumigraph. Threshold amounts of DNA may result in weak bands, and some bands could be missed because they are too weak to be observed.

73. Although the polymerase chain reaction can amplify DNA from the nucleus of a single cell, chance effects may result in one allele being amplified much more than another. To avoid preferential amplification, a lower limit of about ten to fifteen cells' worth of DNA has been determined to give balanced amplification. PCR tests for nuclear genes are designed to yield no detectable product for samples containing less than about 20 cell equivalents (100–200 pg) of DNA. This result is achieved by limiting the number of amplification cycles.

74. The great sensitivity of PCR for the detection of DNA, even under these "safe" conditions, is illustrated by the successful genetic typing of DNA extracted from fingerprints. Roland A.H. Van Oorschot & M.K. Jones, *DNA Fingerprints from Fingerprints*, 387 NATURE 767 (1997).

75. *E.g.*, M.R. Wilson et al., *Extraction, PCR Amplification, and Sequencing of Mitochondrial DNA from Human Hair Shafts*, 18 BIOTECHNIQUES 662 (1995). Of course, mitochondrial DNA analysis can be done with other sources of mtDNA.

76. This test entails measuring the amount of a human-specific DNA probe that binds to the DNA in the extract. This test is particularly important in cases where the sample extract contains a mixture of human and microbial DNA. Vaginal swabs, for example, are expected to contain microbial DNA from the vaginal flora as well as human DNA from the female and sperm donor. Similarly, samples that have been damp for extended periods of time often contain significant microbial contamination; indeed, in some cases, little or no human DNA can be detected even though the extract contains significant amounts of DNA.

77. Boiling a sample for a few minutes releases DNA, and this DNA is used directly for PCR without first characterizing the DNA. The boiling step usually is conducted in the presence of a resin that absorbs inhibitors of PCR.

result is obtained, and if the controls (small samples of known DNA) have behaved properly, then the sample had enough DNA.

§ 11–2.4.2 Was the Sample of Sufficient Quality?

The primary determinant of DNA quality for forensic analysis is the extent to which the long DNA molecules are intact. Within the cell nucleus, each molecule of DNA extends for millions of base pairs. Outside the cell, DNA spontaneously degrades into smaller fragments at a rate that depends on temperature, exposure to oxygen, and, most importantly, the presence of water.[78] In dry biological samples, protected from air, and not exposed to temperature extremes, DNA degrades very slowly. In fact, the relative stability of DNA has made it possible to extract usable DNA from samples hundreds to thousands of years old.[79]

RFLP analysis requires relatively non-degraded DNA, and testing DNA for degradation is a routine part of the protocol for VNTR analysis. In RFLP testing, a restriction enzyme cuts long sequences of DNA into smaller fragments. If the DNA is randomly fragmented into very short pieces to begin with, electrophoresis and Southern blotting will produce a smear of fragments rather than a set of well-separated bands.[80]

In contrast, PCR-based tests are relatively insensitive to degradation. Testing has proved effective with old and badly degraded material such as the remains of the Tsar Nicholas family (buried in 1918, recovered in 1991)[81] and the Tyrolean Ice Man (frozen for some 5,000 years).[82] The extent to which degradation affects a PCR-based test depends on the size of the DNA segment to be amplified. For example, in a sample in which the bulk of the DNA has been degraded to fragments well under 1,000 base pairs in length, it may be possible to amplify a 100 base-pair sequence, but not a 1,000 base-pair target. Consequently, the shorter alleles may be detected in a highly degraded sample, but the larger ones may be missed.[83] As with RFLP analysis, this

---

78. Other forms of chemical alteration to DNA are well studied, both for their intrinsic interest and because chemical changes in DNA are a contributing factor in the development of cancers in living cells. Most chemical modification has little effect on RFLP analysis. Some forms of DNA modification, such as that produced by exposure to ultraviolet radiation, inhibit the amplification step in PCR-based tests, while other chemical modifications appear to have no effect. George F. Sensabaugh & C. von Beroldingen, *The Polymerase Chain Reaction: Application to the Analysis of Biological Evidence, in* FORENSIC DNA TECHNOLOGY (M.A. Farley & J.J. Harrington eds., 1991).

79. This has resulted in a specialized field of inquiry dubbed "ancient DNA." ANCIENT DNA: RECOVERY AND ANALYSIS OF GENETIC MATERIAL FROM PALEONTOLOGICAL, ARCHAEOLOGICAL, MUSEUM, MEDICAL, AND FORENSIC SPECIMENS (B. Hermann & S. Hummel eds., 1994); Svante Paaobo, *Ancient DNA: Extraction, Characterization, Molecular Cloning, and Enzymatic Amplification*, 86 PROC. NAT'L ACAD. SCI. USA 1939 (1989).

80. Practically speaking, RFLP analysis can yield interpretable results if the bulk of the

DNA in a sample exceeds 20,000–30,000 base pairs in length. Partial degradation of the DNA can result in the weakening or loss of the signal from large restriction fragments. This effect is usually evident from the appearance of the restriction fragment banding pattern. Another indication of degradation is smearing in the background of the banding pattern. If there is evidence that degradation has affected the banding pattern, the statistical interpretation of a match should account for the possibility that some allelic bands might not have been detected.

81. Peter Gill et al., *Identification of the Remains of the Romanov Family by DNA Analysis*, 6 NATURE GENETICS 130 (1994).

82. O. Handt et al., *Molecular Genetic Analyses of the Tyrolean Ice Man*, 264 SCIENCE 1775 (1994).

83. For example, typing at a genetic locus such as D1S80, for which the target allelic sequences range in size from 300 to 850 base pairs, may be affected by the non-amplification of the largest alleles ("allelic dropout").

possibility would have to be considered in the statistical interpretation of the result.

Allelic dropout of this sort does not seem to be a problem for STR loci, presumably because the size differences between alleles at a locus are so small (typically no more than 50 base pairs). If there is a degradation effect on STR typing, it is "locus dropout": in cases involving severe degradation, loci yielding smaller PCR products (less than 180 base pairs) tend to amplify more efficiently than loci yielding larger products (greater than 200 base pairs).[84]

Surprising as it may seem, DNA can be exposed to a great variety of environmental insults without any effect on its capacity to be typed correctly. Exposure studies have shown that contact with a variety of surfaces, both clean and dirty, and with gasoline, motor oil, acids, and alkalis either have no effect on DNA typing or, at worst, render the DNA untypable.[85]

Although contamination with microbes generally does little more than degrade the human DNA,[86] other problems sometimes can occur with both RFLP[87] and PCR-based analyses.[88] Nevertheless, there are procedures that identify or avoid these anomalies.[89] Therefore, the validation of DNA typing systems should include tests for interference with a variety of microbes to see if artifacts occur; if artifacts are observed, then control tests should be applied to distinguish between the artifactual and the true results.

84. J.P. Whitaker et al., *Short Tandem Repeat Typing of Bodies from a Mass Disaster: High Success Rate and Characteristic Amplification Patterns in Highly Degraded Samples*, 18 BIOTECHNIQUES 670 (1995).

85. Dwight E. Adams et al., *Deoxyribonucleic Acid (DNA) Analysis by Restriction Fragment Length Polymorphisms of Blood and Other Body Fluid Stains Subjected to Contamination and Environmental Insults*, 36 J. FORENSIC SCI. 1284 (1991); R.A.H. van Oorschot et al., *HUMTHO1 Validation Studies: Effect of Substrate, Environment, and Mixtures*, 41 J. FORENSIC SCI. 142 (1996). Most of the effects of environmental insult readily can be accounted for in terms of basic DNA chemistry. For example, some agents produce degradation or damaging chemical modifications. Other environmental contaminants inhibit restriction enzymes or PCR. (This effect sometimes can be reversed by cleaning the DNA extract to remove the inhibitor.) But environmental insult does not result in the selective loss of an allele at a locus or in the creation of a new allele at that locus.

86. Michael B.T. Webb et al., *Microbial DNA Challenge Studies of Variable Number Tandem Repeat (VNTR) Probes Used for DNA Profiling Analysis*, 38 J. FORENSIC SCI. 1172 (1993).

87. Autoradiograms sometimes show many bands that line up with the molecular weight sizing ladder bands. (The "ladder" is a set of DNA fragments of known lengths that are placed by themselves in one or more lanes of the gel. The resulting set of bands provides a benchmark for determining the weights of the unknown bands in the samples.) These extra bands can result from contamination of the sample DNA with ladder DNA at the time the samples are loaded onto the electrophoresis gel. Alternatively, the original sample may have been contaminated with a microbe infected with lambda phage, the virus that is used for the preparation of the sizing ladder.

88. Although PCR primers designed to amplify human gene sequences would not be expected to recognize microbial DNA sequences, much less amplify them, such amplification has been reported with the D1S80 typing system. A. Fernandez–Rodriguez et al., *Microbial DNA Challenge Studies of PCR-based Systems in Forensic Genetics*, 6 ADVANCES IN FORENSIC HAEMOGENETICS 177 (1995).

89. Whatever the explanation for the extra sizing bands mentioned *supra* note 87, the lambda origin of the bands can be demonstrated by an additional probing with the ladder probe alone or with a human specific probe without the ladder probe. Likewise, the spurious PCR products observed by Ferdinand–Rodriguez et al., *supra* note 88, can be differentiated from the true human PCR products, and the same authors have described a modification to the D1S80 typing system that removes all question of the non-human origin of the spurious PCR products. A. Fernandez–Rodriguez et al., *D1S80 Typing in Casework: a Simple Strategy to Distinguish Non-specific Microbial PCR Products from Human Alleles*, 7 PROGRESS IN FORENSIC GENETICS 18 (1997).

§ 11–2.4.3   Does a Sample Contain DNA from More than One Person?

DNA from a single individual can have no more than two alleles at each locus. This follows from the fact that individuals inherit chromosomes in pairs, one from each parent.[90] An individual who inherits the same allele from each parent (a homozygote) can contribute only that one allele to a sample, and an individual who inherits a different allele from each parent (a heterozygote) will contribute those two alleles.[91] Finding three or more alleles at a locus therefore indicates a mixture of DNA from more than one person.[92]

Some kinds of samples, such as post-coital vaginal swabs and blood stains from scenes where several persons are known to have bled, are expected to be mixtures. Sometimes, however, the first indication the sample has multiple contributors comes from the DNA testing. The chance of detecting a mixture by finding extra alleles depends on the proportion of DNA from each contributor as well as the chance that the contributors have different genotypes at one or more loci. As a rule, a minor contributor to a mixture must provide at least 5% of the DNA for the mixture to be recognized.[93] In addition, the various contributors must have some different alleles. The chance that multiple contributors will differ at one or more locus increases with the number of loci tested and the genetic diversity at each locus. Unless many loci are examined, genetic markers with low to moderate diversities do not have much power to detect multiple contributors. Genetic markers that are highly polymorphic are much better at detecting mixtures. Thus, STRs and especially VNTRs are sensitive to mixtures.

§ 11–2.5   Laboratory Performance

DNA profiling is valid and reliable, but confidence in a particular result that is establishing that a suspect is (or is not) the source of a sample depends on the quality control and quality assurance procedures in the laboratory and the handling and nature of the samples that are compared.

§ 11–2.5.1   Quality Control and Assurance

Quality control refers to measures to help ensure that a DNA-typing result (and its interpretation) meets a specified standard of quality. Quality

---

90. See supra § 11–2.1; infra Chapter 26.

91. Loci on the sex chromosomes constitute a special case. Females have two X chromosomes, one from each parent; as with loci on the other chromosomes, they can be either homozygous or heterozygous at the X-linked loci. Males, on the other hand, have one X and one Y chromosome; hence, they have only one allele at X-linked loci and one allele at Y-linked loci. In cases of trisomy, such as XXY males, multiple copies of loci on the affected chromosome will be present, but this condition is rare and often lethal.

92. On very rare occasions, an individual exhibits a phenotype with three alleles at a locus. This can be the result of a chromosome anomaly (such as a duplicated gene on one chromosome or a mutation). A sample from such an individual is usually easily distinguished from a mixed sample. The three-allele

variant is seen at only the affected locus, whereas with mixtures, more than two alleles typically are evident at several loci.

93. With RFLP testing, alleles from a contributor of as little as one percent can be detected at the price of overexposing the pattern from the major contributor. Studies in which DNA from different individuals is combined in differing proportions show that the intensity of the bands reflects the proportions of the mixture. Thus, if bands in a crime-scene sample have different intensities, it may be possible to assign alleles to major and minor contributors. However, if bands are present in roughly equal proportions, this allocation cannot be made, and the statistical interpretation of the observed results must include all possible combinations.

assurance refers to monitoring, verifying, and documenting laboratory performance.[94] A quality assurance program helps demonstrate that a laboratory is meeting its quality control objectives and thus justifies confidence in the quality of its product.

Professional bodies within forensic science have described procedures for quality assurance. Guidelines have been prepared by two FBI-appointed groups—the Technical Working Group on DNA Analysis Methods (TWGDAM)[95] and the DNA Advisory Board (DAB).[96] The DAB also has encouraged forensic DNA laboratories to seek accreditation,[97] and at least two states require forensic DNA laboratories to be accredited.[98] The American Association of Crime Laboratory Directors–Laboratory Accreditation Board (ASCLD–LAB) accredits forensic laboratories.[99]

[1] Documentation

The quality assurance guidelines promulgated by TWGDAM, the DAB, and ASCLD–LAB call for laboratories to document laboratory organization and management, personnel qualifications and training, facilities, evidence control procedures, validation of methods and procedures, analytical procedures, equipment calibration and maintenance, standards for case documentation and report writing, procedures for reviewing case files and testimony, proficiency testing, corrective actions, audits, safety program, and review of subcontractors. Of course, maintaining even such extensive documentation and records does not guarantee the correctness of results obtained in any

94. For general descriptions of quality assurance programs, see NRC I, *supra* note 35, at ch. 3 ("Ensuring High Standards of Laboratory Performance"); NRC II, *supra* note 37, at ch. 4 (1996).

95. *See* Technical Working Group on DNA Analysis Methods, *Guidelines for a Quality Assurance Program for DNA Analysis*, 22 Crime Laboratory Digest 21 (1995) [hereinafter TWGDAM Guidelines]; 18 Crime Laboratory Digest 44 (1991).

96. *See* Federal Bureau of Investigation, Quality Assurance Standards for Forensic DNA Testing Laboratories, July 15, 1998 [hereinafter DAB Standards]; *see also Recommendations of the DNA Commission of the International Society for Forensic Haemogenetics Relating to the Use of PCR-based Polymorphisms,* 64 Vox Sang. 124 (1993); *1991 Report Concerning Recommendations of the DNA Commission of the International Society for Forensic Haemogenetics Relating to the Use of DNA Polymorphism,* 63 Vox Sang. 70 (1992).

Under the DNA Identification Act of 1994, Pub. L. No. 103–322, 108 Stat. 2065 (codified at 42 U.S.C. § 13701 (1994)), to qualify for federal laboratory improvement funds, a forensic DNA laboratory must meet the quality assurance standards recommended by the DAB and issued by the director of the FBI. The DAB membership includes molecular geneticists, population geneticists, an ethicist, and representatives from federal, state, and local forensic DNA laboratories, private sector DNA laboratories, the National Institute of Standards and Technology, and the judiciary. Its recommendations closely follow the 1995 TWGDAM guidelines.

97. DAB Standards, *supra* note 96, at 1 (preface).

98. N. Y. Executive Law § 995–b (McKinney 1999); Cal. DNA and Forensic Identification Data Base and Data Bank Act of 1998, Cal. Penal Code § 297 (West's 1999).

99. *See* American Society of Crime Laboratory Directors–Laboratory Accreditation Board, ASCLD–LAB Accreditation Manual, Jan.1997. As of mid–1998, ASCLD–LAB had accredited laboratories in Australia, New Zealand, and Hong Kong as well as laboratories in the United States and Canada. The ASCLD–LAB accreditation program does not allow laboratories to obtain accreditation only for particular services—a laboratory seeking accreditation must qualify for the full range of services it offers. This constraint has slowed some forensic DNA labs from seeking accreditation. As an interim solution, the National Forensic Science Technology Center (NFSTC) has an agreement with ASCLD–LAB to perform certification audits on DNA sections of laboratories for compliance with DAB and ASCLD–LAB standards; this service is available to private sector DNA laboratories as well as government laboratories.

particular case. Errors in analysis or interpretation might occur as a result of a deviation from an established procedure, analyst misjudgment, or an accident. Although case-review procedures within a laboratory should be designed to detect errors before a report is issued, it is always possible that some incorrect result will slip through. Accordingly, determination that a laboratory maintains a strong quality assurance program does not eliminate the need for case-by-case review.

[2] Validation

The validation of procedures is central to quality assurance. "Developmental" validation is undertaken to determine the applicability of a new test to crime-scene samples; it defines conditions that give reliable results and identifies the limitations of the procedure. For example, a new genetic marker being considered for use in forensic analysis will be tested to determine if it can be typed reliably in both fresh samples and in samples typical of those found at crime scenes. The validation would include testing samples originating from different tissues—blood, semen, hair, bone, samples containing degraded DNA, samples contaminated with microbes, samples containing DNA mixtures, and so on. Developmental validation of a new marker also includes the generation of population databases and the testing of allele and genotype distributions for independence. Developmental validation normally results in publication in the scientific literature, but a new procedure can be validated in multiple laboratories well ahead of publication.

"Internal" validation, on the other hand, involves the verification by a laboratory that it can reliably perform an established procedure that already has undergone developmental validation. Before adopting a new procedure, the laboratory should verify its ability to use the system in a proficiency trial.

Both forms of validation build on the accumulated body of knowledge and experience. Thus, some aspects of validation testing need be repeated only to the extent required to verify that previously established principles apply. One need not validate the principle of the internal combustion engine every time one brings out a new model of automobile.

[3] Proficiency Testing

Proficiency testing in forensic genetic testing is designed to ascertain whether an analyst can correctly determine genetic types in a sample the origin of which is unknown to the analyst but is known to a tester. Proficiency is demonstrated by making correct genetic typing determinations in repeated trials, and not by opining on whether the sample originated from a particular individual. Proficiency tests also require laboratories to report random-match probabilities to determine if proper calculations are being made.

An internal proficiency trial is conducted within a laboratory. One person in the laboratory prepares the sample and administers the test to another person in the laboratory. An external trial is one in which the test sample originates from outside the laboratory—from another laboratory, a commercial vendor, or a regulatory agency. In a declared (or open) proficiency trial the analyst knows the sample is a proficiency sample. In contrast, in a blind (or more properly "full-blind") trial, the sample is submitted so that the analyst does not recognize it as a proficiency sample.[100] It has been argued that full-blind trials provide a better indication of proficiency because the analyst will not give the trial sample any special attention.[101] On the other hand, full-blind proficiency trials for forensic DNA analysis entail considerably more organizational effort and expense than open proficiency trials. Obviously, the "evidence" samples prepared for the trial have to be sufficiently realistic that the laboratory does not suspect the legitimacy of the submission. A police agency and prosecutor's office have to submit the "evidence" and respond to laboratory inquiries with information about the "case." Finally, the genetic profile from a proficiency test must not be entered into regional and national databases.[102]

The DAB recommends that every analyst regularly undergo external, open proficiency testing[103] and that the laboratory take "corrective action whenever proficiency testing discrepancies [or] casework errors are detected."[104] Certification by the American Board of Criminalistics as a specialist in forensic biology DNA analysis requires one proficiency trial per year. Accredited laboratories must maintain records documenting compliance with required proficiency test standards.[105]

§ 11–2.5.2 Handling Samples

Sample mishandling, mislabeling, or contamination, whether in the field or in the laboratory, is more likely to compromise a DNA analysis than an error in genetic typing. For example, a sample mixup due to mislabeling reference blood samples taken at the hospital could lead to incorrect associa-

100. There is potential confusion over nomenclature with regard to open and blind trials. All proficiency tests are blind in the sense that the analyst does not know the composition of the test sample. In some disciplines, any trial in which the analyst receives "unknowns" from a tester is referred to as a blind trial. With regard to proficiency testing in the forensic area, however, the convention is to distinguish "open" and "blind" trials as described here.

101. *See, e.g.*, Barry C. Scheck, *DNA and Daubert*, 15 Cardozo L. Rev. 1980 (1994). Another argument for the full-blind trial is that it tests a broader range of laboratory operations, from submission of the evidence to the laboratory through the analysis and interpretation stages to the reporting out to the submitting agency. However, these aspects of laboratory operations also can be evaluated, at much less cost, by mechanisms such as laboratory audits and random review of case files.

102. The feasibility of mounting a national, full-blind proficiency trial program is under study as a part of the DNA Identification Act of 1994, Pub. L. No. 103–322, 108 Stat. 2065 (codified at 42 U.S.C. § 13701 (1994)). The results of this study, funded by the National Institute of Justice, are to be reported to the

DAB with subsequent recommendations made to the director of the FBI.

103. Standard 13.1 specifies that these tests are to be performed at least as frequently as every 180 days. DAB Standards, *supra* note 96, at 16. TWGDAM recommended two open proficiency tests per year per analyst. TWGDAM Guidelines, *supra* note 95.

104. DAB Standards, *supra* note 96, at 17 (standard 14.1).

105. Proficiency test results from laboratories accredited by ASCLD–LAB are reported also to an ASCLD–LAB Proficiency Review Committee. The committee independently reviews test results and verifies compliance with accreditation requirements. ASCLD–LAB specifies the vendors whose proficiency tests it accepts for accreditation purposes. Since accreditation can be suspended or withdrawn by unacceptable proficiency trial performance, the proficiency test vendors must meet high standards with respect to test-sample preparation and documentation. Yet, in some instances vendors have provided mislabeled or contaminated test samples. *See* TWGDAM & ASCLD–LAB Proficiency Review Committee, *Guidelines for DNA Proficiency Test Manufacturing and Reporting*, 21 Crime Laboratory Digest 27–32 (1994).

tion of crime-scene samples to a reference individual or to incorrect exclusions. Similarly, packaging two items with wet blood stains into the same bag could result in a transfer of stains between the items, rendering it difficult or impossible to determine whose blood was originally on each item. Contamination in the laboratory may result in artifactual typing results or in the incorrect attribution of a DNA profile to an individual or to an item of evidence. Accordingly, it is appropriate to look at the procedures that have been prescribed and implemented to guard against such error.

Mislabeling or mishandling can occur when biological material is collected in the field, when it is transferred to the laboratory, when it is in the analysis stream in the laboratory,[106] when the analytical results are recorded, or when the recorded results are transcribed into a report. Mislabeling and mishandling can happen with any kind of physical evidence and are of great concern in all fields of forensic science. Because forensic laboratories often have little or no control over the handling of evidence prior to its arrival in the laboratory, checkpoints should be established to detect mislabeling and mishandling along the line of evidence flow.[107] Investigative agencies should have guidelines for evidence collection and labeling so that a chain of custody is maintained. Similarly, there should be guidelines, produced with input from the laboratory, for handling biological evidence in the field. These principles remain the same as in the pre-DNA era.[108]

TWGDAM guidelines and DAB recommendations require documented procedures to ensure sample integrity and to avoid sample mixups, labeling errors, recording errors, and the like. They also mandate case review to identify inadvertent errors before a final report is released. Finally, laboratories must retain, when feasible, portions of the crime-scene samples and extracts to allow reanalysis.[109] However, retention is not always possible. For example, retention of original items is not to be expected when the items are large or immobile (for example, a wall or sidewalk). In such situations, a swabbing or scraping of the stain from the item would typically be collected and retained. There also are situations where the sample is so small that it will be consumed in the analysis.[110]

106. *E.g.*, United States v. Cuff, 37 F.Supp.2d 279, 283 (S.D.N.Y.1999).

107. NRC II, *supra* note 37, at 80–82.

108. Samples (particularly those containing wet stains) should not be packaged together, and samples should be dried or refrigerated as soon as possible. Storage in the dry state and at low temperatures stabilizes biological material against degradation. George Sensabaugh, *Biochemical Markers of Individuality, in* FORENSIC SCIENCE HANDBOOK 338, 385 (Richard Saferstein ed., 1982). The only precaution to have gained force in the DNA era is that evidence items should be handled with gloved hands to protect against handling contamination and inadvertent sample-to-sample transfers.

109. Forensic laboratories have a professional responsibility to preserve retained evidence so as to minimize degradation. *See* TWGDAM Guidelines, *supra* note 95, at 30 (para. 6.3). Furthermore, failure to preserve potentially exculpatory evidence has been treated as a denial of due process and grounds for suppression. People v. Nation, 26 Cal.3d 169, 161 Cal.Rptr. 299, 604 P.2d 1051 (Cal. 1980). In *Arizona v. Youngblood*, 488 U.S. 51, 109 S.Ct. 333, 102 L.Ed.2d 281 (1988), however, the Supreme Court held that a police agency's failure to preserve evidence not known to be exculpatory does not constitute a denial of due process unless "bad faith" can be shown. In *Youngblood*, the police had failed to refrigerate a victim's underwear, precluding the serologic testing of semen then available. DNA testing of the underwear conducted nearly two decades later showed that Youngblood was not the source of the stain. *See* Barbara Whitaker, *DNA Frees Inmate Years After Justices Rejected Plea*, N.Y. TIMES, Aug. 11, 2000.

110. When small samples are involved, whether it is necessary to consume the entire sample is a matter of scientific judgment.

Assuming appropriate chain-of-custody and evidence-handling protocols are in place, the critical question is whether there are deviations in the particular case. This may require a review of the total case documentation as well as the laboratory findings.[111]

As the 1996 NRC report emphasizes, an important safeguard against error due to mislabeling and mishandling is the opportunity to retest original evidence items or the material extracted from them.[112] Should mislabeling or mishandling have occurred, reanalysis of the original sample and the intermediate extracts should detect not only the fact of the error but also the point at which it occurred. It is even possible in some cases to detect mislabeling at the point of sample collection if the genetic typing results on a particular sample are inconsistent with an otherwise consistent reconstruction of events.[113]

Contamination describes any situation in which foreign material is mixed with a sample of DNA. Contamination by non-biological materials, such as gasoline or grit, can cause test failures, but they are not a source of genetic typing errors. Similarly, contamination with non-human biological materials, such as bacteria, fungi, or plant materials, is generally not a problem. These contaminants may accelerate DNA degradation, but they do not contribute spurious genetic types.[114]

Consequently, the contamination of greatest concern is that resulting from the addition of human DNA. This sort of contamination can occur three ways:[115]

1. The crime-scene samples by their nature may contain a mixture of fluids or tissues from different individuals. Examples include vaginal swabs collected as sexual assault evidence[116] and blood stain evidence from scenes

---

111. Such a review is best undertaken by someone familiar with police procedures, forensic DNA analysis, and forensic laboratory operations. Case review by an independent expert should be held to the same scientific standard as the work under review. Any possible flaws in labeling or in evidence handling should be specified in detail, with consideration given to the consequence of the possible error.

112. NRC II, *supra* note 37, at 81.

113. For example, a mislabeling of husband and wife samples in a paternity case might result in an apparent maternal exclusion, a very unlikely event. The possibility of mislabeling could be confirmed by testing the samples for gender and ultimately verified by taking new samples from each party under better controlled conditions.

114. Validation of new genetic markers includes testing on a variety of non-human species. The probes used in VNTR analysis and the PCR-based tests give results with non-human primate DNA samples (apes and some monkeys). This is not surprising given the evolutionary proximity of the primates to humans. As a rule, the validated test systems give no results with DNA from animals other than primates, from plants, or from microbes. An exception is the reaction of some bacterial DNA samples in testing for the marker D1S80.

Fernandez–Rodriguez et al., *supra* note 88. However, this could be an artifact of the particular D1S80 typing system, since other workers have not been able to replicate fully their results, and an alternative D1S80 typing protocol gave no spurious results. S. Ebraham et al., *Investigation of the Specificity of the STR and D1S80 Primers on Microbial DNA Samples*, Presentation B84, 50th Annual Meeting of the American Academy of Forensic Sciences, San Francisco, Feb.1998.

115. NRC II, *supra* note 37, at 82–84; NRC I, *supra* note 35, at 65–67; G.F. Sensabaugh & E.T. Blake, *DNA Analysis in Biological Evidence: Applications of the Polymerase Chain Reaction, in* 3 FORENSIC SCIENCE HANDBOOK 416, 441 (Richard Saferstein ed., 1993); G.F. Sensabaugh & C. vonBeroldingen, *The Polymerase Chain Reaction: Application to the Analysis of Biological Evidence, in* FORENSIC DNA TECHNOLOGY 63, 77 (M.A. Farley & J.J. Harrington eds., 1991).

116. These typically contain DNA in the semen from the assailant and in the vaginal fluid of the victim. The standard procedure for analysis allows the DNA from sperm to be separated from the vaginal epithelial cell DNA. It is thus possible not only to recognize the mixture but also to assign the DNA profiles to the different individuals.

where several individuals shed blood.[117]

2. The crime-scene samples may be inadvertently contaminated in the course of sample handling in the field or in the laboratory. Inadvertent contamination of crime-scene DNA with DNA from a reference sample could lead to a false inclusion.[118]

3. Carry-over contamination in PCR-based typing can occur if the amplification products of one typing reaction are carried over into the reaction mix for a subsequent PCR reaction. If the carry-over products are present in sufficient quantity, they could be preferentially amplified over the target DNA.[119] The primary strategy used in most forensic laboratories to protect against carry-over contamination is to keep PCR products away from sample materials and test reagents by having separate work areas for pre-PCR and post-PCR sample handling, by preparing samples in controlled air-flow biological safety hoods, by using dedicated equipment (such as pipetters) for each of the various stages of sample analysis, by decontaminating work areas after use (usually by wiping down or by irradiating with ultraviolet light), and by having a one-way flow of sample from the pre-PCR to post-PCR work areas.[120] Additional protocols are used to detect any carry-over contamination.[121]

In the end, whether a laboratory has conducted proper tests and whether it conducted them properly depends both on the general standard of practice and on the questions posed in the particular case. There is no universal checklist, but the selection of tests and the adherence to the correct test procedures can be reviewed by experts and by reference to professional standards, such as the TWGDAM and DAB guidelines.

117. Such mixtures are detected by genetic typing that reveals profiles of more than one DNA source. *See supra* § 11–2.4.3.

118. This source of contamination is a greater concern when PCR-based typing methods are to be used due to the capacity of PCR to detect very small amounts of DNA. However, experiments designed to introduce handling contamination into samples have been unsuccessful. *See* C.T. Comey & B. Budowle, *Validation Studies on the Analysis of HLA–DQα Locus Using the Polymerase Chain Reaction*, 36 J. Forensic Sci. 1633 (1991). Of course, it remains important to have evidence handling procedures to safeguard against this source of contamination. Police agencies should have documented procedures for the collection, handling, and packaging of biological evidence in the field and for its delivery to the laboratory that are designed to minimize the chance of handling contamination. Ideally, these procedures will have been developed in coordination with the laboratory, and training in the use of these procedures will have been provided. Similarly, laboratories should have procedures in place to minimize the risk of this kind of contamination. *See* DAB Standards, *supra* note 96; TWGDAM Guidelines, *supra* note 95. In

particular, these procedures should specify the safeguards for keeping evidence samples separated from reference samples.

119. Carry-over contamination is not an issue in RFLP analysis since RFLP analysis involves no amplification steps.

120. Some laboratories with space constraints separate pre-PCR and post-PCR activities in time rather than space. The other safeguards can be used as in a space-separated facility.

121. Standard protocols include the amplification of blank control samples—those to which no DNA has been added. If carry-over contaminants have found their way into the reagents or sample tubes, these will be detected as amplification products. Outbreaks of carry-over contamination can also be recognized by monitoring test results. Detection of an unexpected and persistent genetic profile in different samples indicates a contamination problem. When contamination outbreaks are detected, appropriate corrective actions should be taken, and both the outbreak and the corrective action should be documented. *See* DAB Standards, *supra* note 96; TWGDAM Guidelines, *supra* note 95.

§ 11–2.6 Interpretation of Laboratory Results

The results of DNA testing can be presented in various ways. With discrete allele systems, it is natural to speak of "matching" and "non-matching" profiles. If the genetic profile obtained from the biological sample taken from the crime scene or the victim (the "trace evidence sample") matches that of a particular individual, then that individual is included as a possible source of the sample. But other individuals also might possess a matching DNA profile. Accordingly, the expert should be asked to provide some indication of how significant the match is. If, on the other hand, the genetic profiles are different, then the individual is excluded as the source of the trace evidence. Typically, proof tending to show that the defendant is the source incriminates the defendant, while proof that someone else is the source exculpates the defendant.[122] This section elaborates on these ideas, indicating issues that can arise in connection with an expert's testimony interpreting the results of a DNA test.

§ 11–2.6.1 Exclusions, Inclusions, and Inconclusive Results

When the DNA from the trace evidence clearly does not match the DNA sample from the suspect, the DNA analysis demonstrates that the suspect's DNA is not in the forensic sample. Indeed, if the samples have been collected, handled, and analyzed properly, then the suspect is excluded as a possible source of the DNA in the forensic sample. Even a single allele that cannot be explained as a laboratory artifact or other error can suffice to exclude a suspect.[123] As a practical matter, such exclusionary results normally would keep charges from being filed against the excluded suspect.[124]

In some cases, however, DNA testing is inconclusive, in whole or in part. The presence or absence of a discrete allele can be in doubt, or the existence or location of a VNTR band may be unclear.[125] For example, when the trace evidence sample is extremely degraded, VNTR profiling might not show all the alleles that would be present in a sample with more intact DNA. If the quantity of DNA to be amplified for sequence-specific tests is too small, the amplification might not yield enough product to give a clear signal. Thus, experts sometimes disagree as to whether a particular band is visible on an autoradiograph or whether a dot is present on a reverse dot blot.

122. Whether being the source of the forensic sample is incriminating depends on other facts in the case. Likewise, whether someone else being the source is exculpatory depends on the circumstances. For example, a suspect who might have committed the offense without leaving the trace evidence sample still could be guilty. In a rape case with several rapists, a semen stain could fail to incriminate one assailant because insufficient semen from that individual is present in the sample.

123. Due to heteroplasmy, a single sequence difference in mtDNA samples would not be considered an exclusion. *See supra* § 11–2.2 note 30. With testing at many polymorphic loci, however, it would be unusual to find two unrelated individuals whose DNA matches at all but one locus.

124. *But see* State v. Hammond, 221 Conn. 264, 604 A.2d 793 (Conn.1992).

125. *E.g.,* State v. Fleming, 698 A.2d 503, 506 (Me.1997) ("The fourth probe was declared uninterpretable."); People v. Leonard, 224 Mich.App. 569, 569 N.W.2d 663, 666–67 (Mich. Ct.App.1997) ("There was a definite match of defendant's DNA on three of the probes, and a match on the other two probes could not be excluded."). In some cases, experts have disagreed as to whether extra bands represented a mixture or resulted from partial digestion of the forensic sample. *E.g.,* State v. Marcus, 294 N.J.Super. 267, 683 A.2d 221 (N.J.Super.Ct.App.Div.1996).

Furthermore, even when RFLP bands are clearly visible, the entire pattern of bands can be displaced from its true location in a systematic way (a phenomenon known as *band-shifting*).[126] Recognizing this phenomenon, analysts might deem some seemingly matching patterns as inconclusive.[127]

At the other extreme, the genotypes at a large number of loci can be clearly identical, and the fact of a match not in doubt. In these cases, the DNA evidence is quite incriminating, and the challenge for the legal system lies in explaining just how probative it is. Naturally, as with exclusions, inclusions are most powerful when the samples have been collected, handled, and analyzed properly. But there is one logical difference between exclusions and inclusions. If it is accepted that the samples have different genotypes, then the conclusion that the DNA in them came from different individuals is essentially inescapable. In contrast, even if two samples have the same genotype, there is a chance that the forensic sample came—not from the defendant—but from another individual who has the same genotype. This complication has produced extensive arguments over the statistical procedures for assessing this chance or related quantities. This problem of describing the significance of an unequivocal match is taken up later in this section.

The classification of patterns into the two mutually exclusive categories of exclusions and inclusions is more complicated for VNTRs than for discrete alleles. Determining that DNA fragments from two different samples are the same size is like saying that two people are the same height. The height may well be similar, but is it identical? Even if the same person is measured repeatedly, we expect some variation about the true height due to the limitations of the measuring device. A perfectly reliable device gives the same measurements for all repeated measurements of the same item, but no instrument can measure a quantity like height with both perfect precision and perfect reproducibility. Consequently, *measurement variability* is a fact of life in ascertaining the sizes of VNTRs.[128]

The method of handling measurement variation that has been adopted by

126. *See* NRC II, *supra* note 37, at 142 ("[D]egraded DNA sometimes migrates farther on a gel than better quality DNA ....."). Band-shifting produces a systematic error in measurement. Random error is also present. *See infra* § 11–2.6.1.

127. *See* NRC II, *supra* note 1, at 142 ("[A]n experienced analyst can notice whether two bands from a heterozygote are shifted in the same or in the opposite direction from the bands in another lane containing the DNA being compared. If the bands in the two lanes shift a small distance in the same direction, that might indicate a match with band-shifting. If they shift in opposite directions, that is probably not a match, but a simple match rule or simple computer program might declare it as a match.").

At least one laboratory has reported matches of bands that lie outside its match window but exhibit a band-shifting pattern. It uses monomorphic probes to adjust for the band-shifting. On the admissibility of this procedure, compare

Caldwell v. State, 260 Ga. 278, 393 S.E.2d 436, 441 (Ga.1990) (admissible as having reached the "scientific stage of verifiable certainty") and State v. Futch, 123 Or.App. 176, 860 P.2d 264 (Or.Ct.App.1993) (admissible under a *Daubert*-like standard), *with* Hayes v. State, 660 So.2d 257 (Fla.1995) (too controversial to be generally accepted), State v. Quatrevingt, 670 So.2d 197 (La.1996) (not shown to be valid under *Daubert*), and People v. Keene, 156 Misc.2d 108, 591 N.Y.S.2d 733 (N.Y.Sup.Ct. 1992) (holding that the procedure followed in the case, which did not use the nearest monomorphic probe to make the corrections, was not generally accepted).

128. In statistics, this variability often is denominated "measurement error." The phrase does not mean that a mistake has been made in performing the measurements, but rather that even measurements that are taken correctly fluctuate about the true value of the quantity being measured.

most DNA profilers is statistically inelegant,[129] but it has the virtue of simplicity.[130] Analysts typically are willing to declare that two fragments match if the bands appear to match visually, and if they fall within a specified distance of one another. For example, the FBI laboratory declares matches within a ±5% *match window*—if two bands are within ±5% of their average length, then the alleles can be said to match.[131]

Whether the choice of ±5% (or any other figure) as an outer limit for matches is scientifically acceptable depends on how the criterion operates in classifying pairs of samples of DNA. The ±5% window keeps the chance of a false exclusion for a single allele quite small, but at a cost: The easier it is to declare a match between bands at different positions, the easier it is to declare a match between two samples with *different* genotypes. Therefore, deciding whether a match window is reasonable involves an examination of the probability not merely of a false exclusion but also of a false inclusion: "[t]he match window should not be set so small that true matches are missed. At the same time, the window should not be so wide that bands that are clearly different are declared to match."[132] Viewed in this light, the ±5% match window is easily defended—it keeps the probabilities of *both* types of errors very small.[133]

§ 11–2.6.2 Alternative Hypotheses

If the defendant is the source of DNA of sufficient quantity and quality found at a crime scene, then a DNA sample from the defendant and the forensic sample should have the same profile. The inference required in

129. *See* NRC II, *supra* note 8, at 139 ("[T]he most accurate statistical model for the interpretation of VNTR analysis would be based on a continuous distribution. . . . If models for measurement uncertainty become available that are appropriate for the wide range of laboratories performing DNA analyses and if those analyses are sufficiently robust with respect to departures from the models, we would recommend such methods. Indeed, . . . we expect that any problems in the construction of such models will be overcome, and we encourage research on those models."). Forcing a continuous variable like the positions of the bands on an autoradiogram into discrete categories is not statistically efficient. It results in more matching bands being deemed inconclusive or non-matching than more sophisticated statistical procedures. *See, e.g.,* D.A. Berry et al., *Statistical Inference in Crime Investigations Using Deoxyribonucleic Acid Profiling*, 41 Applied Stat. 499 (1992); I.W. Evett et al., *An Illustration of Efficient Statistical Methods for RFLP Analysis in Forensic Science*, 52 Am J. Hum. Genetics 498 (1993). Also, it treats matches that just squeak by the match windows as just as impressive as perfect matches.

130. NRC II, *supra* note 1, at 139.

131. The FBI arrived at this match window by experiments involving pairs of measurements of the same DNA sequences. It found that this window was wide enough to encompass all the differences seen in the calibration experiments. Other laboratories use smaller percentages for their match windows, but comparisons of the percentage figures can be misleading. *See* D.H. Kaye, Science in Evidence 192 (1997). Because different laboratories can have different standard errors of measurement, profiles from two different laboratories might not be considered inconsistent even though some corresponding bands are outside the match windows of both laboratories. The reason: there is more variability in measurements on different gels than on the same gel, and still more in different gels from different laboratories. *See* Satcher v. Netherland, 944 F.Supp. 1222, 1265 (E.D.Va.1996).

132. NRC II, *supra* note 37, at 140. Assuming that the only source of error is the statistical uncertainty in the measurements, this error probability is simply the chance that the two people whose DNA is tested have profiles so similar that they satisfy the matching criterion. With genotypes consisting of four or five VNTR loci, that probability is much smaller than the chance of a false exclusion. *Id.* at 141.

133. NRC II, *supra* note 37, at 140–41; Bernard Devlin & Kathryn Roeder, *DNA Profiling: Statistics and Population Genetics, in* 1 Modern Scientific Evidence: The Law and Science of Expert Testimony § 18–3.1.2, at 717–18 (David Faigman et al. eds., 1997).

assessing the evidence, however, runs in the opposite direction. The forensic scientist reports that the sample of DNA from the crime scene and a sample from the defendant have the same genotype. To what extent does this tend to prove that the defendant is the source of the forensic sample?[134] Conceivably, other hypotheses could account for the matching profiles. One possibility is laboratory error—the genotypes are not actually the same even though the laboratory thinks that they are. This situation could arise from mistakes in labeling or handling samples or from cross-contamination of the samples.[135] As the 1992 NRC report cautioned, "[e]rrors happen, even in the best laboratories, and even when the analyst is certain that every precaution against error was taken."[136] Another possibility is that the laboratory analysis is correct— the genotypes are truly identical—but the forensic sample came from another individual. In general, the true source might be a close relative of the defendant[137] or an unrelated person who, as luck would have it, just happens to have the same profile as the defendant. The former hypothesis we shall refer to as kinship, and the latter as coincidence. To infer that the defendant is the source of the crime scene DNA, one must reject these alternative hypotheses of laboratory error, kinship, and coincidence. Table 1 summarizes the logical possibilities.

Table 1.

Hypotheses that Might Explain a Match Between Defendant's DNA and DNA at a Crime Scene[138]

IDENTITY:	same genotype, defendant's DNA at crime scene
NON–IDENTITY:	
lab error	different genotypes mistakenly found to be the same
kinship	same genotype, relative's DNA at crime scene
coincidence	same genotype, unrelated individual's DNA

Some scientists have urged that probabilities associated with false positive error, kinship, or coincidence be presented to juries. While it is not clear that this goal is feasible, scientific knowledge and more conventional evidence can help in assessing the plausibility of these alternative hypotheses. If

---

134. That the defendant is the source does not necessarily mean that the defendant is guilty of the offense charged. Aside from issues of intent or knowledge that have nothing to do with DNA, there remains, for instance, the possibility that the two samples match because someone framed the defendant by putting a sample of defendant's DNA at the crime scene or in the container of DNA thought to have come from the crime scene. *See generally, e.g.,* United States v. Chischilly, 30 F.3d 1144 (9th Cir.1994) (dicta on "source probability"); Jonathan J. Koehler, *DNA Matches and Statistics: Important Questions, Surprising Answers,* 76 Judicature 222 (1993). For reports of state police planting fingerprint and other evidence to incriminate arrestees, see John Caher, *Judge Orders New Trial in Murder Case,* TIMES UNION (Albany), Jan. 8, 1997, at B2; John O'Brien & Todd Lightly, *Corrupt Troopers Showed No Fear,* THE POST-STANDARD (Syra-

cuse), Feb. 4, 1997, at A3 (an investigation of 62,000 fingerprint cards from 1983–1992 revealed 34 cases of planted evidence among one state police troop).

135. *See supra* § 11–2.3.

136. NRC I, *supra* note 35, at 89.

137. A close relative, for these purposes, would be a brother, uncle, nephew, etc. For relationships more distant than second cousins, the probability of a chance match is nearly as small as for persons of the same ethnic subgroup. Devlin & Roeder, *supra* note 133, § 18–3.1.3, at 724. For an instance of the "evil twin" defense, see Hunter v. Harrison, 1997 WL 578917 (Ohio Ct.App.1997) (unpublished paternity case).

138. *Cf.* N.E. Morton, *The Forensic DNA Endgame,* 37 JURIMETRICS J. 477, 480 (1997) (Table 1).

laboratory error, kinship, and coincidence can be eliminated as explanations for a match, then only the hypothesis of identity remains. We turn, then, to the considerations that affect the chances of a reported match when the defendant is not the source of the trace evidence.

[1] Error

Although many experts would concede that even with rigorous protocols, the chance of a laboratory error exceeds that of a coincidental match,[139] quantifying the former probability is a formidable task. Some commentary proposes using the proportion of false positives that the particular laboratory has experienced in blind proficiency tests or the rate of false positives on proficiency tests averaged across all laboratories.[140] Indeed, the 1992 NRC Report remarks that "proficiency tests provide a measure of the false-positive and false-negative rates of a laboratory."[141] Yet, the same report recognizes that "errors on proficiency tests do not necessarily reflect permanent probabilities of false-positive or false-negative results,"[142] and the 1996 NRC report suggests that a probability of a false-positive error that would apply to a specific case cannot be estimated objectively.[143] If the false positive probability were, say, 0.001, it would take tens of thousands of proficiency tests to estimate that probability accurately, and the application of an historical industry-wide error rate to a particular laboratory at a later time would be debatable.[144]

Most commentators who urge the use of proficiency tests to estimate the probability that a laboratory has erred in a particular case agree that blind proficiency testing cannot be done in sufficient numbers to yield an accurate estimate of a small error rate. However, they maintain that proficiency tests, blind or otherwise, should be used to provide a conservative estimate of the false-positive error probability.[145] For example, if there were no errors in 100 tests, a 95% confidence interval would include the possibility that the error rate could be almost as high as 3%.[146]

Instead of pursuing a numerical estimate, the second NAS committee and individual scientists who question the value of proficiency tests for estimating case-specific laboratory-error probabilities suggest that each laboratory document all the steps in its analyses and reserve portions of the DNA samples for independent testing whenever feasible. Scrutinizing the chain of custody, examining the laboratory's protocol, verifying that it adhered to that protocol, and conducting confirmatory tests if there are any suspicious circumstances

139. *E.g.*, Devlin & Roeder, *supra* note 133, § 18–5.3, at 743.

140. *E.g.*, Jonathan J. Koehler, *Error and Exaggeration in the Presentation of DNA Evidence at Trial*, 34 Jurimetrics J. 21, 37–38 (1993); Barry C. Scheck, *DNA and* Daubert, 15 Cardozo L. Rev. 1959, 1984 n.93 (1994).

141. NRC I, *supra* note 35, at 94.

142. *Id.* at 89.

143. NRC II, *supra* note 37, at 85–87.

144. *Id.* at 85–86; Devlin & Roeder, *supra* note 133, § 18–5.3, at 744–45. Such arguments have not persuaded the proponents of estimat-

ing the probability of error from industry-wide proficiency testing. *E.g.*, Jonathan J. Koehler, *Why DNA Likelihood Ratios Should Account for Error (Even When a National Research Council Report Says They Should Not)*, 37 Jurimetrics J. 425 (1997).

145. *E.g.*, Koehler, *supra* note 134, at 228; Richard Lempert, *After the DNA Wars: Skirmishing with NRC II*, 37 Jurimetrics J. 439, 447–48, 453 (1997).

146. *See* NRC II, *supra* note 37, at 86 n. 1.

can help to eliminate the hypothesis of laboratory error,[147] whether or not a case-specific probability can be estimated.[148] Furthermore, if the defendant has had a meaningful opportunity to retest a sample but has been unable or unwilling to obtain an inconsistent result, the relevance of a statistic based on past proficiency tests might be questionable.

[2] Kinship

With enough genetic markers, all individuals except for identical twins should be distinguishable, but this ideal is not always attainable with the limited number of loci typically used in forensic testing.[149] Close relatives have more genes in common than unrelated individuals, and various procedures for dealing with the possibility that the true source of the forensic DNA is not the defendant, but a close relative have been proposed.[150] Often, the investigation, including additional DNA testing, can be extended to all known relatives.[151] But this is not feasible in every case, and there is always the chance that some unknown relatives are included in the suspect population.[152] Formulae are available for computing the probability that any person with a specified degree of kinship to the defendant also possesses the incriminating genotype.[153] For example, the probability that an untested brother (or sister) would match at four loci (with alleles that each occur in 5% of the population) is about 0.006; the probability that an aunt (or uncle) would match is about 0.0000005.[154]

147. *E.g.*, Jonathan J. Koehler, *On Conveying the Probative Value of DNA Evidence: Frequencies, Likelihood Ratios, and Error Rates*, 67 U. Colo. L. Rev. 859, 866 (1996) ("In the *Simpson* case, [l]aboratory error was unlikely because many blood samples were tested at different laboratories using two different DNA typing methods."); William C. Thompson, *DNA Evidence in the O.J. Simpson Trial*, 67 U. Colo. L. Rev. 827, 827 (1996) ("the extensive use of duplicate testing in the *Simpson* case greatly reduced concerns (that are crucial in most other cases) about the potential for false positives due to poor scientific practices of DNA laboratories").

148. *See* Margaret A. Berger, *Laboratory Error Seen Through the Lens of Science and Policy*, 30 U.C. Davis L. Rev. 1081 (1997).

149. *See, e.g.*, B.S. Weir, *Discussion of "Inference in Forensic Identification"*, 158 J. Royal Stat. Soc'y ser. A 49 (1995) ("the chance that two unrelated individuals in a population share the same 16–allele [VNTR] profile is vanishingly small, and even for full sibs the chance is only 1 in very many thousands.").

150. *See* Thomas R. Belin et al., *Summarizing DNA Evidence When Relatives are Possible Suspects*, 92 J. Am. Stat. Ass'n 706, 707–08 (1997). Recommendation 4.4 of the 1996 NRC report reads:

If possible contributors of the evidence sample include relatives of the suspect, DNA profiles of those relatives should be obtained. If these profiles cannot be obtained, the probability of finding the evidence profile in those relatives should be calculated with [specified formulae].

NRC II, *supra* note 37, at 6.

151. NRC II, *supra* note 37, at 113.

152. When that population is very large, however, the presence of a few relatives will have little impact on the probability that a suspect drawn at random from that population will have the incriminating genotype. *Id.* Furthermore, it has been suggested that the effect of relatedness is of practical importance only for very close relatives, such as siblings. J.F.Y. Brookfield, *The Effect of Relatives on the Likelihood Ratio Associated with DNA Profile Evidence in Criminal Cases*, 34 J. Forensic Sci. Soc'y 193 (1994).

153. *E.g.*, Brookfield, *supra* note 152; David J. Balding & Peter Donnelly, *Inference in Forensic Identification*, 158 J. Royal Stat. Soc'y Ser. A 21 (1995); Ian W. Evett & Bruce S. Weir, Interpreting DNA Evidence: Statistical Genetics for Forensic Scientists 108–18 (1998); Morton, *supra* note 138, at 484; NRC II, *supra* note 37, at 113. *But see* NRC I, *supra* note 35, at 87 (giving an incorrect formula for siblings). Empirical measures that are not directly interpretable as probabilities also have been described. Belin et al., *supra* note 150.

154. The large discrepancy between two siblings on the one hand, and an uncle and nephew on the other, reflects the fact that the siblings have far more shared ancestry. All

[3] Coincidence

Another rival hypothesis is coincidence: The defendant is not the source of the crime scene DNA, but happens to have the same genotype as an unrelated individual who is the true source. Various procedures for assessing the plausibility of this hypothesis are available. In principle, one could test all conceivable suspects. In principle, one could test all conceivable suspects. If everyone except the defendant has a non-matching profile, then the conclusion that the defendant is the source is inescapable. But exhaustive, error-free testing of the population of conceivable suspects is almost never feasible. The suspect population normally defies any enumeration, and in the typical crime where DNA evidence is found, the population of possible perpetrators is so huge that even if all its members could be listed, they could not all be tested.[155]

An alternative procedure would be to take a sample of people from the suspect population, find the relative frequency of the profile in this sample, and use that statistic to estimate the frequency in the entire suspect population. The smaller the frequency, the less likely it is that the defendant's DNA would match if the defendant were not the source of trace evidence. Again, however, the suspect population is difficult to define, so some surrogate must be used. The procedure commonly followed is to estimate the relative frequency of the incriminating genotype in a large population. But even this cannot be done directly because each possible multilocus profile is so rare that it is not likely to show up in any sample of a reasonable size.[156] However, the frequencies of most alleles can be determined accurately by sampling the population[157] to construct *databases* that reveal how often each allele occurs.[158] Principles of population genetics then can be applied to combine the estimated

their genes are inherited through the same two parents. In contrast, a nephew and an uncle inherit from two unrelated mothers, and so will have few maternal alleles in common. As for paternal alleles, the nephew inherits not from his uncle, but from his uncle's brother, who shares by descent only about one-half of his alleles with the uncle.

155. In the United Kingdom and Europe, mass DNA screenings in small towns have been undertaken. *See, e.g.,* Kaye, *supra* note 131, at 222–26. The strategy has been employed in the United States as well. *See* Edward J. Imwinkelried & D.H. Kaye, *DNA Typing: Emerging or Neglected Issues,* 413 Wash. L. Rev. 76 (2001).

156. NRC II, *supra* note 37, at 89–90 ("A very small proportion of the trillions of possible profiles are found in any database, so it is necessary to use the frequencies of individual alleles to estimate the frequency of a given profile."). The 1992 NRC report proposed reporting the occurrences of a profile in a database, but recognized that "such estimates do not take advantage of the full potential of the genetic approach." NRC I, *supra* note 35, at 76. For further discussion of the statistical inferences that might be drawn from the absence of a profile in a sample of a given size,

see NRC II, *supra,* at 159–60 (arguing that "the abundant data make [the direct counting method] unnecessary.").

157. Ideally, a probability sample from the population of interest would be taken. Indeed, a few experts have testified that no meaningful conclusions can be drawn in the absence of random sampling. *E.g.,* People v. Soto, 21 Cal.4th 512, 88 Cal.Rptr.2d 34, 981 P.2d 958 (Cal.1999); State v. Anderson, 118 N.M. 284, 881 P.2d 29, 39 (N.M.1994).

Unfortunately, a list of the people who comprise the entire population of possible suspects is almost never available; consequently, probability sampling from the directly relevant population is generally impossible. Probability sampling from a proxy population is possible, but it is not the norm in studies of the distributions of genes in populations. Typically, convenience samples are used. The 1996 NRC report suggests that for the purpose of estimating allele frequencies, convenience sampling should give results comparable to random sampling, and it discusses procedures for estimating the random sampling error. NRC II, *supra* note 37, at 126–27, 146–48, 186.

158. In the formative years of forensic DNA testing, defendants frequently contended

allele frequencies into an estimate of the probability that a person born in the population will have the multilocus genotype. This probability often is referred to as the *random match probability*. Three principal methods for computing the random match probability from allele frequencies have been developed. This section describes these methods; the next section considers other quantities that have been proposed as measures of the probative value of the DNA evidence.

[a] The Basic Product Rule

The basic product rule estimates the frequency of genotypes in an infinite population of individuals who choose their mates and reproduce independently of the alleles used to compare the samples. Although population geneticists describe this situation as *random mating*, these words are terms of art. Geneticists know that people do not choose their mates by a lottery, and they use "random mating" to indicate that the choices are uncorrelated with the specific alleles that make up the genotypes in question.[159]

In a randomly mating population, the expected frequency of a pair of alleles at each locus depends on whether the two alleles are distinct. If a different allele is inherited from each parent, the expected single-locus genotype frequency is twice the product of the two individual frequencies.[160] But if the offspring happens to inherit the same allele from each parent, the expected single-locus genotype frequency is the square of the allele frequency.[161] These proportions are known as *Hardy-Weinberg* proportions. Even if two populations with distinct allele frequencies are thrown together, within the limits of chance variation, random mating produces Hardy–Weinberg equilibrium in a single generation. An example is given below.[162]

that the size of the forensic databases were too small to give accurate estimates. To the extent that the databases are comparable to random samples, confidence intervals are a standard method for indicating the amount of error due to sample size. *E.g.*, David H. Kaye, *DNA Evidence: Probability, Population Genetics, and the Courts*, 7 HARV. J. L. & TECH. 101 (1993).

159. *E.g.*, NRC II, *supra* note 37, at 90:

In the simplest population structure, mates are chosen at random. Clearly, the population of the United States does not mate at random; a person from Oregon is more likely to mate with another from Oregon than with one from Florida. Furthermore, people often choose mates according to physical and behavioral attributes, such as height and personality. But they do not choose each other according to the markers used for forensic studies, such as VNTRs and STRs. Rather, the proportion of matings between people with two marker genotypes is determined by their frequencies in the mating population. If the allele frequencies in Oregon and Florida are the same as those in the nation as a whole, then the proportion of genotypes in the two states will be the same as those for the United States, even though the population of the whole country clearly does not mate at random.

160. In more technical terms, when the frequencies of two alleles are p_1 and p_2, the single-locus genotype frequency for the corresponding heterozygotes is expected to be $2p_1p_2$.

161. The expected proportion is p_1^2 for allele 1, and p_2^2 for allele 2. With VNTRs, a complication arises with apparent homozygotes. A single band on an autoradiogram might really be two bands that are close together, or a second band that is relatively small might have migrated to the edge of the gel during the electrophoresis. Forensic laboratories therefore make a "conservative" assumption. They act as if there is a second, unseen band, and they use the excessively large value of $p_2 = 100\%$ for the frequency of the presumably unseen allele. With this modification, the genotype frequency for apparent homozygotes becomes $P = 2p_1$. If the single-banded pattern is a true homozygote, this $2p$ convention overstates the frequency of the single-locus genotype because $2p$ is greater than p^2 for any possible proportion p. For instance, if $p = 0.05$, then $2p = 0.10$, which is 40 times greater than $p^2 = 0.0025$.

162. Suppose that 10% of the sperm in the gene pool of the population carry allele 1 (A_1), and 50% carry allele 2 (A_2). Similarly, 10% of

Once the proportion of the population that has each of the single-locus genotypes for the forensic profile has been estimated in this way, the proportion of the population that is expected to share the combination of them—the *multilocus* profile frequency—is given by multiplying the single-locus proportions. This multiplication is exactly correct when the single-locus genotypes are statistically independent. In that case, the population is said to be in *linkage equilibrium*.

Extensive litigation and scientific commentary have considered whether the occurrences of alleles at each locus are independent events (Hardy–Weinberg equilibrium), and whether the loci are independent (linkage equilibrium). Beginning around 1990, several scientists suggested that the equilibrium frequencies do not follow the simple model of a homogeneous population mating without regard to the loci used in forensic DNA profiling. They suggested that the major racial populations are composed of ethnic subpopulations whose members tend to mate among themselves.[163] Within each ethnic subpopulation, mating still can be random, but if, say, Italian–Americans have allele frequencies that are markedly different than the average for all whites, and if Italian–Americans only mate among themselves, then using the average frequencies for all whites in the basic product formula could understate—or overstate—a multilocus profile frequency for the subpopulation of Italian–Americans.[164] Similarly, using the population frequencies could understate—or overstate—the profile frequencies in the white population itself.[165]

Consequently, if we want to know the frequency of an incriminating profile among Italian–Americans, the basic product rule applied to the white allele frequencies could be in error; and there is some chance that it will understate the profile frequency in the white population as a whole. One might presume that the extent of the error could be determined by looking to the variations across racial groups,[166] but, for a short time, a few scientists

the eggs carry A_1, and 50% carry A_2. (Other sperm and eggs carry other types.) With random mating, we expect $10\% \times 10\% = 1\%$ of all the fertilized eggs to be A_1A_1, and another $50\% \times 50\% = 25\%$ to be A_2A_2. These constitute two distinct homozygote profiles. Likewise, we expect $10\% \times 50\% = 5\%$ of the fertilized eggs to be A_1A_2 and another $50\% \times 10\% = 5\%$ to be A_2A_1. These two configurations produce indistinguishable profiles—a band, dot, or the like for A_1 and another mark for A_2. So the expected proportion of heterozygotes A_1A_2 is $5\% + 5\% = 10\%$.

Oddly, some courts and commentators have written that the expected heterozygote frequency for this example is only 5%. *E.g.*, William C. Thompson & Simon Ford, *DNA Typing: Acceptance and Weight of the New Genetic Identification Tests*, 75 VA. L. REV. 45, 81–82 (1989). For further discussion, see D.H. Kaye, Bible *Reading: DNA Evidence in Arizona*, 28 ARIZ. ST. L. J. 1035 (1996); D.H. Kaye, *Cross-Examining Science*, 36 JURIMETRICS J. vii (Winter 1996).

163. The most prominent expression of this position is R.C. Lewontin & Daniel L. Hartl, *Population Genetics in Forensic DNA Typing*, 254 SCIENCE 1745 (1991).

164. On average, the use of population-wide allele frequencies overstates the genotype frequencies within defendant's subpopulation. *See* Dan E. Krane et al., *Genetic Differences at Four DNA Typing Loci in Finnish, Italian, and Mixed Caucasian Populations*, 89 PROC. NAT'L ACAD. SCI. 10583 (1992); Stanley Sawyer et al., *DNA Fingerprinting Loci Do Show Population Differences: Comments on Budowle et al.*, 59 AM. J. HUM. GENETICS 272 (1996) (letter). This mean overestimation occurs because (1) the use of population-wide frequencies rather than subpopulation frequencies underestimates homozygote frequencies and overestimates heterozygote frequencies, and (2) heterozygosity far exceeds homozygosity.

165. The use of the population-wide allele frequencies usually overstates genotype frequencies in the population as a whole, thereby benefitting most defendants. *See* Kaye, *supra* note 158, at 142.

166. On the problems in defining racial populations, compare C. Loring Brace, *Region Does Not Mean "Race"—Reality Versus Con-*

insisted that variations from one ethnic group to another within a race were larger than variations from one race to another.[167] In light of this literature[168] courts had grounds to conclude that the basic product rule, used with broad population frequencies, was not universally accepted for estimating profile frequencies within subpopulations. Yet, few courts recognized that there was much less explicit dissension over the ability of the rule to estimate profile frequencies in a general population.[169] Particularly in *Frye* jurisdictions, a substantial number of appellate courts began to exclude DNA evidence for want of a generally accepted method of estimating profile frequencies in both situations.[170]

[b] The Product Rule with Ceilings

In 1992, the National Academy of Sciences' Committee on DNA Technology in Forensic Science assumed arguendo that population structure was a serious threat to the basic product rule and proposed a variation to provide an upper bound on a profile frequency within any population or subpopulation.[171] The interim ceiling method uses the same general formulas as the basic product rule,[172] but with different values of the frequencies. Instead of

vention in Forensic Anthropology, 40 J. FORENSIC SCI. 171 (1994), with Kenneth A.R. Kennedy, *But Professor, Why Teach Race Identification if Races Don't Exist?*, 40 J. FORENSIC SCI. 797 (1995).

167. *Compare* Lewontin & Hartl, *supra* note 163, at 1745 ("there is, on average, one-third more genetic variation among Irish, Spanish, Italians, Slavs, Swedes, and other subpopulations than there is, on average, between Europeans, Asians, Africans, Amerindians, and Oceanians."), *with* Richard C. Lewontin, *Discussion*, 9 STAT. SCI. 259, 260 (1994) ("all parties agree that differentiation among [major ethnic groups] is as large, if not larger than, the difference among tribes and national groups [within major ethnic groups]."). Other population geneticists dismissed as obviously untenable the early assertions of greater variability across the ethnic subpopulations of a race than across races. *E.g.*, B. Devlin & Neil Risch, *NRC Report on DNA Typing*, 260 SCIENCE 1057 (1993); N.E. Morton et al., *Kinship Bioassay on Hypervariable Loci in Blacks and Caucasians*, 90 PROC. NAT'L ACAD. SCI. 1892 (1993) (gene frequencies cited by Lewontin & Hartl are atypical, and "[l]ess than 2% of the diversity selected by Lewontin and Hartl is due to the national kinship to which they attribute it, little of which persists in regional forensic samples.").

168. The literature on genetic differences across the globe is reviewed in, *e.g.*, Devlin & Roeder, *supra* note 133, § 18–3.2.1, at 711–28 (suggesting that this body of research indicates that the extent of the variation across subpopulations is relatively small).

169. *See* Kaye, *supra* note 158, at 146. The general perception was that ethnic stratifica-

tion within the major racial categories posed a problem regardless of whether the relevant population for estimating the random match probability was a broad racial group or a narrow, inbred ethnic subpopulation.

170. *See* cases cited, Kaye, *supra* note 158. Courts applying *Daubert* or similar standards were more receptive to the evidence. *E.g.*, United States v. Jakobetz, 955 F.2d 786 (2d Cir.1992), *aff'g*, 747 F.Supp. 250 (D.Vt.1990); United States v. Bonds, 12 F.3d 540 (6th Cir. 1993), *aff'g*, United States v. Yee, 134 F.R.D. 161 (N.D.Ohio 1991); United States v. Chischilly, 30 F.3d 1144 (9th Cir.1994); United States v. Davis, 40 F.3d 1069 (10th Cir.1994).

171. *See* NRC I, *supra* note 35, at 91–92; *id.* at 80 ("Although mindful of the controversy, the committee has chosen to assume for the sake of discussion that population substructure may exist and provide a method for estimating population [genotype] frequencies in a manner that adequately accounts for it."). The report was unclear as to whether its "interim ceiling principle" was a substitute for or merely a supplement to the usual basic product rule. Years later, one member of the committee opined that the committee intended the latter interpretation. Eric S. Lander & Bruce Budowle, *Commentary: DNA Fingerprinting Dispute Laid to Rest*, 371 NATURE 735 (1994). In any event, the interim ceiling principle was proposed as a stopgap measure, to be supplanted by another ceiling principle that could be used after sampling many "[g]enetically homogeneous populations from various regions of the world." NRC I, *supra*, at 84.

172. Applied to a single racial group like whites, the basic product rule estimates the frequency of the multilocus genotype as the

multiplying together the allele frequencies from any single, major racial database, the procedure picks, for each allele in the DNA profile, the largest value seen in *any* race.[173] If that value is less than 10%, the procedure inflates it to 10%. Those values are then multiplied as with the basic product rule. Thus, the ceiling method employs a mix-and-match, inflate, and multiply strategy. The result, it is widely believed, is an extremely conservative estimate of the profile frequency that more than compensates for the possibility of any population structure that might undermine the assumptions of Hardy–Weinberg and linkage equilibria in the major racial populations.[174]

[c] The Product Rule for a Structured Population

The 1996 NRC Report distinguishes between cases in which the suspect population is a broad racial population and those in which that population is a genetically distinct subgroup. In the former situation, Recommendation 4.1 endorses the basic product rule:

> In general, the calculation of a profile frequency should be made with the product rule. If the race of the person who left the evidence-sample DNA is known, the database for the person's race should be used; if the race is not known, calculations for all the racial groups to which possible suspects belong should be made.[175]

product of the single-locus frequencies, and it estimates each single-locus frequency as $2p_1p_2$ for heterozygotes or as a quantity exceeding p^2 for homozygotes, where p refers to frequencies estimated from the database for that race.

173. Actually, an even larger figure is used—the upper 95% confidence limit on the allele frequency estimate for that race. This is intended to account for sampling error due to the limited size of the databases. NRC I, *supra* note 35, at 92.

174. *See, e.g.*, NRC II, *supra* note 37, at 156 ("sufficiently conservative to accommodate the presence of substructure . . . a lower limit on the size of the profile frequency"); NRC I, *supra* note 35, at 91 ("conservative calculation"). This modification of the basic product rule provoked vociferous criticism from many scientists, and it distressed certain prosecutors and other law enforcement personnel who perceived the 1992 NRC report as contributing to the rejection of DNA evidence in many jurisdictions. *See, e.g.*, D.H. Kaye, *DNA, NAS, NRC, DAB, RFLP, PCR, and More: An Introduction to the Symposium on the 1996 NRC Report on Forensic DNA Evidence*, 37 JURIMETRICS J. 395, 396 (1997). The judicial impact of the NRC report and the debate among scientists over the ceiling method are reviewed in D.H. Kaye, *The Forensic Debut of the National Research Council's DNA Report: Population Structure, Ceiling Frequencies, and the Need for Numbers*, 34 JURIMETRICS J. 369 (1994) (suggesting that because the disagreement about the ceiling principle is a dispute about legal policy rather than scientific knowledge, the debate

among scientists does not justify excluding ceiling frequencies).

By 1995, however, many courts were concluding that because a consensus that ceiling estimates are conservative had emerged, these estimates are admissible. At the same time, other courts that only a short while ago had held basic product estimates to be too controversial to be admissible decided that there was sufficient agreement about the basic product rule for it to be used. *See* State v. Johnson, 186 Ariz. 329, 922 P.2d 294, 300 (1996); State v. Copeland, 130 Wash.2d 244, 922 P.2d 1304, 1318 (1996) ("Although at one time a significant dispute existed among qualified scientists, from the present vantage point we are able to say that the significant dispute was short-lived."); D.H. Kaye, *DNA Identification in Criminal Cases: Lingering and Emerging Evidentiary Issues, in* PROCEEDINGS OF THE SEVENTH INTERNATIONAL SYMPOSIUM ON HUMAN IDENTIFICATION 12 (1997).

In 1994, a second NAS committee was installed to review the criticism and the studies that had accumulated in the aftermath of the 1992 report. In 1996, it reported that the ceiling method is an unnecessary and extravagant way to handle the likely extent of population structure. NRC II, *supra*, at 158, 162.

175. NRC II, *supra* note 37, at 5. The recommendation also calls for modifications to the Hardy–Weinberg proportion for apparent homozygotes. The modifications depend on whether the alleles are discrete (as in PCR-based tests) or continuous (as in VNTR testing). *Id.* at 5 n. 2.

"For example," the committee wrote, "if DNA is recovered from semen in a case in which a woman hitchhiker on an interstate highway has been raped by a white man, the product rule with the 2p rule can be used with VNTR data from a sample of whites to estimate the frequency of the profile among white males. If the race of the rapist were in doubt, the product rule could still be used and the results given for data on whites, blacks, Hispanics, and east Asians."[176] However, "[w]hen there are partially isolated subgroups in a population, the situation is more complex; then a suitably altered model leads to slightly different estimates of the quantities that are multiplied together in the formula for the frequency of the profile in the population."[177] Thus, the committee's Recommendation 4.2 urges that:

> If the particular subpopulation from which the evidence sample came is known, the allele frequencies for the specific subgroup should be used as described in Recommendation 4.1. If allele frequencies for the subgroup are not available, although data for the full population are, then the calculations should use the population-structure equations 4.10 for each locus, and the resulting values should be multiplied.[178]

The "suitably altered model" is a generalization of the basic product rule. In this *affinal model*, as it is sometimes called,[179] the "population-structure equations" are similar to those for multiplying single-locus frequencies. However, they involve not only the individual allele frequencies, but also a quantity that measures the extent of population structure.[180] The single-locus frequencies are multiplied together as in the basic product rule to find the multilocus frequency. Although few reported cases have analyzed the admissibility of random match probabilities estimated with the product rule for structured populations, the validity of the affinal model of a structured population has not been questioned in the scientific literature.

The committee recommended that the population-structure equations be used in special situations,[181] but they could be applied to virtually all cases. The report suggests conservative values of the population-structure constant might be used for broad suspect populations as well as values for many

176. *Id.* at 5 (note omitted). *See also* C. Thomas Caskey, *Comments on DNA-based Forensic Analysis*, 49 AM. J. HUM. GENETICS 893 (1991) (letter). For a case with comparable facts, see United States v. Jakobetz, 747 F.Supp. 250 (D.Vt.1990), *aff'd*, 955 F.2d 786 (2d Cir.1992).

177. *Id.* at 5.

178. *Id.* at 5–6.

179. Devlin & Roeder, *supra* note 133, § 18–3.1.3, at 723.

180. NRC II, *supra* note 37, at 114–15 (equations 4.10a & 4.10b); *see also* papers cited, Devlin & Roeder, *supra* note 133, § 18–3.1.3, at 723 n.37. This quantity usually is designated θ or F_{ST}. *See generally* Evett & Weir, *supra* note 153, at 94–107, 118–23, 156–62.

181. The report explains that the recommendation to use the population-structure equations "deals with the case in which the person who is the source of the evidence DNA is known to belong to a particular subgroup of a racial category." NRC II, *supra* note 37, at 6. It offers this illustration:

> For example, if the hitchhiker was not on an interstate highway but in the midst of, say, a small village in New England and we had good reason to believe that the rapist was an inhabitant of the village, the product rule could still be used (as described in Recommendation 4.1) if there is a reasonably large database on the villagers.
>
> If specific data on the villagers are lacking, a more complex model could be used to estimate the random-match probability for the incriminating profile on the basis of data on the major population group (whites) that includes the villagers.

Id..

partially isolated subpopulations.[182] The population-structure equations always give more conservative probabilities than the basic product rule when both formulae are applied to the same database, and they are usually conservative relative to calculations based on the subpopulation of the defendant.[183]

In a few situations, however, very little data on either the larger population or the specific subpopulation will be available.[184] To handle such cases, Recommendation 4.3 provides:

> If the person who contributed the evidence sample is from a group or tribe for which no adequate database exists, data from several other groups or tribes thought to be closely related to it should be used. The profile frequency should be calculated as described in Recommendation 4.1 for each group or tribe.[185]

Similar procedures have been followed in a few cases where the issue has surfaced.[186]

[d] Adjusting for a Database Search

Whatever variant of the product rule might be used to find the probability of the genotype in a population, subpopulation, or relative, the number is useful only insofar as it establishes (1) that the DNA profile is sufficiently discriminating to be probative, and (2) that the same DNA profile in the defendant and the crime scene stain is unlikely to occur if the DNA came from someone other than the defendant. Yet, unlikely events happen all the time. An individual wins the lottery even though it was very unlikely that the particular ticket would be a winner. The chance of a particular supertanker running aground and producing a massive spill on a single trip may be very small, but the Exxon Valdez did just that.

The apparent paradox of supposedly low-probability events being ubiquitous results from what statisticians call a "selection effect" or "data mining." If we pick a lottery ticket at random, the probability p that we have the winning ticket is negligible. But if we search through all the tickets, sooner or later we will find the winning one. And even if we search through some smaller number N of tickets, the probability of picking a winning ticket is no

---

182. *Id.* at 115 ("typical values for white and black populations are less than 0.01, usually about 0.002. Values for Hispanics are slightly higher...."), 116 ("For urban populations, 0.01 is a conservative value. A higher value— say 0.03 could be used for isolated villages."); *cf.* Devlin & Roeder, *supra* note 133, § 18–3.1.3, at 723–24 ("For [VNTR] markers, thetabar is generally agreed to lie between 0 and .02 for most populations.").

183. Devlin & Roeder, *supra* note 133, § 18–3.1.3, at 723.

184. *See, e.g.*, People v. Atoigue, 1992 WL 245628 (D.Guam App.Div.1992), *aff'd without deciding whether admission of DNA evidence was error*, 36 F.3d 1103 (9th Cir.1994) (unpublished).

185. NRC II, *supra* note 37, at 6. The committee explained that:

This recommendation deals with the case in which the person who is the source of the evidence DNA is known to belong to a particular subgroup of a racial category but there are no DNA data on either the subgroup or the population to which the subgroup belongs. It would apply, for example, if a person on an isolated Indian reservation in the Southwest, had been assaulted by a member of the tribe, and there were no data on DNA profiles of the tribe. In that case, the recommendation calls for use of the product rule (as described in Recommendation 4.1) with several other closely related tribes for which adequate databases exist.

Id.

186. *See supra* § 11–1.1.1.

longer p, but Np.[187]

Likewise, there may be a small probability p that a randomly selected individual who is not the source of the forensic sample has the incriminating genotype. That is somewhat like having a winning lottery ticket.[188] If N people are included in the search for a person with the matching DNA, then the probability of a match in this group is not p, but some quantity that could be as large as Np.[189] This type of reasoning led the second NRC committee to recommend that "[w]hen the suspect is found by a search of DNA databases, the random-match probability should be multiplied by N, the number of persons in the database."[190]

The first NAS committee also felt that "[t]he distinction between finding a match between an evidence sample and a suspect sample and finding a match between an evidence sample and one of many entries in a DNA profile databank is important."[191] Rather than proposing a statistical adjustment to the match probability, however, that committee recommended using only a few loci in the databank search, then confirming the match with additional loci, and presenting only "the statistical frequency associated with the additional loci . . . ."[192]

A number of statisticians reject the committees' view that the random match probability should be inflated, either by a factor of N or by ignoring the loci used in the databank search.[193] They argue that, if anything, the DNA evidence against the defendant is slightly stronger when not only has the defendant been shown to possess the incriminating profile, but also a large number of other individuals have been eliminated as possible sources of the crime scene DNA.[194] They conclude that no adjustment is required.

At its core, the statistical debate turns on how the problem is framed and what type of statistical reasoning is accepted as appropriate. The NAS committees ask how surprising it would be to find a match in a large database if the database does not contain the true source of the trace evidence. The

---

187. If there are T tickets and one winning ticket, then the probability that a randomly selected ticket is the winner is $p = 1/T$, and the probability that a set of N randomly selected tickets includes the winner is $N/T = Np$, where $1 \le N \le T$.

188. The analysis of the DNA database search is more complicated than the lottery example suggests. In the simple lottery, there was exactly one winner. In the database case, we do not know how many "winners" there are, or even if there are any. The situation is more like flipping a coin N times, where the coin has a probability p of heads on each independent toss.

189. *See* NRC II, *supra* note 37, at 163–65. Assuming that the individual who left the trace evidence sample is not in a database of unrelated people, the probability of at least one match is $1-(1-p)^N$, which is equal to or less than Np.

190. NRC II, *supra* note 37, at 161 (Recommendation 5.1). The DNA databases that are searched usually consist of profiles of offenders convicted of specified crimes. *See, e.g.*, Boling v. Romer, 101 F.3d 1336 (10th Cir.1996); Rise

v. Oregon, 59 F.3d 1556 (9th Cir.1995); Jones v. Murray, 962 F.2d 302 (4th Cir.1992); Landry v. Attorney General, 429 Mass. 336, 709 N.E.2d 1085 (Mass.1999) (all rejecting constitutional challenges to compelling offenders to provide DNA samples for databases).

191. It used the same Np formula in a numerical example to show that "[t]he chance of finding a match in the second case is considerably higher, because one . . . fishes through the databank, trying out many hypotheses." NRC I, *supra* note 35, at 124.

192. *Id.* The second NAS Committee did not object to this procedure. It proposed the Np adjustment as an alternative that might be useful when there were very few typable loci in the trace evidence sample.

193. *E.g.*, Peter Donnelly & Richard D. Friedman, *DNA Database Searches and the Legal Consumption of Scientific Evidence*, 97 Mich. L. Rev. 931 (1999); authorities cited, *id.* at 933 n.13.

194. *Id.* at 933, 945, 948, 955, 957; Evett & Weir, *supra* note 153, at 219–22.

more surprising the result, the more it appears that the database does contain the source. Because it would be more surprising to find a match in a test of a single innocent suspect than it would be to find a match by testing a large number of innocent suspects, the NAS committees conclude that the single-test match is more convincing evidence than the database search match.

The critics do not deny the mathematical truism that examining more innocent individuals increases the chance of finding a match, but they maintain that the committees have asked the wrong question. They emphasize that the question of interest to the legal system is not whether the database contains the culprit, but whether the one individual whose DNA matches the trace evidence DNA is the source of that trace, and they note that as the size of a database approaches that of the entire population, finding one and only one matching individual should be more, not less, convincing evidence against that person.[195] Thus, instead of looking at how surprising it would be to find a match in a group of innocent suspects, the "no-adjustment" school asks how much the result of the database search enhances the probability that the individual so identified is the source. They reason that the many exclusions in a database search reduce the number of people who might have left the trace evidence if the suspect did not. This additional information, they conclude, increases the likelihood that the defendant is the source, although the effect is indirect and generally small.[196]

§ 11–2.2.3   Measures of Probative Value

Sufficiently small probabilities of a match for close relatives and unrelated members of the suspect population undermine the hypotheses of kinship and coincidence. Adequate safeguards and checks for possible laboratory error make that explanation of the finding of matching genotypes implausible. The inference that the defendant is the source of the crime scene DNA is then secure. But this mode of reasoning by elimination is not the only way to analyze DNA evidence. This section discusses two alternatives that some statisticians prefer—likelihoods and posterior probabilities. In the next section, we review all the statistics that relate to rival hypotheses and probative value and consider the legal doctrine that must be considered in deciding the admissibility of the various types of presentations.

[1]   Likelihood Ratios

To choose between two competing hypotheses, one can compare how probable the evidence is under each hypothesis. Suppose that the probability of a match in a well-run laboratory is close to 1 when the samples both contain only the defendant's DNA, while the probability of a coincidental match and the probability of a match with a close relative are close to zero. In these circumstances, the DNA profiling result strongly supports the claim that the defendant is the source, for the observed outcome—the match—is many times more probable when the defendant is the source than when someone else is. How many times more probable? Suppose that there is a 1% chance that the laboratory would miss a true match, so that the probability of

---

195. *See, e.g.,* Donnelly & Friedman, *supra* note 193, at 952–53.   **196.** *Id.* at 245.

its finding a match when the defendant is the source is 0.99. Suppose further that $p = 0.00001$ is the random match probability. Then the match is 0.99/0.00001, or 99,000 times more likely to be seen if the defendant is the source than if an unrelated individual is. Such a ratio is called a *likelihood ratio*, and a likelihood ratio of 99,000 means that the DNA profiling supports the claim of identity 99,000 times more strongly than it supports the hypothesis of coincidence.[197]

Likelihood ratios are particularly useful for VNTRs and for trace evidence samples that contain DNA from more than one person.[198] With VNTRs, the procedure commonly used to estimate the allele frequencies that are combined via some version of the product rule is called *binning*.[199] In the simplest and most accurate version, the laboratory first forms a "bin" that stretches across the range of fragment lengths in the match window surrounding an evidence band. For example, if a 1,000 base-pair (bp) band is seen in the evidence sample, and the laboratory's match window is ±5%, then the bin extends from 950 to 1,050 bp. The laboratory then finds the proportion of VNTR bands in its database that fall within this bin. If 7% of the bands in the database lie in the 950–1,050 bp range, then 7% is the estimated allele frequency for this band. The two-stage procedure of (1) declaring matches between two samples when all the corresponding bands lie with the match window and (2) estimating the frequency of a band in the population by the proportion that lie within the corresponding bin is known as *match-binning*.[200]

As noted earlier in section 2.6.1, match-binning is statistically inefficient. It ignores the extent to which two samples match and gives the same coincidence probability to a close match as it does to a marginal one. Other methods obviate the need for matching by simultaneously combining the probability of the observed degree of matching with the probability of observing bands that are that close together. These "similarity likelihood ratios" dispense with the somewhat arbitrary dichotomy between matches and nonmatches.[201] They have been advocated on the ground that they make better

---

197. *See* NRC II, *supra* note 37, at 100; D.H. Kaye, *The Relevance of "Matching" DNA: Is the Window Half Open or Half Shut?*, 85 J. Crim. L. & Criminology 676 (1995).

198. *See supra* § 11–2.4. Mixed samples arise in various ways—blood from two or more persons mingled at the scene of a crime, victim and assailant samples on a vaginal swab, semen from multiple sexual assailants, and so on. In many cases, one of the contributors—for example, the victim—is known, and the genetic profile of the unknown portion is readily deduced. In those situations, the analysis of a remaining single-person profile can proceed in the ordinary fashion. "However, when the contributors to a mixture are not known or cannot otherwise be distinguished, a likelihood-ratio approach offers a clear advantage and is particularly suitable." NRC II, *supra* note 37, at 129. *Contra* R.C. Lewontin, *Population Genetic Issues in the Forensic Use of DNA, in* 1 Modern Scientific Evidence § 17–5.0, at 703–05 (David L. Faigman et al. eds., 1997); Thompson, *supra* note 147, at 855–56. For an exposition of this

likelihood ratio approach, see Evett & Weir, *supra* note 153, at 188–205.

199. There are two types of binning in use. *Floating bins* are conceptually simpler and more appropriate than *fixed bins*, but the latter can be justified as an approximation to the former. For the details of binning and suggestions for handling some of the complications that have caused disagreements over certain aspects of fixed bins, see NRC II, *supra* note 37, at 142–45.

200. Likelihood ratios for match-binning results are identical to those for discrete allele systems. If the bin frequencies reveal that a proportion p of the population has DNA whose bands each fall within the match window of the corresponding evidence bands, then the match-binning likelihood ratio is $1/p$.

201. The methods produce likelihood ratios tailored to the observed degree of matching. Two more or less "matching" bands would receive less weight when the measured band lengths differ substantially, and more weight

use of the DNA data,[202] but they have been attacked, primarily on the ground that they are complicated and difficult for nonstatisticians to understand.[203]

[2] Posterior Probabilities

The likelihood ratio expresses the relative strength of an hypothesis, but the judge or jury ultimately must assess a different type of quantity—the probability of the hypothesis itself. An elementary rule of probability theory known as *Bayes' theorem* yields this probability.[204] The theorem states that the odds in light of the data (here, the observed profiles) are the odds as they were known prior to receiving the data times the likelihood ratio: *posterior odds = likelihood ratio × prior odds*.[205] For example, if the relevant match probability[206] were 1/100,000, and if the chance that the laboratory would report a match between samples from the same source were 0.99, then the likelihood ratio would be 99,000, and the jury could be told how the DNA evidence raises various prior probabilities that the defendant's DNA is in the evidence sample.[207] It would be appropriate to explain that these calculations rest on many premises, including the premise that the genotypes have been correctly determined.[208]

One difficulty with this use of Bayes' theorem is that the computations consider only one alternative to the claim of identity at a time. As indicated in § 7.2, however, several rival hypotheses might apply in a given case. If it is not defendant's DNA in the forensic sample, is it from his father, his brother, his uncle, et cetera? Is the true source a member of the same subpopulation? A member of a different subpopulation in the same general population? In principle the likelihood ratio can be generalized to a likelihood function that takes on suitable values for every person in the world, and the prior probability for each person can be cranked into a general version of Bayes' rule to yield the posterior probability that the defendant is the source. In this vein, a few commentators suggest that Bayes' rule be used to combine the various

---

when the lengths differ very little. Devlin & Roeder, *supra* note 133, § 18–3.1.4, at 724. And, bands that occur in a region where relatively few people have VNTRs contribute more to the likelihood ratio than if they occur in a zone where VNTRs are common.

202. *See* NRC II, *supra* note 37, at 161 ("VNTR data are essentially continuous, and, in principle, a continuous model should be used to analyze them."); authorities cited, *id.* at 200; A. Collins & N.E. Morton, *Likelihood Ratios for DNA Identification*, 91 PROC. NAT'L ACAD. SCI. 6007 (1994); Devlin & Roeder, *supra* note 133, § 18–3.1.4, at 724.

203. *E.g.*, Lewontin, *supra* note 198, § 17–5.0, at 705. For discussion, see *supra* § 11–1.

204. *See supra* SCIENCE IN THE LAW: STANDARDS, STATISTICS AND RESEARCH ISSUES, Chapter 5 (Appendix).

205. Odds and probabilities are two ways to express chances quantitatively. If the probability of an event is P, the odds are P/(1–P). If the odds are O, the probability is O/(O + 1). For instance, if the probability of rain is 2/3,

the odds of rain are 2 to 1: (2/3) / (1–2/3) = (2/3) / (1/3) = 2. If the odds of rain are 2 to 1, then the probability is 2/(2 + 1) = 2/3.

206. By "relevant match probability," we mean the probability of a match given a specified type of kinship or the probability of a random match in the relevant suspect population. For relatives more distantly related than second cousins, the probability of a chance match is nearly as small as for persons of the same subpopulation. Devlin & Roeder, *supra* note 133, § 18–3.1.3, at 724.

207. For further discussion of how Bayes' rule might be used in court with DNA evidence, see, *e.g.*, Kaye, *supra* note 158; NRC II, *supra* note 37, at 201–03.

208. *See* Richard Lempert, *The Honest Scientist's Guide to DNA Evidence*, 96 GENETICA 119 (1995). If the jury accepted these premises and also decided to accept the hypothesis of identity over those of kinship and coincidence, it still would be open to the defendant to offer explanations of how the forensic samples came to include his DNA even though he is innocent.

likelihood ratios for all possible degrees of kinship and subpopulations.[209] However, it is not clear how this ambitious proposal would be implemented.[210]

§ 11–2.7   Novel Applications of DNA Technology

Most routine applications of DNA technology in the forensic setting involve the identification of human beings—suspects in criminal cases, missing persons, or victims of mass disasters. However, inasmuch as DNA technology can be applied to the analysis of any kind of biological evidence containing DNA, and because the technology is advancing rapidly, unusual applications are inevitable. In cases in which the evidentiary DNA is of human origin, new methods of analyzing DNA will come into at least occasional use, and new loci or DNA polymorphisms will be used for forensic work. In other cases, the evidentiary DNA will come from non-human organisms—household pets,[211] wild animals,[212] insects,[213] even bacteria[214] and viruses.[215] These applications are directed either at distinguishing among species or at distinguishing among individuals (or subgroups) within a species. These two tasks can raise somewhat different scientific issues, and no single, mechanically applied test can be formulated to assess the validity of the diversity of applications and methods that might be encountered.

Instead, this section outlines and describes four factors that may be helpful in deciding whether a new application is scientifically sound. These are the novelty of the application, the validity of the underlying scientific theory, the validity of any statistical interpretations, and the relevant scientific community to consult in assessing the application. We illustrate these considerations in the context of three unusual applications of DNA technology to law enforcement:

209. *See* Balding & Donnelly, *supra* note 153.

210. A related proposal in Lempert, *supra* note 145, suffers from the same difficulty of articulating the composition of the suspect population and the prior probabilities for its members. Professor Lempert reasons that "the relevant match statistic, if it could be derived, is an average that turns on the number of people in the suspect population and a likelihood that each has DNA matching the defendant's DNA, weighted by the probability that each committed the crime if the defendant did not." *Id.* at 458. He concludes that although this "weighted average statistic" does not directly state how likely it is "that the defendant and not some third party committed the crime," it is superior to "the 'random man' match statistic" in that it "tells the jury how surprising it would be to find a DNA match if the defendant is innocent." *Id.*

211. Ronald K. Fitten, *Dog's DNA May Be Key in Murder Trial: Evidence Likely to Set Court Precedent*, Seattle Times, Mar. 9, 1998, at A1, *available at* 1998 WL 3142721 (reporting a trial court ruling in favor of admitting evidence linking DNA found on the jackets of two men to a pit bull that the men allegedly shot and killed, along with its owners).

212. For example, hunters sometimes claim that they have cuts of beef rather than the remnants of illegally obtained wildlife. These claims can be verified or refuted by DNA analysis. *Cf.* State v. Demers, 167 Vt. 349, 707 A.2d 276, 277–78 (Vt.1997) (unspecified DNA analysis of deer blood and hair helped supply probable cause for search warrant to look for evidence of illegally hunted deer in defendant's home).

213. Felix A.H. Sperling et al., *A DNA-Based Approach to the Identification of Insect Species Used for Postmortem Interval Estimation*, 39 J. FORENSIC SCI. 418 (1994).

214. DNA testing of bacteria in food can help establish the source of outbreaks of food poisoning and thereby facilitate recalls of contaminated foodstuffs. *See* Jo Thomas, *Outbreak of Food Poisoning Leads to Warning on Hot Dogs and Cold Cuts*, N.Y. TIMES, Dec. 24, 1998.

215. *See* State v. Schmidt, 771 So.2d 131 (La.Ct.App.2000) (where a physician was convicted of murdering his former lover by injecting her with the AIDS virus, and the state's expert witnesses used PCR-based analysis to identify HIV strains).

- Although federal law prohibits the export of bear products, individuals in this country have offered to supply bear gall bladder for export to Asia, where it is prized for its supposed medicinal properties. In one investigation, the National Fish and Wildlife Forensic Laboratory, using DNA testing, determined that the material offered for export actually came from a pig absolving the suspect of any export law violations.[216]

- In *State v. Bogan*,[217] a woman's body was found in the desert, near several palo verde trees. A detective noticed two seed pods in the bed of a truck that the defendant was driving before the murder. A biologist performed DNA profiling on this type of palo verde and testified that the two pods "were identical" and "matched completely with "a particular tree and "didn't match any of the [other] trees," and that he felt "quite confident in concluding that" the tree's DNA would be distinguishable from that of "any tree that might be furnished" to him. After the jury convicted the defendant of murder, jurors reported that they found this testimony very persuasive.[218]

- In *R. v. Beamish*, a woman disappeared from her home on Prince Edward Island, on Canada's eastern seaboard. Weeks later a man's brown leather jacket stained with blood was discovered in a plastic bag in the woods. In the jacket's lining were white cat hairs. After the missing woman's body was found in a shallow grave, her estranged common-law husband was arrested and charged. He lived with his parents and a white cat. Laboratory analysis showed the blood on the jacket to be the victim's, and the hairs were ascertained to match the family cat at ten STR loci. The defendant was convicted of the murder.[219]

§ 11–2.7.1 Is the Application Novel?

The more novel and untested an application is, the more problematic is its introduction into evidence. In many cases, however, an application can be new to the legal system but be well established in the field of scientific inquiry from which it derives. This can be ascertained from a survey of the peer-reviewed scientific literature and the statements of experts in the field.[220]

Applications designed specially to address an issue before the court are more likely to be truly novel and thus may be more difficult to evaluate. The studies of the gall bladder, palo verde trees, and cat hairs exemplify such

216. Interview with Dr. Edgard Espinoza, Deputy Director, National Fish and Wildlife Forensic Laboratory, in Ashland, Oregon, June 1998. Also, FDA regulations do not prohibit mislabeling of pig gall bladder.

217. 183 Ariz. 506, 905 P.2d 515 (Ariz.Ct. App.1995).

218. Brent Whiting, *Tree's DNA "Fingerprint" Splinters Killer's Defense*, Ariz. Republic, May 28, 1993, at A1, *available in* 1993 WL 8186972; *see also* C.K. Yoon, *Forensic Science—Botanical Witness for the Prosecution*, 260 Science 894 (1993).

219. *DNA Testing on Cat Hairs Helped Link Man to Slaying*, Boston Globe, Apr. 24, 1997, *available in* 1997 WL 6250745; Gina Kolata, *Cat Hair Finds Way into Courtroom in Canadian Murder Trial*, N.Y. Times, Apr. 24, 1997, at A5; Marilyn A. Menott–Haymond et al., *Pet Cat Hair Implicates Murder Suspect*, 386 Nature 774 (1997).

220. Even though some applications are represented by only a few papers in the peer-reviewed literature, they may be fairly well established. The breadth of scientific inquiry, even within a rather specialized field, is such that only a few research groups may be working on any particular problem. A better gauge is the extent to which the genetic typing technology is used by researchers studying related problems and the existence of a general body of knowledge regarding the nature of the genetic variation at issue.

applications in that each was devised solely for the case at bar.[221] In such cases, there are no published, peer-reviewed descriptions of the particular application to fall back on, but the analysis still could give rise to "scientific knowledge" within the meaning of *Daubert v. Merrell Dow Pharmaceuticals, Inc.*[222]

The novelty of an unusual application of DNA technology involves two components—the novelty of the analytical technique, and the novelty of applying that technique to the samples in question. With respect to the analytical method, forensic DNA technology in the last two decades has been driven in part by the development of many new methods for the detection of genetic variation between species and between individuals within a species. The approaches outlined in the appendix[223] for the detection of genetic variation in humans—RFLP analysis of VNTR polymorphism, PCR, detection of VNTR and STR polymorphism by gel and capillary electrophoresis, respectively, and detection of sequence variation by probe hybridization or direct sequence analysis—have been imported from other research contexts. Thus, their use in the detection of variation in nonhuman species and of variation among species involves no new technology. DNA technology transcends organismal differences.

Some methods for the characterization of DNA variation widely used in studies of other species, however, are not used in forensic testing of human DNA. These are often called "DNA fingerprint" approaches. They offer a snapshot characterization of genomic variation in a single test, but they essentially presume that the sample DNA originates from a single individual, and this presumption cannot always be met with forensic samples.

The original form of DNA "fingerprinting" used electrophoresis, Southern blotting, and a *multilocus probe* that simultaneously recognizes many sites in the genome.[224] The result is comparable to what would be obtained with a "cocktail" of single-locus probes—one complex banding pattern sometimes analogized to a bar-code.[225] Probes for DNA fingerprinting are widely used in genetic research in nonhuman species.[226]

With the advent of PCR as the central tool in molecular biology, PCR-based "fingerprinting" methods have been developed. The two most widely

---

221. Of course, such evidence hardly is unique to DNA technology. *See, e.g.*, Coppolino v. State, 223 So.2d 68 (Fla.Ct.App.), *appeal dismissed*, 234 So.2d 120 (Fla.1969) (holding admissible a test for the presence of succinylcholine chloride first devised for this case to determine whether defendant had injected a lethal dose of this curare-like anesthetic into his wife).

222. 509 U.S. 579, 590, 113 S.Ct. 2786, 125 L.Ed.2d 469 (1993) ("to qualify as 'scientific knowledge,' an inference or assertion must be derived by the scientific method").

223. *See infra* Appendix Table A–1.

224. The probes were pioneered by Alec Jeffreys. *See, e.g.*, Alec J. Jeffreys et al., *Individual-specific "Fingerprints" of Human DNA*, 316 Nature 76 (1985). In the 1980s, the "Jef-

freys probes" were used for forensic purposes, especially in parentage testing. *See, e.g.*, D.H. Kaye, *DNA Paternity Probabilities*, 24 Fam. L. Q. 279 (1990).

225. As with RFLP analysis in general, this RFLP fingerprinting approach requires relatively good quality sample DNA. Degraded DNA results in a loss of some of the bars in the barcode-like pattern.

226. *E.g.*, DNA Fingerprinting: State of the Science (S.D.J. Pena et al. eds., 1993). The discriminating power of a probe must be determined empirically in each species. The probes used by Jeffreys for human DNA fingerprinting, for instance, are less discriminating for dogs. A.J. Jeffreys et al., *DNA Fingerprints of Dogs and Cats*, 18 Animal Genetics 1 (1987).

used are the *random amplified polymorphic DNA* (RAPD) method[227] and the *amplified fragment length polymorphism* (AFLP) method.[228] Both give bar code-like patterns.[229] In RAPD analysis, a single, arbitrarily constructed, short primer amplifies many DNA fragments of unknown sequence.[230] AFLP analysis begins with a digestion of the sample DNA with a restriction enzyme followed by amplification of selected restriction fragments.[231]

Although the "DNA fingerprinting" procedures are not likely to be used in the analysis of samples of human origin, new approaches to the detection of genetic variation in humans as well as other organisms are under development. On the horizon are methods based on mass spectrometry and hybridization chip technology. As these or other methods come into forensic use, the best measure of scientific novelty will be the extent to which the methods have found their way into the scientific literature. Use by researchers other than those who developed them indicates some degree of scientific acceptance.

The second aspect of novelty relates to the sample analyzed. Two questions are central: Is there scientific precedent for testing samples of the sort tested in the particular case? And, what is known about the nature and extent of genetic variation in the tested organism and in related species? *Beamish*, the Canadian case involving cat hairs, illustrates both points. The nature of the sample—cat hairs—does not seem novel, for there is ample scientific precedent for doing genetic tests on animal hairs.[232] But the use of STR testing to identify a domestic cat as the source of particular hairs was new. Of course, this novelty does not mean that the effort was scientifically unsound; indeed, as explained in the next section, the premise that cats show substantial microsatellite polymorphism is consistent with other scientific knowledge.

§ 11–2.7.2   Is the Underlying Scientific Theory Valid?

Neither *Daubert* nor *Frye* banishes novel applications of science from the courtroom, but they do demand that trial judges assure themselves that the underlying science is sound, so that the scientific expert can be found to be presenting scientific knowledge rather than speculating or dressing up unscientific opinion in the garb of scientific fact.[233] The questions that might be

227. J. Welsh & M. McCelland, *Fingerprinting Genomes Using PCR with Arbitrary Primers*, 18 NUCLEIC ACIDS RES. 7213 (1990); J.G.K. Williams et al., *DNA Polymorphisms Amplified by Random Primers Are Useful as Genetic Markers*, 18 NUCLEIC ACIDS RES. 6531 (1990).

228. P. Vos et al., *AFLP: A New Technique for DNA Fingerprinting*, 23 NUCLEIC ACIDS RES. 4407 (1995).

229. The identification of the seed pods in *State v. Bogan*, 183 Ariz. 506, 905 P.2d 515 (Ariz.Ct.App.1995), was accomplished with RAPD analysis. The general acceptance of this technique in the scientific community was not seriously contested. Indeed, the expert for the defense conceded the validity of RAPD in genetic research and testified that the state's expert had correctly applied the procedure. *Id.* at 520.

230. Primers must be validated in advance to determine which give highly discriminating patterns for a particular species in question.

231. Both the RAPD and AFLP methods provide reproducible results within a laboratory, but AFLP is more reproducible across-laboratories. *See, e.g.,* C.J. Jones, et al., *Reproducibility Testing of RAPD, AFLP and SSR markers in Plants by a Network of European Laboratories*, 3 MOLECULAR BREEDING 381 (1997). This may be an issue if results from different laboratories must be compared.

232. *E.g.,* R. Higuchi et al., *DNA Typing from Single Hairs*, 332 NATURE 543, 545 (1988). Collection of hair is non-invasive and is widely used in wildlife studies where sampling in the field would otherwise be difficult or impossible. Hair also is much easier to transport and store than blood, a great convenience when working in the field.

233. *See Daubert v. Merrell Dow Pharm's., Inc.,* 509 U.S. 579, 590, 113 S.Ct. 2786, 125

asked to probe the scientific underpinnings extend the line of questions asked about novelty: What is the principle of the testing method used? What has been the experience with the use of the testing method? What are its limitations? Has it been used in applications similar to those in the instant case—for instance, for the characterization of other organisms or other kinds of samples? What is known of the nature of genetic variability in the organism tested or in related organisms? Is there precedent for doing any kind of DNA testing on the sort of samples tested in the instant case? Is there anything about the organism, the sample, or the context of testing that would render the testing technology inappropriate for the desired application?[234] To illustrate the usefulness of these questions, we can return to the cases involving pig gall bladders, cat hairs, and palo verde seed pods.

Deciding whether the DNA testing is valid is simplest in the export case. The question there was whether the gall bladders originated from bear or from some other species. The DNA analysis was based on the approach used by evolutionary biologists to study relationships among vertebrate species. It relies on sequence variation in the mitochondrial cytochrome b gene. DNA sequence analysis is a routine technology, and there is an extensive library of cytochrome b sequence data representing a broad range of vertebrate species.[235] As for the sample material—the gall bladder—such cells may not have been used before, but gall bladder is simply another tissue from which DNA can be extracted.[236] Thus, although the application was novel in that an approach had to be devised to address the question at hand, each segment of the application rests on a solid foundation of scientific knowledge and experience. No great inferential leap from the known to the unknown was required to reach the conclusion that the gall bladder was from a pig rather than a bear.

The DNA analysis in *Beamish* required slightly more extrapolation from the known to the unknown. As indicated in the previous section, the use of cat hairs as a source of DNA was not especially novel, and the very factors that reveal a lack of novelty also suggest that it is scientifically valid to test the DNA in cat hairs. But we also observed that the use of STR typing to distinguish among cats was novel. Is such reasoning too great a leap to constitute scientific knowledge? A great deal is known about the basis and extent of genetic variation in cats and other mammals. In particular, microsatellite polymorphism is extensive in all mammalian species that have been studied, including other members of the cat family. Furthermore, by testing

L.Ed.2d 469 (1993) ("The adjective 'scientific' [in Rule 702] implies a grounding in the methods and procedures of science. Similarly, the word 'knowledge' connotes more than subjective belief or unsupported speculation."). In *Frye*, the courts determines validity indirectly, using general acceptance as the dispositive consideration. In this section, we discuss the broader inquiry mandated by *Daubert* ,which includes the criterion of general acceptance in the scientific community.

234. *But cf.* NRC I, *supra* note 35, at 72 (listing seven "requirements" for new forensic

DNA tests to achieve "the highest standards of scientific rigor").

235. If the bear cytochrome b gene sequence were not in the database, it would be obligatory for the proponents of the application to determine it and add it to the database, where it could be checked by other researchers.

236. There is a technical concern that the DNA extracted from a gall bladder might contain inhibitors that would interfere with the subsequent sequence analysis; however, this merely affects whether the test will yield a result, and not the accuracy of any result.

small samples from two cat populations, the researchers verified the loci they examined were highly polymorphic.[237] Thus, the novelty in using STR analysis to identify cats is not scientifically unsettling; rather, it extends from and fits with everything else that is known about cats and mammals in general. However, as one moves from well studied organisms to ones about which little is known, one risks crossing the line between knowledge and speculation.

The DNA testing in *State v. Bogan*[238] pushes the envelope further. First, the genetic variability of palo verde trees had not been previously studied. Second, it was not known whether enough DNA could be extracted from seed pods to perform a genetic analysis. Both of these questions had to be answered by new testing. RAPD analysis, a well-established method for characterizing genetic variation within a species, demonstrated that palo verde trees were highly variable. Seed pods were shown to contain adequate DNA for RAPD analysis. Finally, a blind trial showed that RAPD profiles correctly identified individual palo verde trees.[239] In short, the lack of pre-existing data on DNA fingerprints of palo verde trees was bridged by scientific experimentation that established the validity of the specific application.

The DNA analyses in all three situations rest on a coherent and internally consistent body of observation, experiment, and experience. That information was mostly pre-existing in the case of the gall bladder testing. Some information on the population genetics of domestic cats on Prince Edward's Island had to be generated specifically for the analysis in *Beamish*, and still more was developed expressly for the situation in the palo verde tree testing in *Bogan*. A court, with the assistance of suitable experts, can make a judgment as to scientific validity in these cases because the crucial propositions are open to critical review by others in the scientific community and are subject to additional investigation if questions are raised. Where serious doubt remains, a court might consider ordering a blind trial to verify the analytical laboratory's ability to perform the identification in question.[240]

---

237. One sample consisted of nineteen cats in Sunnyside, Prince Edward Island, where the crime occurred. *See* Commentary, *Use of DNA Analysis Raises Some Questions* (CBS radio broadcast, Apr. 24, 1997), transcript *available in* 1997 WL 5424082 ("19 cats obtained randomly from local veterinarians on Prince Edward Island"); Marjorie Shaffer, *Canadian Killer Captured by a Whisker from Parents' Pet Cat*, BIOTECHNOLOGY NEWSWATCH, May 5, 1997, *available in* 1997 WL 8790779 ("the Royal Canadian Mounted Police rounded up 19 cats in the area and had a veterinarian draw blood samples"). The other sample consisted of nine cats from the United States. *DNA Test on Parents' Cat Helps Put Away Murderer*, CHI. TRIBUNE, Apr. 24, 1997, *available in* 1997 WL 3542042.

238. 183 Ariz. 506, 905 P.2d 515 (Ariz.Ct. App.1995).

239. The DNA in the two seed pods could not be distinguished by RAPD testing, suggesting that they fell from the same tree. The

biologist who devised and conducted the experiments analyzed samples from the nine trees near the body and another nineteen trees from across the county. He "was not informed, until after his tests were completed and his report written, which samples came from" which trees. *Bogan*, 905 P.2d at 521. Furthermore, unbeknownst to the experimenter, two apparently distinct samples were prepared from the tree at the crime scene that appeared to have been abraded by the defendant's truck. The biologist correctly identified the two samples from the one tree as matching, and he "distinguished the DNA from the seed pods in the truck bed from the DNA of all twenty-eight trees except" that one. *Id.*

240. *Cf. supra* note 239. The blind trial could be devised and supervised by a court-appointed expert, or the parties could be ordered to agree on a suitable experiment.

§ 11–2.7.3   Has the Probability of a Chance Match Been Estimated Correctly?

The significance of a human DNA match in a particular case typically is presented or assessed in terms of the probability that an individual selected at random from the population would be found to match. A small random match probability renders implausible the hypothesis that the match is just coincidental.[241] In *Beamish*, the random match probability was estimated to be one in many millions,[242] and the trial court admitted evidence of this statistic.[243] In *State v. Bogan*,[244] the random match probability was estimated by the state's expert as one in a million and by the defense expert as one in 136,000, but the trial court excluded these estimates because of the then-existing controversy over analogous estimates for human RFLP genotypes.[245]

Estimating the probability of a random match or related statistics requires a sample of genotypes from the relevant population of organisms. As discussed in section 11–7, the most accurate estimates combine the allele frequencies seen in the sample according to formulae that reflect the gene flow within the population. In the simplest model for large populations of sexually reproducing organisms, mating is independent of the DNA types under investigation, and each parent transmits half of his or her DNA to the progeny at random. Under these idealized conditions, the basic product rule gives the multilocus genotype frequency as a simple function of the allele frequencies.[246] The accuracy of the estimates thus depends on the accuracy of the allele frequencies in the sample database and the appropriateness of the population genetics model.

[1]   How Was the Database Obtained?

Since the allele frequencies come from sample data, both the method of sampling and the size of the sample can be crucial. The statistical ideal is probability sampling, in which some objective procedure provides a known chance that each member of the population will be selected. Such random samples tend to be representative of the population from which they are drawn. In wildlife biology, however, the populations often defy enumeration, and hence strict random sampling rarely is possible. Still, if the method of selection is uncorrelated with the alleles being studied, then the sampling

---

241. *See supra* § 11–2.6.

242. David N. Leff, *Killer Convicted by a Hair: Unprecedented Forensic Evidence from Cat's DNA Convinced Canadian Jury*, Bio-world Today, Apr. 24, 1997, *available in* 1997 WL 7473675 ("the frequency of the match came out to be on the order of about one in 45 million," quoting Steven O'Brien); *All Things Considered: Cat DNA* (NPR broadcast, Apr. 23, 1997), *available in* 1997 WL 12832754 ("it was less than one in two hundred million," quoting Steven O'Brien).

243. *See also* Tim Klass, *DNA Tests Match Dog, Stains in Murder Case*, Portland Oregoni-an, Aug. 7, 1998, at D06 (reporting expert testimony in a Washington murder case that "the likelihood of finding a 10–for–10 match in

the DNA of a randomly chosen dog of any breed or mix would be one in 3 trillion, and the odds for a nine-of–10 match would be one in 18 billion").

244. 183 Ariz. 506, 905 P.2d 515 (Ariz.Ct. App.1995).

245. *Id.* at 520. The Arizona case law on this subject is criticized in D.H. Kaye, Bible *Reading: DNA Evidence in Arizona*, 28 Ariz. St. L.J. 1035 (1996).

246. More complicated models account for the population structure that arises when inbreeding is common, but they require some knowledge of how much the population is structured. *See supra* § 11–2.6.

procedure is tantamount to random sampling with respect to those alleles.[247] Consequently, the key question about the method of sampling for a court faced with estimates based on a database of cats, dogs, or any such species, is whether that sample was obtained in some biased way—a way that would systematically tend to include (or exclude) organisms with particular alleles or genotypes from the database.

[2]   How Large is the Sampling Error?

Assuming that the sampling procedure is reasonably structured to give representative samples with respect to those genotypes of forensic interest, the question of database size should be considered. Larger samples give more precise estimates of allele frequencies than smaller ones, but there is no sharp line for determining when a database is too small.[248] Instead, just as pollsters present their results within a certain margin of error, the expert should be able to explain the extent of the statistical error that arises from using samples of the size of the forensic database.[249]

[3]   How Was the Random Match Probability Computed?

As we have indicated, the theory of population genetics provides the framework for combining the allele frequencies into the final profile frequency. The frequency estimates are a mathematical function of the genetic diversity at each locus and the number of loci tested. The formulas for frequency estimates depend on the mode of reproduction and the population genetics of the species. For outbreeding sexually reproducing species,[250] under conditions that give rise to Hardy–Weinberg and linkage equilibrium, genotype frequencies can be estimated with the basic product rule.[251] If a species is sexually reproducing but given to inbreeding, or if there are other impediments to Hardy–Weinberg or linkage equilibrium, such genotype frequencies may be incorrect. Thus, the reasonableness of assuming Hardy–Weinberg equilibrium and linkage equilibrium depends on what and how much is known about the population genetics of the species.[252] Ideally, large population

247. Few people would worry, for example, that the sample of blood cells taken from their vein for a test of whether they suffer from anemia is not, strictly speaking, a random sample. The use of convenience samples from human populations to form forensic databases is discussed in, *e.g.*, NRC II, *supra* note 37, at 126–27, 186. Case law on the point is collected *supra* § 11–1.

248. The 1996 NRC Report, *supra* note 37, at 114, refers to "at least several hundred persons," but it has been suggested that relatively small databases, consisting of fifty or so individuals, allow statistically acceptable frequency estimation for the common alleles. A new, specially constructed database is likely to be small, but alleles can be a assigned a minimum value, resulting in conservative genotype frequency estimates. Ranajit Chakraborty, *Sample Size Requirements for Addressing the Population Genetic Issues of Forensic Use of DNA Typing*, 64 HUMAN BIOLOGY 141, 156–57

(1992). Later, the NRC committee suggests that the uncertainty that arises "[i]f the database is small . . . can be addressed by providing confidence intervals on the estimates." NRC II, *supra* note 37, at 125.

249. Bruce S. Weir, *Forensic Population Genetics and the NRC*, 52 AM. J. HUM. GENETICS 437 (1993) (proposing interval estimate of genotype frequency); *cf.* NRC II, *supra* note 37, at 148 (remarking that "calculation of confidence intervals is desirable," but also examining the error that could be associated with the choice of a database on an empirical rather than a theoretical basis).

250. Outbreeding refers to the propensity for individuals to mate with individuals who are not close relations.

251. *See supra* § 11–2.6.

252. In *State v. Bogan*, 183 Ariz. 506, 905 P.2d 515 (Ct.App.1995), for example, the biologist who testified for the prosecution consulted

databases can be analyzed to verify independence of alleles.[253] Tests for deviations from the single-locus genotype frequencies expected under Hardy–Weinberg equilibrium will indicate if population structure effects should be accorded serious concern. These tests, however, are relatively insensitive to minor population structure effects, and adjustments for possible population structure might be appropriate.[254] For sexually reproducing species believed to have local population structure, a sampling strategy targeting the relevant population would be best. If this is not possible, estimates based on the larger population might be presented with appropriate caveats. If data on the larger population are unavailable, the uncertainty implicit in basic product rule estimates should not be ignored, and less ambitious alternatives to the random match probability as a means for conveying the probative value of a match might be considered.[255]

A different approach may be called for if the species is not an outbreeding, sexually reproducing species. For example, many plants, some simple animals, and bacteria reproduce asexually. With asexual reproduction, most offspring are genetically identical to the parent. All the individuals that originate from a common parent constitute, collectively, a clone. The major source of genetic variation in asexually reproducing species is mutation.[256] When a mutation occurs, a new clonal lineage is created. Individuals in the original clonal lineage continue to propagate, and two clonal lineages now exist where before there was one. Thus, in species that reproduce asexually, genetic testing distinguishes clones, not individuals, and the product rule cannot be applied to estimate genotype frequencies for individuals. Rather, the frequency of a particular clone in a population of clones must be determined by direct observation. For example, if a rose thorn found on a suspect's clothing were to be identified as originating from a particular cultivar of rose, the relevant question becomes how common that variety of rose bush is and where it is located in the community.

In short, the approach for estimating a genotype frequency depends on the reproductive pattern and population genetics of the species. In cases involving unusual organisms, a court will need to rely on experts with

with botanists who assured him that palo verde tree were an outcrossing species. *Id.* at 523–24.

253. However, large, pre-existing databases may not be available for the populations of interest in these more novel cases. Analyses of the smaller, ad hoc databases are unlikely to be decisive. In *Beamish*, for instance, two cat populations were sampled. The sample of nineteen cats from Sunnyside, in Prince Edward Island, and the sample of nine cats from the United States revealed considerable genetic diversity; moreover, most of the genetic variability was between individual cats, not between the two populations of cats. There was no statistically significant evidence of population substructure, and there was no statistically significant evidence of linkage disequilibrium in the Sunnyside population. The problem is that with such small samples, the statistical tests for substructure are not very sensitive; hence, the failure to detect it is not strong proof that either the Sunnyside or the North American cat population is unstructured.

254. A standard correction for population structure is to incorporate a population structure parameter F_{ST} into the calculation. Such adjustments are described *supra* § 11–2.6. However, appropriate values for F_{ST} may not be known for unstudied species.

255. The "tree lineup" in *Bogan* represents one possible approach. Adapting it to *Beamish* would have produced testimony that the researchers were able to exclude all the other (28) cats presented to them. This simple counting, however, is extremely conservative.

256. Bacteria also can exchange DNA through several mechanisms unrelated to cell division, including conjugation, transduction, and transformation. Bacterial species differ in their susceptibility to undergo these forms of gene transfer.

sufficient knowledge of the species to verify that the method for estimating genotype frequencies is appropriate.

§ 11–2.7.4   What Is the Relevant Scientific Community?

Even the most scientifically sophisticated court may find it difficult to judge the scientific soundness of a novel application without questioning appropriate scientists. Given the great diversity of forensic questions to which DNA testing might be applied, it is not possible to define specific scientific expertises appropriate to each. If the technology is novel, expertise in molecular genetics or biotechnology might be necessary. If testing has been conducted on a particular organism or category of organisms, expertise in that area of biology may be called for. If a random match probability has been presented, one might seek expertise in statistics as well as the population biology or population genetics that goes with the organism tested. Given the penetration of molecular technology into all areas of biological inquiry, it is likely that individuals can be found who know both the technology and the population biology of the organism in question. Finally, where samples come from crime scenes, the expertise and experience of forensic scientists can be crucial. Just as highly focused specialists may be unaware of aspects of an application outside their field of expertise, so too scientists who have not previously dealt with forensic samples can be unaware of case-specific factors that can confound the interpretation of test results.

Appendix

1. Structure of DNA

DNA is a complex molecule made of subunits known as *nucleotides* that link together to form a long, spiraling strand. Two such strands are intertwined around each other to form a double helix as shown in Figure A–1. Each strand has a "backbone" made of sugar and phosphate groups and nitrogenous *bases* attached to the sugar groups.[1] There are four types of bases, abbreviated A, T, G, and C, and the two strands of DNA in the double helix are linked by weak chemical bonds such that the A in one strand is always paired to a T in the other strand and the G in one strand is always paired to a C in the other.[2] The A:T and G:C *complementary base pairing* means that knowledge of the sequence of one strand predicts the sequence of the complementary strand. The sequence of the nucleotide base pairs carries the genetic information in the DNA molecule—it is the genetic "text." For example, the sequence ATT on one strand (or TAA on the other strand) "means" something different than GTT (or CAA).

1. For more details about DNA structure, see, for example, ANTHONY J.F. GRIFFITHS ET AL., AN INTRODUCTION TO GENETIC ANALYSIS (6th ed.1996); ELAINE JOHNSON MANGE & ARTHUR P. MANGE, BASIC HUMAN GENETICS 95 (2d ed. 1999).

2. The bonds that connect the complementary bases are known as *hydrogen bonds*.

Figure A–1

A Schematic Diagram of the DNA Molecule. The bases in the nucleotide (denoted C, G, A, and T) are arranged like the rungs in a spiral staircase

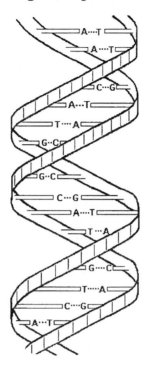

2. DNA Probes

A sequence specific oligonucleotide (SSO) probe is a short segment of single-stranded DNA with bases arranged in a particular order. The order is chosen so that the probe will bind to the complementary sequence on a DNA fragment, as sketched in figure A–2.

Figure A–2

A Sequence-specific Probe Links (Hybridizes) to the Targeted Sequence on a Single Stand of DNA

targeted sequence

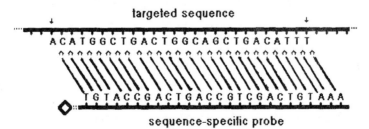

sequence-specific probe

3. Examples of Genetic Markers in Forensic Identification

Table A–1 offers examples of the major types of genetic markers used in forensic identification.[3] As noted in the table, simple sequence polymorphisms,

3. The table is adapted from Committee on DNA Forensic Science: An Update, National Research Council, The Evaluation of Forensic DNA Evidence 74 (1996) [hereinafter NRC II].

some VNTR polymorphisms, and nearly all STR polymorphisms are detected using PCR as a starting point. Most VNTRs containing long core repeats are too large to be amplified reliably by PCR and are instead characterized by *restriction fragment length polymorphism* (RFLP) analysis using *Southern blotting*. As a result of the greater efficiency of PCR-based methods, VNTR typing by RFLP analysis is fading from use.

Table A–1
Genetic Markers Used in Forensic Identification

Nature of variation at locus		
Locus example	Method of detection	Number of alleles
Variable number tandem repeat (VNTR) loci contain repeated core sequence elements, typically 15–35 base pairs (bp) in length. Alleles differ in the number of repeats and are distinguished on the basis of size.		
D2S44 (core repeat 31 bp)	Intact DNA digested with restriction enzyme, producing fragments that are separated by gel electrophoresis; alleles detected by Southern blotting followed by probing with locus-specific radioactive or chemiluminescent probe	At least 75 (size range is 700–8500 bp); allele size distribution is essentially continuous
D1S80 (core repeat 16 bp)	Amplification of allelic sequences by PCR; discrete allelic products separated by electrophoresis and visualized directly	About 30 (size range is 350–1000 bp); alleles can be discretely distinguished
Short tandem repeat (STR) loci are VNTR loci with repeated core sequence elements 2–6 bp in length. Alleles differ in the number of repeats and are distinguished on the basis of size.		
HUMTHO1 (tetranucleotide repeat)	Amplification of allelic sequences by PCR; discrete allelic products separated by electrophoresis on sequencing gels and visualized directly, by capillary electrophoresis, or by other methods	8 (size range 179– 203 bp); alleles can be discretely distinguished
Simple sequence variation (nucleotide substitution in a defined segment of a sequence)		
DQA (an expressed gene in the histocompatibility complex)	Amplification of allelic sequences by PCR; discrete alleles detected by sequence specific probes	8 (6 used in DQA kit)
Polymarker (a set of five loci)	Amplification of allelic sequences by PCR; discrete alleles detected by sequence-specific probes	Loci are bi-or tri-allelic; 972 geno-typic combinations
Mitochondrial DNA control region (D-loop)	Amplification of control-sequence and sequence determination	Hundreds of sequence variants are known

4. Steps of PCR Amplification

The second National Research Council report provides a concise description of how PCR "amplifies" DNA:

> First, each double-stranded segment is separated into two strands by heating. Second, these single-stranded segments are hybridized with primers, short DNA segments (20–30 nucleotides in length) that complement and define the target sequence to be amplified. Third, in the presence of the enzyme DNA polymerase, and the four nucleotide building blocks (A, C, G, and T), each primer serves as the starting point for the replication of the target sequence. A copy of the complement of each of the separated strands is made, so that there are two double-stranded DNA segments. The three-step cycle is repeated, usually 20–35 times. The two strands produce four copies; the four, eight copies; and so on until the number of copies of the original DNA is enormous. The main difference between this procedure and the normal cellular process is that the PCR process is limited to the amplification of a small DNA region. This region is usually not more than 1,000 nucleotides in length, so PCR methods cannot, at least at present, be used [to amplify] large DNA regions, such as most VNTRs.[4]

Figure A–3 illustrates the steps in the PCR process for two cycles.[5]

4. NRC II, *supra* note 3, at 69–70.

5. The figure is adapted from figure 1–6 in COMMITTEE ON DNA TECHNOLOGY IN FORENSIC SCIENCE, NATIONAL RESEARCH COUNCIL, DNA TECHNOLOGY IN FORENSIC SCIENCE 41 (1992) [hereinafter NRC I].

Figure A–3

The PCR Process

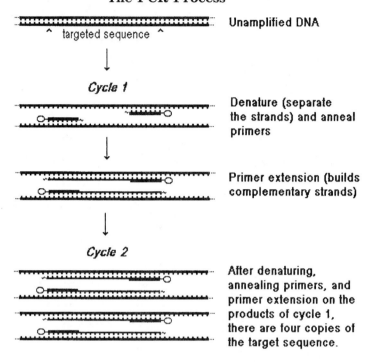

In principle, PCR amplification doubles the number of double-stranded DNA fragments each cycle. Although there is some inefficiency in practice, the yield from a 30–cycle amplification is generally about one million to ten million copies of the targeted sequence.

5. Quantities of DNA in Forensic Samples

Amounts of DNA present in some typical kinds of evidence samples are indicated in Table A–2. These are approximate, and the quantities of DNA extracted from evidence in particular cases may vary somewhat.[6]

---

6. The amounts in the table are given in nanograms (ng) or ng per milliliter (ng/mL). A nanogram is one billionth (1/1,000,000,000) of a gram.

Table A–2
DNA Content of Biological Samples[7]

Type of Sample		DNA Content	Success Rate
Blood		20,000–40,000 ng/mL	
	stain 1 cm x 1 cm	ca. 200 ng	>95%
	stain 1 mm x 1 mm	ca. 2 ng	
Semen		150,000–300,000 ng/mL	
	on post-coital vaginal swab	0–3000 ng	>95%
Saliva		1000–10,000 ng/mL	
	on a cigarette butt	0–25ng	50–70%
Hair			
	root end of pulled hair	1–750 ng	>90%
	root end of shed hair	1–12 ng	<20%
	hair shaft	0.001–0.040 ng/cm	
Urine		1–20 ng/mL	
Skin cells			
	from socks, gloves, or clothing repeatedly used		30–60%
	from handled objects (e.g., a doorknob)		<20%

ng = nanogram, or 1/1,000,000,000th of a gram; mL = milliliter; cm = centimeter; mm = millimeter

7. Adapted from NRC I, *supra* note 5, at 28 (with additions).

Glossary

Adenine (A). One of the four bases, or nucleotides, that make up the DNA molecule. Adenine only binds to thymine. See Nucleotide.

Affinal Method. A method for computing the single locus profile probabilities for a theoretical subpopulation by adjusting the single locus profile probability, calculated with the product rule from the mixed population database, by the amount of heterogeneity across subpopulations. The model is appropriate even if there is no database available for a particular subpopulation, and the formula always gives more conservative probabilities than the product rule applied to the same database.

Allele. In classical genetics, an allele is one of several alternative forms of a gene. A biallelic gene has two variants; others have more. Alleles are inherited separately from each parent, and for a given gene, an individual may have two different alleles (heterozygosity) or the same allele (homozygosity). In DNA analysis, the term is applied to any DNA region (whether or not it constitutes a gene) used for analysis.

Alu Sequences. A family of short interspersed elements (SINEs) distributed throughout the genomes of primates.

Amplification. Increasing the number of copies of a DNA region, usually by PCR.

Amplified Fragment Length Polymorphism (AMP–FLP). A DNA identification technique that uses PCR-amplified DNA fragments of varying lengths. The DS180 locus is a VNTR whose alleles can be detected with this technique.

Antibody. A protein (immunoglobulin) molecule, produced by the immune system, that recognizes a particular foreign antigen and binds to it; if the antigen is on the surface of a cell, this binding leads to cell aggregation and subsequent destruction.

Antigen. A molecule (typically found in the surface of a cell) whose shape triggers the production of antibodies that will bind to the antigen.

Autoradiograph (Autoradiogram, Autorad). In RFLP analysis, the x-ray film (or print) showing the positions of radioactively marked fragments (bands) of DNA, indicating how far these fragments have migrated, and hence their molecular weights.

Autosome. A chromosome other than the X and Y sex chromosomes.

Band. See Autoradiograph.

Band Shift. Movement of DNA fragments in one lane of a gel at a different rate than fragments of an identical length in another lane, resulting in the same pattern "shifted" up or down relative to the comparison lane. Band-shift does not necessarily occur at the same rate in all portions of the gel.

Base Pair (bp). Two complementary nucleotides bonded together at the matching bases (A and T or C and G) along the double helix "backbone" of the DNA molecule. The length of a DNA fragment often is measured in numbers of base pairs (1 kilobase (kb) = 1000 bp); base pair numbers also are used to describe the location of an allele on the DNA strand.

Bayes' Theorem. An elementary formula that relates certain conditional probabilities. It can be used to describe the impact of new data on the probability that a hypothesis is true.

Bin, Fixed. In VNTR profiling, a bin is a range of base pairs (DNA fragment lengths). When a database is divided into fixed bins, the proportion of bands within each bin is determined and the relevant proportions are used in estimating the profile frequency.

Bins, Floating. In VNTR profiling, a bin is a range of base pairs (DNA fragment lengths). In a floating bin method of estimating a profile frequency, the bin is centered on the base pair length of the allele in question, and the width of the bin can be defined by the laboratory's matching rule (e.g., ± 5% of band size).

Binning. Grouping VNTR alleles into sets of similar sizes because the alleles' lengths are too similar to differentiate.

Blind Proficiency Test. See Proficiency Test.

Capillary Electrophoresis. A method for separating DNA fragments (including STRs) according to their length. A long, narrow tube is filled with an entangled polymer or comparable sieving medium, and an electric field is applied to pull DNA fragments placed at one end of the tube through the medium. The procedure is faster and uses smaller samples than gel electrophoresis, and it can be automated.

Ceiling Principle. A procedure for setting a minimum DNA profile frequency proposed in 1992 by a committee of the National Academy of Science. One hundred persons from each of 15–20 genetically homogeneous populations spanning the range of racial groups in the United States are sampled. For each allele, the higher frequency among the groups sampled (or 5%, whichever is larger) is used in calculating the profile frequency. Cf. Interim Ceiling Principle.

Chip. A miniaturized system for genetic analysis. One such chip mimics capillary electrophoresis and related manipulations. DNA fragments, pulled by small voltages, move through tiny channels etched into a small block of glass, silicon, quartz, or plastic. This system should be useful in analyzing STRs. Another technique mimics reverse dot blots by placing a large array of oligonucleotide probes on a solid surface. Such hybridization arrays should be useful in identifying SNPs and in sequencing mitochondrial DNA.

Chromosome. A rod-like structure composed of DNA, RNA, and proteins. Most normal human cells contain 46 chromosomes, 22 autosomes and a sex chromosome (X) inherited from the mother, and another 22 autosomes and one sex chromosome (either X or Y) inherited from the father. The genes are located along the chromosomes. See also Homologous Chromosomes.

Coding DNA. A small fraction of the human genome contains the "instructions" for assembling physiologically important proteins. The remainder of the DNA is "non-coding."

CODIS (Combined DNA Index System). A collection of databases on STR and other loci of convicted felons maintained by the FBI.

Complementary Sequence. The sequence of nucleotides on one strand of DNA that corresponds to the sequence on the other strand. For example, if one sequence is CTGAA, the complementary bases are GACTT.

Cytosine (C). One of the four bases, or nucleotides, that make up the DNA double helix. Cytosine only binds to guanine. See Nucleotide.

Database. A collection of DNA profiles.

Degradation. The breaking down of DNA by chemical or physical means.

Denature, Denaturation. The process of splitting, as by heating, two complementary strands of the DNA double helix into single strands in preparation for hybridization with biological probes.

Deoxyribonucleic Acid (DNA). The molecule that contains genetic information. DNA is composed of nucleotide building blocks, each containing a base (A, C, G, or T), a phosphate, and a sugar. These nucleotides are linked together in a double helix—two strands of DNA molecules paired up at complementary bases (A with T, C with G). See Adenine, Cytosine, Guanine, Thymine.

Diploid Number. See Haploid Number.

D-loop. A portion of the mitochrondrial genome known as the "control region" or "displacement loop" instrumental in the regulation and initiation of mtDNA gene products.

DNA Polymerase. The enzyme that catalyzes the synthesis of double-stranded DNA.

DNA Probe. See Probe.

DNA Profile. The alleles at each locus. For example, a VNTR profile is the pattern of band lengths on an autorad. A multilocus profile represents the combined results of multiple probes. See Genotype.

DNA Sequence. The ordered list of base pairs in a duplex DNA molecule or of bases in a single strand.

DQA. The gene that codes for a particular class of Human Leukocyte Antigen (HLA). This gene has been sequenced completely and can be used for forensic typing. See Human Leukocyte Antigen.

DQα. The antigen that is the product of the DQA gene. See DQA, Human Leukocyte Antigen.

EDTA. A preservative added to blood samples.

Electrophoresis. See Capillary Electrophoresis, Gel Electrophoresis.

Endonuclease. An enzyme that cleaves the phosphodiester bond within a nucleotide chain.

Environmental Insult. Exposure of DNA to external agents such as heat, moisture, and ultraviolet radiation, or chemical or bacterial agents. Such exposure can interfere with the enzymes used in the testing process, or otherwise make DNA difficult to analyze.

Enzyme. A protein that catalyzes (speeds up or slows down) a reaction.

Ethidium Bromide. A molecule that can intercalate into DNA double helices when the helix is under torsional stress. Used to identify the presence of DNA in a sample by its fluorescence under ultraviolet light.

Fallacy of the Transposed Conditional. See Transposition Fallacy.

False Match. Two samples of DNA that have different profiles could be declared to match if, instead of measuring the distinct DNA in each sample, there is an error in handling or preparing samples such that the DNA from a single sample is analyzed twice. The resulting match, which does not reflect the true profiles of the DNA from each sample, is a false match. Some people use "false match" more broadly, to include cases in which the true profiles of each sample are the same, but the samples come from different individuals. Compare True Match. See also Match, Random Match.

Gel, Agarose. A semisolid medium used to separate molecules by electrophoresis.

Gel Electrophoresis. In RFLP analysis, the process of sorting DNA fragments by size by applying an electric current to a gel. The different-sized fragments move at different rates through the gel.

Gene. A set of nucleotide base pairs on a chromosome that contains the "instructions" for controlling some cellular function such as making an enzyme. The gene is the fundamental unit of heredity; each simple gene "codes" for a specific biological characteristic.

Gene Frequency. The relative frequency (proportion) of an allele in a population.

Genetic Drift. Random fluctuation allele frequencies from generation to generation.

Genetics. The study of the patterns, processes, and mechanisms of inheritance of biological characteristics.

Genome. The complete genetic makeup of an organism, comprising 40,000–100,000 genes in humans.

Genotype. The particular forms (alleles) of a set of genes possessed by an organism (as distinguished from phenotype, which refers to how the genotype expresses itself, as in physical appearance). In DNA analysis, the term is applied to the variations within all DNA regions (whether or not they constitute genes) that are analyzed.

Genotype, Single Locus. The alleles that an organism possesses at a particular site in its genome.

Genotype, Multilocus. The alleles that an organism possesses at several sites in its genome.

Guanine (G). One of the four bases, or nucleotides, that make up the DNA double helix. Guanine only binds to cytosine. See Nucleotide.

Hae III. A particular restriction enzyme.

Haploid Number. Human sex cells (egg and sperm) contain 23 chromosomes each. This is the haploid number. When a sperm cell fertilizes an egg cell, the number of chromosomes doubles to 46. This is the diploid number.

Haplotype. A specific combination of linked alleles at several loci.

Hardy–Weinberg Equilibrium. A condition in which the allele frequencies within a large, random, intrabreeding population are unrelated to patterns of mating. In this condition, the occurrence of alleles from each parent will be independent and have a joint frequency estimated by the product rule. See Independence, Linkage disequilibrium.

Heteroplasty. The condition in which some copies of mitochondrial DNA in the same individual have different base pairs at certain points.

Heterozygous. Having a different allele at a given locus on each of a pair of homologous chromosomes. See Allele. Compare Homozygous.

Homologous Chromosomes. The 44 autosomes (non-sex chromosomes) in the normal human genome are in homologous pairs (one from each parent) that share an identical set of genes, but may have different alleles at the same loci.

Human Leukocyte Antigen (HLA). Antigen (foreign body that stimulates an immune system response) located on the surface of most cells (excluding red blood cells and sperm cells). HLAs differ among individuals and are associated closely with transplant rejection. See DQA.

Homozygous. Having the same allele at a given locus on each of a pair of homologous chromosomes. See Allele. Compare Heterozygous.

Hybridization. Pairing up of complementary strands of DNA from different sources at the matching base pair sites. For example, a primer with the sequence AGGTCT would bond with the complementary sequence TCCAGA on a DNA fragment.

Independence. Two events are said to be independent if one is neither more nor less likely to occur when the other does.

Interim Ceiling Principle. A procedure proposed in 1992 by a committee of the National Academy of Sciences for setting a minimum DNA profile frequency. For each allele, the highest frequency (adjusted upward for sampling error) found in any major racial group (or 10%, whichever is higher), is used in product-rule calculations. Cf. Ceiling Principle.

Kilobase (kb). One thousand bases.

Linkage. The inheritance together of two or more genes on the same chromosome.

Linkage Equilibrium. A condition in which the occurrence of alleles at different loci are independent.

Locus. A location in the genome, i.e., a position on a chromosome where a gene or other structure begins.

Mass Spectroscopy. The separation of elements or molecules according to their molecular weight. In the version being developed for DNA analysis, small quantities of PCR-amplified fragments are irradiated with a laser to form gaseous ions that traverse a fixed distance. Heavier ions have longer times of flight, and the process is known as "matrix-assisted laser desorption-ionization time-of-flight mass spectroscopy." MALDI–TOF–MS, as it is abbreviated, may be useful in analyzing STRs.

Match. The presence of the same allele or alleles in two samples. Two DNA profiles are declared to match when they are indistinguishable in genetic type. For loci with discrete alleles, two samples match when they display the same set of alleles. For RFLP testing of VNTRs, two samples match when the pattern of the bands is similar and the positions of the corresponding bands at each locus fall within a preset distance. See Match Window, False Match, True Match.

Match Window. If two RFLP bands lie with a preset distance, called the match window, that reflects normal measurement error, they can be declared to match.

Microsatellite. Another term for an STR.

Minisatellite. Another term for a VNTR.

Mitochondria. A structure (organelle) within nucleated (eukaryotic) cells that is the site of the energy producing reactions within the cell. Mitochondria contain their own DNA (often abbreviated as mtDNA), which is inherited only from mother to child.

Molecular Weight. The weight in grams of one mole of a pure, molecular substance.

Monomorphic. A gene or DNA characteristic that is almost always found in only one form in a population.

Multilocus Probe. A probe that marks multiple sites (loci). RFLP analysis using a multilocus probe will yield an autorad showing a striped pattern of thirty or more bands. Such probes rarely are used now in forensic applications in the United States.

Multilocus Profile. See Profile.

Multiplexing. Typing several loci simultaneously.

Mutation. The process that produces a gene or chromosome set differing from the type already in the population; the gene or chromosome set that results from such a process.

Nanogram (ng). A billionth of a gram.

Nucleic Acid. RNA or DNA.

Nucleotide. A unit of DNA consisting of a base (A, C, G, or T) and attached to a phosphate and a sugar group; the basic building block of nucleic acids. See Deoxyribonucleic Acid.

Nucleus. The membrane-covered portion of a eukaryotic cell containing most of the DNA and found within the cytoplasm.

Oligonucleotide. A synthetic polymer made up of fewer than 100 nucleotides; used as a primer or a probe in PCR. See Primer.

Paternity Index. A number (technically, a likelihood ratio) that indicates the support that the paternity test results lend to the hypothesis that the alleged father is the biological father as opposed to the hypothesis that another man selected at random is the biological father. Assuming that the observed phenotypes correctly represent the phenotypes of the mother, child, and alleged father tested, the number can be computed as the ratio of the probability of the phenotypes under the first hypothesis to the probability under the second hypothesis. Large values indicate substantial support for the hypothesis of paternity; values near zero indicate substantial support for the hypothesis that someone other than the alleged father is the biological father; and values near unity indicate that the results do not help in determining which hypothesis is correct.

pH. A measure of the acidity of a solution.

Phenotype. A trait, such as eye color or blood group, resulting from a genotype.

Polymarker. A commercially marketed set of PCR-based tests for protein polymorphisms.

Polymerase Chain Reaction (PCR). A process that mimics DNA's own replication processes to make up to millions of copies of short strands of genetic material in a few hours.

Polymorphism. The presence of several forms of a gene or DNA characteristic in a population.

Point Mutation. See SNP.

Population Genetics. The study of the genetic composition of groups of individuals.

Population Structure. When a population is divided into subgroups that do not mix freely, that population is said to have structure. Significant structure can lead to allele frequencies being different in the subpopulations.

Primer. An oligonucleotide that attaches to one end of a DNA fragment and provides a point for more complementary nucleotides to attach and replicate the DNA strand. See Oligonucleotide.

Probe. In forensics, a short segment of DNA used to detect certain alleles. The probe hybridizes, or matches up, to a specific complementary sequence. Probes allow visualization of the hybridized DNA, either by radioactive tag (usually used for RFLP analysis) or biochemical tag (usually used for PCR-based analyses).

Product Rule. When alleles occur independently at each locus (Hardy–Weinberg equilibrium) and across loci (linkage equilibrium), the proportion of the population with a given genotype is the product of the proportion of each allele at each locus, time factors of two for heterozygous loci.

Proficiency Test. A test administered at a laboratory to evaluate its performance. In a blind proficiency study, the laboratory personnel do not know that they are being tested.

Prosecutor's Fallacy. See Transposition Fallacy.

Protein. A class of biologically important compounds made up of smaller units (amino acids). The order of the certain base pairs in DNA determines which amino acids, and hence, which proteins are made within a cell.

Quality Assurance. A program conducted by a laboratory to ensure accuracy and reliability.

Quality Audit. A systematic and independent examination and evaluation of a laboratory's operations.

Quality Control. Activities used to monitor the ability of DNA typing to meet specified criteria.

Random Match. A match in the DNA profiles of two samples of DNA, where one is drawn at random from the population. See also Random Match Probability.

Random Match Probability. The chance of a random match. As it is usually used in court, the random match probability refers to the probability of a true match when the DNA being compared to the evidence DNA comes from a person drawn at random from the population. This random true match probability reveals the probability of a true match when the samples of DNA come from different, unrelated people.

Random Mating. The members of a population are said to mate randomly with respect to particular genes of DNA characteristics when the choice of mates is independent of the alleles.

Recombination. In general, any process in a diploid or partially diploid cell that generates new gene or chromosomal combinations not found in that cell or in its progenitors.

Reference Population. The population to which the perpetrator of a crime is thought to belong.

Replication. The synthesis of new DNA from existing DNA. See Polymerase Chain Reaction.

Restriction Enzyme. Protein that cuts double-stranded DNA at specific base pair sequences (different enzymes recognize different sequences). See Restriction Site.

Restriction Fragment Length Polymorphism (RFLP). Variation among people in the length of a segment of DNA cut at two restriction sites.

Restriction Fragment Length Polymorphism (RFLP) Analysis. Analysis of individual variations in the lengths of DNA fragments produced by digesting sample DNA with a restriction enzyme.

Restriction Site. A sequence marking the location at which a restriction enzyme cuts DNA into fragments. See Restriction Enzyme.

Reverse Dot Blot. A detection method used to identify SNPs in which DNA probes are affixed to a membrane, and amplified DNA is passed over the probes to see if it contains the complementary sequence.

Sequence–Specific Oligonucleotide (SSO) Probe. Also, Allele–Specific Oligonucleotide (ASO) Probe. Oligonucleotide probes used in a PCR-associated detection technique to identify the presence or absence of certain base pair sequences identifying different alleles. The probes are visualized by an array of dots rather than by the electrophoretograms associated with RFLP analysis.

Sequencing. Determining the order of base pairs in a segment of DNA.

Short Tandem Repeat (STR). See Variable Number Tandem Repeat.

Single–Locus Probe. A probe that only marks a specific site (locus). RFLP analysis using a single-locus probe will yield an autorad showing one band if the individual is homozygous, two bands if heterozygous.

SNP (Single Nucleotide Polymorphism). A substitution, insertion, or deletion of a single base pair at a given point in the genome.

Southern Blotting. Named for its inventor, a technique by which processed DNA fragments, separated by gel electrophoresis, are transferred onto a nylon membrane in preparation for the application of biological probes.

Thymine (T). One of the four bases, or nucleotides, that make up the DNA double helix. Thymine only binds to adenine. See Nucleotide.

Transposition Fallacy. Confusing the conditional probability of A given B [P(A|B)] with that of B given A [P(B|A)]. Few people think that the probability that a person speaks Spanish (A) given that he or she is a citizen of Chile (B) equals the probability that a person is a citizen of Chile (B) given that he or she speaks Spanish (A). Yet, many court opinions, newspaper articles, and even some expert witnesses speak of the probability of a matching DNA genotype (A) given that someone other than the defendant is the source of the crime scene DNA (B) as if it were the probability of someone else being the source (B) given the matching profile (A). Transposing conditional probabilities correctly requires Bayes' Theorem.

True Match. Two samples of DNA that have the same profile should match when tested. If there is no error in the labeling, handling, and analysis of the samples and in the reporting of the results, a match is a true match. A true match establishes that the two samples of DNA have the same profile. Unless the profile is unique, however, a true match does not conclusively prove that the two samples came from the same source. Some people use "true match" more narrowly, to mean only those matches among samples from the same source. Compare False Match. See also Match, Random Match.

Variable Number Tandem Repeat (VNTR). A class of RFLPs due to multiple copies of virtually identical base pair sequences, arranged in succession at a specific locus on a chromosome. The number of repeats varies from individual to individual, thus providing a basis for individual recognition. VNTRs are longer than STRs.

Window. See Match Window.

X Chromosome. See Chromosome.

Y Chromosome. See Chromosome.

References on DNA

John M. Butler, Forensic DNA Typing: Biology and Technology Behind STR Markers (2001).

Ian W. Evett & Bruce S. Weir, Interpreting DNA Evidence: Statistical Genetics for Forensic Scientists (1998).

Elaine Johnson Mange & Arthur P. Mange, Basic Human Genetics (2d ed. 1999).

National Research Council Committee on DNA Forensic Science: An Update, The Evaluation of Forensic DNA Evidence (1996).

National Research Council Committee on DNA Technology in Forensic Science, DNA Technology in Forensic Science (1992).

CHAPTER 12

PARENTAGE TESTING

Table of Sections

A. LEGAL ISSUES

B. SCIENTIFIC STATUS

Westlaw Electronic Research

See Westlaw Electronic Research Guide preceding the Summary of Contents.

A. LEGAL ISSUES

§ 12–1.0   THE LEGAL RELEVANCE OF PARENTAGE TESTING

§ 12–1.1   Introduction

Parentage testing is a part of popular culture. Exhumation for paternity testing of the remains of French actor Yves Montand provoked national indignation.[1] Star players throughout the National Basketball Association are

§ 12–1.0

1. Craig R. Whitney, *Yves Montand's Body Exhumed In Paternity Case*, N.Y. TIMES, Mar. 12, 1998.

being forced to give blood samples—and, in many cases, to pay substantial child support—as a result of private suits.[2] Taxicabs in New York City and billboards in Chicago, Los Angeles, Atlanta and other large cities advertise toll-free numbers of laboratories that offer mail-order tests to concerned men, women, and children.[3]

Such developments reflect the importance of genetic testing in ascertaining parentage. Cases of disputed paternity are notoriously difficult to decide on the basis of traditional legal evidence. A paternity suit is often a battle of conflicting stories told by persons now hostile to one another. The relevant acts are carried on in private, and the possibility of perjury is all too real.[4] Valid scientific testing for paternity provides a welcome degree of objectivity and accuracy in parentage determinations[5]—not only in civil suits to establish parental rights and responsibilities,[6] but also in matters of citizenship,[7] crime,[8] slander,[9] estates,[10] and insurance.[11]

2. Grant Wahl & L. Jon Wertheim, *Paternity Ward*, Sports Illustrated, May 4, 1998, at 62.

3. Pam Belluck, *Everybody's Doing It: Paternity Testing for Fun and Profit*, N.Y. Times, Aug. 3, 1997.

4. As Justice Brennan wrote more than 50 years ago, "in the field of contested paternity . . . the truth is so often obscured because social pressures create a conspiracy of silence or, worse, induce deliberate falsity." Cortese v. Cortese, 10 N.J.Super. 152, 76 A.2d 717, 719 (N.J.Super.Ct.1950); *see also* Ira M. Ellman & D.H. Kaye, *Probabilities and Proof: Can HLA and Blood Group Testing Prove Paternity?*, 54 N.Y.U. L. Rev. 1131, 1134 (1979).

5. *See, e.g.,* Department of Social Serv. v. Thomas, 660 So.2d 163, 165 (La.Ct.App.1995) ("scientific testing provides persuasive and objective evidence").

6. *See, e.g.,* Clark v. Jeter, 486 U.S. 456, 465, 108 S.Ct. 1910, 100 L.Ed.2d 465 (1988) (equal protection challenge to statute of limitation in an action to secure child support for illegitimate child); Rivera v. Minnich, 483 U.S. 574, 107 S.Ct. 3001, 97 L.Ed.2d 473 (1987) (preponderance of evidence standard is constitutionally permissible in establishing paternity); Mills v. Habluetzel, 456 U.S. 91, 102 S.Ct. 1549, 71 L.Ed.2d 770 (1982) (one-year statute of limitation on paternity suits to identify the natural father of an illegitimate child denies equal protection to illegitimate children); Little v. Streater, 452 U.S. 1, 101 S.Ct. 2202, 68 L.Ed.2d 627 (1981) (due process entitles indigent defendant in action to obtain child support for illegitimate child to blood grouping tests at public expense). *But cf.* Michael H. v. Gerald D., 491 U.S. 110, 109 S.Ct. 2333, 105 L.Ed.2d 91 (1989) (conclusive presumption of husband's paternity for child born in wedlock is constitutional).

7. *See, e.g.,* Alec J. Jeffreys & John F.Y. Brookfield, *Positive Identification of an Immi-*

gration Test–Case Using Human DNA Fingerprints, 317 Nature 818 (1985); A.R. Davis, Note, *Are You My Mother? The Scientific and Legal Validity of Conventional Blood Testing and DNA Fingerprinting to Establish Proof of Parentage in Immigration Cases,* 1994 B.Y.U. L. Rev. 129 (1994).

8. See cases cited *infra* § 12–6.

9. King v. Tanner, 142 Misc.2d 1004, 539 N.Y.S.2d 617 (Sup. Ct., Westchester Co., 1989) (affidavit concerning DNA justifies summary judgment in slander action); *cf.* A.T. v. M.K., 145 Misc.2d 525, 547 N.Y.S.2d 510 (Fam. Ct., Westchester County, 1989) (no collateral estoppel in paternity suit as a result of summary judgment in action for slander over the attribution of paternity).

10. Lach v. Welch, 1994 WL 271518 (Conn.Super.Ct.1994) (the problems of proof that led courts to hold that paternity actions did not survive the death of the putative father have been alleviated by HLA and especially DNA testing of the child and the deceased relatives, so an action against the estate may be brought to permit an illegitimate child to share in the estate); Sardy v. Hodge, 264 Ga. 548, 448 S.E.2d 355 (Ga.1994) (statute creating a rebuttable presumption of paternity for a 97% "probability of paternity" and allowing illegitimate child to inherit even though not declared to be a child during the father's lifetime would not be applied retroactively to allow exhumation of father for DNA testing); In re Estate of Janis, 157 Misc.2d 999, 600 N.Y.S.2d 416 (Surr.Ct., N.Y. County, 1993) (denying non-marital child's order for exhumation to allow DNA testing to establish right to inherit), *aff'd*, 210 A.D.2d 101, 620 N.Y.S.2d 342 (App.Div.1994); Batcheldor v. Boyd, 108 N.C.App. 275, 423 S.E.2d 810 (N.C.Ct.App. 1992) (proper to order exhumation to perform DNA test for paternity on behalf of alleged heir); Alexander v. Alexander, 42 Ohio Misc.2d 30, 537 N.E.2d 1310 (Ohio Co. Probate

For the better part of this century, such testing has been available. By examining red blood cell antigens and enzymes, HLA types, serum proteins, chromosomes, and most recently, fragments of DNA itself, skilled workers can subject allegations of paternity to rigorous testing. Part B, on the scientific status of parentage testing, describes such procedures. This Part describes and comments on some of the legal issues that have arisen when parties offer the tests in evidence in civil and criminal cases.

§ 12–1.2 The Movement Toward Admissibility

Historically, the legal response to scientific parentage testing has been timid and clumsy.[12] Although the first red blood cell groups, comprising the ABO system, were discovered in 1901, decades passed before blood test evidence was admitted in court.[13] At first, even blood tests excluding the defendant as a possible father were deemed inadmissible, but by the late 1940s, the common law generally accepted the use of ABO typing to exclude a man as the biological father.[14] Even so, it firmly rejected the use of this genetic system to establish paternity.[15] The simple ABO tests could exclude, on average, only about 13.4% of the population. A test that usually placed the defendant within the majority of the male population who might have fathered the child was relevant, but not especially probative.[16] Given the risk that the jury would overvalue the scientific evidence, the lopsided common law rule was understandable.[17]

As the number and power of genetic tests that could be applied to determine parentage grew, the traditional rule began to crumble under the

Ct.1988) (permitting disinterment for "a DNA test" by an illegitimate child claiming an inheritance), *aff'd*, 54 Ohio App.3d 77, 560 N.E.2d 1337 (Ohio Ct.App.1989).

11. Tipps v. Metropolitan Life Ins. Co., 768 F.Supp. 577 (S.D.Tex.1991) (Cellmark's multilocus VNTR probes showed that claimant of insurance policy was not the daughter of the deceased and therefore not entitled to any payments under the policy); Killingsworth v. City of Wichita, 16 Kan.App.2d 801, 830 P.2d 70 (Kan.Ct.App.1992) ("wholly dependent child" entitled to death benefits under workers' compensation statute included a natural child who had filed paternity action before the death and whose paternity was proved by "DNA test results"); *cf.* Ellington v. Shalala, 1995 WL 103756 (N.D.Ill.1995) (application for surviving child benefits denied pursuant to the Social Security Act despite 1983 immunogenetic tests indicative of paternity).

12. *See* 1 McCoRMICK ON EVIDENCE § 205 (5th ed., John W. Strong ed., 1999).

13. In parentage proceedings, courts initially questioned the general acceptance of serological methods, *See, e.g.*, Huntingdon v. Crowley, 64 Cal.2d 647, 51 Cal.Rptr. 254, 414 P.2d 382 (Cal.1966) (lack of general acceptance justified exclusion); State v. Damm, 62 S.D. 123, 252 N.W. 7, 12 (S.D.1933) (same).

14. However, even unchallenged exclusions were not determinative in all jurisdictions. *See, e.g.*, Hanson v. Hanson, 311 Minn. 388, 249 N.W.2d 452, 453 (Minn.1977) (reviewing the weight accorded to exclusionary test results).

15. *See* Moore v. McNamara, 201 Conn. 16, 513 A.2d 660 (Conn.1986); Flippen v. Meinhold, 156 Misc. 451, 282 N.Y.S. 444, 446 (N.Y.City Ct.1935) (reporting that "[n]o case has been found in which blood grouping tests have been deemed admissible for the purpose of establishing paternity" and declining to order blood tests for this purpose).

16. *See* Commonwealth v. English, 123 Pa.Super. 161, 186 A. 298, 300 (Pa.Super.Ct.1936) (explaining that "in 14 3/4 per cent. of the cases examined the blood grouping test can exonerate, but in no case does it incriminate"); *Flippen*, 282 N.Y.S. at 446 ("If the test shows a negative result, it would seem to be conclusive proof of nonpaternity, but the positive would simply indicate the possibility of paternity. It would be improper to draw an inference of paternity where merely the possibility is shown; where different inferences may be drawn from a proven fact, no judicial determination may be based thereon.").

17. *See Moore*, 201 Conn. 16, 513 A.2d 660; Commonwealth v. Beausoleil, 397 Mass. 206, 490 N.E.2d 788 (Mass.1986); Ellman & Kaye, *supra* note 4, at 1136.

weight of cases[18] and specialized statutes.[19] Laboratories usually accompanied their inclusionary findings with impressive "probabilities of paternity"— statistics that went largely unchallenged. In the 1980s, some eighty years after the Nobel Prize-winning discovery of the ABO system and thirty years after another Nobel Prize-winning discovery of the HLA system, admission of expert testimony supplying a quantitative measure of the chance that the defendant is the father became routine.[20] Indeed, statutes in most jurisdictions mandate a presumption in favor of paternity when this statistic reaches specified values,[21] and appellate courts have begun to reverse trial judges for giving insufficient weight to the laboratory results.[22]

Although the admissibility of many types of genetic tests to prove as well as to disprove claims of paternity is no longer in doubt,[23] issues as to the admissibility of still newer tests and of probability calculations continue to arise.

§ 12–1.3 New Tests

As new scientific tests for parentage are implemented, courts determine their admissibility under the generally applicable standards for admitting scientific evidence or under special statutes that mandate admissibility. Opinions from various epochs can be found rejecting ABO blood grouping,[24] Kell– Cellano tests,[25] HLA tests,[26] and chromosome banding.[27] Over time, however,

18. *See* Ellman & Kaye, *supra* note 4.

19. *E.g.*, Mastromatteo v. Harkins, 419 Pa.Super. 329, 615 A.2d 390 (Pa.Super.Ct.1992) (DNA paternity test admissible under statute); *see generally* D.H. Kaye & Ronald Kanwischer, *Admissibility of Genetic Testing in Paternity Litigation: A Survey of State Statutes*, 22 FAM. L.Q. 109 (1988).

20. *E.g.*, Clark v. Jeter, 486 U.S. 456, 108 S.Ct. 1910, 100 L.Ed.2d 465 (1988) ("court ordered blood test ... showed a 99.3 percent probability that Jeter is Tiffany's father").

21. *E.g.*, Gregory F.W. v. Lori Anne B., 162 Misc.2d 411, 617 N.Y.S.2d 276 (Fam.Ct., Monroe County, 1994) (describing amendment to N.Y. Fam. Court Act § 532, which states that "[i]f the results of such blood genetic marker or DNA test or tests indicate at least ninety-five percent of paternity, [their] admission shall create a rebuttable presumption of paternity...."). Tenn. Code § 24–7–112(b)(2)(B) provides that:

> An individual is conclusively presumed to be the father of a child if blood, genetic, or DNA tests show that the statistical probability of paternity is ninety-nine percent or greater. A rebuttable presumption of the paternity of an individual is established by blood, genetic, or DNA testing showing a statistical probability of paternity of that individual at ninety-five percent (95%) or greater.

The need for such statutes is questioned, and the phrasing of several of them criticized in D.H. Kaye, *Presumptions, Probability, and Paternity*, 30 JURIMETRICS J. 323 (1990).

22. *See infra* § 12–1.4.

23. *See, e.g.*, McCORMICK, *supra* note 12.

24. State v. Damm, 62 S.D. 123, 252 N.W. 7 (S.D.1933) (medical sciences not shown to be sufficiently agreed on "the transmissibility of blood characteristics").

25. Huntingdon v. Crowley, 64 Cal.2d 647, 51 Cal.Rptr. 254, 414 P.2d 382 (Cal.1966) (Kell–Celano test not generally accepted as giving accurate results).

26. Phillips ex rel. Utah State Dep't of Social Serv. v. Jackson, 615 P.2d 1228 (Utah 1980).

27. *E.g.*, Cobey v. State, 73 Md.App. 233, 533 A.2d 944 (Md.App.1987) (error under *Frye* to admit Olson's quinacrine staining to incriminate defendant in rape resulting in aborted pregnancy). The scientific literature on chromosome banding includes G. Bujdoso, E. Somogyi & V. Bergou, *The Use of Chromosomes in Paternity Actions*, 25 FOR. SCI. INT. 35 (1984); J. Janasson et al., *HL-A Antigens and Heteromorphic Fluoescence Characters of Chromosomes in Prenatal Paternity Investigation*, 236 NATURE 313 (1972); Y. Nakagome et al., *Pitfalls in the Use of Chromosome Variants for Paternity Dispute Cases*, 37 HUM. GENETICS 255 (1977); Olson, *Human Chromosome Variation: The Discriminatory Power of Q-band Heteromorphism (Variant) Analysis in Distinguishing Between Individuals, with Specific Application to Cases of Questionable Paternity*, 38 AM. J. HUM. GENETICS 235 (1986); Hiroshi Shoino et al., *Chromosome Heteromorphisms and Paternity Testing*, 6 AM. J. FOR. MED. & PATHOLOGY 199 (1985).

some of what was new and questionable becomes old and established. Judicial notice of scientific acceptance or acceptability can follow, and there no longer is any serious dispute over the ability of most immunogenetic tests of red and white blood cells, electrophoresis of serum proteins and enzymes, and DNA typing to ascertain whether a man could be the father of a particular child.[28]

The latest and, by far, the most important addition to the armamentarium of paternity testing comes from procedures developed by molecular biologists to characterize fragments of DNA. Most litigation over the admissibility of these DNA tests has not centered on the use of these techniques in parentage testing, but rather on efforts to match traces of semen, blood or other biological material to a defendant suspected of rape, murder, or other offenses.[29] As section 12–2 observes, there are significant differences between DNA testing in such "stain work" and in parentage testing.

Most cases on paternity tests that employ DNA analysis hold the results of properly conducted tests admissible under the common law of evidence, the Uniform Rules, or specialized statutes.[30] However, some of these opinions have not recognized that the various DNA-based paternity test procedures[31] are a new development,[32] and the application of the special statutes for paternity tests to DNA analysis has been in doubt in some jurisdictions. For example, before 1994, New York apparently did not allow DNA test results to establish paternity unless they were combined with HLA testing.[33] Moreover, some of the well-publicized controversy emanating from the stain work cases has spilled over to the paternity area. Thus, the Illinois Court of Appeals held in *Franson v. Micelli*[34] that VNTR paternity tests leading to a paternity index of over 29 million were inadmissible under *Frye* because of the speculation about the importance of population structure that had been voiced in the criminal context.[35]

28. *See, e.g.,* 1 McCormick, *supra* note 12, § 205.

29. *See supra* § 11–1.

30. *See, e.g.,* District of Columbia ex rel. J.A.B. v. W.R., Jr., 60 U.S.L.W. 2175 (D.C.Super.Ct.1991) (DNA test for paternity test performed by Roche labs is not made admissible by statute passed before DNA analysis was available, but the technique is generally accepted and therefore the results are admissible); King v. Taylor, No. 02A01–9504–CV–00091, 1995 WL 607558 (Tenn.Ct.App.1995) (upholding retroactive application of Tenn. Code. Ann. § 24–7–112(b)(2)(A) (1994), which provides that "[i]n any proceeding where the paternity of an individual is at issue, the written report of blood, genetic, or DNA test results by the testing agent concerning the paternity is admissible without the need for any foundation testimony or other proof of the authenticity or accuracy of the test unless a written objection is filed. . . .").

31. For a description of the early techniques, some of which have been abandoned, see D.H. Kaye, *DNA Paternity Probabilities*, 24 Fam. L.Q. 279 (1990).

32. Department of Social Services ex rel. Wolf v. McCarty, 506 N.W.2d 144 (S.D.1993)

(unspecified DNA paternity tests properly admitted, in part because "DNA testing has previously been recognized by this Court in Matter of A.J.H., 363 N.W.2d 196 (S.D.1985) and Matter of F.J.F., 312 N.W.2d 718 (S.D.1981).").

33. *See* Gregory F.W. v. Lori Anne B., 162 Misc.2d 411, 617 N.Y.S.2d 276 (Fam.Ct., Monroe County, 1994) (describing amendments to statute to authorize admission of DNA evidence to establish paternity). The statute is N.Y. Fam. Court Act § 532 (McKinney 1995 Interim Update). Many statutes now explicitly cover "DNA tests." *E.g.,* Tenn. Code § 24–7–112(a)(1) ("Tests for determining paternity may include any blood, genetic, or DNA test utilized by an accredited laboratory."). Whether these statutes will be applied to PCR-based tests not in existence when the statutes were modified remains to be seen.

34. 269 Ill.App.3d 20, 206 Ill.Dec. 399, 645 N.E.2d 404 (Ill.Ct.App.1994), *vacated on other grounds and appeal dismissed*, 172 Ill.2d 352, 217 Ill.Dec. 250, 666 N.E.2d 1188 (1996).

35. In addition to the criminal cases concluding that the controversy over population structure demonstrates a lack of general acceptance of DNA random match probabilities un-

§ 12–1.4   Weight of the Tests

Although properly performed testing for parentage with suitable genetic tests is admissible, the weight to be accorded the results and how they should be presented to the factfinder still can be sources of contention. Generally, the courts speak effusively of the probative value of genetic testing,[36] but the traditional rule is that they must be considered along with the nongenetic evidence in the case.[37] Even so, the trend is to give greater weight to the scientific findings. Indeed, on occasion, lower courts have been reversed for giving insufficient weight to test results establishing paternity.[38] In addition, in some jurisdictions genetic testing is powerful enough to rebut the presumption that a husband is the father of a child born in wedlock. In *Minton v. Weaver*,[39] for example, the Indiana Court of Appeals treated as clearly erroneous a jury finding of nonpaternity where a DNA test of another man indicated

der *Frye*, the opinion refers to "flaws in the method of determining statistical probability calculations" identified by defendant's expert, Dr. Pravatchai Boonlayangoor. 645 N.E. 2d at 406. The supposed "flaws" are that there is "very little difference" between a paternity index of 29 million and an index of 200, that too many VNTR probes (five, instead of one, two, or three) were used, and that a data base of 5,000 (instead of "at least 100,000") was used. *Id*. In light of these "flaws" and the possibility of population structure, the expert concluded that "it is more likely than not that defendant is not the father of plaintiff's child." *Id*. These views are idiosyncratic at best.

36. *See, e.g.,* Tuan Anh Nguyen v. Immigration and Naturalization Serv., 533 U.S. 53, 121 S.Ct. 2053, 150 L.Ed.2d 115 (2001) (referring to the"virtual certainty of a biological link that modern DNA testing affords").

37. *See, e.g.,* City and County of San Francisco v. Givens, 85 Cal.App.4th 51, 101 Cal. Rptr.2d 859 (Cal.Ct.App.2000) (upholding trial court finding of nonpaternity where the paternity index was 1290 and the associated "probability of paternity" was 99.92%, but "the defendant here presented what the trial court found to be 'clear and convincing evidence' that he did not have access to the mother"); D.M.J. v. B.G.B., 576 So.2d 537, 539 (La.Ct. App.1990) (upholding trial court's failure to find paternity "in light of other evidence" than expert testimony that "there was a 99.60% probability that the defendant was the father" where a biostatistician testified that the calculation did not account for sampling error, did not have "a reliable sample for random man" and did not distinguish between "probability of paternity" and "relative chance of paternity"); Chisolm v. Eakes, 573 So.2d 764 (Miss.1990) (allowing jury verdict of nonpaternity to stand despite an HLA test showing a "probability of 99.59649% that Dale Eakes was the father," and observing that "[a]s long as defendant in a paternity action has a right to a jury trial, and absent some statutory pronouncement, paternity test results, even those showing a high probability of paternity, cannot be conclusive

as a matter of law"); Smith v. Shaffer, 511 Pa. 421, 515 A.2d 527, 529 (Pa.1986) (blood test result of 99.99% is not conclusive of paternity, and it was error to grant new trial on the strength of this evidence alone); *cf*. Zearfoss v. Frattaroli, 435 Pa.Super. 565, 646 A.2d 1238, 1243 (Pa.Super.Ct.1994) (discussing Pennsylvania cases on the effect of a high probability of paternity and holding that it was error to grant summary judgment for the mother because "the finder-of-fact (be it jury or judge) [has] it within its prerogative to hold for the putative father/defendant and against the natural mother/plaintiff in a paternity action, regardless of the introduction of one or multiple blood tests (be they of the H.L.A. or D.N.A. variety) establishing a 99.99% probability of paternity, if the other facts are supportive of such a verdict.").

38. *See, e.g.,* Department of Social Serv. v. Thomas, 660 So.2d 163, 164–65 (La.Ct.App. 1995) (trial court's failure to find paternity given the evidence on the record, which included a paternity index of 16,500, was "manifest error"); Commissioner of Social Serv. v. Hector S., 216 A.D.2d 81, 628 N.Y.S.2d 270 (App.Div. 1995) (noting "the more modern trend toward admissibility and greater weight given to these genetic marker test results, rather than considering them as just another factor equal to the cloudy testimonial recollections of the parties," the appellate division held that the trial court erred in failing to find paternity because "the 'staggering' genetic marker test results in this highly unusual case were sufficiently persuasive despite petitioner's cloudy and somewhat contradictory testimony as to her sexual activity and menstrual history."); *cf*. Department of Human Serv. v. Moore, 632 So.2d 929 (Miss. 1994) (holding that it was error for the trial judge to instruct the jury that a probability of paternity of 99.99% (and a paternity index of 22,473,773) merely demonstrated that "out of the black male population it is biologically possible for the Defendant to be the father").

39. 697 N.E.2d 1259 (Ind.Ct.App.1998).

a "99.97% probability that the man is a child's father"[40] and there was "uncontradicted evidence that the man had sexual intercourse with the mother at the time the child must have been conceived."[41] This information, the court wrote, is an "example of the type of direct, clear, and convincing evidence which can rebut the marriage presumption."[42]

Increasing reliance on genetic testing also comes from statutes that create a rebuttable presumption of paternity when the test results point to the alleged father.[43] Precisely what is required to overcome the presumption is unclear, but considerably more than the uncorroborated testimony of the alleged father may be needed.[44]

Of course, a conclusive presumption would make genetic testing determinative. Some states have adopted such laws,[45] and the Uniform Parentage Act of 2000 is structured to bring about this result.[46] In *Tennessee Department of Human Services v. Hooper*,[47] however, the Tennessee Court of Appeals held that a conclusive presumption went too far—that statute, the court reasoned, violated the due process clause by depriving putative father of a "meaningful opportunity to be heard." The court of appeals relied on cases like *Vlandis v. Kline*[48] for the view that "permanent irrebuttable presumptions have long been disfavored under the Due Process Clause." In *Vlandis*, the Supreme Court struck down a state law that irrevocably classified a person as a nonresident for the purpose of tuition at a state university if that person resided out of state before applying to the university. The majority wrote: "since Connecticut purports to be concerned with residency in allocating the rates for tuition, [it] is forbidden by [due process] to deny an individual the resident rates on a basis of a permanent presumption of non-residence, when the presumption is not necessarily or universally true.... Rather, standards of due process require that the State allow such an individual the opportunity to

---

40. *Id.* at 1260.

41. *Id.*

42. *Id. But see* N.A.H. v. S.L.S., 9 P.3d 354 (Colo.2000) ("best interest of the child" standard must be used to resolve a conflict between the statutory presumptions of paternity for the husband as opposed to the other man with a large paternity index); State v. Dorsey, 665 So.2d 95 (La.Ct.App.1995) (a paternity index of 2,075,119 to one, together with mother's testimony that she had sex one time with putative father and that he was father of her child, did not justify overturning Family Court's finding of nonpaternity).

43. *See supra* note 21. The final impetus for these statutes came from the Welfare Reform Act of 1996, 42 U.S.C. § 666(a)(5)(G), which requires these laws as a condition for federal financial assistance to states.

44. *See* City and County of San Francisco v. Givens, 85 Cal.App.4th 51, 101 Cal.Rptr.2d 859 (Cal.Ct.App.2000) (relying on " 'clear and convincing evidence' that the alleged father did not have access to the mother"); County of El Dorado v. Misura, 33 Cal.App.4th 73, 38 Cal. Rptr.2d 908 (Ct.App.1995) ("evidence of the mere existence of other, untested, men is insuf-

ficient of itself to rebut the statutory presumption of paternity based on genetic testing," so trial court erred in not finding paternity); Isabella County Dep't of Social Serv. v. Thompson, 210 Mich.App. 612, 534 N.W.2d 132 (Mich. Ct.App.1995) (applying Michigan presumption of paternity statute and finding that father failed to present "substantial evidence" to rebut bursting bubble type of presumption); Spaw v. Springer, 715 A.2d 1188 (Pa.Super.Ct.1998) (relative credibility does not amount to the clear and convincing evidence required to rebut the statutory presumption of paternity triggered by a "virtually unassailable" probability exceeding 99%).

45. *E.g.*, TENN.CODE ANN. § 24–7–112(b)(2) (Michie 1994) ("An individual is conclusively presumed to be the father of a child if blood, genetic, or DNA tests show that the statistical probability of paternity is 99% or greater.").

46. *See infra* § 12–1.6.

47. Tennessee Department of Human Serv. v. Hooper, 65 U.S.L.W. 2712, 1997 WL 83669 (Tenn.Ct.App. 1997) (unpublished).

48. 412 U.S. 441, 93 S.Ct. 2230, 37 L.Ed.2d 63 (1973).

present evidence showing that he is a bona fide resident entitled to the in-state rates."[49]

The irrebuttable presumption cases, however, have long been viewed as "puzzling and unjustifiable."[50] Never consistently applied, the doctrine received its "death blow"[51] 25 years ago, in *Weinberger v. Salfi*,[52] when the Supreme Court upheld a duration-of-relationship Social Security eligibility requirement for surviving wives and stepchildren of deceased wage earners. According to the majority opinion, "Congress [could] rationally conclude not only that generalized rules are appropriate to its purposes and concerns, but also that the difficulties of individualized determinations outweigh the marginal increments of precise effectuation of congressional concern which they might be expected to produce."[53]

§ 12–1.5   The "Probability of Paternity"

The "probability of paternity" has generated divergent opinions.[54] The problem revolves around the fact that this probability is not derived strictly from the laboratory results and studies of the frequencies of the various genetic characteristics in the population.[55] Implicitly or explicitly, it incorporates a "prior probability" traditionally assumed to have the value one-half.[56] This "prior probability" must somehow be estimated from other evidence in the case. The posterior "probability of paternity" derived by combining the genetic test results with the prior probability of one-half can be called W_{50}, to distinguish it from the probability of paternity that a juror starting from a different point might derive.[57] Whether a computation based on a prior probability of one-half is appropriate in a given case is open to debate,[58] and the relationship (or lack of it) between W_{50} and the other evidence in the case

49. *Id.* at 452.

50. Gerald Gunther & Kathleen M. Sullivan, Constitutional Law 915 (13th ed.1997) (describing the criticism).

51. *Id.*

52. 422 U.S. 749, 95 S.Ct. 2457, 45 L.Ed.2d 522 (1975).

53. Although *Hooper* ignores the Court's repudiation of the irrebuttable presumption doctrine, there is an argument that might support its application to conclusive presumptions of paternity. Perhaps the rule in *Vlandis* warranted the stricter scrutiny because it implicated the fundamental right to interstate travel, while *Salfi* involved only the disbursement of public monies. More generally, it has been suggested that the doctrine retains some vitality "in situations where intermediate or strict scrutiny [is] independently warranted either by the involvement of a sensitive classification or by the presence of an important liberty or benefit." Laurence H. Tribe, American Constitutional Law § 16–34, at 1622–23 (1988). Under this view, if the right not be falsely adjudicated a father is of sufficient constitutional importance, the doctrine could be applied to invalidate the presumption.

54. See 1 McCormick, *supra* note 12, § 211.

55. That information is captured by the paternity index. *See infra* § 12–2.

56. *See* Ellman & Kaye, *supra* note 4. When the prior probability is 50%, the prior odds are one, and the posterior probability of paternity, W, equals the paternity index, PI. For example, if W = 90% for prior odds of 50%, then the PI must the corresponding posterior odds of 9. (A probability of 90% corresponds to odds of 90 to 10, or 9.) The relationship between the probability of paternity and the paternity index is not always understood by the courts. For example, in *Drake ex rel. Atwood v. Apfel*, 2001 WL 705784 (N.D.Tex. 2001), the district court wrote that "[t]he 90% probability of Robert being Ryan's father far exceeds 100 on the paternity index accepted at the Institutional [sic] Conference on Parentage Testing at Arlie [sic] House, Virginia, in May 1982." As we have just seen, however, the PI for a 90% probability is only 9.

57. *See* D.H. Kaye, *The Probability of an Ultimate Issue: The Strange Cases of Paternity Testing*, 75 Iowa L. Rev. 75 (1989).

58. For comprehensive criticism of the undisclosed use of a prior probability of one-half, see *id.*

has confused more than one court.[59]

Some states will not allow the test results to be admitted to prove paternity unless they are accompanied by the paternity probability, but because of the difficulty of interpreting W_{50}, they require this probability to exceed some threshold such as 0.95.[60] Another state permits the probability to be introduced in all situations, but only if it is presented, not as a single number, but as a chart or table of values for a series of prior probabilities ranging from zero to one.[61] Still other states allow the admission of W_{50}, but require independent proof of intercourse.[62] Most states, however, have not focused on the precise meaning of the "probability of paternity" and the limitations of W_{50}.[63]

Nevertheless, the criticism of W_{50} may be becoming academic. The full panoply of conventional genetic tests and DNA tests can produce posterior probabilities well in excess of 0.99 for virtually *any* plausible prior probability in the ordinary case. As a result, it has been suggested that

> [W]e are approaching the point where explicit statistical analysis can be relegated to the background. Today, exclusions rarely are interpreted in terms of a paternity index or a probability of paternity, presumably because these numbers are so close to zero as to give no more guidance to a judge or jury than a simple statement that if the test results are correct, then it is practically impossible for the tested man to be the father. Likewise, an inclusion for which the paternity index is clearly astronomical perhaps may be more profitably described as demonstrating that it is practically impossible for the putative father to be anything but the biological father.[64]

59. *E.g.,* Cole v. Cole, 74 N.C.App. 247, 328 S.E.2d 446 (N.C.Ct.App.) (reconciling a W_{50} of 95.98% with testimony that due to a vasectomy, the defendant was sterile and "the likelihood of his becoming fertile after the vasectomy was 'one in a million'"), *aff'd,* 314 N.C. 660, 335 S.E.2d 897 (N.C.1985).

60. Commonwealth v. Beausoleil, 397 Mass. 206, 490 N.E.2d 788 (Mass.1986) (probability of paternity must be at least 95%); Kofford v. Flora, 744 P.2d 1343 (Utah 1987) (same). This rule is criticized in Kaye, *supra* note 57.

61. Plemel v. Walter, 303 Or. 262, 735 P.2d 1209 (Or.1987), discussed in D.H. Kaye, Plemel *as a Primer on Proving Paternity,* 24 WILLAMETTE L.J. 867 (1988). Of course, experts may chose to present the values of W that correspond to various prior probabilities in jurisdictions that accept less complete presentations. *See, e.g.,* State v. Jackson, 320 N.C. 452, 358 S.E.2d 679 (1987) (geneticist testified to W of 93.4% for "weak" outside evidence 99.31% "at the median level," and 99.96% "at the high range," and stated on cross-examination that "weak" meant a prior probability of 0.1).

62. In re M.J.B., 144 Wis.2d 638, 425 N.W.2d 404 (Wis.1988); *Beausoleil,* 490 N.E.2d 788 (1986); *Kofford,* 744 P.2d 1343 (1987). For criticism of this requirement, see *infra* § 12–1.4.

63. *See, e.g.,* Brown v. Smith, 137 N.C.App. 160, 526 S.E.2d 686 (N.C.Ct.App.2000). *State v. Spann,* 130 N.J. 484, 617 A.2d 247 (N.J.1993), is an exception to this generalization. In that case, described more fully in § 12–1.7, the New Jersey Supreme Court discussed the "probability of paternity" at some length. It stated in dictum that the ad hoc restrictions adopted in cases such as *Commonwealth v. Beausoleil,* 397 Mass. 206, 490 N.E.2d 788 (1986), are "questionable" and that "[b]ased on our understanding of the issue, we would reject those limitations." 617 A.2d at 254. In their place, the court favored presenting the probability of paternity "for a varying range of such prior probabilities, running, for example, from .1 to .9." 617 A.2d at 254.

64. Kaye, *supra* note 31, at 303–04; *see also* State v. Spann, 130 N.J. 484, 617 A.2d 247 (1993):

> As a practical matter, the complex issues raised by admitting evidence of HLA test results in paternity and criminal cases are likely to become less and less important, indeed totally irrelevant, once acceptable scientific standards permit a broader forensic use of DNA "fingerprinting." It is generally accepted that DNA identifying techniques will exclude from consideration the DNA sequences of all but identical twins, making

§ 12–1.6   The Uniform Parentage Act of 2000[65]

The National Conference of Commissioners on Uniform State Laws (NCCUSL) revised the Uniform Parentage Act in 2000 to "facilitate[] modern methods of testing for parentage [and] the enforcement of child support."[66] The UPA in effect, creates an exception to the hearsay rule for a written laboratory report, for it specifies that "a record of a genetic-testing expert is admissible as evidence of the truth of the facts asserted in the report unless a party objects to the report within (14) days after its receipt and cites specific grounds for exclusion."[67]

In keeping with modern practice and much recent legislation, the Act goes well beyond admissibility. It makes an exclusion conclusive,[68] and it makes most inclusions conclusive as well. The latter result follows from what the Act denotes as a presumption. Section 505(a) states that "a man is rebuttably identified as the father of a child if the genetic testing complies with this [article] and the results disclose that: (1) the man has at least a 99 percent probability of paternity, using a prior probability of 0.50, as calculated by using the combined paternity index obtained in the testing; and (2) a combined paternity index of at least 100 to 1."[69] However, the act deviates from most current statutes in that once triggered, the presumption ordinarily cannot be rebutted by anything other than additional genetic testing.[70] Because most cases either produce exclusions or a paternity index of 100 or

DNA testing the functional equivalent of a fingerprint.

Id. at 262 (citations omitted);1 MᴄCᴏʀᴍɪᴄᴋ, *supra* note 12, § 211.

65. Harry Tindall, who chaired the NCCUSL drafting committee, and George Maha, who was a scientific "observer" for the committee, generously commented on a draft of our discussion of selected features of the new UPA. They disagree with several of the conclusions presented here.

66. A Few Facts About The Uniform Parentage Act (2000), available at *http://www.nccusl.org/nccusl/uniformact_factsheets/uniformacts-fs-upa.asp* (last visited June 18, 2001). Although no state has adopted the Act yet, it has the endorsement of the ABA Family Law Section, National Child Support Enforcement, Association, American Academy of Adoption Attorneys, National Association of Public Health Registrars, and it has been introduced in the legislatures of Maryland, Minnesota, Texas, and West Virginia. *Id.*

67. Uɴɪꜰ. Pᴀʀᴇɴᴛᴀɢᴇ Aᴄᴛ § 621(a) (2000). The section does not specify what should be allowed as grounds for exclusion. Section 621(b) provides that:

A party objecting to the results of genetic testing may call one or more genetic-testing experts to testify in person or by telephone, videoconference, deposition, or another method approved by the court.

68. § 631(4) ("Unless the results of genetic testing are admitted to rebut other results of genetic testing, a man excluded as the father of a child by genetic testing must be adjudicated not to be the father of the child."). However, § 507 provides that "[t]he court or the support-enforcement agency shall order additional genetic testing upon the request of a party who contests the result of the original testing." This provision allows parties who doubt the results of a test to demand and receive further testing (at their expense). *See id.* ("If the previous genetic testing identified a man as the father of the child . . ., the court or agency may not order additional testing unless the party provides advance payment for the testing.").

69. With modern parentage testing and fresh samples from a mother, child, and putative father, these thresholds are easily attained. However, in the rare case in which the PI is below 100, section 631(3) provides that "the court may not dismiss the proceeding. In that event, the results of genetic testing, and other evidence, are admissible to resolve the issue of paternity."

70. *See* § 505(b) ("A man identified under subsection (a) as the father of the child may rebut the genetic testing results only by other genetic testing . . . which: (1) excludes the man as a genetic father of the child; or (2) identifies another man as the possible father of the child."); § 631(2) ("a man identified as the father of a child under Section 505 must be adjudicated the father of the child").

more,[71] the effect will be to make the genetic evidence conclusive in nearly all cases.

The Act's presumption is unusual for several reasons. First, it is not clear why a true presumption is needed. If the probability of paternity actually were above 99%, why would the factfinder need to be told that the law presumes paternity? How often do courts fail to find paternity in the absence of clear and convincing evidence that contradicts the expert's report that it is virtually certain that the defendant is the father?[72]

Second, assuming that a presumption is needed because factfinders often are ignoring or underweighting the genetic evidence, specifying it in terms of *both* W_{50} and the likelihood ratio (known as the "paternity index," or PI) is peculiar. If the PI is 100 and the prior odds are 1, then the posterior odds are 100.[73] These odds correspond to $W_{50} = 100/101 = .990099009900....$ Thus, the actual threshold is not .99, but a slightly larger number. It would be simpler to create a presumption in response to a large value of the PI alone.[74] Nevertheless, the redundancy will not cause a problem in practice, since it is functionally equivalent to a presumption based on a PI of 100 alone. In addition, giving both figures may help courts that are more familiar with the probability than the index.[75]

The Act also contains idiosyncratic definitions of the "probability of paternity" and the "paternity index." Section 102(16) describes the PI as "the likelihood of paternity." However, the PI is not a likelihood or a probability. It is a ratio of two likelihoods. For example, a PI of 1,000 does not mean that the "likelihood of paternity" is 1,000. It means that it is 1,000 times more likely to observe the genetic data for a true father than for a random draw from the gene pool. The definition recognizes that a ratio is involved, but its description of the numerator and denominator is as garbled as the description of what they represent.[76]

71. *See* Parentage Testing Standards Program Unit, American Association of Blood Banks, Annual Report Summary for 1998, 3 ("The overall exclusion rate for 1998 was 28.3% for all labs reporting data."), 4 (only one laboratory responding to survey even reports a case resolved with a paternity index below 100), 5 ("typical PIs" are 1,000, or even 5,000).

72. Some lawyers complain of "local justice" that ignores science, and a smattering of cases that fail to find paternity despite a large paternity index can be found. *See, e.g.*, Minton v. Weaver, 697 N.E.2d 1259 (Ind.Ct.App.1998) (reversing such a finding); In re J.W.T., 945 S.W.2d 911 (Tex.Ct.App.1997) (same); In re E.G.M., 647 S.W.2d 74 (Tex.Ct.App.1983) (same).

73. *See infra* § 12–2.5.

74. The Act's approach is comparable to creating a presumption that an air conditioner is working if the temperature in a Texas motel room in August is below a certain temperature. One could define the temperature on the Centigrade scale or on the Fahrenheit scale. Either one would be fine. It would be odd to write a law that used both—and it would be odder still

to use even slightly different temperatures on each scale—to create the presumption.

75. *See e.g., Drake ex rel. Atwood v. Apfel*, 2001 WL 705784 (N.D.Tex.2001) (writing that a paternity probability of 90% "far exceed[s]" a paternity index of 100).

76. The numerator is said to be "(A) the likelihood that the tested man is the father based on the genetic markers of the tested man, mother, and child, conditioned on the hypothesis that the tested man is the true father of the child." Of course, if one conditions on the hypothesis that "the tested man is the true father," then the likelihood that "the tested man is the father based on the genetic markers" (or anything else) is 1. Likewise, the denominator is said to be "(B) the likelihood that the tested man is not the father, based on the genetic markers of the tested man, mother, and child, conditioned on the hypothesis that the tested man is not the father of the child and that the true father is from the same ethnic and racial group as the tested man." Again, if the tested man is not the father, then the likelihood that the likelihood that the tested man is not the father also is one. Conse-

Section 102(18) defines probability of paternity as "the measure, for the ethnic or racial group to which the alleged father belongs, of the probability that the individual in question is the genetic father of the child, compared with a random, unrelated man of the same ethnic or racial group, expressed as a percentage incorporating the paternity index and a prior probability." This, too, is syntactically awkward and semantically obscure. In the end, however, these definitions may not cause a serious problem, if only because experts will not use them in computing the critical PI or W_{50}.

Third, triggering a presumption without attending to the thoroughness of the testing leaves open the possibility that a presumption will arise from testing at only one or two loci. Such testing could produce a PI exceeding 100, but the test would lack power to exclude a sibling, and the likelihood ratio with respect to the hypothesis that such a close relative of the tested man is the father could be considerably less than 100. Presumably, the section of the Act requiring testing "of a type reasonably relied upon by experts in the field of genetic testing" and the use of accredited laboratories will guarantee that a sufficient number of loci are investigated.[77]

Finally, as noted earlier, the presumption is unique in that once triggered, it ordinarily cannot be rebutted by anything other than additional genetic testing. If the additional test is positive for another man, § 504(c) requires the court to order still more genetic tests until one man is excluded.[78] Thus, in the guise of a rebuttable presumption, the Act dictates the outcome of virtually all paternity cases.[79] Genetic testing will be used in every contested civil paternity case. With modern testing, it should always be possible either to exclude a man or to obtain a PI of far more than 100. When this occurs, the Act ensures that the case will be disposed of on the basis of the

quently, the paternity index as defined by the Act is always 1/1 = 1. The difficulty lies in the references to the likelihood that the tested man is or is not the father. The terms involved in the paternity index pertain to the data conditional on the hypotheses, and the data consist simply of the genotypes of the trio.

77. § 503(a) ("Genetic testing must be of a type reasonably relied upon by experts in the field of genetic testing and performed in a testing laboratory accredited by: (1) the American Association of Blood Banks, or a successor to its functions; (2) the American Society for Histocompatibility and Immunogenetics, or a successor to its functions; or (3) an accrediting body designated by the federal Secretary of Health and Human Services.").

78. § 505(c) reads: "Except as otherwise provided in Section 510, if more than one man is identified by genetic testing as the possible father of the child, the court shall order them to submit to further genetic testing to identify the genetic father." The § 510 exception is for the case of monozygotic twins. Because identical twins are genetically indistinguishable, further genetic testing would be pointless. Nevertheless, § 510(a) states that "[t]he court may order genetic testing of a brother of a man identified as the father of a child if the man is commonly believed to have an identical brother

and evidence suggests that the brother may be the genetic father of the child." Apparently, the court is given this power to verify that the "man [who] is commonly believed to [be] an identical brother" really is a twin. If such testing of relatives is useful, though, the court should have the authority to order it whenever a defendant raises the possibility that a close relative is the father of the child whose parentage is questioned.

Paragraph (b) assumes that the identical twins both are tested. It provides that "[i]f each brother satisfies the requirements as the identified father of the child under Section 505 without consideration of another identical brother being identified as the father of the child, the court may rely on nongenetic evidence to adjudicate which brother is the father of the child." Although it is hard to imagine how a genetic test that produces a PI exceeding 100 for one twin would not yield the same value for the other, the end result is reasonable—the finder of fact must rely on nongenetic evidence to decide which of two genetically identical individuals is the father.

79. Under § 631(2), "Unless the results of genetic testing are admitted to rebut other results of genetic testing, a man identified as the father of a child under Section 505 must be adjudicated the father of the child.".

scientific evidence. When this comes to pass, the law will have moved 180 degrees, from an initial distrust of blood test evidence to a final reliance on genetic testing as conclusive evidence of paternity.

§ 12–1.7 Criminal Cases

From time to time, the parentage testing methods that are ubiquitous in civil cases are brought to bear in criminal investigations of incests,[80] rapes,[81] homicides involving missing bodies,[82] and other offenses.[83] The scientific issues do not change,[84] but some courts seem to find the "probability of paternity" more disturbing in this context.[85] In *State v. Hartman*,[86] the Supreme Court of

80. *See, e.g.,* State v. Thompson, 503 A.2d 689 (Me.1986) (sexual relationship with daughter began at age 11 and culminated in birth of child four years later; HLA, red blood cell, and serum protein tests produced W_{50} of 99.46%); E.G. Reisner & P. Reading, *Application of Probability of Paternity Calculations to an Allegedly Incestuous Relationship*, 28 J. Forensic Sci. 1030 (1983).

81. *See, e.g.,* People v. White, 211 A.D.2d 982, 621 N.Y.S.2d 728 (N.Y.App.Div.1995) (defendant's probability of paternity based on VNTR testing of aborted fetus admissible in light of decision in DNA case involving simple semen stain but no paternity issue); State v. Jackson, 320 N.C. 452, 358 S.E.2d 679 (1987) (error to introduce geneticist's testimony that defendant accused of statutory rape of eleven-year-old girl "probably is the natural father of the child" based "entirely on genetic evidence" from HLA and serum protein tests; given the "testimony concerning the paternity index and the evidence of defendant's access before it, the jury was in as good a position as [the expert] to determine whether the defendant was 'probably' the father").

82. *See, e.g.,* State v. Pioletti, 246 Kan. 49, 785 P.2d 963 (Kan.1990) ("DNA analysis introduced at trial [of man accused of killing and cremating his ex-wife] indicated that blood found on the door of the crematory was probably that of the offspring of [the ex-wife's] parents. The test indicated a 99.999% probability of parenthood."); State v. Davis, 814 S.W.2d 593 (Mo.1991) (husband shot his wife and secretly put her car in storage; Cellmark DNA test showed likelihood ratio for blood stain in wife's car being from mother of the couples' two children to be 510 and 190,000, respectively; admissible under general acceptance standard where defendant presented no opposing expert testimony and declined to introduce tests he had Lifecodes perform); William D. Haglund et al., *Identification of Decomposed Human Remains by Deoxyribonucleic Acid (DNA) Profiling*, 35 J. Forensic Sci. 724 (1990) (first published report of using VNTR profiling of suspected parents and decomposed female body found in a park to establish the identity of the remains).

83. Davis v. State, 476 N.E.2d 127 (Ind.Ct. App.1985) (criminal neglect of newborn).

84. Proof of kinship in criminal cases sometimes involves laboratory techniques never before seen in civil paternity or criminal identity testing. *See* Charles M. Strom & Svetlana Rechitsky, *Use of Nested PCR to Identify Charred Human Remains and Minute Amounts of Blood*, 43 J. Forensic Sci. 696 (1998) ("reverse paternity" analysis gave a probability of identity of 98% that the remains in defendant's garage came from the body of his wife in *State v. Huff*, No. 93 CF136 (Ill. App.)). Suggestions for analyzing novel DNA methods or applications are given in the previous chapter.

85. Several cases also raise the broader concerns over the effect of population structure. In *State v. Sivri*, 231 Conn. 115, 646 A.2d 169 (Conn.1994), Cellmark compared blood found in the trunk of a car with blood from parents of missing woman. One allele in each pair at three loci could be matched to each parent; one allele at a fourth probe matched the father, but the other matched neither parent. Dr. Robin Cotton testified that the non-matching allele "most likely represented a mutant gene inherited from the mother, which happens about 5 percent of the time." Apparently treating the possibility of a mutation as if were an established fact, however, Dr. Lisa Forman testified that using the "product rule," the probability that a random Caucasian would have the same three matching alleles as the mother was 1/1,400 and 1/26,000 for the father. Dr. Lawrence Mueller testified for the defendant that linkage equilibrium has never been established and that the available evidence is to the contrary. Dr. Kenneth Kidd testified to the existence of equilibrium, and the trial court admitted the DNA evidence. The Supreme Court of Connecticut remanded for a determination of "whether the probability calculations ... conform to the criteria set out in the [1992 NRC] Committee report, or, if not, whether the evidence nevertheless passes appropriate scientific evidence standards." The dispute over population structure also was dispositive in Commonwealth v. Lanigan,413 Mass. 154, 596 N.E.2d 311 (Mass.1992). These consolidated cases included charges of multiple rape, assault, and incest filed against a man

Wisconsin overturned a rape conviction because it believed that there was something circular in using a prior probability of one-half:

> Although we have concluded that the probability of exclusion and the paternity index are admissible in criminal proceedings, we are not convinced that a defendant's probability of paternity is also admissible. [T]he calculation of a defendant's probability of paternity is typically based upon a 50 percent prior probability which arbitrarily assumes a 50 percent likelihood that the defendant is the father.... In other words, the probability of paternity is calculated based upon the assumption "that the mother and putative father have engaged in sexual intercourse at least once during the period of possible conception." [Citation omitted.] Because the probability of paternity assumes that sexual intercourse has occurred, it is improper to use this statistic to prove that sexual intercourse has occurred.[87]

This argument cannot be correct. Although a prior probability of 50% may be inapposite in a given case and can obscure the meaning of the resulting posterior probability, relying on a high W_{50} to infer intercourse is not circular. A prior probability of 50% does not necessarily presuppose that the defendant definitely engaged in intercourse. Of course, one might assume that he did—and that the probability of a child resulting from such intercourse is 50%, and that the probability of intercourse with anyone else that would produce a child is 50%. But one might also assume a 62.5% probability of defendant's intercourse, an 80% probability of an offspring given such intercourse, and a 50% probability that intercourse with anyone else that would produce a child.[88] In general, the use of a prior probability of paternity merely entails a *probability* of intercourse; realistically, and contrary to the court's analysis, this probability does not have the value of 100%.[89]

In *State v. Spann*,[90] the Supreme Court of New Jersey also reversed a conviction because of the manner in which the expert presented W_{50}. The

and his son. One alleged victim who delivered a child testified before a grand jury that she had sexual intercourse only with the defendants. DNA analysis of blood samples from the victim, her child, and the men proved that the younger man could not have been the father, and that the older man had alleles that were "2,500 times more likely ... if he were the father of the child than if he were not the father." The Supreme Judicial Court affirmed the exclusion of these results, pointing to "[t]he national call for considered, conservative approaches to DNA testing, ... and the absence of such an approach in the present cases...." *Id.* at 316.

86. 145 Wis.2d 1, 426 N.W.2d 320 (Wis. 1988).

87. *Id.* at 326.

88. If the probability of intercourse with the defendant is $P(I)$ and the probability of a child given such intercourse is $P(C \& I)$, then the probability of a child resulting from defendant's intercourse with the victim is $P(C \& I) = P(I) \times P(C|I)$. The first illustration used $P(I) = 1$ and $P(C|I) = 1/2$. The second used

$P(I) = 5/8$ and $P(C|I) = 4/5$. More generally, if, without considering the genotypes of the mother, child, and possible fathers, the probability of a child having resulted from intercourse with some other man is $\frac{1}{2}$, then the prior probability that the defendant is the father is $\frac{1}{2}$, and the probability of his intercourse with the victim is easily derived from the formula for the joint probability $P(C \& I))$ given above. Setting $P(C \& I) = 1/2$, it follows that $P(I) = (1/2) / P(C|I) = 1 / [2 P(C|I)]$.

89. The result in note 88 is easily generalized. If the prior probability is some number P_0, then the probability of intercourse is $P(I) = P_0 / P(C|I)$. This value for $P(I)$ need not (and rarely will) be 1—a mathematical fact that supports the dictum of the New Jersey Supreme Court that "[t]he calculation—Bayes' Theorem—if valid, does not depend on any particular degree of confidence in the fact of intercourse." State v. Spann, 130 N.J. 484, 617 A.2d 247, 261 (N.J.1993). For further criticism of the *Hartman* court's reasoning, *see* Kaye, *supra* note 57.

90. 130 N.J. 484, 617 A.2d 247 (N.J.1993).

defendant was a guard at a county jail. He was convicted of sexual assault as a result of his conduct with a woman incarcerated on a detainer from the Immigration and Naturalization Service. The victim had given birth to a child apparently conceived during her detention in the jail, and HLA tests showed an exclusion probability of 99%[91] and a W_{50} of 96.55%.[92] The expert testified to these numbers, and, using a convention adopted by the paternity testing community, also testified that it was "very likely" that defendant was the father. On cross-examination, defense counsel established that the 96.55% figure presupposed a prior probability of 50%, but the expert characterized this premise as "neutral," "purely objective," and "one of the beauties of the test."[93] The prosecutor argued in summation that "guilt ... is proved to a mathematical certainty by carefully applying an objective scientific technique to the hard facts of this case."[94]

The state supreme court held that the prosecution's portrayal of W_{50} was unfair and that the failure to explain what effect other prior probabilities would have had on the probability of paternity was misleading.[95] Taking pains to avoid upsetting the use of paternity probabilities in civil cases,[96] and expressing hesitation about venturing into deep and murky waters,[97] however,

---

91. The probability of exclusion is the proportion of the population of men who could be excluded as possible fathers of the child in light of the test results for the mother and child. A probability of exclusion of 99% leaves 1% of the male population included as biologically possible fathers. On the admissibility of the probability of exclusion in civil cases, see, for example, Kaye, *supra* note 57.

92. The court believed that the two numbers were inconsistent: "Our understanding of the mathematics suggests that the actual exclusionary figure used was not 1% but rather 3.57%. Had she in fact used a 1% exclusionary figure, the probability of paternity would have been 99.01%, not 96.55%." 617 A.2d at 251 n. 2. The court's calculation, however, assumes that the paternity index is 100. Later in the opinion, the court correctly observes that the exclusion probability is not the sole factor that determines the value of the paternity index. Id. at 255. The reason is simple. Among the 1% of the male population with the paternal alleles, some men have HLA types such that they are more likely to transmit the paternal alleles to the child than other men. *See, e.g.,* Kaye, *supra* note 57. Depending on the HLA types of the mother, child, and alleged father, an inclusion probability of 1% can give rise to a W_{50} of 96.55%.

93. 617 A.2d at 252.

94. *Id.* at 249.

95. This omission gave the jury "no idea what to do with the probability of paternity percentage if its own estimate of probabilities ... was different from .5." *Id.* at 253.

96. The court expressly left open the question of whether such "guidelines" should apply to civil parentage determinations. *Id.* at 265 ("We do not intend by this opinion to compli-

cate or make more difficult the accomplishment of the apparent intent of the Legislature, namely, to enable the State or the mother to readily establish paternity through the use of both the exclusionary percentage and the probability of paternity opinion. That issue is not now before us.").

97. The court declined to decide whether a variable probability of paternity should be admissible, noting that "[o]pinions based on Bayes' Theorem are far from universally accepted for forensic purposes, especially in criminal cases." Id. at 257. Indeed, the court complained that "[t]he intensity and complexity of the dispute is mind boggling on occasion for those other than mathematical experts," and it pointed to what it thought were contradictions or changes in the position of one author. *Id.* at 257.

However, the articles that the court cites as inconsistent present a coherent view. They maintain that statistical decision theory provides the most satisfactory interpretation of the law's burden of persuasions [D.H. Kaye, *Apples and Oranges: Confidence Coefficients Versus the Burden of Persuasion*, 73 CORNELL L. REV. 54 (1987)], that most statisticians use "frequentist" procedures for estimating the values of population parameters or testing hypotheses more often than they employ Bayesian methods [David H. Kaye, *The Numbers Game: Statistical Inference in Discrimination Cases*, 80 MICH. L. REV. 833 (1982)], that in civil parentage disputes a Bayesian presentation of the posterior probability as a function of the prior probability should be admissible [Ira Ellman & David Kaye, *Probabilities and Proof: Can HLA and Blood Group Testing Prove Paternity?*, 54 NYU L. REV. 1131 (1979)], and that the costs of Bayesian presentations of blood-

the court remanded for "a full hearing"[98] to determine whether presenting the paternity probability as a function of the prior probability rather than as the single value, W_{50}, would be admissible.[99]

The Connecticut Supreme Court was less circumspect in evaluating the admissibility of paternity probabilities in criminal cases. In *State v. Skipper*,[100] the defendant was charged with various offenses arising from a sexually abusive relationship that he initiated with the eight-year-old daughter of a neighbor and that lasted for seven years, when she became pregnant. DNA VNTR testing performed on the aborted fetus, the girl, and the defendant resulted in a paternity index of 3,496 and a corresponding W_{50} of 99.97%.[101] Unlike *Spann*, the use of the 50% prior probability was never disclosed, even on cross-examination.[102] Instead, an expert "explained" that "[t]he calculation is that the paternity index divided by the paternity index plus one, gives you the percentage. It's simply a conversion of the paternity index to the percentage. So, it's 99.97 is basically 3500 to 1, which is odds ... expressed as a percentage."[103]

The court held that this expert evidence was inadmissible and reversed the defendant's conviction. Notwithstanding the expert's obfuscation, the court recognized that the undisclosed prior probability of 50% entails a "substantial probability of intercourse,"[104] and it held that "[t]he assumption that there is a substantial possibility that the defendant had intercourse with the victim, however, raises serious concerns in sexual assault cases. It is antithetical to our criminal justice system to presume anything but innocence at the outset of a trial."[105]

Although even under this reasoning, it might be permissible to introduce a paternity probability based on a very small prior probability (which would

stain and other such trace evidence (but not necessarily paternity tests) in criminal cases outweigh the benefits [D.H. Kaye, *The Admissibility of "Probability Evidence" in Criminal Trials* (pt. 2), 27 JURIMETRICS J. 160, 172 (1987)]. In more recent work, however, Professor Kaye has supported the use of Bayes' rule in criminal cases involving DNA evidence. *See, e.g.*, David H. Kaye, *DNA Evidence: Probability, Population Genetics, and the Courts*, 7 HARV. J. L. & TECH. 101 (1993).

98. 617 A.2d at 257.

99. In dictum, the court stated that "the expert's testimony should be required to include an explanation to the jury of what the probability of paternity would be for a varying range of such prior probabilities, running, for example, from .1 to .9." *Id.* at 254. Among other things, the court also suggested that both the probability of exclusion and the paternity index should be admissible (*id.* at 264), that testimony of the probability of paternity should be presented by an expert "qualified ... as a mathematician" (*id.* at 264), and that "[n]o verbal predicate should be stated in any way...." *Id.* at 264.

100. 228 Conn. 610, 637 A.2d 1101 (Conn. 1994).

101. The *Skipper* court incorrectly describes the ratio as "indicating that only one out of 3497 randomly selected males would have the phenotypes compatible with the fetus in question." *Id.* at 1103–04. The mistake here is the same as in *Spann*—the paternity index does not depend on just the probability of inclusion.

102. *Id.* at 1104 n. 12 ("no testimony was elicited from the expert indicating that a 50 percent prior probability of paternity was used in calculating the probability of paternity percentage.").

103. *Id.* at 1105 (quoting testimony of Kevin McElfresh of Lifecodes Corporation).

104. *Id.* at 1107.

105. *Id.* The opinion goes on to state that "[b]ecause Bayes' Theorem requires the assumption of a prior probability of paternity, i.e., guilt, its use is inconsistent with the presumption of innocence in a criminal case such as this, in which Bayes' Theorem was used to establish the probability of paternity, i.e., that the defendant was the father of the product of conception of an alleged sexual assault." *Id.* at 1107.

not involve a "substantial probability of intercourse,")[106] the opinion suggests that any nonzero prior probability—no matter how small—undermines the presumption of innocence:

> Whether a prior probability of 50 percent is automatically used or whether the jury is instructed to adopt its own prior probability, when the probability of paternity statistic is introduced, an assumption is required to be made by the jury before it has heard all of the evidence—that there is a quantifiable probability that the defendant committed the crime.[107]

The *Skipper* opinion, however, fails to explain why or how the presumption of innocence means that the prior probability is zero.[108] Indeed, a prospective juror who professes an absolute, unshakeable belief in the defendant's innocence—which is what a prior probability of zero amounts to—should be excused for cause.[109] Given the absurdity of the court's assumption, several commentators have suggested that the presumption of innocence means something much weaker. The conventional understanding is that it

---

106. For example, if the prior odds were only 1/500, the posterior odds for a paternity index of 3500 still would be 3500 × 1/500 = 70. Odds of 70 to 1 correspond to a probability of paternity of 70/71 = 98.59%.

107. *Id.* at 1107–08 (footnote omitted). The court continues opaquely:

> In fact, if the presumption of innocence were factored into Bayes' Theorem, the probability of paternity statistic would be useless. If we assume that the presumption of innocence standard would require the prior probability of guilt to be zero, the probability of paternity in a criminal case would always be zero because Bayes' Theorem requires the paternity index to be multiplied by a positive prior probability in order to have any utility. "In other words, Bayes' Theorem can only work if the presumption of innocence disappears from consideration."

Id. at 1108 (quoting Randolph Jonakait, *When Blood Is Their Argument: Probabilities in Criminal Cases, Genetic Markers, and, Once Again, Bayes' Theorem*, 1983 U. Ill. L. Rev. 369, 406, 408).

108. In a footnote, the court writes:

> Permitting the jury to derive its own prior probability to arrive at a corresponding probability of paternity, however, still implicates the presumption of innocence. See, e.g., L. Tribe, "Trial by Mathematics: Precision and Ritual in the Legal Process," 84 Harv. L. Rev. 1329, 1368–75 (1971). "It may be supposed that no juror would be permitted to announce publicly in mid-trial that the defendant was already burdened with, say, a sixty percent probability of guilt—but even without such a public statement it would be exceedingly difficult for the accused, for the prosecution, and ultimately for the community, to avoid the explicit recognition that, having been forced to focus on the question, the rational juror could hardly

> avoid reaching some such answer. And, once that recognition had become a general one, our society's traditional affirmation of the 'presumption of innocence' could lose much of its value." *Id.* 1370.

637 A.2d at 1108 n. 18. But Professor Tribe never explains what might be lost by recognizing "in mid-trial" that there is a non-zero probability that a defendant is guilty.

Having failed to justify its assumption that the presumption of innocence means that the prior probability of guilt is exactly zero, the court alludes to another amorphous but important concept—reasonable doubt:

> Moreover, allowing the jury to adopt a prior probability and, hence, arrive at a probability of guilt, raises concerns in criminal cases regarding the burden of proof of guilt beyond a reasonable doubt. In adopting a prior probability of guilt and viewing the corresponding probability of paternity on a chart, the jury is left "with a number that purports to represent [its] assessment of the probability that the defendant is guilty as charged. Needless to say, that number will never quite equal 1.0, so the result will be to produce a quantity ... which openly signifies a measurable ... margin of doubt...."

Id. (quoting Tribe, *supra*, at 1372). Again, the argument seems incomplete. Why the requirement of proof beyond a reasonable doubt bars some measurable doubt remains mysterious. *See* Daniel Shaviro, *Statistical-Probability Evidence and the Appearance of Justice*, 103 Harv. L. Rev. 530 (1989).

109. Memorandum from Bernard Robertson to bayesian-evidence@massey.ac.nz, July 29, 1994, reprinted in Ronald J. Allen et al., *Probability and Proof in* State v. Skipper: *An Internet Exchange*, 35 Jurimetrics J. 277, 283 (1995).

means that the mere fact of an indictment or information is not evidence and may not be considered supportive of guilt; hence, if the government adduces insufficient evidence at trial to permit a reasonable jury to conclude beyond a reasonable doubt that defendant is guilty as charged, the "presumption" is not overcome, and defendant is entitled to a directed verdict of acquittal.[110] Another interpretation that pours more content into the phrase is that *ab initio*, "the defendant should be thought no more likely than anyone else to be guilty."[111]

Despite the flimsiness of the court's reasoning, the type of testimony about the "probability of paternity" given in *Skipper* presents a strong case for exclusion. Not only was the use of the prior probability of 50% undisclosed on direct examination, but W_{50} was presented as if it involved no prior probability—merely "odds ... expressed as a percentage." As we have seen, however, the court's rejection of a more careful presentation, in which the expert displays the impact of the test results on a range of prior probabilities[112] is much less convincing.

Thus, other courts have not been persuaded by *Skipper* to banish the paternity probability from the criminal realm. In *Griffith v. State*.[113] A woman institutionalized at the Lubbock State School became pregnant and bore a child. She was so profoundly retarded that she was unable to communicate the identity of the father. Paternity tests excluded four of the five male employees who would have had contact with her during the relevant time period. The probability of exclusion exceeded 99.99%; moreover, the non-excluded man had a paternity index of 14,961 and a W_{50} greater than 99.99%. He objected unsuccessfully to the introduction of the last figure. The state's expert, a molecular biologist, testified that the use of a prior probability of one-half was "standard," "neutral," and consistent with the presumption of innocence. Indeed, the biologist maintained that one-half was an unrealistically low value for the prior probability.

The Texas Court of Appeals accepted the dubious "neutrality" justification for the use of the prior probability of one-half.[114] Despite this disappointing feature of the opinion, the court correctly recognized that the presumption of innocence does not dictate a prior probability of zero, that a nonzero prior

110. *See, e.g.,* 9 JOHN H. WIGMORE, EVIDENCE IN TRIALS AT COMMON LAW § 2511 (Chadbourn rev.1981).

111. Memorandum from D.H. Kaye & David J. Balding to bayesian-evidence@massey.ac.nz, Aug. 8, 1994, reprinted in Allen et al., *supra* note 105, at 292, 293; *see also, e.g.,* A.P. Dawid, *The Island Problem: Coherent Use of Identification Evidence, in* ASPECTS OF UNCERTAINTY 159, 169 (P.R. Freedman & A.F.M. Smith eds., 1994) ("the presumption of innocence is fully in accord with Bayesian reasoning; before any evidence is adduced, we should treat the defendant as exchangeable with all other members of the population").

112. A variation would be to report how small the prior probability would have to be to keep the posterior probability below, say, 99%.

For a paternity index of 3500, the posterior odds $W/(1 - W)$ are 3500 times the prior odds. Therefore, to keep the posterior probability below 99% (and the posterior odds below 99/1), the prior odds would have to be less than 99/3500. The corresponding prior probability is $99/(99 + 3500) = 2.78\%$. Unless the other evidence in the case suggests that the prior probability is smaller than 3%, the paternity probability exceeds 99%.

113. 976 S.W.2d 241 (Tex.App.1998).

114. It also wrote that this value was generally accepted "in the scientific community of molecular biology." However, molecular biology has nothing to do with assigning prior probabilities of paternity, and few molecular biologists even would know what the phrase means.

does not assume intercourse, and that the use of Bayes' rule is not inherently incompatible with due process. Rejecting contrary dicta in *Skipper* and related cases, it upheld the conviction for sexual assault.

Following *Griffith*, the Court of Appeals for the Sixth Circuit in *Lyons v. Stovall*,[115] was confronted with a rape of a profoundly retarded and physically disabled resident of a state home for the mentally retarded. The rape had occurred in 1983, and the state introduced evidence that two sets of HLA tests excluded all but one of the male workers at the home. The paternity index for the nonexcluded employee was 304 for one set of tests and 429 for the other.[116] The experts reported the associated probabilities of paternity as being 99.9% and 99.76%.[117] The appellate court's opinion implies that the experts did not disclose that these figures assumed a prior probability of one-half.[118]

Defendant was convicted of first-degree criminal sexual assault and sentenced to a term of ten to 25 years' imprisonment. After unsuccessfully appealing in the state courts, he filed for a writ of habeas corpus in the United States District Court for the Eastern District of Michigan, claiming that his "rights to the presumption of innocence and to trial by jury [were] eviscerated because of the introduction of highly prejudicial testimony and argument regarding the purported statistical probability of petitioner's paternity."[119] The district court granted the petition, but a divided court of appeals reversed on procedural grounds. One judge observed that "the resolution of the merits of Petitioner's claim is far from clear as indicated by the case law from the several jurisdictions which allow the use of the statistical data in question,"[120] but another concurred only "in the end result,"[121] and the third would have affirmed the district court in its conclusion that the introduction of the "probability of paternity" deprived the defendant of due process.[122] In sum, it seems fair to say that the law on the admissibility of the "probability of paternity" in criminal cases remains muddled.

---

115. 188 F.3d 327 (6th Cir.1999), cert. denied, 530 U.S. 1203, 120 S.Ct. 2197, 147 L.Ed.2d 233 (2000).

116. Apparently, the experts incorrectly represented that these figures were "the odds that this man is the father of this child compared to any other man in the population who might have been able to contribute the requisite genes." *Id.* at 330. As explained *infra* § 12–2.5, a paternity index is a ratio of conditional probabilities for the genetic data; it is not a statement of the relative likelihoods of any hypotheses as to who was the father. The defendant did not object to this testimony.

117. *Id.* at 331.

118. *Id.* ("The experts made it known to the jury that the probability of paternity percentages were calculated on the underlying mathematical assumption that Petitioner had

had sexual intercourse with Ms. McKenzie; that the percentages had to be viewed and weighed by the jury in light of the other evidence admitted; and that if it were a known fact that Petitioner did not have sexual intercourse with the victim, the value of the probability of paternity would be zero percent.").

119. *Id.*

120. *Id.* at 344.

121. *Id.* (concurring opinion).

122. *Id.* at 347 (dissenting opinion, pointedly observing, at 350, that "Because the *Teague* issue is dispositive of this case, there is no reason to address any other potential issues. To the extent that any opinions do so they offer only personal observations of the authoring judge.").

B. SCIENTIFIC STATUS

by

Jeffrey W. Morris* & David W. Gjertson**

§ 12–2.0 THE SCIENTIFIC STATUS OF PARENTAGE TESTING

§ 12–2.1 Introduction

Establishing familial relationships via laboratory tests of genetic markers has important social and legal applications in such areas as disputed paternity and maternity, kidnaping, adoption, immigration, inheritance, interchange of infants at birth, and identification of human remains from a battlefield or disaster site. Resolving disputed claims of paternity is by far the most common and fastest growing application. In 1968, 10% of live U.S. births were registered as illegitimate.[1] By 1982, that number had increased to 17%,[2] and recent estimates exceed 30% of the annual births.[3] Over 250,000 paternity cases are resolved by genetic testing each year.[4]

Any human trait that is fully expressed at birth, remains constant throughout life,[5] and is inherited in a regular and reproducible manner can be used to investigate parenthood. Even before Mendel defined the gene, racial and other anthropological measures such as body build had been used to exclude paternity. Reliance on such physical characteristics, however, suffers from two drawbacks. First, transmission of these traits is unpredictable and difficult to quantify due to complex interactions involving many genes. Second, and perhaps more importantly, these traits are readily apparent. A mother could rationally bring an accusation of paternity against one man among several possibilities because he most closely physically resembles her child, but it would be an exercise in circular reasoning for others to use the similarity to corroborate her allegation.

Modern parentage testing therefore relies on chemical characteristics of tissues (usually blood) that are invisible to the naked eye and that follow simple patterns of inheritance. This chapter describes these genetic markers (Section 2). It discusses the genetic principles underlying paternity testing (Section 3), characterizes various types of laboratory tests and test-selection criteria (Section 4), and explains the probability of paternity (Section 5), including the principles and assumptions underlying the calculations (Section

* Jeffrey W. Morris, M.D., Ph.D., is the former Director, Long Beach Genetics and Clinical Associate Professor of Pathology, University of California, Irvine. He serves as a member of the Parentage Testing Ancillary Committee, College of American Pathologists and is a past Chairman, Committee on Parentage Testing of the American Association of Blood Banks.

** David W. Gjertson, Ph.D., is Associate Professor of Biostatistics and Pathology, UCLA, and chair of the Parentage Testing Unit of the Standards Program Committee of the American Association of Blood Banks.

§ 12–2.0

1. CURT STERN, PRINCIPLES OF HUMAN GENETICS (3d ed.1973).

2. Fred Schutzman, Interests of the Office of Child Support Enforcement, U.S. Department of Health and Human Services, in INCLUSION PROBABILITIES IN PARENTAGE TESTING 7 (R.H. Walker ed., 1983).

3. Stephanie J. Venture et al., *Births: Final Data for 1998*, 48 NATIONAL VITAL STATISTICS REPORTS 8 (2000).

4. The American Association of Blood Banks annual survey reported 280,510 cases for 1999. *See* AABB PARENTAGE TESTING STANDARDS PROGRAM UNIT, ANNUAL REPORT SUMMARY FOR 1999, at 3 (available in pdf format by clicking on "1999 Annual Report Summary" at http://38.200.9.76/About_the_AABB/Stds_and_Accred/stdsandaccred.htm).

5. A constant trait is unaffected by age, disease, or other environmental conditions.

6). Finally, Section 7 compares and contrasts testing to resolve disputed paternity and testing to identify the perpetrator of a crime.

§ 12–2.2   Genetic Markers Used in Parentage Testing

The modern incorporation of blood traits into the process of determining fatherhood began with the discovery in 1900 of ABO markers (blood types)[6] and the establishment in 1910 that these factors were inherited.[7] The ABO system is one of six red cell systems used by paternity laboratories. The genetic markers for these systems are located on the surface of red cells and evoke an immunological response if exposed to individuals not possessing the cell's markers. This property defines an "antigen." One immunological response is production of an "antibody," a complex molecule that interacts in a lock and key fashion with its eliciting antigen. Antibody-antigen reactions can be used in the laboratory for diagnostic purposes. Use of a specific antibody can determine the presence or absence of its corresponding antigen, and *vice versa*.[8] These antigens are usually detected by "agglutination," a reaction in which red cells suspended in a liquid collect into clumps when the corresponding antibody is added to the liquid.

To illustrate its inheritance at an elementary level, the ABO system can be conceived as having three different forms of the genes (alleles): A, B, and O. Each individual has a pair of alleles (one from each parent), so there are six possible genetic combinations: AA, BB, OO, AO, BO, and AB. Genetic combinations make up an individual's "genotype," so that the ABO system has the six possible genotypes. The A and B alleles code for the A and B antigens, respectively. The O allele codes for neither. (It is thus a "silent" or "null" allele, although special methods can detect its presence.)

An individual's expression (e.g., antigens on a cell's surface) of a genotype is called a "phenotype." Testing of red cells with two specific antibodies, anti-A and anti-B, discriminates four ABO phenotypes: type A (reacts with anti-A but not anti-B), type B (reacts with anti-B but not anti-A), type AB (reacts with both), and type O (reacts with neither). Individuals with phenotypes AB and O have genotypes AB and OO, respectively. But type A individuals may be genetically AA or AO, and type B individuals BB or BO. As a rule, genotype completely specifies phenotype, but not necessarily the converse. Paternity and identity laboratories detect expressions of an individual's genetic make-up—they determine phenotypes.

Today, a laboratory's repertoire of blood tests are of two types. Traditional tests are called "HLA-based evaluations" and include tests for markers on the red cells (ABO and others) and white cells (HLA)[9] as well as red cell

---

6. K. Landsteiner, *Zur Kenntnis der Anti-fermentativen Lytischen und Agglutinierenden Wirkungen des Blutserums und der Lymphe*, 28 ZENTRALBL. BAKT. 357 (1900).

7. E. von Dungern & L. Hirszfeld, *Ueber Vererbung Gruppenspezifischer Strukturen des Blutes*, 6 ZTSCHR. IMMUNITATSFORSCH 284 (1910). Accounts of early medicolegal applications of blood tests are summarized by A.S. Wiener in several reviews: BLOOD GROUPS AND BLOOD TRANSFUSIONS (1935); RH-HR BLOOD TYPES: APPLICATIONS IN CLINICAL AND LEGAL MEDICINE AND ANTHROPOLO-

GY (1954); *Forensic Blood Group Genetics: Critical Historical Review*. 72 N.Y. STATE J. MED. 810 (1972).

8. An antibody-antigen reaction is responsible for a transfusion reaction when mismatched blood is administered.

9. HLA stands for "Human Leukocyte Antigens." These antigens are found not just on the surface of leukocytes (white blood cells), but on most types of cells. They serve to identify one's own cells. The immune system, which

enzyme markers and serum protein markers.[10] In general, methods for the detection of such markers and their inheritance patterns are firmly established and accepted by most courts throughout the world.[11] Such tests have led to the successful resolution of hundreds of thousands of paternity disputes.

Nevertheless, traditional testing is limited to genetic variations (polymorphisms) expressed in the tested tissue (the blood). Of several dozen such tests, only HLA is individually powerful enough to resolve most cases.[12] By contrast, each tissue in the body contains a complete complement of DNA coding for all traits—an estimated 30,000 pairs of genes[13]—whether or not those traits are expressed in the tissue sampled—as well noncoding regions.[14] As a result, tests of DNA markers have largely supplanted the classical tests. The newer DNA-based tests generally are more powerful, less expensive, and easier to perform. They require Fewer tests are needed to achieve for the same level of results, and a smaller quantity of blood can be drawn.

The best established and most widely used DNA tests detect restriction fragment length polymorphisms (RFLPs) by cleaving DNA with enzymes (restriction endonucleases) that recognize specific nucleotide sequences. The majority of RFLPs display genetic diversity by variations in the number of tandem repeats (VNTRs)—units of a core sequence of DNA.[15] Markers are detected with radioactive, chemiluminescence or colormetric DNA probes using the Southern method.[16]

will attack foreign material, does not attack cells that have the proper HLA types, and HLA matching is a standard procedure in the transplantation of most organs. For discussion of their use in parentage, see Paul I. Terasaki, *Resolution by HLA Testing of 1000 Paternity Cases Not Excluded by ABO Testing*. 16 J. Fam. L. 543 (1978).

10. Reviews of the applications of these tests to paternity can be found in Eloise R. Giblett, Genetic Markers in Human Blood (1969); C.L. Lee, *Current Status of Paternity Testing*, 9 Fam. L.Q. 615 (1975); Herbert F. Polesky, Paternity Testing (1975); R R. Race & Ruth Sanger, Blood Groups in Man (6th ed.1975); N.J. Bryant, Disputed Paternity: The Value and Application of Blood Tests (1980); Handbook for Forensic Individualization of Human Blood and Bloodstains (B.W. Grunbaum ed., 1981); Charles Salmon et al., The Human Blood Groups (1984); Susan D. Rolih & W. John Judd, Serological Methods in Forensic Science (1985).

11. *See, e.g.*, J.P. Abbott et al., *Joint AMA–ABA Guidelines: Present Status of Serologic Testing*, 10 Fam. L.Q. 247 (1976); D.H. Kaye & Ronald Kanwischer, *Admissibility of Genetic Testing in Paternity Litigation: A Survey of State Statutes*, 22 Fam. L.Q. 109 (1988).

12. *See* Table 2.

13. *See* J. Craig Venter et al., *The Sequence of the Human Genome*, 291 Science 1304, 1317–21 (2001).

14. While there is little or no variability among individuals in most genes, there is sufficient variation to make each of us genetically unique (except for identical twins). In addition, some noncoding regions are highly variable. For practical purposes, DNA testing can distinguish virtually all people from one another. *See supra* Chapter 11.

15. *See* P.E. Smouse & R. Chakraborty, *The Use of Restriction Fragment Length Polymorphisms in Paternity Analysis*, 38 Am. J. Hum. Genetics 918 (1986). Y. Nakamura et al., *Variable Number of Tandem Repeat (Markers) for Human Gene Mapping*, 235 Science 1616 (1987). Still other RFLPs, such as the genes of the D14S1 marker (pAW101 probe), are thought to exhibit variability by rearranging internal DNA segments of varying length. A.R. Wyman & R. White, *A Highly Polymorphic Locus in Human DNA*, 77 Proc. Nat'l Acad. Sci. 6754 (1980). Differences among individuals in the lengths of their DNA fragments (or, equivalently, their size, measured in number of nucleotide base pairs) are inherited characteristics that can be recognized by altered mobility of bands on gel electrophoresis. *See supra* Chapter 25.

16. E.M. Southern, *Detection of Specific Sequences Among DNA Fragments Separated by Gel Electrophoresis*, 98 J. Molecular Biology 503 (1975).

More recently, another class of VNTR loci that differ by two to six base-pair-repeat units has been used for parentage analysis. These loci are called STRs (Short Tandem Repeats) and are detected using PCR (polymerase chain reaction) methodologies.[17]

There has been controversy surrounding DNA tests to identify trace evidence such as blood or semen stains in criminal cases. Several reports have questioned the "product rule"—multiplying frequencies of matching genetic markers within and across loci to estimate the frequency of phenotypes in the general population that match the trace evidence.[18] Generally, application of the product rule hinges on the absence of any significant population substructure arising through inbreeding of group members within some defined population.[19] Numerous papers have addressed this issue and indirectly gauged the degree of band dependence in forensic identification cases.[20] In

17. A. Edwards et al., *DNA Typing and Genetic Mapping with Trimeric and Tetrameric Tandem Repeats*, 49 AM. J. HUM. GENETICS 746 (1991). K. Mullis et al., *Specific Enzymatic Amplification of DNA in Vitro: The Polymerase Chain Reaction*, 51 COLD SPRING HARBOR SYMPOSIA ON QUANTITATIVE BIOLOGY 263 (1986). The major advantages of STR-based markers compared to RFLP-based markers for parentage testing are (1) the test methods are more amenable to automation (e.g., detection via capillary electrophoresis using the ABI PRISM® series of genetic analyzers), (2) the DNA products are generally of discrete and separable lengths, and (3) the conditions of sample storage are not usually critical. A major disadvantage of STR markers is that the number of alleles (usually 6 to 12) per system is less than those of the longer VNTRs (which have at least 20 discernable alleles), and, thus, individual STR systems have lower probabilities of exclusion. *See* Table 2. Typically, laboratories need to select test batteries of 8 to 10 STR systems to provide an average power of exclusion above 99%. Because of the more limited polymorphism of STR loci, several marker systems may be amplified together or mixed prior to electrophoresis as long as the amplification conditions are compatible and the fragment sizes between loci do not overlap. Usually triplex or quadraplex systems of STRs can be assembled, and each multiplex provides an average power of exclusion similar to a single VNTR system.

18. E.S. Lander, *DNA Fingerprinting on Trial.* 339 NATURE 501 (1989); J.E. Cohen et al., *Forensic DNA Tests and Hardy–Weinberg Equilibrium*, 253 SCIENCE 1037 (1991); R.C. Lewontin & D.L. Hartl, *Population Genetics in Forensic DNA Typing*, 254 SCIENCE 1745 (1991).

19. By analogy, suppose the perpetrator of a burglary is identified as a blue-eyed blonde, and a suspect arrested for attempting to sell the stolen merchandise matches the description. The significance of this match cannot be assessed without an estimate of the probability of a match by chance, i.e., the frequency of blue-eyed blondes in the population. Ideally,

surveys that jointly determine eye color and hair color would be available to provide a direct answer. However, suppose the only available data is that one in ten individuals is blonde and one in ten individuals is blue-eyed. If the traits were independent (if blue-eyed individuals were no more or less likely than non-blue-eyed persons to have blonde hair regardless of the population surveyed), then the frequency of blue-eyed blondes would be $1/10 \times 1/10 = 1/100$. But when both traits are concentrated in Caucasian individuals of European origin, the blue-eyed blondes are more frequent than 1 in 100. As a rule, the frequency of genetic markers, including those tested in paternity and identity laboratories, differ among races—human populations are said to have "structure." Structure is addressed by using race-specific data bases. Moreover, within Europeans, blonde hair and blue eyes are concentrated in Nordic populations; the simple product rule used above might thus be inapplicable even within race-specific data bases. Again, as a rule, the frequency of genetic markers (including those tested in paternity and identity laboratories) differ among ethnic groups within a race; human populations are thus said to have "substructure." The relevant question is whether substructure has a *significant* effect on the accuracy of the product rule. In most situations, the effect is quite minor. *See supra* Chapter 11.

20. While substructure is present, a large body of evidence indicates that it is largely inconsequential because there is less variability *within* races than *between* them. Also, the recently debated issue of population substructure in relation to DNA tests in disputed identity belies the fact that the existence of substructure has been known for generations. L. Hirschfield & H. Hirshfeld, *Serological Differences Between the Blood of Different Races: The Result of Researches on the Macedonian Front*, 1 LANCET 675 (1919). In regard to disputed paternity, it was well addressed prior to introduction of DNA technology. *See, e.g.,* K. Hummel & M. Claussen, *Exclusion Efficiency and*

paternity suits, direct validation of independence is possible given the fact that just two or three DNA systems are generally sufficient to provide convincing evidence for or against parentage. Studies assessing the use of the product rule for DNA-based paternity studies have demonstrated its validity.[21]

§ 12–2.3　Genetic Principles of Paternity Testing

The red cell antigen system MN[22] serves as a classic model to explain the basic genetic principles that underlie paternity testing.[23] Naturally occurring

Biostatistical Value of Conventional Blood Group Systems in European and Non–European Populations: Suitability of Central European Tables for Non–German Speaking Populations, in Biomathematical Evidence of Paternity 96–108 (K. Hummel & J. Gerchow eds., 1981). Current papers regarding the use of the product rule in forensic identification cases include B. Devlin et al., *No Excess of Homozygosity at Loci Used for DNA Fingerprinting,* 249 Science 1416 (1990); R. Chakraborty & K. Kidd, *The Utility of DNA Typing in Forensic Work,* 254 Science 1735 (1991); N.E. Morton, *Genetic Structure of Forensic Populations,* 89 Proc. Nat'l Acad. Sci. USA 2556 (1992); B.S. Weir, *Population Genetics in the Forensic DNA Debate,* 89 Proc. Nat'l Acad. Sci. USA 11654–59 (1992). Evaluations of the effect of substructure have also been performed. *E.g.,* N.E. Morton, *Kinship Bioassay on Hypervariable Loci in Blacks and Caucasians,* 90 Proc. Nat'l. Acad. Sci. USA 1892–96 (1993). For additional discussion, *see supra* Chapter 11.

21. Validation studies use databases that include the results of several genetic tests on each person represented in the database. They count the number of matches of each genetic type and of combinations of the types to determine whether the frequencies of the combinations are as predicted by the product rule. Due to the limited size of available databases, such direct validation is limited to matching frequencies of one in thousands or, at best, one in tens of thousands, but this is more than adequate for disputed paternity. *E.g.,* J.W. Morris & D.W. Gjertson, *The Paternity Index, Population Heterogeneity, and the Product Rule,* in 5 Advances in Forensic Haemogenetics 435 (W. Bar et al. eds., 1993); D.W. Gjertson & J.W. Morris, *Assessing Probability of Paternity and the Product Rule in DNA Systems,* 96 Genetica 89 (1995).

Of course, DNA-based tests are not without difficulties. Although accuracy in VNTR measurement can be enhanced using densitometers and computer processing, inherent limitations on the resolution in electrophoresis systems causes bands to have shape and width; thus, measurement error can never be zero. Limits in gel resolution cause ambiguous allelic assignments since RFLP bands can be closely spaced and overlapping. Typically, these measurement errors are 0.6–3% of band size. To handle this uncertainty, one must

create either statistically-based matching criteria or incorporate modeling assumptions into the analysis. Incorporating measurement variability into forensic and genetic analyses has been the subject of a number of recent scientific reports. *See* D.W. Gjertson et al., *Calculation of Probability of Paternity Using DNA Sequences,* 43 Am. J. Hum. Genetics 860 (1988) (formally incorporated allele measurement error into disputed paternity analysis). Other important discussions on the biostatistical evaluation of DNA studies include: adaptation of mixture lane experiments by J.W. Morris et al., *Biostatistical Evaluation of Evidence from Continuous Allele Frequency Distribution Deoxyribonucleic Acid (DNA) Probes in Reference to Disputed Paternity and Disputed Identity,* 34 J. Forensic Sci. 1311 (1989); estimation of VNTR distributions and probabilities in forensic identification and paternity cases by B. Devlin et al., *Estimation of Allele Frequencies for VNTR Loci,* 48 Am. J. Hum. Genetics 662 (1991), and B. Devlin et al., *Forensic Inference from DNA Fingerprints,* 87 J. Am. Stat. Ass'n 337 (1992); extended models for correlated measurement errors by D.A. Berry, *Inferences Using DNA Profiling in Forensic Identification and Paternity Cases,* 6 Stat. Sci. 175 (1991); D.A. Berry et al., *Statistical Inference in Crime Investigations Using Deoxyribonucleic Acid Profiling,* 41 Applied Stat. 499 (1992); and multilocus minisatellite probe techniques by I.W. Evett et al., *Paternity Calculations from DNA Multilocus Profiles,* 29 J. Forensic Sci. Soc'y 249 (1989), and A.J. Jeffreys et al., *The Efficiency of Multilocus DNA Fingerprint Probes for Individualization and Establishment of Family Relationships, Determined from Extensive Casework,* 48 Am. J. Hum. Genetics 824 (1991).

22. *See* Race & Sanger, *supra* note 10, for a complete description of the MN system. As mentioned above, tests of DNA markers have largely supplanted traditional tests. However, the MN system remains a useful model. The genetic principles apply when analyzing discrete-allele systems such as STRs as well as RFLP systems via "matched-binned" criteria, and they form the underlying framework when using the more rigorous analytic procedures mentioned *supra* note 21.

23. Extensive reviews of population genetics can be found in W.F. Bodmer & L.L. Cavalli-

antibodies for this blood group are of two main types—anti-M and anti-N. Agglutination of these substances with antigens on the surface of red blood cells divides individuals into three groups: (1) MN's, which react with both antibodies; (2) M's, which react with only anti-M; and (3) N's, which react with only anti-N.[24] The three phenotypes and represent visible expressions of an inherited genotype comprised of maternal and paternal contributions.[25]

Family studies of the MN system have shown that the mode of inheritance for these groups is "simple" or "direct," meaning that the groups are governed by single genes obeying Mendel's two laws.[26] Mendel's first law dictates that the alternate forms of genes (here, the alleles M and N) have no permanent effect on one another when present in the same individual, but segregate unchanged during cell division by passing into different gametes (ova or sperm). Mendel's second law states that genes on different chromosomes assort independently. For example, an MN individual (who has inherited an M allele from one parent and a N allele from the other) will transmit each allele 50% of the time. From a phenotypic M individual who has inherited the M allele from both parents (i.e., is a homozygote, MM), the M allele will assort 100% of the time. Similarly, the N allele will assort 100% of the time from a genotypic NN individual.[27]

The final population genetic principle needed to understand the MN system was derived simultaneously by G. H. Hardy and W. Weinberg in 1908.[28] It states that the processes of sexual reproduction do not, in and of themselves, alter the frequencies of alleles. Suppose that the allele M occurs in the population with relative frequency p, and N occurs with frequency q. These frequencies will remain constant in every generation if mating is random and mutation, selection, immigration and emigration do not occur.[29]

Sforza, Genetics, Evolution and Man (1976); Benjamin Lewin, Genes (3d ed.1987); C.C. Li, First Course in Population Genetics (1978); Stern, supra note 1; B.S. Weir, Genetic Data Analysis (1990).

24. Strictly speaking, groups that react with neither antibody also exist; however, individuals with these groups are rare so that they can be ignored, at least for illustrative purposes.

25. The genetic contribution of each parent is called the "haplotype."

26. Later, it was shown that the genes for the MN system are located on the chromosome adjacent to the genes for another red cell antigen system Ss, with two alleles S and s. This close physical proximity means that, while each parent transmits either M or N and either S or s to each offspring, transmission occurs as a unit (as MS, NS, Ms or Ns), and these units are transmitted unchanged through many generations. Consequently, an individual who expresses both alleles for each genetic system (i.e., who has phenotype MNSs) may be genetically either MS/Ns or Ms/NS. Additionally, because genes for MN and Ss systems are inherited as a unit, the probability of inheriting M or N is not independent of the probability of inheriting S or s. In other words, the product rule does not hold when combining the two systems. Such genetic markers are said to be "linked," and biostatistical estimations must treat these two genetic systems as a single unit. As noted, the linkage described is physical due to the adjacent location of the genes. Other physically-linked genetic systems include the red cell antigen system Rh (Dd, Cc and Ee) and the HLA system (A locus, B locus). Linkage may also be due to clustering of traits within populations and subpopulations. See supra note 19.

27. Assortment or transmission probabilities are not so easily derived for systems like the ABO system, which has recessive silent or null genes, or the HLA system, which has linked alleles. See Weir, supra note 9.

28. G.H. Hardy, Mendelian Proportions in a Mixed Population, 28 Science 49 (1908); W. Weinberg, Über den Nackweis der Vererburg beim Menschen, 64 Jahresh. Verein f. Vaterl Naturk. Wurttemb 368–82 (1908) (English translation in Papers on Human Genetics (S.H. Boyer ed., 1963)).

29. The principle can be illustrated by listing the possible mating types and deriving the distributions of genotypes in the next generation for each such mating type. The frequency of each genotype is determined by the distribution of alleles in a defined population. Since

Such a population, in which frequency of genetic types does not change from generation to generation, is said to be in Hardy–Weinberg equilibrium. A corollary to this principle is that if mutation, selection, or the mixing of two populations does produce a stable new allele, say , then the three alleles M, N and will reach Hardy–Weinberg equilibrium after just one generation of random mating.

These three genetic rules result in the principles of parentage testing. To begin with, identification of the genetic markers of mother and child permits deduction of the paternal contribution to the child. A failure to identify this contribution in the tested man constitutes a genetic inconsistency (an "exclusion"), and accumulated inconsistencies result in an opinion of non-paternity (the tested man is said to be excluded). Opinions of nonpaternity are unqualified but never 100% certain because of the possibility of exceptions to the Mendelian rules of inheritance, such as mutations, and because of the possibility of laboratory error. Nevertheless, in many states and for many years, opinions of non paternity have been admissible,[30] and in some states an unchallenged, categorical opinion of non paternity settles the issue.[31]

there are only two possible alleles, $p + q = 1$, and the distribution of possible genotypes is derived from the binomial theorem: $(p + q) = p + 2pq + q$. The quantity p is the frequency of genotype MM, 2pq is the frequency of MN, and q is the frequency of NN. Thus, the frequency of mating type MM $\times$ MM equals $(p)(p) = p^4$ so long as mating is random. The outcomes and frequencies of all such matings are given in Table 1.

Table 1
Frequencies of Genotypes in the MN System in Offspring,
by Mating Type

Mating types			Distribution of genotypes in offspring		
Mother $\times$	Father	Frequency	MM	MN	NN
MM	MM	p^4	1	0	0
	MN	$2p^3q$	½	½	0
	NN	p^2q^2	0	1	0
MN	MM	$2p^3q$	½	½	0
	MN	$4p^2q^2$	¼	½	¼
	NN	$2pq^3$	0	½	½
NN	MM	p^2q^2	0	1	0
	MN	$2pq^3$	0	½	½
	NN	q^4	0	0	1

Thus, the frequency with which children of genotype MM is produced is

$$P(MM) = 1 \times p^4 + \tfrac{1}{2} \times 2p^3q + \tfrac{1}{2} \times 2p^3q + \tfrac{1}{4} \times 4p^2q^2 = p.$$

Likewise,

$$P(MN) = \tfrac{1}{2} \times p^3q + 1 \times p^2q^2 + \tfrac{1}{2} \times 2p^3 q + \tfrac{1}{2} \times 4p^2q^2 + \tfrac{1}{2} \times 2pq^3 + 1 \times p^2 q^2 + \tfrac{1}{2} \times 2pq^3 = 2pq, \text{ and}$$

$$P(NN) = \tfrac{1}{4} \times 4p^2q^2 + \tfrac{1}{2} \times 2pq^3 + \tfrac{1}{2} \times 2pq^3 + 1 \times q^4 = q.$$

Taking account of the fact that there are two alleles per person, we conclude that the relative frequency of each allele in the next generation is as follows:

$$P(M) = (2p^2 + 2pq)/2 = p^2 + p(1-p) = p, \text{ and}$$

$$P(N) = (2pq + 2q^2)/2 = (1-q)q + q^2 = q.$$

30. *See, e.g.,* D.H. Kaye & Ronald Kanwischer, *Admissibility of Genetic Testing in Paternity Litigation: A Survey of State Statutes,* 22 *Fam. L. Q.* 109 (1988).

31. This was the approach taken in section 4 of the Uniform Act on Blood Tests to Determine Paternity (UABT), proposed by the Commissioners on Uniform State Laws in 1952, and incorporated in section 10 of the Uniform Paternity Act, adopted by the Commissioners in 1960. For some time, however, adoption of this provision was not widespread. *See* Ira Mark Ellman & David Kaye, *Probabilities and Proof: Can HLA and Blood Group Testing Prove Paternity?,* 54 NYU L. Rev. 1137 (1979).

By contrast, when the man matches the paternal contribution deduced from the genetic markers of the mother and child, a categorical opinion is not possible because genetic markers are not unique. However, to the extent that a match by chance is unlikely, the tested man is implicated. The evaluation of the evidence thus depends on the frequency of markers in the population. The extent to which paternity is proved can be expressed mathematically, as we discuss in Section 12–2.5. Because our legal system is uncomfortable with mathematical and statistical arguments,[32] however, introduction of genetic evidence to prove rather than disprove paternity is of relatively recent onset.[33]

§ 12–2.4 Selection of Genetic Tests

All else being equal, a test or test battery should efficiently eliminate nonfathers and not eliminate fathers. The statistic that measures the power of a test to exclude nonfathers is the probability of exclusion (PE).[34] The PE is the probability for a test to eliminate a falsely accused man, given the mother-child genetic markers. Specifically, the formula for PE depends on the set of paternal markers of the child, which is determined by the phenotypes of the mother and child. Suppose that in the MN system the mother is type M, and the child is MN. This implies that N is the paternal marker. Let Q be the probability that N appears as an allele in the phenotype of a randomly selected individual of a given racial background. Then $Q = 1-(1-q)^2$, where q is the frequency of N in that race, and the exclusion rate is $PE = 1-Q$. If $q = 0.44$, then $Q = 0.69$, and $PE = 0.31$, implying that 31% of wrongfully accused men would be excluded as the father by the MN blood test, for this mother and child.

Another version of PE is the average, or mean PE. It is defined as the weighted average over all mother-child marker constellations. It is important because laboratories are guided to select genetic systems with high mean PEs, and some courts use it as an overall measure of accuracy. The mean PEs for some genetic systems are listed in Table 2.

Table 2

Average exclusion rates (AER) of paternity tests
for Caucasians, by genetic system

Classical genetic systems	AER Source
White blood cells	
HLA	0.93 [1]
Red blood cells	
ABO	0.14 [1]
MNSs	0.30 [1]
Rh	0.26 [1]
Kidd	0.19 [2]
Kell	0.04 [2]
Duffy	0.07 [2]

32. *See, e.g.,* Charles Nesson, *The Evidence or the Event? On Judicial Proof and the Acceptability of Verdicts*, 98 HARV. L. REV. 1357 (1985); Laurence Tribe, *Trial by Mathematics: Precision and Ritual in the Legal Process*, 84 HARV. L. REV. 1329 (1971).

33. *See* Kaye & Kanwischer, *supra* note 30.

34. Synonyms are "exclusion probability" and "exclusion rate."

Classical genetic systems	AER Source
Red cell enzymes and serum proteins	
Adenylate Kinase	0.03 [2]
6–Phosphogluconate Dehydrogenase	0.02 [2]
Adenosine Deaminase	0.04 [2]
Phosphoglucomutase$_1$	0.25 [2]
Red Cell Acid Phosphatase	0.24 [2]
Glutamic Pyruvate Transaminase	0.19 [2]
Esterase D	0.09 [2]
Glyoxalase$_1$	0.19 [2]
Haptoglobin	0.18 [2]
Transferrin	0.13 [2]
Group Specific Component	0.27 [2]
Properdin Factor B	0.19 [2]
DNA systems	
VNTRs, Probe/locus (enzyme)	
pAC256/D17S79 (PstI)	0.79 [3]
pa3'HVR/D16S85 (PvuII)	0.92 [4]
YNH24/D2S44 (HaeIII)	0.90 [5]
TBQ7/D10S28 (HaeIII)	0.92 [5]
EFD52/D17S26 (HaeIII)	0.91 [5]
SLI1335/D1S339 (HaeIII)	0.95 [5]
STRs	
HUMCSF1P0	0.56 [6]
HUMTHOX	0.35 [6]
HUMTH01	0.54 [6]
HUMvWA	0.64 [6]
D16S539	0.47 [6]
D7S820	0.59 [6]
D13S317	0.44 [6]
D5S818	0.45 [6]

Sources
1. D.W. Gjertson et al., *Empirical Paternity Exclusion Rates*, 8 AM. J. FORENSIC MED. & PATHOLOGY 123 (1987)
2. C. SALMON ET AL., THE HUMAN BLOOD GROUPS (1984)
3. I. Balazs et al., *Human Population Genetic Studies of Five Hypervariable DNA Loci*, 44 AM. J. HUM. GENETICS 182 (1989)
4. R.W. Allen et al., *Application of DNA Probe Technology to Paternity Testing: Characteristics of an Informative Probe (pa3'HVR) Derived from a Locus Linked to the Alpha Hemoglobin Gene Complex*, 29 TRANSFUSION 477 (1989)
5. J.W. Morris, *Paternity Index Calculations in Single Locus Hypervariable DNA Probes: Still More Validation Studies*, in PROCEEDINGS FROM THE THIRD INTERNATIONAL SYMPOSIUM ON HUMAN IDENTIFICATION 177 (1992).
6. A.M. Lins et al., *Development and Population Study of an Eight-locus Short Tandem Repeat (STR) Multiplex System*, 43 J. FORENSIC SCI. 1 (1998)

As Table 2 indicates, many genetic systems have, individually, a limited power to exclude nonfathers. Nevertheless, if the test systems are independent, use of the product rule allows the results to be combined, yielding a cumulative PE of

$$PE_{CUM} = 1 - (1 - PE_1)(1 - PE_2)(1 - PE_3) \dots (1 - PE_N) \qquad (1)$$

The power of combining independent results is substantial. For example, combining ten tests, each with a PE of 0.2 (typical of red cell antigen and serum protein and enzyme systems) yields $PE_{CUM} = 1 - (1-0.2)^{10} = 1 - (0.8)^{10} = 89\%$. When combined with HLA typing (PE = .93, Table 2), such conventional marker systems yield a cumulative PE exceeding 99%: $PE_{CUM} = 1 - (1 - .89)(1 - .93) = 99.2\%$. Combining four tests, each with a PE of 0.9 (as seen with some VNTR DNA systems, Table 2) yields $PE_{CUM} = 1 - (1 - 0.9)^4 = 1 - (0.1)^4 = 99.99\%$. Such a DNA test battery would fail to exclude only 1 out of every 10,000 nonfathers.

§ 12–2.5   Evaluation of the Significance of a Paternity Match

It is not sufficient, when the tested man matches the mother and child, to summarize the evidence by quoting the PE (or equivalently, its complement, the probability of a match by chance). Suppose two men (unrelated to each other and the mother) are named as possible fathers in a paternity case. All agree that the child's father is one of the two men, the men had equal access, and no other evidence distinguishes the men. The four individuals undergo genetic testing. For the sake of illustration, we assume that only the MN system is tested[35] with the following results: mother is M, child is MN, Mr. A is MN, and Mr. B is N. Because the child has an N that did not come from the mother, N is the paternal marker, and because both men possess N, neither is excluded.

Suppose we have 100 such two-man cases, each resulting in the birth of one child. Without specifying the child's type and assuming that each man has equivalent fertility, 50 children would be fathered by the MN man (like Mr. A) and 50 by the NN man (like Mr. B). From our evaluation of mating types,[36] we note that 25 of the 50 children produced by the MN men (like Mr. A) would be type MN while all 50 of the children produced by the NN men (like Mr. B) would be type MN. Thus, 75 children would be produced who have the type MN of the child in our hypothetical case. But 1/3 of these 75 would be produced by men of Mr. A's type, and 2/3 by men of Mr. B's type. Men of Mr. B's type are twice as likely to produce such a child than men of Mr. A's type. Therefore, all else being equal (in accord with our hypothetical), the odds are 2 to 1 that Mr. B is the father.

We may obtain the same result computing the probability of producing a child, alternatively by Mr. A and Mr. B, and compare them. Let X be the chance that a mating of Mr. A and the mother would produce the child, and let Y be the chance that a mating of Mr. B and the mother would produce the child. From the mating array in Table 1, Mr. A's MN type mated with the mother's M type yields the child's MN type with probability ½, so X = 50%. Mr. B's N type mated with the mother's M type yields the child's MN type with probability 1, so Y = 100%. Since each man was equally likely before testing paternity, we give an equal weight of ½ to X and Y, and we conclude that the probability of paternity (sometimes denoted W) for Mr. A is $W_A = ½$

35. Normally, enough tests are conducted such that one man would be excluded and, by the process of elimination, the other man would be the father.

36. *See supra* note 29.

(X) / [½(X) + ½(Y)] = ⅓, and the probability of paternity for Mr. B, is W_B = ½ (Y) / [½(X) + ½(Y)] = ⅔. Mr. B is twice as likely to be the father as is Mr. A.[37]

Even if Mr. B does not show up for his blood test, we can still compute the probabilities. A randomly selected Caucasian would have a 44% chance of transmitting the N allele to an offspring.[38] Thus, Mr. B's unknown-but-random type mated with the mother's M type yields the child's MN type with probability 0.44, so Y = 44%. Since the information for Mr. B has changed, W for Mr. A becomes W_A = (½)(50%) / [(½)(50%) + (½)(44%)] = 53%.

Now, in a typical case Mr. B. is not specifically named. However, if the putative father's denial of paternity is true, another man must be the father. This unknown man, like the unavailable Mr. B, has markers known to us only in the statistical sense.[39] To finish the example, suppose that the mother had named just one man, Mr. A with type MN, as the father of her child. Then Mr. A's W would equal 53% if the paternity probability for Mr. A was 50% prior to testing, as it was in the case where the mother named both Mr. A and Mr. B.

Being based on the probabilities that a given mating would produce an offspring of the child's type, the calculation requires both application of Mendel's laws of inheritance and gene (marker) frequency tables.[40] If X is the probability of the observed phenotypes of the mother, child and alleged father under the hypothesis of paternity, if Y is the probability under the hypothesis of nonpaternity, and if the ratio of these probabilities is the "paternity index" PI = X/Y, then the probability of paternity can be written as

$$W = PI / [PI + 1]^{[41]} \qquad (2)$$

In our sample calculation, the MN system did not significantly change the tested man's chance of being the true father. W = 53% is only slightly higher

---

37. Note that W_A + W_B = 1; one of the men must be the father as specified by our hypothetical. This example demonstrates that the PE, which is based only on the markers of mother and child, and would not distinguish between the tested men, is an incomplete statistic with regard to "inclusionary" chances. See M.P. Baur et al., *No Fallacies in the Formulation of the Paternity Index*, 39 AM. J. HUM. GENETICS 528 (1986); R.C. Elston, *Probability and Paternity Testing*, 39 AM. J. HUM. GENETICS 112 (1986); M.R. Mickey et al., *Empirical Validation of the Essen–Möller Probability of Paternity*, 39 AM. J. HUM. GENETICS 123 (1986) (discussing the optimal properties of W for deciding paternity).

38. The transmission probability for a gene from a randomly selected, but untested, individual is simply its frequency in the population. This is a direct result of Hardy–Weinberg equilibrium from one generation to the next.

39. For this reason, the alternative father is sometimes labeled the "random man."

40. For complicated genetic systems such as the ABO system, where a single genotype cannot be unambiguously deduced from the phenotype, the likelihood of each of the consistent genotypes for the child also is determined by allele frequency tables for a defined population.

41. Essen–Möller and his mathematical colleague, Quensel, derived a version of this formula (generally known as the Essen–Möller formula). See E. Essen–Möller, *Die Beweiskraft der Ahnlichkeit im Vaterschaftsnachweis—Theoretische Grundlagen*, 68 MITT. ANTHROP. GES. (Wien) 9–53 (1938). They arrived at the relationship W = X/(X+Y), which has the equivalent form W = (X/Y) / [X/Y + 1]. Gurtler defined X/Y as the paternity index (PI), yielding the modern formulation of the Essen–Möller equation given in the text. H. Gurtler, *Principles of Blood Group Statistical Evaluation of Paternity Cases at the University Institute of Forensic Medicine Copenhagen*, 9 ACTA. MED. LEG. SOC'Y (Liege) 83 (1956). Twenty-three years after Essen–Möller published his formula, Ihm showed that the formula can be derived from a straightforward application of a theorem introduced by Thomas Bayes in 1763. P. Ihm, *Die Mathematischen Grundlagen, vor Allem fur die Statistische Auswertung des Serologischen und Antropologischen Autachtens, in* DIE MEDIZINISCHE VATERSCHAFTSBEGUTACHTUNG MIT BIOSTATISTISCHEM BEWEIS 128 (K. Hummel ed., 1961).

than the prior chance of 50%. The result suggests examining another genetic system (where the mother-child phenotypic pair would be more discriminating) or conducting many independent tests until the true father constellation becomes rare. If multiple, independent genetic markers are used in the diagnosis, the resulting probability of paternity W_{CUM} is given by a variation of the product rule $W_{CUM} = PI_{CUM} / [PI_{CUM} + 1]$, where the cumulative PI for the series of independent tests is $PI_{CUM} = PI_1 \times PI_2 \times PI_3 \times \ldots \times PI_N$. In what follows, PI will denote the evaluation of the genetic evidence, whether from one test or many.

Equation (2) assumes that the evidence other than the blood tests is equally balanced for and against paternity—that prior to the blood tests, the paternity of the tested man was a 50:50 proposition. Such an assumption, made by the laboratory *in vacuo*, sometimes is justified on the basis that it is "neutral." A better justification is that the assumption is made to illustrate the significance of the genetic evidence, which is summarized by the PI.

To make this point clear, some laboratories present values of W under a variety of assumptions about the strength of the nongenetic evidence. If the other evidence showed that paternity of the tested man were impossible, the prior probability of paternity would be zero. If it showed that his paternity were certain, the prior probability would be 100%. In the real world, we can be confident that the nongenetic evidence will not yield certainty. In any real case, the prior probability is greater than 0% but less than 100%. A formula known as Bayes' theorem gives the probability of paternity W as a function of PI (that comes from the genetic evidence) and the prior probability (that comes from the non-genetic evidence). Using "Prior" to stand for the prior probability, the formula is

$$W = (PI \times Prior) / [(PI \times Prior) + (1 - Prior)] \tag{3}[42]$$

Table 3 illustrates how different assumptions about the nongenetic evidence (expressed in terms of the prior probability) and different strengths of the genetic evidence (PI) influence the probability of paternity W. Presentation of W at various prior probabilities facilitates evaluation of evidence in cases in which there is more than one alternative father or the possible fathers differ in fertility or access. The genetic evidence, summarized by the PI, does not establish the probability of paternity. Instead, it *changes* the probability of paternity. When the PI exceeds 1,000, even a prior probability as small as 1% results in a probability of paternity in excess of 90%.

Table 3
Effect of PI and Prior Probability
on Probability of Paternity
Prior Probability

		1%	10%	Prior Probability 25%	50%	75%	90%
	10	9.2%	52.6%	76.9%	90.9%	96.8%	98.9%
	25	20.2%	73.5%	89.3%	96.2%	98.7%	99.6%
PI	50	33.6%	84.7%	94.3%	98.0%	99.38%	99.8%
	100	50.0%	91.7%	97.1%	99.0%	99.7%	99.9%
	1000	91.0%	99.0%	99.7%	99.9%	99.97%	99.99%

42. Notice that when the prior probability = 50%, $W = (PI)(\frac{1}{2}) / [(PI)(\frac{1}{2}) + (\frac{1}{2})] = PI / (PI + 1)$, the Essen–Möller result.

§ 12–2.6 Principles and Assumptions Underlying W

§ 12–2.6.1 General Principles and Assumptions

In parentage testing, the task of the laboratory is to perform the appropriate tests accurately and to provide a biostatistical evaluation of the results. To use this information correctly, the judge or jury needs to understand the fundamental principles and assess the assumptions underlying the evaluation. At the most fundamental level is the premise that the laws of genetics and mathematics have been correctly applied to yield a valid opinion. Next, this opinion is based on assumptions that can be broadly categorized as specific, empirical and changeable. Specific assumptions include undisputed maternity, accurately identified subjects, and accurate lab results. Empirical assumptions involve a gene's frequency in a defined population.[43] Frequency tables are compiled from case work and are sorted on the basis of race or ethnicity. Changeable assumptions include randomness of mating (where possible fathers are not related to the mother or to each other),[44] race, and prior probability.

For RFLP DNA systems, race is introduced to define a population of possible fathers in the formulation of PI. Gene frequencies are usually uncommon in each race or ethnic group, but occasionally vary markedly from one racial group to the next. For DNA systems with low frequencies of mutation and silent genes, the races of the mother and tested man are irrelevant; race enters into the calculation only as regards other possible fathers.[45] In practice, a subject's race is assigned by interview, and the alternative father's race is equated with that of the putative father. Our casework provides some justification for this practice. We have found a strong concordance in race among men who are tested when a mother identifies two or more men as possible fathers. More importantly, the court can consider the physical characteristics of the child and question any assumption about the race of the alternative father. In some cases, it is useful to tabulate PI based on various assumptions about the race of the father. In general, such analyses indicate that the assumptions have only a modest effect on W.

43. The need to estimate population frequencies on the basis of samples can introduce sampling error. However, Selvin has shown that large uncertainties in gene and haplotype frequencies may produce substantial variation in PI, but for PI in the range of 100 or more, W is not substantially affected. S. Selvin, *Some Statistical Properties of the Paternity Ratio*, in INCLUSION PROBABILITIES IN PARENTAGE TESTING 77 (R.H. Walker ed., 1983); *cf. supra* Table 3.

44. As a general rule, mating is random. J.W. Morris & D.W. Gjertson, *Population Genetics Issues in Disputed Parentage*, in PROCEEDINGS FROM THE FOURTH INTERNATIONAL SYMPOSI-

UM ON HUMAN IDENTIFICATION 63 (1993). Methods have been developed to handle exceptional cases, such as incest and possible fathers who are related to each other (e.g., brothers). J.W. Morris et al., *The Avuncular Index and the Incest Index*, in 1 ADVANCES IN FORENSIC HAEMOGENETICS 607 (1988).

45. This is a property of any single-locus autosomal codominant genetic system, like the MN system. The example in section 12–2.5 of the PI in the MN system shows how only the race of other possible fathers affects the biostatistical evaluation.

With respect to the prior probability, the laboratory lacks prior information except for the plaintiff's (usually the state's or mother's) accusation of paternity, and the defendant's (usually the tested man) denial of fatherhood. Monitoring the distribution of W in casework provides information on the average prior probability.[46] For any given battery of tests, dividing the rate at which tested men are excluded by the rate at which nonfathers are excluded produces estimates of the mean prior probability of nonpaternity. Such estimates usually range from 20% to 30%, so that, typically the prior probability of paternity is 70% to 80%.[47] In any case, the laboratory may choose to present W at a variety of different prior probabilities and leave it to the court to assign W. As shown in Table 3, once the PI reaches 100, W is substantial for virtually all prior probabilities.

§ 12–2.6.2 The Product Rule

The product rule, which assumes that the test results are independent, is used to combine results from different genetic tests. It is used to compute the cumulative PE as well as the cumulative PI (and, therefore, cumulative W). The product rule has not been controversial in paternity testing.[48]

§ 12–2.7 Differences Between Disputed Paternity and Disputed Identity

The use of DNA tests in establishing identity in criminal cases on the basis of blood, semen, or other biological material gave rise to scientific and legal controversy.[49] In contrast, use of DNA tests in establishing paternity has been practically free of scientific controversy, and whatever legal controversy exists is due to efforts to extrapolate from the use of DNA tests in criminal cases to the different use of similar tests in paternity cases. The subdued level of controversy is due partly to the gradual introduction of DNA work in paternity testing. Before DNA methods, powerful batteries of conventional genetic markers for paternity were in use. Classical tests often produced high PIs, and the impact of DNA testing is merely to provide still higher PIs.

On the other hand, for criminalists with a very limited armory of conventional genetic tests for "stainwork," DNA testing has been revolutionary. It is producing evidence in cases where none existed before, and the evidence is far more incriminating than anything previously possible. In

---

46. *See, e.g.,* Mickey et al., *supra* note 37; J.W. Morris, *Experimental Validation of Paternity Probability*, 29 Transfusion 281 (1989) (letter to the editor).

47. For additional analysis of the assignment of prior probabilities, see R.F. Potthoff & M. Whittinghill, *Maximum-likelihood Estimation of the Proportion of Nonpaternity*, 17 Am. J. Hum. Genetics 480 (1965); K. Hummel et al., *The Realistic Prior Probability from Blood Group Findings for Cases Involving One or More Men. Part II. Determining the Realistic Prior Probability in One-man Cases (Forensic Cases) in Freiburg, Munich, East Berlin, Austria, Switzerland, Denmark, and Sweden, in* Biomathematical Evidence of Paternity 81 (K. Hummel & J. Gerchow eds., 1981); M.P. Baur et al., *The Prior Probability Parameter in Pa-*

ternity Testing: Its Relevance and Estimation by Maximum Likelihood, in Lectures of the Ninth International Congress of the Society for Forensic Hemogenetics 389 (1981).

48. Nevertheless, we have devised a method to determine PI and therefore W across genetic loci without using the product rule. Gjertson & Morris *supra* note 21; Morris & Gjertson, *supra* note 21. In effect, we are directly counting "blue-eyed blondes" (*see supra* note 19). This enables validation studies of the product rule, and, when performed on a case-by-case basis, it eliminates objections raised by skeptics of validation studies.

49. *See, e.g.,* D.H. Kaye, *DNA Evidence: Probability, Population Genetics, and the Courts*, 7 Harv. J. L. & Tech. 101 (1993); *supra* Chapter 11.

addition, attitudes (both pro and con) towards DNA testing in the scientific and legal communities have been shaped, in part, by attitudes regarding the criminal justice system in general and capital cases in particular. The report of a committee of the National Research Council on forensic DNA technology recommended using "conservative" statistical estimates to accompany the introduction of novel DNA evidence in criminal trials.[50] By contrast, partly because there is no voiced opposition to the proposition that parents should support their children, no argument has arisen to support extremely "conservative" interpretations of inclusionary DNA evidence in civil paternity suits. Beyond this, disputed paternity and disputed identity differ in three areas—technical, genetic, and computational.

§ 12–2.7.1 Technical Differences

Forensic stains can be of limited size, and the testing procedure itself is destructive. Critical tests sometimes cannot be repeated or reproduced. Since the source of the stain is the core of the issue, a claim that the source is from a single individual, or even from a human, may be contested. As DNA is subject to modification due to adverse conditions, and such modification may complicate interpretation, prosecution and defense may offer strikingly different versions of the stain's history.

None of these issues arises in the typical paternity matter, as blood or other tissue samples may be taken under controlled conditions from individuals who can be positively identified by some combination of eyewitnesses, photographs, or fingerprints. The history of the specimen can be completely known. In addition, the specimens typically are generous, permitting retesting at will, by the original laboratory or referral to another laboratory. Moreover, if there is any doubt about the source of the tested samples,[51] the entire process can be repeated.

Of course, some technical issues are common to both disputed identity and disputed paternity cases. For example, specimens should be properly labeled and the chain of custody on transport to the laboratory should be documented. Once specimens reach the laboratory, processing, testing and interpretation should be performed in a standard and verifiable manner. In practice, this means that proper written procedures should be developed, and strict compliance with these procedures should be documented in every case. Appropriate scientific controls are required and performance and results of such controls should also be documented.[52] Standardization of test procedures within each laboratory leads naturally to exchange of information between laboratories and, thus, to standards promulgated and adopted by the appropriate scientific community. Such uniform standards permit and encourage formal peer review including the inspection and accreditation of laboratories.

Both the paternity and forensic (stain) community have evolved uniform standards and accreditation programs, but at a different pace due to historical

---

50. National Research Council Committee on DNA Technology in Forensic Science, DNA Technology in Forensic Science (1992).

51. Alleged fathers have been known to have a friend substitute for them when blood is drawn.

52. A "control" is a known specimen—one for which the outcome of testing can be accurately predicted. If the "control" (tested alongside an unknown specimen) gives the expected result, it provides assurance that the test procedures for the unknown specimen are functioning properly.

antecedents. Parentage testing has its origins in the medical field. Hospital transfusion services and community blood banks possessed the necessary expertise in red cell antigen testing technology forty years ago. The professional oversight organization for such medical laboratories is the American Association of Blood Banks (AABB), which has inspected and accredited laboratories for decades. Development of newer technologies with added power like enzyme and protein systems and HLA gave rise to increased demand for paternity services and the routine use of results in the courtroom. The AABB published standards and accredited laboratories for paternity testing beginning in 1984, years before the use of DNA technology. Later, it was a straightforward process to include DNA technology into the standard of the AABB and other agencies.[53]

In comparison, standards and accreditation of forensic laboratories for disputed identity have lagged. Such facilities developed from police and prosecution-oriented crime laboratories and from entrepreneurial biotechnology companies, without any strong, central oversight organization. The National Research Council committee report was critical of the slow development of proper standards and proficiency testing for forensic applications of DNA.[54] The committee strongly recommended the establishment of an active professional organization to oversee and enforce standards. The DNA Identification Act of 1994 mandated the FBI to establish the necessary advisory boards.

Lacking the organizational mechanisms to ensure technical quality that have been implemented in the paternity context, the criminal identification laboratories have found their work challenged on technical grounds. Such challenges are sometimes vigorous and acrimonious. Comparable issues rarely arise in disputed paternity trials. As we have noted, paternity specimens are generous and renewable. Therefore, one can objectively and dispassionately address all technical concerns by redrawing and retesting the case in an independent laboratory. This opportunity makes the courtroom an inefficient and inappropriate forum to challenge this aspect of a paternity test.

§ 12–2.7.2   Genetic Differences

In criminal stainwork, the question is the source of the specimen. Answering this question involves traits that are consistent during each individual's life but that vary considerably among individuals, so that a mismatch is to be expected if the person tested is not the source of the stain. Beyond this, however, genetics is largely irrelevant. By contrast, in disputed parentage work, the question is the source of the genetic markers in the child. Genetics is at the heart of the issue. Accordingly, for resolving disputes over parentage, genetic systems should be not only highly differentiated among individuals but also inherited in a regular and reliable pattern. Mutations, which are exceptions to the regular rules of inheritance, have been reported for virtually all classical genetic tests. Mutations have also been reported in DNA systems. Because mutations (and random errors in the laboratory) are

---

53. *See, e.g.,* AABB, STANDARDS FOR PARENTAGE TESTING LABORATORIES (2d ed.1994). The American Association of Histocompatibility and Immunogenetics (ASHI) also publishes standards and accredits for parentage testing, but ASHI's involvement in DNA technology generally is limited to HLA detection.

54. NATIONAL RESEARCH COUNCIL COMMITTEE ON DNA TECHNOLOGY IN FORENSIC SCIENCE, *supra* note 50.

expected to cause false *mismatches*, rather than false matches,[55] laboratories usually require two or more mismatches to exclude a man from paternity. But when a man matches a child, one can be confident that mutations as well as random laboratory error have not occurred.[56] In this sense, a match is a self-validating result.[57] Since contested paternity actions usually involve a match, random laboratory error and mutations rarely are an issue at trial.

§ 12–2.7.3 Computational Differences

The defendant in a criminal stain case has, for each DNA test, two markers—one maternal and one paternal. Again, however, the genetics are irrelevant. The important point is whether both markers match those in the stain. By contrast, in disputed paternity a match for the tested man usually involves a match only to a single paternal marker.[58] For the same genetic system, therefore, a stain match is much more incriminating than a paternity match.[59] Moreover, since the stain match is double, the product rule is required for even a single system's results. The use of just a few powerful DNA tests can produce matching frequencies of one in millions or even one in billions for stain cases. Direct validation of these astronomical results is currently not possible, because of the limited size of the data bases. By contrast, the same test battery for paternity cases yields matching frequencies on the order of one in a hundred or one in a thousand; these frequencies produce PIs in the hundreds or thousands. Available data bases have permitted validation of the PI product rule for such moderate estimates. Further-

55. J.W. Morris & C. Brenner, *Blood Stain Classification Errors Revisited*, 28 J. Forensic Sci. 49 (1988).

56. For current test batteries (traditional or DNA), a nonfather is expected to mismatch in multiple genetic systems. For each system, there are typically multiple genes (alleles). For a nonfather to match by error or mutation, typically the following three conditions are necessary: the errors or mutations must be multiple; the errors or mutations must occur *only* in the systems that would otherwise mismatch (if they occurred in a system that matches by chance, another mismatch would result); and for each of the normally mismatching genetic systems where there is an error or mutation, that error or mutation must *specifically* be from the nonmatching allele to the paternal allele (an error or mutation from a non-paternal allele to another non-paternal allele has no practical consequence). Thus, not just any mutation or error will do. *See, e.g.,* W. Martin et al., *Zur Anwendung des Verfahrens Nach Schulte–Monting und Walter Bei der Statistischen Auswertung von Blutgruppenbefunden*, 23 Aerztl. Lab. 369 (1977); W. Martin, *Consideration of "Silent Genes" in the Statistical Exclusion of Blood Group Findings in Paternity Testing, in* Inclusion Probabilities in Parentage Testing 245 (R.H. Walker ed., 1983); M.R. Mickey et al., *Paternity Probability Calculations for Mixed Races, in* Inclusion Probabilities in Parentage Testing 325 (R.H. Walker ed., 1983)

(examining on a theoretical basis, the effects of silent genes and mutations in the biostatistical evaluation of paternity). As a practical matter, since AABB standards require that genetic loci used for paternity testing have low mutation rates (typically less than 0.5% for DNA loci), W is generally unaffected by mutation, especially for PIs greater than 100.

57. False matches can occur in stain cases as a result of one kind of nonrandom error. One explanation for a match of suspect to stain is that, instead of testing suspect and stain, the suspect (or stain) was run twice! In disputed paternity, however, a tested man is expected to match only one of the markers of the child. If a man and child were to type identically, the laboratory would be alerted to the possibility of error.

58. A match at the single marker not present in the mother but found in the child is all that is necessary.

59. For a typical result in a VNTR DNA test system in which all marker frequencies are near 5%, the frequency of a stain match by chance is given by the Hardy–Weinberg equation of $2pq = 1/200$, while the typical paternity match would occur by chance with approximate frequency of $2p = 1/10$, a 20–fold difference in strength of evidence. For two such systems, there would be a 400–fold difference, and for three such systems, an 8,000–fold difference in strength of evidence.

more, moderate PIs can be computed without use of the product rule.[60]

In stain cases, the race of a donor of the stain (other than the suspect) is analogous to the race of the other possible fathers in a paternity case, but there is no child to assist in determining the reasonableness of assumptions of race in stain cases. Typically, matching frequencies are given based on a variety of different assumptions of race.

Finally, there is one computational similarity between stain cases and paternity cases. Biostatistical estimates depend critically on the assumption that other possible stain donors (or other possible fathers) are not related to the tested man.

§ 12–2.8   Conclusion

Until recently, the resolution of disputed paternity was strictly a legal matter resting primarily on testimony of highly interested parties. In practice, judges and juries usually presumed that a man living with or married to the mother was the father. By and large, the traditional evidence has been replaced by scientific tests. Today, genetic markers in blood and DNA patterns tend to be dispositive. In our experience, over 99% of current laboratory casework is resolved without trial. In other words, disputed paternity has become essentially a scientific matter.

This chapter has described the scientific principles used to resolve disputed paternity,[61] and we have compared the use of DNA in paternity and forensic cases. With its long history of scientific resolution by classical genetic systems and its gradual incorporation of DNA typing, paternity testing has avoided most of the serious controversy surrounding DNA's other forensic applications. Paternity laboratories have cooperated with existing agencies to develop and adopt proper standards that regulate testing and reporting of both exclusionary and quantified "inclusionary" opinions from genetic markers. The existing standards were applicable to DNA paternity testing. Finally, the fact that blood samples are ample and taken under controlled, witnessed conditions permits paternity laboratories to provide test results that can be reproduced to eliminate any doubts over the accuracy of the findings.

---

60. *See supra* text accompanying notes 18–21.

61. The general genetic and statistical concepts can be (and have often been) extended to other issues of biological relationships such as grandpaternity, maternity, and siblingship.

Index

References Are to Sections, Segmented by Chapter

You might also consult this work's table of contents as a finding device. The table of contents lists every section included in the work and the page number where each topical section is to be found. This is most useful when you know within what chapter or for what subject heading you are searching. The summary of contents that precedes the table of contents may be similarly used.
